CAVENDISH

THE EXPERIMENTAL LIFE

CAVENDISH

THE EXPERIMENTAL LIFE

by

Christa Jungnickel

and

Russell McCormmach

Bucknell

Publisher's Cataloging-in-Publication
(Provided by Quality Books, Inc.)

Jungnickel, Christa.
Cavendish : the experimental life / by Christa Jungnickel and Russell McCormmach.–Rev. ed.
p. cm.
Includes bibliographical references and index.
LCCN: 99-60985
ISBN: 0-8387-5445-7
1. Cavendish, Henry, 1731–1810. 2. Chemists–Great Britain–Biography. 3. Cavendish, Charles, Lord, 1692 or 3–1783. 4. Politicians–Great Britain–Biography. 5. Fathers and sons–Great Britain. I. McCormmach, Russell. II. Title.

QD22.C4J86 1999 540'.92 [B]
QBI99-231

for
Albert L. McCormmach
and
Marie Peetz McCormmach

The new edition of this biography is dedicated as well to

Robert Deltete
and
Marvin Sparks

Nothing is more fantastic, ultimately, than precision.
—Robbe-Grillet on Kafka

TABLE OF CONTENTS

LIST OF ILLUSTRATIONS

PREFACE AND ACKNOWLEDGMENTS

THIS BOOK IS A REVISION OF *CAVENDISH*, published in 1996. My wife and coauthor, Christa Jungnickel, a most exacting scholar and writer, died eight years ago, before we could complete our biography, though not before we had collected most of the original sources for it and had written various sections. I assembled *Cavendish* from these sections, but as they had been written independently by two persons, some as long ago as thirty years, the result was highly uneven, a substantial book which was at the same time incomplete and unsatisfactory. The work in hand corrects the faults of the former, incorporates a large number of new sources, and offers a more satisfying and in some respects new interpretation of the person of Henry Cavendish. *Cavendish, The Experimental Life* is a thoroughgoing and extensive revision of our biography.

Part 4 of this book is entirely new, an edition of Henry Cavendish's scientific letters. Known in his day for his taciturnity, Cavendish does to some extent reveal himself through his letters. We trust that our biography will not be confused with the unpopular Victorian genre, "life and letters," to which England's prime ministers and other notables have been subjected. Readers may wish to consult the letters independently of the earlier parts of the biography, and we have edited them accordingly.

A number of persons have read all or parts of the manuscript of the first or second edition of our biography. They have helped to ensure that our portrait of Cavendish and his world is a faithful likeness. The readers cannot, of course, be considered responsible for any persisting flaws in the book. We express our debt of gratitude to our readers and to others who in one form or another have given encouragement and advice: Mark Bonthrone, William H. Brock, I. Bernard Cohen, Arthur L. Donovan, Mordechai Feingold, John Gascoigne, Charles C. Gillispie, Jan Golinski, Peter Harman, Patrick Henry, Ingrid Hofmaster, Sean Kissane, Carmen Mayer-Robin, David Philip Miller, Betty Mohr, Joseph F. Mulligan, Rosemarie Ostler, Jean Luc Robin, Richard Sorrenson, and Mary Lou Sumberg.

We thank Sean Goodlett, who had a large part in preparing the Cavendish letters written in French, and who assisted in other ways in preparing the edition of letters.

We have been aided in our study of Cavendish by many archivists, and in another place we acknowledge permissions. Here we thank Peter Day, Keeper of Collections at Chatsworth, and his associates Michael Pearman and Charles Nobel.

We thank the American Philosophical Society for publishing the first edition of this biography in its series of Memoirs, for bestowing on it the John Frederick Lewis Award, and for granting permission to publish a second edition.

–Russell McCormmach
November 1998

CAVENDISH

THE EXPERIMENTAL LIFE

THE PROBLEM OF CAVENDISH

HENRY CAVENDISH, 1731–1810, is described in superlatives. They are often of praise or wonder. Regarding matters of intellect and fortune, he is called the "the wisest of the rich and the richest of the wise."[1] In his dedication to science, he is compared with "the most austere anchorites," who were "not more faithful to their vows."[2] His accomplishment is likened to the highest example: since the death of Newton, England has suffered "no scientific loss so great as that of Cavendish."[3] Superlatives of another kind are used as well. Cavendish is a man of a "most reserved disposition," of a "degree bordering on disease."[4] Cavendish was, to be sure, one of the greatest scientists of his century, one of the richest men of the realm, a scion of one of the most powerful aristocratic families, a scientific fanatic, and a neurotic of the first order. These things being the case, it would seem that Cavendish's biographers are called upon to paint a psychological portrait of a tormented genius. We have, however, taken a different approach, which we now explain.

Until we looked closely at the life of his father, Lord Charles Cavendish, 1704–83, we did not have a firm understanding of Henry's life. Coming from a family of politicians, Lord Charles predictably entered public life as a politician. While he was active in politics, he also pursued science as a side interest, at a certain point leaving politics to devote himself primarily to science. His direction

[1] J. B. Biot, "Cavendish (Henri)," *Biographie Universelle*, vol. 7 (Paris, 1813), 272–73, on 273.

[2] Georges Cuvier, "Henry Cavendish." This biography from 1812 is translated by D. S. Faber in *Great Chemists*, ed. E. Faber (New York: Interscience Publishers, 1961), 227–38, on 236.

[3] Humphry Davy, quoted in John Davy, *Memoirs of the Life of Sir Humphry Davy, Bart.*, 2 vols. (London, 1836), 1:222.

[4] Henry, Lord Brougham, "Cavendish," in his *Lives of Men of Letters and Science Who Flourished in the Time of George III*, 2 vols. (London, 1845–46) 1:429–47, on 444. Thomas Thomson, *The History of Chemistry*, 2 vols. (London, 1830–31) 1:337.

was continued by his son Henry, who made a complete life within science. The scientific calling of Lord Charles and Henry Cavendish found public expression in the work of the Royal Society of London.

From the perspective of the larger society, Lord Charles might have been seen as overstepping the bounds of his station in life. Drawn to experiment, and especially to the instruments of experimental science, he was a technical man. His aristocratic contemporary Lord Chesterfield made what many would have perceived as a sensible judgment for the time when he censored the architectural expert Lord Burlington for having more technical competence than his rank permitted.[5] Be that as it may, within the Royal Society both rank and scientific competence were honored, and Lord Charles and his son Henry were an outstanding example of their union in the eighteenth century. By the time Henry joined Lord Charles in the Royal Society, it had been in existence for a century. The Society, a legacy of the scientific revolution, had its hallowed traditions, but it retained a measure of its revolutionary potential in English society, as we see in the lives of Lord Charles and Henry Cavendish. Lord Charles found support in the Royal Society for his move from a traditional aristocratic career in politics to the uncommon life of an aristocrat *seriously* dedicated to science; his son Henry began where his father left off, on a course of experimental and observational science in close association with the Royal Society. In its membership, the Royal Society was selective, but in its understanding of science, it offered an acceptable avenue of *public* service; in this capacity, the Society facilitated the transition from politics to science in our branch of the Cavendish family. Owing to the Society, the scientific lives of Lord Charles and Henry Cavendish were, in part, public careers.

Lord Charles Cavendish's attention to the affairs of the Royal Society was extraordinary by any standard: for some fifteen years in the middle of his life, with the exception of the secretaries, no members of the Society gave of themselves more than he did. (In fifteen of the sixteen years between 1748 and 1763 in which he served on the council of the Society, he attended 106 regular meetings, missing only 9, several of which absences were occasioned by the near fatal accident of his youngest son, Frederick.) The importance of Lord Charles to the history of science lies not in any one achievement but in his forty years of organizational work in science. Having made no great discovery, he has entered the history of science as, at most, a footnote, but in a biography of the discoverer Henry Cavendish, Lord Charles Cavendish necessarily appears with nearly equal importance. Lionel Trilling's stricture that "every man's biography is to be understood in relation to his father"[6] may not be a practical guide for all biographers, but for biographers of Henry Cavendish, it is indispensable. We have written this book as a biography of father and son.

---

[5] Dorothy Marshall, *Dr. Johnson's London* (New York: John Wiley & Sons, 1968), 219.

[6] From Lionel Trilling's introduction to *The Portable Matthew Arnold*, ed. L. Trilling (New York: Viking, 1949), 15.

Historians of science know of Cavendishes earlier than Lord Charles. Richard Cavendish, one of the Cavendishes of Suffolk from whom the Devonshires descended, was an Elizabethan politician and student–for twenty-eight years he was a student at Cambridge and Oxford–who translated Euclid into English and wrote poems including (and in spirit foreshadowing our Henry Cavendish) "No Joy Comparable to a Quiet Minde," which begins, "In lothsome race pursued by slippery life . . ."[7] The namesake of one of our Cavendishes, Charles Cavendish, a seventeenth-century politician, was an important man of science, who solved mathematical problems, performed experiments, improved telescopes, and corresponded with inventors of new world systems. This Charles was "small and deformed," but he had a beautiful mind. In a time of violent controversy, he advocated cooperation as the way to truth, subscribing to Descartes' maxim, "to strive to vanquish myself rather than fortune and to change my desires rather than the order of the world."[8] This Charles and his older brother William, duke of Newcastle, who had a scientific laboratory, were friends of Thomas Hobbes, the philosopher who envisioned a state of war of each against all, and who also wrote the most original scientific philosophy in England. Hobbes tutored and influenced three generations of the other main branch of the Cavendishes, the earls, not yet dukes, of Devonshire. He moved in the great houses of the Cavendishes, Chatsworth and Hardwick Hall, both of which our Lord Charles knew well. In the Cavendish library, he found the true university that he had not found in Oxford.[9]

By Charles Cavendish's time, science was not exclusively a male preserve: Margaret Cavendish, duchess of Newcastle, wrote a number of good popular books on the microscope and other scientific interests. She demanded to be admitted as a visitor to the Royal Society, and in general she behaved in such an original and independent manner that she, the first scientific lady in England, was known as "Mad Madge."[10] In Henry Cavendish's time, Margaret Cavendish Bentinck, duchess of Portland, also of the Newcastle branch of the family, was a correspondent of Rousseau and a passionate collector; at her death, the sale of her natural history collection took thirty-eight days.[11] As if handing on the torch, in the year Henry Cavendish was born, 1731, Charles Boyle, earl of Orrery died.

[7] Henry Cavendish's forebear also wrote that "The enemies of Grace, do lurke under the prayse of Nature." Richard Cavendish, *The Image of Nature and Grace, Conteyning the Whole Course, and Condition of Man's Estate* (London, c. 1570). "Cavendish, Richard," *DNB* 3:1266–67.

[8] Jean Jacquot, "Sir Charles Cavendish and His Learned Friends. A Contribution to the History of Scientific Relations between England and the Continent in the Earlier Part of the 17th Century. I. Before the Civil War. II. The Years of Exile," *Annals of Science* 8 (1952): 13–27, 175–91, on 13, 187, 191.

[9] Samuel I. Mintz, "Hobbes, Thomas," *DSB* 6:444–51, on 444–45.

[10] Gerald Dennis Meyer, *The Scientific Lady in England 1650–1760* (Berkeley: University of California Press, 1955), 1–15, quote on 14.

[11] David Elliston Allen, *The Naturalist in Britain: A Social History* (London: Allen Lane, 1976), 29.

Nephew of the first duke of Devonshire, this earl was related to the great seventeenth-century chemist Robert Boyle. The same earl gave his name to George Graham's machine to show the motions of the heavenly bodies, the "orrery," the embodiment of the scientific world view of our Cavendishes.[12] Other early scientifically inclined Cavendishes include three important Fellows of the Royal Society: the third earl of Devonshire; the first duke of Devonshire, who was tutored by the secretary of the Royal Society Henry Oldenburg; and the youngest son of the first duke, Lord James Cavendish.[13] English aristocrats who actively pursued science were few indeed, and if a titled family was destined to distinguish itself in the eighteenth century, it was surely the house of Cavendish.

Our Cavendishes descended from two revolutions, one political and the other scientific. The Cavendish who became the first duke of Devonshire took a leading part in the revolution of 1688–89, which deposed one king, James, and replaced him with another, William. Referred to as the "Glorious Revolution," this change may not seem all that revolutionary when compared with subsequent political upheavals,[14] but to the British of the eighteenth century, it was the epitome of a radical change in human affairs. Joseph Priestley, a scientific colleague of Henry Cavendish's and also a friend of revolutions, said of this "revolution under king William" that before the French and American "revolutions," it "had perhaps no parallel in the history of the world," and for support he cited the philosopher David Hume's view that this revolution "cut off all pretensions to power founded on hereditary right; when a prince was chosen who received the crown on express conditions, and found his authority established on the same bottom with the privileges of the people."[15]

For his part in the revolution, Devonshire was honored by the victorious court. He and his descendants, who included Lord Charles, recognized a clear-cut duty: to uphold the revolutionary settlement and to give desirable shape to its aftermath.

Science, which had been an occasional interest of various earlier Cavendishes, became for Lord Charles an alternative to politics. Having served a respectable number of years in parliament, he redirected his public activities without changing their essential nature and motivation. The Royal Society offered Cavendish a public setting in which he could continue to exercise his highly developed sense of duty. The evidence of continuity in his life is as un-

[12] "Boyle, Charles, Fourth Earl of Orrery," *DNB* 2:1017.

[13] A. Rupert Hall, "Oldenburg, Henry," *DSB* 10:200–3, on 200.

[14] If the revolution is not viewed as "glorious" in the whig sense, as the "harbinger of liberal England," its significance may be seen to have an "even greater global magnitude." Editors' "Preface," *The World of William and Mary: Anglo-Dutch Perspectives on the Revolution of 1688–89*, ed. Dale Hoak and Mordechai Feingold (Stanford: Stanford University Press, 1996), vii–x, on vii–viii.

[15] On this point, Joseph Priestley's *Lectures on History and General Policy* (London, 1826) is quoted and discussed in I. B. Cohen, "The Eighteenth-Century Origins of the Concept of Scientific Revolution," *Journal of the History of Ideas* 37 (1976): 257–88, on 263–64.

dramatic as it is indisputable: he moved his committee work from the House of Commons to the Royal Society. If committees are more often associated with stoic endurance than with high endeavor, they are nevertheless the level of organization in scientific and learned institutions in which necessary tasks get done, and where colleagues get to know one another well and decide who has good judgment and who takes responsibility.[16] Lord Charles's conscientious work as a committeeman and even more as a councillor of the Royal Society singles him out as one of the most important men of science in London. Lord Charles was middle aged when he turned from assisting in the governing of the nation to assisting in the governing of the national scientific society. Thanks to his example, by the time his son Henry came of age, the parallel avenues of politics and science open to a Cavendish were clear. Henry could choose between them at the outset, and the history of science was changed as a result.

By the middle of the eighteenth century, the new political notion of revolution as a radical change rather than a cyclical return was applied to science, and with specific reference to Sir Isaac Newton's *Mathematical Principles of Natural Philosophy*, or *Principia.*[17] Almost to the year, the political revolution of 1688-89 coincided with the publication of that book, an event which has often been singled out as a culmination of the scientific revolution. The *Principia* was the single most important book of science for Henry Cavendish.

Today we still speak of *the* scientific revolution, but when we do, we recognize it as a long and complex historical process, one which did not consist solely of a preparation for the mathematical principles of mechanics and the gravitational system of the world as laid down in the *Principia.* Human understanding of the vastly more complicated operations of chemistry and of life underwent profound reinterpretations as well, and the subtle art of experiment was immensely enriched by advances in techniques and instruments. That ingenious master of experimental apparatus Robert Hooke was not less important than Newton in preparing the way for Lord Charles and Henry Cavendish. The same can be said of that eminent model of experimental persistence and perspicacity, Robert Boyle (who, as an aristocrat working in experimental science and shaping the Royal Society, was the model for Lord Charles and Henry Cavendish in another sense). Newton himself was, of course, a great experimental as well as mathematical scientist. Together, the scientific example of Boyle, Hooke, and Newton and the political settlement of the revolution of

[16] Lewis Thomas, a redoubtable committeeman of science, has remarked in various places on the indispensability and value of committees and on the inescapable disruptiveness of human individuality in the work of committees. For example, in *The Youngest Science: Notes of a Medicine-Watcher* (New York: Viking, 1983), 171; "On Committees," in *The Medusa and the Snail: More Notes of a Biology Watcher* (New York: Viking, 1979), 94–98. Although Cavendish served on committees throughout his sixteen years in the House of Commons, we note that his committee work fell off with time.

[17] Cohen, "Eighteenth-Century Origins," 264.

1688–89 go far to make intelligible the remarkable lives of Lord Charles and Henry Cavendish.

Having made Newton's *Principia* a prominent marker in this introduction, we can envision the brickbats flying. For thirty years or more, historians of science have reacted against the idolatry of Newton, arguing that the eighteenth century should be regarded as a time of originating scientific energies of its own.[18] We concede the point; nevertheless, in following the tracks of the Cavendishes, we repeatedly encounter Newton, though with Lord Charles we are less certain than we are with his son. Henry Cavendish was educated at Cambridge at a time when Newton's *Principia* dominated the curriculum, and although his greatest contributions to science were experimental, he was also a theoretical scientist who grasped the new experimental fields in Newton's "mathematical way."[19] New instruments, apparatus, and experimental techniques were invented in the eighteenth century, but not everything about science had to be invented. The *Principia* was Henry Cavendish's luminous if ever-receding ideal. For his purposes, the *Principia* was still, after a century, the model of science at its best. Cavendish incorporated a living Newton, not an icon, and if by the measure of his ambition, he failed to produce a single work as great as the *Principia*, he did superb research in the process. For the record, we do not subscribe to the view that science in the eighteenth century consisted of filling in the blanks left by Newton's incomplete natural philosophy.

In the accepted usage of his time, Henry Cavendish was a "Newtonian philosopher," but to call him that does little more than to place him in the eighteenth century. That imprecision was implied by the prominent mathematician Charles Hutton at the close of the eighteenth century in his *Mathematical and Philosophical Dictionary,* where he identified five meanings of "Newtonian philosophy," each held by numbers of subscribers, to which we could probably add several more meanings. Newton's legacy was, Hutton wrote, "as multivaried and as diverse as the interests of his apostles and their world cared to make it." We prefer to call Cavendish not a Newtonian philosopher but, as his contemporaries sometimes did, a "natural philosopher." For this term, which today is not without its own multiple meanings, we draw again on Hutton's *Dictionary* for a contemporary description: the natural philosopher is one whose study of nature is characterized by an "enlarged comprehension, by which analogies, harmonies,

[18] This by now historiographic commonplace was once fresh, serving as an important corrective; for example, R. W. Home, "Out of a Newtonian Straitjacket: Alternative Approaches to Eighteenth-Century Physical Science," in *Studies in the Eighteenth Century.* IV: *Papers Presented at the Fourth David Nichol Smith Memorial Seminar, Canberra 1976,* ed. R. F. Brissenden and J. C. Eade (Canberra: Australian National University Press, 1979), 235–49.

[19] Newton's expression, quoted and discussed in Henry Guerlac, "Where the Statue Stood: Divergent Loyalties to Newton in the Eighteenth Century," in *Aspects of the Eighteenth Century,* ed. E. R. Wasserman (Baltimore: The Johns Hopkins University Press, 1965), 317–34, on 323.

and agreements are described in the works of nature, and the particular effects explained; that is, reduced to general rules."[20]

Lord Charles and Henry Cavendish present their biographers with a difficult problem. The practical concerns and the private reserve of the Cavendish family ensured that every scrap of paper having to do with property was saved, but little else, and certainly little that could be regarded as personal. We have Lord Charles Cavendish's business correspondence but not his private letters. Henry Cavendish's business correspondence is preserved too, but otherwise, for such a prominent man, his surviving correspondence is meager. In his case, we suspect that there may not have been much. Virginia Woolf approached her biography of Roger Fry with the question, "How can one make a life of six cardboard boxes full of tailors' bills, love letters, and old picture postcards?"[21] The answer is, as she went on to show, that it is not easy but not impossible either. Henry Cavendish, whose cardboard boxes contain nothing so personal as even tailors' bills, let alone love letters, presents his biographers with an even harder task. How can they make a life from a fifty-year record of observations of thermometers and magnetic needles? It is neither easy nor straightforward, but once again, as we hope to show, it can be done. Cavendish's scientific papers are, in their way, as revealing of his nature as personal letters are of a lover's nature.

When Cavendish died, his unpublished scientific papers passed to his principal heir, Lord George Cavendish. They evidently remained with Lord George's family until his grandson became the seventh duke of Devonshire in 1858, when they were removed to the ancestral house of the Devonshires, Chatsworth, where they remain.[22] The papers, which consist of experimental and observational memoranda, calculations, and studies in various stages of writing, are voluminous, and to Cavendish's biographers, an embarrassment of riches, posing hazards of their own. We have tried to heed Henry Adams's advice to biographers, "proportion is everything,"[23] while at the same time we have accepted that Cavendish's life *was* his science. The distinction between biography and history of science can be fine, and Cavendish's biography calls

---

[20] Entries for "Newtonian Philosophy" and "Philosophy" in Charles Hutton, *Mathematical and Philosophical Dictionary*, vol. 2 (London, 1795), 157, 227. Larry Stewart, *The Rise of Public Science: Rhetoric, Technology, and Natural Philosophy in Newtonian Britain, 1660–1750* (Cambridge: Cambridge University Press, 1992), 387. Simon Schaffer, "Natural Philosophy," in *The Ferment of Knowledge: Studies in the Historiography of 18th-Century Science*, ed. G. S. Rousseau and R. Porter (Cambridge: Cambridge University Press, 1980), 53–91.

[21] Quoted in Susan Sheets-Pyenson, "New Directions for Scientific Biography: The Case of Sir William Dawson," *History of Science* 28 (1990): 399–410, on 399.

[22] *Treasures from Chatsworth, The Devonshire Inheritance.* A Loan Exhibition from the Devonshire Collection, by Permission of the Duke of Devonshire and the Trustees of the Chatsworth Settlement, Organized and Circulated by the International Exhibitions Foundation, 1979–1980, p. 67.

[23] Quoted in John A. Garraty, *The Nature of Biography* (New York: Knopf, 1957), 247.

for a balancing act. We could not have written this book without Cavendish's unpublished scientific papers, and we have relied extensively on them, but at the same time we have tried not to lose a sense of proportion, and with it the man.

A selection of Cavendish's manuscripts has been published, though only one group of them, the electrical, with anything approaching completeness. The electrical manuscripts were examined by a series of experts in that branch of physics. The earl of Burlington loaned the manuscripts to William Snow Harris, who described them in detail in an "Abstract." They were "more or less confused as to systematic arrangement," not "finished Philosophical Papers," Snow Harris said, but they showed clearly that "Mr Cavendish had really anticipated all those great facts in common Electricity which were subsequently made known to the Scientific World through the Investigations and writings of the celebrated Coulomb and other Philosophers."[24] Primarily to show how much of the modern subject Cavendish had anticipated, Snow Harris included extracts from Cavendish's papers in a revision of his textbook on electricity.[25] In 1849 on a visit to Snow Harris, William Thomson examined Cavendish's electrical manuscripts.[26] Concluding that they should be published in their entirety, Thomson, together with several other men of science, put the case to the duke of Devonshire. In 1874 the duke placed the manuscripts in the hands of the first Cavendish Professor of Experimental Physics, James Clerk Maxwell, who for the next five years repeated Cavendish's experiments, transcribed the manuscripts, and prepared a densely annotated and nearly complete edition of Cavendish's unpublished electrical papers together with his two published electrical papers.[27] This extraordinary edition, *The Electrical Researches of the Honourable Henry Cavendish*, was published in 1879 by Cambridge University Press only a few weeks before Maxwell's death.[28] At about the same time as his electrical manuscripts, Cavendish's chemical manuscripts came to the attention of the scientific world, in this case in connection with a resurrected priority dispute over the discovery of the composition of water. To document his defense of Cavendish's claim, in 1839 Vernon Harcourt appended a selection of Cavendish's chemical manuscripts to his published presidential address to the British Association for the Advancement of Science. Harcourt understood that an edition of Cavendish's

[24] William Snow Harris, "Abstract of M.S. Papers by the Hon H. Cavendish." This twenty-five-page abstract, which describes the contents of twenty packets of manuscripts on electricity and four packets on meteorology, is in the Royal Society, MM.16.125.

[25] William Snow Harris, *Rudimentary Electricity*, 4th ed. (London, 1854).

[26] S. P. Thomson, *The Life of William Thomson, Baron Kelvin of Largs*, 2 vols. (London, 1901) 1:218.

[27] Maxwell's correspondence in 1873 concerning the Cavendish papers is published in *The Scientific Letters and Papers of James Clerk Maxwell*, vol. 2: *1862–1873*, ed. P. M. Harman (Cambridge: Cambridge University Press, 1995), 785–86, 839, 858–59.

[28] *The Electrical Researches of the Honourable Henry Cavendish, F.R.S.*, ed. J. C. Maxwell (1879; reprint, London: Frank Cass, 1967).

papers was then being planned.[29] In fact, there had been intermittent discussion of such a plan from the time of Cavendish's death, but for one reason or another it had been put off, as it would continue to be long after Harcourt. In due course, with further delays caused by World War I, in 1921 Cambridge University Press reprinted Maxwell's edition of the electrical papers and published a new, companion volume containing the rest of Cavendish's published papers from the *Philosophical Transactions* together with a small selection of scientific manuscripts from outside the field of electricity, the two volumes appearing as *The Scientific Papers of the Honourable Henry Cavendish, F.R.S.* [30] The selection of manuscripts to be included in the companion volume was made by the general editor and chemist Sir Edward Thorpe, together with four other experts from physics, astronomy, and geology.

Copious as Cavendish's scientific manuscripts are, they are by no means complete. A case in point is the experiment that goes by his name, his weighing of the world: if as with so many of his researches, he had not published it, we would know nothing of its existence. His scientific papers, as they have come down to us, do not mention it. Or to take an example of another kind: a French colleague wrote to Richard Kirwan that Cavendish had made a discovery about the magnetism of metals that "merits great attention."[31] The surviving manuscripts on magnetism by Cavendish, which are primarily about earth-magnetic instruments and magnetical bars, do not tell us what he was referring to. In recent years, important scientific manuscripts of Cavendish's, the existence of which had been unknown to scientists and scholars, have been made public. We have no doubt that many others once existed; we hope that they too may one day come to light.

There are two book-length biographies of Cavendish, both written by chemists. The recent one, by A. J. Berry, provides a readable summary of Cavendish's papers but gives little more than what the editors of the collected papers do, and it does not present anything new about Cavendish's life.[32] Berry would seem to have confirmed what the editor-in-chief of the collected papers,

---

[29] W. Vernon Harcourt, "Address," *British Association Report*, 1839, pp. 3–45, on p. 45. The address is followed by an "Appendix," pp. 45–68, containing extracts of Cavendish's papers on heat and chemistry, which in turn is followed by some sixty pages of lithographed facsimiles.

[30] *The Scientific Papers of the Honourable Henry Cavendish, F.R.S.*, 2 vols. (Cambridge: Cambridge University Press, 1921). The subtitle of the first volume edited by Maxwell and revised by Joseph Larmor is *Electrical Researches.* The subtitle of the second volume under E. Thorpe's general editorship is *Chemical and Dynamical.* Hereafter, this work is cited as *Sci. Pap.* 1 and 2.

[31] Louis-Bernard Guyton de Morveau to Richard Kirwan, 28 Feb. 1786, in Louis-Bernard Guyton de Morveau and Richard Kirwan, *A Scientific Correspondence During the Chemical Revolution: Louis-Bernard Guyton de Morveau and Richard Kirwan, 1782–1802*, ed. E. Grison, M. Goupil, and P. Bret (Berkeley: Office for the History of Science and Technology, University of California at Berkeley, 1994), 142–47, on 146.

[32] A. J. Berry, *Henry Cavendish: His Life and Scientific Work* (London: Hutchinson, 1960).

Thorpe, said of Cavendish's "personal history": little is known of it, "nor is there much hope now that more may be gleaned," since it is doubtful that "there is much more to learn" about this "singularly uneventful" life.[33] Cavendish's earlier biographer, George Wilson, however, wrote an original account of his subject in a highly unusual form of biography, to which we now turn.[34]

If ever a biography violated Adams's advice about proportion, it was Wilson's *The Life of the Honourable Henry Cavendish.* Cavendish's "life," in the ordinary sense of the word, occupies only two chapters, the first and the fourth, which comprise fifty pages out of a total of nearly five hundred pages. The "life" in the *Life* was attached to a book with a different purpose, which was to put to rest the controversy over who deserved credit for discovering the composition of water. The controversy, which had simmered briefly in Cavendish's lifetime, was fanned to white heat in the middle of the nineteenth century by a French *éloge* of James Watt. Dealing almost exclusively with the water controversy, Wilson's account has elements of a detective story and legal drama, his principal subject being not Cavendish but a contest of honor. Apart from polemics, the book is a highly useful work in the history of chemistry, though it does not seem to have been used that way. What it has been used for is its "life" of Cavendish.

Wilson's biography was published by and at the request of the Cavendish Society. Founded in 1846, the Society was one of a number of early nineteenth-century subscription printing clubs, this one for chemical works, named after Henry Cavendish no doubt because of the furor going on then.[35] In addition to the water controversy and the subscription printing club, there was another reason for Wilson's *Life.* In the middle of the nineteenth century, a call went out for biographies of scientists, presumed to be a neglected category of eminent Britons. Believing that scientists and men of letters gave their age "greater glory than the statesmen and warriors,"[36] in 1845 Lord Brougham published biographical sketches of Cavendish and several other scientists. In 1848 the historian of the Royal Society, Charles Richard Weld, condemned the lack of a biography of the late president of the Society, Sir Joseph Banks, as a "reproach to scientific England," confident that if Banks had been a military man or a romantic hero, his biography would long since have been written.[37] In 1843 Wilson began collecting materials for a book on the lives of the British chemists; although he never published this book, he did complete three biographical essays intended for it. Of one of his subjects, William Hyde Wollaston, he said that if he had been a

[33] From Thorpe's "Introduction" to *Sci. Pap.* 2:1.

[34] George Wilson, *The Life of the Honourable Henry Cavendish* (London, 1851).

[35] W. H. Brock, "The Society for the Perpetuation of Gmelin: the Cavendish Society, 1846–1872," *Annals of Science* 35 (1978): 599–617, on 604–5.

[36] Brougham, *Lives of Men of Letters and Science* 1:xi.

[37] Charles Richard Weld, *A History of the Royal Society* . . . , 2 vols. (London, 1848; Arno Press, 1975), 2:116–17.

German, "some patient, painstaking fellow-countryman would long ago have put on record all that could be learned concerning his personal history"; or had he been a Frenchman, "an eloquent Dumas or Arago would have read his *éloge* to the assembled men of science in the French capital." But Wollaston's "fate as an Englishman, is to have his memory preserved (other than by his own works) only by one or two meagre and unauthenticated sketches, which scarcely tell more than that he was born, lived some sixty years, published certain papers, and died." In the book about the life of a chemist he did publish, Cavendish's, in 1851, Wilson regretted that "no other European nation has so imperfect a series of biographies of her philosophers, as Britain possesses." There was not even a good biography of Newton, Wilson said, let alone biographies of recent British scientists, such as Thomas Young, John Dalton, and Wollaston, and only now was there a biography of Cavendish.[38] That Wilson included a "life" at all in his book on Cavendish would seem to have been due to his sympathy with the prevailing desire for biographies of scientists.

When Wilson applied to the Cavendish family for the loan of Henry Cavendish's manuscripts, he said that he had delayed asking because he understood that Lord Burlington was going to write an account of Cavendish's discoveries. (The earl of Burlington, we should explain, was an extinct title resurrected as a courtesy title for Henry Cavendish's heir, Lord George Cavendish, thereafter going to the eldest son of the eldest son of the duke of Devonshire.) This Lord Burlington was the forty-eight-year-old William Cavendish, who would go on to become the seventh duke of Devonshire. Scientifically gifted, he had posted second wrangler in the competitive mathematical examinations at Cambridge and first Smith's Prizeman, returning to Cambridge in 1861 to succeed Prince Albert as chancellor. The richest of all the dukes, in 1870 he drew upon his wealth to build a laboratory for experimental physics at Cambridge, where its first professor, Maxwell, would repeat Cavendish's experiments for his edition of Cavendish's electrical papers. The laboratory was going to be called the Devonshire Physical Laboratory after the seventh duke, but it was named the Cavendish Laboratory instead, after Henry Cavendish according to one account,[39] though this version of the naming has been called into question.[40] The duke did not write an in-house study of Cavendish's work after all, but he established one of the world's greatest physical laboratories, which bears the name Cavendish.

---

38 George Wilson, *Religio chemici. Essays*, ed. J. A. Wilson (London, 1862), 254. Wilson, *Cavendish*, 15.

39 John Pearson, *The Serpent and the Stag: The Saga of England's Powerful and Glamourous Cavendish Family from the Age of Henry the Eighth to the Present* (New York: Holt, Rinehart and Winston, 1983), 214.

40 Peter Harman, the editor of Maxwell's papers, has kindly informed us that he has found no documentation of the switch in name from Devonshire to Cavendish. The name Cavendish may stand for the family. Personal communication. J. G. Crowther too has written that he does not think that Maxwell regarded the laboratory as a memorial to Henry Cavendish: *The Cavendish Laboratory 1874–1974* (New York: Science History Publications, 1974), 35.

Wilson told the future duke that he had been studying Cavendish's works for ten years, that he admired Cavendish's character, and that he intended to do him justice in the water controversy.[41] Burlington let Wilson see the manuscripts. They proved useful to Wilson in vindicating Cavendish of any wrongdoing in the water controversy, but they did not give Wilson the materials he needed to fashion a portrait of the person of Cavendish. For this purpose, Wilson relied largely on short accounts of Cavendish's life published, in most cases, soon after his death, and on first-hand accounts that he and a colleague elicited from older Fellows of the Royal Society and former neighbors of Cavendish's. The accounts of Cavendish at the end of his life, as Wilson noted, were conflicting, as we might expect, given that the words and actions of a person approaching death were then believed to be particularly revealing. But Wilson found the accounts of the rest of his life, taken in their totality, to be largely consistent and compelling, as we do, even as we must recognize that most of them were anecdotal and dependent on recollections of events that occurred at least forty years earlier. Guided by these accounts, Wilson tried to understand his man, tried to "become for the time Cavendish, and think as he thought, and do as he did." But as he closed on his subject, he conflated it with the remorse he felt on devoting so much time and effort to "so small a matter." Like all of his past efforts, this effort Wilson saw as "bleak and dark," and the image of the man he distilled from the accounts of Cavendish corresponds.[42]

Wilson kept his promise to Burlington to portray Cavendish as a man of exemplary probity; but there is more to character than honesty, and Wilson did not admire much of what he saw. Wilson, a deeply religous man, was then contemplating writing a "Religio Chemici" along the lines of Sir Thomas Browne's "Religio Medici," and in the year following the publication of his biography of Cavendish, he published a biography of the physician John Reid, a man of "Courage, Hope, and Faith," whom he greatly admired. Wilson tried to penetrate to where Cavendish's courage, hope, and faith lay, his heart, only to discover that Cavendish was a "man without a heart."[43] In the *Life*, Wilson said that Cavendish was "passionless," "only a cold, clear Intelligence, raying down pure white light, which brightened everything on which it fell, but warmed nothing." Francis Bickley, chronicler of the Cavendish family, concluded from Wilson's *Life* that "there is something pathetic about such an existence as Henry Cavendish's, so fruitful and yet so utterly barren."[44] Sir Edward Thorpe, the general editor of

---

[41] George Wilson to Lord Burlington, 15 Mar. 1850, Lancashire Record Office, Miscellaneous Letters, DDCa 22/19/5.

[42] The quotations are from a letter Wilson wrote at the time, included in his sister's biography, Jessie Aitken Wilson, *Memoir of George Wilson* (London and Cambridge, 1862), 340–41.

[43] Ibid., 338, 342–43. Wilson completed several chapters of his projected book on chemistry and religion. They were brought out after his death in a volume of essays bearing the title *Religio chemici*; note 38 above.

[44] Francis Bickley, *The Cavendish Family* (London: Constable, 1911), 207.

Cavendish's *Scientific Papers*, wrote to a fellow editor that Cavendish was "not a man as other men are, but simply the personification and embodiment of a cold, unimpassioned intellectuality."[45] Cavendish's recent biographer, Berry, quoting Wilson, speaks of Cavendish's "striking deficiencies as a human being."[46] Wilson is entitled to his image of Cavendish, but we should point out that in addition to being Wilson's conviction, that image is a mid-nineteenth-century Romantic cliché, echoing Keats's Appolonius, whose cold mathematical philosophy denied the imagination by subjecting the rainbow and other mysteries to its "rule and line," thereby conquering them and emptying them of their charm. We have dwelled this long on Wilson's biography because it has provided the standard portrait of Cavendish for nearly a hundred and fifty years. Wilson accomplished what few biographers do: he made his subject vivid and memorable. We admire Wilson's biography of Cavendish, and in our own, we make extensive use of the accounts of Cavendish on which he based his portrait. But we have consulted a much wider range of sources than Wilson did, and so our portrait naturally shows differences from his. In addition, times have changed and biographies with them. Our interpretation of Cavendish departs markedly from Wilson's.

We can, it would seem, at least agree on the appearance of Henry Cavendish, since there is only one image. It is an ink-and-wash sketch, from which Wilson had an engraving made for his biography. Cavendish is shown walking with something of a slouch, possibly a family trait, for Joseph Farington observed that a "peculiar awkwardness of gait is universally seen" in the Cavendishes.[47] Cavendish was an immensely wealthy man, but one would not know it from the sketch, which shows him in a rumpled coat and long wig, both long out of date. The physical scientist Thomas Young, who knew Cavendish in his later years, said that he always dressed in the same way, presumably as in this picture.[48] (Young also described Cavendish as tall and thin, which is where agreement ends; another contemporary, the chemist Thomas Thomson, described Cavendish as "rather thick" and his neck as "rather short."[49]) The circumstances under which this picture was executed make one of the best stories about Cavendish, and one there is no reason to doubt. When earlier he had been approached to sit for a portrait, perhaps for the meeting room of the Royal Society, Cavendish had given a blunt refusal. But William Alexander, a draughtsman from the China embassy, succeeded by subterfuge; with the help of a confederate,

---

[45] Sir Edward Thorpe to Sir Joseph Larmor, 7 Feb. 1920, Larmor Papers, Royal Society Library, 1972.

[46] Berry, *Cavendish*, 22.

[47] "Joseph Farington's Anecdotes of Walpole, 1793–1797," in *Horace Walpoles's Correspondence*, 48 vols., ed. W. S. Lewis (New Haven: Yale University Press, 1937–83) 15:316–17.

[48] Thomas Young, "Life of Cavendish," *Encyclopaedia Britannica*, Supplement, 1816–24; in *Sci. Pap.* 1:435–47, on 444.

[49] Ibid. Thomson, *The History of Chemistry*, 2 vols. (London, 1830–31) 1:339.

John Barrow, he was invited as a guest to the Royal Society Club, at which Cavendish dined once a week. As advised, Alexander sat at one end of the table close to the peg on which Cavendish invariably hung his gray-green (or faded violet) coat and three-cornered hat, both of which Alexander surreptitiously sketched. He then sketched Cavendish's profile, which he later inserted between the hat and coat in the finished portrait. Cavendish, of course, was not shown it, but people who knew him were, and they recognized him. The artist left the sketch at the British Museum, where Wilson obtained it.[50] It is a wonderful portrait, and part of the wonder is that it ever came into existence in the first place.

"I desire" was one of Cavendish's favorite expressions. His life was filled with desire, and to a greater extent than most persons, what he desired he could have. For he was perfectly placed: born an aristocrat when the aristocracy was in high tide, he could expect his desires to be taken seriously. Because he was not a peer, he escaped the meaningless aspects of privilege, the time-consuming duties, rituals, and display; he was free to choose inherently more rewarding pursuits, while at the same time he could feel as confident of his place in society as if he were a peer. (Cavendish's diffident behavior in particular social settings was an entirely different matter.) What he desired more than anything else, we know, was to understand the natural world. Given his enviable position, he could separate the rewards of scientific work from those of society at large, which were in any event given to him without having to desire them, an advantage which lent his life its peculiar direction and intensity.

Owing to the near total absence of personal sources, we have had to rely upon other kinds of evidence in coming to know Cavendish. To form our image of him, to draw the human face between the three-cornered hat and the crumpled greatcoat, we have placed him in all of the settings in which we know he appeared.

This biography opens in the 1680s, when science began to dominate educated thought in Western Europe.[51] It ends just over a century later, at the beginning of the nineteenth century. The period it covers was one of transition from scientific "virtuosi" to professional scientists. It also witnessed great advances in scientific techniques and the beginnings of great new fields of investigation. Lord Charles Cavendish, a master of scientific instruments and of the art of experiment, took up challenging problems in the new fields, and his son Henry Cavendish explored them systematically with exacting experimental technique and mathematical theory. In terms of the Cavendish family, the period covered by this biography begins when the rooms of the great Cavendish house, Chatsworth, resounded with the sound of the pugnacious first duke of Devonshire's clanking sword, and it ends when the tone of those same rooms was set by the Proustian languor of the fifth

[50] John Barrow, *Sketches of the Royal Society and Royal Society Club* (London, 1849), 146–47.

[51] Margaret C. Jacob, *The Cultural Meaning of the Scientific Revolution* (Philadelphia: Temple University Press, 1988), 105.

duke of Devonshire. Where the first duke saw a world to conquer, the fifth duke saw the already conquered world in which his comfort was well secured. The fifth duke was no fool. He recognized that his cousin, Henry Cavendish, saw a different world, though he may not have recognized it as a new world to conquer, demanding of Henry what had been demanded of the first duke, hard work. (By "conquer," in the borrowed sense, we mean to understand and to command the workings of nature, ruled by the authority of natural laws.) The fifth duke got it nearly right when he ordered his wife, Georgiana, duchess of Devonshire, to stay away from Henry Cavendish's laboratory (it would seem she did not obey) on the grounds that "He is not a gentleman–*he works*."[52] Henry Cavendish and before him his father, Lord Charles, belonged to what Sir Benjamin Brodie called the "working men of science."[53] In this biography, we show what it meant for two gentlemen, first, Lord Charles Cavendish and then the Honorable Henry Cavendish, to *work* in science.[54]

[52] Bickley, *Cavendish Family*, 202.

[53] On the membership of the Royal Society in Henry Cavendish's day: Sir Benjamin Brodie to Charles Richard Weld, 7 Apr. 1848, quoted in Weld, *History of the Royal Society* 2:153–54, on 153.

[54] *Work* in the setting of professional science is the theme of Christa Jungnickel and Russell McCormmach, *Intellectual Mastery of Nature: Theoretical Physics from Ohm to Einstein*, 2 vols. (Chicago: University of Chicago Press, 1986).

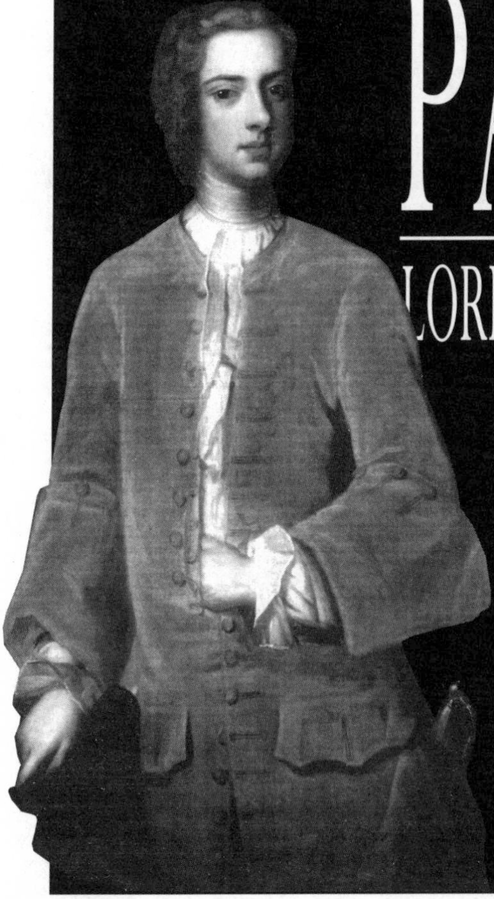

PART ONE

LORD CHARLES CAVENDISH

CHAPTER 1

THE DUKES

IN THE SPRING OF 1691, two young English aristocrats on a grand tour of the Continent met in Venice and apparently liked one another well enough to begin a correspondence after they parted.[1] The older of the two was Henry de Grey, Lord Ruthyn, then not quite twenty; the younger, the nineteen-year-old William, Lord Cavendish. Forty years later, in 1731, they were to become the grandfathers of Henry Cavendish, although William did not live long enough to know of this grandson.

The eldest sons of propertied English earls, the two young men, accompanied by tutors and servants, met as seasoned travelers despite their youth. William Cavendish had already been abroad for over two years, Henry de Grey for over a year.[2] William was on his way to Rome, Henry returning from there. Both of them were no doubt acquiring the rudiments of their later great interest in the arts and architecture, but letters about their travels do not show any youthful ardor for the beauties of Italy, Switzerland, or Holland. In Rome, William Cavendish and his younger brother Henry did "little or nothing . . . that was worth giving your Lordship an account of."[3] From Padua, Frankfurt, or The Hague, they reported seeing friends or missing them, as they crisscrossed the Continent, but said not a word about the finer

[1] William Cavendish to Henry de Grey, 30 May/9 June 1691 and 23 December 1691. Bedfordshire Record Office, Wrest Park Collection, L 30/8/14/1–2.

[2] One of William Cavendish's first stops on the Continent was Brussels. From there he wrote to his mother-in-law, Lady Russell, that he was about to continue on his tour, and she approved, "for to live well in the world; 'tis for certain most necessary to know the world well." *Letters of Lady Rachel Russell; from the Manuscript in the Library at Woburn Abbey*, 5th ed. (London, 1793), 415–16. Henry de Grey, as "Lord Ruthven," had been issued a pass on 16 April 1690 "to travel abroad for purposes of study." G. E. C. (George Edward Cokayne), *The Complete Peerage of England Scotland Ireland Great Britain and the United Kingdom: Extant, Extinct, or Dormant*, vol. 3 (Gloucester: Alan Sutton, 1982), 176–78.

[3] Henry Cavendish to Henry de Grey, 7/19 May 1691, Bedfordshire Record Office, Wrest Park Collection, L 30/8/21/1.

things of classical civilization these young English barbarians had been sent abroad to experience.

What did interest them was the war threatening between England (and its allies) and France, and the dynastic quarrels that were giving rise to it. The war might affect their travel plans, as it did Henry de Grey's, but, more important, it was to be fought to secure the rights to power and property of certain European ruling families; that was the usual purpose of wars then, and understandably a matter of concern to aristocrats of high rank like young Cavendish and Grey. "The Elector of Brandenburg has declared, that he will fullfill the Promise he made to the Duke of Lorrain, at the siege of Bonn, *to maintain the interests of his children* and to contribute to their restoration. The Emperor and all the allys have declared the same thing," William Cavendish reported to Henry de Grey in the summer of 1691.[4] Concern for the dynastic interests of the ruling family that an aristocrat chose to ally himself with was very much a concern for the interests of his own family. That was why William Cavendish was ready to risk his life in battle in 1691 and why his father had risked *his* life only three years earlier to secure the interests in England of the Protestant branch of the Stuarts.

In 1688, William Cavendish's father, the earl of Devonshire, had joined six other English aristocrats in the risky business of inviting William of Orange to the British throne, even though that throne was then rightfully occupied by James II and could some day be legally claimed by James's son, who had just been born. If their scheme of deposing James had misfired, they might have suffered the fate of traitors. But luck was with them, and with the succession of William and his Stuart wife, Mary, to the crown, the earl ensured abundantly the survival of the Cavendish family in political power and in the enjoyment of their property. In 1691, in the spring in which William and Henry met in Venice, the earl of Devonshire outshone "most of the Princes," including the elector of Brandenburg, with his "magnificent" establishment at the royal congress at The Hague, to which he had accompanied King William as lord steward. Three years later, in 1694, the royal couple rewarded his services by raising the earl to duke of Devonshire, the highest rank short of royalty.[5]

The Cavendishes rose to their title relatively quickly, in not much more than a century, and they prepared for it by a steady accumulation of landed property until they were among the richest landowners in England. Along the way, they used some of their money to buy first a baronetcy and then an earldom when the political shifts of the seventeenth century from monarchy to commonwealth and back prompted the granting of royal favors. They remained loyal to the Stuarts–being prudent enough to make their peace with the commonwealth as

---

[4] William Cavendish to Henry de Grey, 30 May/9 June 1691. Italics added.

[5] John Pearson, *The Serpent and the Stag: The Saga of England's Powerful and Glamourous Cavendish Family from the Age of Henry the Eighth to the Present* (New York: Holt, Rinehart and Winston, 1983), 68–71. Francis Bickley, *The Cavendish Family* (London: Constable, 1911), 170–74.

well–until under Charles II such loyalty was no longer in their financial and political interest.[6]

KENT

If the dynastic concern of the Cavendishes was to further strengthen their newly found hold on the top rung of the social ladder, the Greys' was to reclaim their former footing. The Greys had been earls of Kent since the fifteenth century, Henry de Grey's father the eleventh of the line. But Henry's branch of the family had succeeded to the title and estates only in the middle of the seventeenth century, beginning with a country rector with a very large family who was too poor and too old to take his seat in the House of Lords. His successor, Henry's grandfather, did enter politics, but on the wrong side, as it turned out, adopting the cause of parliament against the king. After the restoration of the Stuarts, the Greys prudently kept their distance from court and parliament. In any case, their most pressing need was still to secure their estate and finances; at court or in government in those troubled years, they would only have risked making enemies or spending money that they could not afford. Taking big chances, as the earl of Devonshire had on behalf of William of Orange, was acceptable to a prudent man only if he had power, and power then derived from landed property. In that regard, the Greys were not the Cavendishes' betters or even equals. Nor would they take chances with the life of their heir. Instructing Henry to leave Holland before the king arrived there for his campaign, Henry's father wrote to him: "It would be expected you should go to the campaign with him, and not to do it would be took ill both from your father and you." So Henry traveled on to Geneva, safe from the king, and from there, against his cautious parents' wishes, into Italy.[7]

For ten years after his return from the Continent in 1691, Henry de Grey lived the life of a well-to-do private gentleman, taking up neither of the usual two occupations of young aristocrats, the military or parliament.[8] His public life began almost simultaneously with the reign of Queen Anne. At her coronation, Henry's father carried one of the swords of state; four months later, in August of 1702, his father died suddenly in the middle of a game of bowls, leaving Henry his heir, on his way to the House of Lords as earl of Kent. A nonpolitical man, Kent stood for neither power, party, nor principle, unlike his friend Devonshire, who sought and acquired political power and served the whig cause with a fierce loyalty. Kent's political career had only this in common with Devonshire's, great

---

[6] Pearson, *Serpent and Stag*, 61.

[7] Joyce Godber, *Wrest Park and the Duke of Kent, Henry Grey (1671–1740)*, 4th ed. (Elstow Moot Hall: Bedfordshire County Council Arts and Recreation Department, 1982), 2–3.

[8] Thomas Wentworth, *The Wentworth Papers, 1705–1739. Selected from the Private and Family Correspondence of Thomas Wentworth, Lord Raby, Created in 1711 Earl of Strafford, of Stainborough, Co. York*, ed. James J. Cartwright (London, 1883), 134.

ambition, which in Kent's case took the form of self-interested maneuvering at court. For his long, faithful services at court, Anne elevated him to duke.

If Henry de Grey had any brothers, they died young, for soon the love and hope of his family focused on him. He responded by developing into an affectionate young man, good natured and easygoing. Once he had a family of his own, his concern for his wives–after his first wife died, he remarried–and his children was reflected in their letters to him, full of warmth and appreciation. He was not especially gifted in anything, but he had sufficient intelligence and curiosity to inform himself on a wide range of subjects, including science, as his substantial library attests. He had sufficient vanity to aspire to important positions at court, lacking only the drive to work for such positions by seeking political power. "A quiet mind is better than to embroil myself amongst the knaves and fools about either Church or State," he wrote in a moment of disappointment.[9] He sought offices in the courtier's way, by gaining favor with influential people and then using his connections to request honors and positions. The offices he accepted were administrative rather than political, requiring abilities well within his reach, drawing on skills he was already exercising in the running of his estates. He attended the House of Lords dutifully even after he came to dislike the burden in his middle years.[10] He displayed the same level-headed estimate of his abilities in his later years, when his chief occupation came to be his estate at Wrest Park; on its agriculture and its gardens, he informed himself thoroughly, and he planned and directed the work on his properties with considerable and lasting success. His enemies at court–political opponents who wanted the positions he held, or rivals for royal favors–gave Henry de Grey the name "The Bugg";[11] they meant to ridicule him, implying in this way that he was pompous and proud, pretending to quality, but their description must be admitted to have some truth to it. A good-looking man, he spent the money necessary to cut a fine figure; his annual clothes bills ran higher than those of his wife and several daughters combined, not only while he held high office at court and needed expensive formal apparel, but long before, as a young man about town. On his tomb, he had himself sculpted wearing a Roman toga over a strong, muscular body, his curly hair cropped close to the head, resembling in face and attire Laurent Delvaux's statue of George I, undeniably betraying a certain vanity. A large family portrait painted about five years before his death shows him to be, on the contrary, a relatively short, slender man whose simple velvet coat is decorated

[9] Duke of Kent to Prior, 26 July 1710, quoted in Ragnhild Hatton, *George I, Elector and King* (Cambridge, Mass.: Harvard University Press, 1978), 121.

[10] "Memoir of the Family of De Grey," Bedfordshire Record Office, Wrest Park Collection, L 31/114/22, 23, vol. 2, p. 99.

[11] The earl of Godolphin to the duchess of Marlborough, [24 Apr. 1704], John Churchill, duke of Marlborough, *The Marlborough-Godolphin Correspondence*, 3 vols., ed. H. L. Snyder (Oxford: Clarendon Press, 1975), 1:284.

only with what appears to be the garter and ribbon. Far from posing as the patriarch in his own home, he has yielded center stage to his mother-in-law, the countess of Portland, who was governess of the royal children; he stands rather meekly by her side, receiving from her a cup of tea.[12] His pride lay in his "ancient and noble" family, as he called it, which he hoped, in vain, as it turned out, to continue through his five sons. Not one of them survived him. He achieved a dukedom for his family in 1710, but he ended without an heir to inherit it; he could only look forward to its extinction with his death. All that remained for him to do was to build an ostentatious marble mausoleum, which although pompous, also evokes his struggle against so much disappointed hope.

For at least ten years, beginning in 1736, the Kent estate served as a lecture theater in the physical sciences and an observatory of the heavens. In those years the duke of Kent and, after his death in 1740, the duchess of Kent employed Thomas Wright as a scientific teacher. This is the famous astronomer who was first to delineate the structure of the Milky Way, publishing his finding in 1750 as *An Original Theory or New Hypothesis of the Universe*. Born into an artisan family, self-taught in astronomy, Wright made his living by teaching science, mathematics, and surveying; publishing on these subjects; and surveying the estates of the aristocracy. His pupils included Jemima, duchess of Kent, and Kent's daughters, Ladies Sophia de Grey and Mary de Grey (but not Anne de Grey, who married Charles Cavendish), his son-in-law Lord Glenorchy, and his granddaughter Jemima, the future marchioness de Grey. He taught the Kent women geometry, navigation, surveying, and no doubt other subjects from his ambitious curriculum. Residing for months at a time at Wrest Park, Wright probably did surveying there as well as teaching, for the duke was constantly building, and the duchess, Wright noted in his diary, surveyed all the garden and made plans for it. We know that Wright designed a rustic, thatched cold bath for the marchioness de Grey at Wrest Park.[13] Wright also carried out his own astronomical studies at Wrest Park, in 1736, for example, communicating to the Royal Society his observations taken there of the eclipse of Mars by the moon.[14] Lord Charles and Henry Cavendish no doubt became acquainted with Thomas Wright at Wrest Park and in London on his visits to the Grey side of the family. Wright was still teaching the Kents when Henry Cavendish was fifteen. When the duke of Kent died, his "Closet" included a surveying instrument described as a "Spirit Level with a Telescope Light two foot long by Wright" together with a variety of other mathematical instruments.[15]

---

[12] *Conversation Piece at Wrest Park*, around 1735. Illustration 3, p. 28.

[13] David Jacques, *Georgian Gardens: The Reign of Nature* (London: B. T. Batsford, 1983), 70.

[14] Entries from Thomas Wright's diary, in Edward Hughes, "The Early Journal of Thomas Wright of Durham," *Annals of Science* 7 (1951): 1–24, on 13–22. His observations at Wrest Park are reported in Royal Society, JB 15:371 (28 Oct. 1736).

[15] Bedfordshire Record Office, Wrest Park Collection, L 31/184.

Occupying one hundred and twenty acres, enclosed by a two-mile gravel walk, the elegant garden at Wrest Park contained mementos of friends and of royalty whom the duke had served or admired, which included statues of King William (put up because the duke was a "good Whig") and of Queen Anne (put up because he was a "good Servant"). Standing in a corner of the garden was a pyramid inscribed with the years of the beginning and end of the duke's proud improvements of the estate. The larger setting, the park, was eight hundred acres, enclosed by a grass walk, with plantations of lemon and orange, irregular clusters of "venerable" oak, canals containing fat carp and pike, an obelisk eighty-six feet high, extensive lawns, a pavillion, a greenhouse, a bowling green, statues, vases, a temple of Diana, falls, ridings, and herds of deer. In the distance, cottages and churches could be seen, including a church resembling a picturesque ruined castle. The grand house of the estate was approached by a broad, tree-flanked avenue lying in the park. This description is from a letter written at Wrest Park in 1743, three years after the duke's death, by Thomas Birch, a literary man who thought that the best room in the house was the library.[16] Wrest Park with its wealth of books and with its artful blend of geometrical precision and natural grandeur would have been a familiar scene to Henry Cavendish. Kent's legacy to Lord Charles and Henry Cavendish was a breadth of cultural interests outside politics and pride in the standing of his family, symbolized by his creation, Wrest Park.

DEVONSHIRE

Growing up in the shadow of the "Great Duke of Devon"–his contemporaries spoke of the first duke of Devonshire as if he were already a legend–Henry Cavendish's other grandfather, William Cavendish, the future second duke of Devonshire, could have been crushed completely. The first duke was a willful, flamboyant man who defied and created kings, picked violent quarrels at the drop of a hat,[17] and rebuilt one of England's finest great houses, Chatsworth. In any event, the son grew up to be more mature, better balanced, more reasonable, and on the whole a much more solid and, one suspects, more intelligent man than the father, and, of course, much less exciting. About the second duke there are none of the stories about duels and mistresses, street fights and defiance of all authority that make the first duke so fascinating. Up to a point, young William, reasonably enough, allowed his life to be directed by his father: at sixteen, he was married to fourteen-year-old Rachel Russell, the daughter of Lord William Russell, Devonshire's former political ally and friend and now "martyr"

---

[16] Draft of a letter by Thomas Birch from Wrest Park, 28 Sep. 1743, BL Add Mss 4326B, ff. 180–82.

[17] Great Britain, Historical Manuscripts Commission, *Report on the Manuscripts of the Marquess of Downshire, Preserved at Easthampstead Park, Berks.* vol. 1: *Papers of Sir William Trumbull*, part 1 (London: His Majesty's Stationery Office, 1924), 60, 240, 268–69, 271–72, 276.

to the whig cause.[18] As soon as William came of age, he followed his father into politics, in his early years serving as a Member of Parliament. He even imitated his father's boldness, taking initiatives and speaking frequently for his principles in the House of Commons, on one occasion going so far as to challenge an opponent. But when he spoke, he spoke his own mind, not his father's, and in addressing conflicts, he was much more likely to use reason, persuasion, and compromise than the sword. "His mansion was not a rendevous for the assemblies of foppery," it was said of him: "none were permitted to partake of the . . . refined . . . pleasures of his house . . . but the ingenious, the learned, the sober, the wise."[19] He was not really that proper, but he did value learning and cool judgment, and in an environment of courtly intrigue and political passions, he impressed the duke of Marlborough as a "very honest man" and a man who "governs himself by reason."[20] George I, according to Lady Cowper, thought so, too: he was one of only two men in the kingdom whom the king had found to be "very honest, disinterested."[21]

Of his relationship with his family we get a glimpse only now and then. On his continental tour, as a newly married boy, too young yet to be allowed to live with his wife, he wrote considerate letters to his mother-in-law, Lady Rachel Russell, to which she replied: "I can have no better content in this world than to have your Lordship confirm my hope that you are pleased with your so near relation to us here, that you believe us kind to you, and value our being so."[22]

The boy's thoughtfulness and good breeding made his high expectations all the more agreeable. Writing about William and Rachel's marriage, Lady Russell sensibly remarked: "We have all the promising hopes that are (I think) to be had; of those I reckon riches the least, though that ingredient is good if we use it rightly."[23] William and Rachel Cavendish used their riches responsibly and tried to teach their children to do the same. Rachel apparently was the one to deal with the children. "I must needs tel you y^t y^r father can by noe means allow you to goe on in this way," she admonished their second son James for gambling while on tour abroad, "& soe he bids me tel you, ye expences of y^r travels have been very great already without y^s addition, more I believe then is allow'd to most

[18] Lois G. Schwoerer, *Lady Rachel Russell: "One of the Best of Women"* (Baltimore: The Johns Hopkins University Press, 1988), 161–63.

[19] Hiram Bingham, *Elihu Yale: The American Nabob of Queen Square* (New York: Dodd, Mead, 1939), 308.

[20] The duke of Marlborough to the earl of Godolphin, 14/25 June 1708, in *Marlborough-Godolphin Correspondence* 2:1011.

[21] George I quoted by Lady Cowper, 10 July 1716, in Mary, Countess Cowper, *Diary of Mary Countess Cowper, Lady of the Bedchamber to the Princess of Wales, 1714–1720*, ed. C. S. Spencer Cowper (London, 1864), 115.

[22] Lady Russell to William, Lord Cavendish, 5 Oct. 1688, *Letters of Lady Rachel Russell*, 410.

[23] Lady Rachel Russell to Dr. Fitzwilliam, 29 June 1688, *Letters of Lady Rachel Russell*, 399.

elder brothers, & tho I hope y^r father is able to make you very easy in y^r fortunes yet you may consider ye more you spend abroad soe much ye less you will have at home whare it wou'd doe you more credit & I should think be more for y^r owne satisfaction to spend y^r money amongst y^r friends then strangers."[24] Lord James never learned the value of careful husbandry of his means, but, as we shall see, his younger brother Lord Charles, accompanying him on this trip, learned it very well. Like many of his well-to-do contemporaries, William, their father, did spend some of his fortune on works of art; however, even as a collector he managed to enrich the family fortune. Whether from frugality or good taste, he avoided the more expensive but often second-rate large works and instead acquired one of the finest collections of old master drawings, including works by Raphael, Dürer, Holbein, Rubens, Van Dyck, and Rembrandt.[25]

William's reliance on reason and integrity, a quality apparently shared by his wife, also is reflected in their family life. "I have always taken you to have a very good understanding," Rachel wrote to James; "if you make but a right use of that, you will know what is most for y^r owne good."[26] They encouraged their children to think for themselves. In the matter of an allowance, for example, Rachel twice asked James what he might need while he was abroad, his parents reserving the right to disagree with him: "I thought I was right to aske y^r opinion as to ye sum, concluding I knew you soe well y^t if I shou'd happen to think it too much, you wou'd not take it ill y^t I told you soe."[27] Their difference of opinion resulted in a compromise, with James sending pleasing reports of his economy to his parents. With regard to the boys' travels, too, "y^r father in that wo'd be willing to do what he thought was most agreeable to y^r own inclinations . . . you may let me know what y^r own thoughts are."[28] In a future son-in-law, William and Rachel valued that he was said to be "very sober & of an extreem good character wch is above every thing elce."[29] This sensible family life not only nurtured love and respect but also the clear thinking and the level-headed assumption of responsibility of Lord Charles Cavendish.

From the time he returned from his continental tour until his death in 1729, William Cavendish, from 1707 the second duke of Devonshire, continuously devoted his life to public service at the highest level of government. To the whig interest, he brought not only his own political but also his wife's strong personal desire. Rachel Russell had been brought up not to forget the injustice done her family by her father's execution in 1683 at the hands of the Stuarts. Nine years

[24] Rachel, duchess of Devonshire, to Lord James Cavendish, [late 1722 or early 1723], Devon. Coll.

[25] Pearson, *The Serpent and the Stag*, 87–88.

[26] Rachel, duchess of Devonshire, to Lord James Cavendish, [late 1722 or early 1723].

[27] Rachel, duchess of Devonshire, to Lord James Cavendish, 20 Mar. 1723, Devon. Coll.

[28] Rachel, duchess of Devonshire, to Lord James Cavendish, 13 Feb. 1724, Devon. Coll.

[29] Rachel, duchess of Devonshire, to Lord James Cavendish, [late 1722 or early 1723].

DUKES, DUCHESSES, AND PROPERTIES

1. Henry de Grey, Duke of Kent. By Amiconi? Reproduced by permission of the Bedfordshire Record Office.

2. Jemima Crewe, Duchess of Kent. First wife of the Duke. By Riley. Reproduced by permission of the Bedfordshire Record Office.

3. *Kents*. Conversation Piece at Wrest Park. *By Silsoe, around 1735. Left to right: Mary de Grey, William Bentinck, Barbara Godolphin, Lord Berkeley, Charles Bentinck, Earl of Clanbrassil, Countess of Portland, Duke of Kent, Jemima Campbell (later Marchioness de Grey), Sophia de Grey, Duchess of Kent, Elizabeth Bentinck, Countess of Clanbrassil, Viscountess Middleton. Reproduced by permission of the Bedfordshire Record Office.*

4. *Wrest Park. The duke of Kent's garden at his country house in Bedfordshire. Photograph by the authors.*

5. *No. 4 St. James Square. The duke of Kent's house in London. Reproduced by permission of the Greater London Record Office.*

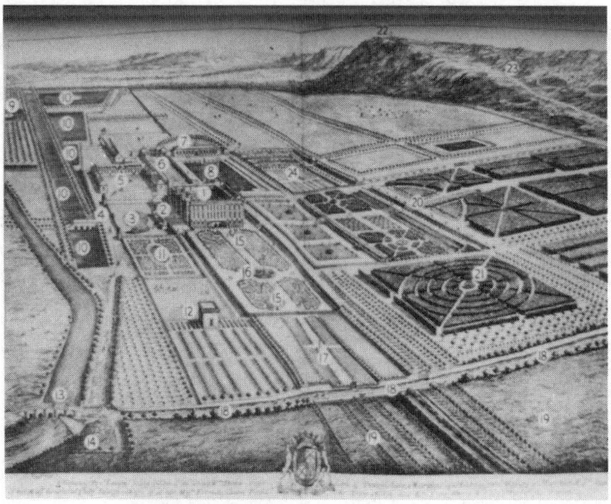

6. Chatsworth. The great Cavendish country house in 1699, five years after William had been raised to the duke of Devonshire and five years before Lord Charles was born. Drawing by L. Kniff, engraved and published in Kip, Nouveau Théatre de la Grande Bretagne, *1716, pl. 17; reproduced in Francis Thompson,* A History of Chatsworth. Being a Supplement to the Sixth Duke of Devonshire's Handbook *(London: Country Life Limited, 1949), 52.*

7. Chatsworth House. Photograph by the authors.

8. Devonshire House. Picadilly. Demolished. Among aristocratic mansions in London, this town house of the dukes of Devonshire was uncommon for being detached rather than terraced. Reproduced by permission of National Monuments Record: RCHME (C) Crown Copyright.

9. William Cavendish, Second Duke of Devonshire. By Charles Jervas. Devonshire Collections, Chatsworth. Reproduced by permission of the Chatsworth Settlement Trustees. Photograph Courtauld Institute of Art.

10. Rachel Russell, Duchess of Devonshire. Wife of the Second Duke. By M. Dahl. Devonshire Collections, Chatsworth. Reproduced by permission of the Chatsworth Settlement Trustees. Photograph Courtauld Institute of Art.

old at the time of her father's trial and execution, she had been taken by her mother to see her father imprisoned at the Tower.[30] Her mother had later written about her: "Those whose age can afford them remembrance, should, methinks, have some solemn thoughts for so irreparable a loss to themselves and family."[31] Attending the proclamation of William and Mary as king and queen, Rachel pronounced herself "very much pleased" to see them take the place of "King James, my father's murderer."[32] Lady Russell tried to turn the family's suffering for the whig cause to her son-in-law's political advantage. Soon after William Cavendish's return in 1691, his "friends," including Lady Russell, exerted their influence to have him stand for member of parliament for Westminster. Lady Russell warned off other potential whig candidates, reminding them of their political debts: "I believe the good his father did in the House of Commons . . . will be of advantage to this [William Cavendish's candidacy]. And it will not hurt his interest that he is married to my Lord Russell's daughter."[33] The Russell name was then thought so great a guarantee of political success that in 1695 two of the principal government whigs unsuccessfully tried to talk Lady Russell into letting her fifteen-year-old son stand for parliament, certain that he would be elected and bring in another whig with him.[34]

That year her oldest son, William, began his parliamentary career as member for Derbyshire, his home county. The Russells, like the Cavendishes, had received official recognition for their services the year before, when William's father was raised to a duke and Rachel's grandfather, William Russell, became the first duke of Bedford, an honor that would have gone to her father if he had lived.

The revolution of 1688–89 elevated the Cavendish family and at the same time gave it political direction. The Declaration of Rights of 1689, enacted as the Bill of Rights, prescribed the religion of the monarch, limited his prerogative powers, increased the powers of parliament, and in general discouraged the prospects of despotic monarchy.[35] The Declaration had left open to dispute the exact relations between king and parliament, and William Cavendish, as marquess of Hartington, stood over the gaps. (The duke of Devonshire had a subsidiary title marquess of Hartington, which his eldest son was allowed to borrow as a courtesy title.) Hartington's actions in the House of Commons suggest the

[30] Mary Berry, *Some Account of the Life of Rachael Wriothesley Lady Russell . . .* (London, 1819), 36.

[31] Lady Rachel Russell to her daughter Rachel Russell, [1687], in *Some Account . . . Lady Russell*, 81.

[32] Rachel, duchess of Devonshire, to a friend, Feb. 1689, in *Some Account . . . Lady Russell*, 93–96, on 95.

[33] Lady Rachel Russell to Mr. Owen, 23 Oct. 1691, in *Letters of Lady Russell*, 532–34, on 533.

[34] William L. Sachse, *Lord Somers: A Political Portrait* (Manchester: Manchester University Press, 1975), 107.

[35] Lois G. Schwoerer, "The Bill of Rights, 1689, Revisited," in *The World of William and Mary: Anglo-Dutch Perspectives on the Revolution of 1688–89*, ed. D. H. Hoak and M. Feingold (Stanford: Stanford University Press, 1996), pp. 42–58, on pp. 47, 57.

political identity he created for himself. Rarely participating in committee work on so-called private bills, which dealt with local problems such as bridge repair and individual estates, he preferred to address general questions, for example, the king's request to retain a large army after the peace of Ryswick. He opposed the request, as did parliament, on the grounds that it was forbidden by the Bill of Rights as a threat to English liberty.[36] At the beginning of the eighteenth century, the criticism of government was redirected toward the king and his ministers for corrupting parliament, which itself was now seen as a threat to liberty.[37] William extended his concern with rights of the House of Commons to the "Rights and Liberties" of "all the Commons of England," asserting the subject's right to address the king for calling, sitting, and dissolving parliament, his right to a speedy trial on every charge including impeachment, and his right to vote as standing above the privileges of the House. In the House of Commons, William came to be closely associated with Robert Walpole.[38] William subsequently moved to the House of Lords as the second duke of Devonshire when his father died in 1707, having ordered inscribed on his tomb, "Here lies William duke of Devonshire, a faithful subject of good princes, and an enemy to tyrants."

Although this is not the place to discuss in detail the career of the second duke of Devonshire, we believe it is important to give the reader an idea of it, since it enters into our understanding of his son Lord Charles and his grandson Henry Cavendish. First, his, the second duke's, public position determined theirs; for them, and for all those with whom they came into contact, their being a Cavendish was a matter of no small significance. Second, the nature of the duke's career reveals much about his understanding of his public role and obligations. Lord Charles Cavendish brought similar attitudes to his own public service, whether it was in politics or in science, and we see them in his son Henry as well. Although in his scientific work, Henry Cavendish would not have had in mind specifically his family's political principles, there is nonetheless a similarity of aspirations; if the Cavendishes secured the ancient rights and laws of the kingdom, why should not a Cavendish aim as high in any other endeavor, including the search for the fundamental ruling laws of nature?

At the time Cavendish entered science, the whig cause with which his family was identified was nearly spent, and in a very general sense, power in society was coming to be determined less by custom and more by rule over nature, which included the experimental manipulation of nature. As human progress was seen to depend less on traditional authority and increasingly on the "authority of

---

36 Henry Horowitz, *Parliament, Policy and Politics in the Reign of William III* (Newark: University of Delaware Press, 1977), 250.

37 Schwoerer, "The Bill of Rights," pp. 49, 57.

38 Horowitz, *Parliament*, 302–3. *Cobbett's Parliamentary History of England. From the Norman Conquest, in 1066, to the Year 1803*, vol. 6: *Comprising the Period from the Accession of Queen Anne in 1702, to the Accession of King George the First in 1714* (London, 1810), cols. 256–57, 301.

experiment," landed families such as the Cavendishes had a vested interest in the world of Henry Cavendish. As improvers of their estates, which comprised gardens, farms, mines, and investments in technical properties such as canals, they were unwitting Baconians.[39] Through their work in and for science, Lord Charles, in the second half of his life, and Henry, throughout his life, were not as removed from the practical concerns of their family as might first appear. The fifth duke of Devonshire, a man of conventional opinions, may have had a glimmering of it, even as he judged Henry Cavendish, his working cousin, to be the black sheep of the family.

[39] Larry Stewart, *The Rise of Public Science: Rhetoric, Technology, and Natural Philosophy in Newtonian Britain, 1660–1750*, (Cambridge: Cambridge University Press, 1992), 253, 384–85, 391–93.

CHAPTER 2

POLITICS

EARLY YEARS AND EDUCATION

Lord Charles Cavendish was born in July or August of 1704.[1] He joined three sisters and two brothers in the nursery of William and Rachel Cavendish, Lord and Lady Hartington. At least three more girls and one more boy were born into the family during the next few years.

When Charles was three, his paternal grandfather, the first duke of Devonshire, died, and his father took possession of the title and of the extensive properties of the Devonshires. The new Devonshire House at Piccadilly, the grand Derbyshire House of Chatsworth, Hardwick Hall in Nottinghamshire, and several other houses could now all be called home by the Cavendish children, even if they did not live in all of them. For a while their homes also included Southampton House, the London residence of their maternal grandmother, Lady Rachel Russell. They visited the houses of their other Russell relatives: Woburn Abbey in Bedfordshire, their mother's girlhood home; Stratton House in Hampshire, their grandmother Russell's country estate; and Belvoir Castle in Leicestershire.[2]

[1] We deduce Lord Charles's probable birthdate from several facts: he became a member of the House of Commons in 1725, and the standard practice for the son of an aristocratic family was to enter an election right after his majority. Corresponding to the assumption that he was therefore born in 1704, we have a remark in a letter by the duchess of Queensberry to Lady Hartington, Lord Charles's mother, dated 4 July [1704], Devon. Coll., no. 94.1: "I believe before now the wedding is over in your family and I hope the next news we hear from it will be your having follow'd my example in bringing a son," which suggests that Lady Hartington was expecting a child soon. The order of births of the other Cavendish children, for some of whom the birthdates are known, make an earlier date not very likely. Neither does the fact that Charles received independent means of support from his father only a week before his election to parliament in April 1725, since if he had been 21 already, he would have already been receiving a regular annuity. Devon. Coll., L/19/31.

[2] Lois G. Schwoerer, *Lady Rachel Russell, "One of the Best of Women"* (Baltimore: The Johns Hopkins University Press, 1988), 222. Schwoerer lists the Russell family homes and refers to Lady Russell's closeness to her children. Various family letters from this period and later refer to members of the family visiting one another.

Inside their various substantial four walls, the Cavendishes enjoyed informal relationships. Unlike many other aristocratic families, for example, the duke of Kent's, Lord Charles's family did not use formal titles for one another. In their letters, even after they were adults, Charles's sisters referred to their mother as "mama," not "her Grace," the title appropriate for a duchess, and they wrote of "brother Charles" rather than "Lord Charles" and of "Granmama Russell" rather than "Lady Russell." Charles's sister Elizabeth suggests the warmth of those relationships when, in 1721, after the deaths of their eldest sister, Mary, and their youngest brother, John, she wrote to another brother James, who was abroad, about Charles, who was about to join him: "It was some comfort to have one of you, but when both are gone I shall find great change when I consider I was once happy in ye company of so many brothers and s^{s}; but it is a thought I cannot bear to think of."[3]

Of his siblings, two brothers, William and James, and four sisters, Mary, Rachel, Elizabeth, and Anne, survived into adulthood with Charles. Their earliest education was probably under the care of tutors and governesses. Their grandmother, Lady Rachel Russell, who on her mother's side was of Huguenot origins, had advocated using the French refugees as tutors in the 1680s.[4] Later she entertained some negative views of the instruction offered by French tutors, but she nevertheless took considerable trouble to find one for her grandchildren by another daughter.[5] The Cavendishes may have followed her lead, since the whole family continued the close connection with their Ruvigny relatives, now settled in Greenwich and parts of Hampshire.[6] At any rate, when James and Charles toured the Continent in 1721–24, they did so under the care of a Frenchman, a Mr. Cotteau.[7] The Cavendish daughters were educated to interests as commonsensical as their brothers. On her honeymoon, Rachel reported to her brother James on a visit to the Derby silk mills, "thought to be one of the finest inventions that ever was seen of the kind."[8] Elizabeth was even more impetuous and independent than Rachel, if we can judge from the few extant letters. Seeing her life as "idle," she wrote to James: "I only wish I was your brother instead of your sister and then I would have bin partaker with you in your travels." Forced to remain behind, she informed her brothers of the politics of the day. Looking at it from the heights of her father's position in the House of Lords and in Walpole's government, she

---

[3] Lady Elizabeth Cavendish to Lord James Cavendish, 13 Feb. [1721] and 24 April [1721], and Lady Rachel Morgan to Lord James Cavendish, 26 September [1723]. Devon. Coll., nos. 166.0, 166.1, and 167.0, respectively.

[4] Mary Berry, *Some Account of the Life of Rachael Wriothesley Lady Russell* . . . (London, 1819), 73.

[5] Schwoerer, *Lady Rachel Russell*, 227.

[6] Ibid. Samuel Smiles, *The Huguenots: Their Settlements, Churches, and Industries in England and Ireland* (New York, 1868), 208–11, 314.

[7] Rachel Cavendish, duchess of Devonshire, to Lord James Cavendish, about 1722, 20 March, 12 July, and 11 Nov. 1723, and 13 Feb. 1724. Devon. Coll., nos. 30.10, 30.11, 30.12, 30.13, and 30.14, respectively.

[8] Lady Rachel Morgan to Lord James Cavendish, 26 September [1723].

approved of a minister who did not enrich himself by his office, and she reported the birth of a prince causing "very great" joy among the people as a political advantage, the birth coming "very seasonably to stir up ye spirit of loyalty in ye people who are in a general dissatisfaction with ye king and parliament who they think don't go ye way to redrys their grivances caus'd by ye south sea."[9]

The Cavendish boys received only the beginnings of their education at home. Their grandmother, Lady Rachel Russell, was of the opinion that "our nobility should pass some of their time" at a university, noting that among them university education "has been for many years neglected,"[10] a view which was shared by her daughter and son-in-law Devonshire, who sent their eldest son, the sixteen-year-old William, to Oxford in 1715, entering him at New College. As a member of a whig family in a tory citadel, William joined with other whigs, only to find their group the target of a mob. In 1717, two months after they were attacked, he was granted the degree of Master of Arts and left Oxford. The family biographer comments on how quickly a duke's son could attain that degree; considering that prudence was a characteristic trait of the Cavendish family and, in particular, of Lord William's parents, his political adventures and his leaving Oxford may have been related.[11] His brothers, in any case, were not sent to a university.

Lord Charles and Lord James began their formal schooling at Eton, where they were entrusted to Dr. Andrew Snape, headmaster from 1711 to 1720, on the recommendation of Robert Walpole, their father's friend and political ally. In 1718, for which there exists a "Bill of Eton Schole," Charles, then fourteen, was in the fifth year, a grade in the Lower School known as Lower Greek, and James was two years ahead of him.[12] Neither boy finished the entire course, which for Charles would have required another five years. Both were heading in a direction other than the university, for which they probably were not prepared in their knowledge of ancient languages in any case. Young noblemen, as the advice given to the father of one of them in 1723 shows, had other options: "Tho' he does not ply his book close," this father was told about his son, it may not proceed from the want of capacity and inclination "but rather from his studying in

9 Lady Elizabeth Cavendish to Lord James Cavendish, 24 April [1721].

10 Lady Rachel Russell to John Roos (Manners), 5 Nov. 1692, in *Letters of Lady Rachel Russell; from the Manuscript in the Library at Woburn Abbey* . . . 5th ed. (London, 1793), 550.

11 Joseph Foster, *Alumni Oxonienses: The Members of the University of Oxford, 1715–1886* . . ., 4 vols. (London, 1891) 1:231. Francis Bickley, *The Cavendish Family* (London: Constable, 1911), 189–90.

12 R. A. Austen Leigh, *Eton College Lists 1678–1790* (Eton: Spottiswoods, 1907), xxiv–xxvii, 14–18. J. H. Plumb, *Sir Robert Walpole,* vol. 1: *The Making of a Statesman* (London: The Cresset Press, 1956), 253. H. C. Maxwell Lyte, *A History of Eton College 1440–1884* (London, 1889), 286–87. The "lower master" of the lower school in 1718 was Francis Goode, who held that position from 1716 to 1734, succeeding Thomas Carter. There were four lower school assistants that year, Thomas Thackeray, Adam Elliot, John Burchett, and Charles Willats, most of whom were drawn from King's College, Cambridge, but Burchett was from Peterhouse. *Eton College Lists,* xxxv. It was customary at Eton for the "sons of wealthy persons to have private tutors," who were not the same as the assistant masters. Lyte, *History of Eton College,* 4th ed. (London, 1911), 284.

the dead languages, which he has not been well grounded in. I have knowen severall instances of this and if it be the case or perhaps his being too much indulged in sloth when younger, I do not see why either of them should be a reason for breaking off his studies. He can read in Italian and French most of the things that are necessary for a gentleman, and tho' he should not give a very close application, something usefull will stick; and who knows but by degrees he may come to like what he now has ane aversion to. Were he mine, I would make him spend some time at Geneva in the studie of the law, should it be only to keep him from being imposed upon by pettyfoggers. Historie and geometry are accomplishments fitt for a gentleman and surely he can never serve his country or famely without knowledge, and geometry, if he give in to it, will at all times be ane amusement when he cannot be more profitably imploy'd. When he has made a tolerable progress in these, it will not be amiss that he make a tour in France and Italy that he may learn from observation what he has not gote by reading."[13]

The reference was to the by now obligatory grand tour that began in France, perhaps passed through Holland and Switzerland, and then settled down to a residence in Italy, home of Rome and the Renaissance. No Englishman could pretend to an education or any degree of sophistication without this tour, two or three years abroad being the rule, a just compensation for having been born in backwater England.[14] Some formal study might be combined with the sightseeing and cultural exposure. Lords Anthony and Henry de Grey, the sons of the duke of Kent and the brothers of Lord Charles's future wife, Lady Anne, had followed this course several years earlier. Now the sons were doing their duty: in 1716, as Lord Henry was planning to go to Geneva, Lord Anthony sent him advice from Venice: "Att Geneva you will find several persons that will be very helpful to you I don't doubt, and I shall send a letter or two to some of the best I knew there who are of the best familys, men who are pretty well acquainted with the world and whose conversations will be agreble as well as instructive, that shall wait upon you and do any service that lies in their power as soon as ever you arrive; there are like wise some of the young men I was acquainted with who will be ready enough to introduce you into any other company you shall like or care for. I suppose you intend to study a little of the Civil Law there; the person I had and who is accounted one of the best is Mr Guip a diligent and Studious man and likewise understanding in History and Chronology." Having followed his own stay in Geneva with travels in Italy, Lord Anthony displayed in the remainder of his letter that he had profited from the lessons in history, having become a careful observer of "antiquities."[15]

---

[13] Great Britain, Historical Manuscripts Commission, *Report on the Manuscripts of Lord Polwarth, Formerly Preserved at Mertoun House, Berwickshire*, ed. H. Paton, vol. 3 (London: His Majesty's Stationary Office, 1931), 287–88.

[14] J. H. Plumb, *Men and Centuries* (Boston: Houghton Mifflin, 1963), 55–60.

[15] Anthony de Grey, Earl of Harrold, to Lord Henry de Grey, about 1716, Bedfordshire Record Office, Wrest Park Collection, L 30/5.

Lord James Cavendish, whose later exploits suggest an early interest in horsemanship and an active life, was probably, and quite appropriately, intended for the military. By 1721, he had gone from Eton to the "academy" in Lorraine, and Lord Charles was then about to join him. Two years later, Lord James was writing to his mother from Geneva,[16] with the likelihood that he continued his education in both Lorraine and Geneva.

The "Académie d'Exercises" at Nancy, the capital of Lorraine, had been established in 1699, soon after Lorraine had been taken back from the French and reconstituted a duchy by the Treaty of Ryswick of 1697. Although the dukes of Lorraine were allowed no army of their own, their military academy attracted young foreign aristocrats, some carrying "the greatest names of Europe." By 1713 the academy had added a course in public law to its curriculum, and Duke Leopold himself established one in natural law. The academy had the purpose of educating cadets for the court guards, the only military body aside from a civilian militia still remaining to the dukes. This close association with the court affected the location of the academy. In 1702, at the start of the War of the Spanish Succession, the French had reoccupied Nancy, forcing Leopold to withdraw with his court to his castle at Lunéville, a building then too ancient to be suitable for an eighteenth-century ducal residence. Leopold replaced the old structure with a large, new residence, which gradually became the official capital of the dukedom even after Nancy had been freed of the French again in 1714. In 1719 a fire temporarily set back this development by destroying the ducal apartments at Lunéville, apparently forcing the court back to Nancy for a short time. It was during this period that Lord James Cavendish joined the academy. Seeing an opportunity for further building, Duke Leopold added a "cabinet des herbes," a good library, and a physical cabinet to his Lunéville residence. Under the influence of Newton's physics and determined to do his own experimenting, he constructed some of the necessary instruments himself and bought the rest, a beautiful and expensive collection from London. In the spring of 1721, just before Lord Charles joined his brother in Lorraine, the duke moved his military academy from Nancy to Lunéville,[17] bringing it into the immediate neighborhood of the scientific facilities he had assembled there.

[16] Lady Elizabeth Cavendish to Lord James Cavendish, 13 Feb. and 24 April [1721]. Rachel Cavendish, duchess of Devonshire, to Lord James Cavendish, 11 Nov. [1723].

[17] Michel Parisse, Stéphane Gaber, and Gérard Canini, *Grandes dates de l'histoire lorraine* (Nancy: Service des Publications de l'Université de Nancy II, 1982), 43. Michel Antoine, "La cour de Lorraine dans l'Europe des lumières," 69–76, and Claude Collot, "La faculté de droit de l'Université de Pont-à-Mousson et de Nancy au XVIIIe siècle," 215–26, both papers in *La Lorraine dans l'Europe des lumières. Actes du colloque organisé par la Faculté des lettres et des sciences humaines de l'Université de Nancy, Nancy, 24–27 octobre 1966.* Series *Annales de l'Est.* Memoire 34. (Nancy: Faculté des lettres et sciences humaines de l'Université, 1968), 70–72, 218. Edmond Delorme, *Lunéville et son arrondissement* (Marseilles: Laffitte Reprints, 1977), 3, 17, 18, 111. Pierre Boyé, *Les Chateaux du Roi Stanislas en Lorraine* (Marseilles: Laffitte Reprints, 1980), 3–4.

Lord Charles Cavendish left London for his education and tour abroad in March 1721, undoubtedly with another party traveling to Paris, since he was to be met there by his brother Lord James's valet, and as the seventeen-year-old son of a duke he would not have been sent off alone.[18] Expected to be with James by mid-April, he instead stayed on in Paris for three weeks longer than planned. As Lord Anthony de Grey had informed his brother a few years earlier, in Paris there were "many things" to be "observed." "You will not stay long there perhaps the first time only see a little of the Town. . . . You wont ommitt however the sight of the most principal things, as the Louvre, the Tuilleries, Place Vendosme & Victoire, Place Royal, the Luxemburg, the Church of Notre dam, L'hotel des invalides, Versailles, Trianon."[19] Both his initial visit to Paris and his stay there with Lord James for several months in 1723–24 came at a favorable stage in English-French relations, during the regency of the duke of Orléans and immediately after. The friendly climate toward England at court was accompanied by a resurgence of cultural life in Paris as, following the death of Louis XIV in 1715, the French aristocrats returned from Versailles to Paris.[20] The flourishing arts, operas, theater, and other entertainments lured so many of the British to Paris in these years that the resident at Paris, Thomas Crawford, complained in 1723 that we "should have had the halfe of the people of England" there if it had not been for the unsafe conditions of the roads; "this town began to be full of London apprentices that came running over here with their superfluous money instead of going to Tunbrige," an English resort.[21] The regency was also marked by another interest of the duke of Orléans, this one much closer to Lord Charles's eventual concerns, the natural sciences and the "improvement of the implements and appliances of the mechanical arts."[22] René Antoine Réaumur, the regent's protégée at the Paris Academy of Sciences, published his important study of the iron and steel industry in Paris in 1722, which may well have come to Lord Charles's attention, given the practical bent of his family and their ownership of Derbyshire lead mines.[23] As a Cavendish, indeed, he may have enjoyed even more direct exposure to the Parisian scientific world, but we have no evidence for that.

[18] Lady Elizabeth Cavendish to Lord James Cavendish, 13 Feb. [1721]. One party bound for Paris which Lord Charles might have joined was that of the English ambassador in France, Sir Lucas Schaub, a young man of thirty-one, who planned to leave London for Paris on 23 Feb./6 March. That plan, given that the trip took four to five days if all went smoothly, would have put him in Paris in the second week of March, the time when Lord James was to send his valet to meet Lord Charles. In the event, Schaub did not leave London until March 1/12, which may account for the delay in Lord Charles's plans, too. *Manuscripts of Lord Polwarth* 3:49, 52.

[19] Anthony de Grey, earl of Harrold, to Lord Henry de Grey, about 1716.

[20] James Breck Perkins, *France under the Regency with a Review of the Administration of Louis XIV* (Boston and New York, 1892), 374–96, 554–57, 559–62.

[21] Thomas Crawford to Lord Polwarth, 9 Oct. [28 Sep.] 1723, in *Manuscripts of Lord Polwarth* 3:308–9, on 309.

[22] Perkins, *France under the Regency*, 556.

[23] J. B. Gough, "Réaumur, René-Antoine Ferchault de," *DSB* 11:327–35, on 328.

After Paris, if he proceeded as planned, Lord Charles joined Lord James at Lunéville, and for nearly two years after that, until late in 1722 or early in 1723, his activities and whereabouts can only be conjectured. Given the pattern of his brother's stay abroad, Lord Charles may very well have spent a year at Lunéville. During the winter of 1722–23, the brothers were traveling together with a tutor, probably in the south. Lord James had been tempted into gambling, prompting his mother to point out to him that the "right use" of their travels should be "seeing what is most curious in ye places you pass thru & making y^r^ observations upon 'em." The following March, Lord James was staying with a prince and princess, an "expensive enuff" way of life, his mother comments in a discussion of his allowance. Neither the duchess's letter to Lord James in March nor another one in the middle of July refers to Lord Charles, making it likely that Lord Charles spent some time on his own in Geneva, from where he had written to his mother that summer or fall.[24]

The Académie de Calvin in Geneva had attracted not only the sons of the duke of Kent, but also the sons of several great English and Scottish families, including the Cavendishes. In 1723, four professors at the academy offered courses in civil and natural law and in philosophy, including, apparently, natural philosophy, since one of its students, the later mathematician Gabriel Cramer, had only recently completed a thesis on sound and next year would compete for the chair of philosophy; he received a share in the chair of mathematics instead, with the assignment of teaching algebra and astronomy.[25] If Lord Charles did not meet Cramer at the academy that year, he may have become acquainted with him through Cramer's brother Jean, the new professor of civil and natural law, who was only twenty-two at the time. At any rate, when Gabriel Cramer visited London sometime between 1727 and 1729, he was easily received into the circle of mathematicians and Fellows of the Royal Society connected with Lord Charles.[26]

[24] Rachel Cavendish, duchess of Devonshire, to Lord James Cavendish, late 1722 or early 1723, and 20 Mar. 1723.

[25] Charles Borgeaud, *Histoire de l'Université de Genève. L'Académie de Calvin 1559–1798* (Genève: Georg, 1900), 442, 641–42. According to the registers of students, the Cavendishes who attended the Geneva academy were Lord Charles Cavendish's great-grandfather William Cavendish, who was accompanied there by his tutor Thomas Hobbes, the philosopher, and Lord Charles's grandfather William Cavendish, the later first duke of Devonshire. However, the registers are not complete, particularly not on foreign noblemen, who might have stayed in Geneva only a few months. Anthony de Grey, earl of Harrold, who studied law in Geneva for a while, for example, does not appear in the register; the absence of Lord Charles's name there is no indication that he did not attend the academy or study with a private teacher in Geneva. Sven Stelling-Michaud and Suzanne Stelling-Michaud, ed., *Le livre du recteur de l'académie de Genève*, vols. 1–3 (Genève: Droz, 1959–72). On the registers: Michael Heyd, *Between Orthodoxy and the Enlightenment. Jean-Robert Chouet and the Introduction of Cartesian Science in the Academy of Geneva* (Boston: Martinus Nijhoff, 1982), 245–47.

[26] Cramer and Lord Charles Cavendish were exact contemporaries. Cramer's travels were a part of his appointment at Geneva and intended for his further education. The scientists he met in England included Nicholas Saunderson, Halley, Sloane, De Moivre, and Stirling. Phillip S. Jones, "Cramer, Gabriel," *DSB* 3:459–62, on 459.

In November of 1723 Lords James and Charles Cavendish were together again, having only just arrived in Paris. Their stay in France required a doubling of their allowances, each now getting £100 annually, and advice about greater caution on the roads: "be very carefull now you are in France," their mother wrote, "how you travel, & also of being out late in ye streets wch they tel me is very dangerious, murthers being there soe common."[27] They spent the winter there, still under the care of Mr. Cotteau, with their mail reaching them through the banker Jean Louis Goudet. In February 1724, when the end of their tour was in sight, they appealed to their parents to stay a few months longer. "Relating to y^{r} return into England," the duchess wrote, "I believe y^{r} father in that wo'd be willing to do what he thought was most agreeable to y^{r} own inclinations. Mr Cotteau writs word you imploy y^{r} time so well, that he thinks it might be for y^{r} advantage if you stay'd in France some months longer, but in y^{r} next you may let me know what y^{r} own thoughts are, y^{r} coming back by Holland is what I believe my L^{d} designes if you like it."[28] Lords Charles and James had their way. They also followed their father's plan of returning home by way of Holland, a detour that very nearly cost Lord Charles his life. On 24 September that year, in "blowing Stormy weather," Captain Gregory of the Katherine Yacht at Ostend "about Three in the afternoon was unhappily Surprized by a Passage Boat oversetting just under my Stern, in which were Two of his Grace the Duke of Devonshire's Sons, viz the Lord James and Charles, with their Governor and Servants, who by the assistance of my People were all most miraculously Saved, particularly Lord Charles, who Sunk under my Counter, and was carried by a very Strong Tide between me and another Ship under water, till he got as far forward as my Stern, where he arose, and got hold of my Shoar fast, from whence we Saved his Lordship, though almost Spent." Lords James and Charles had been on their way to Calais, which suggests that they were coming from Holland, probably The Hague. After losing "most of their Baggage and Apparel, except what they had Ordered to Calais," in the accident, the Cavendish brothers decided to stay with Captain Gregory for the crossing. The captain's report of the accident reached their father by courtesy of the admiralty on 5 October.[29] Lords Charles and James undoubtedly followed close behind, Charles having been abroad for three and a half years.

HOUSE OF COMMONS

In 1725, the year after his return from his tour of the Continent, Lord Charles was elected to the House of Commons. Taking his seat as a Member

[27] Rachel Cavendish, duchess of Devonshire, to Lord James Cavendish, 11 Nov. [1723].

[28] Rachel Cavendish, duchess of Devonshire, to Lord James Cavendish, 13 Feb. [1724].

[29] J. Burchett to William Cavendish, duke of Devonshire, 5 Oct. 1724, with the enclosure of a "Copy of a Letter from Captain Gregory of the Katherine Yacht to Mr Burchett dated the 25th of September 1724 O. S. from Ostend," Devon. Coll., no. 179.0.

of Parliament for Heytesbury, Wiltshire,[30] in the parliamentary session of 1725–26, he joined all but two of the adult males of his family: his eldest brother, Lord Hartington, his uncle Lord James Cavendish, his two brothers-in-law, Sir Thomas Lowther and Sir William Morgan, and a first cousin. The two exceptions were his father, who as duke of Devonshire sat in the House of Lords and was then lord president of the privy council, and his brother Lord James Cavendish, who was in the military, putting off his brief stint in the Commons by fifteen years, until just before his death. Lord Charles Cavendish could have had no doubt about what was expected of him. To get a proper image of the inevitability of that particular blueprint for an aristocrat's life it should be noted that except for his uncle, Lord Charles and his relatives in the Commons were all under thirty, he being the youngest then at twenty-one. This dense representation in the Commons of an aristocratic family like the Cavendishes was only partly due to politics; apart from his father's close association with Robert Walpole, the head of the current whig administration, Lord Charles was in the Commons as a representative of his family's private interest. Very suitably, therefore, he made his first appearance in the Journal of the House of Commons in April of 1726 in connection with a private bill drawn up by his brother concerning the estate of his brother-in-law Sir Thomas Lowther, who had petitioned the Commons that his family be granted the inheritance of Furness monastery in Lancashire, establishing permanently an old family claim.[31] In the same year Cavendish dealt with another private bill that was at the same time about a matter of public importance, and it was also his first parliamentary exposure to a technical problem. The bill followed a long series of parliamentary acts providing for the draining of the Bedford Level fens, a huge tract of marshland to the south and west of The Wash in eastern England. In the seventeenth century, Francis Russell, fourth earl of Bedford, and his son and successor, William, later first duke of Bedford (Lord Charles Cavendish's ancestors), had organized about eighty landowners into a corporation of "adventurers" to finance the draining of these plains, which were still common land, in return for a portion of the resulting farmland. Having invested more in this undertaking and also profited more than any of the other members of the corporation, the Russells were still at the head of it in 1726, but the present duke was then a minor and the project was in the hands of his uncle and guardian, the duke of Devonshire. For Lord Charles Cavendish, it even had a direct connection, since as a younger son he derived income from his mother Rachel Russell's interest in the Russell estates. With the methods then in place to drain the Bedford Level, the new farmland was frequently flooded, and the bill with which Lord Charles

[30] Romney Sedgwick, *The House of Commons 1715–1754*, 2 vols. (New York: Oxford University Press, 1970) 1:536.

[31] Great Britain, Parliament, *House of Commons Journals* (*HCJ*) 20:600–70. Entries from 4 Mar. 1726/27 to 19 Apr. 1726.

Cavendish was involved was a proposal to reduce flooding by constructing a new, steeper "outfall."[32]

Re-elected in 1727, but from the large constituency of Westminster instead of small Heytesbury,[33] Cavendish's involvement in the House's activities increased in 1728 and 1729, only to be followed by four years of personal problems arising especially from his wife Anne's struggle with tuberculosis, which kept him away from his duties much of the time. When, in 1733, his wife died, Cavendish immersed himself in his duties in the Commons. The regular problems of Westminster were typical of cities: repairing streets in "ruinous Condition," clearing them of the "Filth and Dirt" that covered them, and keeping them safe at night.[34] In 1729, for example, Cavendish and his colleagues crafted a bill to correct the ill effects of having several different privately owned "waterworks" lay water lines and cover them with pavement that was neither level nor strong and lasting enough.[35] A few weeks later he and his fellow Member of Parliament William Clayton were ordered "to bring in a Bill for appointing a better nightly Watch, and regulating the Beadles . . . and for better enlightening the Streets, and publick Passages."[36] He worked on such problems for Westminster again in 1736 and 1737 though he had left this constituency.[37] Westminster was at times difficult to represent because it was the seat of parliament and because it was contiguous with London. Popular dissatisfaction with local or national matters sometimes took on tangible form; the streets bills in 1729, for example, brought out a great crowd, whose complaints the Commons refused to hear. During these years the city was in vehement opposition to much of Walpole's administrative program, as in 1733, when Walpole's handling of the proposed excise on tobacco brought not only local opponents but also the London mob to Westminster; Members of Parliament complained of a "tumultuous Crowd" who "menaced, insulted, and assaulted" them as they left the House. By order of the Commons, Cavendish and Clayton had to notify the high bailiff of Westminster that such actions constituted a crime and an infringement on the privileges of the Commons.[38]

---

[32] Samuel Wells, *The History of the Drainage of the Great Level of the Fens, Called Bedford Level: With the Constitution and Laws of the Bedford Level Corporation*, 2 vols. (London, 1830) 1:424–26, 661–62, 744–45. 4 Mar. 1726 (1725) and 10 May 1726 *HCJ* 20:599, 697. H. C. Darby, "The Draining of the Fens, A.D. 1600–1800," in *An Historical Geography of England before A. D. 1800*, ed. H. C. Darby (Cambridge: Cambridge University Press, 1936), 444–64, on 456–59.

[33] Sedgwick, *House* 1:285. 21 July 1727, St. Margaret's Vestry, Minutes 1724–1733, Westminster City Archives, E 2419.

[34] 4 Feb. 1729 (1728), *HCJ* 21:208.

[35] 19 Feb. 1729 (1728), *HCJ* 21:229.

[36] 10 Apr. 1729, *HCJ* 21:313.

[37] 16, 25 Mar. 1736 (1735) and 14, 21 Feb. 1737 (1736), *HCJ* 22:633, 652, and 22:746, 756.

[38] 12, 13 Apr. 1733, *HCJ* 22:115–16. Plumb, *Walpole* 2:262–71.

11. *House of Commons, 1741–42. From an engraving by Benjamin Cole, after John Pine, 1749. Lord Charles Cavendish represented several successive constituencies in the Commons between 1725 and 1741. Frontispiece, Romney Sedgwick,* The History of Parliament: The House of Commons 1715–1754, *vol. 1 (New York: Oxford University Press, 1970).*

After representing Westminster for seven years, Cavendish was elected Member of Parliament for Derbyshire, his last constituency, one which he also served for seven years. At Westminster, like his predecessors there, Lord Charles Cavendish had been elected with whig support. Derbyshire, however, had long been in the hands of the tories; Cavendish was the first whig to be elected for the county since his father had lost the seat over thirty years before, and Cavendish's election was close.[39] His fellow Member of Parliament there was in fact a tory, Nathaniel Curzon, a lawyer and land- and mine-owner who voted consistently against the administration.[40] Other counties in the area, such as Lancashire, Cheshire, and Yorkshire, were also represented by tories, even ardent Jacobites. Cavendish was often not nominated to committees dealing with matters of concern to Derbyshire, although, as its representative, he could not be excluded from such committees, since the speaker of the House had the obligation to add to a committee any member who had a legitimate interest in the matter in question.[41] Cavendish was very actively engaged in only a few private acts initiated by his constituency in Derbyshire, altogether drawing up only four bills for them, but he worked on a number of private acts that benefited Derbyshire even if they did not deal with the county directly.

The subject of these private acts was road repair. The administration of English roads had been undergoing an important change from the beginning of the century. As the uses of the roads evolved from mainly local foot and animal traffic to through traffic for carriages and wagons, the roads were gradually converted into turnpikes, forcing the principal users to contribute to their upkeep. At the initiative of the local parishes responsible for road maintenance, and other interested parties, parliament passed private acts establishing trusts responsible for setting up, financing, and maintaining the new turnpikes. The earliest of these had been along the main roads leading to London, two of which, the Great North Road and the road from London to Manchester, by the 1730s had already been turnpiked over considerable distances, and in some areas, the original turnpike trusts were already up for renewal. For Derbyshire coal trade, industry, and agriculture, it was important to complete the turnpiking of these roads and the east–west roads lying between them as well.[42]

---

39 Sedgwick, *House* 1:223. In his first run for a seat from Derbyshire, Cavendish's vote was 2,081, the runner-up tory Curzon's, 2,044, and the third candidate, the loser Harper's, 1,795. Places where the Cavendishes owned property, such as Normanton, gave almost all their votes to Cavendish. Other places such as Thornhill and Pilsley, just outside Chatsworth, gave him virtually no votes. *A Copy of a Poll Taken for the County of Derby, The 16th, 17th, 18th, and 20th Days of May, 1734 before George Mower, Esq.; High-Sheriff for the Said County* (Derby, n.d.). Devon. Coll., 95/81.

40 Sedgwick, *House* 1:599.

41 P. D. G. Thomas, *The House of Commons in the Eighteenth Century* (Oxford: Clarendon Press, 1971), 58.

42 Sidney and Beatrice Webb, *English Local Government: The Story of the King's Highway* (London: Longmans, Green and Co., 1920), 70. William Albert, *The Turnpike Road System in England 1663–1840* (Cambridge: Cambridge University Press, 1972), 31–43.

In 1735 Cavendish had himself assigned to his first turnpike committee, this one dealing with the part of the London-Manchester road closest to London.[43] Three years later he and Curzon drew up the act that was to close the longest stretch of that road yet to be turnpiked, thirty-nine miles between Loughborough and Hartington, in Leicestershire and Derbyshire, respectively.[44] Altogether he worked on twelve private acts for turnpikes either on or near the two important highways and in addition on five turnpike bills for roads west and southwest of London.[45] To no other subject did he devote as much work; his interest is strongly confirmed by his related committee work on repairing bridges, above all, by the decade of work he devoted to the building of Westminster Bridge.

For the entire sixteen years Cavendish served in parliament, Walpole was prime minster; Cavendish stepped down in 1741, Walpole in 1742. If Cavendish felt a family loyalty to Walpole, he did not always vote with Walpole. In 1725, the year Cavendish entered parliament, William Pultney broke with Walpole,[46] and there is at least the suggestion that Cavendish sympathized with Pultney's opposition whigs. In any event, Cavendish had other important interests to serve, namely, his family's, of course, but also Westminster's. His interests would seem to have been closer to the commercial and financial interests of the city than to those of the country (he sold his country home in 1736 and moved to the city) and the colonies, as is borne out by the episode of Walpole's excise tax on tobacco in 1733. Walpole almost fell from power because of it, with Cavendish doing nothing to help him. Walpole's tax was in the interest of Virginia growers, who had long resented control over their business by the London tobacco brokers. There was violent opposition to this tax in the city. Walpole's bill passed by a narrow vote, whereupon the city raised a petition against it, and Walpole's majority melted away, though he did manage to get the Commons to refuse to hear the petition. Walpole survived but not without a riot outside the Commons. Cavendish supported the bill in the beginning, but then he voted with the opposition on the city's petition against it. The king, who strongly sided with Walpole on this bill and regarded opposition to it as treason, called Lord Charles Cavendish "half mad" and Lord James Cavendish, who voted as Lord Charles did, a "fool."[47]

Cavendish's political career ended in 1741 not by defeat but by choice. Whether he sensed it or not, he left politics at about the time his family could dispense with his services. Up to the mid-1740s, but not beyond, the outcome of

[43] 18 Apr. 1735, *HCJ* 22:469.

[44] 9, 20 Mar. 1738 (1737), *HCJ* 23:73, 107.

[45] Information from *HCJ*.

[46] Plumb, *Walpole* 2:122–24, 127.

[47] Plumb, *Walpole* 2:250–71. Thomas, *House of Commons*, 68–71. John, Lord Hervey, *Memoirs of the Reign of George the Second from His Accession to the Death of Queen Caroline*, ed. J. W. Croker, vol. 1 (London, 1884), 200. Sedgwick, *House* 1:537.

the revolution of 1688–89 remained in question, for until then the tories were predominantly a Jacobite party ready to ally with France to restore the Stuart dynasty. Thereafter, the vigilance of the Devonshires could be relaxed, and Lord Charles Cavendish could with clear conscience consider another path.

As we will see, the Royal Society largely assumed the place that the House of Commons had occupied in Cavendish's life. He followed his own bent, for his political activities and associations did not in any obvious way point him in the direction of science. Of the roughly two hundred Members of Parliament with whom he served on committees during his sixteen years in the Commons, only a few were Fellows of the Royal Society, at most a dozen, with maybe another half dozen becoming Fellows after he had left parliament, and none were to become close scientific associates of his. Elected to the Royal Society about two years after he was elected to the Commons, Cavendish served on the council of the Society for the first time in 1736. He did not serve again until the year after he left parliament; thereafter he served on the council almost without interruption for twenty-five years.

GENTLEMAN OF THE BEDCHAMBER

The duke of Kent was gentleman of the bedchamber to George I, and in 1728 his future son-in-law Lord Charles Cavendish was appointed to the same position, only to the prince of Wales, Frederick. Cavendish was indeed a "gentleman," though as son of the duke of Devonshire he was referred to as "lord" of the bedchamber.[48] With this position, Cavendish was a consort to the person who stood next in line for the throne, required to be in attendance for much of the day when it came his turn. The activities surrounding the prince at court could be tedious and stupid, but Frederick had a serious interest in the arts, in music as a passable cellist, and in painting as a collector of works by Old Masters. Although he probably had little more interest in science than his father, George II, which was practically none, he was willing to be seen in the company of men of science, attending a meeting of the Royal Society at which experiments were performed.[49] Known for his rakehelly living, the prince would have had little in common temperamentally with his studious gentleman of the bedchamber, Lord Charles Cavendish, but the relations between the two young men evidently were good, for Cavendish's second son was named Frederick after the prince, who served as his godfather.

---

[48] John Edward Smith and W. Parkinson Smith, *The Parliamentary Representation of Westminster from the Thirteenth Century to the Present Day*, vol. 2 (London: Wightman, 1923), 272. James Douglas, earl of Morton, who became president of the Royal Society while Cavendish was a member, had held a parallel position at court, as lord of the bedchamber. "Douglas, James, Fourteenth Earl of Morton," *DNB* 5:1236–37, on 1236.

[49] Michael De-la-Noy, *The King Who Never Was: The Story of Frederick, Prince of Wales* (London: Peter Owen, 1996), 107, 115–16, 127, 194.

As it turned out, this prince did not live long enough to become king, but long enough to be a political force in his own right and the scandal of the reign. Frederick was born in Hanover in 1707 and remained there until December 1728, when he was brought suddenly to England because word was received at court that he was about to marry the princess royal of Prussia. The marriage had been negotiated and sanctioned by George I, but in 1727 Frederick's father, now George II, called off the marriage. Although he submitted, the prince detested his father for keeping him dependent, and when he married, with his father's approval, Princess Augusta, daughter of Frederick, duke of Saxe-Gothe, he turned this marriage into a weapon against his father. Competing with the king for popularity in the country, the prince formed an opposition court, welcoming into his household ambitious young men like Pitt, Lyttleton, and the Grenvilles, and he developed an intense dislike for his father's favorite minister, Robert Walpole. Confronted with the prince's passionate rebellion, the king drew the line in 1738; thereafter no one who paid court to the prince of Wales or his wife was admitted to the king's presence at any of the royal palaces.[50] Lord Charles Cavendish, however, had left the prince's service long before his banishment, having resigned in October 1730.[51]

[50] Duke of Grafton to [Theophilus, earl of Huntington], 27 Feb. 1738, in Great Britain, Historical Manuscripts Commission, *Report on the Manuscripts of the Late Reginald Rowden Hastings, Esq., of the Manor House, Ashby de la Zouche*, 4 vols. (London: His Majesty's Stationary Office, 1928–47) 3:22.

[51] Entry on 17 Oct. 1730 in *The Historical Register*, vol. 15: *The Chronological Diary* (London, 1730), 64.

CHAPTER 3

SCIENCE

DE MOIVRE CIRCLE

Technically speaking, Lord Charles Cavendish was a commoner, but he was nevertheless a member of the highest circle of the British aristocracy, and as such he had been brought up to the values of the aristocracy, including the principal value of "duty of service."[1] To an aristocrat such as Lord Charles, the only acceptable form of occupation (aside from administrating, but definitely not farming, his property) was public service, usually either in government or in the military, or possibly in the church. It came down to a narrow but attractive choice of occupations. The Cavendishes had served in some of the highest offices at court and in the government for almost half a century, and Lord Charles Cavendish, as we have seen, followed their example as soon as he reached maturity. Other interests, in the arts, architecture, belles lettres, various areas of scholarship, or natural science, no matter how expertly pursued, had to keep the outward appearance of an aristocrat's private indulgence, at best to be shared with friends. To publish scholarly or scientific writing for income was out of the question for Lord Charles.

The occupational limitations of the aristocracy affected Lord Charles Cavendish's work in science and his reputation, or lack of it, as a scientist. For many years he carried out scientific investigations that were valued and used by other scientists–he was even awarded the Royal Society's Copley Medal–but he published nothing except the one piece of work for which he received the medal. But he could and did contribute publicly to science in the same manner in which he had served in government: as a "parliamentarian" of science, a member of the Royal Society who served on its councils and committees, and as a member of boards and committees of other institutions. He became one of the most

[1] John Cannon, *Aristocratic Century. The Peerage of Eighteenth-Century England* (Cambridge: Cambridge University Press, 1984), 34.

important of the official representatives of science of his time in Britain, and its untiring servant. His qualifications were his scientific talent, practical ability, long parliamentary experience, and the Cavendish name. He was a good example of a kind of scientific practitioner who was useful in eighteenth-century British science but who did not survive into the later organization of science.

In 1725, the year after he returned from his Continental tour, Cavendish became a Member of Parliament, but since he was so very young, completely inexperienced, and relatively unknown, he entered slowly into the work of the Commons. As he was also relatively free of family duties, he had time to continue his education. His teacher, or one of his teachers, was almost surely the great mathematician Abraham De Moivre.

De Moivre's friend Matthew Maty drew up a list of his eminent mathematical friends: Newton, Edmond Halley, James Stirling, Nicholas Saunderson, Martin Folkes, and, on the Continent, Johann I Bernoulli and Pierre Varignon. (To this list we add from other sources William Jones[2] and Brook Taylor,[3] and there were still others.) Maty also listed De Moivre's pupils or, to use the exact French word, *disciples*: Lord Macclesfield, Charles Stanhope, George Lewis Scott, Peter Davall, James Dodson, and Cavendish.[4] (John Colson should be included among his pupils, and no doubt others.)[5]

Since Maty gave only last names, we must decide which "Cavendish" he intended. Writing in the late 1750s, Maty would not have meant Henry Cavendish, who had only recently come down from Cambridge and was not yet a Fellow of the Royal Society. Nor, we believe, is it likely that he would have had in mind William Cavendish, duke of Devonshire, for the judgment Maty wished his readers to make of De Moivre was of his standing among accomplished mathematicians and not within society at large. There are two likely possibilities, Lord Charles Cavendish and his uncle Lord James Cavendish. Both were active in the Royal Society, and both were proposed for membership in the Society by De Moivre's good friend, the eminent mathematician William Jones.[6] Both also subscribed to De Moivre's *Miscellanea analytica de seriebus et quadraturis*; published in 1730, this was the first mathematical or scientific book to which Lord Charles subscribed. The duke of Devonshire was also a subscriber to this book, and it is conceivable that Lord Charles and Lord James were both pupils of De Moivre

[2] De Moivre called William Jones his "intimate friend" in the preface to his book *The Doctrine of Chances; or, A Method of Calculating the Probability of Events in Play* (London, 1718), x.

[3] De Moivre called Brook Taylor his "Worthy Friend" in his *Doctrine of Chances*, 101. He had a correspondence with Brook Taylor, described in Ivo Schneider, "Der Mathematiker Abraham de Moivre (1667–1754)," *Archive for History of Exact Sciences* 5 (1968):177–317, on 196–97.

[4] Matthew Maty, *Mémoire sur la vie et sur les éscrits de Mr. Abraham de Moivre* (The Hague, 1760), 39.

[5] In the foreword to his first book, *Animadversiones*, De Moivre referred to John Colson as one of his pupils, noted by Schneider, "Abraham de Moivre," 189.

[6] Lord James Cavendish was proposed for membership in the Royal Society on 19 Mar. 1718/19, and was admitted on 16 Apr. 1719. Royal Society, JB 11:311, 326.

12. Abraham De Moivre. Painting by Joseph Highmore, 1736. Reproduced by permission of the President and Council of the Royal Society.

and that various Devonshires were as well. (De Moivre called at the Devonshire house in London, possibly in the capacity of mathematical tutor; see below.) Because of the reasonable certainty that by "Cavendish," Maty meant Lord Charles Cavendish, and, in any event, because of the evidence it provides of the mathematical education of the Cavendish family, we include the following brief discussion of De Moivre.

The friends and pupils of De Moivre spanned two generations: De Moivre was Newton's junior by twenty-five years and Lord Charles's senior by about the same number of years. Many of De Moivre's friends and pupils were prominent in the Royal Society: Newton, Folkes, and Macclesfield were presidents; Cavendish, Jones, Davall, Scott, and Stanhope were members of the council; Halley was a paid corresponding secretary and also editor of the *Philosophical Transactions*; and Taylor, like Maty, was a secretary. De Moivre's pupils, in part through De Moivre, had a living connection with the great scientists of the recent past. To judge by their work, De Moivre encouraged in them a wide-ranging response to the problems of quantity, both scientific and practical, of the early eighteenth century. There was a social connection too: Cavendish, we know, met privately as well as publicly with Folkes, Macclesfield, Jones, Davall, and Stanhope. There are grounds for believing that De Moivre fostered a sense of connection between his pupils, as he evidently brought them together at social evenings and later kept them "together as a kind of clique." Maty noted works published by De Moivre's pupils in his *Journal Britannique*.[7] They appeared together in other connec-

[7] Uta Janssens, *Matthieu Maty and the Journal Britannique, 1750–1755* (Amsterdam: Holland University Press, 1975), 17. Augustus De Morgan, "Dr. Johnson and Dr. Maty," *Notes and Queries* 4 (1857): 341.

tions as well.[8] If we leave aside the foreigners named by Maty, we are directed to a select few mathematicians within the larger group of British mathematicians in the early eighteenth century with whom Cavendish came to be connected. For convenience, we will speak of a "De Moivre circle," whose members will give us an idea of the mathematical setting in which, we believe, Lord Charles Cavendish completed his education.

The learned world of London, which Cavendish would enter, had recently been greatly enriched by an influx of Huguenot refugees, who were forced to leave France after the revocation of the edict of Nantes. Within the Cavendish family, as we have seen, the Huguenot Ruvignys settled in Greenwich, a prophetic location, and encouraged other refugees to follow their example.[9] De Moivre and his father, one of a number of Huguenot surgeons and physicians to seek asylum in England, were naturalized in 1686;[10] Abraham was then nineteen and a student of mathematics.

In De Moivre's mind, his arrival in England became so closely identified with his discovery of Newton's work that although two or three years elapsed between the two events, to him they seemed simultaneous. For biographers of Lord Charles and Henry Cavendish, it is gratifying that De Moivre first encountered Newton's work in the house of the earl of Devonshire. It was probably in 1689, when Newton spent a good deal of time in London as a member of the Convention Parliament for Cambridge, and when Devonshire enjoyed the fruits of the revolution as a prominent member of parliament and of the court of William and Mary. De Moivre first saw Newton as Newton was leaving Devonshire's house after presenting the earl with a copy of his *Principia*. Shown into the antechamber where Newton had just left his book, De Moivre picked it up expecting to read it without difficulty, but he found that he understood nothing at all. De Moivre felt that all of his mathematical studies so far, which he had considered entirely up to date, had really taken him only to the threshold of a new direction.[11] He

[8] Most of them appeared together, for example, among the subscribers to De Moivre's republication of his mathematical papers from the *Philosophical Transactions, Miscellanea analytica de seriebus et quadraturis* (London, 1730). The list of subscribers could serve as a guide to British mathematics and its patrons in the early eighteenth century.The book is dedicated to Folkes.

[9] Mary Berry, *Some Account of the Life of Rachael Wriothesley Lady Russell* . . . (London, 1819), 73.

[10] Father and son, "Abraham and Daniel de Moavre," are listed as being in England as of 16 Dec. 1687, in a request to the attorney or solicitor general to prepare a bill for royal signature making them free denizens of the kingdom. *Lists of Foreign Protestants, and Aliens, Resident in England 1618–1688*, ed. W. Durrant Cooper (London, 1862), 50. Samuel Smiles, *The Huguenots: Their Settlements, Churches, and Industries in England and Ireland* (New York, 1868), 235–38.

[11] Maty, *Mémoire*, 6–7. Although the *Principia* was published in the summer of 1687, there is no evidence that Newton came to London to distribute copies of it at that time. Moreover, it would have been of no advantage to either Newton or De Moivre that summer to seek Devonshire's patronage, since he was then so much out of favor at court; in 1688 Devonshire took refuge at Chatsworth to avoid being arrested by the king. By 1689, however, James II had been displaced by William and Mary, at whose court Devonshire had a great deal of influence.

promptly mastered the new mathematics, however, with the result that Newton is said to have referred persons asking him about his work to De Moivre, who knew it better than he did.[12] Through the astronomer Edmond Halley, De Moivre was properly introduced to Newton and as well to the scientific society of London, which led to his election to the Royal Society. He made himself available to Newton in a variety of capacities: he sent news and results of Newton's work to colleagues abroad;[13] he took charge of Newton's publications;[14] he defended Newton;[15] and he kept philosophical company with Newton at the Rainbow coffeehouse and elsewhere.[16] De Moivre's own work drew heavily on Newton's, as he acknowledged by dedicating his masterwork, a treatise on probability, *Doctrine of Chances*, to Newton. This friend of Newton, Halley, and other prominent Fellows of the Royal Society and correspondent of leading mathematicians on the Continent was, we believe, Lord Charles Cavendish's teacher in advanced mathematics.

Mathematical tutoring served a variety of ends. It constituted a finishing school for "gentlemen"; it provided a useful skill for men who sought public office but lacked the advantage of rank;[17] it prepared others who intended to make a living directly from mathematics, such as teachers. It equipped Lord Charles Cavendish for scientific research and administration.

Most of De Moivre's mathematical friends and pupils will enter this biography again; here we will briefly discuss two of them, William Jones and Lord Macclesfield. William Jones, De Moivre's friend, was another mathematics teacher under whom Cavendish may well have studied.[18] Early on, Jones published a book on navigation and another book, a syllabus of mathematics, which drew the attention of Halley and Newton, both of whom became his friends. Elected to the Royal Society in 1712, Jones became one of its most active members. He taught and then tutored in mathematics. He became

---

[12] Ian Hacking, "Moivre, Abraham de," *DSB* 9:452–55, on 452.

[13] For example, concerning copies of Newton's *Principia* promised by De Moivre: letters from Pierre Varignon to Newton, 24 Nov. 1713, and from Johann Bernoulli to Leibniz, 25 Nov. 1713; in *The Correspondence of Isaac Newton,* vol. 6: *1713–1718*, ed. A. R. Hall and L. Tilling (Cambridge: Cambridge University Press, 1976), 42–43, 44–45.

[14] David Brewster, *Memoirs of the Life, Writings, and Discoveries of Isaac Newton,* 2 vols. (Edinburgh, 1855) 1:248. Schneider, "Abraham de Moivre," 212–13.

[15] In Newton's dispute with Leibniz over the invention of the calculus. Hacking, "Moivre," 452.

[16] Frederick Charles Green, *Eighteenth-Century France. Six Essays* (New York: D. Appleton, 1931), 31.

[17] A. J. Turner, "Mathematical Instruments and the Education of Gentlemen," *Annals of Science* 30 (1973): 51–88, on 51–54.

[18] It was Jones's practice to hand out transcripts of Newton's mathematical writings to his pupils; that is the likely source of Lord Charles Cavendish's copy of Jones's transcript of Newton's *Artis Analyticae Specimina sive Geometria Analytica.* Cavendish later loaned his copy of the transcript to the mathematician Samuel Horsley, who was preparing a general edition of Newton's papers. Isaac Newton, *Mathematical Papers of Isaac Newton,* ed. D. T. Whiteside, 8 vols. (Cambridge: Cambridge University Press, 1967–81) 1:xxiii; 8:xxiv, xxvii.

friends with one of his pupils Philip Yorke, later earl of Hardwicke and lord chancellor, traveling with him on his circuit. With another pupil George Parker, later earl of Macclesfield, he had an especially close and enduring association, for years living at Macclesfield's home, Shirburn Castle, where he served as secretary to Macclesfield's father. Jones published a number of original papers in the *Philosophical Transactions*, edited important tracts of Newton's, and served with De Moivre on the committee of the Royal Society on the discovery of the calculus. He intended to write an introduction to Newtonian philosophy but died before he completed it. His library of mathematical books was reputed to be the best in the country. Jones was an important personal and scientific link between Newton and scientific men coming after him, including Lord Charles Cavendish.[19]

Lord Macclesfield was the other aristocrat besides Cavendish to be listed by Maty as a pupil of De Moivre. Macclesfield's father, as lord chancellor, was impeached by the House of Lords under a long list of articles, which taken together specify practically all the ways money can be misused. Before that, at the time he was installed, he was given a pension for his son until his son was old enough to become a teller of the exchequer for life. Like his father, Macclesfield studied law and became a Member of Parliament, but his first love was always the sciences. In addition to studying under De Moivre, he studied under William Jones, and he may have profited from still another Newtonian teacher, since, like Folkes, he studied at Clare Hall when Richard Laughton was there. Becoming a Fellow of the Royal Society at age twenty-five, he was promptly elected to the council, serving there while Newton was still president. In 1752, the year he succeeded Folkes as president of the Royal Society, Macclesfield was instrumental in bringing about a famous practical application of astronomy, a change in the reckoning of history, the calendar. Friends and fellow pupils of De Moivre assisted him: Davall drew up the bill and made most of the tables, and Folkes examined the bill. In the calendar then in use, the new year began on 25 March; in the new style calendar, it began on 1 January, and there was a correction for the accumulated errors in the calendar owing to the precession of the equinoxes, a one-time elimination of eleven days in September. Anyone who doubts the emotional power, as well as the power to bewilder, of numbers, has only to recall Macclesfield's unpopularity, which was visited upon the next generation; when running for a seat in Oxfordshire, his son was met by a mob crying, "Give us back the eleven days we have been robbed of." Macclesfield's private astronomical observatory was said to have had the best equipment of any. He published three papers in the *Philosophical Transactions*, all minor: one about the date of Easter, one about an eclipse of the sun, and one about the temperature

19 "Jones, William," *DNB* 10:1061–62. E. G. R. Taylor, *The Mathematical Practitioners of Tudor and Stuart England* (Cambridge: Cambridge University Press, 1954), 293–94. "Jones (William)," in Charles Hutton, *Mathematical and Philosophical Dictionary*, vol. 1 (London, 1795), 643–44.

of Siberia; his importance for science was as an administrator and patron.[20] Lord Charles Cavendish's quantitative bent found its main outlet in experimental natural philosophy; his importance was, like Macclesfield's, primarily as an administrator, though it was also as mentor to his son Henry Cavendish.

ROYAL SOCIETY

Early in June 1727, De Moivre's friend William Jones proposed the twenty-three year old Lord Charles Cavendish for fellowship in the Royal Society, and two weeks later, on 22 June, Cavendish was formally admitted.[21] At a meeting of the executive council of the Society on that same day, its president, Hans Sloane, raised the question of qualifications for admission of new members. By statute, as a son of a peer, Cavendish was treated as if he were a peer and had to furnish no proof of scientific achievement, ability, or even interest. Under English law, however, the sons of peers were commoners until they inherited the family title. To raise the standards of membership of the Society and reduce the exceptions to the general rules of admission, Sloane proposed to treat all commoners the same way with respect to requirements. The issue came to a head a few months later, in February 1728, when William Jones proposed yet another son of a peer, whereupon the members at large engaged in "Debates arising upon the sense of the Statute with Relation to peers Sons and privy Councellors whether any other Qualifications of such Gentlemen are required to be mentioned or not."[22] In the event, the Society changed some of its requirements for membership, but it let stand those for peers and sons of peers.[23]

Newton died three months before Lord Charles was admitted to the Royal Society. Until the end, Newton was active as president; when he was absent, Folkes or Sloane took the chair in his place. Several members of the council were Newton's friends and, as we have noted, De Moivre's friends too. Halley was especially active in scientific discussions at the meetings. Folkes, Jones, and Bradley were on the council, as were the two secretaries of the Society, the physician and polymath James Jurin, a pupil of Newton's, and John Machin, an astronomer who Newton thought understood his *Principia* best of anyone, and

---

[20] "Parker, Thomas, first Earl of Macclesfield," *DNB* 15:278–82, on 280. "Parker, George, second Earl of Macclesfield," *DNB* 15: 234–35. *Collins's Peerage of England; Genealogical, Biographical, and Historical*, 9 vols., ed. E. Brydges (London, 1812) 4:192–94. Macclesfield, then George Parker, was at Clare Hall apparently under the care of Francis Barnard, who reported to his father in 1716 on his progress; in the same year, Richard Laughton reported to Macclesfield's father about a college election. *Catalogue of the Stowe Manuscripts in the British Museum*, vol. 1 (London, 1895), 548. Charles Richard Weld, *A History of the Royal Society, . . .*, vol. 1 (New York: Arno Press, 1975), 514–16. *A General Index to the Philosophical Transactions, from the First to the End of the Seventieth Volume. Alphabetical Index of the Writers*, ed. P. H. Maty (London, 1787), 696.

[21] Royal Society, JB 13:103 (8 June 1727).

[22] Royal Society, JB 13:175 (8 Feb. 1727/28).

[23] Weld, *History* 1:461.

who with Halley and Jones had been appointed to the committee on the discovery of the calculus. Other council members who had a close association with Newton were Richard Mead, physician and author of a Newtonian doctrine of animal economy; Thomas Pellet, a physician who with Folkes brought out an edition of Newton's *Chronology of Ancient Kingdoms* in the year after Newton's death; Henry Pemberton, who edited the third edition of Newton's *Principia*; and John Conduitt, husband of Newton's niece. Sloane was a physician, natural historian, and good friend of Newton's and Halley's, and like Sloane, several members of the council were physicians with scientific interests: John Arbuthnot, Paul Bussiere, James Douglas, and Alexander Stuart. Roger Gale was a commissioner of excise. The one peer, Thomas Foley, who was repeatedly elected to the council, had an observatory at his country seat near Worcester, from where observations were sent to the Royal Society from time to time. Two members of the council represented a distinctive British contribution to science in the eighteenth century, the making of scientific instruments: John Hadley, who was first to develop the reflecting telescope introduced by Newton, and who later introduced a reflecting octant based on a proposal by Newton; and George Graham, to whom Bradley later said that his own success in astronomy had "principally been owing."[24] The governance of the Royal Society was entrusted to the makers of scientific instruments as well as to their users and to a good number of able mathematicians. This diverse and, by and large, eminent group of scientific men on the council enlarged Cavendish's world in 1727. Later he would serve with seven of them on councils of the Society.

Historians are divided over the question of the quality of science in the Royal Society in the eighteenth century,[25] but there would seem to be no doubt that from the standpoint of experimental science, 1727 was an auspicious year for the Society. That year Stephen Hales brought out *Vegetable Staticks*, the most impressive demonstration yet of the promise of Newton's philosophy to elucidate a new experimental domain of facts. Educated at Cambridge, where he began experimenting on animal physiology, Hales continued his scientific studies while earning his living as a provincial cleric. His primary inspiration was Newton's *Opticks*. With the help of Newton's speculations in the Queries of that book about forces of attraction and repulsion between particles, Hales investigated the composition of plants and the air "fixed" in plants. In early 1727 the chapter of *Vegetable Staticks* dealing with air was read to the Royal Society, revealing that Hales had gone beyond his original enquiry into plants to conclude that air is in "all Natural Bodys" and is "one of the Principal Ingredients or Elements in the Composition of them." His experiments on fixed air helped lay the foundations of pneumatic

---

[24] Bradley quoted, 1747, in E. G. R. Taylor, *The Mathematical Practitioners of Hanoverian England, 1714–1840* (Cambridge: Cambridge University Press, 1966), 120–21.

[25] Richard Sorrenson, "Towards a History of the Royal Society in the Eighteenth Century," *Notes and Records of the Royal Society of London* 50 (1996): 29–46, on 29–30.

chemistry, the field in which Lord Charles Cavendish's son Henry would make his greatest reputation. The full significance of *Vegetable Staticks* could not have been foreseen–it was to encourage a generation of experimentalists–but it was appreciated from the beginning, and Hales was included in the council of the Royal Society at the next election at the end of 1727. Newton, who had presided during the final reading of Hales's chapter on air, died five weeks later, shortly before his handpicked experimenter, J.T. Desaguliers, demonstrated experiments from that chapter.[26] On the day Cavendish was elected to the Society, Desaguliers performed one of these experiments.

We can suggest the range of subjects touched on at the meetings of the Royal Society. Within a year of Cavendish's election, Desaguliers announced that Stephen Gray intended to bring before the Society experiments showing that rubbed glass communicates its electrical quality to any body connected to it by a string; Cavendish pursued this new field of electrical conduction.[27] Two weeks before Cavendish's election, Desaguliers reported on his invention to remove unhealthy air from coal mines, demonstrating it with a working model; it was the Sir Godfrey Copley's Experiment, which would be replaced by the Copley Award, an honor which Cavendish received.[28] Britain was a maritime nation, a fact of which the Royal Society was regularly reminded, in particular with regard to techniques of navigation; Cavendish would become involved in questions of navigational instruments at the Royal Society. The atmosphere posed equally daunting problems, both practical and scientific; the weather was one of Cavendish's major and persisting interests. From the side of medicine, there were reports of stones, cataracts, and aneurisms, and from the side of natural history, there were accounts of coconuts, cinnamon, and poison snakes. Two-headed calves and other monstrous productions were as commonly displayed at meetings as they were rarely found in nature. Investigative reports of singular natural disasters such as earthquakes were heard as often as opportunity permitted. In general, the Society served its members as a great clearinghouse for scientific news. Apart from certain formalities–correspondence read, books received, and guests introduced–the meetings were kept reasonably lively by the variety of their proceedings.

---

[26] Stephen Hales, *Vegetable Staticks: or, An Account of Some Statical Experiments on the Sap in Vegetables . . . . Also, a Specimen of an Attempt to Analyze the Air* . . . (London, 1727). Henry Guerlac, "Hales, Stephen," *DSB*: 6:35–48, on 35–36, 41–43. References to the reading of Hales's discourse on air and to Desaguliers' repetition of experiments from it in Royal Society, JB 13:44 (2 Feb. 1726/27), 45 (9 Feb. 1726/27), 48–50, quote on 48–49 (16 Feb. 1726/27), 70 (13 Apr. 1727), 74 (20 Apr. 1727), 83 (4 May 1727), 103 (8 June 1727), 144 (16 Nov. 1727). Newton's death caused the cancellation of the Society's meeting on 23 March 1726/27: Royal Society, JB 13:62.

[27] Royal Society, JB 13:330 (1 May 1729).

[28] Royal Society, JB 13:93 (28 May 1727). J. T. Desaguliers, "An Attempt Made Before the Royal Society, to Shew How Damps, or Foul Air, May Be Drawn Out of Any Sort of Mines, &c. by an Engine Contriv'd by the Reverend J. T. Desaguliers, L.L.D. and F.R.S.," *PT* 35 (1727): 353–56.

The contents of the *Philosophical Transactions of the Royal Society of London* were not identical with what transpired in the meetings of the Society, but they do give some notion of it. In the decade of the 1720s, when Cavendish entered the Society, the numbers of papers appearing in the journal on natural history and on mixed mathematics (scientific fields with mathematical content but not pure mathematics) were about equal, together accounting for about half of the total number of papers. Medicine came next, accounting for about a fifth of the papers, then experimental natural philosophy and anatomy, each with above a tenth, and there were a few other categories such as speculative natural philosophy, pure mathematics, and antiquities. Combined, the two categories to which Cavendish's work belonged, mixed mathematics and experimental natural philosophy, accounted for one third of the papers, a proportion which did not change much over the next fifty years, into the time when Lord Charles's son Henry was active in the same areas.[29] A fairly typical meeting of the Society, on 27 February 1728/29, was noted in a private journal kept by John Byrom, Fellow of the Royal Society and frequent attender: "Vernon there from Cambridge; Dr. Rutty read about ignis fatuus; humming bird's nest and egg, mighty small; Molucca bean, which somebody had sent to Dr. Jurin for a stone taken out of a toad's head; Desaguliers made some experiments about electricity."[30] That night there was something for everybody.

When Lord Charles Cavendish became a Fellow, the Society wore two crowns, one scientific and one royal. We begin with the scientific: Newton had just died, but he lived on in the causes that continued to be championed in his name. Thomas Derham wrote to the Society from Rome about a book by an Italian that "pretends" to refute propositions in Newton's *Opticks*; Desaguliers responded to the perceived danger. The dispute over whether the measure of force is as the velocity, as Newton said, or as the square of the velocity, as foreign mathematicians said, was settled by Desaguliers (he thought) by experiment, and was clarified by Jurin, who regarded it as a dispute arising from an ambiguity in the meaning of the word "force." Andrew Motte presented to the Society his English translation of Newton's *Principia*, and William Jones was asked to give the society an account of it.[31] As for the royal crown, in the year that Newton

[29] Sorrenson, "Towards a History of the Royal Society," 37. From another source, there is a similar estimate. Physics, including mechanics, meteorology, and various border subjects, accounted for about a third of the papers appearing in the *Philosophical Transactions.* The absolute numbers of papers are very small. John L. Heilbron, *Physics at the Royal Society During Newton's Presidency* (Los Angeles: William Andrews Clark Memorial Library, 1983), 43.

[30] John Byrom, *The Private Journal and Literary Remains of John Byrom,* ed. R. Parkinson, 2 vols. in 4 parts (Manchester, 1854–57), vol. 1, part 1, p. 334 (27 Feb. 1728/29). Royal Society, JB 13:303–7 (27 Feb. 1728/29).

[31] Royal Society, JB 13:175–76 (8 Feb. 1727/28), 242 (4 July 1728), 251 (24 Oct. 1728), 252 (31 Oct. 1728), 257 (7 Nov. 1728), 262 (14 Nov. 1728), 339–40 (22 May 1729), 341 (5 June 1729).

died, King George I died, and his successor to the throne, George II, agreed to succeed him as well in the role of patron of the Royal Society. The change in monarchs entailed considerable protocol, such as carrying the charter book to St. James's for the royal signature, making an address, and paying compliments to the queen. There was also a change of heir to the crown, the new prince of Wales, Frederick, becoming a member of the Royal Society, an honor which was commemorated by the dedication to him of the volume of the *Philosophical Transactions* for 1728. That year Lord Charles Cavendish became gentleman of the bedchamber to Frederick.[32]

Directly below the rank of royalty, within the dukedom of the Devonshires, there was about to be another succession, but for the time being, Lord Charles's father, the second duke of Devonshire, was still alive. The duke was the owner of a great magnet, which turned up in discussion at the Royal Society a few months after Cavendish was elected. Supported in a fine mahogany case and raised by screws, this magnet had prodigious force, as Folkes bore witness, having seen it lift "more than its own weight."[33] In 1730 the magnet was produced again, this time by Desaguliers, who lifted 175 pounds with it, among other experiments he performed before the Society.[34] With this, the "famous Great Loadstone of his Grace the Duke of Devonshire," we conclude our account of Lord Charles Cavendish's introduction to the Royal Society. Borrowing from eighteenth century writers who used magnets to represent bodies pulling other bodies toward them, symbolizing "dominating figures,"[35] we take the great Devonshire loadstone, with its remarkable powers, to have a double meaning, one physical and the other political, and to imply yet another meaning, a scientific one, anticipating the careers of the duke's son and grandson, Lord Charles and Henry Cavendish.

In the remainder of this biography, we discuss the working lives of Lord Charles and Henry Cavendish in their principal workplace away from home, the Royal Society. In no records we have seen did either father or son say what the Royal Society meant to him. We believe, however, that they would have agreed with William Heberden, Lord Charles's close friend who drafted Henry's certificate for membership, on the importance of scientific societies for the improvement of science. Encouraged to learn that the king of France had just instituted a medical society, Heberden wrote to Charles Blagden that "the knowledge of other parts of nature has increased more, by means of such societies, within the last hundred years, than it had done from the age of Aristotle to the time of their foundation."[36]

---

[32] Royal Society, JB 13:86 (11 May 1727), 114 (6 July 1727).

[33] Royal Society, JB 13:314 (13 Mar. 1728).

[34] Royal Society, JB 13:454 (9 Apr. 1730).

[35] Patricia Fara, *Sympathetic Attractions: Magnetic Practices, Beliefs, and Symbolism in Eighteenth-Century England* (Princeton: Princeton University Press, 1996), 189.

[36] William Heberden to Charles Blagden, 9 Dec. 1778, Blagden Letters, Royal Society, H.22.

FAMILY AND FRIENDS

MARRIAGE AND MONEY

In January 1728/29, Lord Charles Cavendish married Lady Anne de Grey, daughter of the duke of Kent. Lord Charles was in his middle twenties instead of in his middle thirties, a more common age for younger sons of nobility to marry,[1] and Lady Anne, who was born in 1706, was two years younger. We know nothing of the affection between Charles and Anne, but certainly wealth, rank, and respectability would have been considerations in this match, and perhaps there was an enduring family connection, too, for at the beginning of the previous century, Henry Grey, earl of Kent, had married Elizabeth, granddaughter of Sir William Cavendish of Chatsworth.[2]

We begin this account of the new family with what we can speak of with confidence, money. Younger sons of the aristocracy customarily received £300 a year, which is what Lord Charles had been receiving from his father since 1725. His father intended for the annuity to be raised to £500 at his death, but he moved the plan ahead starting with Lord Charles's marriage. In addition his father granted him the interest on £6,000 and eventually the capital itself.[3]

[1] Lawrence Stone, *The Family, Sex and Marriage in England 1500–1800*, abr. ed. (Harmondsworth: Penguin Books, 1982), 42.

[2] George Edward Cokayne, *The Complete Peerage of England, Scotland, Ireland, Great Britain and the United Kingdom: Extant, Extinct, or Dormant*, vol. 3 (Gloucester: A. Sutton, 1982), cols. 173–74.

[3] This financial detail would seem to settle the birthdate or, at least, the year of birth of Lord Charles Cavendish, on which we were indefinite earlier. On 6 April 1725 his father gave him the annuity; we think he was twenty-one on this occasion, which would suggest that his birthday was on or near 6 April 1704. But that is not right, since from a letter dated 4 July 1704 we learn that his mother was expecting a baby soon, in July. Lord Charles needed an income in April because he was about to be returned as M.P. for Heytesbury on 13 April that year. The £500 and £6,000 were determined by an earlier settlement of 1678. Devonshire Coll., L/19/31 and L/19/33.

The marriage settlement[4] involved land as well as money. In eighteenth-century society, in which "men were measured by their acres,"[5] nothing could compare with ownership of land for imparting a sense of independence. Following a practice that had been more common in the seventeenth century than in the eighteenth, the second duke of Devonshire devolved property on Lord Charles and his heirs: tithes, rectories, and lands in Nottinghamshire and in Derbyshire. Having been promised them in 1717, Lord Charles received the rents in 1728 and the lands the following year. At the beginning the rents brought in over £1,000 a year, and after the enclosures of the 1760s and 1770s they increased considerably.

Before his marriage, Lord Charles evidently kept a residence in Westminster,[6] but now he and Lady Anne needed a proper home of their own. Securities worth £12,000 and £10,000–Lord Charles's due from his mother's estate and Lady Anne's portion–were transferred to the trustees of their marriage settlement, who raised a sum for the purchase of the estate of George Warburton. This consisted of three manors, Putteridge, Lilley, and Hackwellbury, together with several farms, located directly north of London, at about half the distance of Cambridge, in the adjacent counties of Bedford and Hertford. From the properties that came with Putteridge, the manor in which Lord Charles and Lady Anne lived, they would have received rents. We have no reason to doubt that Lord Charles and Lady Anne planned to stay at Putteridge and raise their family there, in which case had it not been for Lady Anne's early death, the still countrified site of Putteridge would be hallowed ground in the history of science.[7]

There was another provision of the marriage settlement from which Lord Charles would benefit: after the duke of Kent died–he died in 1740–Lord Charles would receive interest on £12,000 left to Lady Anne's trustees. From his mid-twenties, we estimate, Lord Charles Cavendish could count on a disposable annual income of at least £2000, and this income grew. We get an idea of what this income meant from Samuel Johnson, a professional man who rarely made above £300, who said that £50 was "undoubtedly more than the necessities of life require." A gentleman could live comfortably on £500 and a squire on £1,000.[8] Cavendish's income enabled him to live well, invest in stock, acquire books, and support his scientific pursuits. It permitted his son Henry to do like-

[4] H. J. Habakkuk, "Marriage Settlements in the Eighteenth Century," *Transactions of the Royal Historical Society* 32 (1950):15–30, on 15–16, 18, 20–24.

[5] J. H. Plumb, *Men and Centuries* (Boston: Houghton Mifflin, 1963), 72. Devon. Coll., L/19/33.

[6] The residence was probably substantial. Cavendish appeared on the poor rolls of Westminster Parish of St. Margaret's in 1728; he paid 5.5.0 annually, which is what the duke of Kent paid and a quarter of what the duchess of Devonshire paid. Westminster Public Libraries, Westminster Collection, Accession no. 10, Document no. 343.

[7] Devon. Coll., L/19/33 and L/5/69.

[8] George Rudé, *Hanoverian London, 1714–1808* (Berkeley: University of California Press, 1971), 48, 61.

wise and at the same time lay the foundations of his fortune. Within the conventional financial arrangements of wealthy English families of the time, the Cavendishes and the Greys combined to create what was in effect a scientific endowment for Lord Charles and Henry Cavendish.

When Lord Charles and Lady Anne moved to Putteridge, Lord Charles had an active life in the city, at court and in parliament, but also in science; around the time of his marriage, he began to serve on committees of the Royal Society.[9] A portrait of Lord Charles Cavendish shows a handsome young man of slender build and medium complexion, with a long, narrow face, a long nose, full lips, prominent eyes, and an alert expression. We have two portraits of Lady Anne, one of her together with two sisters, and one of her by herself and somewhat older. She is slender with a round face, wideset intelligent eyes, high rounded eyebrows, and straight nose. At the time of these portraits she was evidently in good health, which was not to last.

There is evidence that Lady Anne was not strong before her marriage,[10] and in any case, in the winter a year later, she was ill. Sophia, duchess of Kent, her stepmother, wrote to her father, the duke, that she had just dined at the Cavendishes: "Poor Lady Anne does not seem so well as when I saw her last. Her spirits are mighty low and she has no stomach at all. She has no return of spitting blood nor I don't think she coughs more than she did so that I hope this is only a disorder upon her nerves that won't last."[11] The next winter, 1730–31, was bitterly cold, colder–William Derham, F.R.S., wrote to the president of the Royal Society–than the winter of 1716, when the Thames froze over.[12] That winter, we believe, Lord Charles and Lady Anne went abroad, possibly in the company of his brother Lord James.[13] From Paris, Lady Anne wrote to her father that in Calais she had been very ill with a "great cold" and that she had been blooded and kept low to prevent fever. She did not expect to see much of Paris for fear of being cold, and in any case they were about to leave the city for Nice.[14]

---

9 On 17 July 1729, Cavendish was appointed to a committee to inspect the library and the collections and deliver reports; it met every Thursday from 24 July until 6 November 1729, and on 11 December it was ordered to continue its work. Minutes of Council, Royal Society 3:28–30, 34–36, 39, 55–56, 114–16.

10 In the summer before Lady Anne's marriage, the house accounts for the duke of Kent repeatedly record "Chair hire for Lady Ann." None of the duke's other daughters required chairs then. "July 1728. House Account. To ye 28 December 1728," Bedfordshire Record Office, Wrest Park Collection, L 31/200/1.

11 Sophia, duchess of Kent to Henry, duke of Kent, 21 Feb. 1729/30, Bedfordshire Record Office, Wrest Park Collection, L 30/8/39/5.

12 William Derham, "A Letter . . . Concerning the *Frost* in *January*, 1730/1," *PT* 37 (1731; published 1733): 16–18.

13 At least Lord James was abroad at the same time as Lord Charles. On 10 October 1731, Lord James "came to Town from France." *Weekly Register*, October 16, 1731. BL Add Mss 4457, f. 76.

14 Lady Anne Cavendish to Henry, duke of Kent, 4 Nov. [1730], Bedfordshire Record Office, Wrest Park Collection, L 30/8/11/1.

The combination of sun and sea has given Nice a reputation for being well suited for people convalescing from acute lung ailments,[15] and in all likelihood, Lord Charles and Lady Anne went there for the weather and the waters because of Anne's health. They would probably not have gone there as conventional tourists, for although Nice did become popular with English tourists, that did not happen until the second half of the eighteenth century. In 1731 Charles Cavendish was the only Englishman to stay in Nice who did not have commercial or diplomatic ties there. The only permanent English resident was the consul, who did double service as a spy on the French.[16] About three months after leaving Paris, Lady Anne conceived, and in Nice, on Sunday, 31 October 1731, she gave birth to her first child, named after her father, Henry de Grey. No birthplace could be less predictive: beginning life in a sleepy Mediterranean town of about sixteen thousand inhabitants situated amongst olive groves, Henry Cavendish grew up to be one of the most confirmed Londoners ever.

Before Henry's birth, Lord Charles asked the British consul at Turin to help get permission from the duke of Savoy for "one of the Vaudois Protestant Ministers" to come to Nice to baptize the infant. No doubt Lord Charles had learned that the closest region in which the Protestant religion could be practiced was the valleys of the Vaudois in Piedmont. There is a satisfying family connection here, even if it is likely to be only coincidental: the Vaudois Protestants, historically a persecuted group, kept in close touch with another such group, the Huguenots, to whom, through the Ruvignys, Lord Charles Cavendish was related. Cyprian Appia, who with his brother acted as chaplain in the British embassy in Turin, and who had studied at Oxford and was ordained as an Anglican priest, was sent to Nice on 15/26 October 1731. The express condition was that the "baptism should be performed in a manner as little publick as well might be," reflecting the reserve of Lord Charles and Lady Anne, a trait which would be intensified in Henry Cavendish.[17]

The next stage of Lord Charles and Lady Anne's marriage is short and ends sadly. A year and a half had passed since their departure from England, and they were now back in France, in Lyon, from where in the summer of 1732 Lady Anne wrote to her father about her health and happiness. It was with her usual perfected penmanship, the letters large, uniform, and inclined at precisely the same angle, but her hand was unsteady, like that of an elderly person. Nevertheless, her letter home begins with reassurances: her fever had not returned, and she

[15] "Nice," *Encyclopaedia Britannica* (Chicago: William Benton, 1962) 16:414–15.

[16] Henri Costamagna, "Nice au XVIIIe siècle: présentation historique et géographique," *Annales de la Faculté des Lettres et Sciences Humaines de Nice,* no. 19, 1973, pp. 7–28, on p. 26. Daniel Feliciangeli, "Le développement de Nice au cours de la seconde moitié de XVIIIe siècle. Les Anglais à Nice," ibid., pp. 45–67, on pp. 55–56. Anon., *Les Anglais dans le Comté de Nice et en Provence depuis le XVIIIme siècle* (Nice: Musée Massena, 1934), 72.

[17] Sugiko Nishikawa. "The Vaudois Baptism of Henry Cavendish," *Proceedings of the Huguenot Society of Great Britain and Ireland* 26 (1997): 660–63.

was so far recovered that she and Lord Charles were going to Geneva the next day, a three-day trip. If she handled that well, they would stay there only two or three days and then go directly to Leyden. She did not know when they could return to England. Lady Anne closed the letter with word of her baby, Henry. "I thank God," she wrote, "my boy is very well and his being so very strong and healthy gives me a pleasure I cannot easyly express."[18]

The Cavendishes were going to Leyden to see the great teacher and healer Hermann Boerhaave. Although Boerhaave was nearing the end of his career at the University of Leyden, where he taught medicine and, until recently, botany and chemistry, in 1732 he was still lecturing on the theory and practice of medicine and giving clinical instruction. He had written influential treatises on medicine and was, by many accounts, the most famous physician in the world, if not the most famous scientist since Newton. His ties with British medicine and, in general, with British science were close. From all parts of the world but especially from Britain, students came to Leyden to attend his lectures: of the nearly two thousand students enrolled in Leyden's medical faculty, fully one third were English-speaking. British physicians who had studied under Boerhaave consulted him when their treatment of aristocratic or otherwise important patients had not succeeded. Prominent British travelers went to Leyden to see Boerhaave, often but not always about their health.[19] For his part, Boerhaave was an ardent admirer of British experimental philosophy and one of the first exponents of the Newtonian philosophy in Europe. He was elected to the Royal Society in 1730. For all these reasons, it was natural for the well-informed Lord Charles Cavendish and Lady Anne to seek out Boerhaave's services. Lady Anne told her father that they thought it would be right for Dr. Boerhaave to "see me pretty often in order to make a right judgment of my illness." Since no other letters by her have been found, we do not know what Boerhaave said and prescribed.[20] Tuberculosis was a common disease for which medicine then, of course, had no cure.

At some point Lord Charles and Lady Anne returned to England. Three months after her consultation with Boerhaave, Lady Anne was well enough to conceive again, and on 24 June 1733 she delivered another son, Frederick, named after his sponsor, the prince of Wales. The next we hear is that Lady Anne Cavendish died at Putteridge on 20 September 1733.[21] She was twenty-seven.

[18] Lady Anne Cavendish to Henry, duke of Kent, 22 June [1732], Bedfordshire Record Office, Wrest Park Collection, L 30/8/11/2.

[19] Bolingbroke wrote to his half-sister Henrietta, "I was yesterday at Leyden to talk with Doctor Boorehaven, and am now ready to depart for Aix-la-Chapelle." Letter of 17 Aug. 1729, in Walter Sydney Sichel, *Bolingbroke and His Times: The Sequel* (New York: Greenwood, 1968), 525.

[20] Lady Anne Cavendish to Henry, duke of Kent, 22 June [1732]. G. A. Lindeboom, *Boerhaave and Great Britain* (Leiden: E. J. Brill, 1974), 18; "Boerhaave, Hermann," *DSB* 2:224–28.

[21] Four days later, on 24 Sep. 1733, Lady Anne Cavendish was buried in the Grey family vault at Flitton. "Extracts from the Burial Register of Flitton," Bedfordshire Record Office, Wrest Park Collection, L 31/43.

THE SCIENTIFIC BRANCH OF THE FAMILY

13. *Lord Charles Cavendish. By Enoch Seeman. Devonshire Collections, Chatsworth. Reproduced by permission of the Chatsworth Settlement Trustees. Photograph Courtauld Institute of Art.*

14. *Lady Anne de Grey. Wife of Lord Charles Cavendish. By J. Davison. Reproduced by permission of the Bedfordshire Record Office.*

15. *The Honorable Henry Cavendish. Graphite and gray wash sketch by William Alexander. Beneath the sketch is written, "Cavendish Esqr. F.R.S. Trustee of the British Museum. 1812." The figure measures ten centimeters. Reproduced by permission of the Trustees of the British Museum.*

Henry was not quite two years old, Frederick was three months, and Lord Charles was around twenty-nine. In Lord Charles's station, remarriage was uncommon, and he would live for fifty years as a widower.

Although for Lady Anne, a person in her twenties, life expectancy was over sixty in the eighteenth century, life then at any age was precarious. Hygiene was unknown, medicine was largely helpless, and death was indifferent to privilege. Henry and Frederick Cavendish grew up with one parent, which was a common fate under the prevailing conditions of life.[22]

FAMILY OF THE GREYS

As a widower, Lord Charles kept in touch with Lady Anne's family. For this important fact, we are indebted to Thomas Birch, who enjoyed the patronage of a branch of that family, the Yorkes. Philip Yorke, first earl of Hardwicke, engaged Birch as tutor to his oldest son, also named Philip. He then kept Birch on, from 1735, as a secretary with light duties, which left Birch with plenty of time for his calling, which was writing.[23]

In 1740, the younger Philip married Jemima Campbell, grandaughter of the duke of Kent. That same year the duke died, whereupon Jemima became marchioness de Grey and baroness Lucas of Crudwell. In the years to come, in the off-season, Philip and Jemima lived at the duke of Kent's great estate at Wrest Park in Bedfordshire, and the rest of the time in Kent's townhouse on St. James Square. No match for his self-made father the lord chancellor, Philip rejected his ample opportunities for high political office, withdrawing into his chief pleasure in life, literature. In temperament he was personable, languid, and reserved; and in health he was not robust. He spent much of the day dressing, visiting, and reading long letters from Birch.[24]

Birch was personally close to the younger Philip Yorke, serving as his secretary, literary assistant, and eyes and ears in the world. Although Wrest Park appears frequently at the head of Birch's letters, his principal assignment was London, from which watch he kept his patron informed on literary affairs and also on science. Given Yorke's friends and membership in the Royal Society, Birch expected him to take an interest in, for instance, the test of John Harrison's chronometer for determining longitude on a journey to Jamaica. Jemima Yorke evidently took an interest in science, for we find Birch writing to her about the contents of the *Philosophical Transactions*.[25] When Philip and Jemima Yorke were in

[22] Stone, *Family*, 46–48, 54, 58–59.

[23] Albert E. Gunther, *An Introduction to the Life of the Rev. Thomas Birch D.D., F.R.S., 1705–1766* (Halesworth: Halesworth Press, 1984), 8, 35.

[24] Gunther, *Birch*, 41. L. B. Namier and John Brooke, *The History of Parliament: The House of Commons 1754-1780*, vol. 3: *Members K-Y* (London: Her Majesty's Stationary Office, 1964), 681.

[25] There are many letters from Thomas Birch to Philip Yorke reporting on scientific news between 1747 and 1762 in the Birch correspondence in the British Library, Add Mss 35397 and 35399. Thomas Birch to Jemima, marchioness de Grey, 12 Aug. 1749, BL Add Mss 35397, ff. 200–1.

London, Birch would join them for weekly breakfasts at St. James Square.[26] The duchess of Kent was usually there along with Mary and Sophia de Grey and other members of the Grey family, including in-laws Lords Glenorchy and Ashburnham. In the presence of Birch, Lord Charles Cavendish visited the Greys often in 1741 and 1742 and less often over the next ten years, and sometimes he brought along his son Henry to visit with his maternal grandmother and aunts and uncles.[27] Henry Cavendish may not have had a memory of his mother, but his father made certain that he knew the other dukedom from which he descended.

GREAT MARLBOROUGH STREET

Five years after his wife died, in 1738, Lord Charles Cavendish sold Putteridge together with the rest of his country estate. For the trustees to be empowered to make the sale, an act of parliament had to be passed, and for that, a reason had to be given for wanting to sell it. Putteridge, Cavendish said, was too remote from the rest of his estate, whatever he meant by that. No doubt he wanted to move into the city, where his political, scientific, and social life lay. Parliament directed the trustees to sell the estate for the best price possible.[28]

It would seem that the property sold for about what it had cost, and the price of the house he bought in its place that same year, 1738, was only one tenth of that: for the absolute purchase of a freehold in Westminster, he paid £1,750.[29] The location was near Oxford Road, at the corner of Great Marlborough and Blenheim, both streets named to commemorate military action of the duke of Marlborough: a stone tablet in the wall read "Marlborough Street, 1704."[30] But later when rockets were observed in the middle of Great Marlborough Street, it was not to commemorate victory but to determine Lord Charles Cavendish's longitude from Greenwich.[31]

---

26 Gunther, *Birch*, 35–39.

27 We have no idea of the frequency of Lord Charles Cavendish's visits to his wife's family. We do know that he *and* Birch were at the Grey's together twenty-six times between 1741 and 1751. On two of the occasions, Henry Cavendish came with Lord Charles; Henry was nine and ten at the time. Thomas Birch Diary, BL Add Mss 4478C.

28 "An Act for Discharging the Estate Purchased by the Trustees of Charles Cavendish . . . from the Trusts of his Settlement, and for Enabling the Said Trustees to Sell and Dispose of the Same for the Purposes Therein Mentioned," Devon. Coll.

29 "Assignment of Two Messuages in Marlborough Street from the Honorable Thomas Townshend Esq to His Right Honble Lord Charles Cavendish," 27 Feb. 1737/38, Chatsworth, L/38/35. London County Council, *Survey of London*, ed. F. H. W. Sheppard, vol. 31: *The Parish of St. James Westminster*, part 2: *North of Piccadilly* (London: Athlone, 1963), 251–56.

30 E. Beresford Chancellor, *The Romance of Soho; Being an Account of the District, Its Past Distinguished Inhabitants, Its Historic Houses, and Its Place in the Social Annals of London* (London: Country Life, 1931), 207.

31 "Explosions of Rockets Observ'd at Lord Charles Cavendish's. The Middle of Gr. Marlbro' St." Canton Papers, Royal Society, vol. 2, p. 13.

16. *No. 13 Great Marlborough Street. Demolished. Lord Charles Cavendish's house from 1738 to the end of his life. Henry Cavendish lived here with his father, and after his father's death he leased the house. View of the back premises in Blenheim Street. From a watercolor sketch by Appleton, 1888 . Reproduced by permission of Westminster City Archives.*

17. *Map of Great Marlborough Street. Detail from Horwood's survey c. 1792–99 updated to 1813. The plan of house No. 13, on the corner of Great Marlborough and Blenheim, shows a building at the end of the property, designated No. 1 Blenheim Street, either with a divided garden between it and the main house or with two buildings at the rear. From accounts of the time, we conclude that Henry Cavendish lived in a rear building and Lord Charles in the main house.*

The inhabitants of Great Marlborough Street were gentlemen and tradesmen, evenly balanced. In appearance, Great Marlborough Street was a rather atypical London street, long, straight, and broad, with a touch of Roman-like grandeur. It had its drawbacks, too, opening onto no vistas, its houses solid but undistinguished, giving the street a uniform, rather boring appearance. The house that Cavendish bought, number 13, was unusual in one respect; it was, in fact, *two* houses, as it had been since around 1710, when John Richmond, who had actually fought at Blenheim and had risen to the rank of general, had leased and joined the then separate houses. Following the general's death in 1724, the house went on the market as two houses in one. From a newspaper advertisement the next year, we get an idea of its size and layout. The property was forty-five feet wide and two hundred feet deep. Behind the house was a garden, at the end of which was an apartment with a passageway to the house. The apartment was described as "beautiful" and "newly built" in 1725.[32] Adjoining the apartment were coach houses and stabling. Horwood's London map from the 1790s shows the arrangement: either there were two conjoined buildings at the end of the property or the garden was divided into two, half belonging to the house and half to the rear apartment; in either case the apartment in the rear then had a separate address, number 1 Blenheim Street. It had its own plumbing, an underground kitchen, and four rooms on the single floor above. We suppose that as an adult Henry Cavendish lived in this apartment. Parallel to Great Marlborough Street and running behind the house was a back street, Marlborough Mews (in 1799 Blenheim Mews), giving access to stables and living quarters adapted from stables. Thomas Thomson described Henry Cavendish's apartment as converted stables, which if true would not have been uncommon.[33] When Henry acquired the property on Great Marlborough Street, he had a valuation made of its rental value; the evaluator, Hanscombe, included the "back building coach house & stables."[34] Persons who, like Cavendish, lived on the north side of Great Marlborough Street were assessed rates for that street and, beginning in 1774, also for the south side of the back mews, which was the back side of their properties. Cavendish had an assessment based on a rent of ninety pounds for Great Marlborough Street; his house being double and also end-of-row, his assessment was more than double that of the other occupants on his side of the street. He also had two assessments based on rents of ten pounds each for the mews. No assessment was assigned to

[32] *Parish of St James Westminster*, part 2: *North of Piccadilly*, 256.

[33] Thomson said that Henry's "apartments were a set of stables, fitted up for his accommodation." George Wilson, *The Life of the Honourable Henry Cavendish* (London, 1851), 159. Since Thomson was only nine when Henry Cavendish moved away from Great Marlborough Street, he would not have seen Cavendish's living quarters but only heard about them.

[34] "Hanscombs Valuation of House in Marl. Street," July 1784, Devon. Coll., L/31/45.

Blenheim Street, with its entrance to the rear premises of Cavendish's property. There is evidence that Henry and his father maintained partially separate establishments, but we find that the ratebooks do not list Henry Cavendish until the year his father died. From an official standpoint, Henry lived with his father, who paid the rates. In the ratebook for June 1783, two months after Lord Charles died, Lord Charles's name still appears beside the two assessments for the mews, but now Henry's name is listed for Great Marlborough Street; notations in the book suggest that the premises on the mews and the main house were both empty.[35]

Two years after Lord Charles Cavendish bought the house on Great Marlborough Street, in 1740, he was elected to the local governing body of the parish, the vestry of St. James, Westminster. The vestry dealt with every kind of practical problem of civil life: road repair, paving, night watch, workhouses, petitions for the commons, rates, levies, grants, and accounts. No detail was too small; the vestry approved a new umbrella for ministers attending burials in the rain. It was characteristic of Cavendish to turn up faithfully at vestry meetings, held as needed, roughly once a month. A few other members attended as regularly too, and these included persons he was either related to, such as Philip Yorke, or met with on boards of other institutions, such as Lord Macclesfield from the Royal Society. Cavendish served his parish for thirty-three years, attending his last meeting in early 1783, the year he died.[36]

Like the house, the life of science on Great Marlborough Street was double. Here Lord Charles Cavendish lived most of his life and Henry Cavendish most of his, and here they, together and individually, carried out experimental, observational, and mathematical researches in all parts of natural philosophy.

The wider setting for the scientific activity on Great Marlborough Street was greater London, which included Westminster. At around the time Cavendish bought his house, one sixth of the people of England either lived

---

[35] Ratebooks Great Marlborough Street/Blenheim Street, parish of St. James Westminster Archives, film nos. D64, D72, D87, D673, D683, D708, D1102–1110, D1260–1265. In the year before his father died, Henry Cavendish took a house in Hampstead, and that year he made an inventory of silverware, plates, pans, coffee pots, lamps, and so on; beside some entries, he wrote "CC," beside others "H," standing, we suppose, for Charles Cavendish and for Henry. Because of the year, we doubt that the initials stood for Clapham Common and Hampstead. "An Inventory of Silver Plate Belonging to the Hon[ble] Henry Cavendish Delivered to the Care of Geo. Dobson Feb[y] the 7th 1782," Chatsworth, L/86/comp. 1.

[36] Minutes of the Vestry of St. James, Westminster, D 1760–1764, Westminster City Archives, from Cavendish's election to the vestry on 26 Dec. 1740 (D 1760, p. 145) to his last meeting on 13 Feb. 1783 (D 1764, p. 518). Cavendish had other duties in the parish; he was a trustee, for example, of the King Street Chapel (also known as Archbishop Tenison's Chapel) and its school and met with other trustees at the end of year to pass the accounts. Great Britain, Historical Manuscript Commission, *Report on the Manuscripts of the Earl of Egmont. Diary of the First Earl of Egmont, Viscount Percival*, vol. 3 (London: His Majesty's Stationery Office, 1923), 270 (4 Jan. 1742/3), 306 (4 Jan. 1744/5).

or had once lived in greater London. In his son Henry's lifetime, owing to an influx from the provinces and from abroad, its population rose to nearly a million. Whereas the filth, poverty, and drunkenness of eighteenth-century London are faithfully depicted in Hogarth's prints, the city's lure is equally well depicted in Boswell's London journals. London meant wealth, power, and patronage, an opportunity to rise in the world. It was the seat of national government, a great port city, the commercial center of a colonial system, headquarters of great trading companies, and the financial capital of the world. Whether a Londoner was rising or was, like a Cavendish, already at the top, he had access to every convenience known to civilization. Westminster could boast of almost four hundred distinct trades, among which were those of special interest to Lord Charles and Henry Cavendish, the flourishing scientific instrument and book trades. The resident of London was in the center of the world, yet whenever he felt that the world was too much with him, he had only to step back out of the street to find himself inside his own house, his castle "in perfect safety from intrusion." For a man like Henry Cavendish, who was interested in the great world and at the same time was a shy homebody, it was no small recommendation of London that there "a man is always *so near his burrow*."[37]

For most of Lord Charles Cavendish's life and for a good part of Henry's, London was the center of scientific activity in Britain. Even though in the second half of the eighteenth century, when much of the important scientific activity took place elsewhere, in the Scottish university towns and in the rising industrial towns such as Birmingham and Manchester, London remained "intellectually pre-eminent," a "magnet for men with scientific and technical interests," the "Mecca of the provincial mathematical practitioner."[38] Over half of the British men of science of the eighteenth century who enter the *Dictionary of Scientific Biography* worked mainly in or near London.[39] The city was large enough to be home to numbers of experts in every part of science, yet compact enough for persons of common interests to meet frequently in societies, coffee houses, and private homes. Scientifically interested and interesting visitors from the provinces and from abroad were warmly welcomed into these circles. To paraphrase Johnson, as Lord Charles and Henry Cavendish might have, anyone who was tired of London was tired of science.

---

[37] Quoting an acquaintance on the importance of living in London: James Boswell, *The Life of Samuel Johnson LL.D.*, 3 vols. (New York: Heritage, 1963), 3:73. Rudé, *Hanoverian London*, 4–7, 25, 28, 32–33.

[38] A. E. Musson and Eric Robinson, *Science and Technology in the Industrial Revolution* (Toronto: University of Toronto Press, 1969), 57. E. G. R. Taylor, *The Mathematical Practitioners of Hanoverian England 1714–1840* (Cambridge: Cambridge University Press, 1966), 14.

[39] *Dictionary of Scientific Biography*, 15 vols., ed. C. C. Gillispie (New York: Charles Scribner's Sons, 1970–78).

FRIENDS AND COLLEAGUES

Although it was open to national membership, even international, the Royal Society was the Royal Society *of London.* For the Londoner Lord Charles Cavendish, the Society was the center of his scientific activity. Apart from his family, Cavendish's friends, so far as we know, were almost all Fellows of the Royal Society. Although the membership of the Society reflected the structure of the wider society,[40] its operations were relatively unaffected by social distinctions.[41] Cavendish's friendships within the Society were based not on aristocratic ties but on mutual interests, his birth being no impediment to his association with persons from other walks of life.

Many of Cavendish's friends also belonged, as he did, to the Royal Society Club. Originally named the Society of Royal Philosophers, its members usually referred to it simply as "the Society." The Society, or Club, undoubtedly had a predecessor, but if Cavendish had been a member of the earlier club, as has been asserted, it remains that he was not elected to the new one, the Royal Society Club, until eight years after its founding in 1743.[42] From the beginning, the Club included close friends of Cavendish, such as William Watson, William Heberden, and Birch, and members of the De Moivre circle, such as Folkes, Davall, Scott, and Stanhope. The occasion of Cavendish's election was the fatal illness of Folkes, the president of the Club, who was also the president of the Royal Society. This was at the end of 1751, when the regular time for electing new members to the club was many months off. As vice president, Cavendish had already taken Folkes's place in the Royal Society, and the Club wanted Cavendish to take Folkes's place there too. There was an expectation that Cavendish would become the next president of the Society.[43] Cavendish's election was made an exception, and in January 1752 he assumed the chair at the Royal Society Club.[44]

---

[40] Cavendish, as son of a peer, as we have seen, was admitted under a special rule of privilege; persons from the lower orders were not admitted at all; and "rich Philosophers can only afford to pay" its admission fee of twenty-two guineas. John Smeaton to Benjamin Wilson, 7 Sep. 1747, quoted in Larry Stewart, *The Rise of Public Science: Rhetoric, Technology, and Natural Philosophy in Newtonian Britain, 1660–1750* (Cambridge: Cambridge University Press, 1992), 251.

[41] Richard Sorrenson, "Towards a History of the Royal Society in the Eighteenth Century," *Notes and Records of the Royal Society of London* 50 (1996): 29–46, on 33, 35.

[42] T. E. Allibone argues that the Royal Society Club was continuous with "Halley's Club," for which he has a few pieces of evidence, but for his assertion that Lord Charles Cavendish was probably a member of "Halley's Club" he offers none, and so this lead we are unable to follow up. T. E. Allibone, *The Royal Society and Its Dining Clubs* (Oxford: Pergamon Press, 1976), 45, 97. An opposing view of Halley's part in the origins of the Club is Archibald Geikie, *Annals of the Royal Society Club: The Record of a London Dining-Club in the Eighteenth and Nineteenth Centuries* (London: Macmillan, 1917), 6–9. Lord Charles Cavendish was elected to the Club on 25 July 1751 and became a member on 9 January 1752.

[43] See note 52 and accompanying text in the chapter "Public Activities."

[44] Royal Society Club, Minutes for 28 Nov. 1751. Cited in Allibone, *Royal Society and Its Dining Clubs*, 44–45.

For convenience, the Club met on the afternoon of the same day the Royal Society met, Thursday. Members of the Club did not also have to be members of the Royal Society, but normally they were, and the president of the Club was the president of the Society. Its membership was fixed at forty, though members could bring guests; when Cavendish was admitted, the usual number of members and guests at a dinner was about twenty in the winter and fourteen in the summer. The dinners, which were heavy (fish, fowl, red meat, pudding, pie, cheese, and alcohol), were held for the first three years at Pontack's and then, throughout Cavendish's membership, at the Mitre Tavern on Fleet Street. The Club provided a fuller opportunity than did the formal meetings of the Royal Society for members to discuss science and to express their friendship. Cavendish belonged to the Club for twenty years and dined with it often, but he did not attend the yearly business meetings with any particular regularity, unlike Watson, Birch, Heberden, and several other friends, and for that matter, unlike his son Henry, who was a member later.[45]

The Royal Society Club was certainly the most prestigious, and probably the largest, of the learned clubs in eighteenth-century London, of which there were many. Meeting to discuss science, literature, politics, business, or whatever interests drew men together, London clubs often had a more or less formal membership, with rules and dues, but often too they were informal, certain persons simply forming the habit of appearing during particular hours at certain coffeehouses. Folkes dined not only at the Royal Society Club but also at a club of his own, which met at the Baptist Head in Chancery Lane. Another society of scientific and literary men met at Jack's Coffee House on Dean Street, Soho, and later at Old (or Young) Slaughter's Coffee House on St. Martin's Lane, where in his later years De Moivre solved problems of games of chance for money.[46] Birch met with groups at Tom's Coffee House and at Rawthmell's Coffee-House on Henrietta Street, Covent Garden, later the place of origin of the Society of Arts. At Rawthmell's, Lord Charles Cavendish and a Lord James Cavendish (either Charles's brother or his scientifically inclined uncle) joined Birch and other Fellows of the Royal Society, such as William Jones, Richard Graham, John Colson, Daniel Wray, John Machin, and Thomas Pellet.[47] We do not know at which coffeehouses, other than the Mitre and Rawthmell's, Lord Charles Cavendish might

[45] Minute Books, Royal Society Club, in the Royal Society Library. Cavendish resigned from the Club at the annual meeting in 1772, though he continued to take an interest in it, making it a gift of venison five years later. 9 Sep. 1779, Minute Book of the Royal Society Club, Royal Society, 7.

[46] Thomas Birch Diary, BL Add Mss 4478C, 19 Oct. 1736. W. Warburton to Thomas Birch, 27 May 1738, in John Nichols, *Illustrations of the Literary History of the Eighteenth Century*, 8 vols. (London, 1817–58) 2:86–88, on 88. Bryant Lillywhite, *London Coffee Houses. A Reference Book of Coffee Houses of the Seventeenth, Eighteenth, and Nineteenth Centuries* (London: George Allen and Unwin, 1963), 280–81, 369–70, 421–23, 595.

[47] *The Private Journal and Literary Remains of John Byrom*, ed. R. Parkinson, vol. 2, part 1 (Manchester, 1856), 221, 280, 322.

have been found, but we do know several of those where Henry Cavendish could have been, a subject we come to later.

Coffeehouses and taverns provided clubs with a measure of privacy in their supper rooms, but these were noisy places at best. Private houses provided quieter, more intimate settings for small groups. Lord Willoughby, a prominent Fellow of the Royal Society, presided both over a club that met at a tavern–a life insurance society based on the principles of the De Moivre student and mathematician James Dodson, which met at the White Lion Tavern–and over a club that met alternately in his and Birch's houses.[48] Another group met at Lord Macclesfield's.[49] Lord Charles Cavendish, and his son Henry, belonged to a circle that met in a private house located in the Strand. Little is known about it except that Cavendish's good friends William Heberden, William Watson, and Israel Mauduit also belonged, along with several others. Most of the members were, like Heberden and Watson, physicians: George Baker, Richard Huck Saunders, and John Pringle. Two others, John Ross and Peter Holford, completed the circle, insofar as its membership is known.[50] The main interest that brought these men together was probably science, though in general outlook, there would seem to have been a commonality, too, which might be called a spirit of enlightened protest and reform. Upon becoming Bishop of Exeter, the antiquarian John Ross advocated the extension of tolerance to dissenters in the House of Lords.[51] Israel Mauduit, of Huguenot descent, was a nonconformist, and a writer on religious freedom and politics. John Pringle, president of the Royal Society from 1772, made it his lifework to reform medicine and sanitation in the military.[52] George Baker determined that in his county, Devonshire, drinkers of cider were being poisoned by lead; denounced as a faithless son, Baker nevertheless got his fellow Devonians to stop using lead vats, and he went on to clarify the whole subject of lead poisoning.[53] Watson and Huck Saunders were among the twenty-nine "rebel Licentiates" who joined John Fothergill in urging the Royal College of

[48] Lillywhite, *London Coffee Houses*, 745. Beginning in 1754, a group met every Sunday at Willoughby's house until spring, when it moved to Birch's house; this alternation was kept up for years. The regular members were Watson, Heberden, Israel Mauduit, James Burrow, Daniel Wray, and several other Fellows of the Royal Society with whom Cavendish met socially; he might be expected to have belonged, but he did not. Thomas Birch Diary, 19 May 1754 passim.

[49] Request to be "admitted to the private meetings, of several learned Gentlemen, at Lord Macclesfield's and Lord Willoughby's." Rodolph De Vall-Travers to Thomas Birch, n.d. [4 April 1757], BL Add Mss 4320, f.9.

[50] Andrew Kippis's life of the author published in John Pringle, *Six Discourses, Delivered by Sir John Pringle, Bart. When President of the Royal Society; on Occasion of Six Annual Assignments of Sir Godfrey Copley's Medal. To Which Is Prefixed the Life of the Author. By Andrew Kippis, D.D. F.R.S. and S.A.* (London, 1783), lxiii–lxiv. Kippis says that the group met at Mr. Watson's. This Watson he identifies as a grocer, so he cannot be William Watson.

[51] "Ross or Rosse, John," *DNB* 17:266–67.

[52] "Pringle, Sir John," *DNB* 16:386–89, on 388.

[53] "Baker, Sir George," *DNB* 1:927–29, on 928.

Physicians to admit more readily as Fellows physicians who did not have an M.D. from Cambridge or Oxford.[54] Heberden, from within the College of Physicians, sided with Fothergill, Watson, and Huck Saunders. Heberden had already been a thorn in the side of the College of Physicians with his denunciation of mithridatum, a presumed antidote to poisons, as an ineffective farrago, which the College nonetheless kept in its pharmacopia until late in the century, when his former pupil George Baker took over the presidency. Like Birch, Heberden was a fervid whig, a Wilkite, and a supporter of petitioning clergy.[55] Science, it would appear, provided Cavendish not only an outlet for his intellectual and administrative energies but also the company of men who worked for improvement in a wide range of endeavors.

Cavendish met with scientifically inclined friends in other houses as well, including his own house on Great Marlborough Street. We have a record of fifteen dinners he hosted between 1748 and 1761, to which a total of thirty-two guests came, and to which Charles's son Henry may be added. Birch was at all of these dinners, necessarily, for our knowledge of them comes from Birch, who kept a social calendar in the form of a diary.

Cavendish is first mentioned in Birch's diary in 1730, as if he were public news: "Ld Ch Cavendish resigns."[56] The reference is clearly to Cavendish's resignation as gentleman of the bedchamber to the prince of Wales. Birch's first mention of any personal contact with Cavendish was six years later, in 1736. Their connection then was probably rather formal, since in that entry, and in an entry a year later, Birch identified Cavendish as the brother of the duke of Devonshire.[57] The occasion for this early contact was Birch's scholarship, for Birch recorded that Cavendish gave him original papers concerning his grandfather William Russell, who, Birch noted, was beheaded in Charles II's reign.[58] Here Charles was acting as a representative of the great Cavendish and Russell families, but he and Birch did become close personal friends.

A letter from Birch to Philip Yorke in 1750 gives us a glimpse of Cavendish's social life. Cavendish invited Birch and six other "Bretheren of the Royal Society" to a "small Party," at which he offered a "philosophical Entertainment of an artificial Frost by a Solution of Sal Ammoniac in common Water," after which he provided "what was equally relish'd, a very good Dinner."[59] (This particular

[54] Dorothea Waley Singer, "Sir John Pringle and His Circle–Part I. Life," *Annals of Science* 6 (1949): 127–80, on 161–62.

[55] Humphry Rolleston, "The Two Heberdens," *Annals of Medical History* 5 (1933): 409–24, 566–83, on 412–13, 567–68.

[56] Thomas Birch Diary, 12 Oct. 1730.

[57] Thomas Birch Diary, 29 June 1736 and 1 Aug. 1737.

[58] Thomas Birch Diary, 1 Aug. 1737.

[59] Thomas Birch to Philip Yorke, 18 Aug. 1750, BL Add Mss 35397. The guests were Birch, Folkes, Heberden, Watson, Thomas Wilbraham, and Nicholas Mann.

experiment on artificial frost foreshadowed Henry Cavendish's later researches on freezing solutions.) If Cavendish performed experiments at his other dinners, we do not know, but it was not an unheard of entertainment at the time. Earlier that same year, Cavendish agreed to come to dinner at Martin Folkes's house, to which John Canton was invited along with his magnetic bars. Cavendish, Folkes told Canton, was "very curious" to see Canton perform his experiment, which Cavendish could do "more at ease" at Folkes's house than he could at the Society. The next year, when Folkes was ill, Cavendish presided at the Royal Society and gave an undoubtedly well-prepared, "excellent discourse" on Canton's artificial magnets, for which Canton received the Copley Medal.[60]

Let us look at who came to dinner at Cavendish's house. On 21 October 1758 Cavendish had eight dinner guests, all professional men, all but one middle aged, some but not all married. They were mutual friends, not people Cavendish brought together for introductions. Besides Birch, two others at that dinner, Watson and Heberden, also came to most of the other dinners at Cavendish's. The guests were all active Fellows of the Royal Society, though with the exception of Birch, who was secretary of the Society, they were not then on the council; it is possible that the social evening was combined with a meeting for a specific purpose, perhaps relating to the Royal Society. Cavendish, the only aristocrat, at fifty-four was the next-to-oldest member of the party. His senior by two years, Thomas Wilbraham had long been practicing medicine in London and was then physician to Westminster Hospital. Birch was fifty-two, like Cavendish a long-time widower, with an adult daughter about thirty. Watson was forty-three and married, or at least he had been married, with a son of about fourteen and a daughter. Having started out as an apothecary, Watson was now practicing as a physician, and in the minutes of the meetings of the Royal Society, he had just begun to be listed as "Dr. Watson." Heberden was forty-eight, another widower, with a son about five who was probably living at home. Earlier Heberden had lectured on medicine in Cambridge, but for the past ten years he had been practicing in London. Israel Mauduit at fifty was a rich bachelor, who liked to entertain at home himself. Samuel Squire was about forty-five, married, and probably with children by now (he eventually had three). Indebted to the duke of Newcastle for advancement, this ambitious clergyman was about to rise higher, to bishop. Gowin Knight, at forty-five and apparently unmarried, was then devoting himself to the mariner's compass and to his new duties as principal librarian of the British Museum. The only young man in the company was John Hadley, twenty-seven, who that year had been elected to the Royal Society. Hadley was still trying to find his place in the world, dividing his time between Cambridge, where he was professor of chemistry, and London, where he was soon to settle and become physician to St. Thomas's Hospital. These were men of liberal outlook and so far as we know

[60] Royal Society, JB 20:571–73 (30 Nov. 1751).

their political leaning, whig. Some of them were university men, some–including the accomplished Birch and Watson, and the host, Cavendish himself–were not.

Attending Cavendish's dinner were several very good scientific men–only the year before, Cavendish had been awarded the Copley Medal, as had two of his guests earlier, Watson and Knight–but this dinner was not, scientifically speaking, particularly high-powered. Certain of Cavendish's guests were primarily interested in antiquities, which made the party a mix like the membership of the Royal Society itself. Only Watson had published extensively in the *Philosophical Transactions*, on a varity of subjects, including his professional field, medicine, but also electricity, on which he had important papers. Knight's papers on magnetism were just that year coming out in a collection. Heberden had published four papers on miscellaneous topics, one, a human calculus, falling within his professional field, medicine. Birch too had published four papers, one on Roman inscriptions belonging to his field, history. Half of the guests were, like Cavendish himself, one-paper men. Wilbraham had published a medical account of an hydrophobia. Hadley's one paper was yet to come, on a mummy examined in London. Mauduit's paper was on a wasp's nest. Squire's was on a person who had been dumb for four years and had recovered his tongue upon experiencing a bad dream. Since the dinner guests were all men of learning, some, like Birch, had substantial publications outside of the *Philosophical Transactions*.

Over the period for which we have a record, 1748 to 1762, Cavendish and Birch also dined at Heberden's and Stanhope's houses as often as at Cavendish's, and at Watson's, Lord Macclesfield's, and Yorke's about half as often.[61] With Birch, together with other men of science and learning, Cavendish dined two hundred times, at houses and also often at the Mitre with the Royal Society Club.[62] What brought Cavendish and the others together was, apart from conviviality, a common public life including, if not centering on, the Royal Society.

Cavendish was especially close to three of the colleagues we have discussed, Birch, Heberden, and Watson. Birch was an historian, biographer, and cleric, who met the scientific men more than halfway. Halley signed Birch's certificate at the Royal Society, which read that Birch was "well versed in Mathematics and Natural Philosophy."[63] When Pierre Bayle's biographical dictionary was translated into English in 1710, London publishers planned a revision that would do more justice to English notables, and Birch, at age twenty-six, was invited to be one of its three editors. Appearing in ten volumes between 1734 and 1741, three volumes of which

[61] Birch's Diary records dinners in which Cavendish was present at the homes of fourteen persons, all but one of whom were Fellows of the Royal Society. The names are familiar: in addition to those mentioned above, they include Josiah Colebrooke, Samuel Squire, Mark Akenside, Philip Yorke, Daniel Wray, and William Sotheby.

[62] This count of two hundred is from Birch's Diary. It is a minimum number, since Birch made his entries hastily, not always giving the names of everyone he dined with. Cavendish's name was probably among those sometimes omitted.

[63] Gunther, *Birch*, 13–19.

FRIENDS AND COLLEAGUES

18. *Thomas Birch. Painting by J. Wills, engraving by J. Faber, Jr. Reproduced by permission of the Trustees of the British Museum.*

19. *William Watson. Painting by L. F. Abbot. Reproduced by permission of the President and Council of the Royal Society.*

20. *William Heberden. Painting by Sir William Beechey. Courtesy of the Royal College of Physicians.*

were dedicated to presidents of the Royal Society, this work contained biographies of English scientific notables such as Newton and Flamsteed, written by Birch, who consulted with persons who had known them: Halley, Bradley, and Jones. Birch's most important literary contribution to science was his biography of the seventeenth-century chemist Robert Boyle, to whom he was drawn for his religious and scholarly knowledge as well as for his scientific work, a combination of interests Birch himself had.[64] In his account of Boyle, Birch implied the importance for one's scholarly work of living near other scholars, as Boyle did at Oxford, and as Birch himself did in London, meeting with them in its coffeehouses, salons, and institutions of learning.[65] In 1757, he completed a history of the Royal Society. He had intended to bring it up to date to 1750, but in four volumes he did not get past the seventeenth century, which is where he left it. He prepared his history from the original journals, registers, letters, and council minutes, reproducing many of these materials, chronicling the Society meeting by meeting; his method of history was the method of science, as he understood it, the bringing together of facts.[66] Birch, who depended on clerical livings, and who was chaplain to the College of Physicians, cited Newton in notes to his sermons.[67] An irrepressible conversationalist, Birch was "brisk as a bee," according to Johnson, a connoisseur of conversation.[68] An historian who wrote of science to praise it, a man of facts, convivial and energetic, Birch was a welcome addition in scientific circles.

Like Birch, Heberden, a physician, met the men of science more than halfway. One of his goals was to make the College of Physicians a medical version of the Royal Society, a proper scientific body. He used his influence in the College–in which he took on the duties of councillor, censor, and elect, one of the powerful senior fellows who chose the president from among themselves–to establish a committee of papers and a journal modeled and named after the Royal Society's *Philosophical Transactions*, the *Medical Transactions*. He was himself a man of science. Consistent with his belief that until a Newton appeared in the science of the animate world to discover the "great principle of life," medicine had only one recourse, experience, he regarded his job as the patient and laborious assembling of facts; a painstakingly accurate observer, he made no large generalizations (or discoveries). Despite his admonitions to physicians to publish, he himself was reluctant to do so. His high reputation was based on his practice and his knowledge of the classics, a combination in irreversible decline. Upon being asked what physician he wanted in his final illness, Johnson called for Heberden, "the last of

64 Thomas Birch, *The Life of the Honourable Robert Boyle* (London, 1744), 304–7.

65 Birch, *Boyle*, 113–14.

66 Thomas Birch, *The History of the Royal Society of London for Improving of Natural Knowledge, from Its First Rise* . . . , 4 vols. (London, 1756–57).

67 C. Barton to Thomas Birch, 19 Sep. 1754, BL Add Mss 4300, f. 174. Thomas Birch's Sermons, vol. 7, f. 188, BL Add Mss 4232C.

68 "Birch," *DNB* 2:531.

our learned physicians."[69] More than any other member, Watson made the meetings of the Royal Society rewarding, keeping it abreast of major developments in science. For his role as informant, he was well equipped, equally capable of giving the Society a thorough exposition of Franklin's work in electricity and Linnaeus's work in botany. Forceful, knowledgeable (because of his remarkable memory, he was referred to as the "living lexicon of botany"), a good judge of men, Watson entered energetically into the administration of the Royal Society as he did into that of the other institutions he served, which were more or less the same ones that Birch, Heberden, and Cavendish served.[70]

We learn more about Cavendish's friendships and associations by looking at his activity in the Royal Society. Although there is no record of how he voted on candidates considered for admission to the Society, we know which candidates he recommended and the members with whom he signed recommendations.

Even before a candidate was proposed for membership, he was usually canvassed by the council. The candidate had then to be formally recommended by three or more members, who drew up a sheet with their signatures, the candidate's name, address, and profession, and a brief description of his qualifications for membership. This sheet would be dated and posted by one of the secretaries in the meeting room for the period of several ordinary meetings before the candidate was put to the vote. An exception was made for peers and their sons and various dignitaries, for whom only one recommender was required. Election was by two-thirds of those present.[71] To further a candidate's chances, other members could add their signatures to the sheet. Ten, not an uncommon number, signed Henry Cavendish's certificate in 1760. Occasionally there was a groundswell of enthusiasm for a candidate, as there was for Captain James Cook, whose certificate was signed by twenty-five members, including Henry Cavendish. Certain members constantly put up candidates, and on them falls a good share of responsibility for the early rapid growth of the Society. In the first forty years the number of ordinary members tripled to three hundred, and the number of foreign members grew even faster, rising to almost half the number of ordinary members.[72] During the twenty-five years that Lord Charles

[69] Humphry Rolleston, "The Two Heberdens," 414, 417. Audley Cecil Buller, *The Life and Works of Heberden* (London, 1879), 16, 21–22. William Munck, *The Roll of the Royal College of Physicians of London. Comprising Biographical Sketches of All the Eminent Physicians Whose Names Are Recorded in the Annals*, 2d ed., 4 vols. (London, 1878) 2:159–64. William Heberden, *Commentaries on the History and Cure of Diseases*, 2d ed. (London, 1803), 483, and appendix, "A Sketch of a Preface Designed for the Medical Transactions, 1767," 486–94.

[70] "Watson, Sir William," *DNB* 20:956–58.

[71] 20 Aug. 1730, Minutes of Council, copy, Royal Society 3:51, 77. We have consulted two sources of the Royal Society's Minutes of Council: copies in the Royal Society Library, and microfilm of University Publications of America. To distinguish between the two sources, where our reference is to the copies in the Royal Society Library, we write "copy."

[72] Royal Society, Certificates 3:237 (23 Nov. 1775). Henry Lyons, *The Royal Society 1600–1940: A History of Its Administration under Its Charters* (Cambridge: Cambridge University Press, 1944), 125–26.

Cavendish recommended candidates, the growth of the Society markedly slowed. Cavendish's own contribution was moderate: between 1734 and 1766, he recommended twenty-eight candidates, fewer than one a year.

Birch, who recommended a large number of candidates, on the order of a half dozen a year, signed recommendations with Cavendish more often than any other member, nineteen times.[73] Next came Folkes with ten recommendations in common with Cavendish, then Watson and Wray, each with nine. This agreement is probably not surprising, since Birch, Watson, and Wray, as we have seen, were good friends of Cavendish. Then came Jones, of the De Moivre circle, Cavendish's own recommender, then Burrow, and then Willoughby. There was only one person who signed often with Cavendish with whom he does not seem to have had outside connections, John Machin, professor of astronomy at Gresham College and secretary of the Royal Society; Machin died in 1751, early in this account, and he was in poor health in his last years, which may explain his absence. It should be noted that Cavendish joined Sloane in his early recommendations until Sloane retired as president in 1741. Among Cavendish's ninety-three co-signers, most of the other familiar names appear too, though with less frequency: Heberden, Bradley, Stanhope, De Moivre, Macclesfield, Scott, Jurin, Davall, and Richard Graham, to name several.

If we now turn from Cavendish's co-signers to the candidates he recommended, we get another indication of his associations. In 1753 the council resolved that candidates were to be known "personally" to their recommenders, a practice which in the past had usually been followed though not invariably.[74] We can be reasonably certain that Cavendish was on a personal basis with most if not all of the persons he recommended. Seventeen of the certificates he signed said that the candidates were proficient in the sciences, designated variously as natural philosophy, experimental philosophy, natural knowledge, natural history, philosophical knowledge, philosophy, and different branches of science; six certificates mentioned mathematics, three useful learning, two mechanics, and another two astronomy. Seven of the candidates were said to be distinguished in literature or polite learning, though never that alone. There were a few other accomplishments: antiquities, architecture, medicine, anatomy, musical theory, and (not very helpful) learning and knowledge. Two candidates were professors at Cambridge and Oxford, about whom nothing more needed to be given than the names of their professorships, which in their cases were astronomy and experimental philosophy. For one other candidate no explanation was given other than his position, under-librarian at the British Museum, an institution in which Cavendish was an officer. Recommenders of foreign members of the Society did not have to know the candidates personally but they did have to know

[73] In 1748–60, Birch recommended seventy-six candidates. Royal Society, Certificates.

[74] 10 May 1753, Minutes of Council, copy, Royal Society 4:118–19.

their work. Cavendish recommended three French candidates, one an astronomer, the other two known as authors of a commentary on Newton's *Principia.* It is clear that the persons Cavendish helped gain entry into the Royal Society favored the physico-mathematical sciences, as might be expected, but they were not narrowly identified with particular areas. This dimension of generality is to be expected, given the composition of the Society. Every candidate Cavendish recommended was elected, with the exception of the first, a surgeon, whose rejection may have been due to a suspicion of surgeons in the Society;[75] in 1734 Cavendish joined Sloane, two others, and John Stevens, one of the surgeons to the prince of Wales, in a recommendation of John Wreden, another surgeon to the prince of Wales, both of whom Cavendish probably would have known, since he recently had been gentleman of the bedchamber to the prince of Wales. That, in general, a recommendation by Cavendish was useful to a candidate there can be little doubt. When Joseph Priestley, who unlike Cavendish had to make his living, which he did in part by the sale of his books, was informed that membership in the Royal Society would encourage sales of his book on the history of electricity, he discussed his prospects and strategy with his friend John Canton. Priestley expected that not only Canton but Watson and Richard Price would support his candidacy, constituting the necessary minimum number of three recommenders, and "If L. C. Cavendish could be prevailed upon to join you," he told Canton, "I should think the rest would be easy." (Canton, it would seem, refused to approach Lord Charles Cavendish on the technical ground that Priestley was not a "personal acquaintance" of his.)[76]

SORROWS AND RICHES

As he grew up, Frederick Cavendish–Fredy, his family called him[77]–followed in his older brother Henry's footsteps, at a two-year interval, first attending Hackney Academy and then Peterhouse, Cambridge. In the year after Henry Cavendish came down from Cambridge, in his next to final year at Cambridge, Frederick Cavendish had a bizarre accident, falling from an upper window in one of the courts and striking his head. There is no indication of what he was doing in that window. Riotous behavior at Cambridge was common enough, prompting Thomas Gray to change his living quarters and affiliation, from Peterhouse, Frederick's college, to Pembroke across the street. Or like father, like son, perhaps

[75] Maurice Crosland, "Explicit Qualifications as a Criterion for Membership of the Royal Society: A Historical Review," *Notes and Records of the Royal Society of London* 37 (1983): 167–87, on 171.

[76] Joseph Priestley to John Canton, 14 Feb. 1766, Canton Papers, Royal Society, 2:58. Priestley was elected that year without the help of Cavendish, Benjamin Franklin joining the other three instead. Joseph Priestley to Richard Price, 8 Mar. 1766, in *A Scientific Autobiography of Joseph Priestley (1738–1804)*, ed. R. E. Schofield (Cambridge, Mass.: M.I.T. Press, 1966), 17–19, on 19.

[77] Henry Cavendish referred to "Fredy's" letters and expenses in "Papers in Walnut Cabinet," Cavendish Mss Misc.

Frederick was in his window trying Franklin's experiment on lightning. Whatever the cause, the fall was serious, leaving Frederick's life in the balance for a time and his head with a deep indentation as a reminder of it.[78] The accident happened in late July or early August 1754; by mid-August Frederick was "mending, but not out of danger."[79] That summer Lord Charles Cavendish had been dining frequently with his scientific friends, but then for four and a half months he dropped out, due in part to Frederick's condition.[80] In mid-October, Thomas Birch wrote to Lord Charles to say that his friends hoped that "Mr. Frederick Cavendish's Recovery" would soon allow Lord Charles to join them "in town."[81] Frederick did gradually regain his health, but his brain was permanently impaired.

Of how Frederick occupied himself in the years after his accident, there is no account. However, thanks to the legal and financial ties that bound in the eighteenth century, we have his father's view of Frederick's mental "state." As was the custom with marriage settlements, the younger son Frederick's eventual prosperity was looked after by his mother, who at her death in 1733 left him her one quarter share of the duke of Kent's Steane estate, which was sold and converted into stock that was placed in the hands of trustees. In 1772 the last surviving trustee, Lord William Manners, died, and his son, John, did not want the inherited trusteeship. This meant that Lord Charles Cavendish had to choose new trustees, who would have to be persuaded of the legality of the way the trust had been used in the past. Cavendish wrote up a case for his practice, submitting it for legal opinion. He had been receiving the profits from the Steane estate and after its sale the dividends from stock. His justification was that because of Frederick's accident, "it was manifestly improper to pay the money to him" during his minority. Frederick was then thirty-nine, and "even now," Cavendish said, "it appears to be doubtful whether it is prudent to do it." Cavendish had spent the earnings from the trust on the "maintenance & education" of Frederick, the "expense of which greatly exceeded the income of the estate, except in some of the first years of F's life." The legal opinion he solicited, however, held that the trustees had no power to permit him to receive that money for the purpose he gave, for it was a father's duty to support his child. In the eyes of the law, then, although it was not put this way, Cavendish had been stealing from his disabled son, and he and his heirs (who would be Henry Cavendish) were accountable to Frederick for the money taken from him. Despite this ruling, the new trustees chosen by Cavendish, all members of the family, agreed to let him continue to

[78] Lord Charles Cavendish's legal case involving his marriage settlement and Frederick's expenses, 30 Apr. 1773. Devon. Coll., L/114/32. "Memoirs of the Late Frederick Cavendish, Esq.," *Gentlemen's Magazine* 82 (1812): 289–91, on 289.

[79] Lord Hartington to the duke of Devonshire, 17 Aug. 1754. Devon. Coll., no. 260.119.

[80] Lord Charles Cavendish hosted a dinner at his house on 17 July 1754; the next time he dined with this circle was at Stanhope's house, on 2 December of that year. Thomas Birch Diary.

[81] Thomas Birch to Lord Charles Cavendish, 17 Oct. 1754, BL Add Mss 4444, f. 180.

accept all dividends and interest from the funds in their name. Henry Cavendish as well as Lord Charles was a party to the new–but in effect old–financial arrangements for Frederick's support. Several lawyers became involved, but in the documents we have seen, there is no suggestion that Frederick himself was unhappy with his father. What we have learned is that in Lord Charles's judgment, his son Frederick was incompetent.[82]

Henry and Frederick Cavendish made a visit to Paris at some time or other. Travel abroad after leaving the university was the standard way for a young man to complete his education, and we can imagine that Henry combined this course with an effort to include Frederick in the world. This journey by the two brothers is the occasion of the earliest anecdote about Henry Cavendish. At a hotel in Calais, the brothers passed a room in which a corpse was laid out for burial; neither said anything, but the next day on the road to Paris, this conversation took place. " 'Fred. C., *loq.*–Did you see the corpse?' 'Henry C., *res.*–I did.' "[83] This (Pinteresque) fragment would suggest both Henry's taciturnity and a reserve between the brothers, for which there is other evidence. Frederick and Henry's relationship was cordial but distant.

Lord James, the brother with whom Lord Charles had travelled abroad as a youth, was the older of the two, but he deferred to Charles in family affairs, asking Charles to dispose of his mother's estate and giving him power of attorney in all matters of their joint executorship.[84] Lord James's military life took him away, to Ireland and elsewhere; later he was a Member of Parliament for Malton. He died in 1714, at age thirty-eight.[85]

Lord Charles's eldest brother, William, who was interested in art, evidently also had some interest in science, in which case there would have been an additional bond between the brothers. William was elected to the Royal Society in 1747, and he subscribed to a number of scientific books to which Lord Charles also subscribed, for example, books by De Moivre in 1730, Roger Long in 1742, and Colin Maclaurin in 1748.[86] Charles kept accounts with William,[87] and he served him as

[82] "Copy Case Between Father and Son with Mr. Perryn," 30 Apr. 1773. Lord Charles Cavendish to S. Seddon, 27 and 29 July 1772. "Discharge from the Right Honourable Lord Charles Cavendish to John Manners Esqr as to Trusts for his Lordship and the Honourable Henry Cavendish & Frederick Cavendish His Sons." Devon. Coll., L/14/32. The new trustees were Philip Yorke, earl of Hardwicke, and Lord Charles's nephews Lords Frederick and George Augustus Cavendish.

[83] George Wilson, *The Life of the Honourable Henry Cavendish* (London, 1851), 18, 173.

[84] Lord James Cavendish to Lord Charles Cavendish, 25 Mar. 1727 and 23 Aug. 1732, Devon. Coll., no. 34/2.

[85] *Gentleman's Magazine* 11 (1741): 609.

[86] Subscriber lists in Abraham De Moivre, *Miscellanea analytica de seriebus et quadraturis* (London, 1730); Roger Long, *Astronomy, In Five Books*, vol. 1 (Cambridge, 1742); Colin Maclaurin, *An Account of Sir Isaac Newton's Philosophical Discoveries* (London, 1748).

[87] Lord Charles Cavendish, "Account between My Br. Devonshire & Me. June 18. 1733," Devon. Coll., 86/comp 1.

a political go-between,[88] but they led very different lives, due in part to temperament and in part to their order of birth. William and Charles started out the same way, as Members of Parliament, but Charles left politics and William did not and realistically could not. After his father's death in 1729, William, as third duke of Devonshire, sat in the House of Lords, where he rarely spoke, and when he did it was with such a soft voice that no one could hear him. Not a leader of the party and not a fighter, William accepted high office without high ambition. Like his father, he was a friend of Walpole and did well by the friendship. Walpole made him lord privy seal, then lord lieutenant of Ireland, a responsible, highly lucrative job because of its immense patronage. Local government was the basis of political power in the eighteenth century, and the lord lieutenant of a county was the highest local official, though the lord lieutenancy of Ireland had a trace of derogation; in any event, William carried out this job competently for seven years. William did favors for Walpole in kind, helping to keep him in office.[89] William was a hard drinker, a gambler, not overly smart, and distinctly lazy. He was also cautious and duty-bound, family traits which could be regarded as strengths. Johnson, who rarely saw anything he could admire in a whig, saw in William a man who was "unconditional . . . in keeping his word," a man of "honor."[90] The record we have of Charles's relationship with his brother William has entirely to do with money or property. That was so even during the Jacobite rebellion of 1745, when the pretender, Prince Charles Edward Stuart, landed in Scotland from France, raised an army, and advanced south. The rebels reached as far as Derby, menacing Chatsworth. By subscription, William raised a regiment in Derbyshire to stop the invasion. In London, Charles was William's surrogate banker and advisor; unless William's medals at Chatsworth were "sent out of the Kingdom" (which speaks of the peril of the dynasty, as Lord Charles saw it), he did not think they could be saved if the French landed, since there would be a rising right there.[91] Nothing, as

[88] In a dispute over appointments between the duke of Devonshire and the duke of Newcastle, duke of Devonshire to Hartington, 8 and 20 May, 15 and 24 June 1755. Devon. Coll., nos. 163.51, 163.52, 163.60, and 163.62.

[89] J. H. Plumb, *Sir Robert Walpole* (London: Cresset, 1956–60), 1:42–43, 235–36, and 2:280.

[90] John Pearson, *The Serpent and the Stag: The Saga of England's Powerful and Glamourous Cavendish Family from the Age of Henry the Eighth to the Present* (New York: Holt, Rinehart and Winston, 1983), 89–91; quotation from Johnson on 90.

[91] William, Lord Hartington to Dr. Newcome, 14 Dec. 1745; Lord Charles Cavendish to the duke of Devonshire, undated, Devon. Coll., nos. 260.58 and 211.3; John Whitaker to Dickenson Knight, undated [1745]; R. Knight to Dickenson Knight, undated [Dec. 1745]; John Holland to Ralph Knight, undated [1745], in Great Britain, Historical Manuscripts Commission, *Report on the Manuscripts of Sir William Fitzherbert, Bart., and Others* (London: Her Majesty's Stationery Office, 1893), 164–65. William, duke of Devonshire to Robert Wilmot, 25 Oct. 1745, in Great Britain, Historical Manuscripts Commission, *Report on the Liang Manuscripts Preserved in the University of Edinburgh*, vol. 2 (London: His Majesty's Stationary Office, 1925), 349. Richard Burden to [Viscount Irwin], 7 Dec. 1745, Great Britain, Historical Manuscripts Commission, *Report on Manuscripts in Various Collections*. Vol. 8: *The Manuscripts of the Hon. Frederick Lindley Wood; M. L. S. Clemens, Esq.; Philip Unwin, Esq.* (London: His Majesty's Stationary Office, 1913), 138.

it turned out, had to be done, since the prince was forced to retreat and the revolt ended in 1746.

William had confidence in his youngest brother. Two years after succeeding to the dukedom, William made out his will, in which he left to William Manners and others his horses but named twenty-seven-year-old Charles Cavendish and his wife, Anne, and Robert Walpole trustees for his seven children.[92] Of his four sons, three entered politics, all staunch whigs and allies of Fox, and one entered the military, which by then was an uncommon career for a Cavendish. The youngest son, Lord John, who was Henry Cavendish's age and went through school with Henry, held cabinet posts; of the sons he was by far the most determined in politics. But the oldest son, William, was the most determined in love, and in so being, he knitted together the two greatest aristocratic families in science, Robert Boyle's and Henry Cavendish's. When he was twenty-eight, William picked for his wife the sixteen-year-old Charlotte Boyle, a distant relation of the seventeenth-century chemist. From the point of view of the Cavendish fortune, she was a prize, the sole heir of the immensely rich Lord Burlington. (There is a legend that Henry Cavendish was brought up in Burlington House in Piccadilly, but it seems rather improbable.)[93] But the Burlington family was talked about not because of its wealth but because of its scandals, which decided William's mother, herself a commoner before becoming duchess of Devonshire, against the match. The duke supported his son, the marriage took place, and the third duke's own marriage fell apart as a consequence. The practical result of all this turmoil was that the already fabulous Cavendish estate nearly doubled in value.[94] To William's sorrow, his wife did not live long enough to become duchess, and he himself did not live many years after becoming the fourth duke. Lord Charles Cavendish was the responsible family intermediary, meeting several times with the third duke's lawyer in connection with his son's marriage to Charlotte Boyle.[95]

The third duke of Devonshire died in 1755, and for a time his will was lost. Lord Charles found it, written on a sheet of letter paper and almost worn out, not showy, in keeping with everything else about the plain third duke; with the disposition of property now clarified, life could go on.[96] Like his eldest son, the

[92] Duke of Devonshire, "My Will," 1 Oct. 1731. Devon. Coll., no. 163.95.

[93] Royal Society, *The Record of the Royal Society of London*, 4th ed. (London: Royal Society of London, 1940), 65. By the time the Boyles and the Cavendishes became in-laws (for the second time) and the Cavendishes thereby acquired Burlington House, Henry Cavendish was about to begin his university studies.

[94] Pearson, *The Serpent and the Stag*, 93–103.

[95] Lord Charles Cavendish's involvement is reflected in the statement of expenses rendered to the third duke by Hutton Perkins, the duke's lawyer, on 13 May 1748. Devon. Coll., no. 313.1.

[96] R. Landaff to the fourth duke of Devonshire, 6 Dec. 1755; Thomas Heaton to the fourth duke of Devonshire, 6 Dec. 1755. Devon. Coll., nos. 356.5 and 432.0. Theophilus Lindsey to Earl of Huntington, 24 Dec. 1755. Great Britain, Historical Manuscripts Commission, *Report on the Manuscripts of the Late Reginald Rawdon Hastings, Esq., of the Manor House Ashby de la Zouche*, 4 vols. (London: His Majesty's Stationary Office, 1928–47) 3:111–14, on 113.

third duke's daughters made notable marriages. Lady Rachel married the famous Horace Walpole's cousin and namesake. Lady Carolina married William Ponsonby, second earl of Bessborough, who at the time was secretary to the third duke as lord lieutenant of Ireland; to their son, the third earl of Bessborough, Henry Cavendish would leave a sixth of his great fortune.[97] Lady Elizabeth married John Ponsonby, of the same family, and to make up her dowry the duke, who was rich in property but short of cash, borrowed from Lord Charles Cavendish.[98]

Lord Charles Cavendish assumed various obligations for the women of his family. Together with his uncle Lord James, he served as executor of the estate of his aunt Lady Elizabeth (Cavendish) Wentworth.[99] In 1723, after his daughter Diana died in childhood, the second duke of Devonshire set aside lands to raise dowries for each of his three surviving daughters, Rachel, Elizabeth, and Anne. Rachel and Elizabeth were about to be married at the time, and their brother Charles was named representative for Anne, who was without prospect and never did marry. In time everyone was paid off in cash with interest to keep the properties within the Cavendish estate,[100] but Charles had to talk hard to bring Anne around to the logic of it, she being "extreamly jealous, & fearful of being injured."[101]

Like all of the second duke's daughters who did not die prematurely, Anne lived a long life, to seventy. Rachel, who married Sir William Morgan of Tredegar of a family of big landowners and country whigs, had four children, and lived upwards of eighty.[102] Charles kept in touch with Rachel's family: when her daughter Elizabeth married William Jones of Llanarthy, Charles was a party to

---

97 Entries for the second and third earls of Bessborough, in *Collins's Peerage of England* 7:266–67. Francis Bickley, *The Cavendish Family* (London: Constable, 1911), 207.

98 "Bond from His Grace the Duke of Devonshire to the R[t] Hon[ble] Lord Charles Cavendish," 22 Sep. 1743, Devon. Coll., L/44/12.

99 "Probate of the Will of L[y] Eliz. Wentworth 1741," Devon. Coll., L/43/13. Lady Elizabeth was the widow of Sir John Wentworth of Northempsall. Seven years later, Lords Charles and James Cavendish were released from any further claim on them as executors by another Lady Wentworth, Dame Bridget of York: "L[y] Wentworths Release to Lady Betty Wentworths Executors March 5 1748." But Lord Charles kept a notebook for Lady Betty Wentworth's personal estate for twenty years, from 1741 to 1761. After 1748 Lords Charles and James regularly received a small dividend from two hundred shares of South Sea stock. After Lord James's death, his part went to Richard (Chandler) Cavendish and, eventually, to Lord Charles.

100 "Deed to Exonerate the Estate of the Duke of Devonshire from the Several Portions of Six Thousand Pounds . . . to be Directed to Be Raised for Lady Rachel Morgan, Lady Elizabeth Lowther and Anne Cavendish the Three Surviving Daughters of William Second Duke of Devonshire," 28 July 1775. Devon. Coll., L/19/67.

101 Lord Charles Cavendish to John Heaton, 28 Aug. 1775, draft, and "Account of Deeds to Be Executed by Lord Charles Cavendish." Devon. Coll., 86/comp. 1.

102 *Collins's Peerage of England* 1:356. *The Victoria History of the County of Hertford* (Folkestone and London: University of London, Institute of Historical Research, 1971) 2:190. Geoffrey Holmes, *British Politics in the Age of Anne* (London: Macmillan, 1967), 222.

the settlement.[103] In 1723 Charles's sister Elizabeth married the Member of Parliament for Lancaster, Sir Thomas Lowther, whose family together with the Musgraves "controlled the nerve centre of political power in the two border counties of Cumberland and Westmoreland."[104] The Lowther connection drew Charles into a legal fog worthy of Dickens.

Frequently Lord Charles saw his sister Lady Elizabeth at Chatsworth or at Holker, the great Lowther house in Lancashire, edged with magnificent gardens, set on a wooded, hilly park on Morecambe Bay.[105] Charles was named godfather to Elizabeth's second child.[106] Then the troubles began. The spunky Elizabeth, who wished she had been a boy so she could have gone abroad with Charles and James, went insane. In 1737 she was placed in the hands of physicians "to try what effect it will have upon her to make her of better behaviour."[107] It evidently had none. Her husband, Sir Thomas, a kind but improvident man, lapsed into heavy drinking and debt. In 1745 he died without a will, and his and Elizabeth's one surviving child, William, was placed under the guardianship of Lord Charles Cavendish, the duke of Devonshire, and Lord Lonsdale.[108] For Elizabeth, "Lady B," his insane sister and now widow, he paid a fee to the best doctors in London, Drs. Richard Mead and Edward Wilmot, another to her apothecary, and still other bills to other persons; she did not live long after he took charge of the estate.[109] Soon after Thomas, another Lowther died, his cousin John, leaving most of his estate to Thomas and Elizabeth's child, William, and Charles had now to sort out the details of this property as well. Charles kept on friendly terms with William, his former ward, now of age, inviting him to dinner at his house with scientific friends in 1753.[110] That year Sir William was appointed lord lieutenant of Westmorland,[111] and two years later he was elected

---

[103] Articles on the marriage of William Jones and Elizabeth Morgan, daughter of Lady Rachel Morgan, to which Lord Charles Cavendish was a party, 4 July 1767: Devon. Coll., L/43/16.

[104] *The London Diaries of William Nicolson Bishop of Carlisle 1702–1718*, eds. C. Jones and G. Holmes (Oxford: Clarendon Press, 1985), 3.

[105] Sir Thomas Lowther to Sir James Lowther, 12 Aug. and 5 Sep. 1726, and 11 July 1734. Cumbria County Record Office, Carlisle, D/Lons./W. Bundles 30 and 37. *The Victoria History of the County of Lancaster*, ed. W. Farer and J. Brownbill, vol. 8 (London: Constable, 1914), 270–72.

[106] Sir Thomas Lowther to Sir James Lowther, 8 Aug. 1728, Cumbria County Record Office, Carlisle, D/Lons/W, Letters, 39: Misc. Letters & Papers, 1728–39.

[107] Sir James Lowther to John Spedding, 16 June 1737; quoted in J. V. Beckett, "The Lowthers at Holker: Marriage, Inheritance and Debt in the Fortunes of an Eighteenth-Century Landowning Family," *Transactions of the Historic Society of Lancashire and Cheshire* 127 (1977): 47–64, on 51.

[108] Court appointment of Lord Charles Cavendish as administrator of Sir Thomas Lowther's estate: Devon. Coll., L/31/11. Lord Charles Cavendish to John Fletcher, 18 July 1745; Edward Butler to John Fletcher, 16 May 1745. Lancashire Record Office, DDca 22/5 and 22/3/1.

[109] Lord Charles Cavendish, third notebook, in Devon. Coll., L/43/14. Elizabeth Lowther died in 1747, according to Beckett, "The Lowthers at Holker," 51.

[110] Thomas Birch Diary (5 June 1753).

[111] Beckett, "The Lowthers at Holker," 51.

a Member of Parliament. Then suddenly, in 1756, while attended by Drs. Heberden and Shaw, Sir William died of scarlet fever. William in the meantime had acquired immense riches from his distant uncle Sir James Lowther of Whitehaven, who died in 1755.[112] This Lowther was the fourth Lowther to die in just over ten years; the wealth piled up, and Sir William brought a fortune close to the bosom of the Cavendishes, which was seen as a kind of family coup.[113] Sir William was only twenty-eight when he died, with no successor; his will directed his estate to go to certain people and the work of distributing it to Lord Charles Cavendish, who was entitled to residual plunder.[114]

The great portion of the wealth of the deceased Sir William was reverted by the will of the deceased Sir James Lowther to another James Lowther, the future first earl of Lonsdale, who was not yet of age. The sudden fortune of this young man prompted Horace Walpole to fear that England was becoming the "property of six or seven people."[115] Cavendish, as Sir William's executor, was soon in conflict with young James Lowther. His overseeing of the Lowther properties—manors, farms, colleries, iron pits, lead mines, fire engines, timber, even a fishery—was an immense job, which now became compounded by a lawsuit. Kathrine Lowther, James's mother, thought that Cavendish was unreasonable and hard, and she may have had a point. It is clear that Cavendish hoped to profit from a technicality arising from the close deaths of Sir James and Sir William Lowther. Cavendish was not only Sir William's sole executor, he was also sole executor of Sir James, since the original executor, Sir William, had died almost immedately after Sir James. Charles claimed that Sir James's residual estate passed through Sir William to him. He also claimed £30,000 in New South Sea Annuities, which were put in trust to finance the transfer of Sir William's estate to young James. Charles argued that these funds were his because the transfer of estates could not take place in the specified time for the reason that James was not of age.[116] Charles, that is, claimed property that fell through the legal net; for in neither will was he the intended beneficiary. The case was debated, council on

---

112 Sir James Lowther's will of 1754, Devon. Coll., L/31/17.

113 Henry Fox wrote to Hartington, who in two months would become the fourth duke of Devonshire, "I must wish y^{r} Lordship Joy of the very great Acquisition made by your near Relation S^{r}. W. Lowther, which I am credibly informed, is 4,000£ a year in Land, Coal Mines bringing in 11,000£ a year, & not less than 400,000£ in Money. Sr James Lowther has 100,000£ & an Estate in Middlesex, not a great one." Letter of 4 Jan. 1755. Devon. Coll., no. 330.30.

114 What was not specified in the will went to Lord Charles Cavendish, the sole executor. "Inventory of Wrought Plate from Holker" is a long list of flatware and holloware. The numbers alongside the items are in Henry Cavendish's hand. Devon. Coll., 86/comp. 1.

115 Horace Walpole to Montague, 20 Apr. 1756, *Horace Walpole's Correspondence*, 48 vols., ed. W. S. Lewis (New Haven: Yale University Press, 1941), 9:183–87, on 185.

116 Kathrine Lowther to James Lowther, 8, 11, 15, 19 July 1756; "Heads of What Is Agreed on between Ld Charles Cavendish & Sir James Lowther," n.d. Cumbria Record Office, Carlisle, Archive, D/Lons/L1/61 and 62.

both sides was heard, and the judge declared that the colleries and so forth belonged to young James, and as well the £30,000, and that Cavendish was to pay over to young James the interest on those annuities. Charles lost completely.[117]

The Lowther affair occupied as many pages of notation and probably as much time as Lord Charles Cavendish's scientific experiments. The dispute in the end was entirely impersonal on Cavendish's part, and precisely for that reason, it gives us an insight into his person. His involvement came about because of his sister, who had married a Lowther, but it became more than a family duty; it became an unexpected opportunity. Cavendish, who was already well off, came to believe that he was going to be made rich into the bargain. At the same time he was aware that he was in a delicate position, since any worldly goods that came to him were denied to another, the last in this seqence of Lowthers, the still-living (and still minor) James. The Lowther riches were intended to go to a Lowther, as was right and proper. Lord Charles Cavendish had been invited in as an administrator, but because he was also something of an interloper, he took pains to make clear that his claim on William's personal estate did not arise out of greed: "I do not desire to have a farthing more than I have a right to." We have to take this man of principle at his word: what was his was his by *right*, and so by "law as well as from the principles of justice," he was "intitled" to a full disclosure of the extent and value of the estate, a matter in which he believed he had not been treated with "strict justice." For his part, he intended to "act with perfect openness & candour."[118] The expressions he used, "strict justice" and "perfect openness," are like those, as we will see, that his son Henry would use, applying equally to personal conduct, business, politics, and science.

Try as he might, Lord Charles did not grow rich through the Lowthers, but he did become rich–rather his estate was enriched–through another line of the family. Elizabeth Cavendish was a younger first cousin of Charles, whose father was Lord James Cavendish (Lord Charles's uncle, not his brother of the same name), a Fellow of the Royal Society, who had an interest in mathematics and natural philosophy,[119] and whose mother was Anne Yale, daughter of Elihu, a rich diamond merchant and governor of Fort St. George in Madras, after whom Yale University is named. In 1732 Elizabeth married the politician Richard Chandler, son of Edward Chandler, bishop of Durham, just a year after Lord James's other child, William, had married another Chandler, Barbara. As a man of wide

117 "Sr W. & Sr J. Lowthers' Wills & Papers Relating to Law Suit between L.C.C. & Sr J. Lowther." Devon. Coll., no. 31/17. Cavendish appealed the decision concerning the £30,000.

118 Lord Charles Cavendish to William Richardson, 26, 29 June and 27 July 1756. Lancashire Record Office, DDca, 22/7.

119 Lord James Cavendish and Lord Charles Cavendish together recommended Gowin Knight for fellowship in the Royal Society for his "mathematical and Philosophical knowledge," 24 Jan. 1745, Royal Society, Certificates, vol. 1, no. 14, f. 297.

learning, with a very substantial library, Richard Chandler probably had interests in common with Lord Charles Cavendish.[120] In 1751 Elizabeth's father and brother both died, and her mother had died earlier, leaving only her and Richard Chandler to continue that branch of the family. That year Richard took his wife's name and was known from then on as Richard Cavendish. Richard Cavendish died before Elizabeth, leaving her sole owner of a house in Piccadilly and a great deal more real estate and, in addition, a large sum in securities and mortgages.[121] Having no children, she originally intended to leave her real property to the duke of Devonshire and the rest of her estate to her only living male first cousin on the Cavendish side, Lord Charles. Shortly before her own death, however, she changed her will, cutting off the duke (her second cousin) and naming as co-executor with Lord Charles Cavendish the prominent lawyer and politician Lord Charles Camden. The two executors were to hold the Piccadilly house in trust, but otherwise, as far as Lord Charles was concerned, the will was practically the same. Lord Charles took upon himself the task of executing the will, which, except for the land and specific requests, left everything to him:[122] £75,000 in 3 percent consolidated bank annuities (consols), £22,000 in 3 percent reduced bank annuities, and £47,000 in mortgages. Elizabeth Cavendish's will was brought to court in May 1780, and three and a half years later, shortly after the death of Lord Charles, the fortune it had bequeathed to Charles Cavendish became the property of his son Henry, who thereby became, in due course, the "richest of the wise."[123]

---

[120] Richard Chandler's library evidently encompassed all subjects, including science; it contained books by Newton, Boyle, Hooke, and a good many eighteenth-century scientific writers. *A Catalogue of a Large, Valuable, and Elegant Collection of Books; Including the Libraries of the Late Richard Cavendish, Esq.; the Rev. Dr. Jortin, and Several Other Curious Parcels Lately Purchased. . . . The Sale Will Begin in February 1771. . . . By Benjamin White, at Horace's Head, in Fleet Street, London.*

[121] The round figure of £30,000 turned up again, this time in a promise by the duke of Devonshire to repay that amount to Lady Elizabeth. The duke's promise is in a formal letter enclosed in the document, "The Duke of Devonshire to Lord Charles Cavendish and Mr. [Dudley] Long, Lease for a Year, 15 June 1772." Devon. Coll., L/19/64.

[122] Lady Elizabeth Cavendish's will, 26 Feb. 1778. Devon. Coll., L/31/37. In a codicil of 31 Jan. 1779, she removed her real property from the duke of Devonshire, substituting Dudley Long.

[123] "Lord Camden and the Honourable Henry Cavendish Assignment and Deed of Indemnity," 31 Dec. 1783, Devon. Coll., L/31/37. Also "Copy of Mr Pickerings Letter to Mr Wilmot," 26 Apr. 1780, ibid., L/86/ comp. 1.

PUBLIC ACTIVITIES

PUBLIC LIFE

Lord Charles Cavendish had administrative skills that were valued in arenas outside of politics and science, in the founding and working of new organizations. The people he worked with there were in many cases the same people he worked with in politics and science. In the first section of this chapter, we briefly describe a number of Cavendish's affiliations; each was to an organization having a technical dimension. We begin with his work for a hospital.

For twenty years Robert Walpole kept the country in peace and prosperity, during which time several hospitals were established, Westminster in 1720, Guy's in 1724, and others. These were hospitals in the usual sense of the word. In addition there was a new charitable hospice for unwanted children, the Foundling Hospital. Inspired by foundations for this purpose in Amsterdam, Paris, and elsewhere, the Foundling Hospital was the culmination of an arduous and heartfelt campaign by Thomas Coram on behalf of "great numbers of Helpless Infants daily exposed to Destruction." The Hospital was incorporated by royal charter in 1739 in a ceremony attended by bankers and merchants from the city and by six dukes and eleven earls, who set the tone of the endeavor. The charter was received by the president of the Hospital, the duke of Bedford, a relative of Cavendish's. Cavendish's brother, the duke of Devonshire, and his father-in-law, the duke of Kent, were named in the charter as original governors, and Cavendish himself was elected governor later that year.[1] The Hospital was first located in a leased house, but soon it acquired a new building, set in the fields, the location of most of the other new institutions of eighteenth-century London. The interior of the building was adorned with paintings; elegant concerts were held there.[2]

---

[1] R. H. Nichols and F. A. Wray, *The History of the Foundling Hospital* (London: Oxford University Press, 1935), 16, 19. Roy Porter, *English Society in the Eighteenth Century* (Harmondsworth: Penguin, 1982), 302–3.

[2] John Summerson, *Georgian London*, rev. ed. (Harmondsworth: Penguin, 1978), 119–20.

This fashionable charity needed administrators who were both able and hardened to the task, for conditions of life in an eighteenth-century foundling hospital were appalling. During the first four years the Hospital admitted children indiscriminantly, whether or not they were true foundlings–exposed and deserted children who would otherwise die–nearly a hundred a week at times. Of the roughly fifteen thousand children received then, over ten thousand did die, a mortality rate of about 70 percent. From the provinces, infants were transported under barbaric conditions to the Hospital, where they were dumped, sparing parish officials the trouble and expense of maintenance. To avoid the cost of burial, parents abandoned their children there, more dead than alive. The administrators of the Hospital had to deal with the consequences of their policy and ultimately with the policy itself.

The Hospital could call upon the best medical opinion in London. Hans Sloane, president of the Royal Society, and Richard Mead, both of whom were named in the charter, were among the leading physicians who volunteered their expensive services. William Watson, an expert on infectious childhood diseases, distinguished himself in the Hospital's crusade to prevent the devastations of smallpox, then a disease primarily of children under three.[3]

In 1747 Cavendish became a vice-president of the Hospital, replacing Folkes, who had been so named in the charter.[4] The job of vice-president was not ceremonial; Cavendish spent long hours at the Hospital, week in and week out, over decades.

With the desire to put its children to work, the Foundling Hospital turned for help to the whitefish industry. In 1753 the Society of Free British Fisheries agreed to buy as much Yarmouth Shale as the foundlings could braid. It turned out to be considerable, and a workshop for the purpose was laid out in a converted kitchen in the Hospital, which was proudly opened to the public so that it could observe the children at work.[5] Cavendish was active at both ends of this arrangement, as a governor of the Foundling Hospital and as a member of the council of the Society of Free British Fisheries.[6]

Incorporated by an act of parliament in 1750, the Society was a London-based company modeled after the great chartered trading companies. Its promoters reasoned that since Britain was situated in the "midst of one continuous Herring Shoal," what British fisheries needed to compete successfully with the

---

[3] Ruth K. McClure, *Coram's Children: The London Foundling Hospital in the Eighteenth Century* (New Haven: Yale University Press, 1981), 205–18. William Watson, *An Account of a Series of Experiments Instituted with a View of Ascertaining the Most Successful Method of Inoculating the Smallpox* (London, 1768). Charles Creighton, *A History of Epidemics in Britain*, vol. 2: *From the Extinction of the Plague to the Present Time*, 2d ed. (London: Frank Cass, 1965), 500, 514.

[4] Nichols and Wray, *Foundling Hospital*, 354, 413.

[5] Nichols and Wray, *Foundling Hospital*, 131.

[6] *Collins's Peerage of England. Geneological, Biographical, and Historical*, 9 vols., ed. E. Brydges (London, 1812), 1:356.

Dutch, who then dominated the trade in herring, was the "Power and united Strength" of a trading company. The anticipated benefits for the nation of a flourishing whitefish industry were many: it would empower the kingdom against France by ensuring a supply of seamen, improve its moral character by eliminating the uncivilized practice of impressing seamen, rebuild the economy in depressed regions like the Highlands, and provide work for the unemployed and for children in charity schools. The Society was permitted to own ships, build warehouses and wharfs, carry naval staples, regulate trade, and raise a capital sum for these purposes in the form of joint stock paying three percent.[7]

The officers of the Society, elected for three years, included a governor, a president, and a council. We do not know when Lord Charles Cavendish was elected to the council, but we can imagine why he was there. Sir James Lowther, who owned a fishery and a fleet of ships, belonged to the Society; in the list of nearly seventy charter members, his name came second, following that of the Lord Mayor of London. Cavendish was not a charter member of the Society, but he may have become a member when Sir James (and Sir William) Lowther died.[8] As a councilor of the Society, Cavendish would have been performing both a family and a public duty.

Closer to Cavendish's scientific and scholarly interests was the British Museum with its natural history collection and library. Readers of books lacked a proper public institution in London. Cavendish, a reader who did not depend on public libraries since he had his own very substantial library, donated countless hours to the British Museum as a public service. The Universities of Oxford and Cambridge had libraries, cathedrals had them, and there were a few specialized libraries, such as the one for law at the Inns of Court and the Royal Society's own; even a few small public libraries had been established in London in the seventeenth century; but most readers could not readily lay their hands on a given book. By this yardstick of civilized society, England was decidedly a backward cousin to European countries. Italy had

[7] Francis Grant, *A Letter to a Member of Parliament, Concerning the Free British Fisheries* (London, 1750), 37. Anon., *The Fisheries Revived: or, Britain's Hidden Treasure Discovered* (London, 1750), 13, 46. Anon., *The Vast Importance of the Herring Fishery, &c. to These Kingdoms: As Respecting the National Wealth, Our Naval Strength, and the Highlanders. In Three Letters Addressed to a Member of Parliament* (London, [1750]). Mr. Horsley, *A Translation of the Dutch Placart and Ordinance for the Government of the Great Fishery* (London, 1750).

[8] Sir James Lowther died five years after the founding of the Society. The original members of the Society are listed in *A Bill Intitled an Act for the Encouragement of the British White Herring Industry* (London, 1750). The third member listed, after Sir James Lowther, was Nathaniel Curzon, Lord Charles Cavendish's earlier fellow Member of Parliament from Derbyshire, the county of the duke of Devonshire. In a general way, Lord Charles's concern with fisheries was a concern of his landowning family, for land and water came together: the duke from time to time was party to legal cases involving fisheries, evidently fisheries of the "several" kind, in which the owner is the owner of the soil where the water flows. Stuart A. Moore, *A History of the Foreshore and the Law Relating Thereto . . .*, 3d ed. (London, 1888), 720–21. By a Trader in Fish, *The Best and Most Approved Method of Curing White-Herrings, and All Kinds of White-Fish* (London, 1750), 16.

had important public libraries since the fifteenth century; in Prussia, Berlin had had a great public library since the late seventeenth century; in France the royal library in Paris had been open to the public since 1735, and the Mazarin library there was nearly as large; and other great European cities such as Vienna and Munich had their major public libraries.[9] With the assistance of Cavendish, London belatedly acquired an important public library in the form of the British Museum.

In the usual British manner of addressing social needs, a public library in London came about through private not government initiative. Its benefactor was Hans Sloane, a great collector of both natural history objects and books. When Sloane stepped down from the presidency of the Royal Society in 1741, the secretary Cromwell Mortimer dedicated a volume of the *Philosophical Transactions* to him. Mortimer referred to Sloane's "noble and immense Collection" and to his large library of books on natural history and medicine, inflated by Mortimer to the "most complete in the Universe."[10] Sloane's collections lived on after him as an institution.

Sloane died in 1753, leaving to the nation his natural history collection and library, for a price. Parliament accepted the offer, raising the necessary money by way of a lottery. Sloane's trustees bought Montagu House to hold his legacy, to which were added the Cottonian Collection and the Harleian Manuscripts. Open and free to "all studious and curious Persons,"[11] Montagu House was occasionally referred to as Sloane's Museum, but it would be known as the British Museum.

Sloane's will did not name Cavendish as one of the original trustees, but it included him in a long list of "visitors," starting with the king and the prince of Wales, who were charged with watching over Sloane's possessions.[12] To get from the dignitaries to the working staff–the librarian and underlibrarians–parliament approved a complicated plan. A manageable but still large number of persons selected from the larger number of trustees and visitors were directed to elect fifteen persons. These so-called "elected trustees" were to appoint a standing committee to meet regularly with the staff and take responsibility for the management of the Museum. Eleven of the fifteen elected trustees were fellows of the Royal Society, one of whom was Cavendish, who was also named to the standing committee. Other members of the committee included Cavendish's brother-in-law

---

[9] Edward Miller, *That Noble Cabinet: A History of the British Museum* (Athens, Ohio: Ohio University Press, 1974), 25.

[10] Dedication on 31 Dec. 1741, just a month after Sloane's resignation: *PT*, vol. 41. for 1739 and 1740, published in 1744.

[11] Arundell Esdaile, *The British Museum Library: A Short History and a Survey* (London: George Allen & Unwin, 1946), 18.

[12] Sloane's printed will: BL Add Mss 36269, ff. 39–54. A handwritten list in 1753 of additional trustees includes Cavendish, f. 57.

Philip Yorke and colleagues from the Royal Society–Watson, Birch, and Lord Macclesfield.[13]

Cavendish was involved in every stage of preparation for the opening of the Museum in 1759. The standing committee examined Sloane's insects, birds, and other animals, finding some in good condition and others in a predictable state of decay. They compared the contents of Sloane's cabinets with catalogs in forty-nine volumes, and they made comparable inspections of Sloane's books. By 1755 Cavendish's name sometimes headed the list of trustees at the general meetings, despite the number of peers who could come and whose names would have preceded his had they come. Attendance at the weekly committee meetings dropped to five or so, but Cavendish always came, and when Macclesfield did not come, Cavendish presided, or at least he headed the list of persons attending; in the six months from May to November 1755, Cavendish attended thirty-four meetings of the standing committee, at twenty of which he presided.[14] Cavendish was a man of public affairs with broad intellectual interests and administrative skills, who could be counted on absolutely. That was not the least of the reasons why his services were valued at the British Museum and, in general, in the affairs of the learned world of London.

Montagu House, which earlier had almost been acquired by the Foundling Hospital, was located at the north end of town on Bloomsbury Square. This square was highly fashionable, home to rich physicians such as Sloane and Mead. The original house, designed in the French style for Ralph, later first duke of Montagu, by Robert Hooke, the versatile curator of experiments of the Royal Society, had burned down, and the duke had replaced it with a similar house resembling a contemporary Parisian *hôtel.* Its imposing facade, colonnades, entrance topped by a cupola, with wings extending to the front to form a grand courtyard, and interior of spacious and lofty apartments with paintings on the walls gave this mansion a grandeur befitting a great library and scientific collection in the British metropolis. Given the load it was to bear, of equal significance was the sober evaluation by the standing committee, to which Cavendish belonged, that the house was a "Substantial, well built Brick Building." Seven and a half acres of garden came with it, to which Cavendish's friend and fellow trustee William Watson devoted loving care.[15]

The collections of the British Museum were dedicated to the "Advancement and Improvement of Natural Philosophy and Other Branches of Speculative Knowledge." The scientific ambition of the Museum was clearly evident in the

[13] A. E. Gunther, "The Royal Society and the Foundation of the British Museum, 1753–1781," *Notes and Records of the Royal Society of London* 33 (1979): 207–16, on 209–10.

[14] Thomas Birch's minutes of the meetings of the Trustees of the British Museum: BL Add Mss 4450, ff. 1 and following. Minutes of the General Meetings and the Standing Committee Meetings of the Trustees of the British Museum, ibid., 4451, ff. 3 and following.

[15] Miller, *Noble Cabinet,* 50–54.

21. *Royal Society. Through Lord Charles Cavendish's time, the Royal Society met at Crane Court, the meeting room of which is shown here. The Society had long departed when this print was made. P. Stopford del., J. W. Lowry fo., John W. Parker, 445 West Strand, June 1848. Frontispiece to the first volume of Charles Richard Weld,* A History of the Royal Society, *2 vols. (London, 1848).*

22. *Foundling Hospital. Demolished. Print by S. Vale, published in 1749. Lord Charles Cavendish was a governor of this institution from the year of its charter, 1739. From a contemporary print. Reproduced by permission of the Greater London Record Office.*

23. *British Museum.* Top: Entrance to the Old British Museum, Montagu House. *Lord Charles Cavendish became a trustee of the Museum at its first election, 1753. Henry Cavendish was elected a trustee in 1773. Visitors are seen entering from the left; through one of the two arched gateways on the right can be seen visitors on the staircase and stuffed animals on the landing. The statue is of Sir Joseph Banks, former president of the Royal Society.* Bottom: Staircase of the Old British Museum, Montagu House. *Visitors are shown on the stairs and on the landing looking at stuffed animals. The giraffes seem to be outgrowing Montagu House, which was in a sense the truth, for by the time this painting was made, most of the contents of the overcrowded and dilapidated Montagu House had been removed to the new home of the Museum. Watercolors by George Scharf, the elder, 1845. Reproduced by permission of the Trustees of the British Museum.*

24. *Westminster Bridge.* Westminster from the North East. *By Samuel Scott. Westminster Bridge is shown in an early stage of construction. Lord Charles Cavendish was an active bridge commissioner from 1736 to 1749, the eve of its opening. Reproduced by permission of the Governor and Company of the Bank of England.*

25. *Westminster Bridge.* Westminster Bridge, London, with the Lord Mayor's procession on the Thames, *1747. By Canaletto. Westminster Bridge is nearly finished; final construction can be seen at the far right. Reproduced by permission of the Yale Center for British Art, Paul Mellon Collection.*

qualifications expected of the head of staff, who was, however, called "principal librarian" rather than "keeper of the collections," the title of a handler of books rather than of specimens: he was to be studious, learned, educated as a physician, versed in mathematics, a judge of inventions, able to carry on conversation with the learned in their fields, and competent to write and speak French and Latin and correspond with foreigners.[16] There were disqualifying criteria, too, which were not mentioned.[17] Gowin Knight, the choice for principal librarian, presented himself as a physician who had devoted the greatest part of his life to the "pursuit of natural Knowledge";[18] the evidence, his powerful artificial steel magnets, he brought with him to the British Museum, requesting that a passage five feet wide be appropriated from two rooms to house them.[19] Matthew Maty, De Moivre's friend, who was appointed underlibrarian, and who one day would become principal librarian, had accomplishments equally impressive: he had taken an M.D. under Boerhaave at the University of Leyden, he had studied natural philosophy and mathematics, he had wide-ranging foreign connections as editor of the *Journal Britannique*, and he spoke French and Dutch.[20] Soon after joining the staff of the British Museum, Maty was elected secretary of the Royal Society. Another underlibrarian was Charles Morton, physician to the Middlesex and Foundling Hospitals, who like Maty had taken his M.D. at the University of Leyden; he would become secretary of the Royal Society, and he too would one day become principal librarian.[21] A third underlibrarian, James Empson, was in charge of Sloane's natural history collection. As each underlibrarian had an assistant, the staff was sizable and, in William Watson's opinion, "unexceptionable." Its "disposition," however, was another matter, as librarians and assistants were not on speaking terms, and insubordination was rampant. The poet Thomas Gray, one of the first users of the library of the British Museum, said that "the whole society, trustees and all, are caught up in arms," and he

[16] "Qualifications and Duty Required in the Principal Librarian," BL Add Mss 4449, f. 108. "Rules Proposed to Be Observed in Making the Collections of Proper Use to the Publick by Way of Resolutions in a General Meeting of the Trustees," ibid., f. 115.

[17] Emanuel Mendes da Costa applied for an underlibrarian's job at the British Museum, with these credentials: he was a long-time Fellow of the Royal Society, an expert on fossils, and fluent in all of the main languages. Letter to Lord Hardwicke, 4 Feb. 1756, BL Add Mss 36269, ff. 100–1. William Watson considered Da Costa to be eminently qualified, but his "religion is an unsurmountable object." Letters to the archbishop of Canterbury, 21 June 1756, and Lord Hardwicke, 22 June 1756, BL Add Mss 36269, ff. 139–42, 144–45. Da Costa would not have been surprised. A few years later he asked Thomas Birch if it was "obnoxious to the Society that I (as by Profession a Jew) can put up for Hawksbee's place" in the Royal Society. Letter of 17 Jan. 1763, BL Add Mss 4317, f. 113.

[18] Gowin Knight to Lord Hardwicke, 22 Sep. 1754, BL Add Mss 36269, ff. 29–30.

[19] BL Add Mss 36269, f. 134.

[20] J. Jortin to Lord Hardwick, n.d. and 12 Feb. 1756, BL Add Mss 36269, ff. 104–6.

[21] "Morton, Charles," *DNB* 13:1047–48.

compared the rebellious factions to "fellows of a college."[22] Watson analyzed the conflict in terms of talent and turf.[23]

For a time a two-month reservation was required to secure a seat in the dark space in the basement that was the reading room, but before long the room proved ample; after the Museum had been open a few months, Thomas Gray found himself one of only five readers, the others being the antiquarian William Stukeley and three hacks copying manuscripts for hire.[24] In its first year, it should be noted, alongside Gray, men of science such as Watson, Heberden, and John Hadley visited the reading room.[25] Readers were admitted for six months at a time upon recommendation; members of the Royal Society and other learned bodies were admitted without recommendation. Eventually, the library became the national library, and the natural history collection evolved into a great research center. This successful institution had no more assiduous early administrator than Lord Charles Cavendish.

Cavendish's own researches were directed to questions of basic science, but he was interested in applications of science too, and as we might expect, he had an appropriate affiliation. Elected a member of the Royal Society of Arts on 8 June 1757, he continued his membership until his death. Founded three years before, the Society stimulated hopeful applications of knowledge by awarding prizes from money donated by public-spirited supporters of progress. Given its aims, its membership naturally overlapped considerably with that of the Royal Society: of the eleven founding members of the Society of Arts, four were Fellows of the Royal Society, and in 1768 the president and all ten vice-presidents of the Society were Fellows of the Royal Society. Lord Macclesfield, Franklin, Knight, Heberden, and Watson, to name several of Cavendish's friends, were members, and it was Watson who proposed Cavendish. The Society attracted a strong aristocratic patronage as well; relatives of Cavendish's belonging to it included the dukes of Devonshire and Bedford, the earls of Besborough and Ashburnham, Viscount Royston, and Lord George Cavendish. Cavendish would have felt at home in the Society of Arts, and although he was not active in it in the way that he was in the Royal Society and the British Museum, it is indicative of the breadth of his public interests that in 1760 he was

---

[22] Edmund William Gosse, *Gray*, new ed. (London: Macmillan, 1906),142.

[23] The underlibrarians were naturalists, and their assistants were antiquarians, an unworkable combination, it turned out. The different parts of the British Museum required different talents, which had to be properly assigned, Watson pointed out: "We have an extensive collection of the productions of nature & of art; a very large medical & philosophical library; as well as one relating to antiquities, & a vast collection of coins." The friction among the staff was rooted in this fact: "it must require a great length of time for any person to have a competent knowledge of any one branch of the museum & unless he be acquainted with it, he will be but little qualified to instruct others." The proper persons had to be matched up with the proper subjects. Typical good sense from William Watson to the archbishop of Canterbury, 21 June 1756.

[24] Gosse, *Gray*, 141–42.

[25] "Persons Admitted to Reading Room Jan. 12. 1759 to May 11. 1763," BL Add Mss 45867.

appointed to special committees for judging competitions in the fine arts, technology, and agriculture.[26]

The bridging of the Thames at Westminster was a highly conspicuous application of knowledge of materials, structures, and machines. The early eighteenth century saw both the rapid improvement of roads through turnpiking and the beginning of bridge building on a large scale. The urgency was due to the growth of London, the largest city in the world, the demands of which on the still largely agricultural nation were vast and insatiable. Herds of cattle were driven down turnpikes and over bridges to feed the concentrated mass of humanity on the banks of the Thames. Here and there streets of the city led to stairs down to the river, where cursing boatmen ferried paying passengers to the opposite bank. London Bridge, the only bridge in the city, was medieval, dangerous, congested, and built up with houses. Ideas for improving transportation in London by a second, modern bridge had been discussed since Elizabethan times, but they were successfully resisted by impecunious monarchs, fierce watermen defending their livelihood from ruin, and parties expressing fears such as commercial competition, armed rebellion, and the falling down of London Bridge once it was neglected for a rival.[27]

Renewed interest in a new bridge took the form of two petitions to parliament in 1721, leading to a committee and a bridge bill, but the House of Commons dropped it, probably for political reasons, since Walpole, who favored the bridge and was on the committee, was well hated by then.[28] When in 1736 another petition for a bridge was submitted to the House of Commons, the resulting committee, which could hear testimony of any kind, chose to hear technical testimony, undoubtedly hoping in this way to avoid the commercial controversy which had upset bridge plans in the past. J. T. Desaguliers, the curator of experiments for the Royal Society, addressed the committee on the "proper Instruments for boring the Soil under the River Thames."[29]

The Westminster Bridge Bill of 1736 set up a large body of commissioners, about 175 in number. Although a good proportion of them were Members of Parliament, they also included such an obviously useful person as the director of the Bank of England as well dukes, bishops, and admirals, who were useful in other, more or less obvious ways. In addition there were a good many Fellows of the Royal Society, Lord Charles Cavendish one of them. The first meeting was held

---

[26] 26 Mar., 9 and 30 Apr. 1760, Minutes of the Society, Royal Society of Arts, 5. Derek Hudson and Kenneth W. Luckhurst, *The Royal Society of Arts, 1754–1954* (London: John Murray, 1954), 6. *A List of the Society for the Encouragement of Arts, Manufactures, and Commerce* (London: Printed by Order of the Society, by William Adlard, April 6, 1768).

[27] R. J. B. Walker, *Old Westminster Bridge: The Bridge of Fools* (Newton Abbot: David and Charles, 1979), 12–32.

[28] Walker, *Westminster Bridge*, 44–49.

[29] 16 Feb. 1736 (1735), *HCJ* 22:569.

in June 1736, at which time the commissioners viewed the models of the bridge that had been exhibited in the Commons, and they set up a lottery with the Bank of England to finance the construction.[30]

The Royal Society was kept informed; Thomas Innys exhibited before it a model of his invention of a machine for laying the foundation of the piers of the new bridge. To decide on technical matters of this sort, in June 1737 the bridge commissioners formed a committee of thirteen, the so-called committee of works. Cavendish was appointed to it, as were several other Fellows of the Royal Society, though William Kent, the eminent architect, was perhaps the only member of the committee with obvious qualifications.[31] Now both a commissioner and a committeeman for the bridge, Cavendish took his duties with his customary seriousness.

At the beginning the works committee resolved to consider only wooden bridges since they were cheaper than stone ones, but all the same the committee and the commissioners took an interest in the stone-bridge advocate Charles Labelye, whose method of laying the foundations of the piers would work for either a timber or a stone superstructure.[32] Labelye had credentials different from those of his competitors, the best known of whom all came from a background in architecture and seemed to have had no engineering experience. He was not an architect at all but evidently was experienced in engineering and surveying, for the Commons treated him as an expert "engineer," calling on him to testify on the bridge before their own petition committee along with J. T. Desaguliers. Like Desaguliers, who claimed him as his "disciple" and "assistant,"[33] Labelye was of Huguenot origins. Educated in Geneva, he settled in England, where he became involved in such projects as draining the fens and improving harbors.[34] Not himself a Fellow of the Royal Society, he was friends with a good number of men of science who were. In the midst of building the bridge, he sent the president of the Royal Society, Folkes, a calculation having to do with the card game whist.[35] The prospect of a gambling bridge-builder could be upsetting, but Labelye was only carrying out an exercise in De Moivre's subject, the doctrine of chances. Labelye was a good enough mathematician for Desaguliers to publish his investigation of the *vis*

---

[30] Walker, *Westminster Bridge*, 63–67.

[31] Besides Cavendish, three others on the committee had been Fellows of the Royal Society since the 1720s. They were the chairman of the committee, Joseph Danvers, M.P., a lawyer by training and now a landowner; David Papillon, M.P., practicing lawyer; Thomas Viscount Gage, M.P., from 1743 master of the household to the prince of Wales. Walker, *Westminster Bridge*, 79, 86 n.7.

[32] 5 Aug. 1737, Minutes of the Committee of Works, vol. 1: Aug. 1737–Sep. 1744, Public Record Office, Kew, Work 6/39. 31 Aug. 1737 and 3 May 1738, Bridge Minutes.

[33] 16 Feb. 1736 (1735), *HCJ* 22:569. J. T. Desaguliers, *A Course of Experimental Philosophy*, 2 vols. (London, 1744), 2:506.

[34] Walker, *Westminster Bridge*, 83–86.

[35] Charles Labelye to Martin Folkes, 22 Mar. 1742/41, Folkes Correspondence, Royal Society.

viva controversy in mechanics.[36] The "foreigner" Labelye was hired by the commissioners to build stone foundations for a bridge that still could be made of wood or stone.[37] Eventually the commissioners decided that a bridge made partly of wood was unacceptable; the dignity of Westminster and London demanded that it be built entirely of stone.

At a meeting of the commissioners in August 1738, Cavendish heard a report about violent opposition to the construction of the bridge. Labelye was then putting in place the pile-driving engine to lift and drop the heavy ram. Angered over the threat of losing their trade to the bridge, watermen ran their barges into the boats moored beside the engine. Thereupon the commissioners advertised the part of the bridge act that legislated the death penalty for anyone found guilty of sabotaging the bridge works. That done, the new engine was tried without incident and found to work. In December of that year, Richard Graham, surveyor and comptroller of the bridge works, brought the designer of the engine, the watchmaker James Vauloué, and his model to a meeting of the Royal Society. Vauloué did not follow up the invitation to write an account of it for the Royal Society, but when his friend Desaguliers published the second volume of his *Course of Experimental Philosophy* in 1744, he included a description and drawing of the mighty engine, and Labelye too published an account of it. When in January 1739 the foundation for the first pier was finished, the earl of Pembroke laid the first stone "with great Formality, Guns firing, Flags displaying."[38] Eleven years later, the bridge was opened to traffic.

Technical problems dogged construction all the way, the most damaging of which was the sinking of the bridge. It was supposed to bear 1,200 tons, but when it was loaded with 250 tons of cannon as a test, it sank.[39] "Westminster-Bridge continues in a most declining Way," Thomas Birch wrote to Philip Yorke.[40] People stayed up late to be able say "What kind of a Night the Bridge has had."[41] The hitherto unhappy watermen burst into cheers as they watched the bridge sink as much as four inches in a night.[42] Possibly it was sabotaged, but whatever the cause the subsiding pier had to be rebuilt, requiring extra years. The wait was worth it. Spanning twelve hundred feet, built of Portland and Purbeck stone, Westminster Bridge was a monument to engineering and architectural grace.[43]

This first Westminster Bridge lasted only about a century, a brief life compared with the six hundred years of London Bridge, but that was not owing to

---

[36] Charles Labelye to J. T. Desaguliers, 15 Apr. 1735, published in Desaguliers, *Course* 2:77, 89–91.

[37] Walker, *Westminster Bridge*, 82.

[38] Walker, *Westminster Bridge*, 91–95. Desaguliers, *Course* 2:417–18.

[39] Thomas Birch to Philip Yorke, 11 June 1748, BL Add Mss 35397, ff. 114–15.

[40] Thomas Birch to Philip Yorke, 18 June 1748, BL Add Mss 35397, f. 116.

[41] Thomas Birch to Philip Yorke, 19 Sep. 1747, BL Add Mss 35397, ff. 74–76.

[42] Thomas Birch to Philip Yorke, 12 Sep. 1747, BL Add Mss 35397, ff. 72–73.

[43] Summerson, *Georgian London*, 113–16.

faulty construction. Once Westminster Bridge was built, the rickety condition of London Bridge gave rise to alarm. Labelye advised removing some of its piers, but they had acted as a dam, and when they were removed, tides eroded the river bed and ground away at the piers of Westminster Bridge. Labelye's beautiful bridge had to be replaced.[44]

Halfway into the construction, Labelye wrote that the bridge commissioners "have nothing, and can expect nothing, but Trouble for their Pains," and that he admired their selfless "publick Spirit" and "Patience."[45] Labelye was right about Cavendish, who devoted a large effort to the bridge while at the same time carrying out his parliamentary duties and also his duties on the council of the Royal Society. In 1739, in the third year of the bridge, for example, Cavendish served on twenty-four committees of parliament, and he also went to nineteen meetings of the Westminster Bridge commissioners. In the middle years of the construction, he rarely missed a meeting of the commissioners or the works committee. In addition he came fairly regularly to a third kind of meeting, that of a small committee of accounts for the bridge, often chairing the meeting.[46] In 1744 he attended twenty-five out of twenty-six meetings of the commissioners and eighteen out of nineteen meetings of the works committee; this was his most conscientious year, but other years came close to this one. He was involved in much of the quiet work in the building of Westminster Bridge, employing the combination of political, administrative, technical, and accounting skills he brought to his organizational work for the Royal Society.

SCIENTIFIC ADMINISTRATION

We begin this discussion of Lord Charles Cavendish's administrative work by recalling some basic facts about the running of the Royal Society around the time of his election. By a royal charter of 1663, the Society was constituted a self-governing corporation. Every St. Andrew's Day, November 30th, the members elected from their own number a council of twenty-one, from whom they elected a smaller number of officers: president, treasurer, and two secretaries. The president chose one or more vice-presidents to sit in for him when he was absent. To ensure that the council did not become fixed and at the same time to give it continuity, ten of its members were newly elected each year while eleven were kept on from the old council. The entire government of the Society was invested in the council and president, who were assisted by a person responsible for foreign correspondence and translations of foreign papers. New members were elected by two-thirds of the members

---

[44] Samuel Smiles, *Lives of the Engineers. Harbours–Lighthouses–Bridges. Smeaton and Rennie*, rev. ed. (London, 1874), 70–71, 140–42.

[45] Charles Labelye, *The Present State of Westminster Bridge* (London, 1743), 24–25.

[46] Minutes of the Committee of Accounts, vol. 1: 1738–1744, Public Record Office, Kew, Work 6/41.

who were present at the meeting, and the election of officers was by simple majority.[47]

Having been a member for eight years, Cavendish was elected to its council for the first time in 1736. He was elected again in November 1741, and for the next twenty years he was on the council every year with the exception of 1753, when family business called him away. He served four more non-consecutive terms on the council, his last in 1769, in which year he served on the council together with his son Henry. Henry would have an even longer record of service; combined, their membership on the council would span seventy-three years, with some interruptions. For many years Lord Charles was also a vice-president.

The Royal Society was now in its third home, in Crane Court, a quiet, central location. The front of the house faced a garden, the back a long, narrow court. Up one flight of stairs and fronting the garden was the meeting room, about the size of a modern living room.

The Society as a whole met weekly, except during Christmas and Easter and the long recess in late summer, about thirty times a year in all. How often the council met depended on how busy the Society was and on the energy of the current officers. Ordinarily it met six or fewer times a year toward the end of Folkes's presidency in the late 1740s, and eight to ten times under Lord Macclesfield's in the 1750s, but it met twenty-two times in 1760 during preparations for observing the transit of Venus the following year. Presidents before Newton rarely came to council, but Newton came all the time, changing the day of the meetings of the council to accommodate his schedule. His precedent was followed, with decreasing rigor, by his successors: Sloane missed only 8 out of 105 council meetings in his fifteen years as president; his successor, Folkes, missed one-quarter of his; and Folkes's successor, Macclesfield, missed about one-third of his. Cavendish's first term on the council was under Sloane's presidency, and he missed a good many meetings, perhaps because he found that the council conflicted with his political duties. The year he stepped down from parliament he returned to the council, and his attendance picked up; for the next six years he came to two out of three meetings, and after that he was almost never to miss a meeting. Frequently only a half dozen members attended council meetings, a meager number considering that it included the two secretaries and usually the president; ten or so constituted a fair turnout, but whatever the number, in his later years Cavendish was bound to be one of them. To give an idea of his commitment: in the five years from January 1748 through November 1752, he attended all twenty-seven meetings; in the eight years from December 1753 through November 1761, out of eighty-seven meetings, he attended seventy-eight (at least, since he may only have been late sometimes, and not listed). Only two Fellows came oftener, the two secretaries of the Society, who had no choice short of neglecting their duties: Peter

[47] 20 Aug. 1730, Minutes of Council, copy, Society, 3:50–61.

Davall from 1747, and Thomas Birch from 1752. One other councilor came with great regularity over a long period, the barrister James Burrow, who like Charles Cavendish sometimes acted as temporary president of the Society during a vacancy.[48]

Cavendish's contribution to the running of the Royal Society is more remarkable when his rank is considered. The minutes of the council always listed Cavendish first after the president, except when Lord Macclesfield (before he was president) was there, and later Lord Morton; this protocol ceased after 1760 when the councilors were listed alphabetically. At this time about one-seventh of the membership of the Royal Society was aristocratic,[49] and the proportion was increasing.[50] As an aristocrat who supported science, Cavendish was not unusual. What set him apart was his solicitous attention to the affairs of the Society.

During his long service in the Royal Society, Cavendish did not, so far as we know, initiate changes in the way things were done. He was more likely to second a motion than to make one. He was content to be vice-president and be of service to the president. When Folkes was sick in 1752, he took the chair, and it was he who informed the Society that Folkes was stepping down; this was one of the rare times he did make a motion, if only to return thanks to Folkes.[51] What Cavendish did not do was to step into Folkes's shoes. Thomas Birch wrote to Philip Yorke shortly before Folkes resigned: "when we proceed to a new choice [of president], Lord Macclesfield will have no Competitor, for Lord Charles Cavendish has lately declar'd to Mr. Watson his Resolution not to accept the Presidentship."[52] Cavendish, a natural choice, did not want to preside over the Society.

Early in 1752 Lord Macclesfield asked the council to consider the way papers were chosen for publication in the *Philosophical Transactions*. Earlier there had been a committee of papers, but it had not decided which papers were to be published.[53] One of the secretaries had run the journal, making the decisions on his own though probably taking into consideration requests by individual members. The pertinent secretary at this time was the physician

[48] Information from the Royal Society, Minutes of Council.

[49] Bound with the Minutes of the Committee of Papers is a printed membership list for the Royal Society in 1749. The total British membership then was around 340, and of these around 45 were aristocratic, counting bishops and persons like Cavendish with the courtesy title "Lord."

[50] Richard Sorrenson, "Towards a History of the Royal Society in the Eighteenth Century," *Notes and Records of the Royal Society of London* 50 (1996): 29–46, on 36.

[51] Royal Society, JB 21:195–96 (30 Nov. 1752).

[52] Thomas Birch to Philip Yorke, 14 Oct. 1752, quoted in David Philip Miller, "The 'Hardwicke Circle': The Whig Supremacy and Its Demise in the Eighteenth-Century Royal Society," to appear in *Notes and Records of the Royal Society of London*. We are indebted to the author for thoughtfully sending us a preprint of his article.

[53] Cavendish was present on 30 Oct. 1749: "At a Committee for Reviewing the Papers." "Minutes of the Royal Society," vol. 2, Birch Collection, BL Add Mss 4446.

Cromwell Mortimer, under whose oversight the journal had emphasized antiquarian interests.[54]

The *Philosophical Transactions* had been recently criticized for publishing thin material. The critic John Hill, a writer on natural history and on various subjects outside of science, stepped up his criticisms after having failed in his bid to become a member of the Royal Society. Singling out for ridicule papers on natural history appearing in the journal, he proposed that the Society form a committee to decide on papers to be read or published. There were influential members of the Society, such as William Watson, who agreed with Hill that the standard of papers could be improved.[55]

For the "credit and honour of this society," Lord Macclesfield said, decisions about publication henceforth would be made by a committee. The council declared that the president, the vice-presidents, and the two secretaries were to be on the committee and that no decisions on papers could be made without a quorum of five. For advice on particular papers, authorities outside the committee could be brought in by request of a majority of the committee. In committee, any paper was to be read in full if a member desired it, and then without "debate or altercation." Finally a vote was to be taken by ballot, so as to "leave every member more at liberty to fully declare his opinion."[56] Since the decision to publish a paper was a recognition not every author received, the new committee had a sensitive assignment. Lord Macclesfield (correcting himself) said that the Society had not "usually meddled" in the selection of papers to be published. That it had meddled at various times in various ways, he now conceded; what was going to change was that it would meddle in a systematic and accountable way. Cavendish joined Macclesfield in proposing amendments, and on 26 March 1752 the new statutes were passed by the council.[57] With Cavendish in the chair, Philip Yorke proposed that for the time being the council would be the "committee of papers," and that was agreed to.[58] The *Philosophical Transactions* was now under the direction of the council and for the "sole use and benefit of the society, and the Fellows thereof."[59] The readers of the journal were informed of the change in an advertisement. In April 1752, the committee convened for the first time, Cavendish presiding. Lord Macclesfield came to the first three meetings but then dropped out; at the end of the year when he became the new president of the

[54] Charles Brazerman, *Shaping Written Knowledge: The Genre and Activity of the Experimental Article in Science* (Madison: University of Wisconsin Press, 1988), 137.

[55] Kevin J. Fraser, "John Hill and the Royal Society in the Eighteenth Century," *Notes and Records of the Royal Society of London* 48 (1994): 43–67, on 44, 48–51. John Hill, *Review of the Works of the Royal Society of London* . . . (London, 1751).

[56] 23 Jan. and 15 Feb. 1752, Minutes of Council, copy, Royal Society, 4:49–53.

[57] 20 Feb., 19 and 26 Mar. 1752, Minutes of Council, copy, Royal Society, 4:55, 64, 71–75, 83.

[58] 27 Feb. 1752, Minutes of Council, copy, Royal Society, 4:64–65.

[59] 19 Mar. 1752, Minutes of Council, copy, Royal Society, 4:76.

Royal Society, he started coming again. Cavendish chaired all of the meetings but one through November 1752.

Although now a committee rather than a secretary decided on which papers were to be published, the latter continued to screen papers presented to the Society in the first place. The role of the secretary in controlling access to the Society can be seen in the exchange of letters between Thomas Birch and Samuel Bamfield. Bamfield had a theory of astronomy that disagreed with Newton's, and he wanted to have it read to the Society; Birch refused. Bamfield suggested that another member might see the truth of his theory; Birch recommended that he read John Keill. Bamfield then tried to dedicate his work to Macclesfield and have Macclesfield look at it; Birch denied him.[60]

The work of the committee of papers was demanding. In the years just before 1740 the number of papers reached a peak of well over a hundred per year on the average. After that, the number fell off, but slowly, and the load remained great through Cavendish's years on the committee. It should be noted that the number of papers is not a particularly good measure of the committee's work, since as the papers became fewer, they became longer, tending to the interpretative syntheses of facts of Henry Cavendish's time.[61] At the time the committee of papers was formed, there was a backlog, which the committee went through chronologically, beginning with January of the previous year, 1751, taking several meetings to get through that year. In its first meeting the committee approved sixteen papers for publication, in its second meeting, fifteen, and in its third, twenty-four. Daniel Wray, who began coming at the second meeting, wrote to Philip Yorke of their "diligence, as members of the Committee of Papers,"[62] and we can believe it.

The committee of papers met four to six times a year, usually attended by about four Fellows in addition to the two secretaries, who were required to be there, and the president, when he came. In 1753 Cavendish was not on the council and committee, owing to family affairs. When he returned to the council in 1754, he attended every meeting of the committee, as remained his habit in the years following. He was the most faithful member of this committee. After Cavendish, Burrow came most often to the meetings, Watson and Bradley came occasionally, and other members came and went. Cavendish set an example for his son Henry, who was to be an unfailing laborer for this committee in his time.[63]

To evaluate critically every paper that came before the Royal Society was an excellent way to keep abreast of what went on in science, but we believe that

---

[60] Letters between Samuel Bamfield and Thomas Birch c. 1761–64, BL Add Mss 4300.

[61] Raymond Phineas Stearns, *Science in the British Colonies of America* (Urbana: University of Illinois Press, 1970), 97–98. Brazeman, *Shaping Written Knowledge*, 81.

[62] Daniel Wray to Philip Yorke, 5 July 1752, Hardwicke Papers, BL Add Mss 35401, f. 157.

[63] Rough notes of the meetings of the Committee of Papers taken by Thomas Birch, one of the secretaries, in "Minutes of the Royal Society," vols. 1 and 2, Birch Collection, BL Add Mss 4445 and 4446.

Cavendish's main motivation was service to the Society. In the middle of the eighteenth century, in a variety of ways the Society rationalized its procedures, eliminating unnecessary duplication of records,[64] and making "Considerable Progress" in "methodizing" the several orders of council "relative to the offices of Clerk, Librarian, Keeper of the Repository, Housekeeper, Mace-bearer and Porter."[65] Procedures that applied to the *Philosophical Transactions* were especially important, since its contents were the public record of the Society, and the external authority of the Society largely rested upon them. Publication decisions arrived at by an editorial committee made up of men who were active in science and in the Society were likely to be competent and fair. Cavendish helped get the committee off to a conscientious start in its first year.

From the summer of 1760 to early 1763, the council of the Society was almost exclusively occupied with observations of the transit of Venus in 1761, energized as never before by the complexity of this project. Halley had foretold the transit and recommended that it be observed as a means of measuring the distance of the earth from the sun, the standard length by which the distances of the other bodies of the solar system were expressed. Preparations had to be made long in advance, since to obtain the necessary views of Venus crossing the solar disc, observers had to be selected, equipped, and sent to widely separated locations on the earth. The Society sought help from the East India Company, the admiralty, the treasury, and the king. Nevil Maskelyne and Robert Waddington were sent to St. Helena, and Charles Mason and Jeremiah Dixon were sent to Bencoolen, though they were forced to stop at the Cape of Good Hope instead. Other nations participated in this worldwide project of unprecedented size. Sixty-two observing stations were involved. The Royal Society received reports from far and near, publishing twenty of them in its *Philosophical Transactions*.[66] During this flurry of activity, Cavendish sometimes sat in the president's chair. His dependability is evident from a comment on his rare absence: the secretary of the Society Thomas Birch wrote to Philip Yorke in connection with selecting observers for Bencoolen that he was unable to call a council owing to the "Absence of the President & all his Vice-Presidents, even Lord Cha. Cavendish himself, who is, I presume, at Chatsworth." In addition to dealing with all of the matters that came before the council having to do with the expeditions, he was involved in the scientific work on various levels, from the

[64] On keeping records of all sorts: "Proposal Concerning the Papers of the Royal Society," by Macclesfield, presumably, BL Add Mss 4441. The Society eliminated unnecessary duplication and classification in its record keeping: it was found that papers presented before the Society ended up in two kinds of books, while only one, the minutes of ordinary meetings, was needed. 12 July 1742, Minutes of Council, copy, Royal Society, 3:285.

[65] 1 Feb. 1763, Minutes of Council, copy, Royal Society, 5:1.

[66] Weld, *History of the Royal Society* 2:11–19. A. Pannekoek, *A History of Astronomy* (New York: Interscience, 1961), 284–87. J. D. North, *The Norton History of Astronomy and Cosmology* (New York: W. W. Norton, 1995), 352–54.

examination of a faulty instrument to the writing of a synopsis of the completed observations of the transit.[67]

While the project for observing the transit of Venus was in progress, John Harrison's clock for finding longitude at sea came before the council, which recommended a trial on a voyage to Jamaica.[68] Soon after the transit of Venus, two of the observers, Charles Mason and Jeremiah Dixon, were commissioned by the Royal Society to measure a degree of latitude between Maryland and Pennsylvania.[69] Cavendish played a role in both of these activities; indeed, there was little of significance done officially at the Royal Society in the middle of the eighteenth century in which Cavendish was not fully involved.

Meetings of the council typically had to do with money: payment of bills from printers, bookbinders, solicitors, and instrument-makers; payment of debts; payment of insurance on the houses owned by the Society; payment of salaries. Besides dealing with these matters routinely as they came up in council, Cavendish went over them all again; nearly every year he was appointed one of a committee of auditors of the treasurer's accounts. Cavendish was on call as an all-purpose, responsible Fellow of the Royal Society, as his son Henry would be after him.

Cavendish was also active in the administration of the Royal Observatory. There were decisions to be made about regulations[70] and, above all, about equipment. In 1765, by warrant from the king, the president of the Royal Society together with other Fellows of the Royal Society were charged with making tours of inspection of the instruments of the Observatory.[71] Cavendish was one of several Fellows who regularly made "visitations" to Greenwich to determine which repairs were needed and to estimate the expense; in this capacity again, his son Henry would follow in his footsteps. As late as 1781, two years before his death, Cavendish was still discharging the Royal Society's obligations, reminding the president that the publication of the Greenwich observations was long overdue.[72]

---

[67] 27 May 1762, Minutes of Council, copy, Royal Society, 4:333–34. Thomas Birch to Philip Yorke, Viscount Royston, 6 Sep. 1760, 20 June 1761, BL Add Mss 35399, ff. 153, 207.

[68] 25 June 1761, Minutes of Council, copy, Royal Society, 4.

[69] 25 Oct. 1764, Minutes of Council, copy, Royal Society, 4:45.

[70] Lord Morton to Thomas Birch, 24 Sep. 1764, BL Add Mss 4444.

[71] Upon the death of the astronomer royal, James Bradley, in 1762, his executors removed his observation books from the Royal Observatory, claiming them as private property. In 1763, Maskelyne addressed the Royal Society on the subject of their recovery. To reimpose its authority, the Royal Society requested a new warrant from the king. The new warrant of 1765 appointed the president and council of the Society to be the visitors of the Royal Observatory.

[72] "Visitations of Greenwich Observatory, 1763 to 1815," Royal Society, Ms. 600, XIV.d.11, ff. 6 passim. Cavendish to Banks, 19 May 1781.

Cavendish's private interest in books and manuscripts together with his accounting skills found a public outlet in the Royal Society, where he served as one of the inspectors of the library. His skills were badly needed. The library was described at the time by the clerk of the Society, Emanuel Mendes da Costa, as unkempt: "At present the books weigh less than the filth that covers them." Examining the state of the great Norfolk collection of books and manuscripts, Cavendish and his fellow inspectors reported that the catalog of the collection was faulty in titles and dates, that "there is a deficincy of several whole centuries of numbers" in the catalog, that numbers on books did not agree with numbers in the catalog, that "different volumes of the same work stand on different shelves, and have very different numbers," that "different books have the same number," that "many of the books are so ill arranged, as to the sizes of them, that they cannot be placed upright on the shelves," that many had spoiled bindings or broken wooden covers, and that many more were "very much worm-eaten." As for the rest of the books in the library, their catalog had ceased over twenty-five years before, whereas since that time nearly a thousand books and pamphlets had been donated to the library, the record of which was in the journals of the Society. The problems were so severe that the inspectors recommended making an entirely new catalog for the Norfolk collection, updating the catalog of the rest by going through the journals, altering the shelves or rearranging the books, and rebinding those books that were not so far deteriorated as to be beyond repair. Owing to the inspections, some of the defects of the library were corrected. The library was very much worth the attention of the inspectors and the expense to the Society of maintaining it. In size it compared with an excellent private library, around ten thousand volumes; that was just the size of Henry Cavendish's private library later in the century.[73]

Elected during Sloane's presidency, Cavendish served through Folkes's, Macclesfield's, and Morton's. In 1768, while the council was absorbed in preparations for a second transit of Venus the following year, Morton died. Like Macclesfield before him, Morton was an astronomer and thus an appropriate president under these circumstances, but the next president was the antiquarian James West. Having served as the Society's treasurer for thirty-two years, West held the office of president for only four years, but it was long enough for Henry Cavendish to have formed a negative opinion of his performance.[74] Ten days

---

[73] Andrew Coltee Ducarel to Thomas Birch, 13 Oct. 1763, Birch Correspondence, BL Add Mss 4305, 4:57. "I compute about 10000 vol to whit the Norfolk 500 MSS & 3000 printed. The Society Library about 6000 printed books only": Emanuel Mendes da Costa to William Borlase, 9 July 1763, E. Da Costa Correspondence, BL Add Mss 28535, 2:150. Reports of the inspectors of the "Libraries of the Royal Society," 6 June 1768, 6 Apr. 1769 and 25 July 1770, Minutes of Council, Royal Society, 5:308, 6:25–26, 62–65.

[74] Henry Cavendish's opinion is reported in Charles Blagden to Sir Joseph Banks, 22 Dec. 1783, original letter in Fitzwilliam Museum Library, copy in BM(NH), DTC 3: 171–72. We return to this point in the chapter dealing with Henry Cavendish's politics.

after Morton died, Daniel Wray wrote to Lord Hardwick, F.R.S., that "*Lord Charles* is deaf to all our prayers; and will not *preside* over us."[75] Cavendish was in his early sixties, in good health, and on the council, but he did not want to be president. His feelings on the subject were the same as when Folkes had stepped down nearly fifteen years earlier.

SCIENCE

Lord Charles Cavendish's earliest recorded work in science was done in conjunction with James Bradley, an astronomer of world renown. In June 1728 at Bradley's observatory at Wansted, Cavendish made zenith observations with a telescope designed to detect the parallax of the fixed stars.[76] The instrument had been in place for less than a year, and after Bradley himself, and then Halley, Cavendish was the next person to make observations with it. In the course of looking for an annual parallax later that year, Bradley made his great discovery of the aberration of light from the stars.

With his zenith instrument, Bradley observed small stellar motions which he knew were too large and in the wrong direction to be caused by parallax. They were, he decided, the resultants of the motion of the earth in its orbit and the motion of light. In his announcement of Bradley's discovery to the Royal Society, Halley said that the "three Grand Doctrines in the Modern Astronomy do receive a Great Light and Confirmation from this one Single Motion of the Stars Vizt. The Motion of the Earth. The Motion of Light and the immense distance of the Stars."[77] Bradley had, in fact, provided the first direct evidence of the motion of the earth, that is, of the Copernican theory, and the twenty-four-year-old Lord Charles Cavendish had had a connection, however brief, with this great work of observation and reasoning in astronomy.

26. *James Bradley. Reproduced by permission of the President and Council of the Royal Society.*

We assume that Cavendish learned about observations and instruments from Bradley. Cavendish was able to return the favor several years later after Bradley had moved from Wansted to Oxford. Oxford was only a few miles from Macclesfield's home at Shirburn castle, where Bradley reg-

[75] Daniel Wray to Lord Hardwick, 22 Oct. 1768, in George Hardinge, *Biographical Anecdotes of Daniel Wray* (London, 1815), 137. Next month, James West presided over them as president.

[76] James Bradley, *Miscellaneous Works and Correspondence of the Rev. James Bradley, D.D. F.R.S.*, ed. S. P. Rigaud (Oxford, 1832), 237.

[77] Royal Society, JB 13:260–62, on 261–62 (14 Nov. 1728).

ularly made observations. When Bradley became a candidate to succeed Halley as astronomer royal, Macclesfield exerted his influence. Since his voting had put him out of favor at court, Macclesfield had to proceed indirectly. To build scientific support for Bradley, Macclesfield wrote to William Jones to ask him to enlist Folkes and Lord Charles Cavendish.[78]

We learn of Cavendish's next recorded observations from a passing remark by his friend William Watson: in the severe cold of 1739, the thermometer in Cavendish's room sank to twenty-five degrees; Cavendish, Watson said, then placed his thermometer outside the window and some distance from it, observing a low one night of thirteen degrees.[79] From this account, it would seem that in 1739 Cavendish had a self-registering thermometer for low temperatures, though he did not publicize such an instrument until nearly twenty years later.

Cavendish described his self-registering thermometers in the *Philosophical Transactions* in 1757, by which time he had been working in science for thirty years. Lord Macclesfield, then president of the Society, proposed Cavendish as the Copley Medalist, a choice which the council unanimously (and routinely) approved. In so honoring Cavendish, Macclesfield may have been influenced by Cavendish's social standing as well as by the scientific merits of his work,[80] but as the medal was awarded customarily for an experimental contribution, including instrumentation, it is not clear that in that year a more deserving work was passed over; William Lewis continued to bring his important experiments on platina before the Society,[81] but he had received the Copley Medal in 1754 for earlier experiments in this series. In any case, in his address to the Society on the occasion, Macclesfield chose to bring together the Copley Medalist's scientific and social eminence: Lord Charles Cavendish was as conspicuous for "his earnest desire to promote natural Knowledge, and his Skill and abilities together with his continual Study and endeavour to accomplish . . . his desire" as he was for his "high Birth and eminent Station in life." Because of Cavendish's "excess of Modesty" and a seeming insensibility of "his own extraordinary Merit," the "Society, and consequently the public," had been deprived "of many important discoveries as well as considerable improvements made and contrived by his Lordship, in Several Instruments and Machines necessary for trying Experiments and deducing proper consequences from the Same; and also of the results of various usefull and instructive Experiments that he has been pleased to make in private, with that accuracy and exactness which are peculiar to his Lordship, and which few besides

[78] Lord Macclesfield to William Jones, 13 Jan. 1741/42; Lord Macclesfield to Lord Hardwicke, 13 Jan. 1741/42, in Bradley, *Miscellaneous Works*, xlvi.

[79] William Watson, ". . . Some Account of the Late Cold Weather," *PT* 57 (1767): 443–50, on 444.

[80] Yakup Bektas and Maurice Crosland, "The Copley Medal: The Establishment of a Reward System in the Royal Society, 1731–1839," *Notes and Records of the Royal Society of London* 46 (1992): 43–76, on 52.

[81] Royal Society, JB 22:506, 520 (17 and 31 Mar. 1757).

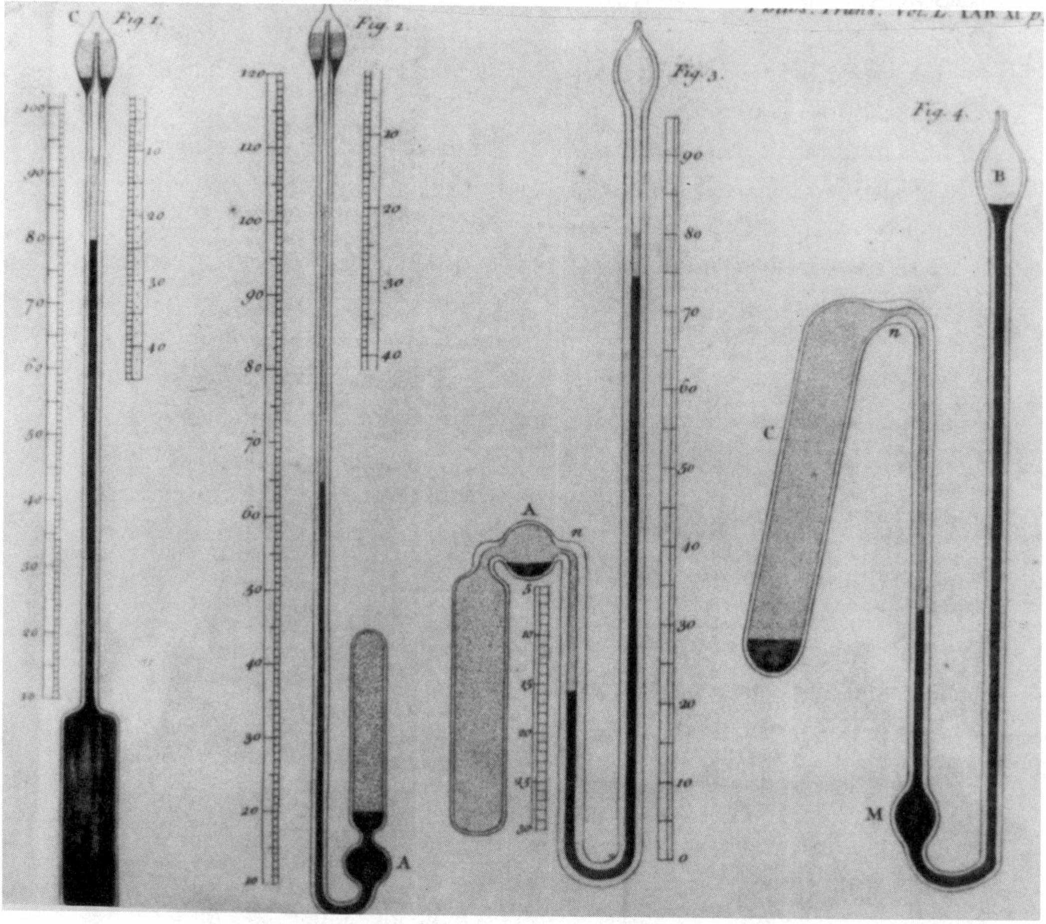

27. Lord Charles Cavendish's Thermometers. The thermometer in Fig. 1 shows the greatest degree of heat. It differs from ordinary thermometers only in that the top of the stem is drawn into a capillary tube, which ends in a glass ball C. The cylinder at the bottom and part of the stem are filled with mercury (dark part of the figure), showing the ordinary degree of heat. Above the mercury is spirit of wine (dotted part of the figure), which also fills the ball C almost to the top of the capillary tube. When the mercury rises with temperature, some spirit of wine is forced out of the capillary tube into the ball. When the mercury falls with a fall in temperature, a space at the top of the capillary tube is emptied of spirit of wine. A scale laid beside the capillary tube measures the empty length, which is proportional to the greatest degree of heat that has been registered. Fig. 2 is an alternative construction. Fig. 3 shows a thermometer for giving the greatest degree of cold. Fig. 4 shows how the instrument can be made more compact, as would be desirable if it were to be sunk to the bottom of the sea or raised to the upper atmosphere by a kite. "A Description of Some Thermometers for Particular Uses," Philosophical Transactions *50 (1757): 300.*

himself have a just right to boast of."[82] Within their lofty phrasing, Macclesfield's observations were accurate. In that age of aristocracy, Cavendish was, as Macclesfield said, an "Ornament" to the Royal Society as well as a zealous promoter of natural knowledge. What Macclesfield called Cavendish's "modesty" could with equal right be called his "confidence." Given his rank and his competence, he did not need to (any more than Macclesfield needed to) publish his researches; indeed, if he had published them, he might have betrayed an *im*modesty. It was enough that at times he made his results available to his colleagues in the Royal Society. As Macclesfield said, Cavendish had not kept his work entirely to himself; else how should Macclesfield know? With a naturalness not easily accessible to those who had to advance themselves in the world, Cavendish could live an approximation to the cooperative scientific life envisioned by the utopians of the previous century.

Unlike his own work, which he kept to himself or communicated privately to individuals or, at most, allowed a colleague to mention publicly, Cavendish's work for the Royal Society was public. He accepted elected offices, other than president, committee appointments, and scientific as well as administrative assignments. His first scientific work for the Society concerned longitude at sea. In 1714, in response to a petition, a parliamentary committee took testimony, including Newton's, in light of which it recommended that a reward be offered for a practical method of determining longitude. That year parliament passed an act that specified rewards of up to £20,000, and authorized a body of twenty-two persons, known as the Board of Longitude, to examine proposals. In principle, a well-known alternative to the lunar method of finding longitude at sea was a seaworthy and accurate clock. John Harrison, at first with his brother James, built a series of clocks for this purpose. His first clock overcame disturbing variations of heat, moisture, friction, and fluidity of oil so perfectly that its error was less than one second a month for ten years running. This wonderfully accurate machine was, however, a delicate pendulum. His second clock, built for shipboard, kept good time while undergoing violent motions simulating storms. To encourage him, the Board of Longitude granted him sums of money, and in 1741 Cavendish was one of twelve Fellows of the Royal Society who recommended that Harrison continue to be so encouraged. Of interest here are the persons Cavendish came together with on the committee, Fellows selected, in most cases, for their authority in matters of accuracy: mathematicians De Moivre and his circle, Folkes, Jones, Macclesfield; astronomers Bradley and Halley; instrument-makers John Hadley and George Graham; the widely

82 The Copley Medal was awarded to Lord Charles Cavendish "on account of his very curious and useful invention of making Thermometers shewing respectively the greatest degrees of heat and cold during the absence of the observer." Royal Society, JB 23:638–48, on 638–39 (30 Nov. 1757).

informed James Jurin; and Cambridge professors Robert Smith and John Colson. In 1763, on the eve of a second trial run of Harrison's latest clock, Cavendish was appointed by an act of parliament to another committee on the subject. From what became a lifework and prolonged legal battle, and with the help of Cavendish and other Fellows of the Royal Society, in the end Harrison was awarded most of the money he demanded and in addition a Copley Medal from the Royal Society. British ships in return got a reliable instrument for determining longitude; Captain Cook used Harrison's clock on his voyage to the South Seas in 1772, justifying the claims of precision made for it.[83]

In 1742 Cavendish accepted another assignment having to do with measurement. The goal this time was to compare the Royal Society's weights and measures with those kept by the Academy of Sciences in Paris: measurements were becoming decisive in experimental work, and depending upon the country in which they were made, they were expressed in the English foot or the French toise, lengths marked off on metal standards and deposited in various archives. The project was expanded to include a comparison of the Royal Society's standards with other standards in England. The instrument-maker George Graham carried out the experiments in the presence of a delegation from the Royal Society, which, other than being smaller, was almost the same as the committee that had investigated Harrison's clock. Of the seven witnesses, five we have discussed in connection with De Moivre: Folkes, who was president then, Macclesfield, Jones, Peter Davall, and Cavendish. The other two were the instrument-maker Hadley and the secretary Cromwell Mortimer. Cavendish, we recognize, was in his element, that of "accuracy and exactness."[84]

For our last example of Lord Charles Cavendish's scientific work in committee, we turn to his experiments on the compressibility of water. The experi-

[83] The act of 1763 altered the original act of 1714 offering the prize. The other members of the new committee were Lord Morton, Lord Willoughby, George Lewis Scott, James Short, John Michell, Alexander Cumming, Thomas Mudge, William Frodsham, and James Green. Only the instrument-maker Short and the watch-makers Frodsham and Green were satisfied with Harrison's explanation. Cavendish was also appointed by the Board to another committee; John Bird deputized for him this time. Taylor, *Mathematical Practitioners of Hanoverian England*, 126, 170, 172. "Some Account of Mr. Harrison's Invention for Determining the Longitude at Sea, and for Correcting the Charts of the Coasts. Delivered to the Commissioners of the Longitude, January 16th 1741–2," given in [John Harrison], *An Account of the Proceedings, in Order to the Discovery of the Longitude* (London, 1763), 7–8, 19, 21. Humphry Quill, *John Harrison: The Man Who Found Longitude* (London: Baker, 1966), 5–6, 120–22, 139–46, 186, 221.

[84] "An Account of the Proportions of the English and French Measures and Weights, from the Standards of the Same, Kept at the Royal Society," *PT* 42 (1742): 185–88. "An Account of a Comparison Lately Made by Some Gentlemen of the Royal Society, of the Standard of a Yard, and the Several Weights Lately Made for Their Use; with the Original Standards of Measures and Weights in the Exchequer, and Some Others Kept for Public Use, at Guild-Hall, Founders-Hall, the Tower, &c.," *PT* 42 (1742): 541–56. *Select Tracts and Table Books Relating to English Weights and Measures (1100–1742)*, ed. H. Hall and F. J. Nicholas, Camden Miscellany, vol. 15 (London: Office of the Society, 1929), 40.

ments originated with John Canton, a schoolmaster best known for his work on electricity, which had earned him a Copley Medal. His new experiments were highly exacting, and the interpretation he put on them contradicted a well-known finding of the Florentine Accademia del Cimento a hundred years before. There arose, in a sense, a dispute between scientific societies, even if one was defunct.

Canton's apparatus was transparently simple: a narrow glass tube open at one end and closed at the other with a hollow glass ball an inch and a quarter across. The ball together with a few inches of the tube was filled with mercury and placed in a water bath. The bath was heated until the mercury rose to the top of the tube, at which time the tube was hermetically sealed. When the mercury had cooled to its original temperature, Canton observed that it stood about a half inch higher than before. The only difference before and after the expansion of the mercury was that the pressure of the atmosphere over it had been removed. Water, Canton concluded, is compressible. He published his experiments in the *Philosophical Transactions* in 1762. Two years later he published a sequel in which he extended his experiments to other liquids, and in which he reported a new, "remarkable property" of water, its greater compressibility in winter than in summer.[85]

Doubts were raised about Canton's experiments in the *Monthly Review*, which was not a scientific journal but which nevertheless reviewed critically the contents of the *Philosophical Transactions*. By the time the journal commented on Canton's second paper, the Royal Society had honored Canton with his second Copley Medal; the journal hinted that it was to the Society's dishonor.[86]

The new president of the Society, the earl of Morton, asked the secretary Thomas Birch if it was "necessary every year to give the Medal." He also asked for the account of the "Experiment, by the Accademia del Cimento which pretends to establish the opinion that water is incompressible."[87] The question of awarding a second Copley Medal to Canton for his experiments on the compressibility of water was moved in council, but in "conversation" some Fellows expressed objections. Concerned for the "honour of the Society," the council appointed a committee to repeat Canton's experiments at the expense of the Society and to report back to the council.[88] The president was directed to inform the

[85] John Canton, "Experiments to Prove that Water is Not Incompressible," *PT* 52 (1762): 640–43; "Experiments and Observations on the Compressibility of Water and Some Other Fluids," *PT* 54 (1764): 261–62. John Canton to Benjamin Franklin, 29 June 1764, in *The Papers of Benjamin Franklin*, vol. 11, ed. L. W. Larabee (New Haven: Yale University Press, 1959), 244–46, on 245.

[86] *The Monthly Review* 29 (1763): 142–44, and 33 (1765): 455–56, on 456.

[87] Earl of Morton to Thomas Birch, 6 and 17 Nov. 1764, BL Add Mss 4315, f. 13, 16.

[88] Besides Cavendish, the committee consisted of the president, Matthew Raper, John Ellicott, James Short, William Watson, Israel Mauduit, and Charles Morton. 28 Nov. 1764, Minutes of Council, copy, Royal Society, 4:57. Francis Blake, Edward Delaval, Benjamin Franklin, and George Lewis Scott were added to the committee: 21 Feb. 1765, ibid., 4:62–63. 17 June 1765, ibid., 4:109.

Society that any objections to Canton's experiments had to be submitted in writing if they were to be considered by the committee. In June 1765 the council ordered the instruments for the committee, which was assisted in its experiments by the instrument-makers John Bird, James Ferguson, and Edward Nairne.[89] Being summer, the Society was in recess, and many of the committee members were out of town. Those who remained–Cavendish, Franklin, Watson, Heberden, and Ellicott–met four times in July to perform experiments in the Museum of the Society. At the beginning of August, the clerk of the Society, Emanuel Mendez da Costa, informed the president, Lord Morton, that the attending members of the committee were convinced of Canton's conclusion, but since they were "all friends to the experiments," he anticipated a "contest," especially since the experiments were of such "nicety." In November, after the Society had resumed its meetings, some of the experiments were performed a second time before a larger committee.

This larger committee contained a principal skeptic of Canton's claims, Francis Blake, an Oxford mathematician, who was an active, highly regarded member of the Society. Blake raised this and that question about Canton's experiments, but his concern appeared to have rested on an appeal to authority backed up by what seemed to him common sense. In the Florentine experiment, water was subjected to great pressure without, evidently, causing any change in its bulk, whereas in Canton's experiment, an observable change was alleged to have resulted from a very slight pressure. Which account was Blake to credit? As requested, Blake put his question to the council in writing.[90]

In a paper drawn up for the council, Cavendish stated and answered the objections to Canton's experiments.[91] The first objection went to the heart of the matter, the conflict with the Florentine experiment. Experiment is authority, Cavendish said, in effect, and experiment can overrule experiment. In response to Blake's objections, Cavendish wrote a separate paper, which he began by making the same point: "The authority of the most able experimenters is of no weight, when it appears that their experiments were made in such a way, as could not possibly show so small a degree of compressibility as Mr Canton has discovered."[92] There had been progress in the art of experiment in the century since the Florentines; Canton's skill in showing "so small a degree of compressibility"

---

[89] John Bird is referred to in Cavendish's memoranda on the experiments. James Ferguson was paid for his work: 10 July 1766, copy, Royal Society, Minutes of Council 5:161. Edward Nairne was also appointed according to Lord Morton: 30 Nov. 1765, Royal Society, JB 25:655.

[90] Francis Blake, "Remarks and Queries Recommended to the Consideration of the Right Honourable the Earl of Morton," Canton Papers, Royal Society, 3.

[91] Canton Papers, Royal Society. These objections are contained also in a much longer (eleven-page) paper, which would also seem to have been written by Cavendish, though the copy in the Canton Papers is not in his handwriting.

[92] Lord Charles Cavendish, "Observations on Mr Blake's Objections to Mr Canton's Experiments," Canton Papers, Royal Society.

was proof of that, as was, in its way, Cavendish's follow-up experiments. We have the Canton controversy to thank for the only surviving record of Cavendish's experimental work. Preserved in Canton's papers are Cavendish's measures and computations, which he sent Canton to review, having annotated them throughout with "by my measure," and signed the bottom of every sheet; the impression given by Cavendish's experimental work is one of great thoroughness and accuracy, characteristics equally of his son Henry's, of which we have ample record. In November 1765 the council resolved that the hypothesis of the compressibility of water accounts for Canton's experiments and that no other appears to do so as satisfactorily, and it voted to award Canton the Copley Medal for 1764.[93] Two days later, at the anniversary meeting of the Society, Morton announced the award of the Medal to Canton, and although in his address he brought up the controversy, he did not describe the ensuing experiments carried out at the Society, since Cavendish had written a "full and accurate Account" of them and of the "Theory deducible from them."[94] Cavendish's paper was read at the next general meeting of the Society.[95]

Of Canton's exquisitely precise experiment, the historian of the Royal Society, Charles Richard Weld, wrote that Lord Charles Cavendish had given the Society a "warm and able" defense.[96] In his address on the Copley Medal, Lord Morton referred to the extraordinary work on Canton's experiments by that "Noble Member of the Society," Lord Charles Cavendish, who was "eminent for his great Abilities, and deep knowledge in all the branches of science that come before him."[97]

"It were to be wished, that this noble philosopher would communicate more of his experiments to the world, as he makes many, and with great accuracy." This reference to Lord Charles Cavendish is contained in a letter written in 1762 by one who was competent to judge, Benjamin Franklin.[98] Franklin was expressing his admiration for Cavendish's experiment on the conduction of electricity by heated glass. The subject of electrical conduction had been expanded by the discovery of the Leyden jar, or electrical capacitor, an instrument which delivered

---

93 21 and 28 Nov. 1765, Minutes of Council, Royal Society, 5:131–32.

94 Lord Morton's address on 30 Nov. 1765: Royal Society, JB 25:647–64, on 656. The award of the Copley Medal did not bring the work of the committee to an end; two and a half weeks later the council resolved that an experiment on the compressibility of water proposed by Lord Morton be resumed. 19 Dec. 1765, Minutes of Council, copy, Royal Society, 5:148.

95 Lord Charles Cavendish, "A Paper Delivered to Mr. da Costa for the Use of the Committee on Mr. Canton's Experiments," dated 21 Oct. 1765, and "Appendix to the Paper on Mr. Canton's Experiments," dated 5 Dec. 1765, Royal Society, JB 25:668–79. The material is also in the Canton Papers, Royal Society, 3.

96 Charles Richard Weld, *A History of the Royal Society*, 2 vols. (London, 1848) 2:32.

97 30 Nov. 1765, Royal Society, JB 25:656.

98 Benjamin Franklin to Ebenezer Kinnersley, 20 Feb. 1762, in *The Papers of Benjamin Franklin*, vol. 10, ed. L. W. Labaree (New Haven: Yale University Press, 1966), 37–53, on 42.

far greater quantities of electricity than did the unaided electrical machine. The insulating and conducting properties of glass had acquired particular interest after Franklin had shown that the whole power of the Leyden jar is concentrated in the glass of the jar and not in the metallic foil coating it. By his experiment, Cavendish showed that when glass is heated to four hundred degrees or higher, it becomes a conductor of electricity.

In 1747 William Watson invited members of the Royal Society to join him in an experiment on electrical conduction, the scale of which, miles literally, was a measure of his enthusiasm for the subject. This inspired experiment was made possible by the Leyden jar, the "explosion" of which could communicate shocks over long distances. Watson thought that a powerful Leyden jar might send a shock across the River Thames, and to try that idea Watson and "many others" assembled at the new Westminster Bridge (to which Cavendish had recently devoted so much work), across which a wire connected to a Leyden jar was laid. The river and the bodies of the experimenters completed an electrical circuit, whereby upon discharging the Leyden jar, Watson and his associates felt shocks in their wrists and elbows. The circuit was progressively lengthened until finally the experimenters moved from the river onto dry land, at Shooters' Hill. Using signals and watches, they concluded that electrical conduction is "nearly instantaneous." In their experiments, which lasted for weeks, twenty-five Fellows of the Royal Society took part, Lord Charles Cavendish among them, as were others of the De Moivre circle, Folkes, Stanhope, Davall, Jones, and Scott. Bradley was there, and so were many of the leading instrument-makers. For this "Body of Philosophers," the outdoor experiments in the middle of summer were an outing as well as an enquiry into nature; Stanhope brought venison pastry and French wine.[99] The experiments were financed by and "made by the order and for the service of the [Royal] Society,"[100] and Watson published an account of them in the *Philosophical Transactions*.[101]

Lord Charles Cavendish also assisted Watson in his private researches on electricity. In a paper in 1752, Watson described an apparatus made by Cavendish for the conduction of electricity through a vacuum. To discover if the vacuum transmits electricity, Watson had to make do with the imperfect vacuum obtained by an air pump until Cavendish solved the problem with an apparatus that achieved a Torricellian vacuum and an electrical circuit at once. Bending a narrow glass tube seven and a half feet long into a parabolic shape, Cavendish filled the tube with mercury and placed its ends in basins of mercury; the mercury in the two arms of the parabola descended until the level stood about thirty inches above the basins, leaving a vacuum at the top. Bringing up a wire from an electrical machine, Cavendish caused electricity to pass through the vacuum in a "continued arch of

---

[99] Thomas Birch to Philip Yorke, 15 Aug. 1747, BL Add Mss 35397, ff. 70–71.

[100] 17 Oct. 1748, Minutes of Council, copy, Royal Society, 4:15.

[101] William Watson, "A Collection of the Electrical Experiments Communicated to the Royal Society," *PT* 45 (1748): 49–120.

lambent flame." Cavendish, Watson observed, joined a "very complete knowledge" of science with that of making apparatus. Of "this noble lord," Watson said that his "zeal for the promotion of true philosophy is exceeded by none."[102]

Of Lord Charles Cavendish's apparatus, the ultimate in simplicity was his sealed vessel for converting water to vapor: a small quantity of water was introduced above the mercury in a barometer, which was enlarged into a ball on top.[103] We will have occasion to refer to Lord Charles's experiments with this apparatus, but here we will give his son's opinion of them. In a memorandum probably intended for his instrument-maker Edward Nairne, Henry Cavendish wrote, "My father's experiments on which what I said concerning the turning of water into vapour are founded seem so convincing as to leave no doubt of the truth of it."[104]

Henry Cavendish's scientific manuscripts record Lord Charles's measurements of the tension of aqueous vapor over a wide range of temperatures.[105] From the same source we know that Lord Charles did experiments on the bulk of water over a wide range of temperatures,[106] that he measured the depression of mercury in glass tubes of different sizes,[107] that he measured the expansion of mercury with heat,[108] that he probably did chemical experiments,[109] and that he made astronomical observations together with Henry.[110] From other sources we

---

[102] William Watson, "An Account of the Phaenomena of Electricity in Vacuo, with Some Observations Thereupon," *PT* 47 (1752): 362–76, on 370–71.

[103] Henry Cavendish, "Theory of Boiling," Cavendish Mss; *The Scientific Papers of the Honourable Henry Cavendish, F.R.S.*, vol. 2: *Chemical and Dynamical*, ed. E. Thorpe (Cambridge: Cambridge University Press, 1921), 356–62, on 355–56.

[104] This two-sheet memorandum concerns the simple additivity of air pressure and the pressure of water vapor in a receiver. Cavendish Mss IV, 4.

[105] Lord Charles Cavendish's values of vapor tension, given in inches of mercury, are reproduced in an editor's note, in *Sci. Pap.* 2:355.

[106] In connection with government taxes on spirits, Henry Cavendish supplied a table of the bulk of water at degrees of heat from 25 to 210 degrees. "From the Experiments of Lord Charles Cavendish, Communicated by Mr. Henry Cavendish. March 1790," Blagden Collection, Royal Society, Misc. Notes. In the same connection, Henry Cavendish communicated the weight of a cubic foot of water, "the result of my father's experiment." Henry Cavendish to Charles Blagden, undated [probably 1790], Royal Society.

[107] Ibid., 653. S. P. Laplace, *Mécanique Céleste*, trans. N. Bowditch, vol. 4 (Boston, 1839), 1004. Henry Cavendish included his father's table of the depression of mercury in his report on the meteorological instruments of the Royal Society in 1776: "An Account of the Meteorological Instruments Used at the Royal Society's House," *PT* 66 (1776): 75–401; in *Sci. Pap.* 2:112–26, on 116.

[108] Thomas Young, *A Course of Lectures on Natural Philosophy and the Mechanical Arts,* 2 vols. (London, 1807) 2:391.

[109] Here and there Henry Cavendish referred to his father's chemicals; for example, 16 June 1781, "Experiments on Air," Cavendish Mss II, 5:56.

[110] Packet of astronomical observations from 1774, in Lord Charles Cavendish's hand, with Henry Cavendish's observations added, and kept by Henry in his own papers. Cavendish Mss Misc. We know of Lord Charles Cavendish's interest in astronomy from sources other than his son, too; for example, William Ponsonby, Viscount Duncannon to the duke of Devonshire, 24 Jan. 1744/43, Devon. Coll.: "I have not had an opportunity lately of seeing Lord Charles, but I make no doubt of his Lordship having made proper observations on the Comet, which appears here in great Splendor."

know that he computed tables of errors of time for William Ludlam, an astronomer at Cambridge,[111] that he made meteorological observations with Heberden,[112] and that he kept a meteorological journal.[113] Although we have only a fragmentary record of Lord Charles's experiments and observations, we know that he made many and that his contemporaries regarded him as a highly competent investigator.

[111] Lord Charles Cavendish, "Difference to Be Subtracted from Sidereal Time to Reduce It to Mean Time." This and two other tables of calculations on errors of time, in William Ludlam, *Astronomical Observations Made in St. John's College, Cambridge, in the Years 1767 and 1768: With an Account of Several Astronomical Instruments* (Cambridge, 1769), 145–48.

[112] In 1769 Lord Charles Cavendish's good friend the physician William Heberden published a paper in the *Philosophical Transactions* comparing the rainfall at the bottom of a tall building with that at the top. Benjamin Franklin had an explanation, which he put in a letter and in which he referred to the experiments of Heberden and Lord Charles Cavendish, both "very accurate experimenters." Franklin to Thomas Percival, undated [probably June 1771], in *The Papers of Benjamin Franklin*, vol. 18, ed. W. B. Willcox (New Haven: Yale University Press, 1974), 155–57, on 155.

[113] Letters from William Borlase to Thomas Hornsby in 1766 and to Charles Lyttleton in 1767, quoted in J. Oliver, "William Borlase's Contributions to Eighteenth-Century Meteorology and Climatology," *Annals of Science* 25 (1969): 275–317, on 293. William Heberden included Lord Charles Cavendish's readings of the greatest cold at night for twenty years, as he recorded them at Great Marlborough Street, in "A Table of the Mean Heat of Every Month for Ten Years in London, from 1763 to 1772 Inclusively," *PT* 78:66.

PART TWO

THE HONORABLE HENRY & LORD CHARLES CAVENDISH

CHAPTER 1

EDUCATION OF HENRY CAVENDISH

A FEW WEEKS after Henry Cavendish's death, a neighbor of his on Bedford Square, the medical scientist John Walker, wrote to the botanist James Edward Smith: "You will have heard that we have lost Mr. Cavendish,–a man of a wonderful mind, more nearly approaching that of Newton than perhaps any individual in this country since his time." Walker said that Cavendish had been "educated and trained by his father from very early youth to scientific pursuits."[1] Of Cavendish's unique, private education and training in science by his father we know only the outcome, but of his formal education we can say something about goals and methods.

HACKNEY ACADEMY

It was from tutors, no doubt, that Henry Cavendish received his early education. We know that the tutor to one of his first cousins was paid one hundred pounds a year,[2] and we assume that a comparable investment was made in Henry's education. With respect to his further education, his father had to choose between a public and a private school. Since he himself had gone to a public school, he might have been expected to send his son to one, especially since that was increasingly the practice among the aristocracy, who regarded

[1] John Walker to James Edward Smith, 16 Mar. 1810, *Memoir and Correspondence of the Late Sir James Edward Smith, M.D.*, 2 vols., ed. Lady Smith (London, 1832), 170–71. We assume that this John Walker was the physician of that name who published on geography, natural history, and physiology, and who was best known for his unceasing promotion of vaccination. "Walker, John (1759–1830)," *DNB* 20:533.

[2] Henry Cavendish's aunt Rachel Cavendish married Sir William Morgan of Tredgar. They had two sons, William and Edward, born a few years before Henry Cavendish, and one of these "Master Morgans" had a tutor who received one hundred pounds per annum. This is according to Lord Charles Cavendish in an account for his widowed sister, undated [1740], Devon. Coll., no. 167.1.

public schools as the proper training ground for "public life." Most of the English peerage was educated either at Eton, which is where Lord Charles had gone, or at Westminster, schools which had acquired a reputation as a "nursery for statesmen." But perhaps his sons, Henry and Frederick, did not look to him like future statesmen. Or perhaps he did not have happy memories of his own schooling, though we note that on at least one occasion, he returned to Eton to attend the public exercises. Or perhaps he belonged to the trend in eighteenth-century England of fathers taking greater interest in their children, one indication of which was their selection of private schools with their masters serving as surrogate fathers. Whatever his reasoning, he sent his sons to a private school.[3]

There were a good many private schools to choose from, most of them conveniently located in the suburbs of London.[4] They offered a variety of curriculums; the school selected by Lord Charles, one of the so-called "academies," Hackney Academy, emphasized modern subjects, which may have been its main attraction to him. The largest of the academies, with an enrollment of about one hundred, Hackney was also the oldest, founded in 1685, and the most fashionable in eighteenth-century England.[5]

Located two miles northeast of London, the village of Hackney with a thousand or so householders was best known as a place where rich Londoners built country seats. Between London and Hackney the traffic was so heavy that "hackney" had become the general word for coaches of the type used there. With its magnificent playing fields and clean air, Hackney Academy enjoyed a reputation for healthy living, and like other private schools, it was thought to answer the standard complaint about the public schools, their rampant sexuality.[6] The school to which Lord Charles sent his sons was, in short, modern, healthy, and safe.

There were other considerations, too; for one, Hackney attracted a certain kind of clientele, not day students from the lower middle class or the crafts, as some academies did, but strictly boarding students, who came from the upper middle and upper classes, in particular, from wealthy whig families.

[3] Of the peers about the same age as Lord Charles Cavendish, forty-six attended Eton and thirty-one Westminster; of those about the age of Henry Cavendish, fifty-three attended Eton and seventy-eight Westminster. From John Cannon, *Aristocratic Century: The Peerage of Eighteenth-Century England* (Cambridge: Cambridge University Press, 1984), 40, 43–44. H. C. Maxwell Lyte, *A History of Eton College 1440–1884*, rev. ed. (London, 1889), 287. Randolph Trumbach, *The Rise of the Egalitarian Family: Aristocratic Kinship and Domestic Relations in Eighteenth-Century England* (New York: Academic Press, 1978), 292.

[4] Trumbach, *Rise of the Egalitarian Family*, 265.

[5] Nicholas Hans, *New Trends in Education in the Eighteenth Century* (London: Routledge & Kegan Paul, 1951), 63–66, 70.

[6] William Thornton, *The New, Complete, and Universal History, Description, and Survey of the Cities of London and Westminster . . . Likewise the Towns, Villages, Palaces, Seats, and Country, to the Extent of Above Twenty Miles Round*, rev. ed. (London, 1784), 481. Daniel Lysons, *Environs of London; Being an Historical Account of the Towns, Villages, and Hamlets, Within Twelve Miles of That Capital*, vol. 2: *County of Middlesex* (London, 1795), 450–51. Trumbach, *Rise of the Egalitarian Family*, 266.

28. Hackney. William Thornton, The New, Complete, and Universal History, Description, and Survey of the Cities of London and Westminster . . . Likewise the Towns, Villages, Palaces, Seats, and Country, to the Extent of Above Twenty Miles Round, rev. ed. *(London, 1784), facing p. 488.*

Ten years before Lord Charles sent his son Henry to Hackney, the hard-headed Lord Hardwicke had sent his son Philip Yorke there to get a good modern education. Other whig peers who patronized Hackney included the duke of Grafton, the earl of Essex, the earl of Grey, and the duke of Devonshire, who sent his son Lord John Cavendish there at the same time that his brother Lord Charles sent Henry. Evidently the first Cavendishes to attend Hackney, Lord John and Henry were soon to be joined by Henry's brother, Frederick. They in turn were followed by the sons of the next, the fourth, duke of Devonshire, Lord Richard and Lord George Henry Cavendish, as Hackney settled in as a Cavendish tradition.[7]

We may approach our subject, the education of a student who would become a great scientist, by looking at the persons who ran Hackney Academy. The Newcomes were a family of teachers, Anglican clergy, and Cambridge graduates with an interest in science. The first of the Hackney Newcomes, Henry, a good classical scholar and strict disciplinarian, was still headmaster when Henry Cavendish was there. Henry Newcome and his son Peter, who later became headmaster himself, were friends of the duke of Kent's family,

[7] Hans, *New Trends*, 72, 243–44.

dining with them at St. James Square.[8] Lord Charles recommended Peter Newcome for membership in the Royal Society, as one skilled in mathematics and polite literature, in 1742, just as he entered his son Henry at Hackney. Cosigners of the certificate included the Hackney graduate Yorke, Thomas Birch, and Daniel Wray, strongly suggesting that Peter Newcome was one of Cavendish's circle.[9] While Henry Cavendish was at Hackney, Newcome joined Lord Charles and other Fellows of the Royal Society in Watson's experiments on the conduction of electricity across the Thames, and a year after Henry left Hackney, Newcome published his observations on an earthquake felt at Hackney in the *Philosophical Transactions*.[10] The connection between the Cavendishes and the Newcomes was ongoing: many years after he had finished at Hackney, and shortly before he was elected to the Royal Society, Henry Cavendish was invited by Peter Newcome to a meeting of the Society as his guest.[11] Newcome was well regarded in the Royal Society, in 1763 and 1764 serving on its council.[12] We find clear connections between Lord Charles Cavendish's scientific interests and Hackney.

Normally students were admitted to Hackney at age seven, but Henry Cavendish did not enter until he was eleven, in 1742, pursuing an advanced course, in which he was instructed in subjects that would apply to his later studies and work: mathematics, natural sciences, French, and Latin. At age seventeen, the usual leaving age for students going on to the university, Henry Cavendish, like all of the other Cavendishes and like most of the other students at Hackney, proceeded directly to the university, which in his case was Cambridge.

PETERHOUSE, CAMBRIDGE

From the fourteenth century to the time Henry Cavendish entered Cambridge, twenty Cavendishes had graduated from this university.[13] The first of the dukes of Devonshire to get a university education, however, was the third duke, who went to Oxford (briefly) and not Cambridge, though he sent his two sons to Cambridge, and his only surviving brother, Lord Charles, likewise sent his two sons to Cambridge. The eldest, Henry, having just turned eighteen, entered

---

[8] Thomas Birch Diary, BL Add Mss 4478C, frequent entries beginning in 1740.

[9] Royal Society, Certificates, 1:260 (25 Nov. 1742). The other signers were James Jurin, Benjamin Hoadley, John Ward, and Thomas Walker. Newcome was elected on 24 Feb. 1743.

[10] William Watson, "A Collection of the Electrical Experiments Communicated to the Royal Society," *PT* 45 (1748): 49–120, on 62. Newcome reported the earthquake as it was felt by persons at his house in Hackney, who included the son of John Hadley, the great instrument-maker. "A Letter from Mr. Peter Newcome F.R.S. to the President, Concerning the Same Shock Being Felt at Hackney, Near London," *PT* 46 (1750): 653–54; read 29 Mar. 1750.

[11] Royal Society, JB 23:711 (10 Jan. 1760).

[12] Minutes of Council, copy, Royal Society, 5.

[13] John and J. A. Venn, *Alumni Cantabrigiensis* . . . , pt. 1: *From the Earliest Times to 1751*, vol. 1 (Cambridge: Cambridge University Press, 1954).

St. Peter's College, or Peterhouse, Cambridge, on 24 November 1749.[14] The first Cavendish to go to that particular Cambridge college, he remained in regular attendance there for three years and three months.

29. *Peterhouse. From David Loggan,* Cantabrigia Illustrata *(Cambridge, 1688).*

At the time, the chancellor of the university was the duke of Newcastle, a minister of state, and a distant relative of our Cavendishes. When the master of Peterhouse died, Newcastle lobbied hard for a whig, a fellow of Peterhouse, Edmund Keene. A close overseer of his sons' education, Lord Charles was on familiar terms with Keene at Peterhouse, as he was with the Newcomes at Hackney. While Henry Cavendish was at Peterhouse, Keene dined with Cavendish's friends, Birch, Heberden, Wray, Mann, and Squire, and on at least one occasion Keene dined with Birch and Cavendish.[15] Although Peterhouse was not particularly favored by the nobility, it was fashionable with the upper classes for a time in the middle of the eighteenth century.[16] Henry Cavendish, his brother Frederick, and his cousin Lord John, and soon after them a relative James Lowther, all went to Peterhouse, which like Hackney, became a family tradition.

The overall attendance at the university at the time Henry Cavendish entered was small and declining, but the proportion of students who were, like Cavendish,

[14] George Wilson, *The Life of the Honourable Henry Cavendish* (London, 1851), 17.

[15] 6 June 1747, 17 May 1751, 18 and 22 Feb. 1752, Thomas Birch Diary.

[16] D. A. Winstanley, *Unreformed Cambridge: A Study of Certain Aspects of the University in the Eighteenth Century* (Cambridge: Cambridge University Press, 1935), 193. Winstanley says that at midcentury, Peterhouse was "much patronized" by the aristocracy, but it should be noted that of peers born in 1711–40, Henry Cavendish's period, only three went to Peterhouse. By contrast, nine went to Clare, eight to King's, seven to Trinity, and six to St. John's. In attendance at Cambridge, in 1740–59, when Henry Cavendish was there, out of twenty-seven peers' sons, again only three were at Peterhouse. Cannon, *Aristocratic Century*, 48–51.

aristocratic was rising.[17] Classed roughly by their station in life, students entered, in ascending order, as sizars, pensioners, fellow-commoners, or noblemen. Sizars, who were the poorest and were charged the lowest fees, and who were really a college charity, were sons of poor clergy, small farmers, petty tradesmen, and artisans. The majority of students were pensioners, who were better off, commonly sons of more prosperous clergy and professional men, but without distinction of birth. Noblemen paid the highest fees, and since they did not have substantial privileges beyond those of fellow-commoners, they often settled to be fellow-commoners.[18] Henry Cavendish entered Cambridge as a fellow-commoner.

Other than for his ability and application to serious study, Cavendish could be said to be typical of fellow-commoners. They were occasionally older men who simply liked university life, but most of them were young men of independent means, often scions of country families and commercial magnates if not of nobility. Comprising just over ten percent of the student population in the eighteenth century, they were a conspicuous minority, inclining to fine dress, sometimes appearing with their own servants, and in any case able to afford to hire poor students to wait on them. They were equivalent to the fellows of the college in that they were admitted to the fellows' table, common room, and cellar, where they could smoke clay pipes and drink Spanish and French wine. They were usually excused from performing the college exercises required of humbler undergraduates and of attending lectures by the college tutors.[19] To judge by Cavendish's later habits, the extravagances of some of the other fellow-commoners did not happen to be his, but his privileges were the same as theirs, including freedom to spend most of his time as he wished.

At the time Cavendish entered, Peterhouse had between thirty and forty students, not all of whom were in residence. During the years he was there, 1749 through 1752, over fifty students were admitted, of which thirteen were fellow-commoners, most of whom later went into politics; the rest were sizars and pensioners, most of whom became clerics.[20] None but Cavendish became notable for any scientific achievement.

Very few eminent British men of science were, as Cavendish was, upper class.[21] By education, too, Cavendish was unusual; the fraction of eminent

---

[17] Cannon, *Aristocratic Century*, 45.

[18] Thomas Alfred Walker, *Peterhouse* (Cambridge: W. Heffer, 1935), 76–78. Edmund Carter, *The History of the University of Cambridge, from Its Original, to the Year 1753* (London, 1753), 5, 29.

[19] Winstanley, *Unreformed Cambridge*, 198. Walker, *Peterhouse*, 78.

[20] The numbers given here are based on Thomas Alfred Walker, *Admissions to Peterhouse or S. Peter's College in the University of Cambridge. A Biographical Register* (Cambridge: Cambridge University Press, 1912). They are less precise but more accurate than those given in the first edition of our *Cavendish*, but the point remains the same, Cavendish's typical course as a fellow-commoner.

[21] Hans, *New Trends*, 34, groups Delaval with Cavendish and Boyle as the three eminent scientists, out of 680 British scientists, who were "sons of peers." Cavendish was not, of course, the son of a peer, but the point is made of the rarity of aristocrats in this company.

British scientists in his time who had a Cambridge or Oxford education was small and steadily falling.[22] Still there were a few young men of future scientific achievement at Cambridge, one of whom was Edward Delaval, younger brother of a peer from an ancient Northumberland family, who would become a chemist, a recipient of the Royal Society's Copley Medal and of another gold medal from the Manchester Literary and Philosophical Society. Because of Delaval's scientific interest, his station, his residence (his college, Pembroke, was across the street from Peterhouse), and his voice (which was resounding, a family trait, earning him the local name of "Delaval the loud"), Cavendish could not have failed to know him or about him; he was to receive his Copley Medal in the same year as Cavendish.[23] One year younger than Cavendish, Nevil Maskelyne, a student at Trinity College, would go on to a distinguished career in astronomy, first as assistant to James Bradley and then in Bradley's post of astronomer royal; he was to become one of Cavendish's most valued colleagues. At Cambridge and also of about the same age as Cavendish were the promising but short-lived chemist John Hadley, the capable practical astronomer Francis Wollaston, and Francis Maseres, an "excellent mathematician," according to a colleague.[24] Hadley was a guest in the Cavendish home and a recommender of Henry Cavendish for membership in the Royal Society, and Cavendish was first to sign the certificates recommending both Wollaston and Maseres for membership in the Royal Society.[25] Of eventual importance to Cavendish as a friend and colleague was another young man at Cambridge, John Michell. Having graduated the year before Cavendish entered Cambridge, Michell was a fellow of Queen's College, where he gave lectures and did experimental work.

The poet Thomas Gray, who resided at Peterhouse not long before Cavendish, described Cambridge fellows as sleepy and drunken and fellow-commoners as their imitators, and in his letters from Cambridge he constantly referred to the stupor of the place. Undoubtedly, there was a measure of truth in his observation, but fellows also had an excuse for their apathy, since they had little to occupy them officially. At an earlier time, they had given lectures, but by

---

22 Hans, *New Trends*, 34, estimates that the proportion of Oxford and Cambridge graduates dropped from 67 percent in the seventeenth century to 20 percent at the end of the eighteenth century. Hans's figures do not have precise meaning, since they are based on rather arbitrary definitions, but the large percentage of scientific practitioners in Henry Cavendish's time who were not Oxford or Cambridge graduates is significant.

23 The name was given to Delaval by his friend Thomas Gray. Robert Ketton-Cremer, *Thomas Gray: A Biography* (Cambridge: Cambridge University Press, 1955), 142–43. Two years older than Cavendish, Delaval took his M.A. and became a fellow of Pembroke. "Delaval, Edward Hussey," *DNB* 5:766–67.

24 William Ludlam, *The Rudiments of Mathematics; Designed for the Use of Students at the Universities: Containing an Introduction to Algebra, Remarks on the First Six Books of Euclid, the Elements of Plain Trigonometry* (Cambridge, 1785), 7.

25 Royal Society, Certificates, 3:65 (Francis Wollaston's announced candidacy, 3 Jan. 1769) and 3:104 (Francis Maseres's announced candidacy, 31 Jan. 1771).

the middle of the eighteenth century their teaching duties had largely fallen away, while their fellowships were becoming sinecures. College lecturers still performed when Cavendish was there, but the practice was on the way to extinction. The motivation to do any work had to come from within, and while there were fellows who had a love of learning and teaching, even a few who were great scholars, most of them contributed little or nothing.[26] The exceptions were the fellows who were also tutors, who did serious, regular teaching. Peterhouse had two tutors, both formerly hard-working sizars at the college, both vicars, neither of whom left a mark as a scholar. The university had a small number of professors, whose teaching was increasingly marginal, as the tutors of the colleges took over their subjects. Lord John Cavendish, Henry Cavendish's first cousin, was also assigned to the same pair of tutors, though he brought his own private tutor, and Henry might have brought his own too.

If fellow-commoners wanted to leave with a degree they had "to keep the statutory two acts and opponencies and to sit for the Senate House Examination," though these exercises were usually circumvented by a procedure known as "huddling."[27] But since a degree was unlikely to make any difference in their lives, they usually left without one, as Henry Cavendish did in February 1753. The suggestion has been made that he objected to the religous tests,[28] which were stringent, but if that was his reason for not graduating, he left no record of it, then or later. The most likely reason he left without a degree was that he did not even consider taking one but simply followed tradition, as did most of the thirteen fellow-commoners at Peterhouse during Cavendish's stay, only five of whom took degrees, and three of these were Masters of Arts only.[29]

The examination that Cavendish did not take was then on its way to becoming the famous Cambridge mathematical tripos. Beginning in the year Cavendish would have taken it, 1753, the list of examinees was divided into wranglers and senior and junior optimes, with lively competition for a high position on it. No doubt if he had elected to take it, Cavendish would have done well on the examination, owing to its mathematical content: John Green, bishop of Lincoln, writing in 1750 while Cavendish was a student, observed that at Cambridge, "Mathematics and natural philosophy are so generally and exactly understood, that more than twenty in every year of the Candidates for a Batchelor of Arts Degree, are able to demonstrate the principal Propositions in [Newton's] *Principia*; and most other Books of the first Character on those subjects."[30]

---

[26] Winstanley, *Unreformed Cambridge*, 256–61. Thomas Gray to Horace Walpole, 31 Oct. 1734, *Horace Walpole's Correspondence*, vol. 13, pt. 1, pp. 58–59.

[27] Winstanley, *Unreformed Cambridge*, 199.

[28] Wilson, *Cavendish*, 17, 181.

[29] Walker, *Admissions*, 292–306.

[30] John Green, *Academic*, 1750, p. 23, quoted in Christopher Wordsworth, *Scholae Academicae. Some Account of the Studies at the English Universities in the Eighteenth Century* (1877; reprint, London: Frank Cass, 1968), 73.

With the emphasis on mathematics at Cambridge, there were naturally some very able mathematical teachers, such as John Lawson of Sidney Sussex College, who was mathematical lecturer and then tutor when Cavendish was a student.[31] Given the very general purposes of mathematical education, students who distinguished themselves in mathematics would as a rule go on to careers other than in mathematics. If Cavendish *had* taken a degree, his competition in the examinations of 1753 would have included William Disney and Thomas Postlethwaite, both of whom became writers on religion and made their careers in Cambridge. Disney, first wrangler, later regius professor of Hebrew, published against Gibbon's history of the Roman Empire and for the superiority of religous duties over worldly considerations.[32] Postlethwaite, third wrangler, later master of Trinity College, published one work, a discourse on Isaiah, while retaining his reputation as one of the best mathematicians in the university.[33] In the previous year, 1752, the second wrangler was Henry Boult Cay, who for a time was a fellow of Clare College before becoming a barrister at the Middle Temple; Cavendish probably knew this wrangler as a student, for later he brought him as his guest to the Royal Society Club.[34] Mathematical achievement at Cambridge was not an indicator of future scientific interest; none of the above three wranglers, Disney, Postlethwaite, or Cay, became a member of the Royal Society. Under Dr. Law, Keene's successor as master of Peterhouse, Cavendish's college produced its first senior wrangler, Robert Thorp, who became co-editor with John Jebb and George Wollaston of a selection from Newton's *Principia*, which became a standard edition in the university, *Excerpta quaedam e Newtoni Principiis* . . .[35] In the next century a number of famous physicists, William Thomson, Peter Guthrie Tait, and James Clerk Maxwell, studied at Peterhouse, with its famous tripos coaches William Hopkins and E. J. Routh.

Whereas Lord Charles Cavendish learned mathematics by private lessons from mathematicians who were Newton's associates, Henry Cavendish learned it at Cambridge, if not elsewhere. At the very least, we can say that whether or not he had a mathematically adept tutor or attended lectures on mathematics, for over three years he was exposed to the mathematical tradition of Cambridge and to the books on mathematics and natural philosophy listed in the various editions of the student guide at Cambridge.[36] Cavendish was not the only eminent

---

31 "Lawson, John," *DNB* 11:736–37.

32 John Nichols, ed., *Illustrations of the Literary History of the Eighteenth Century*, 8 vols. (London, 1817–58), 6:737.

33 "Postlethwaite, Thomas," *DNB* 42:204–5.

34 Minute Book, Royal Society Club, Royal Society, 5 (5 Mar. 1767 and 30 June 1768). Henry Boult Cay is under his father John Cay's entry in the *Dictionary of National Biography*.

35 Walker, *Peterhouse*, 95; *Admissions to Peterhouse*, 73, 119.

36 Daniel Waterland, *Advice to a Young Student. With a Method of Study for the Four First Years* 1706–40; reported in Wordsworth, *Scholae Academicae*, 78–81, 248–49, 330–37.

experimentalist of the second half of the eighteenth century who was exposed to mathematics at Cambridge–there was the chemist William Hyde Wollaston at the end of the century, for example–but there were very few of them. Cavendish's combination of experimental and mathematical approaches in science was highly uncommon.

In the introduction, we discussed Lord Charles and Henry Cavendish in relation to two revolutions, one political and one scientific. The education that Henry received at the University of Cambridge can be related to those revolutions. Newton's main influence in Cambridge was exerted through his physical theories, the route to which was mathematics,[37] and it has been argued that one of the reasons for the appeal of Newton at Cambridge, leading to the emphasis on mathematics there, was a change in the Church of England owing to the revolution of 1688–89. Devoted principally to training clergy, Cambridge became a stronghold of low-church latitudinarians and whigs, to whom Newtonianism had a particular appeal for the support it gave to the argument from design for the existence of a Creator.[38] It is certainly the case that Cavendish was indoctrinated in a scientific orthodoxy originating in the scientific revolution in an institution sympathetic to the revolutionary political settlement. For some three odd years, Cavendish lived and breathed Newtonianism.

The one record we have of Cavendish's thinking while he was at the university conveniently brings together our major themes, education, politics, and science. Frederick, prince of Wales, after holding court in opposition to his father, George II, for nearly fifteen years, died while still waiting for his chance at the throne. Frederick had wanted to become chancellor of Cambridge in 1748, but his father opposed his wish, and the university took the safe course, selecting Newcastle instead.[39] Frederick's death offered the university an opportunity to honor him in memory as it had denied him in life. Cambridge published a deluxe edition of academic exercises to which Cavendish contributed. His poem, "Lament on the Death of Most Eminent Frederick, Prince of Wales," was written in Latin and met the standards of the day, which were not particularly high, inspiring Horace Walpole to make a play on words: "We have been overwhelmed with lamentable Cambridge and Oxford dirges on the Prince's death."[40] The premature death of a prince was an appropriate occasion to reflect on the fragility of life, and Cavendish dutifully wrote that tears are fruitless, the thistle and the lily alike flourish, and death plays no favorites. But the middle stanza is not conventional, for here we hear the voice of the future scientific investigator, the "intimate" of nature:

[37] W. W. Rouse Ball, *A History of the Study of Mathematics at Cambridge* (Cambridge, 1889), 74–76.

[38] John Gascoigne, *Cambridge in the Age of the Enlightenment: Science, Religion and Politics from the Restoration to the French Revolution* (Cambridge: Cambridge University Press, 1989), 145, 147.

[39] Ibid., 104–6.

[40] Horace Walpole to Sir Horace Mann, 18 June 1751, *Horace Walpole's Correspondence*, vol 20, part 4, pp. 260–61.

while nature may mock us, Cavendish wrote, it "does lay bare hidden causes, and the wandering paths of the stars."[41] Such were the circumstances of Cavendish's first publication and probably his last poem. His preferred way of speaking of the hidden causes of nature was in the unadorned language of science.

LEARNING SCIENCE

As the university was dominated by its colleges, its teaching was dominated by its tutors in their colleges and not by the small number of professors of the university. In critical and historical accounts of the university in the eighteenth century, the professors have fared poorly. They sometimes deserved to be dismissed, but it can be said on their behalf that their teaching was becoming increasingly irrelevant to most students as their subjects were being taken over by the tutors. They were deprived of the usual incentive to lecture, though some of them took this form of teaching seriously all the same, and almost all of them brought out textbooks. From the standpoint of Henry Cavendish, the man of science, the professors are of particular interest, since unlike the tutors, who taught all subjects, the professors stood for specialized learning. William Heberden recalled that in his student days at Cambridge, around 1730, Professor Saunderson lectured on Newton, geometry, and algebra while the college lecturers largely ignored these subjects, and that the publications on natural philosophy by the professors Robert Smith and Thomas Rutherforth drew attention to their subjects and spread their teaching in the university.[42] Of importance to us here are certain professors who wrote on subjects of interest to Cavendish.

Whether or not Cavendish heard Cambridge professors lecture, he most certainly knew their textbooks and their common desire to build science on Newton's example. Just what a scientifically minded student like Cavendish made of it was, ultimately, up to him. Just as Cavendish had to start somewhere, so must we: in this chapter we examine textbooks written by professors for use at Cambridge. In this way we learn, as students in Cavendish's day learned, the approved way of studying nature.

The power of mathematics to describe nature was impressively demonstrated by Newton in his *Principia*, or *The Mathematical Principles of Natural Philosophy*. First published in 1687, this work appeared in three editions in Newton's lifetime, the last in 1726.[43] The complementary power of the experimental

---

[41] Henry Cavendish, "Luctus," in Cambridge University, *Academiae Cantabrigiensis Luctus in Obitum Frederici celsissimi Walliae Principis* (Cambridge, 1751).

[42] Heberden quoted in Wordsworth, *Scholae Academicae*, 66–67. Gascoigne, *Cambridge*, 175.

[43] The editors of the three editions of Newton's treatise, generally referred to by the short Latin title *Principia*, were Halley in 1687, Roger Cotes in 1713, and Henry Pemberton in 1726. In 1729 an English translation was brought out by Andrew Motte. A recent edition is *Sir Isaac Newton's Mathematical Principles of Natural Philosophy and His System of the World*, 2 vols., rev. F. Cajori (Berkeley and Los Angeles: University of California Press, 1962). Also see I. B. Cohen, *Introduction to Newton's Principia* (Cambridge: Cambridge University Press, 1971), vii, 7.

30. Sir Isaac Newton. Portrait by G. Kneller, engraving by A. Tardieu. Courtesy of Smith Image Collection, Van Pelt-Dietrich Library, University of Pennsylvania.

enquiry into nature was as persuasively demonstrated in Newton's optical researches, collected in his treatise *Opticks*, which also appeared in three editions, between 1704 and 1717/18. This work concluded with speculations, which were expanded in each edition; their purpose was to stimulate others to carry forward the investigation of nature in Newton's mathematical and experimental way, and they were regarded as the most important part of the book by Newton's followers in the eighteenth century.[44] Cavendish's library contained all editions of the *Principia* and the *Opticks*.

Through the two treatises, Newton's principal physical writings were widely accessible, but his published mathematical writings at the time of his death amounted to a few scattered tracts, which by no means revealed the extent of his researches. In the beginning of the *Principia*, he introduced the mathematical ideas his readers needed to understand what followed, and to the first edition of the *Opticks* he appended two Latin treatises on curves and their quadrature, which later came out in English translation. His followers would publish other of his mathematical writings, the existence of which was known, since he lent out his mathematical manuscripts. William Whiston, Newton's successor at Cambridge, published Newton's *Arithmetica Universalis* in 1707, and in 1711 William Jones edited short works by Newton on fluxions and infinite series, under the title *Analysis per Quantitatum Series, Fluxiones ac Differentias* . . . Newton's method of fluxions was published in

[44] The editions were the first, in 1704, in English; the second, in 1706, in Latin; and the third, in 1717/18, in English again. Isaac Newton, *Opticks; or a Treatise of the Reflections, Refractions, Inflections and Colours of Light*, based on the 4th ed. of 1730 (New York: Dover Publications, 1952). I. B. Cohen, "Newton, Isaac," *DSB* 10:42–101, on 59.

English translation by John Colson, holder of Newton's Lucasian chair in Henry Cavendish's time. Roger Smith, the Plumian professor of astronomy and experimental philosophy then, discovered more mathematical manuscripts by Newton, though he did nothing with them.[45] Newton was gone but his works were discussed and published as if he were still among the living.

The *Principia* laid down the laws of matter in motion and the law of universal gravitation, from which Newton deduced the motions of the planets, comets, moon, and tides.[46] Its sweeping deductive power was the basis of its appeal.[47] The laws of motion were presumed to contain all of the relations between matter, motion, and force in the sense that all of the theorems of geometry are contained in the axioms of that subject. In addition to gravitation, other forces were known to exist, which had yet to be described. The "whole burden of philosophy," Newton wrote, was to observe the motions of bodies and from them to deduce the forces acting and then to deduce from these forces the other phenomena of nature.[48]

The phenomena of the *Principia* were mainly empirical laws and astronomical observations. Newton kept his discussion of experiments separate from the mathematical development, relegating them to "scholiums," the purpose of which was to make certain that the mathematical propositions were not "dry and barren."[49] Newton reported exacting experiments of his own on pendulums, but he revealed himself as the proven master of experimental enquiry as the author of the *Opticks*.

Like the *Principia*, the *Opticks* begins with definitions and axioms, but a glance at its pages reveals that it contains an orderly progression of experiments and that it ends with a series of questions. It argues for a new understanding in optics, which Newton had earlier announced in the *Philosophical Transactions*: the white light of the sun is compounded of heterogeneous colored rays, and colors are original and immutable qualities of light, quantitatively distinguishable by their different degrees of refrangibility upon passing through transparent substances. For the explanation of the bending and reflecting of light by bodies, Newton looked to the subject of his earlier treatise, forces and motions. Between

45 D. T. Whiteside, in his edition of Isaac Newton, *Mathematical Papers of Isaac Newton*, 8 vols. (Cambridge: Cambridge University Press, 1967), 1:xv–xvi, xxv, 33.

46 The discussion that follows of Newton's *Principia* and *Opticks* is taken largely from the section "Newton's Science," in Russell McCormmach, "The Electrical Researches of Henry Cavendish," Ph.D. diss. (Case Institute of Technology, 1967), 5–29.

47 C. Truesdell, "A Program Toward Rediscovering the Rational Mechanics of the Age of Reason," *Archive for History of Exact Sciences* 1 (1960): 1–36, on 6.

48 Newton, *Mathematical Principles*, 1:xvii–xviii.

49 Ibid., 2:397.

the rays of light and bodies, a force acts, and although for some conclusions it is unnecessary to know "what kind of Force," that was an important question, and to answer it, "both [light and bodies] must be understood."[50] Newton did not have a finished "Theory of Light," only the beginning of one. The sixteen "queries" of the first edition suggested Newton's expectation of how the enlarged science of optics would appear when completed. He looked to the promise of the *Principia*, to the derivation of motion from force, but optics was more difficult than astronomy; whereas the bodies of the solar system move in ellipses and parabolas, light passing near bodies has a "motion like that of an Eel."[51]

Heat, one of the consequences of the action of light on bodies, is the subject of nearly half of the first set of queries in Newton's *Opticks*. By the law of action and reaction, the third of Newton's laws of motion, the reflection, refraction, inflection, and emission of light by bodies induce an agitation of the small parts of the bodies; this agitation, an internal vibration of bodies, constitutes heat for Newton.[52] Cavendish, as we will see, was a staunch supporter and developer of what he called "Newton's theory of heat."

The rest of the first set of queries have to do with the action of bodies on light, the optic nerve, and the physiology of color vision. In the second edition of the *Opticks*, Newton added several more queries, which give the fullest statement of his expectations for the mechanics of the forces between the particles of bodies and of those of light. He added a final set of queries on the ether to the third edition. Backed by Newton's authority, the queries of the *Opticks* proved to be a source of new paths (and of deadends) in science for readers throughout much of the eighteenth century.

Even if only its early propositions had to be mastered, Cambridge students found the *Principia* difficult, which gave their teachers useful activity. They lectured, tutored, and wrote textbooks for learners. At whatever level Cavendish studied the *Principia* at Cambridge, in his later scientific work, he revealed his mastery of the main fields of that book, leaving a great many manuscripts on mathematics, mechanics, and astronomy. The manuscripts on astronomy contain many mathematical studies of lenses, connecting his work with Newton's other physical treatise, the *Opticks*.

William Whiston, one of the first to lecture on Newtonian science at Cambridge, wrote several textbooks still in use at Cambridge when Cavendish was there. An ambitious man of wide interests and strong commitments, Whiston's discovery of Newton came as a revelation. After he had studied mathematics at Cambridge and had taken holy orders, he returned to Cambridge, there to join

---

[50] Newton, *Opticks*, 82, 276.

[51] Ibid., 339.

[52] Ibid.

the "poor wretches," as he recalled in his *Memoirs*, who were still studying Descartes's fictions. He had actually heard Newton lecture without understanding a word. It was upon reading a paper by the astronomer David Gregory that Whiston became aware that Newton's *Principia* was the work of a "*Divine Genius.*" With "immense pains" and "utmost zeal," Whiston tackled the *Principia* on his own.[53] He then published *A New Theory of the Earth*, which he submitted and dedicated to Newton, "on whose principles it depended, and who well approved of it." From Newton's explanation of comets, Whiston demonstrated the book of Genesis: the earth, originally a sun-bound comet, was struck by another comet, causing the Deluge and at the same time its present elliptical path and diurnal rotation. These cosmic events were the expression of God's will, but the agency was Newton's universal gravitation.[54] When Newton left Cambridge for his post at the mint in London, he arranged for Whiston to succeed him as Lucasian professor of mathematics. Whiston published his lectures at Cambridge on astronomy and on natural philosophy, the latter being the first extensive commentary on Newton's *Principia*. With Newton's approval he published Newton's lectures on universal arithmetic, or algebra. There Newton wrote that arithmetic and algebra make "one perfect science," with algebra distinguished by its "universal" character, its generality giving it power over particular arithmetic for solving "the most difficult problems."[55] Whiston eventually fell out of favor with Newton (and Cambridge), but Newton had done much for him, placing him at Cambridge and showing him his favor for many years. Whiston reciprocated by implementing Newtonian studies at Cambridge.[56] The local tradition to which Henry Cavendish was heir was underway.

While he was Lucasian professor, Whiston let the young scholar Nicholas Saunderson lecture on the same material, Newton's *Universal Arithmetic, Principia,* and *Opticks*. Blind virtually from birth, Saunderson demonstrated, his

---

[53] William Whiston, *Memoirs of the Life and Writings of Mr. William Whiston. Containing Memoirs of Several of His Friends* . . . (London, 1749), 37.

[54] William Whiston, *A New Theory of the Earth* . . . , 5th ed. (London, 1737); *Memoirs*, 43. Jacques Roger, "Whiston, William," *DSB* 14:295–96.

[55] Whiston's edition of Newton's lectures appeared in Latin in 1707 and was translated by the mathematician Joseph Raphson, *Universal Arithmetick; or, A Treatise of Arithmetical Composition and Resolution* . . . (London, 1720). Newton presented his subject according to his method in teaching: "in learning the sciences, examples are of more use than precepts." Most of the problems Newton discussed are geometrical, but some are mechanical; for example, problems 12 and 16, on elastic collisions and the position of a comet. References to the Raphson translation, pp. 1–2, 80, 117, 191.

[56] Whiston published his astronomical lectures in 1707: *Praelectiones Astronomicae*, translated in 1715 as *Astronomical Lectures, Read in the Publick Schools of Cambridge* . . . These lectures speak of "attraction" and Newton's theory of the moon, but they are not so much a Newtonian text as the astronomical preparation for Newton's philosophy, which Whiston promised to give next term. He published his lectures on natural philosophy in 1710, *Praelectiones Physico-Mathematicae*, translated in 1716 as *Sir Isaac Newton's Mathematic Philosophy More Easily Demonstrated.* Maureen Farrell, *William Whiston* (New York: Arno, 1981), 200. Rouse Ball, *History*, 83–85, 94–95. "Whiston, William," *DNB* 21:10–14. Whiteside, Newton's *Mathematical Papers* 1:xvi.

publisher said, how far the faculties of the imagination and memory could compensate for the want of a sense, and the mathematician Roger Cotes thought that his "want of sight" was an "advantage" as well as a disadvantage. He was a kind of prodigy and living experiment of the Enlightenment, definitely a source of local wonder, as he was able to distinguish a fifth part of a musical note, estimate the size of a room from the sounds in it, tell the difference between genuine and false medals by touch, and, most important, gain great proficiency in higher mathematics. Elected Whiston's successor in the Lucasian chair, Saunderson had good relations with the scientific circle associated with Newton: Cotes, Jones, De Moivre, Machin, John Keill, and others. Like Whiston, Saunderson's importance was not as an original mathematician but as an industrious teacher of the new mathematics and natural philosophy at Cambridge. Saunderson did not publish any books himself, but soon after his death, his lectures on fluxions and algebra were published. When Cavendish entered Cambridge, various of Saunderson's lectures in manuscript were still in circulation, parts of which had been published under others' names. In the middle of Cavendish's time at Cambridge, several of Saunderson's manuscripts presenting work by Newton and Cotes were brought together as *The Method of Fluxions . . . and an Explanation of Sir Isaac Newton's Philosophy*. Ten years later his *Elements of Algebra for Students* was published. Long after Cavendish had left Cambridge, Saunderson's lectures could still be promoted as the best presentation for university students.[57]

Saunderson revered Newton, whose work he made the basis of his teaching. The *Method of Fluxions* begins abruptly with a proposition about triangles, the sides of which are identified with Newtonian forces. Saunderson's subject, fluxions, was the new, powerful mathematics of motion: fluxion $\dot{x}$, in the familiar wording, is the velocity of a flowing quantity x. In his lectures Saunderson referred to experiments, but for the most part he treated only the mathematical part of natural philosophy, uniting fluxions, algebra, geometry, and mechanics into one seemingly inseparable subject. His teaching conveyed a way of thinking about nature, the lesson a Cambridge student in the middle of the eighteenth century would have drawn from reading his lectures.[58]

---

[57] Rouse Ball, *History*, 86. "Saunderson or Sanderson, Nicholas," *DNB* 17:821–22. Roger Cotes to William Jones, 25 Nov. 1711, and Nicholas Saunderson to William Jones, 4 Feb. 1713/14, Stephen Jordan Rigaud, ed., *Correspondence of Scientific Men of the Seventeenth Century*, vol. 1 (reprint, Hildesheim: Georg Olms, 1965), 261–62, on 261; 264–65, on 265.

[58] Nicholas Saunderson, *The Method of Fluxions Applied to a Select Number of Useful Problems: Together with the Demonstration of Mr. Cotes's Forms of Fluents in the Second Part of His Logometria; the Analysis of the Problems in His Scholium Generale; and an Explanation of the Principal Propositions of Sir Isaac Newton's Philosophy* (London, 1756), ix-x, 79, 81, and Advertisement. "Saunderson," *DNB* 17:821. Like Newton's lectures, Saunderson's were a set of examples, which was how they were described by the Cambridge astronomer William Ludlam, who knew them firsthand, having been one of Saunderson's pupils engaged in reading sections of Newton's *Principia*. William Ludlam, *The Rudiments of Mathematics; Designed for the Use of Students at the Universities . . .* (Cambridge, 1785), 6.

Upon Saunderson's death in 1739, the aging De Moivre (who looked to one observer as if he were "fit for his coffin . . . a mere skeleton") and Whiston (who wanted to return but was not taken seriously) were passed over for the mathematical schoolmaster John Colson as the new Lucasian professor.[59] Besides teaching, Colson had taken a modestly active part in the science of his day; his principal scientific claim to the Lucasian chair was his publication three years before of the tract Newton had wanted to publish but for which there was no market, *The Method of Fluxions and Infinite Series.* Long circulated in Cambridge, Newton's manuscript was translated from Latin into English by Colson, who warmly dedicated the publication to William Jones.[60] The Cambridge diarist and antiquarian William Cole described Colson as a "plain honest man of great industry and assiduity."[61] If he disappointed people at Cambridge, as Cole said he did, it was not by his lack of original mathematics but "by his lectures." In Colson, Cambridge had acquired a known quantity: he remained what he had always been, essentially a teacher.

However minor Colson's accomplishments as a mathematician, his enthusiasm for his subject and its inventor cannot be faulted. His words in the annotated edition of Newton's *Method of Fluxions* stand out among Newtonian panegyrics: Newton was the "greatest master in mathematical and philosophical knowledge, that ever appear'd in the world," and his doctrine of fluxions was the "noblest effort that ever was made by the human mind." Unlike Newton's other mathematical writings, which were "accidental and occasional," his *Method* was intended as a text for "novices and learners," a goal about which the teacher Colson could become enthusiastic. Colson made clear the distinction between textbook and original work and between a teacher like himself and an inventor like Newton, yet he implied that the beginner could comprehend the work of the greatest thinker of all time, false encouragement perhaps for many of his auditors and readers, but not for Cavendish. Colson's edition of Newton was at once a textbook, an indoctrination into mathematical Newtonianism, and a polemic,

---

[59] Quotation about De Moivre's age and infirmity from William Cole's diary, quoted in "Colson, John," *DNB* 4:801–2, on 801. From 1709 until he was named Lucasian professor, John Colson taught at Sir Joseph Williamson's Mathematical School in Rochester. He has been confused with a relative of the same name who headed a mathematical school in London from 1692; early on, the younger John Colson may have taught at that school too. R. V. and P. J. Wallis, *Biobibliography of British Mathematics and Its Applications*, part 2: *1701–1760* (Newcastle upon Tyne: Epsilon Press, 1986), 29.

[60] In 1738 Colson translated from the French a theoretical paper by Alexis Clairaut on the figure of the planets for the *Philosophical Transactions*. Before that, he had published two mathematical papers of his own on algebra and another on spherical maps in the same journal. One of the algebra papers had been translated into Latin and appended to the 1732 Leyden edition of Newton's *Arithmetica Universalis*. "Colson," *DNB* 4:801–2. Rouse Ball, *History*, 100–1. Whiteside, in Newton's *Mathematical Papers* 1:xv; vol. 8: *1697–1722* (Cambridge: Cambridge University Press, 1981), xxiii.

[61] Quoted in "Colson," *DNB* 4:801.

with Colson eagerly enlisting in the ranks of Newton's supporters, defending Newton and attacking his critics.[62]

For the learner of fluxions and infinite series, there was Newton's own presentation, and there was Colson's. If Newton's was terse, Colson's was prolix; Newton's treatment of infinite series occupied twenty pages, Colson's "perpetual comment" ninety-eight.[63] Colson assumed little of his reader, patiently explaining what he regarded as the greatest difficulty for a beginner, the notion of a vanishing quantity, expanding freely on the text, giving copious examples, and writing not as a mathematician but as an eternally patient teacher who repeated the obvious as well as the essential. We cannot know if Cavendish read Colson's commentary as well as Newton's text, but if he did, he read two observations that might stimulate a beginning mathematical student. One is that Newton had not said the last word on the subject: improvements in the method of fluxions had been made since Newton, and the subject was capable of further perfection. The other observation has to do with Newton's general method, that of analysis, which proceeds from the known to the unknown; analytics is the "art of invention," a method of discovery.[64]

We turn now from the professors of mathematics to the professors of astronomy and experimental philosophy, whose chair was endowed in 1704 by the archdeacon of Rochester, Thomas Plume. Its two subjects were the subjects of Newton's two books, the *Principia* and the *Opticks*, and in timing it coincided with the beginning of the Newtonian school at Cambridge.

The acceptance of Newton at Cambridge began soon after Newton had left the university for London. Richard Bentley, the new master of Trinity College, was greatly impressed by the new science.[65] Not himself a man of science, he was a good judge of men who were and of their needs. Wanting to make Trinity a center of "Newtonian philosophy," he had a laboratory built for Newton's friend John Francis Vigani, who had lectured on chemistry at Queens' College. Recognizing the scientific talent of Roger Cotes while the latter was a student at Trinity, Bentley introduced Cotes to Newton and Whiston. With their help, in 1706 Bentley secured the new Plumian professorship for his young colleague Cotes. He raised a subscription for an astronomical observatory to be built over Trinity's entrance gate and for neighboring rooms to be assigned to "Bentley's man,"

[62] Colson's comments in *The Method of Fluxions and Infinite Series . . . By the Inventor Sir Isaac Newton . . . To Which Is Subjoined, a Perpetual Comment. . . .* (London, 1736), ix–xii, xx, 335–36.

[63] Colson's work may be compared with that of John Stewart, professor of mathematics at the University of Aberdeen, who published a translation of two mathematical tracts by Newton with commentary, the two tracts occupying fifty-four pages of Stewart's book, the rest of the 497 pages plus introductory matter being Stewart's commentary. *Sir Isaac Newton's Two Treatises: Of the Quadrature of Curves, and Analysis by Equations of an Infinite Number of Terms, Explained. . . .* (London, 1745).

[64] Colson, *Method of Fluxions*, 1, 144.

[65] Rouse Ball, *History*, 75. Gascoigne, *Cambridge*, 149, 155.

Cotes, and to Cotes's assistant, his cousin Robert Smith. He arranged for Whiston of Clare College to have rooms in Trinity next to the gate under Cotes's observatory.[66] Trinity set a precedent for other colleges; Bentley, more than any other person, was responsible for the eventual dominance of the Newtonian school of science and mathematics at Cambridge.

Bentley bore the expense of a new edition of Newton's *Principia* in 1713 and was himself going to edit it, but sensibly he saw to it that the task was assigned to a proper mathematician, Cotes. Cotes's preface to that edition became a cardinal document in the dissemination of Newtonian thought. Three years later, Cotes died suddenly. At thirty-three, he had published only two papers, one of which Robert Smith included in a posthumous edition in 1722 of Cotes's mathematical manuscripts, *Harmonia Mensurarum.* Of Cotes's exceptional promise we have Newton's often quoted observation, "Had Cotes lived we might have known something."[67]

Among other important results, Cotes's *Harmonia Mensurarum* contained the "earliest attempt to frame a theory of errors." Led to the theory of errors by his interest in practical astronomy and its instruments, Cotes made mathematically rigorous the limits of errors arising from the imperfections of the senses and of instruments.[68] Observers could calculate which errors were negligible and which were not and take steps to minimize the latter. Cavendish was interested in this subject, leaving several mathematical papers on it, and in his experimental work he showed a thorough understanding of the theory of errors.

With Whiston, Cotes gave experimental lectures in natural philosophy in the observatory at Trinity. They were among the first experimental lectures to be given anywhere in England. After Whiston's expulsion from Cambridge, Cotes continued the lectures by himself, and after Cotes's death, Robert Smith took them over. In 1738 Smith published Cotes's lectures. Unlike Cotes's *Harmonia Mensurarum*, which was written in terse Latin and intended for a select audience of skilled mathematicians, his *Hydrostatical and Pneumatical Lectures* was written in English for a wide audience. Readers could understand the limited mathematics, Smith said, "with as much ease and pleasure, as in reading a piece of history." Unable to leave it at that, Smith added mathematical notes of his own.[69] The

66 "Bentley, Richard," *DNB* 2:306–14, on 312. A. Rupert Hall, "Vigani, John Francis," *DSB* 14:26–27. James Henry Monk, *The Life of Richard Bentley D.D.*, 2d ed., 2 vols. (London, 1833) 1:202–4. Whiston, *Memoirs*, 133. Ronald Gowing, *Roger Cotes–Natural Philosopher* (Cambridge: Cambridge University Press, 1983), 8, 14.

67 J. M. Dubbey, "Cotes, Roger," *DSB* 3:430–33. "Cotes, Roger," *DNB* 4:1207–9. Roger Cotes, *Harmonia Mensurarum, sive Analysis & Synthesis per Rationum & Angulorum Mensuras Promotae: Accedunt alia Opuscula Mathematica*, ed. R. Smith (Cambridge, 1722). Rouse Ball, *History*, 90.

68 Gowing, *Cotes*, 91–93.

69 Smith added descriptions of experiments and drawings of apparatus. "The Editor's Preface," in Roger Cotes, *Hydrostatical and Pneumatical Lectures*, ed. Roger Smith (London, 1738). For his joint course of experiments with Cotes, Whiston wrote half of the lectures, but he did not publish his. "Cotes," *DNB* 4:1029.

second edition of Cotes's lectures was published in Cambridge in 1747, two years before Cavendish entered Cambridge University.

Cotes's published lectures were concerned mainly with pneumatics but also with hydrostatics, both subjects relying on that most precise of instruments, the balance. Gravitation, the force to which the balance responds, is the force that holds the Newtonian world together, and it gave Cotes's lectures their coherence as well. Gravity, Cotes wrote, "is a property of so universal an extent" that even "air, which as I shall afterwards shew, may be weighed in the ballance." Cotes made clear that his primary inspiration was Newton. He referred to the *Principia* to explain the physical properties of air, its weight, elasticity, and role as the medium of sound. He referred to the *Opticks* to point the direction of science: "Whoever will read those few pages [the last query] of that excellent book [*Opticks*], may find there in my opinion, more solid foundations for the advancement of natural philosophy, than in all the volumes that have hitherto been published upon that subject."

Cotes concluded the four-week course on hydrostatics and pneumatics with a lecture on Boyle's "factitious airs." These were airs, or gases, contained in bodies, which could be freed by fire, explosion, dissolution, putrefaction, and fermentation. At the time of the lectures–before Stephen Hales's experiments–Boyle's were the "best and almost only trials which have yet been made concerning factitious airs." Cotes described Boyle's extraction of airs from a variety of substances, animal, vegetable, and mineral, and by a variety of means, as by mixing iron with the acids aqua fortis and spirit of wine. Cotes presented factitious airs not as a closed subject for a textbook but as a new, hardly begun subject full of experimental challenge. By introducing factitious airs, Cotes extended the exact science of pneumatics to a vast, largely unknown field of gaseous phenomena attending chemical actions.[70] We know that Cavendish read Cotes's lectures, since he cited them in his first publication, which was on, not by chance, factitious air. Cavendish's physical approach to pneumatic chemistry was foreshadowed by Cotes's.

In 1716 Robert Smith was elected to succeed Cotes. Smith was twenty-seven, and for the next forty-four years he was Plumian professor. He was also master of Trinity College after Bentley, and like his predecessor he promoted science in Cambridge in every way he could. To encourage Richard Watson, later professor of chemistry at Cambridge, Smith appointed him to a scholarship, urged him to read Saunderson's *Fluxions* and other mathematical books, and gave him, Watson said, "a spur to my industry, and wings to my ambition." Israel Lyons, later mathematician and astronomer, who then lived in Cambridge, showed such promise that Smith offered to put him through school. Smith published Cotes's works, completed the observatory Cotes had begun, and gave Trinity a bust of

[70] Cotes, *Lectures*, 5, 123, 187, 201–3.

Cotes and money to erect a monument to him, carrying an epithet by Bentley. He left huge benefactions to the college, to the university, and to science, which included funds for his own Plumian professorship and other funds for annual prizes, the Smith Prizes, to go to the two commencing bachelors of arts who had done the best work in mathematics and natural philosophy. Smith presented the college with the statue of Newton by Roubilliac.[71] As a student, Cavendish would have been aware that the Plumian professor was one of the founders of Newton's science at Cambridge.

Given the emphasis on Newton's *Principia* at Cambridge, the holders of the Lucasian and Plumian professorships might have been mathematical astronomers and developers of rational mechanics, but this was not the case. The most important scientific publication to come out of Cambridge was strongly Newtonian, but its subject was optics: Robert Smith's *A Compleat System of Opticks*. We know that this work was in the Cavendish library at Great Marlborough Street, since Lord Charles Cavendish subscribed to it.[72]

When Smith published his *Opticks*, Newton's *Opticks* was nearly thirty-five years old. Newton's was a scientific work, and though the early experiments on the analysis of white light into colored rays were accessible to learners, the rest of his book addressed the most difficult problems of the interaction of light and matter. Newton's *Opticks* raised questions and suggested answers that were not always consistent, and in general it lacked the conclusiveness of a textbook.

By contrast Smith's *Opticks* was a proper textbook. His account of Newton's optics was selective, overlooking Newton's second thoughts and hesitations, and omitting what did not fit. He cited Newton's queries where they supported his system, ignoring their grammatical form and treating them as if they were assertions not questions.

[71] "Smith, Robert," *DNB* 18:517–19. Winstanley, *Unreformed Cambridge*, 150. R. W. T. Gunther, *Early Science in Cambridge* (Oxford: Clarendon Press, 1937), 61. Rouse Ball, *History*, 91. Monk, *Life of Bentley* 2:168. Robert Willis and John Willis Clark, *Architectural History of the University of Cambridge, and of the Colleges of Cambridge and Eton* (Cambridge, 1886), 2:600. Richard Watson, *Anecdotes of the Life of Richard Watson, Bishop of Landaff*. . . , 2d ed., vol. 1 (London, 1818), 14. In 1758 Lyons dedicated to Smith his *Treatise on Fluxions*, which was used in teaching at Cambridge alongside texts on the same subject by Newton, Saunderson, and others.

[72] Robert Smith, *A Compleat System of Opticks in Four Books, viz. A Popular, a Mathematical, a Mechanical, and a Philosophical Treatise. To Which Are Added Remarks upon the Whole*, 2 vols. (Cambridge, 1738). The 340 subscribers included members of Lord Charles Cavendish's mathematical circle, such as Lord Macclesfield, De Moivre, and Folkes (who subscribed for twelve copies); Cambridge mathematicians and physical scientists, such as John Colson, Roger Long, Nicholas Saunderson, Charles Mason, John Rowning, and Richard Davies; Scottish professors of mathematics and physical science, such as Colin Maclaurin, Robert Simpson, John Stewart, and Robert Dick; and London instrument-makers, such as George Graham, James Short, and Jonathan Sissons. Ten years before its publication, in 1728, Smith first advertised for subscribers for his optical treatise, and if that was when Cavendish subscribed, it was just as he entered the Royal Society. He paid thirty shillings each for the two volumes of the book. Alice Nell Walters, "Tools of Enlightenment: The Material Culture of Science in Eighteenth-Century England," Ph.D. diss., University of California at Berkeley, 1992, p. 7.

Since Smith's purpose was to present optics as a "system," he could not leave unanswered the question of the nature of light. In giving his answer, he followed Newton, but he was more decisive than Newton had been. Newton inclined toward the corpuscular view of light, but he speculated freely on alternative, or supplementary, forms of explanation involving an ether. Smith acknowledged that Newton's ether could explain the phenomena of light equally well, but he used only Newton's streaming corpuscles and the intense forces with which they interacted with corpuscles of bodies at intimate distances. For this interpretation he had ample support, since by the second decade of the eighteenth century, the corpuscular theory of light was widely subscribed to in principle. Because Smith's *System of Opticks* came to be recognized as the main authority on Newtonian optics after Newton's own *Opticks*, in some respects supplanting it, it further entrenched the corpuscular theory as the dominant theory of light in eighteenth-century Britain.[73] Cavendish fully accepted the corpuscular theory, and nowhere in his writings, published and unpublished, did he use the word that characterized the alternative theory, "ether."

Smith illustrated the indispensable role of instruments in optics by giving a history of astronomy, beginning with Galileo, from whom astronomy acquired its essential, modern instrument, the telescope. He traced the history to Bradley's great observational discoveries incidental to his work on the cosmological problem, the occasion for Lord Charles Cavendish's first recorded scientific observations. He told of the excellent London scientific instrument-makers, such as George Graham, a man of "extraordinary skill," whose help he had solicited in writing this book.[74] He included papers on refracting telescopes by Huygens, and he discussed Huygens' long, highly magnifying refracting telescopes, which Henry Cavendish borrowed from the Royal Society and erected at his house. He treated the human eye as an optical instrument, constructing a "tolerable eye" from two hemispheres filled with water,[75] and he appended an essay on indistinct vision by his friend and colleague at Trinity, the Bentley protégé James Jurin.[76] Indistinct vision interested Cavendish, who corresponded with the astronomer William Herschel on the subject.

Smith's *Opticks* was comprehensive if not monumental. It included not only theory, mathematics, experiments, the construction and use of instruments, and history but also the theory of knowledge. In discussing how we come by our ideas of things by sight, he took up the question the astronomer Samuel Molyneux asked of the philosopher John Locke: would a blind man who sud-

---

[73] Henry John Steffans, *The Development of Newtonian Optics in England* (New York: Science History Publications, 1977), 48, 50, 53; G. N. Cantor, *Optics after Newton: Theories of Light in Britain and Ireland, 1704–1840* (Manchester: Manchester University Press, 1983), 33–34.

[74] Smith, *Opticks*, 332.

[75] Smith, *Opticks*, 25.

[76] James Jurin, "An Essay upon Distinct and Indistinct Vision," appended to Smith's *Opticks*, 115–70.

denly regained his sight be able to distinguish a globe from a cube by sight alone? To this question the philosophers had given a negative answer, which was apparently confirmed by the recent experience of just such a man reported in the *Philosophical Transactions*. Unpersuaded by the philosophers, Smith had a ready subject at hand, his colleague the Lucasian professor, the blind mathematician Nicholas Saunderson. Saunderson agreed with Smith that by "reason," the blind man upon regaining his sight could tell the globe from the cube.[77] The answer, whether correct or not, that Smith and Saunderson gave to the question about the blind man was an inference from the experimental philosophy: in knowing the world, experience is reflected upon by reason.

Smith published one more scientific book, this one concerned with the sense of hearing, *Harmonics, or the Philosophy of Musical Sounds*. As in optics, in music Smith set out to make a system from within the experimental philosophy, and like his former book, his book on music was well received, becoming a standard text; George Lewis Scott, one of De Moivre's pupils, recommended it to Edward Gibbon as "the principal book of the kind."[78]

Like natural philosophy, music had recently undergone great changes. The monodic idea had become well established, and with it so had the harmonic as opposed to the contrapuntal approach to musical composition, with its emphasis on chords and the modern notion of key. By the use of a definite key and of modulation between keys, unity could be achieved in long expressive melodies. But there was a problem with this: although the modulation between closely related keys could be carried out satisfactorily, the same could not be said of the modulation between remoter keys, as demanded for greater contrast. The first workable solution came with the introduction of an octave scale of twelve tones, the half steps of which were precisely equal.[79]

These several, related innovations–the sense of key, modulation between keys, and equal temperament–made possible the extended musical forms of the early eighteenth century. Robert Smith enters musical history at this point with his *Harmonics*, with which he intended to provide a full understanding of temperament. Ancient musical theorists such as Ptolemy had considered only perfect consonances, and the scales they built upon them necessarily contained imperfect consonances, disagreeable to the ear. By distributing the largest imperfections in certain concords over the others, the modern theorists improved upon, tempered, the ancient scales, with the result that the imperfect concords were less offensive although there were more of them. Smith did not adopt the

---

77 Smith, *Opticks*, 42–43, and "The Author's Remarks upon the Whole," at the end of the book, on 28–29.

78 Robert Smith, *Harmonics, or the Philosophy of Musical Sounds*, 2d ed. (Cambridge, 1759). First edition in 1749. "Smith," *DSB* 12:477. "Smith," *DNB* 18:519.

79 Donald N. Ferguson, *A History of Musical Thought*, 2d ed. (New York and London: Appleton, Century, Crofts, 1935), 272–78.

well-tempered scale, as promoted by Bach in the *Well-Tempered Clavichord*, but addressed the problem starting with the "first principles of the science." He redistributed the imperfections of the ancient scales in such a way as to make the imperfect consonances all equally "harmonious." For this "scientific solution" of the artistic problem, Smith constructed a theory of imperfect consonances, the first ever; it was his acoustical version of indistinct vision in optics.[80]

As in optics, in harmonics, theory held an important place for Smith. In the ancient world musicians no doubt followed their ear rather than the "theories of philosophers," Smith said, arriving at temperament "before the reason of it was discovered, and the method and measure of it was reduced to regular theory"; but the ear was no longer sufficient, and the theory was imperfect, which was Smith's starting point. Smith, an expert performer on the violin-cello, had a musical ear but he did not need one in harmonics. He needed only scientific theory, as he explained: a person without a musical ear could tune an organ to any temperament and to "any desired degree of exactness, far beyond what the finest ear unassisted by theory can possibly attain to." It was the same in optics: Smith's colleague, the blind mathematician Saunderson, taught Newton's theory of colors.[81]

Because he was an experimental philosopher, Smith confirmed his mathematical theory by practice. One experiment was done by the Cambridge organist, another by the clock-maker John Harrison, who played the bass-viol. Musical instruments and scientific instruments became one and the same in Smith's investigation, and as his theory required that instruments be modified, he was helped by "two of the most ingenious and learned gentlemen in this University," John Michell, who became a good friend of Henry Cavendish's, and William Ludlam, to whom Lord Charles Cavendish supplied astronomical calculations. Smith's system was an improvement over other systems of temperament, but in the end the modification of instruments it called for made it impractical.[82]

Smith and his musically talented scientific colleagues belonged to a tradition of scientists with an interest in music going back to Pythagoras and coming down to Huygens and Newton. The tradition of the curriculum worked in favor of the combination of music and science: music had been grouped with astronomy and the parts of mathematics in the quadrivium, and there was much that was still medieval about Cambridge. The contemporary curriculum, with its dual emphasis on mathematics and the classics, also was reflected in Smith's *Harmonics*, in which he quoted early writings on music, often at length and in Latin and Greek.

---

80 Smith, *Harmonics*, v–vii.

81 Ibid., viii–ix, 33–35.

82 Ibid., ix–xiv. "Smith," *DSB* 12:477.

Smith lived in the Enlightenment, a word which referred generally to a felt need for clarity. Like musicians of "delicate ear," in listening to a performance Smith preferred to listen to a single string rather than unisons, octaves, and multiple-part music. He called this a preference for "distinctness and clearness, spirit and duration" over "beating and jarring" and "confused noise." When he listened to a harpsichord, he heard only single strings instead of the multiplicity of strings that most people heard. He quoted from his other book, *System of Opticks*, from Jurin's account there of what happens when a person comes out of a strong light into a closed room: at first the room appears dark, but in time the eye accommodates to the darkness and the room appears light. Jurin's observation applied to sounds too. The discernment of clarity within a confusion of sound and the recovery of vision in darkness symbolized the natural philosopher's quest. In his primary capacity as a teacher of science, Smith was provided with an implicit image by his music. Musicians at first disliked Smith's retuned organ despite its improved harmony, but musicians, like scientists, could be educated, and in time they could no longer stand the "coarse harmony" of organs tuned the old way. Smith's esthetics was an esthetics *understood* by mathematics, experiment, and theory.[83]

Designer of instruments, experimenter, and mathematical theorist, Robert Smith was the complete natural philosopher. Of all persons teaching scientific subjects at Cambridge, with the exception of John Michell, he was closest to the kind of scientist Cavendish would become. We would like to think that Cavendish became acquainted with Smith at Cambridge, but that event seems unlikely. They were not in the same college, and Smith probably did not lecture any longer, and by then he was ill, irascible, and reclusive.[84] It is, however, virtually certain that Cavendish knew Smith through his books on optics and music. Cavendish's theoretical views on optics were the same as Smith's. Smith's book on harmonics came out in 1749, the year that Cavendish entered Cambridge, and as we discuss later in this chapter, Cavendish was probably drawn to music.

Smith's professorship was designated for astronomy as well as for experimental philosophy, but Cambridge acquired another professorship for astronomy all the same, this one joining astronomy to mathematics, specifically to geometry, which made equally good sense. Thomas Lowndes left funds for establishing a salaried professorship of astronomy and geometry, an important recognition of astronomy at Cambridge during the time Cavendish was there. In 1750 Roger Long, master of Pembroke Hall, was named the first Lowndean professor. Cavendish would have known about Long, who stood out as a tory in a predominantly whig Cambridge, and as an autocrat constitutionally

[83] Smith, *Harmonics*, 171–72, 210.

[84] "Smith," *DNB* 18:518.

destined to be at cross purposes with the people around him, He constantly feuded with the fellows of his college, especially over the right of veto, which he exercised with willful frequency. Like his Plumian colleague Smith, Long was a skilled musician, who presented the king and queen with a musical instrument of his own invention, the "lyrichord." In his field of astronomy, Long was renowned as an inventor of immense machines never before seen in Cambridge, which actually served the purposes of education. Some of these Long described in his *Astronomy,* a standard text in the university when Cavendish arrived there. The frontispiece of the first volume illustrates an early construction, a glass celestial sphere known to a "great number of people" and, Long complained, imperfectly copied by several. The book describes another of his machines, a narrow ring twenty feet across on which the constellations of the zodiac and the ecliptic were inscribed, treating the viewer, who sat in the middle, to a panoramic view of this important bit of the heavens. Long wrote of his wish to build the ultimate apparatus, a "planetarium," which would rotate around a platform of spectators. He later built and installed at Pembroke his "great sphere," a revolving globe eighteen feet across, capable of holding thirty people. Designated the "Uranium," this consummate lecturer's planetarium provided the frontispiece of the second volume of Long's *Astronomy.* Long was assisted by Richard Dunthorne, formerly his footboy, who held the butlership at Pembroke, and who published a number of valuable books and papers on the motions of the moon, comets, and the satellites of Jupiter.[85] Long himself made observations, drawn to the great questions of the science, such as the distances of the fixed stars and their possible motions, concluding after "long and careful scrutiny," incorrectly as it happened, that stars do not move. He knew the active astronomers, such as Bradley, under whose vertical telescope he lay with his head on a cushion (as we assume Lord Charles Cavendish had done). But Long's main contribution to astronomy in Cambridge in Cavendish's time was his teaching, and his lecture-text was his main publication.[86]

In *Astronomy,* Long used mathematics sparingly, but he was emphatic on the point that astronomy was quantitative in observation and in theory, and in his account of astronomy he accordingly began with the subject of quantity in all of

---

[85] Wordsworth, *Scholae Academicae,* 249. "Dunthorne, Richard," *DNB* 6:235–36.

[86] The first volume of Long's *Astronomy, In Five Books* was published in Cambridge in 1742. The second volume did not appear until twenty-two years later, in 1764, for reasons of which, Long said, "it would be of no service to the public to be informed." These reasons had in part to do with his interest in music, as a letter from Cambridge noted: "Dr. Long advances, but slowly, in his astronomical work; tho' ye larger part of his 2d vol. is I believe printed. But he keeps amusing himself . . . with alterations in musical instruments, of wch he is very fond." J. Green to Thomas Birch, 29 Jan. 1760, BL Add Mss 4308, ff. 192–93. Only in 1784, after Long's death, was the remaining part of the book published. Long, *Astronomy* 1:ix-x, and 2:iii, 637–38. "Long, Roger," *DNB* 12:109. Rouse Ball, *History,* 105. Gunther, *Early Science in Cambridge,* 164–67. Ketton-Cremer, *Gray,* 83–84. "Dunthorne, Richard," *DNB* 6:235–36. On Long's observations, *Astronomy* 2:637–38.

its manifestations in astronomy. His descriptive treatment of astronomy was, like his machines, grand if not grandiose; in contrast to the usual perfunctory single chapter on the fixed stars, his book devoted many chapters to their immense distances and other cosmic properties. He placed astronomy within natural philosophy, the study of the bodies that comprise the universe. Since the gravitational force was known but the forces of light, magnetism, and electricity were not, gravitational astronomy was far more advanced than the other parts of natural philosophy, Long explained. Newton's *Principia* "gave an entirely new face to theoretical astronomy." This science had been "raised, at once, to a greater degree of perfection than could have been hoped for from the united labours of the most learned men, for many ages, by the amazing genius of one man–the immortal *Newton*!"[87] The great instrument-makers, especially the British, supplied the observers who kept astronomy advancing after Newton. Because Lord Charles Cavendish was a subscriber to Long's *Astronomy*, Henry Cavendish is certain to have seen it at home if not at Cambridge, and he might have attended the flamboyant lectures on which it was based. After Cambridge, Cavendish had his own observatory, where he studied the heavens using instruments and mathematics.

Whatever technical field a student pursued with the help of writings by Cambridge professors, he learned that Newton had given it its present shape. Newtonianism at Cambridge was comprehensive, in that regard acting as Aristotelianism had earlier, impressing a unity of thought on a diversity of endeavors. The best single forum for bringing forward that unity was lectures on natural philosophy. The regius professor of divinity, Thomas Rutherforth, taught Newtonian natural philosophy and published on it as well as on religion, and he used his membership in the Royal Society to promote sales of his books.[88] In 1748, the year before Cavendish entered Cambridge, Rutherforth published the lectures he gave at St. John's College, *A System of Natural Philosophy*.[89] Throughout, Rutherforth used geometrical arguments, even managing to convey a notion of infinitesimal reasoning while at the same time not assuming the most rudimentary knowledge of quantity; he explained that a fraction decreases as its denominator increases.[90] He had an engaging, self-deprecating honesty, asking forgiveness for the errors and inexactitude in his efforts to communicate to persons unfamiliar with the more profound parts of mathematics. Being no particular expert himself, he gave the impression that he was writing for persons not much below his own level of understanding. Wordy, with frequent asides and sarcasms,

---

[87] Long, *Astronomy* 2:717–18.

[88] Thomas Rutherforth to Thomas Birch, 30 Jan. and 6 Feb. 1742/43, BL Add Mss 4317, ff. 305–6, 308.

[89] Thomas Rutherforth, *A System of Natural Philosophy, Being a Course of Lectures in Mechanics, Optics, Hydrostatics, and Astronomy; Which Are Read in St Johns College Cambridge*, 2 vols. (Cambridge, 1748). "Rutherforth, Thomas," *DNB* 17:499–500.

[90] Rutherforth, *System of Natural Philosophy*, 23.

Rutherforth's text reads like the spoken popular lectures they probably were. His was not one of the best elementary textbooks on Newtonian natural philosophy, but it was competent at the level of its intended audience.[91] Its list of subscribers was long, numbering about a thousand, of whom about a third were identified with Cambridge. (That Lord Charles Cavendish did not subscribe to this book does not surprise us.) The text and its local support are testimony of the prestige of Newtonianism at Cambridge.[92]

For completeness, we should point out that when Cavendish was at Cambridge, the Jacksonian professorship of natural philosophy had not yet been established. The Woodwardian professor of geology, Charles Mason (not the Charles Mason of the Mason-Dixon line, whom we will meet later), was a Fellow of the Royal Society, who took an interest in a miscellany of scientific questions, but he, like all the early holders of that chair, did not lecture, and although he was in charge of a collection of fossils of potential interest to Cavendish, and made extensive geological observations, he was unlikely to have contributed to Cavendish's education.[93] The professorship of chemistry was held by John Mickleborough, who like his predecessor Vigani was an ardent advocate of Newtonian chemistry. Twenty-five years before Cavendish became a student, Mickleborough could excuse his delay in answering letters on the grounds that because he was "now engaged in a course of Chemistry here, I can think of nothing but calcinations, sublimations, distillations, precipitations, &c.," but after 1741 he evidently did no more lecturing on chemistry, and neither did anyone else (to our knowledge) until after Cavendish had left Cambridge.[94] It is noteworthy, however, that in his lectures Mickleborough introduced a force of repulsion, a kind of Newtonian force also adopted by John Rowning and Stephen Hales, other prominent fellows in the early eighteenth century at Cambridge, where it became something of a tradition; Cavendish no doubt was aware of this tradition even if he never heard the lectures, and in his own scientific work he incorporated it.

Before we leave the subject of the contribution of Cambridge to Henry Cavendish's education in science, we return briefly to John Colson. He probably did not lecture, but he went to a great deal of trouble to see that good scientific and mathematical texts were available to students. After becoming Lucasian

[91] Robert E. Schofield, *Mechanism and Materialism: British Natural Philosophy in an Age of Reason* (Princeton: Princeton University Press, 1970), 97.

[92] Wordsworth, *Scholae Academicae*, 66–67.

[93] Indicative of Mason's range of interests and of his few papers in the *Philosophical Transactions* are the "hints" about melting iron and about a burning well in a letter he sent to the president of the Royal Society at about the time Cavendish entered Cambridge: Charles Mason to Martin Folkes, 22 Jan. 1746/47, Wellcome Institute, Martin Folkes Papers, Ms.5403. Winstanley, *Unreformed Cambridge*, 168–69.

[94] John Mickleborough to Dean Moss in 1725, in Nichols, *Illustrations*, 4:520. Wordsworth, *Scholae Academicae*, 188–89. L. J. M. Coleby, "John Mickleburgh, Professor of Chemistry in the University of Cambridge, 1718–56," *Annals of Science* 8 (1952): 165–74, on 167, 169–70.

professor, he translated into English several books from several languages, which included Peter van Musschenbroek's *Elements of Natural Philosophy*, the subtitle of which is *Chiefly Intended for the Use of Students in Universities.*[95] The reason Colson gave for making this translation was that there was need for a complete "system" of natural philosophy in English, and he thought that Musschenbroek's was the best. Musschenbroek drew on Continental sources such as Descartes and Leibniz (concerning whom Colson disagreed with Musschenbroek), but his principal source was the "very many and great discoveries of the illustrious *Newton* (the glory of *England*, to whom no age has produced an equal)." Musschenbroek thought that mathematics was the best preparation for natural philosophy, a view which corresponded with the curriculum at Cambridge. Like Colson, he gave encouragement to aspiring students, for although physics was now on a "firm basis" through observation and experiment, there were always problems to solve, and if we cannot solve them, he said, we can "excite other diligent enquirers into nature, that are to come after us." That most puzzling field of electricity would grant its genius "eternal fame," and his name would be struck on public monuments; as if to confirm his prophecy, in the year after the publication of Colson's translation of his text, Musschenbroek himself made a great discovery in electricity, that of the Leyden jar. Natural philosophy, Musschenbroek said, "can never be exhausted."[96]

Colson recognized a kindred spirit in Musschenbroek, who at the time of Colson's translation was professor of mathematics and astronomy at the University of Leyden, and whose main publications were extensions of his lectures in ever larger books. His predecessor at Leyden had been Willem Jacob 'sGravesande, another systematizer and writer of textbooks whose *Mathematical Elements of Natural Philosophy, Confirmed by Experiments: or, an Introduction to Sir Isaac Newton's Philosophy* had been translated from the Latin into English by J. T. Desaguliers in 1720–21. Although 'sGravesande's strength as a teacher was in his use of experiments to support scientific truths, like Musschenbroek he recognized the importance of mathematics for natural philosophy, warning that anyone who went about that subject in "any other way, than by mathematical Demonstrations, will be sure to fall into Uncertainties at least, if not into Errors," Newton having demonstrated in the *Principia* the "great use of mathematics in Physics, as no one before him ever penetrated so deeply into the Secrets of Nature." Musschenbroek and 'sGravesande had both studied at the University of Leyden when its most successful teacher Hermann Boerhaave was lecturing

[95] Colson translated Petrus van Musschenbroek's *Elements of Natural Philosophy* from Latin in 1744; from French he translated Jean Antoine Nollet's *Lectures in Experimental Philosophy* in 1748; from Italian he translated Maria Gaetana Agnesi's *Analytical Institutions* in 1801; and he edited the third edition of Brook Taylor's *Linear Perspective, or a New Method of Representing Justly All Manner of Objects as They Appear to the Eye* in 1749. We have already discussed his translation from Latin of Newton's *Method of Fluxions.*

[96] Musschenbroek, *Elements of Natural Philosophy*, translator's advertisement, iii–v, xi, 6.

there. These three professors made Leyden the capital of Newtonianism on the Continent, not through their research, which was minimal, but through their ample teaching. The experimental philosophy had replaced stable certainty with change, they said, and they encouraged their students to discover new truths using the experimental way aided by mathematical demonstration.[97] When Cavendish was a student, Leyden was probably a better place to learn natural philosophy than Cambridge, but it was not necessary to be in Leyden to learn from it. Translated texts by Musschenbroek, 'sGravesande, and Boerhaave were recommended reading at Cambridge, and they strongly influenced texts by British writers, just as theirs were influenced by British texts. 'sGravesande presented natural philosophy following the "Example of the *English*," by experiments, which had "a kind of Connexion one with another"; Musschenbroek, in his presentation of optics, said that Robert Smith's *Opticks* "has gone beyond all the rest in this science."[98] At both universities the emphasis was on Newtonian philosophy, and at both the professors were primarily teachers and not researchers. Colson, Smith, and Long may not have been as influential in their teaching as Musschenbroek, but they regarded their work in much the same way. For a wide and perceptive reader like Cavendish, the experimental approach of the Leyden authors would have supplemented the mathematical emphasis at Cambridge, and there would have seemed no contradiction; 'sGravesande, who taught by the experimental method, believed that mathematics was the true foundation of natural philosophy.

In broad outline we have sketched the scientific tradition at Cambridge insofar as it was represented by the texts of its early and mid eighteenth-century professors. When Cavendish entered the ranks of scientific researchers, he was a master of mathematical methods and concepts of science within a certain Newtonian framework, and the connections between this framework and Cambridge education are many, significant, and unlikely to be mere coincidence.

GIARDINI ACADEMY

If there was an early musical influence on Henry Cavendish, it came from his mother's side of the family. The duke and first duchess of Kent had a love of music, the duke combining this interest with his political career when as lord chamberlain he worked to bring Italian opera to London. Later, in 1719, the duke was one of the original subscribers to the Royal Academy of Music, and he (but not the duke of Devonshire) became one of its twenty directors.[99] There is a paint-

[97] Edward G. Ruestow, *Physics at Seventeenth and Eighteenth-Century Leiden: Philosophy and the New Science in the University* (The Hague: Martinus Nijhoff, 1973), 7–8, 115–21, 135–39.

[98] D. J. Struik, "Musschenbroek, Petrus van," *DSB* 9:594–97. A. Rupert Hall, "'sGravesande, Willem Jacob," *DSB* 5:509–11. 'sGravesande, *Mathematical Elements of Natural Philosophy*, ix, xv. Musschenbroek, *Elements of Natural Philosophy*, 159.

[99] Otto Erich Deutsch, *Handel: A Documentary Biography* (New York: DaCapo Press, 1974), 91, 102.

ing of the Kent family showing them being musically entertained,[100] and we know that the Yorkes and the Greys attended concerts at the Rotunda.[101] Had Henry Cavendish shown any musical interest, he would surely have been encouraged.

Evidence of Henry Cavendish's interest in music is sketchy. There is a mathematical study by him, "On Musical Intervals."[102] There is a reference to a musical event in Cavendish's laboratory notes on pneumatic chemistry: in 1782 he used his eudiometer–the instrument for measuring the "goodness" of air–to compare the good air of Hampstead, one of the benefits of Hampstead, to which Cavendish had just moved, to the used "Air from Oratorio."[103] More to the point, the auction catalogue of the contents of Cavendish's house at Clapham Common at the time of his death listed a grand piano-forte.[104] According to a story, which on the face of it seems unlikely but which probably contains a core of truth, Cavendish came together with Michell, Herschell, Priestley, and others over musical entertainment.[105] We know for certain that a good number of Cavendish's scientific colleagues were accomplished in music. In describing a "water-worm" that propagated after being cut to pieces, the French scientist René Antoine Réaumur said the worm was "of the Thickness of the Treble String of a Violin," a remark which suggests an intimate knowledge of music and its instruments in the eighteenth century.[106]

We think that Cavendish's education included education in music. He would have recognized the need. The professional musician Charles Burney, Cavendish's contemporary and fellow member of the Royal Society, said that music and the other arts are "governed by laws," and in mastering them the individual advanced nearer perfection "by the assistance of thousands, than by the mere efforts of his own labour and genius."[107]

---

100 Illustration 3, p. 28.

101 A. E. Gunther, *An Introduction to the Life of the Rev. Thomas Birch D.D. F.R.S., 1705–1766* (Halesworth: Halesworth Press, 1984), 62. Great Britain, Historical Manuscripts Commission, *Report on the Manuscripts of the Earl of Egmont. Diary of Viscount Percival Afterwards First Earl of Egmont*, vol. 1: *1730–1733* (London: His Majesty's Stationary Office, 1920), 93, 227; vol. 2: *1734–1738* (London: His Majesty's Stationary Office, 1923), 30.

102 Cavendish Mss VI(a), 28.

103 This entry is unclear as to Cavendish's part. It begins with a comparison of "air caught by [the instrument-maker Edward] Nairne in 2d gallery of Drury Lane playhouse Mar. 15 1782 with air of Hampstead of Mar. 16." It follows with "Air from Oratorio about same time." "Experiments on Airs," Cavendish Mss II, 5:189.

104 *A Catalogue of an Assortment of Modern Household Furniture . . . the Genuine Property of a Professional Gentleman; which Will Be Sold by Auction by Mr. Squibb, at His Great Room Saville Passage, Saville Row, on Wednesday, December 5, 1810, and Two Following Days, at Twelve O'Clock.* Item 45 is a grand piano-forte, by Longman and Broderip, in a mahogany case.

105 "Michell, John," *DNB* 13:333–34, on 333.

106 René Antoine Réaumur, "An Abstract of What Is Contained in the Preface to the Sixth Volume of Mons. Reaumur's History of Insects . . . ," *PT* 42 (1742/43): xii–xvii, on xv.

107 Charles Burney, "Account of an Infant Musician," *PT* 69 (1779): 183–206, on 186, 205.

Given the limited evidence of Cavendish's interest and education in music, in this discussion (as in our earlier discussion of De Moivre), we proceed tentatively. The name Henry Cavendish appears on a list of subscribers to the musical academy of Felice Giardini, and we think that this Henry Cavendish is our subject. Arriving in London in 1751, for ten years beginning in 1755 Giardini adapted Italian operas for the King's Theatre. Later he composed quartets and concertos for strings and a successful English oratorio, *Ruth.* Like Lord Charles Cavendish, Giardini was a governor of the Foundling Hospital, where Handel gave concerts, and where Giardini proposed establishing a musical academy. By the time Cavendish was (if we are right) in contact with him, Giardini was the preeminent violinist in London. Johnson sympathized with Giardini when he learned that the man did not make more than seven hundred pounds a year despite his superior ability.[108] To do even this well, which to be sure made him modestly wealthy, Giardini had to combine activities, one being to run an academy by subscription. In 1758 or 1759, Henry Cavendish along with sixteen others agreed to continue to meet as an "academy" in the coming year as they had in the last, only under new terms, probably having to do with Giardini's finances. The members of the academy agreed to pay eight pounds, half up front and the rest when the academy had met twenty times. It was left to the subscribers whether they were to meet in the morning or the evening; if in the morning, as they had been meeting, breakfast would be provided, if in the evening, lighting.[109] Thirteen of the seventeen, including Cavendish, had already paid their advance, and if all paid up, Giardini would would have earned around one hundred and thirty-five pounds, less out-of-pocket expenses, a good installment on his seven hundred or so pounds for the year.

The subscribers were young and of both sexes, including husbands and wives and persons with various family connections; two of them, George Manners and Lady Granby, were related to Cavendish. At least three of the subscribers were pupils of Giardini: William Hamilton, Isabella Carlisle, and Frances Pelham. Carlisle and Pelham were accomplished singers, who arranged private concerts. Hamilton, having begun lessons with Giardini in the year the Italian arrived in London, was an expert violinist, one of the rare amateur musical gentlemen who could compare in skill with amateur musical ladies.[110] Hamil-

[108] R. H. Nichols and F. A. Wray, *The History of the Foundling Hospital* (London: Oxford University Press, 1935), 247. Roger Fiske, *English Theatre Music in the Eighteenth Century* (London: Oxford University Press, 1973), 284–286.

[109] Great Britain, Historical Manuscripts Commission, *Report on Manuscripts in Various Collections*, vol. 8: *The Manuscripts of the Hon. Frederick Lindley Wood; M. L. S. Clements, Esq.; S. Philip Unwin, Esq.* (London: His Majesty's Stationery Office, 1913), 188–89.

[110] Brian Fothergill, *Sir William Hamilton: Envoy Extraordinary* (New York: Harcourt, Brace & World, 1969), 29. Horace Walpole to George Montagu, 17 May 1763, *Horace Walpole's Correspondence with George Montagu*, vol. 2, ed. W. S. Lewis and R. S. Brown, Jr. (New Haven: Yale University Press, 1941), 69–74, on 73. Horace Walpole to William Cole, 5 Feb. 1780, *Horace Walpole's Correspondence with the Rev. William Cole*, vol. 2, ed. W. S. Lewis and A. D. Wallace (New Haven: Yale University Press, 1937), 186–89, on 187.

ton's first wife, Catherine, who performed with approval before Mozart, was also one of the subscribers to Giardini's academy.

Hamilton,[111] Cavendish's almost exact contemporary, who now is remembered as the husband of Lord Nelson's mistress Emma, was known in his day as a solid diplomat, a learned antiquarian, and a good student of volcanoes. When as envoy to the court of Naples Hamilton leased the Villa Angelica to be closer to his favorite volcano, he arranged a music room, which Catherine described as "right facing Vesuvius, which now and then is kind enough to play whilst I too am playing." The other night it had sent up fiery red stones, "but we went right on playing, just as you would have done if you heard a pop-gun in the street." (Acknowledging a connection between science and art, the secretary and the president of the Royal Society complimented Hamilton on his investigations of the eruptions of Vesuvius, remarking on that "beautifully dreadful phenomenon," that "grand & terrible scene.")[112] In 1794 Sir Joseph Banks wrote to Sir William Hamilton in Naples to compliment him on his description of the recent eruption of Vesuvius: "Cavendish in particular who you know is little given to talking & not at all to flattery says it is very valuable addition to the theory of volcanoes & that tho he does not on any account wish to derogate from the merit of your former papers this is certainly the most valuable one we have receivd from you."[113] What exactly transpired when Hamilton and Cavendish came together in Giardini's academy is unclear, but it undoubtedly had to do with listening together, and it very likely involved performing together.

Giardini, Burney wrote in his history of music, "formed a morning *academia*, or concert, at his house, composed chiefly of his scholars, vocal and instrumental, who bore a part in the performance." This we take to be a description of the academy to which Henry Cavendish subscribed. Knowing that at least some of his fellow subscribers were pupils of Giardini, and were serious and talented, we recognize that Cavendish may have been one of Giardini's "scholars," and moreover that he may have performed before an audience at the academy.[114] It is hard to imagine the shy and taciturn Cavendish singing[115] or performing on an

---

[111] Hamilton has helped us date the agreement between Giardini and the subscribers to his academy. By our reckoning, it was made after Hamilton's marriage in 1758 and before December 1759.

[112] Matthew Maty to William Hamilton, 26 July 1770; John Pringle to William Hamilton, 2 May 1768, BL Add Mss 42069, ff. 81 and 61.

[113] Sir Joseph Banks to Sir William Hamilton, 30 Nov. 1794, BL, Egerton 2641, pp. 155–56.

[114] In Italy a private concert by dilettantes was called an "accademia," which may have been Giardini's meaning. This information is given in a work from the time, Charles Burney, *Present State of Music in France and Italy* (London, 1771), quoted in *Horace Walpole's Correspondence*, vol. 18: *With Sir Horace Mann*, vol. 2, ed. W. S. Lewis, W. H. Smith, and G. L. Lam (New Haven: Yale University Press, 1954), 13, n. 16a. Charles Burney, *A General History of Music. From the Earliest Ages to the Present Period (1789)*, vol. 2 (1789; reprint, New York: Harcourt, Brace), 1012–14.

[115] At least two of Cavendish's fellow subscribers were singers, "Lady Carlisle and Miss Pelham." Burney, *General History*, 1014. Stanley Sadie, "Music in the Home II," in *The Blackwell History of Music in Britain*, vol. 4: *The Eighteenth Century*, ed. H. Diack Johnstone and Roger Fiske (Oxford: Basil Blackwell, 1988), 313–56, on 320.

instrument, but stutterers have been known to be famous orators, and using scientific instruments Cavendish "performed" experiments before competent audiences at the Royal Society.

If, as we think, Cavendish did pursue an advanced education in music, as he did in science, there are reasons why he might have chosen to do so with Giardini. First, Giardini was a well-known teacher: in Thomas Mortimer's *The Universal Director* of 1763, he was listed not as a violinist but as a teacher of singing and harpsichord. Second, from Giardini's arrival in London, the "standards" of London concerts rose, coming to equal those of the best in Europe. He eliminated from performances all possible extraneous ornaments, among other changes. We find parallels in Cavendish's scientific practice.[116]

Cavendish's wonderfully concentrated inner life was directed outward, toward nature, but if we are right about his music, his inner life was not exclusively so directed. The main task of music, as it was understood in the eighteenth century, was to imitate not nature but the feelings, and of all the arts, music was considered the one that spoke most directly to the emotions.[117] Through music Cavendish would have had access to an expression of feelings, perhaps replacing the (for him so difficult) spoken and otherwise conventionally acted out expression of feelings.

---

[116] Simon McVeigh, *Concert Life in London from Mozart to Haydn* (Cambridge: Cambridge University Press, 1993), 14, 197, 220.

[117] *Music and Aesthetics in the Eighteenth and Early-Nineteenth Centuries*, ed. P. le Huray and J. Day (Cambridge: Cambridge University Press, 1981), 3 ff.

SCIENCE

HENRY CAVENDISH'S FAMILY is said to have been greatly disappointed that he did not pursue an ordinary public career, and that his father accordingly treated him in a niggardly fashion.[1] The first half of this statement is plausible. Politics was the life blood of the family, and politics left Henry cold. This, we should remember, was at a time when sons of peers and even sons of sons were practically duty-bound to enter the House of Commons.[2] To appreciate how extraordinary Henry's public career as an unsalaried, nearly full-time servant of the Royal Society might appear to his contemporaries, consider that in the same year that he entered the Royal Society, the House of Commons had five Manners, five Townshends, four Cavendishes, and, in general, an ample representation of aristocratic youngblood. The allegation, however, that Lord Charles was one of the family members who disapproved of Henry's course in life runs up against certain known facts, chief among them being that Lord Charles brought his son into his scientific circle from an early age. As to the charge of niggardliness, we have little evidence to go on. Since Henry did not marry, there was no settlement in writing, and we have not found any other written agreement between father and son. According to one source, until he was forty Henry received an annuity of only £120, though living at home as he did, he could have got by on it. Thomas Thomson said that Henry's annuity was £500,[3] which was the annuity Lord Charles received from his father at the time of his marriage. Lord Charles was very careful with money, and he may even have been tight, but it seems unlikely that he would have punished his son for following his own example. Lord Charles had left politics for (what we take to have been for him) a more fulfilling life in science and in other learned activities. Bypassing politics entirely, Henry directly entered science, which provided

[1] George Wilson, *The Life of the Honourable Henry Cavendish* (London, 1851), 161.

[2] L. B. Namier, *The Structure of Politics at the Accession of George III*, 2 vols. (London: Macmillan, 1929) 1:5.

[3] Thomas Thomson, *The History of Chemistry*, vol. 1 (London, 1830), 336.

him with an even fuller life than it had his father. There is no reason to think that his father tried to coerce him into a form of public life for which he was so clearly unsuited. On the contrary, there is every reason to think that his father supported him completely.

INTRODUCTION TO SCIENTIFIC SOCIETY

In the summer of 1753, soon after completing his studies at Cambridge, Henry Cavendish, together with his brother Frederick, accompanied their father to William Heberden's house for dinner. A number of friends and colleagues of Lord Charles's were there: Thomas Birch, William Watson, Daniel Wray, Nicholas Mann, and the physician and poet Mark Akenside, whom Lord Charles had recommended for fellowship in the Royal Society for his knowledge of natural philosophy.[4] Frederick, whose accident occurred the following year, did not come to any more of these collegial dinners, but Henry came with his father to at least twenty-six of them.[5] The most frequent of Henry's hosts was Heberden, though dinner was sometimes held at Yorke's house and occasionally at Watson's, Stanhope's, Wray's, and Cavendish's own house.[6] Lord Charles saw to it that his son Henry was well-known to his scientific associates.

Fellows of the Royal Society commonly introduced their sons to other members by bringing them as guests to the meetings.[7] Lord Charles first brought Henry as his guest in June 1758, by which time he had already introduced Henry to many of the active Fellows of the Royal Society at his dinners. As a guest Henry came to eighteen meetings of the Royal Society all told, the last in March 1760, and at fifteen of these meetings he came as a guest of his father. On the three other occasions he came at the invitation of Birch, a friend of the family, of Peter Newcome, the teacher at Henry's school at Hackney, and of Michael Lort, who had connections with the family.[8] The year before Henry began coming to the meetings, Lord Charles had received the Copley Medal of the Society, and as vice-president he presided over almost half of the meetings to which he brought Henry as his guest. Henry could feel reassured in this new public world of science.

On 31 January 1760, Henry Cavendish was proposed for Fellowship in the Royal Society by Lord Willoughby, Lord Macclesfield, and James Bradley, an

---

[4] 25 Aug. 1753, Thomas Birch Diary, BL Add Mss 4478C, f. 235.

[5] Again with the proviso that Birch also attended the dinners. Thomas Birch Diary.

[6] Henry Cavendish came with his father to dinner at Heberden's twelve times.

[7] Examples from around this time: John Canton, Jr., was a guest of John Canton, and Johnathan Watson, Jr., was a guest of Johnathan Watson. Entries for 26 Mar. and 9 July 1767, Royal Society, JB 26.

[8] Royal Society, JB 23 (1757–60). Michael Lort, an antiquarian, who in 1759 was appointed professor of Greek at Cambridge. Since he was not yet himself a Fellow of the Royal Society, he must have had the right to invite guests as a university professor. Lort was a good friend of the Cavendish in-law Philip Yorke, and he is also said to have been librarian to the duke of Devonshire.

appropriate combination of rank and skill. Over the next three months, the certificate of recommendation, which was written by Heberden, was signed by six more Fellows: Daniel Wray, Thomas Birch, Thomas Wilbraham, John Hadley, Samuel Squire, and William Watson. All of them, we note, were members of Lord Charles Cavendish's dining circle, with whom Henry too had dined. With that impressive endorsement, and with the qualifications given on the certificate, Henry Cavendish was balloted and unanimously elected on 1 May 1760.[9] What the certificate said was that Cavendish had "a great regard for Natural Knowledge" and that he was "studious of its improvement." General though the description was, it was of a kind often given,[10] and in his case the generality was probably fitting, as he would become known as a universal natural philosopher.

Just as at the Royal Society, at its dining society, the Royal Society Club–the official name was still the Society of Royal Philosophers, changing only in 1794–prospective members were customarily brought as guests before they became elected members. This was the case with Henry Cavendish, though he was proposed for, as opposed to elected to, membership before he had actually attended a dinner. There was no need for him to make himself known to the members, since he knew them already from his father's dinners, whose guests were the same persons who frequently attended the dinners of the club: Watson, Birch, Heberden, Knight, Willoughby, Davall, Squire, Wray, Burrow, Colebrooke, Peter Newcome, Akenside, and the president of the Royal Society, who also presided over the dinners, Lord Macclesfield.[11] On 10 November 1757, at a dinner which Lord Charles attended, Lord Macclesfield recommended Henry Cavendish for membership in the Club.[12] Henry was ballotted according to his place in line, which meant waiting two years, though that was a readily circumvented formality. While he was waiting, he was repeatedly invited to dinners as a guest of his father and treated as if he were a member from the time of his proposal. As it so happened, the timing was perfect, for he was elected to membership in the Club on 31 July 1760, just two months after he was elected to the Royal Society. Henry Cavendish was then twenty-nine and certainly not a ward of his father; although he continued to accompany his father to the Club, his father did not attend regularly anymore, leaving Henry to come on his own.

At his first dinner as a member, on 14 August 1760, Henry paid his admission fee of one pound one shilling together with three shillings for the dinner that day. He sat down at four o'clock in the Mitre Tavern before the following

---

9 Royal Society, Certificates, vol. 2, no. 10, f. 198; Cavendish was proposed on 31 Jan. 1760. Royal Society JB, 23: 845 (1 May 1760).

10 Maurice Crosland, "Explicit Qualifications as a Criterion for Membership of the Royal Society: A Historical Review," *Notes and Records of the Royal Society* 37 (1983): 167–87, on 173–74.

11 Minute Book, Royal Society Club, Royal Society, 4 (1760–64).

12 Archibald Geikie, *Annals of the Royal Society Club: The Record of a London Dining-Club in the Eighteenth and Nineteenth Centuries* (London: Macmillan, 1917), 63.

choices: nine dishes of meat, poultry, and fish, two fruit pies, plum pudding, butter and cheese, and wine, porter, or lemonade.[13] In 1780 the meetings were moved to the Crown & Anchor Tavern on the Strand, closer to the new location of the Royal Society in Somerset House. Cavendish may have known the Crown & Anchor in another connection: this tavern with its great ballroom had long been the site of the fortnightly concerts of the Academy of Ancient Music, as it would continue to be until 1784, combining excellent music with food and drink.[14]

Over the next fifty years, science and food were closely linked in Cavendish's public life. In the first year of his membership in the Royal Society Club, he came to about half of the dinners, sixteen, but after that he came to nearly all of them. A dozen or so members and guests made up the usual dinner party, but there was considerable fluctuation; on 23 April 1767, a day on which the meeting room of the Club was appropriated by the Society of Antiquaries, another arrangement was made, and only one member of the Club turned up for it; he was Cavendish, who brought with him a guest, Nevil Maskelyne. In 1777 the treasurer made an error in scheduling a dinner on Christmas, but Cavendish came anyway, along with two others. Unlike the Royal Society with its vacation and recesses, the Club met every Thursday throughout the year, and Cavendish sometimes attended every dinner. In 1809 he attended fifty-one dinners, and in January and February of 1810, the last two months of his life, he came every time up to the last fortnight.[15] Cavendish felt sufficiently comfortable in his Club that he took charge at the general meeting one year in the absence of the president.[16]

31. *Crown & Anchor. 1743. In this tavern on the Strand at the top of Arundel Street, Cavendish dined with the Royal Society Club on Thursdays. Courtesy of Westminster City Archives.*

[13] 14 Aug. 1760, Minute Book, Royal Society Club, Royal Society.

[14] Robert Elkin, *The Old Concert Rooms of London* (London: Edward Arnold, 1955), 51–52.

[15] Geikie, *Annals of the Royal Society Club*, 73–74, 80, 95, 97. Hector Charles Cameron, *Sir Joseph Banks, K.B., P.R.S. The Autocrat of the Philosophers* (London: Batchworth, 1952), 172.

[16] 25 July 1782, as recorded in the Minutes Books of the Royal Society Club.

SCIENCE AT THE ROYAL SOCIETY

In Cavendish's time, scientific books were writen for students at the university. Other books were written for a general audience. Still others were written to serve as practical manuals. Robert Smith wrote a textbook on optics; Colin Maclaurin wrote a book popularizing Newtonian science; John Michell wrote a book on a method for making artificial magnets. In addition, original work often first appeared, or reappeared in books. Benjamin Wilson published a book giving a new explanation of electricity; Benjamin Franklin published a collection of his letters on electricity from the *Philosophical Transactions.* A scientific investigator of Cavendish's stature would normally have been expected to publish at least one book over the course of his career.

However, as did a small number of his colleagues, notably William Herschel and John Canton, Cavendish published no books but only papers, and he published in only one place, a journal for all of science, the century-old *Philosophical Transactions* of the Royal Society. He turned to that journal even though his fields, experimental and mathematical natural philosophy, were decidedly not its strong point; only 10 percent of the papers of that journal were experimental, and a much smaller proportion were theoretical.[17] Since the era of scientific specialization only began toward the end of his life, he did not have a wide choice of journals, but we believe that his exclusive patronage of the *Transactions* originated in his steadfast commitment to the affairs of the Royal Society.

At Cambridge, Cavendish studied the mathematical methods of natural philosophy, but he had to learn the practice of science elsewhere, at home under his father's guidance, using his father's instruments and publications. His primer, the *Transactions,* came regularly into his father's house during the years he was a student at Cambridge. Beginning in the year Henry came home from Cambridge for good, Lord Charles served on the Royal Society's committee of papers, passing judgment on every paper appearing in its journal. As we have with textbooks in use at Cambridge, we examine the *Transactions* with a view to learning, as Cavendish learned, how to proceed as a researcher and author in science in the middle of the eighteenth century.

In the seventeenth century, the meaning of "experiment" could be as general as "any made or done thing"; the goal of experiment then was usually to discover or to solve a debate; and the argument it supported was usually inductive. By the time Cavendish entered science, the meaning of experiment had narrowed; experiment was often undertaken to prove a hypothesis or a theory or to solve a problem. Before Cavendish was through, experiment would be undertaken to prove a general claim or test a general belief. On the way, experimental papers grew more argumentative, corroborative, and investigative.[18]

The Royal Society's strictures against fanciful language in reporting scientific facts were honored but not strictly observed. In an exchange of letters in the

---

[17] Richard Sorrenson, "Towards a History of the Royal Society in the Eighteenth Century," *Notes and Records of the Royal Society of London* 50 (1996): 29–46, on 39–40.

[18] Charles Brazeman, *Shaping Written Knowledge: The Genre and Activity of the Experimental Article in Science* (Madison: University of Wisconsin Press, 1988), 66–68.

Philosophical Transactions, the electrical experimenter Georg Matthias Bose conceded that by his "style and expressions," he had "embellished a little" the account of an experiment. His correspondent, William Watson, took him to task: "The language of philosophers should not be tainted with the licence of the poets; their aim in the communicating their discoveries to the world, should be simple truth without desiring to exaggerate." Nature, the thing itself, was cause enough for "admiration."[19] Spare writing can have a force of its own, even eloquence. Cavendish's writing had that quality, and because his writing was the same whether the subject was phlogiston or farming, as scientific authors go, he was a natural. Few wrote as plainly as Cavendish; Bose was not unusual, only chastened.

Most of the papers in the *Philosophical Transactions* appeared in English, though papers in Latin from abroad were not uncommon and were rarely translated, a reflection of British education and the continuing use of Latin as a universal language of scholars. Papers in French, Spanish, and other modern European languages were translated, again reflecting British education and also British insularity.[20] Later in the century, the council of the Society resolved to meet foreigners halfway, ordering that papers communicated in foreign languages be printed in the original language in small type at the bottom of the page containing the English translation. In a further development along these lines, English translations might be relegated to an appendix and, on occasion, omitted.[21] Fortunately, there were always Fellows who were willing and able to translate, and like most readers of the journal, Cavendish was in their debt.

Authors in the *Philosophical Transactions* were identified. As the later president of the Society Sir Joseph Banks explained to a contributor, by the "name" of an author the Society did not mean a "bare signature but such additions local and professional as may lead any one of us at once to a knowledge of the person intended by it."[22] The "additions," however, did not include terms like "botanist." To know the author's scientific field, the reader had to infer it from context or else read another paper that mentioned him. Authors sometimes referred to one another by highly specialized terms such as "electrician," at other times by less specialized ones such as "chemist," and occasionally by very broad ones such as a person who pursued "natural history." Someone interested in minerals was likely to be called not a "mineralogist" but a "naturalist" or a "natural historian,"

---

[19] William Watson, "A Letter . . . Declaring That He as Well as Many Others Have Not Been Able to Make Odours Pass Thro' Glass by Means of Electricity . . . ," *PT* 46 (1750): 348–56, on 355–56.

[20] An exception was a paper sent to the instrument-maker James Short, translated from the Latin: Joseph Steplin, "An Account of an Extraordinary Alteration in the Baths of Toplitz in Bohemia. . . . ," *PT* 49 (1755): 395–96.

[21] 20 May 1773, Minutes of Council, Royal Society. In 1780, a paper in Swedish by Carl Peter Thunberg and one in Italian by Felice Fontana were printed in the body of the journal, their English translations in an appendix.

[22] Draft letter by Sir Joseph Banks, 28 Dec. 1791, Banks Correspondence, Kew.

terms which also applied to a person interested in, say, stones from a rhinoceros's stomach. "Philosopher" meant someone who was scientifically knowledgeable.[23] This general term was sometimes qualified; Cavendish was called a "natural philosopher." At the head of his articles in the *Philosophical Transactions*, he was identified by rank and membership, "the Hon. Henry Cavendish, F.R.S."

The Royal Society remained in awe of its most illustrious president, Newton. As a point of honor it was quick to defend him from criticisms perceived as partisan, but there was a subtle change. When Lord Charles Cavendish entered the Royal Society, references to Newton in the *Philosophical Transactions* were generally to praise. Twenty years later when his son Henry was at college, references to Newton were always respectful, but they were tempered and occasionally critical. Halley, in his ode prefixed to the *Principia*, wrote of Newton's "own divinity," of a thinker "nearer to the gods no mortal may approach," but to Henry Cavendish and his contemporaries Newton was definitely mortal, capable of error, and occasionally in need of correction. Thomas Simpson, mathematics teacher at the Royal Military Academy at Woolwich and the principal contributor of mathematics to the *Philosophical Transactions* at this time, solved a problem in inverse fluxions (integration); conscious that his solution differed from Newton's, he acknowledged that it was "impossible to disagree without being under some apprehensions of a mistake."[24] (Concerning the precession of the equinoxes Cavendish wrote in a letter, "As well as I remember Newton as you said really made a mistake from not considering this.")[25] If foreigners pointed out Newton's mistakes, it was a different matter; an Italian who claimed to have discovered six errors in Newton's *Principia* was attacked by the home guard.[26] Alexis Claude Clairaut, who had maintained that Newton's inverse-square law of gravitation was inexact, made a public retraction, but that did not spare him. Having detected an absurdity in Clairaut's reasoning, Patrick Murdock wrote a paper to dispel the erroneous view that Newton's propositions on the motions of the moon were "mere mathematical fictions, not applicable to nature"; on the contrary, Murdock said, Newton's work was "fully confirmed and verified."[27] Clairaut wrote a kind of apology for the *Philosophical Transactions*, in which he said that he had not intended to disparage Newton. Newton had not thought it impossible to be "opposed by experience," but in their zeal some people did not distinguish "between the different ways of opposing that great

---

23 *PT* 46 (1750): 118, 126, 250–55, 362, 369, 589.

24 Thomas Simpson, "Of the Fluents of Multinomials, and Series Affected by Radical Signs, Which Do Not Begin to Converge Till After the Second Term," *PT* 45 (1748): 328–35, on 333.

25 Henry Cavendish to Nevil Maskelyne, 29 Dec. 1784, draft, Cavendish Mss New Correspondence.

26 James Short, "An Account of a Book, Intitled, P. D. Pauli Frisii Mediolanensis, &c. Disquisitio mathematica . . . Printed at Milan in 1752 . . . ," *PT* 48 (1753): 5–17, on 14–15.

27 Patrick Murdock, "A Letter . . . Concerning the Mean Motion of the Moon's Apogee . . . ," *PT* 47 (1751): 62–74, on 62–63, 74.

man's sentiments"; still, if the Royal Society wished, Clairaut would be willing to reword his disagreement with Newton.[28] The disagreement turned on assumptions about the density of the earth, a subject in which Cavendish took great interest. Criticism of Newton could be turned to praise. Euler too had once believed that Newton's theory conflicted with observations of the motion of the moon but he did no longer; Clairaut's retracted claim, he said, had not been damaging but on the contrary had given "quite a new lustre to the theory of the great Newton."[29]

Euler did, however, pick a quarrel with Newton, which had to do with aberration in refracting telescopes, thought to arise from two sources, the different refrangibility of different colors, and the shape of the eyeglass. The latter was a matter of craft, the former was believed to have no remedy. Newton was cited as the authority for this discouraging conclusion about aberration, and though in principle Newton had not ruled out the possibility of an achromatic lens, he had not succeeded in constructing one and had come to doubt its practicability.[30] Euler believed that Newton was wrong on this point, and he corrected him in letters to the *Philosophical Transactions* containing his prescription for making achromatic refracting telescopes. The English optical instrument-maker John Dolland gave the rejoinder this time, deferring to Newton, "that great man," who had proved that it was impossible to eliminate aberration.[31] Dolland would change his mind; his polemic with Euler led him to make experiments with results that differed "very remarkably" from those in Newton's *Opticks*. By combining different kinds of glass, Dolland constructed achromatic lenses, which greatly improved refracting telescopes, and for this bold heterodoxy he was awarded the Copley Medal in 1758. The problem of indistinctness of images in refracting telescopes was still not completely solved, however, and Cavendish would investigate it thoroughly. Thomas Melvill was more speculative in his disagreement with Newton. He rejected Newton's explanation that different refrangibilities were owing to different sizes or densities of the particles of light of different colors. Newton had been misled by an "analogy" between the refraction of light and the gravity of bodies, Melvill said; the true cause of different refrangibilities was

[28] Alexis Claude Clairaut, "A Translation and Explanation of Some Articles of the Book Intitled, *Theorie de la Figure de la Terre . . . ,*" *PT* 48 (1753): 73–85, on 82–83.

[29] "Extract of a Letter from Professor Euler, of Berlin, to the Rev. Mr. Caspar Wetstein, Chaplain to Her Royal Highness the Princess Dowager of Wales," *PT* 47 (1753): 263–64.

[30] D. T. Whiteside, ed., *The Mathematical Papers of Isaac Newton* (Cambridge: Cambridge University Press, 1969) 3:442–43.

[31] "Letters Relating to a Theorem of Mr. Euler . . . for Correcting the Aberrations in the Object-Glasses of Refracting Telescopes," *PT* 48 (1753): 287–96. One letter was by James Short; the others were Leonhard Euler, "Letters Concerning a Theorem of His, for Correcting the Aberrations in the Object-Glasses of Refracting Telescopes"; John Dolland, "A Letter . . . Concerning a Mistake in M. Euler's Theorem for Correcting the Aberrations in the Object-Glasses of Refracting Telescopes."

the different velocity of particles of light of different colors. As this serious challenge to Newton had observational consequences, the Royal Society ordered James Short to investigate them and report back; Melvill's hypothesis was found not to stand up.[32] Henry Eeles combined his explanation of the ascent of vapors with an even broader criticism of Newton. Defending his "hypothesis" of the fluid of fire against the disapproval of "our great modern philosopher" of the use of hypotheses in general, Eeles made the apt observation that Newton himself had used hypotheses in his queries in the *Opticks*. Even gravitation, he said, would not have occurred to Newton without an hypothesis. Since "supposition must always precede the proof," if an hypothesis is rationally founded, it should be tested, for that is how science advances.[33] In various researches of his, Cavendish confidently spoke of his "hypothesis." Newton at mid century was still the immortal Newton, but attitudes could be conflicting on his authority on this or that point.

Scientific conclusions had to be supported by facts, of course, but on the question of whether greater trust was to be placed in observation or in theory, the answer was not always observation. The following discussion of the limits of observational accuracy is taken from papers by the instrument-maker and astronomer James Short and the mathematician Thomas Simpson. Short set out to clarify the disagreement between the observed shape of the earth and Newton's gravitational theory of its flattening at the poles. Critics of Newton's theory such as Clairaut had erred, Short said, in regarding their observations as absolutely exact (Clairaut denied that he placed too much certainty in observations), whereas other observers such as Boscovich had erred in thinking that observations were too inexact to draw any conclusions. When theory and observation were compared, theory could not be faulted until the disparity with observation was greater than the errors attributed to the instrument used and to its user. Newton had a just appreciation of such limits; he calculated the ratio of the two diameters of the earth to be 229 to 230, that is, to three figures, not to four or more figures, which would have been sham accuracy. It would be "absurd" for an observer to compute an angle to a second or a length to a part of an inch if the instrument could only measure to a degree or a foot. Mathematical results were rigorously true, but observations had "certain limits." The error of the instrument was itself one of the "*data*." Short urged observers to follow the "judicious caution" of Newton and also to read Cotes's treatise on the subject of errors.[34] Thomas Simpson proved that it was better to make

[32] T. Melvill, "A Letter . . . to the Rev. James Bradley . . . With a Discourse Concerning the Cause of the Different Refrangibility of the Rays of Light," *PT* 48 (1753): 261–70, on 262.

[33] Henry Eeles, "Letters . . . Concerning the Cause of the Ascent of Vapour and Exhalation, and Those of Winds; and of the General Phaenomena of the Weather and Barometer," *PT* 49 (1755): 124–49, on 124–25.

[34] Short, "An Account of a Book," 5–7.

many observations than only a few and that by taking a mean of them, the chance of making small errors was reduced and the chance of great ones was almost eliminated. This method was used by astronomers, and Simpson urged all experimenters to adopt it.[35] The understanding of errors was highly sophisticated by the time of Cavendish, though in practice it was often ignored.[36] Cavendish was unusual in that he routinely assessed the limits of accuracy of every investigation.

For a fact to be established by experiment, the experiment had to be repeatable. William Watson said of an experiment purporting to prove that electricity communicates odors through glass that the experiment must succeed in Venice and Leipzig, as this one did, but also in Wittemberg, Paris, Geneva, Turin, and London, where it did not.[37] A friend of the original experimenter and six Fellows of the Royal Society met at William Watson's house to repeat the experiment.[38] The original experimenter might himself repeat his experiment. John Canton repeated his experiment with powerful artificial magnets before the president of the Royal Society, who then informed the Society of what he had witnessed.[39]

For a fact to be established by observation instead of by experiment, independent observations were obviously desirable. Peter Newcome of Hackney Academy reported that six persons in his house felt an earthquake upstairs but no one downstairs. The same experience was reported by another person in another house, but that report was not as valuable, since it "depends indeed upon the perception of a single person; whereas his [Newcome's] is verified by the sensations of six different ones."[40] Testimonials by witnesses were solicited and weighed. The mental capacity of witnesses was considered relevant to the testimony, as were their profession, wealth, and rank.[41] The author of a paper on a bright rainbow said that he heard about similar rainbows from "intelligent persons."[42] Another

---

35 Thomas Simpson, "A Letter . . . on the Advantage of Taking the Mean of a Number of Observations, in Practical Astronomy," *PT* 49 (1755): 82–93.

36 Sorrenson, "Towards a History of the Royal Society," 42–43.

37 Watson, "A Letter . . . Declaring That He as Well as Many Others Have Not Been Able to Make Odours Pass Thro' Glass by Means of Electricity . . . ," 349. Steven Shapin, "The House of Experiment in Seventeenth-Century England," *Isis* 79 (1988): 373–404, on 399.

38 William Watson, "An Account of Professor Winkler's Experiments Relating to Odours Passing through Electrified Globes and Tubes . . . ," *PT* 47 (1751): 231–41, on 237–38.

39 John Canton, "A Method of Making Artificial Magnets Without the Use of Natural Ones . . . To Which Is Prefixed the President's Report," *PT* 47 (1751): 31–38, on 32–33.

40 Peter Newcome, "A Letter . . . Concerning the Same Shock Being Felt at Hackney, near London," *PT* 46 (1750): 653–54. James Burrow, "A Letter . . . Concerning the Same Earthquake Being Felt at East Sheen, Near Richmond Park in Surrey," *PT* 46 (1750): 655–56.

41 Shapin, "The House of Experiment in Seventeenth-Century England," 398–99.

42 Peter Davall, "A Description of an Extraordinary Rainbow Observed July 15, 1748," *PT* 46 (1749): 193–95, on 195.

author heard about earthquakes from "a very sensible Scotchman"[43] and a woman with "superior" judgement, accuracy, veracity, and a title.[44] The president of the Royal Society was assured that observers of an earthquake were not "mean, ignorant, or fanciful" but truthful, "rational and just."[45] When a great storm struck a village, the reporter took two reliable men with him to the spot to observe, the local physician and clergyman.[46] The dimensions of an "extraordinary" young man, two feet seven inches tall and twelve or thirteen pounds, were confirmed by eight witnesses, all "of figure and fortune" in the neighborhood.[47] In the cases above, reliability became an issue in part because of the uniqueness of the phenomenon, which unlike an experiment could not be reproduced, though the young man presumably could be measured again. But the character of witnesses came up in accounts of experiments too. An experimenter who was assisted by untrustworthy servants became "very delicate in the choice of the persons who I was desirous should be admitted to our experiments"; he would never again use "either children, servants, or people of the lower class."[48] Persons Cavendish invited to witness his experiments were Fellows of the Royal Society, whose reliability was normally beyond question.

Observers sometimes gathered to examine instruments jointly[49] or to collaborate in making observations.[50] No one was more active in cooperative scientific ventures in the middle of the eighteenth century than James Short. At his house, Short, with three other persons observed the occultation of Venus by the moon,[51]

---

[43] James Burrow, "An Account of the Earthquake on Thursday Morning, March 8, 1749, as Seen in the Inner Temple Garden, by Robert Shaw (a Very Sensible Scotchman) Then at Work There," *PT* 46 (1750): 626–28, on 626.

[44] Lady Cornwallis told James Burrow of her experience of an earthquake: James Burrow, "Part of a Letter . . . Concerning an Earthquake Felt Near Bury St. Edmund's in Suffolk . . . ," *PT* 46 (1750): 702–5, on 703.

[45] William Barlow, "Concerning a Shock of an Earthquake Felt at Plymouth, about One O'Clock in the Morning, between the 8th and 9th of Feb. 1749–50," *PT* 46 (1750): 692–95, on 693.

[46] William Henry, "An Account of an Extraordinary Stream of Wind, Which Shot Thro' Part of the Parishes of Termonomungan and Urney, in the County of Tyrone, on Wednesday October 11, 1752," *PT* 48 (1753): 1–4, on 1.

[47] John Browning, "Extract of a Letter . . . Concerning a Dwarf," *PT* 47 (1751): 278–81, on 279.

[48] Abbé Nollet, "Extract of a Letter . . . Accompanying an Examination of Certain Phaenomena in Electricity . . . ," *PT* 46 (1749): 368–97, on 377.

[49] John Smeaton, "An Account of Some Experiments upon a Machine for Measuring the Way of a Ship at Sea," *PT* 48 (1754): 532–46, on 535, 537, 539–40.

[50] The subject here is the parallax of Mars, determined by observations at two places on earth, in France and in England. "A Letter from Monsieur de L'Isle, of the Royal Academy of Sciences at Paris, to the Reverend James Bradley . . . ," *PT* 48 (1754): 512–20.

[51] The other observers at Short's were John Bevis, John Pringle, and the duke of Queensbury. John Canton observed the event at his house too. John Bevis, "An Occultation of the Planet Venus by the Moon, in the Day-Time, Observed in Surrey-Street, London, April 16, 1751. O. St.," *PT* 47 (1751): 159–63. Bradley also observed it, as written up by James Short, "Mr. John Bradley's Observation of the Occultation of Venus by the Moon," *PT* 47 (1751): 201–2.

and at his and another house, he with two others observed the transit of Mercury, while at five more locations observations of this event were made by still others.[52] To observe an eclipse of the sun, an excursion was made to Lord Morton's castle north of Edinburgh by Short, Morton, and a French astronomer who had come from Paris for the purpose. This excursion was only part of a wider effort in Scotland to observe the eclipse, coordinated by cannon fired from Edinburgh Castle; bad weather obscured it in Edinburgh, but observations were made at Morton's and at nine other locations in Scotland.[53]

In the middle of the eighteenth century, scientific observations were preferably made with instruments, though the occasional meteor or earthquake was experienced directly, as the observer had no choice in the matter. In their reports, investigators referred to the instruments they used and to the makers of the instruments. James Short, himself a maker of instruments, praised a fellow instrument-maker: John Smeaton had "best air-pump I ever saw, all of his own invention and construction."[54] Unusual capabilities of instruments were unfailingly mentioned. In measuring the expansion of metals with his pyrometer, Smeaton claimed an accuracy of one four-thousandth part of an inch, and repeated measurements with it differed by no more than one twenty-thousandth part of an inch. This sensibility, Smeaton said, "exceeds any thing I have met with."[55] Excellent instruments were expensive and often unique, circumstances which encouraged borrowing; upon learning that Smeaton's air-pump was being used for electrical experiments by William Watson, Short went to Watson's house to use it for a mechanical experiment. The *Philosophical Transactions* contained many papers on instruments, which were invariably illustrated by detailed, scaled drawings. In his account of his pyrometer, Smeaton said that its construction and use were clearer from the drawing than "from many words."[56]

The value of instruments was obvious–almost; from Norwich, a keeper of records of the weather complained that many people in his neighborhood judged the weather only by their "outward senses," without resorting to the thermometer, and accordingly they made mistakes, such as putting the hottest day in June when it was in July.[57] In astronomy the value of instruments had long since been demonstrated, though James Bradley thought that the point was still worth mak-

[52] The other observers were Jonathan Sisson, John Bird, John Smeaton, John Canton, and Lord Macclesfield. James Short, "Observations of the Transit of Mercury over the Sun, May 6, 1753," *PT* 48 (1753): 192–200.

[53] James Short, "An Eclipse of the Sun, July 14 1748 . . . ," *PT* 45 (1748): 582–97, on 592.

[54] James Short, "An Account of an Horizontal Top, Invented by Mr. Serson," *PT* 47 (1752): 352–53.

[55] John Smeaton, "Description of a New Pyrometer, with a Table of Experiments Made Therewith," *PT* 48 (1754): 598–613, 600.

[56] Smeaton, "Description of a New Pyrometer," 600, 605.

[57] William Arderon, "Extract of a Letter . . . Concerning the Hot Weather in July Last," *PT* 46 (1750): 573–75, on 574.

ing in the middle of the eighteenth century. Not long ago, Bradley said, astronomy had seemed perfected and no further progress was expected, a conclusion based on the instruments at hand, the telescope and the pendulum clock, and on the theory of "our great Newton." Bradley had shown that this confidence was misplaced. First he discovered the aberration of light, and then recently he discovered another annual change in the place of the stars, nutation or nodding of the axis of the earth, perceptible only because, he said, "of the exactness of my instrument." The pull of the moon on the equator of the earth was understood theoretically, but the nutation of the earth had not been foreseen. This object lesson in science demonstrated the "great advantage of cultivating this, as well as every other branch of natural knowledge, by a regular series of observations and experiments." The "more exact the instruments are . . . and the more regular the series of observations is . . . the sooner we are enabled to discover the cause of any new phaenomenon." Bradley advised astronomers to begin by examining the correctness of their instruments,[58] a practice in which he himself had set the example. No astronomer before him had so thoroughly examined his instruments in search of error; this he had done both by studying the instruments individually and by comparing them one with the other.[59] Entirely in Bradley's spirit, Henry Cavendish examined instruments in both of these ways and in every branch of physical science; and as Bradley recommended, he cultivated experimental fields comprehensively. Bradley, with whom Lord Charles Cavendish began his scientific work, and who proposed Henry Cavendish for membership in the Royal Society, was important to Henry's education in science.

By the middle of the eighteenth century, quantitative observations might appear in reports on any subject in the *Philosophical Transactions*: a measured draught given to, and the blood taken from, a patient;[60] a bill of mortality;[61] the path of a stroke of lightning;[62] the heat of a cave.[63] Henry Miles, a clergyman with a wide-ranging interest in quantities–he communicated a measurement of the "bigness" of a fungus, 210th part of an inch[64]–published an unusual paper for the *Philosophical Transactions*, a philosophical essay. His topic was quantity: prompted by a treatise by Thomas Reid in which ratios were applied to virtue,

---

[58] James Bradley, "A Letter . . . Concerning an Apparent Motion Observed in Some of the Fixed Stars," *PT* 45 (1748): 1–43, on 1–4.

[59] Allan Chapman, "Pure Research and Practical Teaching: The Astronomical Career of James Bradley, 1693–1762," *Notes and Records of the Royal Society of London* 47 (1993): 205–12, on 209.

[60] George Bayly, "A Letter . . . of the Use of the Bark in the Small-Pox," *PT* 47 (1751): 27–31.

[61] James Dodson, "A Letter . . . Concerning an Improvement of the Bills of Mortality," *PT* 47 (1752): 333–40.

[62] Henry, "Account of an Extraordinary Stream of Wind."

[63] William Arderon, "An Account of Large Subteranneous Caverns in the Chalk Hills Near Norwich," *PT* 45 (1748): 244–47.

[64] Henry Miles, "A Letter . . . Concerning the Green Mould on Fire-Wood; With Some Observations of Mr. Baker's upon the Minuteness of the Seeds of Some Plants," *PT* 46 (1750): 334–38.

Miles set out to determine which things were properly subject to mathematical proof, and thus beyond dispute. Miles, who believed that affections and appetites could not be reduced to quantity, identified quantity with "measures," which required a "standard," so that "all men, when they talked of it, should mean the same thing."[65] As quantity referred to anything short of affections and appetites, so did measures and standards. The physician John Pringle, who would become president of the Royal Society, laid down "standards" in his quantitative ranking of salts by their power to resist putrefaction.[66] Cavendish was a quantitative experimentalist, who invented and routinely used standards.

The balance and the thermometer acquired a new importance in science because of their use in quantitative chemistry; by contrast, in the model quantitative science, astronomy, the thermometer played a useful but subordinate role and the balance none at all unless perhaps in making instruments. Pneumatic chemistry, as Cavendish would soon show, depended on the balance for distinguishing different species of air by their specific gravities. As if to point the way, at the time Cavendish prepared to enter Cambridge, at Cambridge Richard Davies published a history of tables of specific gravities, which had "manifold applications . . . for the purposes of Natural Philosophy." Davies began with the "great author," Newton, who determined specific gravities with the "most scrupulous care and exactness" in his optical inquiries; he included George Graham, James Dodson, and John Ellicott with his "exquisite assay-scales"; and he concluded with himself and his sensitive hydrostatical balance built by Francis Hauksbee.[67] The physician Cromwell Mortimer, who studied the effects of chemical remedies in diseases, set out the uses of the thermometer in chemistry, that "most extensive Branch of Experimental Philosophy." Chemistry suffered from the unrepeatability of its experiments, the reason being, Mortimer said, the failure of chemists to record the heat: the chemist's laboratory should be equipped with "various Sorts of Thermometers, proportion'd to the Degree of Heat he intends to make use of," and the chemist should keep track of the time the heat is applied, observing "his Clock with as much Exactness as the Astronomer."[68] Cavendish's most important experimental work was done in

[65] Henry Miles, "An Essay on Quantity; Occasioned by Reading a Treatise, in Which Simple and Compound Ratios Are Applied to Virtue and Merit, by the Rev. Mr. Reid," *PT* 45 (1748): 505–20, on 506.

[66] John Pringle, "A Continuation of the Experiments on Substances Resisting Putrefaction," *PT* 46 (1750): 525–34.

[67] Richard Davies, "Tables of Specific Gravities, Extracted from Various Authors, with Some Observations upon the Same," *PT* 45 (1748): 416–89, on 416, 428.

[68] Cromwell Mortimer, "A Discourse Concerning the Usefulness of Thermometers in Chemical Experiments; and Concerning the Principles on Which the Thermometers Now in Use Have Been Constructed; Together with the Description and Uses of a Metalline Thermometer, Newly Invented," *PT* 44 (1746/47): 672–95, on 673. This paper was first read in 1735 and printed later with revisions.

chemistry, in which he recorded thermometer readings as needed, and in which he worked with as much "exactness" as his instruments permitted.

Electricity was the liveliest experimental science at the time. In the *Philosophical Transactions* for 1748, Stephen Hales reported watching electrical experiments performed in London, noting that in this "new field of researches there are daily new discoveries made."[69] In 1753 Emanuel Mendes da Costa observed that electricity was "now a days the chiefest occupation of philosophers."[70] Cavendish's father was active in experimental electricity, collaborating with William Watson, who introduced the Royal Society to the device that transformed the field, the Leyden jar.[71] Watson gave the Society an account of Franklin's book on electricity, consisting mainly of letters to his English correspondent, all or parts of which had been read at the Royal Society. Watson said that the book showed Franklin to have "a head to conceive, and a hand to carry into execution"; nobody, Watson said with characteristic generosity, knew electricity better than Franklin.[72] There was a sense among investigators that they were no longer working on the periphery of the subject but were disclosing the "nature" of electricity and its "general principles" and "laws"; they talked of "quantities" of electricity.[73] Twenty years later, drawing on the work of Watson and Franklin, Henry Cavendish pursued experimental and mathematical researches on the quantities, principles, and laws of electricity.

The contents of the *Philosophical Transactions* reflected a new and widespread interest in electrical effects out-of-doors, in the great laboratory of nature. Franklin proposed investigating lightning, speaking of the "Philadelphia experiment."[74] Watson together with several Fellows of the Royal Society tried to draw elecricity during a thunderstorm; they failed, but others, such as John Canton and John Bevis, succeeded.[75] Daring experiments on lightning were reported to the Royal Society from Philadelphia, Paris, and elsewhere around the world.

---

69 Stephen Hales, "Extract of a Letter . . . Concerning Some Electrical Experiments," *PT* 45 (1748): 409–11, on 410.

70 Emanuel Mendes da Costa to William Stukeley, 9 Nov. 1753, in John Nichols, *Illustrations of the Literary History of the Eighteenth Century* . . . , 8 vols. (London, 1817–58) 4:503.

71 William Watson, "A Sequel to the Experiments and Observations Tending to Illustrate the Nature and Properties of Electricity," *PT* 44 (1747): 704–49, on 709 ff.

72 William Watson, "An Account of Mr. Benjamin Franklin's Treatise, Lately Published, Intituled, Experiments and Observations on Electricity, Made at Philadelphia in America," *PT* 47 (1751): 202–11, on 210.

73 John Ellicott, "Several Essays Towards Discovering the Laws of Electricity," *PT* 45 (1748): 195–224, 196, 221–22.

74 Benjamin Franklin, "A Letter . . . Concerning an Electrical Kite," *PT* 47 (1752): 565.

75 William Watson, "A Letter . . . Concerning the Electrical Experiments in England upon Thunder-Clouds," *PT* 47 (1752): 567–70. John Canton, "Electrical Experiments, with an Attempt to Account for Their Several Phaenomena; Together with Some Observations on Thunder-Clouds," *PT* 48 (1753): 350–58. There were many more papers at this time on lightning experiments.

Lightning was new insofar as it was explained by an electrical hypothesis, but otherwise it belonged to the general class of violent events, which were a staple of the *Philosophical Transactions*, as they were of life in the eighteenth century. Incidents of thunder and lightning with their attendant "melancholy accidents" were regularly reported. Lightning struck a ship in a "violent manner, disabling most of the crew in eye and limb."[76] The mainmast of another ship was shattered when a "large ball of blue fire" rolled over the water and exploded, "as if hundreds of cannon had been fired at one time."[77] In a valley, in the "violence of the storm," a cloudburst and flash flood threw up "monstrous stones," which were "larger than a team of ten horses could move."[78] A meteor that looked like a "black smoky cloud" split an oak, and its "whirling, breaks, roar, and smoke, frightened both man and beast."[79] Clouds and auroras were seen to turn "blood-red."[80] Plagues of locusts "hid the sun," and undeterred by "balls & shot," they "miserably wasted" the land.[81] Victims of the "black vomit" experienced delirium "so violent" that they had to be tied down so that they did "not tear themselves in pieces."[82] Bitten by a mad dog, a horse in its agony gave off breath "like smoke from a chimney-top," with "much blood scatter'd up and down the stable."[83] An experimental dog was held in a poisonous vapor on the floor of a grotto, "tortured for three minutes," then revived. After being given a South American poison, a "great number of living animals" were "seized with a sudden and almost universal palsy" before they died.[84] Children were carried away by contagion, in the course of which a

[76] William Borlase, "An Account of a Storm of Thunder and Lightning in Cornwall," *PT* 48 (1753): 86–93. John Waddell, "A Letter . . . Concerning the Effects of Lightning in Destroying the Polarity of a Mariner's Compass," *PT* 46 (1749): 111–17, on 111–12.

[77] Mr. Chalmers, "An Account of an Extraordinary Fireball Bursting at Sea," *PT* 46 (1749): 366–67, on 366.

[78] John Lock, "An Account of a Surprising Inundation in the Valley of St. John's Near Keswick in Cumberland, on the 22d Day of August 1749, in a Letter from a Young Clergyman to His Friend," *PT* 46 (1749/50): 362–66.

[79] Thomas Barker, "An Account of an Extraordinary Meteor Seen in the County of Rutland, Which Resembled a Water-Spout," *PT* 46 (1749): 248–49.

[80] Henry Miles, "A Letter . . . Concerning an Aurora Borealis Seen Jan. 23. 1750–51," *PT* 46 (1749/50): 346–48, on 348. William Stukeley, "The Philosophy of Earthquakes," *PT* 46 (1750): 731–50, on 743.

[81] "An Account of the Locusts, Which Did Vast Damage in Walachia, Moldavia, and Transilvania, in the Years 1747 and 1748 . . . . by a Gentleman Who Lives in Transilvania," *PT* 46 (1749): 30–37, on 30–31.

[82] "Extract of So Much of Don Antonio De Ullöa's F.R.S. Account of His Voyage to South America, as Relates to the Distemper Called There Vomito Prieto, or Black Vomit," *PT* 46 (1749–50): 134–39, on 135.

[83] John Huxham, "A Letter . . . Containing an Account of an Horse Bit by a Mad Dog," *PT* 46 (1750): 474–78, on 474, 478.

[84] Abbé Nollet, "Extract of the Observations Made in Italy . . . on the Grotta de Cani," *PT* 47 (1751): 48–61, on 53. F. D. Herrisant, "Experiments Made on a Great Number of Living Animals, with the Poison of Lamas, and of Ticunas," *PT* 47 (1751): 75–92, on 90.

five-year-old girl was observed to cough up a "large quantity of white rotten flesh" in her so "violent a death."[85] In Constantinople the plague was ravaging, becoming "most violent" when the weather was hottest.[86] Very few persons escaped the "small-pox sooner or later in life," with its "very terrible consequences."[87] When limbs were amputated, agaric was plugged into the severed arteries, eliminating the usual method of needle and ligature, the most painful part of amputations and sometimes the cause of death.[88] The fright and misery would be brought to an end only because the world was going to end, according to astronomical calculation, by spiraling toward the sun and on its way "necessarily be burnt."[89] Among Cavendish's scientific papers is an extract from a letter by a ship's captain who examined a sloop that had just been struck by lightning. The mast was split from head to heal and a man seven feet from it received a shock which was "as if all his bones in his body was shaking."[90]

In the laboratory the violence of nature was simulated, and if in the laboratory it was moderated, it was violence all the same, and dangerous; lacking apparatus with effective safety features, investigators sometimes had been "intimidated" and "deterred," in "danger of being hurt."[91] The Leyden jar manufactured a form of lightning and was itself the inspiration for the electrical understanding of lightning and of thunder as well.[92] The "violent explosion of glass drops" in the laboratory was likened to volcanoes.[93] Henry Cavendish was drawn to investigate experimentally the regular course of nature rather than its singular and dramatic events, but he could not overlook the potential violence of the laboratory.

---

85 John Starr, "An Account of the Morbus Strangulatorius," *PT* 46 (1750): 435–46, on 439.

86 Mordach Mackenzie, "A Further Account of the Late Plague at Constantinople . . . ," *PT* 47 (1752): 514–16.

87 Rich Brooke, "A Letter . . . Concerning Inoculation," *PT* 47 (1752): 470–72, on 470.

88 Joseph Warner's account in "Experiments Concerning the Use of the Agaric of Oak in Stopping of Haemorages," *PT* 48 (1754): 588–98.

89 Leonhard Euler, "Part of a Letter . . . Concerning the Gradual Approach of the Earth to the Sun," *PT* 46 (1749): 203–5, on 204.

90 Extract from a letter from Captain Richard Nairne at Quebec, 13 July 1775, Cavendish Mss X(b), 3.

91 For these quotations, we go outside the time when Cavendish was at the university to when he began his electrical and chemical experiments at home: C. L'Epinasse, "Description of an Improved Apparatus for Performing Electrical Experiments, in Which the Electrical Power Is Increased, the Operator Intirely Secured from Receiving Any Accidental Shocks, and the Whole Rendered More Convenient for Experiments than Heretofore," *PT* 57 (1767): 186–91, on 188; Peter Woulfe, "Experiments on the Distillation of Acids, Volatile Alkalies, &c. Shewing How They May Be Condensed without Loss and How Thereby We May Avoid Disagreeable and Noxious Fumes," *PT* 57 (1767): 517–36.

92 Henry Eeles, "A Letter . . . Concerning the Cause of Thunder," *PT* 47 (1752): 524–29. Eeles took exception to the standard analogy between fired gunpowder and thunder; he had an up-to-date explanation based on the fire observed in electrical experiments.

93 Claude Nicolas Le Cat, "A Memoir on the Lacrymae Batavicae, or Glass-Drops, the Tempering of Steel, and Effervescence, Accounted for by the Same Principle," *PT* 46 (1749): 175–88, on 187.

"To avoid being hurt" by a bottle in which he exploded gases, he manipulated his apparatus by a string at a safe distance.[94]

Reading the *Philosophical Transactions* was not a quieting experience. Many of the medical papers described extreme pathologies and monstrous productions in more or less ordinary language, which did not spare the reader. "Letters" from a participant or observer or victim at the scene began, "I was much surprised," and then went on to relate the disturbing details. The most frightening event of all to read about was an earthquake. The year 1750 "may rather be called the year of earthquakes, than of jubilee," one Fellow of the Royal Society observed. These earthquakes occurred as if on command of the Royal Society, their center thought to be London, "the place to which the finger of God was pointed."[95] Henry Cavendish was in his second year at the university when an entire issue of the *Philosophical Transactions* was devoted to earthquakes, to the "natural philosophical understanding" of such "wonders."[96] Presented as an appendix to the regular issues, the earthquake issue consisted of fifty-seven papers submitted to the Royal Society dealing with four earthquakes felt in England and on the Continent in 1750. The earthquakes that year were only a harbinger of the great earthquake of 1755, which destroyed Lisbon and, of importance to us, prompted John Michell to explain earthquakes from first scientific principles.

Half of the observers reporting on earthquakes in the *Philosophical Transactions* were Fellows of the Royal Society, who also collected testimony and communicated letters from others. Fellows or otherwise, reporters of earthquakes rarely observed the direction, time, and duration of the shock; it is noteworthy that none of the observations of 1750 were made by astronomers. As earthquakes go, those of that year were not severe–Gowin Knight thought it was worth reporting that in a neighbor's house a "firkin of butter" was thrown from a shelf[97]–but witnesses nonetheless experienced them as "violent." People thought first of gunpowder, cannon, the explosion of a magazine or powder mill or a mine, or lightning.[98] In his house, Martin Folkes, along with Lord Macclesfield and other visitors, were "strongly lifted up, and presently set down again," while the coachmen standing outside Folkes's door feared that the house would come down on their

---

[94] Henry Cavendish, "Three Papers, Containing Experiments on Factitious Air," *PT* 56 (1766); *The Scientific Papers of the Honourable Henry Cavendish, F.R.S.*, vol. 2: *Chemical and Dynamical*, ed. E. Thorpe (Cambridge: Cambridge University Press, 1921), 77–101, on 82.

[95] William Stukeley, ". . . Concerning the Causes of Earthquakes," *PT* 46 (1750): 657–69, on 669; "The Philosophy of Earthquakes," 732.

[96] Simon Schaffer, "Natural Philosophy and Public Spectacle in the Eighteenth Century," *History of Science* 21 (1983): 1–43, on 17–18.

[97] William Cowper, ". . . Of the Earthquake on March 18, and of the Luminous Arch, February 16. 1749," *PT* 46 (1750): 647–49, on 648. Gowin Knight, "An Account of the Shock of an Earthquake, Felt Feb. 8. 1749–50," *PT* 46 (1750): 603–4, on 604.

[98] Smart Lethieullier, ". . . Of the Burning of the Steeple of Danbury in Essex, by Lightning, and of the Earthquake," *PT* 46 (1750): 611–13.

heads.[99] Gowin Knight's house "shook violently," and the duke of Newcastle's servant came to Knight to tell him what had happened at his house, and that all the way from London Bridge the people were frightened.[100] Animals were frightened too: a cat was startled, a dog was terrified, cows and sheep were alarmed, fish were disturbed, a horse refused water, and crows took flight.[101] Sensations were described variously, such as "falling into a fit."[102] Roger Pickering, a close observer of the weather and natural curiosities, gave a detailed account of his sensations while lying in bed when the quake occurred; a clergyman, he also gave his reflections, which led him beyond the "secondary causes" of the quake to the grandeur and majesty of the "Lord of Nature."[103]

Just what these "secondary causes" were was the scientific question of the day, to which various answers were given, two of which were published together with the collected reports of the earthquake in the *Philosophical Transactions.* Stephen Hales, another clergyman, said that both the ordinary and the extraordinary events of nature were caused by God, but that they did not lie outside natural explanation for that reason. After describing his sensations while lying in bed during a tremor, he explained them by referring to experiments from his *Statical Essays*: an earthquake is caused by the explosive lightning of a sulphureous cloud close to the earth, at a time when sulphureous vapors are rising from the earth in greater quantity than usual.[104] Another explanation of earthquakes was given by another clergyman, William Stukeley, who after a perfunctory consideration of the religious view, turned to the subject of interest in the *Philosophical Transactions*, the physical causes. Rejecting subterranean vapors, he attributed earthquakes to "electrical shock, exactly of the same nature as those, now become very familiar, in electrical experiments." With reference to Franklin, Stukeley said that the "little snap, which we hear in our electrical experiments," is the same snap, only magnified, that we hear in thunderstorms. When a cloud rises from the sea and discharges its contents on the earth, an earthquake results. Having gotten to know the "stupendous powers" of electricity by experiment, he turned to electricity to explain the "prodigious appearance of an earthquake."[105] Stukeley's and Hales's causes of earthquakes, electricity and vapors (or gases), were the two main experimental subjects in Britain in the second half of the eighteenth century, and they were two of Henry Cavendish's great experimental fields (heat was a third).

---

99 Abraham Trembly, "Extract of a Letter, Concerning the Same," *PT* 46 (1750): 610–11, on 611.

100 Knight, "An Account of the Shock of an Earthquake Felt Feb. 8 1749–50," 603.

101 *PT* 46 (1750): 618, 621, 651, 682.

102 Thomas Birch, "An Account of the Same," *PT* 46 (1750): 615–16, on 616.

103 Roger Pickering, " . . . Concerning the Same," *PT* 46 (1750): 622–25, on 625.

104 Stephen Hales, "Some Considerations on the Causes of Earthquakes," *PT* 46 (1750): 669–81, on 677.

105 William Stukeley, "On the Causes of Earthquakes," *PT* 46 (1750): 641–46, on 642–44; "Concerning the Causes of Earthquakes," 663; "The Philosophy of Earthquakes."

The catastrophic Lisbon earthquake in 1755 filled the last roughly hundred pages of the volume of the *Philosophical Transactions* for that year and much of the next year's. Unlike accounts of the earlier earthquakes of 1750, these dwelled on loss of life and physical destruction. This earthquake would not be the last scourge of humanity to prove a stimulus to science. The most important response was John Michell's paper on the cause of the earthquake "So Fatal to the City of Lisbon" and on earthquakes in general, printed in the *Philosophical Transactions* for 1760.[106] We will move ahead a few years after Cavendish had left Cambridge, to 1760, to consider this paper, since it more than any other set the standard for Cavendish in his search for a comprehensive physical understanding of the earth.

Michell and Cavendish's acquaintanceship began no later than the year of Michell's paper on earthquakes in 1760. That year, at Cavendish's first dinner as a member of the Royal Society Club, Michell was present as a guest, and in later years Cavendish often brought Michell as his own guest.[107] In 1760 Michell and Cavendish were both elected Fellows of the Royal Society, and in that same year before their elections, Michell's paper on the causes of earthquakes was read in five consecutive meetings of the Society. Cavendish was present at all five of these meetings, three times as a guest of his father.[108] Michell's subject, the earth's interior, linked his and Cavendish's interests thereafter.

For most of his life Michell was a clergyman, but in his paper on earthquakes he made no reference to providence or any other religious idea. He disagreed with both Hales and Stukeley, who located the cause of earthquakes above the earth. Volcanoes were proof that fires could exist underground, without contact with the air, and by analogy Michell reasoned that volcanoes and earthquakes had the same cause, pent-up water vapor falling into underground fires. The elastic force of heated vapor exceeded even gunpowder in producing "sudden and violent effects." Conceiving of the earth not as "heaps of matter casually thrown together" but as "uniform strata," Michell developed a mechanical theory of the propagation of waves through the elastic substance of the earth's crust: in sufficient quantity, vapor proceeding from the subterraneous fire could insinuate itself between the strata, lifting the earth as it passed.[109] By the same principles that explained the motions of the heavenly bodies, the motions of the earth could be explained. Set in motion by the expansive force of steam, the elastic, stratified earth presented a dynamical phenomenon, which was explicable by the laws of

[106] John Michell, "Conjectures Concerning the Cause, and Observations upon the Phaenomena of Earthquakes; Particularly of That Great Earthquake of the First of November, 1755, Which Proved So Fatal to the City of Lisbon, and Whose Effects Were Felt as Far as Africa, and More or Less throughout Almost All Europe," *PT* 51 (1760): 566–634.

[107] 14 Aug. 1760, Minute Book of the Royal Society Club, Royal Society, 4.

[108] The meetings were on 28 Feb., 6, 13, 20, and 27 Mar. 1760. Royal Society, JB, 23:795, 799, 802, 806, and 809.

[109] Michell, "Conjectures," 582, 594.

motion. What Michell proposed was more than a theory of earthquakes; it was an exact science of the earth.

When we look at the empirical support that Michell brought to his theory, we recognize in it a vindication of the motivating ideals of the Royal Society. The natural histories that Bacon expected from Salomon's House had been tried many times by the Royal Society, often without much benefit, but the natural histories of earthquakes led to science. Michell was able to derive the cause of earthquakes, he said, because of the bounty of facts about the earthquake of 1755, many of which were collected by the Royal Society and in a separate publication on the history and science of earthquakes. Michell's paper of 1760 is replete with references to the *Philosophical Transactions*, most from volume 49 but some earlier. Michell's use of histories was sophisticated; he acknowledged that observations were often carelessly made and reported, but the "concurrent testimonies" of so many persons established the main point. He selected accounts having the "greatest appearance of accuracy" and took a "mean" of them in computing the time, location, and depth of the Lisbon earthquake.[110]

Michell's paper has another connection with the founding ideals of the Royal Society through its references to the experiences of artisans, such as their disastrous experience in casting a cannon in a damp mold, resulting in an explosion of the "greatest violence."[111] The explosion of coal damp in mines was powerful but not powerful enough for earthquakes, Michell said. For that, water had to be converted into steam, and the steam engine was Michell's example, taken from the world of artisans.

Like earthquakes, the weather was regarded as a great force of nature, and when a tremor occurred, thermometer and barometer readings before, during, and after might be noted.[112] The Royal Society received frequent accounts of the weather, both of its extreme manifestations and of its normal variations. The barometer reading, the rainfall, the temperature, usually including the mean and the highest and the lowest, were reported from far and near, from Madeira, Dublin, Charles-Town, and Tooting. James Jurin's method of recording temperature was still practiced, but standardization in meteorology remained a remote ideal. Temperatures might be given in Fahrenheit, Réaumur, and in relationship to the heat of human blood.[113] The clergyman Henry Miles wrote about the thermometer, an instrument which Newton had considered and which several others had tried to bring to "greater Perfection," observing that it was now widely agreed that thermometers made with mercury worked the best.[114] The

[110] Ibid., 629.

[111] Ibid., 594–95.

[112] Henry Miles, " . . . On the Same," *PT* 46 (1749): 607–9.

[113] Arderon, "Extract of a Letter . . . Concerning the Hot Weather in July Last."

[114] Henry Miles, "A Letter . . . Concerning Thermometers, and Some Observations of the Weather," *PT* 46 (1750): 1–5.

credibility of the mercury thermometer was implicitly put to the test in the extreme climate of Siberia, in which Johann Georg Gmelin recorded temperatures as low as minus 120 degrees Farhenheit, which he said was scarcely believable "had not experiments, made with the greatest exactness, demonstrated the reality of it."[115] Commenting on Gmelin's temperatures, William Watson used nearly the same words: the observations, however "extraordinary," were "scarce to be doubted," since they were made with "all possible exactness" and agreed with readings made by others under his direction in different parts of Siberia.[116] Beginning with this remarkable weather report, Henry Cavendish made a fundamental study of the contraction of mercury on freezing, thereby clarifying the behavior of thermometers made with mercury at the same time that he clarified the climates of the earth.

The naturalist William Arderon, who published frequently on the weather in Norwich, kept a record of the constant temperature in a cavern under nearby hills, which he compared with the mean of the hottest and coldest temperatures above ground, finding them almost identical, and noting that the temperature of the Norwich cavern was within a degree of that of the cave beneath the Paris Observatory.[117] Cavendish extended worldwide this method of measuring the average climate. George Graham noted that the magnetic variation at London was not regularly published,[118] and although Cavendish kept a regular record of it, he did not publish it either. Auroras were a regular feature of the journal,[119] and Cavendish published his analysis of an aurora.

Some investigators worked in both the physical and the life sciences, or they brought the physical sciences to bear on the problems of the life sciences. To William Watson, known for his electrical researches, the study of living nature had the same goal as the study of the physical world, to learn the "general laws" of nature. A strong advocate of Linnaeus, Watson published on the sex of plants, the discovery of which, he thought, was as important as that of the circulation of the blood in animals.[120]

The Royal Society's Croonean Lectures in 1747 were given by the physician Browne Langrish, who explained muscular motion by Newton's attracting and repelling forces, giving credit, and dedicating his lectures, to Stephen Hales,

---

[115] John Fothergill's extracts from Gmelin, "An Account of Some Observations and Experiments Made in Siberia . . . ," *PT* 45 (1748): 248–62, on 260.

[116] William Watson, "A Comparison of Different Thermometrical Observations in Sibiria," *PT* 48 (1753): 108–9.

[117] Arderon, "An Account of Large Subterraneous Caverns."

[118] George Graham, "Some Observations, Made During the Last Three Years, of the Quantity of the Variation of the Magnetic Needle to the Westward," *PT* 45 (1749): 279–80, on 280.

[119] John Martyn, "A Letter . . . Concerning an Aurora Borealis Seen February 16. 1749–50," *PT* 46 (1750): 345.

[120] William Watson, "Some Observations upon the Sex of Flowers," *PT* 47 (1751): 169–83, on 179, 182–83.

whose "indefatigable Researches into Nature" showed that particles of air are attracted to solids; Langrish's "scheme" was based on "those Hints which Sir Isaac Newton has given us in the Queries at the End of his incomparable Book of Opticks."[121] The physician Charles Morton published a paper on the same subject, muscular motion, which he, a follower of the "Newtonian, which is the philosophy of nature," laid out in observations, experiments, lemmas, and scholia, according to the example of Newton's *Principia.* Following tradition, Morton regarded his subject as belonging to "natural philosophy."[122] Henry Cavendish did research in all parts of physical science, but not beyond; unlike his friend Watson, he did not do research on plants and animals to understand *their* laws.

Honoring Bacon's ideal of a scientific society that worked to "relieve the necessities of human life,"[123] the Royal Society received a good many papers that were at least partly directed to utilitarian concerns. At the time Cavendish was studying at the university, the *Philosophical Transactions* included papers on mechanical power, manufactures, gunnery, navigation, medicine and health, and the prevention of disasters. John Smeaton showed the Royal Society a tackle of twenty pulleys small enough to fit into the pocket, and with another block of twenty pulleys, he offered an Archimedian-like demonstration of a single person lifting a gun and carriage aboard a naval ship.[124] Smeaton and the Royal Society naturally took an interest in the extraordinary mechanical power generated by steam.[125] William Brownrigg investigated salt-making with lemmas and propositions. William Watson hoped that Brownrigg would do what the Royal Society's historians of salt-making had not, overcome Britain's disadvantage in this trade; Brownrigg, Watson said, was distinguished "both as a chemist, and as a philosopher," and his book on salt-making had "national importance."[126] John Mitchell gave a Baconian history of potash-making, which in England, he said, was "practised only by the vulgar, and neglected and overlooked by the learned;" no nation could do without potash, an essential ingredient in soap, dye, bleach, and glass, and England was a nation that did not know how to make it right.[127]

121 Browne Langrish, "Three Lectures on Muscular Motion," supplement to *PT* 44 (1747): i, 7–8.

122 Charles Morton, "Observations and Experiments upon Animal Bodies, Digested in a Philosophical Analysis, or Inquiry into the Cause of Voluntary Muscular Motion," *PT* 47 (1751): 305–14, on 308.

123 William Watson's expression, from his abstract and review, "An Account of a Treatise by Wm. Brownrigg . . . ," *PT* 45 (1748): 351–72, on 372.

124 John Smeaton, "A Description of a New Tackle, or Combination of Pullies," *PT* 47 (1752): 494–97.

125 John Smeaton, "An Engine for Raising Water by Fire; Being an Improvement of Savery's Construction, to Render It Capable of Working Itself, Invented by Mr. De Moura of Portugal, F.R.S.," *PT* 47 (1752): 436–38.

126 Watson, "An Account of a Treatise by Wm. Brownrigg," 352.

127 John Mitchell, "An Account of the Preparation and Uses of the Various Kinds of Pot-Ash," *PT* 45 (1748): 541-63, on 541.

In Newgate prison, infectious fevers killed convicts and, more serious, officers of courts of justice who were exposed to convicts during trials; to achieve "purity of air" there, it was decided to install a ventilator built by Stephen Hales.[128] On Hales and Lord Halifax's recommendation, Captain Henry Ellis also installed Hales's ventilators in his ship, which caused candles to burn better and bells to ring louder and slaves and other cargo to hold up better.[129] Electrical healing was more often the product of enthusiasm than of repeatable experiments, and claims for it were received with caution, but that electricity had some medical virtue seemed evident to nearly everyone at the time, including the skeptical William Watson, who acknowledged that the administration of a "large quantity" of electricity "greatly heats the flesh, and quickens the pulse," conferring on a susceptible patient "very great advantages."[130] Bills of mortality documented the relative unhealthiness of various places, useful knowledge for "many excellent purposes," including the calculation of annuities on lives, in which a great part of the "real estates of these kingdoms" was vested.[131] Spring waters had medical uses, and sea water might be converted to fresh water.[132] Improvements were made in navigation, such as in the mariner's compass, the invention of which, Gowin Knight said, had "probably been of more general and important use to human society, than the invention of any one instrument whatsoever."[133] To celebrate the recent peace, six thousand rockets were fired in Green Park without incident, thanks to Stephen Hales's recommendation of spreading a layer of dirt or fine gravel over the wood floor to prevent fire.[134] The supreme destructive power remained the province of nature: the *Philosophical Transactions* published many papers on lightning and on their defense, lightning rods. In this rare, direct application of science, Cavendish became involved through the Royal Society.

---

[128] John Pringle, "An Account of Several Persons Seized with the Goal-Fever, Working in Newgate; and of the Manner in Which the Infection Was Communicated to One Intire Family," *PT* 48 (1753): 42–54, on 42.

[129] Henry Ellis, "A Letter to the Rev. Dr. Hales . . . ," *PT* 47 (1751): 211–16.

[130] William Watson, "An Account of Dr. Bianchini's Recueil d'experiences faites à Venise sur le medicine electrique," *PT* 47 (1752): 399–406, on 406.

[131] James Dodson, "A Letter . . . Concerning an Improvement of the Bills of Mortality," 333–34.

[132] John Bond, "A Letter . . . Containing Experiments on the Copper Springs in Wicklow in Ireland, and Observations Thereon," *PT* 48 (1753): 181–90. William Watson, "An Account of Mr. Appleby's Process to Make Sea-Water Fresh; With Some Experiments Therewith," *PT* 48 (1753): 69–71.

[133] Gowin Knight, "A Description of a Mariner's Compass," *PT* 46 (1750): 505–12. John Smeaton, "An Account of Some Improvements of the Mariner's Compass, in Order to Render the Card and Needle, Proposed by Doctor Knight, of General Use," *PT* 46 (1750): 513–17.

[134] Stephen Hales, "A Proposal for Checking in Some Degree the Progress of Fires," *PT* 45 (1748): 277–79. At the end of the issue, the secretary Cromwell Mortimer made an addition to Hales's paper, reporting that the engineers followed Hales's plan in the building they erected for the fireworks, p. 382.

Reflecting eighteenth-century British education, astronomy and classics were frequently joined in the *Philosophical Transactions*. The antiquarian William Stukeley referred to Thales's account of a solar eclipse, reminding scholars of the "admirable use to be made of astronomy in ascertaining matters of history."[135] There was a tradition of astronomical reasoning in history, and just as in science, in chronology Newton now received gentle criticism.[136] A Jesuit who had worked out a chronology of ancient China proposed to do the same for Chinese astronomy.[137] Henry Cavendish contributed to a related interest with his study of the Hindu calendar.

Nearly all of the scientific problems Henry Cavendish worked on during his long career were ones addressed in the *Philosophical Transactions* at the time he was studying at the university. Through his manner of treating problems and not his invention of them, he left his stamp on science.

135 William Stukeley, "An Account of the Eclipse Predicted by Thales," *PT* 48 (1753): 221–26, on 222.

136 Ibid. George Costard, "A Letter . . . Concerning the Year of the Eclipse Foretold by Thales," *PT* 48 (1753): 17–26, on 19.

137 "Extracts of Two Letters from Father Gaubil, of the Society of Jesus, at Peking in China," *PT* 48 (1753): 309–17.

EARLY RESEARCHES

THE EARLIEST DATE in Cavendish's scientific manuscripts is 1764, twelve years after he had left the university and four years after he had been elected to the Royal Society; he was thirty-three. William James's observation that "in most of us, by the age of thirty, the character has set like plastic"[1] applies to Cavendish, if we take his "character" to imply a steadfast devotion to science. The ongoing development of our subject is of a life *within* science.

CAVENDISH'S CORRESPONDENT

The earliest contributions to the *Philosophical Transactions* were letters to its founder, Henry Oldenburg. Over time, the pretense of letters was dropped. The genre of the scientific paper began to emerge, as authors increasingly wrote for their readers instead of the editor. With the committee of papers in 1752, the editor further withdrew.[2] Nevertheless, when Cavendish began reading the *Philosophical Transactions*, authors often communicated their reports as letters, and referred to them as "letters" rather than "papers," though they addressed them usually not to the editor but to the president of the Society or to a member who was knowledgeable in the subject. Sometimes a letter from the author would be published as a preface to the paper. The overlap of letters and journals provides the background of Henry Cavendish's earliest surviving scientific reports, which he addressed to a person he did not name, referring in them only to "you."

If Henry Cavendish was as excessively shy when he was young as he was later, "you" might well have been his father. There are other possibilities. One is the long-time family friend William Heberden. Having lectured on chemistry at Cambridge, Heberden would have been a competent reader, and as we discuss

[1] Paul T. Costa, Jr. and Robert R. McCrae, "Set Like Plaster? Evidence for the Stability of Adult Personality," in *Can Personality Change?*, ed. T. F. Heatherton and J. L. Weinberger (Washington, D.C.: American Psychological Association, 1994), 21–40, on 21–22.

[2] Charles Brazeman, *Shaping Written Knowledge: The Genre and Activity of the Experimental Article in Science* (Madison: University of Wisconsin, 1988), 130, 137.

below, Cavendish's first published chemical research was carried out at Heberden's request. Like Lord Charles, Heberden would have been approachable. Another possible correspondent is a classmate of Cavendish's at Cambridge, John Hadley. Hadley died suddenly while Cavendish's experiments were in progress, but if Cavendish had been in the practice of writing reports of his experiments for Hadley to read, he might have continued to do so, using the same format in writing to "you." Another possibility is the London apothecary Timothy Lane. Still other possibilities are Lord Charles's collaborator William Watson, who together with Heberden and Hadley signed Henry Cavendish's certificate at the Royal Society; the schoolmaster John Canton, who with Cavendish, Heberden, and Watson signed the certificate for Lane; and John Michell, with whom Cavendish would later have a known association. The earliest surviving personal letter by Cavendish is addressed to Canton, establishing that he and Canton discussed electricity together. Cavendish, of course, could have had more than one scientific correspondent, or he could have had none. Considering that his papers contain no responses to his early researches, he might not have sent his reports to anyone but simply adopted the form of the letter-report as he knew it from the *Philosophical Transactions.*

If Cavendish did actually correspond, and we assume that he probably did, and if there were several correspondents, they most likely included Hadley and Lane. Nephew of the great instrument-maker of the same name, John Hadley was one of only two London chemists Cavendish referred to in his first chemical writings. The other chemist was William Lewis, and although Lewis began gathering information on the physical and chemical properties of air at the right time, 1765–70,[3] he could not have been Cavendish's correspondent, or at least not his only one.[4] We know that Cavendish learned about Hadley's work firsthand, since his reference to Hadley was to an unpublished work by him, which had to do with the distillation of metals with salts, as did Cavendish's earliest work.[5] The year Cavendish came down from Cambridge, Hadley stayed on as a fellow of Queens' College. In 1756 he was appointed successor to Mickleburgh as professor of chemistry, in which capacity he did what not all Cambridge professors did, he lectured.[6]

---

[3] F. W. Gibbs, "A Notebook of William Lewis and Alexander Chisholom," *Annals of Science* 8 (1952): 202–20, on 203.

[4] That is evident from the way Lewis is referred to in Cavendish's report to his chemical correspondent.

[5] Hadley's work appears in a footnote to part 4 of Cavendish's paper on factitious air in 1766. The first three parts were published, the fourth withheld. "Experiments on Factitious Air. Part IV. Containing Experiments on the Air Produced from Vegetable and Animal Substances by Distillation," *The Scientific Papers of the Honourable Henry Cavendish, F.R.S.,* vol. 2: *Chemical and Dynamical,* ed. E. Thorpe (Cambridge: Cambridge University Press, 1921), 307–16, on 313.

[6] John Twigg, *A History of Queens' College, Cambridge, 1448-1986* (Woodbridge, Suffolk: Boydell Press, 1987), 212–13. "Hadley, John," *DNB* 8:879–80, on 879. John Hadley, *A Plan of a Course of Chemical Lectures* (Cambridge, 1758). Hadley gave lectures for two consecutive years. Beyond the syllabus of his lectures, he published nothing on chemistry.

He published the plan of his lectures in 1758, and a manuscript from 1759 containing the substance of the lectures is preserved at Cambridge.[7] We can see that his views and Cavendish's were close. Hadley based his course on the work of foreign chemists, in particular, Marggraf and Macquer, who were the source of Cavendish's first chemical problems. Hadley also gave attention to Hales's and Black's work on "fixed air," long before Black's work was acknowledged in print by other chemists; Black's work was the starting point of Cavendish's first published paper on chemistry. Hadley also gave much attention in his lectures to mineral water, and he evidently began his own investigation of it, writing to the secretary of the Royal Society that the analysis of mineral water was "very difficult & would lead into very extensive chemical enquiries," and his own papers on it were "not of consequence enough to be printed";[8] mineral water was the subject of Cavendish's second chemical publication. Hadley and Cavendish were both interested in the new field of latent heat as well. In the late 1750s and early 1760s, they would have had much in common. The chemistry professorship at Cambridge did not pay a living. Desiring a proper profession and income, in 1758 Hadley obtained permission from his college to study medicine and hold a "Physick Fellowship." He came to London frequently, where he regularly saw Cavendish at the Royal Society and its dining club, and as we have seen, he was a friend of Cavendish's father and a guest at the Cavendish home. He invited his and Cavendish's Cambridge classmate, the mathematician Francis Maseres, to hear John Michell's paper on earthquakes read at the Royal Society.[9] He brought himself forward as a candidate to succeed Davall as secretary of the Royal Society.[10] He solicited the support of Hardwick and Newcastle for an appointment, which he received in 1760, as assistant physician at St. Thomas's Hospital.[11] In 1763 he became physician to the Charterhouse and a Fellow of the College of Physicians. Just as he was becoming established, he suddenly died of fever at the Charterhouse in 1764 at the age of thirty-three. Henry Cavendish lost an able scientific colleague, and his early direction as a chemist may have owed something to this friendship.[12]

---

[7] The manuscript of the lectures is in the library of Trinity College. It is discussed in L. J. M. Coleby, "John Hadley, Fourth Professor of Chemistry in the University of Cambridge," *Annals of Science* 8 (1952): 293–301.

[8] John Hadley to Thomas Birch, 13 Sep. 1762, BL Add Mss 4309 p.9.

[9] Hadley planned to take Francis and John Maseres and Mr. Hatrell to the reading, but he could not make it and asked Birch to take them instead. John Hadley to Thomas Birch, 13 Mar. [1760], BL Add Mss 4309, p.3.

[10] Henry Hadley to Thomas Birch, 13 Oct. 1759, BL Add Mss 4309, p.1. Thomas Birch to Philip Yorke, 13 Oct. 1759, BL Add Mss 35399, p.115.

[11] John Hadley to Newcastle, 16 Dec. 1758, BL Add Mss 32886, p.352. Hadley to Hardwicke, 1 Jan. 1760, BL Add Mss 35596, p.73.

[12] "Hadley," *DNB* 8:879.

Timothy Lane was a London apothecary who published two papers in the *Philosophical Transactions*, one on electricity in 1766 and the other on mineral water in 1769. The subjects and the timing correspond to Cavendish's interests; in 1766 Cavendish was interested in electricity,[13] and in 1767 he published his paper on mineral water. Lane took up the problem of mineral water where Cavendish left it, tying it closely to pneumatic chemistry; before publishing his experiments, he submitted them privately to Cavendish for judgment. The learned world, Lane said, "had great reason to hope for many other new and useful experiments" from Cavendish. Lane spoke of Cavendish's "known accuracy," which is what Lane was known for, too, having published in 1766 an account of an electrometer for introducing into electricity a "much greater degree of precision"; with "tolerable accuracy," his electrometer could measure the "quantity" of electric fluid stored in a Leyden jar.[14] Cavendish used Lane's electrometer in his electrical researches. In 1769, Cavendish invited Lane to five meetings of the Royal Society before his election the following year.[15] The Royal Society extended a scientific exchange that had already been established between Lane and Cavendish, which may well have included Cavendish's scientific reports written to be read by "you."

Hadley and Lane were capable of serving as a sounding board for Cavendish's experimental work but probably not for his mathematical theory. At the bottom of the last page of a carefully drafted paper on the motion of sounds, Cavendish added a note addressed to "you," mentioning another demonstration, "which if you have a mind I will shew you."[16] This reader would have had to be mathematically proficient. John Michell was such a reader, and among Cavendish's papers there are several unpublished results of Michell's.[17] If it were not for his geographical and cultural distance, the professor of natural philosophy at the University of Dublin, Hugh Hamilton, would be another candidate for Cavendish's reader. Of about the same age as Cavendish, Hamilton revealed a remarkably similar combination of mathematical and experimental interests.[18] Cavendish cited him with approval in his

[13] Roderick W. Home, "Aepinus and the British Electricians: The Dissemination of a Scientific Theory," *Isis* 63 (1972): 190–204.

[14] Timothy Lane, "A Letter . . . on the Solubility of Iron in Simple Water, by the Introduction of Fixed Air," *PT* 59 (1769): 216–27, on 216; "Description of an Electrometer Invented by Mr. Lane; with an Account of Some Experiments Made by Him with It," *PT* 57 (1767): 451–60, on 451.

[15] Cavendish brought Lane to meetings of the Royal Society on 20 Apr., 4 and 11 May, 8 June, 9 Nov. 1769; Lane was elected the next year. Royal Society, JB 26 (1767–70).

[16] "On the Motion of Sounds," Cavendish Mss VI(b), 35:10.

[17] "Concerning the Spinning of Tops by Mr Mitchell," Cavendish Mss VI(b), 18. Misplaced among Cavendish's magnetic papers is an experiment on strength of materials: "Exper. of Mitchell," ibid., IX, 13. In a journal by Cavendish recording a visit to Michell is a table of strata compiled by Michell: ibid., X(a), 3.

[18] Hugh Hamilton, *Philosophical Essays on the Following Subjects: On the Principles of Mechanics. II. On the Ascent of Vapours . . . III. Observations and Conjectures on the Nature of the Aurora Borealis, and the Tails of Comets* (Dublin, 1766).

"Plan of a Treatise on Mechanicks" for his departure from Newton's laws of motion.

Cavendish left one clue concerning the identity of his correspondent on heat. Comparing bismuth with two other metals, Cavendish said that bismuth differed from them by not "transmitting" heat as fast. He commented on his choice of words: "I forbear to use the word conducting as I know you have an aversion to the word, but perhaps you will say the word I use is as bad as that I forebear."[19] Water, air, and other fluids are conducted through pipes. If heat, as Cavendish believed, is not a fluid like water or air, "conduction" applied to heat could suggest false ideas. It would seem that Cavendish's correspondent agreed with him on the nature of heat. Since the fluid theory of heat was the prevalent theory, the circle of Cavendish's potential correspondents is not large. Nevertheless, in the absence of more revealing documents, we can only speculate about the identity of Cavendish's correspondent or correspondents.

ARSENIC

By the time of his earliest surviving chemical researches, Cavendish had been going to meetings of the Royal Society for seven years, and he had heard few reports on chemistry and little if anything of real substance. Of the chemical authors mentioned in Hadley's syllabus of his lectures on chemistry at Cambridge in 1758, with the exception of the Scottish chemist Joseph Black, all were foreign. The Londoner Henry Cavendish, who was just then setting out on his chemical researches, would have consulted foreign authors as a matter of course.

Cavendish's scientific manuscripts contain an experimental study of arsenic (arsenious oxide),[20] written for "you," and described ominously by one commentator as "Notes on some experiments with arsenic for the use of friends."[21] Cavendish did not say why he carried out this study, but we know that his point of departure was the French chemist Pierre Joseph Macquer's discovery and naming of "neutral arsenical salt" (potassium arsenate), which appeared in two

[19] "Experiments to Show That Bodies in Changing from a Solid State to a Fluid State Produce Cold and in Changing from a Fluid to a Solid State Produce Heat," Cavendish Mss Misc.; *Sci. Pap.* 2:348–51, on 350.

[20] The earliest chemical work by Cavendish for which there is an apparently complete record consists of the following: a bundle of fifty-nine numbered pages of laboratory notes on arsenic, with index; a carefully written, probably final, twenty-five page version of the account; and nineteen unpaginated pages constituting a rough draft. Cavendish Mss II, 1(a); II, 1(b); and II, 1(c). A brief description and analysis of these papers is given by Thorpe in *Sci. Pap.* 2:298–301. The date Dec. 1764 appears on p. 27 of the laboratory notes. The unnamed reader of the work is referred to as "you": "as you tell me you have tried yourself," and the "particulars of this exper. which I showed you before," II, 1(b):20, 25.

[21] Quoted in John Pearson, *The Serpent and the Stag: The Saga of England's Powerful and Glamorous Cavendish Family from the Age of Henry the Eighth to the Present* (New York: Holt, Rinehart and Winston, 1983), 118.

papers in the Paris Academy of Science's *Mémoires* in 1746 and 1748.[22] Macquer's work on arsenic was noticed in Britain; Hadley, as we mentioned, took an interest in it.[23]

In addition to Macquer's way of obtaining the neutral arsenical salt, Cavendish tried his own, dissolving arsenic in spirit of nitre (nitric acid), and then adding pearl ashes (potassium carbonate). He made a discovery: what combined with the alkali to form the neutral salt was an acid, but not any known acid, a new acid, "arsenical acid" ("if you will allow me to call it by that name").[24] Capable of neutralizing alkalies, this new substance had "all the properties of an acid," which Cavendish qualified with an implicit acknowledgment of the fatal reputation of arsenic, "unless perhaps it should fail in respect of taste which I have not thought proper to try."[25]

In going from a first draft to a revised draft, or letter-report, of his account of his researches on arsenic, Cavendish made revealing changes of wording. Whereas in the first draft he expressed his opinions, such as his differences with Macquer, forcefully, in the subsequent version he toned them down. Even in the semi-privacy of a correspondence, this man of strong feelings on scientific questions was guarded.

Ever since Wilson's biography, Cavendish has been described as a calculating machine, and although it is a caricature, he was that too, a man who made quantitative observations and copious calculations. He filled his laboratory notes with numbers standing for weights, expressed in ounces and their breakdown into drams and grains, or for specific gravities, the index of concentration, or for proportions of reactants. In connection with his measures, Cavendish spoke of "saturation," a term in use for the point at which acids in combination with other bodies lose their acidity, and also a term used to describe solutions in which a solvent has dissolved as much of a substance as it can. Cavendish's skill in quantitative work is fully evident in this early chemical research, in which he worked with uncommonly small amounts of substances, ounces instead of the familiar pounds, the mark of a skilled chemist. He had no need to perform experiments on a large scale, the purpose of which was to accomodate the "coarseness of tools, and clumsiness of operators."[26]

---

22 Pierre Joseph Macquer, "Researches sur l'arsenic. Premier mémoire," and "Second mémoire sur l'arsenic," *Mémoires de l'Académie Royale des Sciences*, 1746 (published 1751), pp. 223–36, and 1748 (published 1752), 35–50. Macquer later described this work in 1766 in his *Dictionary of Chemistry Containing the Theory and Practice of that Science . . .* , 2 vols., trans. J. Keir (London, 1771). The article "Neutral Arsenical Salt" is in vol. 2, pp. 666–67. Shortly before Cavendish's researches on the subject, Macquer's work was described in English in an annotation by William Lewis to his translation of Caspar Neumann, *The Chemical Works . . . Abridged and Methodized. With Large Additions, Containing the Later Discoveries and Improvements Made in Chemistry and the Arts Depending Thereon* (London, 1759), 143.

23 Coleby, "John Hadley," 301.

24 Cavendish, "Arsenic," Cavendish Mss II, 1(b):10.

25 Ibid. II, 1(b):13.

26 Charles Blagden, "Report on the Best Method of Proportioning the Excise upon Spiritous Liquors," *PT* 80 (1790): 321–45, on 340.

CHEMICAL LABORATORIES

32. *Chemical Laboratory. Copy of engraving by S. Wate(sp), P. C. Canot sculp. This idealized laboratory with metallurgical furnaces is from Lewis's* Commercium Philosophico-Technicum *(London, 1756). Courtesy of Smith Image Collection, Van Pelt-Dietrich Library, University of Pennsylvania.*

33. *Chemical Laboratory. Photograph of engraving, Deutsches Museum. From Denis Diderot's* Dictionnaire raisonne des arts et metiers*, 1780. Courtesy of Smith Image Collection, Van Pelt-Dietrich Library, University of Pennsylvania.*

In any experiment, he usually began with carefully measured quantities of substances, which he then combined and performed various operations on, and the products he obtained he would again weigh. Having once obtained the products, however, he would put them through a series of tests, "small experiments," as he called them, in which he did not record, and probably did not measure, the quantities involved. In his investigation of neutral arsenical salt, measurements and descriptions alike gave Cavendish indications of what was going on amidst the fumings, the shootings of crystals, and the other manifestations of chemical and physical activity.[27] To the extent that there was a difference between weighing and seeing, the former could be more accurate than the latter: "as well as could be judged by the eye," Cavendish wrote of one arsenic observation, a kind of qualification he did not make about weighing. Yet in his chemical work, his senses were fully engaged. By smell, he distinguished between the various acids and their products. He felt and observed textures: dry, hard, thin jelly, gluey, thick, stiff mud, lump. With colors, he made the greatest number of distinctions: milky, cloudy, yellow, pale straw, reddish yellow, pale madeira, red, reddish brown, dirty red, green, bluish green, pearl color, blue, and transparent, turgid, and muddy. No poet paid greater attention to his sensations than Cavendish did to his, even though, perhaps unlike the poet, he would not have considered his description of them as intuitively guided, independent of reason. Cavendish's notes on arsenic were the journal of a complete man, one of reason and of feeling, one whose whole being was, just then, concentrated on arsenic.

Under "complete," we include the thinking man, whose final goal was understanding. In the last draft of his paper, Cavendish devoted the longest section, roughly half of the whole paper, to theoretical conjectures together with experiments. The experiments he presented first, naturally, for by this time a priori theoretical conjectures were not regarded as the way to advance chemistry. But his underlying theoretical ideas did not arise inductively from his experiments; they came from the same place as his problem of arsenic, from the chemical literature of his day.

Although in the middle of the eighteenth century chemistry was still closely tied to pharmacy, medicine, metallurgy, and manufactures, it also had a fundamental scientific direction. One of its scientific sources was German, associated with Georg Stahl and his predecessor Johann Becher. Stahl gave the name "phlogiston" to the oily earth given off in combustion and presumed present in every combustible body, and although phlogiston was one of four elements of Stahl's chemistry (the other three being water, mercury, and another kind of earth), because of its ubiquitous presence in chemical processes of interest, his chemistry came to be known by the name "phlogiston." The other scientific source was associated with Boyle, Newton, and Boerhaave, who regarded chemistry as a branch of physical science.[28] After

---

[27] Henry Guerlac characterizes chemistry as a qualitative science using quantitative techniques in "Quantification in Chemistry," *Isis* 52 (1961): 194–214, on 196.

[28] Maurice Crosland, "The Development of Chemistry in the Eighteenth Century," *Studies on Voltaire* 24 (1963): 369–441, on 408, 440.

CHEMISTS

34. *Georg Ernst Stahl. Engraving. Courtesy of Smith Image Collection, Van Pelt-Dietrich Library, University of Pennsylvania.*

35. *The Honorable Robert Boyle. Engraving. G. Vertue, del. & sculp. 1739. I. Kersseboom, pinx. Courtesy of Smith Image Collection, Van Pelt-Dietrich Library, University of Pennsylvania.*

Newton, those who approached chemistry in this way thought of the attraction of chemical substances as analogous to the attraction of the earth and the moon, though many chemists, including Cavendish, preferred the name "affinity" to that of "attraction."[29] There were unsuccessful attempts to express this understanding mathematically, but for the most part, chemists used it as a guide in their researches, which they conducted experimentally. Cavendish adopted the physical approach to chemistry, which by this time had incorporated, or appropriated, the combustible principle, phlogiston, from Stahlian chemistry. Having made this traditional distinction between physical and chemical approaches to chemistry, we need to qualify it; for at this time the distinction between physics and chemistry was not always sharply drawn. For example, the distinction was clear in the case of the analysis of salts, but it was not in the study of the gaseous state of matter or in the study of thermal and electrical phenomena. In this chapter we discuss only Cavendish's early chemical researches, but we should point out that there are important connections between them and his early, practically concurrent researches in mechanics, heat, and electricity.

At the time Cavendish took up chemistry, the phlogiston theory had long been familiar in Germany, but in Britain and France it was just taking hold.[30] Macquer's text on theoretical and practical chemistry, translated in 1758, and William Lewis's translation of Caspar Neumann's writings in 1759 were the earliest accounts of phlogiston in English.[31] At the heart of the phlogiston theory was a unified explanation of combustion and of the calcination of metals, the latter being the transformation of metals by intense heating or by chemical combination into a powder having the properties of an earth. Metals, like ordinary combustibles, were thought to contain phlogiston in combination with another constituent, and just as when combustibles are burned their phlogiston separates and flies off, when metals are dissolved in acids they lose their phlogiston, the evidence for which is obvious to the senses in the form of flames and fumes. If a metal is deprived of its phlogiston by an acid and reduced to its calx, the reasoning went, the pure metal can be restored, if sometimes with difficulty, by combining the calx with an inflammable substance from which it extracts the lost phlogiston. Either by its presence or its absence, phlogiston determines most chemical reactions, and by keeping a balance sheet on phlogiston, the chemist could foresee the outcome of chemical processes. The experimental proof of

---

[29] A. M. Duncan, "Some Theoretical Aspects of Eighteenth-Century Tables of Affinity–I," *Annales of Science* 18 (1962): 177–94, on 184–85.

[30] Thomas L. Hankins, *Science and the Enlightenment* (Cambridge: Cambridge University Press, 1985), 95.

[31] W. A. Smeaton, "Macquer, Pierre Joseph," *DSB* 8:618–24, on 619. Macquer's *Élémens de chymie théorique* (Paris, 1749) and *Élémens de chymie pratique* (Paris, 1751) were brought out in English translation by Andrew Reid in 1758 as *Elements of the Theory and Practice of Chemistry*. Nathan Sivin, "William Lewis (1708–1781) as a Chemist," *Chymia* 8 (1962): 63–88, on 73. Neumann, *The Chemical Works . . .*

phlogiston seemed incontrovertible, which is why the physical school of chemistry needed it no less than did the Stahlian. Indispensable as it was as a chemical concept, phlogiston as a thing was elusive; it was widely believed to be the "least accurately known" of all chemical substances or principles, incapable of being isolated and studied on its own.[32]

"The only difference," Cavendish said, between arsenic and arsenical acid–between what he began with and what he ended with–is that the acid "is more thoroughly deprived of its Phlogiston."[33] Identifying arsenic with other "metallic substances," which by the phlogiston theory are rich in phlogiston, he accounted for the changes that arsenic undergoes in becoming the neutral salt and the acid by the readiness with which the attacking acid, spirit of nitre, unites with phlogiston.[34]

Before we discuss Cavendish's first publication in chemistry two years later, we need to discuss briefly his only other early surviving chemical research, done probably about the same time as his research on arsenic. This was on tartar, a hard, thick crust deposited on the sides of casks of wine, red or white depending on the color of the wine.[35] Tartar crystallizes upon evaporation, forming another crust, "cream of tartar," an acid. Cavendish's interest in tartar seems to have been in determining the amount of alkali in cream of tartar (potassium hydrogen tartrate), and in the soluble tartar (normal potassium tartrate). The stimulus no doubt was a publication in 1764 by the German chemist Andreas Sigismund Marggraf, who showed that despite its reputation as an acid, tartar contains an alkali.[36] A pupil of Caspar Neumann's and renowned for his precision, Marggraf has been called the "beginner of chemical analysis."[37] A great admirer of Marggraf, John Hadley said in his Cambridge lectures that Marggraf was the master of his science, the "most uncommonly Eminent whether we consider his ingenuity in Contriving, his practical Skill in conducting his Experiments, or his Sagacity and judgment in the Conclusions he draws from them."[38]

---

32 Thomas Thomson, *The History of Chemistry*, vol. 2 (London, 1831), 250–63. Macquer, *Dictionary* 2:516.

33 Cavendish Mss II, 1(b):16. Cavendish made the acid or, in effect, the same thing, the neutral arsenical salt, three ways: distilling arsenic with nitre, dissolving arsenic in concentrated nitric acid, and heating arsenic with fixed alkali. All three ways had the same rationale: the effect of exposing a metal (for that is how he regarded arsenic) to an acid, or to heat and open air, was to deprive it of its phlogiston.

34 Macquer wrote: "Nothing can equal the impetuosity with which nitrous acid joins itself to phlogiston." *Dictionary of Chemistry* 1:11.

35 Cavendish did two sets of experiments, describing them on numbered sheets: "old experiments on tartar," 10 ff., and "new experiments on tartar," 24 ff. plus 6 more sheets. Cavendish Mss II, 2(a) and 2(b), respectively.

36 Thorpe, in *Sci. Pap.* 2:301. Cavendish "discovered the true nature of cream of tartar (potassium hydrogen tartrate) and its relation to soluble tartar (normal potassium tartrate)": J. R. Partington, *A Short History of Chemistry*, 3d ed. (London: Macmillan, 1957), 104.

37 Thomson, *History of Chemistry* 1:271.

38 Coleby, "John Hadley," 295.

Both tartaric acid and arsenical acid later became known to chemists through publications by the Swedish chemist Carl Wilhelm Scheele, who became celebrated for his discoveries of acids.[39] If Cavendish had published his researches on these subjects, he would have come before the chemical world as an accomplished analytical chemist, one who had gone beyond Marggraf, who "did not attempt numerical results."[40] As it happened, he came before the chemical world as the other type of investigator of importance for eighteenth-century chemistry, a pneumatic chemist. Because of his surviving early chemical manuscripts, we can see how he moved from being the one to being the other.

FACTITIOUS AIR

"Air," "effervescence," "vapors," and "fumes" are words that appear throughout Cavendish's writing on arsenic. Likewise the spectacular aerial effects of experimenting on tartar were widely remarked on at the time, for example, by Hadley, who discussed Hales's production of "fixed air" from the action of acids on tartar. In his *Treatise on Air* in 1781, Tiberius Cavallo gave quantitative examples of the abundant production of fixed air from cream of tartar and salt of tartar; he took figures from Cavendish's first published work on pneumatic chemistry.[41] So powerful was the release of air from tartar that vessels used in the distilling burst into slivers.[42] Air, as Hales had shown, is a chemically active substance, and referring to air as a constituent that passes from substance to substance and sometimes flies off, Cavendish took into account the weight of air in his analytical studies of arsenic and tartar. He did not yet collect air and study it in its own right, but he was already halfway to pneumatic chemistry. Cavendish continued on that course in his first chemical analysis to appear in print. William Heberden's brother, Thomas, had collected an alkali from the lip of a volcano, a place where brimstone might be expected but not a salt like the one he found. From experiments "made and communicated to me by the Hon. Henry Cavendish," William Heberden laid down, and set off in quotation marks, a set of propositions about the salt in question. Cavendish found that this salt differed from the vegetable alkali in that it crystallized without the addition of "fixed air." Here, in a footnote, he cited Black's experiments on magnesia alba. These experiments together with Hales's earlier experiments on air released from bodies provided the foundation of eighteenth-century pneumatic chemistry. In this chemi-

[39] Karl Wilhelm Scheele, "On Arsenic and Its Acid," in *The Chemical Essays of Charles-William Scheele*, trans. with additions by T. Beddoes (London, 1786), 143–86. Partington, *History* 2:729. Thomson, *History of Chemistry* 2:63.

[40] Thomson, *History of Chemistry* 1:271–73.

[41] Tiberius Cavallo, *Treatise on the Nature and Properties of Air, and Other Permanently Elastic Fluids . . .* (London, 1781), 594–96, 606–8.

[42] Antoine Laurent Lavoisier, *Essays on the Effects Produced by Various Processes on Atmospheric Air; with a Particular View to an Investigation of the Constitution of the Acids*, trans. T. Henry (Warrington, 1783), 7.

cal examination of a mineral for his friend Heberden, Cavendish may have been encouraged to begin, if he was not already set upon, his course as a pneumatic chemist.[43]

We need to say more about Black's work. In 1756 Black published an enlarged, English version of his medical thesis at the University of Edinburgh, "Experiments upon Magnesia Alba, Quicklime, and Some Other Alcaline Substances." The origin of this, Black's only major publication, was practical, the medical problem of urinary-tract stones, but in it Black dealt only briefly with the medical virtues of magnesia and extensively with its chemistry. Twenty-seven years old and already a master of the chemical art, Black had an advantage Cavendish did not, a great teacher of chemistry, William Cullen, who regarded chemistry as a branch of natural philosophy with laws as fixed as those of mechanics. Black, who informed himself of the wider world of chemistry, was, like Cavendish, an admirer of Macquer, recommending his text to his students. He was also an admirer of Marggraf, a reason for, or a reflection of, the closeness of Black's and Cavendish's work in chemistry. Black told Cullen that he would rather have written Marggraf's works than anything else in the library of chemistry. Showing his knowledge of the chemist's standard practice, Black determined, for example, the place of magnesia in Geoffroy's table of affinities, but his originality in chemistry began with his observation that when subjected to fire, magnesia lost a great proportion of its weight and that the lost portion was air. His experiments on magnesia led him to the nature of quicklime, that most caustic of substances. Its causticity is inherent in the alkali, Black concluded, made manifest when the alkali is deprived of its air. He showed that this same air, "fixed air" (not an original term), is found in other alkalis and that it is chemically distinct from common air, a novel claim. Like Hales, whom he acknowledged, and like Cavendish, Black did not begin his investigation with air but concluded with it. Like Hales and others, he had observed chemists operating upon a substance when part of it "vanished from their senses," and he intended to study the vanishing part, air, in its own right; he did not get to it, however, leaving the field to Cavendish and others. More than anyone before him, Black used the chemical balance to advantage, and in this too Cavendish was to follow in Black's footsteps.[44]

---

43 William Heberden, "Some Account of a Salt Found on the Pic of Teneriffe," *PT* 55 (1765): 57–60. This paper was read at the Royal Society on 7 Feb. 1764.

44 Henry Guerlac, "Black, Joseph," *DSB* 2:173–83; "Joseph Black and Fixed Air. A Bicentenary Retrospective, with Some New or Little Known Material," *Isis* 48 (1957): 124–51, 433–56. William Ramsay, *The Life and Letters of Joseph Black, M.D.* (London: Constable, 1918), 4–5, 14–15. The observation that inspired Black's and his followers' enquiry was that "chemists have often observed, in their distillations, that part of a body has vanished from their senses, notwithstanding the utmost care to retain it; and they have always found, upon further inquiry, that subtile part to be air, which having been imprisoned in the body, under a solid form, was set free and rendered fluid and elastic by the fire." Joseph Black, *Experiments upon Magnesia Alba, Quicklime, and Some Other Alkaline Substances* (1756; reprint, Edinburgh: Alembic Club Reprints, No. 1, 1898), 16.

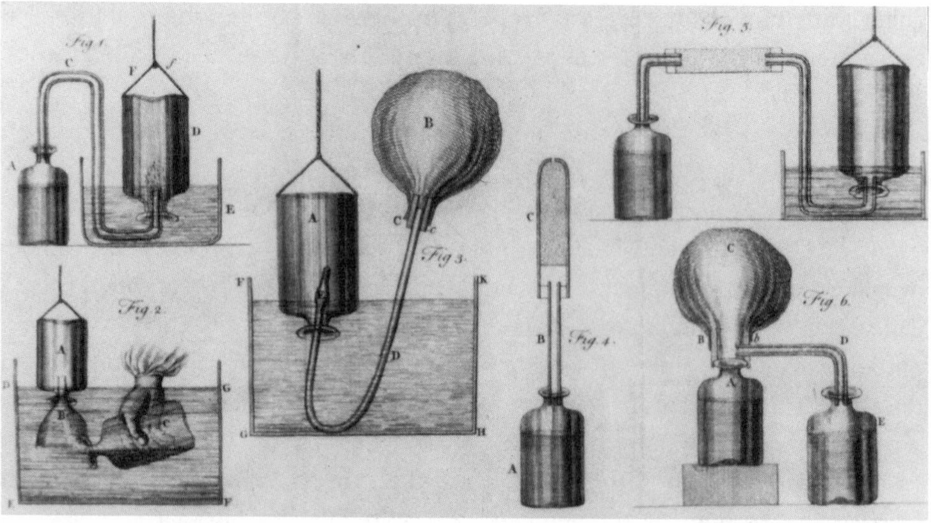

36. *Factitious-Air Apparatus. Fig. 1 shows Cavendish's technique for filling a bottle D with air. The bottle containing water is inverted in the vessel of water E; the air to be captured is generated by dissolving metals in acids and by other means in bottle A. Cavendish's measure of quantity of air is the weight of the water it displaces in D. Fig. 2 shows how he transfers air from one bottle to another. Fig. 3 shows how he withdraws air from a bottle by means of a bladder. The speckled substance in Figs. 4 and 5 is dry pearl ash, through which air is passed to free it from water and acid. "Three Papers, Containing Experiments on Factitious Air,"* Philosophical Transactions *56 (1766): 141.*

Cavendish's first scientific publication under his own name came in 1766, his second in 1767, both appearing in the *Philosophical Transactions.* Recall that this was a journal for all of the sciences; and so it was entirely reasonable that his first publication should be preceded by a paper by John Michell on the determination of a degree of longitude at the equator and a paper on an uncommonly large hernia and followed by an account of the Polish cochineal and four more papers about animals. Cavendish's second paper found itself in similar mixed company: one paper preceding his was an account of men "eight feet tall, most considerably more," observed near the Straits of Magellan, in the country of Patagonia, in 1764; another was an account of a locked jaw and a paralysis cured by electricity; the paper following his was about a meteor and the one after that about swarms of gnats, seen at Oxford.

Cavendish's first scientific publication was, in fact, three papers published as one, as the title indicates, "Three Papers, Containing Experiments on Factitious Air." The first paper was read at the Royal Society on 29 May 1766, just before the long summer recess, the remaining two at successive meetings on 6 and 13 November right after the recess. Cavendish drafted a fourth paper but withheld it. The papers, the three published ones and the unpublished fourth, formed a series; the experiments they reported were related to each other by subject, methods, apparatus, and theoretical logic. Each is about a certain kind of factitious air produced by a certain kind of process: inflammable air from metals and acids; fixed air from alkalis and acids or calcination; mixed airs from organic substances by fermentation and putrefaction; other mixed airs from organic substances by distillation. Within the text, the divisions are called "parts" rather than "papers"; adopting that terminology, we refer to the publication as one paper with several parts.

Cavendish's first paper presented a highly systematic investigation of an entire experimental field, that of factitious air. Instead of using the term "factitious" air to characterize the field, he might have used "fixed," since the usual meaning of "fixed air" then was any sort of air contained in bodies. But he wanted to retain a specific meaning for "fixed air," the air that Black had studied. To avoid confusion Cavendish borrowed Boyle's expression "factitious air" for the general case. By "factitious air," Cavendish meant "any kind of air which is contained in other bodies in an unelastic state, and is produced from thence by art."[45]

Part one of Cavendish's paper is about a new factitious air, our inflammable gas hydrogen. His techniques for collecting and transferring airs can most readily be grasped by looking at his drawings, which we reproduce here. His usual method of measuring the "quantity of air" was by collecting the air in a bottle and observing a mark on the side of it, which gave the weight of water required to fill the bottle to that level. In either spirit of salt (hydrochloric acid) or dilute oil of vitriol (sulphuric acid), he dissolved each of three metals, zinc, iron, and tin, and he investigated the air that was then released. He determined that it was permanently elastic, insoluble in water, and explosive when lit in the presence of common air. He measured the density of several samples and compared it with the density of common air and of water; calculating a mean value, he concluded that the air was "8700 times lighter than water." He determined that the air was capable of holding "1/9 its weight of moisture," and that "its specific gravity in that state is 7840 times less than that of water."[46] These figures and others served to specify the physical properties of a new substance, to which Cavendish gave the name "inflammable air." On the day the first part of Cavendish's paper was read, the secretary of the Royal Society wrote in the "Journal Book" that "it is impossible to do Justice to the Experiments under the title 'On Inflammable Air' without reciting them wholly."[47] We agree with the secretary.

Part two of Cavendish's paper is about "fixed air," our carbon dioxide, the factitious air released by alkalies upon being dissolved in acid or calcined. As he had with inflammable air, Cavendish examined fixed air for elasticity, solubility,

---

45 Cavendish, "Three Papers, Containing Experiments on Factitious Air," *PT* 56 (1766): 141–84; in *Sci. Pap.* 2:77–101, on 77.

46 Cavendish, "Three Papers," 85–86.

47 29 May 1766, Royal Society, JB 25:876.

and combustibility. Though permanently elastic, fixed air, Cavendish found, had properties distinct from those of inflammable air and common air. It did not support fire, and it was soluble in water, for which reason Cavendish collected it over mercury or caught it directly. In fact it proved to have varying solubilities in water, which suggested to Cavendish that "fixed air obtained in marble consists of substances of different natures." He determined the weight of fixed air "in the same manner" as he had that of inflammable air. He determined its quantity in several alkaline substances, the results of which he expressed in terms of a standard, marble; he found that a parcel of volatile sal ammoniac, for example, "contains more fixed air, in proportion to the quantity of acid that it can saturate, than marble does, in the proportion of . . . 217 to 100."[48]

Cavendish's point of departure in part three was the work on fermented and putrefied substances by the Irish physician David Macbride. In 1764 Macbride published a book of experiments designed to show that fixed air is the cement of living bodies and that a putrefying body is one which has lost its cement. He took his understanding of air from Hales, but he also cited Black, the first to do so in print if only just before Cavendish (in his contribution to Heberden's paper).[49] Cavendish looked to see if fermentation and putrefaction yielded any factitious airs other than Black's fixed air. Air from fermented sugar he found to be fixed air, though by examining its solubility, he found that it, like the fixed air from marble, "consists of substances of different nature."[50] The air he obtained from putrefying gravy broth and raw meat he found to be a mixture of fixed air and inflammable air, neither pure.

The fourth part, which Cavendish carefully drafted for publication but then did not submit, again treats vegetable and animal substances, this time wood, tartar, and hartshorn.[51] Cavendish distilled these substances, obtaining a mixture of inflammable and nonflammable airs.[52] His laboratory notes indicate that he returned to this subject later but with no more conclusiveness.

Cavendish's study of factitious air reveals his great caution. The inflammable air produced by putrefaction was "nearly of the same kind" as the inflammable air from metals but "not exactly the same" or else mixed with "some air heavier than it."[53] An intended addendum to part one, a fuller version of his the-

[48] Cavendish, "Three Papers," 89, 91, 93.

[49] E. L. Scott, "The 'Macbridean Doctrine' of Air; an Eighteenth-Century Explanation of Some Biochemical Processes Including Photosynthesis," *Ambix* 17 (1970): 43–57, on 44–49.

[50] Cavendish, "Three Papers," 98.

[51] This unpublished paper is printed, "Experiments on Factitious Air. Part IV. Containing Experiments on the Air Produced from Vegetable and Animal Substances by Distillation," in *Sci. Pap.* 2:307–16.

[52] The mixture contained marsh gas, carbonic oxide, and hydrogen. Thorpe, in *Sci. Pap.* 2:315–16.

[53] Cavendish, "Three Papers," 100.

ory of the solution of metals in acids from his arsenic paper, is just as tentatively expressed, "I have not indeed made sufficient experiments to speak quite positively as to this point."[54] Another form of caution was patient foresight: Cavendish inverted a flask of fixed air over mercury "upwards of a year."[55] His caution can be recognized in other ways. He repeated his experiments and took the mean of the results. He estimated accuracies: in determining how much fixed air water absorbs, his accuracy was "about three or four 1000th parts of the whole bulk of air introduced."[56] He used the correct number of places of numbers, claiming no greater accuracy for his conclusions than was justified by his measurements; he gave the specific gravities of inflammable and fixed airs to three places, which was the maximum accuracy for measurements of that sort.[57]

Because of the importance of phlogiston in the ensuing debates in chemistry, we conclude this discussion of Cavendish's early work in chemistry with his view of the subject. In his paper of 1766, Cavendish wrote that when certain metals and acids react, the phlogiston of the metals flies off "without having its nature changed by the acid" and "forms inflammable air."[58] Thomas Thomson, chemist and historian of chemistry, understood Cavendish to mean that inflammable air from metals was pure phlogiston.[59] Vernon Harcourt, a somewhat later chemist who studied Cavendish's work historically, concluded that Cavendish identified phlogiston with inflammable air "as early as 1766, or very soon after": Cavendish found that there was more than one species of inflammable air, but since the one he obtained from zinc and iron had a constant specific gravity and was constant in its combining properties, "*his Phlogiston* therefore *was* hydrogen and nothing else."[60] We are inclined to agree with Thomson and Harcourt. To many of Cavendish's contemporaries, phlogiston was another of the special weightless fluids, but it almost certainly was not regarded that way by Cavendish. He rejected the two leading directions of speculation in natural philosophy at that time: that of an all-pervading ether, and that of imponderable fluids. He never spoke of the ether; he denied that heat is a fluid; he believed that light has weight; he never referred to magnetic fluids. He accepted electricity as a fluid distinct from ordinary matter, but he never referred to it as imponderable. He never referred to phlogiston as "something" incapable of being isolated and studied in

---

[54] "On the Solution of Metals in Acids. Digression to Paper on Inflammable Air," in *Sci. Pap.* 2:305–7, on 305.

[55] Cavendish, "Three Papers," 88.

[56] Ibid., 89.

[57] William Nicholson's comments in his translation of the notes by French chemists to the French edition of Richard Kirwan, *An Essay on Phlogiston, and the Constitution of Acids*, new ed. (London, 1789), vii–ix.

[58] Cavendish, "Three Papers," 79.

[59] Thomson, *History of Chemistry* 2:340.

[60] W. Vernon Harcourt, Presidential Address, *British Association Report*, 1839, pp. 3–45, on p. 28.

its own right. The identification of phlogiston in its elastic state with inflammable air is consistent with Cavendish's natural philosophy and with the experiments he reported in his paper of 1766.

We realize that a counterargument can be made. To begin with, there is Cavendish's always-cautious wording: in 1766 he wrote that phlogiston "forms" (not "is") inflammable air. We note too that there was no contemporary response, and that chemists who later identified phlogiston with inflammable air did not credit Cavendish with the idea. In a more explicit manner than Cavendish, Richard Kirwan asserted ("proved") the identity of phlogiston and inflammable air in 1782. Having explained the origin of inflammable air from the solution of metals in acids much as Cavendish did, Kirwan went on to interpret the difference between phlogiston contained in metals and phlogiston as inflammable air in a way that Cavendish would have rejected, by calling upon the material theory of heat: in its two states, fixed and free, phlogiston has different proportions of Black's "elementary fire."[61] A year later, guided by experiments of his own, Joseph Priestley also identified phlogiston and inflammable air.[62] But by this time Cavendish had reformulated his understanding of phlogiston in light of his experiments on water and air. What exactly Cavendish thought about the relationship between phlogiston and inflammable air at the time of his first paper we may never know for certain, and Cavendish himself may have believed that his experiments were not decisive on this point. We do know that for the next twenty years he carried out experiments within phlogiston chemistry, and that phlogiston, whatever its exact constitution, served him well.

Following the work of Black, in his first published paper Cavendish helped discredit the ancient idea of a single, universal air. For two kinds of air, inflammable and fixed, he gave a complete analysis, demonstrating that these two species of air differ from common air, and in the case of inflammable air obtained from certain metals, he determined that it was a single, uniform substance, elastic phlogiston. Black later explained why Cavendish did not recognize that fixed air too was a single substance like inflammable air, but the incompleteness of his analysis of this and other kinds of air only revealed the difficulty and challenge of the field; it did not detract from his accomplishment, which was the "first attempt by chemists to collect the different kinds of air, and endeavour to ascertain their nature";[63] it was Cavendish, Thomas Thomson wrote, who "first began the true investigation

[61] Richard Kirwan, "Continuation of the Experiments and Observations on the Specific Gravities and Attractive Powers of Various Saline Substances," *PT* 72 (1782): 179–236, on 195–97.

[62] Joseph Priestley, "Experiments Relating to Phlogiston, and the Seeming Conversion of Water into Air," *PT* 73 (1783): 398–434, on 400.

[63] A. L. Donovan, *Philosophical Chemistry in the Scottish Enlightenment: The Doctrines and Discoveries of William Cullen and Joseph Black* (Edinburgh: University of Edinburgh Press, 1975), 219. J. R. Partington, *A History of Chemistry*, vol. 3 (London: Macmillan, 1962), 316.

of gases," extending the "bounds of pneumatic chemistry, with the caution and precision of a Newton."[64]

Cavendish's study of factitious air offered the chemists who followed him a wealth of methods for collecting, transferring, and measuring air and for isolating and characterizing different kinds of air, a "model to future experimenters."[65] Cavendish opened an avenue to the new field of pneumatic chemistry.

In the following year, 1767, Cavendish published an analysis of mineral water obtained from Rathbone-Place.[66] Produced by a spring, the water until a few years before had been raised by an engine for public distribution in the neighborhood immediately north of Soho Square. Now a pump remained, from which Cavendish drew his sample, which was "foul to the eye," and on which a "scurf" formed upon standing. The occasion for Cavendish's analysis of this unappealing water was evidently a paper in the *Philosophical Transactions* in 1765 by William Brownrigg, a physician in Whitehaven who studied the bad air from James Lowther's coal mines. Brownrigg reported that spa water in Germany released fixed air when it was heated.[67] Looking to see if the same was true of Rathbone-Place water, Cavendish arrived at this conclusion: the reason for the suspension of earth in Rathbone-Place water was its combination with more than its normal amount of fixed air.[68] His finding on solubilities (of certain bicarbonates) can in this sense be seen as a continuation of his study of fixed air; it was also the first analysis of a mineral water that could claim "tolerable accuracy."[69] Cavendish concluded his analysis by examining three other London waters, including water from a pump near his house on Great Marlborough Street.

Writing about the analysis of waters a few years later, the Swedish chemist Tobern Bergman said that it was "one of the most difficult problems in chemistry" because there were so many impurities in the water and their quantities were so small.[70] For these reasons, it was the kind of problem to show off Cavendish's skills as a chemist. But these had already been demonstrated, and acknowledged: for his work the year before on factitious air, he had been awarded the Copley Medal of the Royal Society.

---

64 Thomson, *History of Chemistry* 1:343 and 2:1.

65 Ibid., 1:343.

66 "Experiments on Rathbone-Place Water," *PT* 57 (1767): 92–108; in *Sci. Pap.* 2:102–11.

67 William Brownrigg, "An Experimental Enquiry into the Mineral Elastic Spirit, or Air, Contained in Spa Water; as Well as into the Mephitic Qualities of this Spirit," *PT* 55 (1765): 218–35. J. Russell-Wood, "The Scientific Work of William Brownrigg, M.D., F.R.S. (1711–1800).–I," *Annals of Science* 6 (1950): 436–47, on 436–38, 441.

68 Cavendish, "Experiments on Rathbone-Place Water," 107.

69 Thomson, *History of Chemistry* 2:344.

70 Tobern Bergman, "Of the Analysis of Waters," in his *Physical and Chemical Essays*, vol. 1, trans. with notes by E. Cullen (London, 1784), 91–192, on 109.

In 1766, together with Cavendish, two others received the Copley Medal, Brownrigg for his analysis of mineral water, which we have discussed, and Edward Delaval for his study of the colors of metal films. Delaval, who had been a student at Cambridge when Cavendish was there, was now a fellow of his college, Pembroke Hall, and a chemist. Experimenting with thin metal deposits on glass, Delaval showed that metals differ in color in the order of their density, a kind of study which could be labeled chemical optics.[71] The year 1766 was the year of the chemists.

WORKPLACE

By all accounts, Cavendish cut a somewhat awkward figure in public. He did not do so at home, however, where everything was made to fit. Furnished in the taste of the scientific revolution, with instruments and books, his home was the location of his chosen life.

We conclude our discussion of Cavendish's early researches with their setting, his workplace. The gentleman's double house on Great Marlborough Street, with its elegant stairs leading off the entrance and its rooms used for entertaining, was unlikely to have been used also as a chemical laboratory reeking of fumes. If Henry Cavendish carried out his chemical researches at home, as seems likely, the location would have been either the stables or the separate apartment on the grounds behind the main house, and most likely in the former. Since we know that his father had chemicals, a laboratory in some form was undoubtedly already in place for Henry. By the time he wrote his earliest papers on chemistry, he had an elaborate chemical establishment. Few visitors entered his laboratory, and although neither those who did nor Cavendish himself left a description of it, we know in general what it had to be like. It would not have been located in the underground rooms of the separate building behind the main house, for in the dampness there, metals would have rusted, furnaces collected mold, salts turned watery, and labels fallen off bottles. The laboratory would have been in a ground floor room or, as it has been suggested, in a room in or above the stables. In either case the room had openings to the outside at each end to admit fresh air and clear away poisonous vapors.

The equipment in Cavendish's laboratory would have varied according to the experiments he was making, but we can form a general picture of what was there. There was a chimney high enough to walk under and wide enough to walk in front of. Beneath it were various furnaces and probably a double bellows to fan the flames from gentle heat to red hot. Ready at hand, suspended on hooks, would have been pokers, pincers, tongs, shovels, and pans, much as in a kitchen of that day. Near the chimney was an anvil along with hammers

[71] Edward Delaval, "A Letter . . . Containing Experiments and Observations on the Agreement between the Specific Gravities of the Several Metals, and Their Colours When United to Glass, as Well as Those of Their Other Preparations," *PT* 55 (1765): 10–38.

and a range of other tools. Lining the walls were shelves for containers, chemicals, and bins for storing bulk charcoal, sand, and quicklime. Since acids, alkalis, metals, and earths had to be as pure as possible, standing in a corner of the laboratory was a lead or stone "fountain" with a drain pipe for cleaning vessels after each use, no doubt by an "assistant." In the center of the room was a large table for chemical operations not requiring high heat. On it, we suppose, were scales, mortars and pestles, filtration paper, corks, stirrers, and, not least, pencils, pens and ink, and a stack of small sheets of paper for keeping notes of what happened.[72] From Cavendish's manuscripts, we can be specific about what he required to carry out his early researches. Heat entered into most of the operations: roasting, calcining, dissolving, subliming, evaporating, and distilling. There was a sand pot for distilling at "sand heat" and for holding bottles. His sources of heat were lamps, a forge, and a reverberatory furnace designed to direct the flame back on the heated substance. The latter furnace he placed high into the chimney in anticipation of "obnoxious" fumes. Other operations included precipitating, crystallizing, filtering, deliquescing, and weighing. Cavendish's scales were of high quality, since for him weighing was the method of chemical precision. He had at hand an elaborate collection of containers, some metal, some earthen, most glass. There were open flasks, Florence flasks (having long, narrow necks), retorts (having downward bending necks for distilling), receivers (flasks for retaining condensates and distillates), adaptors (for connecting retorts and receivers), pipkins (small pots and pans), bottles of various sizes, and copper pipes. There was a lead crucible for keeping the bottom of another crucible placed in it cooler than the top, a kind of inverted double-boiler. There was another crucible designed by Cavendish for use in the reverberatory furnace, complete with a set of aludels (pear-shaped pots open at the bottom as well as the top and made to fit over one another for subliming). Cavendish's apparatus was made for the purpose, to which he added a humble coffee cup for calcining. His reagents were many: solvents, acids, solutions of metals in acids, alkalis, neutral salts, and solutions and treated papers for testing acids and alkalis. Cavendish's chemical experiments depended on a sizable investment in chemical apparatus and supplies. The chemist James Keir may have had Cavendish in mind when he gave as one reason for the emergence of chemistry as a science its recent cultivation by "persons who employ the advantages attending rank, opulence, leisure, and philosophical minds."[73]

[72] We have been guided in our sketch of Cavendish's laboratory by the entry "Laboratory (Chemical)" in Pierre Joseph Macquer's *Dictionary of Chemistry,* published in 1766, just after Cavendish had begun his recorded chemical experiments. Macquer's laboratory was intended for the "philosophical chemist," and with his list of reagents, it sufficed for "any chemical experiment." See note 22, above.

[73] James Keir, "Preface," p. iii, in his translation in 1771 of Macquer's *Dictionary of Chemistry.*

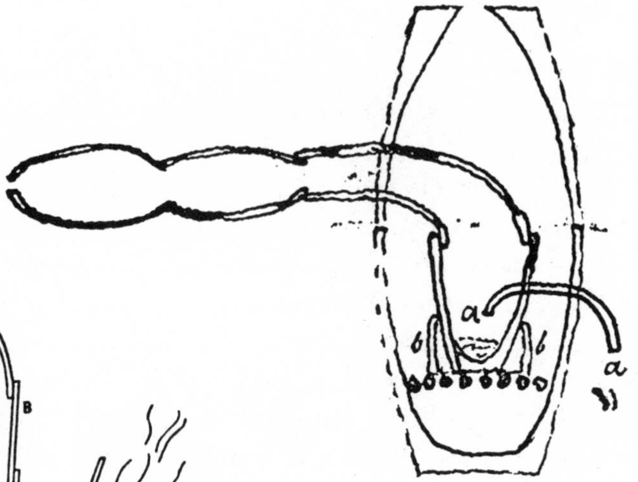

Fig. 2.

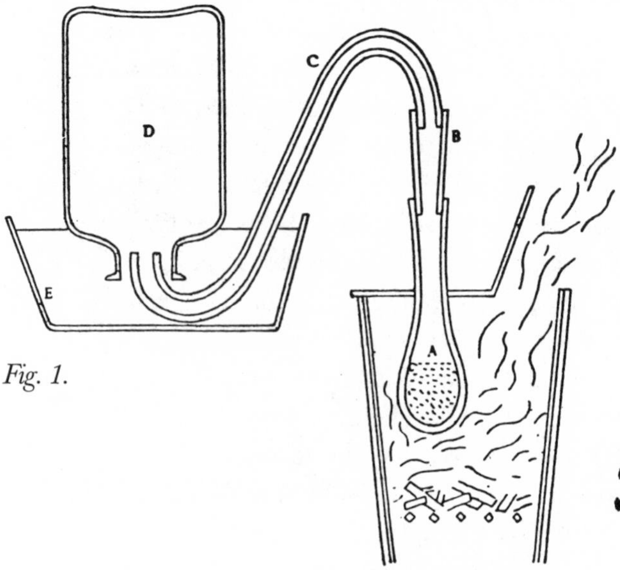

Fig. 1.

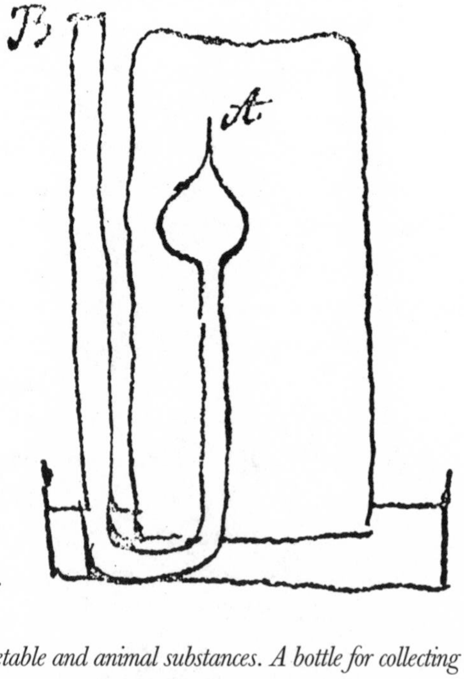

Fig. 3.

37. *Laboratory Apparatus. Fig. 1. Apparatus for distilling vegetable and animal substances. A bottle for collecting air, D, is filled with water and then inverted into vessel E filled with water. Cavendish,* Sci. Pap. *2:308. Fig. 2. Apparatus for subliming arsenic in a crucible, with a set of aludels attached, placed within a reverberatory furnace. Cavendish Scientific Manuscripts II, 1(b):21. Fig. 3. Apparatus for measuring the expansion of air with heat; the bent tube contains mercury and air. Reproductions by permission of the Chatsworth Settlement Trustees.*

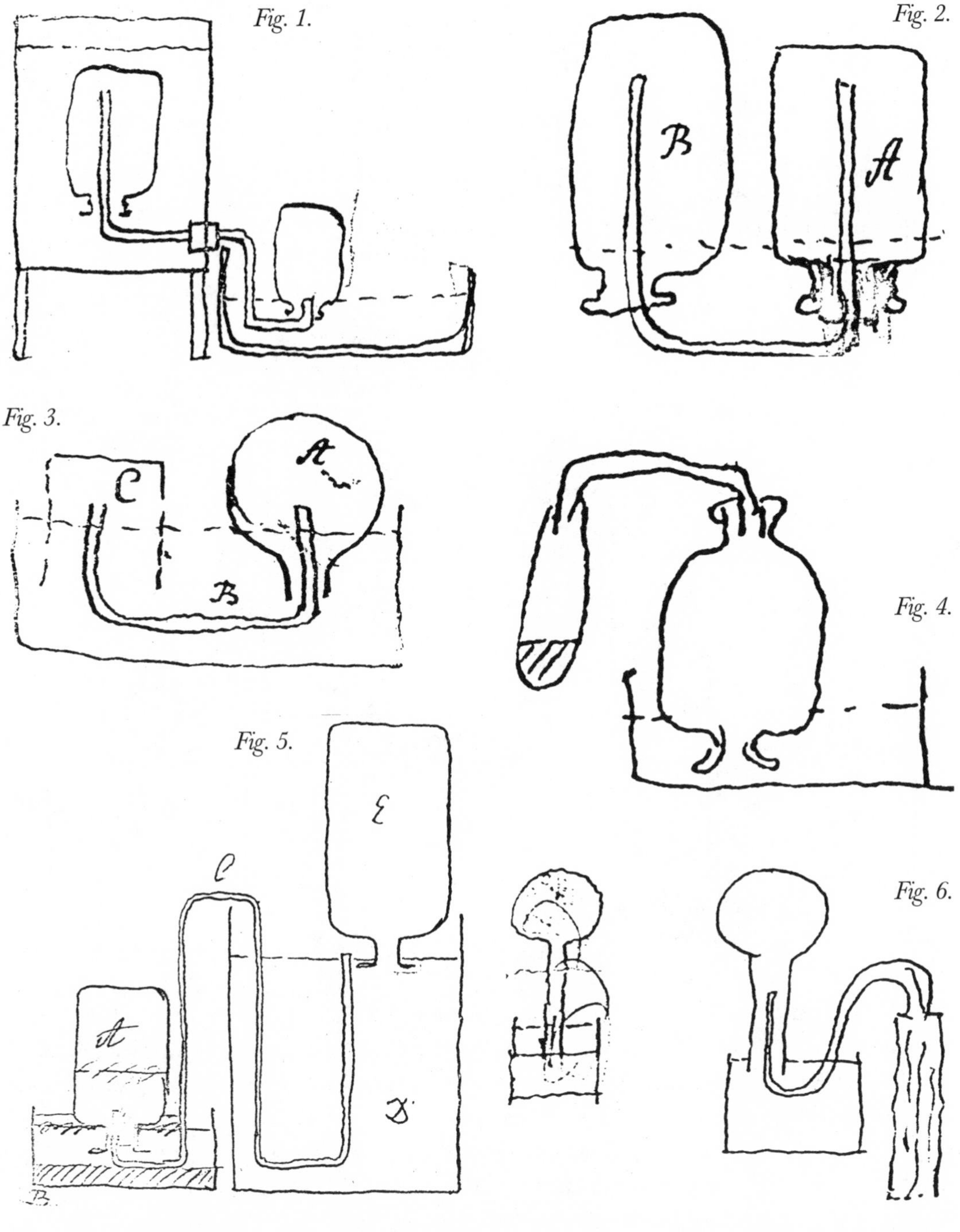

38. *Laboratory Apparatus. Fig. 1. Apparatus to decide if heavier airs in a mixture of airs settle to the bottom. The mixture is contained in the bottle on the left, and as water is gradually let into it, different samples are caught in bottles on the right. Cavendish Scientific Manuscripts II, 5:102. Fig. 2. Apparatus for eudiometer experiments. Bottle B is filled with nitrous air, bottle A with common air. Ibid., 42. Fig. 3. Apparatus for the diminution of air by burning sulphur. Ibid., 61. Fig. 4. Apparatus for capturing air upon boiling burnt charcoal with spirit of nitre. Ibid., 345. Fig. 5. Apparatus to determine if fixed air is produced by mixing common or dephlogisticated air in bottle A with nitrous air in bottle E. Ibid., 5. Fig. 6. Apparatus to determine the effect on the volume of dry air by saturating it with moisture. Cavendish Scientific Manuscripts Misc. Reproductions by permission of the Chatsworth Settlement Trustees.*

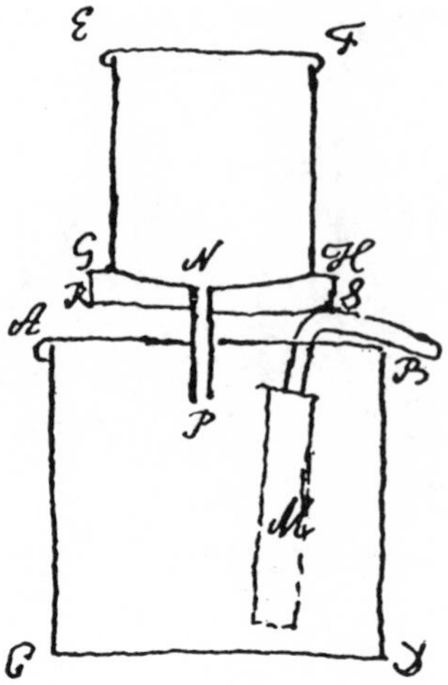

Fig. 1.

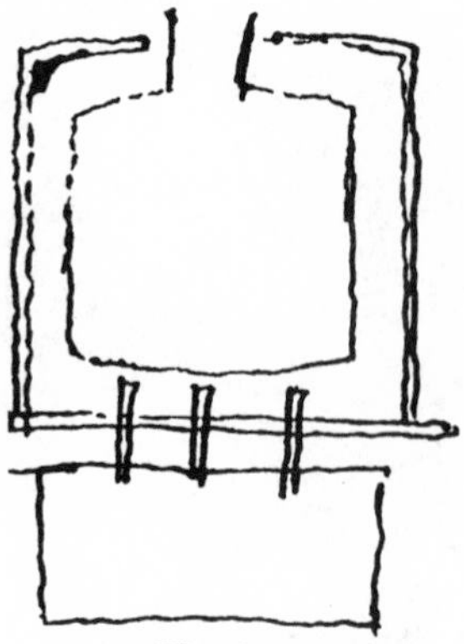

Fig. 2.

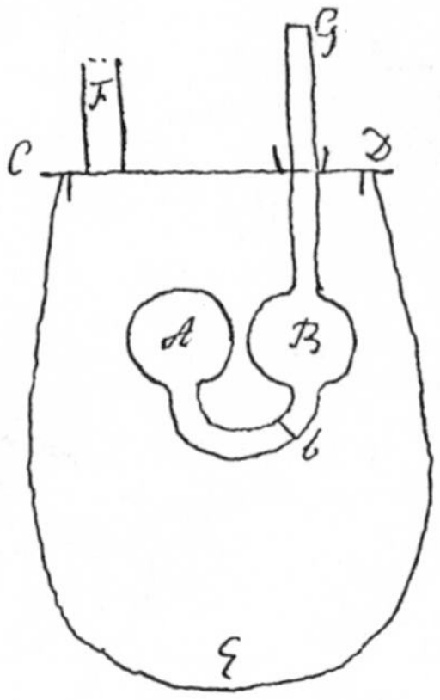

Fig. 3.

Fig. 4.

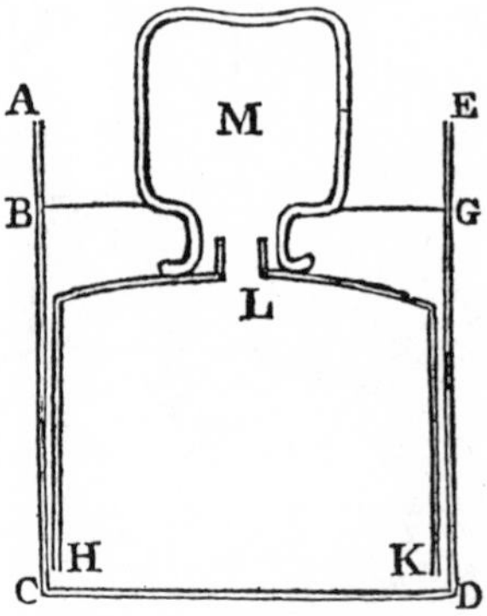

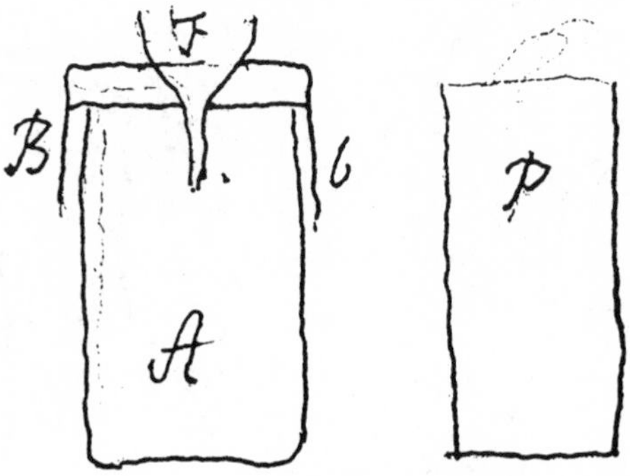

Fig. 5.

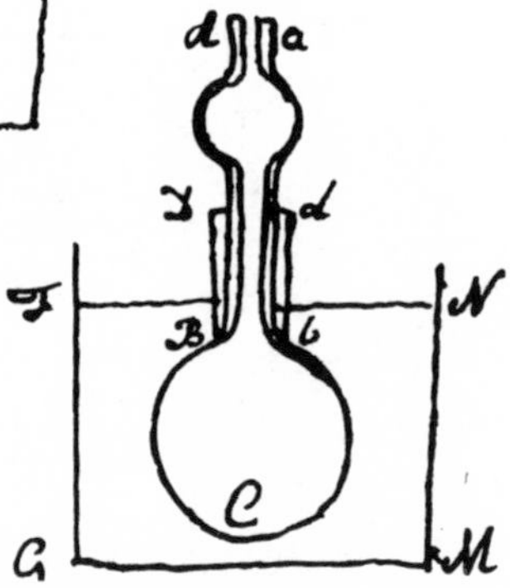

Fig. 6.

39. *Laboratory Apparatus. Fig. 1. Apparatus for experiments on the heats of mixtures. Through the cylindrical funnel on top, hot water is added to cold water in the pan below; M is a stirrer. Cavendish Scientific Manuscripts, untitled paper on experiments on specific and latent heats, p. 2. Fig. 2. Apparatus for determining the time of evaporation of boiling water. The water is contained in a tin bottle surrounded by an insulated tin frame and placed over a spirit lamp. Cavendish Scientific Manuscripts III(a), 9:42. Fig. 3. Apparatus to decide if the heat at which water becomes steam is the same as the heat of the steam. The ball A, which contains a little water and otherwise is filled with mercury to b, is exposed to steam and to the boiling water. Ibid., 1:1. Fig. 4. Apparatus for collecting air discharged from pump water when it is boiled; the pump water is in ACDE, the air in M. Cavendish,* Sci. Pap. *2:105. Fig. 5. Apparatus to find the weight of fixed air in calcareous earth. Acid is poured through the funnel onto a sample of earth contained in cylindrical glass A; after effervescence, the plug P is drawn in and out of the empty part of A to drive out any residual fixed air. Cavendish Scientific Manuscripts II, 5:379. Fig. 6. Apparatus to determine if the electrical charge of coated glass is the same whether hot or cold. The glass bulb C is filled with mercury as is the surrounding vessel, rendering it a Leyden jar, the charge of which is tested while a thermometer is dipped into the mercury at different heats. Cavendish,* Electrical Researches, *opposite p. 180. Reproductions by permission of the Chatsworth Settlement Trustees.*

Fig. 1.

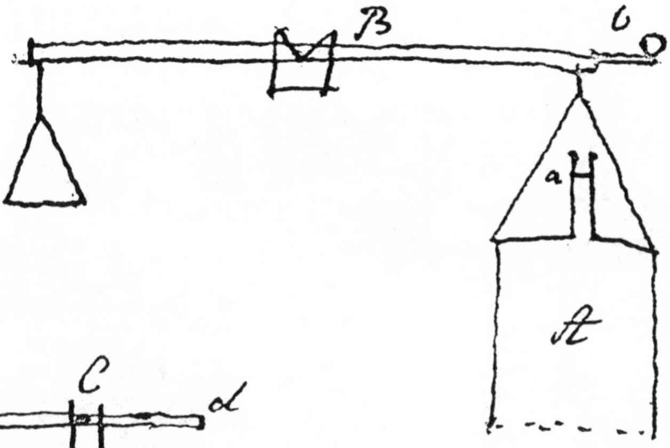

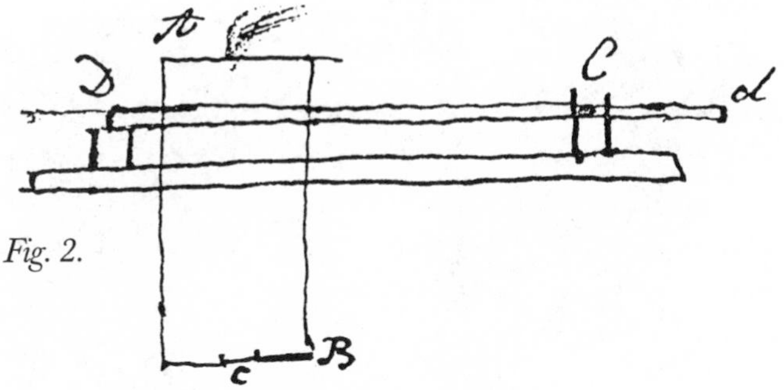

Fig. 2.

Fig. 3.

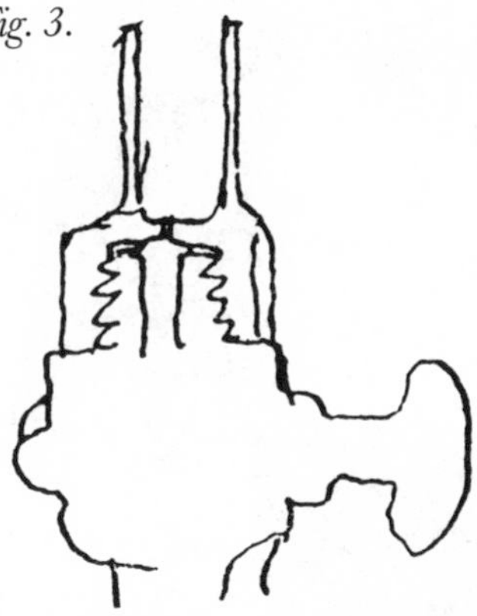

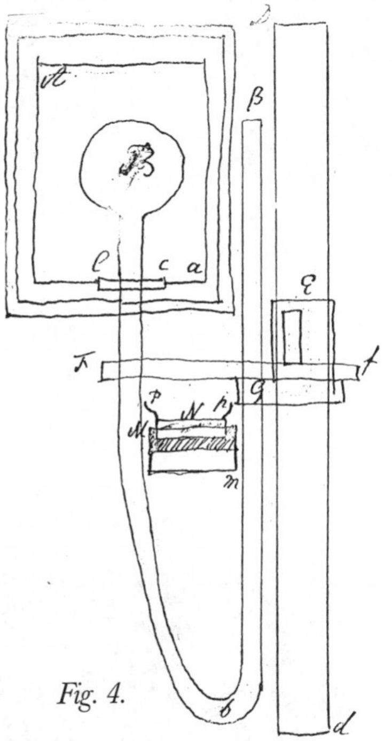

Fig. 4.

40. *Laboratory Apparatus. Fig. 1. Apparatus to test if the vis inertiae of phlogisticated air is the same in proportion to its weight as that of common air. The method requires finding the time in which a given quantity of air contained in A passes through a small hole at the top under a given pressure. Fig. 2. Apparatus for measuring the strength of the detonation of inflammable air with other airs. Air is admitted into the brass cylinder AB and electrically fired, lifting the pivoted board Dd to which it is fixed. Cavendish Scientific Manuscripts II, 5:130. Fig. 3. Apparatus for measuring the cold produced by the rarefaction of air. The brass cap is screwed over the cock of the condensing glass of an air pump. The ball of a thermometer is fitted into the cylinder of the cap, a small hole at the bottom of which allows the escaping condensed air to blow on the bulb. Cavendish Scientific Manuscripts III(a), 8:11. Fig. 4. Apparatus for finding the "force of steam," or tension of acqueous vapor, at heats below 212 degrees, a variation of the apparatus shown in illustration 39, Fig. 3. A small amount of water stands above the mercury in Bb, and the force of steam is determined by a comparison of the height of an ordinary barometer with the height of the barometer with a small amount of water. Ibid., 1:40. Reproductions by permission of the Chatsworth Settlement Trustees.*

INSTRUMENTS FROM THE OBSERVATORY

Fig. 1.

Fig. 2.

Fig. 3.

41. *Instruments from the Observatory. Fig. 1. Telescope with a twenty-five-inch tube, made of brass, on a pillar with tripod stand, with a steadying rod and rack and screw for adjusting the elevation, signed "Berge London late Ramsden." Known for his astronomical instruments, John Berge was principal workman for and then successor to the instrument-maker Jesse Ramsden. Taylor,* Mathematical Practitioners, *255. Fig. 2. Telescope stand. Fig. 3. Four-foot refracting telescope with wooden tube, in its case. By Dolland, probably Peter. Mary Holbrook,* Science Preserved: A Directory of Scientific Instruments in Collections in the United Kingdom and Eire *(London: Her Majesty's Stationery Office, 1992), 114. The small telescope, Fig. 1, is no doubt the one described in the auction catalog of Cavendish's collection, item no. 6, as an old telescope with a stand and brass rack-work. Most likely the large stand and telescope shown here also belonged to Henry Cavendish. Photographs taken by the authors at Chatsworth. Reproduced by permission of the Trustees of the Chatsworth. Settlement.*

For a few chemical laboratories of the time, there exist drawings. We do not have one of Cavendish's, but we have the next best, sketches he made of various apparatus. We reproduce some of these to give an idea of what would have greeted the reader had he been admitted into Cavendish's workplace. Or what would have greeted her: John Davy recalled that a lady of rank–he thought she was the duchess of Gordon, but we suspect she was the duchess of Devonshire–upon visiting Cavendish at Clapham expressed surprise at seeing a long row of utensils; they turned out to be objects used in the crystallization of saline solutions.[74] The auction catalog of Cavendish's instruments listed thirty-one bottles along with retorts, tubes, and the like. Since Cavendish's laboratory probably had to be versatile, we include several sketches of apparatus for fields outside of chemistry.

We do not know if there was also an observatory at Great Marlborough Street, but we suspect that there was a transit room, and there definitely were astronomical instruments. Before he was through, Cavendish had sufficient instruments to equip a good observatory of the time. The auction catalog of his collection lists eleven telescopes. We include photographs of a few instruments perhaps left over from the sale.

---

[74] Wilson, *Cavendish*, 178–79.

CHAPTER 4

TOOLS OF SCIENCE

INSTRUMENTS

Instruments, mathematics, and theory are principal tools of science, and like the good craftsman he was, Cavendish kept his tools sharp. We begin this discussion with scientific instruments.

By Cavendish's time, the craft of instrument-making was highly advanced. Aided by improvements in mechanics, materials, and the graduation of scales, instrument-makers kept up with (and stimulated) the demand for ever more exacting instruments.[1] Living in a city with a flourishing trade in instruments, Cavendish could conveniently inspect, buy, and commission the thermometers and so on that he needed for his research. At some point his need for an instrument-maker became sufficiently persistent that he employed one of his own.

All instruments were imperfect in their infancy, J. A. Deluc said, and although they never achieved perfection, they approached ever nearer to it; the ordinary watch became Harrison's precise timekeeper, the ordinary balance became the precise scales of the chemist.[2] The gradual approach to perfection was for the instrument-maker Jesse Ramsden a guide to practice: "I always incline to improve rather than invent," he said, except where he was convinced that the imperfection of an instrument arose from the principle of construction.[3] Cavendish was an improver of instruments, not an inventor.

There had long been instruments for the weather, such as the weather vane, the rain catch, and even a crude indicator of humidity, but by now it was

---

[1] Maurice Daumas, "Precision of Measurement and Physical and Chemical Research in the Eighteenth Century," in A. C. Crombie, ed., *Scientific Change; Historical Studies in the Intellectual, Social, and Technical Conditions for Scientific Discovery and Technical Invention, from Antiquity to the Present* (New York: Basic Books, 1963), 418–30, on 418, 426–30.

[2] Jean André Deluc, "Account of a New Hygrometer," *PT* 63 (1773): 404–60, on 430–32.

[3] Jesse Ramsden, "The Description of Two New Micrometers," *PT* 69 (1779): 419–31, on 419.

understood that the science of the weather, meteorology, required instruments that measured. Beside the barometer, the most important of these was the thermometer,[4] which was the subject of Cavendish's first assignment from the Royal Society in 1766. Thermometers had begun to be calibrated for improved accuracy, but in their adjustment they still showed wide variation.[5] Cavendish found that the best-made thermometers differed in their readings of the boiling point of water by two or three degrees.[6] Astronomical precision in meteorology was not regarded as important or obtainable,[7] but a disparity that large was unacceptable. Cavendish's assignment was to determine if the boiling point of thermometers is affected by the rapidity of boiling and by the immersion of the thermometers either in the water or in the steam above the water. By experiment he concluded that the rapidity of boiling was not a factor and that steam provided a "considerably more exact method" of adjusting the boiling point.

The Royal Society called upon Cavendish's skill with meteorological instruments again in 1773, this time to draw up a plan for taking daily meteorological readings.[8] The first thing in the morning and again at midday, the clerk of the Society was instructed to read the barometer and nearby indoor and outdoor thermometers, and every morning he was to measure how much rain had fallen, every afternoon estimate the wind, and one fortnight a year consult the dipping needle four times a day. With regard to the thermometer, the clerk was also expected to calculate a rather complicated series of means of readings. Cavendish proposed that all of this information be printed at the end of the last part of the *Philosophical Transactions* for each year; this was done, in nine columns, including one for the date.[9] So that the members did not have to wait until the end of the year to learn what the weather was, the clerk was ordered to post the previous week's record in the public meeting room of the Society.[10]

---

[4] Richard Kirwan, *An Estimate of the Temperature of Different Latitudes* (London, 1787), iii.

[5] William E. Knowles Middleton, *A History of the Thermometer and Its Use in Meteorology* (Baltimore: The Johns Hopkins University Press, 1966), 65, 75, 115, 127.

[6] Henry Cavendish, "Boiling Point of Water. At the Royal Society, April 18, 1766," *The Scientific Papers of the Honourable Henry Cavendish, F.R.S.*, vol. 2: *Chemical and Dynamical*, ed. E. Thorpe (Cambridge: Cambridge University Press, 1921), 351–53.

[7] William E. Knowles Middleton, *The History of the Barometer* (Baltimore: The Johns Hopkins University Press, 1964), 132.

[8] The council ordered the clerk of the Society to make daily observations of the weather "with the instruments to be procured for that purpose, & proper accomodations under the inspection of the Hon Henry Cavendish." 22 Nov. 1773, Minutes of Council, Royal Society, 6:194.

[9] "Meteorological Journal Kept at the House of the Royal Society, by Order of the President and Council," *PT* 67 (1777): 357–84.

[10] "The following scheme drawn up by the Hon Henry Cavendish for the regulating the manner of making daily meteorological observations by the Clerk of the Royal Society . . .," 9 Dec. 1773, Minutes of Council, Royal Society, 6:197–200.

In 1776, at a time when the council was preoccupied with instruments, those of the Royal Observatory[11] and its own,[12] and expanding the instruments used for the Society's meteorological register,[13] Cavendish was named head of a committee to review the entire body of meteorological instruments of the Society. The committee included William Heberden, who kept a meteorological journal; Nevil Maskelyne and Alexander Aubert, who as astronomers necessarily concerned themselves with the weather and also constantly with instruments; Samuel Horsley, regarded by some as the "head of the English mathematicians,"[14] and an astronomer and avid observer of the weather; the secretary of the Society Joseph Planta; and the most important member other than Cavendish, Deluc, the Swiss meteorologist who had recently settled in London, and who had published an influential work calling for the perfection of thermometers.[15] Two important publications came out of the study of the Society's meteorological instruments: a paper by Cavendish in 1776 and one by the committee the following year. With regard to the adjustment of the mark for the boiling point of water on thermometers, Cavendish wrote: "It is very much to be wished, therefore, that some means were used to establish an uniform method of proceeding; and there are none which seem more proper, or more likely to be effectual, than that the Royal Society should take it into consideration, and recommend that method of proceeding which shall appear to them to be most expedient."[16] The recommendation by the committee was drawn largely from Cavendish's report three years earlier.[17] The method of adjusting the boiling point and also the freezing point on the scale of a thermometer was made standard on the authority of the Royal Society. The resulting thermometer was referred to as a "standard."[18]

In his account of the instruments of the Society, Cavendish discussed the "error of observation" and the "error of the instrument," first considerations in

---

[11] Cavendish, Maskelyne, Aubert, Shepherd, and Wollaston were appointed to a committee to examine two new equatorial sectors, which had imperfections due to the neglect of the instrument-maker. 14 Sep. and 12 Oct. 1775, Minutes of Council, Royal Society, 6:273, 275.

[12] Cavendish, Aubert, Nairne, and Maskelyne were appointed to a committee to "examine into the state of the Society's instruments." 14 Nov. 1776, Minutes of Council, Royal Society, 6:303.

[13] The council ordered that once-daily observations with John Smeaton's hygrometer be added to the Society's meteorological observations. 16 Nov. 1775, Minutes of Council, Royal Society, 6:279.

[14] John Playfair, *The Works of John Playfair*, ed. J. G. Playfair, 4 vols. (Edinburgh, 1822) 1:appendix no. 1, "Journal," lxxix.

[15] Middleton, *History of the Thermometer*, 116–17, 127. Douglas W. Freshfield and H. F. Montagnier, *The Life of Horace Bénédict De Saussure* (London: Edward Arnold, 1920), 176–77.

[16] Henry Cavendish, "An Account of the Meteorological Instruments Used at the Royal Society's House," *PT* 66 (1776): 375; *Sci. Pap.* 2:112–26, on 115.

[17] Signed by Cavendish (listed first), Heberden, Aubert, Deluc, Maskelyne, Horsley, and Planta: "The Report of the Committee Appointed by the Royal Society to Consider of the Best Method of Adjusting the Fixed Points of Thermometers; and of the Precautions Necessary to Be Used in Making Experiments with Those Instruments," *PT* 67 (1777): 816–57.

[18] Deluc, "Account of a New Hygrometer," 430.

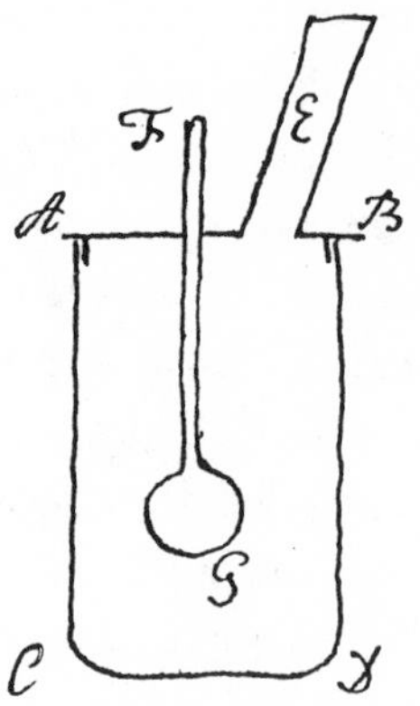

42. *Apparatus for Adjusting the Boiling Point. The committee of the Royal Society, of which Cavendish was chairman, conducted experiments to determine the regularity of the boiling point. ABCD is the pot, AB the cover, E the chimney to carry off steam, FG the thermometer fitted tightly to the cover. The stem of the thermometer as well as the ball are immersed in steam, not water, in accord with Cavendish's recommendation. The committee recommended this apparatus, including an almost identical drawing, in its published report. Cavendish et al., "The Report of the Committee Appointed by the Royal Society to Consider of the Best Method of Adjusting the Fixed Points of Thermometers; and of the Precautions Necessary to Be Used in Making Experiments with Those Instruments,"* Philosophical Transactions *6 (1777):816–57, opposite 856. The drawing by Cavendish is in Cavendish Scientific Manuscripts III(a), 2. Reproduced by permission of the Trustees of the Chatsworth Settlement.*

rendering meteorology a more exact science. "Accuracy" in the recording of the weather was accomplished in part by the indoor and outdoor placement of the instruments, by raising the funnel collecting rain above the roof of the Society's house where there seemed "no danger of any rain dashing into it," and by sheltering the hygrometer from the rain, locating it "where the Sun scarce ever shines on it," but leaving it open to the wind.[19] It was accomplished too by taking the mean of observations; by applying corrections, such as Cavendish's corrections for the thermometer if the stem is cooler than the bulb and Deluc's corrections of the barometer by the thermometer; and by referring to a table giving capillary depressions of the mercury standing in the tube of the barometer. That table, Cavendish pointed out, was made by his father.[20]

Anyone who studies Cavendish's papers on meteorology must be impressed by the tenacity with which he compared his instruments among themselves and with those belonging to the Royal Society and to Nairne and others. For ten years he compared hygrometers. This instrument was a subject of much experimentation, and inventors of hygrometers disputed among themselves so heatedly that Charles Blagden spoke of their "open war."[21] Yet they agreed that the "essential point" about the hygrometer was that all "observers might understand each other, when mentioning degrees of humidity."[22] Smeaton put it best: the goal was to construct hygrometers that, like good thermometers, were "capable of speaking the same language."[23]

[19] Cavendish, "An Account of the Meteorological Instruments," 117.

[20] Ibid., 116–17.

[21] Charles Blagden to Henry Cavendish, 23 Sep. 1787, Cavendish Mss X(b), 14.

[22] Deluc, "Account of a New Hygrometer," 405.

[23] John Smeaton, "Description of a New Hygrometer," *PT* 61 (1771): 198–211, on 199.

43. Register Thermometer. Photograph by the authors. Cavendish's original instrument is in the Royal Institution, a gift of Sir Humphry Davy. Alcohol contained in a large tube expands with heat, causing mercury in the U-end of the tube to move. Through a cord attached to an ivory slip on the surface of the mercury, a hand moves across the circular scale graduated in degrees of heat. This hand in turn moves light friction hands, which remain at the maximum and minimum heats for any one setting of the instrument. A description of the instrument together with an engraving of it is in George Wilson, The Life of the Honourable Henry Cavendish *(London, 1851), 477–78.*

Cavendish tried "Smeaton's" hygrometer used by the Royal Society, and other hygrometers, which he labelled variously "Nairne's," "Harrison's," "Coventry's," "common," "old," "new," "4-stringed," and "ivory." The general type of instrument he studied was the hydroscopic hygrometer, which either weighed the water (Cavendish's weighed the increase in weight of dry salt after moist air was passed over it) or measured the change in dimensions of a moistened substance, such as the contraction of strings; Cavendish preferred the latter method, in contrast to our preference today for weighing. He roasted, salted, wetted, and stretched the moisture-absorbing strings, and he mixed vapors from acids and alkalis with air to see if what we might call pollution made a difference. At times he made readings daily, morning and evening, as often as every twenty minutes, in warm rooms and cold rooms, often together with thermometer readings.[24] If this activity sounds obsessive, it nevertheless went to the heart of the work of science. Cavendish's colleagues did much of the same sort of thing; in a paper on hygrometers, Deluc wrote that he was giving an "account of twenty years assiduous labour in *hygronomy*, mostly occasioned by the anomalies of the *hygroscopic threads*."[25] In any experimental investigation, the reliability of instruments and their method of use were an inseparable part of the scientific argument. For Cavendish and his colleagues, an unexamined instrument was not worth using.[26]

[24] Henry Cavendish, "Hygrometers," Cavendish Mss IV, 5. This manuscript consists of seventy-seven numbered pages of laboratory notes and an index.

[25] Jean André Deluc, "A Second Paper on Hygrometry," *PT* 81 (1791): 1-42, on 40.

[26] The Lowndean professor at Cambridge, William Lax, wrote that no instrument was to be trusted without "previous examination." "On a Method of Examining the Divisions of Astronomical Instruments," *PT* 99 (1809): 232–45, on 233.

The work of the maker of scientific instruments and that of their user went hand in hand.[27] Cavendish no doubt made some of his instruments, probably some of the hygrometers he compared, but most of his instruments were made by highly skilled instrument-makers. Living at the time of world-renown of London instrument-makers, Cavendish was free to devote his labors to research.[28] His colleague George Shuckburgh paid appropriate tribute to the craftsmen of science when he spoke of the "singular success with which this age and nation has introduced a mathematical precision, hitherto unheard of, into the construction of philosophical instruments."[29] In his living quarters at Greenwich Observatory, in addition to a bust of Newton, the astronomer royal Nevil Maskelyne exhibited prints of the builder of the great eight-foot mural quadrant for Greenwich, John Bird, and of the inventor of the achromatic telescope used at Greenwich, John Dolland.[30]

MATHEMATICS

Instruments were aids in making experiments and observations, upon which science depended for its facts. But, as the mathematician Colin Maclaurin wrote in his book on Newton's discoveries, experiments and observations alone would not have enabled Newton to infer causes from effects or to explain effects by causes; for that Newton needed "sublime geometry."[31]

Mathematics, the mathematics teacher and instrument-maker Benjamin Martin wrote, is "the science or doctrine of *quantity*."[32] As such, in the practice of science, mathematics is the intellectual tool that complements the material tool, the instruments of measurement.

Cavendish's manuscripts on mathematics are as numerous as his manuscripts on astronomy or magnetism or mechanics. Certain of them are concerned with mathematical problems having no connection with experimental or observational science. One paper deals with prime numbers.[33] Several papers deal with topics relating to De Moivre's subject: the probability of winning more than losing in a game, the probability of throwing a certain number with a certain number of dice, the possible ways of paying a sum with coins of different

---

[27] E. G. R. Taylor, *The Mathematical Practitioners of Hanoverian England 1714–1840* (Cambridge: Cambridge University Press, 1966), 43, 58.

[28] Ibid., 43.

[29] George Shuckburgh, "On the Variation of the Temperature of Boiling Water," *PT* 69 (1779): 362–75, on 362.

[30] 29 July 1785, "Visitations of Greenwich Observatory, 1763 to 1815," Royal Society, Ms. 600, XIV.d.11, f. 36.

[31] Colin Maclaurin, *An Account of Sir Isaac Newton's Philosophical Discoveries* . . . (London, 1748), 8.

[32] Benjamin Martin, *A New and Comprehensive System of Mathematical Institutions, Agreeable to the Present State of the Newtonian Mathesis*, 2 vols. (London, 1759–64) 1:1.

[33] Henry Cavendish, "On Prime Numbers," Cavendish Mss VI(a), 8.

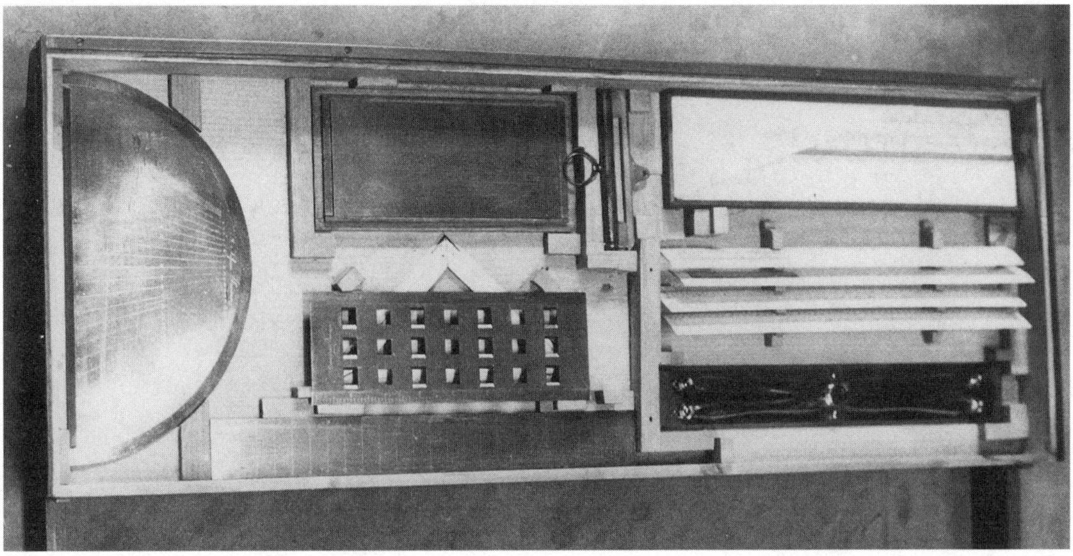

44. *Mathematical Instruments. The instrument cases in this and the next illustration are drawers that fit into a cabinet belonging to Henry Cavendish. There are many scales and rulers, a brass globe map projection, an ivory triangle, and so on, bearing the names of well-known instrument-makers: Jesse Ramsden, Jonathan Sisson, John Morgan, and Fraser, presumably William Fraser. Photograph by the authors. Devonshire Collections, Chatsworth. Reproduced by permission of the Chatsworth Settlement Trustees.*

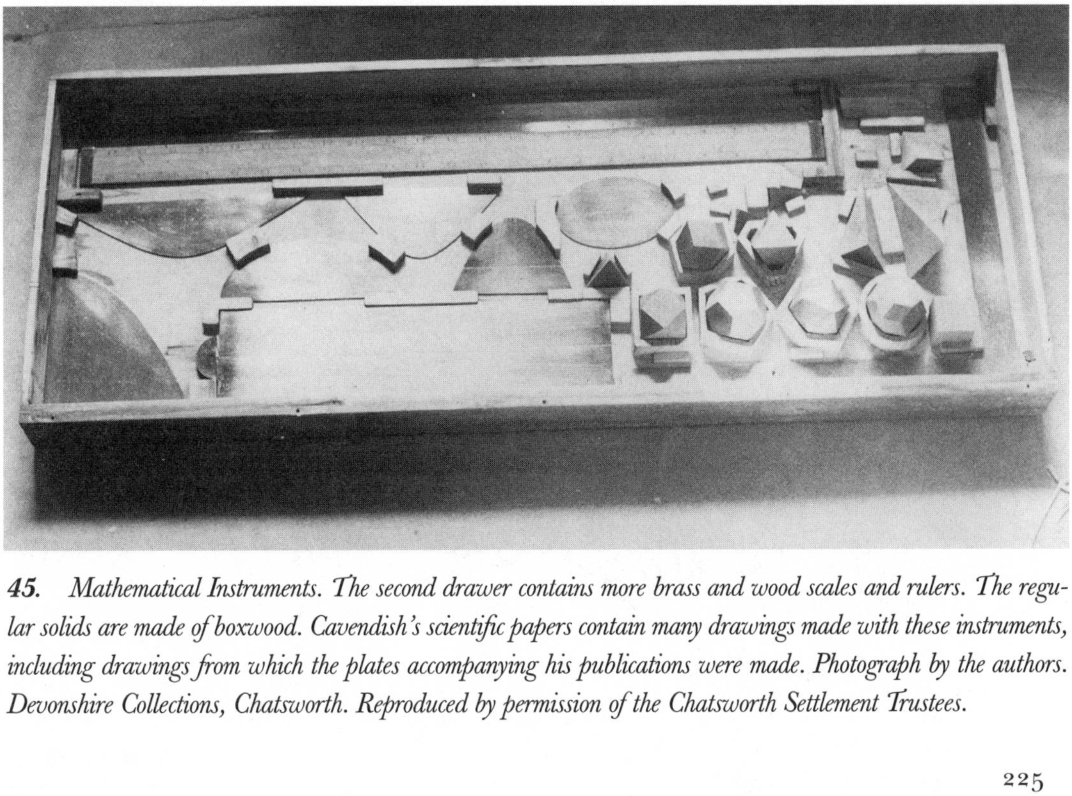

45. *Mathematical Instruments. The second drawer contains more brass and wood scales and rulers. The regular solids are made of boxwood. Cavendish's scientific papers contain many drawings made with these instruments, including drawings from which the plates accompanying his publications were made. Photograph by the authors. Devonshire Collections, Chatsworth. Reproduced by permission of the Chatsworth Settlement Trustees.*

46. *Pantograph. This tool for copying a drawing to a predetermined scale was made by Sisson, either Jonathan or, more likely, his son Jeremiah. It has a walnut case, and it definitely belonged to Henry Cavendish; for it bears the name of the instrument in his handwriting. The photograph was taken by the authors at Chatsworth and is reproduced by permission of the Chatsworth Settlement Trustees.*

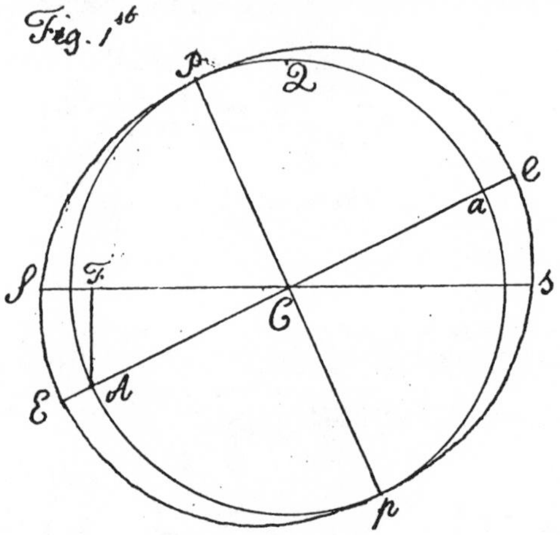

47. *Drawings. Figs. 1–4 belong to a carefully drafted manuscript, "Precession of Equinoxes," Cavendish Scientific Manuscripts VIII, 9. Reproduced by permission of the Chatsworth Settlement Trustees.*

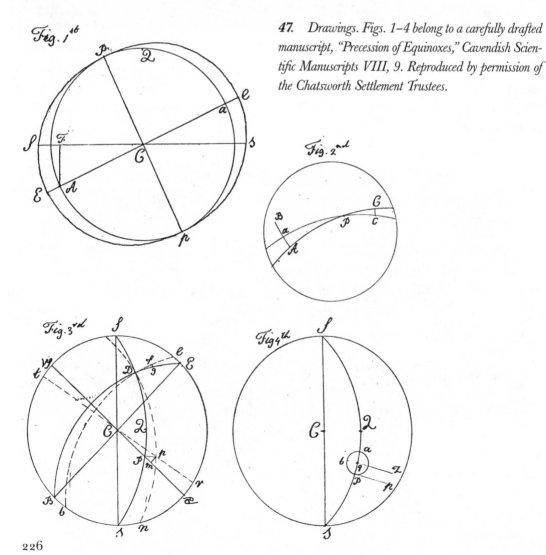

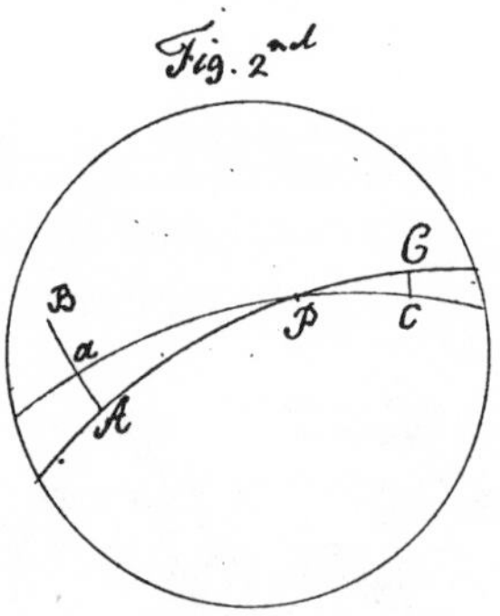

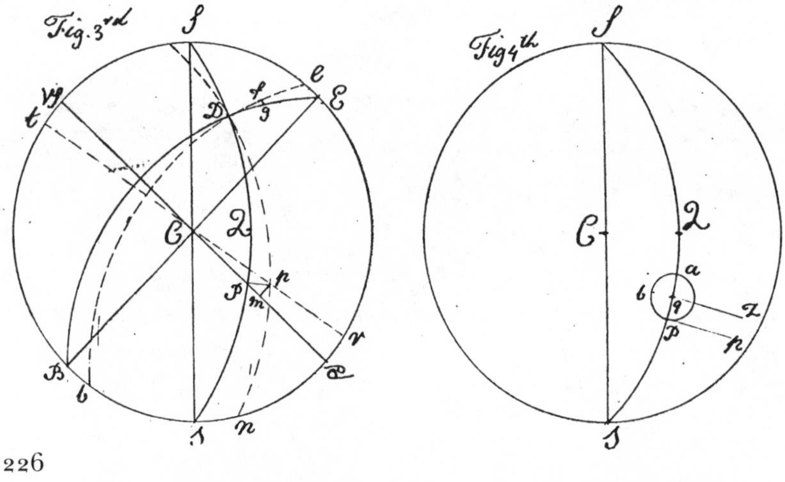

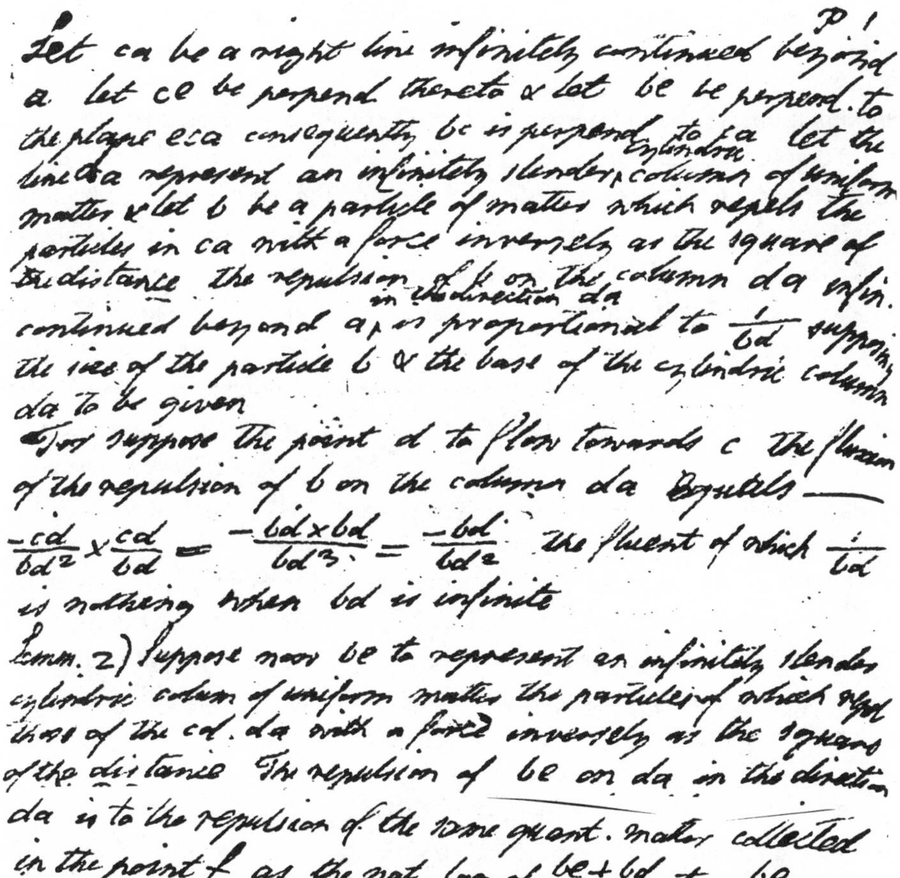

P 1

Let ca be a right line infinitely continued beyond a. let ce be perpend. thereto & let be be perpend. to the plane eca consequently bc is perpend. to ca let the line da represent an infinitely slender cylindric column of uniform matter & let b be a particle of matter which repels the particles in ca with a force inversely as the square of the distance the repulsion of b on the column da infin. continued beyond a, in the direction da is proportional to $\frac{1}{bd}$ supposing the size of the particle b & the base of the cylindric column da to be given

For suppose the point d to flow towards c the fluxion of the repulsion of b on the column da equals

$$\frac{-\dot{cd}}{bd^2} \times \frac{cd}{bd} = -\frac{bd \times \dot{bd}}{bd^3} = \frac{-\dot{bd}}{bd^2}$$

the fluent of which $\frac{1}{bd}$ is nothing when bd is infinite

Lemm. 2) Suppose now be to represent an infinitely slender cylindric column of uniform matter the particles of which repel those of the col. da with a force inversely as the square of the distance The repulsion of be on da in the direction da is to the repulsion of the same quant. matter collected in the point f as the nat. log. of $\frac{be+bd}{ed}$ to $\frac{be}{fd}$

For ~~supposing the line~~ by the last lemma the repulsion of ~~all~~ the matter in be collected in the point f on the col. da ~~may be represented by~~ is proportional to $\frac{eb}{fd}$ & supposing the line eb to flow the fluxion of the repulsion of it da is proportional to $\frac{\dot{eb}}{bd} - \frac{\dot{eb}}{\sqrt{eb^2+ed^2}}$ the fluent of which is the nat. log of $\frac{eb+bd}{ed}$ & is equal to nothing when eb is nothing

Coroll. 1) If be is very great in respect of ed bd differs very little from be & therefore the repulsion of be on da is to the repulsion of the same quantity of matter collected in f very nearly as N.L $\frac{2be}{ed}$ to $\frac{be}{fd}$

48. *Mathematical Notations. This page shows Cavendish's use of fluxions, the Newtonian form of the calculus. Here Cavendish derives an expression for the repulsion of a particle of matter on an infinitely thin column of matter, assuming the force to vary inversely with the square of the distance. Cavendish Scientific Manuscripts I, 1. Reproduced by permission of the Chatsworth Settlement Trustees.*

denominations, and annuities on lives.[34] There are papers on parts of mathematics that had applications in the physical sciences, such as the binomial theorem, the multinomial theorem, infinite series, and the construction and solution of algebraic equations.[35] There are also papers on subjects with a direct bearing on Cavendish's work in the laboratory and the observatory, such as Newton's rule of interpolating, the accuracy of taking the mean of observations, triangular forms that reduce the effects of errors of measurement, and errors of instruments.[36] Most of the mathematical papers deal with problems in plane or spherical geometry, some of which had clear scientific implications, for example, a curve drawn with reference to three points.[37] Many of Cavendish's mathematical papers were written late in life, when he was doing less experimental work.[38] He published none of his work on mathematics, and that raises the question of why he did it. Doubtless solving mathematical problems gave him satisfaction, but we think there was more to it. Since he applied mathematics extensively in his scientific researches in astronomy, the earth sciences, mechanics, and other fields, we liken his mathematical exercises to his constant handling and comparing of instruments.

THEORY

Newton placed his "sublime geometry" in the service of his "experimental philosophy." According to the eighteenth-century Newtonian James Hutton, to perform an intelligent experiment was to inquire into the "truth of a conceived proposition." We would say "preconceived"; for Hutton continued, for science to be "actually advanced," there has to be a "certain theory" in the mind of the experimenter.[39]

Among Cavendish's favorite expressions were "as I know by experience," "by strict reasoning," "with tolerable certainty," and "according to the theory." Taken together they go far to characterize his scientific belief: the right combination of experience and reason leads to theories of nature that have a good likelihood of being "true." To arrive at "theories," embodying laws of nature, was the final goal.

Theories in turn lead to experimental and observational advances, to new facts about nature. Looked at in this way, in addition to being endpoints of

[34] Cavendish Mss VI(a), 1, 23, 46, 48.

[35] Cavendish Mss VI(a), 15, 16, 21, 22, 24, 27.

[36] Cavendish Mss VI(a), 6, 34, 45. The paper on the probable error of instruments does not have a catalog number. The problem it addresses is to determine the probability of the sum of the errors of two instruments given the error of any one instrument.

[37] Cavendish Mss VI(a) 17, 36.

[38] The mathematical manuscripts are never dated, but the watermarks on the paper give occasional indications. In the manuscripts on Braikenridge's surfaces and on the loci of third-order equations, some of the sheets bear watermarks from 1797 to 1804.

[39] James Hutton, *A Dissertation upon the Philosophy of Light, Heat, and Fire. In Seven Parts* (London, 1794), 3.

research, theories are, like instruments and mathematics, tools of investigation in the scientist's work kit.[40]

In the Royal Society, facts were valued over hypotheses; "speculation or mathematical theorizing was conspicuous by its absence" in the *Philosophical Transactions*.[41] In light of the prevailing skepticism toward theories, to propose a new theory was a serious step, especially for someone as cautious as Cavendish. He developed a theory of boiling, which he did not make public. Neither did he make public his theory of metals and acids within the framework of the phlogiston theory. He had theoretical notions about the cause of chemical reactions at the level of particles and forces, but he was far from being able to develop this approach sufficiently to give chemistry its theory. He worked out only two general theories, one of which he published. The theory he did not publish was on heat; the theory he did publish was on electricity.

Cavendish's theories of electricity and heat originated in an existing theory, that of mechanics. His authority on this subject was Newton's *Principia*. To a competent reader like Cavendish, it was evident that this book was not the final word on the subject.[42] Among his earliest writings was a plan of a treatise on mechanics. There, like Newton, he treated force as a primitive concept, but he departed from Newton on the laws of motion. The first two laws "contain all we know of the properties of matter relating to motion," Cavendish wrote; the law of the equality of action and reaction, "called by Sr I. N. the 3rd law of motion but improperly," was "merely a property of the doctrine of pressures."[43] Cavendish's most productive departure from the *Principia* was his use of Leibniz's *vis viva* as the measure of the force of moving bodies. Identifying heat with the motion of the particles of bodies, he described the system of particles with the help of vis viva; the *Principia*, by contrast, did not give equations of motion for systems of more than two particles.[44] He looked at the problem of the spinning top, which lay outside the scope of the *Principia*.[45] He studied the efflux of fluid from a vessel, a problem which Newton

[40] These "tools" were related. Mathematics had its instruments. Instruments had their "theory." Benjamin Martin reminded any person who was using an instrument without knowing its rationale or theory that he was working "in the dark"; just as the "*Science* of any Profession consists in the Theory." *The New Art of Surveying by the Goniometer* (London, 1766), Preface.

[41] Richard John Sorrenson, "Towards a History of the Royal Society in the Eighteenth Century," *Notes and Records of the Royal Society of London* 50 (1996): 29–46, on 37, 40.

[42] Clifford Truesdell, "A Program toward Rediscovering the Rational Mechanics of the Age of Reason," *Archive for the History of Exact Sciences* 1 (1960): 1–36, on 6–9.

[43] "Plan of a Treatise on Mechanics," Cavendish Mss VI(b), 45:13, 16

[44] "Remarks on the Theory of Motion," Cavendish Mss VI(b), 7; in *Sci. Pap.* 2:415–30. "Heat," Manuscript Division, Pre-Confederation Archives, Public Archives of Canada, Ottawa, M G 23, L 6.

[45] Truesdell, "Program," 9. "Concerning the Spinning of Tops by Mr Mitchell," Cavendish Mss VI(b), 18. In a footnote to this paper, Cavendish wrote: "This point (on which the analysis of the top's motion rests) is what is known by the name of the center of percussion. How I came not to take notice of it I do not know."

had treated incompletely.[46] He analyzed the precession of the equinoxes; on that subject, Newton was believed to have made a flat error.[47] To Newton's theories of fluids, which were largely wrong,[48] Cavendish gave critical attention: the motion of water waves "as Sr I. N. has described it . . . is not the case"; "Sr I. Ns demonstration concerning sound . . . does not agree with experiment."[49] Cavendish incorporated his criticism of Newton's theory of the elastic fluid of air in his published theory of electricity, to which we now turn.

Newton informed the Royal Society that if glass is rubbed on one side, its opposite side will attract and repel bits of paper with an irregular and persisting motion.[50] Agitated bits of paper might not seem all that impressive, but Newton sensed that electricity plays a large role in nature. In the *Principia* he wrote of a "certain most subtle spirit which pervades and lies hid in all gross bodies." He speculated that this ether might account for the forces of electric bodies and beyond that for light, cohesion, animal sensation, and willed commands. To learn the laws of "this electric and elastic spirit," Newton said, more experiments were needed.[51]

As experimental techniques were developed for detecting, generating, and accumulating electrical charges, Newton's prophecy of the importance of electricity in the scheme of things seemed borne out. Fifty years after Newton, the insightful student of the Leyden jar William Watson observed that electricity was an "extraordinary power" that "cannot but be of very great moment in the system of the universe."[52] On the eve of Cavendish's researches on electricity, Joseph Priestley observed that electricity was "no local, or occasional agent in the theatre of the world"; rather it played a "principal part in the grandest and most interesting scenes of nature."[53] Watson and Priestley were essentially repeating what Newton had said, only now with a good deal more evidence. Scientific expectations ran high; by the 1760s electrical researchers had begun to associate electricity with a force acting over sensible distances according to a determinable law, the starting point of a systematically quantified field of electricity. For several years Cavendish gave nearly undivided attention to this new

---

46 Truesdell, "Program," 19–20. Cavendish, "On the Motion of Water Running Out from a Hole in the Bottom of a Vessel," Cavendish Mss VI(b), 26.

47 "Precession of Equinoxes," Cavendish Mss VIII, 9.

48 Truesdell, "Program," 9.

49 "Concerning Waves," "On the Motion of Sounds," Cavendish Mss VI(b), 23, 35.

50 Reported in Joseph Priestley, *The History and Present State of Electricity, with Original Experiments* (London, 1767), 12–14.

51 Isaac Newton, *Sir Isaac Newton's Mathematical Principles of Natural Philosophy and His System of the World*, 2 vols., trans. A. Motte, rev. F. Cajori (Berkeley and Los Angeles: University of California Press, 1962), 2:547.

52 William Watson, "An Account of the Phenomena of Electricity in Vacuo," *PT* 47 (1752): 363–76, on 375–76.

53 Priestley, *The History of Electricity*, xii.

force of nature. He planned to publish a book on it, taking as his model Newton's *Principia*.

For its unity, simplicity, and grandeur, the ether held a strong appeal to Newton's followers, though in the middle of the century in Britain, progress in the exact understanding of electricity and other experimental fields was brought about primarily with the aid of the related concept of specific fluids. Hermann Boerhaave's doctrine of elementary fire was an influential intermediary between the ether and the hypothetical fluids of electricity, magnetism, light, and heat.[54] Assumed to be weightless, particulate, and active, these fluids all bore the characteristic of Boerhaave's fire: they were bodies "*sui generis*, not creatable, or producible *de novo*."[55]

In his *History of Electricity*, Priestley wrote that English electricians and most foreign ones too had adopted Benjamin Franklin's fluid theory of positive and negative electricity. Priestley's own opinion was that the basic features of the theory were as "expressive of the true principles of electricity, as the Newtonian philosophy is of the true system of nature in general."[56] Franklin defined a body to be "positive electrified if it has more than its "normal" quantity of electric fluid, "negatively" electrified if it has less. The usefulness of his terms is evident in his analysis of the Leyden jar: one side of the jar is electrified positively in exact proportion as the other side is electrified negatively; the same amount of fluid enters one side as flows out the other. Franklin's analysis turns on the quantity of electric fluid, and although quantity alone is insufficient to explain all electrical phenomena, it does afford a reasonable understanding of most instances of attraction and repulsion of electrified bodies.

"Thoughts Concerning Electricity," Cavendish's first electrical theory,[57] cannot be earlier than 1767, since it cites Priestley's *History of Electricity*, which was published that year. Cavendish rejected the commonly held idea of electric "atmospheres" surrounding bodies. He introduced the concept of "compression" or, as we would say, "pressure" of the electric fluid. This concept, Maxwell observed, is equivalent to the modern concept of "potential";[58] that is, it plays the role in Cavendish's fluid theory of electricity that the potential plays in the modern theory of electricity. Cavendish used Franklin's terms "positive" and "negative," but he gave them a different meaning, associating them not with the

---

[54] I. B. Cohen, *Franklin and Newton: An Inquiry into Speculative Newtonian Experimental Science and Franklin's Work in Electricity as an Example Thereof* (Philadelphia: American Philosophical Society, 1956), 214–34.

[55] Hermann Boerhaave, *A New Method of Chemistry; Including the Theory and Practice of That Art: Laid Down on Mechanical Principles, and Accommodated to the Uses of Life. The Whole Making a Clear and Rational System of Chemistry*, 2 vols., trans. P. Shaw and E. Chambers (London, 1727) 1:233.

[56] Priestley, *History of Electricity*, 160, 455.

[57] Maxwell calls it the first "form of Cavendish's theory": *Sci. Pap.* 1:397–98. The paper, "Thoughts," is on 110–17.

[58] Ibid., 111.

quantity of electricity but with his concept of compression: a body is "positively" or "negatively" electrified according to whether the fluid in it is more or less compressed than it is in its natural state. Recognizing the need for two quantitative concepts, Cavendish introduced another pair of opposing terms: a body is "overcharged" or "undercharged" if it contains more or less fluid than it does in its natural state. "Thoughts," which in the early parts is carefully drafted, ends inconclusively. Cavendish questioned how far his idea of an electric fluid "diffused uniformly through all bodies not appearing electrical," the repulsion of its particles extending "to considerable distances," "will agree with experiment." He wrote, "I am in doubt." The mathematical investigation accompanying "Thoughts" broke off in midsentence. Cavendish changed theories. His new theory was again based on an expansive electric fluid, and it again dispensed with electric atmospheres, but it had a greater complexity of forces. He published this second theory of electricity in the *Philosophical Transactions* in 1771.

To Cavendish a theory rested upon an hypothesis about nature made credible by its experimental or observational consequences, as drawn out by the theory. He introduced his second theory of electricity with this hypothesis: "There is a substance, which I call the electric fluid, the particles of which repel each other and attract the particles of all other matter with a force inversely as some less power of the distance than the cube: the particles of all other matter also, repel each other, and attract those of the electric fluid, with a force varying according to the same power of the distance."[59] By Cavendish's hypothesis, there is an electric force of repulsion between the particles of ordinary matter, which explains the repulsion of undercharged bodies, the major problem with Franklin's explanation, and the hypothesis includes a statement about the mathematical form of the law of force.

In his theory of 1771, Cavendish made some changes in terminology, speaking of "positive" and "negative" electrification or "degree" of electrification instead of his earlier, more graphic "compression," but the concept is the same, fluid pressure. He introduced the term "saturation," which he was then using in chemistry, to describe the normal or natural state. In chemistry it meant that affinities were rendered inactive in a chemical union, and in electricity it meant that attractive and repulsive forces were equal and no net electrical activity was manifest. Cavendish spoke of the electric fluid and common matter as "contrary" matters, behaving in some respects like acids and alkalies, or like factitious airs and the bodies containing them; the main difference in these comparisons is that the electrical fluid is free to move inside conducting bodies and is prevented from running out of those bodies by the nonconducting air outside them. Any departure from the saturated state causes a body to be "overcharged" or "undercharged," as before.

---

[59] Cavendish's paper was read at two meetings of the Royal Society, 19 Dec. 1771 and 9 Jan. 1772. "An Attempt to Explain Some of the Principal Phaenomena of Electricity, by Means of an Elastic Fluid," *PT* 61 (1771): 584–677; *Sci. Pap.* 1:33–81, on 33.

Following the example of the *Principia*, Cavendish laid out his scientific argument with definitions, propositions, and lemmas. He analyzed the electrical content of mathematically treatable bodies such as spheres, cylinders, discs, and parallel plates in a state of electrical equilibrium, connected by "canals," or wire-like threads of matter through which the electric fluid can freely move. For convenience of calculation, he assumed that the fluid in the canals is incompressible.

At the time that Cavendish published his electrical paper, at Cambridge the Plumian professor of astronomy and experimental philosophy Anthony Shepherd was giving a course of lectures on experimental philosophy, ordering his lectures on electricity under the heading "Mechanics."[60] To develop his theory of electricity, Cavendish drew on propositions from the principal work on mechanics from his student days at Cambridge. Referring to Newton's derivation of Boyle's law from the *Principia*, Cavendish compared his electrical fluid with an elastic fluid of the kind he had recently investigated in chemistry, air. Assuming that particles attract and repel with a force inversely as the *n*th power of the distance, and in some cases assuming that *n* is 2, as it is in the case of the force of gravity, he analyzed the behavior of his electrical fluid in a large variety of experimental arrangements. He carried through the analysis using Newton's fluxional calculus. With evident help from Newton, Cavendish demonstrated as rigorously as he could the consequences of his hypothesis. His paper was an essay in the difficult and still rudimentary science of fluid mechanics.[61]

Having developed the theory in the first half of his paper, in the second half Cavendish applied it to experiments done by others. Given his experimental skill, he might have been expected to give experiments of his own, but at the time his paper was read to the Royal Society, in late 1771, he had just begun making them. The next chapter will show that his electrical theory was indeed a tool for exploring a new realm of facts.

In the opening paragraph of his paper on electrical theory, Cavendish referred to Aepinus's *Tentamen theoriae electricitatis et magnetismi*, published in 1759. Only after he first wrote his paper, Cavendish said, did he learn that his hypothesis was not "new," that Aepinus had used "the same, or nearly the same" hypothesis as he had, and that Aepinus's conclusions from it agreed nearly with his own. Cavendish noted that he had "carried the theory much farther" and had treated the subject in a "more accurate" manner. This remark is all that Cavendish said about Aepinus's theory in print. On 23 June of an unspecified year, Cavendish wrote to John Canton to say that Canton need not apply to Priestley for a copy of the *Tentamen*, since Cavendish had just come across it in

---

60 Anthony Shepherd, *The Heads of a Course of Lectures in Experimental Philosophy Read at Christ College* (Cambridge, 1770?), 3.

61 The indispensable "canals" communicating electric fluid were derivative of the canals of fluid mechanics. Cavendish used "canals" in his theory, for example, of the progagation of sound in air: "On the Motion of Sounds," Cavendish Mss VI(b), 35.

a London bookstore.[62] The background of Cavendish's letter is the following interaction between Cavendish, Canton, Priestley, and Franklin. In April 1766 Franklin sent Priestley a copy of the *Tentamen* to help him in preparing his *History of Electricity*. Not owning the *Tentamen* and wanting to consult it, Cavendish asked Canton, a friend of Priestley's, to ask Priestley if he would send the book to Canton "for Mr. Cavendish."[63] Then Cavendish saw the book at a bookstore and cancelled his request to borrow it. Roderick Home argues convincingly that the above exchanges all took place in 1766.[64] That was five and a half years before Cavendish's paper on electrical theory was read to the Royal Society. We must suppose that Cavendish pursued his own work in electricity with such confidence that he could ignore his own library, even where he had gone to the trouble to add to it a specific work. He preferred to make an original experimental investigation of an interesting question rather than to read everything that had been said on it by others. We are inclined to credit Cavendish with an extraordinary determination to know but not necessarily with an encyclopedic knowledge of what other people knew.

We have assumed that when Cavendish came across Aepinus's book, he bought and read it then, but perhaps he did not. In 1766 Cavendish was in the middle of his researches in chemistry, and he may have put the book aside or delayed its purchase.[65]

The principal interest of the Aepinus episode is what it reveals about electrical work in Britain at the time. Aepinus was well known in Britain. In 1762, for instance, a large shipment of publications from the St. Petersburg Academy was received in London, which included "Professor Aepinus's Dissertations," with instructions for them to be distributed to twenty-seven persons.[66] Canton, Franklin, Benjamin Wilson, and perhaps other electrical experimenters in London were familiar with Aepinus's *Tentamen*,[67] yet it is entirely conceivable that

[62] Henry Cavendish to John Canton, 23 June [1766], Canton Papers, Royal Society, Correspondence, vol. 2.

[63] John Canton to Benjamin Franklin, [1766], *The Papers of Benjamin Franklin*, vol. 19, ed. W. R. Wilcox (New Haven: Yale University Press, 1969), 544.

[64] Roderick W. Home, "Aepinus and the British Electricians: The Dissemination of a Scientific Theory," *Isis* 63 (1972): 190–204. Cavendish's assertion that he learned of Aepinus's hypothesis only after completing his paper was puzzling to us. In the first edition of *Cavendish*, we questioned Home's conclusion, but we have reconsidered the matter in light of our rethinking about Cavendish; we now find Home's evidence and reasoning to be convincing. We had assumed that Cavendish's knowledge of the scientific literature was thorough, but we are less certain of that point now. Ten years after the fact, he told Blagden that "when [he] wrote his paper on attraction [weighing the world], he shewd his ignorance of what had been done by others." 8 June 1809, Charles Blagden Diary, Royal Society, 5:328 (back).

[65] This suggestion was made by Home in a private communication.

[66] Daniel Dumaresque to Thomas Birch, 25 Sep. 1762, BL Add Mss 4304, p. 79.

[67] Home, "Electricians," 201.

Cavendish would not have heard any discussion of Aepinus's electrical theory. Joseph Priestley's revisions of his *History of Electricity* left unchanged his erroneous discussion of Aepinus's theory,[68] suggesting that his electrical colleagues were insufficiently knowledgeable about the theory to point out Priestley's error.

Aepinus's theory was first discussed extensively in print in English only a half century later, by John Robison. Because of its mathematical nature, Robison said, Aepinus's theory was the first to tread in Newton's footsteps.[69] Robison was also a great admirer of Cavendish's electrical theory, but his praise came too late to make any difference to Cavendish, Aepinus, or the science of electricity.

---

[68] Personal communication from Robert E. Schofield.

[69] John Robison, *A System of Mechanical Philosophy,* 4 vols., ed. with notes by D. Brewster (Edinburgh, 1822), 4:109.

ELECTRICITY

HENRY CAVENDISH carried out his electrical experiments, as he had his early chemical experiments, while living with his father on Great Marlborough Street. We know roughly the size of the room in which he did them, for he calculated the inductive influence of it on his apparatus, regarding the room as a sphere sixteen feet in diameter, "about its real size."[1] We can imagine the room as containing various electrical instruments, some delicate like Lane's and Henley's electrometers, some massive like Cavendish's great battery of Leyden jars, which was similar to Priestley's in 1767, the first large battery.[2]

CAPACITY

If Cavendish had followed his paper on electrical theory with further publications, the next of his "papers" would have given the "first experiment," a proof of the mathematical law of the electric force.[3] Several attempts had been made to determine directly the law of electric force by experiment, and there had also been Priestley's inference of the law of electric force from the electric-cup experiment based upon a well-known theorem of the *Principia*, which states that there is no force in the interior of a gravitating shell if the force of gravitation obeys the inverse-square law. Other electricians gave different explanations of the electrified cup; John Canton told Priestley that it contained no "mystery."[4] Only Cavendish, it seems, followed up Priestley's line of reasoning.

---

[1] Henry Cavendish, *The Scientific Papers of the Honourable Henry Cavendish*, vol. 1: *The Electrical Researches*, ed. J. C. Maxwell, rev. J. Larmor (Cambridge: Cambridge University Press, 1921), 169. Maxwell's 1879 edition was reprinted by Frank Cass in 1967, cited here as *Electrical Researches*.

[2] William D. Hackmann, *Electricity from Glass: The History of the Frictional Electrical Machine 1600–1850* (Alphen aan den Rijn: Sijtoff & Noordhoff, 1978), 99–100.

[3] Cavendish, *Electrical Researches*, 142. The discussion in this chapter is drawn from Russell McCormmach, "The Electrical Researches of Henry Cavendish," Ph.D. diss. (Case Institute of Technology, 1967), especially chapter 4, "Cavendish's Electrical Experiments," and chapter 5, "Conclusion," 322–497.

[4] John Canton to Joseph Priestley, 10 Jan. 1767, Canton Papers, Royal Society, Correspondence 2.

Cavendish demonstrated mathematically that if the intensity of the electric force falls off as the inverse square of the distance from the electric source, the redundant electric fluid on an electrified sphere lies entirely on its outer surface. He made two conducting globes of slightly different sizes, placing one inside the other and connecting them electrically. Upon electrifying the outer globe, he found that the inner one was not electrified, in agreement with the inverse-square law. The rough instrument he used for detecting electricity on the inner globe–a simple pair of pith balls suspended by linen threads–he made into an instrument of relatively high accuracy by his method. By reducing the charge of the Leyden jar to one-sixtieth of its original strength and applying it to the globe, he found that the pith balls barely separated. With that measure of the sensitivity of his apparatus, he knew that the "quantity of redundant electricity communicated to the globe in this experiment was less than $1/60^{th}$ part of that communicated to the hemispheres in the former experiment," and he concluded that there was no reason to believe that the "inner globe is at all overcharged." He expressed this result in a more meaningful form: the electric force varies inversely as some power of the distance between $2 + 1/50$ and $2 - 1/50$, from which he concluded that there is "no reason to think that it differs at all from the inverse duplicate ratio."[5] That is, if the inverse power of the distance of the law of electric force were $2 + 1/50$ or $2 - 1/50$, Cavendish would have detected a charge on the globe. Cavendish repeated the experiment, replacing the globe within a globe by a parallelepiped within a parallelepiped, thereby ruling out his result as an artifact of the sphere. Then he showed experimentally that just as the law of gravitation depends not only on the distance between two bodies but also on the quantities of matter in them, the electric force between two bodies depends also on the quantities of redundant electric fluids in them.[6]

Charles Augustin Coulomb established the inverse-square law of electric force directly using a torsion balance, and in due time the law went into history as "Coulomb's law." It would seem that no one knew of the hollow-globe experiment before Cavendish's unpublished papers were studied in the nineteenth century. Charles Blagden, Cavendish's colleague who knew his work best, wrote to Heberden in 1787 that Coulomb had just demonstrated that the force of electricity acts "exactly according to the square of the distance."[7] Blagden was obviously ignorant of Cavendish's earlier proof.

The hollow-globe experiment has been discussed perhaps more than any other unpublished experiment in science. One reason for this is the principle of the experiment, which allows scientists to improve indefinitely on Cavendish's

---

[5] Henry Cavendish, "Experimental Determination of the Law of Electric Force," *Sci. Pap.* 1:124.

[6] Henry Cavendish, "Whether the Force with Which Two Bodies Repel Is as the Square of the Redundant Fluid, Tried by Straw Electrometers," *Sci. Pap.* 1:189–93.

[7] Charles Blagden to William Heberden, 10 June 1787, draft, Blagden Letters, Royal Society, 7:66.

49. Battery of Leyden Jars. The box is labelled "JCM" [James Clerk Maxwell], "Electrical Apparatus belonging to Henry Cavendish." Photograph by the authors. Devonshire Collections, Chatsworth. Reproduced by permission of the Chatsworth Settlement Trustees.

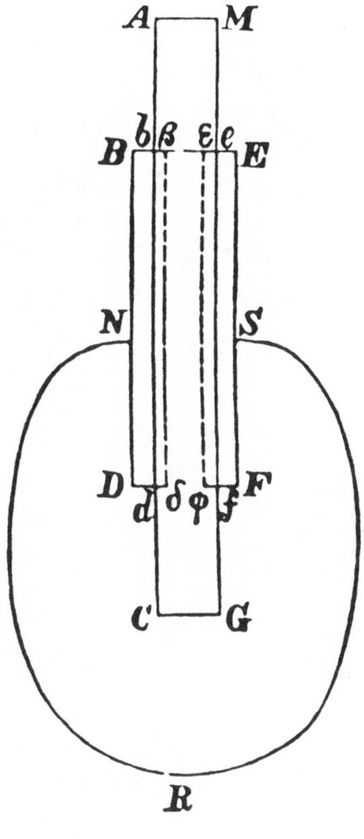

50. Leyden Jar. Cavendish analyzed the phenomena of the Leyden jar, or condensor, using this diagram. ACGM stands for a plate of glass seen edgeways, on either side of which are plates of conducting matter, such as metal foil. The dotted lines indicate the possible penetration of the electric fluid into the glass from the conducting plates. To charge the Leyden jar, one conducting plate is electrified, the other grounded. If a canal (wire) NRS is connected to the two conducting plates, the redundant electric fluid passes from one to the other, "and if in its way it passes through the body of any animal, it will by the rapidity of its motion produce in it that sensation called a shock." "An Attempt to Explain Some of the Principal Phaenomena of Electricity, by Means of an Elastic Fluid," Philosophical Transactions *61 (1771): 623.*

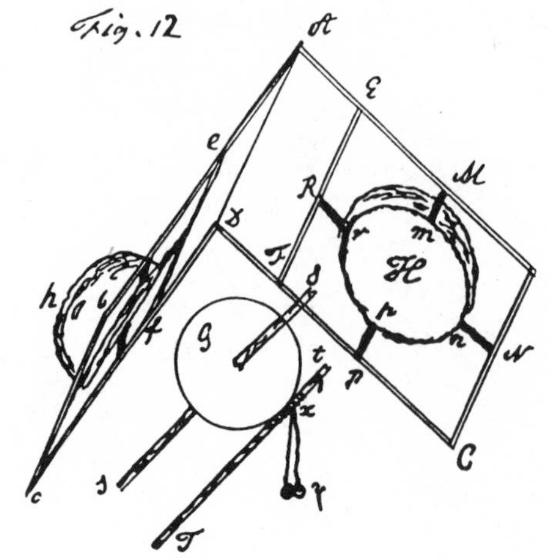

51. *Apparatus for Determining the Electric Force. With this apparatus Cavendish demonstrated the distance dependency of the law of electric force. His drawing of it shows a hinged wooden frame that when closed brings together two hemispherical shells around but not touching an inner globe. The globe, which is 12.1 inches in diameter, is suspended by a stick of glass. The hemispheres and the inner globe are covered with metal foil, and a metal connection is made between the two. When the frame is closed, the hemispheres are electrified with a Leyden jar. Then the metal connection is removed by a string from outside, and the frame is opened. A pair of pith balls, shown in the drawing, is brought against the inner globe. Cavendish found that the pith balls do not separate, showing that no electricity has been communicated to the inner globe. By a theorem from Newton's* Principia, *Cavendish concluded that the electrical force obeys the inverse-square law of the distance. "Experimental Determination of the Law of Electric Force," Cavendish Scientific Manuscripts I, 7(a);* The Electrical Researches of the Honourable Henry Cavendish, *ed. J. C. Maxwell (Cambridge, 1879), 104. Reproduced by permission of the Chatsworth Settlement Trustees.*

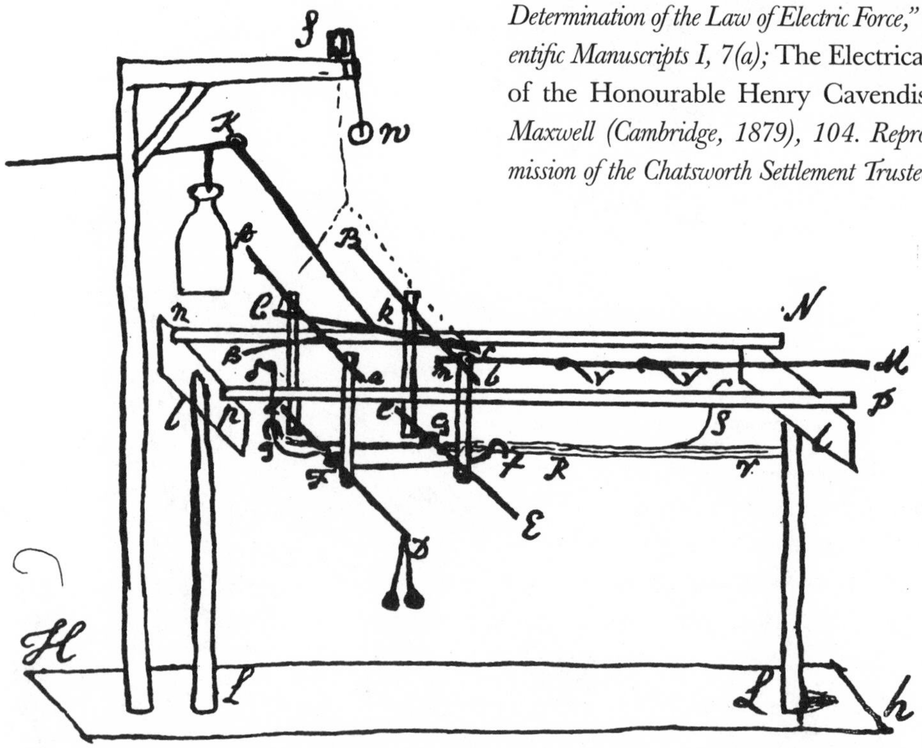

52. *Apparatus for Determining Charges. Standing on the floor, this seemingly rickety contrivance of wood and glass sticks, wires, and Leyden jar is actually portable and described by Cavendish as compact. Two plates coated on both sides in the manner of a Leyden jar are electrified together, one plate serving as a standard; then a communication is made between the upper coating of one plate and the lower coating of the other; if the original charges of the two plates are the same, the pith balls at D, serving as the electrometer, will not separate, but if the charges are different, they will.* Ibid., *145. Reproduced by permission of the Chatsworth Settlement Trustees.*

53. Electrical Machine. Made by Edward Nairne, stamped at the base "Nairne's/Patent/Medico-Electrical/ Machine," this instrument belonging to Henry Cavendish was presented to the Cavendish Laboratory at Cambridge by the duke of Devonshire around 1928. It consists essentially of a glass cylinder with a turning handle and two metal cylinders, which contain Leyden jars. There are also a leather pad, a square of silk, and a brass discharging rod with a glass handle. Courtesy of the Whipple Museum of the History of Science, Cambridge, England.

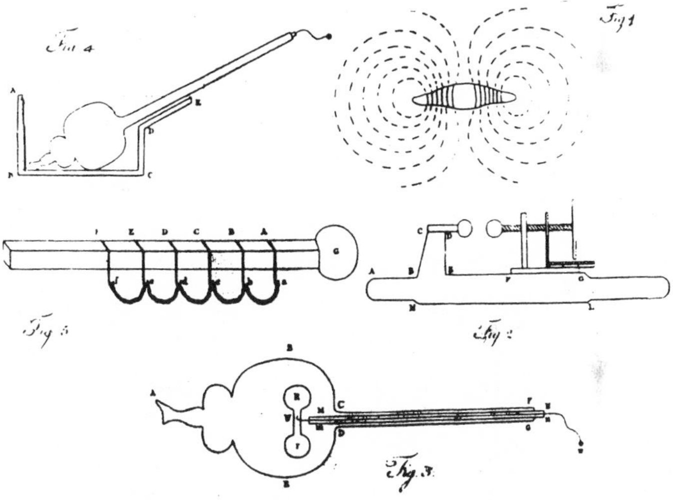

54. Artificial Electric Fish. In Fig. 1, the solid line is the outline of an electric fish, or "torpedo," immersed in water. The dotted lines are the direction of flow of the electric fluid. Should a person place his hands on the top and bottom of the fish or even only in water in the vicinity of the top and bottom, some fluid will flow through him. Cavendish's use here of the idea of lines of current did not become established in science until the next century. Fig. 2 is Cavendish's handheld modified version of Timothy Lane's electrometer, made of brass and wood, indicating the distance a spark flies. Not shown is the pith-ball electrometer used to estimate the strength of a charge. Resembling a stringed musical instrument, the drawing in Fig. 3 is the artificial torpedo. Cut to the shape of the fish, a piece of wood 16¾ inches long and 10¾ inches wide with a handle 40 inches long is fitted with a glass tube MNmn. A wire passing through the tube is soldered at W to a strip of pewter, which represents the electric organs. The other side of the apparatus is fitted exactly the same way, with tube, wire, and pewter. With the exception of the handle, the whole is wrapped with a sheet of sheepskin leather. Fig. 4 shows the apparatus immersed in a vessel of salt water. Fig. 5 shows a device for testing if the shock of the artificial torpedo can pass through chain. Through the wires and the body of the artificial fish, Cavendish discharged portions of his great battery of forty-nine extremely thin-walled Leyden jars. Leonid Kryzhanovsky, "The Fish Tale of Early Electricity," Electronics World and Wireless World *99 (1993): 119–21. The drawing appears in Henry Cavendish, "An Account of Some Attempts to Imitate the Effects of the Torpedo by Electricity,"* Philosophical Transactions *66 (1776): 196–225; in* The Electrical Researches, *ed. J. C. Maxwell, pp. 194–215, on p. 196.*

limits of accuracy. A century after Cavendish, at Cambridge, Cavendish's hollow-globe experiment was repeated with an electrometer capable of detecting a charge thousands of times smaller than Cavendish's straw electrometer could; the conclusion was that the electric force varies inversely as some power of the distance between 2 + 1/21600 and 2 - 1/21600.[8] Since Cavendish, the electrification of concentric conducting shells "has been at the heart of the most sensitive tests" of that law.[9] Another reason for the interest in Cavendish's experiment is historical and philosophical. Why did Cavendish assume that the law of electric force has the mathematical form of an inverse power of the distance?[10] Do Cavendish's and Maxwell's claims for the accuracy of the experiment stand up?[11] How did Cavendish control the errors of the experiment?[12] Why did he not publish his experiment?[13]

The hollow-globe experiment and its sequel not only determined the law of electric attraction and repulsion but also served "in some measure" to confirm the "truth" of the theory as a whole. For the location of the redundant electric fluid on or extremely near the surface of a body would "by no means" have been expected without the theory. Cavendish's subsequent experiments, in which he assumed the inverse-square law of electric force and canals of incompressible electric fluid, provided "great confirmation" of the "truth of the theory."

The latter experiments were carried out on the charges of bodies of various sizes and shapes, connected by slender wires. They were experiments on what came to be called the electrical "capacities" of bodies, a new activity in electrical science owing to his theory. His method depended upon the leading idea of the theory, the "degree of electrification": electrically connected bodies of various shapes and sizes carry different charges at the same degree of elec-

---

8 The experiment was done by Donald MacAlister in 1877 and 1878 under Maxwell's direction. James Clerk Maxwell, "On the Unpublished Electrical Papers of the Hon. Henry Cavendish," *Proc. Camb. Phil. Soc.* 3 (1877): 86–89, on 87.

9 Ross L. Spencer, "If Coulomb's Law Were Not Inverse Square: The Charge Distribution inside a Solid Conducting Sphere," *Americal Journal of Physics* 58 (1990): 385–90, on 385.

10 Laplace gave the first proof that for there to be no force inside a uniform hollow globe, the only function of the distance it can have is the inverse square, as noted by Maxwell in *The Electrical Researches of the Honourable Henry Cavendish* (London, 1879), 422. Laplace's proof still does not rule out other possible forces consistent with Cavendish's experiment; the point is discussed in Jon Dorling, "Henry Cavendish's Deduction of the Electrostatic Inverse Square Law from the Result of a Single Experiment," *Studies in the History and Philosophy of Science* 4 (1974): 327–48, on 335–36, 341–42.

11 Ronald Laymon, "Demonstrative Induction, Old and New Evidence and the Accuracy of the Electrostatic Inverse Square Law," *Synthese* 99 (1994): 23–58.

12 Cavendish's hollow-globe experiment and his subsidiary experiments have been likened to a "Russian doll with experiment inside of experiment." Jean A. Miller, "Enlightenment: Error and Experiment, *Henry Cavendish's Electrical Researches*," M.A. diss. (Virginia Polytechnic and State University, Blacksburg, 1997), 71.

13 Leonid Kryzhanovsky, "Why Cavendish Kept 'Coulomb's' Law a Secret," *Electronics World and Wireless World* 98 (1992): 847–48.

trification; the ratio of these charges is therefore physically meaningful and, Cavendish showed, measurable. As he had in chemistry, in electricity he introduced standard measures, here a conducting globe of 12.1 inches diameter, the same globe he had used in the hollow-globe experiment, and "trial plates," which were pairs of rectangular tin sheets that could be slid across one another to vary the area of the rectangle. He expressed the charge of a body as the charge of a globe of the same capacity at the same degree of electrification. With his careful technique, he obtained highly precise measurements of electrical capacities using a simple pith-ball electrometer or a "more exact" version of it made of stiff wheaten straws and cork balls instead of linen threads and pith balls. He found the ratio of the capacity of a circular disc to that of a sphere of the same diameter to be $^1/_{1.57}$; the theoretically calculated value today is $^1/_{1.570}$ . . .[14]

Despite the dreadful reputation of Leyden jars, in his experiments on electrical capacities Cavendish's Leyden jars were "extremely weakly" charged to reduce the loss of electricity running into the air and over the surface of nonconductors. Before giving an account of his experiments, he discussed the "accuracy" that could be expected of them. To partially compensate for an "error" in the use of trial plates arising from unknown causes, "for greater security" he always took multiple observations, comparing "each body with the trial plate 6 or 7 times." To reduce the error of the observer, he was careful to place his eye always at the same distance from the electrometer. In an experiment on a very weak Leyden jar constructed of air instead of glass, he placed his little finger on one of the plates, feeling a "small pulse," and upon varying the experiment, he was unable to "perceive any difference in the feel." His "assistant," who was turning the electrical machine, was asked to try the experiment, and he also felt no difference. Cavendish gave close attention to the "error of the experiment," concerned that the differences between his results and the theory were not owing to an "error in the theory." That the differences were "so small" he regarded as a "strong sign that the theory is true."[15]

Another "Part" of the "work" dealt with experiments on the charges of plates of glass and other nonconductors coated in the manner of Leyden jars. For these experiments, Cavendish again introduced trial plates, in this case plates with circular coatings of foil which were themselves simple Leyden jars. He determined the thickness of the plates with a Bird dividing engine. In a qualitative way Cavendish's theory explained Leyden jars perfectly well, as he had shown in his published paper of 1771, but now Cavendish was doing quantitative electricity, and Leyden jars nearly ended his career as a mathematical electrician. When he

[14] Cavendish, *Electrical Researches*, 119–21, 141–42. R. J. Stephenson, "The Electrical Researches of the Hon. Henry Cavendish, F.R.S.," *The American Physics Teacher* 6 (1938): 55–58, on 56.

[15] Cavendish, *Electrical Researches*, 121, 127, 135, 254.

discovered that the measured charge of a glass Leyden jar was eight times greater than the charge predicted by his theory, a discrepancy which could not be written off as experimental error, he wrote in the manner of understatement, "This is what I did not expect before I made the experiment." He was afraid that the "reader" might suspect that there was "some error in the theory,"[16] and although he convinced himself that there was not, it took a great many experiments and all his theoretical ingenuity. To explain why the glass of the Leyden jar acted as if it were eight times thinner than it actually was, he supposed that glass has a structure of nonconducting and conducting parts, arranged in alternating layers, the thickness of any one conducting layer of glass being "infinitely small," and the total thickness of the nonconducting parts being one-eighth the thickness of the conducting parts.[17] Lest the explanation seem entirely ad hoc, Cavendish made an "analogy between this and the power by which a particle of light is alternately attracted and repelled many times in its approach towards the surface of any refracting or reflecting medium." At this point he directed the reader to John Michell's explanation of Newton's so-called fits of easy reflection and transmission of light, according to which each particle of a refractive or reflecting medium is surrounded by a great many equal intervals of attraction and repulsion alternately succeeding one another.[18] In experimenting with different kinds of glass and other nonconducting substances, Cavendish made a fundamental discovery, which Faraday would rediscover, that of specific inductive capacities. Like the thermal properties of different substances–in the 1760s Cavendish had made a fundamental investigation of specific and latent heats–the electrical properties of different substances vary quantitatively and characteristically. As he had in heat, in electricity Cavendish made discoveries by his quantitative experiments without any theoretical anticipation. Within the context of experiments undertaken to explore the consequences of his electrical theory, his experimental technique in itself proved to be a tool of discovery.

CONDUCTION

Conduction was only slightly represented among the "principal phaenomena" of electricity in Cavendish's paper of 1771. By 1773 he had changed his mind, or at least his direction; from then on all of his electrical experiments had to do with conduction. Since current electricity was still undiscovered, Cavendish had to rely on transient discharges of Leyden jars, and to measure the effect he made himself into his own principal instrument. In other kinds of experiments, Cavendish's primary sense was variously sight, hearing, and occasionally smell and taste, but in his experiments on electrical conduction, it was touch or, to be

---

[16] Henry Cavendish, "Experiments on Coated Plates," *Sci. Pap.* 1:151–88, on 175, 180.

[17] Ibid., 176.

[18] Michell's account was reported in Joseph Priestley's *History and Present State of Discoveries Relating to Vision, Light, and Colours*, 2 vols. (London, 1772) 1:309–11.

more specific, an electrically stimulated sensation in the skin of the hands and in the internal nerves of the wrists and elbows. His technique was to insert himself into the electric circuit by holding a piece of metal in each hand and touching one piece to the knob of a Leyden jar and the other piece to one end of a tube containing a conducting solution, while the other end of the conducting solution was connected by a wire to the other side of the Leyden jar. The glass tubes containing his solutions were about a yard long, calibrated, with wires inserted at each end as electrodes. To vary the resistance of a solution, he slid one of the wires, thereby changing the effective length of the solution. For the purpose of comparing one conducting solution with another, he prepared a series of six equally charged Leyden jars, which he then discharged alternately through the two solutions (and himself), adjusting the wire in one of the tubes until the shocks of the two solutions were as nearly equal as he could judge. In this way, with "truly marvelous" discrimination, he obtained conductivities consistent with one another and remarkably close to those obtained by later experimenters using the galvanometer, the instrument invented forty years later for the purpose.[19]

Cavendish explained electrical conduction as he had electrical equilibrium, by the fluid mechanics of the matter of electricity, attributing the shock he felt with his hands to the combined effect of the quantity of electric matter discharged and its velocity. He experienced the force of electricity in motion as the direct electrical analog of momentum, the Newtonian measure of the force of ordinary matter in motion. In passing through matter–wires, solutions, and flesh–the electric fluid encountered "resistance." Following the practice of fluid mechanics, Cavendish assumed that the resistance varied as some power of the velocity. His experiments to determine that power yielded the value one or values close to it. It has been pointed out that if Cavendish's velocity is interpreted as strength of current, or current per unit area, he came upon what would later be known as Ohm's law.[20]

By an oblique route, Cavendish revealed to the public his understanding of electrical conduction. Long before Luigi Galvani's work at the end of the eighteenth century, animal electricity had been recognized and studied, but its identity with common electricity had yet to be experimentally demonstrated. With Cavendish's help, an electric fish called the "torpedo" was shown to be capable of delivering shocks with common electricity.

Known in antiquity and in the Renaissance as a magical fish, the torpedo retained its occult aura even into the eighteenth century but not beyond the experiments of the 1770s.[21] The fish enters the history of modern physics with

---

19 Maxwell's "Introduction," *Electrical Researches of the Honourable Henry Cavendish*, xxvii–lxvi, on lvii–lviii.

20 Maxwell made this observation in Cavendish, *Sci. Pap.* 1:25.

21 Brian P. Copenhaver, "Natural Magic, Hermeticism, and Occultism in Early Modern Science," in *Reappraisals of the Scientific Revolution*, ed. D. C. Linberg and R. S. Westman (Cambridge: Cambridge University Press, 1990), 261–301, on 278–79.

the Dutch physicist Petrus van Musschenbroek, who likened its shock to the one he felt upon discharging a Leyden jar through his body. He suggested that the torpedo was an electric fish, and the name stuck.[22] The torpedo is one of a number of fishes capable of delivering a shock, the most formidable of which is a South American eel, the *Electrophorus electricus*, called "Gymnotus." This large, otherwise almost blind, sluggish fish with small teeth and no spines or scales was said with some exaggeration to be able to kill men and horses. From America the Royal Society received reports that the Gymnotus gives a "true electric shock," that its shock is "wholly electrical."[23] The identification of the singular power of the Gymnotus with electricity may be one reason why John Walsh began to experiment on the torpedo, an electrical fish in the nearby seas.[24] From La Rochelle, France, where he went on a torpedo hunt, Walsh wrote to Benjamin Franklin that he found the torpedo's effect to be "absolutely electrical."[25] The back and breast of the fish were found to have different electricities, like the sides of a Leyden jar, leading Walsh to wonder if its effect could be exactly imitated by one. To learn more about his fish he enlisted the services of the anatomist John Hunter. Dissecting a specimen, Hunter was impressed by what he found: each of the pair of electrical organs of the torpedo had about 470 prismatic columns, and each column was divided by horizontal membranes, 150 to the inch, forming tiny spaces filled with fluid.[26] Hunter presented the Royal Society with male and female specimens of this wonderfully structured animal. Walsh submitted a paper to the Royal Society: of the torpedo, he wrote that "*the Leyden phial contains all his magic power*."[27]

The case for the electrical nature of the torpedo had not yet been made to everyone's satisfaction. There were solid grounds for doubt: the torpedo could not produce a spark or separate pith balls, basic signs of the presence of electricity. One who doubted was the electrician William Henly, who at about the same time as Cavendish made an "artificial torpedo" of conducting materials. It exhibited "no attraction or repulsion of light bodies, no snap, no light, nor indeed any sensation." Henly argued that the real torpedo was

---

[22] Leonid N. Kryzhanovsky, "The Fishy Tale of Early Electricity," *Electronics World and Wireless World* 99 (1993): 119–21, on 119.

[23] Hugh Williamson, who had done experiments on the fish in Philadelphia in 1773, was now in London: "Experiments and Observations on the Gymnotus Electricus or Electric Eel," *PT* 65 (1775): 94–101. From Charleston, Alexander Garden wrote that several specimens of the fish were going to be sent to England: "An Account of the Gymnotus Electricus, or Electric Eel," *PT* 65 (1775): 102–10.

[24] R. T. Cox, "Electric Fish," *American Journal of Physics* 11 (1943): 13–22, on 14. W. Cameron Walker, "Animal Electricity before Galvani," *Annals of Science* 2 (1937): 84–113, on 88–90.

[25] John Walsh to Benjamin Franklin, 12 July 1772, quoted in John Walsh, "Of the Electric Property of the Torpedo," *PT* 63 (1773): 461–80, on 462.

[26] John Hunter, "Anatomical Observations on the Torpedo," *PT* 63 (1773): 481–89, on 484–85.

[27] John Walsh, "Of Torpedos Found on the Coast of England," *PT* 64 (1774): 473.

in the same predicament as the artificial one, incapable of delivering an "*electrical shock*."[28]

Cavendish, Walsh said, was the "first to experience with artificial electricity, that a shock could be received from a charge which was unable to force a passage through the least space of air."[29] Since Cavendish had not published his electrical experiments, Walsh had to have received this information from him by request. In 1774 Walsh was awarded the Copley Medal for his experiments on the electrical nature of the torpedo. On the occasion, the president of the Royal Society, John Pringle, said that "between lightning itself and the Leyden Phial there is no specific difference, nay scarcely a variety, as far as is known, why then should we unnecessarily multiply species and suppose the torpedo provided with one different from that which is everywhere else to be found?"[30]

In 1776 Cavendish published his experiments on an artificial torpedo.[31] A main objection to the idea that the torpedo possesses electricity was that its shock is delivered underwater where the electric fluid has easier channels than through the victim's (or the experimenter's) body. That criticism was based on the commonly held but incorrect view that all of the electric fluid flows along the "shortest and readiest" path. The paths it actually takes depend on the relative resistances of all of the paths available to it. The reason, Cavendish explained, why a person holding a wire with both hands, thereby forming a parallel circuit with the wire, does not feel a shock when a discharge is sent along the wire is that the resistance of the body is so much greater than that of the wire that only an insensible fraction of the discharge passes through the body. To explain how a fish could throw a great shock and yet not produce a spark, Cavendish noted that the length of spark from a battery of Leyden jars varies inversely as the number of jars in the battery. He believed that the electric organs of the torpedo were equivalent to a great number of Leyden jars connected like a battery: these living jars were weakly electrified, but because of their great number, they could store a large quantity of electricity. Cavendish answered another common objection with this observation: the discharge of the torpedo is completed so quickly that a pair of pith balls in contact with the animal does not have time to separate. To prove the correctness of his explanations, Cavendish built his artificial torpedoes. His first was cut out of wood in the shape of the fish, but it did not conduct as well as Cavendish thought the real fish did; he built a second one by press-

---

28 William Henly to William Canton, 14 Mar. 1775, Canton Papers, Royal Society, Correspondence 2:104.

29 Walsh, "Torpedo," 476.

30 John Pringle, *A Discourse on the Torpedo Delivered at the Anniversary Meeting of the Royal Society, November 30, 1774* (London, 1775). Quoted in Dorothea Waley Singer, "Sir John Pringle and His Circle.– Part III. Copley Discourses," *Annals of Science* 6 (1950): 248–61, on 251.

31 Henry Cavendish, "An Account of Some Attempts to Imitate the Effects of the Torpedo by Electricity," *PT* 66 (1776): 196–225; in *Sci. Pap.* 1:194–210.

ing together shaped pieces of thick leather like the "soles of shoes" to represent the body and attaching thin plates of pewter to each side to imitate the electric organs. With glass-insulated wires he connected the pewter plates to a battery, encasing the whole in sheepskin leather soaked in salt solution, the stand-in for the skin of the torpedo. Discharging different numbers of Leyden jars through the artificial torpedo and placing his hands on or near it, he found that the sensations agreed with descriptions of the shock of the real torpedo.

So that others could experience his artificial torpedo, Cavendish invited into his laboratory a number of interested persons: the torpedo anatomist Hunter; Lane, whose electrometer Cavendish was using; Nairne, whose battery and coated glass plates he was using; Priestley, who was in London on a visit; and Thomas Ronayne.[32] The latter, a skeptic, had said of Walsh's electrical hypothesis of the torpedo that he would have to "give up his reason" to believe that the tissues of the fish could accumulate enough electricity to deliver a shock; he left Cavendish's laboratory a believer, we presume, since Cavendish recorded in his notes of the visit, "Mr Ronayne felt a small shock."[33] Cavendish explained that the battery of the real fish was superior to his, powerful as his was.[34] From Hunter's observations, Cavendish calculated that the torpedo had nearly fourteen times the electrical capacity of even this battery. Cavendish concluded that "there seems nothing in the phenomena of the torpedo at all incompatible with electricity."[35]

Cavendish was not to have the last word on this subject, since the Voltaic battery would provide a better model for the electric organs of fishes than the Leyden jar battery, and Davy, Faraday, and others would perform the definitive researches on the electrical character of the several kinds of electrical fish.[36] Although Cavendish thought that it was likely that the electric fish contained something "analogous" to the Leyden jar battery, he also considered that there might be no such thing, and in envisioning the possibility that the electric fluid is not stored but gradually transferred by a small "force" through the substance and over the surface of the body of the fish, he anticipated the Voltaic battery and the associated fundamental concept of electromotive force.[37] (We realize that we run the risk of becoming tiresome by frequently noting Cavendish's anticipation of later discoveries. That he did so, however, has been a persistent reason for the wonder with which the world has come to regard him.)

After his paper on the torpedo, through early 1777, Cavendish continued to experiment on the conductivity of solutions, using a given salt solu-

---

[32] The guests are named in Cavendish's laboratory notes for 27 May 1775. Ibid., 313.

[33] Ibid. Letter from William Henly to John Canton, 21 May 1775, Canton Papers, Royal Society; quoted in Cavendish, *Electrical Researches*, xxxvii.

[34] Maxwell's note in Cavendish, *Electrical Researches*, 299.

[35] Cavendish, *Electrical Researches*, 213.

[36] Maxwell's note in Cavendish, *Electrical Researches*, 435–37.

[37] Cox, "Electric Fish," 21–22.

tion as a standard measure. In 1781 he returned briefly to the subject for a last time.

THE WORK

We close this account of Cavendish's electrical experiments with a discussion of the "work," the book he intended to publish, and of the response to the part of it he did publish.[38] With the reading of his paper on electrical theory to the Royal Society in 1771, Cavendish was recognized as an authority on electricity. In the following year he was appointed to an ongoing committee of the Royal Society to protect the powder magazines at Purfleet from destruction by lightning. In response to a request by the government, the Royal Society volunteered its best local electricians, Watson, Franklin, Wilson, and, its most recent arrival, Cavendish.[39] In 1773 this committee paid a visit to Purfleet to confirm that the lightning conductors were erected according to their instructions;[40] in 1777 Cavendish was appointed to another committee with the same purpose;[41] in 1796 Cavendish and Charles Blagden were appointed as a committee to reexamine the state of the conductors at Purfleet.[42] In 1801 Cavendish was appointed to a committee with the related assignment of determining the proper floor covering to reduce frictional electricity at powder magazines and works.[43]

---

38 Cavendish, *Electrical Researches*, 172. As an article, the "work" would have been long: the material to be included occupies 104 pages of the Maxwell edition of Cavendish's electrical researches, and it would have expanded into nearly twice that number of pages in the *Philosophical Transactions.* The 1771 paper was itself long, taking up forty-nine pages in the Maxwell edition and ninety-four in the *Philosophical Transactions*, by far Cavendish's longest publication. It is likely that at some point Cavendish abandoned his original idea of publishing another article in the *Philosophical Transactions* and set out instead to write a book. Maxwell thought that Cavendish was working on a book, in *Sci. Pap.* 1:13.

39 26 Aug. 1772, Minutes of Council, Royal Society 6:144–49. This was the second committee on lightning conductors; the first, in 1769, was without Cavendish, who had not yet published on electricity. The second committee, with Cavendish, gave a report and recommendations. Wilson dissented from the opinion of the report and did not sign it. Also on the committee was the clerk of the Royal Society, John Robertson, who was a skilled scientific investigator but had done no published work in electricity. Cavendish's name appears first in the list of committee members as authors of the published report: "A Report of the Committee Appointed by the Royal Society, to Consider of a Method for Securing the Powder Magazines at Purfleet," *PT* 63 (1773): 42–47. Wilson's dissenting opinion follows on p. 48.

40 22 Nov. 1773, Minutes of Council, Royal Society 6:193.

41 In 1777 there was a third committee with an almost entirely new membership, with the exception of Cavendish. On it were the specialists in electrical instruments Nairne, Henly, and Lane, the other British scientist to bring forward a general, mathematical theory of electricity, Charles Stanhope, Lord Mahon, and the electrical experimenter, Priestley. This third committee reported on the dissident Wilson's recommendation for rounded instead of pointed lightning conductors, a controversy ideally suited for the talents of Swift, if he had been around to know of it. Henry Lyons, *The Royal Society, 1660–1940: A History of Its Administration under Its Charters* (New York: Greenwood, 1968), 193.

42 17 Mar. 1796, Minutes of Council, Royal Society 8:82.

43 11 June and 12 Nov. 1801, Minutes of Council, Royal Society 8:185, 190–92.

While Cavendish's electrical theory drew the attention of the Royal Society, it generated no evident interest among electrical researchers. The next paper on electricity to be published in the *Philosophical Transactions* after Cavendish's was about a new electrometer by William Henly, which made use of a cork ball turning over a graduated scale. Priestley, the author of the paper, said that the electrometer was capable of measuring "both the precise degree of the electrification of any body, and also the exact quantity of a charge before the explosion."[44] Henly's electrometer was an excellent instrument for investigating the experimental consequences of Cavendish's mathematical theory. Cavendish, in fact, put it to that use, but apparently no one else did. In 1812, the year of Simon Denis Poisson's great mathematical theory of electricity, and forty years after Cavendish's theory, Thomas Thomson wrote in his *History of the Royal Society*:

> The most rigid and satisfactory explanation of the phenomena of electricity, which has hitherto appeared in any language, is contained in a very long, but most masterly paper of Mr. Cavendish, published in the Philosophical Transactions for 1771. It is very remarkable, and to me an unaccountable circumstance, that notwithstanding the great number of treatises on electricity which have appeared since the publication of this paper, which is, beyond dispute, the most important treatise on the subject that has ever been published, no one, so far as I recollect, has ever taken the least notice of Mr. Cavendish's labours, far less given a detailed account of his theory. Whether this be owing to the mathematical dress in which Mr. Cavendish was obliged to clothe his theory, or to the popular and elementary nature of the treatises which have been published, I shall not pretend to determine; but at all events it is a thing very much to be regretted.[45]

Thomson's impression is confirmed by George Green, who came across Cavendish's "excellent paper" in a search of the literature after finishing his important essay of 1828 on the electrical potential functions; he noted that Cavendish's theory "appears to have attracted little attention."[46]

One of the reasons it received little attention was that British researchers in the new experimental fields were not mathematical theorists. Moreover, around the time of Cavendish's publication, electricity was no longer in the forefront, as it had been fifteen years before, and the same can be said of the topics within electricity that Cavendish addressed. His "principal" phenomena–the attraction and repulsion of bodies, electric induction, the Leyden jar, and the electrification

[44] Joseph Priestley, "An Account of a New Electrometer, Contrived by Mr. William Henly, and of Several Electrical Experiments Made by Him," *PT* 62 (1772): 359–64, on 359; read 28 May 1772.

[45] Thomas Thomson, *History of the Royal Society from Its Institution to the End of the Eighteenth Century* (London, 1812), 455.

[46] George Green, *An Essay on the Application of Mathematical Analysis to the Theories of Electricity and Magnetism* (Nottingham, 1828), v.

of air—were thought to be adequately understood. Priestley's *History of Electricity* contained his own investigations of phenomena that were not adequately understood, and in his queries in that book he suggested the nature of the problems that interested Cavendish's contemporaries; these had mainly to do with the connections between electricity and light, sound, heat, and chemistry. Typical of the direction of thought then was Henly's belief that light, fire, phlogiston, and electricity were "only different modifications of one and the same principle."[47] Although Cavendish would certainly have accepted connections between these agents, his work was not directed to them.

Cavendish did not publish his electrical experiments for reasons more complicated than simple neglect. What had begun as a second paper for the *Philosophical Transactions* became a large treatise on electricity, and although he seems to have been satisfied with several of his subsequent electrical researches, he may well have been dissatisfied with the treatise. His discovery of the influence of chemical substances on the capacity of Leyden jars may have been one source of dissatisfaction, and the relationship of his experiments on conduction to his theory is unclear.

Cavendish had begun his electrical researches after his initial publication on factitious air, which earned him a Copley Medal. After his paper on electrical theory a few years later, there was no sign that anyone recognized that this was the beginning of a work that might stand beside Newton's. He never again published a theoretical paper.

Since Cavendish's electrical researches were by no means the only ones that he would lay aside after preparing them for publication, his change of heart did not have entirely to do with the subject of electricity. William Heberden, who wrote the certificate for Cavendish's membership in the Royal Society, wrote a paper (which he did not publish) on the advantages of writing but not publishing. Writing, he said, "enlarges the mind and improves the taste," a sufficient reason for going to the trouble. The writer, however, if he "has already established a reputation, loses it as soon as he ventures to give anything to the public." The happiest writer, Heberden thought, was one who wrote "always with a view to publishing, though without ever doing so."[48] For a person who relished controversy as little as Cavendish did, his good friend Heberden's advice might have seemed not only witty but wise.

---

[47] William Henly, "Experiments and Observations in Electricity," *PT* 67 (1777): 85–143, on 135.

[48] William Heberden, "Upon Composition, Authors, and Their Works in General, Either of Genius or Science," quoted in Humphry Rolleston, "The Two Heberdens," *Annals of Medical History* 5 (1933): 409–24, 566–83, on 417–18.

LEARNED ORGANIZATIONS

ROYAL SOCIETY

At the time Cavendish entered the Royal Society, in 1760, its membership was stable, as it had not been before and would not be after. During the twenty years centering on 1760, the average number of ordinary members was virtually constant, around 355, whereas it had grown by nearly one-quarter in the thirty years after Cavendish's father had joined. The foreign membership was now at its maximum, around 160, 40 percent larger than it had been thirty years before; thereafter it slowly declined owing to a deliberate policy of the Society to stop the escalation of this honorary segment of its membership.[1]

Cavendish acted to perpetuate but not inflate the membership. Throughout his fifty years in the Society, he recommended a new member every year or two, somewhat over thirty all told. The first time he signed a certificate, he did so together with his father, whose name appears first; that was the only time father and son made a recommendation in common. Lord Charles Cavendish made only four more recommendations after 1760. Four of the first five candidates Cavendish recommended were Cambridge men. His first, in 1763, was Anthony Shepherd, who had recently been appointed the Plumian professor of astronomy and experimental philosophy at Cambridge. Shepherd was ten years older than Cavendish, but the other three were Cavendish's age, previously fellow students

[1] On 19 Dec. 1765 the council resolved to admit no more than two foreign members a year until their number fell to eighty. Excluded from this limit were sovereign princes and their sons, ambassadors, foreigners living in England, and presidents of foreign academies of science. The council passed a series of other resolutions on the subject, the most important being that no foreigner could be admitted in shorter time than six months and that he had to be recommended by three foreign and three domestic members. 19 Dec. 1765 and 6 Feb. 1766, Minutes of Council, copy, Royal Society, 5:146–48, 153–54.

at Cambridge. They were the mathematician and barrister Francis Maseres, the astronomer and cleric Francis Wollaston, and the antiquarian and diplomat John Strange.[2]

A further indication of the connection between Cambridge and Cavendish's scientific life in London is the list of guests he brought to the Royal Society Club. Starting in 1766 the Club identified guests with the members who brought them, and we see that Cavendish's first five guests after that year were all educated at Cambridge. One of them was William Ludlam, who was a little older than Shepherd, then a fellow of St. John's College, Cambridge, but soon to vacate his fellowship to accept a rectory. Ludlam published a book of astronomical observations made at St. John's in 1767–68, including an account of several astronomical instruments together with calculations made for him by Lord Charles Cavendish; independently of his son Henry, Lord Charles also invited Ludlam to the Club as a guest.[3] Another guest was John Michell, the Woodwardian professor of geology at Cambridge, who in 1767, the year Henry invited him to the Club, left Cambridge to become rector of Thornhill in Yorkshire.[4] The three other guests of Henry's were his age, having been fellow students of his at Cambridge, John Strange, Henry Boult Cay, a fellow of Clare College, Cambridge, and Wilkinson Blanshard. Cay, who was soon to vacate his fellowship to practice as a barrister of the Middle Temple,[5] was elected a member of the Club, even though he was not a member of the Royal Society. Blanchard, a Fellow of the Royal Society and of the College of Physicians and physician to St. George's Hospital, was also elected to the Club.

A useful source of information about Cavendish in the Royal Society is the certificates book. Cavendish's recommendations of candidates for membership in the Royal Society are a mirror of his life in science. After his first recommendations of candidates with Cambridge affiliations, his next, in 1769, was of Timothy Lane, who was then working in electricity and chemistry, as was Cavendish. Cavendish's first foreign candidate was the electrical researcher Jean-Baptiste Le Roy in 1772.[6] In the mid 1780s Cavendish, together with Charles Blagden,

[2] Royal Society, Certificates. With dates of proposal: Anthony Shepherd, 2:242 (19 Jan. 1763); John Strange, 2:343 (early Jan. 1766); Francis Wollaston, 3:65 (3 Jan. 1769); Francis Maseres, 3:104 (31 Jan. 1771).

[3] 14 May 1767, Minute Book, Royal Society Club, 5. William Ludlam, *Astronomical Observations Made in St. John's College, Cambridge in the Years 1767 and 1768: With an Account of Several Astronomical Instruments* (London, 1769). "Ludlam, William," *DNB* 12:254–55.

[4] 4 June 1767, Minute Book, Royal Society Club, 5. "Michell, John," *DNB* 13:333–34.

[5] 14 May 1767, 30 June 1768, and 16 Feb. 1769, Minute Book, Royal Society Club, 5. Henry Boult Cay is included in the entry for his father, "Cay, John," in the *Dictionary of National Biography*. Archibald Geikie, *Annals of the Royal Society Club: The Record of a London Dining-Club in the Eighteenth and Nineteenth Centuries* (London: Macmillan, 1917), 91, 100.

[6] Royal Society, Certificates: Timothy Lane, 3:73 (6 May 1769); Jean-Baptiste Le Roy, 3:161 (5 Sep. 1772).

undertook several tours of Britain, making industrial and geological observations, and investigating specimens from ovens and minerals from the earth. The candidates Cavendish recommended at this time included James Watt, who is identified in the certificates book as the inventor of the new steam engine and the author of a paper on chemistry in the *Philosophical Transactions*; James Keir, the former glass and now alkali manufacturer, who is identified as the author of a paper on the crystallization of glass and as the editor of a dictionary of chemistry; and James Lewis Macie (James Smithson) and Philip Rashleigh, both identified with chemistry and mineralogy. Cavendish's recommendation of the foreign geologist Horace Bénédict de Saussure belongs to this group, too.[7] In the late 1780s, when Cavendish's chemical publications came to an end and he evidently abandoned the phlogiston theory of chemistry, he welcomed into the Royal Society as foreign members the leaders of the triumphant anti-phlogistic chemistry: its inventor Antoine Laurent Lavoisier, and his colleagues, L. B. Guyton de Morveau and Claude Louis Berthollet.[8] In the same period, the late 1780s, Cavendish synthesized his wide-ranging experimental and theoretical work in heat, and it was then that he recommended the Swedish master of that subject, Johan Carl Wilcke.[9] In 1789 Cavendish recommended Pierre Simon de Laplace for his work in mathematics and astronomy, and every foreign member after that, with one possible exception, ten all told, were also known for their work in mathematics and astronomy, which were the same fields that Cavendish was then diligently pursuing. This sizable foreign group consisted of Joseph Louis Lagrange, Jean-Baptiste Joseph Delambre, Joseph Mendoza y Rios, Gregorio Fontana, David Rittenhouse, J. H. Schröter, Joseph Piazzi, Franz Xaver von Zach, W. Obers, and Carl Friedrich Gauss.[10] We postpone to the end of this section our discussion of the large group of world travelers recommended by Cavendish.

Of the almost one hundred Fellows of the Royal Society who joined Cavendish in recommending candidates, only a few appear with him on more than one certificate: Nevil Maskelyne appears on half of the certificates, and after him, in decreasing frequency, come the keeper of the natural history department of the British Museum Daniel Solander, William Watson, James Burrow, and William Heberden. Several of these persons are carryovers from co-signers with Cavendish's father.

[7] Royal Society, Certificates: James Watt, 5 (24 Nov. 1785); James Keir, 5 (8 Dec. 1785); James Lewis Macie (James Smithson), 5 (19 Apr. 1787); H. B. de Saussure, 5 (3 Apr. 1788); Philip Rashleigh, 5 (29 May 1788).

[8] Royal Society, Certificates: L. B. Guyton de Morveau, 5 (3 Apr. 1788); A. L. Lavoisier, 5 (3 Apr. 1788); Claude Louis Berthollet, 5 (30 Apr. 1789).

[9] Royal Society, Certificates, 5 (30 Apr. 1789).

[10] Royal Society, Certificates: Pierre Simon de Laplace, 5 (30 Apr. 1789); Joseph Louis Lagrange, 5 (5 May 1791); Joseph Delambre, 5 (5 May 1791); Joseph Mendoza y Rios, 5 (11 Apr. 1793); Gregorio Fontana, 5 (10 July 1794); David Rittenhouse, 5 (6 Nov. 1794); J. H. Schröter, 5 (19 Apr. 1798); Joseph Piazzi, 6 (17 Nov. 1803); Franz Xaver von Zach, 6 (17 Nov. 1803); W. Obers, 6 (17 Nov. 1803); Carl Friedrich Gauss, 6 (17 Nov. 1803).

In November 1765 Henry Cavendish was elected to the council of the Royal Society,[11] the first of thirty-four times, and like his father, he rarely missed a meeting. In his first year on the council, other than for the two secretaries, Henry Cavendish attended with greater regularity than any other member. For the next twenty years he was on the council about half of the time; for the last twenty-five years, through 1809, he was on the council every year. His service on special committees appointed by the council was nearly as consistent.[12] He was extensively involved in the two great projects initiated by the Society during his time, the observation of the transit of Venus in 1769 and the experiment on the attraction of mountains in 1774. He drew up plans for a voyage of discovery to the Arctic; he worked on changes in the statutes of the Society and on the printing of the *Philosophical Transactions*; he was appointed to committees concerned with the state of the instruments of the Royal Society and the Royal Observatory; and he was on committees called into being by requests of the government. He was appointed to twenty-three committees, more or less,[13] and he took on assignments for the Society that did not involve a committee but at most an instrument-maker to work with him. Altogether, Cavendish worked with about sixty Fellows on special committees. Since the work of the Society was spread around, usually other Fellows appeared on only one committee with him, the exceptions being Nevil Maskelyne, the astronomer royal, and the astronomer Alexander Aubert, who was an expert on meteorological as well as astronomical instruments.[14]

In addition to serving on one-time committees, Henry Cavendish, like his father, was often elected one of the annual auditors of the treasurer's account. The first time was during his first year on the council, 1766, when he served with two stalwart members, James Burrow and George Lewis Scott; Cavendish reported to the council in the name of the three auditors, a degree of prominence he could accept.[15] The treasurer's balances were small, but that did not diminish the responsibility of the auditors; Cavendish was joined in subsequent years by other reliable members such as Maskelyne and Benjamin Franklin.

Like his father, Cavendish served regularly on the committee of papers,[16] which attracted able men, regardless of their own habits in the matter of publication; some of them, such as Maskelyne and William Herschel and Cavendish himself, were themselves authors of many papers in the *Philosophical Transactions*,

---

[11] Royal Society, JB 25:663 (30 Nov. 1765).

[12] From a survey of the Minutes of Council, copy, Royal Society, 5–7 (1763–1810).

[13] It depends on how one counts. Committees were often renewed, becoming virtually new committees with the same or a redefined task.

[14] Cavendish served on eight committees with Maskelyne and as many with Aubert.

[15] 24 Nov. 1766, Minutes of Council, Royal Society, 5:152. One week later, on 30 Nov. 1766, p. 156, Cavendish reported for the three auditors.

[16] From a survey of the bound volume of minutes of the Royal Society's committee of papers, 1 (1780–1828).

but others, such as Aubert, published nothing or next to nothing. In addition to attending the meetings of the committee, which took place monthly as needed, the members had homework. On any particular paper, the committee would make one of several decisions: to print, not to print, to withdraw, or to postpone. If postponed, the paper might be referred to one or two members; this happened to Cavendish, and among his papers we find studies of his own that originated this way. In the case of strong disagreement over a given paper, the matter could be taken up by the council of the Society. That was done in 1789: Cavendish gave the council his reasons why a paper that the committee had ordered to be printed in the *Philosophical Transactions* should not be printed; the council then recommended to the committee that it "reconsider their former vote on the subject of the said paper."[17]

In 1766 the council began its painstaking preparations to observe the transit of Venus of 1769, the second of these rare, paired transits, which offer an accurate measure of the sun's distance. Only four years earlier, the Society had at last completed its work on the 1761 transit, with rather disappointing results. At the time, the secretary of the Society Thomas Birch wrote to Philip Yorke that the observations of the transit "differ so considerably from each other . . . that it is question'd, whether the Credit of the Conclusions to be drawn from them will not be much weaken'd: and I am apprehensive that our Astronomers, if not Astronomy itself, will suffer a little in Reputation." Pride as well as science called for a repetition of the measurement. Having learned from their errors in 1761, astronomers planned their observations for 1769 with meticulous care. Evidently the first study of the new transit to be brought before the council was a letter by Henry Cavendish to Lord Morton, president of the Society, on the best places in the world to observe the transit.[18] The success of the project depended critically on the selection of stations. Lord Charles Cavendish, as we have seen, did considerable work on the first transit; Henry Cavendish did so, beginning to end, on the second.

While he was still in the midst of his chemical experiments on air, Cavendish studied the observations of the earlier transit of Venus of 1761. There was a connection of sorts. At the time of the first transit, the effect of the atmosphere of Venus had not been considered, with the result that the reported times of contacts of Venus and the sun were discordant.[19] By making different assumptions

---

[17] The paper proposed a new and easy method for determining the difference of longitude. 19 Feb. 1789, Minutes of Council, Royal Society, 7:310.

[18] Thomas Birch to Philip Yorke, Viscount Royston, 13 June 1761, BL Add Mss 35399, f. 202. Henry Cavendish to Lord Morton, 9 June 1766; in Henry Cavendish, *The Scientific Papers of the Honourable Henry Cavendish*, vol. 2: *Chemical and Dynamical*, ed., E. Thorpe (Cambridge: Cambridge University Press, 1921), 435–36. 19 June, Minutes of Council, Royal Society, 5:46–47. Cavendish would later be appointed to a committee of eight to consider places for observing the transit. 12 Nov. 1767, ibid., 5:172.

[19] H. Spencer-Jones, "Astronomy through the Eighteenth Century," in *Natural Philosophy*, published by the *Philosophical Magazine* in 1948, pp. 10–27, on p. 16.

about the elastic fluid constituting the atmosphere of Venus, Cavendish computed the errors of observation owing to the refraction of light passing through it from the sun to the earth.[20] Before Cavendish was done with his work on the transit of Venus of 1769, he had written over 150 pages.[21] As it turned out, the observations of the second transit did not result in an unambiguous figure for the distance of the sun, but the accuracy of the estimate was markedly improved; the project was a major achievement of measuring science.

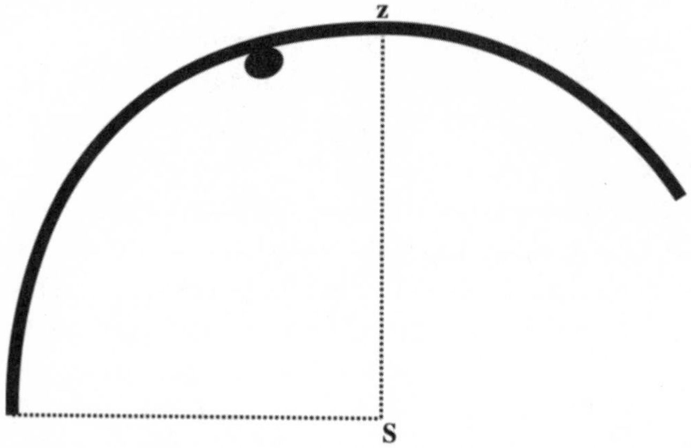

55. Transit of Venus. On the Island of Maggeroe, on the North Cape of Europe, the transit of Venus of 1769 was observed by William Bayley, who was sent there by the Royal Society. The event was partly obscured by clouds but not completely, as is shown by his drawing (which has been redrawn for this book). "Astronomical Observations Made at the North Cape, for the Royal Society," Philosophical Transactions *59 (1769): 262–66, on 266.*

In a letter in 1771 from Maskelyne to Cavendish, we first learn of Cavendish's participation in the other great project of the Royal Society in the second half of the eighteenth century, the experiment on the attraction of mountains to determine the density of the earth;[22] the letter contained two theorems for calculating the gravitational attraction of mountain-like geometrical solids.[23] On the face of it, the experiment on the attraction of mountains seems remote from the Society's recent concern with the transits of Venus, but the goals were

[20] Henry Cavendish, "On the Effects Which Will Be Produced in the Transit of Venus by an Atmosphere Surrounding the Body of Venus," Cavendish Mss VIII, 27.

[21] In addition to "Thoughts on the Proper Places for Observing the Transit of Venus in 1769," his letter to Morton, and "On the Effects . . . of an Atmosphere," Henry Cavendish wrote these studies: "Computation of Transit of Venus 1761, 1769," "Method of Finding in What Year a Transit of Venus Will Happen," "Computation of Transit of 1769 Correct," and "Computation for 1769 Transit," Cavendish Mss VIII, 30–33.

[22] The discussion of the attraction of mountains is based on Russell McCormmach, "The Last Experiment of Henry Cavendish," in *'No Truth Except in Details': Essays in Honor of Martin J. Klein*, ed. A. J. Kox and D. M. Siegel (Dordrecht: Kluwer Academic Publishers, 1995), 1–30.

[23] Nevil Maskelyne to Henry Cavendish, 10 Apr. 1771, Cavendish Mss VIII, 4.

much the same: they were to measure the earth in relation to its home in the universe, the solar system, by determining a standard in each case, a distance in the first and a quantity of matter in the second. The distances of the planets were expressed in terms of the distance of the earth from the sun; likewise, the densities of the sun and some of the planets were known only relatively, so that the density of the earth had to be known to know the density of the other bodies.[24] In the experiment on the attraction of mountains, the mean density of the earth is deduced from measurements of the "deviation of the plumb line at the bottom of a mountain by taking the meridian altitudes of stars."[25]

In the middle of 1772, Maskelyne proposed the experiment to the Royal Society, and the council appointed a committee to consider it and to call on the treasurer as needed.[26] In a letter to Cavendish at the beginning of 1773, Maskelyne said that he had made a copy of Cavendish's rules for computing the attraction of mountains, which were "well calculated to procure us the information that is wanted."[27] In a paper written for his fellow committeeman Benjamin Franklin, Cavendish explained what sorts of mountains are best. The want of attraction of a valley, he said, is as good as the attraction of a mountain and perhaps better.[28] In the middle of 1773, the committee reported to the council on its resolutions, and given the extensive planning Cavendish had done on the experiment, it was appropriate that Cavendish should be the one to make the report.[29] Cavendish was, in effect, the head of the committee. Charles Mason, as directed by the committee, was sent on horseback into the Scottish Highlands to look for mountains and valleys suitable for the experiment. In early 1774, the committee decided on Schehallien, a 3,547-foot granite mountain in Perthshire[30] made to Cavendish's

---

[24] Charles Hutton, "An Account of the Calculations Made from the Survey and Measures Taken at Schehallien, in Order to Ascertain the Mean Density of the Earth," *PT* 68 (1778): 689–788, on 784. B. E. Clotfelter, "The Cavendish Experiment as Cavendish Knew It," *American Journal of Physics* 55 (1987): 210–13, on 211.

[25] Henry Cavendish, "Paper Given to Maskelyne Relating to Attraction & Form of Earth," Cavendish Mss VI(b), 1:19.

[26] Nevil Maskelyne, "A Proposal for Measuring the Attraction of Some Hill in This Kingdom by Astronomical Observations," *PT* 65 (1772): 495–99. 23 July 1772, Minutes of Council, copy, Royal Society, 6:145.

[27] Nevil Maskelyne to Henry Cavendish, 5 Jan. 1773, Cavendish Mss X(b); published in full in *Sci. Pap.* 2:402. Having made his copy, Maskelyne returned Cavendish's "Rules for Computing the Attraction of Hills." The preliminary version of that paper is Henry Cavendish, "Thoughts on the Method of Finding the Density of the Earth by Observing the Attraction of Hills," Cavendish Mss VI(b), 2, 6.

[28] Henry Cavendish, "On the Choice of Hills Proper for Observing Attraction Given to Dr Franklin," Cavendish Mss VI(b), 3:5.

[29] 24 June and 29 July 1773, Minutes of Council, copy, Royal Society, 6:180, 185–86. The committee which met on 18 July to approve the resolutions consisted of Cavendish, Barrington, Horsley, Maskelyne, Watson, and the secretaries Maty and Morton.

[30] 27 Jan. 1774, Minutes of Council, Royal Society, 6:206–8.

56. *Schehallien. Photograph of the mountain, with its advantageous geometry for determining the average density of the earth. A. J. Berry,* Henry Cavendish: His Life and Scientific Work *(London: Hutchinson, 1960), opposite p. 81.*

order: big, regular, detached, with a narrow base in the north-south direction on either side of which observations could optimally be taken. The committee selected Maskelyne as their experimenter. His Greenwich assistant Reuben Burrow determined the size and shape of the mountain; Maskelyne observed forty-three stars from it. When the experiment was done, Cavendish and C. J. Phipps went over Burrow's scarcely legible papers from the field.[31]

On the basis of the experiment and Newton's "rules of philosophizing," Maskelyne told the Royal Society in July 1775 that "we are to conclude, that every mountain, and indeed every particle of the earth, is endued with the same property [attraction], in proportion to its quantity of matter," and further that the "law of the variation of this force, in the inverse *ratio* of the squares of the distances, as laid down by Sir Isaac Newton, is also confirmed."[32] For this work, Maskelyne was awarded the Copley Medal in 1775. In his address on the occasion, the president of the Society, John Pringle, said that now the Newtonian system is "finished" and that every man must become a Newtonian.[33] Maskelyne's and Pringle's conclusions could have come as no surprise to Cavendish, who in any case was interested in the quantity the experiment addressed, the mean den-

[31] 6 and 27 Apr. 1775, Minutes of Council, Royal Society, 6:267–69.

[32] Nevil Maskelyne, "An Account of Observations Made on the Mountain Schehallien for Finding Its Attraction," *PT* 65 (1775): 500–42, on 532.

[33] John Pringle, *A Discourse on the Attraction of Mountains, Delivered at the Anniversary Meeting of the Royal Society, November 30, 1775* (London, 1775); the remark on the Newtonian system comes at the end of the discourse.

sity of the earth. That quantity had to wait for the calculations of the mathematician Charles Hutton, who had been hired by Maskelyne for the task. Not until 1778 did Hutton finish his paper of some hundred pages of "long and tedious" figuring. To explain why it took him so long, Hutton said that new methods of calculation had to be invented, and Cavendish had supplied him with some of these. The calculation gave the ratio of the attraction of the earth to the attraction of the mountain. The ratio had two values: one was computed by assuming that the density of the mountain is the same as the density of the earth, which came out 9933 to 1; the other was computed using Maskelyne's observations of the plumb line, 17,804 to 1. The quotient of the two ratios, 17,804 to 9,933, is 9 to 5, the quantity by which the mean density of the earth exceeds that of the mountain. Hutton pointed out that the density of the mountain was unknown, but he nevertheless expressed the result in a more satisfying form: by assuming that the mountain is "common stone," the density of which is 2½, the "mean density of the whole earth is about 4½ times the density of water." Newton's best guess was that the density of the earth is between 5 and 6 ("so much justness was even in the surmises of this wonderful man!"). Reminding his readers that this experiment was the first of its kind, Hutton hoped that it would be repeated in other places.[34]

There is a legend that Maskelyne threw a bacchanalian feast for the inhabitants of the region near Shehallien.[35] It is hard to picture the stodgy Maskelyne taking part in this affair and impossible to picture Cavendish, but of course Cavendish was not there. Just as he did not travel to observe the transit of Venus, he did not go to Scotland to observe stars from a mountain; he planned the experiment from his home on Great Marlborough Street in London.

A related activity of the Royal Society from which Cavendish likewise stayed home was voyages of discovery, although he was fully involved in the scientific preparations for them. In the second half of the eighteenth century the world was still incompletely explored by Europeans. In the wake of James Cook's southern voyages, the Royal Society proposed, and the king agreed to, a voyage to the far north, the primary object of which was to settle the practical question of the existence of a shorter route to the East Indies across the North Pole, the hopefully designated Northwest Passage. The Society anticipated that such a voyage would also be of service to the "promotion of natural knowledge," the "proper object" of the Society.[36] C. J. Phipps was put in command of two frigates, joined by the astronomer Israel Lyons. As a member of the Royal Society's committee for this

---

[34] Hutton, "An Account of the Calculations," 689–90, 750, 766, 781–83, 785.

[35] Derek Howse, *Nevil Maskelyne: The Seaman's Astronomer* (Cambridge: Cambridge University Press, 1989), 137–38.

[36] After Daines Barrington, F.R.S., had spoken with the secretary Lord Sandwich, the council of the Royal Society ordered the secretary to write to him proposing a northern voyage with practical and scientific ends. 19 Jan. 1773, Minutes of Council, copy, Royal Society, 6:160–61.

voyage,[37] Cavendish drafted instructions for the use of his father's self-registering thermometer for taking the temperature of the sea at various depths, as recommended in his publication of 1757. He worked out the corrections required to bring the accuracy of his father's thermometer up to date; these were quoted by Phipps in his account of the expedition, *A Voyage Towards the North Pole*.[38] On this voyage no opportunity for advancing the Royal Society's knowledge of the earth was overlooked. The Board of Longitude had a stake in it too; to improve the art of navigation, the Board provided Phipps with instruments for experiments. The physical sciences were well represented on this expedition, but not to the exclusion of the life sciences. Watching over the interests of the latter, the president of the Society, Sir Joseph Banks, provided Phipps with instructions on how to draw up an account of natural history. The wide-ranging scientific responsibilities of Phipps and his crew were demanding to say the least: in addition to conducting their vessels through perilous waters, they took time to observe the refraction of light, measure the height of mountains using a barometer and a theodolite, study icebergs, determine the specific gravity of ice, survey coasts using a megameter, record magnetic variation and dip, record the temperature, pressure, and humidity of the air, observe the acceleration of a pendulum to give the figure of the earth, distill sea water, compare a variety of timekeepers, and make astronomical observations all the way. Phipps's expedition was a traveling observatory and laboratory of the earth, or as Cavendish might have envisioned it, the Royal Society under sail.[39]

Around the time of Phipps's journey, there was keen interest at the Royal Society in the scientific exploration of the far north. During the transit of Venus in 1769, the Society sent the astronomer William Bayley to the North Cape, the northernmost projection of Norway. The Society also sent the astronomer and mathematician William Wales, who was a sailing companion of Bayley's, and the astronomer Joseph Dymond to Hudson Bay, where they made extensive meteorological as well as astronomical observations in connection with the transit. In

[37] 22 and 29 Apr. 1773, Minutes of Council, copy, Royal Society, 6:172–73. The instructions for Phipps's voyage were drawn up by Cavendish, Nevil Maskelyne, Samuel Horsley, Mr. Montaine, and Matthew Maty. Charles Richard Weld, *A History of the Royal Society*, 2 vols (1848; reprint, New York: Arno Press, 1975), 2:72.

[38] Henry Cavendish, "Rules for Therm. for Heat of Sea," twenty-four numbered pages with much crossing out, Cavendish Mss III(a), 7. "To Make the Same Observations on the Flat Ice or Fields of Ice as It Has Been Called," part of a ten-page manuscript, ibid., Misc. There is a second draft of the instructions about ice fields among Cavendish's Journals, ibid., X(a). See the section "Entire Globe" in part 3, chapter 6, "Earth." Cavendish's instructions for the use of his father's thermometer are quoted in Constantine John Phipps, *A Voyage Towards the North Pole, Undertaken by His Majesty's Command, 1773* (London, 1774), 145.

[39] On Lord Charles Cavendish's thermometer, Phipps, *Voyage*, 27, 32–33, 142. The first seventy-six pages of *Voyage* are a narrative of the journey, with its perils; at one stage, the two ships, Carcass and Racehorse, were icebound and thought lost, about to be abandoned. The bulk of the account, from p. 79 to p. 253, is appendices containing experiments and observations.

1776, Cook made a journey to the north, with Bayley aboard, carrying Cavendish's instructions. The next year Richard Pickersgill made a northern journey carrying Cavendish's directions for use of the dipping needle.[40]

Beginning in 1773, if not earlier, Cavendish incorporated the Hudson's Bay Company into his network of sources of information; its northern remoteness afforded an opportunity to study nature in deep freeze. In December of that year, as an acknowledgment of its "considerable and repeated benefactions," the council of the Royal Society moved to send the Company a collection of meteorological instruments with instructions for its officers to measure the weather and report back to the Society, with the secretary of the Society Matthew Maty to serve as intermediary.[41] Three days after the motion, Maty wrote to Cavendish, acknowledging Cavendish's "hints" about the observations to be made at Hudson Bay, and asking him where the instruments were to be placed in that icy climate; because the rain gauge, in particular, could only be used in summer, Maskelyne had proposed that the snow be collected on the frozen river, and Maty wanted to know what Cavendish thought about the suggestion.[42]

The great trading companies, together with the admiralty, were, in effect, a part of the method of science in eighteenth-century Britain. Like the Hudson's Bay Company, the East India Company offered remote observations to the scientific men of London. Cavendish, the scientific gatekeeper, received observations from voyages between England and the East Indies for communication to the Royal Society.[43] To an observer in Madras, no doubt at Fort St. George, headquarters of the East India Company, Cavendish gave directions for making scientific observations. Among his papers copied in his own hand is a weather journal from Madras.[44] To nearly the end of his life, he received scientific communications from that part of the world.

One of Cavendish's close friends in the Royal Society was a professional voyager, the first hydrographer for the East India Company and later the first hydrographer for the admiralty, Alexander Dalrymple. A man of great energy and versatility, Dalrymple was an explorer, chartmaker, navigator, surveyor, commander, geographer, author of the first English book on nautical surveying, and

[40] See letter 1, part 4 of this book. Cavendish Mss IX, 41, 43.

[41] 23 Dec. 1773 and 20 Jan. 1774, Minutes of Council, copy, Royal Society, 6:206, 208.

[42] Matthew Maty to Henry Cavendish, 26 Dec. 1773, Cavendish Mss X(b), 2.

[43] Robert Barker, "An Account of Some Thermometrical Observations Made at Allahabad in the East-Indies, in Lat. 25 Degrees 30 Minutes N. During the Y 1767, and Also During a Voyage from Madras to England in the Y 1774, Extracted from the Original Journal by Henry Cavendish," *PT* 65 (1775): 202–6. Alexander Dalrymple, "Journal of a Voyage to the East Indies, in the Ship Grenville, Capt. Burnet Abercrombie, in the Year 1775," Communicated by the Hon. Henry Cavendish, *PT* 68 (1778): 389–418. Dalrymple took measurements with thermometers and barometers made by Nairne and Blunt, and he made observations with a dipping needle, and in his report he gave a long extract on the instrument by Cavendish (p. 390).

[44] "Journal of Weather at Madras," for 1777–78, Cavendish Mss Misc.

the moving spirit behind the "second British Empire."[45] Thoroughly scientific in his approach to oceanic exploration, he had a keen interest in scientific instruments, especially chronometers. Cavendish, who was always greeted warmly by Dalrymple in letters to him, named him a trustee of his property, left him a legacy in his will, and repeatedly lent him money.[46] Cavendish no doubt thought he was amply rewarded in the news of the world Dalrymple regularly brought him.

Persons who brought back scientific information from the ends of the earth had a particular appeal to Cavendish, who invited them as his guests at the Royal Society and the Royal Society Club. In the certificates book of the Society, we find that he recommended at least ten persons who were known for their wide travels as well as their learning. One of them was a ship's captain, James Horsburgh, who like Dalrymple would be appointed hydrographer to the East India Company. Dalrymple met Horsburgh in London, introducing him to men of science there, including Henry Cavendish. From Bombay in 1805, Horsburgh sent Cavendish a paper on meteorological readings to be read at the Royal Society and subsequently to be published in the *Philosophical Transactions*. Dalrymple wrote to Horsborgh of his intention to propose to Cavendish, Maskelyne, and Aubert that they join him in recommending Horsborgh as Fellow of the Royal Society. That was done according to plan, only Aubert did not sign the certificate since he died that year.[47] Other world travelers recommended by Cavendish included Josias Dupré, who as secretary for the East India Company at Fort St. George at Madras had appointed Dalrymple as his deputy, preparing the way for the latter's career; Robert Barker, a Member of Parliament, formerly in the service of the East India Company as "Commander in Chief in Bengal, being curious in natural History";[48] Samuel Davis, "of Bhagalpur in the East Indies," who as a civil servant in Benares was an active member of the Asiatic Society, publishing in its journal on the "astronomical computation of the Hindus"; James Cook, at the time the "successful conductor of two important voyages for the discovery of unknown countries by which geography & natural history have been greatly advantaged & improved"; James King, "Captain in the Royal Navy, lately

[45] W. A. Spray, "Alexander Dalrymple, Hydrographer," *American Neptune* 30 (1970): 200–216, on 200–1. Howard T. Fry, *Alexander Dalrymple (1737–1808) and the Expansion of British Trade* (London: Frank Cass, 1970), xiii–xvi, xx–xxi.

[46] Cavendish loaned Dalrymple £500 in each of several years, 1783, 1799, 1800, and 1807. Dalrymple borrowed from Cavendish to pay off other debts due immediately: Alexander Dalrymple to Henry Cavendish, 2 July 1807. Upon Dalrymple's death, his administrator asked Cavendish to tell him how much was owed him. The matter was still pending a few years later when Cavendish died. "27 Dec 1811 Principal Money and Interest This Day Received of Alex. Dalrymple Esq. Exctr. 2873.3.5." Devon. Coll., L/31/64 and 34/64.

[47] James Horsburgh, "Abstract of Observations on a Diurnal Variation of the Barometer between the Tropics," *PT* 95 (1805): 177–85. "Horsburgh, James," *DNB* 9:1270–71. Fry, *Dalrymple*, 253–55. Royal Society, Certificates: James Horsbugh, 6 (21 Nov. 1805).

[48] Royal Society, Certificates: Robert Barker, 3:209 (15 Dec. 1774); Josias Dupré, 4:23 (25 Feb. 1779). "Barker, Sir Robert," *DNB* 1:1128–29.

returned from a Voyage of Discoveries in the South Seas"; Isaac Titsingh, "long resident in various parts of the East, particularly Japan"; William Bligh, "Post Captain in H.M.'s Navy . . . whose Voyages to the Pacific Ocean have established his character as an able Navigator, whilst they enriched our Westindian Colonies with the most valuable productions of the South Sea Islands"; John Thomas Stanley, "who has lately made a voyage to Iceland for the improvement of natural knowledge"; and John Hunter, Henry Cavendish's personal physician who had recently returned from Jamaica, where he had served as superintendent of military hospitals, and was soon to bring out his most important publication, a book on the diseases of the army in Jamaica.[49] These were worldly men whom Cavendish recommended as regular members of the Royal Society over a period of thirty years. By and large, London Fellows ran the Society, but Cavendish did not want the Society to consist of people like himself, Londoners who rarely left town. As we have seen he helped to bring into the Society persons who had direct experience of the wider world, who brought with them fresh perspectives and new information, ensuring the Society of a vigorous scientific life and counteracting parochial tendencies.

The meeting place of the Royal Society at Crane Court was cramped, and when Joseph Banks became president in 1778, he approached the government for better quarters, a prospect which the Society had been considering for some years. Cavendish was appointed to a committee to meet with the architect about fitting up apartments in the new home of the Society in Somerset House.[50] Having examined the meteorological instruments of the Society a few years before and advised on their use at Crane Court, he was charged with seeing to the best relocation of these instruments.[51] True to form, in his report to the council he was particularly concerned with the "error" of a thermometer, and proposed setting it some feet away from the sunlit wall, hardly "any eye sore," though he preferred a window of the room where the Antiquaries met, if they "would permit it."[52] Subsequently, he was appointed to the committee to direct the keeping of the Meteorological Journal.[53] Better located than Crane Court, Somerset House had more space, too, though it was not exactly spacious.[54] In the meeting room,

---

[49] Royal Society, Certificates: James Cook, 3:237 (23 Nov. 1775); James King, 4:56 (23 Nov. 1780); John Hunter, 5 (12 Jan. 1786); John Thomas Stanley, 5 (29 Apr. 1790); Samuel Davis, 5 (28 June 1792); Isaac Titsingh, 5 (22 June 1797); William Bligh, 6 (19 Feb. 1801).

[50] 16 Mar. 1780, Minutes of Council, copy, Royal Society, 6:397.

[51] 6 July 1781, Minutes of Council, Royal Society, 6:439.

[52] 2 Aug. 1781, Minutes of Council, Royal Society, 7:79–81. The Society's concern with placing the meterological instruments continued, leading to a committee of Cavendish, Alexander Aubert, William Heberden, Jean André Deluc, William Watson, and Francis Wollaston: 12 Feb. 1784, ibid., 7:158.

[53] 19 Jan. 1786, Minutes of Council, Royal Society, 7:240. The committee consisted of Cavendish, Chambers, Aubert, Richard Kirwan, and Sir George Shuckburgh.

[54] D. C. Martin, "Former Homes of the Royal Society," *Notes and Records of the Royal Society of London* 22 (1967): 12–19, on 16.

57. *Royal Society.* The Meeting Room of the Royal Society at Somerset House 1780–1857. *Painting by Frederick William Fairholt, engraving by H. Melville. Henry Cavendish came regularly to meetings in this room for the last thirty years of his life. Reproduced by permission of the President and Council of the Royal Society.*

the president sat in a grand, high-backed chair, like a judge, well above the table at which the secretaries sat, while the ordinary members sat on hard benches with rail backs resembling pews. For the last thirty years of his life, Cavendish came regularly to this meeting room, where he sat beneath the paintings of illustrious past members, crammed on the walls one above another. (By refusing to sit for a painting, he insured that he would not be exhibited on those walls helplessly exposed forever to the prying eyes of strangers.) The next move of the Society was not until 1857, when its new home was Burlington House in Piccadilly, which had belonged to the Cavendishes.

BRITISH MUSEUM

In 1773 Henry Cavendish joined his father as a trustee of the British Museum, elected to succeed Lord Lyttleton. For ten years he came to the biweekly meetings of the standing committee of the trustees with his father, a commitment which was both substantial and unusual, since rarely as many as six trustees attended these meetings. The committee prepared reports for consideration at the general meetings of the trustees, held three or four times a year, to which seldom as many as a dozen came, often not enough for a quorum. In addition to the Cavendishes, the few other trustees who attended frequently included their friends from the Royal Society and their relatives: Banks, Wray, Watson, Pringle, Yorke (now Lord Hardwicke), and Lord Bessborough.[55]

The standing committee had a wide range of responsibilities, mostly having to do with routine business, such as paying bills and performing audits, but there was also an unpredictable element. The committee routinely gave permission for visitors to copy documents and draw birds but also to examine human monsters under the inspection of an officer of the Museum. It heard standard complaints about the cold of the medals room and the damp of the reading room, but also about the infighting of the several librarians; the committee ordered them to stop quarreling and be amicable.[56] It laid out money to buy or to subscribe to important works of science for the library, such as Robert Smith's *System of Opticks* and Samuel Horsley's edition of Newton's works.[57] It noted gifts of books and collectibles. Just before Henry Cavendish was elected a trustee, the committee ordered thanks to John Walsh and John Hunter for two specimens of the electric eel,[58] and two years later, just as Cavendish was beginning his experiments on an artificial torpedo, Walsh presented another electric eel, the organs of which had been laid open by Hunter, and in addition Hunter presented a transverse section of an electric eel.[59] Occasionally gifts were substantial: in 1773 Banks presented his large collection of Icelandic sagas, and Rockingham presented his large collection of animals preserved in spirit in seventy-two glasses, to which he added seventeen more glasses the next year. But most gifts were isolated curiosities of the sort that were often written about in the *Philosophical Transactions*, a six-legged pig, a frog preserved in amber, the head of a sea horse, and–presented by Lord Charles Cavendish–a "curious Specimen of a double Egg."[60] Stuffed birds from the Cape of Good Hope, serpents from the East Indies, shells from Labrador, insects from Jamaica, a gun and powder horn from Bengal, Captain Cook's artificial curiosities from the South Sea islands, and much more from Britain's colonial extremities and seafaring way of life piled up in the British Museum.[61]

---

[55] Henry Cavendish was elected trustee on 8 Dec. 1773. His record of attendance is in the minutes of the British Museum: Committee, vols. 5 to 9; General Meeting, vols. 3 to 5.

[56] The order for amicable personal relations was made on 9 May 1777. Committee Minutes of the British Museum, BL, 6.

[57] 31 July and 11 Sep. 1778, Committee Minutes of the British Museum, BL, 6.

[58] 23 Apr. 1773, Committee Minutes of the British Museum, BL, 5.

[59] Walsh's gift was in Jan. or Feb. 1775, and Hunter's was on 16 June 1775, Diary and Occurrence-Book of the British Museum, BL Add Mss 45875, p. 6.

[60] Meeting on 13 Sep. 1776, Committee Minutes of the British Museum, BL, 6.

[61] Ibid., 3 ff.

First Lord Charles Cavendish, then Lord Charles and Henry Cavendish together, and then Henry Cavendish gave conscientious attention to the affairs of the British Museum for over fifty years. Through this central, public institution for books and collections, they expressed their desire to serve the public and the cause of learning.

SOCIETY OF ANTIQUARIES

In the same year that he became a trustee of the British Museum, 1773, Cavendish was elected a Fellow of the Society of Antiquaries of London. Described as a gentleman of "great Abilities, & extensive knowledge," but appropriately with no mention of accomplishments in antiquarian scholarship, Cavendish was recommended by Heberden, Wray, Burrow, Josiah Colebrook, Daines Barrington, and Jean Louis Petit, all of whom were also members as well of the Royal Society.[62] Macclesfield, Birch, Banks, and other colleagues of Cavendish's from the Royal Society were also members of the Society of Antiquaries, indicative of the large overlap in the membership of the two societies.[63]

The Society, which originated with a group who met in a coffeehouse to discuss history and genealogy, was formally created, or re-created, in 1717. The leading spirit of the Society in its early years was the physician William Stukeley, an accomplished antiquarian, the "Archdruid of this age,"[64] who was also a prominent member of the Royal Society. Early on there was an attempt to merge the Antiquarian Society and the Royal Society, but the stronger desire was for separateness and equality. In 1751 Martin Folkes, who was at the same time president of the Society of Antiquaries and president of the Royal Society, pushed through a reform establishing a council and officers for the Society of Antiquaries in exact imitation of those for the Royal Society, and in that year the Society was granted a royal charter.[65] In other ways too it imitated the Royal Society, acquiring a dining club, a journal, and a committee of papers. Fellows of the Royal Society, it would seem, sometimes acted in concert in the politics of the other society, and it no doubt worked the other way too.[66] Of

---

[62] Cavendish was proposed on 21 Jan. 1773 and elected on 25 Feb. 1773. Minute Book, Society of Antiquaries, 12:53, 580.

[63] Of the twenty-one members of the council of the Society of Antiquaries in 1760, eleven were also Fellows of the Royal Society, and of its ordinary membership, forty-four more were Fellows of the Royal Society. "A List of the Society of Antiquaries of London, April 23, MDCCLX," BL Egerton 2381, ff. 172–75.

[64] "William Stukeley, M.D.," in William Munk, *The Roll of the Royal College of Physicians of London. Comprising Biographical Sketches of All the Eminent Physicians Whose Names Are Recorded in the Annals*, 4 vols. (London, 1878) 2:71–74, on 74.

[65] Joan Evans, *A History of the Society of Antiquaries* (Oxford: Oxford University Press, 1956), 442.

[66] Peter Davall to Thomas Birch, 22 Apr. 1754, BL Add Mss 4304, vol. 5, f. 126. Daniel Wray to Thomas Birch, 7 Mar. 1753, BL Add Mss 4322, f. 111.

the officers and council members of the Society of Antiquaries, a large proportion were also Fellows of the Royal Society, who were often not the most productive scholars of antiquities. At the time the Society of Antiquaries received its charter, a member wishing to make public new discoveries in antiquities might consider doing so through either the Royal Society or the Society of Antiquaries. Francis Drake, F.R.S. and F.S.A., told Charles Lyttleton, F.R.S. and future president of the Society of Antiquaries, that he had had better success communicating discoveries of antiquities to the Royal Society than to the Society of Antiquaries, and that he was inclined to follow that guide with his present subject, a Roman altar, as he did, publishing his paper on it in the *Philosophical Transactions*.[67] James Burrow, F.R.S. and F.S.A., sent a paper to Thomas Birch, F.R.S. and F.S.A., saying that he always intended it for the Society of Antiquaries and "never entertained the least thought of communicating it to the Royal Society, since it cannot pretend to be of any use towards the advancement of *natural* knowledge," but because of an opinion of the committee of papers, he was sending it to the Royal Society after all.[68] The division between the topics belonging to the Royal Society and those belonging to the antiquaries was evidently clear in principle to Burrow, but in practice it was not sharply drawn. As was the case with the Royal Society, the Society of Antiquaries also had interests in common with the British Museum, an institution which drew support from the "antiquarian milieu."[69]

The duty of the Society of Antiquaries was clear: it was to record "Antient Monuments," such as cities, roads, churches, statues, tombs, utensils, medals, deeds, letters, and whatever other ruins and writings supported the "History of Brittish Antiquitys."[70] But the meaning to be derived from such objects was a matter of judgment and strong feeling. By the time Cavendish joined the Society, its minutes recorded long papers, which reveal contemporary views on the direction of the field. There was, for instance, a paper on the history of Manchester, written on a "rational plan," which promised to rise above the parochialism of the usual town histories, above the "private" histories of single towns, to illuminate the "general polity" of towns and the "general antiquities" of the entire kingdom and to lay open the causes and circumstances of "any momentous events" affecting Manchester. Antiquaries could already condemn antiquarianism in the

[67] Francis Drake to Charles Lyttleton, 26 Jan. 1756, Correspondence of C. Lyttleton, BL Stowe Mss 753, ff. 288–89.

[68] The Royal Society's committee of papers sent Burrow's paper to the secretary of the Royal Society, having drawn red lines through the passages that Burrow had expressly addressed to the Society of Antiquaries. James Burrow to Thomas Birch, 18 June 1762, Birch Correspondence, BL Add Mss 4301, vol. 2, p. 363.

[69] David Philip Miller, "The Royal Society of London 1800–1835: A Study in the Cultural Politics of Scientific Organization," Ph.D. diss. (University of Pennsylvania, 1981), 46.

[70] In Stukeley's hand, in the first minute book of the Society, quoted in Joan Evans, *A History of the Society of Antiquaries* (Oxford: Oxford University Press, 1956), 58.

later pejorative meaning of the term.[71] Other papers from this time made a moral point: a history of cockfighting corrected the "errors" of the modern writers, but its purpose was to show the perversion of cockfighting from a religious and political institution for instilling valor to the present-day pastime founded on cruelty, finding it offensive to humanity that "rational & civiliz'd minds" could take enjoyment in this spectacle.[72]

In 1770 the Society of Antiquaries introduced its own journal, the *Archeologia*, an occasion for a clear and forceful statement of the purpose of the Society by its director, Richard Gough. The chartered antiquaries had as their object not their "own entertainment" but the communication of their "researches to the public." Belonging to the modern "age wherein every part of science is advancing to perfection," antiquaries had a duty to make the proper use of their facts: "*history*" was not a poetic narration but a "regular" inquiry into the records and proofs of the past.[73]

Apart from their common cause, "science," "knowledge," and "truth," and their common membership, the Society of Antiquaries and the Royal Society had a common work. Because science had its own antiquities, both societies had a concern with the history and biography of science.[74] History and natural history were both collecting activities,[75] and between history and astronomy, both dating activities, there was a lively interaction.[76] Antiquaries were interested in views of Pompeii and the like, and there was now interest in the Gothic as well as in the Classic, but there was also interest in contemporary history, so strongly marked by science and technology, such as in the history of the Royal Society of Arts, to which Lord Charles and Henry Cavendish belonged.[77]

---

[71] John Whitaker, "The History of Manchester," 6 Dec. 1770, Minute Book, Society of Antiquaries, 11.

[72] Samuel Pegge, "A Memoir on Cockfighting . . . ," 12 and 19 Mar. 1772, Minute Book, Society of Antiquaries, 11.

[73] Richard Gough on the purpose of the Society of Antiquaries' publication, in volume 1, 1770, of *Archeologia.*

[74] There are many letters from members of the Royal Society to John Ward, professor of rhetoric at Gresham College, F.R.S. He published frequently on antiquities in the *Philosophical Transactions*, and he was president of the Society of Antiquaries. For example, Ward had a correspondence about collecting the scientist Robert Boyle's letters for the benefit of the Royal Society: Henry Miles, F.R.S., to Ward, 10 Feb. 1741/42 and 13 June 1746, Letters of Learned Men to Professor Ward, BL Add Mss 6210, ff. 248, 249–50.

[75] In connection with a natural history of fossils, Emanuel Mendes da Costa wrote to John Ward to ask if certain Roman vases were made of marble or porcelain. Letter of 13 Nov. 1754, Letters of Learned Men to Professor Ward.

[76] Concerned with Homer's placement of Troy, John Machin wrote to John Ward: "My whole time has been employed in tedious and irksome calculations to adjust and settle the moons mean motion, in order to make a proper use of the eclipse at the death of Patroculus." 23 Oct. 1745, ibid., ff. 230–31.

[77] This "history of the rise and progress of the Society for the Encouragement of Arts, Manufactures & Sciences" was read at the meetings of 1 and 8 June 1758. The paper was kept in a folio with the purpose of entering "occurrences of our own time." Emanuel da Costa, "Minutes of the Royal Society and the Society of Antiquaries," BL, Egerton Mss 2381, ff. 57–58.

Henry Cavendish became a member of the Society of Antiquaries at a time when the membership was rapidly expanding, having nearly doubled in the ten years before his election.[78] The "well-rounded gentleman" often had accomplishments in antiquities,[79] and many of the new members came from the upper classes, including the nobility. A good number came from science too: in the same year as Cavendish, Benjamin Franklin and John Pringle were elected. There is the suggestion that wealthy and learned persons entered the Society to receive its new journal, *Archeologia*.[80] Many Fellows of the Royal Society published in the antiquaries' journal, among them those who recommended Cavendish for membership in the Society of Antiquaries: Barrington, Colebrooke, and Wray. Cavendish took particular interest in papers in *Archeologia* having to do with India; his own paper on the Hindu calendar fitted either that journal or the *Philosophical Transactions*, which was where he published it.

Henry Cavendish's membership in the Society of Antiquaries together with that in the Royal Society and his trusteeship in the British Museum were inscribed on the plate of his coffin, but to Cavendish the affiliations were not of equal importance. He dedicated himself to the affairs of the Royal Society and the British Museum, whereas he took on no responsibilities in the Society of Antiquaries. He entered the record only once and then as an intermediary, submitting drawings of an Indian pagoda in the name of his scientific friend Alexander Dalrymple.[81]

There had been a plan to bring together in the same meeting place the Society of Antiquaries, the Royal Society, the British Museum, and the Royal Academy of Painting, Sculpture and Architecture, but the British Museum moved into Montagu House in 1754, and the year before the Society of Antiquaries took over a former coffeehouse in Chancery Lane. Twenty years later, in the year Cavendish was elected to the Society of Antiquaries, the Royal Society began planning its apartments for its new location, Somerset House. Cavendish, who was much involved with that move, agreed with others on the council of the Royal Society that it would be a "great inconvenience" to have any apartments in common with the Society of Antiquaries, or even a common staircase, for their "publick apartments . . . will be understood by all Europe, as meant to confer on them an external splendor, in some measure proportioned to the consideration in which they have been held for more than a century."[82] The architect William Chambers

[78] Membership was 173 in 1764 and 290 in 1774. Evans, *History*, 148.

[79] Miller, "The Royal Society of London," 14.

[80] Evans, *History*, 150.

[81] Henry Cavendish to William Norris, undated. This letter, which is in the library of the Society of Antiquaries, has to do with an extract by Alexander Dalrymple from a journal in the possession of the East India Company, evidently referring to: "Account of a Curious Pagoda Near Bombay . . . ," drawn up by Captain Pyke in 1712, and communicated to the Society of Antiquaries on 10 Feb. 1780 by Dalrymple; published in *Archeologia* 7 (1785): 323–32.

[82] 10 May 1776, Minutes of Council, Royal Society, 6:293.

informed the Royal Society that no entrance, hall, staircase, or anteroom could be contrived "suitable to the splendor of the Royal Society" except what it must have in common with the Society of Antiquaries,[83] but in this vote of the council, Cavendish came down on the side of the Royal Society.

83 18 May 1776, Minutes of Council, Royal Society, 6:294.

CHAPTER 7

MAN OF PROPERTY

LEAVING HOME

Lord Charles Cavendish appears on the ratebooks for his house on Great Marlborough Street until his death in 1783, after which Henry is listed.[1] That house was now called his "town house," since the year before he rented a second, country house in Hampstead.[2]

William Thornton's guide to London and the countryside surrounding it, published in 1784, gives us an idea of Hampstead at the time Cavendish moved there. Located north of London, this village "was once very small, but by the increase of buildings is now of considerable extent. Many of the citizens of London have fine houses here, because the situation is not only delightful, but the air is esteemed exceeding wholesome. . . . At the north extremity of the village is a heath or common, which is adorned with many handsome buildings, and is so elevated, as to command one of the most extensive prospects of the kingdom."[3] Fashionable Hampstead offered Londoners a vista and an escape from city stench and squalor.

In the late seventeenth century, Hampstead had begun to change from a rural to an urban village. A mineral spring was opened there, giving it a reputation for healthiness as well as a good income from its water, which was recommended by physicians who drank it themselves. A popular spa early in the eighteenth century, Hampstead remained a resort, though its continuing growth owed to prosperous Londoners, such as Cavendish, taking up residence there.[4] Cavendish's

---

1 12 June 1783, Paving Ratebooks, Great Marlborough Street/Marlborough Mews, Westminster Archives, D 1260.

2 Cavendish's first appearance in the ratebooks was on 3 Jan. 1782. "Hampstead Vestry. Poor Rate," Holborn Public Library, London.

3 William Thornton, ed., *New, Complete, and Universal History, Description, and Survey of the Cities of London and Westminster . . . Likewise the Towns, Villages, Palaces, Seats, and Country, to the Extent of Above Twenty Miles Round*, rev. ed. (London, 1784), 482.

4 Alex J. Philip, *Hampstead, Then and Now. An Historical Topography* (London: George Routledge, 1912), 45–46. F. M. L. Thompson, *Hampstead: Building a Borough, 1650–1964* (London: Routledge & Kegan Paul, 1974), 20–22, 24.

HAMPSTEAD

58. No. 34 Church Row, Hampstead. Cavendish lived at the end of this row next to the church for almost four years, from 1782 to 1785. But for the automobiles, this street with its church and terraced houses looks much as it did then. Photograph by the authors.

59. Hampstead Bearings. From a lower room in his country house at Hampstead, Cavendish took bearings in the direction of London. With a theodolite he recorded the angular positions of prominent objects such as trees, houses, hills, and church steeples falling within an arc of about sixty degrees. On a map of London and environs, published by R. Phillips on 1 May 1808, we have drawn Cavendish's lines of sight.

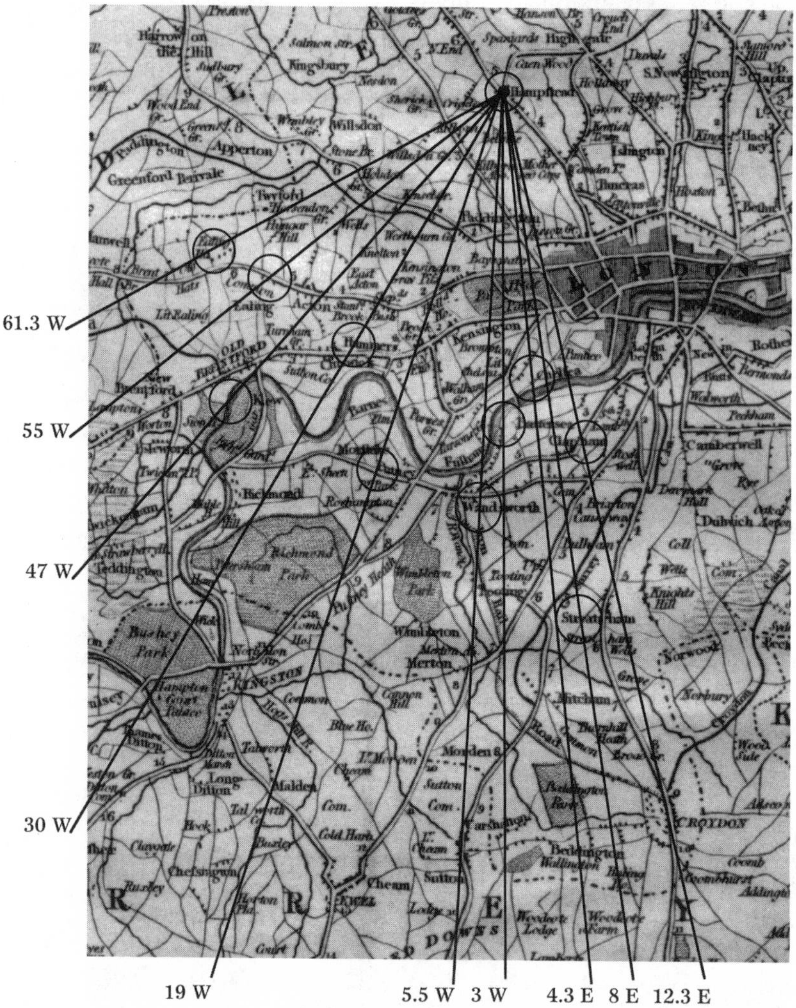

1. *New houses on the road to Clapham.*
2. *Streatham steeple.*
3. *Chelsea steeple.*
4. *Battersea steeple.*
5. *Wandsworth steeple.*
6. *Fulham steeple.*
7. *Putney steeple.*
8. *Hammersmith steeple.*
9. *Kew Chapel.*
10. *Acton steeple.*
11. *Ealing steeple.*

From a folder labeled in Cavendish's hand "Bearings," in Cavendish Scientific Manuscripts Misc.

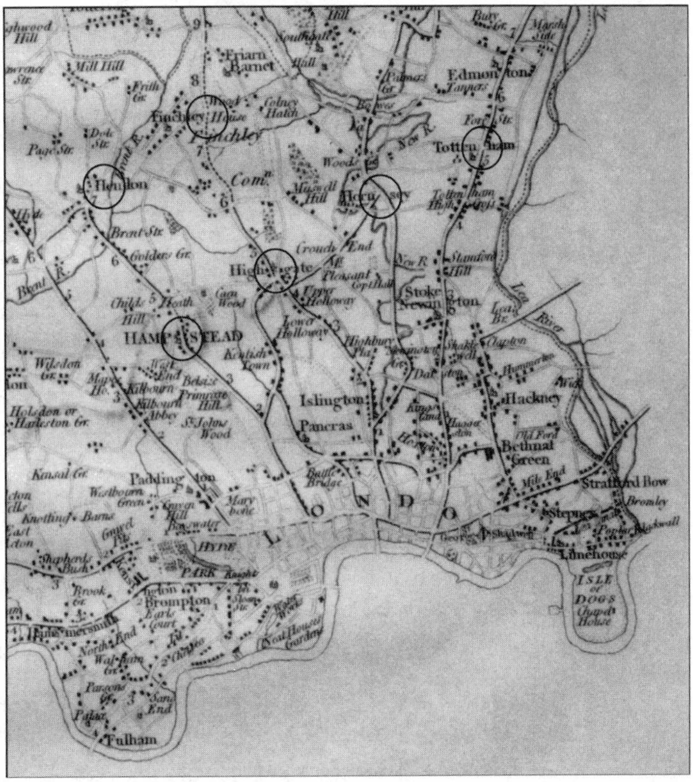

60. *Hampstead Environs. From his house at Hampstead, Cavendish made trips into the surrounding countryside, noting mile stones and other markers, such as churches and villages, which we indicate by circles on this map of the portion of the county Middlesex directly north of London. Locations and mileages are from several miscellaneous sheets in the Cavendish Scientific Manuscripts at Chatsworth.*

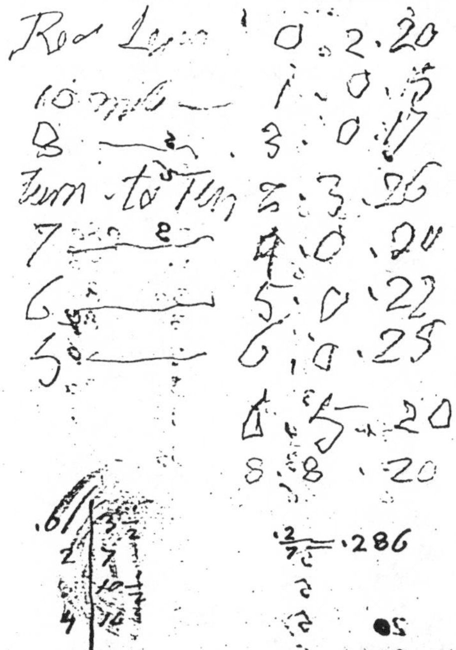

61. *Mileage Counter. This page was obviously written by Cavendish while moving, the unsteadiness of his hand giving an idea of what travel was like then. The abbreviated place names are Red Lyon, about 8 1/2 miles from his home, and Finchley Church, about two miles closer. Cavendish recorded several of his local journeys with a measurer, 35 revolutions equalling 1/10th of a mile. Between places marked on the map of the previous illustration, this table gives the distance in miles as measured by Cavendish. We are not certain what his means of conveyance was when he took these measures, but we know that he had an "odometer" attached to the wheels of his carriage. Such an instrument could be bought for from seven to ten guineas, and it was believed to be accurate to within one percent. After Cavendish's death, his "way-wiser" passed to the instrument-maker Newman, who presented it to the museum of King's College, London. It was there when Wilson wrote his biography of Cavendish, but our recent inquiry at King's indicates that it is there no longer. As it was made of wood, perhaps it simply disintegrated. Benjamin Vaughan to Thomas Jefferson, 2 Aug. 1788, in* The Papers of Thomas Jefferson, *ed. J. P. Boyd, vol. 13 (Princeton: Princeton University Press, 1956), 459–61, on 460. The sheet of distances from Cavendish Scientific Manuscripts Misc. is reproduced with permission of the Trustees of the Chatsworth Settlement.*

address was 34 Church Row, the street of choice in Hampstead, where visitors congregated and persons of "quality" promenaded. In appearance, the attractive, terraced houses have changed little since Cavendish's day.[5]

Cavendish's scientific activities at home were now divided between two locations, the exact separation of which was an astronomical datum: "Hampstead is 1,82 miles or 10.2 seconds of time west of Marlborough street," he recorded.[6] During his first spring at his new country house, he compared the good air of Hampstead with the foul air of the city.[7] He was assisted by the instrument-maker Edward Nairne, who lived only a few doors away, at 21 Church Row. During his first winter, he busied himself with experiments on the freezing temperature of mercury.[8] From his house, he sighted on the weathercock of the parish church nextdoor, and from the steeple he or an associate surveyed the countryside with a quadrant. The vista from Hampstead was commanding. Cavendish took bearings of the duke of Devonshire's palladian house at Chiswick; of temples, gazebos, and pagodas; and of the steeples at Walton, Battersea, Hammersmith, Stretham, Acton, Paddington, Chelsea, and Ealing, and of the steeple of the church at Clapham Common, on the far side of London, the location of his next country house.[9] Cavendish's final appearance in the Hampstead ratebooks was on 17 September 1785. This first stage of leaving home had lasted three and a half years.

LANDLORD

For over fifty years, Lord Charles Cavendish was responsible for farms and tithes in Nottinghamshire and Derbyshire, which were his for life as a part of his marriage settlement. Living in London, he administered his estate by correspondence with his steward, who was responsibile for watching over his properties; recommending to him repairs, improvements, and the proper rent to charge; informing him about the reliability of existing and prospective tenants and what to do when they caused problems, which included eviction; treating with other landlords and surveyors to settle disputes over enclosures; influencing voting in local elections; and collecting rents. Caught in the middle between his distant employer and the tenants, a steward's life was not easy. He was required to be at

[5] Stabling could be had elsewhere in the village, and coach service into London was very convenient, there being between fourteen and eighteen return trips a day. Barrett, *Annals of Hampstead* 1:279–80. Thompson, *Hampstead*, 25, 56. "Hampstead Vestry. Poor Rate."

[6] Cavendish Mss Misc.

[7] Henry Cavendish, minutes of experiments on air, 15 and 16 Mar. 1782, Cavendish Mss II, 5:189. "Hampstead Vestry. Poor Rate."

[8] 17 Dec. 1782 and 15 Jan. 1783, Charles Blagden Diary, Royal Society, 1. Henry Cavendish to John Michell, 27 May 1783, draft, Cavendish Mss New Correspondence.

[9] Cavendish had help with the observations taken from the Hampstead church steeple, or he helped someone, as the angles were written by another person, 23 and 25 July 1783. The unclassified papers in Cavendish's scientific manuscripts contain a great many sheets of observations of bearings, with dates falling between 1770 and 1792.

once pleader, negotiator, spy, and enforcer. Lord Charles's steward was a man named Cotes, who had come with a weighty recommendation from the "archbishop." This prelate might have been the archbishop of Canterbury, who like Lord Charles was a conscientious trustee of the British Museum, but we suspect he was the archbishop of York, who received money from Cavendish for paying pensions due from the rectory in the parish of Arnold. Cotes was healthy at the beginning, but he soon began to decline irreversibly. Cavendish perceived the "decay of his understanding for some years" without, however, taking any steps. "Out of tenderness," and perhaps also with due respect to the archbishop, Cavendish "could not dismiss him abruptly." He wanted Cotes to resign instead, which Cotes eventually did in 1764. In his place, Cavendish hired Thomas Revill, a choice he almost immediately regretted but which he nonetheless lived with for almost twenty years.[10] Revill abused his predecessor and evidently Cavendish's tenants as well, and Cavendish came to regard him as a "peevish old man," who created more problems than he solved. Two words appear with striking frequency in Cavendish's half of their argumentative correspondence, "just" and "reasonable," positive words he never applied to his steward but to actions his steward did not take and should have taken.[11]

Lord Charles introduced his eldest son to business as he had to science, turning over the management of his estate to Henry in the summer of 1782. Lord Charles did not yet formally make it over, and he continued to participate in its management,[12] but he allowed Henry to receive the income from rents, tithes, and land taxes. Lord Charles's own father had proceeded that way, in the first year turning over the rents to him and in the second year the property itself. The income Henry now received was around £1,600 a year. At age fifty-one, he began his life of well-to-do independence as the administrator of ancestral landed property.

Lord Charles had always made a point of being present when Henry tried something unfamiliar. In 1782 he was seventy-eight, and although he was still active, he may have realized that he was nearing the end. If that was the case, it would have been time to ease his son into the business of running his estate. From Henry's point of view, with the imminent prospect of taking charge of his father's landed properties, it was time to begin leaving home. Land, we think, was equated with independent living for Henry.

Henry Cavendish's life as an absentee landlord gives us insight into his person. Like his father before him, Henry Cavendish had first to settle on a steward. Unsatisfactorily as he had worked out, Revill had an extenuating circumstance. As he had explained to Lord Charles, because of a problem with his

---

[10] Lord Charles Cavendish to Thomas Revill, 5 Sep. and 13 Dec. 1764, draft, Devon. Coll., L/31/20.

[11] Lord Charles Cavendish to Thomas Revill, drafts, 19 Sep. and 3 Dec. 1776, 12 Apr. 1777, 18 Mar. 1778; Revill to Cavendish, 31 Jan. 1765, Devon. Coll., L/31/20 and 34/5.

[12] Henry Cavendish to W. Gould, draft, 30 Dec. 1782, Devon. Coll., L/34/7.

throat, he could scarcely speak and was reduced to communicating by writing, though he was helped in his work by a nephew.[13] Revill's attitude, a mix of servility and arrogance, was understandably exasperating, but his difficulty in speaking no doubt helps explain the roundabout way he went at his work. His new master, Henry Cavendish, who himself had such difficulty in speaking that a defect was suspected, evidently felt no bond of sympathy and neither made nor accepted excuses for Revill's lapses.

The duke of Devonshire was well-served by his agent, J. W. Heaton, who recommended William Gould, citing his "integrity and judgment on country business."[14] Henry Cavendish accordingly settled on Gould as his new steward before turning to the necessary task of firing his father's steward of so many years. Revill had already written to his new master that he wanted to collect the next rents. Cavendish told him not to because he intended to replace him. Revill protested, and in reply Cavendish said that he would not have answered him at all but for Revill's concern that his reputation would suffer. There was no cause for such concern, Cavendish said, since it was "so natural" for someone taking over an estate to entrust it to a steward whose judgment he could rely on. If, however, any doubts about his reputation were to arise on this account, Cavendish would set matters right. Cavendish had meant to end the letter there but changed his mind, adding that although he had no doubt of Revill's fidelity and good intentions, he had good reasons for deploring his actions: "the infirmity of your temper which has made you either quarrel or behave with petulance to so many of those you have had business with & the little information my father could ever get from you concerning the matters under your charge render you very unfit a person to take care of an estate without which cause I should never have thought of employing another steward." To his new steward, Cavendish mentioned Revill's "angry letter," copying out part of his reply to Revill, only in place of "infirmity" of temper substituting his father's expression, "the peevishness of his temper." For a full year, Revill wrote repeatedly to Cavendish to complain of his firing. Cavendish neither answered Revill's letters nor entered them in the index of his correspondence. The standard by which Cavendish judged Revill unfit he held up to his replacement. Gould was to give Cavendish's tenants no cause to complain, and he was readily to give Cavendish any and all information he desired. The first item of business was for Gould to make a complete examination "into the condition of the whole estate."[15]

---

[13] Thomas Revill to Lord Charles Cavendish, 16 Dec. 1764.

[14] W. Gould to J. W. Heaton, 10 June 1782. This letter Heaton forwarded to Cavendish, adding his recommendation of Gould. Henry Cavendish to W. Gould, draft, 8 and 9 Aug. 1782, Devon. Coll., L/34/7.

[15] Henry Cavendish to Thomas Revill, drafts, 16 and 28 Aug. and 5 Sep. 1782; Henry Cavendish to W. Gould, draft, 6 Sep. 1782, Devon. Coll., L/34/7.

In Nottinghamshire and Derbyshire, the Cavendishes had long counted among the big landlords who bought out the landed gentry and took over their manors.[16] Lord Charles and Henry Cavendish's properties were in the neighborhood of the duke of Devonshire's, from which they had been separated off.[17] The duke of Devonshire's main country house was in the area, at Chatsworth, in Derbyshire. Nearby, in Nottinghamshire, was Hardwick Hall, where family estate records were kept, and where Henry Cavendish directed his steward to examine documents concerning his properties.[18] In matters concerning their lands, the Cavendish family kept in touch. When one of Henry Cavendish's properties became available, a prospective tenant approached him through his first cousin Lord John Cavendish.[19] When legislation pended that affected his estate, Cavendish was assisted in parliament by his principal heir, Lord George Cavendish.[20] Legally, physically, and politically, Henry Cavendish's properties were in the country of the Cavendishes.

In the late eighteenth century, the enclosure movement in Britain was in full swing. A property in Nottinghamshire illustrates how Lord Charles and Henry Cavendish became entangled in the complex problems attending enclosure. Under the old pattern of farming, tilled land was parcelled into strips with mixed ownership;, meadows were also parcelled, and pastures were subject to common rights. To meet changing economic needs, this pattern of open arable fields with common rights was replaced by one in which strips were consolidated and common control and use of land were reduced; this device was called enclosure.[21] The practical intent of enclosure, as Lord Charles Cavendish put it with his usual clarity, was to "lay each person's allotment together as much as can be."[22] Before the eighteenth century, most of the land suited for pasture in Nottinghamshire had already been enclosed, but it was only in the eighteenth century that most of the land used for grain was enclosed too, and a third of it was still unenclosed at the end of the century. Because substantial economic gains could be anticipated from enclosure, big landlords and farmers were for it. If the landowners

16 J. D. Chambers, *Nottinghamshire in the Eighteenth Century: A Study of Life and Labour under the Squirearchy*, 2d ed. (London: Frank Cass, 1966), 7.

17 For example, Cavendish received rent from the tithes of Marston in Derbyshire, the greater part of which parish was owned by the duke of Devonshire. W. Gould to Henry Cavendish, 28 Sep. 1782, Devon. Coll., L/34/7.

18 Henry Cavendish to W. Gould, draft, 2 Dec. 1787, Devon. Coll., L/34/7.

19 W. Gould to Henry Cavendish, 20 Aug. 1785; Lord Arundall Gallway to Henry Cavendish, 21 Aug. 1785; Pemberton Milnes to Lord John Cavendish, 24 Aug. 1785; Lord John Cavendish to Henry Cavendish, 25 Aug. [1785]; Henry Cavendish to Lord John Cavendish, draft, n.d. [reply to letter of 25 Aug. 1785]. Devon. Coll., L/34/7.

20 George Bramwell to Thomas Dunn, n.d., enclosed in a letter from Thomas Dunn to Henry Cavendish, 14 Dec. 1790, Devon. Coll., L/34/10.

21 Chambers, *Nottinghamshire*, 141.

22 Lord Charles Cavendish to Thomas Revill, draft, 8[9] Dec. 1776, Devon. Coll., L/34/5.

could not agree–in Nottinghamshire, the principal opposition to enclosure came from small freeholders–an act of parliament might be required to overcome local resistance. All but one of Cavendish's properties were in parishes enclosed by acts of parliament, most of them passed in the decades of the 1770s through the 1790s, which was when the greatest acreage was enclosed by this means in Nottinghamshire. Lord Charles and Henry Cavendish were not dominant landholders in favor of enclosure, and they could not avoid conflict.[23]

Enclosure by parliamentary act followed a regular procedure. With the support of three quarters or more of the landholders, or of one sufficiently big landholder, a petition for permission to bring the bill was presented. If the petition was accepted, interested members of parliament would draw up the bill, which was almost certain to pass without determined opposition. Commissioners were then appointed from among the big farmers and local landlords and one or two outside experts. Their job was to carry out a survey, place the owners' allotments in enclosed fields, see to it that all the improvements specified in the act were built, and look into damage claims. Enclosure was a costly improvement: landowners were out the expense of passing the act, fees for lawyers, surveyors, and commissioners, and the very considerable capital expenses of building fences, drains, roads, and various farm structures.[24]

While Lord Charles Cavendish was still administering the estate, in 1776, the proprietors in the parish of Arnold in Nottinghamshire considered petitioning parliament to enclose their land. Cavendish did not want the petition but since he could not stop it if the proprietors proceeded, with the help of his steward he decided what to insist on so that he would come out unharmed. He was entitled to tithes from the use of the land at Arnold; from his tithe tenant, he received rent twice yearly, the total of which, a little over £100, made Arnold intermediate in value among his properties. In the event of enclosure, Cavendish would be expected to forfeit his tithes in exchange for an allotment of land. Just how much and what kind of land were the question.

Roughly speaking, the parish of Arnold contained sixteen hundred acres of land already enclosed, four hundred of open fields, and thirty of glebe, or clerical, land. In addition, there were about two thousand acres of common land, called the "forest," twenty of which, called a "break," were enclosed in lieu of tithes by agreement between the tithe tenant and the parish. The farmers' use of the break for tillage and the common for keeping sheep was seen as compensation for the tithes they had to pay for their open fields and enclosures.[25] The quantity of land at Arnold and the amounts given over to differ-

[23] Chambers, *Nottinghamshire*, 148, 165, 171–73, 202.

[24] W. Gould to Henry Cavendish, 25 Mar. 1784, Devon. Coll., L/34/7. Chambers, *Nottinghamshire*, 178, 199–200.

[25] W. Gould to Henry Cavendish, 7 and 28 Sep. 1782, 25 Mar. and 24 Nov. 1784, Devon. Coll., L/34/7.

ent uses were imprecisely known, since there had been no survey. Proceeding from incomplete information, Revill made proposals to the proprietors about what share of the common fields and the forest Lord Charles Cavendish should receive in return for giving up his tithes.

Revill's proposals were ill-received by the proprietors of Arnold, whose spokesman called repeatedly on Lord Charles, bringing their objections to him in person. Cavendish wanted them to deal with Revill instead, but they objected to Revill even more than to his proposals. Cavendish was told that "there was such animosity between [Revill] & the people of Arnold" that the proprietors believed that any agreement with him was impossible.[26] Revill was at fault, Cavendish concluded, by asking for more than was "just," and by regarding his proposals as absolute demands, a "peremptory" manner certain to create enemies. Instead of high-handed practice, Cavendish urged reason and negotiation.[27] The matter of the Arnold enclosure languished, but several years later, in 1782, it came up again in the form of a petition for a bill. Having just taken charge of his father's farms, Henry Cavendish faced a local history of bad feeling.[28]

The recent enclosures had been "attended with great detriment and injury to the estate," Henry's new steward Gould told him, by which he meant not the unavoidable "great sums that have been expended on those Inclosures and the Buildings upon them" but the avoidable, absolute loss in the value of the estate, owing, Gould said, mainly to the "shameful negligence and inattention (to call it by no worse a name)" of his predecessor, Revill.[29] The latter kind of injury Cavendish was determined to avoid through the attentiveness of his new steward. Cavendish received hereditary wealth in the form of income from the land, in return for which he was responsible for maintaining the income for the duration of his life. It was his duty and a point of honor to preserve the value of his estate, to which end he entered into a long dispute with the proprietors at Arnold about the amount of land he was entitled to receive in lieu of tithes. In principle, it was land equivalent in rental value to the tithes he would have received from the improved land after enclosure, but the comparison of values was not straightforward. Depending on how it was figured, either the farmers or Cavendish benefited more.

After a meeting of the proprietors at Arnold on parliamentary enclosure in 1784, their spokesman William Sherbrooke wrote to Cavendish to convey their offer of a specified allotment of land to compensate him for the loss of his tithes.[30] Gould calculated the rent Cavendish would receive on this offer,

[26] Lord Charles Cavendish to Thomas Revill, draft, 3 Dec. 1776, Devon. Coll., L/34/5.

[27] Lord Charles Cavendish to Thomas Revill, drafts, 3 and 12 Dec. 1776, Devon. Coll., L/34/5.

[28] Gould forwarded the petition from Arnold in a letter to Cavendish, 28 Sep. 1782.

[29] Gould to Cavendish, 28 Sep. 1782.

[30] W. Sherbrooke to Henry Cavendish, 11 Nov. 1784, Devon. Coll., L/34/7.

using current rents and deducting the interest he would pay for fences and buildings and the vicarial tithes he would go on paying. It came to £169 per year, far below the £250 Gould estimated Cavendish's tithes would bring. Cavendish should accept an allotment of yearly value no less than £360, to be laid out by the commissioners, Gould advised. That value would recognize the expenses Cavendish would incur; it was fair, Gould said, but he felt certain the proprietors would not like it.[31] Neither did Cavendish like it; he explained to his steward that if a specific value were proposed, he would come out a "loser," because the commissioners routinely overvalued land. He wanted the allotment decided Sherbrooke's way (but not at his value), which was for the commissioners to allot him a certain "proportion" of the land. That, Cavendish believed, was a surer measure of the value of the land than money.[32] Gould, of course, accepted his employer's wish, and he advised him accordingly on the proportion of land to ask for. Gould wanted to select the location of the allotment on the forest, but Cavendish thought he was being overly zealous, making unnecessary trouble for the commissioners, who might then be "less disposed to do me justice." Otherwise, Cavendish accepted the proportions Gould had calculated for him. Cavendish did not want enclosure, but he was resigned to it as long as he received his just due.[33] The Arnold proprietors rejected Cavendish's counterproposals. The land Cavendish would receive, Sherbrooke said, would rent for £500, and he knew a man who would pay it. Sherbrooke complained not just about the proposals but about Cavendish's steward as well. Cavendish was told of Gould's refusal to answer letters, to attend the parish meeting, or even to receive a delegation of "very respectable men," thereby exhibiting "all the insolence of delegated authority."[34] Gould, if the proprietors were to be believed, was behaving like Revill. Cavendish did not mention to Gould the proprietors' complaint, which in any event could hardly have been news to him, nor did he advise him on his behavior toward the proprietors. Cavendish, it would seem, had come to accept confrontation as inevitable, and he paid his steward to defend his interests and bear the abuse. He wanted Gould to get more exact information on acreage, rents, and tithes at Arnold, for only then could they "prove" that their proposals were not "unreasonable." Justice in this issue was a matter of knowledge and arithmetic even though the quantities involved could be no firmer than estimates: Cavendish

---

[31] W. Gould to Henry Cavendish, 24 Nov. 1784, Devon. Coll., L/34/7.

[32] Henry Cavendish to W. Gould, drafts, Dec. and 24 Dec. 1784, Devon. Coll., L/34/7.

[33] W. Gould to Henry Cavendish, 31 Dec. 1784; Henry Cavendish to W. Gould, draft, 6 Jan. 1785 and 2 Dec. 1787, Devon. Coll., L/34/7.

[34] Henry Cavendish to W. Sherbrooke, draft, 6 Jan. 1785; W. Sherbrooke to Henry Cavendish, 3 and 18 Feb. 1785. Cavendish also received an anonymous letter from a landholder in Arnold complaining of Gould, Mar. 1785, Devon. Coll., L/34/7.

told Gould that justice all around would be served only if his "estate should be improved in the same proportion as that of the land owners." His duty to his estate was to insure that it received this proportion. His letters to his steward began to look like laboratory notes.[35]

The "affair of Arnold," as Cavendish called it, dragged on for years.[36] Early in 1789 Gould informed Cavendish that enclosure was likely, but a little later he informed Cavendish that it was unlikely because the vicar, a hard bargainer, wanted more for his tithes on turnips and lambs than the proprietors offered him. Then on 11 March 1789, Gould told Cavendish that the landholders intended to go to parliament without the vicar, leaving the old enclosure and the new allotments still subject to vicarial tithes. Gould had arrived at an agreement for Cavendish's allotment of land, which excluded it from vicarial tithes. Cavendish had then to be given additional land equal to the tithes he must pay the vicar. The amount in question came to around £15 a year for Cavendish.[37]

Characteristically, Cavendish pressed Gould for facts on the vicar's turnip tithes[38] to enable him to decide what "part of the turnips are tithable." Cavendish felt acute discomfort if he lacked sufficient reason in making decisions about his estate, even if the amount of money involved was insignificant, as it was in this case. Concerning the vicar's turnip tithes, Cavendish wrote sternly to Gould that he wished Gould had "explained the matter to me clearly." Gould had given Cavendish his recommendations about the turnip tithes without at the same time giving him his "reasons." Henceforth Gould was always to give Cavendish his "reasons."[39]

In its own good time, the Arnold affair came to a close. Following upon the petition, on 2 March the Arnold enclosure bill was ordered, setting in motion an elaborate parliamentary procedure, which was concluded with the royal assent on 13 July. Cavendish saw a draft of the bill at the end of March. With the exception of one proprietor of fifty acres and another of twelve acres, all parties gave their consent to the bill.[40] For Cavendish, as no

35 Henry Cavendish to W. Gould, drafts, 23 Feb. 1785 and n.d. [after 28 Feb.] 1785; Henry Cavendish to W. Sherbrooke, draft, 16 Feb. 1785, Devon. Coll., L/34/7. From Gould's earlier rough estimates, Cavendish calculated that by the terms he requested, he would get £266 annually, which was slightly more than the £233 he calculated for his tithes and rent of break should an enclosure not take place. He wanted better information to refine this calculation. Henry Cavendish to W. Gould, draft, 20 Feb. 1785, ibid.

36 Cavendish to Gould, draft, 2 Dec. 1787.

37 W. Gould to Henry Cavendish, 9 and 21 Feb., 11 and 19 Mar. 1789, Devon. Coll., L/34/12.

38 Henry Cavendish to W. Gould, draft, n.d. [reply to letter of 21 Feb. 1789], Devon. Coll., L/34/12.

39 Ibid.; W. Gould to Henry Cavendish, 19 Mar. 1789.

40 W. Gould to Henry Cavendish, 30 Mar. 1789, Devon. Coll., L/34/12. 2 Mar., 13 May, and 12 June 1789, *Journal of the House of Commons* 44:138, 361, 454, and 456.

doubt for the other landowners, the news from Arnold would be bad before it was good again: in the summer of the following year, Gould told Cavendish that he had collected the rents from all but two of Cavendish's tenants, but he was not remitting them. The entire amount was expended in the Arnold enclosure.[41]

Cavendish's early correspondence concerning his farms reveals him to be new to the business, his father clearly having handled it by himself until then. Once the farms were his responsibility, Cavendish approached their management in the same spirit with which he approached science. He set out to acquire a total familiarity with the facts, from which he reasoned on the basis of general principles, including principles of justice, to conclusions about the actions to take.

Cavendish had a busy life in London with absorbing interests of his own choosing. From the questions he asked of his steward, we get the distinct impression that he never saw his farms. He was burdened with landed property on which he never lived and which gave him trouble for a relatively small income he did not need after the first year. His steward sent him enclosure bills to study, and because he owned so many properties, these bills repeatedly demanded his attention. With regard to an enclosure that had been pending for two years, Cavendish wrote irritably to Gould: "You ought to have informed me of it at the time instead of delaying it till lately & then representing it to me as brought in by surprise & without your knowledge[.] I am very sorry to find that you could act in this manner & hope I shall never see another instance of any thing of the kind."[42] Cavendish suffered irritations like this because they came with his life, and he probably never questioned their inevitability as he never relaxed his vigilance over his property to ensure that it was not injured. He managed his property as a family duty, which if it brought him no joy was nevertheless a source of satisfaction, if not of identity. No matter how far from his family his activities in science took him, in his occupation with landed property, he was at one with them.

DEATH OF LORD CHARLES CAVENDISH

Lord Charles Cavendish was remarkably healthy. He experienced the almost universal malady of that time, "gout," but he was not crippled by it,[43] and to judge by his attendance at meetings, he did not suffer from any protracted illnesses. He came to a meeting of the standing committee of the British Museum

[41] W. Gould to Henry Cavendish, 5 June 1790, Devon. Coll., L/34/12.

[42] Henry Cavendish to W. Gould, draft, 12 May 1789, Devon. Coll., L/34/12. Gould defended himself against Cavendish's "severe reprimand" and gave his reasons. W. Gould to Henry Cavendish, 20 May 1789, Devon. Coll., L/34/12.

[43] Lord Charles Cavendish to Thomas Revill, draft, 2 Mar. 1765, Devon. Coll., L/31/20.

as late as 7 February 1783.[44] He died "on or about" 28 April 1783;[45] by our reckoning, he was nearly seventy-nine. Not yet renowned as the father of Henry Cavendish, his obituary notice in *Gentleman's Magazine* identified him as the great uncle to the present duke of Devonshire, who but for his title was undistinguished. The obituary also said that Lord Charles was ninety, but it got him right when it called him an "excellent philosopher."[46]

For so rich a man, Cavendish's will was extremely brief, as his son Henry's would be too. Unchanged since it was made nearly thirty years before, it left £4,000 to Lord Charles's younger son, Frederick, compensation for what he had skimmed from Frederick's estate, and £1,000 for charity. Everything else belonged to his oldest son and sole executor, Henry.[47] Lord Charles's estate included real property, securities, and the recently inherited, combined estates of three related Cavendishes, Lord James, Richard (Chandler), and Elizabeth.[48]

At some point, probably when he resettled after his father's death, Henry made an inventory of his and his father's papers, which he now classified as *Fathers papers* and *Mine*. He kept all the papers in a tall walnut cabinet with an upper case. Lord Charles's personal papers have all been separated out and evidently lost, but it was unlikely to have been Henry who lost them; rather he classified and stored them under lock and key. Papers that we do not have but that Henry did include letters to and from Lord Charles and his family, letters to his wife, Lady Anne, Frederick's letters, Ruvigny papers, poetry, genealogy, mathematical papers, a pocketbook of experiments, measurements (probably meteorological) taken at Chatsworth, and papers on meteorological instruments, refracting telescopes, crystals, artificial cold, and specific gravities. Papers of Lord Charles's that have survived are mainly legal documents having to do with wills, annuities, titles, rents, dividends, suits, and his marriage settlement. Henry's own papers in the combined classification have to do with the same things as his father's, for they came with their way of life, properties and lawyers.[49]

Upon the death of Lord Charles, there was a small, almost imperceptible change in protocol. In his publications in the *Philosophical Transactions*, Henry

---

44 7 Feb. 1783, Committee Minutes, British Museum, 7.

45 Devon. Coll., L/31/37.

46 *Gentleman's Magazine* 53 (1783): 366.

47 Lord Charles Cavendish's will was probated on 28 May 1783. "Special Probate of the Last Will and Testament of the Right Honble Charles Cavendish Esqr Commonly Called Lord Charles Cavendish Deceased," Devon. Coll., L/69/12.

48 Upon Lord Charles Cavendish's death, Lord Camden became the sole surviving executor of the residue of Elizabeth Cavendish's estate. Henry Cavendish promptly applied to him, "being desirous of having" all the wealth in his own hands. "Lord Camden and The Honorable Henry Cavendish, Assignment and Deed of Indemnity, Dated Thirty-First of December 1783," Devon. Coll., L/31/37.

49 "Walnut Cabinet in Bed Chamber," "Papers in Walnut Cabinet," and "List of Papers Classed," Cavendish Mss Misc.

Cavendish's name was no longer preceded by "*Hon.*" Strictly speaking Henry never had a right to the title,[50] "The Honourable" being a courtesy title once removed. From 1783 on, he was Henry Cavendish "Esq." or simply Henry Cavendish; he signed his name H. Cavendish. One year after Lord Charles's death, a friend commented that "no address is requisite to please Mr Cavendish."[51]

Henry Cavendish attended all but two of the dinners of the Royal Society Club in 1783: Lord Charles died at the end of April, and Henry was absent from the first two dinners in May.[52] Writing to Henry Cavendish in late May, John Michell unnecessarily apologized for imposing on him "so soon after the loss of Ld Charles."[53] As to the meaning of the loss to Henry we can only wonder. We believe that no one had been as important as his father to him. We base our belief on several considerations.

From an early age, Henry was trained in science by his father. His father sent him to a secondary school with a modern curriculum and then to a university with a Newtonian curriculum. At both places, his father made contact with the persons in charge. No later than the year after Henry left the university, his father began to bring him to dinners with his friends from the Royal Society. Five years after that introduction, Henry began attending meetings of the Royal Society as a guest of his father. His first recommendation of a candidate at the Royal Society was made jointly with his father. His father was not on the council during Henry's first term, but because the council was elected, their separation perhaps could not be helped; Henry was first elected in 1766, then again in 1767, Lord Charles in 1768, and then Henry and Lord Charles together in 1769. Henry's early scientific researches at home were done with his father's books, journals, and instruments, and he and his father made observations together. Henry joined the same scientific clubs as his father. His father was present at Henry's early attendances at general meetings of trustees and at meetings of the standing committee of the British Museum. In his work at the Royal Society and the British Museum, Henry showed the same extraordinary diligence as his father; Henry had the example of his father before him, and he evidently approved of it, for he

[50] "The Honourable" followed by given name and surname was allowed the sons of earls and the children of viscounts and barons. Other than for a duke, who was called "His Grace," and a marquess, who was called "The Most Honourable," the title "The Right Honourable" was given to all peers as a courtesy. Henry Cavendish was none of these things. His father, however, was sometimes called "The Right Honourable Lord Cavendish," both parts of his title being by courtesy and proper. *Treasures from Chatsworth, The Devonshire Inheritance.* A Loan Exhibition from the Devonshire Collection, by Permission of the Duke of Devonshire and the Trustees of the Chatsworth Settlement, Organized and Circulated by the International Exhibits Foundation, 1979–1980, p. 24. In Lord Charles Cavendish's will, he is given as the "Right Honourable," commonly called "Lord." In Henry Cavendish's will, he is given as "Esquire," commonly called "Honourable."

[51] Charles Blagden to William Cullen, 17 June 1784, draft, Blagden Letterbook, Yale.

[52] They were dinners on 1 and 8 May 1783. Minute Books, Royal Society Club, Royal Society.

[53] John Michell to Henry Cavendish, 26 May 1783, Cavendish Mss New Correspondence.

imitated it. That is the most conclusive evidence of all of his father's importance to him.

Despite Lord Charles's privileges, his life had a very sad aspect. His wife died while he was still in his twenties, leaving him with two tiny boys to raise. While only in his teens, the youngest boy, Frederick, suffered an accident which impaired his brain and left him permanently dependent on Lord Charles. His other son, Henry, must have given early and clear signs of another kind of incompetence, a pathological shyness, which might have left him dependent on his father. Lord Charles, it would seem, shepherded and sheltered his older son until he felt ready to meet the world. He provided Henry with an appropriate education, a place to live and work, and opportunity to meet and become comfortable with persons with scientific interests. Whatever failings as a father Lord Charles may have had, he did certain things right. For science was obviously right for his supremely intelligent and diffident son. The help that Lord Charles gave Henry in establishing an independent life, we have discussed earlier in this chapter.

Direct evidence of Lord Charles Cavendish's intimate life is meager, but we know that he died with the knowledge that his oldest son was in charge of his life and master of his chosen line of work, science. His son had followed in his path and had gone beyond him. Of his achievements, the example and assistance he provided Henry were his greatest and, we trust, his proudest.

Part Three

Henry Cavendish

PERSON

CHARLES BLAGDEN

At about the time of his father's death, Henry Cavendish acquired a close associate, Charles Blagden. Cavendish had known Blagden casually but now their acquaintance deepened. Given Cavendish's habits of privacy, his willingness to allow another person to be regularly in his company is remarkable in itself.

Because of his unique relationship with Cavendish, Blagden holds a particular interest in this biography, but he is interesting in his own right as well. A man of modest means and abilities (unlike his friend Cavendish in both respects), he made for himself a place in science at a time before science was a profession; his association with Cavendish played a part in his ambitions.

In the course of his medical studies at Edinburgh University, where he took his M.D. in 1768, Blagden received a good scientific education. He heard both Joseph Black and William Cullen lecture on chemistry, becoming friendly with the latter, whom he regarded as his teacher. From his side, Cullen regarded Blagden as a "friend" with whom he had "particular intimacy," Blagden being "very much in my family."[1] Blagden does not seem to have been close to Black, but in Blagden's papers there is a copy of Black's lectures, partly in Blagden's hand,[2] and a testimonial by Black that Blagden had attended his lectures.[3] In the year following his graduation, Blagden set up practice in Gloucester, where he kept an electrical machine made by Jesse Ramsden, which he may have used on his patients. He soon acquired a good reputation in Gloucester, but he was

[1] William Cullen to William Hunter, 11 Feb. 1769; quoted in John Thomson, *An Account of the Life, Lectures, and Writings of William Cullen, M.D., Professor of the Practice of Physic in the University of Edinburgh*, 2 vols. (Edinburgh, 1859) 1:555–56, on 555.

[2] Blagden was in Edinburgh in 1765–69. Charles Blagden to William Cullen, 17 June 1784, draft, Yale, Blagden Letterbook. Joseph Black's lectures are in Box 7 of the Blagden Papers at Yale. Henry Guerlac, "Black, Joseph," *DSB* 2:173–83, on 173–74.

[3] Joseph Black to Charles Blagden, 5 Oct. 1769, Blagden Letters, Royal Society.

restless,[4] his sights set on London where, a friend told him, a physician like William Heberden could earn £2,000 to £4,000 a year, maybe more. This friend advised him to remain in the provinces for another four or five years, because few people in London took seriously a physician under thirty.[5] Another friend offered similar advice, at the same time acknowledging that Blagden's happiness lay where all of his "interests centered," in the "great town."[6] By 1772 Blagden was living in London.

In London, Blagden expanded his connections with science. Elected to the Royal Society, he carried out daring experiments in concert with a number of other Fellows. Guided (and protected) by a doctrine he attributed to Cullen, he exposed himself to very high heats, testing the power of the human body to resist them, the subject of his first paper in the *Philosophical Transactions*. With his fellow experimenters, he spent considerable time inside a room heated to temperatures above the boiling point, nearly 260 degrees. Eggs hardened, beef roasted, but Blagden and the other human subjects emerged unharmed, proof, to Blagden, that Cullen was right, that the "body has a power of destroying heat." The heated room was a new "instrument," with promising implications for practical medicine.[7] In 1775, the year of the last of his experiments in a heated room, Blagden made a scientific connection with Cavendish. Now an army surgeon assigned to North America, he was instructed by Cavendish on how to serve science at the same time: on the voyage to America, Blagden was to compare the temperature of the sea with that of the air, and when he got there he was to make observations of the temperature of wells and springs. These directions, Blagden said, "led to my discovery of the heat of the gulf stream" and to a publication in the *Philosophical Transactions*. Finding the temperature of the stream to be several degrees above that of the sea through which it ran, he suggested that seamen carry a thermometer as an aid in navigation.[8] Because of the war, Blagden had little opportunity to make the observations of wells and springs that Cavendish wanted, but he followed events in science as best he could, including its politics, asking Banks why Cavendish was left off the council of the Royal Society in 1778. Longing to resume his life in science, in 1779 he received permission from General Cornwallis to return from America to England. By 1780 Blagden was settled in Plymouth, where he remained for two years working in the military hospital. He

[4] J. Smart to Charles Blagden, 22 Sep. 1769; Henry Cumming to Charles Blagden, 7 Nov. 1769; Jesse Ramsden to Charles Blagden, 23 Nov. 1769; Thomas Curtis to Charles Blagden, 26 Dec. 1769 and 8 Feb. 1770. Blagden Letters, Royal Society, S.11, C.72, R.40, C.77, C.79.

[5] Thomas Curtis to Charles Blagden, 15 Jan. 1770, Blagden Letters, Royal Society, C.78.

[6] J. Smart to Charles Blagden, 24 Feb. 1772, Blagden Letters, Royal Society, S.16.

[7] Charles Blagden, "Experiments and Observations in an Heated Room," and "Further Experiments and Observations in an Heated Room," *PT* 65 (1775): 111–23, 484–94, on 119, 493.

[8] Charles Blagden, "On the Heat of the Water in the Gulf-Stream," *PT* 71 (1781): 334–44, on 334, 341–44. A fuller statement of Cavendish's part is in the draft of a paper in Blagden Papers, Yale, box 2, folder 26.

was back home but he was in Plymouth, which he regarded as "miserable exile."[9] In an ideal life, he told Sir Joseph Banks, president of the Royal Society, he would "live as much as I can among books," and he asked if the Royal Society could make him "Inspector of the Library, or something of that sort," with apartments in or next to the Royal Society in Sommerset Place. Banks said no,[10] leaving Blagden to explore other means of escape. The North Pole voyager Phipps, who had gone with Blagden into the heated room, repeatedly offered his connections in the admiralty to help Blagden's career.[11] Before long Blagden became secretary of the Royal Society through his association with Banks. That office placed him at the center of activities of the Royal Society, and it provided him with a small income, which augmented his income from other sources.

In the summer of 1782 Blagden attended lectures by an "itinerant Philosopher," Dr. Henry Moyes, who was reputed to be a prodigy, but whose knowledge of recent developments Blagden found "extremely inaccurate & defective,"[12] at best scraps from Black's lectures on heat. Blagden scoffed at Moyes's claim that mercury freezes at minus 350 degrees. The day after a lecture and apparently prompted by it, Blagden recorded in his diary "hints" for experiments on heat, "ideas which suggested themselves": in addition to experiments, he speculated "whether heat may not be the cause of all chemical attracting, the different bodies not attracting one another, but attracting the common medium, heat."[13] This way of thinking about heat was decidedly not Cavendish's, but that did not stand in the way, for Blagden was soon making experiments on freezing mixtures with Cavendish.

At some point Blagden moved from Plymouth to London to live with his brother and to make his fortune in the great city. In early 1783 he went on half pay as a physician to the forces.[14] He was now again in regular personal contact with the leading men of science, at the Royal Society and its dining club, at the Monday Club (see below), and at the homes of individuals: William Herschel, Alexander Aubert, and Banks. In the summer of 1782, Blagden began visiting the heads of the Cavendish family, the duke and duchess of Devonshire, often dining with them. In March of that year, he had breakfast at their cousin Henry Cavendish's house, and that fall he began assisting Cavendish in experiments. In keeping with a promise he had made to Cavendish before he left for the war

---

9 Charles Blagden to Sir Joseph Banks, 3 Nov. 1782, copy, BM(NH), DTC 3:205–6.

10 Charles Blagden to Sir Joseph Banks, 19 July 1782, draft; Sir Joseph Banks to Charles Blagden, 19 Aug. 1782, Blagden Letters, Royal Society, B.8a and 9.

11 C. J. Phipps, Lord Mulgrave to Charles Blagden, 1 Mar. 1780, Blagden Letters, Royal Society, P. 35.

12 Blagden to Banks, 19 July 1782.

13 16, 18, 19 July 1782, Charles Blagden Diary, Royal Society, 1.

14 Letter from the war office: FitzPatrick to Charles Blagden, 7 May 1783, Blagden Letters, Royal Society, F.10.

in America, Blagden collected Plymouth air in all kinds of weather, in nine bottles, which he brought to Cavendish in his new house in Hampstead, where they tested it with the eudiometer.[15] In December, with Cavendish, Blagden went over the experiments on extreme cold done at Hudson Bay under Cavendish's direction, and, on "Cavendish's advice," he set about to learn what had been done on that subject "chiefly with a view to quicksilver," which would lead to his history of the freezing of mercury, published in the *Philosophical Transactions* the following year.[16] In his enthusiasm for experimenting on freezing mixtures, he froze a finger white several times,[17] and on 27 February 1783 he recorded that on the previous day Cavendish had frozen mercury. By 1785 Cavendish and Blagden's association was recognized by Banks, who in letters to Blagden asked him to give his compliments to Cavendish. Banks toasted them: "may success attend all your mutual operations."[18]

Blagden and Cavendish were both single and resettling, Cavendish in midlife at fifty-one, and Blagden in a change of career at thirty-four. Cavendish would undoubtedly have been drawn to Blagden for what Boswell called his "copiousness and precision."[19] These were, after all, traits of Cavendish's own. Blagden was knowledgeable in most departments of science, acquainted with a wide circle of men of science, a diligent scientific correspondent, and a linguist who cultivated connections with foreigners. When he became secretary of the Royal Society in 1784, he greatly extended his lines of communication. In 1786 he wrote to Benjamin Thompson in Germany: "It is scarcely possible that any ph[ilosophical] discoveries can be made in England without coming to my knowledge by some channel or another,"[20] and with his foreign connections, he could have said nearly the same about his knowledge of philosophical discoveries abroad. Competent in the use of instruments, he assisted Cavendish in carrying out experiments. Lacking a strong scientific direction of his own, he entered effortlessly into Cavendish's work. He took on editorial responsibilities for the *Philosophical Transactions*, and privately he did the same for Cavendish's papers published in that journal.[21] Blagden had a love of books, he was boundlessly curious, he had an excellent memory for facts, he was a conduit of information about scientific matters from around the world, and he was reliable, loyal, and accessible when Cavendish needed him. It would be hard to invent a man better qualified to be Cavendish's right hand.

[15] Blagden to Banks, 3 Nov. 1782. Entry for 28 Nov. 1782, Charles Blagden Diary, Royal Society, 1.

[16] 17 and 23 Dec. 1782, Charles Blagden Diary, Royal Society, 1.

[17] 25 Feb. 1783 and following entries, Charles Blagden Diary, Royal Society, 1.

[18] Sir Joseph Banks to Charles Blagden, 28 July and 4 Aug. 1785, Blagden Letters, Royal Society, B.35 and 36.

[19] Quoted in Frederick H. Getman, "Sir Charles Blagden, F.R.S.," *Osiris* 3 (1937): 69–87, on 73.

[20] Charles Blagden to Benjamin Thompson, 7 Feb. 1786, draft, Blagden Letterbook, Yale.

[21] Charles Blagden to Henry Cavendish, n.d. [1785], Cavendish Mss X(b), 4.

What Blagden expected in return for his services to Cavendish is less clear. Some favors were simply mutual. Cavendish supplied Blagden with any scientific information he wanted: on claims for a barometric tube made by George Adams, Blagden was skeptical but unsure: "but Mr Cavendish will be here presently, & then I will consult *him*."[22] Blagden's manuscripts contain letters and papers from Cavendish on questions of science pertaining to Blagden's interests. Of ten papers Blagden published in the *Philosophical Transactions*, four originated with Cavendish and two others were done with Cavendish's help.[23] Perhaps most important, Cavendish provided Blagden with a form of patronage. By placing his trust publicly in Blagden, Cavendish helped him to realize a place in the world. Lord Castlereagh gave as Blagden's scientific qualifications that he had several publications in science, that he had been a secretary of the Royal Society, and that he had been "an intimate friend of the late Mr Cavendish."[24]

Blagden considered establishing a medical practice in London, but he lacked the desire or the drive to see it through. He wanted income, and it has been assumed that Cavendish answered his want. Given the social and financial disparity between Cavendish and Blagden, the rumor mills were busy: the chemist Kirwan, who had a wicked pen, wrote to a French colleague that Blagden looked at questions of science only through Cavendish's eyes because Cavendish "is a near relation of the duke of Devonshire and has six thousand pounds sterling yearly income."[25]

Wilson and others have stated that Cavendish settled an annuity of £500 on Blagden.[26] Because an annuity would bear on the relationship between Cavendish and Blagden, we have tried to confirm it. From an examination of Blagden's financial records for the six years 1785–90, we find that in September 1785 he received £7 from Cavendish, and in September 1787, £14; each time Cavendish and Blagden had just returned from one of their journeys, and we assume that Blagden was being reimbursed for small expenses he had been out. Blagden's income came from three sources during the six years for which we have comparable records: his half pay from the army, his salary from the Royal

[22] Charles Blagden to Sir Joseph Banks, 12 Oct. 1786, BL Add Mss 33272, pp. 19–20.

[23] In the ten papers, we omit two in the *Philosophical Transactions*: an extract from a letter by Blagden on the tides at Naples in 1793, and an appendix to Ware's paper on vision in 1813. The repeated involvement of Cavendish in Blagden's scientific work is documented in Blagden's publications and in his papers in which sheets of Cavendish's handwriting are intermixed. Blagden Papers, Yale, box 2, and elsewhere.

[24] Lord Castlereagh to Sir Charles Stuart, 13 July 1819 (copy), Blagden Letters, Royal Society, C.6.

[25] Richard Kirwan to Guyton de Morveau, 9 Jan. 1786, in *A Scientific Correspondence During the Chemical Revolution: Louis-Bernard Guyton de Morveau and Richard Kirwan, 1782–1802*, ed. E. Grison, M Sadoun-Goupil, and P. Bret (Berkeley: Office for the History of Science and Technology, University of California at Berkeley, 1994), 161–64, on 163.

[26] The annuity is asserted by John Blagden Hale, Thomas Thomson, Lord Brougham, and George Wilson, *The Life of the Honourable Henry Cavendish* (London, 1851), 133, 142, 160.

Society, and dividends from his securities, which included and may have consisted entirely of Scotch bonds. There were two exceptional additions to his income. In April 1787 he deposited with his banker Scotch bonds worth £726, after which he paid out £300 and then £598 to Thomas Lewis of Gray's Inn, his brother's solicitor, business agent, and former partner, who also acted for Charles; the £300 sum was paid to Thomas Hale for the use of Charles's brother, John Blagden Hale; we have not found a reference to the larger sum.[27] The other large addition was in September 1789, when he deposited £1,400 from the sale of a house. In none of this do we find evidence of a £500 annuity.

In October 1784 Blagden moved from his lodgings off Great Ormond Street about six blocks northeast of Cavendish's house to a rental house right across the street from Cavendish's, No. 7, Gower Street, Bedford Square.[28] In the spring of 1785, he gave notice to his landlord that he was quiting the premises.[29] He moved into another house on the same street, this one on the same side as Cavendish's, No. 19, Gower Street, Bedford Square. This move was definitely upscale; the rateable value of his new house was double that of his first house and half the value of Cavendish's. Blagden owned this house and after four years sold it.[30] Blagden's papers contain two undated, unaddressed drafts of letters referring to a house, which we have good reason to think were written to Cavendish.

> Just after you were gone Mr Hanscombe called here with the inclosed note, & opened it; he had [-----] before at your house, but having been informed you were gone by to Hamstead came to shew it to me. I am extremely obliged to you for the liberal offer you have made; but as, were I so rich that the sum would be no object to me I should still think it too much for the house, & sho^d probably refuse to give it. I cannot but consider it as totally inequitable that you sho^d give it for me. I therefore do most seriously request that you would refuse to comply with the terms proposed, & wait till an opportunity offers of making a fairer purchase; and in the mean time I will use every means in my power to become reconciled to my present situation.[31]

Blagden referred to Hampstead in this letter, and Cavendish had a country house at Hampstead from 1782 to 1786. If the letter was written to Cavendish,

---

27 Gloucestershire Record Office, D1086, F156.

28 Charles Blagden to John Blagden Hale, n.d., draft, Blagden Letterbook, Yale. In this letter Blagden says that he will move into his house on Gower Street at the end of next week. He mentions that he observed Blanchard's balloon on the day of this letter, which dates it, 17 Oct. 1784.

29 Charles Blagden to Mr. Mountfort, 22 Mar. 1785, draft, Blagden Letterbook, Yale.

30 In 1786 the ratebooks list Blagden at both of his addresses on Gower Street; for that year the rateable value of Blagden's first house was £32 and of his second house £65; Cavendish's house was valued at £120. Rate books for Gower Street: Bloomsbury Division (part 1), p. 11; St Giles in the Fields Division (part 2), pp. 23, 25. For 1789: St Giles in the Fields Division (part 2), pp. 31–32. Camden Archives.

31 Blagden Collection. Misc. Matter–Unclassified, Royal Society.

it was within that period, probably in 1785. The other reference in the letter is to Hanscomb, who was later engaged to build new houses on Cavendish's land at Clapham. Among Blagden's papers is a carpenter's bill from Hanscomb and Fothergill for work done on his, *Blagden's,* house at Clapham in the summer and fall of 1785.[32] It is conceivable that Blagden considered settling at Clapham, where Cavendish intended to do his experimental work. There are no extant rate books for Clapham, but the less inclusive Clapham land tax records have survived, and they contain no listing for Blagden. Nowhere in Blagden's correspondence or other papers is there mention of a house at Clapham. We conclude that Hanscomb's carpenters' bill was incorrectly labeled, intended for Cavendish for work done on his house, with Blagden acting as Cavendish's agent. Cavendish had extensive work done on his new house at Clapham Common in the months covered by the carpenters' bill. The second letter concerns a quarrel between Blagden and Sir Joseph Banks, which would place it in 1789 or 1790.

> The generosity of your conduct in your original offer, in your subsequent present of this house, in your late confirmation of that present, and especially in your further offer when I expected to marry last year, I shall always take a pride in acknowledging.[33]

The mention of the offer to Blagden upon his marriage almost certainly identifies Cavendish as the recipient of this letter. The house that Blagden sold in 1789 was his house on Gower Street, and we believe that it was the "present" referred to in this letter, and that Cavendish was the giver. We know that Cavendish wanted to help Blagden resume his medical practice, a goal which a house would have served more directly than an annuity.

Cavendish and Blagden's association is said to have ended with a formal break, in 1789.[34] The break at that time, as we will see, was in the first instance not between Blagden and Cavendish but between Blagden and Banks. The break in any case was only partial: after 1789 neither Cavendish nor Blagden published any more experimental researches (with the exceptions of Blagden's experiments on levying the excise duty on alcohol the following year and of Cavendish's experiment on the density of the earth ten years later), but they continued to meet to perform experiments at Clapham Common.[35] When Blagden was out of the country, he continued to write to Cavendish with scientific news.[36] When Blagden fell ill while abroad, he had

---

32 Hanscomb & Fothergill, "Carpenters Work Done for Dr Blagden at His House at Clapham," Gloucestershire Record Office, D 1086, F 153.

33 Blagden Collection. Misc. Notes, Royal Society, 224.

34 Wilson, *Cavendish,* 129.

35 Charles Blagden to Sir Joseph Banks, 17 Oct. 1790, BL Add Mss 33272, pp. 91–92.

36 Blagden told Banks to tell Cavendish to expect a letter from him on an excursion to Tivoli. Charles Blagden to Sir Joseph Banks, 11 May 1793, BL Add Mss 33272, pp. 119–20.

his doctor inform Cavendish, who in turn informed Banks.[37] When Blagden wanted support in the Royal Society, Cavendish gave it, as in 1793 when Blagden wanted to stay abroad another year and retain his position as secretary of the Royal Society.[38] As long as Blagden was in London, he and Cavendish continued to meet regularly to the end of Cavendish's life. The change in their relationship was one of degree not of kind, but there definitely was a change; when Cavendish died, Blagden spoke of an earlier time when he had been "intimate with him."[39]

The exact nature of their relationship is hard to define. Both men lived by strict routines but they were able to make an accommodation. To what degree personal warmth made it possible, they did not choose to reveal. Davy characterized them both as "cold & selfish."[40] Cavendish kept any thoughts he had about friendship to himself. Blagden might be expected to have left a personal account; that he did not may be explained by a remark he made about Boswell's account of his and Johnson's tour of the Hebrides: "Most people would be sorry to have a bosom friend, who kept a journal of their conversations, to publish as soon as they should be dead."[41]

MONDAY CLUB

Henry Cavendish's social life took place largely in clubs. From the Restoration in the seventeenth century through the eighteenth century and beyond, men of science congregated, often as clubs, in the coffeehouses and taverns of London.[42] The Royal Society Club was the best known and the best documented of Cavendish's clubs, but from letters to Cavendish and from Blagden's diary we know of other, less formal clubs, which kept no records. Clubs commonly went by the names of the coffeehouses and taverns where their meetings took place. In letters to Cavendish from the 1770s, Alexander Dalrymple sent greetings to their mutual friends at the Mitre and at the King's Head. The King's Head Tavern in Chancery Lane was where Robert Hooke and other Fellows of the Royal Society gathered in the late seventeenth century, but the King's Head was a com-

---

[37] Cavendish had been informed of Blagden's illness a week before, but he did not tell Banks until he had something "more precise." Cavendish described a violent fever but reassured Banks that now there was the "utmost reason" to expect Blagden to recover. He was receiving the "utmost care," and his "head was perfectly clear." Henry Cavendish to Sir Joseph Banks, 23 Sep. 1793, copy, BM(NH), DTC 3:257.

[38] Sir Joseph Banks to Charles Blagden, n.d. [after 11 May 1793], draft, BL Add Mss 33272, p. 121.

[39] 1 Mar. 1810, Charles Blagden Diary, Royal Society, 5:428 (back).

[40] J. Z. Fullmer, "Davy's Sketches of His Contemporaries," *Chymia* 12 (1966): 127–50, on 133.

[41] Charles Blagden to Joseph Banks, 9 Oct. 1785, Banks Correspondence, Kew, 1.210.

[42] A. E. Musson and E. Robinson, *Science and Technology in the Industrial Revolution* (Toronto: University of Toronto Press, 1969), 58. Bryant Lillywhite, *London Coffee Houses. A Reference Book of Coffee Houses of the Seventeenth, Eighteenth and Nineteenth Centuries* (London: George Allen & Unwin, 1963), 22–24.

mon name for taverns.[43] The Royal Society Club met at the Mitre Coffee House on Fleet Street, and later at the Crown & Anchor on the Strand. In letters to Cavendish from the 1780s, John Michell greeted their common friends at the Cat and Bagpipes. The name of this tavern is more original, but all that is known about it is that it was located on Downing Street and was popular.[44]

Henry Cavendish and his father went to some of the same clubs together. First among these was the Royal Society Club. Then, as noted earlier, Henry and his father met in a private house on the Strand. We also noted that his father met with a group at Rawthmell's Coffee House, and we are almost certain that Henry did too. Rawthmell's was on Henrietta Street, in Covent Garden. To settle the time of an inspection of government powder magazines, William Watson asked fellow committeeman Benjamin Franklin to "call in Henrietta Street"; "Mr. Cavendish [chairman of the committee] Seldom fails of coming there."[45]

There were other scientific clubs which Cavendish did not belong to but his friends and colleagues did. One which included Aubert, Nairne, and Kirwan met at the Chapter Coffee House and later at the Baptist Head Coffee House.[46] Another which included Blagden, Banks, Maskelyne, and other associates met at Jack's Coffee House and later at Young Slaughter's Coffee House on St. Martin's Lane.[47] Other clubs met at Banks's house[48] and at Kirwan's house.[49]

A club that Cavendish did belong to was the Monday Club, named after the day of the week it met. The meeting place was the George & Vulture, a coffeehouse located in George Yard, off Lombard Street.[50] This club had been meeting since at least the 1760s.[51] Cavendish came regularly to it for fifteen years or more. When John Pringle returned from Edinburgh to London in 1781, he rejoined the Monday Club, where he met with "such friends as Mr. Cavendish, Dr. Heberden,

[43] From the 1730s, too, we have record of a meeting that included a number of scientific men at a King's Head: *The Private Journal and Literary Remains of John Byrom*, vol. 1, part 2, ed. R. Parkinson, (London, 1855), 556. Seven King's Head taverns are listed under signs of taverns in *Vade Mecum*, and included in Walter Besant, *London in the Eighteenth Century* (London: Adean & Charles Black, 1902), 639–40.

[44] *Notes and Queries*, 9 Nov. 1850, p. 397, quoted in Archibald Geikie, *Memoir of John Michell* (Cambridge: Cambridge University Press, 1918), 58.

[45] William Watson to Benjamin Franklin, 31 July 1772, *Papers of Benjamin Franklin*, vol. 19, ed. W. B. Willcox (New Haven: Yale University Press, 1975), 213.

[46] G. L'E. Turner, "The Auction Sales of the Earl of Bute's Instruments, 1793," *Annals of Science* 23 (1967): 213–42, on 220.

[47] Henry B. Wheatley, *London, Past and Present. A Dictionary of Its History, Associations, and Traditions*, 3 vols. (London, 1891), 2:484. Lillywhite, *London Coffee Houses*, 404.

[48] John Strange to Joseph Banks, 8 Aug. 1788, Banks Correspondence, Kew, 1.315.

[49] Musson and Robinson, *Science and Technology in the Industrial Revolution*, 123.

[50] Lillywhite, *London Coffee Houses*, 160, 201, 699, 792.

[51] Verner W. Crane, "The Club of Honest Whigs: Friends of Science and Liberty," *William and Mary Quarterly* 23 (1966): 210–33, on 213.

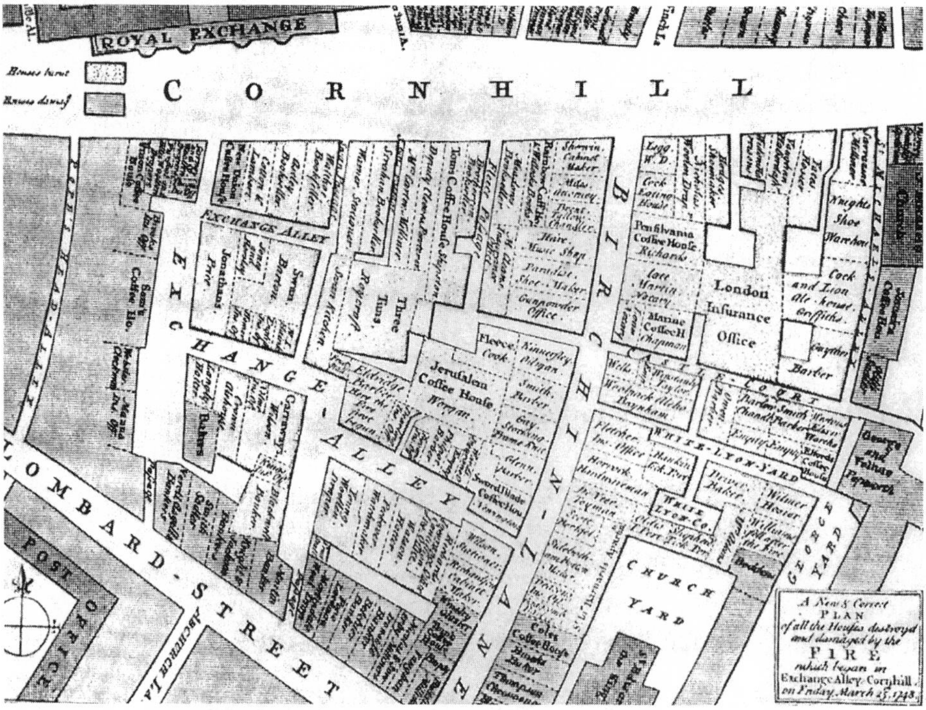

62. *Map of Cornhill. This map was made to show the buildings damaged or destroyed by a fire originating in Exchange Alley in 1748. A good number of coffeeshops relocated but not the George & Vulture off George Yard, shown at the upper right corner of the map. There Cavendish joined his friends on Monday evenings. Aytoun Ellis,* The Penny Universities: A History of the Coffee-Houses *(London: Secker & Warburg, 1956), opposite 94.*

and Dr. Watson."[52] Blagden began coming to it at about the same time, soon after he returned to London, as we know from his diary.[53] Aubert, Dalrymple, Franklin, Phipps, Nairne, and Smeaton were members, all of them associates of Cavendish's, and all of them Fellows of the Royal Society.[54] The discussions at this club were often continuations of those at the Royal Society and the Royal Society Club.[55] Blagden's diary reveals that he and Cavendish often went together to dine at the Monday Club. Upon returning home one night, Blagden noted: "went with him [Cavendish] to Club: I spoke of spirit & independence, & true friends."[56] He did not record what Cavendish said on the subject.

[52] Quotation from the *Annual Register*, 1783, p. 45; in James Sime, *William Herschel and His Work* (New York: Charles Scribner's Sons, 1900), 50.

[53] 1 Jan. 1782, Charles Blagden Diary, Royal Society.

[54] On Franklin and Aubert: Crane, "Club of Honest Whigs," 213. On Dalrymple: 15 June 1795, Charles Blagden Diary, Royal Society, 3:62, and elsewhere. On Phipps, Nairne, and Smeaton: Alexander Aubert to Sir Joseph Banks, 1 July 1789, BL Add Mss 33978, no. 251.

[55] Alexander Aubert to William Herschel, 7 Sep. 1782, Herschel Mss, Royal Astronomical Society, W1/13, A 10. Aubert to Banks, 1 July 1789.

[56] 25 Aug. 1794, Charles Blagden Diary, Royal Society, 3:13.

63. *Sir Charles Blagden. Etching from the portrait by Thomas Phillips. Reproduced by permission of the President and Council of the Royal Society.*

64. *Alexander Dalrymple. Engraving by Rudley from a drawing by John Brown. Frontispiece to* European Magazine *42 (November 1802).*

65. *Alexander Aubert. Engraving by Chapman from a painting by Drummond. Bernard Drew,* The London Assurance. A Second Chronicle *(Plaistow: Curwen, 1949), opposite 149.*

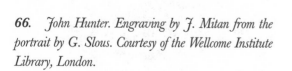

66. *John Hunter. Engraving by J. Mitan from the portrait by G. Slous. Courtesy of the Wellcome Institute Library, London.*

MAN WITHOUT AFFECTIONS?

Having described Cavendish among his friends and colleagues, we return to what was most essential about him, his preference for the *umbratilis vita.* Research and reading, by and large solitary activities, "formed the whole occupation of his life," Blagden wrote. Strong passions were thought to be foreign to him, though if we accept the premise that feeling and thinking are connected, we must recognize that Cavendish's life had an enduring emotional component. Accounts given by persons who knew him agree that his motivation was highly directed and altogether extraordinary. Blagden put it simply: Cavendish had a "love of truth."[57]

We can speak confidently of Cavendish the man of science, but can we speak of Cavendish the *complete* man? In a course on chemistry given in 1855, the lecturer gave an emphatic no to this question. He began the course by warning his students about Cavendish: "It may be fairly asked, why bring such a character forward for examination? . . . Is it enough *not* to be a villain, a debauchee, a murderer? Or, rather, is it not our duty to be *something* that shall create an influence for *positive good* on our fellow-men? To this the answer must be made, that the character of Cavendish is not introduced as a subject of admiration, or for imitation, but rather as a warning to all men who cultivate the intellect, that they do not neglect the social portion of their nature."[58] This lecturer, who regarded Cavendish as a "calculating machine," had read a book published four years before, George Wilson's *The Life of the Honourable Henry Cavendish.*

Wilson's biography is a vivid portrait of Victorian negations, of a man lacking in piety, family, philanthropy, and poetry; estranged from humanity, Cavendish cared only for science. We might agree with Wilson that Cavendish cared only for science, but we do not see that that precluded his humanity. It seems to us that quite the opposite was the case. Science included Cavendish in the world, for it was through science that Cavendish formed relationships with his fellow human beings. Science is foremost a social endeavor.

Davy said that Cavendish was a "great Man with extraordinary singularities." Wilson spoke of Cavendish's "singular oddities of character," of the prominent "peculiarites of his character."[59] Friends were intrigued by his character. "Talk about Mr Cavendish, & explanation of character," Blagden wrote in his diary,[60] but he did not record what that explanation was. After an evening spent in Cavendish's company, Blagden normally noted one or two words in his diary to sum up Cavendish's behavior. "Secluded," his choice of

---

[57] Blagden's anonymous obituary of Cavendish in *Gentleman's Magazine*, Mar. 1810, p. 292.

[58] The introductory lecture to a course on chemistry at the National Medical College by Lewis H. Steiner, *Henry Cavendish and the Discovery of the Chemical Composition of Water* (New York, 1855), 6.

[59] Fullmer, "Davy's Sketches of His Contemporaries," 133. Wilson, *Cavendish*, 167.

[60] 14 July 1795, Charles Blagden Diary, Royal Society, 3:65 (back).

word for his character sketch of Cavendish, is not found in his diary, but the words Blagden did use suggest a desire for seclusion. Occasionally he used words of relief such as "civil," "civiller," and "pleasant to talk with," but mostly they were harsh words such as "melancholy," "forbidding," "odd," "dry," and "sulky." "Sulky," the word Blagden used most often he also occasionally applied to Banks and other companions, but he applied it consistently only to Cavendish. *Sulky*: obdurately out of humor, aloof, passive and silent in fending off approaches.

We group our observations of Cavendish's character under three headings: taciturnity, solitariness, and shyness. We start with taciturnity. According to Lord Brougham, Cavendish "uttered fewer words in the course of his life than any man who ever lived to fourscore years, not at all excepting the monks of La Trappe."[61] Less colorfully, on a visit to London in 1782, John Playfair described Cavendish as one who "speaks with great difficulty and hesitation, and very seldom."[62]

To Wilson the most striking of Cavendish's peculiarities was his "singular love for solitariness."[63] Davy said that Cavendish "lived latterly the life of a solitary." John Barrow said that Cavendish seemed "to consider himself as a solitary being in the world, and to feel himself unfit for society."[64]

Barrow recalled Cavendish's "extreme shyness," as confirmed by "all his habits."[65] Davy said that Cavendish was "afraid of strangers, and seemed, when embarrassed, even to articulate with difficulty."[66] Blagden noted in his diary, "Mr C's great embarrassment, dryness."[67] Thomas Thomson found Cavendish "shy and bashful to a degree bordering on disease; he could not bear to have any person introduced to him, or to be pointed out in any way as a remarkable man." Thomson told a story about a meeting between Cavendish and a visiting Austrian at Banks's house: Cavendish was introduced to the Austrian as a profound and celebrated philosopher, and then he was forced to listen to a flattering speech: "Mr. Cavendish answered not a word, but stood with his eyes cast down, quite abashed and confounded. At last, spying an opening in the crowd, he darted through it with all the speed of which he was master, nor did he stop till he reached his carriage, which drove him directly home." Cavendish had "a most reserved disposition and peculiarly shy habits," Lord Brougham said. "This led to some singularity of

[61] Henry, Lord Brougham, "Cavendish," in *Lives of Men of Letters and Science Who Flourished in the Time of George III* (Philadelphia, 1845), 250–59, on 259.

[62] Wilson, *Cavendish*, 165.

[63] Ibid.

[64] John Barrow, *Sketches of the Royal Society and the Royal Society Club* (London, 1849), 144.

[65] Ibid.

[66] Wilson, *Cavendish*, 167.

[67] 26 May 1794, Charles Blagden Diary, Royal Society, 3:3.

manner, which was further increased by a hesitation or difficulty of speech, and a thin shrill voice. He entered diffidently into any conversation, and seemed to dislike being spoken to. . . . At [the Royal Society, and Banks's weekly conversaziones] I have met him, and recollect the shrill cry he uttered as he shuffled quickly from room to room, seeming to be annoyed if looked at, but sometimes approaching to hear what was passing among others." Encountering Cavendish at Banks's house, W. H. Pepys found him "very attentive to what I was describing. When I caught his eye he retired in great haste, but I soon found he was again listening near me." Pepys was advised by Banks "to avoid speaking to him as he would be offended," but if Cavendish spoke to him, he was to "continue the conversation," as he is "full of information." A chemist who often dined at the Royal Society Club made a similar observation about Cavendish: "If you attempted to draw him into conversation he always fought shy." This advice was given by Dr. Wollaston, who added that "the way to talk to Cavendish is never to look at him, but to talk as it were into vacancy, and then it is not unlikely but you may set him going." Another diner at the Royal Society Club, J. G. Children, approached a group in which Cavendish was in conversation; as soon as his "eye caught that of Cavendish," the latter "instantly became silent: he did not say a word. The fact is he saw in me a strange face, and of a strange face he had a perfect horror." To Wilson, the best example of Cavendish's "excessive shyness" was told to him by a Fellow of the Royal Society who observed Cavendish at Banks's house: "I have myself seen him stand a long time on the landing, evidently wanting courage to open the door and face the people assembled, nor would he open the door until he heard some one coming up the stairs, and then he was forced to go in."[68] Once inside Banks's house, he still stood apart, characterized by Sir Henry Holland, who was there, as the *umbratilis vita*.[69] Cavendish was easy to spot but difficult to meet. He became anxious if a stranger took an interest in him. He discouraged conversation, and if trapped, he ran. His features were strained, his speech excited, his demeanor that of a creature poised for flight. He was reticent, inhibited, awkward, and embarrassed in the presence of strangers, especially if they were of the opposite sex; he was, as we would say, antisocial.

This account of Cavendish's "singular oddities of character" is a good approximation to a contemporary clinical description of extreme shyness together with a measure of bashfulness. Psychologists disagree as to whether or not shyness is a form of social anxiety, but they agree that the shy person experiences anxiety, and that self-consciousness or embarrassment can be highly

---

[68] Wilson, *Cavendish*, 166–70.

[69] Alexander Geikie, *Annals of the Royal Society Club: The Record of a London Dining-Club in the Eighteenth and Nineteenth Centuries* (London: Macmillan, 1917), 225.

disagreeable; the inward manifestation of shyness, the emotional element, is fear or self-consciousness or both.[70]

Cavendish was an anxious man. Lord Brougham said that if spoken to, Cavendish would leave abruptly "as if scared and disturbed"; he described Cavendish's face as "intelligent and mild, though, from the nervous irritation which he seemed to feel, the expression could hardly be called calm." W. H. Pepys said that Cavendish's "speech was hesitating and excited." Similarly Davy described his voice as "squeaking," and "his manner nervous." The best example of Cavendish's social fear, we think, is his hesitancy in front of the door to Banks's house, "evidently wanting courage to open the door and face the people assembled."[71]

Depression often accompanies extreme shyness. Melancholy, William Rowley of the Royal College of Physicians wrote in 1804, "is known by sullenness, taciturnity, meditation, dreadful apprehensions, and despair." So far as we know, Cavendish did not despair, but he certainly did exhibit the other traits listed by Rowley. If Cavendish was afflicted, it was perhaps by what the Reverend Theophilus Lindsey in 1755 called "lowness of spirit," not "real illness," but of "as much reality." The description fits Cavendish, who gave the impression of being, in Lindsey's words, "anxious and pained," the "fate of genius of so fine and delicate an edge."[72]

Low energy is a familiar symptom of depression. Persons of high achievement commonly display more energy than others, but on this point we wonder about Cavendish. He did a great deal of original work in science, much more than his publications would suggest, as we know from his manuscripts, but he also had a great deal of time in which to do it. What Blagden wrote to a colleague in 1790, "Mr Cavendish does not seem to be very busy,"[73] we suspect could have been said of him at other times as well. In response to a correspondence begun by Priestley, Cavendish said that he would send an account of his experiments

---

[70] W. Ray Crozier, "Social Psychological Perspectives on Shyness, Embarrassment and Shame," in *Shyness and Embarrassment: Perspectives from Social Psychology*, ed. W. Ray Crozier (Cambridge: Cambridge University Press, 1990), 53–54. Peter R. Harris, "Shyness and Embarrassment in Psychological Theory and Ordinary Language," ibid., 59–86, on 62. Henk T. Van der Molen, "A Definition of Shyness and Its Implication for Clinical Practice," ibid., 255–85, on 259–60. John R. Marshall, *Social Phobia: From Shyness to Stage Fright* (New York: Basic Books, 1995), 56. Philip G. Zimbardo, *Shyness: What It Is, What to Do About It* (Reading, Mass.: Addison-Wesley, 1977), 109–14. Arnold H. Buss, "A Conception of Shyness," in *Avoiding Communication: Shyness, Reticence and Communication Apprehension*, ed. J. A. Daley and J. C. McCroskey (Beverley Hills: Sage, 1984), 39–49, on 39–42.

[71] Wilson, *Cavendish*, 167–69.

[72] William Rowley, *A Treatise on Madness and Suicide, with the Modes of Determining with Precision Mental Affections, in a Legal Point of View, and Containing Objections to Vomiting, Opium, and Other Mal-Practices, &c. &c.* (London, 1804), 1, 12. Theophilus Lindsey to [Francis, 10th earl of Huntington], 20 Feb. 1755, in Great Britain, Historical Manuscripts Commission, *Report on the Manuscripts of the Late Reginald Rawden Hastings, Esq., of the Manor House, Ashby de la Zouche*, 4 vols. (London: His Majesty's Stationary Office, 1928–47), 3:93–95, on 94.

[73] Charles Blagden to Richard Kirwan, 20 Mar. 1790, draft, Blagden Letters, Royal Society, 7:322.

in the future, "but I am so far from possessing any of your activity that I am afraid I shall not make any very soon."[74] Compared to the energetic Priestley, any person might feel inactive, but for Cavendish this description was self-characterizing. For six months Priestley's second letter went unanswered; Cavendish apologized, "as I make not a tenth part of the exper that you do & as my facility in writing falls short of yours in a still greater proportion I am afraid you will think me a bad correspondent & that the advantage lies intirely on my side."[75] During a political revolt within the Royal Society, Blagden wrote to Banks that Cavendish said that his only objection to assuming leadership was "his unfitness for active exertion."[76] We can say with reasonable certainty that Cavendish was not supercharged.

Taciturnity, solitariness, and shyness, Cavendish's chracterizing behaviors, led persons who knew him to regard him as an alien being. Blagden's diary records a poignant if ambiguous entry, "Conversation about Monday Club. Mr. C[avendish] knew not what to do. Said some men without certain feelings."[77] After Cavendish had left his party at the Monday Club one night, Blagden and Aubert talked about Cavendish and agreed that he had "no affections, but always meant well."[78] A contemporary described Cavendish as the "coldest and most indifferent of mortals."[79] None of these observers would have said that Cavendish was without feelings, only without warmth.

A foreign visitor described Cavendish as "a man so unsociable and cynical that he could stand honorably in the same tub with Diogenes."[80] Unsociable, yes, but cynical Cavendish certainly was not. Normally Cavendish could not be anyone but himself. He could not conceal his feelings, a skill which to most persons comes naturally; from this point of view, Cavendish was not a person without affections but one who was at their mercy.

We return to the image of Cavendish at Banks's door, frozen in place until new arrivals forced him to enter. Who cannot sympathize with that fear? Who cannot also feel a measure of admiration? For on his own, Cavendish had got that far, to Banks's threshold. And he *did* cross it to mingle with the guests, some of whom were likely to be the object of his terror, strangers. He did not allow his

---

[74] Henry Cavendish to Joseph Priestley, n.d. [May or June 1784], draft, Cavendish Mss New Correspondence; published in *A Scientific Autobiography of Joseph Priestley (1733–1804): Selected Scientific Correspondence*, ed. R.E. Schofield (Cambridge, Mass.: M.I.T. Press, 1966), 232–33.

[75] Henry Cavendish to Joseph Priestley, 20 Dec. 1784, draft, Cavendish Mss New Correspondence; published in *A Scientific Autobiography of Joseph Priestley*, 239–40, on 240.

[76] Charles Blagden to Sir Joseph Banks, 5 Apr. 1784, BM(NH), DTC 3:20–21.

[77] 12 Nov. 1795, Charles Blagden Diary, Royal Society, 3:76 (back).

[78] 15 Sep. 1794, Charles Blagden Diary, Royal Society, 3:16 (back).

[79] Wilson, *Cavendish*, 173.

[80] Marsillio Landriani to Alessandro Volta, 9 Oct. 1788, quoted in John L. Heilbron, *Electricity in the 17th and 18th Centuries: A Study of Early Modern Physics* (Berkeley: University of California Press, 1979), 477.

shyness to preclude a public life and a successful career in science. Day in and day out he arrived at the threshold, so to speak, and crossed it, and made his entrances. Had he not been so determined, he might still have pursued science, but it would have been as a reclusive hobby. To work in science required coming into the world and asserting a public presence. What was significant about Cavendish's "character" was his determination to prevail.

Because Cavendish was successful, we might think of his shyness not as a mental and social handicap but as a useful defense, guarding his privacy, and freeing him to carry out his work.[81] Likewise, we might view his solitariness and taciturnity not as a reaction but as an indication of self-sufficiency and maturity.[82] We find Cavendish to be an extraordinarily strong person. We also find him to be a person with whom we can feel a bond of human sympathy.

Cavendish's silent and solitary ways notwithstanding, he was a champion of openness; he placed the utmost value on public knowledge and the exchange of ideas.[83] The Royal Society, with its profession of openness, was a congenial workplace for him. When he held back from publication, it was not from a desire for secrecy. He saw the harm that secrecy caused his colleagues, who became embittered over accusations of stolen ideas. He objected to Michell's request that he keep secret a discovery of an astronomical method and instead persuaded Michell to let him announce it to the world. He persuaded the government to lift the official cloak of secrecy on Charles Hatchett's experiments on alloys carried out under his direction. When asked his opinion of the author of a pamphlet on the dissensions of the Royal Society who wanted to remain anonymous, Cavendish "answered at once & decisively that the only way to make it produce any useful effect was for the author to sign his name"; Cavendish's "opinion, so decisively against its being anonymous," caused the author, Andrew Kippis, to change his mind and sign his name to it.[84] When Martin van Marum criticized Cavendish for not giving him information he had requested about his experiment on nitrous acid in the atmosphere, Cavendish replied vigorously. He published the private letter he had sent to Marum three years before so that readers could judge the (un)fairness of Marum's complaint; Cavendish said that he "should be sorry to be thought to have refused any necessary information" to a colleague wanting to repeat his experiment.[85] To

---

81 Zimbardo, *Shyness*, 12, 16, 20.

82 Anthony Storr, *The School of Genius* (London: A. Deutsch, 1988), 29. Susan Sontag, "The Aesthetics of Silence," in *Styles of Radical Will* (New York: Farrar, Straus and Giroux, 1969), 19–20, 26.

83 Robert R. McCrea and Paul T. Costa, Jr., *Personality in Adulthood* (New York and London: Guilford Press, 1990), 44.

84 Charles Blagden to Sir Joseph Banks, 24 and 26 Oct. 1784, BM(NH), DTC 3:83–86. Andrew Kippis, *Observations on the Late Contests in the Royal Society*.

85 Letter to Marum and surrounding discussion in Cavendish, "On the Conversion of a Mixture of Dephlogisticated and Phlogisticated Air into Nitrous Acid, by the Electric Spark," *PT* 78 (1788): 261–76; *The Scientific Papers of the Honourable Henry Cavendish, F.R.S.*, vol. 2: *Chemical and Dynamical*, ed. E. Thorpe (Cambridge: Cambridge University Press, 1921), 224–32, on 231–32.

take an example from outside science, when Cavendish took over the management of his father's farms he let his steward know that the condition of his job was complete openness. Openness was a significant trait of Cavendish's.

Openness to others, to new experiences, to new ideas, and to criticism is a quality called for alike in an experimental investigator and in an individual who chooses an unconventional path in life. Cavendish pursued a working life as an experimenter, and by so doing he made of his life a kind of experiment. As an experimenter he did not accept nature as given but adapted it to respond to his questions. Likewise he did not accept the life course that was his birthright but adapted it to his interests. To science and to life he brought a questioning attitude and an acceptance of uncertainty. To experiment on nature is to settle for tolerable certainty. To experiment with life's possibilities is to follow a path that has not been completely charted.

Other than both being studious, Lord Charles and Henry Cavendish do not seem to have had very similar personalities. Lord Charles was well rounded, drawn to sports, races, and hunting.[86] Comfortable in society, he confidently assumed the chair at meetings. By contrast, his son Henry felt acute discomfort in ordinary company, and as a rule he did not take charge. Yet in their tireless attention to the affairs of the Royal Society, they were much alike in their actions. Factors in addition to personality such as duty of service and intellectual interest, were decisive in their choice of a common path of life through science.

But personality mattered too. Henry Cavendish went further down the path than his father, and his achievement was greater. This man who was so extraordinarily cautious in all his transactions with society was the circumspect experimenter at home. His awareness of his surroundings took the inward form of an acute self-consciousness. In the laboratory it took the objective form of the "error of the observer" and "corrections" for the totality of extraneous factors influencing the experiment. His "peculiarities" helped in another way too by lending him a formidable dignity, which ensured that people did not impose upon him. He was left to do what was best for him, which was to work in science.

[86] The duke of Newcastle to the duke of Devonshire, 21 Nov. 1745. Lord Hartington to the duke of Devonshire, 23 Dec. 1746. Lord Charles Cavendish to John Manners, 18 June 1772, draft, Devon. Coll., No. 182.32, 260.65, and L/114/32.

PLACES

A MAP OF THE PLACES Cavendish could call home reveals a paramount fact about him: he was a city man. When he lived outside of London as an adult, he was not further away than a suburb, well within sight of the spires of the city. He owned properties in the countryside, but he had no thought of living there. London offered him the civilized amenities and learned company he needed for his chosen way of life.

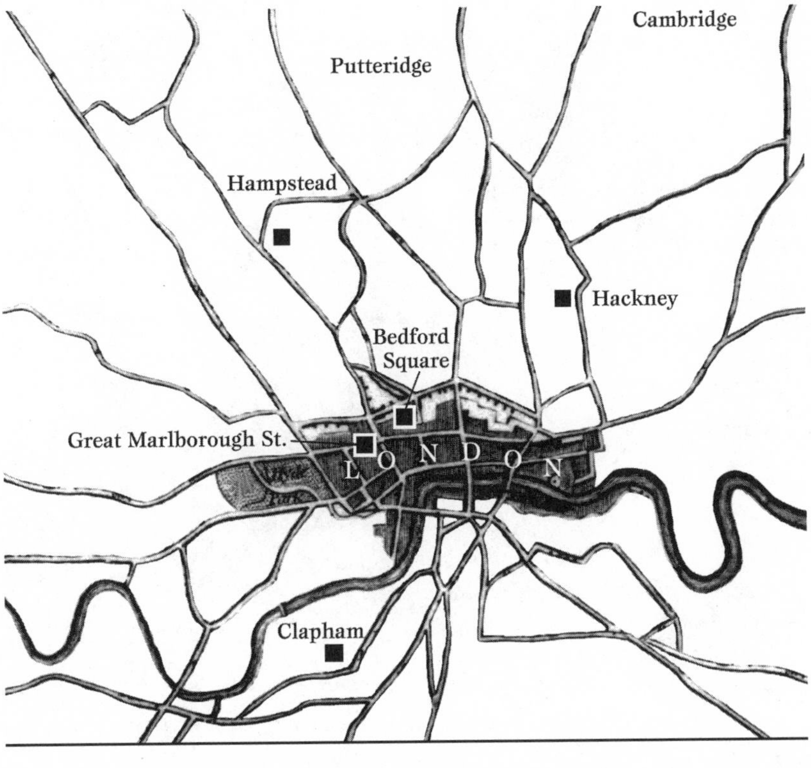

67. *Places Where Cavendish Lived. To the north, off the map at the top, are Cambridge, fifty-odd miles from London, and Putteridge, about half as far.*

68. Map of Cavendish's London. Cavendish's familiar destinations in London are identified by numbers that have been superposed on Plan of London, with Its Modern Improvements, *published by Richard Phillips, on 2 May 1808 or 1809.*

1. *Royal Institution.*
2. *Great Marlborough Street house.*
3. *Sir Joseph Banks's house.*
4. *Bedford Square house.*
5. *British Museum.*
6. *Royal Society.*
7. *Crown & Anchor.*
8. *Edward Nairne's instrument shop.*
9. *George & Vulture.*

BEDFORD SQUARE

As Cavendish had servants to tend to his domestic needs, he had assistants to aid him in his scientific pursuits. Blagden's role we have discussed already. "Richard" turned the globe of the electrical machine or felt the electrical shock, as directed.[1] James Lewis Macie, who later changed his name to James Smithson, founder of the Smithsonian Institution in Washington, D.C., is said to have assisted Cavendish in his chemical researches.[2] We know for certain that Cavendish employed Charles Cullen, son of the Edinburgh professor of medicine, William Cullen. No doubt it was through Blagden, William Cullen's pupil and friend, that Charles came to Cavendish's notice. At one point Blagden wrote to Cullen to say that his son was doing well, though there was a suggestion that he was not, which was probably the reason for the letter. Blagden said that the young man had been totally unfamiliar with a certain book and with Cavendish's studies in general. Four months later, owing to Cavendish's dissatisfaction with his skill and knowledge of books, Charles considered resigning. He accepted Cavendish's criticism, but he also had an excuse, which he hoped would earn him a reprieve: "the moving from Marlboro Street to Bedford Square" had distracted him from his regular work, which he had put off until "after the house was a little more settled."[3] Cavendish was still in the throes of leaving home.

Having taken a country house two years earlier, beginning in 1784 Cavendish rented out his father's house on Great Marlborough Street and the premises on Marlborough Mews to a number of Brookeses, James and Joshua Brookes, Jr. and Sr.[4] He also rented part of the mews to his principal heir, Lord George Cavendish. Joshua Brookes continued the local scientific tradition in a bizarre fashion. Holding a "Theatre of Anatomy" there in 1786–98, Brookes lectured and exhibited bodies of notorious criminals, and in the garden behind the

---

[1] Henry Cavendish, *The Electrical Researches of the Honourable Henry Cavendish*, ed. J. C. Maxwell (1879; reprint, Frank Cass, 1967), 254, 285.

[2] Leonard Carmichael and J. C. Long, *James Smithson and the Smithsonian Story* (New York: G. P. Putnam's Sons with the Smithsonian Institution, 1965), 64. "Smithson, James," *DNB* 18:579–81. If we lack corroborating evidence that Macie assisted Cavendish, we know for certain that Cavendish assisted him. Cavendish also recommended Macie for membership in the Royal Society. Royal Society, Certificates: James Lewis Macie, vol. 5 (19 Apr. 1787).

[3] William Cullen to Charles Blagden, 8 May 1784, Blagden Letters, Royal Society, C.70. Charles Blagden to William Cullen, 17 June 1784, draft, Blagden Letterbook, Yale. Charles Cullen to Charles Blagden, 7 Nov. 1784 and "Monday" [1784], Blagden Letters, Royal Society, C.62 and C.63. Perhaps Charles Cullen did work out, for there is one more letter from him to Charles Blagden, n.d., ibid., C.64, which says that Cavendish finds that Macquer's chemical dictionary with Bergman's notes is almost out of print, and Cullen wonders if he might bring out a new edition. At Cavendish's expense, Cullen translated a pamphlet by Torbern Bergman on the mineral wolfram, a tungstate of iron and manganese, *A Chemical Analysis of Wolfram; and Examination of a New Metal, Which Enters into Its Composition* (London, 1785). Blagden to John Michell, 13 Sep. 1785, draft, Blagden Letterbook, Yale.

[4] Ratebooks for Great Marlborough Street and Marlborough Mews, St James, Westminster, Westminster Archives, D 1263–65.

house, where Lord Charles and Henry Cavendish had measured the earth and the atmosphere with their delicate instruments, Brookes built a vivarium out of huge rocks, where he chained wild beasts.[5]

Cavendish bought another house not many blocks from Great Marlborough Street, on Bedford Square. The house came with family connections: the Russells through the duke of Bedford, and the Cavendishes through the previous owner of the house, Henry's first cousin and parliamentary leader Lord John Cavendish. Located in the west end of London, Bedford Square was laid out in 1775–80, one of the many squares built in the seventeenth and eighteenth centuries, imparting a measure of order to the urban sprawl. These squares were the joint venture of the owner of a large estate and builders, who were granted long-term leases and low ground rent. Typically, the houses had to be of a certain kind and (considerable) expense.[6] Bedford Square is intact today; on each side of it, one can see the original block of nearly uniform, three-storey brick houses, built of specified materials, dimensions, and design. The middle of each block of houses is distinguished by a prominent, stuccoed facade, ornamented with pediments and pilasters, and the entrance doors of the houses are crowned with varied, rounded fanlights.[7] No. 11 Bedford Square, Cavendish's house, is still standing, now used for offices by the nearby University of London. It carries a bronze tablet donated by the duke of Bedford in 1904 identifying it as having once belonged to the chemist Henry Cavendish. In style Cavendish's house is the same as that of the blocks of houses, but it does not physically join them. It is an end-of-row house on the northeast corner of the square, on Gower Street, with its entrance on Montague Place. The neighborhood has long since been densely built up, but when Cavendish moved there, Gower Street quickly ran into the fields.

"I have scarce ever met with a more substantial or better built House, and the whole Edifice is finished with the best materials," an appraiser wrote of Cavendish's house on Bedford Square shortly after his death.[8] The floors of the two main storeys of the house were of Norway oak and the hall and staircase of excellent Portland stone. The dining and drawing rooms had sculptured white marble chimneypieces. All three storeys and the attic for the servants had bowed windows to the back, which, like the veranda, overlooked a deep garden.

---

5 "Henry Cavendish to Mr Joshua Brookes. Counterpart Lease of a Messuage or Tenement with the Apperts No. in Marlborough Street in the Parish of St James Westminster County Middlesex," 1788, Devon. Coll., L/38/35. London County Council, *Survey of London*, ed. F. H. W. Sheppard, vol. 31: *The Parish of St. James Westminster*, part 2: *North of Piccadilly* (London: Athlone, 1963), 256.

6 George Rudé, *Hanoverian London, 1714–1808* (Berkeley: University of California Press, 1971), 11–14. London County Council, *Survey of London*, vol. 5: *The Parish of St. Giles-in-the-Fields*, part 2 (London: London County Council, 1914), 150.

7 *Survey of London*, vol. 5, part 2, p. 150. Rudé, *London*, 14.

8 "Mr. Willock's Valuation of House & Stables in Bedford Square," a letter from John Willock to John Heaton, 30 Dec. 1813, Devon. Coll., L/34/10.

69. *No. 11 Bedford Square. Henry Cavendish appears on the rate books for this town house from 1786 to the end of his life. Photographs by the authors.*

Detached from the house and located at the bottom of the garden were a double coach house and stabling for five horses, which had been converted to another use, while other buildings across a mews had served as equivalent coach houses and stabling.[9]

Cavendish's Bedford Square house is best described as a green, live-in scientific facility. The color scheme of the furnishings was consistent: green moreen window curtains, green transparent canvas-lined mahogany blinds, green chair covers, and firescreens covered with green silk. The furniture was mahogany.[10] The house was said to contain "Museums,"[11] and there is reason to think that Cavendish used it to display his mineral collection; Blagden requested that "specimens" from industrial sites be boxed and sent to Cavendish "direct . . . in Bedford Square."[12] By far the greatest part of the house was given over to books and such fixtures as book users require.[13] With the exception of the dining and back parlor rooms, all of the main rooms had bookshelves. So altered was the house that a sum equal to a quarter of the value of the house would have been required to restore it to a condition "fit for the residence of a family."[14]

In the next section, we discuss Cavendish's books and the use of the Bedford Square house as a semi-public library; here we limit our account to a physical description of the altered premises. The house was entered through a semi-octagonal bay opening onto a hallway and a stairway beyond. To the left of the hallway was the dining parlor, which was used as intended. To the right of the hallway was a room called the lower library with bookshelves consisting of 90 sliding shelves mounted on 20 uprights. The uprights, fitted with plinth and cornice, no doubt extended from floor to ceiling. Off of this library to the right was an adjoining room where a copying machine was located, a double-roller apparatus by Watt & Co., and bookshelves consisting of 14 uprights and 93 sliding shelves. Off this room to the left was an adjoining room, which had 10 uprights, sliding shelves, and a cupboard for maps. The floor plan shows curved stairs leading from the ground floor to the principal floor, which Cavendish evidently gave over entirely to library use. It was here that the main library room was located, with its 28 uprights, 268 sliding shelves, Wedgwood ink stands, high and

---

9 *The Particulars of a Capital Leasehold House and Offices Situate at the North East Corner of Bedford Square . . . Sold by Auction, by Mr. Willock . . . The Twenty-ninth of April, 1814.* Willock to Heaton, 30 Dec. 1814. London County Council, *Survey of London*, ed. L. Gomme and P. Norman, vol. 5, *The Parish of St. Giles-in-the-Fields*, part 2 (London: London County Council), 161–62, and plates 75, 76.

10 "Inventory of Sundry Fixtures, Household Furniture, Plate, Linen &c. &c. the Property of the Late Henry Cavendish Esquire at His Late Residence in Bedford Square. Taken the 2nd Day of April 1810," Devon. Coll., L/114/74.

11 Willock to Heaton, 30 Dec. 1813.

12 Charles Blagden to John Michell, 19 Sep. 1786, draft; Charles Blagden to William Lewis, 10 Nov. 1786, draft, Blagden Letterbook, Royal Society, 7:37, 53.

13 George Wilson, *The Life of the Honourable Henry Cavendish* (London, 1851), 163.

14 Willock to Heaton, 30 Dec. 1813.

low steps, cushioned chairs, desks and table, and a table clock. The next floor, the two-pair floor, also had rooms for books, but they were not equipped with tables and chairs for readers. This private floor held what was called the upper library, and the room adjoining it was reserved for books too, as was a small room to the front of the house. Even Cavendish's bedroom on this floor had a bookcase.[15] This partial list of uprights and shelves is intended to convey a correct notion of what was essential about the Bedford Square house: it was a house of books, with little room for anything else, its "sole furniture" a library.[16] Its owner was a bookish man, who collected books, as rich men did then, and who also read them and lent them out.

If it were not the embodiment of a rare intellectual force, the Bedford Square house might seem to be nothing but so many yards of occupied shelving, a place of utmost *im*personality. But in the selection of books, as we will see, the Bedford Square library expressed the individuality of its owner. Limited as were the other contents of the Bedford Square house, they too were revealing of Cavendish. In the footman's account book for the latter years, amidst entries for the coal merchant, window tax, and breeches-maker are entries for "prints of the moon,"[17] which may have adorned the walls. Cavendish was not an art collector like his grandfathers, but he hung paintings. With one exception the paintings were all of Cavendishes, four three-quarter portraits and one small portrait. In storage he kept ten damaged family portraits. (Other than for one "fixture," a "fine landscape" on a pediment frame,[18] Cavendish's other house, on Clapham Common, apparently contained no art; no paintings were inventoried there.) The paintings in the Bedford Square house, otherwise devoted to science, expressed the other side of the owner: as well as a man of science, he was a proud Cavendish.[19]

Apart from seeing to it that the books were cared for, Cavendish had few needs at Bedford Square, keeping only three servants; besides the porter there was a housemaid and a cook.[20] For a time there was also a librarian. Cavendish sometimes stayed in the city at his Bedford Square house, which was just around the corner from the British Museum and convenient to the Royal Society, and he kept appointments at the house, too.

For the last twenty-five years of his life, Cavendish's scientific life was carried out in his house at Bedford Square and also in his house at Clapham Common. To his houses he devoted the familiar aristocrat's loving attention, but the function of his houses was unfamiliar. They were, in their own terms, "great" houses,

---

15 "Inventory of Sundry Fixtures, Household Furniture, Plate, Linen etc. etc."

16 John Barrow, *Sketches of the Royal Society and Royal Society Club* (London, 1849), 148.

17 Bills paid, 3 Dec. 1806 and 21 Feb. 1810, "Bedford Square. James Fullers Account With the Exec. of Hen: Cavendish Esq. . . . Settled 30 August 1810," Devon. Coll.

18 "About Purchas of House & Furn. at Clapham," 1785, Devon. Coll., 86/comp. 1.

19 "Inventory of Sundry Fixtures."

20 "Wages Due to the Servants at Clapham and Bedford Square," Devon. Coll.

only not in the sense of "piles," as the English call their imposing houses, but of scientific facilities. They were houses of science, which have to be considered together to be properly appreciated.

To keep order in his life in two houses, Cavendish drew up a list of keys under various headings, including the heading "instruments," which gives us some insight into his activities at home. He kept a small but choice selection of instruments at Bedford Square, made by John Bird, Jeremiah Sisson, and Edward Nairne, among others, which were the kinds of instruments to be expected: microscopes, presumably for the minerals kept at Bedford Square, and instruments for taking measurements at a fixed location, such as astronomical telescopes, quadrants, clocks, and magnetic dipping needles.[21] Cavendish kept his large collection of instruments at Clapham Common, where he made most of his observations and experiments.

The division of functions of his two houses was not absolute, but at the end of his life, it was nearly so. In the valuations of the two houses, only at Clapham Common were scientific instruments listed.[22] Far greater than his investment in instruments was his investment in books; the value of his books at Bedford Square was truly enormous, over twice the combined value of the other contents of both houses and twice the value of the Bedford Square house itself.[23] Cavendish's Bedford Square house represented scientific knowledge as recorded in publications, and his Clapham Common house represented scientific knowledge in progress, experiment and observation. Dedicated to his scientific pursuits, Cavendish's two houses complemented one another.

LIBRARY

From his father, Henry Cavendish inherited a large library, which he built upon to the end of his life. In his line of work, a personal library was a strong asset, since scientific books and journals were expensive and not conveniently accessible.

---

[21] The keys are listed under headings L.1 through L.6, which might stand for "London," and "Clapham N° 1" followed by N°s. 2 through 4. The Clapham N°. 1 keys were, he noted, "carried about me." Some or all of them fit Bedford Square locks. The other "N°" keys may have been for Bedford Square or they could have been duplicates for Clapham Common. There is a key for "Observatory," which we know Cavendish had at Clapham Common but which he probably also had at Bedford Square. In any case, the instruments under lock and "N°" keys are of the same type: microscopes and astronomical instruments by excellent instrument-makers, such as Jesse Ramsden, John Dolland, and John Hadley. There were two instruments that do not fit the above description: an air pump and an electrical machine. "Keys at London," Cavendish Mss unclassified.

[22] Under the category of philosophical and astronomical instruments, Clapham Common was listed at £544.19.0 and Bedford Square at nothing. "Extracts from Valuation of Furniture &c.," Devon. Coll.

[23] Cavendish's books at Bedford Square were valued at £7,000. Thomas Payne to John Heaton, 6 Sep. 1810. After Cavendish's death, his Bedford Square house brought £3,530. "29 April &c. 1814 Account Respecting the Sale of a Leasehold House at the North East Corner of Bedford Square," Devon. Coll.

The British Museum acquired scientific books, but its collection was inadequate for Cavendish's needs, as was the library of the Royal Society; in 1773 inspectors of the latter library reported that it was very defective in just those subjects that interested Cavendish, works in natural philosophy and mathematics.[24]

Unlike the Cavendishes, most persons interested in science in the eighteenth century could not afford to buy or to subscribe to many scientific books and journals. They relied in part on substantial private libraries made available to them upon application to their owners. In eighteenth-century England, scientific libraries like Sloane's and Banks's served the purpose of later public libraries, their owners treating their collections as a "public trust on behalf of learning."[25] Following the pattern, Cavendish allowed the library in his house on Bedford Square to be used as a semi-public institution. He was performing a duty of public service.

Earlier Cavendish may have made his collection available at another location. According to his biographer George Wilson, he set apart for his library a "separate mansion in Dean Street, Soho."[26] We are inclined to doubt the house on Dean Street. Joseph Banks's great library in his house on Soho Square is sometimes referred to as his library on neighboring Dean Street, and it is entirely possible that Wilson's source confused the two. The ratebooks for Dean Street, Soho, contain no entries for Cavendish.[27] Sir John Barrow said that Cavendish's library was in his house on Bedford Square.[28] We know for certain that at the end of his life, his library was located there.

The library had a catalog, a take-out register, and a librarian to watch over the books and the patrons and to carry out his master's wishes. To a prospective user of the library, Blagden explained the official policy: "Wishing to promote science by every measure in his power," Cavendish made his library accessible "at all seasons of the year." Blagden made clear that what was accessible was the library and definitely not its owner: Cavendish did not want people even to sit in his library but to "borrow such books as they wish & take them home for a limited

[24] 24 June 1773, Minutes of Council, copy, Royal Society, 6:177.

[25] Raymond Irwin, *The Origins of the English Library* (London: George Allen & Unwin, 1958), 179.

[26] Wilson, *Cavendish*, 163, cites Cavendish's early biographers Cuvier and Biot on the subject of his library. But all that Biot says is that Cavendish located his library two leagues, or five English miles, from his residence so as not to be disturbed by readers consulting it. Five miles is roughly the distance from Clapham to the center of London. Since neither Biot nor Cuvier mentions Dean Street, Wilson supplied this address from unknown sources. Georges Cuvier, "Henry Cavendish," translated from the French by D. S. Faber, in *Great Chemists*, ed. E. Faber (New York: Interscience Publishers, 1961), 227–38, on 237; J. B. Biot, "Cavendish (Henri)," *Biographie Universelle*, vol. 7 (Paris, 1813), 272–73, on 273.

[27] Dean Street entries turn up intermittently through the assessment of the poor rate; entries for the years 1783, 1785, 1790, 1795 contain no reference to Cavendish. From 1781 the ratebooks were split between the wards of King Square, West, and Leicester Fields, West, Westminster Record Office.

[28] Barrow, *Sketches*, 148.

time."[29] To further his policy, books would even be sent to borrowers.[30] Even with these rules in effect, ordinarily it was not Cavendish but his librarian who met the public. The librarian guarded Cavendish's privacy, if imperfectly. When the twenty-one year old Alexander von Humboldt traveled to London in 1790, he applied for permission to use Cavendish's library, which he received together with the advice that under no circumstances was he to talk to Cavendish if he should see him there.[31] There is no record of any incident. But La Blancherie, who was living in London, complained directly to Cavendish about the treatment he received from his librarian. Having requested a history of astronomy, he was told by the librarian that Cavendish had just taken that book to Clapham Common. When he then asked for a biographical dictionary, the librarian told him that Cavendish had taken it too. The librarian told him to come back, as he did, whereupon the librarian told him that Cavendish still had the books and moreover had great need for them. Having been thwarted at the British Museum and now at Cavendish's library, La Blancherie thought that the British nation owed him damages. He said he knew that Cavendish would not authorize this conduct by his librarian but would condemn it.[32] We are inclined to think otherwise.[33]

The first we hear of Cavendish's librarian is in 1785, the year before Cavendish moved to Bedford Square. He was almost certainly a German by the name of Heydinger, who that fall went to the Custom House to receive a chest of books sent by King's Packet to Cavendish from abroad.[34] We hear of him again in 1787 in a similar capacity, this time seeing to it that a new chemical journal from Germany reached Cavendish.[35] This or another librarian was the beneficiary of a unique instance of Cavendish's largess. He lived in Cavendish's house until he left Cavendish's employment, whereupon he moved to the country. Some while later Cavendish was told that his former librarian was in poor health. Cavendish was sorry to hear that. It was then suggested that Cavendish might help him out with an annuity. "Well, well, well, a check for ten thousand pounds, would that do?"[36] The words sound willful but the amount was certainly not arbitrary; £10,000 invested in funds would have earned dividends of £600, a comfortable annuity but not lavish wealth.

The librarian, from what we know, earned his retirement, for despite Cavendish's reputation for clockwork routine, he was not particularly good at

---

[29] Charles Blagden to Thomas Beddoes, 12 Mar. 1788, draft, Blagden Letters, Royal Society, 7:129.

[30] Blagden told Herschel that Cavendish had the books he needed and that Herschel could either look at them in his library or have the books sent to him at Slough. Charles Blagden to William Herschel, 19 May 1786, draft, Blagden Letters, Royal Society, 7:762.

[31] James Thorne, *Environs of London* (London, 1876) 1:111.

[32] Pahin de la Blancherie to Henry Cavendish, 23 Sep. 1794, Cavendish Mss New Correspondence.

[33] See our commentary to La Blancherie's letter in part 4, letter 87, note 7.

[34] Charles Blagden to Sir Joseph Banks, 15 and 30 Sep. 1785, Kew, 1:204 and 1:207.

[35] Charles Blagden to Lorenz Crell, 7 June 1787, draft, Blagden Letters, Royal Society, 7:60.

[36] Wilson, *Cavendish*, 174.

keeping order in his affairs and his things. His books were described as being in a "bad state of arrangement."[37] Very possibly the librarian was hired to put the library in shape so that readers could use it and was then kept on. He prepared a catalog of Cavendish's books and journals, entering it in a great, heavy volume; the entries are in more than one hand, none of them Cavendish's, which might suggest that the catalog was continued by another librarian after the first left. Cavendish did his part by signing the register for every book he borrowed, even if he were only taking it to his other house at Clapham Common.[38] The librarian was useful to Cavendish in another way; Blagden wrote to Cavendish that he hoped that he had got Heydinger to read a letter in German for him.[39] Heydinger may have had a scientific interest of his own; at least twice Cavendish brought him to the Royal Society as his guest.[40]

Thomas Young said that after Cavendish's German librarian died, Cavendish himself devoted one day a week to checking out books.[41] If Cavendish kept up this practice for long, we do not know, but when he died, it appears that he had a librarian, who received a small salary, and who might have dealt with borrowers.[42]

A few years after Cavendish's death, the sixth duke of Devonshire assembled the great Chatsworth library from his own collections and from Cavendish's library, which had been given to him by Cavendish's heir, Lord George.[43] With the possible exception of about 450 books in their original paper covers,[44] Henry Cavendish's library today is bound in leather and dispersed among the other books at Chatsworth, most of them shelved in the beautiful, old Long Gallery. Constituting about one-quarter of the ducal library, Henry Cavendish's books are identified both by his book stamp, a simple *H.Cavendish*, and by his separate catalog number.

The catalog of Cavendish's library is incomplete, going only to the early 1790s, and we know that Cavendish continued to buy books after that time. For

---

[37] Ibid.

[38] Cuvier, "Henry Cavendish," 237. Barrow, *Sketches of the Royal Society*, 148.

[39] The letter was from the German chemist Lorenz Crell. Blagden wrote, "I hope you got Mr. Heydinger to read Crell's letter." Letter of 23 Sep. 1787, Cavendish Mss X(b), 14.

[40] 17 Apr. 1788 and 24 Dec. 1789, Royal Society, JB, 33.

[41] Thomas Young, "Life of Cavendish," originally published in the supplement to the *Encyclopaedia Britannica* for 1818–1824, reprinted in *The Scientific Papers of the Honourable Henry Cavendish, F.R.S.*, vol. 1: *The Electrical Researches,* ed. J.C. Maxwell, rev. J. Larmor (Cambridge: Cambridge University Press, 1921), 435–47, on 445. Young's statement that the librarian died is at variance with the statement about the librarian retiring to the country and Cavendish giving him £10,000; if both statements are true, the latter librarian was not the German.

[42] "Collingwood, the Librarian, One Years Salary Due Xtmas 1811" in "29th May 1812. Taxes &c. for House in Bedford Square," Devon. Coll.

[43] Historical notice by J. P. Lacaita, July 1879, *Catalogue of the Library at Chatsworth*, 4 vols. (London, 1879), 1:xvii.

[44] Listed as "Cavendish Tracts. Draft Catalogue 1966."

this reason we can speak with greater accuracy of the contents of his catalog than of his library. Books in Latin and books in English appear in roughly equal proportions in the catalog, each accounting for about one-third of the total, and books in French come next, and then, in sharply reduced proportions, books in German and in other European languages. The catalog lists about nine thousand titles, representing some twelve thousand volumes,[45] indicating that Cavendish had a large library, but not an immense one for the time. Sloane's library, the foundation of the library of the British Museum, was four times as large, and even Cavendish's seafaring friend Alexander Dalrymple had a larger library.[46] A number of Cavendish's colleagues had substantial libraries, though smaller than his. Nevil Maskelyne's in 1811 contained 757 "lots," the term used in auction catalogs; John Playfair's in 1820, 1,421 lots; Charles Hutton's in 1816, 1,854 lots. Large libraries belonging to professional persons tended to be libraries of physicians with an interest in science; William Cullen's contained 3,010 lots.[47]

Cavendish's library was open to a qualified public, but its contents were not selected with the public in mind.[48] The largest category in the catalogue was natural philosophy, with nearly two thousand titles. Chemical books were not listed separately but under natural philosophy, as were books on most of Cavendish's other main interests, such as mechanics, instruments, and meteorology. In this same category were many books on medicine, anatomy, and animal economy, very few of which were published after Lord Charles died. Mathematics, the second largest category, included in addition to books on pure mathematics, books on natural philosophy in which mathematics was used, such as Newton's *Principia* and *Opticks* and Robert Smith's *System of Opticks*. Astronomy was well-represented. Lord Charles and Henry Cavendish were collectors of rare books, owning first editions of the classic works of science by Copernicus, Brahe, Kepler, and others. In the natural history of life, Cavendish had only slight interest, but he was interested in other parts of natural history, buying many works on mineralogy and geology. He took great interest in books on voyages and travels, which he used in his scientific work. Only about half of the books in the cat-

---

45 R. A. Harvey, "The Private Library of Henry Cavendish (1731–1810)," *The Library* 2 (1980): 281–92, on 284.

46 Part I of the catalog of Dalrymple's library contains 7,190 entries. Part II, containing books on navigation and travel, his specialty, might be even longer. *A Catalogue of the Extensive and Valuable Library of Books; Part I. Late the Property of Alex. Dalrymple, Esq. F.R.S. (Deceased). Hydrographer to the Board of Admiralty, and the Hon. East India Company, Which Will Be Sold by Auction, by Messrs. King & Lochée, . . . on Monday, May 29, 1809, and Twenty-three Following Days, at Twelve O'Clock* (London, 1809).

47 Ellen B. Wells, "Scientists' Libraries: A Handlist of Printed Sources," *Annals of Science* 40 (1983): 317–89, on 338, 354, 362, and 370.

48 Harvey, "Private Library," has tallied books in Cavendish's catalog by subject according to whether they were published before or after 1752, the year Henry finished his university education. The results are not meaningful in the way they are intended. A more useful division for distinguishing Henry Cavendish's interests from his father's is 1783, when Lord Charles Cavendish died.

alog were scientific. The category of poetry and plays was as large as that of mathematics, some eleven hundred volumes. Listed in it were the works by Shakespeare, Dryden, Congreve, Pope, Swift, Gray, and other authors one would expect to find in a literary library. There were some books of poetry published in the 1750s, but after that the entries in this category were mainly of plays. After Lord Charles's death, when Henry alone added to the library, there were no more books of poetry or plays, with the exception of an Indian drama.[49] Henry had a passing interest in history and antiquities–separate headings in the catalog–with several titles having to do with India. His catalog had no division for histories of individual lives, or biographies, but he bought *The Life of Samuel Johnson*, written by James Boswell, a guest at dinners of the Royal Society Club which Cavendish attended.[50] Cavendish may well have met Johnson, who frequented the Crown & Anchor, where the Royal Society Club met. His catalog had no division for moral philosophy, but he bought Adam Smith's *Theory of Moral Sentiments*. We note that his catalog began with astronomy, mathematics, and natural philosophy, subjects which came first in his life.

Often libraries are revealing because of marginalia in their books. Cavendish, however, rarely put a mark in a book; in the third edition of Newton's *Principia*, he (or someone) penciled in a few numbers, and in a speculative treatise on attracting and repelling powers by Gowin Knight, he (or someone) made a couple of pencilled notations.[51] Holding few surprises, Cavendish's library is confirming, not revealing; it tells us that he was interested in the physical sciences and mathematics and not in literature and languages.

CLAPHAM COMMON

After Hampstead, Cavendish's next country address was Clapham Common. The nearby village of Clapham was described in a survey of 1784 as "very large," "straggling," "pleasantly situated," and containing "many country seats belonging to the gentry and citizens of London." It stood on a low hill overlooking the Thames, four miles south of Westminster Bridge, with daily coach service into the metropolis. Good roads made it possible for Clapham inhabitants to go to London by way of London Bridge, do business from one end of the city to the other, and "without being any further from home" return by Westminster

[49] Cálidás, *Sacontula, or the Fatal Ring, an Indian Drama* (London, 1790). Not entered in the catalog (because it was too late) under poetry and plays but found in the Chatsworth library, with Henry Cavendish's stamp, is the related work, *The Loves of Cámarúpa and Cámalutà, an Ancient Indian Tale*, trans. W. Franklin (London, 1793).

[50] Boswell's *Life* is listed under "History" in Cavendish's catalog. Boswell dined at the Royal Society Club twice in 1772, both times with Cavendish in attendance. Archibald Geikie, *Annals of the Royal Society Club: The Record of a London Dining-Club in the Eighteenth and Nineteenth Centuries* (London: Macmillan, 1917), 118.

[51] Gowin Knight, *An Attempt to Demonstrate, That All the Phoenomena in Nature May Be Explained by Two Simple Active Principles, Attraction and Repulsion* . . . (London, 1748), 11–12.

Bridge, completing a triangle. Lysons, in his survey published a few years after Cavendish's move, said that the population of Clapham had increased faster than that of any other parish he had examined. In 1788 the population was 2,477; four years later it was about 2,700, with an average of ten new houses going up each year. Clapham's draw was its magnificent common, which was described to Cavendish as "the most beautiful, the most healthy and highly improved spot of land, not only round the metropolis, but perhaps in the kingdom."[52] This was an interested developer's hyperbole, but the appeal of the common to city dwellers like Cavendish was strong. Bankers, merchants, and other well-to-do Londoners built big houses, often second houses, facing it. The pastoral serenity of the common is captured in a print from 1784 (See Illustration 71, p. 327.) In the foreground it shows footpaths, a man with his dog, a cow, and in the distance across the Long Pond, the new parish church and several substantial houses.[53] The cow in the print calls to mind the only story to have come down in which Cavendish appears as a man of spontaneous action, a hero. He is said to have saved a woman who lived at Clapham from the attack of a mad cow, causing a sensation at Clapham where Cavendish was known to go to lengths to avoid female encounters.[54] There may be more to Cavendish's involvement, for he kept three cows, one of which could have been the mad cow.[55]

With his inheritance, Cavendish had the means to build or buy several great houses and to live in a grand style, but he did not do so. Not lavish estates with large households, for which he had no use, but a well-built, ample country house met his needs. "A tolerable good house, built of red brick," is how it was described a few years after Cavendish moved into it. Clapham Common was not a retreat for the aristocracy; no other Cavendishes lived there, nor did any Russells or Manners. According to a contemporary map identifying the seventy-four houses on Clapham Common by their occupants, only Cavendish was addressed as the "Rt. Hon.," and only one other person had a title, a Lady Tibbs; the others were simply "Mrs." or "Esq."[56]

---

52 Christopher Baldwin to Henry Cavendish, 3 May 1784, "1784–1786. H. Cavendish & C. Baldwin. Correspondence re Sale of Land," Devon. Coll., 86/comp. 1. Daniel Lysons, *The Environs of London: Being an Historical Account of the Towns, Villages, and Hamlets, within Twelve Miles of That Capital*, vol. 1: *County of Surrey* (London, 1792), 169. William Thornton, *The New, Complete, and Universal History, Description, and Survey of the Cities of London and Westminster . . . Likewise the Towns, Villages, Palaces, Seats, and Country, to the Extent of Above Twenty Miles Round* (London, 1784), 478.

53 Thornton *New, Complete, and Universal History*, facing 490.

54 At Clapham, Cavendish was regarded as a "confirmed women-hater," according to Wilson, *Cavendish*, 178.

55 "Mr Cavendish's Executorship Agenda," Devon. Coll.

56 James Edwards, *A Companion from Lincoln to Brighthelmston, in Sussex; Consisting of a Set of Topographical Maps . . .* (London, 1789, 1801), 11. "Perambulation of Clapham Common 1800. From C. Smith's 'Actual Survey of the Road from London to Brighthelmston,'" in J. H. Michael Burgess, *The Chronicles of Clapham [Clapham Common]. Being a Selection from the Reminiscences of Thomas Parsons. Sometime Member of the Clapham Antiquarian Society* (London: Ramsden Press, 1929), opposite 112.

In the first edition of this biography, following the historian of Clapham,[57] we said that Cavendish bought this house from a banker, Henton Brown, claimed to be the first owner. We now know that that is not true. Cavendish was a renter. On 18 June 1785, William Robertson, a merchant of George Yard, Tower Hill, leased the premises on Clapham Common to Cavendish.[58] What Cavendish did buy was furniture to put in the house; drawingroom pieces he bought from his landlord Robertson.[59] The fixtures of the house were over fifty years old; an inventory, made at the time of the sale of the estate in 1732, with annotations by Cavendish, allows us to tour the conventional house before Cavendish converted it into an approximation of a scientific institute. The house had two stories and two "wings," east and west, with at least twenty-one rooms and passageways. There were five bedrooms, including a two-pair "green chamber" and a bedroom used for needlework. There was a yellow damask room, a crimson damask room, a drawing room, a dining room, and a study. The house was fitted throughout with green venetian sun shades. Most rooms had stoves with decorative borders. The fixtures of the kitchen and laundry were made of cast iron, copper, lead, and brick. Outside in the courtyard there was a pigeon house on a pedestal in the courtyard, and the gardens contained a brass sundial on a stone pedestal and carved vases on brick pillars. The grounds also contained stables and a loft. Cavendish's notations show that he had already begun to rearrange the house for his purposes; bookcases in the study had been moved into the front room of the house.[60]

[57] Eric E. F. Smith, *Clapham* (London: London Borough of Lambeth, 1976), p. 78, writes that the first owner of the house was the banker Henton Brown, whose bank failed in 1782, and that the next owner was Cavendish.

[58] Assignment of lease, 18 June 1785, Surrey Deeds (Index), Lambeth Archives, 14.171. The lease was for the "residue of a term of 29 years granted on the expiry of a lease of 22 March 1750 made between William Bridges and Henton Brown." In the land tax records for Clapham, Cavendish is listed as the "occupier" of the property and the proprietor or landlady is given as Lady Rivers. The taxable yearly value was given as £122, and the corresponding assessment as £0.13.6, figures somewhat higher than those for most of Cavendish's neighbors. Clapham land tax schedules for the years 1786, when Cavendish's name first appears, through 1795. Lambeth Archives.

[59] Persons who entered Cavendish's house on Clapham Common were said to have reacted to "its desolate appearance, and its scanty and mean-looking furniture." John Barrow, *Sketches of the Royal Society and Royal Society Club* (London, 1849), 150. Given the use the house was put to, its furnishings undoubtedly looked spare, but that they also looked mean is uncertain. Before he moved in, Cavendish bought a costly drawing-room suite that included ten inlaid satinwood cabriole elbow chairs. Henry Cavendish, "Sundry Drawing Room Furniture &c. of Wm. Robertson's Esqr Appraised to Cavendish Esqr 11th June 1785"; "About Purchas of House & Furn. at Clapham," Devon. Coll., 86/comp.1. The catalog for the auction of Cavendish's furniture on 5–7 Dec. 1810 is confirming of its quality. Previously, we regarded the catalog as restricted to the contents of Cavendish's house at Clapham, but we now think that it included the contents of his house on Bedford Square as well. We conclude from it that, if we make allowance for their owner's scientific obsessions, the furnishings of both of his houses were eminently respectable, befitting his station. *A Catalogue of an Assortment of Modern Household Furniture . . . the Genuine Property of a Professional Gentleman . . .*, Devon. Coll.

[60] "An Inventory of Fixtures in the House Purchased by Mr.Cavendish of Mr. Robertson"; "An Inventory of Fixtures Belonging to Mess^r^ Collinson and Triton of Clapham in Surry to Be Valued to the Purchaser of the Estate, May 13th, 1732," Devon. Coll., 86/comp.1.

CLAPHAM COMMON

70. *Cavendish's House at Clapham Common. Cavendish's country house from 1785 to the end of his life is shown here from the back, in a later, altered version. Demolished. Frontispiece to* The Scientific Papers of the Honourable Henry Cavendish, *2 vols., ed. J.C. Maxwell, Sir J. Larmor, and Sir E. Thorpe (Cambridge University Press, 1921). All rights reserved: Cambridge University Press. Reprinted with the permission of Cambridge University Press.*

71. *View of Clapham Village from the Common. William Thornton,* The New, Complete, and Universal History, Description, and Survey of the Cities of London and Westminster . . . Likewise the Towns, Villages, Palaces, Seats, and Country, to the Extent of Above Twenty Miles Round, *rev. ed. (London, 1784). Facing p. 490.*

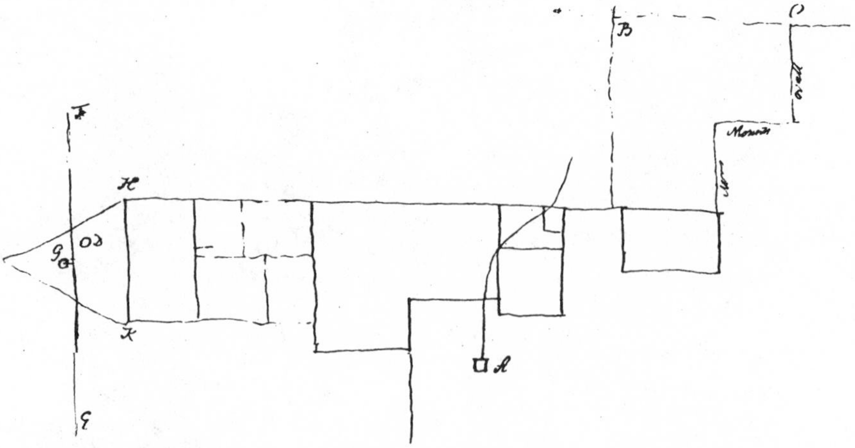

72. *Plan of Drains at Clapham Common. Cavendish's house faces the Common at the bottom of the diagram. The separate building to the right is evidently a greenhouse, formerly containing an outhouse, which Cavendish refers to in his notes on experiments on air. To the left is a basin that becomes a pond, $7\frac{1}{2}$ feet deep, into which the drains from H and K run, and which is filled from the pipe EF, which probably comes from the pond across the road in the Common. G is the valve for letting water into the pond. The other letters stand for: A, a drain sink; B, the gate to the kitchen garden; BC, a drain running from Mrs. Mount's house to the right of what Cavendish has labelled Mrs. Mount's wall; D, a well formerly supplying the pantry or dairy. Water from A eventually runs into a ditch in the field behind the house, and from there it is conducted to the "lane," presumably Dragmire Lane, which bounds Cavendish's property. Next to the pond is a sundial, which Cavendish used as a marker in taking measurements of the basin. Cavendish refers to his walled "court yard," but he does not indicate its location. This diagram was probably drawn up in connection with renovations Cavendish made before moving into the house. "Plan of Drains at Clapham & Measures Relating to Bason," Cavendish Scientific Manuscripts Misc. Reproduced by permission of the Chatsworth Settlement Trustees.*

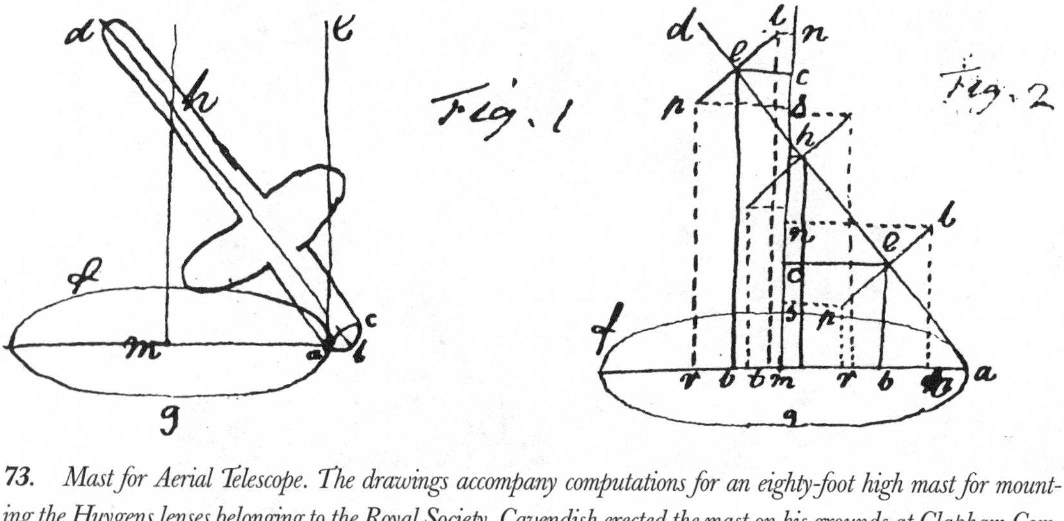

73. *Mast for Aerial Telescope. The drawings accompany computations for an eighty-foot high mast for mounting the Huygens lenses belonging to the Royal Society. Cavendish erected the mast on his grounds at Clapham Common. Cavendish Scientific Manuscripts Misc. Reproduced by permission of the Chatsworth Settlement Trustees.*

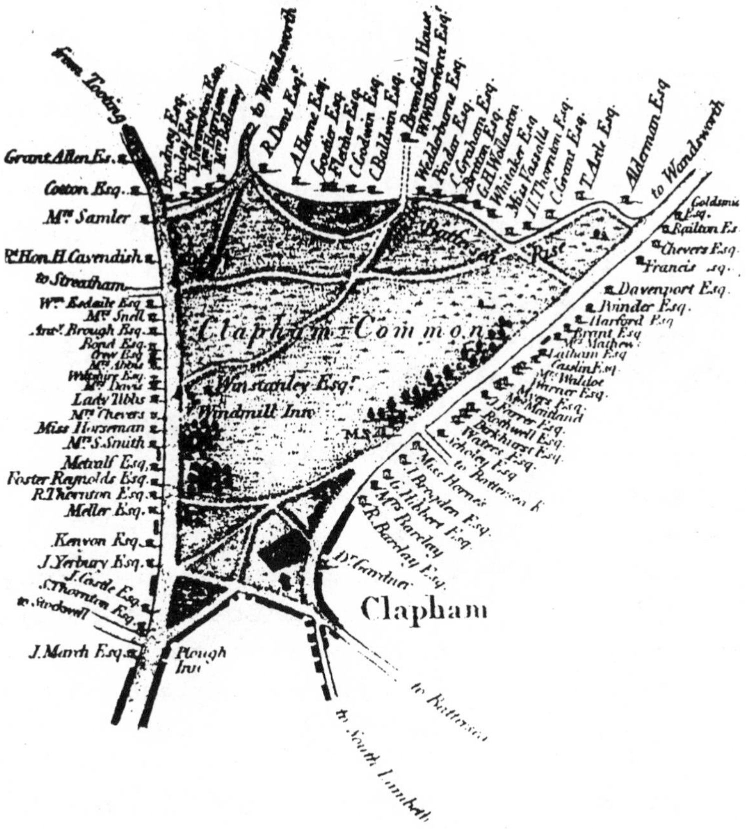

74. Map of Clapham Common. Cavendish's house is on the left side of the Common, fourth house from the top. "Perambulation of Clapham Common 1800. From C. Smith's 'Actual Survey of the Road from London to Brighthelmston.'" The Chronicles of Clapham [Clapham Common]. Being a Selection from the Reminiscences of Thomas Parsons. Sometime Member of the Clapham Antiquarian Society *(London: printed privately by A. V. Huckle & Son, Ltd., The Ramsdan Press, 1929), opposite 112. Reproduced by permission of the Bodleian Library.*

Cavendish's alterations on the house were for privacy and for science, if the two can meaningfully be separated. He is said to have had a back stairs built after having encountered a maid with a broom and pail on the existing stairs.[61] The house left a memorable impression on his contemporaries. Little was set aside for comfort. The upstairs had an astronomical observatory, complete with a "transit-room";[62] the downstairs drawing room was a laboratory and an adjacent room was a forge. The lawn had a wooden platform from which Cavendish

[61] Wilson, *Cavendish*, 170.

[62] "Transit-room" at Cavendish's Clapham Common house appears on the map in William Roy, "An Account of the Trigonometrical Operation, Whereby the Distance between the Meridians or the Royal Observatories of Greenwich and Paris Has Been Determined," *PT* 80 (1790): 111–270, on 261.

climbed a large tree to make scientific measurements. "The whole of the house at Clapham was occupied as workshops and laboratory," the noted London instrument-maker John Newman recalled. Another person observed that "it was stuck about with thermometers, rain-gauges, etc."[63]

No sooner had Cavendish settled into his new house at Clapham Common than he took the first step toward erecting an aerial telescope on the premises. From the Royal Society he borrowed Huygens' lenses of very long focal lengths, for which he built a proper mount. To judge from calculations found among his scientific papers, the mount was a tapered wooden mast eighty feet high, supported by twenty-foot struts planted eleven feet from the base, with a horizontal piece fixed to it.[64] Towering above Cavendish's house, as if a relic of a nostalgic man of the sea, the mast was the most conspicuous feature of Cavendish's scientific setting. A contemporary description of Cavendish's property read: "In a paddock at the back of the house is a mast of a ship, erected for the purpose of making philosophical experiments."[65]

To run his household, Cavendish employed seven regular domestic servants, three of whom were female: housekeeper, housemaid, cook, gardener, coachman, and two footmen. Because his house was not ordinary but a place of science, Cavendish at some point added another servant, a mathematical instrument-maker, whom he paid much more than the others, £65 a year. As Cavendish's way of life did not change over the twenty-five years that he lived in the Clapham house, neither did the complement of servants other than perhaps the instrument-maker, who probably did not live there.[66]

In 1905 Cavendish's house at Clapham Common–it had come to be called "the Cavendish House"–was pulled down and the estate sold, to be replaced by rows of red-brick villas. At a sale near the end of its life, the house was described as "a capital family residence with a suite of well-proportioned reception rooms, elegant drawing room, noble dining room, handsome library, morning room and billiard room, a large conservatory and 17 bedrooms," with grounds "enriched with stately timber of oak, cedar, beech, fir and cypress, laid out with a terrace walk, lake and summerhouse," kitchen garden, greenhouse, orchid house, aloe-house, and vineyards. Cavendish would have been hard-pressed to recognize this showy, sprawling structure as having once been his. Its owners had had very different tastes and had put the house to very different uses. In 1833 it was bought by a developer, who added a big reception room, another servants' wing, and a terrace fronting the garden. Thirty years later it was bought by an art patron,

63 This quotation was from a Fellow of the Royal Society. Wilson, *Cavendish*, 164.

64 The computations for the mast are in Cavendish Mss Misc.

65 Edwards, *A Companion from London to Brighthelmston*, 11.

66 "Account of the Number of Persons Residing in the Parish of Clapham . . . Dtd 18 Feb. 1788," Greater London Record Office, P 95/TRI 1/72. "Wages Due to the Servants at Clapham and in Bedford Square," 1810, Devon. Coll.

who enlarged it to hold a splendid collection of contemporary paintings. By imagining these accretions and the white stucco laid over the original red brick removed, the central block can just be made out in late photographs of the house.

Within the space of three or four years, Cavendish moved out of his father's house on Great Marlborough Street, into and out of a house at Hampstead, and into houses on Bedford Square and on Clapham Common. At the end of 1784, Cavendish told Priestley that having been engaged in "removing my house," he had been kept from making experiments the past summer and had only recently returned to them. He was excusing the six months that had passed since Priestley's last letter to him; the excuse was genuine.[67] Cavendish's subsequent move to Clapham Common left his work in even greater disarray. Because of the need to make repairs on the new house, Cavendish and Blagden's planned scientific journey to Wales had to be postponed by three weeks in June 1785.[68] That September Cavendish refused an invitation to visit Yorkshire, as Blagden explained to the host, John Michell: Cavendish "promises himself that pleasure sometime or other, yet he cannot spare time for another journey this year, as it will give him full employment till winter to bring his new country-house of Clapham into order. He is but just removed thither: & all his pursuits are interrupted till his books, instruments &c can be brought out of the confusion in which they lie at present."[69] The interruptions continued. In November Blagden wrote to Laplace that "Mr. Cavendish will not soon have another paper ready, his apparatus having been deranged by moving to another house." Blagden added hopefully that in his new house, Cavendish would have "conveniences for carrying on his experiments to still greater perfection."[70] Cavendish was fifty-three at the time of his move to Clapham, which was to be the main location of his scientific researches to the end of his life.

LAND DEVELOPER

Several months before he moved to Clapham Common, Cavendish bought fifteen acres of land fronting on the Common. The owner was Christopher Baldwin, a merchant and West Indian landowner, who was also a principal developer of the Common. Baldwin asked more for the land than Cavendish offered but he wanted the sale even more, finally settling for what he was offered.

A year later Cavendish and Baldwin found themselves in conflict over a narrow strip of land, where Baldwin had extended his property into a lane leading

67 Henry Cavendish to Joseph Priestley, 20 Dec. 1784, draft, Cavendish Mss New Correspondence; in Joseph Priestley, *A Scientific Autobiography of Joseph Priestley (1733–1804)*, ed. R. E. Schofield (Cambridge, Mass.: MIT Press, 1966), 239–40, on 239. Cavendish was doing experiments on air, and in the record of these experiments for 1784, none bears a date between March and November. Henry Cavendish, "Experiments on Air," Cavendish Mss II, 5.

68 Charles Blagden to William Lewis, draft, 20 June 1785, Blagden Letterbook, Yale.

69 Charles Blagden to John Michell, draft, 13 Sep. 1785, Blagden Letterbook, Yale.

70 Charles Blagden to P. S. Laplace, draft, 16 Nov. 1785, Blagden Letters, Royal Society 7:733.

off the Common. In his dealings with Baldwin, Cavendish revealed his practical side, which was principled, proud, and unyielding.

Cavendish was told by his lawyer, Thomas Dunn, that Baldwin wanted £60 from him for the legal expenses he incurred over the strip of land. Dunn complained, "I hope I shall never have any business to transact with such another man as long as I live,"[71] Baldwin in turn complained to Cavendish that Dunn did not mind damaging Baldwin to save "a *little* matter to *you*." Baldwin claimed that he was actually out £120 for the closing arrangements, but if Dunn were to be believed Cavendish would file a bill in Chancery against him if he would not take £40. Baldwin in turn would then have to file an action against Cavendish to try to recover the rest of his expenses. Baldwin could not believe that Cavendish wanted to "go through all this" for a "slip of land."[72]

The dispute over the £40 was not yet settled when another problem arose. Dunn had heard that the people of Clapham planned to pull down all fencing on the Common and that Baldwin knew about it. In that event Cavendish "must not give him a farthing for the piece of ground," since it encroached on the Common. Learning of this objection, Baldwin wrote to Cavendish, "In my whole life I never was so heartily tired of any thing as I am of the unmeaning correspondence into which I have been drawn by you and your attorney. . . . I am buried in letters founded in error and ignorance." Baldwin was not going to accept £40, and it was not true that the people of Clapham were going to pull down the fences. It was true, Cavendish told Baldwin; moreover, he was informed that the people of the neighboring parish of Battersea planned to tear down the fences on their common unless the owners paid them a "composition." Cavendish said he was "so confident" of his information that he was no longer prepared to pay Baldwin the £40, but only £40 less the composition. Baldwin warned Cavendish not to stir up the people of Clapham by spreading the idea of tearing down the fences. Cavendish replied that if Baldwin did not accept his offer, £40 less composition, and make over the rights to the property in two or three days, he would take it as refusal and act accordingly.[73]

Cavendish asked for a "direct answer," but Baldwin's answer was anything but direct. He asked about Cavendish's intention to build a fence between their properties. Even before Cavendish bought the fifteen acres from him, Baldwin had sent him "Hints for Consideration," advising him about building fences.[74]

[71] Christopher Baldwin to Henry Cavendish, 7 July [1785]; Henry Cavendish to Christopher Baldwin, draft, n.d. [July 1785]; Thomas Dunn to Henry Cavendish, 6 Sep. 1785, Devon. Coll., 86/comp. 1.

[72] Christopher Baldwin to Henry Cavendish, 19 Sept. 1785, Devon. Coll., 86/comp. 1.

[73] Thomas Dunn to Henry Cavendish, 6 Feb. 1786; Christopher Baldwin to Henry Cavendish, 22 Feb. 1786; Henry Cavendish to Christopher Baldwin, draft, n.d. [after 22 Feb. 1786]; Christopher Baldwin to Henry Cavendish, 27 Feb. 1786; Henry Cavendish to Christopher Baldwin, draft, n.d. [after 27 Feb. 1786], Devon. Coll., 86/comp. 1.

[74] Christopher Baldwin to Henry Cavendish, Midsummer's Day, 1784, Devon. Coll., 86/comp. 1.

Cavendish had not acted. Later Baldwin told Cavendish that his fences were ruined, allowing cattle to enter Baldwin's garden from Cavendish's fields. Baldwin now ordered Cavendish immediately to procure the oak pailing for the fence between their properties. The fence, Cavendish replied, "would have been put up long before now if I had not waited till the dispute about the ground taken in from the common was settled."[75] "I shall observe my agreement about the fence but will not be prescribed to about it nor bear your delays or cavils." Baldwin was to come to Dunn's on Wednesday or Thursday when Cavendish would be there to execute the deed. If he did not come Cavendish would give him nothing for the land. Baldwin wrote back asking Cavendish what he meant by saying he would observe his agreement about the fence. The correspondence between Cavendish and Baldwin came to an end with a flurry of letters, four of them passing between them on one day, the first Saturday in May 1786. Cavendish wrote: "I can not at all conceive what is the cause of this behavior whether you have any private reason for wishing to delay the agreement or whether you distrust my honour about the pailing & wish to make some further conditions about it. If the latter is the true cause you may assure yourself that I will never submit to make any such conditions or explanation with a person who distrusts my honour."[76] A few days later the papers were signed conveying the property to Cavendish.[77] The whole transaction had taken two years.

Both in the original sale of fifteen acres and in the consequent disagreement over the slip of land, Baldwin misjudged Cavendish. Baldwin thought that money was the issue, and for him no doubt it was, especially given his large debts. To Cavendish, the matter of Baldwin's legal expenses, £60 or £40 or £40 less composition, like the matter of the vicar's turnip tithes, was one not of money but of principle. Baldwin's single worst error of judgment was to doubt the honor of Cavendish.

In his correspondence with Baldwin, Cavendish said nothing of his reasons for buying the land. Baldwin thought that Cavendish intended to build on it for himself, and perhaps at first he did. Later Baldwin thought that Cavendish intended to rent the land, in which case he asked to be the renter, but Cavendish turned him down.[78] Cavendish rented Baldwin's former land to three builders at

---

[75] Christopher Baldwin to Henry Cavendish, 8 Feb. [1786]; Henry Cavendish to Christopher Baldwin, draft, n.d. [on or after 8 Feb. 1786], Devon. Coll., 86/comp. 1.

[76] Christopher Baldwin to Henry Cavendish, 3 Mar. 1786, Saturday [1 Apr. 1786], Saturday [1 Apr. 1786]; Henry Cavendish to Christopher Baldwin, drafts, 1 Apr. [1786], n.d. [1 Apr. 1786], Devon. Coll., 86/comp. 1.

[77] Christopher Baldwin to Henry Cavendish, "Lease for a Year," 5 Apr. 1786; "Release of a Piece of Land on Clapham Common," 6 Apr. 1786. At the same time, Baldwin gave up all claim to the original fifteen acres. Christopher Baldwin to Henry Cavendish, "General Release," 6 Apr. 1786. Devon. Coll., L/38/78.

[78] Baldwin to Cavendish, 3 May 1784 and 8 Feb. 1786; Cavendish to Baldwin, draft, n.d. [on or after 8 Feb. 1786].

£200 a year each. By the terms of their lease, they were to spend at least £4,000 within four years to build "good & substantial dwelling houses with convenient stables coach houses" and to spend another £6,000 within eight years for the same purpose. When the buildings were "compleated to the satisfaction" of Cavendish, the builders and Cavendish would join in granting separate leases for the houses with rent payable to Cavendish. Five long-term leases agreeable to his conditions were granted, which brought him a total yearly rent of £200.[79]

Ultimately the money that Cavendish paid Baldwin came from other Cavendishes, and like everything he owned, the Clapham property would one day be returned to other Cavendishes. He named as trustees of his Clapham Common estate his closest scientific colleagues in London, Charles Blagden, Alexander Dalrymple, and Alexander Aubert. The property passed from Henry Cavendish to his brother, Frederick, and from the latter to the duke of Devonshire, who sold it in 1827.[80]

[79] Four leases for buildings and land were signed in 1795, the fifth, to two of the builders themselves, in 1805. A sixth lease, in 1805, was for land only, and it went to the third builder. "Statement of Leases Granted by the Honourable Henry Cavendish of Messuages and Land at Clapham in Surry," Devon. Coll., L/34/10.

[80] "Abstract of the Title of His Grace the Duke of Devonshire to an Estate at Clapham Common in the County of Surrey," Devon. Coll., L/38/78, and L/16/20.

POLITICS

THE PRESIDENT OF THE ROYAL SOCIETY Sir Joseph Banks kept his distance from political faction: "I have never entered the doors of the House of Commons," he told Benjamin Franklin at the time of the American Revolution, "& I will tell you that I have escaped a Million of unpleasant hours & preserved no small proportion of Friends of both parties by that fortunate conduct."[1] But within every group, however disinterested in politics in principle, power can become an issue, a truth which would be brought home to Banks the year after he wrote to Franklin of his unpolitical conduct. Like Banks, Henry Cavendish did not directly participate in national politics, but like Banks and because of Banks, he was drawn into a struggle for power within the Royal Society.

ROYAL SOCIETY

In his *History of the Royal Society*, Charles Richard Weld wrote that it was "painful" for him to turn to the events of 1783 and 1784. He would rather have passed them over in "silence," but duty forbade it. He gave what he regarded as an impartial account of the so-called "dissensions," which "turned the hall of science into an arena of angry debate, to the great and manifest detriment of the Society."[2] The dissensions originated, Weld said, in a widespread resentment of Sir Joseph Banks. President of the Royal Society since 1778, Banks announced at the time of his election his "determination to watch over the applications for admission, and the election by ballot." There being no secret about it, Fellows

[1] Sir Joseph Banks to Benjamin Franklin, 9 Aug. 1782, quoted in A. Hunter Dupree, *Sir Joseph Banks and the Origins of Science Policy* (Minneapolis: Associates of the James Ford Bell Library, University of Minnesota, 1984), 15.

[2] Charles Richard Weld, *A History of the Royal Society*, 2 vols. (London, 1848) 2:151. This discussion of the Royal Society dissensions is taken from Russell McCormmach, "Henry Cavendish on the Proper Method of Rectifying Abuses," in *Beyond History of Science: Essays in Honor of Robert E. Schofield*, ed. E. Garber (Bethlehem: Lehigh University Press, 1990), 35–51. We acknowledge permission by the Associated University Presses to use material from this article.

wishing to elect a new member would likely bring him to one of Banks's breakfasts, and if Banks approved of him, he would then be invited as a guest to a dinner of the Royal Society Club, at which Banks also presided, where he would meet influential members. But if Banks disapproved of the candidate, he would urge individual members to blackball him at balloting time.[3] Banks was not always successful.[4]

For the good of the Society, Banks believed, the members should bring in two kinds of persons, men of science and men of rank. Like the membership at large, the ruling council of the Society contained men of both kinds, and here again, in the elections Banks made clear his likes and dislikes, exposing himself to the charge of packing the council with pliant friends. Banks's forceful interference in elections revealed a pattern, or so certain members thought, which was a bias against men of science, particularly men of the mathematical sciences, and in favor of men of rank. Their dissatisfaction with Banks came to a head in, as Weld termed it, the "violent dissensions, foreign to matters of science," of 1783 and 1784.[5]

In Weld's account and in other historical accounts of the dissensions, Henry Cavendish receives only one brief mention, if any at all. Speeches are quoted at greater or lesser length, but Cavendish is recalled only for his seconding of a motion of approval of Banks as president of the Society.[6] This, to be sure, was the only time Cavendish entered the public record of the dissensions, but there was much more to Cavendish's involvement than this, as there had to be given the eminence of Cavendish in the Society.

To understand Cavendish's part in the dissensions, we need to recall some of the characteristics of the political Cavendishes. A contemporary historian writes of the Cavendishes:

> Much was heard of the "great Revolution families"–of whom some of the proudest, as Sir Lewis Namier has pointed out, were in fact descended from Charles II's bastards. These families–above all, perhaps, the Cavendishes–could not forget that their ancestors had, as it were, conferred the crown upon the king's ancestors, and they did not mean to let him forget it either, for they alluded to it in season and out of season. They looked upon themselves as his creators rather than his creation: one would almost say that they had forgotten that the dukedom of Devonshire itself had been established, less than a century earlier, by the merely human agency of a king.[7]

---

[3] Weld, *History* 2:152–54. Henry, Lord Brougham, "Sir Joseph Banks," in Brougham, *Lives of Men of Letters and Science Who Flourished in the Time of George III*, vol. 1 (London, 1845), 364.

[4] Charles Blagden to Sir Joseph Banks, 30 Oct. 1785, Banks Correspondence, Kew, l.213.

[5] Ibid., 2:153, 170. Henry Lyons, *The Royal Society, 1660–1940: A History of Its Administration under Its Charters* (New York: Greenwood, 1968), 198–99.

[6] Weld, *History* 2:162. Lyons, *Royal Society*, 213.

[7] Richard Pares, *King George III and the Politicians* (Oxford: Clarendon, 1953), 58–59.

Edmund Burke observed in 1771 that "No wise king of Great Britain would think it for his credit to let it go abroad that he considered himself, or was considered by others, as personally at variance with . . . the families of the Cavendishes."[8] George III, Burke also believed, was no wise king. Whereas the first two Georges had had to conciliate the families of, and to reconcile themselves to the principles of, the revolution of 1688–89, George III could take the dynasty for granted. Upon acceeding to the throne in 1760, he immediately set about to break the power of the old whig families. In fact, although it was not entirely obvious at the time, the whig ascendancy had come to an end. Marking this historic turn was the resignation in 1762 of the fourth duke of Devonshire; never again could a Devonshire assume that holding high office was his birthright. At just this time, Henry Cavendish entered the world of science. He did not desire a life in politics; he would have found campaigning difficult and speaking in the commons futile. At best, he might have found assignments in certain committees congenial. He wisely chose for himself a path in science, but he did not for that reason entirely escape politics. From his part in the dissensions of the Royal Society, we get a glimpse of the kind of politician he would have been had he chosen otherwise.

Devonshire House, the Picadilly mansion of the dukes of Devonshire, was the London headquarters of the whigs.[9] The whigs of the 1780s, the so-called New Whigs, were libertarian, passionately opposed to George III's policy on the American colonies, and admiring of Charles James Fox, the most implacable of George III's personal enemies.[10] This whig leader and his king were in fundamental disagreement over power: Fox believed that power was properly exercised only through the king's ministers, whereas George III believed that his ministers were bound by loyalty to uphold his policy. George III rejected Fox's doctrine that the king was to enjoy no personal power, that he was merely to sit on the throne, not to rule from it. In the ensuing constitutional struggle, the government of the kingdom was brought to a standstill. The person of George III was *the* political issue, as John Dunning asserted in his well-known resolution of 1780, which was favored by a parliamentary majority: "That the influence of the Crown has increased, is increasing, and ought to be diminished."[11] The case has been made that the

[8] The plural "families" was used by Burke because there was more than one politically influential Cavendish family. In the sentence quoted, Burke referred to several political leaders in addition to the Cavendishes. Pares, *King George III and the Politicians*, 59.

[9] Whigs are a large part of Hugh Stokes's subject in *The Devonshire House Circle* (London: Herbert Jenkins, 1917).

[10] John Pearson, *The Serpent and the Stag: The Saga of England's Powerful and Glamourous Cavendish Family from the Age of Henry the Eighth to the Present* (New York: Holt, Rinehart and Winston, 1983), 128–29.

[11] Pares, *King George III and the Politicians*, 119–25, 134–35.

years 1783–84 witnessed the greatest "political convulsion" in Britain since the revolution of 1688.[12]

The same years witnessed the dissensions of the Royal Society, in which the president, Joseph Banks, was accused, like George III, of desiring personal rule, and the regular business of the Society was brought to a standstill. While Henry Cavendish's relatives, above all his first cousin and chancellor of the exchequer Lord John Cavendish, were actively concerned with the constitutional convulsion, Henry himself was actively concerned with its counterpart in the Royal Society. Henry was, according to a relative, "very proud of his family name,"[13] and the nature of his activity in the political affairs of the Royal Society was as characteristically "Cavendish" as his slouching gait.

The occasion that gave rise to the convulsion in the Royal Society was a disagreement between the president and his council on the one hand and the foreign secretary, the mathematician Charles Hutton, on the other. Unlike the two regular secretaries of the Society, the foreign secretary was not necessarily on the council. When Hutton was elected to his office in 1779, he happened also to be an elected member of the council, but after 1780, when the dissensions occurred, he was no longer. At a meeting of the council on 24 January 1782, Hutton's responsibility and performance were taken up, the one judged onerous, the other inadequate. Hutton, it was decided, had not dealt with the foreign correspondence with "sufficient punctuality," and he was "by no means adequate to the duties of his office." But he was also overworked and underpaid, which seemed a likely reason for the tardiness. The council resolved that in the future, Hutton should not be expected also to translate foreign articles and extracts from foreign books, and in return he was not to fall behind in the foreign correspondence. Hutton agreed to continue as foreign secretary with this new understanding. Nothing more was heard of the matter publicly until nearly two years later when, at a meeting of the council on 20 November 1783, it was resolved that the foreign secretary of the Society had to live permanently in London. Two members of the council, the astronomer royal Maskelyne and one of the regular secretaries of the Society Paul Maty, dissented from this move, which was obviously directed against Hutton, who as professor of mathematics at the Royal Military Academy of Woolwich could not live in London. Hutton promptly resigned. At the ordinary meeting of the Society on 11 December 1783, it was moved that Hutton be formally thanked for his services as secretary for foreign correspondence, a motion which Banks opposed, and which was vigorously debated. The motion passed by a narrow margin, whereupon Banks duly thanked Hutton. At the following meeting, on 18 December, Hutton delivered, and a secretary read aloud, a written defense of his handling of the foreign correspondence, after which a

[12] John Cannon, *The Fox-North Coalition: Crisis of the Constitution, 1782–4* (Cambridge: Cambridge University Press, 1969), x-xi.

[13] Lady Sarah Spencer quoted in Stokes, *Devonshire House Circle*, 315.

motion was made and carried that Hutton had justified himself, which again was attended by a vigorous debate. The mathematician Samuel Horsley attacked Banks, accusing him of infringing upon the chartered rights of the Society. Horsley said he knew of enough wrongs to keep the Society "in debate the whole winter . . . perhaps beyond the winter."[14]

The prospect of a winter of discontent, spent in acrimonious debate, would have been alarming to Cavendish, who regarded the serious scientific purpose of the Society as inviolable. At this point he became actively–if invisibly to all but a handful of members–engaged in shaping the outcome of the dissensions. His activity is reported in daily letters from Blagden in London to Banks at his country house.

Highly personal in tone, the debates about the leadership of the Society turned on a scientific judgment. The principal question the members addressed was this: had the Society been seriously damaged scientifically and its honor tarnished by its president, Banks? To keep Banks informed about opinion on this question, Blagden delicately inquired into Cavendish's position. Naturally, Banks needed to know where the Society's *scientifically* most eminent member stood.

Banks had various connections other than scientific ones with Henry Cavendish and his family. Banks's grandfather, a Member of Parliament and later sheriff of Lincolnshire, and a Fellow of the Royal Society,[15] gave his vote to Lord Charles Cavendish, whom he was "zealously for," in Lord Charles's successful bid to become Member of Parliament for Derbyshire.[16] Joseph Banks together with several partners extracted lead from Gregory's Mine, paying the duke of Devonshire a portion of the lead ore in compensation.[17] In September 1783, just one month before Charles Hutton was forced out by Banks and his council, Banks received a large private loan from Henry Cavendish.[18]

One side of Banks's understanding of his office as president was, as he put it to Lord Liverpool, "scientific service of the public."[19] Cavendish would certainly have approved of Banks's performance in that regard. The other side of his understanding might be called the "public service of science," and in this regard his performance did not fully satisfy Cavendish, as we will see. But to anticipate the end of this episode, we can say that Cavendish would have agreed

[14] 24 Jan. 1782, Minutes of Council, Royal Society, 7:97–98. Weld, *History* 2:154–60.

[15] J. D. Griffith Davies, "The Banks Family," *Notes and Records of the Royal Society of London* 1 (1938): 85–87.

[16] Joseph Banks II to William Soresby, copy, 12 Mar. 1734; Joseph Banks II to Sam Haslam, 12 Mar. 1734, *Banks Family of Revesby Abbey 1704–1760*, ed. J. W. F. Hill (Hereford: Hereford Times Limited, 1952), 160–61.

[17] "Agreement with the Duke of Devonshire for Continuing to Mine the Gregory Lead Mine in Derbyshire," 3 Feb. 1779, Derbyshire Collections, BL Add Mss 6679, pp. 5–10.

[18] "Sir Joseph Banks to the Honble Henry Cavendish. Bond for 4000 pounds of Interest," 29 Sep. 1783.

[19] Sir Joseph Banks to Lord Liverpool, 18 Nov. 1788, Liverpool Papers, BL Add Mss 38223, 34:273.

with his friend William Heberden that in whatever ways Banks might have fallen short, he exerted and sacrificed himself "in favour of Science."[20]

On Monday, four days after the stormy meeting of the Royal Society, after dining at their scientific club, Cavendish accompanied Blagden to his home, where they discussed the troubles of the Society. That morning Cavendish had gone to see Heberden, and the two of them had arrived at a common position. Blagden reported that Cavendish and Heberden would support Banks, but "just." While Cavendish did not "absolutely refuse a vote of approbation" of Banks, he would "absolutely oppose" any resolution that by its wording would seem to pass censure on Horsley and his friends for what they had done in the past, for they had given no evidence of acting out of any motive other than the good of the Society. Furthermore, the good of the Society required that its members exercise just such scrutiny of their president and council. But Cavendish did not mean for this vigilance to take the form of debates during regular meetings, disrupting the scientific business of the Society. To put a stop to the debates without denying members their rights, Cavendish proposed a resolution that he believed would be passed by a very large majority. From dictation Blagden wrote down the resolution and read it back to confirm the wording:

> That the proper method of rectifying any abuses which may arise in the Society is, by choosing into the council such persons as it is supposed will exert themselves in removing the abuses and not by interrupting the ordinary meetings of the Society with debates.

Blagden did not think that this resolution would have the result Cavendish intended. Horsley would agree that it was the task of a new council to remedy abuses, but he would argue that for the Society to be made aware of the abuses, the debates must continue. Cavendish thought that such an argument from Horsley would carry weight, but there was an effective answer to it. The Society could inform itself of any abuses by holding special meetings for the purpose, and then if Horsley persisted with his interruptions, the Society would be within its rights to censure or even expel him. After his conference with Cavendish, Blagden gave Banks his opinion: the resolution Cavendish proposed was probably the best of any so far, and if to it was added another resolution to the effect that any motion had to be announced at the meeting before it was to be debated, the whole affair might be brought to a speedy and favorable conclusion.[21]

But Cavendish's resolution omitted all mention of support for the incumbent president, Banks, which was something less than Blagden and Banks had hoped from him. Cavendish did not even want to talk to Banks about past councils because he would find it awkward, one obvious reason being that

---

[20] Charles Blagden to Sir Joseph Banks, 23 Dec. 1784, Fitzwilliam Museum Library, Perceval H199.

[21] Charles Blagden to Sir Joseph Banks, 22 December 1783; original letter in Fitzwilliam Museum Library; copy in BM(NH), DTC 3:171–72.

75. Sir Joseph Banks. Painting by Sir Thomas Lawrence, engraving by H. Robinson. Reproduced by permission of the Trustees of the British Museum.

Cavendish had been omitted from them. Cavendish believed that Banks was "a little blameable" on this subject, though he "forgave" him. With Blagden's prompting, Cavendish recalled past presidents he had served under. Banks's predecessor, the physician John Pringle, Cavendish said, had acted like Banks and had given rise to the same complaint about ineffective councils. Pringle's predecessor, the antiquary James West, was "King Log" (from Aesop's fable of the frogs who desired a king to watch over their morals and were thrown an insipid log instead). But West's predecessor, the astronomer and mathematician Lord Morton, handled the affairs of the Society in an unexceptionable way. Cavendish allowed that Banks's method of choosing the candidates for council was fair, but he blamed Banks for not doing as Morton did, which was to "put in people who would have an opinion of their own, without agreeing implicitly with the President in every thing." Cavendish believed that if his resolution carried, it would mean that on election day there would be a contest. He wanted Blagden to reassure Banks that he would support the "House list" on election day unless it was "very exceptionable." He also wanted Blagden to tell Banks that he did not want to be consulted on the list beforehand, as Banks hoped he would. Blagden told Cavendish–Blagden quoted himself to Banks–that "any list that he [Cavendish] can possibly think good, will be sufficient for me."[22]

Through Blagden, Banks asked Cavendish to come to his house the next day, which was Christmas. Cavendish replied, through Blagden, that he could not come. Blagden explained to Banks that it was "possible" that Cavendish had set aside the following day for doing experiments, but most likely he wanted to avoid an "embarrassing conversation" with Banks. Banks was to be reassured that Cavendish was not "hostile" toward him and wanted to remain on good terms.

[22] Charles Blagden to Sir Joseph Banks, 22 December 1783. Charles Blagden to Sir Joseph Banks, Wednesday morning [24 December 1783]; original letter in Fitzwilliam Museum Library; copy in BM(NH), DTC 3:176.

It was only necessary that Banks allow Cavendish to differ with him in opinion at any time "without an open quarrel," which was to repeat what Cavendish wanted of Banks in his dealings with the council.[23]

In conversation with Cavendish, Blagden brought up the principal disrupter of the meetings of the Society, Banks's enemy, Horsley. Blagden quoted Cavendish to convey his exact meaning to Banks. These being the only faithfully recorded spoken words by the reserved Henry Cavendish, they hold an interest of their own.

CAVENDISH: I did not expect any success from the Drs negotiations [Dr. Heberden and, no doubt, Dr. Horsley's]. But whatever violence *they* may express, that is no reason against proceeding with all moderation, as by such conduct the sense of the Society will be ensured against them.

BLAGDEN: I wish you would see Dr. H[orsley] & learn from himself the implacable temper expressed; as I think you would then change the opinion to which you seemed inclined when we conversed last, that those gentlemen might have nothing in view but the good of the Society.

CAVENDISH: I did not say they had nothing else in view, but only that no proof yet appeared of other motives.

At the end of their conversation, Cavendish came around to Blagden's position: he, like Heberden, would approve a vote of confidence in Banks, but only if its wording gave no offense. With this, Blagden declared himself highly satisfied with the results of his mediation.

Blagden informed Banks, "Great opposition is making against you," some members being "decidedly against you even on the subject of the Presidency." So far as he could learn, Blagden said, they intended to put Lord Mahon in Banks's place. The alleged injustice done to Hutton as foreign secretary was only the occasion of the dissensions, their real cause being a "grudge of very old standing," backed by many grievances, William Heberden told Blagden.[24] Banks's opponents charged him with excluding deserving men from the Society because they were not of sufficient social rank, their favorite example being the able mathematician Henry Clark, whom they said was kept out because he was merely a schoolmaster. The membership of the last council they held in derision. The battle line, as they drew it, was between Banks's fancy gentlemen, or "Maccaronis," and the "men of Science."[25]

Heberden did not elaborate on the long-standing grudge, but it certainly included feelings arising from a conflict between the natural historians and the

---

[23] Charles Blagden to Sir Joseph Banks, 24 December 1783; original letter in Fitzwilliam Museum Library; copy in BM(NH), DTC 3:177–79.

[24] Blagden to Banks, 23 and 27 December 1783. *Supplement* to: Friend to Dr. Hutton, *An Appeal to the Fellows of the Royal Society, Concerning the Measures Taken by Sir Joseph Banks, Their President, to Compel Dr. Hutton to Resign the Office of Secretary to the Society for Their Correspondence* (London, 1784), 11, 15.

[25] Blagden to Banks, 27 December 1783. Charles Blagden to Sir Joseph Banks, 28 December 1783, Fitzwilliam Museum Library, Perceval H202.

mathematical practitioners, both groups aspiring to authority within the Society. Banks, himself a natural historian, was thought to favor natural history, as did many of his allies, aristocrats and gentry, who were interested in horticulture and agriculture, and who introduced another element, social rank, into the dissensions.[26]

To a letter to Banks, Blagden attached a postscript dated Monday, 29 December, which read:

> Resolved, That this Society approve of Sir Jos: Banks as their President, and mean to support him in that office.

"Such, my dear friend," Blagden wrote to Banks, "is the resolution Mr C. has just approved at my house." In Blagden's view, the vote on this resolution would sort out Banks's friends from his foes. Cavendish, he added, still thought that the resolution he first proposed would prove necessary, since the Society would not agree that under the present statutes they are forbidden to debate except at the day of elections.[27]

In anticipation of the next meeting of the Society, Horsley told his friends that Banks was going to try to expel him, in that way ensuring, Blagden told Banks, an ample turnout of Horsley's friends.[28] To make certain that his own friends turned out, Banks sent a card to all members of the Society requesting their attendance, and at the meeting on 8 January 1784, some 170 members came, fewer than half of whom attended regularly. From the president's chair, facing the massed assembly, Banks watched as "each side took their station and looked as important as if matters of the utmost consequence to the State were the subject of their deliberation."[29] As planned, the accountant general of the Society, Thomas Anguish, rose to make the motion. The previous two meetings of the Society, he reminded his audience, had been disrupted by debates, and at the second of these, Horsley had threatened to keep the Society debating the rest of the winter, the obvious intent of which was to unseat Banks. The motion Anguish put to the members was the resolution approving of Banks, which Cavendish had earlier approved. Cavendish now seconded the resolution before the Society. Cavendish said nothing in support of it, and there is no evidence that he said anything else during this long night of angry speeches.[30]

---

26 David Philip Miller, "Sir Joseph Banks: An Historiographic Perspective," *History of Science* 19 (1981): 284–92, on 288–89.

27 Postscript dated 29 December 1783, Blagden to Banks, 28 December 1783.

28 Charles Blagden to Sir Joseph Banks, 30 December 1783, Fitzwilliam Museum Library, Perceval H203.

29 Notes of the meeting taken by Banks, quoted in Hector Charles Cameron, *Sir Joseph Banks, K.B., P.R.S.: The Autocrat of the Philosophers* (London: Batchworth, 1952), 134.

30 [Paul Maty], *An Authentic Narrative of the Dissentions and Debates in the Royal Society, Containing the Speeches at Large of Dr. Horsley, Dr. Maskelyne, Mr. Maseres, Mr. Poore, Mr. Glenie, Mr. Watson, and Mr. Maty* (London, 1784), 24–25. *Supplement,* 9.

The first speech was made by Edward Poore, a barrister at law in Lincoln's Inn, who called the motion a dishonorable attempt to evade scrutiny of Banks's conduct by praising it. The attempt would not succeed, he said; it would not stop debate (and did not, as Cavendish and Heberden had predicted). Francis Maseres, cursitor baron of the exchequer and mathematician, said that for the Society to exercise its power of election of the president and council, the Society had first to discuss the question of Banks's "abuse of power." Horsley said that the "abuses are enormous," and he went on about them at such length that Banks's supporters clamored for the question, almost drowning him out with their cries and with a clattering of sticks. As a last resort, Horsley said, "the scientific part of the Society" would secede, which would leave Banks leading his "feeble *amateurs*," his mace standing for the "ghost of that Society in which philosophy once reigned and Newton presided as her minister." Maskelyne, the astronomer royal, said that if it proved necessary to secede, the "*best* Society would be the *Royal* Society in fact, though not in name." The mathematician James Glenie was interrupted before he could finish what he had to say, which was that the present council was incapable of understanding mathematics, mechanics, astronomy, optics, and chemistry, and that the Society as led by Banks, a natural historian, was degenerating into a "cabinet of trifling curiosities," a "virtuoso's closet decorated with plants and shells." When late in the evening the motion was finally put to a vote, it carried 119 to 42, the Society favoring Banks to continue as their president by a three to one margin.[31] This, then, was the outcome of all the meetings, letters, maneuverings, and canvassing. The safest course having been taken by Banks's supporters, the resolution contained no detail; it said nothing about limiting debates, nothing about abuses, nothing about reforms, nothing, that is, that might divide the majority.

The opponents of Banks as well as his supporters claimed that they longed for a return of "tranquility, order, harmony, and accord" and the "instructive business of these weekly meetings, *the reading of the learned papers presented to the Society*."[32] For three consecutive meetings, however, the debates had prevented the reading of all new scientific papers. Only John Michell's great paper on the distance and other measures of the fixed stars, which Cavendish had communicated to the Royal Society, continued to be read at two of these meetings, on 11 and

---

[31] *Narrative*, 26–77. *Supplement*, 9. Royal Society, JB 31:270–71. Despite charges to the contrary, in the Royal Society at this time, the physical sciences looked to be flourishing and appreciated. At the St. Andrew's Day meeting for elections on 1 December 1783, Banks gave a discourse on two Copley Medals, one awarded to John Goodricke for his paper on the variation of the star Algol, the other to Thomas Hutchins for his experiments, which Cavendish directed, on freezing mercury. Entry for 1 December 1783, Royal Society, JB.

[32] *Narrative*, 30, 70.

18 December, while at the third meeting, on 8 January, no papers at all were read.[33]

The main new paper read together with Michell's paper at the next meeting, on 15 January, was itself another strong paper, and though it was not mathematical like Michell's, but experimental, it was written by a mathematical member, Cavendish. This new paper by Cavendish, "Experiments on Air," was destined to be, by many accounts, his most important, containing his discovery of the production of water from the explosion of gases. Following upon three meetings in which the members had listened to speeches contrasting the present, feeble state of the Royal Society with what it had been in Newton's day, and coming one week after Cavendish had seconded the successful motion approving of Banks's presidency, the reading of Cavendish's work at the first opportunity was a power move. Earlier that day, Paul Maty, secretary of the Royal Society and outspoken critic of Banks, wrote to Banks asking him to send papers, as there were not enough for the meeting, and telling him that he refused to read papers he was not prepared for, nor would he come to Banks's house on Soho Square for papers unless a statute was made to command him. Banks wrote back that same day saying that he had read the papers in hand, and he ordered Maty to read Cavendish's paper, sent forthwith.[34]

On 22 January, the council of the Society passed a resolution on debates stating that any motion or question to be ballotted on had to be put in writing and signed by at least six Fellows and delivered to a secretary. It would then be posted in the common room at the next meeting and be ballotted on at the meeting after that. At the next council meeting, Maty moved that the opening words of the resolution be deleted. They read, "That the Meetings of the Society may not be wasted by unprofitable debates contrary to the intent & meaning" of the statutes of the Society. He was voted down.[35]

It would seem that the Society had returned to business-as-usual, but the new statute requiring all motions to be announced in advance did not produce the desired calm. Duly announced was a motion to reinstate Hutton in his office, and it and motions to restrain Banks's interference with elections led predictably to renewed debates in late January and February.[36] At a meeting in March, Maty gave a speech and then went on to read papers, as was his duty.

33 Charles Blagden to Claude Louis Berthollet, 13 January 1784, draft, Blagden Letterbook, Yale. Royal Society, JB 31:265, 268–71. On 27 November 1783, the reading began of the paper by John Michell, "On the Means of Discovering the Distance, Magnitude, &c. of the Fixed Stars, in Consequence of the Diminution of the Velocity of Their Light, in Case Such a Diminution Should Be Found to Take Place in Any of Them, and Such Other Data Should Be Procured from Observations, as Would Be Farther Necessary for That Purpose," *PT* 74 (1784): 35–57.

34 Paul Maty to Sir Joseph Banks, 15 Jan. 1784; Banks to Maty, 15 Jan. 1784, BL Add Mss 33977, 257 and 257(2).

35 22 and 29 Jan. 1784, Minutes of Council, Royal Society, 7:154, 157.

36 Weld, *History* 2:162–64. *Narrative*, 79–134.

Horsley was at that meeting but few of his supporters came, and Banks took hope.[37] Maty, who had "distinguished himself by his violence against Sir Jos. Banks," in Blagden's words, resigned as secretary of the Society.[38] Banks sent another card to all members of the Society on 29 March to inform them of the vacancy and to say that "at his desire," Blagden had declared himself a candidate for the office. Banks's opponents took fresh offense, referring to Banks's card as his permission to elect, or as they put it, the "President's Congé d'Elire."[39]

Following the row over the election of Maty's replacement, new contingency plans were laid, with Cavendish again taking part and for the same reason. On Monday, 5 April, Blagden told Banks that Cavendish and his friend Alexander Dalrymple had accompanied him home that evening to determine the "proper measures for preventing a few turbulent individuals from continuing to interrupt the peace of the R. S." Cavendish was willing to join a committee or to call a meeting to form a plan of action and draft appropriate resolutions. The general idea was that the committee would present the resolutions to the much larger meeting of members, the composition of which was to be decided by the committee. If the resolutions were acceptable to these members, they would be expected to vote for them at such times as the dissensions again interrupted the scientific work of the Society. From a list of members, Cavendish selected seven as being "proper" for drafting the resolutions. Heberden was one of them, and when Blagden said that Heberden probably would not join them, Cavendish offered to go to Heberden the next morning to try to persuade him. Cavendish had nothing against taking the lead except for his general "unfitness for active exertions."[40] That evening Cavendish wrote to Blagden: "It is determined that Mr Aubert & I shall go to D^{r} H[eberden] & see what we can do. If it is to no purpose a larger meeting will be called & very likely some resolution similar to what you mentiond proposed to them."[41]

Despite his general disclaimer, Cavendish took an "active part," Blagden wrote to tell Banks the next day, to "render the R. S. more peaceable." Cavendish had called not only on Heberden but also on Francis Wollaston and Alexander Aubert, and he was going to write to William Watson, all of whom were on Cavendish's list of seven, and he had even called for the meeting to take place in his house and had settled on a time for it.[42]

---

37 Sir Joseph Banks to Charles Blagden, 6 March 1784, Blagden Letters, Royal Society, B.26.

38 Charles Blagden to le comte de C., 14 May 1784, draft, Blagden Letterbook, Yale. 1 Apr. 1784, Minutes of Council, Royal Society, 7:160.

39 Weld, *History* 2:165. *Supplement*, 12.

40 Charles Blagden to Sir Joseph Banks, 5 April 1784, BM(NH), DTC 3:20–21.

41 Henry Cavendish to Charles Blagden, Monday evening [5 April 1784], Blagden Papers, Royal Society, C.26.

42 Charles Blagden to Sir Joseph Banks, 6 April 1784, BM(NH), DTC 3:25–26.

That is the last we hear of Cavendish's efforts to restore peace to the Royal Society. One month later the Society voted for the secretary to replace Maty. Hutton, the deposed foreign secretary and still the primary rallying cause for Banks's opponents, ran against Banks's man, Blagden. The vote was again not close, 139 to 39, in favor of Blagden. Banks in effect had made the election of the secretary a vote of confidence in him, since he endorsed Blagden who had served throughout the stormy times as Banks's proxy.[43]

The turmoil of the Society was reflected in the *Philosophical Transactions*, the printing of which was held up, and Volume 73 for 1783 was a mass of "confusion." Cavendish's paper on Hutchins's experiments on the freezing of mercury was printed out of order because Hutchins's own paper was mislaid by the secretary, Maty. When after much delay Hutchins's paper was found, it was paginated with astericks and then, unaccountably, inserted in the middle of Cavendish's paper. Different copies of the journal had different mistakes. Two years later Blagden was still dealing with the aftermath.[44]

Yet after the event, the dissensions seemed hardly more than a tempest in a teapot to Blagden. He was surprised that foreigners took such interest in that "foolish & trifling affair, as it really was with us."[45] He wrote to a foreign correspondent that the disaffected members of the Society had not only failed in their plan to unseat Banks but in the end had planted him in his seat more firmly than ever.[46] Most important, science had not stopped: to a friend, Blagden wrote that "notwithstanding the interruption given to our business in the Royal Society by some turbulent members . . . several valuable papers have been read, and some discoveries of the first magnitude announced," adding that "of these, the most remarkable was made by Mr Cavendish."[47] Banks received a letter from abroad at this time, beginning with the observation that the Royal Society's dissensions "have made a good deal of noise on the Continent" and that Banks's report that the troubles are "nearly quelled" was welcome news, next observing that Cavendish's discovery of the production of water from air was "one of the greatest steps that have been made" towards understanding the elements.[48]

Although it is true that the dissensions did not flare up again, smoldering resentments continued to the end of Banks's long presidency, in 1820. In late 1785

---

[43] Weld, *History* 2:165–66.

[44] Charles Blagden to le comte de C., 2 April 1784, draft; Charles Blagden to John Michell, 13 Sep. 1785, draft, Blagden Letterbook, Yale.

[45] Charles Blagden to Sir Joseph Banks, 9 August 1788, BL Add Mss 33272, pp. 50–51.

[46] Blagden to le comte de C., 2 April 1784.

[47] Charles Blagden to Charles Grey, 3 June 1784, draft, Blagden Letterbook, Yale.

[48] Henry Cavendish, "Experiments on Air," *PT* 74 (1784): 119–69; reprinted in *The Scientific Papers of the Honourable Henry Cavendish, F. R. S.*, vol. 2: *Chemical and Dynamical*, ed. E. Thorpe (Cambridge: Cambridge University Press, 1921), 161–81; read 15 Jan. 1784. The Abbé Mann to Sir Joseph Banks, 4 June 1784, published in Henry Ellis, ed., *Original Letters of Eminent Literary Men of the Sixteenth, Seventeenth, and Eighteenth Centuries* (London, 1843), 426–29, on 426–27.

Blagden informed Banks about an alternative to the *Philosophical Transactions*, an "opposition Transactions," in which Maskelyne was involved, although Maskelyne denied that it had anything to do with the "late opposition." As far as Blagden had been able to learn, it was a work that Hutton had undertaken to publish twice a year, to which Hutton and his friends would contribute, and it would not be confined to mathematics. Blagden took to calling this project the "*seceeding Transactions*."[49] From 1784 there is evidence of a mathematical club meeting on Fridays every other week, not Thursdays when the Royal Society Club met, at the Globe Tavern on Fleet Street, and to judge by its membership, which included Hutton, Maseres, and Maskelyne, it had characteristics of an opposition dining society.[50] Some dozen years after his dismissal as foreign secretary, Charles Hutton gave an embittered description of the Royal Society in his *Mathematical and Philosophical Dictionary*, beginning the entry "Royal Society of London": "This once illustrious body . . . ," the meeting hour of which had been adjusted to the convenience of "gentlemen of fashion," now consisted mainly of honorary members, who did not usually communicate papers, and those members who did were discouraged "by what is deemed the arbitrary government of the society," and in consequence the *Philosophical Transactions* had "badly deteriorated."[51]

Since under Banks's presidency the council of the Royal Society was dominated by the aristocracy and the gentry,[52] we might expect Cavendish as a matter of course to have been on the council during the dissensions. Before Banks became president of the Royal Society in 1778, Cavendish had frequently sat on the council, but in the years following, 1778–84, he was on it only once. Consequently, he had had no direct part in the Hutton affair, which had occasioned the dissensions. Had he been on the council then, the case against Banks would have been substantially weakened. Banks would never again omit Cavendish's name from the house list. In 1785, the year after the dissensions, Cavendish was elected to the council, as he was every year after that through 1809, just before his death.

As an ordinary member without office, Cavendish had attended the meetings of the Society at which the great debates took place. He seconded, undoubtedly by prearrangement, the motion approving Banks's presidency, nothing more, but that was all that was needed, for Cavendish was not simply another member of the Society. First of all, he was a *Cavendish*, a name which carried an authority of its own. He owed nothing to, and needed nothing

49 Charles Blagden to Sir Joseph Banks, 23 and 30 Oct. 1785, Banks Correspondence, Kew, 1:213–14.

50 Derek Howse, *Nevil Maskelyne: The Seaman's Astronomer* (Cambridge: Cambridge University Press, 1989), 161.

51 Miller, "Sir Joseph Banks," 289. Charles Hutton, *A Mathematical and Philosophical Dictionary*, 2 vols. (London, 1795–96) 2:399–400.

52 David Philip Miller, "The Royal Society of London 1800–1835: A Study in the Cultural Politics of Scientific Organization," Ph.D. diss. (University of Pennsylvania, 1981), 49.

from, Banks, and for him to act from reasons of personal gain or personal loyalty or disloyalty would have been seen as acting out of character. Second, he was universally respected for his achievements in physical science, not natural history, and he was also known to be a good mathematician. If Cavendish had sided with Horsley and his friends, mathematicians who styled themselves as the genuine scientific element of the Society, Banks's credibility would have been damaged. Blagden fully understood this, which is why Cavendish was a key to his stratagems to save Banks's presidency, as his letters to Banks reveal. Cavendish's endorsement of Banks by seconding the crucial motion was a *scientific* answer to Horsley's characterization of Banks's men as feeble amateurs.

To his opponents, Banks showed favoritism to natural history, and considering that Cavendish did work only in natural philosophy, he might be expected to have joined the opposition if he took any side at all. But if we look at Cavendish's actions in the Society, we see that he had always supported natural history, and in that sense he was a predictable ally of Banks's. Cavendish's many recommendations of voyagers of discovery for fellowships in the Royal Society were a show of support for natural history as much as for natural philosophy. As a guest of his at the Royal Society Club, Cavendish brought Daniel Solander, a natural historian who had studied with Linnaeus and who organized the collection at the British Museum, and who was "the constant companion and assistant of Joseph Banks."[53] On many occasions, Cavendish brought to the Royal Society as his guest Solander's successor as Banks's librarian, another natural historian, Jonas Dryander.[54] Cavendish was himself a natural historian from the side of the physical earth sciences, a collector of stones and minerals, which he evidently displayed in cases in his semi-public house on Bedford Square.

Blagden, in a letter of 2 April 1784 in which he referred to the dissensions at the Royal Society, wrote also of the wider political scene, of "our internal operations in politics, & the consequent general election, [which] have set the whole kingdom in a ferment; it is a very interesting scene which the wisest & steadiest among us contemplate not without emotion."[55] Scientific and general politics were frequently compared in the course of the dissensions, the one side complaining of the "ruins of liberty," the other side of Englishmen "apt to be mad with ideas of liberty, ill understood."[56] Again, the one side spoke of the

---

[53] Archibald Geikie, *Annals of the Royal Society Club: The Record of a London Dining-Club in the Eighteenth and Nineteenth Centuries* (London: Macmillan, 1917), 117. Roy A. Rauschenberg, "Solander, Daniel Carl," *DSB* 12:515–17.

[54] Royal Society, JB, vol. 30 (13 Dec. 1781), vol. 31 (16 Jan. 1783). "Dryander, Jonas," *DNB* 6:64.

[55] Blagden to le comte de C., 2 April 1784. Writing to Banks three days later, on 5 April, about the dissensions, Blagden added a postscript concerning the elections in London.

[56] J. Glenie's speech on 8 January, quoted in *Narrative*, 70. Blagden to Berthollet, 13 January 1784.

"levelling spirit and impatience of all government which infects the present age," "the great evil and disease of the times," the other side of the Royal Society as a "republic," according to which all laws decided by the council are to be debated by the entire membership whenever a mover and a seconder wish it.[57] Or again the one side urged a democratic solution to the abuses of the Society, while the other warned of an illegal "democratic infringement on the principles of the constitution," which was "very much like what was passing in another place."[58] The analogy between the Royal Society and parliament was made explicit. When speakers against Banks were shouted down and the question was demanded, Maskelyne said that he had been at other meetings that modeled their debates after the example of parliament, and there the question was not put until everyone had had a chance to speak.[59] The favorite analogy was between Banks as president of the Royal Society and the king or some official. Horsley described Banks's call upon the members to elect Blagden as their secretary as a "nomination by the president, *as their sovereign*, of the person he would have them chuse; which is exactly similar to the proceeding of the king in the nomination of a new bishop."[60] Horsley's colleague Maty said that his view of the presidency of the Royal Society is of a "presidency of bare order, like that of the Speaker of the House of Commons, and in Council the President ought not to lead more than any other person."[61] Banks's opponents talked of his despotism, of his dictatorial ways, of his wish for dominion. The age of absolute monarchs was over, but Banks seemed not to have noticed, they thought. But the supporters of Banks did not wish for an absolute monarch any more than his detractors did, and no one was more definite on this subject than Henry Cavendish.

In explaining Cavendish's behavior to Banks, Blagden drew the appropriate parallel between Cavendish's position in science and that of his relatives in politics. "The sum is," Blagden wrote to Banks, "that like his namesakes elsewhere, he [Cavendish] is so far loyal as to prefer you to any other King, but chooses to load the crown with such shackles, that it shall scarcely be worth a

[57] Blagden to Banks, 28 December 1783. Letter written by Michael Lort to Bishop Percy, 14 February 1784, at the height of the dissensions, quoted in Weld, *History* 2:169. Lort to Bishop Percy, 24 Feb. 1784.

[58] Anguish's speech on 12 February, quoted in *Narrative*, 112.

[59] Maskelyne's speech on 8 January, quoted in *Narrative*, 62. The Royal Society and parliament were occasionally joined in the same person. C. J. Phipps, Lord Mulgrave, who was active both in the debates of the House of Commons and in those of the Royal Society, spoke with Blagden on the subject of the dissensions as much as "his present political agitation would allow." Lord Mulgrave strongly urged Banks and his supporters against temporizing, since discontented men were "never made quiet by coaxing." Blagden, who used the analogy himself, thought that Lord Mulgrave carried the analogy of "H[ouse] of C[ommons] ideas to our Society" further than was justified. Blagden to Banks, 23 December 1783.

[60] Horsley's speech on 1 April, quoted in *Supplement*, 12.

[61] Maty's speech on 12 February, quoted in *Narrative*, 99.

gentleman's wearing."[62] With regard to Cavendish's "grievance" against Banks, Blagden wrote again to Banks, "It is exactly the old story of an absolute Monarchy, whereas he [Cavendish] thinks the Sovereign cannot be too much limited."[63] Putting a positive light on Cavendish's political position, Blagden wrote to Banks after a meeting with Cavendish, "The utmost consequence will be, some diminution of power, but none of dignity."[64] That reassurance was of paramount importance to Banks, who wore the red ribbon of the Order of the Bath to meetings of the Society, believing that the office he held deserved the utmost dignity.[65]

On the importance of the membership of the council of the Royal Society, Henry Cavendish and his father, Lord Charles, were evidently of one mind. As vice-president presiding over a general meeting of the Royal Society, Lord Charles announced, pursuant of the Statute, "how much it imported the Society that Such persons should be chosen of the Council out of whom might be made the best Choice of a President and other officers."[66]

"Mr Cavendish rather wished to have the Presidentship." This sentence appears in a manuscript in the British Library, entitled "Notes of Conversations 1770–1790."[67] The context is evidently the election of a new president of the Royal Society in 1778, the honor going to Banks. Given Cavendish's extreme shyness, the accuracy of this unattributed fragment of conversation is highly questionable. He exercised an authority within the Society, but as we have seen in the episode of the dissensions, he did so quietly and unobtrusively. We give another example here from a more routine confrontation. In 1793 William Charles Wells, an American-born physician then practicing in London and soon to become physician at St. Thomas's Hospital, was a candidate for membership in the Royal Society. There was a party against Wells, and Charles Blagden asked members about him, learning that there was little in his favor and little against him. Blagden looked in Wells's book published the year before, *Upon Single Vision With Two Eyes*, satisfying himself that the candidate was not a "man of mean understanding" nor one "who has confined his attention solely to medicine." That was the "state of things" when at the Royal Society Club Blagden "consulted" Cavendish and also another senior member, both of whom said that no opposition should be made, and "on their authority" all intention of soliciting votes against Wells was "given up."[68]

[62] Blagden to Banks, 22 December 1783.

[63] Blagden to Banks, Wednesday morning [24 December 1783].

[64] Blagden to Banks, 24 December 1783.

[65] Cameron, *Banks*, 158, 200.

[66] 16 Nov. 1752, Royal Society, JB 21:181.

[67] BL Add Mss 35258, f. 15.

[68] Sir Charles Blagden to Sir Joseph Banks, 8 Nov. 1793, BL Add Mss 33272, pp. 127–28. William Dock, "Wells, William Charles," *DSB* 14:253–54.

NATION

If the arena in which Henry Cavendish acted upon his political views was the Royal Society, his manner of acting was nonetheless that of the Cavendishes in parliament. An appropriate Cavendish to bring up for comparison is William Cavendish, the fourth duke and older first cousin of Henry. The fourth duke held high positions in government including, briefly, the position of prime minister in 1756–57. In the political diary he kept, his editors write, he revealed his "complete self-assurance as to his place in the order of the world. He sits in [Privy] Council as naturally as at his dining-room table. Devonshire's assumption was that Great Britain should be governed by an aristocracy, with himself a principal. . . . No maker or unmaker of ministries, he advised Kings about ministers, though his main concern was always to preserve harmony amongst His Majesty's servants." The fourth duke had no intimate friends in political life. "This detachment was natural to him and inevitably confirmed his exalted station. Here however lay the key to Devonshire's usefulness, recognized by everyone. He was the supremely objective man, never led away by passion, completely reliable and so the ideal receiver of confidences." Devoted to work and duty, everything he did he did well.[69] These characteristics of the fourth duke–self-assured, conscientious, withdrawn, competent, and supremely objective–were those, by and large, of the Cavendish family and, in particular, of that member who distanced himself farthest from the active political life of the nation, Henry Cavendish. The family motto *Cavendo tutus*, a play on words meaning "safe by being cautious," was the fourth duke's guide throughout his life, as it was Henry Cavendish's.[70]

Like the fourth duke and like other politicians of his family, Henry Cavendish chose to work in committees rather than to come forward as a leader, a preference which agreed with his understanding that power should be exercised by councils of serious men of independent judgment. He did not want to be president of the Royal Society, of this we are certain, nor did he want to make or depose presidents, but he was always ready to advise presidents as a call of duty, and always in the interest of stability and harmony.

Like his namesakes in government, whatever Henry Cavendish did, he did well, and whatever he did not do well, which included delivering speeches, he did not do at all. He acted constantly in society, only his was not the given society of high fashion and politics, his birthright, but that of his own choosing, the society of scientific men. He acted from his strengths, which were his intelligence, his sense of fairness, and his ability to work with groups to arrive at decisions for common action. His strengths also included, as his participation in the events of

[69] *The Devonshire Diary: William Cavendish, Fourth Duke of Devonshire, Memoranda on State of Affairs, 1759–1762*, ed. P. D. Brown and K. W. Schweizer, Camden Fourth Series (London: Royal Historical Society, 1982) 27:19–21.

[70] George Wilson, *The Life of the Honourable Henry Cavendish* (London, 1851), 190.

1783–84 show, an understanding of political behavior; he was as close an observer of men as he was of natural phenomena.

In his capacity as secretary to the Royal Society, Blagden wrote to correspondents in 1789 to say that there was no science to report, that "everybody's attention seems turned to politics."[71] The next year he wrote that science throughout Europe was languishing and that the Royal Society had heard nothing important since William Herschel's paper on the rotation of Saturn's ring, "the minds of men being turned to greater interests."[72] Two years later on a visit to France, Blagden was mobbed and nearly hanged. Banks wrote to him that in England, "minds are much heated" by the "dreadful state into which reform has placed France," and he trusted that the English people would learn a lesson from it.[73] Kirwan heard that "Mr. Cavendish talks politics," which surprised him because Cavendish had been "silent" during "Ld North's Rump Parliament, in w[h] his family were so much engaged," and which had "agitated the whole Nation."[74] At the George & Vulture, Cavendish was "freer than usual," saying that "minister & measures" had to be changed and that they "should have confidence in Fox."[75] Henry Cavendish stood by his family in politics and by the brilliant and flawed Charles Fox, whose public address was, in effect, Devonshire House in London. Present during a conversation in which it was said of war the sooner the better, Cavendish "said he could scarcely refrain from bursting out."[76] Blagden recorded a number of Cavendish's observations about war, though in each instance the note is so brief that it reveals only the tenor of Cavendish's opinion. But that is sufficient for us to get an impression of Cavendish's view of nations in conflict. Blagden presented Cavendish with the arguments for setting on Prussia while holding out peace. "Never was a nation so mad," Cavendish responded.[77] The only possibility of a combined resistance to the French was by a "fair intelligence" between Prussia and Austria, Cavendish said, to which Blagden replied "impossible," since Austria's goal was to swallow up Prussia.[78] On the report of a new war with America, Cavendish said that the Americans were "now more moderate than their predecessors." Blagden rejected that opinion on the grounds that Americans would hold onto their places at any cost, to which Cavendish "assented & looked in agitation." Blagden said that England had best turn into a

71 Charles Blagden to William Farr, 24 Jan. 1789, draft, Blagden Letters, Royal Society, 7:206. Charles Blagden to M. A. Pictet, 9 Apr. 1789, draft, ibid., 7:223.

72 Charles Blagden to William Farr, 31 July 1790, draft, Blagden Letters, Royal Society, 7:429.

73 Charles Blagden to Sir Joseph Banks, 5 Sep. 1792, BL Add Mss 33272, pp. 107–8. Sir Joseph Banks to Charles Blagden, 19 Feb. 1793, Blagden Letters, Royal Society, B.41.

74 Richard Kirwan to Sir Joseph Banks, 10 Jan. 1789, copy, BM(NH), DTC 6:122–24.

75 16 Mar. 1795, Charles Blagden Diary, Royal Society, 3:50 (back).

76 20 Dec. 1795, Charles Blagden Diary, Royal Society, 3:82 (back).

77 Ibid.

78 30 Nov. 1804, Charles Blagden Diary, Royal Society, 4:286.

nest of pirates and war against all the world, and that England was likely to be at war soon with Russia: "to all this [Cavendish] sadly assented."[79] On two major points Cavendish and Blagden agreed. In the making of a new ministry, in which Cavendish's "family took an active part," Blagden said he was for the old opposition, Fox. To Blagden's remark that all of mankind had gone mad together, Cavendish "thought there was a great diminution of common sense in the world."[80] Taken together, these and other fragmentary comments by Cavendish point to a man who looked to reason in human affairs and did not find much.

If one looks at the dissensions of the Royal Society as a kind of experiment of the Enlightenment, a test of its characterizing beliefs, the outcome is subject to interpretation. But it seems clear that through it all, Cavendish acted consistently upon certain of those beliefs. He trusted that disputes can and ought to be settled by discussion between men who are fair, moderate, informed, and willing to exercise their reason. In the eighteenth century, as in any other, a person who held that expectation of human nature was liable to disappointment.

[79] 15 May 1806, Charles Blagden Diary, Royal Society, 4:442.

[80] 3 Apr. 1804, Charles Blagden Diary, Royal Society, 4:217. This exchange on the unreason of people may not have had to do with politics, but it would apply.

AIR AND WATER

"CHEMISTRY IS THE RAGE IN LONDON AT PRESENT," John Playfair noted in his journal on a visit in 1782.[1] This observation sets the stage for Henry Cavendish's next course of experiments and series of publications.

In Cavendish's period, the major achievement in chemistry was the distinction between various kinds of air, the first step in the chemistry of the gaseous state of matter. We have discussed Cavendish's paper on factitious air, which he published in 1766. When in 1771 the industrial chemist James Keir brought out an English translation of Macquer's five-year-old *Dictionary of Chemistry*, he added material on factitious air from Black, Macbride, and Cavendish. By then for a chemical dictionary to correspond to the "present state of chemical knowledge," it had to include pneumatic chemistry.[2] Two years later the president of the Royal Society, John Pringle, gave a discourse on the history of pneumatic chemistry.[3] In 1781 Tiberius Cavallo surveyed the field in a book of over eight hundred pages, *Treatise on . . . Air.* Pneumatic chemistry was an indispensable branch of chemistry when Cavendish returned to it after his electrical researches.

GOOD AIR

This chapter is concerned with the chemistry of the main components of common air–"dephlogisticated air" (oxygen) and "phlogisticated air" (nitrogen)–and of two other gases, "nitrous air" (nitric oxide) and "inflammable air" (hydrogen). Upon combining different kinds of air, Cavendish and his colleagues observed a large change in volume, the basic understanding of which did not come about until the very end of Cavendish's life. To look

[1] *The Works of John Playfair*, 4 vols., ed. J. G. Playfair (Edinburgh, 1822) 1:xxxv.

[2] Pierre Joseph Macquer, *A Dictionary of Chemistry. Containing the Theory and Practice of That Science . . .*, 2 vols., trans. J. Keir (London, 1771) 1:i, iv.

[3] John Pringle, "A Discourse on the Different Kinds of Air, Delivered at the Anniversary Meeting of the Royal Society, November 30, 1773," *PT* 64 (1774): 1-41, Supplement at the end of the volume.

ahead, in 1809 Joseph Louis Gay-Lussac published his law of combining volumes of gases, according to which gases combine in simple proportions, and their contraction upon combining bears a simple proportion to their original volume; two years later his law received a molecular interpretation by Amadeo Avogadro.

In a paper in the *Philosophical Transactions* in 1772, Priestley reviewed the achievements of pneumatic chemistry, adding to them a new kind of air, nitrous air, the first of his many new airs. Priestley had been guided to this discovery by a conversation with Cavendish;[4] he had also profited from Cavendish's technique of storing water-soluble airs over mercury. Priestley's work on airs in turn stimulated Cavendish to return to the subject, at first in connection with Priestley's new air, nitrous air, the working agent of a new instrument.

"I hardly know any experiment that is more adapted to amaze and surprize than this is," Priestley wrote, "which exhibits a quantity of air, which, as it were, devours a quantity of another kind of air half as large as itself, and yet is so far from gaining any addition to its bulk, that it is diminished by it."[5] Nitrous air was another means, in addition to breathing, burning, and putrefaction, of consuming "good" air. Moreover, this new way of "phlogisticating" air promised a new exactness in the study of air; the decrease in the volume of the mixture of a measured quantity of common air and a measured quantity of nitrous air over water (the products of the reaction being absorbed in the water) measured the goodness of the common air; a better test, Priestley said, than putting mice in it to see how they fared. His method was to mix known quantities of nitrous air and the air to be tested and then to admit the residual air into a graduated tube, which he called a "eudiometer."[6] Priestley's test was soon embodied in a variety of measurers of the goodness of air, or "eudiometers," which were regarded at once as instruments of science and of public health.[7]

Among Cavendish's scientific papers is a bundle of small, carefully indexed sheets, nearly four hundred, labeled "Experiments on Air." Here and there they bear dates, informing us that Cavendish began his new experiments on air in 1778 and effectively ended them in 1786. The account of the first experiment is illustrated with a drawing of a eudiometer, essentially two inverted bottles, one containing dephlogisticated air or common air, the other nitrous air, connected by a siphon. He collected the common air from several gardens: William Watson's, William Heberden's, and his own. He repeated his eudiometer experiment many times, varying the way

---

[4] Joseph Priestley, "Observations on Different Kinds of Air," *PT* 62 (1772): 147–264, on 210.

[5] Ibid., 212.

[6] William H. Pepys, "A New Eudiometer, Accompanied with Experiments, Elucidating Its Applications," *PT* 97 (1807): 247–59, on 248–49.

[7] Tiberius Cavallo, *A Treatise on the Nature and Properties of Air, and Other Permanently Elastic Fluids. To Which Is Prefixed, an Introduction to Chemistry* (London, 1781), 453–57.

the two airs were mixed, the way they were shaken together, and the apparatus. We give one example here to show Cavendish at work. He noted that upon mixing the two airs, a small deposit was formed. This he dissolved and distilled, with these results: the first running was acidic and pungent, the next was tasteless and odorless, and the last left behind "a very small quantity of yellowish sediment" too small to examine. Upon the first two runnings he did auxiliary experiments, in which he tested sediments for inflammability, observed crystals, and noted colors. He did further auxiliary experiments to detect the presence of fixed air (carbon dioxide) in the residuum of the mixed airs. He found that lime water did not become cloudy, the standard test for the absence of fixed air, but to make certain that the lime water was effective and not saturated by nitrous acid, he breathed into it. In this case he saw the expected clouds, but then to test his breath, "lest it might be supposed that the clouds formed in the lime water by breathing through it were owing to a vol. alk. in my breath," he "breathed in like manner through some distilled water" to which he had added a reagent, finding that no clouds were formed thereby. In this test of a test of a test, Cavendish revealed his extraordinarily circumspect awareness of experimental error.

In his first experiments on airs, in the 1760s, Cavendish estimated the combustible portion of common air by the loudness of the explosion when it was detonated with inflammable air, inventing, in effect, a crude sort of eudiometer.[8] The new, potentially exact instrument Cavendish described in 1783 was a variant of the "most accurate" eudiometer invented by the Florentine Felice Fontana.[9] With his eudiometer, Fontana had tested the air in different locations in Europe and in London, concluding that air in different places and at different times was almost the same and that the large differences other observers measured arose from errors in their methods.[10] On this point, chemists were divided. At about the time Cavendish took up the subject, Tiberius Cavallo wrote in his treatise on air that the laws of the *differences* in the purity of common air in different parts of the world were "perhaps the most interesting part of the study of elastic fluids."[11]

Cavendish described two methods of measuring the goodness of air, one by adding nitrous air to the air in question, the other by adding the air in question to nitrous air. Using the latter method, he slowly fed common air into a

[8] George Wilson said this technique might be called an "Acoustic Eudiometer." *The Life of the Honourable Henry Cavendish* (London, 1851), 41.

[9] Henry Cavendish, "An Account of a New Eudiometer," *PT* 73 (1783): 106-35, on 106.

[10] Felice Fontana, "Account of the Airs Extracted from Different Kinds of Waters; with Thoughts on the Salubrity of the Air at Different Places," *PT* 69 (1779): 432–53. Rembert Watermann, "Eudiometrie (1772–1805)," *Technik-Geschichte* 35 (1968): 293–319, on 302–3.

[11] Cavallo, *A Treatise on the Nature and Properties of Air,* 477.

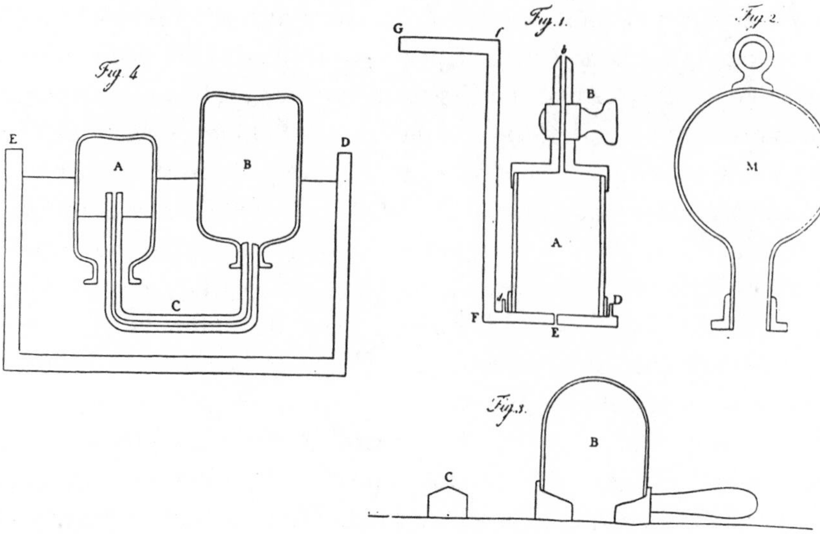

76. *Eudiometer. Fig. 1 shows the main apparatus, a glass cylinder A with brass cap and a cock at the top and an open brass cap at the bottom fitted into a socket of a bent brass holder as "a bayonet is on a musquet." The whole is submerged in a tub of water. Fig. 2 is an inverted bottle for holding air, and Fig. 3 is a standard measure of air. Cavendish's method was to put a certain measure of nitrous air (nitric oxide) into the inverted bottle and a certain measure of common or dephlogisticated air into the glass cylinder. The cylinder was then set on the socket and the bottle over the cock, and the two kinds of air were mixed in the bottle. Fig. 4 shows a different eudiometer. Bottle A contained common air, B nitrous air, which was slowly introduced through tube C into the common air without coming into contact with the water in the tub. "An Account of a New Eudiometer,"* Philosophical Transactions *73 (1783): 134.*

bottle[12] containing nitrous air over water, shaking the bottle all the while.[13] For the "test" of the air, he introduced a "standard" and a scale of measurement: the upper fixed point of the scale was the "standard" 1, which stood for the goodness of common air, the lower fixed point the "standard" 0 of perfectly phlogisticated air (nitrogen). The "standard" of any sample of air was proportional to the quantity of dephlogisticated air (oxygen) in it. Cavendish's use of the word "standard" here was clarified by Blagden in his instructions to Cavendish's translator. "Standard . . . means properly that fixed measure to which others are

[12] The eudiometer Cavendish described in his paper of 1783 was not that which later became known as the "Cavendish Eudiometer," which the Cavendish Society adopted as its emblem in the early nineteenth century. The so-called Cavendish eudiometer was an electrically detonated eudiometer invented by Volta, of a kind Cavendish used in his experiments on the condensation of water; but he never referred to it as a eudiometer. Wilson, *Cavendish*, 42–43. Kathleen R. Farrar, "A Note on a Eudiometer Supposed to Have Belonged to Henry Cavendish," *British Journal for the History of Science* 1 (1963): 375–80.

[13] Jan Golinski, *Science as Public Culture: Chemistry and Enlightenment in Britain, 1760–1820* (Cambridge: Cambridge University Press, 1992), 125.

compared, but in a more general sense is used by us to express the proportion which any thing bears to a fixed measure: thus if a mixture was made of 3 parts of gold & one of base metal, we might say the *standard* of the mixture was 3/4."[14] Cavendish found that the "standard," in this sense, of pure dephlogisticated air was 4.8, a figure he later adjusted to 5. It was not then known that the gases reacting in the eudiometer, our nitric oxide and oxygen, combine in different proportions, the reason for the vastly different purities of air reported from different places. What was known to Cavendish, and to other chemists such as Fontana and Jan Ingenhousz, was that the only way to achieve uniform results was by laying down a uniform procedure, which was the goal of Cavendish's paper.[15] Cavendish gave results from sixty days of trials with his eudiometer of air taken in London and in Kensington, on clear, soggy, and wet days, early in the day and late, from which he concluded that within the error of the measurement, there was no difference in the degree of phlogistication of the air from place to place and time to time. Late in his life, he would read in the *Philosophical Transactions* that his "masterly analysis" of the air in London and Kensington had an "accuracy" that has been "more distinctly perceived the more the science of chemistry has advanced."[16] His measurements, made with "superhuman care," as they have been characterized in recent times, led him to a result which subsequent chemists have translated into terms and quantities corresponding to our understanding of the atmosphere: the concentration of oxygen in the atmosphere is, according to Cavendish, 20.83 percent, which is remarkably near the currently accepted value of 20.95 percent. In making this comparison, it should be noted, Cavendish is credited with a somewhat greater precision than he would likely have claimed.[17]

At the end of his paper on the eudiometer, Cavendish compared its action with the sense of smell. The eudiometer is not like the telescope, an instrument which extends the human senses. On the contrary, the sense of smell can detect "infinitely smaller" quantities of impure air than can be measured by the eudiometer; a person can detect a ten-ounce measure of nitrous air released into a twelve-by-twelve-foot room, an immeasurably small quantity, which would not alter the eudiometer test by more than 1/47,000 part. The nitrous test can show the degree of phlogistication "and that only," a limitation which does not diminish the usefulness of the test but enhances it; for our smell is no "test," Cavendish said, of phlogistication, and there are ways of phlogisticating air that do not

14 Charles Blagden to Bertrand Pelletier, [Nov. 1784], draft, Blagden Letterbook, Yale.

15 Edward Thorpe, "Introduction," *The Scientific Papers of the Honourable Henry Cavendish, F.R.S.*, vol. 2: *Chemical and Dynamical*, ed. E. Thorpe (Cambridge: Cambridge University Press, 1921), 18.

16 Pepys, "A New Eudiometer," 249.

17 Peter Brimblecombe, "Earliest Atmospheric Profile," *New Scientist* 76 (1977): 364–65. Bent Søren Jorgensen, "On a Text-Book Error: The Accuracy of Cavendish's Determination of the Oxygen Content of the Atmosphere," *Centaurus* 12 (1968): 132–34.

impart a smell to it, just as there are ways of imparting a smell that do not phlogisticate.[18] In the last analysis, Cavendish's conclusion is a realistic affirmation of this instrument of measurement in science.

Investigators might come to regard eudiometers as unreliable,[19] but interest in improving them continued, with claims made for their high "precision and accuracy" and "present perfection" toward the end of Cavendish's life.[20] Several years after Cavendish's paper, Count Rumford wanted instruments from England, and Blagden advised him, "Of Eudiometers Mr Cavendish's . . . is undoubtedly preferable to any other."[21] In a discussion with Blagden on a paper about eudiometer tests by Alexander von Humboldt,[22] Cavendish referred to "my paper on Eudiometers," then fifteen years old, in which he had shown that the results of a eudiometer test of common air vary according to the "methods" of mixing that air with the nitrous air. Cavendish was skeptical of Humboldt's experiments, and although he thought that trying the quantity of nitrous air remaining after the mixing had the "appearance" of an improvement, it made the experiment "liable to the error of 2 operations instead of one." "But however that may be, the great difference which he [Humboldt] finds in the purity of common air convinces me that there must be some fault in his method; for though I tried the air of 60 different days, I could not find any difference; & though a faulty method of trying will make the purity of the air appear different at different times when in reality it is not, I do not see how it can make it appear always the same when in reality it is different."[23] Cavendish was confident of his experiments, dubious of the methods of experimenters who achieved results in conflict with his, and in his reasoning devastatingly logical.

Around the time that Cavendish published his work on the composition of air, the balloon was invented, and with it a new kind of adventurer came onto the scene, the "aeronaut." Much about this earliest human flight was derring-do, but there was also an element of science, both in the principles of flight and in the use of flight for making meteorological measurements, and Cavendish took an immediate interest in both. A new field of applied pneumatic chemistry was born.

In fact, Cavendish was regarded as a founding father of balloon flight owing to his first publication on air, in 1766. From Cavendish's description of inflammable air, it was self-evident to Joseph Black that balloons filled with this lighter-than-common air were a practical possibility. Black spoke about it with friends

---

[18] Cavendish, "Account of a New Eudiometer," 144.

[19] Golinski, *Science as Public Culture*, 93.

[20] Pepys, "A New Eudiometer," 259. W. Allen and W. H. Pepys, "On the Changes Produced in Atmospheric Air, and Oxygen Gas, by Respiration," *PT* 98 (1808): 249–81, on 249.

[21] Charles Blagden to Benjamin Thompson, Count Rumford, 27 May 1787, draft, Blagden Letters, Royal Society, 7:55.

[22] Rembert Watermann, "Eudiometrie (1772–1805)," *NTM* 35 (1968): 293–319, on 308–9.

[23] Henry Cavendish to Charles Blagden, 18 Dec. [1798], Blagden Letters, Royal Society, C.24.

and in his lectures, but he did not bother to do the experiment.[24] "Theoretical flying," Blagden said, "has been a topic of conversation among our philosophers as long as I can remember, at least ever since Mr Cavendish discovered the great lightness of inflammable air."[25]

In 1782 the French brothers Joseph and Étienne de Montgolfier experimented with balloons filled with inflammable air and with hot air, and in the following year, they gave a public demonstration of a hot-air balloon.[26] Balloons created a sensation in France and mixed feelings in Britain. Not without a touch of national envy, the British spoke of "Balloon madness" or else of missed opportunity: the French made no scientific observations from their balloons, Banks complained. It was to be hoped, Banks said, that the English would "not rise to the absurd height we have seen in France."[27]

Cavendish took note of the French achievement.[28] The principle of the inflammable-air balloon was fully understood on the basis of weight, but the hot-air balloon raised a question. Evidently to decide if hot air alone caused the balloon to rise or if the balloon also depended on a substance lighter than common air given off by the burning material, Cavendish and Blagden collected the air from burning straw and leather. Determining it to be a mixture of gases heavier, not lighter, than common air,[29] they concluded that hot-air balloons ascend solely because of the rarefaction of air.[30] In practical terms, hot-air balloons were extremely dangerous and clumsy, and Blagden expected nothing of them, but he thought that inflammable-air balloons could bring about an important "revolution . . . in human affairs."[31]

Before long, balloons appeared in the skies above England too, and Cavendish and his friends came out in force to observe them. From Putney Heath, Aubert's observatory in Austin Friar's, and elsewhere, with theodolite and clock, they recorded the paths of Vincenzo Lunardi's balloon in September

---

[24] In a letter from Joseph Black to James Lind, in William Ramsay, *The Life and Letters of Joseph Black, M.D.* (London: Constable, 1918), 77–78.

[25] Charles Blagden to le comte de C., 2 Apr. 1783, draft, Blagden Letterbook, Yale.

[26] W. A. Smeaton, "Montgolfier, Étienne Jacques de; Montgolfier, Michel Joseph de," *DSB* 9:492–94. The early experimentation in France with balloons filled with inflammable air and hot air is discussed in Charles C. Gillispie, *The Montgolfier Brothers and the Invention of Aviation 1783–1784* (Princeton: Princeton University Press, 1983), 15–31.

[27] Sir Joseph Banks to Charles Blagden, 22 Sep. and 12 Oct. 1783, Blagden Letters, Royal Society, B.29–30.

[28] Cavendish's papers contain a testimonial signed by Benjamin Franklin, among others, of a Montgolfier experiment on 21 July 1783, and also an extract, in Blagden's hand, about Montgolfier from the *Journal Encyclopédique*.

[29] Notations in both Blagden's and Cavendish's hand, beginning "Smoke of Straw," Cavendish Mss Misc.

[30] Letter from Charles Blagden 5 Dec. 1783, draft, Blagden Letterbook, Yale.

[31] Charles Blagden to Claude Louis Berthollet, 19 Dec. 1783, draft, Blagden Letterbook, Yale.

1784, and Jean Pierre Blanchard and John Sheldon's balloon the next month.[32] Cavendish was interested in the science of flight, but unfortunately his manuscripts on this subject have been lost.[33]

Balloons offered their passengers "scenes of majestic grandeur," inciting in them an "unknown degree of enthusiastic rapture and pleasure,"[34] but for Cavendish, balloons were a practical means of elevating his scientific observatory thousands of feet above the earth. Through Blagden, he asked the American physician John Jeffries to sample the air during his flight with the French aeronaut Blanchard in November 1784. Jeffries took with him jars filled with distilled water, emptying them at various heights and bottling the air. With the eudiometer, Cavendish tested these samples and compared them with air taken on the ground at Hampstead, establishing that there is little systematic variation in the concentration of delphlogisticated air (oxygen) in the lower atmosphere. He did not publish this finding, the credit for it going to Gay-Lussac for his research twenty years later.[35] We note that Cavendish himself had no more inclination to travel above the earth than across it, but he did have use for aeronauts who went up in balloons.

WATER

In a paper in the *Philosophical Transactions* in 1784, "Experiments on Air," Cavendish reported his experiments on the water deposited by the explosion of common air with inflammmable air. We might expect that just as he and Black had replaced the ancient element air with distinct gases, he would show that the ancient element water was a combination of gases, but that is not what he thought he did. He did not bring into question the elemental notion of water, even as his experiments laid the factual basis for our modern understanding of

[32] Charles Blagden to Sir Joseph Banks, 16 Sep. 1784, Kew, 1.173. Blagden to Banks, 17 and 21 Oct. 1784, copy, Banks Correspondence, BM(NH), DTC 4:75–76,77–78. Alexander Aubert to William Herschel, 13 Sep. 1784, Royal Astronomical Society, Herschel M 1/13. "Path of Balloon," for Blanchard and Sheldon's ascent on 16 Oct. 1784, Cavendish Mss VIII, 24. In Cavendish's hand, "Result of Observations of Balloons," Blagden Collection, Royal Society, Misc. Notes. Archibald and Nan L. Clow, *The Chemical Revolution: A Contribution to Social Technology* (London: Batchworth Press, 1952), 156.

[33] For his sketch of Cavendish in 1845, Lord Brougham borrowed two manuscripts which are now lost: "Theory of Kites" and "On Flying." Their existence and loan to Brougham are noted in Cavendish's manuscripts at Chatsworth.

[34] Thomas Baldwin, *Aeropaidia: Containing the Narrative of a Balloon Excursion from Chester, the Eighth of September, 1785* (London, 1785), 2.

[35] "Eudiometer Results of Air Taken by Dr. Jefferies," and "Test of Air from Blanchard's Balloon," Cavendish Mss II, 9. Thorpe in *Sci. Pap.* 2:22. Jefferies' air samples were numbered, but Cavendish's manuscripts do not contain the explanation of the numbers, and it was believed lost. However, recently it was located in Jefferies' account of his flight, from which the earliest atmospheric profile, the "Cavendish-Jefferies profile," has been reconstructed. It shows that at the various sampling elevations, between one and three kilometers, the amount of oxygen in the air over London was virtually constant. Brimblecombe, "Earliest Atmospheric Profile," 365.

water as a chemical combination of gases. His way of referring to water was ambiguous as to its elemental or compound nature, but the purpose of his paper was to explain the phlogistication of common air, and his discussion of water in this context was unambiguous. Several paths led to Cavendish's experiments with exploding airs and their residue, water. One obvious path was his previous work on airs, in particular his recognition in 1766 of inflammable air as a separate kind of air. Also leading to the new experiments were his his studies of electricity and latent and specific heats. The most direct route to them was his experiments on common air using the eudiometer, which led to the experiments in his paper of 1784. The wider setting was the investigations by Priestley, Lavoisier, and Carl Wilhelm Scheele from the late 1770s of the air lost during phlogistication. Cavendish's immediate stimulus was again the work of Priestley together with his fellow experimenter John Warltire.

The purpose of Cavendish's new experiments was "to find out the cause of the diminution which common air is well known to suffer by all the various ways in which it is phlogisticated."[36] It was a question as important as it was difficult; Priestley had more than one opinion on it, and other chemists had other opinions.[37] Cavendish's answer derived from an experiment he performed in late June or early July 1781, "Explosion of Inflam. Air by El. in Glass Globe to Determine Mr Warltires Experiment."[38] The experiment Cavendish referred to arose, as did his own in response, from a variant of the nitrous air eudiometer invented by Allesandro Volta, the electric-spark eudiometer. The electrical explosion of inflammable and common air was by then a recognized method of phlogisticating air.[39] Warltire, as reported by Priestley, electrically fired a mixture of inflammable and common air in a closed vessel, noting the generation of heat and light and a loss of weight, which Warltire attributed to the escape of a ponderable matter of heat. Warltire and Priestley also noted a deposit of dew inside the vessel, to which they did not attribute fundamental significance.[40] Repeating Warltire's experiment, Cavendish obtained dew and heat but no loss of weight. The latter fact could not have surprised him, since he believed that heat is motion not ponderable matter. Given that he found dew, he could not have been surprised by the heat, since he had found that condensation, the change from an air to a liquid, always generated heat, though what was involved here was more than a simple change of state.[41] If it had not been for Warltire,

[36] Henry Cavendish, "Experiments on Air," *PT* 74 (1784): 119–69; *Sci. Pap.* 2:161–81, on 161.

[37] Cavallo, *Treatise*, 419–20.

[38] Cavendish, "Experiments on Air," Cavendish Mss II, 5:115.

[39] Golinski, *Science as Public Culture*, 135.

[40] Joseph Priestley, *Experiments and Observations Relating to Various Branches of Natural Philosophy* . . . (London, 1781) 2:395–98.

[41] This analysis draws on Russell McCormmach, "Henry Cavendish: A Study of Rational Empiricism in Eighteenth-Century Natural Philosophy," *Isis* 60 (1969): 293–306, on 305.

he probably would have been surprised by the dew itself; in any event he recognized its significance. He observed that all of the inflammable and about one-fifth part of the common air lost their "elasticity" and "condensed" into the dew lining the vessel. This dew had no color, taste, or smell; "in short, it seemed pure water."[42] Cavendish determined that the lost fifth part of the common air was the new air that Priestley had announced in 1774, which was discovered independently by Scheele, "dephlogisticated air," our oxygen. He inferred from the experiments resulting in the condensation of water that dephlogisticated air is "in reality nothing but dephlogisticated water, or water deprived of its phlogiston," and that inflammable air is either "pure phlogiston," as Priestley and Kirwan thought, or in all probability "phlogisticated water" or "water united to phlogiston." When the two airs combine with the help of an electric spark, their water becomes manifest, condensing onto the walls of the container.[43] In this explanation, phlogiston is viewed as elemental, and dephlogisticated and inflammable airs as compounded. To the question of what causes the decrease in common air when it is phlogisticated, Cavendish's answer was that the dephlogisticated part of common air combines with inflammable air and is then no longer air but water.

For completeness, Cavendish identified the other part of atmospheric air, the already phlogisticated air, our nitrogen: phlogisticated air, he said, is nitrous acid united to phlogiston.[44] These several relationships between phlogiston, dephlogisticated air, phlogisticated air, and water constitute Cavendish's understanding of air, which differed markedly from that of certain other chemists.

Finding no role for fixed air in the phlogistication of common air, Cavendish contradicted Kirwan, from whom Cavendish would soon hear.[45] His differences with Watt and Lavoisier were fundamental. In a paper read before the Royal Society, Watt proposed that water is a union of dephlogisticated air and phlogiston, deprived of their latent heat. In his paper the year before on the freezing of mercury, Cavendish had given his differences with Black on the subject of latent heat. Now it came up again in chemistry, and Cavendish again rejected latent heat because he did not believe that heat is a kind of matter instead of motion; even the use of the term "latent" led to "false ideas" in chemistry. He rejected Watt's theory in chemistry evidently because he rejected latent heat.[46] He was circumspectly opposed to Lavoisier's efforts to eliminate phlogiston from chem-

---

[42] Cavendish, "Experiments on Air," 166–67.

[43] Ibid., 171–73.

[44] Ibid., 170–72.

[45] Henry Cavendish, "Answer to Mr. Kirwan's Remarks upon the Experiments on Air," *PT* 74 (1784): 170–77; *Sci. Pap.* 2:182–86. Cavendish's papers contain an extract, in Blagden's hand, of a letter from Kirwan to Crell that appeared in Crell's journal discussing the whole unresolved dispute. "Extract of a Letter from Mr. Kirwan in London to Professor Crell (Chem. Annals. no. VI p. 523. June 1784)," Cavendish Mss X(b), 10.

[46] Cavendish, "Experiments on Air," 173–74.

77. *Eudiometer. The metal eudiometer belonging to Cavendish was presented by Sir Humphry Davy to the Royal Institution, where the authors took this photograph. The instrument is about six inches long and two inches across. The stop-cock on the top served to fill and exhaust the cylinder, the one on the bottom to remove the water resulting from explosions of airs in the cylinder.*

istry and to introduce in its stead oxygen (Cavendish's dephlogisticated air). He conceded that nature seemed to be about equally well explained on Lavoisier's phlogistonless chemistry as his own, but since the "received principle of phlogiston explains all phaenomena," he adhered to it still; there was "one circumstance also, which though it may appear to many not to have much force, I own has some weight with me": on the phlogiston theory, plants give off phlogiston when they are burned, and it seemed obvious to Cavendish that plants are more compounded than their ash; on Lavoisier's theory, the ash, containing oxygen, is the more compounded. But Cavendish thought it would be "very difficult to determine by experiment which of these opinions is the truest."[47] He then raised a difficulty for Lavoisier's view of dephlogisticated air, or oxygen, as the "acidifying principle." For some acids it works, Cavendish said, but not for all, in particular, not for marine acid, or hydrochloric acid,[48] and Cavendish, we know, was right. His otherwise strong paper ended with an admittedly weak defense of phlogiston chemistry, *and* with a strong criticism of Lavoisier's theory of acids. Thomas Thomson thought that if the chemical world had not paid "total inattention" to Cavendish's criticism in 1784, the success of the anti-phlogiston school would not have been as rapid as it was.[49] When Cavendish abandoned the phlogiston theory three years later, as we have reason to think he did, he did not necessarily subscribe to Lavoisier's viewpoint. It is very likely that he accepted the interpretation he gave in his paper of 1784, Lavoisier's hypothesis with Cavendish's "additions and alterations," and no doubt Cavendish exempted Lavoisier's acidifying principle from his own version when he came to reject phlogiston.

[47] Ibid., 179–81.

[48] Ibid., 181.

[49] Thomas Thomson, *The History of Chemistry*, 2 vols. (London, 1830–31) 1:348.

NITROUS ACID

In 1785 Cavendish published a second paper bearing the title "Experiments on Air," which contained a thorough examination of an observation he had made in the first paper: if a trace of phlogisticated air is admitted into a mixture of inflammable and dephlogisticated air and detonated, dilute nitrous acid rather than pure water is deposited. In a new series of experiments he showed that the inflammable air in this experiment is unnecessary; when fired by electricity, phlogisticated air and dephlogisticated air alone yield nitrous acid, and if they are mixed in the right proportions, the gases are entirely consumed, leaving only nitrous acid.[50] Cavendish's explanation was that dephlogisticated air aided by the electric spark reduced phlogisticated air, by depriving it of its phlogiston, to nitrous acid. These experiments paralleled those on the explosion of dephlogisticated air and inflammable air, leaving only water.

Word of Cavendish's new experiments traveled quickly, thanks to Blagden, who described them to Berthollet by letter. Two weeks after Cavendish's paper was read to the Royal Society, Blagden heard from Berthollet that "one part" of his experiments had been repeated in Paris, where they were given another interpretation; Berthollet wrote to Blagden that "we think that Mr Cavendish has combined dephlogisticated air with phlogisticated air, instead of having decomposed the latter."[51] The different interpretations had to do with Cavendish's disagreement with Lavoisier on the formation of acids, which Cavendish had pointed out in his first paper describing his experiments on air.

Three years later Cavendish published another paper on the conversion of dephlogisticated and phlogisticated air into nitrous acid by means of the electric spark. Lavoisier and his colleagues had been unable to repeat Cavendish's experiments, and Cavendish could not imagine why but for "want of patience." Martin van Marum wrote to Cavendish in 1785 of his similar failure to obtain Cavendish's result, even with the help of his new electrical machine, the largest in existence. Cavendish did not know why Marum failed either, though he thought that the apparatus might be faulty.[52] But instead of guessing what went wrong in experiments by others, Cavendish chose to demonstrate what was right in his own. At his request, the clerk of the Royal Society, George Gilpin, repeated the experiments during several days in late 1787 and early 1788. They were witnessed by ten or more Fellows of the Royal Society, most of whom came

[50] Henry Cavendish, "Experiments on Air," *PT* 75 (1785): 372–84; *Sci. Pap.* 2:187–94, on 191.

[51] Berthollet told Blagden that his last letter had created great interest in Paris in Cavendish's "beautiful experiments," and he described their different interpretations. Claude Louis Berthollet to Charles Blagden, 17 June 1785, Blagden Letters, Royal Society, B.126.

[52] Martin van Marum to Henry Cavendish, 6 Jan. 1785; Cavendish to Marum, undated, draft, Cavendish Mss New Correspondence. Cavendish published this letter in his paper, "On the Conversion of a Mixture of Dephlogisticated and Phlogisticated Air into Nitrous Acid by the Electric Spark," *PT* 78 (1788): 261–76; *Sci. Pap.* 2:224–32, on 232.

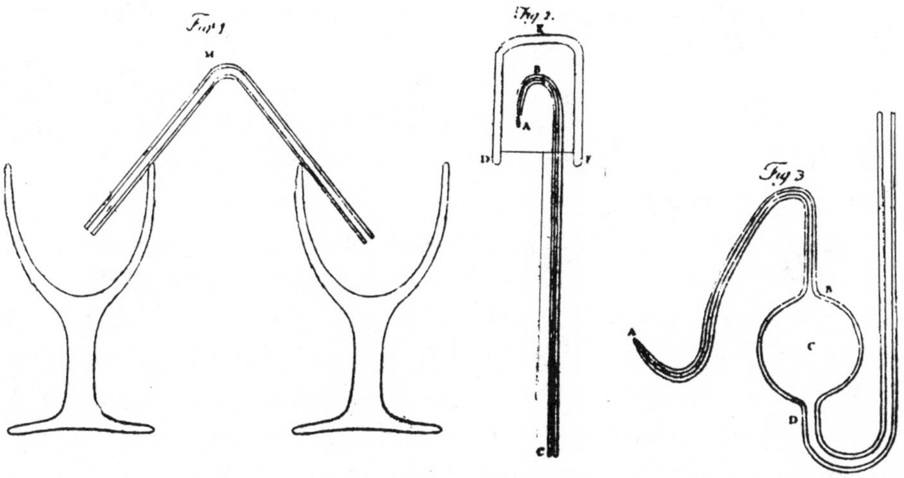

78. *Apparatus for Experiments on Air. For converting phlogisticated air (nitrogen) into nitrous (nitric) acid, a spark is passed through air trapped in the bent tube shown in Fig. 1. The tube, first filled with mercury, is inverted into two glasses containing mercury. Figs. 2 and 3 show small-bore tubes used to insert the nitrous air into the bent tube. "Experiments on Air,"* Philosophical Transactions *75 (1785): 384.*

to each part of the experiments.[53] Gilpin worked Nairne's patent electrical machine a half hour at a stretch, obtaining two or three hundred sparks a minute, whereas Cavendish had only worked his machine for ten minutes at a time, but details of method aside, Gilpin's experiments fully confirmed Cavendish's. These repeated experiments were the substance of Cavendish's last publication in chemistry.

Cavendish's contributions to pneumatic chemistry were widely separated, the first in 1766–67, and the second almost twenty years later, in 1783–85. The earlier contribution was fundamental to the development of chemistry as a science, opening up a field of discovery of new airs, and exhibiting a quantitative approach essential for keeping track of elastic fluids, the nature of which is to escape. The later contribution was just one, however important, of many. By then the field had clear objectives, established techniques, and theoretical directions. Probably what was most important about Cavendish's later papers was their example; to have studied them was to have taken a master class in the art of experiment. Jean Senebier, an experimentalist who published insightful essays on the experimental method, wrote to Cavendish after reading his recent papers on airs, expressing his admiration for Cavendish's "exactitude,"

[53] The witnesses were Banks, Blagden, Heberden, Watson, John Hunter, George Fordyce, J. L. Macie, and Johann Casper Dollfuss; William Higgins and Richard Brockelsby came on a day after an "accident" happened, and Cavendish did not list them in his paper. T. S. Wheeler and J. R. Partington, *The Life and Work of William Higgins, Chemist (1763–1825)* (New York: Pergamon, 1960), 33, 66.

characterizing him as "a master and a great master in the difficult art of making experiments."[54]

ATMOSPHERE

If Cavendish's later work is looked upon as a kind of chemical meteorology, it takes on an additional significance. The title he gave to his two major chemical papers in 1784 and 1785, "Experiments on Air," did not refer to a single, universal air–he did not believe in one–but to common air, the air of the atmosphere. He, along with other leading chemists, understood that this air consisted of two "distinct substances," dephlogisticated air and phlogisticated air, neither of which was understood when Cavendish took up his researches with the eudiometer. He intended his paper of 1784 to "throw great light on the constitution and manner of production of dephlogisticated air."[55] His paper of 1785 had the same objective, only directed to "phlogisticated air": "we scarcely know more of the nature of the phlogisticated part of our atmosphere, than that it is not diminished by lime-water, caustic alkalies, or nitrous air; that it is unfit to support fire, or maintain life in animals; and that its specific gravity is not much less than that of common air"; we do not know if there are "in reality many different substances confounded together by us under the name of phlogisticated air." Cavendish demonstrated that the phlogisticated air of the atmosphere was one substance.[56] By joining his knowledge of pneumatic chemistry, affinity, heat, and electricity, Cavendish clarified the understanding of the atmosphere. In 1785 Blagden sent his brother three papers by Cavendish and Watt, which taken together seemed to Blagden "fully to explain the nature of our atmosphere." Blagden noted that the most important of the three was Cavendish's paper on the origin of nitrous acid (and not the paper on the production of water), for it showed that the greatest part of the atmosphere "is nothing but that acid in aerial form."[57] Likewise Priestley wrote to Cavendish that his experimental work on phlogisticated air was "one of the greatest, perhaps the very greatest, and most important, relating to the doctrine of air."[58]

Daniel Rutherford, Black's and Cullen's student, wrote his medical dissertation in 1772 at the University of Edinburgh on Black's fixed air or, as Rutherford called it, "mephitic air." In the course of his experiments, Rutherford isolated

---

[54] Jean Senebier to Henry Cavendish, 1 Nov. 1785, Cavendish Mss New Correspondence.

[55] Cavendish, "Experiments on Air," 161.

[56] Cavendish, "Experiments on Air," 192–93.

[57] Charles Blagden to Thomas Blagden, 8 Dec. 1785, Blagden Letterbook, Yale.

[58] Joseph Priestley to Henry Cavendish, 30 Dec. 1784, Cavendish Mss New Correspondence. Priestley's letter was in reply to Cavendish's, written late in 1784, which summarized the main points of what would become the published paper of the following year. Henry Cavendish to Joseph Priestley, 20 Dec. 1784, draft, Cavendish Mss New Correspondence. These letters are published in *A Scientific Autobiography of Joseph Priestley (1733–1804)*, ed. R. E. Schofield (Cambridge, Mass.: M.I.T. Press, 1966), 239–42, quotation on 241.

another, similar air, phlogisticated air, our nitrogen. As Rutherford's dissertation was published, he is given credit for discovering nitrogen, but many years earlier Cavendish had studied this air. In a paper written for a correspondent, "you," who had shown him a letter from Priestley on what Priestley called "mephitic air," by which Cavendish understood Priestley to mean air that "suffocates animals," Cavendish said that "in all probability there are many kinds of air which possess this property," and he knew of at least two airs of this kind, Black's fixed air and common air in which something has burned, or "burnt air." Cavendish gave his correspondent the results of an earlier experiment of his, in which he had determined by specific gravity and other characteristics that burnt air was not fixed air. This paper by Cavendish is undated, but Priestley gave a version of it in his paper of 1772.[59]

In his published experiments on phlogisticated air, Cavendish was unable to eliminate a "bubble" in his apparatus, 1/120th part of the whole. This minuscule residue, which Cavendish described as an experimental error, was consequently, and consequentially, noticed by William Ramsay. The occasion was the "water controversy," which had resulted in George Wilson's biography of Henry Cavendish, a secondhand copy of which Ramsay had bought when he was a student. Years later, in the 1890s, Ramsay recalled the pertinent passage and drew it to the attention of Lord Rayleigh, who like Ramsay was concerned with a third-decimal difference in the density of the nitrogen in the atmosphere and the density of the nitrogen produced chemically.[60] Together they determined that Cavendish's residue was a new gas of the atmosphere, the chemically inert argon. Nitrogen, they found, was actually a mixture of nitrogen and argon, a finding which opened up a new epoch in the study of the atmosphere. The discovery of argon inspired Ramsay to write a history of the gases of the atmosphere, in which he observed that of all the experimenters in this field, Cavendish was "undoubtedly the greatest."[61]

As we have seen, Cavendish was guided in his experimental study of the atmosphere by the phlogiston theory, to which he gave his own formulation. His interlocked interpretations of phlogiston, phlogisticated air, dephlogisticated air, nitrous acid, and water provided him with a satisfactory understanding of the atmosphere; we can look upon his experiments on air as a late triumph of the phlogiston theory.

---

[59] Henry Cavendish, "Paper Communicated to Dr Priestley," Cavendish Mss Misc. Scheele too studied this gas, perhaps as early as 1771, but he did not publish on it until 1777. E. L. Scott, "Rutherford, Daniel," *DSB* 12:24–25.

[60] There are two versions of the way Cavendish's experiment came to the notice of Rayleigh. We have given Ramsay's. Rayleigh's is that he was first informed of Cavendish's experiment not by Ramsay but by James Dewar. Morris W. Travers, *A Life of Sir William Ramsay, K.C.B., F.R.S.* (London, 1956), 100–7.

[61] William Ramsay, *The Gases of the Atmosphere: The History of Their Discovery* (London, 1896), 143. Bruno Kisch, *Scales and Weights: A Historical Outline* (New Haven: Yale University Press, 1965), 8.

NEW CHEMISTRY

Had there been no "chemical revolution," the progressive development of techniques in chemistry in the eighteenth century would have taken place all the same. But there was a chemical revolution–an assertion which is accepted by most historians of chemistry even as they disagree about what the revolution was, what its boundaries were, and what place the overthrow of phlogiston had in it[62]–and consequently the historical interest in Cavendish has been largely in relation to that event. Cavendish's substantial contribution to chemisty was not among the conceptual changes that marked the chemical revolution. In contrast to Cavendish, Lavoisier set a course for himself that required a break with the science he learned; from the early 1770s he consciously strove to make a revolution in physics and chemistry, and twenty years later he had done just that, or, depending upon one's interpretation, he had completed the first part of the revolution. A change of this magnitude in chemistry required a number of developments, the most obvious of which was pneumatic chemistry, which replaced the idea of elementary air with that of chemically active, distinct gases, or the gaseous state. Lavoisier's chemistry was built around the new understanding of gases. Cavendish's production of water from gases was important for Lavoisier, who recognized that it implied that water is a compound. That gave him the answer to the critical question of what happens when metals are dissolved in acids: the inflammable air, or hydrogen, that is released does not come from the metals, as the phlogiston theory taught, but from the dissociated water. The same experiments did not, and could not, persuade Cavendish of the new chemistry, since he had a reasonable explanation of the experiments in terms of phlogiston. He did not accept at face value the increase in weight of burned and calcined bodies–these bodies lost phlogiston yet gained weight–the various attempts at explaining which gave Lavoisier strong arguments for the absurdity of phlogiston. In order to build as well as destroy, Lavoisier had to work out a new understanding of chemical compounds and a new nomenclature to express it, and he had to win disciples. These things, of course, he did. His *Traité élémentaire de chemie* in 1789 would instruct the next generation of chemists in the new chemistry.[63]

Cavendish had strong feelings about the changes Lavoisier was bringing about, as we know from private remarks in a correspondence between Blagden and Cavendish when Blagden was away from London on the French and English triangulation project in 1787. The French crossed the Channel bearing antiphlogistic chemical publications including a copy for Cavendish of the new

---

62 Arthur Donovan, "Introduction," in *The Chemical Revolution: Essays in Reinterpretation*, ed. A. Donovan, ser. 2, vol. 4 of *Osiris*, published in 1988 by the History of Science Society, 5–12, on 5–6. Robert Siegfried, "The Chemical Revolution in the History of Chemistry," ibid., 34–50, on 34–35.

63 Changes that underlay the chemical revolution are summarized in William H. Brock, *The Fontana History of Chemistry* (London: Fontana, 1992), 84–85.

Méthode de nomenclature chimique written by Lavoisier and his colleagues.[64] Having looked in the book, Cavendish told Blagden that he understood that the proposal for the systematic renaming of the substances of chemistry was a move to impress the new theory on chemistry, for the language and the theory could not be separated. Nothing, Cavendish said, serves "more to rivet a theory in the minds of learners than to form all the names which they are to use upon that theory." If this precedent were to succeed, every chemist with a new theory might present it together with a new language, with the result that no one could understand what was being said without learning the theory. Moreover, every experimental advance in chemical composition would be followed by renaming. A systematic nomenclature did not lead to clarity, as the proposers believed, but to "confusion," a "great mischief." Because traditional names of chemical substances had no connection with their composition, no bias was built into them. Cavendish was not opposed to naming uncommon neutral salts by the names of their components because there were so many of them. Apologizing to Blagden for this uncharacteristic "long sermon" on the "present rage of name-making," Cavendish said that he did not believe that the nomenclature would take hold in any case. It was only a "fashion," a word Cavendish used three times in his "sermon."[65] Blagden's reaction was much the same. The authors of the chemical nomenclature had been seduced by the Linnean natural history, Blagden wrote to Cavendish, a false analogy. The objects studied by natural history remained the same over long periods, but in chemistry discoveries came so rapidly that names would have to change constantly. Like Cavendish, Blagden saw "little danger that the systematic names will be adopted."[66] Cavendish and Blagden were typical of British scientists in their response to the nomenclature. In addition to rational arguments like those Cavendish gave to Blagden, there was a kind of British bluffness about the insistence on familiar language in chemistry. Soon after the nomenclature, another good French idea, the metric system, was proposed, which prompted Cavendish's scientific friend George Shuckburgh to appeal to British "good sense" and "preserve, with the measures, the language of their forefathers": he would "call a yard a yard and a pound a pound."[67]

What is striking about the exchange between Cavendish and Blagden over the nomenclature is that their dissatisfaction with the new chemistry was

[64] From Dover, Blagden wrote to Cavendish in London that he had the book and would hold it if Cavendish planned to join him or forward it to Banks's where Cavendish could pick it up. Because of foul weather, Cavendish did not go to Dover, with the result that he and Blagden discussed the nomenclature by letter. Charles Blagden to Henry Cavendish, 16 Sep. 1787, Cavendish Mss X(b), 13. Charles Blagden to Claude Louis Berthollet, 17 Nov. 1787, draft, Blagden Letters, Royal Society, 7:85. Henry Cavendish to Charles Blagden, n.d. [Sep. 1787], draft, Cavendish Mss Misc.; *Sci.Pap.* 2:324–26.

[65] Cavendish to Blagden, [Sep. 1787].

[66] Charles Blagden to Henry Cavendish, 23 Sep. 1787, Cavendish Mss X(b), 14.

[67] The quotations from George Shuckburgh in 1798 are given in Kisch, *Scales and Weights,* 19.

79. *Joseph Black. Raeburn, pinx. Dean, sculp. Courtesy of the Smith Image Collection, Van Pelt-Dietrich Library, University of Pennsylvania.*

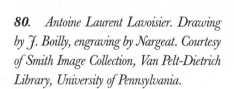

80. *Antoine Laurent Lavoisier. Drawing by J. Boilly, engraving by Nargeat. Courtesy of Smith Image Collection, Van Pelt-Dietrich Library, University of Pennsylvania.*

81. *Joseph Priestley. Leeds portrait of Priestley around 1765. Courtesy of Smith Image Collection, Van Pelt-Dietrich Library, University of Pennsylvania.*

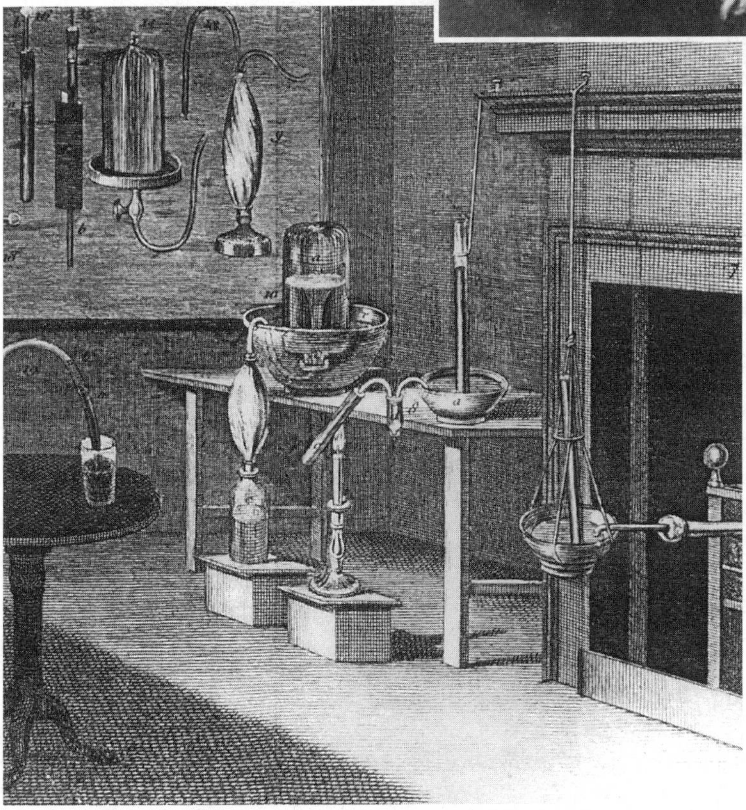

82. Priestley's Chemical and Electrical Apparatus. From Priestley, Experiments and Observations on Air*, vol. 1, 1774. On the right is a clay pipe luted to a gunbarrel for producing inflammable air from chalk.*

83. Karl Wilhelm Scheele. Engraving. Courtesy of Smith Image Collection, Van Pelt-Dietrich Library, University of Pennsylvania.

84. Scheele's Laboratory. Photograph of woodcut by W. Kreuter, Deutsches Museum. Courtesy of Smith Image Collection, Van Pelt-Dietrich Library, University of Pennsylvania.

directed solely at systematic naming and not at all, at least explicitly, at the content of the theory it expressed. Cavendish not only did not oppose systematic chemistry, he insisted on it; whether chemistry had much or little system was a matter of interpretation,[68] but a chemistry that was without internal connectedness would have held no interest for Cavendish. That phlogistic chemistry was a useful "system" was evident to the chemists working within it, as it was to one who had just abandoned it in favor of Lavoisier's new system, L. B. Guyton de Morveau. To Kirwan, an upholder of phlogiston, who had strong theoretical ideas in chemistry, Guyton wrote that until Lavoisier's, Kirwan's "system" was "without doubt both the most scientific and the most ingenious that has been proposed."[69] Cavendish disagreed with some of Kirwan's ideas but not because they were systematic. The kind of system that Cavendish opposed was systematic naming, where it seemed to prejudice the theoretical questions. Other proposals of chemical nomenclature and shorthands around this same time were met with skepticism by Blagden and, we assume, by Cavendish.[70] The fate of phlogistic chemistry did not seem to be the issue with Cavendish. Blagden told Cavendish that Lavoisier had "ably combated the arguments of the phlogistic chemists" who had reported on the nomenclature,[71] as if Blagden excluded Cavendish from the phlogistic chemists, as perhaps he did. Blagden and Berthollet had been in regular correspondence as representatives of their national societies, and by 1785 Berthollet was an antiphlogistonist. That year Blagden wrote to Berthollet that the English had not yet "given up" on phlogiston; he mentioned its warm advocacy by Kirwan, and he explained that "it belongs to the temper & character of the philosophers of this country" to retain a familiar hypothesis "as long as they can explain the phenomena upon it." Of recent work in France, Blagden wrote to Priestley, "I will not say [it] *overturns* the doctrines of ph^{n} but shakes it to its very foundations." With Cavendish, phlogiston was a "doubtful point." Whether the "old hypothesis of p" is right or Lavoisier's that dephlogisticated air is a "simple substance," Blagden told Berthollet, is a "question which I think cannot remain long undecided."[72] To

---

68 William Nicholson thought that chemistry still had "little system," which justified another dictionary of chemistry after Macquer's. Nicholson, *A Dictionary of Chemistry, Exhibiting the Present State of the Theory and Practice of That Science . . .*, 2 vols. in 1 (London, 1795) 1:v.

69 This passage from Guyton's letter is translated by the editors of *A Scientific Correspondence During the Chemical Revolution: Louis-Bernard Guyton de Morveau and Richard Kirwan, 1782–1802*, ed. E. Grison, M. Sadoun-Goupil, and P. Bret (Berkeley: Office for History of Science and Technology, University of California at Berkeley, 1994), 33.

70 "Dr Black has just made a new chl nomenclature: I think he might have been better employed"; J.-H. Hassenfratz's chemical shorthand was thought to serve no "useful purpose" in England; and James Watt risked his reputation with his chemical algebra. Charles Blagden to M.-A. Pictet, 12 Feb. 1790, draft, and James Watt, 6 Dec. 1788, draft, Blagden Letterbook, Royal Society, 7:402 and 7:185.

71 Blagden to Cavendish, 23 Sep. 1787.

72 Charles Blagden to Claude Louis Berthollet, 21 and 24 May and 28 June 1785, draft, Blagden Letterbook, Yale.

William Cullen, Blagden wrote about the "question now warmly agitated relative to the existence of phlogiston"; "whichever of the two systems, Stahl's or Lavoisier's," was adopted, however, Cavendish's experimental work was of equal importance in either.[73] Following Cavendish's lead in 1784, when describing Cavendish's work to others, Blagden gave both explanations, the old and the new. In 1787, in the same letter in which he acknowledged receipt of the *Nomenclature chimique*, Blagden told Berthollet that his memoirs had answered the "principal objections made by the supporters of the old doctrine of phlogiston." The arguments of the new chemistry were so much clearer than those of phlogistic chemistry that the "combat must soon be at an end."[74] In these letters written at the turning point of the chemical revolution, Blagden was expressing his own opinion, but we wonder to what degree, if any, it was in opposition to the opinion of the chemist he worked with daily, Cavendish.

In late 1787, Cavendish was busy disseminating the new chemistry in London. Having received a bundle of Berthollet's antiphlogistic memoirs sent over with the *Nomenclature chimique*, Cavendish dispersed the publications to the "difft gentl for whom they were intended," himself included, "all in the best manner he was able."[75] If Kirwan is to be believed, by the time of the new chemical nomenclature, Cavendish had already given up the old chemistry. In a postscript to a letter to one of the authors of the *Nomenclature chimique*, Guyton de Morveau, Kirwan wrote that "Mr Cavendish has renounced phlogiston." Kirwan did not give his source or elaborate, but what he said is consistent with what Blagden had been saying to and about Cavendish. The date was 2 April 1787, only a few weeks after Marum had told Lavoisier that he rejected phlogiston. Cavendish and Marum were evidently the first two scientists outside of France to abandon the old chemistry,[76] but there would soon be many. The Jacksonian professor at Cambridge, Isaac Milner, saw the handwriting on the wall; in his final lecture, in 1788, he discussed Lavoisier's experiments and commented that the "antient hypothesis of Phlogiston seems overturned at one Stroke, and a new and simple theory substituted in its

---

[73] Charles Blagden to William Cullen, 5 July 1785, draft, Blagden Letterbook, Yale.

[74] Charles Blagden to Claude Louis Berthollet, 17 Nov. 1787, draft, Blagden Letters, Royal Society, 7:85.

[75] Blagden to Berthollet, 17 Nov. 1787.

[76] If, as Kirwan said, Cavendish gave up phlogiston, we still do not know his views on Lavoisier's theory other than for the reservations he referred to at the end of his paper "Experiments on Air." We do, however, know Marum's. To Lavoisier on 26 Feb. 1787, Marum wrote that he had "adopted almost entirely your theory, having rejected phlogiston, which I regard at present as an insufficient and useless hypothesis." To Kirwan on 13 Dec. 1787, Guyton de Morveau wrote: "You know that M. Van Marum has decomposed water by electricity, repeated the experiment with nitrous acid of M. Cavendish, and that he has also abandoned phlogiston." Marum's letter to Lavoisier of 26 Feb. 1787 is quoted, p. 175, n. 8, and Kirwan's letter to Guyton of 2 Apr. 1787 and Guyton's to Kirwan of 13 Dec. 1787 are published, pp. 165–67 and 171–77, in *A Scientific Correspondence During the Chemical Revolution.*

place–a Theory founded on direct and satisfactory Experiments."[77] In 1788–89 the major exponents of the new antiphlogistic chemistry in France were elected as foreign members of the Royal Society. Cavendish signed their certificates, and in the case of the preeminent chemist among them, Lavoisier, Cavendish was the *first* to sign.[78]

In 1788 an English translation of the new nomenclature came out, but its adoption by users of that language was relatively slow, given the British reluctance to use French words or their anglicized versions and, in some cases, to part with phlogiston chemistry. In his treatise on chemistry in 1790, William Nicholson judged the phlogiston and antiphlogiston hypotheses as equally probable; in his dictionary of chemistry in 1795 he said that he regarded the antiphlogistic hypothesis as the most probable, but he did not use the new nomenclature because he did not want to "anticipate the public choice." Priestley never adopted the new language or gave up phlogiston. Black soon gave it up, but he accepted the new language only selectively and invented a partially new one of his own. In the 1790s, however, the French nomenclature was commonly used in Edinburgh and in London.[79] In a letter in 1794 Blagden spoke of Thomas Beddoes's apparatus and the "dephlogisticated dog" inside it; he crossed out "dephlogisticated" and wrote instead "oxygenated." Scientifically correct speech had to be practiced.[80] Late in life, Cavendish used Lavoisier's new names on occasion.[81]

WATER CONTROVERSY

The "water controversy" was a priority dispute arising from the following events. In 1781, as we have seen, Cavendish repeated Warltire's experiment on the electrical detonation of inflammable and dephlogisticated airs, determining that the resulting dew was pure water. He informed Priestley, who repeated the experiments and reported them to Watt. In a letter that circulated among members of the Royal Society, Watt gave his interpretation of the experiments. Hearing about Cavendish's experiments and Watt's conclusions from Blagden on a

---

77 L. J. M. Coleby, "Isaac Milner and the Jacksonian Chair of Natural Philosophy," *Annals of Science* 10 (1954): 234–57, on 256.

78 Royal Society, Certificates, 5 (3 Apr. 1788).

79 William Nicholson, *The First Principles of Chemistry* (London, 1790), viii. Nicholson, *Dictionary of Chemistry*, vii. Maurice Crosland, *Historical Studies in the Language of Chemistry* (London: Heinemann, 1962), 193–206.

80 Charles Blagden to Georgiana, duchess of Devonshire, 4 Jan. 1794, Devon. Coll.

81 In computations made probably around 1800, Cavendish used "hydrogen" and "oxygen": Henry Cavendish, "Experiments on Air," Cavendish Mss II, 5:390. In a letter to Blagden about a paper by Humboldt on the eudiometer, Cavendish used Lavoisier's name for phlogisticated air (our nitrogen) "azote." This was in 1798, some ten years after his fulminations against Lavoisier's new chemical nomenclature. Henry Cavendish to Charles Blagden, 18 Dec. [1798], Blagden Papers, Royal Society.

trip to Paris in 1783, Lavoisier promptly did experiments of his own and wrote up an account of them.[82]

Then, in 1784, Cavendish published the paper in which he identified the product of the explosion of the two airs with water. Cavendish, Watt, and Lavoisier, the principals in the water controversy, had different interpretations of the experiments. If the water controversy had been about these differences, it would have been a controversy of the usual kind in science, but this one was about character.

The Swiss scientist Jean André Deluc, who had been living in England for ten years, was in Paris at the time Cavendish's paper on air and water was read in London, but he heard about it, and when he returned he asked Cavendish for a copy of the manuscript to read. Deluc then wrote to his friend Watt that Cavendish had put forward his "system, word for word," without mentioning Watt. Cavendish, Deluc told Watt, was a plagiarist. Watt, who already believed the worst of Lavoisier, accepted Deluc's judgment about Cavendish.

By not revealing all of what Blagden had told him of Cavendish's and Watt's work, Lavoisier also laid himself open to the charge of plagiarism. Appalled by Lavoisier's representation of Cavendish's work, Blagden took a variety of measures, public and private, to set matters right. Lavoisier stood corrected; after all he did not covet a discovery so much as all of chemistry, and the experiments on water had told him how to get it.[83]

The passion behind the water controversy was decidedly Watt's. He told Deluc that he did not depend on the favor of "Mr. C: or his friends; and could despise the united power of *the illustrious house of Cavendish*, as Mr. Fox calls them."[84] Cavendish was a rich man with a mean spirit, Watt wrote to another correspondent.[85] When Watt saw Cavendish's paper he recognized that their theories were different. In 1785, Watt and Cavendish met in Birmingham, where they discussed steam engines, a subject on which Watt and not Cavendish was the principal authority. That year Cavendish recommended Watt for fellowship in the Royal Society, his name appearing third after Smeaton's and Priestley's in the long list of Watt's supporters. Clearly

[82] The day after Lavoisier repeated Cavendish's experiments, Blagden wrote to Banks that Lavoisier had done so. He said that Lavoisier had Blagden's account of it from Priestley's paper and Cavendish's verbal information. Letter of 25 June 1783, copy, BM(NH), DTC 3:184–86. It seems that word of Priestley's experiments had already reached Paris. Henry Guerlac, "Lavoisier, Antoine-Laurent," *DSB* 8:66–91, on 78.

[83] Our main source here is George Wilson, *The Life of the Honourable Henry Cavendish* (London, 1851), a book primarily about the water controversy. Two later papers on the subject we have also consulted: Sidney M. Edelstein, "Priestley Settles the Water Controversy," *Chymia* 1 (1948): 123–37; Robert E. Schofield, "Still More on the Water Controversy," ibid., 9 (1964): 71–76. Jean André Deluc to James Watt, 1 Mar. 1784, in *Correspondence of the Late James Watt on His Discovery of the Theory of the Composition of Water*, ed. J. P. Muirhead (London, 1846), 42–43.

[84] Jean André Deluc to James Watt, 1 Mar. 1784, in *Correspondence of the Late James Watt*, 48–49.

[85] James Watt to Jean André Deluc, 6 Mar. 1784; James Watt to Mr. Fry of Bristol, 15 May 1784, *Correspondence of the Late James Watt*, 48, 61.

85. *James Watt. Painting by Sir William Beechey, drawing by W. Evans, and engraving by C. Picart. Courtesy of Smith Image Collection, Van Pelt-Dietrich Library, University of Pennsylvania.*

by then there were no lasting hard feelings, certainly not on Cavendish's part.[86]

Much of the controversy revolved around datings of experiments and publications. The datings were genuinely tangled, as this brief summary will show. Soon after Warltire's experiments on the ponderability of heat were published, Cavendish began his experiments on the production of water from the explosion of two airs. Before 26 March 1783 his experiments were communicated to Priestley, and before 24 June they were communicated to Lavoisier. But his experiments were only read to the Royal Society on 15 January 1784. Watt and Lavoisier did their researches later than Cavendish, but since they made their views known earlier, in 1783, they appeared, as Wilson said, "with a *primâ facie* character of priority to him [Cavendish], as claimants of the disputed discovery."[87]

The troublemaker in all of this was Deluc, whose motives are unclear, particularly in light of his long association with Cavendish. When for financial reasons, Deluc left his native Switzerland to settle in England, Cavendish promptly brought him as his guest to a meeting of the Royal Society, a month before his election.[88] Thereafter he and Deluc served together in the Society, performed experiments together, corresponded, and disagreed civilly. Like Deluc, Blagden had a role in the water controversy not as a claimant to the discovery but as an intermediary between the persons who were. As Deluc's complicity was built into his close relationship with Watt, Blagden's was with Cavendish. Blagden's known association with Cavendish was his scientific passport, while at the same time his zealous regard for the reputation of Cavendish made him vulnerable. Latter-day champions of Watt made Blagden a scapegoat, but he was guilty not of the unfairness and venality with which he was charged but only of neglect of his own better interests. Nor was Cavendish guilty of exploiting Blagden's dependent position to get him to commit fraud on his behalf. Priestley was an innocent party in all of this. But with the remote exception of Deluc, there was no malice

86 Royal Society, Certificates, 5 (24 Nov. 1785).

87 Wilson, *Cavendish*, 60–61.

88 Royal Society, JB 28:132 (13 May 1773).

on the part of anyone. When the steps leading to the dispute are examined one by one, as has been done by Wilson and others, this conclusion seems inescapable to us: the basic cause of this "controversy," as distinguished from a scientific disagreement, was the casual way scientific information was communicated in the eighteenth century. The discovery of the nature of water was timely, and the stakes were high, so that otherwise tolerable exchanges by letters, conversations, visits, and meetings, with their indifferent datings, could, with proper incitement, seem darkly suspicious. As it turned out, precisely because there was also disagreement of the usual kind, different interpretations of the same experiments, there was glory to go around.

A second water controversy arose long after the participants in the first were dead. It was prompted by the secretary of the French Academy D. F. J. Arago, who in his *éloge* of Watt asserted that Priestley was the first person to prove that air could be converted into water and that Watt was the first person to understand it.[89] The consequent furor initiated by Harcourt's presidential address at the British Association meeting in 1839 was sustained by a passion of another kind, nationalism. Since the revived controversy was the occasion for Cavendish's unpublished scientific work to begin to be made public, it had that value if perhaps no other.

KEEPING UP WITH CHEMISTRY

In 1784 the German chemist Lorenz Crell launched the *Chemische Annalen*, a monthly journal that replaced the quarterly one he had been editing. Cavendish took evident interest in this journal, which had the support of German chemists and favored, as he still did, the phlogistic approach to chemistry. Cavendish was soon in touch with the editor about subscriptions. It was no simple matter to obtain foreign journals in England in the eighteenth century, as Cavendish's negotiations with Crell bear out.

As a result of the water controversy, Cavendish and the *Chemische Annalen* had gotten off on the wrong foot. Crell published two accounts of the discovery concerning air and water in which Lavoisier was named the discoverer and Cavendish the confirmer. For more information about Cavendish's work, Crell wrote to Banks, who passed the letter to Blagden. The latter replied to Crell with a "short history of the discovery," setting Crell straight by correcting the claims of Lavoisier, who had "suppressed part of the truth." Blagden complimented Crell on the quick publication of translated extracts from Cavendish's paper containing the true discovery and for Crell's correct dating of the paper, 1784, instead of 1783, as the separately printed cover of the paper had erroneously put it. In a note printed with the extracts, Crell graciously acknowledged that he was under an obligation to Cavendish because he, like

[89] As Vernon Harcourt summarized Arago's case, in his Presidential Address, *British Association Report* (1839), pp. 3–45, on p. 15.

others, had made an "error," ascribing the discovery of the production of water to Lavoisier, whereas the "*first Discovery*" belonged to Cavendish. This initial letter from Blagden to Crell included the latest scientific news from Britain, meant to entice Crell to join in a regular scientific exchange between the two countries.[90]

Crell proposed publishing Blagden's short history of Cavendish's discovery, and although Blagden had not intended it for the public, he had no objection, since it was "strictly true." He only hoped that Crell's German translation of it would rather "soften than strengthen the expressions," since however poorly Lavoisier had behaved in this affair, he was "upon the whole a very respectable character & eminent as a philosopher." In keeping with his invitation to Crell, Blagden enclosed scientific news, which had to do with "Mr Cavendish, whose name I shall so often have occasion to mention in this correspondence," but this time it had to do with Cavendish's new work on the freezing of mercury rather than the history of his old work.[91]

The German chemist knew something about Cavendish's rank but little about English titles. "The Honourable Henry Cavendish (not My Lord)," Blagden corrected him, "desires to become one of your subscribers." To this end, Blagden said, Cavendish had given directions to the post office to ensure that he received the journal promptly.[92]

Six months later, Blagden wrote to Crell that the postmaster at Amsterdam had told him that some of Crell's packets were held up because of their large size and were probably irrecoverable. This trouble could have been anticipated, since Banks had gone through it with Crell the year before.[93] Crell had sent the material not by post but by stagecoach or wagon, Blagden said, conveyances which were not "connected with but in opposition to the Post." When Cavendish succeeded in receiving a few issues of the *Chemische Annalen* and its supplement, the *Beiträge*, by post, Blagden instructed Crell to send Cavendish the rest by post as well. However, when after three months the remaining issues had not yet arrived in London, Blagden complained to the post office and then to Crell: "Mr Cavendish pays many times the original value of the work to have it in this manner quick by the post; but the various delays have entirely frustrated that

[90] Among Cavendish's manuscripts is a translation into English, not in Cavendish's hand, of Crell's translation into German of extracts from Cavendish's paper of 1784, with Crell's retraction of his earlier error, "Translation from Mr. L. Crell's Chemical Annals, 1785. part 4. p. 324." Charles Blagden to Lorenz Crell, 28 Apr. 1785, draft, Blagden Letterbook, Yale. Blagden's letter, in English, clarifying the discovery to Crell was translated into German by Crell and translated back into English by Wilson, *Cavendish*, 362–63. Wilson's translation was reproduced by A. J. Berry, *Henry Cavendish: His Life and Scientific Work* (London: Hutchinson, 1960), 81–82.

[91] Charles Blagden to Lorenz Crell, 2 Dec. 1785, draft, Blagden Letters, Royal Society, 7:738.

[92] Charles Blagden to Lorenz Crell, 20 Jan. 1786, draft, Blagden Letterbook, Royal Society, 7:742.

[93] Lorenz Crell to Sir Joseph Banks, [1785], 17 Dec. 1785, 1 May 1786, 4 Mar. 1790, BL Add Mss 8096:69–70, 239–40, 284–85, and 8097:296–97.

object."[94] The post office proved not to be a better way. Two years later the business of delivery was at last settled and the correspondence on that subject ended: "Mr Cavendish finds it more convenient to get the Ch. Annalen," Blagden wrote to Crell, "in the common way, tho' a little later, than to be perplexed with the post office; he . . . will not give you any further trouble on the subject."[95]

There were other complications, for example, the matter of payment for the subscription, of how much and to whom, and Blagden told Crell to send directions and to appoint some person to collect Cavendish's money. Kirwan wanted to subscribe as did Banks, and the journal could not be sent to everyone "through the same channel under one cover." In addition to the journal, there were other publications by Crell that Cavendish wanted: from his German bookseller, Cavendish had ordered Crell's *Auswahl aus den neuen Entdeckungen*, but the bookseller had disappointed him. Crell offered to copy out the material Cavendish wanted, but Cavendish wanted the entire volumes.[96]

To convey scientific publications from Britain to Germany was no simpler. Blagden sent a copy of Cavendish's latest paper to Crell in a packet, which he gave to William Herschel, who was going to Göttingen to erect one of his telescopes. From Göttingen, Herschel forwarded the packet by the nearest conveyance to Helmstadt, where Crell picked it up. Blagden apologized to Crell: "It is extremely difficult to get an opportunity of sending you any thing from England, otherwise you should be furnished sooner with such publications."[97]

The business of Cavendish and Crell was not unrelieved frustration. Cavendish thanked Crell for offering "the Old Hock," and Blagden assured Crell that "we shall endeavour to form such a party of gentlemen as would be required."[98]

EXACTITUDE

After Cavendish's first chemical paper, on factitious air, was read to the Royal Society, thanks were returned to him for his "Accurate paper."[99] In the year he published his last chemical paper, a chemist referred to him as "that most accurate philosopher."[100] Throughout his career, he addressed every problem with

[94] Charles Blagden to Lorenz Crell, 4 July, 12 Aug., and 13 Oct. 1786, drafts; Charles Blagden to Charles Jackson at the post office, 10 Oct. 1786, Blagden Letters, Royal Society, 7:7, 26, 44, and 45. By 4 July, Cavendish had received the first and second issues of the *Annalen* and the fourth issue of volume 1 of the *Beiträge*. On 6 August, he was still waiting for the third through sixth issues of the *Annalen* and the first through the third issues of volume 1 of the *Beiträge*.

[95] Charles Blagden to Lorenz Crell, 4 Apr. 1788, draft, Blagden Letters, Royal Society, 7:137.

[96] Blagden to Crell, 4 July and 12 Aug. 1786.

[97] Blagden to Crell, 4 July 1786.

[98] Charles Blagden to Lorenz Crell, [1786], Yale.

[99] 6 Nov. 1766, Royal Society, JB 25:927

[100] From Kier to Priestley, 26 Mar. 1788, quoted in Priestley, "Additional Experiments and Observations Relating to the Principle of Acidity, the Decomposition of Water, and Phlogiston," *PT* 78 (1788): 313–30, on 327.

"patient industry" and "acute discernment," reluctant to give an opinion on the problem until he had "studied it to the bottom."[101]

Before Lavoisier's "new chemistry" was generally accepted, there was already a new chemistry, which owed considerably to Cavendish. We give an example. When John Hadley left Cambridge to practice medicine in London in 1760, he did not give up his chair, perhaps intending to return. When he died unexpectedly in 1764 and the chair again became available, the person elected to it that year was Robert Smith's protégé Richard Watson. Having placed second wrangler in 1759 and now a fellow of Trinity, Watson's main qualification as professor of chemistry was his willingness to take the impecunious position. He readily conceded that he knew nothing about chemistry, but with the help of an "operator" brought from Paris, he worked hard to learn, and he was soon giving experimental lectures, teaching students privately, and working in his own laboratory, well on his way to becoming a "very competent chemist."[102] His lecturing began in the same year as Cavendish's first published paper, on factitious air, and his approach to chemistry was clearly influenced by the quantitative, physical methods reported in that paper. His *Plan of a Course of Chemical Lectures* makes the connection with Cavendish explicit. He published a number of credible papers in the *Philosophical Transactions*, but about then his life took a more practical turn. In 1771 he was appointed regius professor of divinity with a good income. He became well known as the author of religious works, and although he continued to publish on chemistry too, it was in a popular vein.[103] To a bright, young person like Watson taking up chemistry in the 1760s, the promising direction could be seen as the chemistry of quantitative exactness, as exemplified by Cavendish's work. This was the new chemistry.

Key to Cavendish's success in obtaining accurate results in chemical experiments was his thorough understanding of instruments, which in turn rested upon his mastery of the scientific principles underlying them. For its logogram, the Cavendish Society selected a glass vessel used for synthesizing water from gases.[104] In keeping with its name, the Society might well have chosen another apparatus or instrument: although it lacked the urn-like simple beauty or the controversial relevance of the water vessel, the air pump would have served the purpose. In his experiments on phlogisticated air and nitrous acid, Cavendish needed the best vacuum he

[101] Thomson, *History of Chemistry* 1:339, 345.

[102] J. R. Partington, *A History of Chemistry*, vol. 2 (New York: St. Martin's Press, 1961), 765.

[103] L. J. M. Coleby, "Richard Watson, Professor of Chemistry in the University of Cambridge, 1764–71," *Annals of Science* 9 (1953): 101–23, on 102–7, 121–22. Between 1781 and 1785, Watson published his elementary, popular, and very successful *Chemical Essays* in five volumes. Blagden judged Watson's essays "pleasant, but perfectly flimsy." Charles Blagden to Sir Joseph Banks, 10 Sep. 1784, Correspondence of Sir Joseph Banks, Kew, D 204.

[104] The logogram was of a pear-shaped instrument used for teaching purposes at the time of the publishing society, not of Cavendish's time; Cavendish used a glass globe. Wilson, *Cavendish*, 42. Farrar, "A Note on a Eudiometer Supposed to Have Belonged to Henry Cavendish."

could get, thus a good air pump. His knowledge of the physical principles of the instrument is illustrated by the advice he gave on how to operate it. John Smeaton claimed that his improved air pump gave a rarefaction of 1,000 or 2,000 times instead of the previous limit of under 150. Implicit confidence was placed in his claim until the instrument-maker Edward Nairne discovered a fallacy, to which he was led after obtaining incredible rarefactions of 100,000. By making comparisons with other standard gauges, Nairne saw that the error lay in Smeaton's new gauge–a pear-shaped bulb holding mercury–but Nairne did not know the reason for it. He performed an experiment with the air pump before Smeaton and other interested Fellows of the Royal Society, Cavendish among them. Cavendish explained that the discrepancy was due to water vapor. To get the gauges to agree, he said, the pump must be as free as possible of all traces of water, since Smeaton's gauge did not measure vapor pressure in addition to the air pressure as other gauges did. When Nairne took this precaution, the gauges agreed, and the rarefaction proved to be a believable 600. Cavendish's explanation rested on his father's experiments, which showed that whenever the pressure of the atmosphere on water is reduced to a certain level (which depends on temperature), the water is immediately turned into vapor and is as immediately turned back into water upon restoring the pressure. This change of state affected Smeaton's gauge but not the others.[105] Cavendish's understanding of the physical principles affecting the gage is further shown by his response to a person who doubted his explanation of the erroneous rarefactions. "The objection your friend makes to my manner of accounting for the difference of the 2 gages is a very sensible one & if it were not for a circumstance which I forgot to mention would I believe prevent any more air from being drawn out of the receiver after it was so much exhausted as to be filled chiefly with vapour. This is that while any air is left in the receiver the pressure therein will be greater than if it contained only the vapour of water."[106] The circumstance Cavendish forgot to mention was the principle of partial pressures, which he used in various calculations, but which would only become generally known in the next century with the work of John Dalton.[107]

Another instrument the Cavendish Society could have chosen for its logogram was the float thermometer. As an auxiliary instrument used by Cavendish to calibrate another instrument, his register thermometer, it would have symbolized his exacting methods, and the elegant beauty of its glasswork would have made it an attractive ornament.[108] Or the Society might have chosen the register thermometer itself or almost any other thermometer, the

[105] This clarification of the air pump occurred in 1776. It was described by Nairne in a paper and by Charles Hutton in his entry "Air" in *Mathematical and Philosophical Dictionary*, vol. 1 (London, 1795), 56–57.

[106] The person Cavendish was addressing is not named. Cavendish Mss IV, 4.

[107] S. A. Dyment, "Some Eighteenth Century Ideas Concerning Aqueous Vapour and Evaporation," *Annals of Science* 2 (1937): 465–73, on 473.

[108] Cavendish, *Sci. Pap.* 2:397.

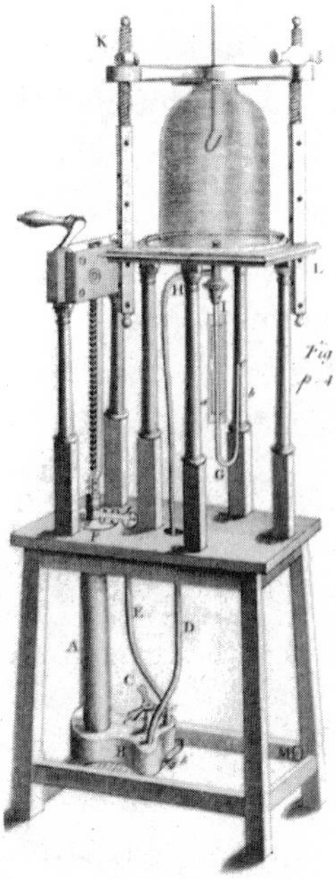

86. Smeaton's Air-Pump. Left-hand figure shows A barrel, B cistern, C handle of cock, D pipe communicating from cock to receiver, E pipe between cock and valve, GI siphon gage. Right-hand figure shows the new gage, the workings of which Cavendish explained on the basis of his father's experiment. The new gage, which Smeaton called the "pear-gage," is a glass holding about a half pound of mercury, held by the brass piece DE, open at A; the graduated tube BC is closed at C. During the exhausting of the receiver, the gage is suspended in it. When the pumping is done, the gage is lowered so that its open end is immersed in a cistern of mercury. The air is then let in, driving the mercury into the gage until the air remaining in it is of the same density as the external air. The rarefaction of the air in the receiver can then be read off from the number of divisions occupied by the air at the top. Cavendish noted that the air trapped in the gage contains water vapor; compressed by the mercury, the vapor at a certain point is turned into liquid water, eliminating the partial vapor pressure and thus allowing readings of unprecedented rarefactions. In other gages of the time, this phenomenon did not occur. The gage is described by its inventor, John Smeaton, "A Letter . . . to Mr. John Ellicott, F.R.S. Concerning Some Improvements Made by Himself in the Air-Pump," Philosophical Transactions *47 (1752): 415–28, on 421; illustration of the air-pump opposite 424. Cavendish's analysis of the pear-gage is given by Edward Nairne,* Philosophical Transactions *67 (1777): 622.*

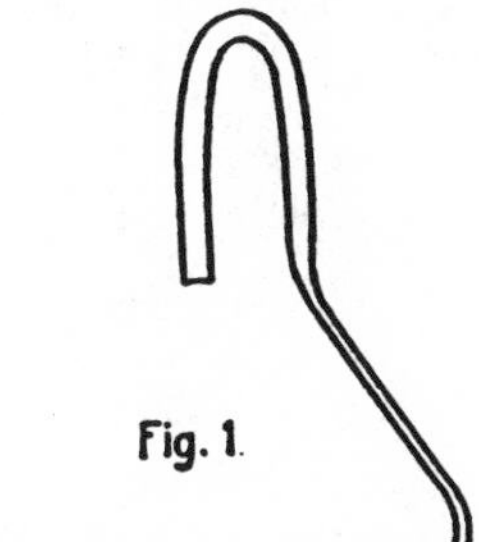

Fig. 1.

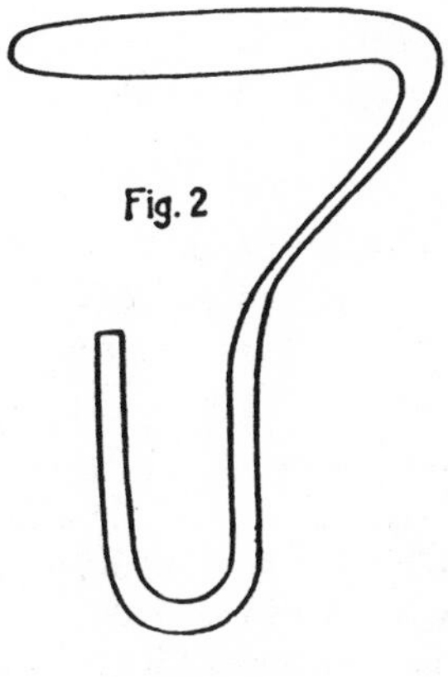

Fig. 2

87. Float Thermometer. This instrument is filled with alcohol with some mercury in the legs; it was used by Cavendish to calibrate his register thermometer; illustration 43. The drawing of the float thermometer from Cavendish's Scientific Manuscripts is reproduced in Cavendish, Scientific Papers *2:397.*

instrument to which Cavendish devoted most attention. When his instrument collection was put up for sale in 1816, it still contained forty-four thermometers.[109] But we think that the logogram best typifying Cavendish's exactness in chemistry would have been the instrument of weighing, the balance. As Blagden said, "quantities can be determined to much greater exactness by weight than by any practicable way of measurement."[110] The determination of weights, William Nicholson wrote, was "half the business of a chemist." We have mentioned that Cavendish owned the first of the great precision balances of the eighteenth century.[111] Built to Cavendish's plan, the balance was housed in a rough wooden case standing about ten feet tall. The beam, made of sheet iron 19½ inches long, was supported by steel knife edges rotating on steel planes, and it was raised and lowered by V-shaped brass supports at the two ends; suspended from the beam by brass universal joints were the weighing pans, measuring about a foot across and placed about two feet beneath the beam. The balance was capable of weighing to an accuracy of five milligrams.[112] It is not dated but the instrument-maker's name is known to be "Harrison," who may have been the John Harrison of chronometer fame, but more likely he was William Harrison, whom Cavendish employed as his private instrument-maker in his later years. The one other great precision balance in Britain, owned by the Royal Society, was built by Jesse Ramsden, under whom Cavendish's instrument-maker, Harrison, had worked.[113] Cavendish's biographer Wilson singled out Cavendish's weighing as the one certainty among the debated events of the "water controversy": "Whatever, then, is doubtful in the Water Controversy, this at least is certain, that Cavendish was the first who observed that when given weights of hydrogen and oxygen are burned together in certain proportions, they are replaced by the same weight of pure water."[114]

When Lavoisier learned of Cavendish's experiments on water, he made his own with the assistance of the great mathematical astronomer P. S. Laplace. So

---

[109] *A Catalogue of Sundry Very Curious and Valuable Mathematical, Philosophical, and Optical Instruments . . . Which Will Be Sold by Auction . . . on Saturday the Fifteenth of June 1816, at Twelve O'clock*, Devon. Coll.

[110] Charles Blagden, "Report on the Best Method of Proportioning the Excise upon Spirituous Liquors," *PT* 80 (1790): 321–45, on 325.

[111] William Nicholson, in his translation of notes by French chemists to the French edition of Richard Kirwan, *An Essay on Phlogiston, and the Constitution of Acids*, new ed. (London, 1789), viii. Maurice Daumas, *Scientific Instruments of the Seventeenth and Eighteenth Centuries*, trans. M. Holbrook (New York: Praeger, 1972), 134–35, 221–23.

[112] Ernest Child, *The Tools of the Chemist* (New York: Reinhold, 1940), 79.

[113] From a list of Henry Cavendish's servants at his death in 1810, we know that his instrument-maker's name was William Harrison, who was sixty-one at that time. He was a source of one of the accounts of Cavendish's death, in Wilson, *Cavendish*, 183. The balances attributed to yet another Harrison, a Thomas Harrison, whom we suspect is confused with Thomas Harris. Mary Holbrook, *Science Preserved: A Directory of Scientific Instruments in Collections in the United Kingdom and Eire* (London: Her Majesty's Stationery Office, 1992), 169.

[114] Wilson, *Cavendish*, 363.

caught up did Laplace become in chemistry that Blagden inquired if what he was told was true, that Laplace "had renounced his mathematical studies, & was applying himself solidly to chemistry."[115] Owing to the balance, chemistry was a science exact enough to engage an astronomer. When he read Cavendish's paper on water, Laplace wrote to Blagden that Cavendish's experiments were "infinitely important" and made with the "precision and finesse that distinguish that excellent physicist."[116] This may be taken as a tribute from one mathematical scientist to another, both of them working in chemistry. "Possessing depth and extent of mathematical knowledge," Sir Humphry Davy said of Cavendish, "he reasoned with the caution of a geometer upon the results of his experiments."[117] The exactitude that distinguished Cavendish's work was also the direction that chemistry was taking in the late eighteenth century, at which time already about a third of chemical publications were quantitative.[118] Cavendish's lasting contribution to chemistry was the impetus he gave to the increasing accuracy of that science. (It probably seems clearer to us than it did to

88. *Chemical Balance. Belonging to Henry Cavendish. Built by "Harrison," probably Cavendish's private instrument-maker William Harrison, this instrument is the earliest of the great precision balances of the eighteenth century. Reproduced by permission of the Royal Institution of Great Britain.*

[115] Charles Blagden to Claude Louis Berthollet, 8 Dec. 1789, draft, Blagden Letterbook, Royal Society, 7:377.

[116] Pierre Simon Laplace to Charles Blagden, 7 May 1785, Blagden Letters, Royal Society, L.181.

[117] Humphry Davy, *Elements of Chemical Philosophy*, vol. 1 (London, 1812), 37.

[118] H. Gilman McCann, *Chemistry Transformed: The Paradigmatic Shift from Phlogiston to Oxygen* (Norwood: Ablex, 1978), 143–46.

Cavendish's contemporaries that his direction was in the best interests of science. British resistance to Lavoisier's antiphlogistic chemistry was partly based on distrust of his claims for quantitative accuracy and even the relevance of those claims to the disputed issues in chemistry, and as well to Lavoisier's geometric model of reasoning in chemistry.)[119]

Measurements, the meaningful and reliable recording of natural events and substances in numbers, presuppose standards. Having determined the "true" specific gravity of gold, Robert Boyle said, the weigher then had a "standard" for estimating the goodness of other specimens of gold.[120] There was another kind of "standard," the standard of practice, such as the calibration of a thermometer. Praising George Martine's reduction of the scales of fifteen thermometers to a single standard, Black envisioned a "universal language" for measuring temperature.[121] Cavendish's work on and with the eudiometer illustrated both kinds of "standards," a scale and a practice, and the use Cavendish made of the instrument also referred to a standard substance: he determined that the composition of common air was constant, the criterion of a standard. Cavendish's introduction of standards in weighing acids and alkalies by introducing equivalent weights is a good example of exactitude in his experimental practice. The concept of equivalent weights gained power with the atomic theory of chemistry, but before then it served Cavendish very well, as before Cavendish it had served others. It went back to the turn of the eighteenth century, to Wilhelm Homberg, whose most important work was his quantitative experiments on the neutralization of alkalies by acids.[122] (Homberg's method was deficient in one respect, which Cavendish's work corrected: it ignored the weight of gases absorbed and given off, as Black pointed out in his work on magnesia alba.[123] James Keir corrected Homberg's table of the equivalent weights of acids, referred to salt of tartar, with numbers he took from Cavendish's 1766 paper on factitious air.)[124] From the start of his chemical researches, Cavendish recorded equivalent weights, introducing the word "equivalent."[125] In his first publication, on factitious air, he compared the weights of different alkalies required to saturate a given quantity of acid to one thousand grains of marble, his standard; by this measure, he ranked alkalies by the quantities of fixed air they contained; where his results were not as accurate as he

[119] Golinski, *Science as Public Culture*, 130–52.

[120] Boyle, quoted in Shapin, *Truth*, 343.

[121] Golinski, *Science as Public Culture*, 47.

[122] Marie Boas Hall, "Homberg, Wilhelm or Guillaume," *DSB* 6:477–78. J. R. Partington, *A History of Chemistry*, vol. 3 (London: Macmillan, 1962), 44–45.

[123] Joseph Black, *Experiments upon Magnesia Alba, Quick-lime, and Other Alkaline Substances*, 1755 (Edinburgh: Alembic Club Reprints, No. 1, 1898), 17–18.

[124] Entry "Acid" in Macquer's *Dictionary of Chemistry*.

[125] Partington, *History of Chemistry* 3:320.

89. Standard Volume Measures for Air. There is a description of them together with a drawing in Cavendish, "An Account of a New Eudiometer," Philosophical Transactions *73 (1783): 106–35, on 128 and plate III. Cavendish said that any inaccuracies he incurred in using these volume measures were insignificant, for he determined the "exact quantity of air used by weight." The measures are in the Royal Institution. Photograph by the authors.*

desired, it was owing to the impurities of the salts he had to work with.[126] By the use of the balance, Cavendish gave to chemistry an ordering, which was one by quantity instead of by nomenclature, free from the theoretical bias he believed implicit in the latter. His equivalent weights prefigured the quantitative laws of chemistry, such as the laws of combining proportions, which belonged to the next stage in the development of chemistry. In chemistry, as in other parts of natural philosophy, Cavendish's insistence on standards gave to his work its characteristic stamp of exactitude.

In a biography, the individual inevitably stands apart. To correct for any distortion of history, we briefly return to Cavendish's world, if only to consider one aspect of it, varieties of exactitude. To chemistry Cavendish brought a marked preference for the quantitative methods of experimental physics, and although his direction did not win unanimous support, it did represent influential opinion in chemistry both in Britain and abroad. His British colleague in chemistry Richard Kirwan studied acids to "measure" the degrees of affinity between them and bases, in his opinion the foundation of "chymistry, considered as a science," to which end he expressed in "numbers" the quantity of acid taken up in the "saturation" of a base.[127] Like Cavendish and a good many other chemists, Kirwan

[126] Henry Cavendish, "Three Papers, Containing Experiments on Factitious Air," *PT* 56 (1766): 141; in *Sci. Pap.* 2:77–101, on 92–94, 96.

[127] Richard Kirwan, "Conclusion of the Experiments and Observations Concerning the Attractive Powers of the Mineral Acids," *PT* 72 (1782): 15, 34, 36, 38.

sought to introduce standards into experimental practice, proposing a method for reducing the specific gravities of bodies at various temperatures to a "common standard."[128] Another British colleague in chemistry, Joseph Black, has been characterized as not so much a chemist as a Newtonian natural philosopher of forces, who sought general laws governing the changes of state of matter by making skillful use of quantifying instruments, the balance and the thermometer.[129] To look abroad, Cavendish's French counterpart, Lavoisier, used a method in chemistry drawn from experimental physics, with its increasing reliance on instruments of quantitative measurement;[130] without measuring and weighing, Lavoisier said, "neither physics nor chemistry can any longer admit anything whatever."[131] Cavendish's closest colleagues, who by and large were not chemists, approached their work with much the same expectations of accuracy. John Michell, the closest of them all, in a brief paper on a new method of measuring longitude used the word "exactness" six times as well as related words such as "accuracy."[132] Writing to Cavendish, Michell said that he wished that there was an instrument–he proposed one–for comparing the brightness of stars, which would serve as a "standard."[133] In another paper, Michell recommended Hadley's quadrant as having a "much greater degree of precision" than any other means for surveying harbors and coastlines.[134] Michell's method of marine surveying was judged superior by Alexander Dalrymple,[135] the hydrographer and expert on instruments, who wrote to his friend Cavendish that longitude taken at sea was "exact" to one degree, an accuracy obtainable after taking the mean of many observations with a Hadley quadrant.[136] Before the Board of Longitude, Cavendish's instrument-maker Edward Nairne demonstrated dipping needles constructed according to Michell's plan, enabling the needles to be adjusted to a "great nicety."[137] Looking to discover the

[128] Richard Kirwan, "Remarks on Specific Gravities Taken at Different Degrees of Heat, and an Easy Method of Reducing Them to a Common Standard," *PT* 75 (1785): 267–71.

[129] A. L. Donovan, *Philosophical Chemistry in the Scottish Enlightenment: The Doctrines and Discoveries of William Cullen and Joseph Black* (Edinburgh: University of Edinburgh Press, 1975), 201, 215, 220–21.

[130] Arthur Donovan, *Antoine Lavoisier: Science, Administration, and Revolution* (Oxford: Blackwell, 1993), 49.

[131] Brock, *The Fontana History of Chemistry*, 117.

[132] John Michell, "Proposal of a Method for Measuring Degrees of Longitude upon Parallels of the Aequator," *PT* 56 (1766): 119–25.

[133] John Michell to Henry Cavendish, 2 July 1783, Cavendish Mss New Correspondence.

[134] John Michell, "A Recommendation of Hadley's Quadrant for Surveying, Especially the Surveying of Harbours, Together with a Particular Application of It in Some Cases of Pilotage," *PT* 55 (1765): 70–78, on 70.

[135] Alexander Dalrymple, *Essay on the Most Commodious Methods of Marine Surveying* (London, 1771), 7.

[136] Dalrymple to Cavendish, n.d. [1777], Cavendish Scientific Mss X(b), 6.

[137] Edward Nairne, "Experiments on Two Dipping-Needles, Which Dipping-Needles Were Made Agreeable to a Plan of the Reverend Mr. Mitchell, F.R.S. Rector of Thornhill in Yorkshire, and Executed for the Board of Longitude," *PT* 62 (1772): 476–80, on 477.

distances of stars by their annual parallax, Cavendish's astronomical colleague William Herschel said that "great improvements of mathematical instrument-makers have hardly left us with anything to desire," permitting measurements of one second of arc; the building of telescopes of "very great perfection" capable of realizing a precision of one second was a challenge to an improver of telescopes like himself.[138] What Cavendish's mathematical colleague Charles Hutton said of weights and measures at the end of the eighteenth century, Cavendish would have said of quantitative units used in science generally: they should be referred to a "standard," "universally the same throughout the nation, and indeed all nations."[139]

Concern with accuracy was at the same time concern with error. If Cavendish seemed preoccupied with error, he was only practicing good science as it was then done. His colleagues dealt regularly with error. Circumspection, they understood, was required of an experimenter. Experiments "rarely leave no room for doubt," William Roy wrote; different experimenters using different instruments and different methods arrive at different results, and it is "not until things have been viewed in every possible light, that the errors, even of our own experiments, are discovered."[140] They recognized the need for humility. Francis Wollaston wrote to William Herschel, "I believe we both of us have the advancement of science too much at heart to decline acknowledging an error." Errors afforded opportunity. Herschel believed that a paper by John Michell was fundamentally in error but also that it was "of the utmost importance, its being contrary to facts being a point of almost as much consequence as its agreeing with them."[141] A maxim of Dalrymple's was that "errors may lead to truth."[142] James Hutton said that errors are not grounds for skepticism; on the contrary, they "contribute for establishing the certainty of science, when these are properly corrected."[143] Cavendish incorporated error into his work by making it an object of investigation. He set about to know the truth of error and thereby contain it. He routinely took precautions to reduce, not unrealistically to eliminate, the "error of the observer," the "error of the instrument," and in general the "error of the experiment." It is within a common world of scientific endeavor in which

138 William Herschel, "Parallax of the Fixed Stars," *PT* 72 (1782): 82–111, on 82–83.

139 Charles Hutton, "Measure," in his *Mathematical and Philosophical Dictionary*, vol. 2 (London, 1796), 89–90.

140 William Roy, "Experiments and Observations Made in Britain, in Order to Obtain a Rule for Measuring Heights with the Barometer," *PT* 67 (1777): 653–770, on 653–54.

141 Francis Wollaston to William Herschel, 22 Mar. 1789, Royal Astronomical Society, Herschel Mss W 1/13, W.193. William Herschel to Samuel Vince, 15 Jan. 1784, Royal Astronomical Society, Herschel Mss W 1/1, 92–95, on 93.

142 Howard T. Fry, *Alexander Dalrymple (1737–1808) and the Expansion of British Trade* (London: Frank Cass, 1970), xiii.

143 James Hutton, *A Dissertation upon the Philosophy of Light, Heat, and Fire. In Seven Parts* (London, 1794), 6.

accuracy was highly valued, errors were examined, standards of measurements and practice were commonly introduced, and instruments were regarded as indispensable means for attaining truth that Cavendish's achievements in chemistry, as in other parts of science, are to be properly understood and evaluated.

If within that world Cavendish is still seen to stand somewhat apart, there are several reasons why. The most important was the uncommon completeness of his scientific knowledge. With his experimental and observational work, he combined skillful mathematical analysis. To understand the operations of nature, he employed "strict reasoning," which for him ideally was "strict mathematical reasoning." It followed that he brought to his researches a zeal for measurement, for the outcome of measurement and the object of mathematical reasoning were one and the same, quantity.[144] For reasoning to have substance as well as be strict, the quantity itself has to be credible, and Cavendish pioneered methods of precise experiment and observation. Here again he used strict mathematical reasoning: by analysing his measurements mathematically, he could state precisely in each investigation what was implied by his objective of "tolerable certainty."

Cavendish's exacting methods had a personal source as well: the great caution with which he approached life in general was manifested in his rigorous analysis of all of the circumstances of an experiment or observation. We tentatively suggest another source, this one social, arising from his class and his family's standing. Measurement, like coinage, has long been a trait of authority and sovereign power. Measures are legislated, and standards that secure them are kept by a central authority. Governments seek to impose uniform measures, ensuring an orderly commerce by providing all parties with a common language. Scientific organizations desire uniform measures for similar reasons. The same measures are used in the activities of civil society as are used in scientific work, and the value placed upon exactness in relation to measures affects both uses: the desirability of exactness in weighing was recognized at the same time in commerce and in science, which was the time in which Cavendish lived. As a member of the ruling class, Cavendish might be expected to have instinctively imbued his work with the common language of authority: number, weight, and measure.[145]

---

[144] Henry Miles, "An Essay on Quantity; Occasioned by Reading a Treatise, in Which Simple and Compound Ratios Are Applied to Virtue and Merit, by the Rev. Mr. Reid," *PT* 45 (1750): 505–20, on 506.

[145] Witold Kula, *Measures and Men*, trans. R. Szreter (Princeton: Princeton University Press, 1986), 18. Kisch, *Scales and Weights*, 8.

CHAPTER 5

MERCURY

COLD

Substances differ in the heat required to raise their temperature by a degree; substances also differ in the heat that they absorb or generate during a change of state, as from solid to liquid. These two facts gave rise to a vigorous experimental field in the middle of the eighteenth century. They were the subject of Cavendish's earliest experiments in heat.[1]

Adair Crawford, a contemporary of Cavendish's, explained the difficulty of performing repeatable experiments in heat: "A change in the temperature of the air in the room, a variation in the time that is employed in mixing together the substances which are to have their comparative heats determined, a difference in the shape of the vessel, or in the degree of agitation that is given to the mixture, will often produce a considerable diversity in the result of the same experiment."[2] The experimenter was faced with "a variety of adventitious circumstances, so minute as to require the most attentive observation." The subject was made to order for an experimenter of Cavendish's caution. As in his experiments in chemistry and electricity, in his experiments in heat he introduced a "standard," allowed "corrections," and took the "mean" of repeated trials. In this way, and with the help of good thermometers, he achieved, in Crawford's words, a "very near approximation to the truth."

We have seen how Cavendish's introduction to pneumatic chemistry depended on Joseph Black's work. Here again, in his introduction to heat, he was informed of Black's work at an early point. As he had his chemical researches, Cavendish wrote up his experiments on specific and latent heats for an unspecified

[1] Henry Cavendish Mss III(a), 9, untitled bundle of 117 numbered small sheets. The earliest date, 5 Feb. 1765, occurs near the end of the record.

[2] Adair Crawford, *Experiments and Observations on Animal Heat, and the Inflammation of Combustible Bodies. Being an Attempt to Resolve These Phaenomena into a General Law of Nature* (London, 1779), advertisement.

reader, "you."[3] The suggestion has been made that he did not write for publication because he did not want to enter into rivalry with Black in a field that Black had staked out for himself.[4] That may be the reason, or part of the reason, but we should note that Cavendish's first publication was in just such a field, factitious air. Rarely does significant work in science fail to bring its author into rivalries of one sort or another. There are additional reasons why Cavendish did not publish his experiments on heat. The experiments raised difficult theoretical problems, which Cavendish tried to resolve, at first without success, and by the time he succeeded, it was too late. Black included specific and latent heats in his lectures on chemistry, which became, in effect, a slow but sure publication. By the 1770s a number of Black's former students were working with his concepts. Around the same time there appeared work on the subject from abroad too, such as Johan Carl Wilcke's. In 1783 Cavendish referred to the rule of latent heat in a discussion of the freezing of water, giving neither argument nor citation, but simply remarking that it was a "circumstance now pretty well known to philosophers."[5]

Cavendish made public his experimental knowledge of heat in the same way he had his experimental knowledge of electricity, not by publishing his comprehensive experiments but by applying the knowledge he had gained from them to a specific question. In electricity it had been the shock of the torpedo; in heat it was the freezing of mercury.

Throughout the eighteenth century, experiments and observations were made on cold temperatures. In the 1720s Daniel Gabriel Fahrenheit froze water in a vacuum, and with a mixture of nitre and ice, he obtained temperatures as low as forty degrees below zero.[6] Around 1750 Lord Charles Cavendish performed experiments with freezing mixtures. In the mid-1760s his son Henry, in a continuation of his experiments on latent heats, examined the cold produced by mixing snow with various chemical reagents, reaching temperatures of around twenty degrees Fahrenheit, and in the next decade he recorded a temperature of twenty-five degrees below zero, using a mixture of snow and aqua fortis.[7]

---

[3] Henry Cavendish, "Experiments on Heat," in *The Scientific Papers of the Honourable Henry Cavendish, F.R.S.,* vol. 2: *Chemical and Dynamical,* ed. E. Thorpe (Cambridge: Cambridge University Press, 1921), 327–47.

[4] George Wilson, *The Life of the Honourable Henry Cavendish* (London, 1851), 446. Douglas McKie and Niels H. de V. Heathcote, *The Discovery of Specific and Latent Heats* (London: Arnold, 1935), 52.

[5] This "circumstance" is "that all, or almost all, bodies by changing from a fluid to a solid state, or from the state of an elastic to that of an unelastic fluid, generate heat; and that cold is produced by the contrary process." Henry Cavendish, "Observations on Mr. Hutchins's Experiments for Determining the Degree of Cold at Which Quicksilver Freezes," *PT* 73 (1783): 303–28; in *Sci. Pap.* 2:145–60, on 150.

[6] Daniel Gabriel Fahrenheit, "Experimenta & Observationes de Congelatione aquae in vacuo," *PT* 33 (1724): 78–84.Cromwell Mortimer, "A Discourse Concerning the Usefulness of Thermometers in Chemical Experiments . . . ," *PT* 46 (1746–47): 672–95, on 682.

[7] Entry for 22 Jan. 1776, minutes of experiments on heat, Cavendish Mss III(a), 9:94–96. "Extract from Nairne," in Cavendish's hand, reporting a temperature of thirty-eight degrees below zero using spirit of nitre and snow, on 14 Jan. 1776. Cavendish Mss Misc.

Much colder temperatures had been obtained. In St. Petersburg in 1759, J. A. Braun with others cooled mercury to the point where it could be hammered and drawn like any other metal, and his colleague F. U. T. Aepinus observed a change in the surface of the mercury in the thermometer tube, a sure indication of contraction upon freezing. There no longer could be any doubt that mercury, the substance once regarded as the essence of fluidity, could be solidified, but beyond that fact little was known for certain about the behavior of mercury at very low temperatures. The *Philosophical Transactions* for 1760 contained an account of artificial cold by Nicolas de Himsel, who said that the Petersburg experiments mostly agreed "in this, that the quicksilver becomes solid, when it falls in the thermometer to 500 degrees, more or less," but they did not "sufficiently agree" to allow "any thing certain" to be deduced.[8] In the same volume, Keane Fitzgerald observed that Himsel's own experiments on the freezing of mercury made the mercury thermometer unfit for measuring great cold.[9] In the journal for 1761, William Watson published an enthusiastic account of Braun's work on this "intirely new" subject.[10]

Not only freezing mixtures but also the natural cold of the Arctic regions could dramatically sink the mercury in thermometers. The natural historian Johann Georg Gmelin recorded a temperature of 120 degrees below zero in Siberia.[11] Pyotr Simon Pallas,[12] who reported a temperature there of minus 70 degrees, also noted that the mercury froze to the glass stem of his thermometer, and that when the mercury began to melt the thermometer stood at minus 45 degrees. Cavendish copied out the parts of Pallas's account of his travels in Siberia dealing with the freezing of mercury.[13]

Cavendish also made a long extract of a paper by Braun, in which Braun told of repeating Fahrenheit's experiments and of being surprised when the mercury in the thermometer fell hundreds of degrees below zero; unable to arrive at a consistent freezing point of mercury, Braun was confident that it could not be at a

---

8 Nicolas de Himsel, "An Account of Artificial Cold Produced at Petersburg," *PT* 51 (1760): 670–79, on 673.

9 Keane Fitzgerald, "A Description of a Metallic Thermometer," *PT* 51 (1760): 823–33, on 833.

10 William Watson, "An Account of a Treatise in Latin, Presented to the Royal Society, Intituled, De admirando frigore artificiali, quo mercurius est congelatus, dissertatio, &c. a J. A. Braunio, Academiae Scientiarum Membro, &c.," *PT* 52 (1761): 156–72. A. W. Badcock, "Physical Science at the Royal Society, 1660–1800. I. Change of State," *Annals of Science* 16 (1960): 95–115, on 100.

11 John Fothergill, "An Account of Some Observations and Experiments Made in Siberia, Extracted from the Preface to the Flora Siberica . . . [by] Gmelin . . . ," *PT* 45 (1748): 248–62, on 258–60. William Watson, "A Comparison of Different Thermometrical Observations in Siberia," *PT* 48 (1753): 108–9.

12 Pyotr Simon Pallas, *Reise durch verschiedenen Provinzen des russischen Reiches in den Jahren 1768–1773*, 2 vols. (St Petersburg, 1771–76).

13 "Account of Freezing of ☿ from Pallas Journey into Siberia," extract in Cavendish's hand, Cavendish Mss III(a), 15.

"less cold than –346" degrees.[14] Braun's experiments were repeated by Thomas Hutchins, governor of Albany Fort, Hudson Bay, using instruments and instructions sent to him by the Royal Society. In the winter of 1774-75, Hutchins froze mercury. Like Braun, he found the experiments inconclusive on the question of the freezing temperature. There seemed to be no instant of freezing, for without changing appearance the mercury continued to fall to below minus 400 degrees. Hutchins asked the Royal Society for more tubes of mercury capable of graduation to *1,000 degrees below zero.*[15]

The reason why Hutchins had got no further was evident to the two persons in Britain who had first clarified to themselves the principles of latent heat, Joseph Black and Cavendish. In a letter in 1779 about Braun's and Hutchins's experiments, Black said that frozen mercury could not record its own freezing temperature. He did not give his reasons for this opinion, but they undoubtedly included the contraction of mercury upon freezing. To get around the difficulty, he proposed a new experimental arrangement whereby the thermometer bulb would be immersed in a mercury bath. Since metals solidify slowly from the outside inward, when the mercury in the bath first froze, the mercury in the bulb would still be liquid, allowing the thermometer to record the freezing temperature. Hutchins informed the Royal Society of Black's proposal, which he made the basis of his next series of experiments. Unknown to Black, Cavendish had already proposed the same apparatus to the president of the Royal Society, Sir Joseph Banks. The apparatus had suggested itself to Cavendish, since the experiment on mercury was a repeat of his many earlier experiments on the freezing of various metals. Black did not publish on this subject, but this time Cavendish did.[16]

The experiments on cold were delegated to a servant of the Hudson's Bay Company; because of its location, the frozen north was a better place than (relatively) warm London. At the time of the transit of Venus in 1769, the Royal Society gave its observers at Hudson Bay detailed instructions on the use of the barometer, since "in so cold a place as Hudson Bay, the barometer will be depressed considerably by the condensation of the mercury by the cold." Cavendish drew

---

[14] This extract, in Cavendish's hand, in Cavendish Mss Misc., is an account of the experiments by several Petersburg academicians following Braun's discovery; in English translation from the French by James Parsons, "An Account of Artificial Cold Produced at Petersburg: By Dr. Himsel. In a Letter to Dr. De Castro, F.R.S.," *PT* 51 (1760): 670–76.

[15] Thomas Hutchins, "An Account of Some Attempts to Freeze Quicksilver, at Albany Fort, in Hudson's Bay, in the Year 1775: With Observations on the Dipping-needle," *PT* 66 (1776): 174–81.

[16] Joseph Black to Andrew Graham on 5 Oct. 1779, published by Thomas Hutchins in "Experiments for Ascertaining the Point of Mercurial Congelation," *PT* 73 (1783): *303–*370, on *305–*306. Black did not know that Cavendish had recommended a similar apparatus to the president of the Royal Society, Sir Joseph Banks. Henry Cavendish, "Observations on Mr. Hutchins's Experiments for Determining the Degree of Cold at Which Quicksilver Freezes," *PT* 73 (1783): 303–28; *Sci. Pap.* 2:145–60, on 149.

up lists of experiments on the freezing of mercury and the expansion with heat of other fluids and showed them to Banks.[17] In the winter of 1781–82, Hutchins compared eight thermometers made by Nairne & Blunt and by Troughton. On one day during that December, after taking a reading every twenty seconds for about an hour in weather colder than twenty degrees below zero, he recorded that he "went away to warm myself," an indication of the rigors of the climate and the limits of endurance of the experimenter.[18] In the course of ten experiments with both natural and artificial cold in which he read three instruments–a mercury thermometer, a spirit thermometer, and the "apparatus"–Hutchins determined the freezing point of mercury. Hutchins's experiments were "very accurate," Cavendish told John Michell.[19] Hutchins said that his "excellent instructions" left him with "nothing to do but to follow them."[20] Cavendish, Blagden said, was the "real author and first mover of the whole business."[21]

Hutchins's paper appeared in the *Philosophical Transactions* for 1783. It was followed by a paper by Cavendish giving his "observations" on Hutchins's experiments. The experiments confirmed Cavendish's hypothesis that the great sinking of mercury in thermometers in extreme cold is due to the great contraction of mercury. If true, the earlier reports of the intense cold produced by freezing mixtures would have been "really astonishing," but they were actually reports about the contraction of mercury. Submerged in freezing mixtures, Hutchins's thermometer fell to 450 degrees below zero, but the cold of the freezing mixture was never less than 46 degrees below zero. Cavendish presented his investigation into the freezing of mercury as a direct continuation of his earlier unpublished experiments on the freezing of lead and tin and on the latent heat of water.[22] The essential point was clearly and simply demonstrated. As the thermometer placed in the container of mercury fell to 40 degrees below zero, where it stayed, the only possible conclusion was that mercury freezes at 40 degrees below zero. Hutchins returned to England and demonstrated his apparatus before Cavendish and Blagden at Cavendish's house in Hampstead.[23] Hutchins then returned the thermometers to

---

[17] 9 June 1768, Minutes of Council, Royal Society, 5:313. There are several drafts of instructions in Cavendish's papers, most of them in Cavendish Mss III(a), 4 and 14. The first group is mainly concerned with Hutchins's experiments published in 1783, though it contains some subsequent instructions sent in 1784. The second group is concerned with the next series of experiments at Hudson Bay Company, conducted by John McNab, published in 1786 and 1788. In addition, there are unclassified papers on the Hudson Bay experiments in the miscellany of Cavendish's manuscripts.

[18] Hutchins, "Experiments," *317.

[19] Henry Cavendish to John Michell, 27 May 1783, draft, Cavendish Mss New Correspondence.

[20] Hutchins, "Experiments," *304.

[21] Charles Blagden, "History of the Congelation of Quicksilver," *PT* 73 (1783): 329–97, on 346.

[22] Cavendish, "Observations," 146, 150–51.

[23] Thomas Hutchins to Charles Blagden, n.d., "Monday Morning," Blagden Letters, Royal Society, H.59.

the Royal Society, where in the best practice of the time, in the presence of witnesses–in addition to Cavendish, they were Banks, Hutchins, Blagden, and Nairne, who made the apparatus–they were examined according to the procedure recommended by the boiling-point committee of 1777. Upon making corrections for the boiling point on Hutchins's thermometers, the adjusted freezing temperature of mercury was declared to be minus 38⅔ degrees or, in round numbers, minus 39 degrees, in remarkably close agreement with the modern value, minus 38.87 degrees. Hutchins probably did not freeze mercury solid, since the mercury in his thermometer did not fall as far as Braun's; from Braun's experiments, however, Cavendish concluded that upon freezing, mercury shrinks by almost 1/23 its bulk, a figure close to modern measurements.[24]

The new understanding of mercury entered the scientific literature at once. In 1782, the Swedish chemist Torbern Bergman published a treatise on mineralogy. In 1783, the year of Hutchins's and Cavendish's publications on mercury, an English translation of Bergman's treatise appeared, *Outlines of Mineralogy*. Under the entry for mercury, Bergman wrote that it "has been erroneously ranked among the brittle metals, for at 654 degrees below 0 it freezes, and then spreads under the hammer like lead. But as such an extreme degree of cold rarely happens unless artificially produced, we cease to wonder why it is always liquid or rather melted." The translator, William Withering, commented that recent experiments at Hudson Bay seemed to

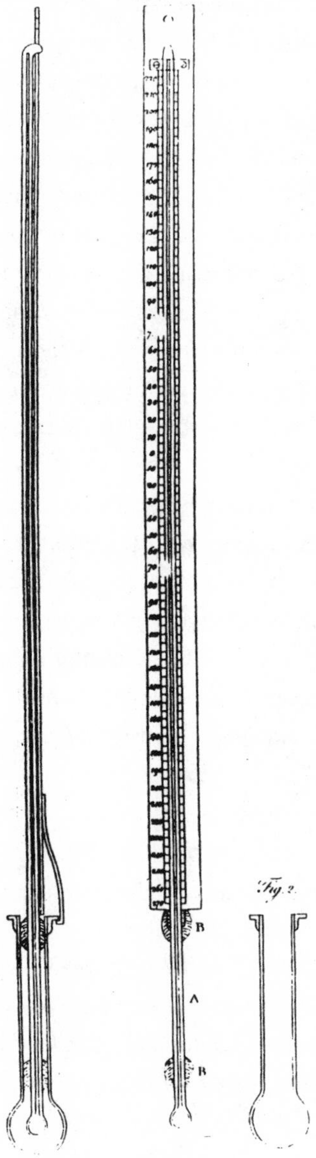

90. *Thermometers for Extreme Cold. The middle figure shows the thermometer with the stem and bulb extending below the scale. The figure on the left gives a side view of the thermometer with the extended stem and bulb inserted into a cylinder holding the mercury to be frozen. Thomas Hutchins, "Experiments for Ascertaining the Point of Mercurial Congelation,"* Philosophical Transactions *73 (1783): *370.*

[24] Cavendish, "Observations," 157.

give the freezing point as 39 degrees below zero, and he altered Bergman's "Table of Metals" accordingly: the "melting heat" of mercury now read, "–39 or –634" degrees Fahrenheit.[25]

Experiments on the freezing of mercury brought together several of Cavendish's interests: the work of the Royal Society, latent heats, the climates of the earth, and the workings of a principal instrument of science, the mercury thermometer. Michell remarked on the latter: "indeed I think you are bound to find us something else in it's stead, having robbed us of so excellent a measure of heat & cold, as the Quicksilver was supposed to be for so many degrees below –39."[26]

Cavendish was not finished with artificial cold. In 1783 he built an apparatus that produced cold by rarefying air mechanically,[27] and over the next few years others did similar experiments; in 1786 Blagden could say that this way of producing cold was "lately much talked of, in consequence of experiments by Mr. Cavendish, Dr. Crawford, & I believe some other gentlemen."[28] Wanting to know the greatest cold that could be produced by a freezing mixture of snow and various chemical solutions, Cavendish requested that more experiments be carried out at Hudson Bay. The experimenter this time was John McNab, master at Henley's House, Hudson Bay, who like Hutchins earned rare praise from Cavendish for his "accuracy." Carried out in weather that reached fifty degrees below zero, McNab's new experiments provided cold "greatly superior" to any yet produced (as opposed to claimed) as well as insight into the "remarkable" way nitrous and vitriolic acids freeze. Cavendish published McNab's experiments in 1786.[29]

In a field which had only just begun to be quantitative, Cavendish reintroduced the "standard" measures he had used in his early chemical experiments: he specified the strength of acids in freezing mixtures by the weight of marble they could dissolve. Corresponding to a range of strengths of the acids at a temperature of sixty degrees, he made a table of specific gravities of the acids, which correspond with modern, theoretical values to the second decimal place.[30] In his attempt to determine the strength of acid requiring the least degree of cold to freeze, he discovered that there were points of "inflexion" (corresponding to various hydrates). Cavendish asked McNab to do another set of experiments on the

---

[25] The disparity between the two numbers for the low reading, –654 and –634, is in the text. Torbern Bergman, *Outlines of Mineralogy*, trans. W. Withering (Birmingham, 1783), 71, 83.

[26] John Michell to Henry Cavendish, 2 July 1783, Cavendish Mss New Correspondence.

[27] Henry Cavendish, "Experiments on Cold by Freezing Mixtures & Rarefaction of Air," Cavendish Mss III(a), 8. Cavendish, *Sci. Pap.* 2:384–89.

[28] Charles Blagden to Erasmus Darwin, 14 Sep. 1786, draft, Blagden Letters, Royal Society, 7:34. Charles Blagden to Mrs. Grey, 30 Jan. 1788, ibid., 7:111.

[29] Henry Cavendish, "An Account of Experiments Made by John McNab, at Henly House, Hudson's Bay, Relating to Freezing Mixtures," *PT* 76 (1786): 241–72; in *Sci. Pap.* 2:195–213, on 195.

[30] The comparison is made by Thorpe, in Cavendish, *Sci. Pap.* 2:59–60.

freezing of acids of varying strengths, which became the subject of Cavendish's last paper on heat, in 1788.[31]

Cavendish published only three papers on heat (or cold, which belongs to the same subject), and all three presented experiments done by others, Hutchins and McNab. Cavendish was content to limit his public contribution to commenting on and drawing inferences from work done in close association with the Royal Society.

HEAT

Blagden began his obituary of Cavendish with the observation that Cavendish had made himself master of "every part of Sir Isaac Newton's philosophy." It is odd that in what follows Blagden failed to mention Cavendish's work on heat, although he made note of all of his other major works. Odd, we say, because in none of Cavendish's other fields was he known to have declared himself publicly a more decided follower of Newton, and also because Blagden had assisted Cavendish in his work on heat. If there is a circumstance that might bear on Blagden's forgetfulness in his obituary of his late friend and colleague, it is that Blagden subscribed to the popular material theory of heat, of which, as we will see, Cavendish held a low, almost contemptuous, opinion.[32]

In 1783 Cavendish determined the freezing point of mercury with the help of the concept of latent heat, as we have seen, but he did not use the word *latent*, deliberately not, because it "relates to an hypothesis depending on the supposition, that the heat of bodies is owing to their containing more or less of a substance called the matter of heat; and as I think Sir Isaac Newton's opinion, that heat consists in the internal motion of the particles of bodies, much the most probable, I chose to use the expression, heat is generated."[33] He rejected Black's "latent heat" in this, his first public mention of the motion theory of heat. This theory was then a contested and for many investigators a dubious theory, and his grounds for saying that it was "much the most probable" he did not give, not here nor elsewhere in print. He did make one more public pronouncement on

---

[31] Henry Cavendish, "An Account of Experiments Made by Mr. John McNab, at Albany Fort, Hudson's Bay, Relative to the Freezing of Nitrous and Vitriolic Acids," *PT* 78 (1788): 166–81; in *Sci. Pap.* 2:214–23.

[32] Draft of Blagden's obituary of Cavendish, Blagden Collection, Royal Society, Misc. Notes, No. 225. The obituary was published in *Gentleman's Magazine* (Mar. 1810), 292. Publicly, Blagden did not commit himself on the theory of heat, but he let Cavendish know that he regarded latent heat as an "elastic fluid." Charles Blagden, "Experiments on the Cooling of Water Below Its Freezing Point," *PT* 78 (1788): 125–46, on 140. Charles Blagden to C. L. Berthollet, 5 June 1786, draft, Blagden Letters, Royal Society, 7:2. An undated draft of a paper by Blagden obviously intended for Cavendish, Blagden Papers, Yale, box 2, folder 23. The discussion of heat in this section draws on Russell McCormmach, "Henry Cavendish on the Theory of Heat," *Isis* 79 (1988): 37–67. We acknowledge permission to use the material: University of Chicago Press, copyright 1988 by the History of Science Society, Inc., all rights reserved.

[33] Cavendish, "Observations," 150–51.

the theory of heat, which again was to object to the expression and hypothesis of "latent heat." It occurred in his paper on air and water the following year, in which Cavendish remarked on a recent paper by James Watt on the same subject. Cavendish's point was again the relationship between words and reality in describing heat. In the passage in question, now remembered not for its content so much as for its part in the water controversy, Cavendish gave his reasons for avoiding Watt's "language," Watt's "form of speaking": "Now I have chosen to avoid this form of speaking, both because I think it more likely that there is no such thing as elementary heat, and because saying so in this instance, without using similar expressions in speaking of other chemical unions, would be improper, and would lead to false ideas; and it may even admit of doubt, whether the doing it in general would not cause more trouble and perplexity than it is worth."[34] The quarrel Cavendish had with the language of heat illustrated a general observation made by the geologist James Hutton in 1794: as in mathematical reasoning, in scientific reasoning terms have to be clearly defined, and scientific language was vaguest in theories of heat, a reason for the inability of investigators to agree on them.[35]

The passage on Watt in 1784 and the footnote on Joseph Black the year before were all that Cavendish in his lifetime was to tell his readers about the nature of heat. The scientific manuscripts he left at his death were found to contain two more references to Newton's theory of heat. One was buried in a corollary to a theorem in a paper on the theory of motion, which begins, "Heat most likely is the vibrating of the particles of which bodies are composed"; the other appeared in an experimental paper on latent and specific heats, which concluded with the observation that certain of his experiments at first seemed to him "very difficult to reconcile with Newton's theory of heat, but on further consideration they seem by no means to be so. But to understand this you must read the following proposition."[36] Unfortunately, there the paper ends, abruptly, without the promised proposition. Until recently these references, two published and two unpublished, were the only known explicit statements by Cavendish on the theory of heat. Since it can be shown that Cavendish's understanding of the nature of heat entered fundamentally into his researches on factitious airs, the production of water, and electricity, as well as his researches on the freezing of mercury and on freezing mixtures in general,[37] what was missing was a fully developed theory of heat, one comparable to his fully developed theory of electricity.

[34] Henry Cavendish, "Experiments on Air," *PT* 74 (1784): 119–53; *Sci. Pap.* 2:161–81, on 173–74.

[35] James Hutton, *A Dissertation upon the Philosophy of Light, Heat, and Fire. In Seven Parts* (Edinburgh, 1794), 7–9.

[36] Henry Cavendish, "Remarks on the Theory of Motion," Henry Cavendish Mss VI(b), 7; *Sci. Pap.* 2:415–30, corollary 2 on 425–26. Henry Cavendish, "Experiments on Heat," ibid., misc.; *Sci. Pap.* 2:327–51, on 351 (the title is not Cavendish's).

[37] Russell McCormmach, "Henry Cavendish: A Study of Rational Empiricism in Eighteenth-Century Natural Philosophy," *Isis* 60 (1969): 293–306.

In 1969 Lord Chesham, a direct descendant of Henry Cavendish's heir Lord George Cavendish, put up for sale several manuscripts by Henry Cavendish, including a theoretical paper, "Heat." This paper was written in two drafts, one a revised, nearly fair copy with some crossings out. It gives, as we would say, a rigorously mathematical, mechanical theory of heat complete with the principle of conservation of energy, the concept of the mechanical equivalent of heat, and applications of the theory to the principal branches of physical science.[38] This paper is a remarkable culmination of Cavendish's experimental and theoretical researches; more than any of his other writings, it testifies to Cavendish's concern with the foundations of natural philosophy.

The idea of heat as motion had received many formulations by Cavendish's time. To the question of just what it is that moves, a variety of answers had been proposed. The vibrating object might be the ordinary particles of bodies, the air and acid sulphur in bodies, the subtle ether, or the fluid of fire. Newton's authority was invoked in support of more than one of these options, but to Cavendish, Newton's theory meant the vibrations of the ordinary particles of bodies. Many of the examples in the queries of Newton's *Opticks* invoked this view of heat, which contributed to the coherence of Newton's natural philosophy as it did to that of Cavendish's.[39]

The hypothesis of the internal vibrations of the parts of bodies offered plausible explanations of, for example, the heat produced by hammering, friction, and the absorption of light, but it seemed incompatible with other phenomena. A seemingly obvious contradiction was the cold produced by mixing sal ammoniac and water and by a variety of chemical reactions. Since the particles of these substances were surely set in motion, it would seem that heat does not attend all motion. Another instance of the same kind was the failure of liquids and gases to generate heat upon being agitated.[40] A major theoretical difficulty was that the heat capacities of bodies were found not to be proportional to their densities, as the motion theory was understood to require. Further difficulties were discussed by the first Jacksonian professor of natural philosophy at Cambridge, Isaac Milner, in lectures he delivered in 1784–88, the time of Cavendish's "Heat." A basic objection was that the vibrations of particles had not been proven to exist. Another objection was

[38] The revised draft of "Heat" consists of forty-three pages of text and notes, one page of diagrams with an accompanying page of explanation, and one page of additions and alterations. The original manuscripts of both drafts of "Heat" are located, under the reference M G 23, L 6, in the Manuscript Division, Pre-Confederation Archives, Public Archives of Canada, Ottawa.

[39] Robert E. Schofield, *Mechanism and Materialism: British Natural Philosophy in an Age of Reason* (Princeton: Princeton University Press, 1970), 13, 37, 48, 77–78, 84–85, 139, 160, 179, 183. Sir Isaac Newton, *Opticks; or a Treatise of the Reflections, Refractions, Inflections and Colours of Light*, 4th ed. (1730; reprint, New York: Dover, 1952), 348–49, 375–406.

[40] William Irvine, "The Nature of Heat," in Irvine, *Essays, Chiefly on Chemical Subjects*, ed. W. Irvine, Jr. (London, 1805), 21–23.

that heat was not observed to be proportional to motion, as it would be if heat were motion. Another was that when oil and grease were used to eliminate friction, heat seemed to be eliminated too, although motion was communicated to the particles. There were still more objections, Milner noted. Heat was observed to pass slowly through bodies, as a liquid might, rather than rapidly, as motion does. Again in contradiction with experience, the motion theory of heat implied that heat should not spread at all, since the quantity of motion of a system of particles is unaffected by their mutual actions and collisions. The observed passage of heat across a vacuum could not be explained by motion since there are no intervening particles to be set in vibration. The liberation of heat during the solidification of a liquid was inconceivable on the view of heat as motion; so was the generation of cold upon evaporation. In general the motion theory seemed incompatible with latent heat, since latent motion was no motion. The objections were many, but Milner had answers, for as it happened, he was a believer in the motion theory and a critic of the opposing material theories. "The arguments against this [motion] Theory have of late Years been esteemed so numerous and weighty that it has almost been given up by Philosophers," but it had been given up "a little too precipately," and Milner wished that "somebody else had endeavoured to shew the truth" of it by contrasting it with the fashionable material fluid theories of heat.[41]

The difficulties of the motion theory could be seen as one general difficulty: new mechanical ideas for the theory had not kept pace with the rapid experimental development of the science of heat in the late eighteenth century, whereas the material theory of heat had developed together with the experimental science.[42] Heat was one of a number of fluids that had come to characterize British speculative natural philosophy from about the middle of the eighteenth century.[43] The fluid of heat was usually taken to be imponderable, subtle, and closely associated with fire, and its particles were usually assumed to repel one another and to be attracted to the particles of ordinary substances. The theory of this expansive fluid was readily grasped, easy to apply, plausible, predictive,

[41] L. J. M. Coleby, "Isaac Milner and the Jacksonian Chair of Natural Philosophy," *Annals of Science* 10 (1954): 234–57, on 242–52.

[42] Robert Fox, *The Caloric Theory of Gases from Lavoisier to Regnault* (Oxford: Clarendon, 1971), 19, 22–23.

[43] J. L. Heilbron, *Weighing Imponderables and Other Quantitative Science around 1800*, Supplement to *Historical Studies in the Physical and Biological Sciences,* vol. 24, pt. 1 (Berkeley: University of California Press, 1993), 5–33. Schofield, *Mechanism and Materialism*, 157–90; P. M. Heimann, "Ether and Imponderables," in *Conceptions of Ether: Studies in the History of Ether Theories, 1740–1900*, ed. G. N. Cantor and M. J. S. Hodge (Cambridge: Cambridge University Press, 1981), 61–83, on 67–73. Arthur Quinn, "Repulsive Force in England, 1706–1744," *Historical Studies in the Physical Sciences* 13 (1982): 109–28, on 127; Douglas McKie and Niels H. de V. Heathcote, "William Cleghorn's *De igne* (1779)," *Annals of Science* 14 (1958): 1–82. Fox, *Caloric Theory*, 19–20, 22, 25.

and supported by leading authorities of the day. Black was thought to hold the fluid theory, as were his students William Cleghorn, William Irvine, and Adair Crawford.

Investigators rarely needed to declare themselves for one theory of heat or the other, since they could carry out their experiments very well without doing so. A case in point is Lavoisier and Laplace's joint paper in 1783, a classic study in the emerging science of calorimetry. Lavoisier almost certainly held the material theory of heat; what Laplace thought is uncertain, and he was later to hold the material theory, but in any event it was he who described the motion theory in their joint paper. Side by side with the motion theory, the authors described the material theory, without deciding between the two. Cavendish read Lavosier and Laplace's paper on heat,[44] but he did not follow their example of remaining uncommitted to one or the other theory: twice in print he rejected the material theory of heat, as we have seen, and he gave his arguments for the motion theory in a paper he planned for publication, "Heat."

Black and his followers had the common difficulty of being unable to form an idea of the internal motions of bodies that could account for the phenomena of heat. Even in the case of friction, which offered the strongest support for the motion theory, it was hard to envision the motions responsible. Black's main complaint against the motion theory, however, was that none of its supporters had shown how to apply it to the entirety of the phenomena of heat.[45] The same complaint could not have been made about the material theory, at least not after Cleghorn's work. Cavendish set out to supply what was missing from the side of the motion theory. "Heat" is a systematic presentation of Newton's theory of heat together with comprehensive supporting evidence drawn from many parts of physical science. With this fundamental theory, so far as we know his last, Cavendish brought the mechanical understanding of heat to a level that would not be surpassed for over a half century.

Before continuing further, we need to clarify a point of mechanics we touched on earlier in this book. We assume that by the time Cavendish left Cambridge, he was thoroughly familiar with Newtonian mathematical principles of natural philosophy. For the purposes of this discussion it is sufficient to recall that in Newtonian mechanics, the measure of the quantity of motion of a body is the product of the mass and velocity of the body, or momentum. At some point, undoubtedly at Cambridge, Cavendish became familiar with another formulation of mechanics originating with Leibniz. In it the quantity of motion of a body is taken to be *vis viva*, the product of the mass and the square of its velocity, which is proportional to our kinetic energy. Leibniz and his followers regarded *vis viva* as a quantity that is conserved, one incapable of

[44] Charles Blagden to Antoine Laurent Lavoisier, draft, 15 Sep. 1783, Blagden Letterbook, Yale.

[45] Schofield, *Mechanism and Materialism*, 186–87. Irvine, *Essays*, 22.

disappearing without giving rise to a comparable effect, an equal quantity of latent or potential motion. This understanding was well-suited for the treatment of a range of mechanical problems, but it encountered difficulties in the treatment of collisions between bodies. From experience it was known that collisions are never perfectly elastic, implying that *vis viva* is lost, but because the belief in conservation was firm, the missing *vis viva* was regarded as only apparently lost, continuing on in hidden forms such as the compression of bodies or the motion of parts internal to bodies. Leibniz proposed the latter explanation, but he did not identify the hidden *vis viva* with heat, even though in his day heat was commonly believed to be the internal motion of bodies. It would seem that the conceptual problems of treating heat as a quantity made this identification difficult.[46]

In a paper that has been labeled by others "Remarks on the Theory of Motion," Cavendish discussed the usefulness of *vis viva* as a "way of computing the force of bodies in motion." For most questions arising in "philosophical enquiries," he acknowledged that the usual and most convenient way of computing the forces was Newton's momentum and that *vis viva* was usually reserved for solving problems concerning machines for "mechanical" purposes. The mechanical engineer John Smeaton wrote about *vis viva* for fellow engineers, and he gave his writing on the subject to Cavendish for comment.[47] But *vis viva* had "philosophical" uses, too, Cavendish said, as he went on to show. Instead of "*vis viva*," he preferred to speak of the "mechanical momentum"[48] of bodies in motion; by this choice of terminology, referring to both ways of computing the force of moving bodies as species of "momentum," he drew on his conviction that the choice was a question of convenience, not of fundamentals.[49] Force itself was fundamental, not the way it was measured. Assuming that forces are "central" and that no force is lost by friction and inelastic collisions, he laid down a very general law of conservation of mechanical momentum and "additional momenta," or potential mechanical momentum; we would call it the law of conservation of energy. He extended the conservation law to encompass lost force by identifying heat with the mechanical momentum of the invisible vibrations of the particles of the large bodies of our experience. He acknowledged

---

[46] Erwin N. Hiebert, *Historical Roots of the Principle of Energy Conservation* (Madison: State Historical Society of Wisconsin, 1962), 80–93. P. M. Heimann, "'Geometry and Nature': Leibniz and Johann Bernoulli's Theory of Motion," *Centaurus* 21 (1977): 1–26.

[47] The paper Smeaton gave Cavendish to comment on was probably "New Fundamental Experiments upon the Collision of Bodies," *PT* 72 (1782): 337–54. John Playfair, *The Works of John Playfair*, 4 vols., ed. J. G. Playfair (Edinburgh, 1822) 1:lxxxiii.

[48] Bernoulli first and then Smeaton called it "mechanic force." Newton did not treat this measure of force and thus gave it no definition. W. H. Wollaston, "The Bakerian Lecture on the Force of Percussion," *PT* 96 (1806): 13–22, on 16.

[49] P. M. Heimann and J. E. McGuire, "Cavendish and the *Vis viva* Controversy: A Leibnizian Postscript," *Isis* 62 (1970): 225–27.

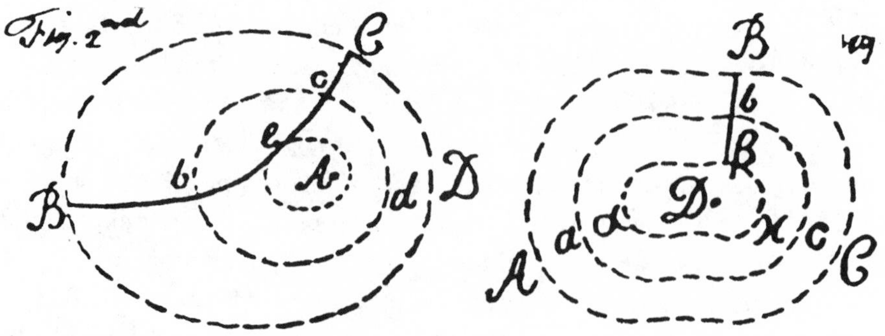

91. *Forces. The dashed lines represent forces of attraction and repulsion of constant intensity surrounding bodies or particles of matter, or force centers, A and D. BC in Fig. 2 and Bb in Fig. 3 are the paths of a second attracting and repelling body or particle. With the aid of these diagrams and a proposition from Newton's* Principia, *Cavendish argued for his general law of conservation of the sum of "real" and "additional" "mechanical momenta" (our kinetic and potential energy). It has been pointed out that Cavendish was struggling here with our concept of equipotential curves. "Remarks on the Theory of Motion," Cavendish Scientific Manuscripts VI(b), 7:plate 3; Cavendish,* Scientific Papers *2:430.*

that there were phenomena–the heats involved in fermentation, dissolution, and burning–that he did not know how to explain by his theory of heat. In "Remarks," he did not introduce the concept of latent heat, leading us to think that it was written before his experiments on latent and specific heats, probably in the early 1760s. "Heat," which covers the same ground as "Remarks" but goes far beyond that paper, would then have been written about twenty-five years later, in the late 1780s.

Cavendish began the new theoretical work, "Heat," with a purely mechanical investigation; his propositions paralleled those in "Remarks on the Theory of Motion," only here he developed them more thoroughly. He divided *vis viva,* defined as the mechanical effect of a body in motion, into two kinds, "visible" and "invisible." The visible was the *vis viva* of the center of mass of a body undergoing progressive motion or of the body undergoing rotation or both; the invisible was that of the particles of the body moving among themselves; and the total *vis viva* of the body was the sum of both. He further divided the invisible *vis viva* into two parts: one was "active"; the other was inactive, with the potential for becoming active. His symbol *s*, standing for the active, is the actual *vis viva* of all of the particles constituting the body; his symbol *S* stands for one half the sum of the *vis viva* that each particle would acquire by the attraction or repulsion of every other particle in falling from infinity to its actual position within the body. Assuming that the attractions and repulsions between particles are always the same at the same separations and different at different separations, he derived the law of conservation of *vis viva*, active and inactive; the quantity $s - S$ cannot change as a result of the motions of the particles among one another.

Next Cavendish identified the mechanical quantities occurring in the propositions about *vis viva* with the quantities occurring in heat. "Heat," according to his "hypothesis," "consists in the internal motion of the particles of which bodies are composed"; this motion is vibratory, the particles being bound close to their place by attracting and repelling forces. He identified the "active heat" of the body with the active, actual *vis viva*, s, and the "latent heat" with the potential *vis viva*, $-S$, and consequently the "total heat" with $s - S$, the conserved quantity. "Sensible heat" is what Cavendish called the heat of a body as given by a thermometer; it is related to the active and latent heats through the constitution of the body. With these definitions, Cavendish had a complete technical vocabulary for the theory of heat.[50]

The first test of Cavendish's theory of heat was its ability to account for the phenomena of heat itself. When two bodies, isolated and unequally heated, are brought into contact, one gives up heat and the other acquires it until the sensible heat of each is the same. In the exchange the total heat given up must be the same as the total heat received, but just how this heat is divided between the active and latent heats in the two bodies depends on the weights of the bodies and on "some function either of the size of their particles or of any other quality in them," for example, the frequency of vibration of the particles.[51] The distinctions, based on experimental knowledge, between sensible, total, active, and latent heats enabled Cavendish to explain the phenomena of specific heats, the subject of his earliest experiments in heat.

Having secured the vibrational theory of heat within its own field, heat, Cavendish then applied it to other parts of physical science, first to optics. "There can be no doubt," Cavendish said, that light is a body consisting of extremely small particles emitted from luminous bodies with extremely high velocity. When these particles are reflected from a body, they are not reflected by a single particle or by a few particles of that body but by a great quantity of its matter, so that according to mechanical principles no perceptible *vis viva* is communicated to the body. The same explanation applies to the case of refracted light. But where light is absorbed, its particles are reflected back and forth within the body until their velocity is no greater than that of the particles of the body, "so that their *vis viva* will be equally distributed between the body & them" and the absorbing body will thereby acquire sensible heat.[52] Light falling upon a body that does not have a mirror surface heats the body.

---

[50] Cavendish did not formally introduce a term for "specific heat," though he mentioned the "capacities for heat" of bodies. Cavendish, "Heat," 11–12, 24, 41.

[51] Ibid., 14–16.

[52] Ibid., 18–20.

To calculate the *vis viva* of light, Cavendish turned to an experiment by John Michell to "ascertain the momentum of light." This experiment was widely regarded as proof that light really does consist of streaming material particles.[53] Inside a box with a window to the sun was a thin sheet of copper fastened to one end of a horizontal wire and balanced by a weight at the other end. Rays of the sun were concentrated and directed by a concave mirror so that they struck the copper plate perpendicularly, resulting in a rotation of the wire.[54] From the observed speed of rotation and other details of the experiment, and from the assumption that the light was perfectly reflected from the copper, Cavendish calculated the *vis viva* of the sunlight falling each second on 1½ square feet of surface. He translated this result into its mechanical effect: the rate of *vis viva* of sunlight falling on that surface exceeded the work done by two horses, that is, over two horsepower.[55]

A plate of glass is heated more than a plate of polished metal when exposed to a fire or the sun. But since the metal absorbs more light than the glass, according to Cavendish's theory it ought to be heated more than the glass. To resolve this apparent conflict with the theory, Cavendish referred to recent experiments by Carl Wilhelm Scheele and Horace Bénédict de Saussure on the newly discovered "heat rays." Cavendish assumed that heat rays, like light rays with which they commingle in various proportions, are material particles emitted by hot bodies, and although their velocity is not known, they too must communicate *vis viva.* But heat rays differ from light rays, too; not only do they not excite the sensation of vision, but they are absorbed by glass and are efficiently reflected by polished metals, which is just the reverse of the behavior of light. It is the heat rays, then, and not the accompanying light rays, that warm the glass preferentially. These new invisible rays enabled Cavendish to reconcile the facts with his theory of heat; if the rays did not exist, the theory would fail.[56]

According to the vibrational theory, bodies are warmed when they emit light and radiant heat, but since the repulsion by bodies of the particles of light and radiant heat is accomplished by a relatively great amount of matter, the *vis viva* of recoil in the bodies is too small to detect. The theory, however, is confirmed by the familiar observation that as a body grows hotter, it emits more light and heat. The particles of light and radiant heat are bound to their natural places in a body by the forces of attraction and repulsion of the particles of the body, and when the latter particles are set in brisk vibration, the particles of light and radiant

[53] G. N. Cantor, *Optics after Newton: Theories of Light in Britain and Ireland, 1704–1840* (Manchester: Manchester University Press, 1983), 57.

[54] Joseph Priestley, *The History and Present State of Discoveries Relating to Vision, Light and Colours*, 2 vols. (London, 1772), 1:387–89. Cantor, *Optics after Newton*, 57. S. G. Brush and C. W. F. Everitt, "Maxwell, Osborne Reynolds, and the Radiometer," *Historical Studies in the Physical Sciences* 1 (1969): 103–25.

[55] Cavendish, "Heat," 22.

[56] Ibid., 23–24.

heat are moved into positions where they experience violent repulsion, flying off from the body as free light and radiant heat.[57]

Heat can be produced mechanically, for example, by friction and hammering, and Cavendish showed how this effect too agrees with the theory. Since a violent force is required to produce heat, the particles of the heated body must be displaced or even torn away at its surface, and that in turn alters the latent heat of the body, giving rise to sensible heat. The same displacement or tearing away of particles is responsible for the loss of elasticity in the collision of two bodies or in the bending of a body. Cavendish's analysis here of the forces of particles was more problematic than in some other applications of the theory, but on the basic point of the theory, he was "certain": if any visible *vis viva* is lost by the rubbing, striking, or bending of bodies, these bodies must acquire an "augmentation of total heat equivalent thereto."[58]

Electricity is the field that Cavendish had developed with the greatest theoretical and experimental thoroughness, devoting the labor of a decade to it without, however, having closely examined the heat produced by electricity in motion. Now, he said, he was going to "argue upon the principles laid down in my paper concerning the cause of electricity," his paper of 1771, to derive a formula for the *vis viva* of electric fluid discharged by a Leyden jar through a wire. He doubted that the particles of the electric fluid, because of their extreme lightness, could communicate sufficient *vis viva* to the particles of the wire to account for the violent heat of the wire. His explanation of the violent heat is that the electric discharge displaces the particles of the wire, greatly diminishing its latent heat. The heat caused by electric discharge is consistent with the theory, "though," Cavendish said, "it is an effect which I should not have expected."[59]

As the final application of his theory, Cavendish discussed the expansion and change of state of bodies with heat. When a body is heated, he reasoned, the increased vibrations of its particles alter their mutual attractions and repulsions, which in turn alter the size of the body. When the vibrations become great enough, the attractions and repulsions of the particles vary sufficiently for the body to change its form and properties entirely, which is what happens in evaporation and in melting: the increased vibrations of the particles diminish their adhesion, making bodies more fluid. By the same reasoning, Cavendish explained why chemical decomposition and combination are promoted by heat.[60]

Experiment was never distant from theory for Cavendish, and in three places in "Heat" he made a note to himself to do an experiment suggested by the theory, and in the rough draft of the paper he noted a fourth experiment to try. In one place he said that he wanted to determine if "friction is as much diminished

[57] Ibid., 25–26.

[58] Ibid., 26–31, on 31.

[59] Ibid., 32–38, on 41.

[60] Ibid., 38–39.

by oil & grease as the heat is" (recalling one of Milner's objections to the motion theory of heat). In another, he said that he was concerned about the diminution of the latent heat of a wire during an electric discharge. In another, he said that he intended to expose various equally dark bodies to sunlight to determine that the total heat acquired by different bodies from the sun's rays is the same. In the rough draft of "Heat" he commented on this last experiment: "If it should prove that different bodies do not receive the same total heat from the ⊙s light it would be difficult to reconcile with this hypothesis. But then it seems as difficult to reconcile it with the supposition of heat being a material substance except that as those hypotheses are less capable of being brought to the test of strict reasoning it is easier for those gentlemen to find loop holes to escape by."[61]

The experiments Cavendish envisioned all bore on "this hypothesis," the fundamental, contested hypothesis that heat is motion. His intention is especially clear from another proposed experiment that appears in the discussion of the heat caused by the impulse of light and of Michell's experiment to determine the momentum of sunlight: "Exper. to determine the *vis viva* necessary to give a given increase of sensible heat to a given body by alternately exposing a thermometer in the ⊙ & shading."[62] Whether or not Cavendish performed such an experiment, or any other experiments with the same goal, we do not know. In any event, the proposed experiment involved the calculation of a mechanical equivalent of heat for a given substance. Determinations of the equivalence of heat and work would be made systematically by others in the middle of the nineteenth century, when they would provide the foundation for the development of the mechanical theory of heat, or thermodynamics.

Cavendish was interested in the reality of the vibrations constituting heat, as he revealed in the rough draft of "Heat," where he gave a more complete statement of the above experiment. From the determination of the *vis viva* equivalent to an increase of sensible heat in a body, and by supposing that the total heat in a body at one thousand degrees is double that at zero degrees, he could "guess at the velocity with which the particles of a body vibrate."[63]

The "Conclusion" of "Heat" begins: "It has been shewn therefore by as strict reasoning as can be expected in subjects not purely mathematical, that if heat consists in the vibrations of the particles of bodies, the effects will be strikingly analogous, & as far as our experiments yet go, in no case contradictory to the phenomena." By showing that it is fully sufficient to explain the phenomena, Cavendish made a strong case for the hypothesis that the vibrations of the particles of bodies constitute heat. "To put the matter in a stronger light," he said, it "seems certain that the action of such rays of light as are absorbed by a body

61 Cavendish, "Heat," rough draft, 15. The experiment on exposing dark bodies to sunlight is proposed in "Heat," 24.

62 Cavendish, "Heat," 22.

63 Cavendish, "Heat," rough draft, 12.

must produce a motion & vibration of its particles; so that it seems certain that the particles of bodies must actually be in motion." Given, then, that the vibrations certainly exist, there must be effects corresponding to them, and these are "analogous to most of the phenomena of heat and disagree with none." The hypothesis is not only sufficient, it is necessary.[64]

With these concluding remarks Cavendish let rest the case for Newton's theory of heat, having implicitly answered the main criticisms of it. He showed that the hypothetical vibrations can account not only for the heat of friction, for example, for which a motion theory would seem to be well-suited, but also for heats, such as those accompanying changes of state, for which the material theory seems especially well suited. In each application of the theory, Cavendish suggested the possible motions and configurations responsible. He thereby showed that, unlike earlier presentations of the motion theory, his could not be faulted for lack of clear ideas of the mechanism. By logical and where possible mathematical arguments Cavendish proceeded from a precise hypothesis and from accepted mechanical principles to a demonstration of the "striking" analogy between the effects of insensible vibrations and the perceptible phenomena of heat. He judged his theory to be a strong, good theory, not "of that pliable nature as to be easily adapted to any appearances."[65]

Cavendish was not yet finished. In the nearly fair copy of "Heat" he had not yet said a word about one of its most obvious motivations, the material theory, which for Cavendish failed to meet the criteria defining a strong, good theory. He reserved his judgment of the opposing theory to the end of the "Conclusion": given the evidence for the existence of internal vibrations, he wrote, there was no reason to "have recourse to the hypothesis of a fluid, which nothing proves the existence of." He continued:

> The various hypotheses which have been formed for explaining the phenomena of heat by a fluid seem to shew that none of them are very satisfactory; & though it does not seem impossible that the fluid might exist endued with such properties as to produce the effects of heat; yet any hypothesis of such kind must be of that unprecise nature, as not to admit of being reduced to strict reasoning, so as to suffer one to examine whether it will really explain the phenomena or whether it will not rather be attended with numberless inconsistencies & absurdities. So that though it might be natural for philosophers to adopt such an hypothesis when no better offerd itself; yet when a theory has been proposed by Sr I.N. which, as may be shewn by strict reasoning, must produce effects strongly analogous to those observed to take place, & which seems no ways inconsistent with any, there can no longer be any reason for adhering to the former hypothesis.[66]

[64] Cavendish, "Heat," 40, 43.

[65] Ibid., 41–42.

[66] Ibid., 42.

Cavendish did not criticize the material theory in general, or any of its variants in particular, for specific failures; he criticized it only for the kind of theory it was, prone to inconsistency, absurdity, and imprecision. He presented the Newtonian theory as a closed circle of reasoning, so compelling in its logic, comprehensiveness, and agreement with experience, that the alternative material theory, indeed, any alternative theory, must be unreasonable.

Three times in the conclusion of "Heat" Cavendish used the expression "strict reasoning," a phrase which captures the spirit in which Cavendish studied nature. He had used it before in his other great theoretical work: "The method I propose to follow," he wrote in the introduction to his published electrical theory of 1771, "is, first, to lay down the hypothesis; next, to examine by strict mathematical reasoning, or at least, as strict reasoning as the nature of the subject will admit of, what consequences will flow from thence," and finally to compare these consequences with experiment.[67] The method he used in the theory of heat was the same.

"Heat" carries no date, but it was certainly written after 1783.[68] During the years 1783–88 Cavendish worked most intensively on heat and on the closely related subject of pneumatic chemistry. With the exception of his first publication, in 1766, all of his publications on pneumatic chemistry appeared then, as did all of his publications on heat. As we have seen, in 1783 Cavendish rejected Black's term "latent heat" because of the theory of heat it implied, and four years later, he rejected another terminology for the same kind of reason: this was the terminology proposed in the *Méthode de nomenclature chimique*, which implied Lavoisier's theory of chemistry, and which included among the elements of chemistry, the matter of heat, "caloric." The "long sermon" Cavendish gave Blagden about the mischief caused by the new chemical nomenclature and, in general, the "present rage of namemaking" he took to heart when writing "Heat."

[67] Henry Cavendish, "An Attempt to Explain Some of the Principal Phaenomena of Electricity, by Means of an Elastic Fluid," *PT* 61 (1771): 584–677, on 584.

[68] At auction sales, "Heat" was assigned first to the decade 1795–1805 and then to around 1780; the truth probably lies somewhere in between. Cavendish certainly wrote this paper after "Remarks on the Theory of Motion," which mentions only some of the phenomena discussed in "Heat." Also, in "Remarks" Cavendish regarded the cold produced by chemical mixtures as a difficulty for the theory, whereas in "Heat" he no longer did. Most important for this comparison is that in "Heat" Cavendish drew on his knowledge of specific and latent heats, developing the mechanical theory accordingly, whereas in "Remarks" he did not mention them. The connection between "Heat" and Cavendish's experiments on specific and latent heats is direct; for example, the numbered paragraph 7 on p. 16 of "Heat," concerning the heats of chemical mixtures, states in general terms the conclusion on p. 39 of the experimental notes on heat, Cavendish Mss III(a), 9. Christie's sales catalog assigned the first dating primarily on the basis of the watermarks on the paper, in which the name J. Cripps alternates with Britannia in a crowned circle, assuming that the earliest recorded mark of James Cripps was in 1792. Cavendish did use the J. Cripps stationery several times in the 1790s and 1800s, but he also used it earlier, in the 1780s (the earliest appearance being manuscript pages A3 through A5 of "Experiments on Air," Cavendish Mss II, 10, published in the *Philosophical Transactions* in 1785). "Heat" reappeared at Dawsons of Pall Mall. It was noted that James Cripps, father and son, made paper from 1753 to 1803, and based on references to other authors in the manuscript, another dating was proposed, around 1780.

He now used the standard terminology of mechanics, "*vis viva*," rather than his own "mechanical momentum." By the same token, he used Black's terminology for heat because it was now standard: in his early writings on heat he used expressions such as "heat is generated," but in "Heat" he systematically used "latent heat," while giving it an interpretation within the Newtonian heat theory.

Fortunately, Cavendish left more specific clues as to the approximate time when he wrote "Heat." In the manuscript, he mentioned the work of several of his contemporaries. He cited Joseph Priestley's history of optics, but that book appeared early, in 1772. He cited the names, but not the publications, of Scheele and Saussure for their researches on radiant heat. Cavendish closely followed Scheele's work–which, like his own, joined the sciences of heat and pneumatic chemistry–and the reference in "Heat" shows his familiarity with Scheele's only book, which appeared in English translation in 1780.[69] Cavendish's mention of Saussure no doubt refers to the second volume of his travels in the Alps, which came out in 1786.[70] The absence of citations to work done in the 1790s may be taken as indirect evidence for an upper limit for the dating of this manuscript.[71]

For these reasons, we would place "Heat" in the late 1780s. As to the immediate stimulus for writing the paper, Cavendish said nothing. In 1785 George Fordyce published an experimental paper in the *Philosophical Transactions* demonstrating the loss of weight by ice upon melting. Since ice lost weight as it gained heat, Fordyce speculated that heat might be a body possessing absolute levity, though he was inclined to believe that heat was a completely general quality like attraction, only its opposite.[72] If Fordyce's experiments, and Crawford's too, were proven right, Blagden told Laplace, they would work an "extraordinary revolution in our ideas."[73] That was recognized by Benjamin Thompson, who in 1787 repeated Fordyce's experiments, convincing himself that they were wrong and that heat could not be a material substance.[74] Cavendish had earlier witnessed

69 Cavendish, "Heat," 23. Cavendish's source is undoubtedly the experiments on "heat rays" and light using polished metal and glass, discussed in Carl Wilhelm Scheele, *Chemical Observations and Experiments on Air and Fire*, 1777, trans. J. R. Forster, with notes by Richard Kirwan (London, 1780), 72–74, 92–98.

70 Cavendish, "Heat," 23. Here Cavendish's source is no doubt Saussure's account of the experiments he did with M. A. Pictet on the reflection of "obscure heat" emitted by hot, but not red-hot, bodies in *Voyages dans les Alpes*, vol. 2 (Neuchâtel, 1786), 354–55.

71 For example, Pierre Prevost's experiments on heat rays and Count Rumford's on the mechanical production of heat, belonging to the 1790s, would have been relevant to Cavendish's argument, as would be Herschel's experiments on radiant heat from 1800.

72 George Fordyce, "An Account of Some Experiments on the Loss of Weight in Bodies on Being Melted or Heated," *PT* 75 (1785): 361–65, on 364; Coleby, "Isaac Milner," 245.

73 Charles Blagden to Lorenz Crell, 28 Apr. 1785, draft, Blagden Letterbook, Yale. Charles Blagden to Pierre Simon Laplace, 5 Apr. 1785, ibid.

74 Sanborn C. Brown, *Benjamin Thompson, Count Rumford* (Cambridge, Mass.: M.I.T. Press, 1979), 219–220. Fordyce himself in 1787 declared against the view that heat is a "substance." He did not go so far as to say that it is motion, calling it a "quality": George Fordyce, "An Account of an Experiment on Heat," *PT* 77 (1787): 310–17, on 316.

experiments like Fordyce's, and although he did none himself and never discussed the question in print,[75] he was kept informed on pertinent researches in Paris.[76] We do not believe, however, that Fordyce's paper on heat or any other theoretical or experimental paper on heat around 1787 was the occasion for Cavendish to write "Heat"; if it had been, he would have discussed it. Nor, we believe, was the occasion any new theoretical work of his own. "Heat" was not based on a new understanding of his; after all, the central idea, the identification of heat with *vis viva*, had occurred to him long before, at the time of the "Remarks." Nor was the stimulus his own heat experiments, since the experiments crucial to the refinement of the theory, those on specific and latent heats, he had done much earlier.

Another possible stimulus was practical applications of heat, which were abundant at this time. For several years, in the mid-1780s, Cavendish and Blagden made journeys to various parts of Britain, visiting industrial works wherever they went, and making close observations of power machinery such as water wheels and steam engines. The late 1780s were the years of Cavendish's concentrated researches on heat, including, if our dating is right, the theoretical study "Heat." But any stimulus Cavendish received from his industrial tours was, at most, of a general nature. "Heat" contains no practical discussions. To the text immediately following his calculation of the horsepower of light and his proposed experiment to determine the *vis viva* required to produce a given increase of sensible heat in a body, he added this footnote: "If it was possible to make a wheel with float boards like those of a water wheel which should move with ½ the velocity of light without suffering any resistance from friction & the resistance of the air, & as much of the ☉s light as falls on a surface of 1½ sq. feet was thrown on one side of this wheel, it would actually do more work for any mechanical purpose than 2 horses."[77] An implication for the conversion of forces for practical purposes might be read into this, but the example, taken at face value, is a thought-experiment.

One principal reason why Cavendish wrote "Heat," we believe, is that he had recently been doing extensive experimental work on heat, and he wanted to clarify for himself, anew, the theoretical foundations of the subject. His way of clarification was to develop systematically and rigorously the consequences of the fundamental hypothesis and then to compare these consequences with experimental results. Our interpretation is supported by two pages among the unnumbered sheets at the end of the rough draft of "Heat." They contain notes Cavendish made before writing the draft, listing and briefly commenting on the

[75] John Roebuck, "Experiments on Ignited Bodies," *PT* 66 (1776): 509–12. These experiments, witnessed by Cavendish among others, showed an increase of weight in iron and silver upon cooling, a result in agreement with Fordyce's later experiments.

[76] Charles Blagden to Henry Cavendish, n.d., [1785], Cavendish Mss X(b), 4.

[77] Cavendish, "Heat," 22.

phenomena he would discuss there. Some notes are straightforward statements, such as this example of the mechanical equivalent of heat: "Heat from action of ⊙s light" leading to the "calculation of *vis viva* of ⊙s rays & of D° required to commun. given quant. heat." Other notes are tentative, as if Cavendish were posing questions to discuss in the paper to follow. "Heat by friction & hammering. Whether they can give suffic. *vis viva*," to which Cavendish added a footnote suggesting a possible answer to the question: "Perhaps may where much force is concentrated in small space as in boring holes &c but as friction is not produced without tearing the greatest part of heat produced thereby is likely to be owing to other cause." To the note "Heat by emission of light, the light commonly impelled by repulsion of large particles of matter," he added a footnote, "but quere whether this can be the case in flame." He raised other questions: "whether all kinds of force applied should give any vis viva to a body or only suffic. quick motions," and "what is the cause of friction & want of elasticity whether it is not always owing to tearing off of particles or altering their arrangement." The latter question was followed by a proposed experiment on friction. He questioned "why the motion of the particles should cause a body to expand"; unable to "explain" that fact, he suggested that the answer lay in the altered interactions and positions of particles in motion.[78] There is nothing in the wording of Cavendish's questions to indicate that he was in any doubt about the truth of the hypothesis that heat is the vibration of particles.

The wider scientific world, however, had serious doubts about the hypothesis that Cavendish championed. Earlier supporters were seen to waver if not convert. In 1782, in his treatise on natural philosophy, William Nicholson wrote that the view of heat as the vibration of particles was "scarcely hypothetical." To postulate a fluid of heat was tantamount to multiplying causes in violation of the rules of scientific reasoning; moreover, such a fluid demanded scarcely credible, "amazing," properties. But in his treatise on chemistry in 1790, Nicholson left undecided the nature of heat, calling it a "great question" deserving the attention of natural philosophers. So marked was the tide of scientific opinion that Cavendish could mistakenly be thought to subscribe to the fluid hypothesis. In 1786, in a book on the latest advances in heat, light, and pneumatic chemistry, Bryan Higgins wrote that there was no need for him to justify his material view of heat, since Cavendish together with "other distinguished Philosophers have accepted it." If Cavendish took note of Higgins's mistake, he must at the same time have realized that he had not made sufficiently public his view of heat. With "Heat," he intended to set the record straight.[79]

---

[78] Cavendish, "Heat," rough draft, two sequential, unnumbered pages, the first beginning "heat from action of ⊙s light . . ."

[79] William Nicholson, *An Introduction to Natural Philosophy*, 2 vols. (London, 1782) 1:134; *The First Principles of Chemistry* (London, 1790), 6. Bryan Higgins, *Experiments and Observations Relating to Acetous Acid, Fixable Air, Dense Inflamable Air, Oils and Fuel; The Matter of Fire and Light* (London, 1786), 301–2.

In length, "Heat" compares with Cavendish's manuscript "Thoughts Concerning Electricity" and the mathematical propositions belonging to it, the preliminary version of his paper containing a complete electrical theory, which he published in the *Philosophical Transactions* in 1771.[80] Cavendish referred to the first draft of "Heat" as the "foul copy," appending to it several pages of additions and alterations. In a footnote to the second draft, he referred to the "text," to which he provided an apparatus of footnotes. He planned yet another writing in which certain paragraphs would be reordered. "Heat" was not written for a friend, "you," but for publication. In scope and ambition, it would have equalled his paper on electrical theory. Treating the principal experimental fields of natural philosophy, the two papers would have stood side by side as the two great works of theoretical physics in Britain in the second half of the eighteenth century.

We can acquire some insight into Cavendish's direction in the late 1780s by looking at his world then. By this time Cavendish would have seen that the general understanding of physical reality that had guided his researches for twenty years was everywhere under attack or ignored. The ether and the imponderable fluids were now widely understood to have provided the theoretical foundation of a new, unified natural philosophy. Although it was based on a fluid, Cavendish's electrical theory was ignored by his British colleagues, while abroad his theory remained all but unknown.[81] Electrical researchers were commonly interested in the connections between electricity and the ether, chemical action, air, sound, light, and heat; Cavendish's theory was exclusively electrical, concerned solely with the implications of a hypothetical electric fluid together with the law of electric force. The phlogiston theory of chemistry was under attack; by 1784, when Cavendish publicly defended the phlogiston theory, Lavoisier's new understanding of combustion was well advanced, and over the next few years chemists began converting to the new chemistry. In Britain, as we have seen, Cavendish himself was probably the first to abandon phlogiston, in 1787. Pneumatic chemistry, the science which owed most to Cavendish's work, was just then acquiring its caloric theory, according to which the particles of gases were surrounded by a repellent fiery matter, an idea foreign to Cavendish's way of thinking. The beleaguered Newtonian theory of heat was demonstrably superior to its competitor, the material theory, Cavendish was convinced. This conclusion was supported by his researches not only in the science of heat proper but also in the two other sciences in which he had done his most important experimental work, chemistry and electricity. In referring the phenomena of heat to

[80] Henry Cavendish, "Thoughts Concerning Electricity" and "Cavendish's First Mathematical Theory," Cavendish Mss I, 17 and 18, and his published paper of 1771, "An Attempt to Explain Some of the Principal Phaenomena of Electricity, by Means of an Elastic Fluid."

[81] Blagden, upon delivering to Cavendish a gift of René-Just Haüy's new treatise on electricity and magnetism, which contained an electrical hypothesis similar to Cavendish's, observed that the author seemed unaware of Cavendish's fundamental paper of 1771: Blagden to C. L. Berthollet, draft, 11 Sept. 1787, Blagden Letters, Royal Society, 7:69.

forces of attraction and repulsion between the particles of matter, even if he could say nothing more precise about the forces than that they were conservative, Cavendish demonstrated in "Heat" that Newton's direction for advancing natural philosophy was still adequate to the task of accommodating recent experimental work. The above considerations underlay the unusually forceful wording of "Heat."

It is easier to appreciate why Cavendish wrote "Heat" than to decide why he dropped it. Possibly when Cavendish began "Heat," he expected more from it. Founded on the principles of mechanics, his theory of heat was rigorous, but at the stage he left it, he had not yet shown the theory capable of predicting new, quantitatively determinable phenomena. In that important respect, its development was inferior to that of his electrical theory with its impressive predictive powers.

Referring to Cavendish's unpublished papers, Blagden said that "it is to be supposed that he afterwards discovered some weakness or imperfection in them." But if the ideas in "Heat" were imperfect from Cavendish's point of view, the question is only pushed back. What were his standards? "When a theory has been proposed by Sr I. N." and agrees with the facts, Cavendish said of Newton's theory of heat, it is to be accepted. Cavendish had written up his electrical researches as an intended treatise on the force of electricity, an electrical system of the world, in form and substance the electrical sequel of Newton's gravitational system of the world. Heat is an equally fundamental subject; its phenomena are universal, since heat is produced by every kind of force. It is, we believe, against the standards set by Newton in the *Principia* that Cavendish's individual mix of assertion and caution must be viewed.

If we were to reverse the usual terms of the comparison between the two and think of Newton as Cavendish, it would be as if Newton had had no Halley, in which case there might have been no *Principia*, and as if Hooke had outlived Newton, in which case there might have been no *Opticks*. So far as we know, Cavendish perceived no one to be his enemy as Newton did Hooke; he also had no one like Halley to urge him to put his work into finished form. If Cavendish was not the coldest of mortals, as one of his contemporaries said of him, he was by all accounts distant, discouraging any attempt at familiarity. No one would have presumed to tell Cavendish what he ought to do, if anyone knew enough about his work even to harbor the thought. Like his work in electricity, his work in heat–it extended much longer than his work in electricity, over twenty years–was allowed to languish. There is no reason to think that his contemporaries knew what he was about, though perhaps Blagden had an inkling. He published three papers on heat, all of them commentaries on experiments performed by someone else, from which only the most perspicacious reader could have imagined the full experimental and theoretical grasp that informed them.

THE NATURAL PHILOSOPHER

"Philosophy," the geologist and natural philosopher James Hutton wrote, is the aim of "science." Although natural philosophy cannot advance one step without experiment, unless experiment is guided by philosophy, it can produce only endless collections of facts, and that, Hutton said, is not philosophy. "The disposing of one fact, that is, the putting it into its proper place in science or the general order of one's knowledge, is doing more for natural philosophy, than a thousand experiments made without that order of connection or relation which is to inform the understanding." William Enfield, a teacher at Warrington Academy, similarly identified natural philosophy with the ordering of scientific facts within general truths. Honor is bestowed on those who enhance the public store of experimental facts, he said; and "one who proceeds thus far, is an experimentalist; but he alone, who, by examining the nature and absorbing the relations of facts, arrives at general truths, is a philosopher. A moderate share of industry may suffice for the former: patient attention, deep reflection, and acute penetration, are necessary in the latter. It is therefore no wonder, that amongst many experimentalists there should be few philosophers."[82]

If we accept the above characterization of natural philosophy, George Wilson in *The Life of the Honourable Henry Cavendish* excluded Cavendish from the ranks of natural philosophers. He said that Cavendish's universe consisted "*solely* of a multitude of objects which could be weighed, numbered, and measured." He came to this understanding of Cavendish's "Theory of the Universe" after examining his chemical papers closely and his papers on heat and on his journeys cursorily. These papers contained observations and experimental researches in which weighings, thermometer readings, and similar numbers occurred throughout. They were, Wilson believed, the restricted language of a man whose elected vocation was to "weigh, number, and measure as many of those objects as his allotted three-score years and ten would permit." A "calculating engine" was Wilson's characterization of Cavendish's brain.[83] Wilson's judgment has been uncritically repeated ever since, but he was fundamentally in error about his subject.

"It is the business of natural Philosophy," the natural philosopher Hugh Hamilton wrote, "to reduce as many Phaenomena as may be to some general well-known Cause."[84] In all three of Cavendish's major original lines of research, chemistry, electricity, and heat, he held theories of the causes of the phenomena. His chemical researches were guided by the phlogiston theory, which he discussed in his earliest, unpublished chemical writings and in his published ones

[82] Hutton, *Dissertation upon the Philosophy of Light, Heat, and Fire*, xi. William Enfield, *Institutes of Natural Philosophy, Theoretical and Experimental* . . . (London, 1785), vi–vii.

[83] Wilson, *Cavendish*, 185–86.

[84] Hugh Hamilton, *Philosophical Essays on the Following Subjects: I. On the Principles of Mechanics. II. On the Ascent of Vapours . . . III. Observations and Conjectures on the Nature of the Aurora Borealis, and the Tails of Comets* (Dublin, 1766), 36.

as well. The starting point of his electrical researches was his theory of the electric fluid, in the unpublished "Thoughts Concerning Electricity," and in its elaboration and refinement in the published theoretical paper of 1771. His earliest experimental researches in heat followed his unpublished paper treating the theory of heat as the vibrations of particles, "Remarks on the Theory of Motion." All of these theoretical writings belong to the 1760s, we believe, when Cavendish was in his thirties and just setting out as a researcher. For the rest of his career he worked from these theoretical ideas (he apparently gave up phlogiston, but not until after his last publication in chemistry), modifying them as needed, perfecting them, and studying the phenomena in question experimentally.

Cavendish's goal was to understand nature, not to calculate for its own sake. That much is clear from "Heat," though the manuscript does contain calculations. Following the mechanical theorems governing vibrating particles, Cavendish carried through a long calculation for the example of electric discharge and another for Michell's experiment on light. But for the most part the subject of heat did not yet lend itself to extended calculations. The persuasiveness of Cavendish's paper derived from another source, its coherence, comprehensiveness, and strict reasoning, which included mathematical reasoning where it applied. Passing from one branch of natural philosophy to another, he reasoned that Newton's theory did "really explain" the phenomena of heat. "Heat" is a continuous argument for the hypothesis that heat consists of the invisible vibrations of bodies; it is a study in *understanding*.

In developing his case for Newton's theory, which is a theory about nature at the level of the particles of matter, Cavendish repeatedly called on a general standpoint. Elsewhere in his writings he called on it, too, but only in "Heat" did he make explicit his beliefs about the ultimate constituents, his "Theory of the Universe." The discussion occurs in a footnote to the discussion of friction, which in the rough draft is motivated by an observation omitted from the fair copy: "The nature of friction & imperfect elasticity deserves to be considered more accurately." It continues:

> According to Father Boscovich & Mr Michell matter does not consist of solid impenetrable particles as commonly supposed, but only of certain degrees of attraction & repulsion directed towards central points. They also suppose that the action of 2 of these central points on each other alternately varies from repulsion to attraction numberless times as the distance increases. There is the utmost reason to think that both these suppositions are true; & they serve to account for many phenomena of nature which would otherwise be inexplicable. But even if it is otherwise, & if it must be admitted that there are solid impenetrable particles, still there seems sufficient reason to think that those particles do not touch each other, but are kept from ever coming in contact by their repulsive force.[85]

[85] Cavendish, "Heat," rough draft, 18; and Cavendish, "Heat," 28–29.

This is what Cavendish thought the world was made of. He believed that Boscovich and Michell were likely to be right about particles, but it would change nothing in the argument at hand if Newton, who believed in solid impenetrable particles, was right, for in either case, the force of repulsion keeps particles from touching and losing *vis viva.*

John Michell's views were made public by Priestley in 1772 in his history of optics.[86] Roger Joseph Boscovich's views were published in his treatise *Theoria philosophiae naturalis*, which appeared just as Cavendish was beginning his career as a researcher.[87] The Leibnizian and Newtonian elements in Boscovich's theory, such as Leibniz's law of continuity and Newton's attractive and repulsive forces, made his theory compatible with, and useful for understanding, Newton's theory of heat in the form that Cavendish gave to it. In Boscovich's theory, point masses interact through central forces, permitting no friction or inelastic collisions, which destroy *vis viva.* At close separations, particles experience infinite repulsion, at large separations, gravitational attraction, and in between they experience the attractions and repulsions responsible for cohesion, vaporization, and a great variety of other chemical and physical phenomena. Boscovich represented his universal "law of forces" by a continuous curve: above the axis the force is repulsive, below the axis it is attractive, and the points where it passes from repulsion to attraction mark the limit points of cohesion. Particles vibrate about these points when disturbed, and the vibrations continue indefinitely until the particles are again disturbed. The area between the curve and the axis is proportional to *vis viva*, since it measures the action of a force across a distance. Boscovich's theory, with its implied possibility of perpetually vibrating particles accounting for combustion, dissolution, and fermentation, and with its implied conservation law, provided support for Newton's theory of heat, which is why Cavendish introduced it in "Heat."[88]

For Cavendish the world was constituted of force. Force was the basic, irreducible concept of science. Our entire experience of nature testified to its existence and ubiquitous presence. Blagden recorded in his diary that Cavendish "argued that one had no right to say that matter could not act

---

[86] Priestley, *History* 1:309–11, 392–93, 786–91.

[87] Priestley also discussed Boscovich's views in his *History*, but Cavendish would have also known them directly from their author, in his first edition in 1758 of the *Theoria.* Cavendish and Michell met Boscovich on his tour of England, both dining with him at the Royal Society Club on 5 June 1760 and Cavendish with him again on 26 June 1760: Royal Society Club Minute Book, Royal Society, vol. 4.

[88] It makes no difference here that Boscovich himself believed in the matter of fire; Roger Joseph Boscovich, *A Theory of Natural Philosophy*, trans. J. M. Child from the 2d ed. of 1763 (Cambridge, Mass.: MIT Press, 1966), 22–23, 43, 73, 76–96. Boscovich did not have a conservation law and generally regarded *vis viva* as having little significance, which may seem surprising given that his theory readily explains the conservation of *vis viva.* Thomas L. Hankins, "Eighteenth-Century Attempts to Resolve the *Vis viva* Controversy," *Isis* 56 (1965): 281–97, on 294, and on Boscovich, 291–97; on Michell and Boscovich, Schofield, *Mechanism and Materialism*, 236–49.

where it was not: one knew nothing about it but from experience, & experience rather led to believe that it might."[89] And matter, according to the above quotation from "Heat," was nothing other than centers of force. Cavendish, as we have maintained, accepted Newton's view that the main task of philosophy was to determine the forces of nature and their phenomena. The forces responsible for the phenomena of heat pose a problem for the natural philosopher. They act only over short distances, and in Cavendish's time no "universal synthesis of short-range forces" had been established.[90] Nevertheless, as Newton had shown in his derivation of the sine law of refraction for individual rays of light, it was possible to determine rigorously some results of importance in science without knowing "what kind of Force" is acting, instead assuming only very general properties of forces.[91] Cavendish showed that the phenomena of heat can be deduced from a knowledge only of the general nature of the acting forces. Boscovich's forces, which depend on distance and are directed to central points, are forces that satisfy the assumptions of Cavendish's conservation law. It is conceivable that Cavendish's reading of Boscovich gave him his original direction, but for someone as widely informed as Cavendish we doubt that the impetus was so straightforward.[92] Cavendish had mastered Newton's science, but he needed more than Newton gave him to create "Newton's" theory of heat, and important as Leibnizian *vis viva* was for his purposes, that did not give it to him either. Neither did Michell's and Boscovich's views on the nature of matter and force. Rather Cavendish drew on all of these sources and on his and others' experimental investigations of heat, and by strict reasoning he brought them together to make the theory he presented in "Heat."

In the introduction, we give our reasons for preferring to speak of Cavendish as a "natural" philosopher rather than as a "Newtonian" philosopher. But that is not to deny that he was also a Newtonian of a well-defined persuasion. We return to this point even as we call attention to his differences with Newton and to sources other than Newton for his understanding of forces. To characterize fully Cavendish's Newtonianism would be to recapitulate much of what we have said about him from his education at Cambridge onwards. His researches in heat contain his most revealing statement on the subject. "When a theory has been proposed by Sr I. N.," Cavendish wrote, and it is in agreement with experience, it

[89] 22 Nov. 1804, Charles Blagden Diary, Royal Society, 4:284.

[90] Cantor, *Optics after Newton*, 87.

[91] Newton, *Opticks*, 82.

[92] Michell arrived independently at views similar to Boscovich's, and Cavendish may have done so, too, given the theoretical problems he was working on. It has been pointed out that there was a British tradition paralleling Boscovich's views: Cantor, *Optics after Newton*, 71–72; Schofield, *Mechanism and Materialism*, 237–38; P. M. Heimann and J. E. McGuire, "Newtonian Forces and Lockean Powers: Concepts of Matter in Eighteenth-Century Thought," *Historical Studies in the Physical Sciences* 3 (1971): 233–306.

should be accepted. To no other authority did Cavendish give a blanket endorsement like this. In "Heat" he did not weigh the evidence for the competing theories of heat, Newton's and the material, but developed only the former and denounced the latter. If there is the suggestion here of a doctrinaire element in Cavendish's thinking, it remains that the theory of heat as motion would be vindicated in the next century.

Other aspects of Cavendish's Newtonianism, we note, placed him not in the vanguard but in opposition to future developments in science, for example, to the wave theory of light. In America, Francis Hopkinson observed that when he viewed a lamp through a silk handkerchief and moved the handkerchief before his eyes, he saw dark bars which did not move. Hopkinson took his "optical Problem" to the astronomer David Rittenhouse, who performed experiments with a square of parallel hairs, observing that the lines seen through it varied in strength and color. Doubts about Rittenhouse's experiment were expressed at a meeting of the Royal Society. However, "Lord Cavendish," Hopkinson wrote to Thomas Jefferson, performed the experiment and "declared it was truly stated." Cavendish had a high opinion of Rittenhouse, being the first to sign the certificate recommending him for membership in the Royal Society.[93] What Rittenhouse had constructed was, in fact, a diffraction grating, an instrument which would be used to measure the wavelength of light. Only thirteen years later, in 1800, Thomas Young submitted a paper to the Royal Society on the wave theory of light, reopening an old debate, which would lead to the dominant theory of light in the nineteenth century. No doubt Cavendish had an explanation for Rittenhouse's experiment, probably agreeing with Rittenhouse's own, which was that it was an instance of the inflexion of light by bodies as described by Newton; that is, Rittenhouse's experiment was explained by the corpuscular theory of light. Nevertheless, with hindsight, it would seem that Rittenhouse's experiments were a missed opportunity for Cavendish, but then everyone else missed it too.[94] Cavendish continued to hold the corpuscular theory of light after Young's introduction of the wave theory: in, or after, 1804 Cavendish calculated the gravitational bending of light passing near the surface of any body, such as the limb of a star or the edge of a hair.[95]

As Young understood Newton, it was "Newton's opinion, that heat consists in a minute vibratory motion of the particles of bodies, and that this motion is communicated through an apparent vacuum by the undulations of an elastic

[93] 6 Nov. 1794, Royal Society, Certificates, 5.

[94] Francis Hopkinson to Thomas Jefferson, 14 April 1787, in *The Papers of Thomas Jefferson*, vol. 11, ed. J. P. Boyd (Princeton: Princeton University Press, 1955), 288–90. Brooke Hindle, *David Rittenhouse* (Princeton: Princeton University Press, 1964), 276–77. John C. Greene, *American Science in the Age of Jefferson* (Ames: Iowa State University Press, 1984), 158–60.

[95] This calculation is in Cavendish Mss Misc., published in *Sci. Pap.* 2:437. Although it is undated, inspection of the watermark on the paper shows that it could not have been earlier than 1804.

medium, which is also concerned in the phenomena of light."[96] Young's understanding pointed to the physics of the ether, the origin of unified views of nature of the nineteenth century. Cavendish's understanding of Newton did not incorporate the ether. He held to a theoretical view by which the phenomena of nature were seen to have a uniform cause in attractive and repulsive, centrally acting forces. This view, together with mechanical theorems about the appropriate measure of the forces of moving bodies, *vis viva*, permitted him to display a connectedness between the several major domains of phenomena constituting the broad field of experimental natural philosophy.

[96] Thomas Young, *A Syllabus of a Course of Lectures on Natural and Experimental Philosophy* (London, 1802), 149.

CHAPTER 6

EARTH

PHILOSOPHICAL TOURS IN BRITAIN

Active in the planning of voyages and expeditions of others, Cavendish never went on one himself. He did, however, make a number of journeys by carriage within Britain, always in the summer when conditions of travel were at their best. On the first journey we know anything about, Cavendish passed through Oxford to Birmingham and back by way of Towcester, making trials of Nairne's dipping needle at each stop, usually in a garden. Those trials may have been the whole point, for it was 1778, soon after Cavendish's report on the meteorological and magnetic instruments of the Royal Society, and he was still very much involved.[1] Beginning in 1785 Cavendish became a regular and more rounded scientific tourist. This fiftyish man of fixed, secluded habits had recently taken on as his assistant Charles Blagden, who had much to do with Cavendish's adventurous turn.

An inveterate traveler, Blagden recorded his journeys in notes and letters, beginning with a journey he took to Scotland to study at age seventeen.[2] We have his report of a visit to Wales when he was twenty-three and an impressionable if conventional tourist. A follower of Rousseau, the "most eloquent & feeling of men,"[3] he was drawn to abbeys and vistas, but he was also interested in mines, iron works, and "philosophical curiosities." He wanted to know the great world, yet wherever he traveled he was frustrated because people could not answer his straightforward questions about what lay a mile around them–places, routes, departures, and the like. He was astonished at the "extreme stupidity of the

[1] Henry Cavendish, "Trials of Nairne's Needle in Different Parts of England," Cavendish Mss IX, 11:45–54. Dates in the second half of August 1778 are scattered through this record of observations.

[2] Charles Blagden to Sarah Nelmes, 1 Nov. 1765, Blagden Letters, Royal Society, B.159. In other letters in 1767 Blagden gave Nelmes accounts of shorter journeys in Scotland. Nelmes, who lived in Bristol, and Blagden were distant relatives. "Accounts, Bills, Insurance, and Copy of Will of S. Nelmes," Blagden Mss, Royal Society.

[3] Blagden recommended reading Rousseau to a friend. Charles Blagden to Thomas Curtis, 26 July 1771, Blagden Letters, Royal Society, B.162.

people," who were entirely satisfied with their "little world."[4] For several years he served in North America as surgeon in the British army. Then, as a seasoned traveler, soon after his return to Britain he toured Devonshire, where he found the coves and rocks "beautiful" and "romantic," but where he also observed mileages, weather, slate, and clay.[5] His most important journey was from Plymouth to London in 1781, where he soon made his life in science.[6] In the summer of 1783 he visited France, but by then he was already in the service of Cavendish.[7]

Blagden urged Cavendish to travel. In 1785, Blagden wrote to John Michell that he "endeavoured to persuade our friend Mr Cavendish to make you a visit at Thornhill."[8] He did not succeed, but he hoped that he and Cavendish could accept his "kind invitation" next year,[9] as they did. This year they went in another direction, to Wales. Blagden made advance arrangements. He wrote to his brother-in-law William Lewis that he had proposed to Cavendish that they visit his iron works in Glamorganshire and that Cavendish was "very curious." Lewis wrote back promising to show them "all the different Ironstones," and offering his house, but if the "Hammers should be too noisy" he would put them up at another house removed from the pounding.[10] For years after this visit, Lewis sent Cavendish specimens, such as kish (a kind of graphite that separates from iron in smelting), for Cavendish to examine.[11] All along their tour Blagden and Cavendish talked to owners, engineers, agents, and workmen, who gave them information no one else could, and specimens to keep. Blagden reported to Banks that Cavendish "bears the journey remarkably well."[12] Their trip lasted three weeks.

Cavendish and Blagden's journey was by then a well-established custom among experienced travellers in Britain, an industrial version of the Grand Tour. Like Cavendish and Blagden, in the same year, the London chemists William Higgins and William Lewis visited British factories.[13] A favorite stop of tourists was the Soho

[4] Charles Blagden, "Memorandum of a Tour Taken for Four Days Beginning Aug. 18 1771," Blagden Papers, Yale, box 1, folder 3.

[5] Charles Blagden, "Tour of the South Hams of Devonshire," 1780, Charles Blagden Diary, Yale, Osborn Shelves f c 16.

[6] Charles Blagden, "Journey from Plymouth to London 1781," Yale, Osborn Shelves f c 16.

[7] Charles Blagden's memoranda of his trip to France in 1783, Blagden Papers, Yale, box 1, folder 3.

[8] Charles Blagden to John Michell, 25 Apr. 1785, draft, Blagden Letterbook, Yale.

[9] Charles Blagden to John Michell, 13 Sep. 1785, draft, Blagden Letterbook, Yale.

[10] Charles Blagden to William Lewis, 20 June 1785, draft, Blagden Letterbook, Yale. William Lewis to Charles Blagden, 25 June 1785, Blagden Letters, Royal Society, L.46.

[11] Charles Blagden to William Lewis, 10 Nov. 1786 and 6 Nov. 1787, drafts, Blagden Letters, Royal Society, 7:53 and 7:83.

[12] Charles Blagden to Joseph Banks, 31 July 1785, Banks Correspondence, Kew, 1:199.

[13] A. E. Musson and E. Robinson, *Science and Technology in the Industrial Revolution* (Toronto: University of Toronto Press, 1969), 122.

Works outside Birmingham, where Matthew Boulton showed them steam engines.[14] The conventional beginning of the British industrial revolution is 1760, the year Cavendish entered the Royal Society. By the time of his journeys with Blagden, an extraordinary industrial landscape had come into being. He ventured into it with all the curiosity he brought to his studies in electricity, chemistry, and heat. The guests Cavendish invited to the Royal Society Club soon after his 1785 journey reflect his expanded interests: the ceramics manufacturer Josiah Wedgwood, his host John Michell with whom he was in geological correspondence at the time, the mineralogist Charles Greville, and the mineralogical chemist James Macie (Smithson), who himself had just made a geological, mining, and manufacturing tour.[15]

On their first journey, Cavendish and Blagden saw quarrying, cloth manufacture, dying, coal mining, coal-tar manufacture, lime-kilning, coke-making, copper-casting, brass-drawing, and iron-making. They saw iron and steel made into buttons, needles, nails, and ship bolts. They saw slitting and flatting mills, hammers, rollers, cranes, pincers, and iron furnaces standing as high as forty-five feet. The scenes they witnessed at forges were violent with their intense heat and fireworks, as were those at coal pits, some of which were burning. Yet but for a difference of scale, there was an unmistakable similarity between this landscape and Cavendish's serene laboratory. Cavendish accepted Lord Mulgrave's invitation to visit his alum works, "having formerly made experiments himself on the crystallization of alum."[16] The manufacturers used the same chemicals as Cavendish; they brought their materials together by proportionate weights as he did; they were concerned with impurities as he was; they had their hearths and bellows as he had his. He and Blagden brought with them instruments including chemical equipment, with which they tried their own little experiments.[17]

Stopping in Birmingham, Cavendish visited Watt and the industrialist John Wilkinson. Watt, who had invented the separate condenser in the 1760s, had just made another major improvement in the steam engine. This one converted the linear motion of the piston's drive to a rotary motion, which was useful in mills. Cavendish was shown it and also a furnace Watt had contrived for burning smoke, which he intended to apply to the steam engine. Cavendish's papers contain drawings by him of Watt's rotative mechanism and Watt's smoke-burning furnace.[18] At other iron works, Cavendish and Blagden came across Watt's steam

---

[14] Robert E. Schofield, *The Lunar Society of Birmingham: A Social History of Provincial Science and Industry in Eighteenth-Century England* (Oxford: Clarendon Press, 1963), 26–27.

[15] 9 Mar. and 14 Dec. 1786, Minute Book, Royal Society Club, Royal Society, 8. Leonard Carmichael and J. C. Long, *James Smithson and the Smithsonian Story* (New York: G. P. Putnam's Sons, 1965), 68.

[16] Charles Blagden to Lord Mulgrave, 2 Aug. 1786, draft, Royal Society, 7:17.

[17] The journal is in a wrapper labeled in Cavendish's hand, "Computations & Observations in Journey 1785," Cavendish Mss X(a), 4. The journal itself is in another hand.

[18] Henry Cavendish, "Watts Fire Place for Burning Smoke," Cavendish Mss Misc.

engines in use.[19] That fall Watt came to London, to Albion Mills at Black Friars Bridge, where his new smoke-burning furnaces were to be installed. We can imagine that Cavendish was on hand, as we know he went there to inspect plans for a steam engine and a waterwheel.[20]

Cavendish's meeting with Watt took place about a year after the water controversy and Watt's private denunciations of Cavendish. Cavendish's journal does not record that the two men talked about the composition of water, though Watt told Cavendish about scientific experiments he had done with the steam engine on the condensation of steam and the latent heat generated. Earlier that year, when Watt was in London, he was invited as a guest to the Royal Society Club,[21] where he was received "very kindly by Mr. Cavendish and Dr. Blagden, and my old friend Smeaton."[22] Clearly, Cavendish and Watt wished to be on friendly terms.

On this first journey together, Cavendish and Blagden pursued a new active interest of Cavendish's, geology. They made regular observations of strata, rocks, and pebbles surfacing the roads, noting blue, red, and white clay, limestone, granite, sand, and slate along the way. They drew no conclusions but no discouragement either, as they continued to make geological observations on their subsequent journeys.

In early summer of the following year, Blagden's brother, John Blagden Hale, invited Cavendish to join with Blagden on a visit. Blagden told his brother that he had "every reason to believe that he [Cavendish] will not find it convenient to go from home." Blagden conveyed the invitation, but he knew his friend. A week later he wrote to his brother, confirming that Cavendish did "not find it convenient to leave home."[23] He added "at this time": two months later Cavendish and Blagden set out again on a roughly three-week trip, this one much longer than the first, over eight hundred miles to the north of England and back. They went directly to John Michell's house at Thornhill, near Wakefield in Yorkshire,[24] then to Lord Mulgrave's, returning to Michell's where they stayed several more days.[25] In his diary, Blagden wrote: "At Mr Michell's took some altitudes & looked over his fossils. . . . At night looked thro' his telescope: tho' much false light & confused images

[19] "Computations & Observations in Journey 1785."

[20] Charles Blagden to Sir Joseph Banks, 23 Oct. 1785, Banks Correspondence, Kew, 1:212. Cavendish together with Smeaton and Blagden were invited to inspect drawings of a steam engine and a water wheel at a works by the late Albion Mills, after which they observed a water wheel in action at Bow. John Maitland to Sir Joseph Banks, 19 Dec. 1791, BL Add Mss 33979, p. 118.

[21] It was on 24 Feb. 1785. Archibald Geikie, *Annals of the Royal Society Club* (London: Macmillan, 1917), 174.

[22] Watt quoted in Samuel Smiles, *Lives of the Engineers. Harbours–Lighthouses–Bridges. Smeaton and Rennie*, rev. ed. (London, 1874), 169.

[23] Charles Blagden to John Blagden Hale, 13 and 20 June 1786, drafts, Blagden Letters, Royal Society, 7:4, 8.

[24] Charles Blagden to Lord Mulgrave, 2 Aug. 1786, draft, Blagden Letters, Royal Society, 7:17. Charles Blagden to John Michell, 5 Aug. 1786, draft, ibid., 7:21.

[25] Charles Blagden to John Blagden Hale, 14 Sep. 1786, draft, Blagden Letterbook, Royal Society, 7:33.

yet obs'd ♄ with it well: could see the belt plainly; & obs'd an emersion of the 3 sat. much better than it appeared thro' the 2 feet reflector."[26] On Sunday, Blagden went to Michell's sermon, which he had heard or read before; we assume that Cavendish did not hear the sermon, since Blagden did not mention it. Much of their time was spent making–rather wanting to make, since the weather was foul–excursions up mountains with Cavendish's barometer, "a main object" of their tour.[27] Cavendish discussed geology with Michell, and he came away with a treasure, Michell's table of strata, measured to the inch, going down 221 feet.[28] Cavendish's account of this journey is mostly about strata.[29]

92. *Portable Barometer. The ingenious mahogany case opens into a tripod. The barometer is suspended in gimbals. Alongside the (now broken) barometer are two scales, one English and one French. At the bottom near the wooden cistern, there is a thermometer with a correction scale. When inverted for carrying, the instrument measures 43½ inches. Photographed at Chatsworth by the authors. Reproduced by permission of the Trustees of the Chatsworth Settlement. This barometer was certainly Cavendish's, probably the one described in the auction catalog of Cavendish's instruments as a "mountain barometer," and likely the barometer that Cavendish took with him on his journeys outside London to measure the heights of mountains. William Roy, with whom Cavendish collaborated on experiments with barometers, used a portable barometer almost identical to the one at Chatsworth for taking the heights of mountains. Although the Chatsworth barometer is unsigned, we know from Roy that this kind of barometer was made by Jesse Ramsden. The instrument was highly accurate. The height of the mercury column was read to one-five hundredth part of an inch by means of a nonius moved by rackwork. Roy used two such instruments in his experiments, finding them to agree within a few thousandths of an inch. Roy, "Experiments and Observations Made in Britain, in Order to Obtain a Rule for Measuring Heights with a Barometer,"* Philosophical Transactions *67 (1777): 653–787, facing 658.*

[26] 2 Sep. 1786, Charles Blagden Diary, Yale, Osborn Shelves f c 16.

[27] Charles Blagden to Sir Joseph Banks, 13 Aug. 1786, BL Add Mss 33272, p. 1.

[28] Henry Cavendish, "Strata Which Michell Dug Through for Coal," in Cavendish's journal of the 1786 trip, Cavendish Mss X(a), 3:13–14. Michell's table gives thirty levels, coal alternating with various other matter. Down to seventy-seven feet, it gives Michell's own knowledge from two pits near his church at Thornhill; the rest is from other pits.

[29] Cavendish's journal of the journey of 1786, Cavendish Mss X(a), 3.

On the same trip, Cavendish and Blagden toured Lord Mulgrave's alum works, from where alum liquor and related substances were sent to Cavendish in London.[30] In Sheffield they observed file-making and other manufactures "pretty much in detail." They stayed at a place recommended by Michell, the Fortune Inn; which proved to be "the vilest house," Blagden complained to Michell, "at which I had ever the misfortune to put up."[31] They made a special trip to Rotheram, to inquire about plumbago, a substance formed in furnaces during the extraction of iron from its ore. From there they proceeded to Chesterfield, where Cavendish acquired a specimen of kishy iron "for examination." In Chesterfield they also went down a mine; Blagden found the ladders "fatiguing," his legs too short, but he said nothing of Cavendish's discomfort if he experienced any. Cavendish noticed evidence of violence in the mine.[32] "Tempestuous" wind and rain frustrated their plans to climb mountains in the Lake District, forcing them to leave sooner than they had planned, but not before Blagden had caught a glimpse of the "magnificent & beautiful" scene.[33] What Cavendish thought of it he did not say. The closest Blagden came to criticizing Cavendish was in a letter fifteen years later, where he wrote, "When I went to the lakes it was in company with Mr Cavendish, who had no curiosity for several things which it would have given me great pleasure to have seen."[34] A month after their return to London, Blagden wrote to Banks that Cavendish was "making experiments upon the stones we brought home," and on specimens from the industrial works, "which will find him some employment if he critically examines them all."[35]

For the third straight year, in 1787, Cavendish and Blagden set off on a journey, this time to the southwestern corner of England, Cornwall. They picked a route along the seacoast "on account of particular experiments to be done there."[36] They brought with them letters of introduction written by Watt and Boulton among others, giving as their purpose, "a philosophical tour."[37] The Cornish mines being new to them, Cavendish and Blagden went down a tin mine

[30] "Computations & Observations in Journey 1786," Cavendish Mss X(a), 5. The wrapper is labeled in Cavendish's hand, the narrative written in another. "Examination of Substances Sent from Ld Mulgrave's," in "White Book," Cavendish Mss, pp. 7–13.

[31] Charles Blagden to John Michell, 19 Sep. 1786, draft, Blagden Letterbook, Royal Society, 7:37.

[32] Charles Blagden to Sir Joseph Banks, 17 Sep. 1786, BL Add Mss 33272, pp. 9–10.

[33] Charles Blagden to Sir Joseph Banks, 4 Sep. 1786, BL Add Mss 33272, pp. 7–8.

[34] Charles Blagden to Lord Palmerston, 25 Nov. 1800, Blagden Letters, Yale.

[35] Charles Blagden to Sir Joseph Banks, 8[?] Oct. 1786, BL Add Mss 33272, pp. 15–16.

[36] Charles Blagden to William Lewis, 11 July 1787, draft, Blagden Letterbook, Royal Society, 7:338.

[37] Two letters from George Hunt [?], 23 Jan 1787, who was asked to write letters of introduction by his nephew R. Wilbraham, "The bearer of this are Mr Cavendish. . . ." Blagden Papers, Yale, box 1, folder 4. Along the way, too, Blagden solicited letters, such as James Rennell to Rev. Burington, 18 Aug. 1787, "The bearer, Dr Blagden, is my particular friend. . . ." Blagden Letters, Royal Society, R.5. Charles Blagden to James Watt, 23 Aug. 1787, draft, Blagden Letters, Royal Society, 7:349.

a hundred fathoms deep.[38] Blagden found the descent troublesome and little of interest at the bottom except the manner of working, which had to be seen to be understood. On the rest of the trip he and Cavendish contented themselves with seeing what was above ground.[39] They visited Josiah Wedgwood's clay pits for his porcelain manufacture. The previous winter Wedgwood had sent Blagden specimens of feldspar, with the request that Blagden show them to Cavendish and Kirwan.[40] Cavendish and Blagden visited smelters with their strong smell of arsenic and their workmen covered with red dust. They saw great stampers driven by waterwheels, crushing ore, and steam engines emptying mine shafts of water and hauling up ore.[41] They saw pumping machinery improved by Watt, to whom, Blagden thought, the Cornish were indebted to be able to "work their copper mines at all."[42] Cavendish returned home with specimens to subject to "chemical analysis," which Blagden expected would "shew some more light" on how they were formed.[43] Between industrial sites, Cavendish mainly observed strata.[44] Good weather enabled them to go up mountains with their barometer to measure heights.[45] On their return through Devon, Blagden, who had been there before, took "great pleasure in shewing to Mr Cavendish" the "grand beauties of that remarkable coast." Blagden reported to Banks that Cavendish looked "the better for his journey."[46]

Cavendish and Blagden made a side trip to Dartmoor in southwest Devonshire to carry out an elaborate experiment on the changes in the barometer at different heights of hills. The boulder-strewn hills of Dartmoor rise to around two thousand feet.[47] Blagden, who had lived in nearby Plymouth, made the local arrangements, which involved the assistance of three other men and the construction of a small meteorological observatory.[48] The experiment proved inconclusive, but it was carefully executed and it had theoretical significance, and

---

38 Charles Blagden to Mrs. Grey, 14 June 1787, draft, Blagden Letters, Royal Society, 7:324.

39 Charles Blagden to William Watson, 22 Aug. 1787, draft, Blagden Letters, Royal Society, 7:347.

40 Josiah Wedgwood to Charles Blagden, 30 Dec. 1786, Gloucestershire Record Office, D 1086, F 158.

41 Thirty-page journal of the 1787 journey in another's handwriting but with many insertions in Cavendish's hand. Cavendish Mss X(a), 6.

42 Charles Blagden to Mrs. Grey, 28 Aug. 1787, draft, Blagden Letters, Royal Society, 7:351.

43 Charles Blagden to John Michell, 1 Sep. 1787, draft, Blagden Letters, Royal Society, 7:354.

44 Henry Cavendish's journal of the 1787 trip, Cavendish Mss X(a), 7.

45 There are several large sheets of observations taken with the barometer on the 1787 trip, in Cavendish Mss Misc.

46 Charles Blagden to Sir Joseph Banks, 14 Aug. 1787, BL Add Mss 33272. Blagden to Mrs. Grey, 28 Aug. 1787.

47 Brian Le Messurier, ed., *Crossing's Hundred Years on Dartmoor* (reprint; New York: Augustus M. Kelley, 1967), 15.

48 Charles Blagden to William Farr, 12 June 1787, draft, Blagden Letters, Royal Society, 7:67; and other correspondence with Farr around this time.

through it Cavendish revealed his administrative skills as a scientific director with Blagden's indispensable help. This scientific expedition into the wet and windy moors was conceived, planned, and funded by Cavendish.

Cavendish and Blagden made no more journeys together. In the summer of 1788, Blagden went to France, sending back scientific news for Cavendish.[49] So familiar had Cavendish and Blagden become as a traveling pair that the following year Blagden had to correct Deluc, explaining that he was planning a tour of Italy not with Cavendish but with Lord Palmerston.[50]

Cavendish made one more journey, in 1793. Blagden was then living in Europe,[51] and this time it was Banks not Blagden who encouraged Cavendish to travel. Specifically, Banks wanted Cavendish to witness trials of a new steam engine which, alongside the original engine, was working the Gregory lead mine in Derbyshire. As both Banks and the Cavendish family profited from that mine, Cavendish may have made the journey in the interest of both, as a favor to Banks and as a duty to the family, though we suspect that the opportunity of conferring with Watt and Boulton on steam engines was the decisive motive. Banks indeed urged Watt and Boulton to meet with Cavendish at the mine, and in the notes Cavendish kept of the journey, he recorded not only observations of strata, quarries, collieries, and the air from the Gregory mine, but also an experiment by Watt to determine the specific gravity of steam.[52]

Such were Cavendish's purposes in the journeys of his middle years. Setting out from London in different directions, Cavendish explored different corners of the kingdom. Wherever he went, he examined industrial processes and their materials and products, determined the heights of mountains, collected "stones" and noted their physical characteristics and investigated them chemically,[53] and observed the "order of the strata."[54] He was a tourist with an active curiosity and definite tastes: what interested him he pursued tirelessly, and what did not he silently ignored.

By reason of his journeys, Cavendish became one of the new geologists; in Britain in the late eighteenth century, the main spur to geology was precisely what he was doing, crossing large tracks of country making observations of strata.[55]

---

49 Charles Blagden to Sir Joseph Banks, 13 July 1788, BL Add Mss 33272.

50 Charles Blagden to Jean André Deluc, 5 Sep. 1789, draft, Blagden Letters, Royal Society, 7:301.

51 Charles Blagden to Sir Joseph Banks, 11 May 1793, BL Add Mss 33272, pp. 119–20. Henry Cavendish to Sir Joseph Banks, 23 Sep. 1793, copy, BM(NH), DTC 8:257.

52 Sir Joseph Banks to Matthew Boulton, 6 and 18 July, 10 Aug. 1793, Birmingham Assay Office. "Trial of Air Caught in Gregory Mine," Cavendish Mss Misc.

53 Henry Cavendish, "List of Stones with Their Examination," Cavendish Mss Misc.

54 This twenty-one page paper on strata in Cavendish's hand does not have a group number, but it is kept with the travel journals in the Cavendish Mss.

55 Roy Porter, *The Making of Geology: Earth Science in Britain, 1660–1815* (Cambridge: Cambridge University Press, 1977), 119.

When Blagden toured the Continent, he reported to Cavendish on the soils he observed, extending Cavendish's own observations on the other side of the Channel. The guiding thought was expressed by Cavendish's other principal source of geological information, John Michell. In his 1760 paper on earthquakes, Michell noted that level countries show great extents of the same strata: "we have an instance of this in the chalky and flinty countries of England and France, which (excepting the interruption of the Channel, and the clays, sands, &c. of a few counties) compose a tract of about three hundred miles each way."[56] Despite Cavendish's wide-ranging geological observations, he knew that he had arrived at nothing worth publishing. In one place he acknowledged that he was only scratching the surface and that only superficial knowledge could come of it.[57] He would surely have said the same of his knowledge of industrial machinery. His knowledge of the constitution of minerals was extensive but largely happenstance, and again he published nothing of it and showed no inclination even to organize his experiments. The scientific observations Cavendish made during and following his journeys can easily be recognized as belonging to important developments in the science of that time, but there is a sense in which his journeys were summer vacations too, justified by his active curiosity about the natural and the manmade landscapes far from London. A great reader of travels by others, as we know from his library, he was prepared to be enticed out of his study by Blagden and to become himself, for a time, a traveler. His journals do not differ from travel journals commonly kept by others except perhaps in their spareness. They have much in common with the journals of geological and industrial observations of the chemist William Lewis and of Cavendish's colleague Charles Hatchett, and with the geological journals of Saussure and Deluc.[58] It is hard to think of Cavendish enjoying himself, but it seems that he did on these journeys, in his active way, for as his traveling companion observed, he held up well and looked better for them.

The journeys marked a change in the direction of Cavendish's work in chemistry. His experiments in pneumatic chemistry in effect came to an end with his paper on phlogisticated air in 1785, the year he made his first journey with Blagden. In 1786 he began keeping a new record of chemical experiments,

[56] John Michell, "Conjectures Concerning the Cause, and Observations upon the Phaenomena of Earthquakes . . . ," *PT* 51 (1760): 566–634, on 587.

[57] Archibald Geikie, "Note on Cavendish as a Geologist," in *The Scientific Papers of the Honourable Henry Cavendish, F. R. S.*, vol. 2: *Chemical and Dynamical*, ed. E. Thorpe (Cambridge: Cambridge University Press, 1921), 432.

[58] Horace Bénédict de Saussure, *Voyages dan les Alpes, precédés d'un essai sur l'histoire naturelle des environs de Genève*, vol. 2 (Genève, 1786). Jean André Deluc, *Geological Travels*, 3 vols., trans. H. de la Fite (London, 1811). Charles Hatchett, *The Hatchett Diary. A Tour Through the Counties of England and Scotland in 1796 Visiting Their Mines and Manufactures*, ed. A. Raistrick (Truro: D. Bradford Barton, 1967). F. W. Gibbs, "A Notebook of William Lewis and Alexander Chisholm," *Annals of Science* 8 (1952): 202–20, on 211.

an indexed, bound book, which he labeled "White Book No. 1." This book contains a transcription from his laboratory "minutes," some of which are inserted loosely, not yet transcribed, bearing tell-tale chemical stains.[59] The experiments it records go on to 1806; their subject might be called geological and industrial chemistry, but the simpler description of mineralogical chemistry would not be misleading, given the often undifferentiated eighteenth-century use of "mineralogy" to stand for both ores and stones.[60] Though Cavendish published no work of his own on minerals and strata, he left ample record that he made this a serious study in the last quarter of his life. The *Philosophical Transactions* at the turn of the century contained many papers in this field, the challenge of which Richard Chenevix, one of the authors, described: to establish qualitatively the presence of different substances in a specimen required "delicate research," and to determine quantitatively their proportions was the "most difficult operation of analytic chemistry."[61] That challenge Cavendish could not have ignored.

The "White Book" came to light only in recent times. Its scope can be suggested by a few entries: whitish sparkling ore from Hudson Bay, native iron from Mexico, earth from Isle of Man, lava from Mt. Vesuvius, limestone, chalk, clay, and mica. It is a book of the earth, which makes no distinction between the natural and the manmade. Cavendish brought the practices of the scientific revolution to bear on the materials and productions of the industrial revolution. He recorded a large number of scientific experiments on specimens from mines and industrial processes, such as kish from iron furnaces, slag from the purification of copper, finery cinder, and dust from lead smelting furnaces. The engineer James Cockshutt supplied him with specimens of coal and iron, and it is perhaps fitting at this juncture of the two revolutions that the scientist Cavendish wrote up a chemical paper on the making of iron, with recommendations, for the engineer Cockshutt.[62]

The last candidate Cavendish recommended for fellowship in the Royal Society was a geologist, Sir James Hall, in 1806.[63] Known as the "father" of

---

[59] This book has 138 numbered pages; 90 loose sheets are laid between the bound ones. Large blank spaces are left in the book for cross-referencing and later additions. It is a copy book for preserving results of experiments. "White Book No. 1," Cavendish Mss. On p. 59 Cavendish referred to "2d book," which suggests that there once was a "White Book No. 2." We note that Cavendish was still using chemicals belonging to his father: on pp. 61–62, Cavendish took a measure of tincal (an Asiatic crude borax) "of my fathers."

[60] V. A. Eyles, "The Extent of Geological Knowledge in the Eighteenth Century, and Methods by Which It Was Diffused," in *Toward a History of Geology*, ed. C. J. Schneer (Cambridge, Mass.: M.I.T. Press, 1969), 159–83, on 175.

[61] Richard Chenevix, "Analysis of the Arseniates of Copper, and of Iron, Described in the Preceding Paper . . . ," *PT* 91 (1801): 193–240, on 209.

[62] Henry Cavendish, "Paper Given to Cockshutt," inserted loosely in "White Book No. 1."

[63] Royal Society, Certificates, vol. 6 (proposed 20 Feb. 1806).

experimental geology, Hall is remembered especially for his experiments in answer to criticisms of James Hutton's *Theory of the Earth.* A principal criticism of Hutton's theory arose from an early result of pneumatic chemistry. Against his explanation of the formation of limestones by subterranean heat, his critics argued that heat would have calcined the limestone, driving off its fixed air (carbon dioxide) and converting it to quicklime, as Black had taught. Hutton supposed that the great pressure of the earth prevented this action. Using Wedgwood pyrometers to measure temperatures upwards of a thousand degrees, and using a technique of Rumford's for measuring the force of gunpowder to determine very high pressures, Hall proved that Hutton was right. In other experiments, to which he was led in part by observations in a glass factory, Hall proved that fused basalt becomes stony masses when it cools, not just glass as Hutton's critics maintained.[64] We do not know what Cavendish thought of Hutton's theory, but we suspect that he liked it better than he did the theories of Hutton's critics, such as Deluc and Kirwan, who upheld the Mosaic account of Genesis. To these critics, Hutton's idea that the earth has no "vestige of a beginning" was both unintelligible and skeptical.[65] In none of his known work did Cavendish concern himself with origins, and we doubt that his thinking in geology was any different, and it is all but unthinkable that he would have accepted Genesis. Blagden, who joined Cavendish in recommending Hall, thought that the reluctance of foreigners to assign an ancient date to "fossils" was based on religious faith or fear of magistrates or clergy, and that in private many would allow that the "world must be much older."[66] Cavendish gave no evidence of faith and had no reason to fear officials. John Playfair, the foremost exponent of Hutton's theory, said that geology used to explain everything by the "*first origins of things*," which was why it was so long in becoming a science; geology as a science was properly concerned to "*discover the laws*" of the great "revolutions" of the earth.[67] Cavendish would surely have assented to this "scientific" direction of the geology of his day. His recommendation of Hall makes sense to us. Hall pursued a geological science seeking "laws," supported a geological theory that assigned to heat the principal power, did physical and chemical experiments to establish the hypothesis of that theory, and looked to industry to advance his scientific work. His directions corresponded closely with Cavendish's in the last twenty-five years of

---

[64] V. A. Eyles, "Hall, Sir James," *DSB* 6:53–56, on 54.

[65] Jean André Deluc, *An Elementary Treatise on Geology: Determining Fundamental Points in That Science, and Particularly of the Huttonian Theory of the Earth,* trans. H. de la Fite (London, 1809), vi, 24, 63–64. Deluc argued against Hall's experimental conclusions, pp. 359–61. Richard Kirwan, *Geological Essays* (London, 1799), 482. Kirwan, pp. 4–6, said that geological facts are historical, relying on testimony, and that no recourse can be made to experiment.

[66] Charles Blagden to John Michell, 25 Apr. 1785, draft, Blagden Letterbook, Yale.

[67] Playfair quoted in Deluc, *Elementary Treatise,* 11–14.

his life. We return to this point in our discussion below of Cavendish's experiment of weighing the world.

ENTIRE GLOBE

William Roy, who headed the British half of the project to determine the relative locations of the Greenwich and Paris Observatories by triangulation, called for an extrapolation of that project to measure arcs in "different and very remote parts of the globe," from which an accurate judgment of the shape of the earth could be deduced. For help in this worldwide effort, Roy looked to the king, "who loves and cherishes the sciences," to the East India Company, "a Body of Merchants, whose power, as well as opulence, stand at this day unequalled in the mercantile history of the world," to the empress of Russia, "who commands so great a proportion" of the northern latitudes of the world," and beyond.[68] In a similar vein, Cavendish told the astronomer royal that it would "very well become the admiralty to send a vessel to observe the longitudes of such places as are most frequented by our ships as till then the method of finding the longitude at sea will be of very imperfect use," and if they were to do so, they could "tell us the length of the pendulum in many different climates without any additional trouble," leading to an accurate determination of the shape of the earth.[69] Cavendish's wide-ranging curiosity is well conveyed by his instructions to an unnamed traveler; the first part of the following instructions could not have been written earlier than 1777.[70]

> In England the heat of the water in deep wells or quick springs is very nearly equal to the mean heat of the air & it well deserves inquiry whether it is the same in other countries for if it is so it would afford the readiest way of comparing the mean heat of different climates. As your correspondents[71] observations if continued will tell us the mean heat of the air at Madrass I should be very glad if he would also try the heat of the water in the wells of the place the deeper & less exposed to the air the better. It will be sufficient to try it once or twice at opposite seasons of the air but if he would be so good as to try it on 2 or 3 different wells it would be the better. If it is a draw well it will be sufficient to draw up a bucket of water & try the heat with his thermometer. If it is a pump I would recommend to him to pump a few minutes before he tries the heat as the water which comes first is what is containd in the body of the pump which perhaps may be of a different heat from that in the well.

[68] William Roy, "An Account of the Mode Proposed to Be Followed in Determining the Relative Situation of the Royal Observatories of Greenwich and Paris," *PT* 77 (1787): 188–228, on 222–26.

[69] "Paper Given to Maskelyne Relating to Attraction & Form of Earth," Cavendish Mss VI(b), 1:18.

[70] We infer the year 1777 from a manuscript in Cavendish's hand, "Journal of Weather at Madrass," Cavendish Mss Misc.

[71] Alexander Dalrymple, who had just returned from Madras, where he had correspondents, may have been the recipient of this letter of instructions.

I am informed that the usual way of cooling their water at Madrass is to expose it to the open air in porous earthen vessels.[72] I should be very glad if he would now & then try the heat of the water in them at different times of the day & different seasons of the year & also set down the heat of the air at the same time so as to shew how much the water is cooled by the evaporation.

If there should happen to be any Tuffoon while he is there I could wish that he would observe the alterations of the barometer & wind & weather as closely as he conveniently can from the time of the first presages of it to the end & that if he has an opportunity he would endeavour to collect how far it extended & at what time it began & ended at different places & that he will set down any other circumstances which may occur to him that he thinks will tend to make us better acquainted with the nature of those extraordinary phenomena.

The exposition of your correspondents thermometer without doors which was placed under a shady tree seems not quite unexceptionable as I am afraid that the air under the tree may be cooled by the evaporation from the leaves. What confirms me in this opinion is that the therm. without doors was seldom hotter than that within doors in the middle of the day & was commonly considerably cooller in the morning whereas if it had not been for that cause I imagine the thermometer without doors would commonly have been considerably hotter than that within doors in the middle of the day.

All the portable barometers of Ramsden which I have seen have a Vernier division by which we may observe the height to 100^{ths} & 200^{ths} of an inch & have a screw at the bottom by which the quicksilver in the cistern may be adjusted to the proper height. If it would not be too much trouble to your correspondent it would be better if he would set down the height of the barometer to hundredths of an inch & it would be more satisfactory if he would mention whether he frequently adjusts the quicksilver in the cistern or whether he trusts to its remaining always the same. I need not say that if a person would be accurate in his observations he should examine the height of the quicksilver in the cistern frequently.[73]

---

72 In 1776–77 Cavendish carried out many experiments on the changes in temperature of boiled and unboiled water held in glazed and porous pans. "Evaporation," Cavendish Mss III(a), 12. There was considerable scientific interest in the Indian practice of cooling water by evaporation, an illustration of the newly acquired concept of latent heat, which was not thought to be fully explained. Benjamin Franklin, upon witnessing the chemist John Hadley cool a thermometer by dipping the bulb into ether and then letting the ether evaporate, observed: "It is but within these few years, that the European philosophers seem to have known this power in nature, of cooling bodies by evaporation. But in the east they have long been acquainted with it." Letter to John Lining, 17 June 1758, in *The Papers of Benjamin Franklin*, vol. 8, ed. L. W. Larabee (New Haven: Yale Univeristy Press),109. Franklin returned to the subject, observing "that a Man naked, and standing in the Wind, and repeatedly wet with Spirits might be frozen to death in a Summer's Day." Franklin thought that "none of our common Philosophical Principles will serve us in accounting for this." Letter to Cadwallader Colden, 26 Feb. 1763, ibid. 10:204.

73 Cavendish left a space at the bottom of this page, the next paragraph beginning a new page.

To make the same observations on the flat ice or fields of ice as it has been called.[74]

If they find any springs of water in any place where they go ashore to find their heat with the thermometer or if they should not find any springs & they do not think it too much labour to dig a well 6 or more feet deep to find the heat of the ground at the bottom of the well & also at 2 or 3 intermediate depths as this seems the likeliest way of guessing at the mean heat of the climate. The best way of finding the heat of the ground in the well I imagine will be to bore holes into the ground some inches deep wide enough to receive the thermometer & when the thermometer is in to stop up the hole with earth or tow to prevent the outer air from getting to the ball of the thermometer.

Whenever they bring up water from a great depth by the machine for that purpose to save a bottle of the water & also one of the surface water at the same place. I recommend saving bottles of the water rather than examining them at the time as I imagine they may be examined more accurately when you come home than they can be done in the hurry & bustle of the ship.

It is to be wished that they would find the heat (at least near the surface) & save a bottle of the water near home as well as in the northern seas as very few observations have ever been made either of the heat or saltness of the sea. It may be worth while making observations near the surface oftener than they can be expected to make them at great depths.

The endeavour to find if possible whether the ice you meet with is formed at that place or brought to it from a distance & if the ice seems to be formed at the place to observe the nature of the coast as well as you can whether it consists of steep rocks with channels of water between or whether it is a flat shore etc & if it is of the 1st kind whether the channels seem deep enough to float such great masses.

To observe the nature of the ice mountains as exactly as they can for that purpose if they can get near enough to them in their boat to break off some large pieces the higher above the surface of the water the better as there is less danger of their being soaked with salt water & to examine their texture: whether

[74] If the instructions for the observer in India and those for a journey to the far north were written for the same person and at the same time, the journey to the far north could not have been earlier than 1777; that is the earliest year for the instructions for India. In the chapter "Learned Institutions," we point out that in the 1770s Cavendish and the Royal Society took an interest in three voyages to the far north: undertaken in quick succession, they were Captain Phipps's in 1773, Captain Cook's in 1776, and Lieutenant Pickersgill's in 1776. The next major British voyages in quest of a Northwest Passage were led by Charles Duncan in 1790–92. Barrow, *History of Voyages*, 345. Dalrymple promoted Duncan's voyages, and Cavendish's instructions might have been given to Dalrymple to be conveyed to Duncan. However, among the journals Cavendish kept of his travels through Britain, Cavendish Mss X(a), and obviously misplaced there, is a second draft of the instructions for observing on ice. This one is not attached to instructions for an observer in India, suggesting that the two instructions were written for separate occasions; in that event Cavendish's instructions for observing on ice might have been written for one of the earlier northern expeditions above, or for observers at Hudson Bay; see letter 6, p. 541.

they consist of solid ice or of hardend snow or both. To observe whether there are any roots of trees plants or other bodies found in the ice & if any plants are[75] found to ascertain the kind if they can to shew the place of its production. To save a bottle of the water procured by melting them. If they consist of different sorts of ice to save a bottle from each kind that it may be examind whether it has any saltness observing to cut off the outside before they melt it as the outside may become salt by the spray of the sea. If it can be done conveniently it may be worth while to bore a hole into the ice mountain a foot or more deep & wide enough to put the therm. in in order to find its heat. It may [be] of use to find the specific gravity of the ice both as it will serve to shew the nature of it more exactly & as it will enable one to form some guess how far they reach under water. The best way I know of doing this will be to tye a bullet or leaden weight to it with wire sufficient to make it sink in water to hook it on by the wire to a pair of scales & to weigh it first in air & then under water & then in air again. If fresh water could be spared for the experiment it would be better as the salt water dissolves the ice much faster than fresh but if the piece of ice is large I believe it may be tried very well in salt water. For the same reason the colder the water it is weighd in the better. The larger the piece you try also the better. I should think the experiment would be more exact if tried with as large a piece as one could easily lift in salt water than with a piece of a pound weight in fresh water. There is no need of exact scales or of weighing the piece exactly but it should be done as expeditiously as possible. Care must be taken to set down whether it is weighd in salt water or fresh.

I do not at present think of any means of judging whether the ice is formed in the places or whether it is brought from a distance except by observing whether there are many masses of that kind adhering to the shore or whether the[y] are only found floating in the sea with other circumstances of that kind & also by a careful observation of the currents & of the places where you begin & cease to meet with them. But there will very probably occur to you many other circumstances which may be of use towards determining the place & manner of their production.

As a theory frequently enables people to make observations which would otherwise escape them I will hint they may perhaps be formed on shores consisting of rocky islands with narrow channels between by the snow & ice falling from the sides of the rocks into the channels in the winter & filling them up & that in the spring they are forced out by storms & the tides.

If you should stay long enough to see the Aurora Borealis to observe what part of the heavens the Corona points to & whether it agrees with the magnetic pole & also to observe whether there is any irregularity in the dipping needle & if you should be ashore at the time in the horizontal needle.

75 Cavendish wrote "or," meaning "are," we think.

From typhoons in the tropics to icebergs in the arctic, divers phenomena occurring on or near the surface of the earth were subjected to Cavendish's questioning. For answers he looked to persons who traveled to places he would never see. In the next section, we examine a question Cavendish had about the interior of the earth. This question he answered himself without ever leaving home.

WEIGHING THE WORLD

Cavendish lived all of his adult life in and around London in solid houses with servants to guard his privacy. These houses he turned into places of science, where the drama of his life was staged, unseen, internal, and profound.[76]

We begin our discussion of Cavendish's weighing of the world with a point about his way of life; for this we need briefly to look ahead to the end of his life, to an anonymous obituary of Cavendish published in the *Gentleman's Magazine*.[77] The author was Blagden, we know, because his papers contain an otherwise unidentified fragment of the notice in his handwriting. The circumstances are explained in two letters to Blagden from Lord George Cavendish, Henry Cavendish's main heir, and in entries in Blagden's diary. Evidently Lord George had written a sketch of Cavendish's character to go in the papers, and he asked Blagden to "fill it up."[78] Blagden wrote his sketch and showed it to Lord George the next day.[79] Lord George wished that Blagden had altered the part about Cavendish's character, which probably referred to what he himself had written, and he said he would consult with the duke of Devonshire about this family matter.[80] Lord George next wrote to Blagden that the duke of Devonshire had approved his sketch of Cavendish's "character" for the "Publick Papers." In a second letter, written the next day, Lord George informed Blagden that the corrections Blagden meanwhile had sent him had arrived too late, and the notice had already gone to press. (However, the corrections were not too late for *Gentleman's Magazine*). At the bottom of Lord George's letter, Blagden wrote out again the corrections he had requested, two of which are of no consequence here, the third saying that Blagden wanted Cavendish's habits to be called not "retired" but "secluded."[81] "Retired" and "secluded" conveyed much the same impression but with a nuance. "Retired" suggested withdrawn or inactive,

---

[76] The discussion in this chapter is taken from Russell McCormmach, "The Last Experiment of Henry Cavendish," in *'No Truth Except in Details': Essays in Honor of Martin J. Klein*, ed. A. J. Kox and D. M. Siegel (Dordrecht: Kluwer Academic Publishers, 1995), 1–30. We acknowledge permission to use material from this chapter: Copyright Kluwer Academic Publishers 1995; reprinted by permission of Kluwer Academic Publishers.

[77] *Gentleman's Magazine*, March 1810, 292.

[78] 6 Mar. 1810, Charles Blagden Diary, 5:431 (back).

[79] 7 Mar. 1810, Charles Blagden Diary, 5:431.

[80] 8 Mar. 1810, Charles Blagden Diary, 5:431 (back) and 432.

[81] Lord George Cavendish to Sir Charles Blagden, 9 and 10 Mar. 1810, Blagden Letters, Royal Society, C.17 and C.19.

"secluded," shut up.[82] The second word, Blagden decided, was the better word for Cavendish.

The best word to characterize Cavendish's biographers is "bewilderment." Cavendish's scientific manuscripts confront them with studies on virtually every topic in the physical sciences, carried out independently of one another, without rhyme or reason other than with the implicit goal of total understanding. But that is only a first impression, for if the biographers persist, they see that Cavendish's manuscripts fall into large groups, which relate to the goals of the science of Cavendish's time. One such group had to do with researches on the earth, including its gaseous envelope and its location and orientation in the solar system. Another group had to do with researches on general laws and properties of nature. Researches on the earth that were most significant for eighteenth-century science tended to involve numbers of investigators working together, in contrast to researches on general laws of nature, which tended to be done by individuals working on their own. In the several organized researches on the earth in which Cavendish took part, he worked with others while preserving his essential privacy. In his last published experiment, the determination of the mean density of the earth, he worked in seclusion. He brought the earth into his place of privacy, his home, where he experimented on it on his own. Then because he was working in science, he communicated his results. The experiment of weighing the world came to be known to scientists as "the Cavendish experiment."

Cavendish's wish to see the world weighed in the balance is on record in a letter he wrote to John Michell in 1783. He knew that Michell was having difficulty completing a large telescope. He wrote: "if your health does not allow you to go on with that [the telescope] I hope it may at least permit the easier and less laborious employment of weighing the world." Cavendish gave his preference of the two employments: "for my own part I do not know whether I had not rather hear that you had given the exper. of weighing the world a fair trial than that you had finished the great telescope."[83] "Experiments to Determine the Density of the Earth," Cavendish's paper in the *Philosophical Transactions* for 1798, opens with an explanation of his and Michell's connection. "Many years ago, the late Rev. John Michell, of this Society, contrived a method of determining the density of the earth, by rendering sensible the attraction of small quantities of matter; but, as he was engaged in other pursuits, he did not complete the apparatus till a short time before his death, and did not live to make any experiments with it. After his death the apparatus came to the Rev. Francis John Hyde Wollaston, Jacksonian Professor at Cambridge, who, not having conveniences for making experiments with it, in the

[82] "Shut up apart" is an eighteenth-century meaning of "seclude." *Oxford Universal Dictionary*, 3rd rev. ed., 1935, p. 1825.

[83] Henry Cavendish to John Michell, 27 May 1783, draft, Cavendish Mss New Correspondence.

manner he could wish, was so good as to give it to me."[84] When Michell died in 1793, his instruments and apparatus were left to his former college in Cambridge, Queens'.[85] Just how the apparatus came into Wollaston's hands Cavendish does not say, nor does he say who initiated the gift of the apparatus from Wollaston to Cavendish, though from all that passed before, it probably was Cavendish. In any event, Michell, Cavendish, and Wollaston were on familiar terms. Wollaston belonged to a dynasty of men of science and the Church, all of whom, like Cavendish and Michell, had studied at Cambridge.[86] It is entirely reasonable that Michell's apparatus ended up in Cambridge with one of the Wollastons, and that Cavendish knew its whereabouts and was given it to use.

Cavendish was nearly sixty-seven when he weighed the world; his last published experiment had been ten years before, and he would not publish another. The experiment of weighing the world was in reality seventeen "experiments," each consisting of many trials. Cavendish began the first experiment on 5 August 1797, and he completed the first eight experiments by the last week in September. He performed the remaining nine experiments the following year, from the end of April to the end of May. The paper reporting them was read to the Royal Society on 21 June 1798, just three weeks after the last experiment. The long paper with its extensive calculations must have been largely written by the end.

Cavendish began the account of the experiment with these promising words, "The apparatus is very simple." The apparatus, which Cavendish largely rebuilt,

---

84 Henry Cavendish, "Experiments to Determine the Density of the Earth," *PT* 88 (1798): 469–526; in *Sci. Pap.* 2:249–86, on 249.

85 "Michell, John," *DNB* 13:333–34, on 334.

86 Wollaston's father, Francis, born the same year as Cavendish, and a classmate of Cavendish's at Cambridge, took his degree in law but entered the Church instead. Interested in astronomy, he had his own observatory and first-class instruments. With at least that much in common, in 1768 Cavendish brought Francis Wollaston as a guest to a meeting of the Royal Society on 8 Dec. 1768; Wollaston's certificate is dated 3 Jan. 1769 and signed by Cavendish along with Maskelyne and several other prominent members; Wollaston was elected that year. Royal Society, JB 26:1767–1770; Royal Society, Certificates, 3:65; "Wollaston, Francis," *DNB* 21:778–79. One of Francis Wollaston's sons, William Hyde Wollaston, was an eminent chemist. Cavendish proposed him, as he had his father, for membership in the Royal Society. Royal Society, Certificates, 5 (9 May 1793); "Wollaston, William Hyde," *DNB* 21:782–87, on 782. Another of Francis's sons, George Hyde Wollaston, was one of Cavendish's neighbors at Clapham Common, where Cavendish performed his experiment on the density of the earth. "Wollaston of Shenton," *Burke's Genealogical and Heraldic History of the Landed Gentry* (London, 1939), 2479. George Hyde Wollaston's house as well as Cavendish's are on the map of Clapham Common, "Perambulation of Clapham Common 1800," from C. Smith, *Actual Survey of the Road from London to Brighthelmston.* Yet another of Francis's sons was Francis John Hyde Wollaston, Jacksonian Professor of Chemistry, from whom Cavendish received Michell's apparatus. "Wollaston, Francis John Hyde," *DNB* 21:779–80. Michell's association with the Wollastons went back as far as Cavendish's. As a recently elected Fellow of the Royal Society, Michell's first recommendation for a new member, in 1762, was for Francis's youngest brother, George Wollaston, Fellow and Mathematical Lecturer of Sidney-Sussex College, Cambridge. "Wollaston, Francis," 779.

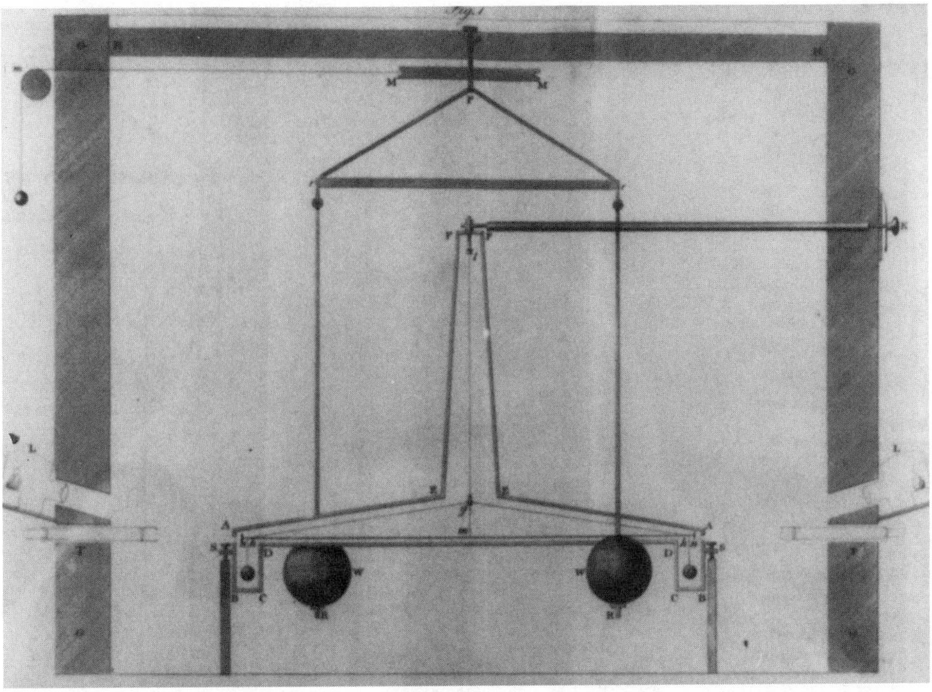

93. Apparatus for Weighing the World. Cavendish's modified version of John Michell's apparatus. The large spheres R are the weights that attract the small spheres suspended from the arm, which in turn is suspended by the fine wire gl. The room in which the apparatus is housed is also shown and as well the arrangements for viewing it from outside the room. "Experiments to Determine the Density of the Earth," Philosophical Transactions *88 (1798): 526.*

is in truth easily described. Its moving part was a six-foot wooden rod suspended horizontally by a slender wire attached to its center, and suspended from each end of the rod was a lead ball two inches across. The whole was enclosed in a narrow wooden case to protect it from air currents. Toward the ends of the case and on opposite sides of it were two massive lead balls, or "weights," each weighing about 350 pounds. The weights could be swung to either side of the case to approach the lead balls inside, and in the course of the experiment this was regularly done. The gravitational attraction between the weights and the balls drew the rod sensibly aside. From the angle of twist of the rod, the density of the earth could be deduced; to achieve this, the force that was needed to turn the rod against the force of the twisted wire had to be known, and for this it was necessary to set the rod moving freely as a horizontal pendulum and to observe the time of its vibrations.

To the modern reader, it may not be obvious how the density of the earth enters the experiment as it is described above. It becomes "obvious" once the formulas for the forces acting in the experiment are written out and the resulting equations are manipulated. Cavendish's reasoning seems roundabout to us

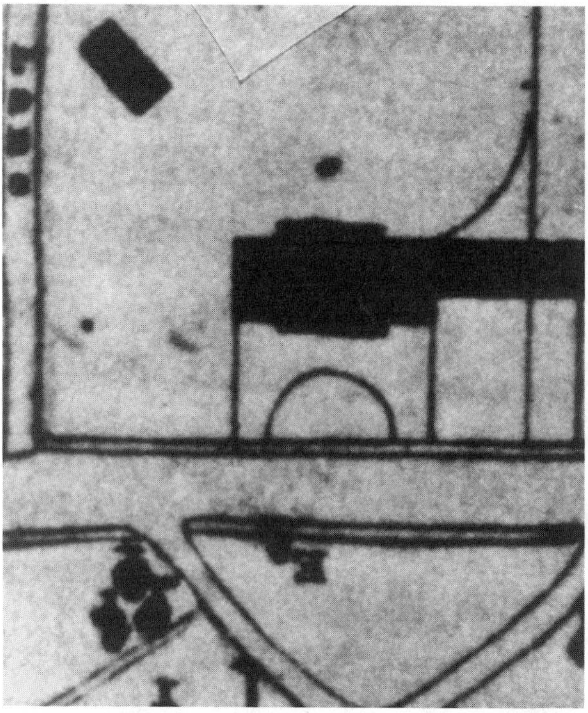

94. Plan of Cavendish's Clapham Property. This detail from "Batten's Plan of Clapham" of 1827 shows the shape of Cavendish's house seventeen years after his death and twenty-nine years after his experiment on the density of the earth. To the left of the house is an outbuilding about fifty-eight by twenty-six feet, the long dimension of which is oriented in the east-west direction. Cavendish referred to the arm of his apparatus as aligned in the magnetic east-west, which suggests that this outbuilding is where Cavendish performed the experiment. This reasoning is given, and this detail from Batten's plan is reproduced, in P. F. Titchmarsh, "The Michell-Cavendish Experiment," The School Science Review, *no. 162 (March 1966): 321–22.*

largely because it is unfamiliar.[87] He worked with ratios rather than with equations. He introduced a theoretical artifice, a simple pendulum, the length of which was one-half the length of the beam of his apparatus. With its help he derived the ratio of the force necessary to apply to each ball to draw the arm aside by one scale division to the force of gravity on the ball; the ratio is expressed in terms of the period of vibration of the arm. He then calculated the ratio of the attraction of the lead weight on a ball to the attraction of the earth on the ball; this ratio is expressed in terms of the mean density of the earth. From these two ratios he derived the number of divisions that the weights cause the arm to be drawn from its natural position; this number is expressed in terms of the period of the arm and the mean density of the earth. Then by substituting the observed divisions and period of oscillation, he deduced the unknown quantity, the density of the earth, which he expressed in terms of the density of water, the standard. The experiment essentially compares the gravitational

[87] What modern accounts usually say Cavendish did, he did not do: he did not derive the universal gravitational constant, though it can be readily derived from the results of his experiment. This is the point of B. E. Clotfelter, "The Cavendish Experiment as Cavendish Knew It," *American Journal of Physics* 55 (1987): 210–13. Cavendish's object was to determine the density of the earth, and there is nothing in his analysis to require the gravitational constant, nor is there any reason why, at that time, he should have regarded it as desirable. The unit of force did not yet exist for expressing $F = GM_1M_2/r^2$, the attraction between two masses, M_1 and M_2, separated by distance r.

attraction of the lead weights on the balls to the gravitational attraction of the earth on the same.

Twenty-five years before Cavendish's experiment, the Royal Society had carried out its own experiment with the same end, the determination of the average density of the earth. At that time it was an open question whether or not a mass the size of a mountain was sufficient to cause a detectable effect. Newton had thought it was not. In his experiment with the torsion balance, Cavendish achieved a detectable effect with weights small enough to fit into an apparatus. Here too Newton had been discouraging, having calculated that if two one-foot spheres of earth-matter were placed only one-quarter inch apart, they would not "come together by the force of their mutual attraction in less than a month's time." But Newton was right about the minuteness of the force: in Cavendish's experiment the gravitational attraction of the weights on the balls was only of the order of one part in 10^8 of the gravitational attraction of the earth on them, that is, of their weight.[88]

Because the smallest disturbance could destroy the accuracy of the "weighing," Cavendish placed the apparatus in a small, closed "room" about ten feet high and as many feet across. From outside the room, Cavendish worked pulleys to swing the weights close to the case to set the rod in motion. He observed the deflection and vibration of the rod by means of telescopes installed at each end of the room. Verniers at the ends of the rod enabled him to read its position to within one-hundredth of an inch. The only light admitted into the room was provided by a lamp near each telescope. Once an experiment was underway, it could not be interrupted until the end; depending on the stiffness of the suspension wire, it might take as long as two and one-half hours.

Because the apparatus was simple and the procedure was straightforward, it might seem that Cavendish's report of the experiment would be brief. It was not, taking up fifty-seven pages in the *Philosophical Transactions*, in length second only to his paper on the theory of electricity. The reason it was so long was the accuracy Cavendish demanded of the experiment. Near the beginning of his paper, where he estimated the minuteness of the gravitational force, Cavendish began his discussion of errors and corrections, and he continued discussing them to the end. The following account is intended to give the reader an idea of Cavendish's experimental practice and through it an idea of the person behind the experiment.

Looking ahead to the conclusion of his analysis of the experiment–that unequal heating of the air was the disturbing force hardest to avoid–Cavendish explained how he located and designed the apparatus to minimize

[88] Sir Isaac Newton, *Sir Isaac Newton's Mathematical Principles of Natural Philosophy and His System of the World*, trans. A. Motte, 2 vols., rev. F. Cajori (Berkeley and Los Angeles: University of California Press, 1962), 2:569–70. Cavendish stated the proportion as one part in 50,000,000, which applied to the 8-inch weights Michell intended to use. For the 12-inch weights Cavendish himself used, the proportion is roughly three times larger, but the order of magnitude of the minuteness remains the same.

this main "source of error." He then gave his "manner of observing," describing his concerns and precautions. He found "some inaccuracy" in the vibration of the arm caused by the resistance of the air, but the "error" caused by the motion of the point of rest he found to be inconsiderable. He determined the time of vibration of the apparatus anew for each separate experiment, in that way minimizing the effect of "accidental attraction, such as electricity" arising from the plates of glass through which the moving arm was observed, which would occasion an "error in the result." To determine the incidental attraction on the arm by the iron rods from which the heavy lead weights were suspended, he removed the weights. When he did, he found a disparity between his observations and his theoretical calculation of the attraction of the iron rods. He attributed the very small excess of the attraction of the rods above their gravitational attraction to "magnetism," but then upon replacing the iron rods by copper ones and still finding the same excess attraction, he concluded that it was due to an "accidental cause." Being unable to "correct" the "error," he calculated that its effect on the final result was no more than one-thirtieth of the whole. With this reassurance he then continued with the main experiments. Next, observing that the attraction of the weights on the balls seemed slowly to increase with time, he suspected a "want of elasticity" in the wire or in something the wire was attached to, but by drawing on his knowledge of the limits of elasticity, and doing experiments on the wire he was using, he decided that this was an unlikely cause; he replaced the wire with a stiffer one nonetheless. His description of elastic after-working, it has been noted, was original, its discovery usually assigned to the late nineteenth century. Finding that the attraction of the weights continued to vary, he suspected magnetism once again; he performed experiments to see if the weights and balls acquired the polarity of the earth, arranging the weights so that they could turn on a vertical axis and rotating them daily, and then replacing the two-inch lead balls with ten-inch magnets and reversing them. The latter substitution is an example of what has been called one of the "grand principles of experimental physics": if a disturbing effect is suspected, the experimenter makes it bigger to see how serious it is. Cavendish decided once again that magnetism was not the source of the error. His next hypothesis was that the cause of the variable attraction was "a difference in temperature between the weights and the case," producing a current of air. Even though he thought that this cause was "improbable," he took the apparatus apart and did new experiments, this time placing lamps beneath the weights and a thermometer next to the case. The effect was large after all, and so he did more experiments, burying thermometers in the weights and viewing them through the telescope by the aid of light reflected from a convex mirror, convincing himself that he had found a major source of this error: overnight the weights did not cool as much as the case, giving rise to convection currents, which pushed the balls toward the sides of the case. He then carried out the remaining experiments to determine the density of the earth.[89]

Cavendish was by no means finished with errors and corrections. In calculating the density of the earth from his data, he made an idealization, according to which the arm and the copper rods holding the weights have no weight, and the weights attract only the nearest ball and the attraction of the case is ignored. He accordingly made *six* "corrections," five of which were not of "much signification," but were "not entirely to be neglected" either. The important correction was the effect of the position of the arm on the attraction between the weights and the balls; this attraction influenced the time of vibration. One of the corrections, that of the effect of the mahogany case on the arm inside it, involved an elaborate analysis, which Cavendish included in the paper as an appendix, even though the "whole force is so small as not to be worth regarding." The solution required infinite series and perhaps had its own interest. In the conclusion of the paper, Cavendish gave a table of results of the seventeen experiments. They were in fairly close agreement, but still their differences were too large to be explained fully by the "error of observation" or by air currents owing to temperature differences. He expressed the final outcome of the experiments as a mean of the results for each of the two wires, finding the two means to be the same. Noting that the extreme results differed from the mean by no more than one-fourteenth of the whole, he concluded that the mean density of the earth was determined "to great exactness" as 5.48 times the density of water.[90]

Cavendish was still not done, for he thought that his readers might object that because the outcome was influenced by the heated currents of air, it could be influenced by another related source, "some other cause, the laws of which we are not well acquainted with," leading to "a considerable error in the result." To put to rest this objection, he reminded his readers that he had done the experiments in various weathers and temperatures. He anticipated yet another objection, this one fundamental: "namely, that it is uncertain whether, in these small distances, the force of gravity follows exactly the same law as in greater distances." His reply was that there was no evidence that the law differs "until bodies come within the action of what is called the attraction of cohesion, and which seems to extend only to very minute distances." In a number of experiments, he placed the balls as close to the case as possible and found no difference. Thus, Cavendish concluded his paper with second and third thoughts about possible factors affecting the accuracy of the outcome.[91]

---

89 Cavendish, "Experiments to Determine the Density of the Earth," 250, 252, 254–55, 259, 263–67. C. W. F. Everitt, "Gravitation, Relativity and Precise Experimentation," in *Proceedings of the First Marcel Grossmann Meeting on General Relativity*, ed. R. Ruffini (Amsterdam: North-Holland, 1977), 545–615, on 548.

90 Cavendish, "Experiments to Determine the Density of the Earth," 277, 280, 283–84.

91 Ibid., 284.

The experiment of weighing the world consisted of observations of matter moving in response to two of the best known forces, gravity and the restoring force of twisted wire, but as we have seen, to achieve the accuracy he desired, Cavendish had to consider nearly all of the forces known to natural philosophy: in addition to gravity and elasticity, they were forces associated with magnetism, electricity, deformation, heat, and cohesion. Cavendish's mastery of the art of experiment incorporated his mastery of natural philosophy.

The astronomer Francis Baily thought that Cavendish wrote his paper "more for the purpose of exhibiting a specimen of what he considered to be an excellent method, than of deducing a result which should lay claim to the full confidence of the scientific world."[92] We are inclined to believe that Cavendish had both ends in view, to exhibit a method and to give a result. By the time he performed the experiment with Michell's apparatus, "a contrivance of this kind for trying small attractions" had already been used by Charles Augustin Coulomb in electricity and magnetism,[93] and so the method was not entirely new. Cavendish's paper on the density of the earth can be compared with other papers by him. His paper on factitious air introduced new methods of studying gases, but it also gave the resulting densities of the gases he studied. His paper on the eudiometer was about an improved method for determining the goodness of air, but it also gave results of tests of the air he made on nearly sixty days. Only one of his papers, his last, on an astronomical dividing engine, would seem to have been solely about a method.

In addition to demonstrating a method and to gaining knowledge of the earth's interior, there was another reason, we believe, why Cavendish did this last major experiment. He had long since completed the principal researches of his middle years in electricity, chemistry, and heat, for which he is famous, and by the end of the eighteenth century, in all of these fields, scientific opinion had moved away from his. But his experiment on gravity was not subject to the vagaries of scientific opinion in the same way. This is not to say that he did not expect criticism. In any case, he got it.

Despite and in part because of his last experiment, Cavendish had not freed himself from the claims of the earlier method of determining the density of the earth, the attraction of mountains. His paper brought a prompt response from Charles Hutton, who just a year or so earlier had called attention to his calculation of the density of the earth in connection with the Royal Society's experiment

---

92 Quoted in P. F. Titchmarsh, "The Michell-Cavendish Experiment," *The School Science Review*, no. 162 (March 1966), 320–30, on 330.

93 Cavendish, "Experiments to Determine the Density of the Earth," 250. Cavendish said that "Mr. Michell informed me of his intention of making this experiment, and of the method he intended to use, before the publication of any of Mr. Coulomb's experiments." From what Cavendish knew of Michell, the torsion balance was independently invented by him and by Coulomb. Coulomb's biographer C. Stewart Gillmor discusses the question of priority in *Coulomb and the Evolution of Physics and Engineering in Eighteenth-Century France* (Princeton, 1971), 163–65.

on the mountain Schehallien.[94] Hutton had been shown a manuscript of Cavendish's paper by Maskelyne, and on the same day that he received a second copy of the paper from the Royal Society, he wrote to Cavendish from the Royal Military Academy in Woolwich where he worked. Cavendish's "ingenious" paper, which made the density of the earth 5.48 that of water, concluded with a paragraph calling attention to the earlier, lower value of 4½, in the "calculation of which" he, Hutton, had borne "so great a share." Anyone who has looked at Hutton's laborious calculations can sympathize with the plaintive note. Hutton thought that Cavendish's wording hinted at inaccuracies in his calculations and seemed to disparage the Royal Society's experiment. That experiment, Hutton reminded Cavendish, had determined not the density of the earth but only the ratio of that density to the density of the mountain, 9 to 5. Hutton had supposed that the density of the mountain is the density of ordinary stone, 2½ times that of water, but the actual density of the mountain was unknown, as Hutton had pointed out at the time. All that was known was that Schehallien was a "mass of stone." Hutton now believed that the density of the mountain was higher, 3 or even 3½, which would then make the density of the earth "between 5 and 6," where Cavendish had put it, and "probably nearer the latter number." The Royal Society had not finished its experiment because it had not determined the density of stone, Hutton said. Even now, he hoped that the Society would finish it, so that "an accurate conclusion, as to the density of the earth, may be thence obtained."[95]

Cavendish believed that he had just drawn that "accurate" conclusion. His value of 5.48 had been determined, as he said in his paper, "to great exactness." Exactness has two possible meanings, one referring to the closeness of 5.48 to the truth of nature, the other to the way Cavendish arrived at 5.48. In this discussion only the latter applies. Cavendish took mean values, considered the spread of the extreme values, and in general estimated the confidence that could be placed in 5.48. At the bottom of Hutton's letter to him, Cavendish drafted a brief response, which is identical to the last paragraph of his published paper. "According to the experiments made by Dr Maskelyne on the attraction of the hill Schehallien the density of the earth is 4½ times that of water." As to which density, his or the Society's, was more to be "depended on," Cavendish did not commit himself, since the Society's determination was "affected by irregularities whose quantity I cannot measure."[96] Nevertheless, at the time, Cavendish's value was more "exact" than Hutton's, even if future determinations of the density of the earth should turn out (they did not) to be closer to Hutton's value.

In 1807 Thomas Young published his lectures on natural philosophy in which he judged Cavendish's experiment to be more accurate than the Royal

---

[94] Charles Hutton, in *Mathematical and Philosophical Dictionary*, vol. 2 (London, 1796), 407.

[95] Charles Hutton to Henry Cavendish, 17 Nov. 1798, Cavendish Mss New Correspondence.

[96] Ibid. Cavendish, "Experiments to Determine the Density of the Earth," 284.

Society's, for the latter relied on conjectures about the internal density of a mountain. Cavendish's result for the mean density of the earth lay halfway between the limits guessed by Newton, between 5 and 6, a "new proof," Young said, of the "accuracy and penetration of that illustrious philosopher."[97] Cavendish's experiment bestowed new honor on Newton.

Hutton had not finished with the problem of determining the density of the earth by the attraction of mountains. In 1780, he had published a paper following up "the great success of the experiment" on Schehallien to "determine the universal attraction of matter," in which he repeated his wish that more experiments of the same kind would be made. In 1811 John Playfair made an investigation of the structure of the rocks of Schehallien, finding three kinds of rock with densities 2.4, 2.7 to 2.8, and 2.75 to 3. Reasoning from these figures that the mean density of the mountain was about 2.75, Hutton calculated a new mean density of the earth, the product of 2.75 and 9/5, or "almost 5." As for the Royal Society's experiment on the attraction of mountains, Hutton said, "we may rest satisfied" with this result. Since Hutton earlier had estimated the density of the mountain to be 2.5, Playfair's measurements raised his calculated density of the earth, but only slightly. Cavendish's figure for the density, 5.48, remained closer to, within one percent of, the accepted value today. It is not quite as close if a later, corrected figure for Cavendish's density is used.[98]

Twenty years after his experiment on weighing the world, Cavendish told Blagden that "when he wrote his paper on attraction, he shewd his ignorance of what had been done by others."[99] In his paper Cavendish acknowledged John Michell but no one else. The experiment rested on a great body of research, which Cavendish did not feel the need to cite. Ever since Newton's *Principia*, astronomers such as Bradley had been studying the motions of bodies under the action of gravitation, and mathematicians such as Maclaurin, Legendre, and Laplace had been elaborating the theory of attraction. Cavendish's experiment continued their work with this difference: it brought the precision of astronomical observation down to earth, to experimental physical science. In addition to studies on attraction, the experiment belonged to another tradition, that of a general science of the earth, a strong interest of both Michell's and Cavendish's. In this connection, it may be seen as a contribution to a new direction, as exemplified by Sir James Hall's work, experimental geology.

---

[97] Thomas Young, *A Course of Lectures on Natural Philosophy and the Mechanical Arts*, 2 vols. (London, 1807) 2:575.

[98] Charles Hutton, "Calculations to Determine at What Point in the Side of a Hill Its Attraction Will be the Greatest, &c.," *PT* 70 (1780): 1–14, on 3. Hutton included Playfair's finding in a revised version of his original paper on the Royal Society's experiment, "The Mean Density of the Earth. Being an Account of the Calculations Made from the Survey and Measures Taken at Mount Shichallin. . . . " In Hutton, *Tracts on Mathematical and Philosophical Subjects* . . ., vol. 2 (London, 1814), 1–68, on 64.

[99] 8 June 1809, Charles Blagden Diary, Royal Society, 5:328 (back).

THE CAVENDISH EXPERIMENT

From Paris Cavendish was asked to repeat his own experiment on the density of the earth. Writing to Banks in 1802, Blagden reported a conversation with Laplace about Cavendish's experiment, which he thought Banks might want to pass along to Cavendish. Laplace said that many people suspected that the attraction that Cavendish measured might involve electricity as well as gravity, and he expressed the wish that "Mr. Cav. would repeat it [the experiment] with another body of greater specific gravity than lead," such as a glass globe filled with mercury or a gold ingot.[100] In his paper Cavendish wrote that he planned to correct a defect in his method "in some future experiments," but so far as we know, he did no more experiments. He did not need to, for others would do them. In the following century, the density of the earth was measured at least six times using Cavendish's method, and twice using the Royal Society's method of the attraction of mountains, and several more times using a different method of the attraction of mountains; it was also done using the seconds pendulum and the common balance.[101]

In time the Cavendish experiment ceased to be regarded as a way to determine the earth's density, even as it continued to be performed. It became instead the experiment to determine "big *G*," the gravitational constant appearing in the law of gravitational force, defined as the strength of attraction between two one-kilogram masses one meter apart. As C. V. Boys explained in 1892: "Owing to the universal character of the constant *G*, it seems to me to be descending from the sublime to the ridiculous to describe the object of this [Cavendish's and now Boys's] experiment as finding the mass of the earth or the mean density of the earth, or less accurately the weight of the earth."[102]

Today, three hundred years after Newton and two hundred years after Cavendish, gravity is still at the center of physical research. To quote from a recent publication by researchers in the field: The "most important advance in experiments on gravitation and other delicate measurements was the introduction of the

[100] Charles Blagden to Sir Joseph Banks, 1 Apr. 1802, BL Add Mss 33272, pp. 172–73.

[101] Clotfelter, "The Cavendish Experiment," 211. Notable repetitions include R. Reich, *Versuche über die Mittlere Dichtigkeit der Erde mittelst der Drehwage* (Freiburg, 1838); Francis Baily, *Memoirs of the [Royal] Astronomical Society of London* 14 (1843): 1–120; C. V. Boys, "On the Newtonian Constant of Gravitation," *PT* 186 (1895): 1–72.

[102] Boys is quoted by Clotfelter on the shift in interest in Cavendish's experiment: "The Cavendish Experiment as Cavendish Knew It," 211. Boys first calculated *G* from the Cavendish experiment, and then from it he calculated the mean density of the earth. Conversely to obtain *G* from the density of the earth, Boys said he could have recalculated the attraction of the earth by viewing it as an ellipsoid of similar shells of equal density, which is the way J. H. Poynting had calculated it in 1892. Boys recommended using a room with a more uniform temperature than Oxford's, a detail which will be appreciated by anyone who knows Oxford and the uniform chill of its rooms. His accuracy was great, despite his room.

torsion balance by Michell and its use by Cavendish. . . . It has been the basis of all the most significant experiments on gravitation ever since."[103]

By its method and example, Cavendish's experiment has had a far-reaching influence on physical science in general. In "Cavendish's skillful hands" the torsion balance has "revolutionized the science of precision measurements"; not only have nearly all of the determinations of "big G" been done with that instrument, but it has been used in "countless other applications, such as seismological measurements and electrical calibration–wherever precise control over very small forces is called for."[104] A contributor to a recent symposium on general relativity traces the "noble tradition of precise measurement to which we are heirs" to Cavendish's experiment, which he calls the "first modern physics experiment."[105]

Weighing the world had a precedent in William Gilbert's experiments on magnetism two hundred years earlier. In *De Magnete*, his classic work in early experimental physics, Gilbert wrote that he had formed "a little load-stone into the shape of the earth," and that he had "found the properties of the whole earth, in that little body," on which he could experiment at will.[106] Gilbert called his little earth-shaped magnet a "terrella," a little earth. We wonder if there was not only a parallel but an association of ideas, for at Chatsworth there is a terrella in a silver mount said to have belonged to Henry Cavendish.[107]

Mountains high on the earth and open to the sky could deflect weights, and the earth could be weighed that way, and Cavendish had helped the astronomers who weighed it that way, but he did not go into the field to take part in the actual experiment. His own experiment with metal spheres, his gravitational terrellas, corresponded to his way of life. He did not need to go out into the world to know it; he could know the world and know it more precisely in his laboratory, using apparatus and reasoning from universal principles. Cavendish stayed at home and looked inside of a room and through a slit in a case, inside of which was the world on his terms.

It has been noted that while there is much talk about the effect of the scientist's personality on science, there is little of the other, perhaps more profound,

---

103 A. H. Cook, "Experiments on Gravitation," in *Three Hundred Years of Gravitation*, ed. S. W. Hawking and W. Israel (Cambridge: Cambridge University Press, 1987), 51–79, on 52. Appropriately, Cook talks of the Cavendish experiment only in connection with *G* and not with the density of the earth. Only recently, he says, has the accuracy of *G* been improved upon over what can be obtained from Cavendish's own experiment, and although in the study of materials we can achieve an accuracy of 1 part in 10^{12}, we still know *G* only to about 1 part in 10^3.

104 Christian von Baeyer, "Big G," *Discover* (March 1996): 96–101, on 98–99.

105 Everitt, "Gravitation, Relativity and Precise Experimentation," 546.

106 Kenelm Digby, 1645, quoted in "Biographical Memoir," in William Gilbert, *De Magnete*, 1600, trans. P. Fleury Mottelay (1893; New York: Dover reprint, 1958), xviii.

107 Mary Holbrook, *Science Preserved: A Directory of Scientific Instruments in Collections in the United Kingdom and Eire* (London: HMSO, 1992), 113.

effect of science on the personality.[108] In Cavendish we see both effects, mutually reinforcing. Cavendish turned away from ordinary society, which he found difficult, and toward nature and its understanding through science, and through science he came into a small society he found to his liking. Those traits that in his casual contact with people gave rise to anecdotes about his eccentricities were precisely the traits that in his scientific work made him extraordinary. To do science, Cavendish did not have to overcome his extreme diffidence but only to adapt it to science. The experiment on the density of the earth, *the* Cavendish experiment, is arguably not Cavendish's most important experiment, but if it is looked at for what it tells about the experimenter–as if it were a diary, which Cavendish did not keep, or a formal portrait, which he did not allow–it is the most revealing of his experiments.

The man who weighed the world was a very private figure and yet a constant companion of men of science. Through the experiment on the density of the earth, Cavendish worked out his private destiny, and at the same time he acted as the able representative of a general development in science. The drive for precision began in his time and has gathered force ever since. Cavendish worked in seclusion at Clapham Common (though in the last two parts of the experiment, Cavendish had George Gilpin, the clerk of the Royal Society, replace him at the telescope), but his experiment belonged to a public world of established scientific problems, instrumental possibilities, and interested, qualified parties.

As a person who loved seclusion, Cavendish was, in fact, an ideal candidate for a man of experiment. By his time, the experimenter had largely ceased to perform experiments in semi-public settings and had instead retreated into his laboratory. There he could control the variables of his experiment by repeating the experiment many times, changing only a single variable to isolate its effect. The single experiment was in that sense a series of experiments, logically connected. By making subsidiary experiments he could examine patiently every source of error and make every necessary correction. He could anticipate every objection, forestalling criticisms by others later. Secluded in his laboratory, Cavendish practiced science as it was then increasingly done. The account of what Cavendish did and experienced in the privacy of his laboratory, the experimental report read to the Royal Society and published in its journal, related the "smaller world of the laboratory to general claims about the regularities of the larger world of nature."[109]

At about the time Cavendish weighed the world, John Playfair wrote that skeptics would have predicted that after the systems of Aristotle and Descartes, Newton's too would pass: "This is, however, a conclusion that hardly any one will

[108] Philip J. Hilts, *Scientific Temperaments: Three Lives in Contemporary Science* (New York: Simon and Schuster, 1982), 11.

[109] Charles Brazeman, *Shaping Written Knowledge: The Genre and Activity of the Experimental Article in Science* (Madison: University of Wisconsin, 1988), 79.

now be bold enough to maintain, after a hundred years of the most scrupulous examination have done nothing but add to the evidence of the *Newtonian system*."[110] Newton's science promised to be timeless. Cavendish's weighing of the world was an experiment conceived as a continuation of Newton's work and executed on the basis of Newton's principles. If the idea of kinetic sculpture had existed in the eighteenth century, Cavendish's torsion balance might have been seen as Newton's proper monument, memorializing the discoverer of eternal truths.

Cavendish's experiment made history, but there was no history in it, as we now explain. Cavendish kept a number of clocks going, comparing them, using them in his researches, and consulting them in his daily life, and by the standard portrait of him, subjecting himself to their rule. Time for him was a measure of events, but it was not a generator of events, a point of view which, more than his phlogistic chemistry, places him in his age. The nature of his interest in time is suggested by his study of the Hindu civil year, which is based on astronomical periodicities, portending nothing new in the world. In his work on heat, Cavendish arrived at the first law of thermodynamics, but he did not state the second, which implies the physical directionality of time. He rarely dated his experiments, nor was there need to, given the kind of questions he asked of nature. His geological observations in the field led him to the chemistry of minerals but not to ideas about an earth evolving in time. His last published experiment, the subject of this chapter, replaced the static chemical balance with the torsion balance, but it was a balance all the same. The secular changes in his readings during the weighing of the world were not a datum but an erratum. The last experiment by this master experimenter was one of the great dynamic experiments of the passing age, and it was in the vanguard of the emerging physics of precision, but it did not point in the direction of the new history of the earth with its dynamic idea of time. The experiment had been conceived in the period when Cavendish was most active, the 1760s to the 1780s, and it was only by chance that it had to wait until the end of the century. From the middle of the eighteenth century, Buffon, Kant, Herschel, and others had envisioned the earth and the heavens as evolving over eons in concordance with Newtonian principles, but it would be scientists who came after Cavendish who would work intensively within a world view strongly imprinted by history.[111] Not eons but short durations, capable of exact measure, were the frame of reference of Cavendish's science; his instruments at the time of their auction contained "a very curious machine for measuring small portions of time."[112] The Cavendish experiment was a replication in the laboratory of the workings of the solar system, and as such it belonged to the classical

[110] Playfair, quoted in Deluc, *Elementary Treatise on Geology*, 14–16.

[111] Stephen Toulmin and June Goodfield, *The Discovery of Time* (New York: Harper & Row, 1965), 125, 266.

[112] Item 20 in *A Catalogue of Sundry Very Curious and Valuable Mathematical, Philosophical, and Optical Instruments* . . . (London, 1816).

Newtonian world view. The system of weights that Cavendish observed was stable too. The same might be said of Cavendish's social and political world, though we can see that it was also passing into history.[113]

Cavendish's era in science was about to be superceded in another respect. A faith in the interconvertibility of the forces of nature would inspire a host of theorists and experimenters, whose discoveries would redraw the map of the physical sciences in the century that followed. This development, we suspect, would not have taken Cavendish by surprise, given his understanding of forces as alternating regions of attraction and repulsion centering on mass points. This understanding, which may be seen to promise interconversions, already linked Cavendish's varied researches. He called on it to rescue his theory of electricity from experimental contradiction. He introduced it into his theory of heat to resolve difficulties with the heat of friction. He did so again in his theory of boiling to explain the "difference of the heat of boiling and ebullition."[114] In a study of the construction of the magnetic dipping needle, he analyzed the error of the needle by assuming that the axis of the needle and the plane on which it rolls "do not actually touch but are kept from one [another] by a repulsive force."[115] In his weighing of the world, he anticipated the objection that over the small distances of his apparatus the gravitational force might follow a different law. Particularly suggestive of work done in the next era of science were Cavendish's studies of heat. He examined experimentally the role of heat in magnetism,[116] electricity,[117] and nearly every other part of experimental natural philosophy. His theoretical work on heat led him to a fully general law of the conservation of force, or energy, the great unifying law of the doctrine of the interconversion of forces. One of the earliest of the interconversions to be discovered was between electricity and chemistry, and we know that Cavendish took great interest in the work in electrochemistry by Humphry Davy at the Royal Institution. The pity is that Cavendish did not live another ten years to learn of Hans Christian Oersted's discovery of a fundamental connection between electricity and magnetism and to tell us what he made of it.

Cavendish was a universal natural philosopher in a time when the discipline of physics was just emerging. In Germany, the early physics journal was the *Annalen der Physik und Chemie*, and when after eight years of operation its founder, F. A. C. Gren, died–this was in 1798, the year of Cavendish's experiment–its

---

113 Historians of science today are inclined to regard the Newtonian world view as a reflection and rationale of the British monarchy after the Glorious Revolution. Margaret C. Jacob, *The Cultural Meaning of the Scientific Revolution* (Philadelphia: Temple University Press, 1988), 109, 112, 123.

114 Cavendish Mss III(a), 5; in *Sci. Pap.* 2:354–62, on 361.

115 Henry Cavendish, "On the Different Construction of Dipping Needles," Cavendish Mss IX, 40:12–14.

116 Henry Cavendish, "Effect of Heat on Magnets," Cavendish Mss IX, 3.

117 Henry Cavendish, "Experiments on Electricity," in *The Electrical Researches of the Honourable Henry Cavendish*, ed. J. C. Maxwell (Cambridge: Cambridge University Press, 1879), 104–93, on 180–81.

new editor L. W. Gilbert wrote a foreword to the journal under the restricted title, *Annalen der Physik.* Explaining that the richest vein of material for his journal would continue to be mined from foreign sources, Gilbert trusted that in his journal, work by the best physicists in Germany would stand side by side with the best work from abroad, such as Cavendish's experiment on the density of the earth with its wonderful "exactness."[118] Cavendish's experiment, in this sense, belongs to the history of physics of the nineteenth and twentieth centuries.

However much Cavendish's workplace resembled a scientific institute, it was not yet one of these modern inventions. The following example of the setting of later Cavendishlike experiments will bring out the difference. In 1878 John Henry Poynting gave an account of experiments "undertaken in order to test the possibility of using the Common Balance in place of the Torsion Balance in the Cavendish Experiment," and in 1891 he reported on his continuing experiments done with the common balance. For his repetition of the Cavendish experiment using a common instead of a torsion balance, he received a grant from the Royal Society, and he was given a workplace in the laboratory at Cambridge named after Henry Cavendish or after his family. James Clerk Maxwell, the first director of the Cavendish Laboratory, gave Poynting permission to do the experiment.[119] Poynting's experiment belongs to physics after it had become an established discipline with its principal home in places of higher learning, complete with institutes, directors, and grants. By contrast, Cavendish did his experiment at home at Clapham Common.

Clapham Common was also the home of the "Clapham Sect" (a term invented after Cavendish was gone), a group of prosperous, well-educated Anglican reformers known as Evangelicals, who worshipped in the local church, Holy Trinity. They were fervently pious, believing in original sin and hellfire, living by the word of God, and working to save themselves, their countrymen, and heathen anywhere. They wanted to breathe life into the Church of England, which they believed had capitulated to shallow eighteenth-century rationalism, with its external morality and calculus of happiness. They kept spiritual diaries, recording their sins at the end of each day. Their meeting place was the oval library in the roomy house on the Common belonging to Henry Thornton, president of the Sunday School Society and chairman of the Sierra Leone Company, and a banker and Member of Parliament. In the 1790s, other Evangelicals moved from London to be nearby. Thornton's cousin William Wilberforce moved there to share his house. John Venn, the rector of Holy Trinity and founder of the Church

[118] L. W. Gilbert, "Vorrede," *Annalen der Physik* 1 (1799): unnumbered page in the three-page foreword. This quotation connects Henry Cavendish with the starting point of Christa Jungnickel and Russell McCormmach, *Intellectual Mastery of Nature*, 2 vols. (Chicago: Chicago University Press, 1986), 1:35.

[119] J. H. Poynting, "On a Determination of the Mean Density of the Earth and the Gravitation Constant by Means of the Common Balance," *PT* 182 (1892): 565–656, on 565–66.

Missionary Society, had the most hospitable house on the Common. Across the Common lived Thornton's somewhat less ardently pious brothers, Samuel and Robert. The Evangelicals' causes were social as well as religious, such as corruption in parliament, barbarity of the criminal code, duelling, bullbaiting, cockfighting, and, their most heartfelt, slavery, against which they fought for sixty years. Wilberforce brought the first bill to outlaw the slave trade in 1789, and it and all subsequent bills failed until 1807, when persistence was at last rewarded; the abolition of slavery itself had to wait considerably longer.[120]

John Venn followed the path of his Evangelical father, Henry, who had held the curacy at Clapham for some years. Before that, Henry had lectured on Greek and geometry as a Fellow of Queens' College at Cambridge. His son John also did well in mathematics at Cambridge, but his main interests were astronomy, mechanics, and optics. John could explain the principles of the thermometer and compass very well; he owned a Dolland telescope and other scientific instruments; he read the *Philosophical Transactions of the Royal Society*. While ministering to souls, he also made a scientific contribution to Clapham, giving lectures on science to his own and his neighbors' children, and introducing Jenner's smallpox vaccination to the whole parish. At Clapham he often saw Isaac Milner, the very capable Jacksonian Professor of Natural Philosophy at Cambridge, who implanted the Evangelical movement at Cambridge and who had won over Wilberforce to evangelicalism.[121] As a student at Cambridge, Venn had been a good friend of Francis John Hyde Wollaston's, who succeeded Milner as Jacksonian Professor, and from whom Cavendish obtained John Michell's apparatus for weighing the world. But like all members of the Clapham Sect, Venn preferred heaven over earth, and in a letter of comfort to Wollaston, who had suffered a personal loss, Venn cautioned his scientific friend that he may have immersed himself in science to the detriment of his duty to Christ: "Alas! How little honour it is to be the best chemist in Europe in comparison with being a useful minister of Christ. What comparison can there be between saving a soul and analysing a salt. . . . Science and amusement and company are useful in their proper places; you know me too well to think that I would declaim against them in general. It is the abuse of them that prevails at Cambridge–an abuse which renders us careless and insensible upon the verge of eternity."[122]

---

[120] John Pollock, *Wilberforce* (London: Constable, 1977), 117–18; Standish Meacham, *Henry Thornton of Clapham, 1760–1815* (Cambridge, Mass.: Harvard University Press, 1964), 27–28; E. M. Forster, *Marianne Thornton. A Domestic Biography* (New York: Harcourt, Brace, 1956), 4–9, 26–63; R. de M. Rudolf, "The Clapham Sect," in *Clapham and the Clapham Sect*, ed. E. Baldwin (Clapham: Clapham Antiquarian Society, 1927), 89–90; Michael Hennell, *John Venn and the Clapham Sect* (London: Lutterworth, 1958), 104–68.

[121] John Gascoigne, *Cambridge in the Age of the Enlightenment: Science, Religion and Politics from the Restoration to the French Revolution* (Cambridge: Cambridge University Press, 1989), 254.

[122] Hennell, *Venn*, 42, 52–53, 143. Foster, *Marianne Thornton*, 35–36, 53.

In the late eighteenth century, society like nature was subject to "experiment." The recent French Revolution was a case in point, William Thornton believed, an "experiment made upon human nature by men insensible of our natural corruption, an experiment by which they expected to show the advantage of a general deliverance from restraint–the superiority of Reason over Revelation. When men are thus left to follow Nature, and are released from their subjection to the laws both of God and of civil society, iniquity will not fail to predominate."[123] The Evangelicals, in all good faith, could themselves support a poorly conceived experiment on society: children from central Africa were brought to Clapham, where they were taught to be civilized in the English way, and for a time the children were seen roaming the Common, invited into the neighboring houses by their curious owners; unaccustomed to the "rigours of the English climate," most of these children died.[124] The logical outcome of the French Revolution, insofar as the inhabitants of Clapham Common were concerned, was Napoleon, who was expected to descend on them momentarily. Evangelicals were not pacifists, and in the year Cavendish made his delicate measurements of gravitating matter at his home on the Common, Venn published *Reflections in This Season of Danger*, in which he declared that "Religion not only permits but enjoins us to defend our property, liberty, and lives against the attacks of violence." The parish was defended by the Clapham militia, commanded by Samuel Thornton.[125] As it turned out, the disturbances of the peace in 1797–98, when Cavendish was doing his experiment, were of the usual kind. The patrol for watching and lighting for the village of Clapham reported that two men were stopped early one Sunday morning in possession of "a bag of cabbages, a pewter pot, and some greenhouse plants."[126]

Another social experiment was underway at Clapham, this one having to do with manners. At a meeting in 1798, the inhabitants of the parish agreed unanimously that in the interests of both the individual Christian and civil society, it was "highly improper, on that Day [Sunday], to exercise our worldly occupations, to travel, except in cases of urgency, or for purposes of benevolence, or to employ our domestics in any thing interfering with their public or private religious duties."[127] There was a call for the prosecution of any violators. Upon Clapham, the Evangelicals imposed what would become the quiet, devout contemplation of the life to come, the Victorian Sunday.

The first full-length biography of Cavendish reflected the concerns of the Victorian Sunday. Its author, George Wilson, who was both a scientist and a deeply religious man, noted that Cavendish's decisive experiment on the com-

123 Meacham, *Thornton*, 65.

124 Pollock, *Wilberforce*, 183–84. Hennell, *Venn*, 241–42.

125 Meacham, *Thornton*, 80. Hennell, *Venn*, 215.

126 "Watching and Lighting Notes, Clapham," 138.

127 *Resolution Agreed to by the Inhabitants of Clapham for the Better Observance of the Lord's Day, 1798.*

position of water was done on a Sunday. We note that Cavendish performed the fifth part of his experiment on the density of the earth on a Sunday, 20 August 1797. Looking for indications of a "doctrinal belief" in Cavendish and finding none, Wilson discussed his "*apparent* irreligiousness." A Fellow of the Royal Society said, "As to Cavendish's religion, he was nothing at all." According to an inhabitant of Clapham, Cavendish "never attended a place of worship."[128] At a dinner of the Royal Society Club, Cavendish brought up Clapham Church, but it was to point out that something there was eaten "thro' by the insects . . . working their way out."[129] The "World to come," Wilson said, did not engross Cavendish's thoughts.

Benevolence and charity, which were essential to the Evangelicals, evidently meant nothing to Cavendish, who reduced them, Wilson said, to a "singular numerical rule": a resident of Clapham informed him that when a person approached Cavendish with a request, he looked over the list for the largest gift, then wrote a check for that amount, no more and no less.[130] We have located the list of Easter offerings from the rector's account book for the years from 1791. In the first year, Cavendish matched the maximum gift on the list, one pound one shilling, as Wilson said. But when the neighbor whose gift he had matched raised his gift to five pounds five shillings, Cavendish stayed with his original one pound one shilling; the neighbor's health may have prompted his generosity, for two years later he was dead.[131] If Cavendish had a "singular numerical rule," he did not apply it foolishly. We note that Cavendish gave to the African Association, a cause dear to the hearts of the Evangelicals. The charities to which Cavendish contributed from January 1806 to January 1807 were, in addition to the above, magdalen (reformed prostitute), asylum, poor people, St. George's Hospital, and St. Giles Charity School; in the last seven months of his life, he gave to forty-eight "poor people," whose names are listed in his porter's account book. If Cavendish's giving was not heartfelt, it was not grudging either.[132]

Caring only for his work, Cavendish might well have appeared to Venn as guilty of the "abuse" of science, but Sundays were actually a workday for Venn as they were for Cavendish, for on Saturday evening and Sunday morning, Venn prepared the sermon he would give that Sunday. Perhaps Venn and Cavendish were not so far apart in their respective forms of work, each an offering of the self in the name of truth. A shy man like Cavendish, Venn's force of personality derived from his otherworldliness, his faith in eternity. Cavendish's this-worldliness was not without its own form of the eternal, his faith in the laws of nature.

---

128 George Wilson, *The Life of the Honourable Henry Cavendish* (London, 1851), 180–82.

129 19 Feb. 1807, Charles Blagden Diary, Royal Society, 5:39.

130 Wilson, *Cavendish*, 188–89.

131 Untitled Clapham rector's account book, 1791–1842, Lambeth Archives, P/C/26, p. 152.

132 "Bedford Square. James Fullers Account with the Exec. of Hen:Cavendish Esq. . . . Settled 30 August 1810," Devon. Coll.

At the end of Cavendish's life, his landlord at Clapham was Samuel Thornton. His house was occupied for a time by John Thornton, the son of Samuel and favorite nephew of Henry Thornton, with whom he worked for missions and Africans.[133] But accounts left by the Evangelicals of their activities do not mention Henry Cavendish, who it would seem did not associate with his neighbors. What caused the Evangelicals to band together at Clapham Common held no interest for Cavendish. In the *Principia,* Newton wrote that the discussion of God "does certainly belong to Natural Philosophy." Cavendish, a hundred years later, did not agree with Newton; if he had, we would know it, since he discussed everything else having to do with natural philosophy. His interests, so far as he left a record, were bound to this earth, not otherworldly. Cavendish, as we have seen, did all in his power to understand the earth in this broad sense.

[133] Eric E. F. Smith, *Clapham* (London: London Borough of Lambeth, 1976), 78. Entry for 1810, Clapham Land Tax Records. Lambeth Archives.

CHAPTER 7

LAST YEARS

BANKS, BLAGDEN, AND CAVENDISH

In 1768 the council of the Royal Society accepted the request of a young man to accompany Captain Cook on his voyage to the South Seas to observe the transit of Venus the next year. Described in the minutes of the council as a "gentleman of large fortune, who is well versed in natural history," he was Joseph Banks, descendant of landed gentry in Lincolnshire with a tradition of public service. On Cook's voyage, Banks brought with him a suite of eight persons, paid for by himself, including Linnaeus's pupil Daniel Carl Solander.[1] Seven years after his return in 1771, at age thirty-five, Banks was elected president of the Royal Society, his principal office in a life of public service.

Banks's assertive presence on Cook's voyage foreshadowed his activity as president of the Royal Society. In that post he exerted an extraordinary personal force in English science. His importance was not as an author of scientific publications but as a scientific patron, administrator, and entrepreneur. Georges Cuvier said of him: "The works which this man leaves behind him occupy a few pages only; their importance is not greatly superior to their extent." Meager as his scientific accomplishment was, Cuvier said, Banks had performed "good service to the cause of Science" in other ways, such as using his influence with men of power.[2] No single activity can sumarize Banks's way of serving, but he may have shown himself to best advantage as host of a Sunday salon at his house. Cavendish went faithfully to these sober, tea-drinking-only socials, held in the civilized setting of Banks's library, which

[1] 9 June 1768, Minutes of Council, Royal Society, 5:314. George A. Foote, "Banks, Joseph," *DSB* 1:433–37, on 434.

[2] David Philip Miller, "The Royal Society of London 1800–1835: A Study in the Cultural Politics of Scientific Organization," Ph.D. diss. (University of Pennsylvania, 1981) 9, 14–16, 19, 43–44, 46–47. Hector Charles Cameron, *Sir Joseph Banks K.B., P.R.S.: The Autocrat of the Philosophers* (London: Batchworth, 1952), 209.

Banks called his "conversaziones," an elegant word for an English at-home. Banks's salon was distinguished for its regularity, intimacy,[3] and diversity; men of science mixed with foreign visitors, world voyagers, and men of fortune and rank. Cavendish, aristocrat and man of science, was doubly welcome at Banks's.

Cavendish publicly gave his approval of Banks in the presidency during the dissensions at the Society, and implicitly he gave it over the thirty-two years he served the Royal Society under Banks. Long accustomed to working together in the Society, and to meeting socially at the Sunday conversaziones and elsewhere, Cavendish and Banks were friendly, but they probably were not friends.

Cavendish and Blagden had a close working relationship, and they were also friends. Someone said of their relationship that in the end it did not "suit,"[4] but the break, if that is the right word, appears to have been in the first instance a break between Blagden and Banks, with Cavendish the affected third party. In early 1788 Blagden wrote to Banks that he intended to resign as secretary of the Royal Society, and on the same day he sent a copy of the letter to Cavendish, explaining that he was taking this step to prevent him and Banks from becoming a "violent mixture."[5] Three days later Blagden wrote to Watson, who evidently had intervened to make peace, that he bore no "ill will" toward Banks and would continue to serve Banks but would stop "short of an absolute sacrifice" of himself.[6] He told Banks that his secretaryship of the Royal Society was the "great misfortune" of his life; he referred to his "reflections" on his "connexion" with Banks, which he said he would send later.[7] Banks replied that he had no idea what Blagden was talking about, whether Blagden's complaints were leveled at him or at the world in general. He had thought they were friends but now he feared they were enemies.[8]

Blagden's unhappiness was multiplied by a task Banks had assigned to him, which was to find a method of determining the correct excise duty on alcoholic beverages. For a time the Swiss chemist Johann Caspar Dollfuss had worked on it, but then Dollfuss left, and his experiments were repeated by George Gilpin, clerk of the Royal Society, who then proposed other experiments for Blagden to make. Recommending that the government set duty strictly by specific gravity, Blagden published the results of the experiments in the *Philosophical Transactions* in

[3] Timothy Holmes, *Sir Benjamin Collins Brodie* (London, 1898), 46, 68.

[4] George Wilson, *The Life of the Honourable Henry Cavendish* (London, 1851), 129.

[5] Letters from Charles Blagden to Sir Joseph Banks, 2 Feb. 1788, draft, and to Henry Cavendish, 2 Feb. 1788, draft, Blagden Letters, Royal Society, B. 38–39.

[6] Charles Blagden to William Watson, Jr., 5 Feb. 1788, draft, Blagden Letters, Royal Society, 7:115.

[7] Charles Blagden to Sir Joseph Banks, 27 Mar. 1789, BL, Add Mss 33272, pp. 56–57.

[8] Sir Joseph Banks to Charles Blagden, n.d. [after 28 Mar. 1789], draft, BL Add Mss 33272, p. 58.

1790.[9] In this work Blagen was greatly assisted by Cavendish,[10] but it nevertheless cost Blagden much time and effort.

Blagden complained that he should have been paid for this work. Banks replied that he had performed many tasks for the government and never thought of reward, but he would look into it if Blagden would tell him what he expected. Blagden's resentment of Banks had been building. From the time he returned from America, Blagden said, Banks had taken him for granted, deceiving him, making him a "tool of his ambition." When Blagden took on the job of secretary to the Royal Society during the dissensions, he believed that Banks would advance him in society, improving his fortune, but Banks did nothing of the kind. Instead Banks discouraged him from pursuing his profession, medicine, and even from marrying, his only purpose being to keep Blagden dependent on him. Banks defended his character and conduct.[11] Blagden's rancor at Banks continued, as did their correspondence until it became tiresome.[12]

Cavendish is said to have accepted Blagden as his associate on the condition that he give up medicine and devote himself to science.[13] The contrary would seem to have been the case. Blagden reminded Banks that in 1784, two years after Blagden had become Cavendish's associate, he had told Banks that "Mr Cavendish wished me to prosecute seriously the profession of physic."[14] At about this time Blagden wrote plaintively to people about "being now quite out of the

[9] Charles Blagden, "Report on the Best Method of Proportioning the Excise on Spirituous Liquors,"*PT* 80 (1790): 321–45. Jesse Ramsden published a pamphlet criticizing the report, *An Account of Experiments to Determine the Specific Gravity of Fluids* (London, 1792). Blagden did the experiments over again to eliminate a source of error, publishing the results in a second paper, "Supplementary Report on the Best Method of Proportioning the Excise upon Spirituous Liquors," *PT* 82 (1792): 425–38. George Gilpin published an immense series of tables, in small print, based on the experiments reported by Blagden: "Tables for Reducing the Quantities by Weight, in Any Mixture of Pure Spirit and Water, to Those by Measure; and for Determining the Proportion, by Measure, of Each of the Two Substances in Such Mixtures," *PT* 84 (1794): 275–382.

[10] "Remarks by Mr Cavendish," Blagden Collection, Misc. Notes, Royal Society, No. 65. Charles Blagden to Henry Cavendish, 12 and 26 Mar. 1790, draft, Blagden Letters, Royal Society, 7:317 and 7:695. Among other kinds of assistance, Cavendish made available his father's table of the expansion of water with heat. "From the Experiments of Lord Charles Cavendish, Communicated by Mr Henry Cavendish. March 1790," Blagden Collection, Misc. Notes, Royal Society, No. 99.

[11] Charles Blagden to Sir Joseph Banks, 28 Mar. 1789, BL Add Mss 33272, p. 59. Sir Joseph Banks to Charles Blagden, 15 July 1789, Blagden Letters, Royal Society, B. 39. Charles Blagden to Sir Joseph Banks, 25 July 1789, draft, Blagden Collection, Royal Society, Misc. Matter–Unclassified. Sir Joseph Banks to Charles Blagden, 31 July 1789, Blagden Letters, Royal Society, B. 40.

[12] Charles Blagden to Sir Joseph Banks, 27 Mar. 1790, BL, Add Mss 33272, p. 73. Sir Joseph Banks to Charles Blagden, n.d., draft, ibid., 73–74. Charles Blagden to Sir Joseph Banks, 28 and 29 Mar. 1790, 3 Apr. 1790, ibid., 75, 77. Sir Joseph Banks to Charles Blagden, n.d., draft, ibid., 80. Charles Blagden to Sir Joseph Banks, 8 Apr. 1790, ibid., 81.

[13] Henry, Lord Brougham, "Cavendish," in *Lives of Men of Letters and Science Who Flourished in the Time of George III*, vol. 1 (Philadelphia, 1845), 250–59, on 258.

[14] Blagden to Banks, 8 Apr. 1790.

practice of physic" and therefore unable to advise on remedies,[15] about being as little familiar with inoculation and other topics of medicine "as if I had never been of the profession."[16] Blagden blamed Banks for encouraging him to abandon his profession and then not advancing and compensating him.

It seems reasonably clear that in 1789 Blagden was on good terms with Cavendish and not with Banks. That summer Blagden contemplated going abroad with friends, Henry Temple, second viscount Palmerston, and his wife, Lady Mary, and possibly staying away the coming winter. His only reservation about that plan had to do with Cavendish's desires: if by being away he would hold up Cavendish in any of his pursuits, he would stay. Cavendish raised one objection, which did not have to do with his desires but with Blagden's: being abroad would interfere with what Blagden had "much more at heart than any object in life,"[17] his return to medicine. Blagden thought his chances at practicing medicine at the resorts were as good as in London, and with Cavendish's blessing, he left with the Palmerstons. Before he did, he sold his house and its furnishings on Gower Street, with the thought that he would never again have a permanent address in England. Persons with messages for him were to be directed to Cavendish's house on Bedford Square. His bureau containing private papers was left in Cavendish's bedroom, and Cavendish was given the key and instructed to open the bureau and keep or burn the papers if Blagden should suffer an accident.[18] Blagden had recently turned forty and his life seemed without direction, as he set out on yet another Continental journey, evidently with gloomy premonitions.

When Blagden considered marriage, Cavendish entered into his plans in an essential way. In 1789 the potential wife was picked out, a Miss Bentinck, and in November of that year Blagden asked his brother to inform him about her. Would she enjoy Blagden's kind of company and "particularly would so far enter into the pursuits of my friend Mr. C. as not to think some portion of time spent in his company tedious? This would be a matter of the utmost consequence to us both. You will easily suppose I do not mean that she should enter into our studies, but simply that she should not find it disagreeable to be present when such matters were the subject of conversation, or when any experiment which had nothing offensive in it, was going on."[19] Blagden contemplated the three of

[15] Charles Blagden to William Farr, 14 Nov. 1785, draft, Blagden Letterbook, Yale.

[16] Charles Blagden to Francoise Delaroche, 1 Dec. 1786, draft, Blagden Letterbook, Yale.

[17] Charles Blagden to Henry Cavendish, Aug. 1789, draft, Blagden Letters, Royal Society, 7:694.

[18] Charles Blagden to his brother, John Blagden Hale, 17 Sep. 1789; "An Inventory of Furniture &c. Taken September 3.1789 at Dr Blagden's House in Gower Stret Appraised & Sold to Hill Esqr.," Gloucestershire Record Office, D 1086, F 155 and F 157. Charles Blagden to William Lewis, 15 Sep. 1789, draft, Blagden Letters, Royal Society, 7:306. Charles Blagden to his brother, 16 Sep. 1789, draft, ibid., 7:309. Charles Blagden to Henry Cavendish, 16 Sep. 1789, draft, Blagden Letters, Royal Society, B. 166.

[19] Charles Blagden to John Blagden Hale, 13 Nov. 1789, draft, Blagden Papers, Yale, box 5, folder 49.

them together, Blagden, his wife, and Cavendish. He was not worried about Cavendish's reaction but hers. Since Blagden knew Cavendish well, his plans to continue his work with Cavendish in the presence of his wife call into question the anecdotal absolute misogyny[20] of Cavendish. In one of his letters of reproach to Banks, referring to his desire to marry, Blagden said that he "had great reason to believe Mr Cavendish would assist me in making such a settlement as the family could not properly object to."[21] Banks, too, had taken into account Blagden's expectations; to justify his use of Blagden's services on the problem of excise duties, he told Blagden in the stilted third-person way they had adopted in their communications with one another that "as the Dr. [Blagden] told me on a former occasion, that if he married Miss Bentinck, Cavendish would make ample settlement on him, equal to the wishes of her family, I little suspected that his time and trouble were to be valued by the hour."[22] From the letters of 1789 and 1790 we see that Cavendish was a friend in need to Blagden.

The draft of a letter by Blagden, which was probably written in 1790, gives us a clear idea of the extent of Blagden's disappointment with Banks. Blagden saw Banks as standing in the way of everything important in his life: his profession, his marriage, and his fortune. The recipient of the letter is Blagden's benefactor, who could well be Cavendish, though he could be Heberden or someone else. To make Banks's "ungenerous, (if not treacherous) conduct the more evident," the letter reads, "let me contrast it with your own. You, to whom I had not had any opportunity of being servicable, seeing how unwisely I neglected my profession, had the goodness not only to advise me to resume it, but likewise to offer that you would bear all the pecuniary risk attending the pursuit, so that my private fortune should at all events remain unimpaired. I am sensible how imprudently I acted in not following your advice; but at that time I had still the weakness to believe Sir J. B.'s professions sincere."[23]

As it turned out Lord Palmerston did not go on to Italy to spend the winter of 1789–90, as planned, and in the late fall Blagden returned to London to resume his job as secretary of the Royal Society. He did not resume his profession, however, and the marriage did not take place either. Out of all that emotional turmoil, nothing much changed in Blagden's life. On the day Cavendish died, Blagden told Banks that Cavendish always knew "what was right for him," that Cavendish was a "true anchor."[24] Blagden admired in Cavendish what he himself seemed to lack.

---

20 Wilson, *Cavendish*, 169–70.

21 Blagden to Banks, 8 Apr. 1790.

22 Banks to Blagden, 27 Mar. 1790.

23 Draft of a letter in the Blagden Collection, Misc. Notes, Royal Society, No. 224. Because of the similarity of content and wording to a letter from Blagden to Banks on 8 Apr. 1790, it is probably from around that time.

24 24 Feb. 1810, Charles Blagden Diary, Royal Society, 5:426.

As Blagden saw it, Cavendish encouraged him in the direction of independence, whereas Banks used him. From Banks's point of view, Blagden got what he apparently wanted, with Banks's help; he, Banks, deserved no blame at all, but if anything credit, and if Blagden did not know or say what he truly wanted, there was nothing Banks could do about that. Neither man showed much insight into their relationship, though Blagden, who experienced what we might call a breakdown, might hardly have been expected to.

After the storm, a surface calm was restored. Banks and Blagden settled for a modus vivendi, but it had an edge. Blagden confided in his diary that "Sir JB came at length, & behavd with his usual cunning & falseness, for éclat."[25] Blagden found the "perverseness & jobbing of Sir JB's manner worse than ever."[26] Banks's moral sentiments were "debased," his character was "odious."[27] People who see one another daily over a long time can irritate one another, but Blagden's censures of Banks seem severe. On his side, Banks could be wounding, as he was when Blagden considered stepping down as secretary of the Royal Society. Blagden had been elected to that post for fourteen successive years, during which time he had burned his eyes out; he could no longer read papers at the meetings, but he wanted to leave open the possibility of resuming the job later. Banks told him to forget it because Blagden's "enemies" would bring up his absences on his travels and accuse him of "not cultivating science with the same ardor as you have formerly done, owing to the habits you have lately adopted of mixing much in the gay circles of the more elevated ranks of society."[28] Blagden replied with indignation that he had "never performed the office so well" as he had last winter.[29] Blagden resigned for good in the winter of 1797.[30]

In late 1790 Blagden excused himself from a trip he had planned to take with his friend Lord Palmerston, the reason being "some experiments at Clapham." Blagden and Cavendish continued to be much together, but their relationship was less close than it had been. From what he could learn, Wilson concluded that the change in their relationship "did not occur till at least 1789," and we agree; as we note above, as late as November 1789 Blagden was concerned how his potential wife would react to his work with Cavendish. We can safely assume that Cavendish did not want to quarrel with Banks, and it might have seemed to him prudent to keep an impartial distance from both parties. We assume also that Blagden too desired distance; Thomson said that Blagden

[25] 28 May 1807, Charles Blagden Diary, Royal Society, 5:73.

[26] 20 Nov. 1806, Charles Blagden Diary, Royal Society, 5:12.

[27] 2 Feb. 1805 and 12 Mar. 1807, Charles Blagden Diary, Royal Society, 4:307 and 5:46.

[28] Sir Joseph Banks to Charles Blagden, 27 Apr. 1797, Blagden Letters, Royal Society, B. 44.

[29] Charles Blagden to Sir Joseph Banks, 27 Apr. 1797, BL Add Mss 33272, pp. 158–59.

[30] He resigned on 30 Nov. 1797. The draft letter of resignation, undated, with no address, begins: "The inflammation of my eyes . . . ." Blagden Collection, Royal Society, Misc. Matter–Unclassified.

"left him,"[31] and that seems correct. It is possible, of course, that the relationship between Blagden and Cavendish would have changed when it did independently of the strain in Blagden's relationship with Banks. The two men, after all, came from different strata of society, and their demeanors could hardly have been more contrasting: Cavendish's bafflingly eccentric, Blagden's flawlessly conventional. With good will on both sides, their friendship must have been trying, especially for Blagden.

Blagden's diary affords glimpses of Cavendish after their break. Blagden rarely recorded what Cavendish said, as he was interested primarily in Cavendish's behavior toward himself. Cavendish's mood affected his own: at the Royal Society, "Cav. at first sulky, then came round; I took no notice"; Blagden "just bowed to Cav. but did not avoid him"; "Cav. a little more familiar & I in return"; "Cav. spoke pretty freely, & I to him";[32] "Talked easily with Cav."; "Cav. talked more to me than usual with greater interest"; "No talk with Cav"; "Cav. looked so sulky I did not choose to speak to him."[33] "Cav. shook kindly my hand; asked if here for any time. I said three months at which he looked disappointed but said nothing."[34] In a moment of truth, or perhaps of frustration, Blagden confided in his diary: "made nothing of C. cannot understand him."[35]

If his relationship with Cavendish did not suit, Blagden's regard for Cavendish did not change. Blagden never doubted that his friend was extraordinary. He told his teacher William Cullen that Cavendish had not only great scientific ability but "the strictest integrity, the most amiable candour & a truly philosophical simplicity of manners."[36] Writing to Banks from Paris, Blagden compared Cavendish with "Laplace, who is as much superior among them here as Mr Cavendish is with us."[37] At Cavendish's death, Blagden wrote to a correspondent in Paris that Cavendish was "by much the best philosopher in my opinion that we have, or have had, in my time, at the R.S."[38]

THE DUCHESS AND THE PHILOSOPHER

Through the Devonshire and Kent dukedoms, Cavendish had an enduring connection with the world independently of Blagden, Banks, and other scientific

[31] Charles Blagden to Lord Palmerston, 8 Oct. 1790, draft, Osborn Collection, Yale, box 63/43. Wilson, *Cavendish*, 129. Thomas Thomson, *The History of Chemistry*, vol. 1 (London, 1830), 338.

[32] 19 May 1803, 15 Jan., 22 Feb., and 19 Mar. 1807, Charles Blagden Diary, Royal Society, 4:153, 5:26, 40, 51.

[33] 30 Nov, 1803, 9 Dec. 1804, 3 Feb. and 9 May 1805, Charles Blagden Diary, Royal Society, 4:187, 289, 308, 333.

[34] 8 May 1803, Charles Blagden Diary, Royal Society, 4:151.

[35] 27 Aug. 1795, Charles Blagden Diary, Royal Society, 3:67.

[36] Charles Blagden to William Cullen, 17 June 1784, draft, Blagden Letterbook, Yale.

[37] Sir Charles Blagden to Sir Joseph Banks, 1 Apr. 1802, BL Add Mss 33272, pp. 172–73.

[38] Sir Charles Blagden to B. Delessert, 20 Mar. 1810, draft, Blagden Letters, Royal Society, D. 44g.

colleagues. For most of Cavendish's adult life, the head of the family was the fifth duke of Devonshire. From Chatsworth, Thomas Knowlton wrote to the naturalist John Ellis, "I wish that our young Duke [the fifth duke was twenty-two] would, like his father, who every day improved in knowledge, take a turn that way."[39] But the young fifth duke would continue not to be like his father, who had been a self-improving man with a highly developed sense of service, and one of the most respected of eighteenth-century British statesmen. The fifth duke was the first of the dukes of Devonshire to resolutely turn his back on politics. He had that much in common with Henry Cavendish, in whom the absence of political desire was clearly an asset in his chosen life. The fifth duke had other traits in common with Henry: he was intelligent, perhaps having "something of the questioning way of Mr [Henry] Cavendish."[40] Still more like Henry, he was reclusive, introverted, awkward, and indifferent to religion, but here the resemblance ends. Since little individual exertion was required of the duke, he made little, preferring to lie in bed until the middle of the afternoon and then to get up only to go to his club. He was dissolute, unfaithful, and, in his dedicated passivity, fascinating.[41] He disapproved of Henry Cavendish, as we have noted, because "*he works*."[42] When Henry Cavendish died, the duke took a passing interest in the inheritance. The duke lived only one year beyond his working second cousin.

The fifth duke and his (first) wife, Lady Georgiana Spencer, had this much in common: like their great friend Charles James Fox, they were both prodigal gamblers.[43] Otherwise the duchess was the duke's temperamental opposite, vivacious, enthusiastic, charming, "her animal spirits were excessive." The duke, by contrast, was said to be a simile for winter.[44]

Like the Cavendishes, the Spencers had sided with the victorious party in the revolution of 1688–89. Taking a greater interest in politics than her husband, the duchess actively supported the cause of Fox and his followers. Known as the queen of London fashion, she also had an avid if unfocussed interest in music, literature, history, and science. With Giardini, she studied music;[45] with a "Philosopher," she studied how to use the globes, buying two for herself from the instrument-maker George Adams;[46] with a "German," she studied chemistry and

[39] Thomas Knowlton to John Ellis, Oct. 1770, in James Edward Smith, *A Selection of the Correspondence of Linnaeus, and Other Naturalists*, 2 vols. (London, 1821), 2:79.

[40] The full quotation is: "Talk with D. about Dss. 10h: had something of the questioning way of Mr Cavendish." This comparison, we realize, could as easily refer to the duchess as to the duke. 4 Sep. 1794, Charles Blagden Diary, Royal Society, 3:15.

[41] John Pearson, *The Serpent and the Stag: The Saga of England's Powerful and Glamourous Cavendish Family from the Age of Henry the Eighth to the Present* (New York: Holt, Rinehart & Winston, 1983), 122–23.

[42] Francis Bickley, *The Cavendish Family* (London: Constable, 1911), 202.

[43] Hugh Stokes, *The Devonshire House Circle* (London: Herbert Jenkins, 1917), 283–88.

[44] Mary Robinson, *Beaux and Belles of England* (London: Grolier Society, n.d.), 301.

[45] Bickley, *The Cavendish Family*, 241.

[46] Duchess of Devonshire to Countess Spencer, 11 Jan. 1783, Devon. Coll., no. 483.

95. Georgiana, Duchess of Devonshire. Lady Georgiana Spencer, first wife of the fifth duke of Devonshire. Painting by Sir Joshua Reynolds. Reproduced by permission of the Chatsworth Settlement Trustees. Photograph Courtauld Institute of Art.

mineralogy;[47] with Blagden she exchanged scientific news; and she took a keen interest in her cousin-in-law Henry Cavendish. Writing to the duchess, Blagden referred to "our friend Mr Cavendish."[48] From abroad the duchess asked Blagden to tell her about "any chemical, mineralogical, or philosophical novelty," and to give her compliments to Cavendish.[49] When she and Blagden happened to both be abroad and meet, they spent an evening in "much talk about chemistry & mineralogy," with Blagden noting in his diary, "Dss of Devonshire said she was quite wild with studies of that nature: asked much about Mr Cavendish & his pursuits"; "much talk with the Dss about Sir Jos. Banks's meetings, Mr Cavendish, &c."[50] The duchess called on Cavendish at his house,[51] and Cavendish called on her. Once when Blagden came to see her at Devonshire House, he found Cavendish there engaged in scientific talk.[52] The duchess and the philosopher were friends.

Wanting to be informed about science and about Henry Cavendish's activities, the duchess overcame his shyness and his alleged misogyny. To get him to talk she only had to keep to the subject of science. Her genuine interest and lively curiosity no doubt did the rest.

---

47 Sir Charles Blagden to Lord Palmerston, 21 Feb. 1794, draft, Yale, Osborn Collection, box 63/43.

48 Sir Charles Blagden to the duchess of Devonshire, 4 Jan. and 6 Mar. 1794, Devon. Coll.

49 Duchess of Devonshire to Sir Charles Blagden, 4 Mar. 1794, Blagden Letters, Royal Society, D.61.

50 "The Diary of Sir Charles Blagden," ed. Gavin De Beer, *Notes and Records of the Royal Society of London* 8 (1950): 65–89, on 76, 80, 83.

51 Once when she called on Cavendish, his servant told her he was not well, and she asked Blagden to find out how he was. Sir Charles Blagden to Sir Joseph Banks, 11 Aug. 1795, BL Add Mss 33272, p. 143. It was not an excuse; Blagden called on Cavendish later that month and found him "decaying: his forehead healing not kindly." 27 Aug. 1795, Charles Blagden Diary, Royal Society, 3:67.

52 1 Sep. 1794, Charles Blagden Diary, Royal Society, 3:14. Cavendish may have acted as a tutor to the duchess: when Blagden arrived at her house, he found "Mr. Cav. there; saw none had notes." The duchess proposed that Cavendish "shew extracts from Js de Physique." On 27 Nov. 1794, Blagden again came across Cavendish at the duchess's: "Met Mr. Cav. there: pleasant talk." Ibid., back p. 33.

PUBLISHED WORK

Cavendish's last five papers in the *Philosophical Transactions* all had to do directly or indirectly with astronomy, though only one of them, his paper on weighing the world, was a major work. One of the other papers was a note about the aurora borealis, a subject which by method and practitioner belonged equally to astronomy and to meteorology. Cavendish discussed three accounts of an uncommon aurora observed in 1786. He encouraged "people to attend to these arches" to help determine if his hypothesis was "true," which was that the aurora consists of parallel rays of light shooting skyward. His "hypothesis" had "some probability in it," but it was not yet a "theory of which I am convinced."[53] His paper was one of six papers, including the three he discussed, on auroras appearing in part 1 of the *Philosophical Transactions* for 1790; it can be seen as a contribution to an effort by the Royal Society to draw attention to these "luminous arches." Another paper by Cavendish was a comment on a recent paper on nautical astronomy by Mendoza y Rios.[54] The two remaining papers were more substantial. One, in 1792, was about the Hindu civil year.[55] Indian astronomy was then an active field among Western scholars, and Cavendish was in touch with several of them. He brought as a guest to the Royal Society Club William Marsden, F.R.S., an Asian scholar who published a paper on Hindu chronology in the *Philosophical Transactions*.[56] Cavendish commented on a paper on Hindu astronomy by Samuel Davis, another Oriental scholar;[57] Davis was subsequently elected to the Royal Society on the recommendation of Cavendish, who appeared first on Davis's certificate.[58] For his own study of Hindu astronomy, Cavendish borrowed almanacs from another Fellow of the Royal Society, the Sanskrit scholar Charles Wilkins. Another indication of Cavendish's interest in the subject was specific additions to his library around this time. He bought a

[53] Henry Cavendish, "On the Height of the Luminous Arch Which Was Seen on Feb. 23, 1784," *PT* 80 (1790): 101–5; *The Scientific Papers of the Honourable Henry Cavendish, F.R.S.*, vol. 2: *Chemical and Dynamical*, ed. E. Thorpe (Cambridge: Cambridge University Press, 1921), 233–35.

[54] Mendoza y Rios was given permission by Cavendish to publish an extract from a letter concerning nautical astronomy, printed at the end his paper "Recherches sur les principaux problèms de l'astronomie nautique," *PT* 87 (1797): 43–122: "Addition. Contenant une methode pour reduire les distances lunaires," 119–22; "Extract of a Letter . . . to Mr. Mendoza y Rios, January, 1795," in Cavendish, *Sci. Pap.* 2:246–48.

[55] Henry Cavendish, "On the Civil Year of the Hindoos, and Its Divisions; With an Account of Three Hindoo Almanacs Belonging to Charles Wilkins, Esq.," *PT* 82 (1792): 383; in *Sci. Pap.* 2:236–45.

[56] William Marsden, "On the Chronology of the Hindoos," *PT* 80 (1790): 560–84. Entry for 17 May 1787, Royal Society Club, Minute Book, Royal Society, 8. In that year, Marsden was elected member of the Club.

[57] Davis asked Banks to show one of his papers to Cavendish, initiating the connection. Samuel Davis to Sir Joseph Banks, 10 Mar. 1791, Banks Correspondence, Kew, 1.38. Blagden forwarded Davis's answers to Cavendish's questions. Charles Blagden to Henry Cavendish, 7 Nov. 1791, draft, Blagden Letterbook, Royal Society, 7:579.

[58] Royal Society, Certificates, 5 (28 June 1792).

number of books on India, and he subscribed to the *Asiatick Researches*, the journal of the Asiatic Society of Calcutta, a society modeled after the Royal Society of London.

Cavendish's last publication was about a method for dividing astronomical instruments. Instrument-makers had watchmakers to thank for their dividing engines, the basis of precision in eighteenth-century science.[59] The success of instrument-makers depended critically on their ability to accurately divide circles and straight lines into equal parts. George Graham's eight-foot mural quadrant at the Royal Observatory was subjected to a painstaking examination by James Bradley, who concluded that it was in error by over fifteen seconds of arc. John Bird replaced it with a quadrant that was accurate to within one second of arc.[60] In work of such precision, Bird was without equal. He never let more than one other person into the room when he was working, since the heat could spoil his divisions. Describing a mural quadrant divided by his method, Bird gave what could be considered the faith of an instrument-maker: "a mean of several observations, made by good observers with accurate instruments, properly adjusted, will always lead us either to the truth itself, or extremely near to it."[61]

As was the practice up to his time, Bird made his divisions by hand. That changed; in the 1770s Jesse Ramsden built a machine to mark divisions, today regarded as his "outstanding invention."[62] His machine used an endless screw to turn a wheel under a cutting point, six revolutions of the screw translating into one degree; the Board of Longitude paid him to publish a description.[63] When he completed a mural quadrant for Milan in 1790, he invited Cavendish among others to see and try it. Ramsden told them that "any common man in his workshop, with good eyes and hands, could, on the same princples, have divided it to equal perfection."[64] He made it sound easy, but dividing was the hardest part of the instrument-maker's work.

Cavendish, who was regarded as an expert on instruments of all kinds, was appointed to a committee of the Royal Society to find out why Ramsden was behind schedule in delivering a seven-foot equatorial circle to the Royal Observatory. At Ramsden's house, Cavendish observed work-in-progress by the master divider, as Ramsden exhibited his "Circle ready for dividing." Cavendish

59 Maurice Daumas, "Precision of Measurement and Physical and Chemical Research in the Eighteenth Century," in *Scientific Change*, ed. A. C. Crombie (New York: Basic Books, 1963), 418–30, on 422.

60 Alan Chapman, "Pure Research and Practical Teaching: The Astronomical Career of James Bradley, 1693–1762," *Notes and Records of the Royal Society of London* 47 (1993): 205–12, on 209.

61 John Bird, *The Method of Dividing Astronomical Instruments* (London, 1767), 13.

62 E. G. R. Taylor, *The Mathematical Practitioners of Hanoverian England, 1714–1840* (Cambridge: Cambridge University Press, 1966), 244.

63 Jesse Ramsden, *Description of an Engine for Dividing Mathematical Instruments* (London, 1777).

64 These are Blagden's words in reporting on the inspection of Ramsden's quadrant to Joseph Banks. 23 Sep. 1790, BL Add Mss 33272, pp. 89–90.

communicated to the Royal Society a paper on dividing circles by another instrument-maker, John Smeaton. The method Smeaton advocated depended not on sight but on contact. To illustrate its superiority, he referred to his pyrometer, an instrument of contact, which was accurate to one sixty-thousandth part of an inch. Any instrument using sight was accurate to only one four-thousandth part; that is, it had only one-fifteenth the accuracy possible with an instrument using contact. Smeaton summed up the importance of the method of dividing circles: "Perhaps no part of the science of mechanics has been cultivated by the ingenious with more assiduity, or more deservedly so, than the art of dividing circles for the purposes of astronomy and navigation."[65] In 1809 Cavendish joined the "ingenious" mechanics with his own method of dividing circles.

Edward Troughton and his older brother, John, were renowned for their dividing instruments, which were used by other instrument-makers, the ultimate compliment. By the beginning of the nineteenth century, Edward Troughton, who now conducted the business alone, had succeeded Ramsden as the foremost instrument-maker in England. In 1807 Cavendish was part of a visitation committee from the Royal Society who agreed with the astronomer royal that observations at the Royal Observatory would have greater accuracy if they were made with a circular instrument as well as with the existing mural quadrant. On the committee's invitation, Troughton recommended a circle six feet in diameter, which was approved by the committee and the council of the Royal Society and forwarded to the Board of Ordnance.[66] In the following year, Troughton delivered a paper to the Royal Society on his method of dividing, for which he was awarded a Copley Medal in 1809.[67] These events are the setting of Cavendish's paper of that year.

As a member of the council Cavendish agreed to give the medal to Troughton,[68] but Cavendish had been critical of Troughton in discussions two years before. Blagden wrote in his diary that "Cav. thought Troughton deficient in judgment, contrives some things very ill."[69] At a later meeting of the commit-

---

[65] 31 July and 25 Sep. 1783, Minutes of Council, Royal Society, 7:143, 146. John Smeaton, "Observations on the Graduation of Astronomical Instruments; with an Explanation of the Method Invented by the Late Mr. Henry Hindley, of York, Clock-Maker, to Divide Circles into Any Given Number of Parts," in *The Miscellaneous Papers of John Smeaton, Civil Engineer, &c. F.R.S. Comprising His Communications to the Royal Society, Printed in the Philosophical Transactions, Forming a Fourth Volume to His Reports* (London, 1814), 170–202, on 170, 186.

[66] Meeting of the committee on 22 Jan. and report of the meeting of the council of the Royal Society on 28 May 1807, "Visitations of Greenwich Observatory 1763 to 1815," Royal Society, Ms. 600, XIV.d.11, ff. 59–62.

[67] A. W. Skempton and Joyce Brown, "John and Edward Troughton, Mathematical Instrument Makers," *Notes and Records of the Royal Society* 27 (1973): 233–49, on 246. Roderick S. Webster, "Troughton, Edward," *DSB* 13:470–71. Edward Troughton, "An Account of a Method of Dividing Astronomical and Other Instruments by Ocular Inspection, in Which the Usual Tools for Graduating Are Not Employed . . . ," *PT* 99 (1809): 105–45.

[68] 16 Nov. 1809, Charles Blagden Diary, Royal Society, 5:389.

[69] 22 Jan. 1807, Charles Blagden Diary, Royal Society, 5:29.

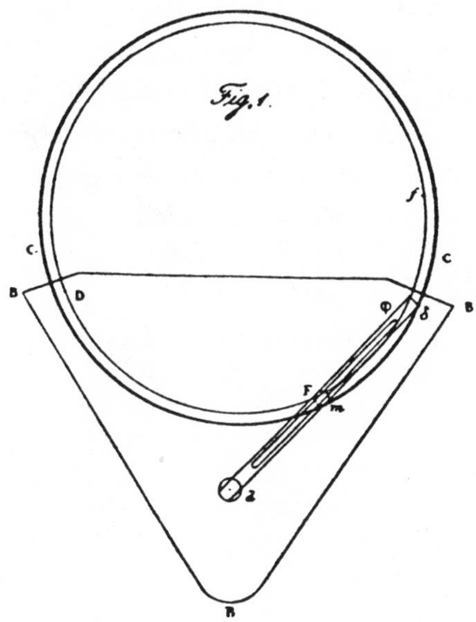

96. Dividing Instrument. From Cavendish's paper, "On an Improvement in the Manner of Dividing Astronomical Instruments," Philosophical Transactions *99 (1809): 221–45.*

tee on instruments for the Royal Observatory, Cavendish spoke against Troughton's "proposed instrument."[70] Cavendish's objection to Troughton was partly based on the four-foot transit instrument he made for the astronomer Stephen Groombridge; the instrument was to plague Troughton for years.[71] The committee reported to the council of the Society that the "instrument recommended by Mr Troughton is the best they are likely to procure under the present circumstances."[72] The less than wholehearted endorsement expressed Cavendish's reservations.

Cavendish carried his reservations further by writing a paper in which he proposed an alternative to Troughton's method. To ease the "great inconvenience and difficulty" of the common method of dividing, Cavendish eliminated the need to set the point of the beam compass in the divisions, which bruised them. The "great objection to the old method of dividing is entirely removed," he said. Troughton had just published an "ingenious method," and it was now up to instrument-makers to decide if his method or Troughton's was best.[73]

Elsewhere in this biography, we have called attention to Cavendish's study of error in the pursuit of accuracy. The dividing circle belonged to the class of instruments which, the astronomer John Pond said, have the advantage that "with them, we may infer with great precision not only the mean probable error, but likewise the greatest possible error to which they are liable."[74] The Lowndian professor of astronomy and geometry at Cambridge University, William Lax, in the paper immediately following Cavendish's in the *Philosophical Transactions* for 1809, spoke of how unsatisfactory it was to make observations of "extreme

[70] 14 May 1807, Charles Blagden Diary, Royal Society, 5:69.

[71] 23 Jan. 1807, Charles Blagden Diary, Royal Society, 5:29. In 1823 the instrument was examined for accuracy to "correct rumours harmful to Mr Troughton." Taylor, *Mathematical Practitioners*, 289.

[72] 28 May 1807, Minutes of Council, copy, Royal Society, 7:503.

[73] Henry Cavendish, "On an Improvement in the Manner of Dividing Astronomical Instruments," *PT* 99 (1809): 221–45; *Sci. Pap.* 2:287–93, on 287.

[74] John Pond, "On the Declinations of Some of the Principal Fixed Stars; with a Description of an Astronomical Circle, and Some Remarks on the Construction of Circular Instruments," *PT* 96 (1806): 420–54, on 421.

accuracy" with an instrument whose "exactness" cannot be judged. No instrument he said, should be trusted without "previous examination," and in his paper, he gave a method for determining the "greatest possible error" of such examination.[75] Troughton, in the third paper on dividing astronomical instruments in the same volume of the *Philosophical Transactions*, made a thorough study of errors, listing six standards and instruments in order of accuracy, expressing their greatest error in parts of an inch:

Sir George Shuckburgh's 5-foot standard	.000165
General William Roy's scale of 42″	.000240
Sir George Shuckburgh's equatorial of 2-foot radius	.000273
Greenwich Observatory quadrant of 8-foot radius	.000465
Alexander Aubert's standard of 5-foot length	.000700
Royal Society standard of 92″	.000795

Troughton was pleased with the high ranking of Roy's scale, since it was used to measure the baseline of the national trigonometrical survey.[76] Troughton's paper is filled with professional pride of the instrument-maker.

Although Cavendish's method of dividing does not seem to have been adopted, it occupies a distinguished place in his biography. As an attempt to improve the method of making the most precise instruments of science, his final contribution to science was about the tools for making the tools for achieving exactness. Besides Troughton, the only other instrument-maker named by Cavendish in his paper was Bird, the most exact of earlier dividers, with whose dictum (cited above) Cavendish would have been sympathetic. At age seventy-eight, with his paper on dividing engines, Cavendish acknowledged the direction of science to which his previous work had given such impetus.

COINAGE OF THE REALM

If Cavendish had lived two hundred years later, he might have been a successful director of a scientific institute. He clearly liked giving directions. His publications on heat, we may recall, were commentaries on experiments he designed for others to carry out. The long series of meteorological observations he planned for Dartmoor were made by others at the site. To scientifically determine the excise duty on spirits, Blagden made extensive experiments on specific gravities under Cavendish's guidance. Cavendish instructed travelers to make observations for determining the average climates of the world. He did the basic plan-

[75] William Lax, "On a Method of Examining the Divisions of Astronomical Instruments," *PT* 99 (1809): 232–45, on 232–33.

[76] Troughton, "An Account of a Method of Dividing," 140.

ning for the two major Royal Society projects of his time: he determined the places on the earth from which the transit of Venus should be observed, and he devised the rules for deciding on the mountain from which to make observations to determine the density of the earth. Shy among strangers, Cavendish interacted fully with scientific persons he knew. He chaired committees of the Royal Society. At home he worked with an assistant. His house at Clapham was a live-in forerunner of a research institute. Owing to a combination of traits–intelligence, dexterity, thorough knowledge, and a sense of fairness–he acquired an authority he did not have to assert. Despite his privileged rank in society, he believed that in scientific affairs authority should be vested in persons distinguished by their competence. He was ambitious but not for himself, always ready to deflect credit to colleagues. He was interested in everything new in science, and at the same time he had a strong direction of his own. He liked to work with young men of science. If Cavendish had an institute under his charge, it would bear his stamp; its members would live and breathe science. But of course if Cavendish had lived two hundred years later, he would not be Cavendish. We have recalled these facts about him to provide the background for certain experiments he directed for the public good in his later years.

In his *Sentimental Journey Through France and Italy*, Laurence Sterne wrote that he had in his pocket "a few king William's shillings as smooth as glass," explaining that "by jingling and rubbing one against another for seventy years together in one body's pocket or another's, they are become so much alike you can scarce distinguish one shilling from another."[77] That description of worn coinage was given in 1768, five years before a large recall of smooth gold coins.

In 1787 Charles Jenkinson directed a committee of the privy council to look into the state of the coins of the kingdom. The committee collected information for years. In 1796 the one man of science on the committee, Sir Joseph Banks, gave Jenkinson a long list of questions about the "extravagant waste" of gold owing to the wear of coins and defects in their manufacture.[78] The next year the war with France strained the finances of Britain; the stock of gold being uncertain, parliament ordered the Bank of England to cease payments of its notes in gold. At the same time the minting of gold coins was cut back, and in 1798 the minting of silver coins was stopped completely.[79]

The industrialist Matthew Boulton and the chemist Charles Hatchett were asked to write reports on the coinage, which were then given to the engineer John Rennie, who was engaged to make a complete study of the mint; the reports were

---

[77] Laurence Sterne, *A Sentimental Journey Through France and Italy*, first published in 1768; introduction by V. Woolf (London: Milford, 1951), 165–66.

[78] Unsigned memorandum by Sir Joseph Banks to the earl of Liverpool, [1796], in Liverpool Papers, BL Add Mss 38422, vol. 233, ff. 320–24, on 321–22.

[79] John Craig, *The Mint: A History of the London Mint from A.D. 287 to 1948* (Cambridge: Cambridge University Press, 1953), 260–62.

also given to Banks and Cavendish. Hatchett's report was found satisfactory, Boulton's not.[80] Cavendish recommended that the necessary experiments on coins be done by Hatchett, "whose accuracy can be relied on."[81] Cavendish was asked to assist Hatchett, and if it would help to persuade him (it was not needed) the king would appoint Cavendish a privy councillor.[82]

97. Coinage Apparatus. This drawing shows the apparatus designed by Cavendish for examining the wear of coins, built for him by the instrument-maker John Cuthbertson. In it, twenty-eight pairs of coins are pressed and rubbed together by turning the crank. Each pair of coins is separately weighted, and the frames holding the top and bottom coins vibrate at different rates to reduce grooving. Charles Hatchett, "Experiments and Observations on the Various Alloys, on the Specific Gravity, and on the Comparative Wear of Gold. Being the Substance of a Report Made to the Right Honourable the Lords of the Committee of Privy Council . . . ," Philosophical Transactions *93 (1803): end of volume.*

In the time of King William, silver coinage was the standard, while notes and coins made of other metal had only conventional value, but for most of the eighteenth century gold had been the de facto standard. In a speech opening the proceedings of the reconstituted committee on coins in 1798, Jenkinson, now earl of Liverpool, advocated the recognition of gold in place of silver as the legal standard.[83] The experiments Cavendish laid out were to decide what kind of gold coin would best resist wear. To replicate the wearing down of coins in Laurence Sterne's pocket, and any other kind of wear arising from their circulation, inge-

[80] Lord Liverpool to Sir Joseph Banks, 10 May 1798, copy, BM(NH), DTC 3:279–80.

[81] Henry Cavendish to Sir Joseph Banks, 28 July and 6 Aug. 1798, copy, BM(NH), DTC 3:19–20, 29. Lord Liverpool to Sir Joseph Banks, 13 Feb. 1799, copy, ibid., 195–96. A report was also given, on Cavendish's urging, by A. Robertson, an Oxford mathematician who did research on coinage; Robertson's report was delivered and read by Cavendish, to whom Liverpool gave his thanks on 12 Apr. 1799: Liverpool Papers, BL Add Mss 38424, vol. 235, f. 55.

[82] Lord Liverpool to Sir Joseph Banks, 7 July 1798, copy, BM(NH), DTC 3:19–20.

[83] "Heads of So Much of Lord Liverpool's Speech at the Council Board . . . Respecting the Coins and Mint of this Kingdom . . . ," Liverpool Papers, BL Add Mss 38423, vol. 234, ff. 402–7.

nious machines for punishing coins were designed by Cavendish and built by the instrument-maker John Cuthbertson, in whose house the experiments were carried out. One machine was a rotating oak container in which a large number of pieces of gold of different ductibility were agitated.[84] Another more complex machine pressed coins together, moving them laterally across one another. The measure of wear was the loss of weight of the coins. In another part of the experiments, thirteen gold alloys were hammered and rolled.

The experiments on coins turned out not to be particularly useful to the government, since they confirmed the practice of the moneyers, who proceeded with their alloys by experience without the aid of science.[85] But they did bring forward new facts of considerable scientific value. Hatchett said that knowledge of metal alloys had not "kept pace with the rapid progress of modern chemistry," being scarcely superior to what Pliny and the ancients knew.[86] As for knowledge of wear, a recent commentator writes, the grasp shown by Cavendish of its complex nature "was masterly; it could have been studied with advantage by investigators a century later."[87]

Hatchett wrote the report for the privy council committee on coins. Cavendish prefaced it with a letter explaining that Hatchett was the sole author because he had done the experiments and was best able to give an account of them.[88] Hatchett's experiments were done with "great judgement & accuracy, & in the manner which to both of us seemed best adapted to the object proposed," Cavendish said.[89] Cavendish then made an appeal to the government to let Hatchett publish his results rather than keeping them a government "secret." No "bad effect" could come of their publication, Cavendish said.[90] Banks supported the appeal, telling Liverpool that Cavendish and Hatchett were anxious that their findings on metallurgy might be anticipated, especially

---

[84] Charles Hatchett to Sir Joseph Banks, 14 Mar. 1800, BL Add Mss 33980, f. 225.

[85] J. C. Chaston, "Wear Resistance of Gold Alloys for Coinage: An Early Example of Contract Research," *Gold Bulletin* 7 (1974): 108–12, on 112. Sir Joseph Banks to Lord Liverpool, 11 May 1801, BL Add Mss 38424, ff. 158–59.

[86] Hatchett, "Experiments and Observations," 193.

[87] Chaston, "Wear Resistance," 112.

[88] Sir Joseph Banks to Lord Liverpool, 11 May 1801, BL Add Mss 38424, ff. 158–59. The report, addressed to Lord Liverpool and the select committee for coins, signed by Hatchett, 28 Apr. 1801, BL Add Mss 38426. The title of the report of the experiments, beginning on f. 25, is "Experiments and Observations on the Various Alloys, on the Specific Gravity, and on the Comparative Wear of Gold."

[89] Cavendish to the Privy Council Committee for Coins, prefacing Hatchett's report signed 28 Apr. 1801, BL Add Mss 38426, f. 1.

[90] Henry Cavendish to Charles Hatchett, 15 Oct. 1802; this letter was enclosed in a letter to Banks by Hatchett, in which Hatchett said that Lord Liverpool was satisfied with Cavendish's opinion on the publishable nature of the material. Banks gave his approval too, which he sent to Lord Liverpool: Charles Hatchett to Sir Joseph Banks, 24 Oct. 1802. Hatchett and Cavendish's desire to see the experiments published was first put to Lord Liverpool by Sir Joseph Banks on 21 Aug. 1801, BL Add Mss 38424, f. 160.

by the French.[91] Hatchett's abridged paper was read to the Royal Society and published in the *Philosophical Transactions.* "At the request of Mr. Cavendish," Hatchett wrote, "I have written the following account; but I should be highly unjust and ungrateful to that gentleman, did I not here publicly acknowledge how great a portion truly belongs to him." The machines and dies were "entirely contrived" by him.[92]

Weights and coinage had been inseparable over the ages. Traditionally the main interest of governments in reliable weights was coinage, as the names of currency indicate, the British "pound," for example.[93] It was fitting that England's most celebrated weigher, the man who weighed the lightest substance, inflammable air, and the heaviest object, the world, should be the one to supervise the weighing of the most valuable substance, gold, to assess its wear.

There was a sense in which coinage and nature posed a similar problem. In his researches Cavendish repeatedly introduced a "standard" by which to measure a certain class of phenomena, and he referred to substances or actions as being in a certain respect "equivalent." The same terms were used to understand the wealth of nations. In a letter to Liverpool on the subject of coinage, Cavendish referred to the "standard" of the fineness of gold;[94] the standard of gold was analogous to the purity of air. Liverpool told his committee on coins that money was the standard of the realm: the "standard coin of every country is the measure of property in it," and it is also the "equivalent" of the property;[95] the equivalence of coins and property was analogous to the equivalence of heat and vis viva. Money, as a measure, differs from all other measures. The problem of coinage came about because the standard for measuring the value of things could not be fixed once and for all; money was an equivalent made of gold, silver, or copper, and the prices of those metals fluctuated. From its dual function of standard measure and equivalent, money acquired the "principal difficulties" that attend it in speculation and in practice.[96]

There was a long-standing tradition of scientific service in the government in matters of coinage. Newton had been master of the mint, and after Newton the connection of the mint with the Royal Society had remained sub-

[91] Banks to Lord Liverpool, 21 Aug. 1801.

[92] Charles Hatchett, "Experiments and Observations on the Various Alloys, on the Specific Gravity, and on the Comparative Wear of Gold. Being the Substance of a Report Made to the Right Honourable the Lords of the Committee of Privy Council . . .," *PT* 93 (1803): 43–194, on 45.

[93] Bruno Kisch, *Scales and Weights: A Historical Outline* (New Haven: Yale University Press, 1965), 6, 9.

[94] Henry Cavendish to Lord Liverpool, 13 July [1798], BL Add Mss 38423, ff. 164–65.

[95] "Heads of So Much of Lord Liverpool's Speech."

[96] Charles Jenkinson, Lord Liverpool, *A Treatise on the Coins of the Realm; in a Letter to the King* (Oxford, 1805), 8–9.

stantial. Most of its masters had been Fellows of the Royal Society.[97] So far as we know, Cavendish was never considered for that job, but of the scientific men of his time he was closest to Newton in stature. No doubt it was as Newton's successor that Cavendish was asked to examine the condition of the nation's coinage. Both the practical importance and the symbolic meaning of the question would have pointed to Cavendish as the appropriate scientific authority. For Cavendish it would have been performing a duty to the public.

ROYAL INSTITUTION

For decades Cavendish served two institutions, the Royal Society and the British Museum, and in the last decade of his life he served a third, the Royal Institution. The last named was the creation of Benjamin Thompson, or as he was then better known, Count Rumford. Having served with the British army in the American Revolution, he retired, but not from his profession. Later at the court of the elector of Bavaria, he served as the head of the army, and there he acquired his title. He also made inventions, per-

98. *Royal Institution.* Distinguished Men of Science Living in Great Britain in 1807–8, *engraving by William Walker around 1862, taken from a drawing by Sir John Gilbert. The setting of this print is the library of the Royal Institution, but the group portrait is artificial. Henry Cavendish sits apart with eyes downcast, perhaps the artists's interpretation. Cavendish's profile and dress are clearly based upon William Alexander's sketch, with these differences: Cavendish's hat is removed; he is seated instead of walking; he faces the other direction; and he is made to appear thirty years younger. Henry Cavendish was a manager of the Royal Institution from 1800. Reproduced by permission of the National Portrait Gallery.*

[97] Chaston, "Wear Resistance," 108. John Craig, "The Royal Society and the Royal Mint," *Notes and Records of the Royal Society* 19 (1964): 156–67, on 161–62.

formed experiments on heat, and conceived of the idea of an institution of mechanics and heat. In 1798 he came to London, where his ideas on kitchens and heating had preceded him, put in place at the Foundling Hospital by the philanthropist Thomas Bernard. Invited by Bernard and the recently formed Bettering Society to draw up a plan, Rumford proposed an institution dedicated to teaching the applications of science and spreading knowledge of inventions. To fund it he organized a subscription whereby a person who gave fifty guineas or more became a perpetual proprietor. There was a quick response, and in 1799 the Royal Institution of Great Britain was launched.[98] The first lecture was announced for March 1800 in a house on Albemarle Street.

Cavendish and the duke of Devonshire paid their fifty guineas about a year after the Institution was founded, by which time it looked respectable.[99] The governing body of the Institution consisted of nine managers, elected initially from the proprietors, and Cavendish promptly became a manager.[100] The meetings of the managers were irregular but frequent and attended as a rule by only three or four managers along with the secretary and treasurer; Cavendish was the most faithful attender. Cavendish was also a conscientious member of the scientific committee of council, a standing committee set up to oversee the syllabus and scientific experiments. In addition to Cavendish, the committee included Blagden, Hatchett, and several other Fellows of the Royal Society.[101]

When the first scientific lecturer, Thomas Garnett, acted independently of Rumford, Rumford got the managers to appoint a small committee consisting of Cavendish, Banks, and himself to supervise the syllabus in the future.[102] In this and other ways Rumford, leaned on Cavendish and Banks to establish his authority.

---

[98] K. D. C. Vernon, *The Foundation and Early Years of the Royal Institution*, 1–4; reprinted from the *Proceedings of the Royal Institution* 39 (1963). W. J. Sparrow, *Knight of the White Eagle* (London: Hutchinson, 1964), 109–10. Sanborn C. Brown, "Thompson, Benjamin (Count Rumford)," *DSB* 13:350–52.

[99] Cavendish became a proprietor on 10 Feb. 1800. The managers, at their meeting on 17 Feb., said that the Royal Institution was "now established on a Basis so firm & respectable, that no Doubt can be entertained of its Success." Royal Institution of Great Britain, *The Archives of the Royal Institution of Great Britain in Facsimile. Minutes of Managers' Meetings 1799–1900*, vols. 1 and 2 (in one volume), ed. F. Greenaway (Ilkley: published in association with the Royal Institution of Great Britain by the Scolar Press Limited, 1971).

[100] He was elected at the annual meeting of proprietors on 1 May 1800. Entry for 5 May 1800, Minutes of the Meetings of Managers, Royal Institution, 2:70.

[101] 31 Mar. 1800, Minutes of the Meetings of Managers, Royal Institution Archive, 2:39–41. The other members of the committee were Major Rennell, Joseph Planta, E. Whitaker Gray, J. Vince, and William Farish. The last two were professors of experimental philosophy and of chemistry at Cambridge. Maskelyne was appointed but declined because he was too busy.

[102] 2 Feb. 1801, Minutes of the Meetings of Managers, Royal Institution, 2:126–27. Vernon, *Foundation*, 18.

The second year saw important changes of staff. On Banks's recommendation, Garnett was replaced by Thomas Young, and on Rumford's recommendation, Humphry Davy was hired as an assistant lecturer in chemistry. Davy ensured the success of the Institution by persistently attracting a fashionable audience to his public lectures and by doing outstanding chemical research.[103]

Rumford's methods were dictatorial and his presence erratic, and as the Royal Institution departed from its original purpose his interest in it flagged; in 1802 this restless man left the Institution for good. The next year the scientific committee was reappointed, with Cavendish, Banks, and Hatchett on it again.[104] That same year the committee recommended as Thomas Young's successor John Dalton, who gave occasional lectures at the Institution.[105] Cavendish did not live quite long enough to see the arrival of the greatest of all the scientists to work in the Royal Institution, Michael Faraday.[106]

Cavendish had long been a subscriber to the Society of Arts without taking part in its affairs, whereas he became fully involved in the affairs of the Royal Institution. The difference likely had to do with the stronger connection to science in the Royal Institution. We know that Cavendish advocated close cooperation between the Royal Institution and the Royal Society, because it was he who seconded Rumford's motion to direct the secretaries of the two institutions to keep one another regularly informed.[107] Cavendish took some interest in the lectures given at the Institution, but probably no more than was required of him as a member of the standing committee; among his papers is a letter from Thomas Young asking his opinion on a question about gearwork for his syllabus, and in his lectures Young gave an explanation of halos around the sun that Cavendish had suggested to him.[108] Cavendish's main interest undoubtedly lay in the scientific research in the laboratory, over which he, Banks, and Hatchett had

---

103 Vernon, *Foundation*, 24.

104 26 May 1803, Minutes of the Meetings of Managers, Royal Institution, 3:137–38.

105 5 Sep. 1803, Minutes of the Meetings of Managers, Royal Institution, 3:151.

106 Three years after Cavendish's death, in 1813, Davy received from Faraday a copy of the notes Faraday took of Davy's lectures at the Royal Institution, the beginning of Faraday's long association with the Institution.

107 The Royal Institution began its own journal. The motion seconded by Cavendish called for the Royal Society to inform the Royal Institution of papers read at its meetings that were suitable for the Royal Institution's journal. It also required that an earlier resolution, on 31 Mar. 1800, of the Royal Institution be communicated to the Royal Society; this concerned the duty of the scientific committee to communicate discoveries to the Royal Society. Entry for 5 Apr. 1802, Minutes of the Meetings of Managers, Royal Institution, 2:260.

108 Thomas Young to Henry Cavendish, 3 Sep. 1801, enclosed in a paper, "On the Shape of the Teeth in Rack Work," Cavendish Mss, VI(b), 31. In Thomas Young's *A Syllabus of a Course of Lectures on Natural and Experimental Philosophy* (London, 1802), paragraph 179, Young acknowledged Cavendish for the demonstration. Sir Joseph Larmor's comment in *Sci. Pap.* 2:410. Thomas Young, *A Course of Lectures on Natural Philosophy and the Mechanical Arts*, 2 vols. (London, 1807) 2:308.

99. *Charles Hatchett. Reproduced by permission of the President and Council of the Royal Society.*

100. *Thomas Young. Painting by Sir Thomas Lawrence, engraving by G. Adcock. Courtesy of Smith Image Collection, Van Pelt-Dietrich Library, University of Pennsylvania.*

__101.__ Sir Humphry Davy. Lonsdale, pinx. Worthington, sculp. Courtesy of Smith Image Collection, Van Pelt-Dietrich Library, University of Pennsylvania.

__102.__ James Louis Macie (Smithson). Tempera on paperboard, miniature portrait by Henri-Joseph Johns, 1816. Reproduced by permission of the National Portrait Gallery, Smithsonian Institution.

charge.[109] Through the last year of his life Cavendish witnessed Davy's experiments and assisted in them.[110]

In a paper read before the Royal Society in 1798, Rumford wrote that the "effects produced in the world by the agency of Heat are probably *just as extensive*, and quite as important, as those which are owing to the tendency of the particles of matter towards each other; and there is no doubt but its operations are, in all cases, determined by laws equally immutable."[111] Heat, then, is as important as gravitation in the scheme of the world. At first Rumford believed that heat is a fluid, but he changed his mind; heat, he came to believe, is the internal vibrations of bodies.[112] From the point of view of the Royal Institution, his new understanding of heat was fortunate. In 1799 the twenty-one year-old Davy published a tract on heat,[113] which came to the notice of Rumford, who recognized ideas in it similar to his own. Thereupon Rumford offered their author a job at the Institution.[114] Garnett, who had studied under Black at Edinburgh University, gave a full account of Black's theory of "latent heat" in his lectures at the Royal Institution. He used the word "caloric" throughout, and although he understood it to be independent of the cause of heat, he spoke of caloric as being "combined" with ordinary matter, suggesting a material theory of heat. Rumford and Garnett had a falling out over another issue, but Rumford may have been dissatisfied with the contents of Garnett's lectures as well.[115] Young, Garnett's replacement, held a view of heat similar to Rumford's, and in their lectures at the Institution, Young and Davy made clear their preference for the vibratory theory. For a time in the Royal Institution, there were several advocates of an unfashionable view of heat: Rumford, at the head of the Institution, the two science lecturers, Davy and Young, and the experimentalist of Rumford's inner circle, Cavendish. Whatever else might be made of this, it is noteworthy that

---

109 Vernon, *Foundation*, 27.

110 John Davy, *Memoirs of the Life of Sir Humphry Davy, Bart.*, 2 vols. (London, 1836) 1:222.

111 Count Rumford, "An Inquiry Concerning the Source of the Heat Which Is Excited by Friction," *PT* 88 (1798): 80–102; in Benjamin Thompson, Count Rumford, *The Complete Works of Count Rumford*, vol. 1 (Boston, 1870), 469–92, on 491.

112 Count Rumford, "An Inquiry Concerning the Weight Ascribed to Heat," *PT* 89 (1799): 179–94.

113 Davy was working in Thomas Beddoes's Pneumatic Institution at the time. Beddoes included Davy's "Essay on Heat, Light, and the Combinations of Light" in a collection in 1799, *Contributions to Physical and Medical Knowledge, Principally from the West of England.* David M. Knight, "Davy, Humphry," *DSB* 3:598–604, on 599.

114 George E. Ellis, *Memoir of Sir Benjamin Thompson, Count Rumford* (Philadelphia, 1871), 486.

115 Thomas Garnett, *Outlines of a Course of Lectures on Chemistry: Delivered at the Royal Institution of Great Britain, 1801* (London, 1801), 15–17, 30–31. He published at the same time *Outlines of a Course of Lectures on Natural and Experimental Philosophy, Delivered at the Royal Institution of Great Britain, 1801* (London, 1801). On his studies at Edinburgh, "The Life of the Author," in Thomas Garnett, *Popular Lectures on Zoonomia, or The Laws of Animal Life, in Health and Disease* (London, 1804), vi–vii.

near the end of his life, Cavendish was in the company of scientists who broadly agreed with him on the nature of heat, a subject on which he had strong theoretical views.[116]

The Royal Institution offered Cavendish a chance both to serve science publicly and to come together with gifted young scientists. Two of the most perceptive biographical accounts of Cavendish were written by Davy and Young, who knew him especially from the Institution. "He was reserved to strangers," Davy said of Cavendish, "but, when he was familiar, his conversation was lively, and full of varied information. . . . He was warmly interested in all new subjects of science."[117]

When Davy arrived at the Royal Institution in 1801, he was received by Rumford, Cavendish, and Banks, who promised him any apparatus he wanted for his experiments.[118] When Cavendish died, his proprietorship in the Institution was inherited by Lord George Cavendish, from whom Davy obtained some of Cavendish's choice chemical apparatus. Five months after Cavendish's death, Davy received permission from the managers to bring this apparatus into the Royal Institution for use in experiments and lectures.[119] The apparatus would have given Davy a perpetual reminder of their original owner: in his chemical treatise published two years after Cavendish's death, Davy observed that Cavendish "carried into his chemical researches a delicacy and precision, which have never been exceeded."[120]

INSTITUTE OF FRANCE

While Rumford was still head of the Royal Institution in late 1801, he wrote to Banks from Paris to inform him confidentially that he, Banks, headed the list of ten foreigners put up by the class of mathematics and physics of the Institute of France, the successor of the Academy of Sciences. Each of the several classes

116 G. N. Cantor has noted the agreement on heat between Rumford, Davy, and Young, in "Thomas Young's Lectures at the Royal Institution," *Notes and Records of the Royal Society* 25 (1970): 87–112, on 90. In contrast to Garnett's noncommittal approach but implied preference for the fluid theory, Young in his lectures at the Royal Institution argued by analogy with sound to the truth of the vibration theory of heat, "Newton's opinion." Thomas Young, *A Course of Lectures on Natural Philosophy and the Mechanical Arts,* 2 vols. (London, 1807) 1:148–49, 656. Davy and Young were concerned to impart in their lectures the new understanding of radiant heat. With praise for Rumford's experiments, Davy explained that vibrating particles of bodies give rise to vibrations in the ether, which in turn communicate vibrations to particles of bodies. Humphry Davy, *A Syllabus of a Course of Lectures on Chemistry Delivered at the Royal Institution of Great Britain* (London, 1802), 50–54. Davy wrote in 1799, "It has then been experimentally demonstrated that caloric, or the matter of heat, does not exist" and that heat is a "peculiar motion, probably a vibration, of the corpuscles of bodies." *The Collected Works of Sir Humphry Davy, Bart.*, ed. J. Davy, 4 vols. (London, 1839) 2:13–14.

117 John Davy, *Memoirs of the Life of Sir Humphry Davy*, 1:222.

118 Humphry Davy to Davies Gilbert, 8 Mar. 1801, in John Ayrton Paris, *The Life of Sir Humphry Davy* (London, 1831), 78.

119 *The Archives of the Royal Institution* 5 (1975): 47, 62 126, 160.

120 Humphry Davy, *Elements of Chemical Philosophy*, vol. 1 (London, 1812), 37

of the Institute proposed candidates for foreign membership to be balloted on at a general meeting, the number to be admitted fixed at twenty-four. Interested parties ranked those in the running much like racehorses.[121]

Rumford reported that after Banks came Maskelyne, Cavendish, Herschel, Priestley, Pyotr Simon Pallas, Alessandro Volta, and three others, in that order. Rumford was himself proposed but in another class. Blagden, who also was in Paris, kept Banks closely posted on the rapidly evolving, rather undignified scene. Not himself a candidate, Blagden joined in the frenzied lobbying for persons who were. Pressing Cavendish's claims with the scientists he knew in the Institute, Blagden fully expected Cavendish to be the first elected after the Institute had fulfilled its duty of electing all the former foreign associates from the defunct Academy.[122] His next letter was less certain. Pallas and Cavendish were tied on the first ballot, and on the second Pallas came off one vote ahead, not because the "people here are so ignorant as to think him superior to Cavendish," but because Pallas was a former associate of the Academy. Volta, whose high reputation was "here, perhaps a little exaggerated," Martin Heinrich Klaproth "deservedly," and Watt were very much in the running. Cavendish might be chosen at the next election, and although there was "no certainty" of it, very much in his favor was the opinion of the First Consul, Napoleon, who took the opportunity of "expressing how much he esteems Mr Cavendish."[123] In his next report, Blagden said that at the coming election, the mathematics and physics class intended to present, first, Cavendish, then Watt, "who ran him pretty hard," and third Paolo Mascagni, Volta being out of the running.[124] This time Blagden was proven right; Cavendish was elected.[125] The Institute listed the foreign members according to their merits in science: Banks was first, Maskelyne next, because of his lunar tables for determining longitude, and then Cavendish.[126] This recognition we liken to the elevation of an earlier political Cavendish to duke of Devonshire.

DAILY LIFE

The latter years of Cavendish's life were years of peril for the nation. He went among the men of science as he had always done, at the Royal Society, at his clubs, and at Banks's house, but the talk was now often about politics,

[121] Count Rumford to Sir Joseph Banks, 22 Nov. 1801, BL Add Mss 8099. Banks had been proposed for the class of mathematics and physics by the botanical section.

[122] Sir Charles Blagden to Sir Joseph Banks, 19 June 1802, copy, BM(NH), DTC 3: 170–74.

[123] Sir Charles Blagden to Sir Joseph Banks, 15 Oct. 1802, BM Add Mss 33272, pp. 204–5.

[124] Sir Charles Blagden to Sir Joseph Banks, 26 Nov. and 6 Dec. 1802, BL Add Mss 33272, pp. 210–13.

[125] Sir Charles Blagden to Sir Joseph Banks, 29 Jan. 1803. Fitzwilliam Museum Library, Perceval H205.

[126] Sir Charles Blagden to Sir Joseph Banks, 1 Feb. 1803, Fitzwilliam Museum Library, Perceval H206.

impending war, and battles rather than about science. In the year Cavendish weighed the world, 1798, the council of the Society put to the ballot and unanimously agreed to the motion to pay £500 to the Bank of England "as a voluntary contribution towards the defence of the country at this critical period."[127] Blagden's diary, our main source of information about Cavendish's comings and goings during these years, is mostly about the general agitation, when it is not about his private agitation over Madame Lavoisier or his difficulty in getting a passport to return to France. There is little on science in it. Even Cavendish was caught up in the events in the world at large. At the Royal Society, Cavendish said "that if Pitt came in against K's inclinations, the K. if quite well, wo^{d} soon find the means of getting him out again"; to Blagden's observation that North Germany was then quiet, Cavendish "still thought Holstein wo^{d} be attacked at some moment."[128] At the Society, when the conversation turned to war, Denmark, and Pitt, Cavendish lifted up his hands.[129]

Toward the end of his life, as at any time during it, what was most conspicuous about Cavendish was his steadfast desire to know and practice science. When given a paper by Herschel to look over, Blagden knew that Cavendish was the "best person" to read it;[130] this was one year before Cavendish died. Two months before he died, Cavendish told Blagden that he had "doubts about some part of Malus's paper, & did not know if understood it."[131] The French physicist Étienne Louis Malus had just begun publishing his important work on optics, and Cavendish was following it. In the last year of his life, Cavendish saw much of Davy; or as Blagden put it, Davy was "intriguing with Cav." Davy thought that he had converted azote (nitrogen) into oxygen, an extraordinary finding if true. Blagden said that "Mr Cavendish has gone thro' the experiment with him [Davy], & detects no source of fallacy." Cavendish was "quite satisfied that the gases convertible," seeing "no way of explaining Davy's expt but by conversion of nitrogen."[132] Cavendish was actively following, and in this case aiding in, Davy's important researches in chemistry. As late as 1806, Cavendish was still doing experiments of his own in chemistry, undertaking a long series on platina.[133] For the rest, Cavendish attended his scientific meetings; in the 1790s his attendance at the council was irregular, but it picked up again in his last decade.

---

127 22 Feb. 1798, Minutes of Council, copy, Royal Society, 7:353.

128 26 Mar. 1804, Charles Blagden Diary, Royal Society, 5:214.

129 1 Dec. 1806, Charles Blagden Diary, Royal Society, 5:15.

130 16 Feb. 1809, Charles Blagden Diary, Royal Society, 5:286.

131 3 Dec. 1809, Charles Blagden Diary, Royal Society, 5:396 (back).

132 Charles Blagden to Richard Chenevix, 1 May 1809, draft, Blagden Letters, Royal Society, C.35. 9 June, 13 and 20 July, Charles Blagden Diary, Royal Society, 5:295, 306, 308.

133 In January 1806, e.g., on platina: "White Book," Cavendish Mss, p. 68.

WEALTH

As in his laboratory, in his domestic arrangements Cavendish preferred simplicity. As far as clothing went, he paid no attention to changing fashions, wearing the same dress year after year. He was said to have had no wardrobe, only one suit of clothes at a time.[134] This estimate must be close, for when Cavendish died the clothing at Clapham Common was evaluated at £37, and at Bedford Square nothing.[135] He did not entertain at home often, and when he did the company, so far as we know, was scientific. What his guests were served was remembered as invariable, one leg of mutton. When on one occasion several guests were expected, Cavendish's housekeeper complained to him that one leg of mutton would be insufficient, and Cavendish replied, "Well, then, get two."[136] We do not know what Lord Charles provided at home, but we do know that at Cambridge, Henry Cavendish ate mutton five days of the week, and mutton was common fare for invited guests; Peter Collinson asked Martin Folkes, president of the Royal Society, and his daughter to visit him and "take a piece of Mutton with me."[137] Under French influence, the composition of English meals is said to have changed. In continuing what he had known as the usual hospitality from his early years, Cavendish might have disappointed guests who had grown accustomed to more divers meals. Cavendish was fixed in his ways but not absolutely rigid. We have the butcher's and fishmonger's bills from the very end of his life, and although leg of mutton would seem to have been the favored dish, Cavendish's housekeeper also ordered beef, loin pork, cod, and oysters.[138] His hospitality is suggested by his wine cabinet at Bedford Square, which at the end of his life held twenty-two bottles of port, tokay, and white wines, and ten dozen empty bottles.[139] His houses contained no objects of art of any value; for taxing purposes, his paintings, portraits of family members, were valued at £13.[140] At Clapham Common he kept a carriage and some farming stock worth somewhat under£200. Only one category of nonscientific possessions stands out. From Lady Elizabeth Cavendish, Lord Charles Cavendish had inherited diamonds, jewels, and coins, which would have passed to Henry. John Barrow said that Cavendish owned an old lady's diamond-beset stomacher appraised

[134] Wilson, *Cavendish*, 188.

[135] "Extracts from Valuations of Furniture &c.," Devon. Coll.

[136] Wilson, *Cavendish*, 164.

[137] Peter Collinson to Martin Folkes, n.d., Folkes Correspondence, Royal Society, Mss 250, vol. 3, No. 55.

[138] "Vouchers to Mrs Stewarts Household," at Clapham Common, Devon. Coll., box 31.

[139] "Extracts from Valuations of Furniture &c."; "Inventory of Sundry Fixtures, Household Furniture, Plate, Linen &c. &c. the Property of the Late Henry Cavendish Esquire at His Late Residence in Bedford Square Taken the 2nd Day of April 1810," Devon. Coll., L/114/74.

[140] "Extracts from Valuations of Furniture &c."

at £20,000. In this as in other details about Cavendish, Barrow probably did not get the facts quite right. When Cavendish died, the legacy duty was 4 percent, an incentive for the heirs to encourage the lowest possible appraisals, but since the total value placed on Henry's possessions of this sort was only £2,000, it seems unlikely that one single item was actually worth £20,000. Cavendish did not spend lavishly, which is the reason his wealth was not squandered.

Apart from his investments, which were enormous, Cavendish's wealth consisted mainly of his Bedford Square house and the contents of it and the contents of his house on Clapham Common. The furniture in each of the houses was valued at around £600, which was close to the value of the instruments at Clapham Common; the great value of the books, £7,000, we have already discussed.

The reason why Henry Cavendish's wealth existed in the first place was that his father was wealthy. The great wealth of Lord Charles and then of Henry Cavendish had three sources: the family settlements and legacies, without which there would have been no wealth at all; financial prudence; and the public debt of the kingdom. In addition to the two revolutions we have discussed, the political and the scientific, Lord Charles and Henry Cavendish were beneficiaries of a third, contemporary "revolution," this one commercial. Certainly one of the major outcomes of the revolution of 1688–89 was a change in the relationship between business and government. In the past, most government borrowing had been on the king's word, which had proven untrustworthy. Parliament took over the responsibility for guaranteeing loans in 1693, from which time a "public debt" can properly be spoken of. The public had sufficient confidence in the financial stability of the country to deposit its money in the Bank of England, which was designated to handle the public debt in part, and to buy shares in it, the "funds." As good land was becoming scarce, public loans appealed as an alternative source of income, with several to choose from. An enormous loan was offered by the South Sea Company and a smaller one by the East India Company, and a substantial loan was offered by the Bank of England, which also issued a group of annuities. The latter contained so-called perpetual annuities, or annuities requiring the government to pay a fixed rate of return in perpetuity. Over the course of the century, most of the public debt–and most of our Cavendishes' wealth–came to be held in annuities of this kind.[141]

The perpetual annuities owned by the Cavendishes were controlled by a new policy introduced in 1751, on the eve of Henry Cavendish's majority. The

141 Alice Clare Carter, *The English Public Debt in the Eighteenth Century* (London: The Historical Association, 1968), 2–9. John Carswell, *The South Sea Bubble*, rev. ed. (London: Alan Sutton, 1993), 8, 12, 18–20.

outstanding loans paying 3 percent, some through the Bank of England and some through the exchequer, were consolidated into a single fund, which was named the "3 per cent Consolidated Annuities," or "consols" for short. Other annuities paying more than 3 percent were united in another fund now paying only 3 percent, which were named "3 per cent Reduced Annuities." Both of these funds were managed by the Bank of England, which paid out interest, or "dividends." The dividends were paid twice yearly; in other words, 3 percent annuities paid 6 percent annually. On stated days the dividends were drawn and signed for; if the owner of the stock was not present, the dividends were deposited through power of attorney with the Bank or the trading companies.[142]

Most of the owners of Bank of England stock lived in and around London. They were a varied lot, with many migrants, Huguenots and Spanish and Portuguese Jews, a good many gentry, gentlemen, and peers, especially dowagers and ladies, corporate bodies such as the colleges of Cambridge, and increasingly spinsters and widows. As the number of investors in the eighteenth century was few, and the majority of these were small investors, most of the stock was held by a very few persons, who included the Cavendishes. Most investors bought stock and kept it, regarding it as gilt-edged, and withdrawing only dividends or else reinvesting them.[143]

The foundations of Lord Charles Cavendish's wealth were modest, principally his income from farms, his annuity, his inheritance, and his due according to the marriage settlement. By the time of his death fifty-five years after the settlement, by accretion, his investments had turned into a reasonable fortune. He held what we would now call a diversified portfolio: between his South Sea annuities, new and old, and his Bank of England stock, consols, and reduced 3 percent annuities, he was worth £159,200. This amount Henry Cavendish inherited in 1783, and it did not yet contain Elizabeth Cavendish's legacy, intended for Lord Charles, but which only appeared in 1784 as an addition to Henry Cavendish's account. Her legacy nearly doubled his wealth, bringing him £48,000 in mortgages and £97,100 in consols and reduced 3 percent annuities. In addition, before his father died, Henry Cavendish held securities in his own name, and although by comparison their value was not as large, it was not negligible either: as of 1776 he had £1,100 in South Sea annuities, and as of 1781 he had £14,000 in reduced 3 percent annuities. Thus, in the year after his father's death, in addition to a considerable sum in mortgages, Henry Cavendish held nearly

142 Eugen von Philippovich, *History of the Bank of England, and Its Financial Services to the State*, 2d ed, trans. C. Meredith (Washington, D.C.: Government Printing Office, 1911), 135. John Clapham, *The Bank of England, A History*, 2 vols. (Cambridge: Cambridge University Press, 1945) 1:77, 97–98. Carter, *English Public Debt*, 10.

143 Carter, *English Public Debt*, 18–19. Clapham, *Bank of England* 1:280–88.

£300,000 in the securities named above (and perhaps some smaller amounts in other securities).[144]

Wilson and Thomson both give an anecdote about Cavendish and his bankers. A large sum of cash, £70,000 or £80,000, depending on who tells it, had accumulated in Cavendish's account, prompting a banker to call on him to ask what to do with it. The banker overheard the following conversation between Cavendish and his servant. "Who is he? Who is he? What does he want with me?" "He says he is your banker, and must speak to you." When the banker was admitted, Cavendish cried, "What do you come here for? What do you want with me?" The banker explained, and Cavendish responded, "If it is any trouble to you, I will take it out of your hands. Do not come here to plague me." "Not the least trouble to us, Sir, not the least; but we thought you might like some of it to be invested." "Well! well! What do you want to do?" "Perhaps you would like to have forty thousand pounds invested." "Do so! Do so, and don't come here and trouble me, or I will remove it."[145] Cavendish's bankers, Messrs. Cornelius Denne and Co, in the Strand, were accustomed to receiving directions by mail from Cavendish, such as, "Please to lay out the sum of twenty six thousand pounds in the purchase of four different stocks as under & charge to my account." In this way Cavendish "made considerable purchases every year of additional stock in the same funds."[146] His directions seem to have been straightforward and consistent; his dividends were reinvested alternately in four securities: new and old South Sea annuities and consols and reduced 3 percent annuities, and primarily in the latter two.[147] His farm rents went directly to his bankers, and his business was transacted through them. He had enough wealth that he did not have to think

144 Lord Charles Cavendish's stock at the time of his death consisted of: Bank of England stock, £25,815; New South Seas Annuities, £47,000; Reduced 3 percent Annuities, £18,285; Consolidated 3 percent Annuities, £62,100; and Old South Sea Annuities, £6,000; which made a total of £159,200. The next year, 1784, Henry Cavendish's bank account was augmented by Elizabeth Cavendish's legacy to Lord Charles Cavendish, which consisted of: Reduced 3 percent Annuities, £22,100; Consolidated 3 percent Annuities, £50,000; and another group of the latter, £25,000; which made a total of £97,100. The earl of Hardwicke deposited £916 in his account in 1783. So to start with, Henry Cavendish had £272,800 from these sources, and he had several thousand pounds in securities in his own name. The above information is from the ledgers of the Bank of England Archive: South Sea Annuities 1776–1793, vol. 154, p. 65; Bank Stock, 1783–1798, No. 59, p. 389, and 1798–1815, No. 64, p. 439; Reduced 3 percent Annuities, Supplement Ledger, 1781–1785, p. 10614, and 1785–1793, pp. 1505, 2242, and 1793–1801, pp. 1727, 1801, and 1803–1807, p. 1937, and 1807–1817, p. 6001; Consolidated 3 percent Annuities, 1782–1788, pp. 3449–50, 3854, 3927, and 1788–1792, pp. 8000, 8619, and 1792–1798, pp. 8000, 8730, and 1799–1804, pp. 8001, 9012, and 1804–1812, p. 8001; South Sea Old Annuities, vol. 79, 1776–1786, p. 90, and vol. 90, 1794–1815, p. 648.

145 Wilson, *Cavendish*, 175–76.

146 Henry Cavendish to Messrs Denne & Co., 25 Mar. 1793, "1790–1816. Accs. & Receipts. Case & Opinions," Devon. Coll., 86/comp. 3.

147 Correspondence from Cavendish's bankers, Devon. Coll., 86/comp 3.

about it, an ideal life which he did not want disturbed by house calls from his bankers.

When occasionally Cavendish himself acted as a banker-in-need to his friends and family, who turned to him for loans, he took little trouble over the business and gave it even less thought. He did not, for example, remember if he had received interest on some money he had lent to a friend; the reason he gave for his uncertainty was that "I am not very regular in my accounts."[148]

To the world, Cavendish's vast wealth has proven as intriguing as his discoveries, as Biot's well-known epigram testifies: Cavendish was "the richest of the wise and the wisest of the rich." Cavendish was "indeed, not less famed in his country for the great accumulation of his property than for his intellectual and scientific treasure."[149] The source of his wealth and how and when he came by it have been stated variously. Thomson said that an aunt who outlived Cavendish's father left Cavendish a great deal of money. Biot said that Cavendish's uncle, a general overseas, returned to England in 1773 to find his nephew neglected by his family, and to make it aright he left his entire fortune to him. Cuvier gave a similar account, adding the detail that the uncle had fought in India. Wilson, who was inclined to accept Cuvier's authority on this point, concluded that Cavendish probably had become wealthy before his father's death.[150] For his *éloge* of Cavendish, Cuvier went directly to Blagden, but he also took details from Biot's biography, which was filled with errors. Blagden let Cuvier know that he had the origin of Cavendish's fortune wrong. Blagden believed that it was Cavendish's father, and he was right.[151] A millionaire when he died twenty-six years later, Henry Cavendish was already one-third of the way there in the year after his father died. We have not found a general from India, who is in any case unnecessary.

In financial matters, as in so many others, Henry Cavendish followed his father's course, investing in gilt-edged securities and almost never touching them. Shortly before his father's death, when he was establishing an inde-

---

148 Cavendish's undated draft of a letter to Alexander Dalrymple's administrator: Devon. Coll., L/34/64.

149 In literal translation, Biot's epigram is wordier: Cavendish was "the richest of all the learned and probably also the most learned of all the rich." J. B. Biot, "Cavendish (Henri)," *Biographie Universelle,* vol. 7 (Paris, 1813), 272–73, on 273. "Cavendish, Henry," *Encyclopaedia Britannica*, 9th ed., vol. 5 (New York, 1878), 271–72, on 271.

150 The alleged uncle who left his fortune to Henry Cavendish in 1773 was repeated in biographical dictionaries including the most important for scientists: "Cavendish, Henry," in J. C. Poggendorff, *Biographisch-Literarisches Handwörterbuch zur Geschichte der exacten Wissenschaften*, vol. 1 (Leipzig, 1863), 406. Thomas Thomson, *History of Chemistry*, vol. 1 (London, 1830), 336–49, on 336. Wilson, *Cavendish*, 158–60.

151 Blagden's correspondent Madame D. Gautier was acquainted with Cuvier's wife. On 30 April 1811 Gautier communicated Cuvier's thanks to Blagden for his information on Cavendish, and after seeing Cuvier's *éloge,* Blagden wrote back, on 20 April 1812, draft, Blagden Letters, Royal Society, G.11 and G.11a. Georges Cuvier, "Henry Cavendish," translated by D. S. Faber, in *Great Chemists*, ed. E. Faber (New York: Interscience Publishers, 1961), 229–38.

pendent life, Cavendish sold a small part of his securities, receiving £8,500 for them, but that was the exception. During the Napoleonic Wars, the government offered a higher return on loans and very substantial bonuses as a percentage on capital on top of the half-yearly dividends,[152] but throughout the entire time after his father's death, Cavendish's account seems to have risen fairly steadily. The figure of £40,000 in the story about Cavendish and his banker is in line; in November 1804, Cavendish reinvested £36,000 in reduced and consolidated annuities, and in July 1805 he reinvested £51,000.[153] When Cavendish died, most of his stocks were selling below par, as was usual. On paper their value was well over £1,000,000; on the market, their value was about £821,000 for stocks and annuities in his own name and about £18,000 for the same in trust. Cavendish owned some of almost every kind of security, but the bulk of his investment was in only two, consols and reduced 3 percent annuities. He still owned the mortgages left to his father by Elizabeth Cavendish, and his banker had about £11,000 cash in hand.[154] Henry Cavendish's fortune compared favorably with some large fortunes in the late eighteenth century, such as Lady Bute's inheritance of £800,000, Lord Bath's legacy of £1,200,000, and Sir Samuel Fludyer's legacy of £900,000.[155]

As Biot said, Cavendish was the richest of the wise, and insofar as his investments were concerned, he was at least one of the wiser of the rich; over the long run, during the years in which he amassed his fortune, he could hardly have managed his inheritance better than to reinvest its earnings in consols and reduced 3 percent annuities, especially since he was a man who had other things to do with his days than to spend them in his counting house.

THE END

In their few surviving letters, Henry and his brother Frederick addressed one another as "Dear Brother," and Frederick closed his letters with "your affectionate brother." Both showed largely unnecessary concern for one another's health, though Frederick was not as well as he let on. Henry was "alarmed" upon hearing on good authority that Frederick was ill, but Frederick reassured him that he had never felt better other than for the gout that cramped his handwriting, keeping

---

152 Clapham, *Bank of England* 2:39–40, 46.

153 Henry Cavendish, bundle of receipts for purchases of annuities, sold at particular discounts, to Messrs. Cornelius Denne & Co., Devon. Coll., 86/comp. 3.

154 Mess. Snow & Co., "Valuation of Property in the Funds," 24 Feb. 1810. Devon. Coll., L/114/74. Cavendish's mortgages were from the duke of Devonshire and Knight Mitchell, and the trust was under the names of Lord Hardwicke, Lord George Cavendish, and Lord Frederick Cavendish.

155 L. B. Namier, *Structure of Politics at the Accession of George III,* 2d ed. (London: Macmillan, 1957), 164.

occupied "as usual visiting my friends or riding out most days."[156] Frederick was still living in Market Street, where he had lived from about age forty, first in the home of a clergyman, then in a small house and later in a larger house of his own, attended by two "confidential domestics." Market Street was a quiet village in Hertfordshire, just across the border from Bedfordshire, near the Benedictine Monastery of St. Albans. There is a brief letter from Henry to Frederick setting a time to meet with him at "St Albans," which may have been an alternative way of referring to his address.[157] Much of his time Frederick spent visiting in the neighborhood, where he was regarded as a harmless eccentric. He was a skillful drawer, given to displaying his portfolios, which he intended to leave to the British Museum (he did not). He had a huge library of classics and literature. Endowed with the remarkable memory of the Cavendishes, he recited poetry with such accuracy that he was called a "living edition." His preferences among the modern poets, such as Thomson, Akenside, and Mason, were thought to be influenced by their politics. Extremely proud of his family, he often quoted the epitaph of the first duke of Devonshire, friend of good princes and enemy of tyrants. With his bag wig, cocked hat, and deep ruffles, Frederick in his later years was a quaint relic. Bookish, whiggish, unfashionable, unmarried, without a profession, proud of his family name, in several respects Frederick resembled his brother, Henry. In other respects he differed; he was drawn to literature and art instead of to science, and to society rather than to solitude; he was described as having a "very social disposition."[158]

Frederick was known to be a soft touch. One of his last letters to Henry is about a young married man who was just getting started and needed £150 to pay off his upholsterer's bill. Frederick asked Henry for this amount, since he did not have it. Henry obliged his brother, who was "confident [it] will do a great deal of good."[159] Frederick had a comfortable income, but he exceeded it and had to ask Henry for money.[160] He needed help with his property taxes, which were (then as now) baffling. Henry was sympathetic: "the printed forms sent both by the comissioners of Income & assessed taxes are intricate & not clearly expressed."[161] Frederick was mindful of his brother's interests: "As I believe you attend a good deal to the observation of the barometer," he sent Henry a careful account of the reading by his barometer that morning. He had read in the paper that Herschel predicted a wet end-of-summer, and Henry, who had read this in the paper too, told his brother

---

[156] Frederick Cavendish to Henry Cavendish, 10 Sep. 1809; Henry Cavendish to Frederick Cavendish, n.d., draft. Devon. Coll., 86/comp. 1.

[157] Henry Cavendish to Frederick Cavendish, n.d. [1784], draft, Cavendish Mss New Correspondence.

[158] "Memoirs of the Late Frederick Cavendish, Esq.," *Gentleman's Magazine* 82 (1812): 289–91.

[159] Frederick Cavendish to Henry Cavendish, 5 and 12 Feb. 1810, Devon. Coll., 86/comp. 1.

[160] Frederick Cavendish to Henry Cavendish, 9 Feb. 1810, Devon. Coll., 86/comp. 1.

[161] Frederick Cavendish to Henry Cavendish, 28 Oct. 1806; Henry Cavendish to Frederick Cavendish, n. d., draft, Devon. Coll., 86/comp. 1.

that Herschel could have said no such thing since he had "too much sense to make predictions of the weather."[162] Henry knew his colleague, who twenty years before complained that the "papers have ascribed to me a foreknowledge of the weather, . . . which I am not so happy as to be in possession of."[163]

Frederick was two years younger than Henry, and he outlived him by two years. The life span in this branch of the Cavendishes was remarkably constant: Lord Charles, Henry, and Frederick all lived to around seventy-nine. Up to the end, Henry Cavendish seemed vigorous, physically and mentally. Cavendish's physician was his good friend John Hunter, whom we hear of for the first time in 1792, when Cavendish was sixty. Blagden went to Clapham Common only to be told, to his surprise, that Cavendish was ill. Blagden responded with sympathy (and perhaps hurt): "If you had chosen that I should wait upon you, I cannot doubt but you would have sent to me."[164] That same day upon learning that Cavendish was being seen by Dr. Hunter, he wrote again to Cavendish to say that he "could not do better" and to ask only if he could visit him "as a friend."[165] Blagden told Banks the next day that he was "engaged to be with Mr Cavendish (who is much disposed) at Clapham."[166] In his discomfort, Cavendish was attended by two friends, Blagden and Hunter. What was wrong with Cavendish we know from another friend, Alexander Dalrymple, who sent a sympathy note to him together with a folk remedy: Dalrymple was "very sorry yesterday to hear that You were prevented from coming amongst us by an attack of the Gravel."[167] Gravel, a common complaint then, meant painful or difficult urination possibly with a deposit of urinary crystals.

Since there was a famous contemporary surgeon and anatomist named John Hunter, we need to point out that Cavendish's doctor was not that John Hunter. He is not well known today, but at the time he was highly regarded for his scientific as well as medical skills. When he was proposed for membership in the Royal Society in 1785, his certificate was signed by twenty-five Fellows of the Royal Society,[168] which was the same number Captain Cook received ten years before in an extraordinary expression of support. Cavendish was one of the signers, along with all of Cavendish's friends, Dalrymple, Aubert, Heberden, Blagden, Nairne, Smeaton, Maskelyne, and others including the other John Hunter.

162 Frederick Cavendish to Henry Cavendish, 10 Sep. and 18 Dec. 1809; Henry Cavendish to Frederick Cavendish, n.d., draft, Devon. Coll., 86/comp. 1.

163 William Herschel to Lord Salisbury, 8 Jan. 1789, Royal Astronomical Society, Mss Herschel, W 1/1, 170–71.

164 Charles Blagden to Henry Cavendish, 12 Mar. 1792, draft, Blagden Letters, Royal Society, 7:624.

165 Charles Blagden to Henry Cavendish, 12 Mar. 1792, draft, Blagden Letters, Royal Society, 7:625.

166 Charles Blagden to Sir Joseph Banks, 13 Mar. 1792, draft, Blagden Letters, Royal Society, 7:626.

167 Alexander Dalrymple to Henry Cavendish, 16 Mar. 1792, Cavendish Mss X(b), 16.

168 12 Jan. 1786, Royal Society, Certificates, 5.

Hunter was then a physician to the army who was, according to his certificate, "well versed in various branches of natural knowledge." At the time of his election to the Royal Society he was thirty-one. A graduate of the University of Edinburgh, his writings on medicine show that he followed the teachings of William Cullen. His dissertation of 1775 was remarkable for its subject, anthropology, but just as he has been eclipsed by his namesake, his dissertation has been eclipsed by a more famous work on the subject appearing in the same year by J. F. Blumenbach.[169] Hunter regarded humans as a species, circumscribed within limits by Divine Wisdom, and the differences among them as varieties; in this respect, humans were just like plants, butterflies, and shell creatures, in which natural history took greater interest. He had no need for the Scriptural explanation of Cain as the father of the blacks, nor need for the Deity to explain differences in mental faculties. He looked instead to "natural causes" to explain differences in human color, stature, parts, and minds. One of the principal natural causes of such differences was "heat," which is where his path first crossed Cavendish's.[170] Before Hunter set sail for Jamaica in 1780 to superintend military hospitals, Cavendish suggested that he observe the heat of springs and wells while he was there. His paper on the subject, appearing in the *Philosophical Transactions* for 1788, gave a full account of Cavendish's hypothesis: the heat of the earth comes solely from the sun, not the from earth's interior; accordingly, precise measurements of the temperature from the interior of the earth, where the temperature remains constant through the seasons, ought to provide the mean temperature of any climate; in this way a few observations of the heat of springs and wells could be as informative as "meteorological observations of several years."[171] Hunter included this discussion in his main publication, *Observations on the Diseases of the Army in Jamaica.*[172] His other publications appeared in medical journals. The judgment on his work is that it did not live up to its early promise. He died at the age of fifty-four, in 1809, the year before his famous patient Cavendish died, and he had not published any new work in over ten years.[173]

---

169 Blumenbach's *De generis humani varietate nativa* was translated by T. Bendyshe and published together with a translation of Hunter's *Disputatio inauguralis quaedam de Hominum varietatibus, et harem causis exponens* . . . (Edinburgh, 1775) in *The Anthropological Treatises of Johann Friedrich Blumenbach . . . and the Inaugural Dissertation of John Hunter, MD. On the Varieties of Man* (London, 1865).

170 Hunter, *On the Varieties of Man*, 365–68, 378.

171 John Hunter, "Some Observations on the Heat of Wells and Springs in the Island of Jamaica, and on the Temperature of the Earth Below the Surface in Different Climates," *PT* 78 (1788): 53–65, on 53, 58, 65. Charles Blagden to William Farr, 21 Jan. 1788, draft, Blagden Letters, Royal Society, 7:107.

172 Hunter included the paper from the *Philosophical Transactions* as an appendix to the second edition of his *Observations on the Diseases of the Army in Jamaica* (London, 1796). The first edition was in the same year as the paper, 1788.

173 Lise Wilkinson, " 'The Other' John Hunter, M.D., F.R.S. (1754–1809): His Contributions to the Medical Literature, and to the Introduction of Animal Experiments into Infectious Disease Research," *Notes and Records of the Royal Society of London* 36 (1982): 227–41, on 235–36.

From Blagden we learn of Cavendish's next illness. Cavendish came faithfully to Banks's open houses, so that when he was absent one Sunday in 1804, Blagden made note of it.[174] A few days later Blagden was informed that Cavendish was ill.[175] This time Cavendish was attended by Everard Home, who informed Blagden that Cavendish had a rupture, nothing more serious; he would need a truss, that was all. Home was about the same age as Hunter, and had served at the same time as Hunter with the army in Jamaica; the two were well acquainted, both active members of a medical club founded in 1783 which met at Slaughter's Coffee House.[176] By the time Cavendish called on his services, Home was eminent both professionally and scientifically. He had succeeded the anatomist John Hunter as surgeon to St. George's, and he was known as a prolific writer on surgical and anatomical subjects. Cavendish would have met him at the Royal Society, where he repeatedly was chosen to give the physiological Croonian lectures.[177] With Home, as with Hunter, Cavendish formed a scientific as well as a medical connection, performing an optical experiment on the cornea in response to a paper by Home.[178] Home would remain Cavendish's physician to the end.

When Cavendish had his rupture, Home told Blagden that the disorder began with a swelling of the legs: "as if old the first time," Blagden wrote in his diary that day.[179] Cavendish was ill on 16 and 17 February, and Blagden went to see him on the 18th, on which day Cavendish made out his final will, though it seems he did not show it to Blagden.[180] Either Home or Blagden, or both, evidently had an insight. Cavendish was seventy-two, and he had an intimation of–perhaps a brush with–death.

On a day when the Royal Society Club met in 1807, Blagden recorded in his diary, "Spoke to Cav. about parallax of fixed stars; it seemed as if he began to forget."[181] Cavendish was seventy-five and perhaps a bit forgetful, but after a

---

[174] 12 Feb. 1804, Charles Blagden Diary, Royal Society, 4:201.

[175] 16 Feb. 1804, Charles Blagden Diary, Royal Society, 4:202 (back).

[176] The Society for the Improvement of Medical and Chirurgical Knowledge, whose leading member was the (other) John Hunter. Wilkinson, "John Hunter," 234.

[177] William LeFanu, "Home, Everard," *DSB* 6:478–79.

[178] In 1795 Blagden sent Cavendish a paper by Home. Evidently the paper contained Home's account of what would have appeared in John Hunter's Croonian Lecture if he had not died before he could give it. Everard Home, "Some Facts Relative to the Late Mr. John Hunter's Preparation for the Croonian Lecture," *PT* 84 (1794): 21–27. Hunter believed that the cornea could adjust itself by its own internal actions to focus the eye at different distances. Cavendish, assisted by Blagden, performed an experiment to detect changes in the convexity of the cornea accompanying changes in the focus, using a divided object-glass micrometer. Entries for 8, 11, and 16 Nov. 1795, Charles Blagden Diary, Royal Society, 3:75 (back), 76, and 77 (back).

[179] 17 Feb. 1804, Charles Blagden Diary, Royal Society, 4:202 (back), 203.

[180] "Copy of the Will of Henry Cavendish Esq.," in "Account of the Executor of Henry Cavendish Esq. as to Money in the Funds," Devon. Coll., L/31/65.

[181] 4 June 1807, Charles Blagden Diary, Royal Society, 5:76.

meeting of the council of the Royal Society in 1809, eight months before Cavendish died, Blagden wrote that he "looked in excellent health."[182]

Within natural philosophy, Cavendish's breadth of competence was extraordinary, but as a sensible and observant man, he recognized that he knew only some things well and that other persons knew other things well. He declined to advise Bristol on its sewage partly on the grounds that "physicians" knew more about health and "engineers" knew more about rivers than he did. Yet he was not drawn to specialized scientific clubs and societies, which had been in existence in London since before his father's time. The Temple Coffee House Botanic Club was formed at the end of the seventeenth century, to which Hans Sloane and a good number of eminent natural historians belonged.[183] John Martyn's botanical society met in the 1720s; by 1740 an entomological society existed; in 1782 the Society for Promoting Natural History was founded. The best-known early mathematical society was the Spitalfields Mathematical Society, which eventually was absorbed by the Royal Astronomical Society.[184] An early chemical society was the Chapter Coffee House Society, which met from 1780. There was Bryan Higgins's short-lived Society for Philosophical Experiments and Conversations, an extension of Higgins's chemical lectures, which in the mid-1790s taught Lavoisier's new chemical nomenclature; Cavendish's friend Thomas Young was one of the subscribers. At the very end of Cavendish's life, a number of small, private chemical societies were founded in and around London: the London Chemical Society, announced in 1807 by Friedrich Accum, a chemical teacher and briefly Davy's assistant at the Royal Institution; the Lambeth Chemical Society, launched around 1809; and the Society for the Improvement of Animal Chemistry.[185] The latter society had a close connection with the Royal Society, as is made clear by the founding resolution at a meeting of the council of the Royal Society in April 1809. The new society was designated an "assistant society," in no sense in competition with the original. To underscore the continuity with the old society, and to add prestige to the new, at the same meeting the council resolved "that Mr Cavendish be requested to allow his name to be added to those of the members of this new society."[186] The meetings took the form of dinners and conversation every three months held alternately at the house of Cavendish's doctor, Home, and at the house of his collaborator, Hatchett. Other members included Davy, William Thomas Brande (who would succeed Davy as professor of chemistry at the Royal Institution), the physician

[182] 8 June 1809, Charles Blagden Diary, Royal Society, 5:328 (back).

[183] David Elliston Allen, *The Naturalist in Britain: A Social History* (London: Allen Lane, 1976), 10.

[184] Gwendoline Averly, "English Scientific Societies of Eighteenth and Early Nineteenth Centuries," Ph.D. diss. (Teeside Polytechnic, 1989), 26–29.

[185] Gwendoline Averley, "The 'Social Chemists': English Chemical Societies in the Eighteenth and Early Nineteenth Century," *Ambix* 33 (1986): 99–128, on 102, 108–9, 113.

[186] 27 Apr. 1809, Minutes of Council, Royal Society, 7:527–31.

William Babington (one of the founders of the Geological Society), and the physician Benjamin Collins Brodie (who was the outstanding pupil of Home).[187] Later the Society turned into a dinner club, but at the beginning it was given to serious scientific discussion. In 1809, the year of its founding, the Society sponsored two papers printed in the *Philosophical Transactions*, one by Home and one by Brande, both electrochemical. Home's paper continued the discussion of the electric eel or torpedo, Cavendish's subject; it is revealing of the changed state of science that Cavendish heard Home describe the torpedo as a "Voltaic battery" instead of Cavendish's battery of Leyden jars, the torpedo having now become a problem of chemistry rather than of electricity.[188]

If Cavendish came to the few meetings of the Society for the Improvement of Animal Chemistry held before his death, he would have been an interested party to the discussions and not a monument. He had given considerable thought to plant and animal substances in his study of putrefaction and fermentation in his first paper on pneumatic chemistry in 1766, and again in his study of the phlogistication of air in 1784. His active interest in living things was directed to what they had in common with unliving things. His young associate James Louis Macie offered him an ideal problem: to determine the density of tabasheer, a rocklike substance found in the joints of tropical bamboo. For the product of a plant, tabasheer had improbable properties. Macie found it to be indestructible by fire, totally resistant to acids, and glasslike when fused with alkali; he concluded, correctly, that it was "siliceous earth." Tiny specimens of tabasheer were given to Cavendish, who took "great care" in weighing them in water.[189]

The society for animal chemistry was the only specialized society Cavendish belonged to. The Society of Civil Engineers, centering on Cavendish's friend John Smeaton, was founded in 1771 and reorganized in 1792; honorary or regular members included friends of Cavendish's such as Banks, Rumford, Hatchett, James Cockshutt, and Charles Greville, but not Cavendish himself. He was not a member of the patriotic Society for the Improvement of Naval Architecture, founded in 1791, which brought together practical men and certain men of science who were close to Cavendish such as Banks, Hatchett, Aubert, Maskelyne, and Hutton.[190] He did not belong to the Linnaean Society, founded in 1788, nor the Mineralogical Society, founded in 1799, nor the Geological Society, founded in 1807. His age might explain his absence, but he was vigorous, and a suggestion was even made that he add to his obligations in science: in 1805 Banks

---

[187] Sir Benjamin Collins Brodie, *Autobiography of the Late Sir Benjamin Brodie*, Bart., 2d ed. (London, 1865),88–92.

[188] Everard Home, "Hints on the Subject of Animal Secretions," *PT* 99 (1809): 385–91, on 386.

[189] James Louis Macie, "An Account of Some Experiments on Tabasheer," *PT* 81 (1791): 368–88, on 370, 384–85, 388.

[190] Averly, "English Scientific Societies," 91, 102–3.

proposed to augment the Board of Longitude and to include Cavendish.[191] The more complete explanation is, we think, that the specialized, national societies, which would eventually include the Chemical Society of London in 1841, belonged to a different era of science. They emerged together with the professional identity of the scientific expert.

To the end, Cavendish was fully active in the work of the Royal Society. He agreed to superintend the construction of an apparatus for measuring the temperature of the depths of the sea. His father had recommended this use for the thermometer he invented over fifty years before. Henry did not have time to oversee the experiment once more.[192] He attended council on 21 December 1809, missing only one meeting, on 15 February 1810. Henry Cavendish died on 24 February 1810.

The Cavendish family had extensive connections with the Church: the duke of Devonshire had the second largest patronage, holding twenty-nine and a half livings,[193] but this was a measure of temporal power, not spiritual inclinations. Lord Charles Cavendish had a scholarly interest in religion, as we gather from books he bought for his library, and he may well have been religious. We know that he contributed to a fund for the Fairchild Sermon, overseen by the Royal Society, and delivered at a certain church in Whitson week on the theme of "The Wonderful Works of God."[194] But if his branch of the family observed religious practices, there is no record of it. As for Henry Cavendish, we have already mentioned George Wilson's conclusion that the "world to come" did not engross him. Although Cavendish "gave no outward demonstration of interest in religion, and did [not] join his fellow men in worshipping God," Wilson "would willingly believe that the 'something particular,' which he told his servant was to engage the undisturbed attention of his last, and solemn, silent hours, was his preparation for the unseen world into which he knew he was about to pass."[195] Wilson may be right, but if he is not, Cavendish would not have been all that remarkable. His physician Home, who was with Cavendish at the end, was a materialist who regarded the mind as an arrangement of matter and denied any difference between man and animal other than in the arrangement of matter. Cavendish's outlook belonged to a rational, secular current of thought of his time, which together with his extreme privacy guaranteed that his religiosity, if he had any, would not be evident to strangers or to his biographers.

---

191 23 Feb. 1805, Charles Blagden Diary, Royal Society, 4:313.

192 Sir Joseph Banks to William Scoresby, Jr., 8 Sep. 1810, copy, Whitby Literary and Philosophical Society.

193 John Cannon, *Aristocratic Century: The Peerage of Eighteenth-Century England* (Cambridge: Cambridge University Press, 1984), 64.

194 Henry Lyons, *The Royal Society, 1660–1940: A History of Its Administration under Its Charters* (New York: Greenwood, 1968), 175–76.

195 Wilson, *Cavendish*, 185.

The several accounts of Cavendish's last days vary but agree in this particular: Cavendish was fully conscious and resigned to the imminent end. The account most at variance with the others was given by Home to John Barrow, who published it long after the event. It is also the most likely. When one of Cavendish's servants came to Home's house to say that Cavendish was dying, Home went directly to Clapham Common, finding Cavendish "rather surprised" to see him. His servant should not have bothered Home, Cavendish said, since he was dying, and there was no point in prolonging the misery. Home stayed all night at Cavendish's bedside. Through it all Cavendish was calm, and shortly after dawn he died.[196]

Home was certainly there, as we know from an entry in Blagden's diary from the time. Heberden would seem to have been there too, as we know from Lord George Cavendish, who as Cavendish's executor paid his as well as Home's fees.[197] This Heberden was William Heberden, son of Charles and Henry Cavendish's old friend, who had died in 1801. The younger Heberden, who was as distinguished as his father, being physician in ordinary to the king and the queen, prescribed neutral salts, which Cavendish could not keep down. At Banks's house, where Blagden learned of Cavendish's death, Home gave him an "affecting account" of Cavendish's death the previous day. There was a "shortness of questionings," Home said; Cavendish "seemed to have nothing to say, nor to think of any one with request." He told Home "it is all over, with unusual cheerfulness, & at parting wished Home good by with uncommon mildness." Cavendish ordered that his main heir, Lord George Cavendish, "be sent for as soon as the breath was out of his body, but not before."[198] Home, who had treated Cavendish six years earlier for a rupture, told Blagden that the rupture had nothing to do with Cavendish's death, even though he evidently had refused to wear a truss. Cavendish had an "inflammation of the colon," which for the past year had caused diarrhea but which in the end obstructed the passage of food.[199] Banks lamented the loss to science, but that was all, he "felt nothing." Blagden, by contrast, was moved, noting in his diary that he "continued all day to feel the effect of this event on my spirits." He also noted that it was a cloudy, threatening day, as if a mirror to his spirits.[200] Two weeks later Blagden watched from his window the "funeral procession of my late friend . . . with much emotion."[201]

[196] John Barrow, *Sketches of the Royal Society and Royal Society Club* (London, 1849), 153–54.

[197] Heberden gave a prescription. 25 Feb. 1810, Charles Blagden Diary, Royal Society, 5:426 (back), 427. Home's fee was £105, Heberden's £21. Lord George Cavendish, "Mr Cavendish's Executorship Agenda," Devon. Coll.

[198] 25 Feb. 1810, Charles Blagden Diary, Royal Society, 5:426 (back), 427.

[199] 4 Mar. 1810, Charles Blagden Diary, Royal Society, 5:429 (back), 430.

[200] 24 Feb. 1810, Charles Blagden Diary, Royal Society, 5:426, 426 (back).

[201] 8 Mar. 1810, Charles Blagden Diary, Royal Society, 5:431 (back), 432.

We now pass to another, all-too-human emotion. Cavendish's fortune was on everyone's mind, including his physician Home's; on the morning Cavendish died, Home had Cavendish's servant give him the keys, with which he prowled through the house opening drawers, trunks, and cupboards looking for treasures, which he found and noted.[202] In a few days the word was out that no will had been found. Blagden had seen it but not "since the time I was intimate with him." Blagden knew that he had been in the will then, and he also thought that Cavendish had probably changed it since.[203] Blagden told the company at Banks's that Cavendish's income was above £40,000 a year. Since Cavendish was not a "person who gave the £40,000 to hospitals," and since he did not spend more than £5,000 a year (so Blagden said), he had to have left a fortune.[204] In time the will was found. Blagden was left £15,000, Dalrymple and Hunter each £5,000, though both of them had died since the last will was made in 1804. These were trifling sums, relatively speaking. Cavendish's wealth came from the family, to whom it reverted. His personal property was left to Lord George (Augustus Henry) Cavendish, his executor. As for the funds, over £800,000, one-sixth went to his second cousin Frederick Ponsonby, the third earl of Bessborough, and five-sixths to Lord George Cavendish and his family; the latter was portioned into two-sixths for Lord George and one-sixth each for Lord George's three sons, William and, still minors, the namesakes of our branch of the family, Henry and Charles. Both Lord Charles and Henry Cavendish had a history of dealing with Lord George over property, and Henry had decided on Lord George as his principal heir long before he died, meeting with him once a year for a half hour or so.[205] At a Sunday soiree at Banks's house, a gossip told Blagden that "Ld Geo Cavendish courtd Henry Cavendish abundantly."[206] Lord George had married sensibly and was rich even by Cavendish standards, but he was not averse to receiving another fortune; Henry Cavendish's legacy had nothing to do with need but only with principle and, within rather narrow limits, preference. The dukedom would eventually revert to Lord George's descendants, an eventuality Henry Cavendish might well have considered.

Apart from his brother, Henry had outlived his own generation of Cavendishes. Of the next generation, there were five prospective male heirs, two of whom Henry named in his will, Lord George Cavendish, who as his main heir probably surprised no one, and Frederick, earl of Bessborough (son of Lady Carolina Cavendish, daughter of the third duke of Devonshire). Cavendish is said to have enriched Bessborough because he was pleased by his conversation,

[202] Barrow, *Sketches*, 154–55.

[203] 1 Mar. 1810, Charles Blagden Diary, Royal Society, 5:428 (back).

[204] 1 and 2 Mar. 1810, Charles Blagden Diary, Royal Society, 5:428 (back), 429.

[205] Wilson, *Cavendish*, 173.

[206] 17 Sep. 1809, Charles Blagden Diary, Royal Society, 5:330.

and that might well have been a factor though certainly not the whole explanation. Bessborough and Cavendish met often at the British Museum, where Bessborough, like Cavendish, was an active trustee, serving on the standing committee and attending meetings regularly. In the last years, they also met at the Royal Institution, where they were both managers. Owing to their family connection, Cavendish and Bessborough also came together at Devonshire House, where Cavendish heard talk about Bessborough's quick and capable drawings of Italy.[207]

The last three male Cavendishes of the next generation were Horatio and George Walpole, sons of Rachel Cavendish, and William Cavendish, the fifth duke of Devonshire. We have no indication that Henry Cavendish associated with Horatio and George Walpole in any way, but we note that the great political connection between the Walpoles and the Cavendishes at the time of the second duke had now been replaced by a connection through marriage. The one obvious Cavendish who was not in Henry's will was, formally speaking, the first and most expectant Cavendish of them all, the tenant for life of the vast family estate, the fifth duke of Devonshire. Lady Sarah Spencer speculated on why Henry Cavendish forgot the duke's existence in his will: perhaps Cavendish "thought that said existence was something of a *disgrace* to the noble name of Cavendish,"[208] as well he might have. The Cavendishes, including Henry Cavendish, were a family of achievement, with the notable exception of the fifth duke. For his part, the fifth duke was "quite convinced" that Cavendish would leave him nothing.[209] Resigned to nothing, the duke was delighted to learn that Cavendish had left his money to the family, specifically to the earl of Bessborough. The duke, however, was "disgusted to see the disposal of so vast a property in a few lines, as if to save trouble."[210] We have seen many wills from the time and none briefer, or clearer, than Henry Cavendish's.

Cavendish, grandson of the duke of Kent, had three living male relatives of his own generation on the Grey side: John, second earl of Ashburnham, who was eighty-six and very infirm; and the brothers John William Edgerton, the seventh earl of Bridgewater, and Francis Henry Edgerton, the future eighth earl of Bridgewater. Cavendish had only one male relative of the next generation on the Grey

[207] Wilson, who also said that Cavendish "was not, I believe," related to Bessborough, missed their family connection, though it was close. Wilson, *Cavendish*, 190. 1 Sep. 1794, Charles Blagden Diary, Royal Society, 3:14.

[208] Lady Sarah Spencer quoted in Hugh Stokes, *The Devonshire House Circle* (London: Herbert Jenkins, 1917), 315.

[209] Letter from the fifth duke's second wife, Elizabeth Foster, to Augustus Foster, 1 Mar. 1810, in *The Two Duchesses. Georgiana Duchess of Devonsire. Elizabeth Duchess of Devonshire. Family Correspondence*, ed. V. Foster (London, 1898), 345.

[210] Quotation from the "Journal" kept by the duchess of Devonshire, in Dorothy Margaret Stuart, *Dearest Bess: The Life and Times of Lady Elizabeth Foster, Afterwards Duchess of Devonshire* (London: Methuen, 1955), 174.

side: George, the future third earl of Ashburnham. The earls of Bridgewater were Fellows of the Royal Society, and Francis Henry, the eighth earl, is well known to historians of science as the founder of the *Bridgewater Treatises*, the authors of which were selected by the president of the Royal Society and the Bishop of London to demonstrate the "Power, Wisdom, and Goodness of God, as manifested in the Creation."[211] This clergyman was strongly interested in science but not in a way that would have brought him and Henry Cavendish together. Lord Charles Cavendish kept a correspondence with his sister-in-law Lady Ashburnham, Jemima de Grey,[212] but we have come upon no record of contact between Henry Cavendish and the Ashburnham or Bridgewater families. Henry Cavendish saw to it that his wealth remained within the Cavendish family; his will made perfect sense, its surprises being minor variations on the standard theme.

Henry's landed property went to his brother, Frederick, after whom it reverted to the duke of Devonshire, from whose predecessor their father, Lord Charles, had acquired it in the first place. In 1784 Frederick made a will, which he did not revise, leaving his personal estate to Henry, but since he outlived Henry, it went instead to his maternal first cousins, the earls of Bridgewater and Ashburnham and Francis Henry Edgerton, above. The earl of Bridgewater executed Frederick's estate.[213]

Lady Sarah Spencer did not regret that the duke of Devonshire gained nothing from Cavendish's death, since he and his heir, Hartington, were "*pretty well* off."[214] On the side of science, however, there was keen disappointment. Some of Cavendish's "warmest admirers have expressed regret that no portion of that vast wealth was appropriated to scientific objects."[215] He had not left money to Davy,[216] and Davy himself had expected it, Blagden thought: "Davy said, Mr. C. has at least remembered one man of science [i.e., Blagden], in a tone of voice which expressed much."[217] There were rumors that even Blagden was disappointed, that he had higher expectations,[218] but there is no indication of this in anything he wrote, including his frank diary. In the days following Cavendish's death, Blagden defended his old friend.

The funeral procession that Blagden watched from his window set out with the body from Clapham Common at seven in the morning on March 8th. Five

---

211 Charles C. Gillispie, *Genesis and Geology: A Study in the Relations of Scientific Thought, Natural Theology, and Social Opinion in Great Britain, 1790–1850* (New York: Harper & Row, 1959), 209.

212 Henry Cavendish, "Papers in Walnut Cabinet," Cavendish Mss Misc.

213 W. Ware to John Heaton, 27 Feb. 1810, Devon. Coll. "Memoirs of the Late Frederick Cavendish," 291.

214 Stokes, *Devonshire House Circle*, 315.

215 "Cavendish," *Encyclopaedia Britannica*, 9th ed., 5:271.

216 5 and 6 Mar. 1810, Charles Blagden Diary, Royal Society, 5:430 (back), 431.

217 8 Mar. 1810, Charles Blagden Diary, Royal Society, 5:431 (back), 432.

218 Lord Brougham, *Lives of Men of Letters and Science*, 258.

private carriages belonging to the duke of Devonshire and to Henry Cavendish's heirs, Lord George Cavendish, Lord Bessborough, and Lord George's oldest son, William Cavendish, traveled northward through London on their way to Derby,[219] where they were met at the gates of the city by twenty-four burghers and twenty-four constables and a retinue of city officials (all of whom were paid to do this) dressed in black. They then proceeded to the Church of All Saints, where Cavendish was buried in the family vault. The pomp and ceremony were invariable for the Cavendish dead, and it was elaborate and expensive. Everything had to be rented, the hearse and coach ornamented with black ostrich feathers and drawn by six horses, eight men on horses, and on and on. The bill for nine days came to about £750.[220]

The scientific colleagues who gathered at Banks's house in the weeks following Cavendish's death had concerns other than his will. There was Cavendish's large library, which passed along with all of his other personal possessions to Lord George. Blagden thought that Cavendish wanted it not to be dispersed but to be kept accessible, as it had been in his lifetime.[221] No doubt there was talk about Cavendish's instruments and apparatus, for Davy was soon to be given his pick of them, while other pieces went to the instrument-maker John Newman of Regent Street, son of the maker of Cavendish's wind-measurer, the remainder being sold at auction by Lord George in 1816.[222] At the time of Cavendish's death, his instruments were valued at £544; at the auction sale, they brought only £159, which is a measure of the depletion of his collection by then.[223] A large part of Cavendish's apparatus was left by Sir Humphry Davy to John Davy; its value lay entirely in its usefulness, being made of fir rather than hardwood and constructed with no regard to appearances.[224]

From the beginning, there was discussion of an edition of Cavendish's published works, but just what to do about his unpublished papers was an open question.[225] Blagden thought that these papers would be found in a state unfit for publication. Lord George wanted Blagden to look over the papers anyway, and

219 Lord Bessborough to Charles Blagden, 7 Mar. 1810, Blagden Letters, Royal Society, B.149.

220 "Mr. Swift's Bill for Expenses Attg the Funeral of Hen: Cavendish Esq.," 29 Aug. 1810, Devon. Coll., L/114/74.

221 3 and 4 Mar. 1810, Charles Blagden Diary, Royal Society, 5:429, 429 (back), 430.

222 Wilson, *Cavendish*, 475. *A Catalogue of Sundry Very Curious and Valuable Mathematical, Philosophical, and Optical Instruments . . . of a Gentleman Deceased . . . On Saturday the Fifteenth of June 1816, at Twelve O'clock*, Devon. Coll.

223 "Extracts from Valuations of Furniture &c.," 1810. *A Catalogue of Sundry Very Curious and Valuable Mathematical, Philosophical, and Optical Instruments. . . .*

224 Wilson, *Cavendish*, 178.

225 This discussion of Cavendish's papers is taken from Russell McCormmach, "Henry Cavendish on the Theory of Heat," *Isis* 79 (1988): 37–67, on 37–38. The first mention of a proposed edition of Cavendish's works appears in the entry for 8 Mar. 1810; other entries on the subject are on 10, 26, and 27 Mar., 5, 8, 9, 11, 12, and 26 Apr., and 24 May 1810, Charles Blagden Diary, Royal Society, 5.

so on 6 April Blagden, Banks, and evidently other interested colleagues met with Lord George at Cavendish's house at Clapham Common to inspect the manuscripts. After spending about four hours on them they decided that the papers were, for the most part, "only mathematics." Blagden returned to Cavendish's house, and for the next two weeks he was kept busy with the papers, after which he reported to Lord George:

> We have now finished the search which your Lordship desired us to make, in the hope of finding, among the papers of the late Mr Henry Cavendish, something which he had prepared & thought fit for printing. Our search has in this respect been fruitless; a result for which we are sorry, though we must confess that it was not unexpected to us; because we knew that Mr Cavendish was always ready to publish whatever he had made out to his full satisfaction. There are some few small scraps, which are transcribed nearly fair, as if he had thought of communicating them to the R.S.: but as it is apparent that they have been laid by, in that state, for a considerable time, it is to be supposed that he afterwards discovered some weakness or imperfection in them, or that they had been anticipated in a manner of which he was not aware when he composed them; in short, that he had some good reason for not giving them to the public. In truth, Mr Cavendish's fame stands so high already in the scientific world, that no papers but of the most perfect kind could be expected to increase it, whilst it might be lowered by anything of an inferior nature.[226]

Blagden and his colleagues firmly recommended against including any of the unpublished papers in the proposed edition of Cavendish's papers, but they expected that dates and circumstances of his discoveries might be found among them that would be useful for the introduction. Since the papers were in "great disorder," some qualified person with time to spare would have to be found to go through them. They could think of only one person, the man whom Cavendish sometimes employed, the clerk of the Royal Society, George Gilpin, but they decided that he was probably too ill. They supposed that Lord George might ask around. Three months after Cavendish's death, Blagden and Banks, between themselves, agreed to postpone plans for an edition of Cavendish's works.

Blagden, Banks, and the others recognized the perils of trying to improve a reputation posthumously, but they were mistaken about the worth of Cavendish's papers. That could hardly have been otherwise, since the papers contained much that was original, and much more than the work of a few hours or a few days was required to appreciate this. Blagden was right in thinking that Cavendish's fame was then so great that no unfinished papers could increase it, but he was wrong about the future. Today Cavendish is nearly as well-known for

---

[226] Sir Charles Blagden to "My Lord" [Lord George Cavendish], n.d., draft, Blagden Collection, Royal Society, Misc. Matter–Unclassified.

what he did not publish as for what he did publish. One eminent scientist after another has studied his manuscripts and has come away in wonder at what he achieved with the instruments and concepts available to him. To them it has seemed as if Cavendish were not of his own century, but of the next.[227]

[227] In 1874, one hundred years after Cavendish had done his experiments on electrical capacity, Maxwell wrote to W. Garnett, his future biographer, that Cavendish's "measures of capacity will give us some work at the Cavendish Laboratory, before we work up to the point where he left it." Quoted in Sir Joseph Larmor's preface to vol. 1 of the 1921 edition of Cavendish's *Sci. Pap.*

CHAPTER 8

CAVENDISH

HENRY CAVENDISH was the preeminent mathematical and experimental scientist in Britain in the century and a half between Newton and Thomson and Maxwell. At the time of his death, he was compared with Newton; with hindsight we make the comparison with Thomson and Maxwell. To a greater degree than any of his countrymen, he realized the possibilities of the physical sciences of his day. We base our assessment both on the research he published and on that which he did not.

We have made the case that in a certain sense Lord Charles's and Henry Cavendish's lives in science began in English dukedoms. We return to this connection, to the qualification English. In England the power of the nobility did not derive from legal rights and royal favors but from ownership of land. Land was kept in the family by marriage settlements, which in turn kept the family intact with an identity that passed from generation to generation.[1] Lord Charles Cavendish and then Henry managed landed property, and although the income from it was trifling in the end–the great wealth of Charles and Henry Cavendish was not land but stocks–the meaning of this small property was not trifling. The property represented the source of the family's place in society, its great landholdings.

The English aristocracy escaped overthrow by revolution, the fate of its Continental counterparts, because English lords themselves had proven ready to undertake revolution to protect their property. Repeated rejections by the aristocracy of attempts by the crown to increase its power culminated in the revolution of 1688–89, which made the state subservient to the landed interest.[2] In the eighteenth century a contented aristocracy acted responsibly, ensuring its survival and establishing, as one commentator has put it, "the tradition of public

[1] H. J. Habakkuk, "England," in *The European Nobility in the Eighteenth Century*, ed. A. Goodwin (London: Adam and Charles Black, 1953), 1–21, on 2.

[2] M. L. Bush, *The English Aristocracy: A Comparative Synthesis* (Manchester: Manchester University Press, 1984), 12.

duty."[3] That tradition contained within it, if implicitly, the direction that Lord Charles and Henry Cavendish gave to their lives.

Younger sons of the aristocracy, if not totally dissolute or dilettantish, ordinarily entered the established professions: politics, the military, and the church. Lord Charles Cavendish had a good income from his family and with it considerable choice, which he exercised by entering first politics and then science. The professions in England had proliferated in the fifty years before Lord Charles, but the new ones were largely improvised and without formal training or standards of entry. At around the time Lord Charles came of age, the professions were harder to define than before, and any experience of what we would call professional solidarity was rare, though esprit de corps could be found here and there.[4] An income could be made from science by teaching or popularizing it, and it served as an adjunct to certain kinds of technical work, but it was not yet generally recognized as a regular occupation. Science was open to interpretation, and like art or gaming or amateur architecture, it could be embraced by an aristocrat as a freely chosen outlet for his energies. Lord Charles's redirection did not take social courage so much as intelligence and imagination in addressing the possibilities of his social world. His work in the Royal Society pointed to science as a world in becoming; in his son Henry's time it was a realized world only waiting to be recognized. Henry Cavendish went beyond his father to engage in the activity that has come to be valued in modern science, advancing the knowledge of nature through published research.

By foregoing a career in politics, Henry Cavendish deprived his family of a reliable vote in parliament for a number of years, but by then his vote was dispensable. What was enduring in the family tradition was a determination to serve. Like his father, Henry lived by his commitments, and nothing in his record suggests that he believed he defied his family by his choice of ends to serve. If he experienced conflict as a result of being both a proud Cavendish and a dedicated man of science, it was not obvious to people who knew him. The basic agreement between his view of the world and his family's is clearly evident in the part he took in the dissensions of the Royal Society in the 1780s.

Personal reserve might be looked upon as a characteristic of eighteenth-century society. "It would be impertinent to say this much of one's private affairs to anybody but a friend who is concerned about them." So wrote a friend to the earl of Huntington.[5] Cavendish's reserve was strong but so was that of some of

---

[3] Edward John B. D. S., Lord Montagu of Beaulieu, *More Equal Than Others: The Changing Fortunes of the British and European Aristocracies* (London: Michael Joseph, 1970), 156–57.

[4] Geoffrey Holmes, *Augustan England. Professions, State and Society, 1680–1730* (London: George Allen & Unwin, 1982), 4, 9. We agree generally with Holmes's point, though when a physician was proposed for fellowship in the Royal Society, the proposal was often by another physician, which suggests an element of association.

[5] Hans Stanley to Francis, tenth earl of Huntington, 8 Feb. 1753, in *Hastings* 3:1.

his associates. In reserve and related traits such as taciturnity and caution, the chemist William Hyde Wollaston and Cavendish were so much alike that, according to George Wilson, they might have been "twin brothers."[6] But to judge by reports from the time, Henry Cavendish was regarded as one of a kind.

The seemingly complete absence of intimacy in Cavendish's life can be taken in either of three ways: he had no "private affairs"; he kept them to himself; or his private affairs *were* science. We are inclined to the latter view. The sights, smells, touches, tastes, and sounds that he experienced in the laboratory were no less (or more) private than the experiences of persons who did not perform experiments on nature. Cavendish's "private affairs" took place in the laboratory, observatory, field, and study. When he chose to, he made them public.

Cavendish was a man of "silent" habits, who had "difficulty in bringing out his words."[7] This form of stinginess poses practical problems, since people who have difficulty talking have difficulty living.[8] We can be certain that Cavendish's silences did not express a disinterest in communicating, a possibility which is ruled out by everything he stood for. The "hereditary taciturnity"[9] of the Cavendishes no doubt encouraged his silences. Taciturnity is correlated with shyness, and it is the personality trait with the strongest genetic basis.[10] But we believe that Henry Cavendish's silences had additional origins.

We have given a number of examples of Cavendish's wariness of words as instruments of deception. Heir to the world of quantity and abstract mathematical relations created by the scientific revolution, he preferred numbers to words as the medium of "strict reasoning" about nature. We can think of Cavendish's silence as an acknowledgment of the inadequacy of common spoken language to represent the world as truthfully and accurately as he would have wished.[11]

When Cavendish spoke, as Playfair noted, it was always "exceedingly to the purpose, and either brings some excellent information, or draws some important conclusion."[12] We have quoted Davy's observation that what Cavendish said was "luminous and profound."[13] Young thought that Cavendish's hesitancy of speech

---

[6] George Wilson, *Religio chemici. Essays,* ed. J.A. Wilson (London, 1862), 294.

[7] Barrow, *Sketches of the Royal Society and Royal Society Club*, 144.

[8] Gerald M. Phillips, "Reticence: A Perspective on Social Withdrawal," in *Avoiding Communication: Shyness, Reticence and Communication Apprehension*, ed. J. A. Daley and J. C. McCrosky (Beverley Hills: Sage, 1984), 51–66, on 52, 65.

[9] Expression used by Henry Holland, quoted in Gwendy Caroe, *The Royal Institution: An Informal History* (London: John Murray, 1985), 39.

[10] Cheek and Briggs, "Shyness," 329. Jerome Kagan, J. Steven Reznick, and Nancy Snidman, "Biological Bases of Childhood Shyness," *Science* 240 (1988): 167–71.

[11] George Steiner, "The Retreat from the Word," in *George Steiner: A Reader* (New York: Oxford University Press, 1984), 283–304, on 284–88.

[12] John Playfair quoted in George Wilson, *The Life of the Honourable Henry Cavendish* (London, 1851), 166.

[13] John Davy, *Memoirs of the Life of Sir Humphry Davy, Bart.*, vol. 1 (London, 1836), 222.

was not a physical defect but an expression of the "constitution of his mind."[14] We suspect that Cavendish spoke precisely and sparingly as a point of conscience. Like the Trappists' vow, his silence was in part a conscious choice, as was his practice of occasionally breaking it.

What Cavendish had to say about science–it was a great deal–he said primarily in writing, not in speech. For him there was clearly an important difference between writing and speaking. To judge from the few fragments of his speech preserved in anecdotes, he was given to repeating himself, at least when agitated. His writing, by contrast, is controlled. Speech is, of course, impermanent, and so can be writing if it is not published, but Cavendish kept what he wrote for fifty years. He valued what he put on paper.

A case has been made that Cavendish's failure to publish more of his work was the result of his class and wealth, which isolated him from the scientists of the industrial age who would otherwise have encouraged him.[15] We agree that his aristocratic connection probably did affect his publishing. In the preceding century, the aristocrat Boyle published a large quantity of scientific writing, and in Cavendish's time Lord Mahon published a good book on the principles of electricity, but it is noteworthy that in the middle of the eighteenth century, highly capable men of science who were also aristocrats–Lord Charles Cavendish, Lord Morton, and Lord Macclesfield–published nothing to speak of; their stronger motivation was to perform a public service as scientific administrators. We also agree that Cavendish was to some extent isolated, but his isolation seems to us not imposed by his position in society so much as self-imposed, and it was selective. He did not isolate himself from scientific company, though he did not form close scientific associations either.

The reasons for Cavendish's reluctance to publish were no doubt complex and depended on the particular work in question, and because he said nothing about his reasons, they will probably never be fully known. In this biography, wherever the subject has come up, we have made a judgment. Certainly Cavendish's standard of excellence played a part. Blagden, who spent days poring over Cavendish's unpublished papers after his death, believed that Cavendish's standard was the primary explanation. Subsequent commentators have noted that Cavendish disliked controversy. Cavendish advised John Michell sensibly enough to make his work promptly and widely known if he wished to receive credit for it. It might seem that he did not always follow his own sound advice unless he was more concerned with avoiding controversy than

[14] Thomas Young, "Life of Cavendish," in *The Scientific Papers of the Honourable Henry Cavendish, F.R.S.,* vol. 1: *Electrical Researches,* ed. J.C. Maxwell and J. Larmor (Cambridge: Cambridge University Press, 1921), 435–47, on 444.

[15] James Gerald Crowther's analysis is provocative, but it is too schematic to be very convincing or helpful. "Henry Cavendish," in *Scientists of the Industrial Revolution: Joseph Black, James Watt, Joseph Priestley, Henry Cavendish* (London: Crescent Press, 1962), 271–340.

he was with receiving recognition. But if we are right, his life of service was directed to the enterprise of science; no number of individual researches, neither his nor his colleagues', would result, for example, in an agreement on the calibration of thermometers. There was no scientific counterpart of Adam Smith's invisible hand by which individuals pursing only their own interests could have advanced the enterprise. For this, coordinated effort and organizational support were needed. Through the Royal Society, Cavendish offered his services unstintingly, and though that did not prevent him from publishing his private researches, his actions strongly suggest that he gave priority to his work for the Society. His day-in, day-out work in the service of science can be regarded as of equal if not of greater importance than the researches he carried out on his own.

The stage of science to which Cavendish belonged is another consideration in drawing any conclusions about his publishing habits. The desire to achieve recognition through published research could be intense, as priority disputes showed, but the understanding that published research was a uniform yardstick by which individual scientific achievement was to be measured was still in the future. Able colleagues of Cavendish's achieved scientific prominence by different main routes: Herschel's was through publication, but Cullen's was by teaching science, Banks's by promoting it, and Aubert's by serving it. Cavendish received recognition for his name, for his service to the Royal Society, for his scientific ability, and for his publications. In truth he did not need to publish at all. Cavendish, we think, would be surprised at the interest we take in what he did and did not publish, and so would some of his colleagues.

For Cavendish, writing was integral to an activity that Blagden said was his sole "amusement": to bring reason to bear on experience of the natural world to get to the truth. Every written account of an experiment or an observation is a record of personal experience, and as such it is potentially the material of biography. If Cavendish's life was about science, the trove of scientific manuscripts he left behind is its faithful record, and his life accordingly is one of the best documented lives of the eighteenth century.

The historian Herbert Butterfield described the civilization that emerged at the end of the scientific revolution as dissolving all traditions before it, "having eyes for nothing save a future of brave new worlds," a civilization "exhilaratingly new perhaps, but strange as Nineveh and Babylon."[16] To his contemporaries, Henry Cavendish appeared strange. That may have had less to do with his "peculiarities" than with his single-minded scientific drive. He devoted his life to building a brave, new scientific civilization, though he would not have described his work in any such terms. His contribution was a by-product of duty of service and a love of truth expressed in the exacting language of science.

[16] Herbert Butterfield, *The Origins of Modern Science*, rev. ed. (New York: Free Press, 1965), 202.

PART FOUR

HENRY CAVENDISH'S SCIENTIFIC LETTERS

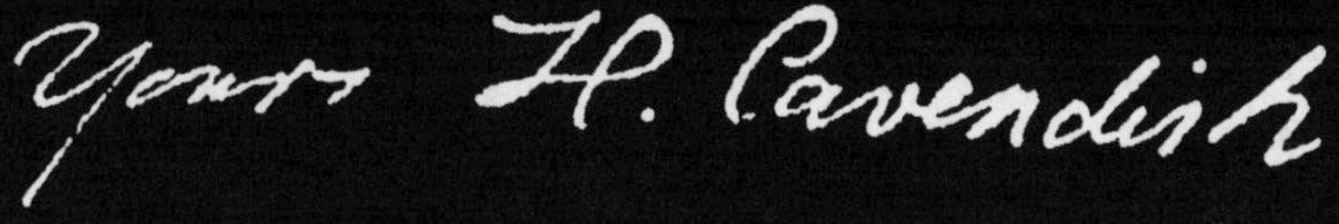

INTRODUCTION

WHILE A CONSIDERABLE NUMBER of Henry Cavendish's scientific manuscripts have been made public, his scientific letters have been relatively ignored. We have found the letters helpful in understanding his life, and we believe that the readers of this biography will too.

At the time of the "water controversy," one or two of Cavendish's letters were introduced as depositions, and since then a number of his letters have been published. This edition includes all previously published letters.

In 1961, some forty letters belonging to Henry Cavendish were found in his brother Frederick Cavendish's box of papers in the Devonshire Collections at Chatsworth. These, together with the smaller number of letters already contained in the Cavendish Scientific Mss of the Devonshire Collections, constitute the majority of his scientific letters. The remaining letters are scattered among several public archives.

At the time of his death, Cavendish's scientific papers were found to be in great disorder, which may help explain why some got saved and others did not. Perhaps too Cavendish did not save systematically. He did not necessarily save the important letters and discard the unimportant; he kept Priestley's letters, but he also kept a letter he would have regarded as crank.

For one who had a long and active public life, Cavendish left few letters. Legendary for his silences in company, he would seem to have felt no more "talkative" at his writing table.

Several of Cavendish's unpublished studies were written in the form of letters to be read by an unspecified "you," but which were in all other respects standard scientific papers, and his editors have published them as such in his *Scientific Papers.* We do not reproduce any of these papers in this edition. There are a substantial number of papers that might be called letters of instructions, often having to do with projects undertaken by the Royal Society, such as scientific expeditions. These too we exclude with one exception, which we include because it is the earliest letter we have by Cavendish.

Authors on occasion wrote to Cavendish to ask him to communicate papers to the Royal Society. John Michell enclosed two letters with a paper of his, one personal and the other public. His main reason for including a public letter, he told Cavendish, was "the greater respect & attention [his paper] will naturally receive from the credit of your patronage." We include here all such "public" letters appearing in the *Philosophical Transactions of the Royal Society*.

Most of Cavendish's letters were "private," usually beginning with "Dear Sir." But even letters written in a form that is unmistakably that of a private letter were not necessarily confidential. They fell somewhere between a conversation and a publication; Joseph Priestley told Cavendish that he was "at liberty to mention the facts [of his letter] to any of your acquaintances." Cavendish published his reply to a private letter from Martin van Marum. Michell began a correspondence with Cavendish by recalling their "little talk" on his last visit to London, and when in the course of the correspondence he ventured on "very random conjectures or consequences," he drew back, withholding what he had to say until his next opportunity to meet with Cavendish; speculative matters were "often much more proper for discussion in the course of conversation, than to stand upon paper, even in an epistolary correspondence only." In this edition we publish all of the known "private" scientific letters of Cavendish's.[1]

We give several facsimile extracts. Cavendish's handwriting had no frills, rarely even punctuation and capitalization. In this regard his letters may be contrasted with Michell's, with their profusion of commas, semicolons, and colons, freely inserted, and with Priestley's, with their profusion of underlinings.

In his letters Cavendish maintained the distance he insisted upon in face-to-face encounters, but that is not to say that he wrote impersonally. On the contrary his letters could not be mistaken for anyone else's, and if they never became intimate, neither did the letters addressed to him. Within the conventions of "epistolary correspondence," as they were accepted by Cavendish's circle, Cavendish was responsive; he was solicitous of the health of his friends, as they were of his. It would be unnecessary to draw attention to Cavendish's humanity except that ever since his first full-length biography, he has been likened to an intelligent robot. We discuss this point in the introduction to the biographical part of this book.

With the exception of business correspondence and a few letters exchanged with his brother, Henry Cavendish's extant letters are about science and only that. He was not one to initiate a correspondence but he could be enticed into one provided the subject was science. Cavendish thanked Priestley for writing to him, saying that he "shall be very glad to be informed of any other experiments you may make." He thanked Michell for the same reason, assuring him that he "shall be very glad to hear of any schemes you are upon." In return, "with pleasure" Cavendish would tell Priestley and Michell about any work he might do. Cavendish's letters to Priestley and Michell were lively but they were few. With

[1] One letter we are unable to publish, Henry Cavendish to Charles Hatchett, 30 May 1802. The Wellcome Institute for the History of Medicine, which holds this letter, informs us that at present it cannot be found. We think that two unaddressed and undated draft letters by Charles Blagden were written to Cavendish; we discuss these letters, which we date 1785 and 1789 or 1790, in the chapter "The Person," but since we cannot be absolutely certain about them, we do not include them in this edition.

his many sources of up-to-date scientific information in London, he may have felt no need to continue an exchange of letters past a certain point.

Cavendish is one of the greatest scientists ever, as he is one of the most unusual personalities of science. By bringing his letters together in this edition, we trust that we will further the understanding of this remarkable man.

EDITORIAL NOTE

TRANSCRIPTIONS OF CAVENDISH'S LETTERS have been made from photoreproductions. Wherever an original letter is not written in the author's hand, the source of the contemporary transcription is given in a footnote. In the case of previously published letters, bibliographic references are given in a footnote.

An effort has been made to strike a balance between faithfulness to the original texts and readability, erring on the side of the former. Spelling, capitalization, raised characters, symbols, and numerical notation are reproduced as they appear. Punctuation is unchanged except for periods, which are added where no terminal punctuation is supplied; where periods are added, the succeeding word is capitalized, beginning a new sentence. On occasions where the absence of a comma makes a sentence confusing, an extra space is inserted. Minor deletions by the author are omitted without comment, except where they are germane to the sense of the letter, in which case they are enclosed within angled brackets <> and placed ahead of the revised text. Longer deletions, if germane, are reproduced in footnotes. Probable readings are enclosed in square brackets. Indecipherable passages are indicated by dashes within square brackets. The number of dashes stands for the number of illegible characters; five dashes, the maximum number, stand for five or more illegible characters [-----]. Interpolations by the author are entered without comment. With the exception of elevated footnote numbers, all editorial insertions in the letters appear within square brackets. If an excerpt rather than an entire letter is reproduced, the omitted parts are indicated by square brackets enclosing ellipses [. . .]. Uncommon or possibly confusing abbreviations are expanded with the use of square brackets, though usually only in their first appearance in a letter. Any questionable readings not explained by the above notations are explained in footnotes. Where words are misspelled the authors' errors are allowed to stand.

Insofar as possible, the physical layout of the letters is preserved. For ease of reference, each letter is preceded by a number, an address, a date, even if the date is repeated in the letter, and the source of the letter. Because all letters are either to or from Cavendish, the address includes only the name of his correspondent. Letters that are undated or are partially dated but are missing the year are given a probable date and enclosed within square brackets, sometimes preceded by qualifiers such as "after."

Letters to Cavendish contained in Charles Blagden's letterbooks we call "drafts" rather than "copies," since they contain corrections characteristic of draft letters. They did, of course, serve as Blagden's copies as well.

Letters written in French are given both in French and in our English translation.

Editorial commentary within footnotes is intended to clarify references in letters to persons, places, and scientific matters, and to provide the letters with a context of personal and public events and of contemporary scientific developments. In order that the letters may be consulted independently of the preceding biographical parts of this book, the footnotes to the letters occasionally repeat information encountered earlier in the book, and the letters are routinely cross-referenced. Subjects brought up in the letters are frequently discussed in the biography, but we do not cross-reference them; the index serves this purpose. Wherever possible, primary sources are cited in the footnotes; where a published source is cited, it is done so only by short title, if the full title is given in the bibliography.

LIST OF LETTERS

CAVENDISH'S CORRESPONDENTS.

Banks, Sir Joseph
Blagden, Sir Charles
Brockelsby, Richard
Brooke, John.
Canton, John
Cavendish, Frederick
Churchman, John
Dalby, Isaac
Dalrymple, Alexander
Deluc, Jean André
Dixon, Jeremiah
Douglas, James, Lord Morton
Farr, William
Franklin, Benjamin
Harrington, Robert
Hatchett, Charles
Herschel, Sir William
Horsburgh, James
Hunter, John
Hutton, Charles
Jenkinson, Charles, Lord Liverpool
La Blancherie, Pahin de
Marum, Martin van
Maskelyne, Nevil
Maty, Matthew
McNab, John
Mendoza y Rios, Joseph de
Michell, John
Mongez, Jean-André
Norris, William
Priestley, Joseph
Senebier, Jean
Vaughan, Benjamin
Vaughan, William
Vivian, Thomas
Walker, Richard
Young, Thomas

HENRY CAVENDISH'S SCIENTIFIC LETTERS

1. TO JAMES DOUGLAS, EARL OF MORTON[1]

[9 JUNE 1766]

From the original draft letter in the Devonshire Collections, Chatsworth[2]

The best way of finding the parallax of the sun from the transit of venus in 1769[3] is by a comparison of the duration of the transit in different places for which purpose it should be observed in such places where the difference of duration is the greatest. The duration is greatest about Tornea[4] & Wardhus[5] in Lapland.[6] It is to be hoped that Swedes and Danes will send observers to those places.[7] The place where the duration is least is in some of the islands supposed to be in the South sea[8] to the south of the Equator, & which would consequently be the best place to compare with Tornea & Wardhus. If observers could be sent there, which I imagine there is no probability of, the next best places are Cape Corrientes in Mexico where the duration is above 16 minutes less than at Tornea & California where the duration is from 16 to 15 minutes less than at Tornea. The Royal Society proposes to send observers to California[9] which is a better place than Cape Corrientes as at this latter place the transit will end so little before sun set that there is great danger of the suns being hid in clouds.

It is very desirable that the transit should be observed also in some place where the duration is of an intermediate length between that at California & the north as it would serve as a check in case of error in either of other observations & besides that would be particularly useful in case the observation should fail at either of the other places. I know of no place so proper for this purpose as Kamptschatka.[10] In the southern part of the peninsula of Kamptschatka the duration is near 8 minutes less than at Tornea & rather more than 8 minutes greater than at the south point at California. So that the difference is sufficient to deduce the parallax very well by comparing the duration at Kamptschatka with that at either of the foregoing places supposing the observation to fail at one of them. I know of no other place proper for this purpose except the north western parts of Hudsons bay where I believe it would be extremely difficult to send observers as ships can hardly get there early enough in the summer to land observers there before the transit & it would be hardly practicable for observers to winter there.[11] Besides that if it was practicable to send observers there it would not be so proper a place as Kamptschatka[12] as the sun is much lower & consequently there is more danger of its being hid in clouds.[13]

---

[1] James Douglas, Earl of Morton (1702–68), astronomer, F.R.S. 1733, from 1764 president of the Royal Society. "Morton," *DNB* 5:1236–37. Cavendish indicated on his draft of the letter that it was given to Dr. Morton, who was the physician Dr. Charles Morton, one of the secretaries of the Royal Society. We think that this is the draft of a letter dated 9 June 1766, addressed to the president, and read to the council of the Royal Society on 19 June 1766. Entry for 19 June 1766, Royal Society, Minutes of Council 5:147. The Royal Society informs us that Cavendish's letter has not been preserved in its archive.

[2] Cavendish Mss VIII, 26. Published in *Sci. Pap.* 2:435–36.

[3] The relative distances of the planets are expressed in terms of the distance of the earth from the sun, the standard unit. As this unit determines all of the distances of the solar system, its accurate measurement was regarded in the eighteenth century as having fundamental significance. The unit can be calculated from a measurement of the distance of any of the planets. The latter can be found from the different positions of the planet as viewed from different places on the earth; this is the method of parallax, and it is the method used in conjunction with observations of the transits of Venus. The closer the planet is to the earth, the more accurate is the measurement of its parallax. When Venus is close, it is between the earth and the sun and occasionally on a direct line. Observers at different latitudes on earth will record slightly different times of ingress and egress of the black disk of Venus as it crosses the bright disk of the sun. From such observations the parallax, and thus the distance, of Venus can be determined, and from it the parallax of the sun, or the distance of the earth from the sun, can be deduced. "Transits" of Venus are relatively rare, but when they do occur, they may do so in pairs only eight years apart. The Royal Society organized a large effort on the occasion of the transit of 1761, with unsatisfactory results. Having learned from this experience, in June 1766 the Society began to prepare for the transit of 1769. In his first year as a member of the council of the Society, Cavendish identified the best places for observing it. The next year Cavendish together with seven other Fellows of the Royal Society were appointed a committee to decide the proper places for observing the transit. Weld, *History of the Royal Society* 2:32. Pannekoek, *History of Astronomy*, 284–87. 12 Nov. 1767, Minutes of Council, Royal Society, 5:172.

[4] Torneå, Sweden, in Cavendish's time. It is Tornio, Finland, now. According to Cavendish's source, the latitude of this northern location is 65° 51′; a modern atlas gives it as 65° 55′.

[5] Wardhus was the English name for Vardøhus, a few degrees east and south of North Cape. Today it is Vardö, Norway. Observations of the transits of Venus in 1761 and 1769 were made at this location. Map facing p. 526 in Michael Roberts, *Gustavus Adolphus: A History of Sweden 1611–32*, vol. 1 (London: Longmans, Green, 1953).

[6] The Royal Society's northern expedition was led by William Bayley, astronomical assistant in the Royal Observatory. The eventual destination was the North Cape of Europe on the Island of Maggoroe, the northernmost tip of Norway, in Lapland; latitude 71° 30′. The Admiralty provided Bayley with passage. Weld, *History* 2:36. Taylor, *Mathematical Practitioners*, 223–24. Bayley, "Astronomical Observations Made at the North Cape, for the Royal Society," *PT* 59 (1769): 262–72. The Royal Society also sent the astronomer Jeremiah Dixon, who with Charles Mason had observed the transit of Venus of 1761, to the island of Hammerfost (Hammerfest) near the North Cape of Europe. Bell, "Dixon," *DSB* 4:131–32. Dixon, "Observations Made on the Island of Hammerfost, for the Royal Society," *PT* 59 (1769): 253–61. Observations were made in Lapland, at Ponoi, latitude 67° 4′1/2, by J. A. Mallet, of Geneva, "Extract of a Letter . . . to Dr. Bevis, F.R.S.," *PT* 60 (1770): 363–67.

[7] The council of the Royal Society resolved to ask Swedish astronomers where they intended to observe the transit. 3 Dec. 1767, Minutes of Council, Royal Society, 5:199. They took observations at Uppsala and Stockholm, and at Cajuneburg, now Kajaani in north central Finland. George Renwick, *Finland To-day* (London: T. Fisher Unwin, 1911), 142. "Observationes Transitus Veneris per Discum Solis, Die 3 Junii, 1769, habitae in Suecia, et Societati Regiae Londinensi communicatae, a Petro Wargentin, ejusdem Societatis Sodali, et Academiae Regiae Scient. Stockholmensis Secretario," *PT* 59 (1769): 327–32.

[8] The Royal Society sent Captain James Cook and Charles Green, astronomical assistant at the Royal Observatory, to the newly discovered (by Europeans) island called "King George's land," Tahiti, in the South Pacific. The Admiralty provided a ship, the *Endeavour*. Not Cook but Alexander Dalrymple was the Society's first choice of observer, described as "having a particular turn for Discoveries and being an able Navigator, and well skilled in Observation." But Dalrymple insisted that he have command of the ship, which the Admiralty found "intirely repugnant" to its rules. The Admiralty instead appointed Cook. Taylor, *Mathematical Practitioners*, 48–49. 19 Nov. 1767, 21 Apr., 5 May, and 23 June 1768, Minutes of Council, Royal Society, 5:177, 293–94, 299, 316–17.

[9] The Society wanted Roger Joseph Boscovich of Pavia to make observations in California on its behalf, but he was unable to go; the person who went instead was the French astronomer Jean-

Baptiste Chappe d'Auteroche, who had observed the earlier transit in 1761. Marković, "Bošković," *DSB* 2:326–32, on 327. Woolf, "Chappe d'Auteroche," *DSB* 3:197–98. "Extract of a Letter, Dated Paris, Dec. 17, 1770, to Mr. Magalhaens, from M. Bourriot; Containing a Short Account of the Late Abbé Chappe's Observation of the Transit of Venus, in California," *PT* 60 (1770): 551–52.

10 Kamchatka Peninsula off the eastern coast of Russia.

11 Hudson Bay was recommended as an observational site by the transit of Venus committee. 3 Dec. 1767, Minutes of Council, Royal Society, 5:199. Despite Cavendish's doubts, the observers were able to spend the winter there. William Wales, a London teacher of mathematics, and the astronomer Joseph Dymond were provided passage by the Hudson's Bay Company to and from Fort Churchill. From there they proceeded to Prince of Wales's Fort on the northwest coast of Hudson Bay, where they successfully carried out observations of the transit of Venus. Taylor, *Mathematical Practitioners*, 49, 248. Willson, *The Great Company*, 34–35. Wales and Dymond, "Astronomical Observations Made by Order of the Royal Society, at Prince of Wales's Fort, on the North-West Coast of Hudson Bay," *PT* 59 (1769): 467–88. Cavendish was right about the cold: Wales reported that in November "a half pint glass of British brandy was frozen solid in the observatory," after which, in January, the "cold began to be extremely intense." The lowest reading at the observatory was minus 43°, only slightly above the freezing temperature of mercury. Wales, "Journal of a Voyage, Made by Order of the Royal Society, to Churchill River, on the North-West Coast of Hudson's Bay; of Thirteen Months Residence in That Country; and of the Voyage Back to England; in the Years 1768 and 1769," *PT* 60 (1770): 100–36, on 123–24.

12 From Kamchatka, as from other places around the world, Cavendish received data for his computations of the 1769 transit of Venus. Cavendish Mss VIII, 33.

13 Cavendish wrote a slightly more technical paper on the subject, labelled in his handwriting, "Given to Council of Society," and titled, "Thoughts on the Proper Places for Observing the Transit of Venus in 1769." After listing "all the places I can find, proper for comparing the duration" of the transit, and giving their coordinates, he wrote that "there are also places where the time of the beginning & end might be compared to advantage. For example between the western parts of England & France (where the transit begins almost the soonest) & cape St Lucar in California, there is a difference of about 7′ in the time of the first internal contact: & between Bombay & St Lucar there is a difference of about 11′ 1/2 in the time of the last internal contact. The difference is not a great deal less between Madrass & St Lucar. . . . To conclude, I think it seems by all means advisable for the Society to send observers to California, & if possible to get it observed in more than one place there; as it appears to be so very conveniently situated, both for observing the duration, & also the beginning & end of the transit. It is to be hoped that the Swedes & Danes will get it observed in the north, & perhaps the Russians in Kamptschatka: especially when they are informed that observations will be made in California to compare with theirs. If they were not to do so I should think it would be worth while for the Society to endeavour to get it observed in Spitsbergen or Hudsons bay, if it should be found practicable. It seems also worth while to get it observed at Bombay or some part of the east indies, especially if the duration should not be observed in the proper places." From this document, we see that Cavendish mentioned England, France, and India to the council, countries he did not mention in his letter to Morton. Cavendish Mss VIII, 29. In Britain the transit was observed at London, Greenwich, Oxford, Shirburn Castle near Oxford, Leicester, Glasgow, Hawkhill and Kirknewton near Edinburgh, and Cavan in Ireland. In France it was observed at Paris and elsewhere. From India observations were communicated by the court of directors of the East India Company. *Philosophical Transactions* for 1769 and 1770.

2. TO JOHN CANTON[1]

23 JUNE [1766][2]

From the original letter in the Royal Society[3]

Marlborough street June 23.

Sir

Since I saw you I have met with Aepini tentamen theoriae electricitatis & magnetismi,[4] which I suppose is the book you spoke of, at Nourses.[5] I am sorry I did not enquire there sooner; but I thought there was so little likelyhood of meeting it there, that I neglected it. I hope however it is not too late to prevent your writing to Dr Priestly[6] for the book.

Your Obedient humble servant
H. Cavendish

---

[1] John Canton (1718–72), London schoolmaster, F.R.S. 1749. "Canton," *DNB* 3:908–9.

[2] The probable year of this letter, 1766, has been settled by Home, "Aepinus and the British Electricians."

[3] Canton Papers 2:31.

[4] Franz Ulrich Theodosius Aepinus (1724–1802), mathematician and natural philosopher, member of the Imperial Academy of St. Petersburg. Heilbron, "Aepinus," *DSB* 1:66–68. Through the Academy he brought out his most important work, *Tentamen theoriae electricitatis et magnetismi,* in 1759. Around the time of this letter, Cavendish began working on an electrical theory of his own; he acknowledged that in the *Tentamen,* Aepinus had put forward an electrical hypothesis "nearly the same" as his own. Henry Cavendish, "An Attempt to Explain Some of the Principal Phaenomena of Electricity, by Means of an Elastic Fluid," *PT* 61 (1771): 584–677, on 584.

[5] London bookshop with which both Cavendish and the Royal Society did business. 19 May 1768, Minutes of Council, Royal Society, 5:303.

[6] Joseph Priestley (1733–1804), F.R.S. 1766, who in 1766 was teaching at the dissenting academy in Warrington, had need of works on electricity for his *History of Electricity.* The book appeared in 1767. In that year Priestley became minister to a Presbyterian congregation in Leeds, where he did his most important scientific work. Schofield, "Priestley," *DSB* 11:139–47, on 139–42.

3. FROM NEVIL MASKELYNE[1]

10 APRIL 1771

From the original letter in the Devonshire Collections, Chatsworth[2]

Greenwich April 10. 1771

Sir,

I have farther reduced and simplified my Theorem expressing the attraction of an hyperbolic wedge which I here send you, as also another for the attraction of a portion of an elliptic cuneus:[3] both which I hope you will find pretty convenient for calculation. I am

Your humble Servant
N. Maskelyne

[. . .][4]

---

1 Nevil Maskelyne (1732–1811), astronomer and cleric, F.R.S. 1758, astronomer royal since 1765. "Maskelyne," *DNB* 12:1299–1301.

2 Cavendish Mss VIII, 4. This brief letter introduces three pages of mathematical studies of attraction.

3 This letter is the earliest record of Cavendish and Maskelyne's collaboration on what would become an independent project of the Royal Society, the measurement of the attraction of mountains.

4 Following Maskelyne's signature are the two theorems: "To find the attraction of a hyperbolic wedge on a particle placed at the common vertex of the two inclined planes"; "The formula of the attraction of a portion of an elliptic wedge on a point placed at the principal vertex of the ellipsis where the common section of the planes lies." On the back, in Cavendish's hand, is a note on the formulas: "express. for Hyp. should be divided by $\overline{n+1}^2$ & that for ellipse by $\overline{1-n}^2$," where n:1 is the ratio of the square of the conjugate axis to the square of the transverse axis of the hyperbola and the ellipse. In a separate paper, Cavendish developed a number of theorems similar to Maskelyne's on the attraction of geometrical bodies approximating to real mountains. "Paper Given to Maskelyne Relating to Attraction & Form of Earth," ibid., VI(b), 1.

To find the attraction of a hyperbolic wedge on a particle placed at the common vertex of the two inclined planes.

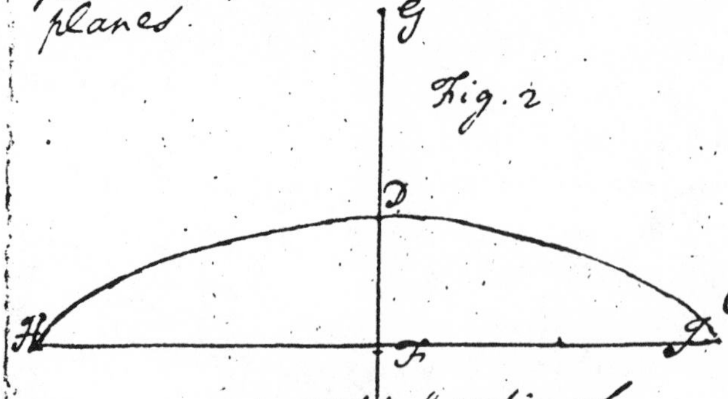

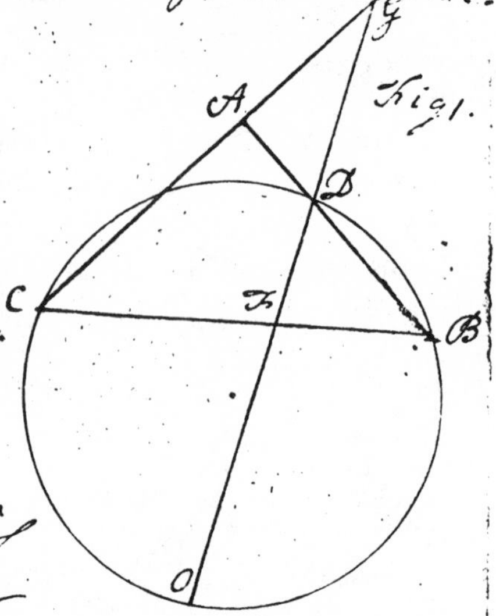

Let CAB be a vertical section of the conical hill, whose base is AOB, D the station of the Observer, DF a section of the cone by a plane perpendicular to the plane CAB; DF will be the axis of an hyperbola HDI fig 2, whose vertex is D, and ~~centre~~ the vertex of the opposite Hyperbola G (the intersection of DF and CA) therefore GD is the transverse axis of the hyperbola. Put $GD = a$ $GF = x$ $HF = y$

$y^2 = \overline{x^2 - ax} \times \frac{CFB}{DFG} = \overline{x^2 - ax} \times n$

[N.B. if a circle be described thro' C, D, B, $\frac{CFB}{DFG} = \frac{FO}{FG} = \frac{n}{1}$]

put d = sine of angle of wedge.

Hence fluxion of attraction of the wedge HDI is =

$2d\dot{x}\sqrt{\frac{nx}{\overline{n+1}\cdot x - a}} = 2d\dot{x}\sqrt{\frac{n}{n+1}} \times \sqrt{\frac{x}{x-b}}$ (putting $b = \frac{a}{n+1}$)

whose fluent is $= 2d\sqrt{\frac{n}{n+1}} \times$ fluent of $\dot{x}\sqrt{\frac{x}{x-b}}$.

F. $\dot{x}\sqrt{\frac{x}{x-b}}$ is $= \sqrt{x \times \overline{x-b}} + b \times \text{Hyp.Log}\,\overline{\sqrt{x-b} + \sqrt{x}} - \frac{1}{2}\text{Hyp.Log.}\,b$

But from this must be substracted (by way of correction) the value of the fluent when $x = a$ or $\sqrt{a^2 - ab} + b \times \text{hyp.log}\,\overline{\sqrt{a-b} + \sqrt{a}} - \frac{1}{2}\text{hyp.log.}\,b$

Therefore the whole attraction of the cuneus is =

$2d\sqrt{\frac{n}{n+1}} \times \sqrt{x \times \overline{x-b}} + 2d\sqrt{\frac{n}{n+1}} \times b \times \text{H.Log}\,\overline{\sqrt{x-b} + \sqrt{x}} - \frac{1}{2}\text{H.Log.}\,b$

103. *Extract on Attraction of Mountains. From Nevil Maskelyne's letter to Henry Cavendish, 10 April 1771. Cavendish Scientific Manuscripts VIII, 4. Reproduced by permission of the Chatsworth Settlement Trustees.*

4. TO BENJAMIN FRANKLIN[1]

4 AUGUST [1772]

From the original letter in the Historical Society of Pennsylvania[2]

Tuesday Aug. 4

Sir

We have agreed to go to Purfleet[3] on friday morning: we propose setting out a ½ an hour past 9; so that I suppose we shall be there about one at latest. I am sorry I could not send you notice sooner; but Dr Watson[4] was not able to fix on a day sooner. As I imagine friday is about the time you thought of coming to town, you perhaps might like to come back from Purfleet with us.[5] If you should and would write me word, I will take care that there shall be room for you.

Your Obedient humble servant
H. Cavendish

[address]:
To
Dr Franklin
At Mr Sargents
at May Place
near Dartford
Kent

---

1 Benjamin Franklin (1706–90), F.R.S. 1756. Cohen, "Franklin," *DSB* 5:129–39, on 129–30.

2 Franklin Papers 6:77. Published in *Papers of Benjamin Franklin* 19:228–29.

3 In 1772 after hearing that lightning had destroyed several powder magazines at Brescia, Italy, together with much of the town, with the loss of many lives, the Board of Ordnance asked the Royal Society for advice about its own unprotected magazines at Purfleet. Cavendish, who the year before had published a paper on electricity, was appointed to a committee to examine the buildings at Purfleet. "A Report of the Committee Appointed by the Royal Society, to Consider of a Method for Securing the Powder Magazines at Purfleet," *PT* 63 (1773): 42–47, on 44. Weld, *History* 2:95.

4 William Watson (1715–87), F.R.S. 1741, physician, natural philosopher, and natural historian, renowned for his electrical experiments, together with Cavendish, Franklin, John Robertson, and Benjamin Wilson, was appointed to the Purfleet committee. Cavendish's name was listed first in the report containing the recommendations of the committee, dated 21 August 1772, delivered to the council on 26 August 1772. Minutes of Council, 6:144–49. Wilson gave a dissenting opinion. Minutes of Council, Royal Society 6:146. "A Report of the Committee Appointed by the Royal Society, to Consider of a Method for Securing the Powder Magazines at Purfleet." "Mr. Wilson's Dissent to Part of the Preceding Report," *PT* 63 (1773): 48. Wilson, "Observations upon Lightning, and the Method of Securing Buildings from Its Effects," ibid., 49–65. "A Letter to Sir John Pringle, Bart. Pr. R.S. on Pointed Conductors," ibid., 66. "Watson," *DNB* 20:956–58.

5 A few days before, Franklin had gone to Kent. From there he went directly to nearby Purfleet on Friday, 7 August, for the meeting of the lightning committee. Editorial note 5 in *Papers of Benjamin Franklin* 19:228–29.

5. FROM NEVIL MASKELYNE

5 JANUARY 1773

From the original letter in the Devonshire Collections, Chatsworth[1]

Greenwich Jan. 5 1773

Dear Sir,

Inclosed I return you your rules & directions for the choice of hills having a considerable attraction;[2] which I have taken the liberty to take a copy of: I think them well calculated to procure us the information that is wanted . . . According to your Table, I should estimate, that the valley, called Glent-Tilt, lying on the N.W. side of the mountain Ben-Glae in Scotland, should produce a defect of attraction on the two opposite sides of 36″, supposing the mean depth 1000 yards, the shape spheroidical and [the] length of the valley 8 miles, the breadth 4 miles (I believe it is less) and the angle which the direction of the valley makes with the meridian 50°. Col. Roy,[3] from whose account these dimensions are taken, says it makes an angle of 50° or more with the true meridian. If the mean density of the earth exceed that at the surface 5 times, there will still remain 7″ attraction. I think the dimensions of this extraordinary valley deserve a more particular inquiry.[4] I shall be obliged to you for a line to acquaint me, whether you found any thing material in those papers of the late Mr Robins, which you examined, that have not been printed;[5] as the proof of Mr Call's[6] paper (making mention of them at the end of his account of the draught of the 12 signs in an indian Pagoda) is now in my hands; & I would add a note about the papers.[7] I am Sir,

Your very humble Servt,

N. Maskelyne

[address]:

To

The Honble Henry Cavendish

at Lord Charles Cavendish's

Great Marlbro' Street.

---

1 Cavendish Mss X(b), 1. Published in *Sci. Pap.* 2:402.

2 See letter 3. In 1772 Maskelyne proposed that the Royal Society measure the deflection of a plumb line by the gravitational attraction of a mountain, leading to a value for the mean density of the earth. "A Proposal for Measuring the Attraction of Some Hill in This Kingdom by Astronomical Observations," *PT* 65 (1775): 495–99; read in 1772. A committee was formed with Maskelyne and Cavendish on it; the other members were Benjamin Franklin, Daines Barrington, Samuel Horsely, Matthew Raper, and William Watson, with Joseph Banks added later. Weld, *History* 2:79. In addition to a number of short studies, Cavendish wrote four long papers on the problem of the choice of hills, or mountains, and valleys for observing attraction: "Paper Given to Maskelyne Relating to Attraction & Form of Earth," "Mr Cavendish's Rules for Computing the Attraction of Mountains on Plumblines," "On the Choice of Hills Proper for Observing Attraction, Given to Dr Franklin," and "Thoughts on the Method of Finding the Density of the Earth by Observing the Attraction of Hills," Cavendish Mss VI(b), 1, 2, 3, 6.

[3] William Roy (1726–90), military engineer, F.R.S. 1767, had made a military survey of Scotland. "Roy," *DNB* 17:371–73, on 371.

[4] The actual experiment was carried out on a mountain rather than a valley. The sum of the deviation on the opposite sides of the mountain amounted to 11.6″. Maskelyne, "An Account of Observations Made on the Mountain Schehallien for Finding Its Attraction," *PT* 65 (1775): 500–42, on 531.

[5] Benjamin Robins (1707–51), military engineer and mathematician, F.R.S. 1727, presented a number of papers to the Royal Society, but only a few of them were published in the *Philosophical Transactions*. Robins's friend Martin Folkes intended to bring out an edition of his works, but he fell ill, and instead Robins's executor James Wilson published a selection of his papers entitled, *Mathematical Tracts of the Late Benjamin Robins*, 2 vols. (London, 1761). Briggs, "Robins," *DSB* 11:493–94.

[6] John Call (1732–1801), military engineer in India. "Call," *DNB* 3:705–6.

[7] Call, who had been secretary to Robins when the latter was chief engineer of the East India Company, offered Robins's manuscripts to the Royal Society. At the request of the Society, Maskelyne together with Cavendish, Matthew Raper, and Samuel Horsley examined the manuscripts, deciding that they contained nothing substantially new on science beyond what had already been printed. John Call, "A Letter . . . to Nevil Maskelyne, F.R.S. Astronomer Royal, Containing a Sketch of the Signs of the Zodiac, Found in a Pagoda, Near Cape Comorin in India," *PT* 62 (1772): 353–56, on 355; read 14 May 1772.

I imagine the best place to make the observations will be on each side the valley of the Tilt just above the steepest part of the ascent in which case I believe the effect may be estimated the same as if the ground was as in the figure

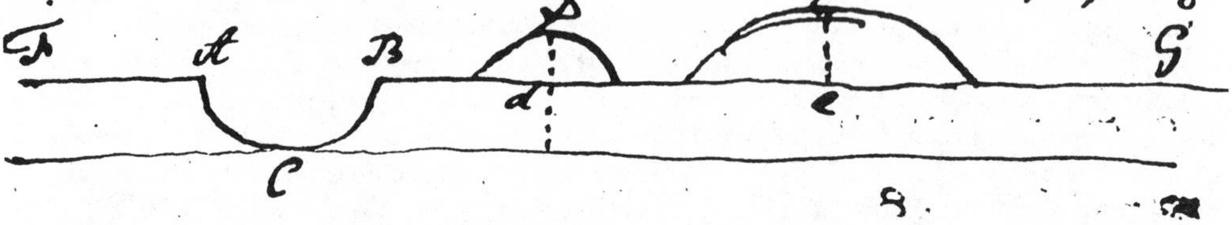

ACB is a valley infinitely continued in length the section across it being a segment of a circle the perpend. height of A/B above C being {1166/1066 feet & AB being 3700 the ground on each side of A & B being continued infinitely on the same height with those points except that there are 2 hills D & E consisting of segments of spheroids the diam. of D/E being 1200/5000 feet their height above B {700/1080 at the distance {BD/BE being {2500/7000

On this supposition the whole effect of ACB

104. *Extract on Attraction of Mountains. "Mr Cavendish's Rules for Computing the Attraction of Mountains on Plumblines," Cavendish Scientific Manuscripts VI(b), 2. Reproduced by permission of the Chatsworth Settlement Trustees.*

6. FROM MATTHEW MATY[1]

26 DECEMBER 1773

From the original letter in the Devonshire Collections, Chatsworth[2]

December 26. 1773.

Dr Maty presents his compliments to Mr Cavendish, is very sorry not to have been at home, when he honoured him with a visit, and sends him one of the forms, which he spoke of, tho' he is sensible it might be rendered still more convenient.

The hints about the observations to be made at Hudson's Bay will be extremely serviceable, and as the ships do not go out before the end of May, the Surgeon[3] who is to undertake them will have sufficient opportunities to receive instructions.[4]

The fixed Barometer seems to be highly preferable to the portable; but I doubt whether it would be easy to keep in the ship the tubes ready filled. It might be worth while for the Gentleman to be taught by Mr. Nairne[5] how to fill the tubes, and he should take with him a sufficient supply both of them and of mercury.

Should not one of the thermometers always be kept out of doors, to ascertain the temperature of the open air?

The rain gage can hardly be used but in summer; and as to the snow D^r^ M[askelyne] would propose to have an Area of two or three square yards of flat ground, if possible on the frozen river, reserved for that purpose. By clearing the snow fallen upon it every week, after having measured the height, one might easily determine the corresponding quantity of water. The snow indeed may not always be equally dense; but that might be ascertained and a Medium fixed.

Mr. Rouelle's paper on fixt air,[6] which D^r^ In[gen-Housz][7] had borrowed last Thursday is now sent to Mr Cavendish.[8]

---

[1] Matthew Maty (1718–76), F.R.S. 1751, since 1765 secretary of the Royal Society, and since 1772 principal librarian of the British Museum. "Maty," *DNB* 13:76–79, on 76–77.

[2] Cavendish Mss X(b), 2.

[3] Evidently Thomas Hutchins; see letter 15, note 3.

[4] Around this time the Royal Society was interested in exploring the northern latitudes. In the summer of 1773, upon the recommendation of the Royal Society, the king directed that an expedition be undertaken in search of a Northwest Passage. At a meeting of the council of the Royal Society on 29 April 1773, Cavendish read a paper with instructions for the expedition. In charge was Constantine John Phipps, captain of one of the two ships making the voyage; Phipps quoted from Cavendish's instructions in his account, *Voyage towards the North Pole*, 145–47. In 1774 the Society proposed to the Admiralty another northern voyage with similar objectives; two years later an expedition set out under the command of Captain James Cook, who carried with him scientific instructions from Cavendish. Weld, *History* 2:69–76. Cavendish Mss IX, 42. In 1776 Lieutenant Richard Pickersgill sailed to Labrador looking for the Northwest Passage, and he too had instructions from Cavendish. Pickersgill, "Track of His Majesty's Armed Brig Lion from England to Davis's Streights and Labrador, with Observations for Determining the Longitude by Sun and Moon and Error of Common Reckoning; Also the Variation of the Compass and Dip of the

Needle, as Observed During the Said Voyage in 1776," *PT* 68 (1778): 1057–62. Cavendish Mss IX, 41. To obtain information about the far north, the Society repeatedly involved the Hudson's Bay Company. With assistance from the Company, the Society sent two observers to Hudson Bay to record the transit of Venus in 1769; see letter 1. The same observers also recorded meteorological information for the Society. Joseph Dymond and William Wales, "Journal of a Voyage, Made by Order, of the Royal Society, to Churchill River, on the North West Coast of Hudson's Bay; of Thirteen Months Residence in That Country; and of the Voyage Back to England"; "Observations on the State of the Air, Winds, Weather, &c. Made at Prince of Wales's Fort, on the North West Coast of Hudson's Bay, in the Years 1768 and 1769," *PT* 60 (1770): 100–136, 137–78. In 1773 the council ordered that meteorological instruments be bought by the Society for the Hudson's Bay Company. 23 Dec. 1773, Minutes of Council, Royal Society, 6:203. Cavendish planned meteorological experiments to be carried out at Hudson Bay by Thomas Hutchins. See letter 15, note 3. In 1774, the council resolved to ask the Board of Longitude for a dipping needle to send to the Hudson's Bay Company. 20 Jan. 1774, ibid., 205–5. The following year Thomas Hutchins reported observations made with the needle at various locations beginning in the Orkney Islands and ending at Albany Fort, Hudson Bay: "Experiments on the Dipping Needle Made by the Desire of the Royal Society," *PT* 65 (1775): 129–38.

[5] Edward Nairne (1726–1806), London instrument-maker. Taylor, *Mathematical Practitioners*, 214.

[6] Probably Hilaire-Marin Rouelle, "Observations . . . sur l'air fixe et sur ses effets dans certaines eaux minerals." Hilaire-Marin Rouelle (1718–79), French chemist. Rappaport, "Rouelle," *DSB* 11:564.

[7] Jan Ingen-Housz (1730–99), F.R.S. 1771, originally of the Netherlands, practiced medicine in London and carried out experiments in pneumatic chemistry. Pas, "Ingen-Housz," *DSB* 7:11–16, on 11–12.

[8] Cavendish would naturally have been interested in Rouelle's paper since he had demonstrated the role of fixed air in the suspension of calcareous earth in mineral water. "Experiments on Rathbone-Place Water," *PT* 57 (1767): 92–108.

7. FROM ALEXANDER DALRYMPLE[1]

[AUGUST 1775]

From the original letter in the Devonshire Collections, Chatsworth[2]

Dr Sir

I sent you from Madeira a Copy of our Journal to that Place,[3] I had made a mistake of 5′ in the Long. & Time Keeper from 12th to 30th May, having been 5′ more E. than I had reckond by a mistake in calculating the error of Time Keeper.[4]

We found the Marine Barometer of very great Use, it prognosticated a very severe gale of wind which we had no other tokens of, but we find that here the S.E. winds however *hard*, raise the Barometer, indeed they always are accompanied by clear weather.[5]

I think if the Stand or Frame of the Dipping needle[6] was, instead of being in two pieces, fixed on a swivel as the Knights Compass,[7] it would be more convenient as it might then be easily turned to find the magnetical meridian which is attended with some inconvenience at present when the Ship does not remain steady in the same direction.

There are scarcely any Cellars in this Country. Their wines are all kept in Storehouses above ground; There is only one Cellar that I could hear of at the Cape Town and Mr Russell promised to carry the Thermometer into it if He could get permission. I shall not fail of sending you his Experiment when I receive it, and any Observations I may be able to make in Springs here if I can find any proper for the purpose.[8]

I beg to be rememberd to all Friends at the Kings Head[9] and Mitre[10] and am with great truth

Dr Sir

Your obliged humble Servant

ADalrymple

Simmons Bay[11]

near the Cape of Good Hope

---

[1] Alexander Dalrymple (1737–1808), hydrographer, F.R.S. 1771. "Dalrymple," *DNB* 5:402–3.

[2] Cavendish Mss X(b), 5.

[3] Dalrymple was on a nine-month journey from London to Madras. For many years he served in India and other parts of Asia as an employee of the East India Company. Having returned to England, in 1775 he was again posted to Madras. On the outward journey, he carried instructions from Cavendish on the use of the dipping needle; these he repeated in his meteorological log, communicated to the Royal Society by Cavendish, "Journal of a Voyage to the East Indies, in the Ship *Grenville*, Captain Burnet Abercrombie, in the Year 1775," *PT* 68 (1778): 389–418, on 390. Part 1 of the *Philosophical Transactions* for 1778, in which Dalrymple's log appeared, contained five other meteorological journals or registers, an indication of the interest in meteorology at the time in the Royal Society.

[4] The timekeeper was made by John Arnold (1736–99), a London instrument-maker who specialized in clocks. Dalrymple, "Journal of a Voyage," 389. Taylor, *Mathematical Practitioners*, 222–23.

[5] The barometers and thermometers used on this voyage were all made by the firm of Nairne and Blunt. Dalrymple, "Journal of a Voyage," 389. Taylor, *Mathematical Practitioners*, 214, 256, 293.

[6] The dipping needle measures the inclination to the horizontal of a magnetic needle suspended at its center of gravity and free to turn in the vertical plane of the magnetic meridian.

[7] Gowin Knight (1713–72), F.R.S. 1745, magnetic experimenter, patented a mariner's compass in 1766. Taylor, *Mathematical Practitioners*, 182. Around the time that Dalrymple wrote to Cavendish about the meteorological and magnetic instruments on board ship, Cavendish made a comprehensive study of the meteorological and magnetic instruments belonging to the Royal Society: "An Account of the Meteorological Instruments Used at the Royal Society's House," *PT* 66 (1776): 375–401. See also letter 10, note 2. The dipping needle was returned with the *Grenville* to London, where it was observed at Deptford and "in a pretty large garden in London, about five miles distant." That garden was almost certainly Cavendish's, free of ironwork, where he tried magnetical instruments for the Royal Society. Dalrymple, "Journal of a Voyage," 390.

[8] In the middle of May 1775 at an earlier stop on the journey to India, at Port Funchal in Madeira Island, Dalrymple was given a probably faulty report of a thermometer reading, taken "in consequence of our request," in a cool cellar. Entry for 15 May 1775, Dalrymple, "Journal of a Voyage." Dalrymple was assisting Cavendish, who requested thermometer readings of cellars, caves, springs, and wells as an indication of average climates. Mr. Russell's thermometer is referred to in Dalrymple, "Journal of a Voyage," 389.

[9] Evidently a meeting place for Cavendish, Dalrymple, and their friends, who perhaps formed a club. "King's Head" is not specific, being one of the most common signs of taverns and coffeehouses in London.

[10] The Royal Society Club met at the Mitre Tavern on Fleet Street. Cavendish was a long-time member; Dalrymple became a member in 1777.

[11] In late August 1775 the *Grenville* anchored at "Symmons Bay" (Simon's Bay), which Dalrymple surveyed, at the Cape of Good Hope. Dalrymple, "Journal of a Voyage." Spray, "Dalrymple," 207.

8. FROM ALEXANDER DALRYMPLE

15 OR 19 FEBRUARY 1776[1]

From the original letter in the Devonshire Collections, Chatsworth[2]

Dr Sir

I have had a copy made of our Journal from England hither but on looking into it I find it so ill-copied that it will require a very careful examination which I cannot at present bestow on it. I must therefore delay sending it 'till the next Conveyance which will sail in about 3 or 4 months.[3]

I beg my Respects to Lord Charles Cavendish[4] and Compliments to all Friends at the Mitre & Kings Head.[5]

Capt Abercromby[6] has carried the Dipping Needle to Bombay with him & has promised to be regular in his Observations.

Upon 2^{d} Thoughts I have tho^{t} it most eligible to send the Journal as it is.

I am with great Esteem

Dr Sir

Your most obliged Hble St

ADalrymple

Fort St. George[7]

15th [or 19th] Feby 1776

---

[1] It is unclear whether Dalrymple wrote 15 or 19.

[2] Cavendish Mss X(b), 7.

[3] Dalrymple was writing to Cavendish from Madras.

[4] Lord Charles Cavendish (1704–1783), Henry Cavendish's father.

[5] See letter 7, notes 9 and 10.

[6] Captain Burnet Abercrombie, of the *Grenville*, on which Dalrymple sailed in 1775; see previous letter, note 3.

[7] East India Company headquarters on the Coromandel coast, at Madras.

9. FROM JEAN ANDRÉ DELUC[1]

19 FEBRUARY 1777

From the original letter in the Devonshire Collections, Chatsworth[2]

Answer of De Luc to Theory of Boiling[3]

Monsieur

Je vous suis extrémement obligé de la peine que vous avez prise de m'exposer la Theorie qui vous fait préfèrer la vapeur de l'eau bouillante, à l'eau bouillante elle-même, pour fixer le point supérieur du Thermomètre.[4] J'ai leu trois fois votre Mémoire[5] avec beaucoup d'attention; car cette matière m'interesse beaucoup. Cependant je vous avouë que je n'y ai pas trouvé des raisons d'abandonner ma Theorie, fondée sur un grand nombre de considérations & d'expériences, & qui me semble expliquer fort bien vos expériences mêmes.[6] Si j'avois assez de loisir, & que vous en eussiez assez vous-même, pour que nous pussions nous engager dans ces discussions de Theorie, elles seroient très agreables pour moi. Mais il faudroit en effet beaucoup de tems; puis qu'il s'agiroit de vous détailler, comment tous les phénomènes que vous allégués, & beaucoup d'autres que votre Theorie expliqueroit encore, s'expliquent de même par la mienne; & de vous exposer ensuite, quels sont les autres phénomènes qu'il me semble que vous n'expliqueriez pas. Tout cela est répondu non seulement dans le Supplement à mon ouvrage qui ne traite que de la chaleur de l'eau bouillante; mais dans le Chap[itre] où j'explique mon opinion sur la cause des variations du Baromètre;[7] & dans mon Memoire sur l'hygromètre.[8] C'est une matière très vaste en un mot; & dans ce moment je suis trop occupé d'autres objets, pour pouvoir embrasser celui-là; d'autant plus que les discussions sur les choses qui ne sont pas susceptibles de démonstrations géomètriques, & qui sont seulement soumises à la probabilité, sont quelquefois sans fin; comme nous le voyons dans presque toutes les parties de la physique systématique.

Heureusement ces discussions Theorétiques ne sont pas nécessaires à notre objet. Dans l'une & l'autre Theorie, la vapeur qui sort de l'eau bouillante doit avoir à très peu près la chaleur de cette eau. Ainsi ce n'est pas de ma Theorie proprement que naissoient mes objections. Je vais m'expliquer plus précisement à ce sujet.

Une de mes objections se trouve avoir un peu de rapport avec votre Theorie. Je craignois que suivant la manière dont le vase seroit fermé, c'est à dire dont l'air extérieur pourroit agir sur la vapeur, le degré de chaleur de celle-ci ne subit quelque changement.

Dans votre Theorie, Monsieur, la vapeur de l'eau bouillante ne peut pas se réfroidir le moins du monde, sans redévenir eau sur le champ. Cependant lorsque dans le petit pot, le *bec* & la cheminée sont ouverts à la fois, la vapeur, sans se condenser, devient sensiblement moins chaude.

Il est vrai que vous dites, que c'est la vapeur *non mêlée avec l'air*, qui se condense tout de suite par la moindre diminution de la chaleur. Mais j'avouë que je ne comprends pas cette distinction: c'est bien toujours par plus ou moins de mélange avec l'air, dans des vases différens ou différemment fermés, que je craignois que la vapeur ne fût pas au même dégré de chaleur dans toutes les expériences, quoiqu'à même hauteur du Baromètre. A cet égard cependant j'avouë, qu'il paroit par plusieurs des expériences que vous nous avez montrées, que d'assez grandes différences dans les circonstances apparentes, n'en ont pas produit de sensibles dans le dégré de chaleur: quoiqu'ensuite, dans les mêmes circonstances apparentes, nous en ayons trouvé.

Mettant à part un moment toute Theorie, il semble que la chaleur de la vapeur de l'eau bouillante, peut difficilement être considérée comme plus fixe que celle de l'eau même; car elles sont tellement mêlées dans la masse avant que la vapeur se dégage, qu'elles paroissent devoir intimément participer à la température l'une de l'autre. Ainsi pour supposer que la vapeur au moment de sa sortie, ait réellement un dégré fixe de chaleur qui lui soit propre, il faut qu'il soit rigoureusement vrai, & démontré par des expériences immédiates, que la vapeur en effet, ne peut être *vapeur*, qu'à ce dégré fixe de chaleur. Or je ne trouve pas que cela découle de votre raisonnement à la page 5, qui me semble être votre preuve principale; il peut y avoir ce me semble d'autres causes de ce phénomène là.

Le couvercle percé, mis sur le vase où l'eau bout, rend aussi le dégré de chaleur de cette eau plus constant pendant l'expérience; il opére à cet égard sur l'eau, comme sur la vapeur même; cela est aisé à concevoir dans toute Theorie, & parconséquent n'en favorise aucune. Il s'agit seulement de savoir, si cette *constance* au moment d'une observation, promet aussi un degré *fixe* en toute observation. Jusqu'ici il me paroit qu'il y a des doutes.

Ma seconde objection étoit, que la chaleur de la vapeur près de la surface de l'eau, seroit peut-être différente dans un vase profond, où la colonne de vapeur seroit grande, que dans un vase moins profond. C'est cette expérience que vous aviez tentée dans la dernière seance; il faudra attendre le résultat.

Enfin je craignois l'effet de la compression des vapeurs dans un vase fermé, dont la cheminée seroit assez étroite pour qu'elles se pressassent au passage: Car alors il n'auroit pu qu'en résulter quelque pression sur l'eau, qui auroit infailliblement augmenté son dégré de chaleur. Mais encore à cet égard vos expériences m'ont rassuré, en me prouvant qu'il pouvoit y avoir assez de variété dans les circonstances apparentes, sans qu'il y eût une compression sensible des vapeurs, ni par conséquent une augmentation de chaleur dans l'eau.

Tenons nous en donc, Monsieur, quant a present du moins, aux essays immédiats, sans nous arrêter aux causes; c'est notre chemin le plus court & le plus sur; & après avoir tout éprouvé, nous retiendrons ce qui nous paroitra le meilleur. J'espère que nous les trouverons enfin, par tous les soins que vous voulez bien prendre.

Je vous renvoyé votre Memoire, supposant que vous serez bien aise de le ravoir. Je vous envoye aussi le vase dans lequel je mets ordinairement mes Thermomètres dans l'eau bouillante, dont peut-être aurons nous occasion de faire usage; & demain j'aurai l'honneur de me rendre chez vous à l'heure indiquée.

Je suis avec beaucoup de consideration

Monsieur

Votre très humble & très obéissant serviteur

J. A. DeLuc

Pimlico le 19 fev[e] 1777

---

[1] Jean André Deluc (1727–1817), Swiss natural philosopher, who settled in England, F.R.S. 1773. Beckinsale, "Deluc," *DSB* 4:27–29.

[2] Cavendish Mss X(c), 5.

[3] This heading is in Cavendish's handwriting. Cavendish did not publish his "Theory of Boiling," but it has since has been published, Cavendish Mss III(a), 5; *Sci. Pap.* 2:354–62. The original paper is contained in a group of manuscripts, which also contains a paper by Cavendish, "Boiling Point of Water. At the Royal Society, April 18, 1766," *Sci. Pap.* 2:351–53, together with several large sheets written partly by Cavendish and partly by someone else, labeled, "Trials of Boiling Point of Different Thermometers at Royal Society." The latter trials contain the date 23 Jan. 1777, which is four weeks before this letter by Deluc to Cavendish.

[4] In 1776 Cavendish published a paper on the Royal Society's meteorological instruments in which he discussed the adjustment of the boiling point of a thermometer, "An Account of the Meteorological Instruments Used at the Royal Society's House," *PT* 66 (1776): 375–401; read 14 Mar. 1776. That year he was appointed head of a committee to review the meteorological and magnetic instruments of the Royal Society. The committee, which included Deluc, agreed with Cavendish that in fixing the upper point of the scale of a thermometer, the bulb should be placed in the vapor above the boiling water. "The Report of the Committee Appointed by the Royal Society to Consider of the Best Method of Adjusting the Fixed Points of Thermometers; and of the Precautions Necessary to Be Used in Making Experiments with Those Instruments," *PT* 67 (1777): 816–57; read 19 June and 28 Dec. 1777.

[5] The "memoir" Deluc referred to in this letter was certainly Cavendish's "Theory of Boiling," which supported his view that steam is more exact than water for adjusting the boiling point of thermometers.

[6] Among Cavendish's miscellaneous manuscripts is "Extracts from De Luc Relating to the Boiling of Water." The extracts begin, "1st theory of evap." and "further theory," followed by results of experiments, all identified by page numbers. According to Deluc, vapor arising from evaporation is of the same nature as the steam from boiling water; he opposed the view that air dissolves water as water does salt. Cavendish, by contrast, was a solutionist, who made a distinction between vapor and steam; the opening words of his theoretical paper read, "There are 2 species of evaporation: 1st that which is performed with a less heat than that of boiling water; and 2ndly that which is called boiling." In three places in his paper, Cavendish referred favorably to Deluc's work on the subject, not to any of their differences, though they were sharp. Cavendish's paper opens with four experimental "principles," and concludes with a "hypothesis" about the nature of forces, one associated with John Michell and Roger Joseph Boscovich. Dyment, "Vapour and Evaporation," 471–73.

[7] *Recherches sur les modifications de l'atmosphère*, 2 vols. (Genève, 1772).

[8] As in his book on the modifications of the atmosphere, in this paper on the instrument for measuring humidity Deluc disagreed with those who regarded air as a solvent, an inappropriate, "chemical" way of speaking. Deluc's physical approach was based upon heat, which he regarded as a fluid; he explained vapor as a union of igneous particles with the particles of water. "Account of a New Hygrometer," *PT* 63 (1773): 404–60, on 458–59. Deluc first published his theory of evaporation in *Researches* (preceding note), then with James Watt's help in an improved form in *Idées sur la météorologie*, 2 vols. (Paris, 1786). This history of his theory was given by Deluc in "On Evaporation," *PT* 82 (1792): 400–24, in which he again denied that air plays any role in evaporation, reaffirming that steam is formed by evaporation and by boiling, and that in both processes, we see "water fly off with latent fire," ibid., 401, 403, 406.

9T. TRANSLATION OF LETTER FROM DELUC.

19 FEBRUARY 1777

From the original letter in the Devonshire Collections, Chatsworth

Answer of DeLuc to Theory of Boiling

Sir

I am extremely obliged for the pains you have taken to introduce me to the theory which makes you favor the vapor of boiling water to the boiling water itself for fixing the upper point of the thermometer. I read your paper three times with much care, for this matter greatly interests me. However, I must confess that I did not find in your paper any reasons to abandon my own theory, founded as it is on a large number of considerations and experiments, and which seems to me to explain very well your own experiments. If I had enough free time, and if you had enough of it yourself, so that we could engage in these discussions of theory, they would be most agreeable to me. But it would be necessary to have, in effect, quite a bit of time considering that what is required is that I show you how all the phenomena, and many others, which you allege your theory could further explain, are explained all the same by mine, and then show you the other phenomena that, it seems to me, you could not explain. All this is answered not simply in the supplement to my work, which treats only the heat of boiling water, but in the chapter where I provide my opinion on the cause of variations in the barometer, and in my paper on the hygrometer. In a word, it is a vast subject; and at this moment I am too occupied with other things to be able to treat it; what is more, the discussions on things which are not susceptible to geometric demonstration, and which are only subject to probability, are sometimes endless, as we see in nearly all parts of systematic physics.

Fortunately, these theoretical discussions are not necessary to our object. In both theories the vapor that rises from the boiling water ought to have approximately the same heat as the water itself. So it is not exactly my theory that gave rise to my objections. I will explain myself more precisely on this subject.

One of my objections relates somewhat to your theory. I was concerned that, depending on the manner in which the vessel was closed (that is to say, the way in which the external air could act on the vapor), the degree of heat of the vapor would undergo some change.

In your theory, Sir, the vapor of the boiling water cannot be cooled in the least without immediately becoming water again. However, when in a little vessel, the *mouth* and its neck are open at the same time, the vapor, without condensing, becomes perceptibly cooler.

True, you state that it is the vapor *unmixed with air* that condenses immediately because of the least diminution of heat. But I own that I do not understand this distinction: it is because there was almost always more or less a mixture of vapor with air in the different or differently sealed vessels that I was afraid that the vapor was not at the same degree of heat in all of the experiments, although the barometer was at the same height. In this regard, however, I admit that it appears that you have shown us in several experiments that large enough differences in the apparent circumstances did not produce any noticeable alteration in the degree of heat; although afterwards, in the same apparent circumstances, we have found some alteration.

Setting aside for a moment all theory, it seems that the heat of the vapor of boiling water can be considered only with difficulty as more fixed than that of the water itself; for they are so mixed in the mass before the vapor emerges that they appear to have no alternative but to influence the temperature of each other. So to suppose that the the vapor at the moment it emerges has in reality a fixed degree of temperature of its own, it is necessary that it be rigorously true, and demonstrated through some immediate experiments, that the vapor in reality can be *vapor* only at this fixed degree of heat. Thus, I do not find that this proceeds from your reasoning on page 5, which seems to me to be your principal proof; it seems to me that there can be other causes for this last phenomenon.

The perforated stopper, placed on the vessel in which the water boils, also renders the degree of heat of this water more constant during the experiment; in this regard it operates on the water as on the vapor itself; this is easy to conceive in any theory, and consequently favors neither. What is at stake is simply knowing if this *constancy* at the moment of an observation promises a *fixed* degree in all other observations as well. Until this is known it appears to me that there are some doubts.

My second objection was that the heat of the vapor near the surface of the water would perhaps be different in a deep vessel, where the column of vapor would be greater than in a shallow vessel. It is this experiment that you had tried in the last meeting; I must await the results.

Finally, I feared the effect of the compression of vapors in an enclosed vessel in which the neck would be narrow enough for the vapors to press into the passage. For the result could only have been pressure on the water, which certainly would have augmented its degree of heat. But again in this regard your experiments reassured me by proving that there could be enough variety in the apparent circumstances without there being a noticeable compression of the vapors nor consequently an augmentation of heat in the water.

Let us then, Sir, proceed with immediate tests without dwelling on causes; this is our shortest and most certain path; and after having tried everything, we will retain what appears to us the best solution. I hope that we will finally find them, by all the pains that you wish to take.

I return your paper, supposing that you will be glad to have it back. I send as well the vessel in which I ordinarily place my thermometers in the boiling water, which perhaps we will have occasion to make use of. And tomorrow I will have the honor to meet you at your residence at the indicated hour.

I am with the highest esteem

Sir

Your very humble and very obedient servant

Pimlico 19 Feb. 1777

J. A. DeLuc

10. FROM ALEXANDER DALRYMPLE

[1777]

From the original letter in the Devonshire Collections, Chatsworth[1]

Dr Sir

I send you the compleat Journal of all my Observations made with your dipping Needle,[2] I have drawn no inferences nor attempted to form any System for many reasons, but not the least cogent is the consideration that where Observations are tacked to a System they are often suspected to be bent to favour the System but where mere matter of fact is given it is not liable to suspicion & may assist with other materials to throw a light on this very curious part of Natural History; I think these Observations sufficiently shew that there is a great Consistency in the Instrum^{t}. & gives good grounds to hope it may be more than a matter of Curiosity here after when a Number of Observations are made in various parts of the Globe.

I am very sorry the Observations at Madrass are incompleat as I perceive I did not change the Poles, and I did not observe this till I quitted the Swallow so that I am affraid Captn. Panton[3] with whom I left your Instrument may omit the Observations there on a Supposition of my having made them. He promises to continue the Observ^{s}. during the remainder of his Voyage back to India & to England in Case of being ordered home when he will deliver you the Instrument.

The Longitudes are by the Time Keeper from the Lizard to the Cape of Good Hope & from the Cape to Madrass. The error at the Cape was 1° 3′ too far E. but if my ☾ Observat^{s} off Trinidada are to be relied on the Difference was then greater. However we can hardly expect to find a Series of Observations of Long. at Sea more exact than to 1° & the Error may be corrected by proportion if you please. The Keeper was out about a degree in Long from the Cape to Fort S George still Eastw^{d}.

I took the Long. of Anjengo as in M. dapre's new Edit^{n} of the Nept. Oriental[4] having no Observa^{s} there but I had many ☾ Observ^{s} at Mocha agreeing so well to gether that I did not scruple to take that as a New point. Unfortunately the T[ime] K[eep]^{er} got out of order before we reached Suez I believe by being ill hung in the Gimbals,[5] as it struck when the Ship pitched at the same time the [---] [-----]. However when I have finished a Sketch of the Red Sea, which I have reserved for my Quarantine Occupation I shall, I hope, be able to fill up that Deficiency tollerably well.

The Long. of Suez I apprehend is very near the truth, for altho' there are two Setts very near 1′ different, yet as the mean of them is exactly the same to 1′ as the mean of the 5 Setts cont^{s} in all 23 distances of ☾ & ⊙ taken different days I apprehend it is well determined. The other Setts were but very few minutes different.

I am not so strenuous an Advocate for the precision of ☾ Observations as Some Men I have met with, tho' I think they will very seldom exceed *a degree* in Error except when Weather or some other Circumstance is obviously unfavourable. The greatest Objection to these Observations was the difficulty of getting so many people as were required for Alt[s] &c. but Necessity the Mother of Invention has taught me to get the better of that for there being no Hadley[6] but mine aboard the French Vessell in which I came accross the Mediteranean. I found it necessary to do: the whole myself in this manner–I rule Columns marking by a line whether the Alt. Upper or Lower Limit & Nearest or furthest Limbs observd in Dist.

HMS	☉̲̅ alt	☾̲̅ alt	or |☾ (☾| or |☉) or ☉| Dist

I take an Alt. of ☉ then an Alt. of ☾ & then 3 distances ☉ & ☾ then another Alt of ☾ & lastly another Alt of ☉ calling *now* at each Observ[n] to a Person who marked with a pencil where the 2[d] Hand of the Watch was at when I called *now* & I wrote down immediately after Observation the time &c. By this means I have the rate of the ☉ & ☾ rising or falling in a given time; I take the Mean Distance as the *Distance* of ☉ & ☾ at the *mean* time of the 3 distances & find the ☉ & ☾ Alt by proportion for that time. These I call a *Sett*, & take as many setts as I can conveniently. This I look upon as a very great advantage as I often found it difficult aboard the M. of War as well as the Grenv[le] to get people without putting them to great Inconvenience but I do not now require an assistant who can even read the figures on the Watch. It is true the Weather has not permitted me to make much use of this *Discovery* but it may be convenient to others or perhaps here after to myself particularly at Land where the Alt. may be taken very exactly by the Artificial Horizon and I apprehend there is no way of determining the Long. more precisely than by the *Mean* of *many* ☾ Distances at Land, with the Hadley on such a Stand as Mr Ludlam describes.[7]

I have found your Needle is liable to rust. Whether this can be prevented by gilding or whether the Needle can be enclosed I leave you to Judge but I apprehend this is a defect very necessary to be remedied–The upright pillars thro' which the Center pins go are loose in the Box & when it hangs they do not always stand perpendicular. This I fancy is the Cause why the Dip was generally greater with the face one way than the other: I perceived it only in the Swallow & endeavourd to keep them upright.

It is very requisite to have a Glass Case which shall protect the Instrument from the Wind when hanging in the Gimbals for it often may be necessary to observe in the open air & I could not contrive any means effectually to screen it from the wind in the Swallow.

It would be a very great advantage if the Needle could *direct itself* to the Magnetic Meridian. *Barlow*,[8] whose Book published above a Century ago on this Subject you have probably seen, says an Inclinatory Needle that *does not* is good for nothing, but I cannot think of any means of doing it *universally* unless the Pillars Circle & Needle could be made light enough to turn round in pivots; I have an indistinct recollection of having heard a paper of M[r] Lorimer's read at the Society[9] in which something of the kind is proposed. However if the Compass is made to turn easy in a Ball Metal Socket I apprehend no very great Inconvenience will attend its confined state; but a Ship frequently yaws about so that it is impossible to set it to the Magnetic Meridian & yours could not be moved without disturbing the Needle.

The great Object is to make this Instrument serve as a Variation Compass[10] as well as an Inclinatory one; if this can be done as easily as I conceive it may, I doubt not they may be generally introduced into the India Shipping and by this means in a very few years a compleat series of Observations be obtained for one half the Globe. A great advantage in the Inclinatory Observations is that they do not require a sight of the Sun which being invisible at a particular hour frequently prevents observations of the Variation and I hope with an Instrument properly made the Dip may be observed at all times.

Altho' there is at present no plague in any part of the Levant I am confined here by Quarantine for 20 days and as my Stay in England may be very short I shall be greatly obliged to you if you will take the trouble to give directions to get two Inclinatory Compasses made for me.

I am so bad a Draughtsman that I am in some doubt whether you will be able to understand my Sketches; they are merely crude ideas leaving it intirely to you & our Friends at the Kings Head.

I apprehend all Compasses ought to have perpendicular Motion in their Socket because the Jerk of a Ship inclines them to spring up which Motion Gimbals will not prevent.

I forgot to mention that the Observations of the Variation in the Grenville were from the Ships Compasses & Observations of the Officers, as also in the Swallow: Nairne by some mistake disappointed me of the Variation Compass which I had ordered before I left England & he has since sent a Boat Compass instead of it; The Observations therefore of the Variation are not *better* than *common* but I have no reason to suppose them *worse* in the Grenville: The Swallow is so full of Iron about the quarter deck that she is a Vessell very ill adapted for Magnetical Observat^{s}. tho' no Care was wanting to avoid its influence as much as possible.

I do not know whether any Observations have been made to determine if the Variation is different when the Needle has its true inclination instead of lying horizontal as all the Variation & steering Compasses do. It may be necessary to correct this defect in case it should be one but I would not wish to encumber the Instrument with unnecessary refinements. The Simplicity of yours & the easiness with which Observations could be made being its great excellence, complex Instruments will never do for Sea but by *complex* I mean with respect to the *Observer* & not the *Maker*.

The Artificial Magnets ought to be in a stronger box for the weight of the Magnets by the motion of the Ship broke that in which yours were contained.

I apprehend the motion may in great measure be taken off by the aid of a Pendulum Ballance, which however is not necessary at all times, but only in rough seas. This you will be much better able to judge of than I am. If you think such a Ballance would be of use, the Stand should be made so as to take to pieces easily &, pack up in a Deal Case, as short as possible & no larger than sufficient to hold it with good Stowage; it will be convenient to have the Legs in 3 parts that the Stand may, by omitting, or using the middle piece be made of a different height as occasion requires. The Artificial Magnets may be packed in this Case which ought not with every thing in it to weigh more than a man can easily carry.

I apprehend the Spread or Span of the lower Gimbals cannot be too small; This Gimbal ring may be made to carry a square frame of sufficient width for the Glass Skreen to rest upon; & the Glass Skreen may be in 4 Sides with a cover to go over a tip to put to gether occasionally & when not wanted may slide into the sides of the Loaded Stand nn.[11]

I have not described the *Sights* because I would postpone them till I get to England: it will be sufficient to make the provision I have mentiond eeee.

I beg you will present my best respects to our Friend Mr Raper[12] & remember me to all Friends at the King's Head & Mitre.

I am

Dr Sir

Your most Obliged Hble Serv

ADalrymple

---

1 Cavendish Mss X(b), 6.

2 Cavendish made exhaustive studies of dipping needles, comparing those made by different instrument-makers, trying them in different locations, observing them near disturbing magnets, examining various constructions, studying their bending, and analyzing the error of the observed dip. Many dates found among these studies fall in the 1770s, at the time of his correspondence with Dalrymple on the subject. Cavendish Mss IX, 43, contains his directions for Dalrymple on the use of the dipping needle. Cavendish was recognized as an expert, having made "many, and very accurate observations . . . with several needles" for the Royal Society in 1775: George Gilpin, "Observations on the Variation, and on the Dip of the Magnetic Needle, Made at the Apartments of the Royal Society, between the Years 1786 and 1805 Inclusive," *PT* 96 (1806): 385–419, on 397.

3 John Alexander Panton was captain of "His Majesty's Sloop of War," *The Swallow*. Dalrymple did not last long in his new post in India; caught up in the politics of the East India Company, he was sent home in 1776. From 14 Oct. 1776 to 10 Jan. 1777, Dalrymple kept a register of the dipping needle on the *Swallow*, as it sailed off the coast of Arabia. Dalrymple, "Journal of a Voyage," 417–18.

4 Jean-Baptiste-Nicolas-Denis d'Après de Mannevillette, *Le Neptune oriental, ou routier general des cotes des Indes orientales et de la China* . . . (Paris, 1745); in 1775 it reappeared in 2 vols.

5 A form of suspension that enables a body, here a clock, to remain level when its support tips.

6 Reflecting quadrant (octant) invented by John Hadley (1682–1744), optical instrument-maker, F.R.S. 1717. Taylor, *Mathematical Practitioners*, 123–24.

7 William Ludlam, *Directions for the Use of Hadley's Quadrant, with Remarks on the Construction of That Instrument* (London, 1771). William Ludlam (1717–88), mathematician and astronomer, was a fellow of St. John's College, Cambridge until 1768, when he accepted a rectory from his college. "Ludlam," *DNB* 12:254–55.

[8] William Barlow or Barlowe (d. 1625), a younger contemporary of William Gilbert, archdeacon of Salisbury, author of *Magneticall Advertisements* (London, 1613, 1616, 1618). Wolf, *History of Science . . . 16th and17th Centuries* 1:298.

[9] J. Lorimer, "Description of a New Dipping-Needle," *PT* 65 (1775): 79–84.

[10] The variation compass measures the angle between a magnetic needle and the geographical meridian. In this compass the magnetic needle is free to turn in the horizontal plane.

[11] "nn" and in the next paragraph "eeee" evidently refer to "sketches" Dalrymple mentions. They have been separated from this letter.

[12] Matthew Raper, F.R.S. 1754, elected member of the Royal Society Club on the same day as Cavendish, may have been ill, for he died a year or two after this letter, on 29 July 1779. Geikie, *Royal Society Club*, 71, 145. Interested in astronomy and antiquity, Raper published several papers in the *Philosophical Transactions*. From time to time he served on the council of the Royal Society; Cavendish had recently served with him on committees of the Society; see letter 5, notes 2 and 7.

Fig. 1.

Fig. 2.

105. *Earth Magnetic Instruments. Fig. 1. Cavendish's dipping needle. Fig. 2. Cavendish's variation needle. Photographs by the authors. By permission of the Science Museum, London/Science & Society Picture Library.*

11. FROM JEAN ANDRÉ DELUC
28 JANUARY 1779

From the original letter in the Devonshire Collections, Chatsworth[1]

A Franeker Université de Frise

1778

X^{bre}. 26 à 11h. du mat. Bar. 30p.813/4 *au pied anglois.* Elevation qui surpasse d'1/4 de ligne la plus grande depuis 8 ans–

29. . . à 6h. du Soir 29.3.–

1779 30. . . 29.8.–

Janv. 1. . . 3h. du Matin . . . . 28.7.1/2 Ce qui, est à 1 ligne près le plus bas point où il aît été dans ces mêmes 8 ans

. . . . 10h. du Soir 29.10 5/8

3. . . 8h. du matin 30.7 1/8

La première Nuit de l'année fut aussi orageuse en Frise qu'en Angleterre, & il y eut des tonnerres & des éclairs.

M. De Luc fait bien des complimens à Monsr Cavendish, sachant qu'il donne attention aux observations Météorologiques, qui se font à la Soc. roy^{le} & ne doutant pas qu'il n'en âit apporté une toute [attention] particulière aux grandes variations du Bar. De la fin de l'année dernière & du commencement de celle-ci, il lui envoye copie des observations faites ces jours là en Frise par le grand Météoronome de Franeker, Monsr le Prof^r Van Swinden.[2]

Ce Prof^r à qui la Meteorologie doit déja tants, & devra toujours davantage, qui surtout a remporté le Prix à l'Ac. des Sc. de Paris sur la meilleure construction des Boussoles, donne une attention particulière à tout ce qui tient au Magnétisme & à toutes les variations diurnes & annuelles de l'aiguille aimantée,[3] & il a témoigné à M De Luc qu'il seroit charmé que quelque amateur à Londres voulut entrer en correspondance avec lui sur cet intéressant sujet.

Pimlico le 28 Janv. 1779

---

[1] Cavendish Mss X(b), 8.

[2] Jan Henrick van Swinden (1746–1823), meteorologist and natural philosopher, professor of philosophy, logic, and metaphysics at Franeker University in the Netherlands. Hackmann, "Swinden," *DSB* 13:183–84.

[3] With Charles Augustin Coulomb, in 1777 Swinden received a gold medal from the Paris Academy for an essay on the magnetic needle. Best known for his precise, patient work in meteorology, he, together with his students at the university, took hourly observations of terrestrial magnetism for ten years. Ibid.

11T. TRANSLATION OF LETTER FROM DELUC
28 JANUARY 1779

From the original letter in the Devonshire Collections, Chatsworth

At Franeker University of Frise

1778

Dec. 26 at 11:00 in the morning Bar. 30p.81¾ *on the English scale.* At a height which surpasses by ¼ of a line the greatest height in 8 years–

29 at 6:00 in the evening 29.3.–

1779 30 29.8.–

Jan. 1 3:00 in the morning 28.7.½ which is nearly within 1 line of the lowest point in these same 8 years

10:00 in the evening 29.10⅝

3 8:00 in the morning 30.7⅛

The first night of the year was as stormy in Frise as in England, and there was thunder and lightning.

M. Deluc sends his compliments to Mr. Cavendish, knowing that he pays attention to meteorological observations that are made at the Royal Society, and not doubting that he takes a most particular interest in the great variations of the barometer. From the end of last year through the beginning of this one, he [Deluc] sends him copies of observations made at that time in Frise by the great meteorologist from Franeker, M. Prof. van Swinden.

This professor, to whom meteorology already owes so much, and will always be indebted to, who moreover won the prize of the Academy of Sciences in Paris for the best construction of compasses takes a particular interest in all that relates to magnetism and all the diurnal and annual variations of the magnetic needle, and he informed M. Deluc that he would be delighted if a London amateur wished to enter into correspondence with him on this interesting subject.

Pimlico 28 January 1779

12. TO WILLIAM NORRIS[1]

[FEBRUARY 1780]

From the original letter in the Society of Antiquaries[2]

Mr Cavendish[3] presents his compliments to Mr Norris & sends him an account with drawings of a curious Pagoda near Bombay which he would be glad if he would read to the Society. It is extracted by Mr Dalrymple of this society from a journal in the possession of the India company.[4] Mr Dalrymple informs him that there is also a description of the same pagoda in the last volume of Neuburg's travels but that description was taken at a time when the building was less perfect than when this account was made & besides that work is in a language very little understood here & has not yet been translated.

---

[1] William Norris (1719–91), secretary of the Society of Antiquaries. "Norris," *DNB* 14:591.

[2] Archive of the Society of Antiquaries of London, c.5.

[3] Like Dalrymple, Cavendish was a Fellow of the Society of Antiquaries. Elected on 25 Feb. 1773, Cavendish does not seem to have been active in the Society; this letter is the only one by him in its records. Minute Book, Society of Antiquaries, 12:580.

[4] In 1779 Dalrymple had been appointed hydrographer to the East India Company. The paper Cavendish forwarded to the Society for Dalrymple was evidently, "Account of a Curious Pagoda Near Bombay, Drawn up by Captain Pyke, Who Was Afterwards Governor of St. Helena. It Is Dated from on Board the Stringer East-Indiaman in Bombay Harbour 1712, and Is Illustrated with Drawings. This Extract Was Made from the Captain's Journal in Possession of the Honourable East-India Company. By Alexander Dalrymple, Esq. F.R. and A.S. and Communicated to the Society, Feb. 10, 1780," *Archaelogia* 7 (1785): 323–32.

13. FROM FREDERICK CAVENDISH[1]

1 MARCH 1780

From the original letter in the Devonshire Collections, Chatsworth[2]

Market Street
Wed. Mar 1st 1780

Dear Brother,

As I know you observe the Aurora Borealis with much attention,[3] I send you an account of one which appeared last Night, and which in some respects was the most remarkable I have known. It had the most perfect Corona I ever beheld, with Radii streaming down on all sides, and overspreading *the whole* Hemisphere. The Corona was situated almost close to the hinder foot of Ursa Major. Very near to the two Stars ω and γ; but rather on that side which is nearest to the Stars Ψ and β and in Line with them. The Aurora was of a pale colour, tho' I am inform'd that before I observ'd it, the Sky was very Red in the Eastern quarter (as describ'd to me) sometimes in a Flush, and sometimes darting up the Heavens. And I myself occasionally observ'd a Flush of Red, in the West, and in other directions; 'tho it was not the general tenour of its' appearance. It was a little tremulous in its' motion, by no means darting quick, as I have sometimes observ'd it; but varying its' Figure sometimes, and sometimes disappearing. The Situation of the Corona was always the same, its' Radii always concentrating in the same Point. Sometimes the Space within the Corona was pretty clear; at other times fill'd nearly, with irregular Streams of luminous matter, hurried confusedly together, darting quick, and again instantly disappearing.

It was near 10.o'Clock when I first perceiv'd it (it had been observ'd by others, an hour or two sooner) but it disappearing soon after, I did not attend to it 'till looking at the Thermometer a little before 12.o'Clock, I found the Aurora exceeding bright. I accordingly took my Plan of the Stars, in order to determine the precise situation of the Corona. I attended to it for near an hour, and am certain as to the Situation I have describ'd.

Give my Duty to my Father. I hope ye are both in good Health.

I am your affectionate
Brother
Frederick Cavendish.

[In Henry Cavendish's handwriting]:

$\left.\begin{array}{r}\text{Altitude}\\ \text{azim.}\end{array}\right\}$ γ about $\begin{array}{l}72^\circ\\ \text{11 East}\end{array}$ at 12 o clock

alt. Ψ about 85 all 4 stars nearly in the same vertical circle

[address]:
Honble Henry Cavendish
at Lord Charles Cavendish's
Great Marlborough
Street
London

---

[1] Frederick Cavendish (1733–1812), Henry's brother. "Memoirs of the Late Frederick Cavendish, Esq.," *Gentleman's Magazine* 82 (1812): 289–91.

[2] Cavendish Mss X(b), 9. Published in *Sci. Pap.* 2:69.

[3] Cavendish later published an analysis of three accounts of an uncommon aurora, "On the Height of the Luminous Arch Which Was Seen on Feb. 23, 1784," *PT* 80 (1790): 101–5.

14. FROM WILLIAM HERSCHEL[1]

[AFTER 26 FEBRUARY 1782][2]

From the original letter in the Royal Astronomical Society[3]

Memorandum for Mr Cavendish

By a letter from the Revd Mr Hornsby[4]- I find that Mr Cavendish has computed several Observations of the Comet made by Dr Maskelyne and Mr Hornsby and that in all these computations my observations differ 2 min: & more *in defect*, when others do not differ more than ½ a minute, almost always much less, and their difference generally *in excess*.[5] From this Mr Hornsby thinks there must be some considerable error in my observations. I could wish Mr Cavendish to be acquainted that there is in my opinion no possibiliy of an error that can amount to more than 5″ in any of my observations except I have marked it as such, and that in general the error is much less than 5″. The reason of the disagreement I imagine is owing to a mistake in the Stars. For as I could not determine the Situation of them otherwise than by an eye draught I suppose either Dr Maskelyne or Mr Hornsby must have taken the wrong stars when they gave Mr Cavendish my observations. I can find my stars at any time & as I shall soon be in Town I hope to shew them to Dr Maskelyne in order that he may settle their places with more precision. The Telescopic stars α β γ &c are so small as not to be visible in my finder, so that it is very easy to mistake them.

---

[1] William Herschel (1738–1822), astronomer, F.R.S. 1781. "Herschel," *DNB* 9:719–25, on 719–20.

[2] The letter Herschel refers to is from Thomas Hornsby, 26 Feb. 1782, Royal Astronomical Society, Mss Herschel, W 1/13, H.29.

[3] Mss Herschel, W 1/1, p. 56. This letter-memorandum is published in part in Lubbock, *Herschel Chronicle*, 106–7.

[4] Thomas Hornsby (1733–1810), astronomer, succeeded James Bradley as Savilian professor of astronomy at Oxford University in 1763. North, "Hornsby," *DSB* 6:511–12.

[5] In March 1781 Herschel discovered what he took to be a faint comet. In May of that year he and Hornsby began corresponding about it, first about Hornsby's efforts to find it, and then about its orbit. The correspondence went smoothly until February of the following year, when Hornsby wrote to Herschel, "I presume you have been informed that Mr Cavendish has computed several obs^ns^ of the Comet made by Dr Maskelyne & myself, as also your first obs^n^. He has determined its mean Distance to be not more than 19 times the Earth's Distance, & not less than 17 or 17½, . . . but in all these Comparisons your obs^n^ differs 2 minutes & more in defect, when the others do not differ more than ½ a minute, almost always much less, & their difference generally in excess. There must therefore I think be some considerable error in your obs^n^." In the meantime A. J. Lexell, in St. Petersburg, announced that the object was not a comet but a planet. It was in fact Uranus, the seventh major planet from the sun, and the first new planet discovered in historical times. It would change Herschel's life, but in his correspondence with Hornsby and Cavendish, he still referred to it as a comet. Cavendish Mss VIII, 8, contains a packet of seventeen sheets from 1781 on the computation of "Hirschel's Planet." On the distance of Uranus from the sun, about nineteen times the distance of the earth, Cavendish was right, but the orbit he calculated was probably off, as he worked with observations taken over less than a year, and the period of the planet is about eighty-four years. Lubbock, *Herschel Chronicle*, 107. Hornsby to Herschel, 24 and 31 Mar., 14 Apr., 14 Oct. 1781, 26 Feb. 1782, Royal Astronomical Society, Mss Herschel, W 1/13, H.25–29. Herschel to Hornsby, 22 May 1781 and 1 Feb. 1782, ibid., W 1/1, pp. 12, 31–33.

15. TO CHARLES BLAGDEN[1]

3 DECEMBER [1782]

From the original letter in the Royal Society[2]

Mr Cavendish presents his compliments to Dr Blagden & returns his paper with many thanks. The thing which struck him as some little difficulty is, that at Jan. 1 8.0 AM the ☿ in the thermometer had been 12 hours below the point of freezing, & must therefore have been frozen solid both in the ball & tube. One would therefore have expected that after this it would either have remained stationary, or if by any means it had been loosened in the tube & put in motion, it would have sunk into the ball; whereas 2 hours after it sunk lower, but not more than 6 degrees.[3]

Tuesday Dec. 3

---

1 Charles Blagden (1748–1820), physician to the army, F.R.S. 1772, from 1784 secretary of the Royal Society. Scott, "Blagden," *DSB* 2:186.

2 Blagden Letters, C.27.

3 The secretary of the Royal Society, Matthew Maty, at the request of the Society, applied to the Hudson's Bay Company to carry out experiments; see letter 6. Thomas Hutchins offered to do the experiments, in the course of which he twice froze mercury in 1775. Hutchins, "An Account of Some Attempts to Freeze Quicksilver, at Albany Fort, in Hudson's Bay, in the Year 1775; with Observations on the Dipping-Needle," *PT* 66 (1776): 174–81, on 176. In 1776, in London, instruments were made to enable Hutchins to continue with his experiments, but owing to some confusion they were not sent until 1781, when Cavendish supplied Hutchins with thermometers, apparatus, and directions. Cavendish Mss III(a), 14c; also *Sci. Pap.* 2:381–84. In the winter of 1781–82, Hutchins resumed his experiments: he made ten altogether, reading three instruments: a mercury thermometer, a spirit thermometer, and an "apparatus" of Cavendish's design, the latter giving the correct reading, −39° Fahrenheit, for the freezing point of mercury. Cavendish was confirmed in his surmise that the rapid fall of the mercury in the thermometer after this point, through hundreds of degrees, was due to the contraction of mercury upon freezing, about 1/23rd of its bulk. In November 1782, Blagden noted in his diary that an account by Thomas Hutchins had arrived, telling of his successful experiments on the freezing of mercury. One month later, he noted that Cavendish advised him, Blagden, to write a history of the whole subject. 23 Nov. and 23 Dec. 1782, Charles Blagden Diary, Royal Society, 1. In the *Philosophical Transactions* for 1783, Hutchins's experiments and Cavendish's analysis of them were published side by side, with Blagden's history appearing immediately after Cavendish's. Hutchins, "Experiments for Ascertaining the Point of Mercurial Congelation," *PT* 73 (1783): *303–*370, on *317. Cavendish, "Observations on Mr. Hutchins's Experiments for Determining the Degree of Cold at Which Quicksilver Freezes," *PT* 73 (1783): 303–28. Charles Blagden, "History of the Congelation of Quicksilver," *PT* 73 (1783): 329–97, on 341–46. See letter 18.

16. FROM JOHN MICHELL[1]

26 MAY 1783

From the original letter in the Devonshire Collections, Chatsworth[2]

Dear Sir;

I have taken the liberty of sending you herewith a paper relating to the subject, upon which I had a little talk with you, when last in London. The fear of being troublesome so soon after the loss of Ld Charles[3] has made me defer sending it for some time, & perhaps I ought still to ask your pardon for sending it so soon, as I have done; but as I dont wish you to give yourself the least trouble about it, till it is perfectly agreable to you, I hope you will be so good as to excuse me, if I am guilty of any impropriety.

Besides having already conversed with you upon the subject of the paper, I send you, & knowing no one more capable of judging properly of it than yourself,[4] I had another reason for wishing to have it come to the Society through your hands, for the sake of the greater respect & attention it will naturally receive from the credit of your patronage. I have, for the same reason, as well as some others, which you will easily guess at, addressed a Letter to you, which stands at the head of it, & which, if the Society should do me the honour to print the paper in their Transactions, I should wish to have printed along with it, to serve as a sort of introduction to it. I imagine there will hardly be time to present it & get it read before the recess:[5] I am not very sollicitous about it, only, if it is defer'd to next Winter, I shall be obliged to you not to let the principle of it go abroad, till the paper itself can come before the Society, for reasons, that will be sufficiently obvious to you. If the Society should think proper to print it, if it is not inconvenient, I should wish to have the Sheets sent to Thornhill to be corrected, in case I should not happen to be in London at the time: Or at least I should wish to know when it is printed, that I may have the opportunity of ordering a few Copies for my own use, to give away to such friends as are not members.

I shall not trouble you with any account about the great Telescope,[6] & other schemes at present, only so far as just to say, that I expect to be able to give it a fair trial in due time, & for the rest, I hope to talk with you farther, some time about this time twelve months, when I propose, if ill health or some other accident does not prevent me, to come to London.[7] Illness & but an indifferent state of health for some months past, have prevented me from getting forwards this Winter, so fast as I otherwise meant to have done: I dont yet look upon myself as perfectly recover'd; but I am much better, than I have been, & keep mending, I hope, dayly. With much respect & esteem, I have

Thornhill (near Wakefield)
26 May 1783

the honour to be, Dear Sir,
Your obedient humble Servt
J. Michell

1 John Michell (1724–93), rector of Thornhill, Yorkshire, F.R.S. 1760. "Michell," *DNB* 13:333–34.

2 Cavendish Mss New Correspondence.

3 Lord Charles Cavendish, Henry's father, died "on or about" 28 April 1783. Devon. Coll., L/31/37.

4 Michell had good reason to expect a sympathetic reading of this, his second and last paper on stars. His two papers were closely related in content, and Cavendish was known to have formed a good opinion of the first, published in 1767. William Watson, Jr., wrote to his friend William Herschel that he was "glad to find that you have lately examined Mr Michel's paper, wch you may remember I first pointed out to your notice. I know that some of the closest & chastest reasoners I am acquainted with approve of it, such as Mr Henry Cavendish." Watson to Herschel, 16 Mar. 1783, Royal Astronomical Society, Mss Herschel, W 1/13, W.24.

5 Michell's paper would not be read until 27 November 1783, after the recess of the Royal Society: "On the Means of Discovering the Distance, Magnitude, &c. of the Fixed Stars, in Consequence of the Diminution of the Velocity of Their Light, In Case Such a Diminution Should Be Found to Take Place in Any of Them, and Such Other Data Should Be Procured from Observations, as Would Be Farther Necessary for That Purpose. By the Rev. John Michell, B.D.F.R.S. In a letter to Henry Cavendish, Esq. F.R.S. and A.S.," *PT* 74 (1784): 35–57.

6 Michell was known to be making a powerful reflecting telescope of short focal length. Michell described it: "The diameter by shrinking in cooling, &c. is not quite 30 Inches, as I at first proposed, but it is full 29½ & the focal length of it, when finished is intended to be no more than ten feet, so that the whole Telescope, when compleated, will not much exceed 12½ or 13 feet though of the Newtonian form." "My great speculum weighd between 3$\overset{a}{4}$0 & 3$\overset{a}{5}$0. It is in the thickest part very near three inches thick, it may indeed in some sense be consider'd, as three inches & quarter thick. It is entirely supported by springs, which are contrived in such a manner, as to make as little inequality as possible in the pressure in different situations, & the whole of the pressure & support will be upon the thickest part of it." Michell to William Herschel, 22 Jan. and 2 April 1781. Royal Astronomical Society, Mss Herschel, W 1/13, M.99 and 101. This telescope would have exceeded Herschel's. Blagden wrote to Michell of "wonders" that the latter performed, "yet yours of so much larger an aperture, having more than double the quantity of light, is an object of constant inquiry to him [Herschel] as well as to your other friends of the Monday Club." Blagden to Michell, 25 Apr. 1785, draft, Blagden Letterbook, Yale. Herschel later would make a mirror almost double the diameter of Michell's, though his most important work was done with his smaller ones.

7 Ever since becoming rector of Thornhill in Yorkshire in 1767, Michell made the long journey to London as often as circumstances permitted, which were not as often as he would have liked. To Herschel he explained, "I have no thoughts of coming to Town this Winter; the expence of such a journey is more than I can afford every year, at least whilest I have Telescopes in hand. . . . I wish it was in my power to see all my friends there once a year & to learn what was going forward in the literary world; but it is necessary to conform oneself to circumstances." Michell to Herschel, 22 Jan. 1781. In the year he began to correspond with Cavendish, 1783, Michell was fifty-nine, and ill health made his traveling plans uncertain. Michell had, however, been to London recently, as he noted in the letter accompanying his paper. In the following year, 1784, after his paper on the stars, he visited London for at least a month and a half, as a guest attending every weekly dinner of the Royal Society Club between 6 May and 24 June. Royal Society Club, Minute Book, Royal Society, vol. 7. Geikie, *Michell*, 20, supposes that Michell had "some appointment or duty which for a number of years took him annually to London."

17. FROM JOHN MICHELL

26 MAY 1783

From the *Philosophical Transactions of the Royal Society of London*[1]

Thornhill, May 26, 1783.

Dear Sir,

The method, which I mentioned to you when I was last in London, by which it might perhaps be possible to find the distance, magnitude, and weight of some of the fixed stars, by means of the diminution of the velocity of their light,[2] occurred to me soon after I wrote what is mentioned by Dr. Priestley in his History of Optics,[3] concerning the diminution of the velocity of light in consequence of the attraction of the sun; but the extreme difficulty, and perhaps impossibility, of procuring the other data necessary for this purpose appeared to me to be such objections against the scheme, when I first thought of it, that I gave it then no farther consideration. As some late observations,[4] however, begin to give us a little more chance of procuring some at least of these data, I thought it would not be amiss, that astronomers should be apprized of the method, I propose (which, as far as I know, has not been suggested by any one else) lest, for want of being aware of the use, which may be made of them, they should neglect to make the proper observations, when in their power; I shall therefore beg the favour of you to present the following paper[5] on this subject to the Royal Society.

I am, &c.

---

[1] This letter to Henry Cavendish was printed at the beginning of John Michell, "On the Means of Discovering the Distance," 35–36.

[2] The principle of Michell's paper is Newton's law of universal gravitation, as laid down in the fourth paragraph of the paper: "Let us now suppose the particles of light to be attracted in the same manner as all other bodies with which we are acquainted; that is, by forces bearing the same proportion to their *vis inertiae*, of which there can be no reasonable doubt, gravitation being, as far as we know, or have any reason to believe, an universal law of nature." Upon this supposition, large stars should attract the light they emit sufficiently to retard the velocity of the light in detectable measure. If a star were very large, with a radius 500 times that of the sun and of the same density as the sun, Michell calculated, it would attract back to itself all of its light, and we would never see it. Michell, "On the Means of Discovering the Distance," 35, 37, 42. The possibility of Newtonian invisible stars was envisioned before Einsteinian black holes of the twentieth century. Simon Schaffer, "John Michell and Black Holes," *Journal for the History of Astronomy* 10 (1979): 42–43. Goodricke's colleague in the observation of variable stars, Edward Pigott, speculated that some stars disappear and that others never have shone. He thought that there might be as many "*unenlightened stars*," which remain in "*eternal darkness*," as visible stars. "An Investigation of All the Changes of the Variable Star in Sobieski's Shield, . . . ; with Conjectures Respecting Unenlightened Heavenly Bodies," *PT* 95 (1805): 131–54, on 152–53.

[3] Joseph Priestley, *The History and Present State of Discoveries Relating to Vision, Light, and Colours*, 2 vols. (London, 1772). The discussion of the proportion that the force by which light is propelled from stars bears to the force of gravity is on 1:786–91. From his calculation of the great disproportion of the two forces, Michell observed, on p. 789, "what an extremely little diminution the velocity of light can suffer by the attraction of the sun."

[4] William Herschel, "Catalogue of Double Stars," *PT* 72 (1782): 112–62.

[5] See last letter, note 5.

18. TO JOHN MICHELL
27 MAY 1783

From the original draft letter in the Devonshire Collections, Chatsworth[1]

27 May 1783

D[ear] S[ir]

I am much obliged to you for your letter[2] & am glad you put your thoughts on this subject upon paper. I talked to S^r J[oseph] B[anks][3] about it as soon as I received it but found that there are so many papers on hand that there will be no possib[ility] of reading it before the recess. I am sorry however that you wish to have the principle kept secret. The surest way of securing merit[4] to the author is to let it be known as soon as possible & those who act otherwise commonly find themselves forestalled by others. But in the present case I can not conceive why you should wish to have it kept secret for when you was last in town you made no secret of the principle but mentiond it openly at our mondays meeting[5] & if I mistake not at other places & I have frequently heard it talked of since then. As to the method you propose for determining whether the vel[ocity] [of] light is diminished (which seems a very good one) I do not remember that you did mention that but as I do not imagine that you was likely soon to make any exper. of that kind yourself I see no reason why you should wish to keep that secret. On the whole I think that instead of your desiring <me> to keep the princ[iple] of the paper secret you ought rather to wish me to shew the paper to as many of your friends as are desirous of reading it.[6]

In Art. 10 you seem to have expressed yourself contrary to your real meaning. You say the dens[ity] of the cent[ral] body remaining the same the vel. of a body falling towards it from an infinite height will always be at the same distance from the point C taken any where without the central body as the sem[i] di[ameter] of the central body. I suppose you mean that it will be so not at the same distance from C but at the same distance in proportion to the sem. di supposing that distance to be greater than the sem. di. If I am right & you will tell me in what manner you would have it alterd I can do it most likely without sending back the paper. It seems not to affect any other part of the paper as in the next coroll[ary] & in art. 16 you refer to it conform[able] to what I suppose to be your true meaning.

I am very glad to hear that you[r] health is better & continuing to mend. We heard before that it had not been well this winter. Whenever you are disposed that way I shall be very glad to hear of any schemes you are upon & of your progress in the telescope. If your health does not allow you to go on with that I hope it may at least permit the easier & less laborious employment of weighing the world[7] & for my own part, I[8] do not know whether I had not rather hear that you had given that exper. a fair trial than that you had finished the great telescope.

Mr Goodrich[9] of Yorkshire has found that the diminution of light of the star Algol returns in a period of $2^d\ 21^h$. The time during which it appears with a diminished lig[h]t is 7^h & the dimin. of light supposed about ⅔. One of the epochs of the greatest obscuration was[10] It has been seen also by Mr Kirwan.[11] 2 different ways of accounting for it have been thought of by spots & by a planet revolving round it. If by the 1st it is necessary to suppose that almost all the luminous part of the star is placed in a small part of that narrow zone which is hid from our eye only 7 hours. If by a planet it is necessary to suppose either that the planet is incompassed with an hazy atm[osphere] bigger than the star or else that the plan. is not much less than the star & that the density of both are several times less than that of the sun. Otherwise the time of obscuration would not be so great.

We have lately had a paper of Mr Hirsch.[12] to shew that the sun & planetary sistem is moving very fast. I forget the direction. His principal argument is that the proper motion of almost all the stars whose proper motion is laid down either in D^r M[askelyne]^s tables[13] or in Mayers posthumous works[14] are in that direction which agrees with this supposition.[15]

Mr Hutch[ins][16] who before froze ☿ at Hudsons bay has given us some very accurate experiments for determining the point at which it freezes. They were made chiefly with an app[aratus] sent by me for that purpose. He has shewn in the most convincing manner that it freezes at 39 below 0 that the very low degrees to which the therm[ometer]s have been made to sink have been owing (as you most likely was aware of) to the contraction of the ☿ in freezing that ☿ as well as water is capable of being coold a little below the freezing point without freezing & jumps suddenly up to it as soon as it begins to freeze that the greatest cold produced by his freezing mixtures was about 45 below 0 though in some of his exp[eriments] the natural cold was near 39. He also froze ☿ by the natural cold & determined its freezing point that way. I have given a paper to the Soc[iety] to explain his exper.[17] & Dr Blag[den] has given a very good account of what has been done about freezing ☿ both by artif[icial] & natural cold.[18] Besides Siberia & Hudsons bay it has been frozen naturally in Sweden & perhaps at Gottingen. I froze it this winter artificially at Hampstead.[19]

---

1 Cavendish Mss New Correspondence.

2 Letter 17.

3 Sir Joseph Banks (1743–1820), botanist, F.R.S. 1766, president of the Royal Society from 1778 to the end of his life. Foote, "Banks," *DSB* 1:433–37.

4 We have given a probable reading of this passage, omitting a "the" and an "of." Cavendish wrote, "The surest way of securing the merit of an invention to the author . . ." He crossed out "an invention," replacing it with "discovery," which he also then crossed out.

5 Monday Club, meeting weekly, on Mondays, at the George and Vulture Tavern, located in George Yard, Lombard Street.

6 Michell followed Cavendish's advice. Letters 19, 20.

7 This is the first we read of "weighing the world," Michell's experiment to determine the average density of the earth by means of a torsion balance. Michell made the apparatus, but he evidently did not do the experiment. After Michell's death, Cavendish acquired the apparatus and rebuilt it,

as he reported in "Experiments to Determine the Density of the Earth", *PT* 88 (1798): 469–526, on 469.

[8] Here Cavendish tried three phrasings before he settled on a fourth: "I had rather hear," "I think I had," and another which is illegible because of the crossings out.

[9] John Goodricke (1764–86), whose name was spelled a number of ways by Cavendish and Michell, to whom it was unfamiliar, was a deaf-mute astronomical prodigy living in York, who had just communicated his first paper to the Royal Society. Cavendish would have heard it read at the meeting of the Society on 15 May, less than two weeks before he wrote to Michell mentioning it. The paper, which was about the periodic variation of the light from the star Algol, was published later that year, for which Goodricke received the Copley Medal of the Society: "A Series of Observations on, and a Discovery of, the Period of the Variation of the Light of the Bright Star in the Head of Medusa, Called Algol," *PT* 73 (1783): 474–92. One of Goodricke's surmises, and one which Michell would develop, was that the variation was owing to the "interposition of a large body revolving round Algol." That Algol is indeed an eclipsing variable was only firmly established a century later. Goodricke's other surmise was that Algol had "some kind of motion of its own, whereby part of its body, covered with spots or such like matter, is periodically turned towards the earth," p. 482. Goodricke's two surmises, including the correct one, were not altogether remarkable, Herschel having included them among the possible causes of the changes of stars in a paper read two months before Goodricke's, "On the Proper Motion of the Sun and Solar System; with an Account of Several Changes That Have Happened Among the Fixed Stars Since the Time of Mr. Flamsteed," *PT* 73 (1783): 247–83, on 259; read 6 Mar. 1783. In the short time remaining to him, Goodricke went on to discover the periodically variable light from two other stars, δ Cephei and β Lyrae, instances of other classes of variable stars. Kopak, "Goodricke," *DSB* 5:467–69.

[10] Cavendish left a space after "was," probably intending to add a number.

[11] Richard Kirwan (1733?–1812), F.R.S. 1780, is best known for his work in chemistry, but he had very broad interests in the physical sciences, including astronomy. Born in Ireland, he was living in London in 1783. Scott, "Kirwan," *DSB* 7:387–90.

[12] William Herschel had been elected to the Royal Society only in 1781, and he had moved from Bath to Datchet, near London, in 1782. Although he had received the Copley Medal for discovering a new planet, Uranus, in 1781, his renown was still recent enough for Cavendish to misspell his name.

[13] Herschel regarded Nevil Maskelyne as an ally who believed as he did that most or all of the stars have a proper motion. Herschel, "On the Proper Motion of the Sun," 260. As a companion to his annual *Nautical Almanac and Astronomical Ephemeris*, Maskelyne published *Requisite Tables*. These two works were Maskelyne's "greatest contribution" to astronomy and navigation. Howse, *Maskelyne*, 85.

[14] Herschel first used an extract given him by J.-J. L. de Lalande of Tobias Mayer's tables of proper motions of stars. Then Alexander Aubert gave him a "scarce edition" of Mayer's original work, the posthumous *Opera inedita Tobiae Mayeri* (Göttingen, 1775). Herschel, "On the Proper Motion of the Sun," 274. Johann Tobias Mayer (1723–62), Göttingen University astronomer. Forbes, "Mayer," *DSB* 9:232–35.

[15] Drawing upon evidence that certain stars had moved, and inferring from the principle of attraction that all stars moved and that the sun therefore must move, and for support citing Michell on the probable motion of the sun, Herschel concluded that the observed proper motion of stars is in part only an "*apparent*" motion, owing to the motion of the sun and its planets with respect to the stars. The motion was in a determinable direction, which Cavendish did not remember, that of the constellation Hercules. "On the Proper Motion of the Sun," 248, 260, 277.

[16] Thomas Hutchins (1730–89), governor of Albany Fort, Hudson Bay. See letter 15, note 3.

[17] Cavendish, "Observations on Mr. Hutchins' Experiments."

[18] Blagden, "History of the Congelation of Quicksilver." See letter 15, note 3.

[19] Using a freezing mixture, Cavendish froze mercury at his house in Hampstead on 26 Feb. 1783, as Blagden recorded the next day. 27 Feb. 1783, Charles Blagden Diary, Royal Society, 1.

19. FROM JOHN MICHELL

2 JULY 1783

From the original letter in the Devonshire Collections. Chatsworth[1]

Dear Sir

I am much obliged to you for your Letter of the 3d Ult,[2] which I received on the Sunday following. Your observation of the mistake I have been guilty of in the 10th Art. is perfectly right, & I owe you many thanks for preventing it from appearing in public, which it probably would have done, in case the Society should do me the honour to print the paper, if you had no been so good as to have given it attention enough to detect it. I will endeavour to correct it below.

Though I had given some obscure hints, about the principle of my paper, to other friends when I was last in London, yet except what I had said to yourself, I apprehended they were too obscure to have the drift of them fully understood; but whether they did or did not give a sufficient clue to it, upon farther consideration, I believe you are right, & shall therefore have no objections to your permitting any one, you think proper to read it; indeed the more people see it the better, if it is divulged at all.

The observation of Mr Goodrick's concerning Algol is a very curious one. The most probable way of accounting for it, that I can think of, & which I should think not very unlikely to be the real case, if it did not require the concurrence of so many circumstances, is as follows. I would suppose, that this star consists in fact of two stars,[3] one a central one much larger than the other, & the other, a smaller one revolving round it in 69 hours, the period assigned for the return of it's darker appearance. I would suppose the bigger star to be luminous, as well as the smaller one, but that it is so much less so, that notwithstanding the difference of size, it produces but half as much light as the other. I would farther suppose, that the satellite revolves in an excentric orbit, whose major axis produced passes through the Earth or nearly so, & that it's perihelion lies on this side. Let us suppose for instance, that the major axis of the ellipse, it revolves in is to it's minor axis in the proportion of 10 to 6, & consequently that the perihelion distance is only 1/9 of it's aphelion distance. Now because the period of the revolving star is only 69 hours, if the central body is of the same density with the Sun, the mean distance of the revolving star, from the centre of the central one must be equal to about eight semidiameters & half of this latter, whose semidiameter therefore must be equal to the fraction 5/8,5 or 0,58823[4] decimal parts of an unit, ten of which are equal to the major axis of the ellipse, in which the satellite revolves, & one to it's perihelion distance from it's principal. If 0,58823 represents the semidiameter of the central star, the double of that quantity or 1,17646 will represent it's whole diameter, & consequently the satellite may be eclipsed during the time it is passing through an arc at the aphelion, which would be subtended by that quantity. Now it will appear upon computation, that the area of a sector contained between two lines drawn from the extremities of an arc, lying equally on each side one of the extremities of the major axis of an ellipse, of the dimensions above supposed, to the farther focus, the subtense of the arc being 1,17646 will be to the whole area of the ellipse, as 112, to 1000 very nearly, which as the whole area of the ellipse corresponds to 69 hours will amount to almost seven hours & three quarters, which is almost three quarters of an hour more than we want; but if we had a mind to make every thing correspond exactly, this might easily be done by supposing the central body a little denser, or the orbit of the revolving body not quite so excentric, or by supposing the major axis, not to point exactly at the Earth, but only nearly so.

If this should happen to be the true solution of the case, the prism may possibly inform us, almost with certainty, that it is so; for supposing the central star should be large enough to affect the velocity of the light emitted from it, & the other not so, the prism would then separate the two stars from each other, & the smaller but more luminous star would entirely disappear for seven hours, the time it should be eclipsed; nay & the proportion of the satellite's diameter to the size of it's orbit might be perhaps discover'd from the time it took up in vanishing, as also whether it began to pass behind the central star nearer to the apsis or farther from it than it emerged as the time of vanishing & reappearing should be one a little shorter or longer than the other: Though the entire disappearance of the satellite for seven hours, when separated from the other, if that might be, would be much the most satisfactory, yet the very speedy diminution, & increase of the light at the beginning & end of the darker appearance of the star, if it is found to be so in fact, would tend very much to make the above hypothesis probable, & would make it almost impossible, that the appearance should be owing to any spot, that is only hid from us for a very little more than the tenth part of a revolution of the star round it's axis; besides that this latter hypothesis is exceedingly encumber'd by the very critical situation, that such a spot must be in, it's extream smallness in comparison to the body, on which it is placed, & the consequently extream brightness it must have, &c. At the same time, if the light is gradually dying away & reviving again for a very considerable time at the beginning & ending of the darker appearance, this would make one more inclined to adopt it, if some other more probable solution could not be thought of; but for the honour of the principle of the paper, I sent you, & for the great entertainment such an appearance would afford to the astronomical world, I am bound to hope, that the appearances may be owing to the cause, I have supposed above, & that the prism may split Algol into two; though I must acknowledge, that I dare not entertain any very sanguine hopes of it's turning out so, there being so many chances against it.

As I imagine the change of brightness in Algol has only been estimated by guess, & not by any certain measure, I cant help wishing, that this star in particular, & indeed as many of the rest of the stars in general, as may be, should have their comparative brightness examined by an instrument, which should not only shew, within very narrow limits, the proportion of light which each affords, & by that means enable us to class them according to their true rank; but also serve, at ever so great a distance of time, as a standard to refer to, so as to find pretty exactly, whether they have undergone any change in that respect. I have formerly observed in my paper on the probable parallax &c. of the fixed stars that something of this kind would be desirable, & the many new facts, that are beginning to come out, with regard to them, seem to make it still more so at present.[5]

In the paper just refer'd to, I supposed the light of the brightest of the fixed stars not to exceed that of the least of those, that are visible to the naked eye, in a greater proportion than that of 1000 to 1. The method, I took to find these proportions, was only sufficient to determine it somewhat grossly, within some moderate limits, which was all, that was wanted for the purpose of that paper. I did it by looking with one eye at a smaller star through a telescope (which I had found by former experiments yielded as much light as was equal to a pencil of about an Inch & one eighth in diameter) & with the other eye naked at a brighter star, limiting the aperture of the pupil by round holes of different sizes pierced in a card, & trying them, till I found one, through which I judged both the stars to appear, as nearly as might be, equally bright; I then compared the size of the hole with the above pencil, & from thence judged of the proportion of their light. If the stars are not so far asunder, as the apparent diameter of the field of the telescope, they may by this method be brought to appear very near together, & be compared with one another tolerably well; but some better method than this, & one that should go to the measuring the quantity of light with some degree of precision, ought to be used for the purpose above mention'd. Now as a hard name adds much to the dignity of a thing, & would perhaps not look amiss in our friend Mr Nairne's catalogue of instruments, I shall take the liberty of christning an instrument for this purpose, an Astrophotometer. The best method of making an instrument of this kind, which occurs to me at present, is by combining the plan of the Helioscope with Monsr Bailly's[6] scheme for making telescopes of different sizes nearly equally good for observing the precise time of the immersions & emersions of Jupiter's satellites;[7] & this I think may be easily enough done by no very complex or expensive addition to a common Telescope, such for instance as a two feet Reflector. By means of the instrument I propose, I would diminish the light of the star till it was just beginning to vanish, which to the same eye, when the sky is equally dark, is I believe a very determinate point, & not a very indeterminate point to the general run of common eyes, that are not very remarkably better or worse than their neighbours. The light of Syrius, when looked at in a night, that has no other light than that of the stars, through a two feet reflector of 4½ Inches aperture, I judge to be somewhere about 50.000 or 60.000[8] times greater than that of the least visible fixed star to the naked eye; it would therefore be necessary to be able to diminish it's light in that proportion by the instrument to bring it to the measure. Now I would propose, that an instrument upon Monsr Bailly's principle (See Ph[ilosophical] Trans[actions] Vol. 63. P. 185)[9] should be fixed upon the mouth of the telescope, which should occasionally either leave the whole aperture open or diminish it through all the intermediate degrees at pleasure, so as to leave only a 50th or 60th part at the last, which, I think, would be a very sufficient extent for that part of the instrument: I would then have next to the eye a Helioscope, consisting, as they usually do, of four reflectors, which, if they are all made of parallel glass planes, which should reflect from both surfaces, would each, according to Monsr Bouguer,[10] reflect about a 10th part of the light, which fell on them, & all the four therefore would reduce the light, that first fell on them, to a 10.000^{dth} part of the whole, which, if I have estimated the light of Syrius properly, would still leave him bright enough to want a farther reduction, by the apparatus at the other end of the telescope, of 4 or 5 degrees in 5 or 6. But perhaps it would be better, to have only one reflecting surface to these glasses, in which case each of them would reflect only about a 20th part of the light that fell upon it, & consequently all the four together only an 160.000^{dth} part; if however, the last glass was to have both surfaces polished, this might possibly bring Syrius within compass; but at least two double surfaces, I think, would do so, especially as, I believe, at an angle of 45° these glasses reflect rather more than a 20th. In order to come at the smaller stars, we should want less diminutions of the light; I would therefore have the helioscopical part of the Astrophotometer, so contrived, as that one might be able to take out any one or more of the glass reflectors, & place metal ones in their stead, at pleasure, by which means, with the help of Monsr Baillys scheme, we should have it in our power pretty accurately to compare different degrees of brightness, from 1 to 100.000 or more, by steps, where no one step should differ from that next to it by a greater quantity, than perhaps 1 in about 20 or 30, & the instrument would give us directly itself the difference of brightness, without having recourse to any hypothesis, by substituting only one metalline speculum at a time, instead of a glass one, or vice versa; for the difference of light occasion'd by such a substitution would not be more than in the proportion of about 12 to 1, whereas the instrument is supposed to be capable of making a difference of 50 or 60 to 1 by diminishing or increasing the aperture, & therefore a star properly chosen would come sufficiently within the limits of it to be visible or made to vanish both with the metalline & glass reflector; & if it was desirable to make the steps still less than in the proportion of 12 to 1, this might be very easily done by first substituting a glass reflector, that reflected from both surfaces, instead of one, that reflected from one surface only, & then a metalline one i[n]stead of this double one.

I certainly did not mention the scheme of the Prism, when I saw you last, not having hit upon it till very lately; for though, when I first thought of the possibility of getting some information about the distance, &c. of the fixed stars from the diminution of the velocity of their light, it naturally occur'd to me, as you will readily suppose, that the change, which would be occasion'd in it's refrangibility on this account, was probably the only means of finding it out; yet the little chance, as I then thought, of this principle being ever made use of to any good purpose, made me bestow very little thought upon any methods of applying it: it did indeed occur to me at that time, that by the difference, which would be occasion'd in the refrangibility of the light, a small difference would be made in the focal length of an object glass; but this difference, I was well aware, was so small, that it would require a very great diminution of the velocity of light to be sensible at all, & at best would be but a very vague measure of it; & being very little interested by what I expected so little from, I gave myself no farther trouble to enquire, whether there might not be some better method of applying the same principle; & it was not till after I had heard of Mr Herschel's discovery of so many double stars, when I was last in London (for I had hardly heard any thing of it before) that I began to think, that possibly the diminution of the velocity of light might now begin to be the foundation of some observations, which might be applied to some good purpose: It was this, which put it into my mind to give the subject a reconsideration, & made me think of communicating it to yourself at the same time. But though I had heard soon after my arrival in town last year, that Mr Herschel had found a great many stars to be double, &c. I was by no means aware, that their number was near so great, as I found it, when I got the last Vol. of the Trans[actions][11] & it was not till after I got that Volume, & when the paper, I sent you, was pretty nearly finished, that I thought of applying the prism, when it occur'd to me, that such an instrument would be a very convenient one for the purpose intended, if any of the vast number of those double stars, &c. should happen to be properly circumstanced, which we may well entertain some hopes is not unlikely to be the case amongst so many.

I have no thoughts of executing either the Prism or Astrophotometer myself at present, nor, if I had, should I have any wish not to have them both as early & as generally known as you please; but I shall more especially, having no intentions of executing either of them myself, be very glad, that any body else should adopt either or both of them, whether exactly upon the plan, I have suggested, or with any improvements or alterations, that yourself or any one else may think proper, & the sooner & more generally they come into use the better, as I may, by that means, have more hopes of living to see some of the improvements, & new discoveries, that may, I hope I may say, probably be made by their assistance in this branch of Astronomy.

Mr Goodrich the author of the observation, you sent me, is wholly unknown to me, nor was I aware, who he was, till after I received your Letter.[12]

Mr Herschel's idea of the Solar System being in motion, I think not at all improbable; but I apprehend it will require both a great many more observations, than we are yet in possession of, & a great deal both of sagacity & industry, when those observations shall have been made, to make out, with any certainty, what part of this motion is owing to ourselves, & what to others. Mr Herschel is as likely to do it, as any body, & the coincidence of several apparent motions argues somewhat in favour of his hypothesis, yet as we cannot reasonably suppose the other systems all quiescent, & our own alone in motion, till I see the particular comparison of all the motions, that have been observed, I would not too hastily entirely acquiesce in it. It would indeed be very desirable, if this matter could be made out pretty clearly, as it might then afford us the means of discovering some time or other a secular parallax, as I have hinted on a former occasion,[13] & by that means give us another step towards discovering the real distance of the stars.

I dont much wonder to hear Mr Herschel has met with an accident in one of his speculums,[14] as well as myself in more than one. Mr Short[15] met with one at least in one of his great speculums, which broke as he was laying it on the tool, he was going to grind it on, & the parts of it were near falling upon his toes. Some parts of this kind of metal whilest cooling, getting fixed before the rest, are, I think I can almost say with certainty, many of them upon the stretch, in consequence of which, unless they are very well annealed, they are very apt to break, sometimes by an accidental discontinuity, produced by very small causes, & in very small parts of the whole; & yet in some cases it will bear a great deal more, than one would suppose such brittle metal capable of. We have made no scruple of hewing some pounds of metal from the speculum, I have at present, with a chizzel, & that pretty nearly as freely, as we should have hewn a piece of stone, in order to save the trouble of grinding it off, which it bore perfectly well, though equally brittle, & no more annealed than those we had broken with what one would have expected much less danger from.

I have it in contemplation, & hope to try the experiment of weighing the world in the course of the Summer, but wont promise too much for fear of performing too little. The other things I have in contemplation are some experiments upon the strength, compressibility, &c. of metals, woods, & stones, for which I have made some preparations; but my natural indolence, without a pretty strong stimulus, & which has been rather encreased by an indifferent state of health for these last twelve months, sometimes, as you know, makes my intended experiments proceed but slowly.

I am much obliged to you for your account of your own & Mr Hutchins's experiments on the freezing of Quicksilver, & shall be very glad to see both what you & Dr Blagden have said upon the subject. I suppose both your accounts are intended for the Transactions.[16] I always had my doubts about the very low degrees, to which the Mercury descended in some of the experiments, where it was frozen; but I did not I own suspect that quite so great a proportion of it was owing to the contraction at the point of fixing. I suppose you must have made use of some other fluid or perhaps metalline thermometers to measure this matter, & indeed I think you are bound to find us something else in it's stead, having robbed us of so excellent a measure of heat & cold, as the Quicksilver was supposed to be for so many degrees below –39.

I had some time since heard that Dr Priestley had made some experiments, by which he apprehended he had converted water into air. I was indeed rather inclined to doubt, though I could not form any determinate judgment upon it for want of knowing the experiments; but of his having found, that he was mistaken, or the extraordinary fact, you allude to, I had not heard any thing, till I received your Letter,[17] nor do I yet know what that fact is.

I have sent you on the next leaf another paragraph, instead of that, in which I had made the mistake, you was so good as to point out to me: it is very little alter'd, as you will see, from the original, but will, I hope, sufficiently correct it, & express what was, or at least ought to have been intended. I have written it, I think, upon the same sized lines, & left margin enough on each side, to pass a part of it on either side between the backs of the other leaves, in order to fasten it to them, which I hoped would give you the least trouble, & the Article in the original you will be so good as to cancel by striking a pen through it.

I ought & meant to have answer'd your Letter much sooner, but have delayed it longer, than I intended, having been from home part of the time, since I received it, & being willing to take a little time to examine both the things abovemention'd, & several others which occur'd in the course of considering the subject; but which however upon examination, I dont think worth sending you, either as being too crude or on account of their looking too far forward into the consequences of observations not yet made, or facts not yet known to exist, & which perhaps do not exist at all, or if they do, may never be known to do so: Very random conjectures or consequences, that would follow from such or such observations, &c. if they should ever be made, are often much more proper for discussion in the course of conversation, than to stand upon paper, even in an epistolary correspondence only.

I must now beg you to accept my best respects, & present my Comp^s to all friends, that may enquire after me, at the Society,[18] Cat & Bagpipes,[19] &c. when you see them. I am,

Thornhill Dear Sir,

2 July 1783

With much respect & esteem

Your obed^t humble Servt

J. Michell

---

1 Cavendish Mss New Correspondence.

2 This letter is in reply to Cavendish's draft letter of 27 May; letter 18. Michell's reference to it as the letter of 3 June is consistent with comments by Michell to matters that are not contained in Cavendish's draft; see note 17 below. Cavendish evidently made additions to the letter he drafted before sending it to Michell a week later.

3 Michell regarded double stars as close-lying, physically bound stars rather than the optical effect of two widely separated stars happening to fall approximately along a straight line to the earth: "it

is highly probable in particular, and next to a certainty in general, that such double stars, &c. as appear to consist of two or more stars placed very near together, do really consist of stars placed near together, and under the influence of some general law." "An Inquiry into the Probable Parallax, and Magnitude of the Fixed Stars, from the Quantity of Light Which They Afford Us, and the Particular Circumstances of Their Situation," *PT* 57 (1767): 234–64, on 249. Herschel, too, was interested in double stars, but for now he remained cautious about their nature, preferring the term "*double-star*" to other terms such as "Companion" and "Satellite" because he thought it was "much too soon to form any theories of small stars revolving round large ones." "Catalogue of Double Stars," 161. Later, for reasons of his own, Herschel would come around to Michell's view of double stars.

[4] That is, $^{5}/_{8.5}$ or 0.58823 in modern notation.

[5] In his paper of 1767 Michell had proposed a catalog of stars on a new plan, classified, as he told Cavendish in his letter, by their true rank, providing a standard for discovering any changes in the stars. He urged astronomers to "enquire into the exact quantity of light, which each star affords us separately, when compared with the Sun; that, instead of distributing them, as has hitherto been done, into a few ill defined classes, they may be ranked with precision both according to their respective brightness, and the exact degree of it." "An Inquiry into the Probable Parallax," 241.

[6] Jean-Sylvain Bailly (1736–93), astronomer, member of the Paris Royal Academy of Sciences, who would become mayor of Paris and eventually be guillotined. Chapin, "Bailly," *DSB* 1:400–2.

[7] Bailly made an extensive study of the inequalities of the four known satellites of Jupiter, leading him to propose a technique for measuring their light, which required placing graduated pasteboard diaphrams in front of the object glass to intercept the light. He pointed out that the diaphrams could be applied to any telescope large enough to view the satellites. His method was not limited to the problem of Jupiter's satellites, as Michell recognized, but was a general method for making precise comparisons of light intensities. Ibid.

[8] Fifty thousand or sixty thousand.

[9] Michell did not cite Bailly's memoir of 1771 on the method of measuring light, published by the Academy of Sciences, but his "Letter to the Rev. Nevil Maskelyne, F.R.S. Astronomer Royal . . . Containing a Proposal of Some New Methods of Improving the Theory of Jupiter's Satellites," *PT* 63 (1773): 185–216, on 185, 203–6.

[10] Pierre Bouguer (1698–1758), a member of the Paris Academy of Sciences, in 1729 published a pioneering work on the comparison of light intensities, or photometry, *Essai d'optique sur la gradation de la lumière*, a much enlarged version of which, entitled *Traité*, was published posthumously, in 1760. Bouguer is regarded as the inventor of the photometer, the progenitor of Michell's Astrophotometer. Middleton, "Bouguer," *DSB* 2: 343–44. *Pierre Bouguer's Optical Treatise on the Gradation of Light*, translated, with Introduction by W.E. Knowles Middleton (Toronto: University of Toronto Press, 1961).

[11] Beginning in 1779, Herschel concentrated on discovering double stars, his interest drawn to these objects as a means for measuring the distance of the stars. By assuming that the fainter member of a double star is sufficiently distant to be regarded as a fixed star, he hoped to determine the distance of the brighter, supposedly nearer member from its annual apparent motion with respect to the fixed star. His catalog contained 269 double and multiple stars, 227 of which were first noted by him. After Herschel had delivered his paper, Sir Joseph Banks gave him a posthumously published memoir by Johann Tobias Mayer, who had observed double stars for another reason, and Herschel found that Mayer had discovered another 31 double stars he had overlooked. Herschel, "Catalogue of Double Stars," 157–58. Hoskin, "Herschel," *DSB* 6:328–36, on 328–30.

[12] See letter 18, note 9.

[13] See last letter, note 15. Michell wrote in his paper of 1767 that the observed apparent change in the position of stars "may be owing either to the real motion of the stars themselves, or to that of the Sun, or partly to the one, and partly to the other. As far as it is owing to the latter (which it is by no means improbable may in some measure be the case) it may be considered as a kind of secular parallax, which, if the annual parallax of a few of the stars should some time or other be discovered, and the quantity and direction of the Sun's motion should be discovered likewise, might

serve to inform us of the distances of many of them, which it would be utterly impossible to find out by any other means." "An Inquiry into the Probable Parallax," 252–53.

[14] Herschel's speculum broke in the winter of 1782–83 owing to the cold. His close friend William Watson, Jr., wrote to him, "I was extreamly sorry to hear by means of your Brother, that you have had the misfortune to break your best 12 Inch Speculum by the frost." In his next letter, Watson added, "after so many hours Labour." Watson to Herschel, 19 Jan. and 16 Mar. 1783, Royal Astronomical Society, Mss Herschel, W 1/13, W.23 and 24.

[15] James Short (1710–68), a well-known London maker and user of astronomical instruments. Taylor, *Mathematical Practitioners*, 190–91.

[16] See letter 15, note 3.

[17] As Priestley's experiments are not mentioned in the draft of Cavendish's letter to Michell, Cavendish must have included them as an afterthought in the letter he sent. In his simplest method of converting water to air, Priestley heated water in an earthen retort. Cavendish, he said, had carried out experiments that were an inverse of his own, reconverting air to water by "decomposing it in conjunction with inflammable air." Priestley was tentative about his hypothesis, but "the experiment with the tobacco-pipe, in which the steam is made red-hot . . . cannot be explained so well on any other hypothesis any more than Mr. Cavendish's experiment on finding water on the decomposition of air." Were he right, the air we breathe would be generated by water. Priestley, "Experiments Relating to Phlogiston, and the Seeming Conversion of Water into Air," *PT* 73 (1783): 398–434, on 421, 426, 428–29, 433–34.

[18] The Royal Society Club was commonly called the "Society."

[19] The Cat and Bagpipes was a popular tavern and chop house on the corner of Downing Street, next to King's Street. *Notes and Queries*, 9 Nov. 1850, p. 397, quoted in Geikie, *Memoir of John Michell*, 58.

20. TO JOHN MICHELL

[12 AUGUST 1783][1]

From the original draft letter in the Devonshire Collections, Chatsworth[2]

Dear Sir

I thank you for your letter[3] & have shown your paper to some of your friends & among them to Dr Maskelyne who has pointed out to me a few things which seem oversights.[4] In the 24th art. you say for the diam[eter] of the central star being as the cube of the distance between that & the revolving star & their distance from the earth being in the simple ratio of their distance from each other the apparent diam. of the central star must be as the square of its real distance from the ⊕ inversely & conseq[uently] the surface of a sphere being as the square of the diam the area of the apparent disc must be as the 4th power of its distance from the ⊕ *inversely*. I suppose the 2 inverselys should be struck out.

In art. 32 we suppose the numbers 21″,29 & 22″,453 & 1″.10‴ should be changed into 33″ 35″,88 & 2″.53‴ & conseq[uently] in art. 33 the numbers 1″.10‴ 2″.10‴ & 10‴ should be changed into 2″.53‴ 3″.53‴ & 1″.53‴ & that having been removed from its place more than the whole distance between them should be alterd for near 3 times the distance.

Dr Mask[elyne] observes that the bending of the ray given by you is only that which a ray falling on the glass with an angle of incidence of 1′ suffers on passing into the glass. In art. 33 also we suppose that the thicker part of the prism should be changed into the thinner. This occurs twice.

In the 4th line of article 8 instead [of] the distances of the points R.r from C we suppose you mean D.d.

On consideration I think the alteration of the focus of a telescope seems a much more accurate way of finding the difference of velocity of light than the prism besides the advantage of being more convenient & universal. I mentiond this to Dr M. who is now of the same opinion, though at first he did not come into it. According to a computation I made if the velocity of light is diminished by only 1/1000 part the focal distance of the object glass in an achromatic should be diminished by 17/10000 of the whole though with a simple object glass it is alterd not quite so much & with a good achrom[atic] Dr M thinks a much smaller alteration can be perceived.

I am afraid however that this shews there is not much likelyhood of finding any stars whose light is sensibly diminished. Dr Maske has purposely looked at several stars with an achrom. but has not found any diff[erence] to be depended on. Mr Hirsch[el] has looked with one at a great many stars & at some on purpose but never perceived any diff. Mr Hirsch. is grinding a prism for this purpose.[5]

I like your Astrophotometer very well & wish that observat[io]n[s] of that kind were made. There is another contrivance which I have formerly thought of for this purpose namely to place a speculum before the object glass of a small telescope turned on its axis so as to alter the angle of reflection & also of being elevated or depressed like the horizon glass of a Hadleys quadrant except that it must be capable of being elevated or depressed so as to cover more or less of the aperture & also of being round on its axis as the index glass is & then to bring 2 stars into the field of the telescope one seen direct & the other by reflection & to elevate or depress the speculum till they appeard equally bright.[6]

The idea (in your hypothesis of Algol) of making the orbit very excentric will serve to account for the time of the obscuration being so great without supposing their density to be small. As to the rest of the hypothesis I imagine you rather wish than think it to be likely. As far as I can learn the light does not diminish rapidly but on the contrary the duration of the full diminution is but small.

We are told by Mr Smeaton[7] that your great speculum is completed & finishd to your satisfaction. I hope there is no mistake in the information.

The substance of Dr Priestleys exper[iment] is as follows. On putting about as much water into an unglazed earthen retort as could be absorbed by the earth & distilling no water came over but only air & in most of his exper. the air was nearly equal in weight to the water used but if he used more water the quantity of air caught was not much greater. The air was in general almost as good as common air. If he used a glass or glazed earthen retort no air was procured. If he fitted a tobacco pipe to the mouth of a glass or other retort & heated the pipe very hot while by heating the body of the retort the steam of the water was made to pass through the hot pipe he also procured a great deal of air. From these exper he supposed that the water was changed into air. But on coming to town he passed the neck of an earthen retort with a little water in it through one end of a glass receiver open at both ends & cemented it close the other end of the receiver being dipt into water. He then heated the body of the retort which as I before said was included in the receiver by Parkers[8] great burning glass in which a great deal of air was caught & at the same time the water rose within the receiver which shewed that while the water oozed out of the retort into the receiver the air passed the contrary way from the receiver into the retort. This was further confirmd by filling the receiver with airs of different kind as the air caught was always of the same kind as that put into the receiver. The force with which the air was sucked into the retort appeard to be very considerable for if the receiver was dipt into ☿ instead of water the ☿ was drawn up if I mistake not consid[erably] more than an inch above the level.

---

[1] The date of this letter is given in letter 23.

[2] Cavendish Mss New Correspondence.

[3] Letter 19.

[4] Following this letter, we reproduce the two sheets of corrections of Michell's paper by Maskelyne, which Cavendish incorporated.

[5] A month after this letter by Cavendish to Michell, Blagden wrote to a colleague that Michell had a hypothesis to explain the variation of the light from Algol and that Michell did "not despair of bringing this hypothesis to the test of experiment." Charles Blagden to Jean-Baptiste Le Roy, 15 Sep. 1783, draft, Blagden Letterbook, Yale. A month later, Blagden reported that astronomers were still unsuccessful in their efforts to detect a difference in the velocity of light coming from different stars, but that they intended to acquire instruments constructed for this purpose. Letter to Claude Louis Berthollet, 24 Oct. 1783, draft, ibid. A year later Blagden sent a copy of Michell's paper to Pierre Simon Laplace, mentioning nothing about observations. Speaking for himself, Cavendish, Maskelyne, and Herschel, and maybe others, he said that Michell's paper "though almost purely speculative, we think extremely curious." Blagden to Laplace, 3 Sept. 1784, draft, Blagden Letterbook, Yale.

[6] Cavendish promptly had a photometer made for him, no doubt on the plan of the one he described to Michell. With it, he and Blagden observed Algol. Blagden reported to Banks that "whether it be that he [Goodricke] made the period too long, or that it is not absolutely uniform, cannot be determined. Mr Cavendish's photometer is not found to answer." Charles Blagden to Sir Joseph Banks, 16, 23, and 30 Oct. 1783, Fitzwilliam Museum Library, Perceval H190, H193, H195.

[7] John Smeaton (1724–92), instrument-maker, engineer, and surveyor, F.R.S. 1753. Taylor, *Mathematical Practitioners*, 218.

[8] William Parker, who with his sons John and Samuel operated a glass manufacturing firm in London, provided Priestley with "every instrument I wanted in glass," including burning lenses. Taylor, *Mathematical Practitioners*, 294. Schofield, in *Autobiography of . . . Priestley*, 367.

106. *Burning Lens. Cavendish used this instrument in his chemical experiments. Photograph by the authors. By permission of the Science Museum, London/Science & Society Picture Library.*

21. FROM NEVIL MASKELYNE TO HENRY CAVENDISH FOR JOHN MICHELL

[12 AUGUST 1783]

From the original memorandum in the Devonshire Collections, Chatsworth[1]

Put a:1 the ratio of the semidiam^r^ of a fixt star to that of the sun: x:1 the ratio of the diminution of its light to the whole velocity of its light at its first emission. $x^2 = \frac{a^2}{494000}$ & $a = 703\sqrt{x}$ Hence a star whose diam^r^ is 7 times that of the sun will diminish its own light by 1/10000th part, which may be perceptible to a good achromatic telescope. The alteration of the focus is 5/3 of the alteration of the velocity of light.–

Page 1. 9 lines from bottom for specific gravity substitute density.
P.3 5 lines from the bottom for R,r read D,d.
P. 12 lines 9 & 12 dele[te], inversely
P. 17 l.7 for 21,29 read 33. & for 22,453 read 35,88.
l. 8 for 1″.10‴ read 2″.53‴
l. 19 for thicker read thinner
l. 22 for 1″.10‴ r. 2″ 53‴
l 23 for 2.10 r 3.53
l. 25 for thicker r. thinner
l. 27 for 10‴ r 1″.53‴
l 28 insert, near 5 times

In p. 17 Mr Michell computes the refraction of the light at the first surface of the prism, supposing the angle of incidence to be 1′, but neglects the refraction at the 2^d^ surface which will be greater. The best way is to calculate the refraction in going out of the prism, supposing its motion within it to be parallel to the base of the prism. This doubled will be the whole refraction of the prism.[2]

---

[1] This two-page list of corrections of Michell's paper by Nevil Maskelyne was folded into the preceding draft letter from Cavendish to Michell, 12 Aug. 1783. Cavendish Mss New Correspondence.

[2] At the bottom of the second side, and upside down, is a calculation in Cavendish's handwriting.

33
35,88
———
2,88 = 2.528

22. TO JOHN MICHELL

4 [OR 3] NOVEMBER 1783[1]

From the original draft letter in the Devonshire Collections, Chatsworth.[2]

Dear Sir

I wrote to you a good while ago to inform you of some oversights in your paper which D^{r} M[askelyne] had pointed out to me but have not received any answer & do not know whether it is owing to your not having received my letter or to your waiting to revise the paper or to any other cause. But as the meetings of the soc[iety] will begin next th[ursday] I desire you will let me know what you would have me do about the paper.

[1] Cavendish noted on this draft letter, "To Michell Nov. 4 1783." Michell referred to this letter as Cavendish's letter of 3 November; see letter 23.

[2] Cavendish Mss New Correspondence.

23. FROM JOHN MICHELL

10 NOVEMBER 1783

From the original letter in the Devonshire Collections, Chatsworth[1]

Dear Sir,

I duely received yours of the 3^d Inst.[2] I was not aware that the Society was to meet so soon as you mention. I apprehended their custom to have been, not to meet till St Andrew's, before when I meant to have thanked you for your favour of the 12th of Aug^st last, & to have requested the favour of you to correct the several blunders, you & Dr Maskelyne have been so good as to point out to me, & for which I think myself much obliged to you both. So many carelessnesses want perhaps more apology, than I have to make for them, but indeed I was in a very indifferent state of health, when I wrote the paper, which made me languid, & disinclined to much application: this, I hope will plead somewhat in my excuse; I think myself however very fortunate in having it fall under the eyes of two such intelligent friends, who have done me the honour to read it with attention enough to detect so many of my mistakes, & prevent their appearing in a more public manner.

If you will be so good as to take the trouble of making the corrections, that are wanting by striking out, interlining, or altering a few words, & figures, as may be necessary, I think there will be no occasion to send the paper back to Thornhill; for it is by no means necessary, that the corrections should be in my own hand writing.

In Art 8th in the 3^d or 4th line from the end, if the copy I sent you agrees with my foul copy, there is wanting the word *inversely* immediately after Sun; this therefore I will be obliged to you to insert, by interlining it, as well as to change the Letters R & r for D & d, agreably to what you observe, they should be.

In Art 24th I must desire you to erase or strike out the two last *inverselys* but one, which as you say are certainly wrong, & the very reverse of what ought to have been.

In Art 31st towards the end, instead of the numbers *31* to *19,4* I think it would be better to say *31,96* to *20*, which are in the same proportion, as the others, but which lead more directly to the numbers, such as they ought to have been. I find, that in my foul copy, I had at first made use of these numbers, & afterwards had changed them to those, that stand at present in the copy, I sent you; my intention was to make the incident ray fall perpendicularly on one side of the Prism, for the sake of the greater simplicity; but, through some inattention, instead of making the angle of incidence at the second surface equal to one minute, as I ought to have done, I made it so at the first surface, which occasion'd the mistake. I would therefore, in Art 32^d, changing the numbers only, but retaining the words as they stand, read "the light with it's velocity undiminished would be turned out of it's way 33″ & with the diminished velocity 35″,88 nearly, the difference between which being almost 2″.53‴ would be," &c.[3]

In Art 33^{d} "*thicker*," in the two places, in which it occurs may, if you please, be changed into thinner, by erasing *ck* & inserting *nn* in it's room; & I must desire you also to erase 1″.10‴ 2″.10‴ & 10‴ & insert in their places 2″.53‴, & 3″.53‴ & 1″.53‴ respectively, as they occur, & instead of "having been removed from it's place more than the whole distance between them" to make it, as you propose, "having been removed from it's place *near three times* the whole distance between them" which may either be done by erasing *more than* & writing *near three* in it's stead & interlining the word *times*, as above, or in any other way you please.

As I have not at present time to give my paper another revisal, as well as to answer the rest of your paper of the 12th Augst without making you wait some time longer before you hear from me, I take the earliest convenient opportunity of answering your last, leaving every thing, but what relates to the corrections of my paper to another opportunity, as I should now be glad to have it read, as soon as convenient & agreable to you; the revisal, it has already undergone, has most probably left no material errors in it, & if any thing should hereafter occur, there will, I suppose, be time enough to make any trifling alterations, before it will be printed, if the Society should think proper to do me that honour.

I received a Letter a few days ago from Dr Maskelyne, which I propose to answer shortly.[4] I am so much out of the way of procuring any intelligence about the meteors, he wished me to enquire after, that I am afraid I shall not be able to be of any service to him upon the occasion; I am however making what enquiries I can, for him.

With due Comp^{s} to yourself & all other friends I am with much respect & esteem,

Thornhill — Dear Sir,
10 Nov 1783 — Your obed^{t} humble Servt
J. Michell

[1] Cavendish Mss New Correspondence.

[2] Letter 22.

[3] In transcribing Michell's notation for seconds and sixtieths of seconds of arc, we have made a change. Beneath the double and triple strokes, he wrote two dots, as he did after the decimal proportion of a second in 35″,88. We have omitted the two dots and have added a period between the seconds and sixtieths of a second, corresponding to the way his numbers were set in the paper in the *Philosophical Transactions*. Thus, in place of 2″53‴ with two dots under the strokes, we put 2″.53‴.

[4] The letter would have enclosed Maskelyne's three-page printed directions for observers of meteors, dated 6 November, *A Plan for Observing the Meteors Called Fire-Balls*.

24. TO CHARLES BLAGDEN

[5 APRIL 1784][1]

From the original letter in the Royal Society[2]

Dear Sir

It is determined that Mr Aubert[3] & I shall go to D^r H[eberden][4] & see what we can do. If it is to no purpose a larger meeting will be called & very likely some resolutions similar to what you mentiond proposed to them.[5] I shall be at home at Hampstead, tomorrow till 12 but would not have you take the trouble to come to me unless there is any thing which you want to talk to me about.

Yours

H. Cavendish

Monday evening

---

[1] This tentative dating is made on the basis of Charles Blagden to Sir Joseph Banks, 5 Apr. 1784 BM(NH), DTC 3:20–21.

[2] Blagden Letters, C.26.

[3] Alexander Aubert (1730–1805), director and from 1787 governor of the London Assurance Company, astronomer, F.R.S. 1772. "Aubert," *DNB* 1:715.

[4] William Heberden (1710–1801), London physician, F.R.S. 1749. "Heberden," *DNB* 7:359–60.

[5] This letter refers to the so-called "dissensions" of the Royal Society of 1783–84, which had to do with a division within the membership on the subject of its president, Sir Joseph Banks. When the disruptions of the meetings of the Society continued even after Banks had received a vote of confidence, Cavendish, together with several other members, considered resolutions for restoring peace.

25. FROM JOHN MICHELL

20 APRIL 1784

From the original letter in the Devonshire Collections, Chatsworth[1]

Dear Sir,

Upon reconsidering the matter, in consequence of what you said in your Letter of the 12 Augst,[2] I found the alteration of the focal distance of an object glass would be a much better measure of any change in the velocity of light, than I was before aware of, & I may very possibly be satisfied, when I come to talk with you upon the subject, that it is preferable to the Prism; nevertheless I own I am yet a little inclined to be partial to the latter, & I have less fear of being any how deceived, in placing some degree of confidence in it; I do not however so far distrust the observations made by Mr Maskelyne with the object glass, as not to be afraid, that the chance of making any discoveries by means of the diminution of the velocity of light, in consequence of the attraction of the bodies, from whence it is emitted, is not so great, as I should be inclined to wish it. But though it would certainly be very agreable to me, if any discoveries should be made by this means, yet I never formed any such very sanguine hopes of it's success, that I shall be greatly disappointed in case nothing should come of it: it is very possible there may be no stars large enough to produce any sensible effect, & it is also just possible, that light (& perhaps too the electrical fluid, which seems to be in some degree allied to it, &c.) may not be so much affected by gravity, in proportion to their vis inertia, as other bodies;[3] but though I am much more inclined to believe this is not the case, yet the singular properties those substances are possessed of, seem to leave a little more room for doubt with respect to them, than other common kinds of matter.

The way I proposed of accounting for the appearances of Algol, I certainly laid no great stress upon, as you supposed: it was necessary so many circumstances should concur, that it was extreamly unlikely they should all happen to exist together, as I believe, I observed, when I mention'd it. The splitting him into two, & the sudden appearance & disappearance of one of the two, together with the time of the obscuration, if it answer'd, might indeed have made the solution somewhat probable; or even the sudden diminution & increase of the light now look a little the same way; but I looked upon the chance, that even the latter of these should turn out so, as extreamly small, & the former as still much more so. At all adventures however, I wish a good set of observations might be made either with the instrument you propose, the Astrophotometer, or any other proper instrument for the same purpose, as I think such observations would probably lead to many discoveries in a field, that is at present almost entirely new. In respect to Algol in particular, it is not unlikely that the degree of the diminution of the light, together with the times, in which it took place, might go [a] great way towards determining, with some degree of probability, to what cau[se] it is owing.

Several other advantages might possibly also be derived from observ[ations] of this kind: A chasm in the general gradation of the light of the stars from the greater ones downwards might help perhaps to point out which stars in general (especially if confirmed by other circumstances) belong to our own group, if such a group exists, agreably to a hint to this purpose, in my former paper on the probable parallax of the fixed stars; &c.[4]

I am much obliged to you for your acc^t of Dr Priestley's experiment; it is indeed a very extraordinary one, nor can I in the least guess at any reason why in the distillation of the water through a porous vessel, the air should be drawn in the contrary way, & especially with so much force; for this, I think, is the fact, if I rightly understand it.

This experiment however puts me in mind of a reason, that occur'd to me some time ago, why perhaps boiling the water previously to setting it in porous vessels, in order to make it freeze, as is practiced in the East Indies,[5] may tend to promote that effect. Not indeed that I see at present any connexion between the two, & yet possibly there may be some distant relationship between them. Water, when exposed to the air, absorbs, as you know, a certain quantity of it, till it has saturated itself with it; now when this air is expelled by boiling, may not the affinity between the water & air, by which they are mutually inclined to unite before the water is sufficiently saturated, tend to accelerate the evaporation in the instance in question, & by that means produce a greater degree of cold? An observation, I have met with (I believe in some of Beaumé's[6] works) seems, I think to increase the probability of this hypothesis: the observation is, that much more liquor will be distilled, all other circumstances being alike, when the worm is of a larger diameter, notwithstanding it communicates freely with the open air in both cases; so that the coming into contact with a greater quantity of air seems to promote the evaporation.

I shall now mention to you an observation of my Brother's,[7] which I saw also myself, & which I think was sufficiently marked for us not to be mistaken in it; of which however, unless we had had more experience of it, or had been aware of it before hand, I would not be too sure, though I verily think we were not deceived in it. In a little pond, we have, in which we keep a few gold & silver fish, during the long haziness, which obtained in the atmosphere last summer, there was a want of transparency in the water, that we had not usually seen at a like time of the year in former seasons, insomuch that, I think, we could have seen these fish as distinctly formerly at the depth of two feet & half, as, during this haziness, at the depth of one foot below the surface, & when this haziness in the air cleared up, the haziness in the water disappeared, if not precisely at the same time yet within at least, we think, four & twenty hours of it, & probably much less.

Soon after I wrote to you last, I was again very indifferent in my health, & continued so for some time; & having delayed writing to you for a good while on this account, & having nothing, that immediately called upon me for an answer, together with a considerable degree of languidness, & perhaps also too much natural disinclination to writing, I still waited somewhat longer, that I might be the better able to give you some farther account of what progress, I had made in my Telescope: the difficulties I have had to encounter, in consequence of having undertaken it upon so large a scale, & the want of the means of procuring more assistance in a country place, as well as the expence, have protracted the finishing it much longer, than probably those, who have not seen the progress of it, will easily be able to account for; I hope however to compleat it in the course of next summer. The account Mr Smeaton had given you, though not exactly right, was not wholly without foundation. I had said, that I had at last got the great speculum ground & polished not much to my dissatisfaction: to have finished it tolerably well, after so many disappointments, as I had before met with, I looked on as a considerable point gained; I had not however succeeded so much to my satisfaction, as not to have hopes of mending it, & I have in fact polished it once over again already, & mean still to have another trial with it in the Summer, promising myself, that I shall yet be able to mend it. The great Speculum being once polished, you will perhaps wonder why the Telescope should not be finished out of hand. Now, if I was to enter into the detail of what I have been doing since, & what I have still to do, before it will be compleated, you would find, that, according to my rate of proceding, there are sufficient reasons why it should not be yet compleated; I have however been able so far to try it, as to have reasonable hopes, I think, of making it tolerably distinct, notwithstanding it's very great aperture & short focus: Whether I shall be able to make it very distinct or not, time must shew, & possibl[y] [to] [suc]ceed very perfectly may exceed my industry or be attended w[ith] [--] more expence, than I can conveniently bestow upon it; but I hope to be able to give it such a trial,[8] as may enable me to judge, whether my scheme is practicable or not, & I may then leave the more perfect completion of it to others, who may have more industry, & be better able to bear the expence of it than I am.

Thus far I had written several months since, when some things occur'd; which made me again put off writing to you from time to time. When I see you, which I now hope will be the beginning of next month,[9] I shall perhaps be able to make some apology for my long silence, of which ill health has indeed been in some measure the cause; at least I shall hope for your pardon, & that my friends will be so good as to take me as they find me, & not imagine, that I have any intention of neglecting or offending them, which is very far from my wishes or intention. I meant to have said a good deal more to you, about various other matters of different kinds; but as I now hope to see you so soon, I will not at present enter into any other subject. With best respects & Comp^s^ as proper to yourself & all other friends, I have the honour to be,

Thornhill
20 April 1784

With much respect & esteem,
Dear Sir,
Your very obed[t] humble Serv[t]
J Michell

[address]:
To
The Hon[ble] Henry Cavendish
Great Marlborough Street
London
Single Sheet

---

[1] Cavendish Mss New Correspondence.

[2] Letter 20.

[3] Michell here acknowledged the commonly held opinion that light, electricity, magnetism, heat, and phlogiston were substances distinct from ordinary matter. Herschel, who had looked so far in vain for starlight with a dimished velocity (letter 20), speculated in the same vein. To the astronomer Samuel Vince, Herschel wrote, "M[r] Michell's excellent Paper [of 1783], if it should not be supported by facts (As I believe I can almost say from my own experiments it will not) must lead us to surmise pretty strongly that light is *not* subject to the common laws of motion; At all events that paper is of the utmost importance, its being contrary to facts being a point of almost as much consequence as its agreeing with them." Letter of 15 Jan. 1784, Royal Astronomical Society, Mss Herschel, W 1/1, pp. 92–95. Michell, in his remark to Cavendish, suggested that he thought not that light might be entirely weightless but that it might not respond to gravitation in the same measure as ordinary bodies. Cavendish would have regarded Michell's speculation as reasonable. Three years earlier, in October 1780, he had done an experiment to examine a similar speculation: "It was tried whether the *vis inertia* of phlogisticated air was the same in proport. to its weight as that of common air." "Experiments on Air," Cavendish Mss II, 5:80–82; in *Sci. Pap.* 2:320–22. An objection to the view of light as a gravitating body was raised by Benjamin Franklin in 1768: by emitting its light, the sun would lose matter; its gravitational force would diminish, and the earth would recede. The objection was answered by the mathematician Samuel Horsley: by making what he believed were reasonable assumptions, he concluded that the loss of matter from the sun was real but imperceptible, only $^1/_{13,232}$ part of its matter in 385,130,000 years. "Difficulties in the Newtonian Theory of Light, Considered and Removed," *PT* 60 (1770): 417–40.

[4] Michell, "Inquiry into the Probable Parallax," 250–54.

[5] There was considerable scientific interest in the Indian practice of cooling water by evaporation. It was commonly believed that water must be boiled to make ice in India, but one observer said that boiling was not done in Benares, where porous pans were sufficient. John Lloyd Williams, "Account of the Method of Making Ice at Benares," *PT* 83 (1793): 56–58.

[6] Antoine Baumé (1728–1804), chemist, member of the Paris Academy of Sciences. McDonald, "Baumé," *DSB* 1:527.

[7] John Michell's late brother Gilbert Michell is mentioned in his will, dated 28 Nov. 1792.

[8] A year later, in August, Smeaton told the London astronomer Aubert that Michell had polished the speculum to his satisfaction. Smeaton hoped soon to see a celestial object with it. Sir Joseph Banks to Charles Blagden, 4 Aug. 1785, Blagden Letters, Royal Society, B.36. Later that month Michell tried the telescope during daylight, as Herschel learned from his friend William Watson, Jr. "Have you heard of the success of M[r] Michel's speculum? My father informed me about a fortnight ago, that M[r] Dalrymple has paid him a visit, & saw the Telescope, & that it performs extreamly well upon day objects." Letter of 8 Sep. 1785, Royal Astronomical Society, Mss Herschel, W 1/13, W.38. In November, Blagden told Lord Mulgrave that Michell was still not fully satisfied with his telescope but that with it letters of $^1/_{10}$th inch could be read at a considerable distance. Draft letter

of 19 Nov. 1785, Blagden Letters, Royal Society, 7:736. A year later Blagden and Cavendish visited Michell, Blagden reporting that the telescope was still imperfect but a "very reasonable instrument." Blagden to Claude Louis Berthollet, 13 Sep. 1786, draft, ibid., 7:29. They had a chance to try it on celestial objects at night: "tho' much false light & confused images yet ob'd ♄ with it well: could see the belt plainly; & obs'd an emersion of the 3 sat. much better than it appeared thro' the 2 feet reflector." Entry for 2 Sep. 1786, Charles Blagden Diary, Yale. For all his work on it, Michell's great telescope did not enrich astronomy. After his death it was bought by Herschel. King, *History of the Telescope*, 91.

[9] Within three weeks, by 6 May, Michell was in London; see letter 16, note 7.

26. FROM JOSEPH PRIESTLEY

13 MAY 1784

From the original letter in the Devonshire Collections, Chatsworth[1]

Dear Sir

According to my promise, I have repeated the experiment with the *lead and mercury*[2] with all the precautions I could think of, and with a result sufficiently agreeable to what I observed before.

Having dissolved two Ounces of lead in mercury, I expelled as much of it in the form of black powder as weighed six Ounces, without even blowing into the phial, either with a pair of bellows, or my mouth. From this I expelled, in a coated glass retort, 4½ Oz measures of air, 2 of which was wholly absorbed by water, leaving a small residuum almost wholly phlogisticated, as also was the common air contained in the neck of the phial and that came over first; my test (with equal quantities of nitrous air) being 1.8. I did not urge this process very far, and there remained 1½ Ounces of blackish powder.

Being satisfied that the fixed air did not come from the bellows, or my breath, I expedited the remainder of the process by blowing with the bellows, which were very clean, and in constant use; and by this means got 18 Ounces more of the black powder, from which, together with what remained of the former process, I expelled 23½ Oz measures of air in six portions, the quantities of which, with what remained after washing in lime water, and the purity of the residuum, are expressed in the following table.

Air received	Residuum	Quality	
5	4	1.6	Equal quantities of nitrous air
5	.75	1.44	
5	.5	0.8	
5	.75	0.8	
2.5	1.1	0.6	Two equal quantities of nitrous air
1.	.5	0.63	
23½	7.6	16	

Both the quantity and the quality of the air seems to depend, in a great measure, on the manner of applying the heat. In all the cases the first phlogiston that is expelled affects the common air contained in the retort, the next seems to contribute to the formation of *fixed air*, and when it is almost wholly expelled, the remaining air comes over pure.

After agitating this mixture some time (viz after about 300 strokes) it grows hot, the *liquid* mass then becoming in part *solid*. This is also the case when I squeeze the mercury out of the coagulated mass in a cloth. It is sometimes as hot as I can well bear to handle.

To give you some idea of the *expedition* of this process, I observed that, towards the end of it, with 400 shakes of the phial (which would take about two minutes, blowing into it after every hundred shakes) I got six Ounces of the black powder, so that the whole took up no great time.

Nothing I well know is so acceptable [to] yo[u] [as] truth; and therefore, if it be agreeable to [you] I [will] send you an account of the result of so[me] other experiments which I am about to make relating to this subject. In the mean time it will give me great satisfaction if you, or Dr Blagden, will inform me what you think of this experiment, and whether you have succeeded in making it.

I am, with great respect,
Dear Sir,
Yours sincerely
J Priestley

Birmingham 13 May 1784
[address]:
The Honble Henry Cavendish Esq
Hampstead
near
London

[1] Cavendish Mss New Correspondence. Published in *Autobiography of . . . Priestley*, 231–32.

[2] By mixing lead and mercury in common air, Priestley several years earlier had come upon an efficient method for cleaning mercury of lead impurities, from which a black mass yielding fixed air (carbon dioxide) resulted. Priestley to Alessandro Volta, 6 June 1777, in *Autobiography of . . . Priestley*, 159–60. Cavendish was puzzled by Priestley's results, especially the fixed air, and he and Priestley must have talked about their differences, leading to the "promise" by Priestley to repeat the experiment and to report on it to Cavendish, the occasion of this first letter of their known correspondence; see next letter.

27. TO JOSEPH PRIESTLEY

[AFTER 13 MAY 1784]

From the original draft letter in the Devonshire Collections, Chatsworth[1]

D. S[ir]

I am much obliged to you for the account of your exper[iments][2] & shall be very glad to be informed of any other experiments that you may make. As soon as I make any more experiments about it myself I will be sure to send you an account of them but I am so far from possessing any of your activity that I am afraid I shall not make any very soon.

I cannot at all conceive what should be the reason of the difference in our experiments the air in mine being not only almost free from fixed air but also about 8 times as great in proportion to the black powder or to the lead employed as in yours.[3] If one could suppose that your powder was mixed with a sufficient quantity of the particles of the cloth in which it was squeezed it would account for both these circumstances but it seems very improbable that that should be

$$\frac{33}{3} \times \frac{18}{23\frac{1}{2}} = \frac{11 \times 18}{24} = \frac{11 \times 3}{4} = 8$$

the case. If it should appear on trial as you seem to suspect that the quality of the air expelled from the same black powder would be different according as the heat was applied slow or quick the heat in both cases being at last raised high enough to expel all the air it would seem a decisive proof that the fixed air was generated in the experiment. You do not say with what heat the powder was urged in your exper. In mine it was sufficient to vitrify the lead.

The heat produced by the shaking & by the squeezing out the ☿ is very curious.

---

[1] Cavendish Mss New Correspondence. Published in *Autobiography of . . . Priestley*, 232–33.

[2] Letter 26.

[3] Priestley found that mercury to which lead or tin was added and which was then agitated in the presence of air deposited a powder consisting mainly of the calx of the added metal, and that the powder sometimes contained fixed air (carbon dioxide). Cavendish discussed these experiments in three publications as well as in his correspondence with Priestley. In each instance Cavendish considered impurities as the likely source of the fixed air and thus the reason for the difference between his results and those of others. "Experiments on Air," *PT* 74 (1784): 119–69; in *Sci. Pap.* 2:162. "Answer to Mr. Kirwan's Remarks upon the Experiments on Air," *PT* 74 (1784): 170–77; in *Sci. Pap.* 2:182–83. "On the Conversion of a Mixture of Dephlogisticated and Phlogisticated Air into Nitrous Acid, by the Electric Spark," *PT* 78 (1788): 261–76; in *Sci. Pap.* 2:232. Cavendish gave a similar explanation for his differences with Richard Kirwan: see letter 35, note 7.

28. FROM JOSEPH PRIESTLEY

16 JUNE 1784

From the original letter in the Devonshire Collections, Chatsworth[1]

Dear Sir,

As you wish to be informed of the progress of my experiments,[2] I shall briefly mention what I have done since my last; stating the *facts* only, as you will be better able than I am to draw the proper *inferences* from them.

Resuming my experiments on the seeming conversion of water into air;[3] I find that a vessel of *chalk* answers as well as one of *clay*. *Mercury* comes thro in the form of a black powder, tho, in the same degree of heat, I cannot with an air pump force a particle of the mercury thro the retort, which, in this, case was made of pipe clay. Alkaline air is transmitted as well as air of other kinds.

Throwing the focus of a burning lens upon shavings of iron, in d^{d} [dephlogisticated] air confined by mercury, both very warm and dry, the air disappeared, no water was found, but some fixed air; and the slag to which the iron was reduced had gained as much weight as that of the air that had vanished. In the open air 24 grains of iron imbibed 5 grains of air, and 24 grains of steel imbibed 7½ grains. After this my lens could not melt it, nor will any acid, except the marine, dissolve it. It is the same thing as the *scales of iron* from a smiths forge.

Throwing the focus of the lens on iron thus saturated with pure air, in inflammable air, confined by mercury, all very dry, the air disappeared, and the iron lost so much weight that the d^{d} air expelled from it would have saturated the inflammable air that disappeared; and in this case as much water was produced as I imagined would have been equal to the weight of the air.

Having mixed a quantity of d^{d} air, and of inflammable air from *iron* in the usual proportion of 1 to 2, I exploded 3½ Ounce measures of it, and found neither water nor fixed air; but using inflammable air from *charcoal*, (which shewed no sign of containing any fixed air) I got ⅘ of an Ounce measure of fixed air, and an evident quantity of *water*.

To prosecute these experiments to advantage I much want a burning lens of greater power than mine. However, I shall d[o] as well as I can, and shall not fail to acquaint you with the results; hoping [to] be favoured with your observations on them, and you are at liberty to mention the facts to any of your acquaintances.

I am, with much respect,

Dear Sir,

Yours sincerely

J Priestley.

Birmingham 16 June 1784

[address]:
The Hon[ble] Henry Cavendish
Hampstead
near
London

---

[1] Cavendish Mss New Correspondence. Published in *Autobiography of . . . Priestley*, 233–34.

[2] Letter 27.

[3] Priestley, "Experiments Relating to Phlogiston."

29. TO CHARLES BLAGDEN

10 SEPTEMBER [NOT BEFORE 1784][1]

From the original letter in the Royal Society[2]

Mr Cavendish is very sorry he should have forgot to send his Coachman to him yesterday but sends him now with this note when he will be at his service till 2 o clock. If the coachman does not find him at home to day he will come to him again to morrow at the same time but if that is an inconvenient day desires he will not stay at home on purpose & on Monday will settle on some other day. Bed. square Sept: 10

[1] The earliest year is determined by Cavendish's address, Bedford Square, to which he moved in 1784.

[2] Blagden Letters, C.20.

30. TO JOSEPH PRIESTLEY

20 DECEMBER 1784[1]

From the original draft letter in the Devonshire Collections, Chatsworth[2]

D. S[ir]

I am very obliged to you for your letter last June[3] & would have acknowledged the favour before had I not delayd it in hopes of sending you an account of some exper[iments] in return but by the trouble of removing my house & one thing or another I was prevented from making any <exper.> all the summer. I have lately however gone on with the exper I told you I was making about the Electric spark.[4] I believe I mentioned to you when in town that on taking the electric spark through impure dephl[ogisticated] air confined by lime water & ☿ no cloud was formed in the lime water & that none was formed also on letting up some fixed air but that on adding to that a little caustic vol[atile] alk[ali] a brown sediment was immediately formed. The 2 last circumstances seemd to shew that an acid was formed in the operation which dissolved the lime & the first circumstance shewd that no fixed air was generated by it. What was the reason of the brown colour of the sediment I do not know unless a little of the ☿ was dissolved. As this [---] some of the phlog[isticated] air with which the deph[logisticated] air was debased was turned into N[itrous] acid. I lately took the spark through a mixture of deph[logisticated] & common air confined between sope leys & ☿ adding fresh air as required till no more would be absorbed. The quantity of sope leys employed was such as ¼ if satur[ated] with nitr[ous] acid would have yielded about ¼ gra. of nitre & the air absorbed containd about 69 of pure deph[logisticated] air & 32 of phlogist[icated] air.

I believe I told you when you was in town that I had just tried an exper of the same kind as this but that by accident & a bad method of trying the sope leys I could not tell whether any nitre was produced or not.

The sope leys after the operation was found to be intirely neutralized & on evap[oration] it yielded a small quantity of saline matter which proved to be true nitre.

Though the exp. & the burning of nitre shews that part of the phlogist[icated] air of the atmosphere consist of the nr. acid united to phlogist[on] yet it might be doubted whether the whole is so & whether there are not rather various different substances confounded together by us under the name of phlogist[icated] air. But from the following exper it should seem as if the whole was of the same kind as on taking the spark through some of the same air confined as before till about 75 parts of phlogist[icated] air were absorbed & after that adding some pure deph. air & continuing the spark till the diminution was nearly ceased & then adding liver of sulphur to absorb the dephlog. air it was reduced to less than one measure. So that out of the 76 parts of phlog. air employed there was only one which was not absorbed or as we may conclude from the former exper turned into nitr acid.[5]

I shall at any time be very glad to hear how you go on in your exper. & will with pleasure send you an account of any thing I do myself but as I make not a tenth part of the exper that you do & as my facility in writing falls short of yours in a still greater proportion I am afraid you will think me a bad correspondent & that the advantage lies intirely on my side.

---

1 Cavendish labeled this draft letter, "to Dr Priestley Dec. 20 1784."

2 Cavendish Mss New Correspondence. Published in *Autobiography of . . . Priestley,* 239–40.

3 Letter 28.

4 "Experiments on Air," Cavendish Mss II, 5. "Diminution of Air by Electric Spark," p. 306, to an entry the day before the date of this letter, p. 323.

5 In his published paper the following year on the phlogisticated air (nitrogen) of the atmosphere, Cavendish repeated his discussion from Priestley's letter and improved the accuracy of the result he reported by an order of magnitude. To Priestley he said that within 1 part in 76, the phlogisticated air of the atmosphere is all of the same kind, capable of being reduced to "nitrous acid." In his laboratory minutes, p. 317, and in his paper, he estimated the "small bubble" remaining in his apparatus as no more than 1/120th part of the phlogisticated air, a residue he treated as the measure of his experimental accuracy. This tiny bubble led through Cavendish's work to the discovery of the inert gases of the atmosphere a hundred years later. "Experiments on Air," *PT* 75 (1785): 372–84; in *Sci. Pap.* 2:193. Travers, *Ramsay,* 100–7.

31. TO NEVIL MASKELYNE

29 DECEMBER 1784[1]

From the original draft letter in the Devonshire Collections, Chatsworth[2]

I am sorry I have neglected so long [to] fulfill my promise of last Thursday about Mr Vinces paper[3] but have been prevented by other matters from attending to it.

If the wheel abd revolves on the center c it is evident from the properties of the lever that any force F applied to the point x in a direction perpendicular to cx will have just as much effect in stopping the motion of the wheel as the force F x cx/ca applied to the point a in the same direction & consequently as friction does not depend on the velocity but acts with the same force on x as on any other particle of the same size the effect of friction on any particle x to retard the motion of the wheel is simply as its distance from the center.[4]

What I suppose led you to think otherwise is that if the wheel is put in motion the effect which the momentum of each particle has in preventing the motion from being stopt is as the square of its distance from the center. For supposing any force to be applied at [point] a so as to retard the motion the diminution of velocity produced in the point x is as cx & consequently the force which must be applied to the point x in order to produce that diminution is also as cx & therefore the force which must be applied to the point in order to have that effect is as the square of cx.

As well as I remember Newton as you said really made a mistake from not considering this in the precession of the equinoxes supposing the force necessary to be applied to the equator in order to move any particle of the earth to be simply as its distance from the axis of motion.[5]

---

[1] Cavendish wrote at the bottom of this draft letter "Dr Maskelyne Dec 29. 1784."

[2] Cavendish Mss New Correspondence.

[3] "On the Motion of Bodies Affected by Friction," *PT* 75 (1785): 165–89; read 25 Nov. 1784. Samuel Vince (1749–1821), mathematician and astronomer, F.R.S. 1786. Having graduated first wrangler and first Smith's prizeman, Vince was then living in Cambridge; later he would be appointed Plumian professor of astronomy and experimental philosophy in the university. "Vince," *DNB* 20:355–56.

[4] Cavendish's statement agrees with Vince's experimental "principles" of the force of friction on moving bodies: the force depends on the surface of contact and not on the velocity.

[5] Like Cavendish and Maskelyne, Vince evidently moved from the problem of friction to that of the precession of the equinoxes and to Newton's reputed error. His next paper on mechanics, "On the Precession of the Equinoxes," *PT* 77 (1787): 363–67, began: "The true cause of the precession of the equinoctial points was first assigned by Sir Isaac Newton; but it is confessed, that he has fallen into an error in his investigation of the effect." Vince argued that the "true solution" could be deduced from Newton's "own principles."

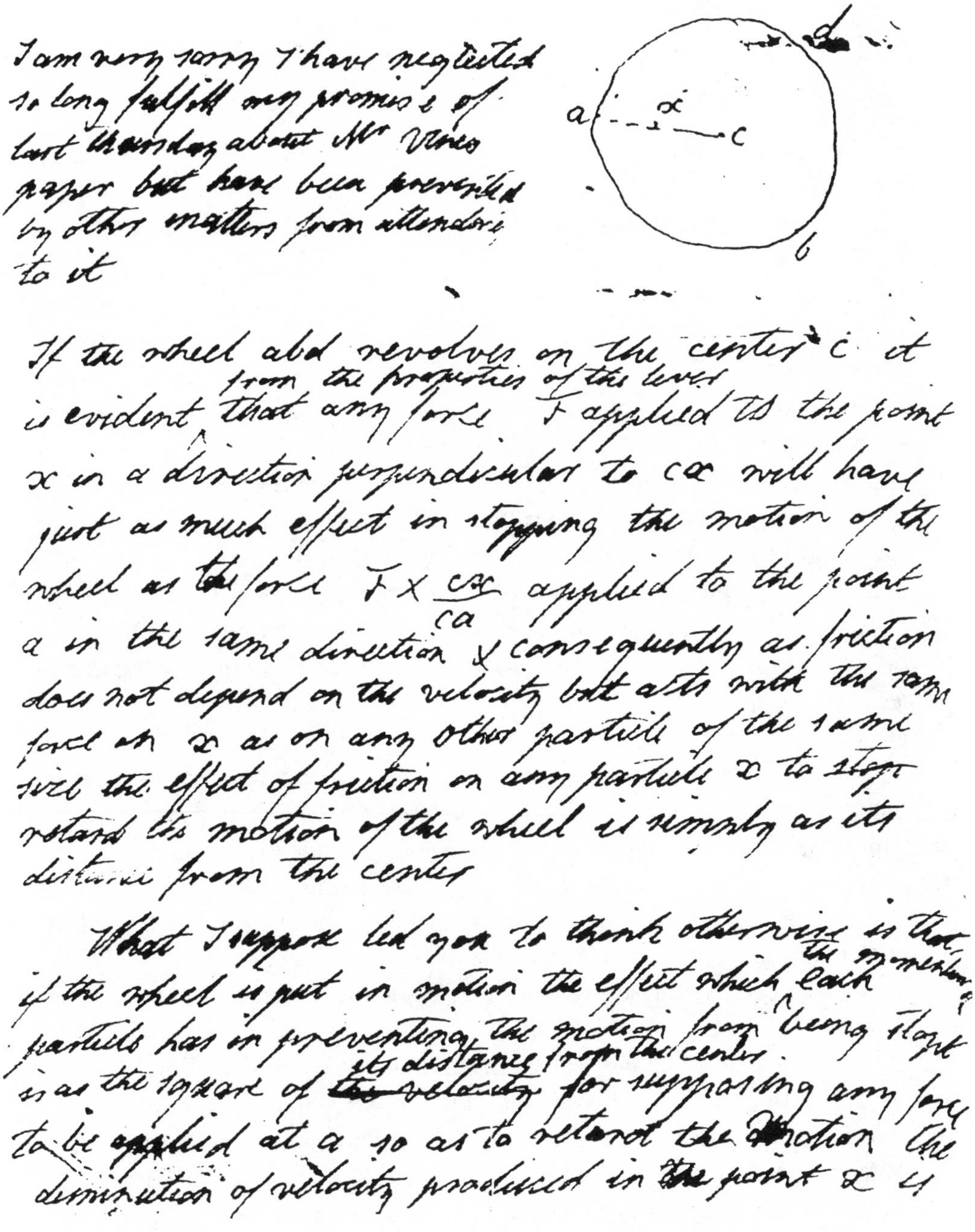

I am very sorry I have neglected so long fulfill my promise of last thursday about Mr Vinces paper but have been prevented by other matters from attending to it

If the wheel abd revolves on the center c it is evident from the properties of the lever that any force F applied to the point x in a direction perpendicular to cx will have just as much effect in stopping the motion of the wheel as the force $F \times \frac{cx}{ca}$ applied to the point a in the same direction & consequently as friction does not depend on the velocity but acts with the same force on x as on any other particle of the same size the effect of friction on any particle x to ~~stop~~ retard the motion of the wheel is simply as its distance from the center

What I suppose led you to think otherwise is that, if the wheel is put in motion the effect which each [the momentum] particle has in preventing the motion from being stopt is as the square of its distance from the center ~~the velocity~~ for supposing any force to be applied at a so as to retard the motion the diminution of velocity produced in the point x is

107. *Extract on Friction of Moving Bodies. Letter from Henry Cavendish to Nevil Maskelyne, 29 December 1784, Cavendish Scientific Manuscripts New Correspondence. Reproduced by permission of the Chatsworth Settlement Trustees.*

32. FROM JOSEPH PRIESTLEY

30 DECEMBER 1784

From the original letter in the Devonshire Collections, Chatsworth[1]

Dear Sir

I am glad that my experiments give you any pleasure;[2] but you greatly overrate both my readiness in making them, and my facility in writing; and may not perhaps consider that my time is likewise much engaged in things of a very different nature.

I am much obliged to you for the account of your experiments on *phlogisticated air*, which I consider as one of the greatest, perhaps the very greatest, and most important, relating to the doctrine of air. You seem, indeed, fully to have proved the existence of the nitrous acid in that kind of air, and consequently to have discovered the true source of *nitre* in all the processes for making it.[3]

Presently after my last to you, I discovered the fallacy of the conclusion from my former experiments, and the truth of your hypothesis, that *water* is a necessary ingredient in *inflammable air*.[5] Iron filings, in their ordinary state, gave air a whole day in a gun barrel, and a common fire, but at length ceased, but the process was renewed by putting water to them–I likewise found that when I had no *wet leather* for my receiver to stand upon, but made every thing as *dry* and as *hot* as possible, I could not disperse more than two grains of charcoal by heat in vacuo.

On this I repeated the *Parisian experiments* only sending steam from a separate boiler, thro a hot *copper cylinder*, containing *iron filings*, or *charcoal*, with the results which they describe; but I see no reason to conclude that the inflammable air, in either of these cases, comes from the *water*. Iron, in this process, yields one half more inflammable air than it does when dissolved in acids, and exactly of the same kind, except that it is free from all offensive smell. In this manner there can be no doubt, but that balloons may be filled with the purest air, in the cheapest manner.

It is remarkable that *iron*, treated in this manner, is one third heavier than it was before, and is, in all other respects, the very same thing with iron saturated with d[d] [dephlogisticated] air. When heated in *inflammable air*, it loses that weight, which is found in *water*, but when heated with *charcoal* it yields no water at all, but an immense quantity of *air* part of which (1/5 at the beginning) is fixed air, and the remainder, tho inflammable, is quite as heavy as common air. The reason of this appears when it is decomposed with d[d] air, for then the fixed air it contains is separated from it. After either of the two processes, the iron is restored to its own final properties.

Steam of water has no effect on *Copper* but sending thro my copper tube, only 4 Ounces of *Spirit of wine in vapour*, it was dissolved, and came in pieces, being converted into a *black powder*. On this I took *earthen tubes*, and putting copper into it, formed a curious combination of copper and spirit of wine. I have done the same with *lead*, and *silver*, and shall try all the metals.

Putting into the earthen tube pieces of other earthen tubes (in order to expose more red hot surface) I convert the whole of *spirit of wine, ether,* and *oil of turpentine* into inflammable air, remarkably different from each other. That from *ether* will not fire with d^{d} air. It burns with a white lambent flame. The pieces of earthen retorts &c with which I fill the earthen tubes, in some of these experiments, are fastened together with a remarkable kind of *charcoal*, the same, I suspect, with that describe[d] in my paper on charcoal. I have great quantities of it, and shall try its electrical properties soon.

With respect to *the seeming conversion of water [into] air*, I find that the transmission of vapour and air depends upon actual *pores*, tho the exper[iment] succeeds with the closest *white marble*. It mus[t] therefore be owing to some kind of *attraction of cohe[sion]* tho I cannot explain it.

I think I told you before, that I convert *alkaline air* into *inflammable*, by heating anything in it red hot.

I shall be obliged to you if you will shew this letter to Dr Heberden, who is pleased to interest himself in my experiments, and to whom I have not written [-----] lately, tho he is already acquainted with many particulars in this letter.

I am, Dear Sir,
Yours sincerely
J Priestley

Birm. 30 Dec^{br} 1784
[address]:
The Honourable Henry Cavendish Esq
Hampstead
near London

---

1 Cavendish Mss New Correspondence. Published in *Autobiography of . . . Priestley*, 240–42.

2 Letter 30.

3 Cavendish, "Experiments on Air," *PT* 75 (1785): 372–84; in *Sci. Pap.* 2:191.

4 Cavendish, "Experiments on Air," *PT* 74 (1784): 119–69; in *Sci. Pap.* 2:173.

33. TO JEAN-ANDRÉ MONGEZ[1]

22 FEBRUARY 1785

From the original draft letter in the Devonshire Collections, Chatsworth[2]

Á Londres ce 22 fevrier
1785–

En lisant, Monsieur, la traduction de mon memoire sur l'air publié dans le journal de Physique, Je fus frappé de le voir datté de janvier 83, comme si la lecture en euts été faite *alors* devant la Société Royale; J'eus recours aux exemplaires détachés imprimés pour l'usage de mes amis, Sur l'un desquels apparemment avoit été faite votre traduction; Je trouvai à mon grand Etonnement, qué l'Imprimeur avoit fait Cette même faute dans toutes les copies, malgré que l'original publié dans les Transactions Philosophiques avoit été datté, comme il devoit l'etre, de Janvier 84. Je Vous serai trés obligé, Monsieur, de vouloir bien faire mention de cette méprise dans le cahier prochain de votre Journal.[3]

Je suis mortifié d'etre dans le cas d'ajouter qu'il s'en faut de beaucoup, que la traduction soit exacte; on a manqué le sens en plusieurs endroits.[4]

J'ai l'honneur d'etre avec des sentimens distingués

Monsieur

Votre trés humble et trés
obeiss[t] serviteur

[address]:

À Monsieur
Monsieur J. A. Mongez le Jeune
&c &c &c
au Bureau du Journal
de Physique
à Paris

---

[1] Jean-André Mongez (1751–88), writer and editor. "Mongez," *Biographie universelle*, new ed., 28:622; Poggendorff 2: cols. 186–87.

[2] Cavendish Mss X(b), 11. Published in French in Wilson, *Cavendish*, 423. The letter is unsigned, and the handwriting belongs to someone other than Cavendish or Blagden, but it is written on Cavendish's stationery, and it is certainly by Cavendish. It is a draft, with crossings-out. According to Wilson, the letter is addressed to "T. A. Mongez, le Jeune," editor of the *Journal de Physique*. But Jean-André Mongez took over the direction of the journal from his uncle F. Rozier in 1780. Gillispie, *Science and Polity in France*, 190. Jean-André was the younger brother of the distinguished archeologist Antoine, the origin, we think, of "le Jeune" in Cavendish's address. Wilson misread the "J" as a "T."

[3] Although the correct date of the reading of Cavendish's paper on the generation of water, "Experiments on Air," was given in the *Philosophical Transactions*, 15 January 1784, in the separate copies of the paper–what we would call reprints or offprints–the year was mistakenly given as 1783. The error was an embarrassment to Cavendish, especially as his paper led to a priority dispute, the "water controversy." The French translation of "Experiments on Air" in the *Journal de Physique*

retained the incorrect date. Despite this letter by Cavendish, the journal did not point out the error, an instance, Wilson says, of "Editorial reluctance to confess error." Wilson, *Cavendish*, 419–24.

[4] The translator was the chemist Pierre-Joseph Pelletier. Blagden offered help, but the translation was a disaster all the same. Blagden was surprised to learn that Pelletier intended to translate Cavendish's second paper, "Experiments on Air." Blagden supposed that Pelletier was anxious to redeem his reputation. Blagden to Pelletier, [Nov. 1784], draft, Blagden Letterbook, Yale. Blagden to Sir Joseph Banks, 3 Sep. 1785, Banks Correspondence, Kew, 1.201.

33T. TRANSLATION OF LETTER TO MONGEZ

22 FEBRUARY 1785

From the original draft letter in the Devonshire Collections, Chatsworth

London 22 February
1785–

In reading, Sir, the translation of my paper on air published in the Journal de physique, I was astonished to see it dated January 83, as if it had been read before the Royal Society *then*; I had recourse to the unbound offprints made for my friends, from one of which apparently your translation was made. I found to my great astonishment that the printer had made this same error in all the copies, despite the fact that the original published in the Philosophical Transactions had been dated as it ought to be, as January 84. I will be very much obliged to you, Sir, should you kindly make mention of this mistake in the next issue of your journal.

I am mortified to have to add that the translation is far from being exact; the sense has been missed in several places.

I have the honor to be with the sincerest of sentiments,

Sir

Your very humble and very
obed[t] servant

[address]:
To
M. J. A. Mongez, Jr.
&c &c &c
at the Office of the Journal
de physique
in Paris

34. FROM CHARLES BLAGDEN

[1784 OR 1785]

From the original letter in the Devonshire Collections, Chatsworth[1]

Dear Sir,

As Mr. Berthollet[2] is appointed my correspondent by the Academy, I consider the inclosed letter[3] as a disavowal on the part of that Body, of M. Lavoisier's[4] pretentions to your discovery.[5] It appears to Sir Jos. Banks in the same light.

You will observe that M. Lavoisier in trying the experiment so much insisted on, of reviving red precipitate with iron, found *no fixed air.* A similar experiment has been made in Germany with copper instead of iron, without obtaining fixed air; but here it is objected that copper having a stronger affinity to phlogiston than iron has, prevented any of it from joining the d[d] [dephlogisticated] air; & that the only decisive experiment would be with Zinc, which has less affinity to phlogiston.

M[r] Herschel is come to town sick; his disease an ague which is now endemic at Datchet.[6] He is now better, but so strongly affected by his illness, as to be afraid of returning to Datchet even when he shall be quite well.

I shall be detained in this part of the town too late today for me to dine in the city; but shall be at home in the evening in case you have any questions to ask: I intend writing to Paris tomorrow.

Your faithful hble Serv[t]
CBlagden.

Monday 1½ p.m.

---

1 Cavendish Mss New Correspondence.

2 Claude Louis Berthollet (1748–1822), chemist, member of the Paris Academy of Sciences, F.R.S. 1789. Kapoor, "Berthollet," *DSB* 2:73–82.

3 The enclosed letter was very likely from Berthollet to Blagden, 19 Mar. 1785, published in its original French in Wilson, *Cavendish*, 345–46.

4 Antoine Laurent Lavoisier (1743–94), chemist, member of the Paris Academy of Sciences, F.R.S. 1789. Guerlac, "Lavoisier," *DSB* 8:66–91.

5 The reference is to the "water controversy." Lavoisier's claims to the discovery of the composition of water are closely analyzed by Wilson, *Cavendish*, 337–47.

6 Location of Herschel's observatory.

35. FROM CHARLES BLAGDEN

[AFTER 2 JUNE 1785]

From the original letter in the Devonshire Collections, Chatsworth[1]

Dear Sir,

Together with the revised proofs of your Paper, and the M.S. I send the first proofs,[2] that you may the more readily perceive some alterations which I thought it expedient to make. Any of them which you shall not approve may easily be changed back again: that which pleases me least is p. 382 l.5 from the bottom; but it is very awkward to make use of such an expression as "*the case*" twice in three lines.

This afternoon I have seen a letter from M. de Morveau,[3] in which he gives an account of a similar experiment to Dr Fordyce's[4] on the effect of heat on the gravity of bodies, and with the same result.[5] That experiment, however, at which M. de Morveau was present, seems to be more ambiguous, because the water was made to boil in the glass vessel hermetically sealed. How could this be? It was also tried with glacial oil of vitriol, & found to answer in the same manner. 9000 grains of water lost 5/4 gr. between boiling and freezing: (whether the act of freezing be included does not appear). M. de Morveau fancies that in a certain vitrified acid of phosphorus he has found an acidifiable basis, which proves the existence of phlogiston, of which he is a most zealous defender; but his reasoning on the subject is sufficiently obscure.[6]

Mr Kirwan has repeated, with great accuracy, the experiment of distilling red precipitate with iron filings; & finds that no fixed air whatever is produced; so that when you, on performing that experiment, found fixed air, it must have proceeded from the foulness of the materials you employed. See Phil. Tr. 1784 p 175.[7] Of all the metals he has tried, Zinc only produced fixed air, by detonation with nitre.

Your faithful humble Servant.

CBlagden.

A life of Bergman,[8] written by himself, is publishing in Sweden. At Dijon they are printing a collection of Scheele's[9] Works, translated into French.[10]

Saturday Night.

---

[1] Cavendish Mss X(b), 4.

[2] Cavendish, "Experiments on Air," *PT* 75 (1785): 372–84; read 2 June 1785.

[3] Louis Bernard Guyton de Morveau (1737–1816), French chemist, F.R.S. 1788. Smeaton, "Guyton de Morveau," *DSB* 5:600–4.

[4] George Fordyce (1736–1802), London physician, F.R.S. 1776. Poggendorff 1: col. 773.

[5] George Fordyce, "An Account of Some Experiments on the Loss of Weight in Bodies on Being Melted or Heated," *PT* 75 (1785): 361–65. Blagden thought that if Fordyce were right in thinking that heat diminishes the gravity of bodies rather than making them heavier, it would produce an "extraordinary revolution in our ideas." Blagden to Lorenz Crell, 28 Apr. 1785, draft, Blagden

Letterbook, Yale. Cavendish, who believed that heat is motion not a fluid, would have been skeptical of Fordyce's conclusion.

[6] Guyton de Morveau was a warm advocate of phlogiston in 1785, but soon, in 1787, he would be converted to Lavoisier's point of view, and he would become one of the authors of the new nomenclature. Smeaton, "Guyton de Morveau," 602.

[7] In the *Philosophical Transactions* of 1784, these three papers appeared back to back: Cavendish's "Experiments on Air," Kirwan's criticism of it, and Cavendish's rejoinder. Cavendish maintained that in all phlogistic processes in which respirable air is consumed, water is produced. Kirwan held to his earlier view that fixed air (carbon dioxide) is generated and absorbed in these processes. In his rejoinder Cavendish argued that in the "most material experiment" of Kirwan's argument–an experiment owing to Priestley in which red precipitate (red oxide of mercury) and iron filings are mixed–fixed air is generated, but it is not generated by the iron. Rather it is separated off from the impurities in the iron, chiefly plumbago. Cavendish, "Experiments on Air"; Kirwan, "Remarks on Mr. Cavendish's Experiments on Air"; Cavendish, "Answer to Mr. Kirwan's Remarks upon the Experiments on Air," *PT* 74 (1784): 119–79, on 174–75. See letter 27, note 3.

[8] Torbern Olof Bergman (1735–84), Swedish chemist, natural philosopher, and natural historian, member of the Stockholm Academy of Sciences, F.R.S. 1765. Smeaton, "Bergman," *DSB* 2:4–8.

[9] Carl Wilhelm Scheele (1742–86), Swedish chemist, member of the Stockholm Academy of Sciences. Boklund, "Scheele," *DSB* 12:143–50.

[10] Carl Wilhelm Scheele, *Mémoires de chymie*, 2 vols., trans. Mme. Guyton de Morveau (Dijon, 1785).

36. FROM RICHARD BROCKLESBY[1]

4 JUNE 1785

From the original letter in the Devonshire Collections, Chatsworth[2]

Tin filings, or grey Calx of Tin calcined by weak Nitrous Acid, & the calx of either rubbed together wth dry Vegetable Alkali emits a strong Volatil Alkali in great quantity. Query how is this produced? Is not the fact deserving attention in Mr Cavendish's investigation of the component principles of elastic fluids?

This was left wth Dr Brocklesbys respects to Mr Cavendish.

4th June 1785

---

[1] Richard Brocklesby (1722–97), London physician, F.R.S. 1746. "Brocklesby," *DNB* 2:1282–83.

[2] Cavendish Mss Misc.

37. FROM JEAN SENEBIER[1]

1 NOVEMBER 1785

From the original letter in the Devonshire Collections, Chatsworth[2]

Pour Monsieur Cavendish

Monsieur

Ilya longtemps que je connois tout le prise de vos travaux et que je desire de vous temoigner le plaisir que me procurent vos belles decouvertes. Vous avés bien voulu me faire present des morceaux précieux que vous avés communiqués à la Societe Royale de Londres. Daignes encore me permettre de vous assurer de ma reconnoissance.

J'ai lu avec toute lattention possible ces deux Memoires[3] que je relirai surement souvent encore. Jy ai admiré la dexterite avec laquelle vous faites vos expériences, lexactitude que vous y apportés, la sagacite avec laquelle vous les imagines pour rendre rigoureuses les conclusions que vous en tirés. Vous etes un maitre et un grand maitre dans lart difficile de faire des experiences.[4] Je me trouverai trop heureux de parvenir a suivre de loin vos excellentes lecons.

Je ne sais si c'est un préjugé, mais il me semble qu'une foule dexperiences tendent a etablir que la combinaison du phlogistique avec lair deflogistiqué forme lair fixe ou bien que les procedés phlogistiquants changent la partie de lair pur qui est dans lair atmospherique en air fixe, et la quantité de cet air fixe produit est trop grande pour lattribuer a la saleté de l'air commun ou de deflogistiqué. Si dans la calcination des Metaux la combustion du soufre ou du phosphore il n'en paroit aucune trace ne seroit ce point parce quil est absorbé par ces corps. Javoue que la combustion de lair inflammable metallique offre une anomalie qui me paroit jusquesa present irreductible a la Loi que j'ai crue pres que générale. Mr Prestley me marque quelques experiences bien propres a confirmer cette opinion. Son *Charbon metallique* ou son Cuivre supersature dephlogistique exposé a laction de la lentille sous un recipient plein d'air dephlogistique le chang[e]ra pres que tout en air fixe. Au reste je ne decide rien. J'attends avec avidité les suites de vos recherches et les responses que vous voudrés peut etre me donner pour dissiper mes doutes.[5]

Vous seres peut etre etonné de ma franchise. Le croires vous Monsieur; je ne puis imaginer encore que toute leau que vous avés obtenue dans la combustion de l'air inflammable, et de lair dephlogistiqué appartint constitutionnellement a ces airs. Je crois bien quune partie de cette eau est constitutionnelle dans l'un des deux airs ou que cette partie est peut etre le produit de la combinaison operée par la combustion. Je nexamine pas cette question mais je crois fort en meme temps qu'une grande partie de cette eau etoit dissoute seulement dans ces deux airs qui l'ont lachée quand ils nont plus pu la retenir et remarques le bien cette eau devoit etre dans ces airs puis qu'ils ont toujours été enfermés par l'eau, agités avec elle et quil est démontre quil faut tres peu de temps pour saturer d'eau lair qui est a meme de s'en saturer. En vain Mr Lavoisier a cru repondre à cette objection dans des experience quil a faites pendant le printemps passé. Il a fait passer ces deux airs saturés d'eau au travers d'un tube rempli dAlkali caustique avant de les bruler, mais il est demontré que ce procèdé ne peut tout au plus dessecher un peu quune tres petite quantite de lair qui passe dabord. LAlkali humecte et tout le reste de lair passe sans se dessecher comme lhygrometre le prouve. Au reste je n'ai point encore fait ce genre d'experience, mais je me dispose à les commencer bientot avec un appareil qui me les facilitera beaucoup, mais encore une fois je vous propose mes doutes Monsieur et je craindrai toujours de me tromper quand je ne me rencontrerai pas avec vous.

Cest ainsi que vous m'inspirés une tres grande defiance sur mes experiences que j'ai publiees dans mes Recherches analytiques sur l'air inflammable.[6] Quand vous aves fait detonner l'air inflammable avec lair deflogistiqué vous n'avés jamais trouvé leau produite par la combustion impregnée de lacide avec lequel vous avés fait lair inflammable. J'ai fait cependant mes experiences après avoir lavé mon air inflammable dans une eau alkalisée lors que je lavois fait avec un acide et je le lavois dans une eau acidulée lors que cet air inflammable avoit ete fait avec un alkali volatil. Cependant dans tous ces cas j'ai cru reconnoitre en brulant lair inflammable avec lair commun, des traces sensibles de la nature saline avec laquelle je lavois fait. Dois je vous ajouter que depuis ces experiences j'en ai fait de nouvelles qui me confirment la composition de lair inflammable et cette confirmation est dautant plus propre a faire impression sur moi qu'elles sont faites par des moyens très differents, et quelles sont une nouvelle maniere d'analyser lair inflammable. Cependant je veux refaire toutes mes experiences. Jaime mieux la verite que mon opinion et je suis bien plus disposé a vous croire qu'a me croire moi meme.

Je vous dirai tout ce que je pense. J'ai été etonné que vous n'ayés pas parlé du lavage repete de l'air inflammable parce que j'ai appris par mon experience quil conservoit longtemps les traces exterieures de la matiere saline avec laquelle je lavois fait.

Si javois pu avoir la lentille que j'attends tous les jours de Mr Parker jaurois fait des experiences tranchantes sur cette matiere, mais jespere quelles sont seulement differées et que je pourrai realiser entierement mes projets sur cette matiere.

Au reste je suis bien charmé de voir que vous n'admettés point comme un Etre réel ce que plusieurs Physiciens appellent *chaleur latente*. Je ne sais voir dans cette denomination que la [peinture] de la faculté qu'ont les corps de s'echauffer par le moyen de leur rapports avec le feu. J'aime voir les agents physiques que j'employe se démontrer a mes sens par des effets sensibles et les belles experiences de Mr Felice Fontana[7] ne laissent aucune espoir de prouver ainsi lexistence de cet Etre nouveau.

Je ne puis mieux croire que l'air inflammable soit le phlogistique de Stahl[8] a moins d'imaginer que la lumiere qui reduit largent dans la lune cornée ne soit aussi de l'air inflammable, mais parce que l'air inflammable dans un etat de decomposition reduit les metaux et ce n'est seulement que dans ce cas quil produit cet effet faudra t'il en conclure que dans son etat de combinaison il produise cet effet. Je ne puis au moins limaginer. Cependant l'air inflammable en se decomposant sur leau noircit largent, mais s'il est enfermé dans un vase bien sec avec du Mercure bien sec il ne lui fait eprouver aucun effet. Mais je marrete. C'est un sujet que je serois appellé a traiter de nouveau.

J'ai lu vos belles experiences sur l'air phlogistiqué. Je ne puis trop vous dir[e] combien elles m'ont etonné. Après la premiere lecture je pouvois a peine croire les resultats que vous avés si habilement decouverte et saisis que les recherches que vous continués surement sur cette matiere importante seront utiles et curieuses. Elles seules peuvent nous faire connoitre l'air que nous respirons, que je serois heureux de pouvoir jouir de vos travaux et detre savant de votre science car jetudie plus pour minstruire que pour instruire les autres et je suis plus sur des idees que je recevrai de vous que de celles que jaurai produites.

Je serai naif avec vous comme je le suis toujours. Permettés moi donc de vous faire cette objection. Si les choses se passent dans la nature comme dans le Tube recourbé ou vous faites eclater letincele electrique dans lair flogistiqué et l'air pur, narrivera t'il pas qu'apres les Coups de Tonnerres il y aura de lacide nitreux produit en abondance et sil y en a n'en appercevroit on pas les traces sur les couleurs bleus des fleurs et par mille autres moyens.

Les procedés flogistiquants qui forment l'air fixe comme par exemple les corps en pourriture favorisent la nitrification. Cependant ce n'est pas ceux qui font l'air flogistiqué, puis quils agissent seulement sur la partie pure de l'air. On n'a pas remarqué que les années orageuses fussent plus favorables a la production du nitre, ou de lacide nitreux, il paroit dans les experiences bien faites qu'on a entreprise pour decouvrir sil y avoit quelque acide mineral dans lair que l'Alkali dont on esperoit la combinaison n'a donné aucune marque qui put la faire soupconner.

Pardonnés moi Monsieur je vous ai ecrit comme un disciple ecriroit à son maitre et soyés sur que ma lettre avec les doutes qu'elle renferme ne sortira pas de mon portefeuille. Je ne publierai jamais que lestime et la consideration respectueuse avec laquelle j'ai lhonneur detre

Monsieur

Votre tres humble et obeis
sant serviteur
Senebier

Geneve ce 1er Novembre 1785

Comme j'ignorois votre adresse j'ai remi ma lettre a un ami qui s'est chargé de vous la faire parvenir ce qui est cause du long delai que j'ai pris pour vous repondre.[9]

La franchise que je vous ai montree ne me permet pas de vous dissimuler un soupçon. Lalkali que vous aves employé quoique vous lappellees *Soap lee* ne seroit il point tiré du Nitre? Et alors il ne seroit pas surprenant que vous eussies obtenu du Nitre car quoi quon fasse on ne peut le debarrasser alors de ce sel neutre. Ou bien votre lessive des savonniers ne seroient elles point faites avec des Cendres tirant de plantes nitreuses? Le scrupule seroit alors moins fondé mais il pourroit avoir lieu. Cette experience est si importante et si delicate que vous devres preparer vous meme votre alkali en le tirant du Tartre par le feu. Et alors il ne resteroit aucun doute.

---

[1] Jean Senebier (1742–1809), Swiss physiologist interested in the exchange of gases in green plants exposed to light. Pilet, "Senebier," *DSB* 12:308–9.

[2] Cavendish Mss New Correspondence.

[3] These would be Cavendish's two papers of 1784 and 1785 entitled "Experiments on Air."

[4] Senebier wrote extensively and thoughtfully on what he commended Cavendish for, the art of experimentation: *Essai sur l'art d'observer et de faire des expériences*, 2d ed., 2 vols. (Genève, 1802).

[5] See Priestley's letter of the previous year, number 28.

[6] *Recherches analytiques sur la nature de l'air inflammable* (Genève, 1784). The British chemist Peter Woulfe, who spent time regularly in Paris, had sent a copy of Senebier's *Recherches analytiques* to Cavendish the previous winter. Charles Blagden to Peter Woulfe, 11 June 1785, draft, Blagden Letterbook, Yale.

[7] Felice Fontana (1730–1805), Italian scientist. Belloni, "Fontana," *DSB* 5:55–57.

[8] Georg Ernst Stahl (1660–1734), German physician and chemist. King, "Stahl," *DSB* 12:599–606.

[9] We do not know if Cavendish replied to this letter, but we suppose that he did. He invited the correspondence by sending Senebier his papers, and he valued Senebier's work. In his handwriting are five pages of notes from Senebier dealing with air from plants, effects of different airs and different light on plants, and the action of light on minerals. Cavendish Mss X(c), 15. Senebier, *Mémoires physico-chymiques, sur l'influence de la lumière solaire pour modifier les êtres des trois règnes de la nature, & sur-tout ceux du règne végétal*, 3 vols. (Genève, 1782).

37T. TRANSLATION OF LETTER FROM SENEBIER

1 NOVEMBER 1785

From the original letter in the Devonshire Collections, Chatsworth

For Mr. Cavendish

Sir

For a long time now I have known the value of your works and have desired to inform you of the pleasure that your beautiful discoveries give me. You were kind enough to give me some important information that you communicated to the Royal Society of London. Please allow me to express again my gratitude.

I read with all possible attention the two papers, which I will surely often reread. I admired in these the dexterity with which you make experiments, the exactitude with which you conduct them, the sagacity with which you conceive them so as to make rigorous the conclusions you draw from them. You are a master, and a very great master, of the difficult art of making experiments. I will be only too happy to follow from a distance your excellent lessons.

I am unsure if this is a prejudice, but it seems to me that a great number of experiments tend to confirm that the combination of phlogiston with dephlogisticated air forms fixed air, or rather that the phlogisticating processes change the portion of pure air in the atmosphere into fixed air, and the quantity of this fixed air produced is too great to attribute it to the impurities of common or dephlogisticated air. If in the calcination of metals or in the combustion of sulphur or of phosphorous no trace of it appears, would this not be because it is absorbed by these bodies? I confess that the combustion of metallic inflammable air offers an anomaly, which appeared to me until now irreducible to the law that I believed nearly general. Mr. Priestley acquainted me with some very proper experiments that can properly confirm this opinion. His *metallic carbon* or his supersaturated dephlogisticated copper exposed to the action of the burning lens under a receiver filled with dephlogisticated air will change it nearly all into fixed air. Yet I can decide nothing. I eagerly await the results of your work and the responses that you will perhaps agree to supply me with in order to dispel my doubts.

You will be perhaps astonished by my frankness. Will you believe me, Sir; I still cannot imagine that all of the water you have obtained in the combustion of inflammable with dephlogisticated air belongs constitutionally to these airs, although I believe that a portion of this water is inherent in one of these airs or that this portion is perhaps the product of the combination produced by the combustion. I do not examine this question, but at the same time I strongly believe that a large part of this water was dissolved only in these two airs, which discharged it when they were no longer able to retain it, and note that this water ought to have been in these airs since they have always been enclosed in water, agitated with it, and it is proven that one needs only a little time to saturate with water the air, which is disposed to be saturated by it. In vain Mr Lavoisier thought to respond to this objection in some experiments he made last spring. He passed these two airs saturated with water through a tube filled with caustic alkali before burning them, but it is proven that this process at most slightly dessicates only the very small quantity of air that first passes. The moist alkali and all the rest of the air pass without being desiccated, as the hygrometer proves. Besides, I have not yet made this kind of experiment, but I am disposed to begin it soon with an apparatus that will help me conduct these experiments. But once again I offer you my doubts, Sir, and I will always be afraid of going wrong when I find myself in disagreement with you.

In much the same fashion, you inspire in me a very great mistrust of my own experiments, which I published in my Recherches analytiques sur la nature de l'air inflammable. When you detonated inflammable with dephlogisticated air, you never found the water produced by the combustion to be impregnated with the acid with which you made the inflammable air. I, however, conducted my experiments after having bathed my inflammable air, when I had made it with an acid, in an alkaline water, and I bathed it in an acidulated water when this inflammable air had been made with a volatile alkali. In all these cases, however, I believed I encountered in burning inflammable air with common air some sensible traces saline nature with which I had made it. Should I add that since making these experiments, I have made new ones that confirm for me the composition of inflammable air, and this confirmation moreover is all the more sufficient to give me the impression that they are made by very different means, and that they are a new way of analyzing inflammable air. Nevertheless, I wish to redo all my experiments. I love truth more than my opinion, and I am more inclined to believe you than myself.

I will tell you all that I am thinking. I have been surprised that you have not spoken of the repeated bathing of the inflammable air, because I learned from my experience that it retained for a long time the external traces of the saline matter with which I made it.

If I had been able to have the lens, which I expect any day from Mr. Parker, I would have made decisive experiments on this matter, but I hope they are only deferred and that I will be able entirely to realize my plans in this matter.

Besides, I am truly delighted to see that you do not regard as a real Being what several physicists call *latent heat.* I can only recognize by this name the portrayal of the property that bodies have of being heated through their relation to fire. I like to see the physical agents I use reveal themselves to my senses by perceptible effects, and the beautiful experiments by Mr. Felice Fontana allow no hope of proving as such the existence of this new Being.

I cannot believe furthermore that inflammable air is the phlogiston of Stahl without imagining that the light which reduces silver in luna cornea is also from inflammable air. But because inflammable air in a state of decomposition reduces metals, and it is only in this case that it produces this effect, must one conclude that in its state of combination, it produces this effect? I at least am unable to imagine it. However, inflammable air, in decomposing over water, blackens silver, but if it is enclosed in a very dry vessel with very dry mercury, it does not result in any effect at all. But I will stop here. This is a subject which I would be called to treat anew.

I read your beautiful experiments on phlogisticated air. I cannot exaggerate how much they surprised me. After the first reading, I was barely able to believe the results that you so skilfully discovered and understood; the researches that you surely continue on this important matter will be useful and interesting. Only they can make known to us the air we breathe. How happy I would be to benefit from your works and to learn from your science, for I study more to instruct myself than to instruct others, and I am more confident of the ideas which I will receive from you than those that I will have produced.

I will be candid with you as I always am. Allow me then to make this objection. If things occur in nature as in the curved tube where you produce the electrical spark in the phlogisticated and pure air, will it not come to pass that after the thunderclaps, nitrous acid will be produced in abundance? And if there is some of it, would not one perceive traces of it in the blue color of flowers and by a thousand other means?

The phlogisticating processes that form fixed air favor nitrification, as with, for instance, putrefying bodies. However, it is not those bodies that make phlogisticated air, since they act only on the pure part of air. No one has observed that stormy years have been more favorable to the production of nitre or nitrous acid. Well-executed experiments, which we have undertaken in order to discover if there is any mineral acid in the air, make it apparent that the anticipated combination of alkali gave no indication that would cause one to suspect its presence.

Pardon me, Sir. I have written to you as a disciple would write to his master, and you may be certain that my letter, with the doubts it contains, will not leave my portfolio. I will only make public the esteem and the respectful consideration with which I have the honor to be

Sir

Your very humble and obedient
servant
Senebier

Geneva 1st November 1785

As I did not know your address I entrusted my letter to a friend who took the responsibility of forwarding it to you, which is the reason for the long delay I have taken in responding to you.

The frankness that I have shown you does not permit me to conceal a suspicion. The alkali that you have used, although you call it *soap lee*, would it not be extracted from nitre? And so it would not be surprising that you should have obtained nitre, for whatever one does one cannot get rid of this neutral salt. Or else, would not your soaps from the manufacturers be made with ashes taken from nitrous plants? The doubt would then be less well-founded, but it could still remain. This experiment is so important and so delicate that you yourself ought to prepare your alkali by extracting it from tartar by fire. Only then would all doubt be expelled.

38. FROM MARTIN VAN MARUM[1]

6 JANUARY 1786[2]

From the original letter in the Devonshire Collections, Chatsworth[3]

a M. Cavendish.
Londres.

Monsieur!

Il y a quelques mois, que M Blagden m'a fait l'honneur de m'envoyer un exemplaire de votres *experiments on air read Juin 2.1785*, pour y trouver l'explication des quelques phenomenes concernant les differentes especes d'air, que j'avois observé dans mes experiences avec la grand machine de Teyler,[4] dont j'ai donné la description cette année. J'avois deja vu la description de vos belles expériences chez M Monge[5] a Paris, quand j'y etois dans le dernier mois d'Aout. Plusieurs Academiciens m'animoient alors de repeter vos expériences avec la grande force de notre Machine Teylerienne. Ayant recu apres votre Memoire par le soin de M. Blagden, j'ai pris la resolution de faire vos experiences aussi tot que j'y trouvais l'occasion: mais comme vous n'avez pas donné la description, a quelle maniere vous avez preparé l'air dephlogistiqué, dont vous vous êtes servi, j'ai commencé l'experience en employant l'air dephlogistiqué produit de mercure précipité rouge. De cet air, bien depuré de son acide, j'ai melé en 2 parties, avec trois parties d'air commun, comme vous avez a present. M Paets van Troostwyk[6] d'Amsterdam, qui est bien connu par ses recherches sur l'air, m'assistoit dans toutes ces experiences. Au lieu de votre syphon je me suis servi d'un tube ab, placé perpendiculairement, dont la partie superieure se etoit perforé par un fil de fer, qui conduisoit le fluide electrique. De cette maniere je pouvois faire passer le rayon electrique de notre machine presque continuellement par un colonne d'air de 3 ou $3\frac{1}{2}$ pouces. Le diametre ou la largeur de cette tube etoit $\frac{2}{12}$ pouce. L'alcali caustique, dont je me suis servi, etoit preparé, suivante votre indication, et avoit la meme force, que celle que vous avez employé; j'en placois $\frac{5}{12}$ pouce sur le mercure. De cette maniere j'ai dissout premierement une colonne d'air d' $8\frac{3}{5}$ pouces, et examinant alors l'alcali, en brulant un petit echantillon de papier que j'en avois impregné, j'observai, qu'il avoit reçu un peu d'acide nitreux; cependant il etoit tres loin d'etre neutralisé. Je continuois l'experience, jusqu'a j'avois dissout encore 14 pouces de la meme melange d'air, dessus le reste du meme liqueur alcaline, qui formoit a present un colonne d'un quart de pouce, et examinant alors de la meme maniere ce liqueur, j'etois fort surpris d'observer, que je m'avois rien gagné. Cet alcali n'avoit reçu plus d'acide nitreux, qu'avant cette repetition.

Ensuite je me suis servi d'air dephlogistiqué produit du minium par l'acide vitriolique. De cet air, bien depure de l'air fixe, j'ai melé sept parties, avec trois parties d'air phlogistiqué, suivant votre indication. De cette melange j'ai dissout $22\frac{1}{4}$ pouces dans le meme tube de $\frac{2}{12}$ pouce de largeur, dessus un colonne d'alcali d'1/8 pouce. Examinant alors cet alcali a la meme maniere, j'observois qu'il avoit reçu un peu d'acide nitreux; mais je n'ai pu decrouvir, qu'il en etoit plus impregné, où qu'il approchoit plus la point de saturation, que dans l'experience precedente.

Apres ces experiences infruc-tueuses j'ai taché d'obtenir d'air dephlogistiqué de la poudre noire formée par l'agitation du mercure avec le plomb, (pour suivre votre experience aussi exacte, qu'il me seroit possible) [--] echauffant ce poudre dans un [cornue] de verre placée dans un bain de sables. M. Cuthbertson,[7] a Amsterdam, (le Mechanicier Anglais, qui a construit notre Machine) s'est chargé avec cette operation. Mais que quoiqu'il a eschauffé ce [cornue], jusqu'il etoit fondu, il n'en a pourtant rien reçu que d'air fixe. Repetant l'experience le resultoit etoit egale.

Je prens la liberte de vous addresser le detail exacte de ces experiences, afin que vous pouvez juger, Monsieur! d'ou vienne, que les resultats de celles çi ne s'accordent avec les votres; et de vous prier, que vous voulez avoir la bonté de m'instruire a quelle maniere je puisse obtenir cet air, que vous avez employé, et si vous pouvez deviner, quelle soit la cause, que l'alcali dans mes experience a reçu si peu d'acide nitreux, quoique la quantité d'air, que j'ai dissout pour saturer cette petite portion dans la deniere experience, etoit si grande.

Puisque je m'interesse beaucoup, Monsieur! de confirmer vos experiences, qui m'ont donné une grande satisfaction, a cause qui repandront beaucoup de lumiere sur plusieurs phenomenes, je vous prie de m'instruire la dessus par votre reponse; Vous m'obligerez donc infinimment Monsieur! de me repondre en peu de tems, d'autant plus, qu'on desire de seavoir de moi, si mes experiences s'accordent avec les votres. Je differerai pourtant d'en parler, puisque je me flatte, que je reussirai mieux, quand j'aurai reçu votre instruction.

J'ai l'honneur d'etre avec une consideration tres distinguée

Monsieur.

votre tres humble &
tres obeissant serviteur
M:V:Marum

Harlem le 6 Janvier
1785
[address]:[8]
Henry Cavendish
Esq. F.R.S. and A.S.
London
Bedford Square

---

[1] Martin van Marum (1750–1837), Dutch physician, botanist, and natural philosopher, member of the Netherlands Society of Sciences, F.R.S. 1798. Muntendam, "Marum," *DSB* 9:151–53.

[2] Marum incorrectly dated his letter a year earlier, 1785 instead of 1786.

[3] Cavendish Mss New Correspondence.

[4] In 1777 Marum was appointed by the Society of Sciences to direct their expanding museum, Teyler's Cabinet of Physical and Natural Curiosities. There, in the physical laboratory of the museum, Marum carried out experiments using a new electrical machine. With disks five and a half feet across, this machine was the largest of its kind in the world. Beginning in 1785, Marum described experiments made using the machine, in three volumes of the proceedings of the Museum, *Verhandelingen uitgeven door Teyler's tweede Genootschap*. Muntendam, "Marum." The personal exchange between Marum and Cavendish was preceded by a letter from Blagden to Marum, "occasioned by the perusal of your magnificent work on the vast electrical machine," in particular, of the part treating the "effects produced by the electric spark or ray in passing through different kinds of air. Now there was lately read before the R.S. of London a Paper by the Honble Mr Cavendish which explains in my opinion to perfect satisfaction, some of the more remarkable phaenomena you obtained in those experiments. As it will not be possible for me to publish that volume of the Phil. Tr. containing this Paper till the winter, & you seem to be now actually employed in such researches with the advantage of a most powerful apparatus, I hope to do an essential service to the cause of Science, by inclosing for you the copy of a memoir which throws so much light on the subject, and so happily points the way to future discoveries." Blagden to Marum, 24 Aug. 1785, draft, Blagden Letterbook, Yale. The preprint that Blagden sent to Marum was Cavendish's paper demonstrating that the phlogisticated part of the atmosphere consists solely of nitrous acid loaded with phlogiston; it was published that winter, "Experiments on Air," *PT* 75 (1785): 372–84.

[5] Gaspard Monge (1746–1818), mathematician, physicist, and chemist, member of the Paris Academy of Sciences, enters the history of the "water controversy," having independently carried out experiments on the synthesis of water in 1783. Although Monge had been informed in a general way about Cavendish's experiments by Charles Blagden, his own experiments were original. He did not, however, as Cavendish did, detect "nitrous acid" in the product of the explosion of airs, the starting point of Cavendish's second publication entitled "Experiments on Air," in 1785 (note 4 above), also the subject of Marum's letter to Cavendish that year. Wilson, *Cavendish*, 350. Taton, "Monge," *DSB* 9:469–78, on 469–72.

[6] Adriaan Paets van Troostwijk (1752–1837) was an Amsterdam merchant, author of many chemical works, and a member of the Dutch Royal Institute of Sciences, Literature, and Fine Arts. Snelders, "Troostwijk," *DSB* 13:468–69.

[7] John Cuthbertson (1745–1851), instrument-maker, in London and in Amsterdam. Muntendam, "Marum," 152. Taylor, *Mathematical Practitioners*, 203.

[8] At the top of the address is written, "To Sir PPB."

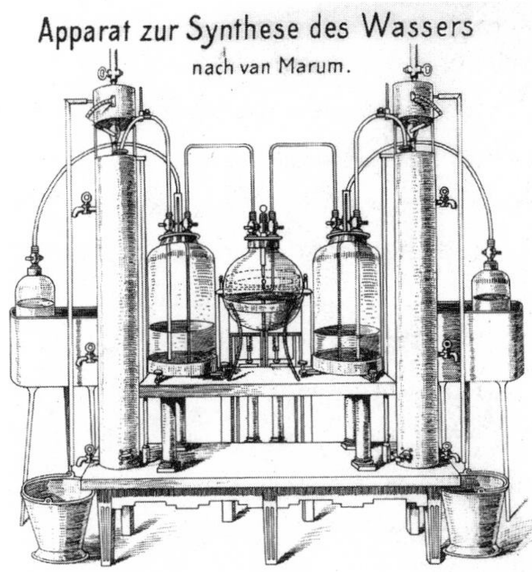

108. *Marum's Apparatus for the Synthesis of Water. At Leyden in 1787, Martin Van Marum repeated the experiment on the synthesis of water from airs. Photograph of drawing at the Deutsches Museum. Courtesy of Smith Image Collection, Van Pelt-Dietrich Library, University of Pennsylvania.*

38T. TRANSLATION OF LETTER FROM MARUM

6 JANUARY 1786

From the original letter in the Devonshire Collections, Chatsworth

To Mr. Cavendish.
London.

Sir!

A few months ago, Mr. Blagden did me the honor of sending me a copy of your *Experiments on Air read June 2. 1785* in order to find the explanation of some phenomena concening different types of air that I have observerd in my experiments with the great Teyler machine, which I described this year. I had already seen the description of your beautiful experiments at Mr. Monge's in Paris when I was there last August. Several academicians encouraged me to repeat your experiments using the powerful Teyler machine. Having afterwards received your paper through Mr. Blagden's kindness, I resolved to conduct your experiments as soon as I found the occasion to do so; but as you have not given the description of the manner in which you prepared the dephlogisticated air you used, I began the experiment by employing dephlogisticated air produced from precipitated red mercury. I mixed 5 parts of this air, well purified of its acid, with three parts of common air, as you presently have. Mr. Paets van Troostwyk of Amsterdam, who is best known for his studies on air, assisted me in all these experiments. Instead of your siphon I made use of a tube ab [see diagram], placed perpendicularly, through the top of which an iron wire was inserted that conducted the electric fluid. In this fashion I was able to make the electric ray from our machine pass nearly continually through a column of air 3 to 3½ inches. The diameter or the width of this tube was 2/12 inches. The caustic alkali that I made use of was prepared as you indicated and had the same strength as that which you employed; I placed 5/12 inches of it over mercury. In this manner, I first dissolved a column of air of some 8⅗ inches, and, examining then the alkali by burning a small sample of paper with which I had impregnated it, I observed that it had received a small amount of nitrous acid; however, it was very far from being neutralized. I continued the experiment until I had dissolved 14 more inches of the same mixture of air over the rest of the same alkaline liqueur, which formed a quarter inch column, and examining this liqueur in the same manner, I was most surprised to observe that I had gained nothing at all. This alkali had not received more nitrous acid than before I repeated the above process.

Next I used dephlogisticated air produced from minium by vitriolic acid. I mixed seven parts of this air, well purified of fixed air, with three parts of phlogisticated air, as you indicated. From this mixture I dissolved 22¼ inches [of air] in the same 2½ inch wide tube over a ⅛ inch column of alkali. Examining this alkali in the same manner, I observed that it had received a small amount of nitrous acid: but I could not learn whether it was more impregnated, or whether it came closer to the point of saturation than in the preceding experiment.

After these unsuccessful experiments I attempted to obtain dephlogisticated air from the black powder formed by the agitation of mercury with lead (in order to follow your experiment as exactly as possible), heating this powder in a glass retort placed in a sand bath. Mr. Cuthbertson of Amsterdam (the English mechanic who constructed our machine) took the responsibility of this operation. But although he heated this retort until it melted, he nevertheless received only fixed air. Repeating the experiment gave the same result.

I take the liberty of sending you the exact detail of these experiments so that you can judge, Sir! where the results of these don't match yours; and to beg of you to have the goodness to instruct me in what manner I can obtain the air that you have employed, and if you can divine what causes the alkali in my experiments to receive so little nitrous acid, even though the large quantity of air I dissolved in order to saturate this small portion in the last experiment was so large.

As I take a great interest, Sir! in confirming your experiments, which have given me a great deal of satisfaction because they shed so much light on several phenomena, I beg you to instruct me on the above topics in your response; I will be infinitely obliged to you, Sir! if you would respond quickly; moreover, many people wish to know from me if my experiments agree with yours. I will postpone, however, speaking of the matter, as I flatter myself that I will be more successful when I will have received your instruction.

I have the honor to be with the sincerest of sentiments

Sir.

your very humble &
very obedient srvant
M:V:Marum

Harlem, 6 January
1785
[address]:[1]
Henry Cavendish
Esq. F.R.S. and A.S.
London
Bedford Square

[1] At the top of the address is written, "To Sir PPB."

39. TO MARTIN VAN MARUM

[AFTER 6 JANUARY 1786][1]

From the *Philosophical Transactions*[2]

To M. Van Marum

Sir,

I received the honour of your letter,[3] in which you inform me of your ill success in trying my experiment on the conversion of air into nitrous acid by the electric spark.[4] It is very difficult to guess why an experiment does not succeed, unless one is present and sees it tried; but if you intend to repeat the experiment, your best way will be to try it with the same kind of apparatus that I described in that Paper. If you will do so, and observe the precautions there mentioned, I flatter myself you will find it succeed. The apparatus you used seems objectionable, on account of the danger of the iron being corroded by absorbing the dephlogisticated air.

As to the dephlogisticated air procured from the black powder formed by agitating mercury mixed with lead, as it was foreign to the subject of the Paper, and as I proposed to speak of it in another place, I did not describe my method of procuring it. As far as I can perceive, the success depends intirely on carefully avoiding every thing by which the powder can absorb fixed air, or become mixed with particles of an animal or vegetable nature, or any other inflammable matter: for which reason care should be taken not to change the air in the bottle in which the mercury is shaken, by breathing into it, as Dr. Priestley did, or even by blowing into it with a bellows, as thereby some of the dust from the bellows may be blown into it. The method which I used to change the air was, to suck it out by means of an air-pump, through a tube which entered into the bottle, and did not fill up the mouth so close but what air could enter in from without, to supply the place of that drawn out through the tube.

I am, &c.

---

[1] Cavendish evidently replied to Marum in the month he received Marum's letter, January, for he labeled Marum's letter, "Van Marum & answer Jan. 1786."

[2] Cavendish published this reply to Marum's letter in "On the Conversion of a Mixture of Dephlogisticated and Phlogisticated Air into Nitrous Acid, by the Electric Spark," read 17 Apr. 1788, *PT* 78 (1788): 261–76; *Sci. Pap.* 2:232. The reason he published it is that Marum, after having received Cavendish's reply to his letter, publicly complained that Cavendish had denied him the information he requested. Cavendish was stung by this criticism. In the paper above, which was about the repetition of the experiment in question, Cavendish defended himself by juxtaposing his letter to Marum alongside Marum's public criticism and letting the reader judge. With regard to the main experiment, Cavendish had given Marum all the information that was in his "power" to give. With regard to the way he had obtained the dephlogisticated air to carry out the experiment, he had "explained on what I imagine the success intirely depends." Cavendish thought that "no one at all conversant in this kind of experiments will think that I did not communicate to him [Marum] my method of procuring that air." Marum, *Premiere Continuation des Expériences, fait par les moyen de la Machine électrique Teylerienne*, published in 1787. Cavendish, "On the Conversion," *Sci. Pap.* 2:230. We

note that two years after Cavendish's paper containing his reply to, and his implicit criticism of, Marum, on 5 Aug. 1790, Cavendish dined with Marum at the Royal Society Club. Minutes of the Royal Society Club, Royal Society. A draft of Cavendish's letter to Marum is in Cavendish Mss New Correspondence. In the draft letter, the "M." is absent from the address. The other differences are punctuation and abbreviations and some crossings-out with rewording. Because there is no significant difference between the draft and the published letter, and since the latter would seem to be definitive, we reproduce it here.

[3] Letter 38.

[4] Cavendish, "Experiments on Air," *PT* 75 (1785): 372–84.

40. TO WILLIAM HERSCHEL

1 JUNE 1786

From the original letter in the Royal Astronomical Society[1]

Bedford square June 1 1786

Dear Sir

I am much obliged to you for the sight of your paper.[2] The experiments with the microscope are very curious, & well deserve attention; but I should be a better judge of their degree of force, if you had mentiond the proportion which the aperture bore to the focal length of the object glass, in those experiments in which the object was seen distinctly, as well as in those in which it was indistinct; which is a circumstance which I cannot supply as the focal length in the former experiments is not set down.

Though Huygenss[3] supposition about the smallness of the pencils is difficult to account for, yet it must be owned that yours is much more so; as his may depend on the manner in which the sensation of the retina is affected by light, which is a subject that we know very little of; whereas in your supposition I think only the refraction of light can be concerned, which is a subject that we know much more of. For this reason it can not be expected that any one should assent to your hypothesis without good proof; & accordingly he will expect that you should shew that the appearances you observed, can not depend on some other cause. For this reason your paper would be much more satisfactory, if you would set down not only the diameter of the pencils & proportion of the aperture to the focal length, but also the magnifying power, & the degree of indistinctness which ought to arise from the aberration & difference of refrangibility in the object glass, & any other circumstances which may be supposed to influence the experiment, or at least to shew that the phenomena could not proceed from those circumstances.

Quere Is not there a mistake in the diameter of the pencil in the 8th experiment?

If nothing happens to prevent it I hope my glasses[4] will be mounted & ready to look through in less than a weeks time. As soon as they are I will let you know.

Your sincerely

H. Cavendish

---

[1] Mss Herschel, W 1/13, C.17. A draft of this letter is in Cavendish Mss New Correspondence.

[2] Herschel had given Cavendish the manuscript of a paper that would be read at the Royal Society three weeks later, on 22 June, and published as "Investigation of the Cause of That Indistinctness of Vision Which Has Been Ascribed to the Smallness of the Optic Pencil," *PT* 76 (1786): 500–507. From the time Herschel began to communicate his work to the Royal Society, he was kept informed of the skepticism with which his claims of high magnification and distinct, "round & well defined" images were received there; the skeptics included Alexander Aubert, Nevil Maskelyne, and Jesse Ramsden. William Watson, Jr., to Herschel, 25 Dec. 1781, 4 and 11 Jan. 1782, Royal Astronomical Society, Mss Herschel, W 1/13, W.13, 14. Herschel to Thomas Hornsby, 1 Feb. 1782, ibid., W 1/1, pp. 31–33. Herschel responded to his critics by publishing his method of

"*experimentally*" determining magnifying powers. "A Paper to Obviate Some Doubts Concerning the Great Magnifying Powers Used," *PT* 72 (1782): 173–78. Herschel's paper of 1786 reported the experiments he made to disprove the optical doctrine that vision grows indistinct when optical pencils shrink to below a fortieth or a fiftieth of an inch across, and that the cause resides in the human eye. Using a microscope of high magnification, Herschel carried out experiments to show that much smaller pencils yield a distinct image, supporting his view that the indistinctness of the images of celestial objects lies not in the human eye but in the instrument. In that event, distinctness can be improved by improving telescopes, as Herschel was constantly doing. We know of Cavendish's interest in Herschel's claims from the story Herschel told his son, John. At a dinner given by Aubert that year, 1786, Cavendish who was seated beside Herschel and maintaining his usual silence suddenly said, "I am told that you see the stars round, Dr. Herschel." "Round as a button," Herschel replied. Cavendish lapsed into silence until near the end of dinner when he said in a doubtful voice, "Round as a button?" "Exactly, round as a button." Lubbock, *Herschel*, 102. Herschel had made his experiments as early as 1778, to which he returned only because of a "late conversation" on the subject with learned friends, to which Cavendish, however succinctly, evidently contributed.

[3] Christiaan Huygens (1629–95), Dutch expert on optics and a leading figure of the scientific revolution. Bos, "Huygens," *DSB* 6:597–613.

[4] Huygens, who is referred to in the letter as the major authority behind the view of optical pencils that Herschel wanted to refute, appears in the letter in another connection, the "glasses." Huygens is credited with having introduced a telescope with increased magnification and diminished aberration or indistinctness, fittingly called an "aerial telescope." This telescope had a very long focal length. Dispensing with the traditional barrel of a telescope, the object-glass was fixed to the top of a tall pole; the observer aligned the eye-piece with the aid of a taut thread. Huygens, through his brother Constantine who was also a telescope builder, presented the Royal Society with three object-glasses of focal lengths 123 feet, 170 feet, and 210 feet. In November Cavendish was given permission to borrow the Huygens glasses and others, to mount which he erected an 80-foot mast on the grounds of his new house at Clapham Common. These glasses had been borrowed before and used as a standard for estimating the progress in telescope-making. The astronomers James Bradley and James Pound had compared the 123-foot one with a Newtonian reflecting telescope made by John Hadley, finding the latter superior not only in manageability, which was to be expected, but also in definition. Five days after the letter from Cavendish to Herschel, Charles Blagden wrote to a colleague that Herschel was looking forward to Cavendish's trial of the Huygens telescope for "comparing the effect with that of his large reflectors." Three weeks later Herschel was still waiting. Blagden wrote to another colleague that Cavendish was going to try the telescopes of longest focal length, and he would let him know if they saw "anything of consequence with them, but probably they are much inferior to Dr Herschel's large reflectors." Blagden added that it was "desirable however to form a just estimate of the tools with which our ancestors worked." Herschel joined the instrument-maker Peter Dolland and others at Clapham Common to participate in the trial. Herschel's reflectors no doubt outperformed the aerial telescopes. Dolland found his "Dwarf," a forty-six inch, triple-lens, achromatic refractor, to be "fairly a match for the Giant." Sampson and Conrady, "Three Huygens Lenses," 289–92. 17 Nov. 1785, Minutes of Council, copy, Royal Society, 7:134. Computations for the mast in Cavendish Mss Misc. King, "Hadley," *DSB* 6:5–6. Blagden to Claude Louis Berthollet, 5 June 1786, draft, Blagden Letters, Royal Society 7:2. Blagden to Benjamin Thompson, 7 July 1786, draft, Blagden Letters, Royal Society, 7:15. Kitchner, *Economy of the Eyes*, 22.

41. FROM WILLIAM HERSCHEL

12 JUNE 1786

From the original letter in the Devonshire Collections, Chatsworth[1]

Sir,

The favour of your observations on my paper[2] ought to have been sooner acknowledged,[3] but I was willing to defer it till I might at the same time give you the additional circumstances mentioned in your letter as likely to shew better what degree of force might be attributed to my experiments. I have written sometime ago to Dr Watson[4] for his Microscope, which I used in these expe^{ts}, that I may have the same object glasses with which some of them were made, in order to ascertain the exact proportion between their apertures & focal lengths. My Brother, who comes from Bath to day, is to bring the Microscope;[5] there will however be hardly any time till my return from Germany for going thro', & properly digesting, a set of experiments.[6]

I forbore assigning a *Physical* cause for the indistinctness arising from an undue proportion between the aperture & focal length contenting myself with hinting only that such an indistinctness would take place when the aperture of an object lens or speculum bears less than a certain ratio to its focal length. If this hint should be fully verified & established, the discovery would be of some value tho' we should never know the *physical* cause, which, however, probably we shall also point out hereafter. As you seem to think that the *refraction* of light can only be concerned I beg leave to remark that many other experiments have already convinced me that something of the same nature takes place in *reflexion*, but this being a subject which will require many further scrutinies I though it best, at the conclusion of the paper, to express my wish that what I had said might be looked upon &c . . .

I am greatly obliged to you for the remark on the dia^{r} of the pencils in the 8th expe^{t}. The words object-lens & eye glass are, by mistake, put one for the other. When that error is corrected the diam^{r} of the pencils will be right. To avoid any ambiguity it will be the best way to say "8 Exp^{t}. I changed the eye-lens for another of ,171 focal length; the object-glass & distance between the two lenses remaining as in the two last experiments; aperture ,02. This gave &c:["]. You find Sir, that this exper^{t} was made in pur[suit] of lessening the pencils by an encrease of [power][7]. In the 3, 4 & 5th they were reduced by [the aperture].[8] In the 6th by power; in the 7th by apert. & power; and in the 8th again, almost as much as conveniently could be done, by power & also partly by aperture. And these six experiments seemed to me, at that time, to suffice. With many acknowledgments for the friendly communication of your Sentiments I have the honour to be with the greatest Esteem,

S^{r} y^{r} most obed^{t} humb Ser^{t}

Wm Herschel

Slough. June 12.86.
[address]:
M^{r}. Cavendish
Bedford-Square
London

---

1 Cavendish Mss New Correspondence. A copy of this letter is in Royal Astronomical Society, Mss Herschel, W 1/1, p. 146.

2 Letter 40.

3 Herschel would have just received a letter from Charles Blagden, who was both an associate of Cavendish's and a secretary of the Royal Society, reminding him that "several days ago Mr Cavendish wrote to you some observations on your Paper relative to the small pencils." In his next letter, Blagden told Herschel that he had entered the corrections in his paper, and he pointed out another mistake in the paper. Three months later Blagden told Herschel that he had sent his paper to the printer, explaining that it had been held back because Herschel, who had been abroad, could not "correct the press." Blagden to Herschel, 10 and 19 June and 16 Sep. 1786, Royal Astronomical Society, Mss Herschel, W 1/13, B.76, 77, 79. Cavendish and Blagden were helpful to Herschel in preparing his paper in yet another way. Blagden looked up references on small pencils in Cavendish's library and informed Herschel that books dealing with the subject by Huygens, Robert Smith, and Joseph Priestley would be waiting for him at Cavendish's library or, if he wished, sent to him at Slough. Blagden to Herschel, n.d., ibid., Mss Herschel, W 1/13, B.78; Blagden to Herschel, 19 May 1786, draft, Blagden Letters, Royal Society, 7:762.

4 William Watson, Jr. (1744–1825?), physician, F.R.S. 1767, living in Bath, was a close friend of Herschel's. Watson is included in his father's entry, "Watson, Sir William," *DNB* 20: 956–58, on 958.

5 A week before Herschel's letter to Cavendish, Watson had written to Herschel that he was forwarding the requested microscope through Herschel's brother. Pleased to learn of Herschel's paper on the smallness of optical pencils, Watson wished that Herschel would write another paper on the telescope, which would not only "remove prejudices which have generally been adopted, but will likewise oblige other astronomers however unwilling they may be to acknowledge the superiority of yours not only as to powers but in respect to distinctness & quantity of light." Watson to Herschel, 5 June 1786, Royal Astronomical Society, Mss Herschel, W 1/13, W.45. William Herschel's brother Jacob lived in England, the two having fled to England when the French occupied Hannover in 1757. Hoskin, "Herschel," 328.

6 Herschel was going to Göttingen to erect one of his telescopes as a gift from the king. Cavendish took advantage of Herschel's trip to help convey his latest paper on chemistry to Lorenz Crell, editor of a German scientific journal, with whom he was having practical difficulties exchanging publications. Charles Blagden to Crell, 4 July 1786, draft, Blagden Letters, Royal Society, 7:12.

7 The letter being torn here, the word "power" is taken from the copy of the letter in the Royal Astronomical Society.

8 The words "the aperture" are from the copy of the letter in the Royal Astronomical Society.

42. FROM JOHN MCNAB[1]

1 SEPTEMBER 1786

From the original letter in the Devonshire Collections, Chatsworth[2]

Albany Fort 1st Septr 1786

Sir

I was duly honoured with your favor containing your Sentiments on the experiments, that they have been acceptable to yourself and the Royal Society yields me inexpressable pleasure.[3]

I have received your Remarks upon them to the Society, for which please to accept my gratefull thanks. It will be a peculiar pleasure in using my utmost endeavours to render the present experiments worthy of your further acceptance, permit me to remain with the highest respect

Sir
Your much obliged
and most Obedient Humble Servant
John McNab

[1] John McNab, surgeon at Henley House and Albany Fort, Hudson Bay. Brown, *Strangers in Blood*, 170.

[2] Cavendish Mss New Correspondence.

[3] Following the experiments on the freezing of mercury by Thomas Hutchins at Hudson Bay, Cavendish wanted further experiments made with freezing mixtures, with the expectation that they could be made to produce an even greater cold. For this purpose Hutchins recommended his colleague at Hudson Bay, John McNab. As he was with Hutchins, Cavendish was well pleased with McNab, publishing two papers based on the experiments McNab carried out under his direction, and praising him for his accuracy and attention. "An Account of Experiments Made by Mr. John McNab, at Henley House, Hudson's Bay, Relating to Freezing Mixtures," and "An Account of Experiments Made by Mr. John McNab, at Albany Fort, Hudson's Bay, Relative to the Freezing of Nitrous and Vitriolic Acids," *PT* 76 (1786): 241–72, and 78 (1788): 166–81.

43. FROM JOHN MICHELL
8 November 1786

From the original letter in the Devonshire Collections, Chatsworth[1]

Dear Sir,

I have received yours of the 6th Inst,[2] & am not sorry to find you have got a man, who you think is likely to suit you pretty well.[3] I should not wish to part with the man I have, till I have got through with several things, I wish to try, at least in a good measure, which I hope will be the case, in a year's or year & half's time, & near the end of that time, if you should wish to change, I would gladly make it convenient to you, either by parting with him a few month's sooner, or keeping him a few months longer; when however I can determine with a little certainty more exactly when I mean to give over, I will give you timely notice that you may do as you like about it.

I have received two Letters from Dr Blagden,[4] which I mean to answer in a little while; but as I am at best but a dilatory correspondent, & there are a good many subjects in them that require to be spoken to, I hope he will not think I forget my obligations, if I should trespass upon his patience a little longer, than he may think I ought to do.

I am very sorry to find I recommended you to so ill managed a house at Sheffield:[5] the last time I was there I was at a friends, & the house had then but just begun, & I knew that it was a handsome new built Inn, in the building of which several of my friends had been concerned in the tontine way, which was the reason of giving it the name, but I had no idea of the badness of it's management, which if I had at all been aware of, I should by no means have thought of recommending any body thither, & shall take care for the future not to recommend any more customers to the same house, till it gets into other hands, & I have some reason to believe it is better managed.

I saw Mr Beatson[6] soon after I received Dr Blagden's first letter, to whom I mention'd your wish of having a specimen of the Black Lead, & which he told me he meant to have sent you, though you had not said any thing farther about it, as soon as the Walkers[7] begin to work again, & he can procure a good sample for you. He desired, I would present his Comps to yourself & Dr Blagden, & expressed great regret that he happen'd not to be at home, when you called there.

I am much obliged to Dr Blagden for a copy of Dr Herschel's paper on small Pencils.[8] I am now perfectly satisfied, that the reason, I gave you at the Society, the first time I heard of the matter, is the true reason, why Mr H[erschel] sees a distinct image, where he imagines it contradicts what was first observed by Mr Hugens,[9] & has since been observed by others af[terwards:] none of Mr H's cases are at all inconsistent with Hugens, who is undoubtedly perfectly right, for a [number of] Mr H's cases are manifestly in instances, where either the rays fall two much diverging on the eye, to be brought to an accurate focus, or they are what may, I think, not improperly be called false pencils, not consisting of little cylinders of parallel rays, when they enter the eye, but the several rays being somewhat inclined to each other in different ways or directions, instead of being collected at the bottom of the eye into an accurate focus or mathematical point are scatter'd over a small circle, which it is necessary they should be, in order to produce distinct vision, according to my paradoxical assertion as it was thought in some of the letters I wrote to Mr Smeaton last year, which you have seen, I believe; but as I mean, when I write to Dr Blagden to be a little more explicit & examine Mr H.'s cases separately, I shall say no more on this subject at present, only that I am glad Mr H. has given them to us, for which I think the optical world is much obliged to him, as it will not only serve to set a very extraordiny fact in the natural history of the eye in a clear light; but enable us to apply it to some useful purposes in some practical matters, where we may avail ourselves of the knowledge of it to our advantage. With best respects & comps as due to yourself Dr Blagden & all other friends, in which all here desire to join, I am, Dear Sir,

Thornhill Yours very sincerely J. Michell

8 Nov 1786

[address]:

To

The Honble Henry Cavendish

at Clapham

near London

---

1 Cavendish Mss New Correspondence.

2 We do not have Cavendish's letter to Michell of 6 November 1786, but we can be certain that it continued their discussions of that summer, when Cavendish and Blagden made a journey to the north of England. They stopped twice at Thornhill to see Michell, staying six days the second time. Entry for 2 Sep. 1786, Charles Blagden Diary, Yale. Blagden to John Blagden Hale, 14 Sep. 1786, draft, Blagden Letters, Royal Society, 7:33.

3 Cavendish hired scientific assistants. Two years earlier, we know, Charles Cullen, son of the Scottish physician and chemist William Cullen, worked for Cavendish in this capacity. Michell, too, evidently had help, for in connection with making the speculum for his great telescope, he referred to "we," and he excused his delay in finishing it, in part, to the difficulty in procuring "assistance" in his rural neighborhood. Charles Cullen to Charles Blagden, 7 Nov. 1784 and "Monday" [1784], Blagden Letters, Royal Society, C.62 and 63. See letters 19 and 25 by Michell.

4 Blagden to Michell, 19 Sep. and 31 Oct. 1786, Blagden Letters, Royal Society, 7:37 and 49.

5 The Fortune Inn, which Blagden characterized as the "vilest house at which I had ever the misfortune to put up." Blagden to Michell, 19 Sep. 1786.

6 William Beatson (1757–1825), together with his cousin Robert Beatson (1750–90), operated a glassworks in Rotherham, near Sheffield. Founded in 1751, since 1783 it was known as W. Beatson & Co. *The Glass Works. Rotherham, 1751–1951* (Rotherham: Beatson, Clark, 1952), 5–10. After visiting Michell, Cavendish and Blagden passed through Rotherham intending to see "Beatson," but he was away. Blagden to Michell, 19 Sep. 1786.

7 Shortly before the glassworks was started in Rotherham, an iron foundry was set up by Samuel Walker, and one of the four businessmen behind the glassworks was Aaron Walker. *Glass Works*, 5. On their journey that summer, Cavendish and Blagden went to Rotheram to inquire about a

"remarkable circumstance" they had learned from Beatson, the production of large quantities of plumbago in the process of extracting iron from its ore in "Messrs. Walkers furnaces." The workmen confirmed that sometimes they had handfulls of plumbago but little then. Being told that a furnace near Chesterfield produced plumbago, Cavendish and Blagden went there next, but again they could not get a large sample. Blagden asked Michell to ask Beatson to send Cavendish one or more pieces of plumbago for analysis. Plumbago, a black, shiny matter, was called "black lead" by Michell, and "kish" by the workmen. At "Walkers furnace at Rotheram," they were disappointed in encountering no plumbago or kish. Cavendish Mss X(a), 3:9. Charles Blagden to Sir Joseph Banks, 17 Sep. 1786, BL Add Mss 33272, pp. 9–10. Charles Blagden to John Michell, 19 Sep. 1786, draft, Blagden Letters, Royal Society, 7:37. Charles Blagden to William Lewis, 26 Sep. 1786, draft, ibid., 7:38. Beatson provided the sample of plumbago, and Cavendish recorded his analysis of it, comparing it with a sample of "kish iron" he brought home from Chesterfield: "Kish or Plumbago from Beatson," in "White Book," Cavendish Mss, pp. 57–58.

[8] Herschel, "Investigation of the Cause of That Indistinctness of Vision Which Has Been Ascribed to the Smallness of the Optic Pencil." Blagden wrote to Michell that "as it will be at least a fortnight before the printing of the Transactions can be finished, & you will probably not receive them till some time after the publication, I send you a proof sheet of Dr Herschel's paper against indistinctness of vision from small pencils, conceiving it to be a subject about which your curiosity is particularly interested." Michell ascribed indistinctness to the smallness of the optical pencil, the view Herschel rejected. Blagden to Michell, 31 Oct. 1786, draft, Blagden Letters, Royal Society, 7:49. Michell responded with a letter on small pencils, which Blagden showed to Herschel, who wrote a letter about it. Blagden did not forward it to Michell on the grounds that the "subject can be more conveniently talked over when we meet, which I hope will be next spring." Blagden to Michell, 14 July 1787, Blagden Letters, Royal Society, 7:341. Cavendish too was interested in Herschel's paper, having given Herschel his criticisms of it before publication; see letters 40 and 41.

[9] Christiaan Huygens.

44. FROM CHARLES BLAGDEN

16 SEPTEMBER 1787

From the original letter in the Devonshire Collections, Chatsworth[1]

Dover Sep. 16, 1787.

Dear Sir,

We know nothing more as yet of M. de Cassini's[2] motions, but the General[3] is of the same opinion as myself that he will very likely come over here with the packet wednesday, & that I shall go to France the following saturday evening.[4] As to the Base it cannot be begun in less than ten days, & probably will not within a fortnight. From the state of the ground near Dover great difficulty occurs in connecting the castle with the triangles to the westward; new points must be sought out, & it is as yet very uncertain whereabout they will be. The General will be very happy to see you whenever you find it agreable, & if that should not be till after I am gone, will inform you himself when the operations actually begin.

Should you come down hither before next saturday I shall be much obliged to you for bringing two small things I left behind: namely, White's Ephemeris,[5] which you will find in the front drawing room of the house in Gower Street,[6] on the shelf of the book-case under my Dictionaries, among the nautical Almanacs; and a posting map of Germany, which lies among other maps, in the same room, between the bureau & the wall. This map of Germany is a worn out dirty thing, folded up nearly square, with some figures in writing upon the outer side of it or folded; the names in the map are in German, but the title at the corner I think is in Latin. If you do not come yourself by saturday, I would beg the favour of you to look these out, and tell my servant to take them to General Roy's house in Argyll Street, to be put down hither with my parcel for him.

To day it is extremely wet, which prevents us from going to look for stations. The General expects the instrument[7] to arrive here tomorrow; & will get it up on the Castle as soon as possible, to observe the pole star the first clear night.

I have here the Nomenclature chymique[8]: if you were to come soon I would keep it till your arrival: otherwise I would return it to Sir Joseph Banks's, where you might command it.

I remain always,

dear Sir

Your very faithful hble

CBlagden.

[address]:

The Hon[ble]

Henry Cavendish

Bedford Square

London

[1] Cavendish Mss X(b), 13.

[2] Jean-Dominique Cassini (1748–1845), director of the Paris Observatory, member of the Paris Academy of Sciences, soon to be elected a foreign member of the Royal Society. Taton, "Cassini," *DSB* 3:106–7.

[3] William Roy, military surveyor, was promoted to major-general in 1781.

[4] These arrangements had to do with the Anglo-French project to determine accurately the relative locations of the Greenwich and Paris Observatories. In 1783 the director of the Paris Observatory C.-F. Cassini de Thury proposed to George III that the English lay down a series of triangles from London to Dover, there to connect with triangles already executed in France. The proposal was passed to Sir Joseph Banks, president of the Royal Society. Banks recommended William Roy to head the English half of the project. In April 1784 Cavendish and Banks met with Roy on Hounslow Heath near the Greenwich Observatory to begin observations on a five-mile baseline for the triangulation. At the time of this letter to Cavendish, a second baseline was about to be measured at Romney Marsh on the southern coast of England. Over 28,000 feet long, the measured length of the second base was found to differ by only "a few inches of the truth." The latter was the length as calculated from the triangulation proceeding from the first baseline on Hounslow Heath. Roy called this confirmation "an instance of exactness as probably never occurred in any former operation of this sort." Roy requested a British commissioner to join the French commissioners in making measurements across the Straits of Dover, thereby joining the English and French triangles. He proposed Blagden, who was duly appointed by the council of the Royal Society. At the time of this letter Blagden was preparing to cross the Straits; he would do so on 25 September. O'Donoghue, *William Roy*, 1, 41. Sir Joseph Banks to Charles Blagden, 13 Oct. 1783, Blagden Letters, Royal Society, B.19. Charles Blagden to Sir Joseph Banks, 12 July 1784 and "Tuesday" [1784], Banks Correspondence, Kew, 167 and 171. Charles Blagden to Benjamin Thompson, 22 May 1787, draft, Blagden Letters, Royal Society, 7:55. 29 June 1787, Minutes of Council, Royal Society, 7:276. William Roy, "An Account of the Measurement of a Base on Hounslow-Heath," *PT* 75 (1785): 385–480, on 389–91; "An Account of the Trigonometrical Operation, Whereby the Distance between the Meridians of the Royal Observatories of Greenwich and Paris Has Been Determined," *PT* 80 (1790): 111–270, on 116, 247.

[5] Robert White, *Atlas Ouranios, The Coelestial Atlas, or, A New Ephemeris: for the Year of Our Lord 1787* (London, 1787).

[6] Blagden's house on Gower Street, close to Bedford Square, only a few doors from Cavendish's.

[7] Believing that instruments of sufficient precision did not yet exist, Roy said that it was necessary to "reinvent them all." Principal among them was a theodolite. This instrument, which Jesse Ramsden was commissioned to build, was accurate to within one second of arc. With it, Roy said, "it is hoped the angles may be determined to a degree of precision hitherto unexampled." O'Donoghue, *William Roy*, 41. Blagden's letters to William Watson, Jr., and to William Farr on 22 Aug. 1787, drafts, Blagden Letters, Royal Society, 7:346–47.

[8] *Méthode de nomenclature chimique, proposée par MM. de Morveau, Lavoisier, Bertholet [sic] & de Fourcroy . . .* (Paris, 1787).

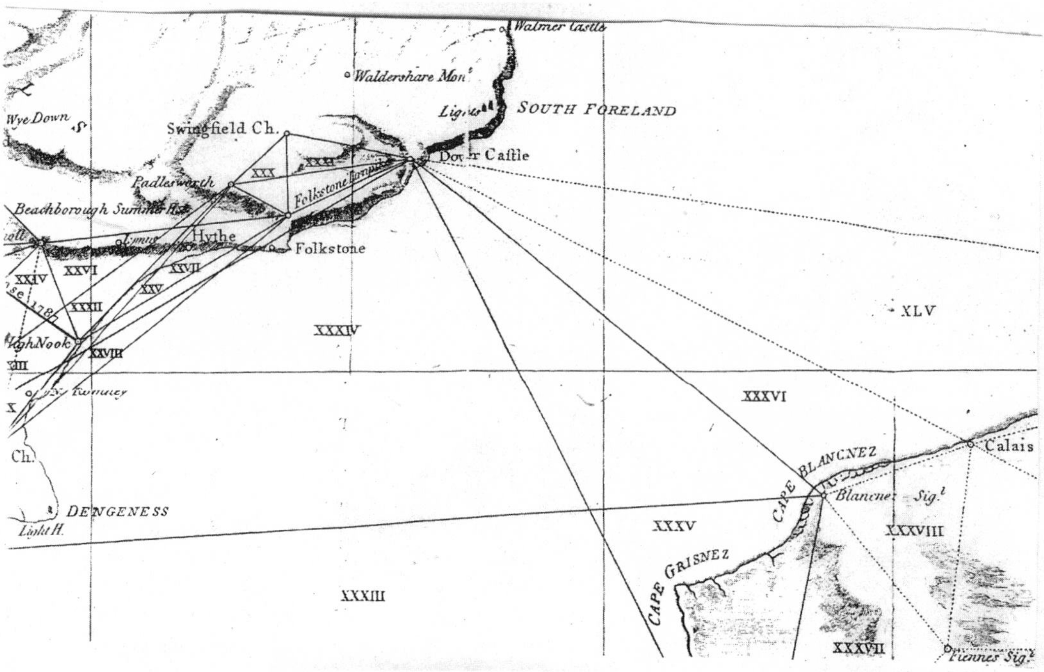

109. *Triangulations at Dover. Detail showing the extension of triangles across the Channel, joining the English and French projects. From the map appended to Roy, "An Account of the Trigonometrical Operation."*

110. *Ramsden's Theodolite. This instrument was the centerpiece of the British half of the Anglo-French triangulation project. Perhaps capitalizing on its fame, the auction catalog of Cavendish's instruments singled out "a most capital theodolite, by* Ramsden.*" Reproduced from the engraving in William Roy, "An Account of the Trigonometrical Operation."*

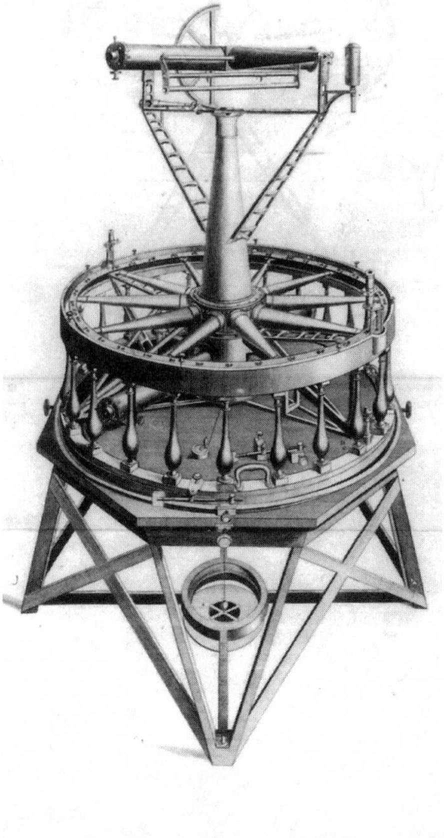

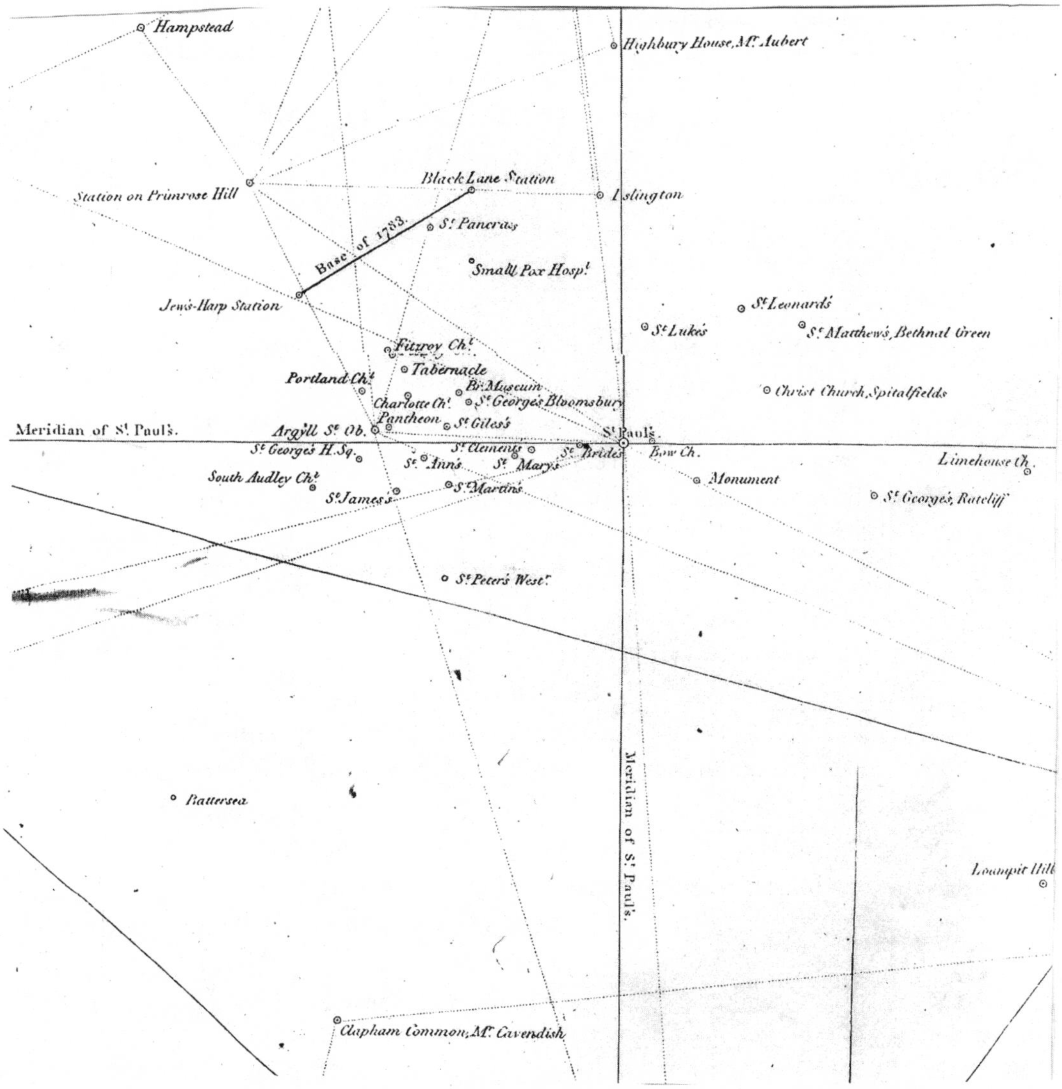

111. *Triangulations around London. Triangles measured by the British surveyors showing their starting point, the base line of 1783 on Hounslow Heath. The purpose of laying down secondary triangles was to improve plans of London and maps of the country. Cavendish's observatory at Clapham Common, shown at the bottom of the map, is one of the stations. Roy's observatory on Argyll Street is shown, as are Aubert's observatories at Highbury House and at Loampit Hill. Greenwich Observatory is just to the upper right of Loampit Hill, off the map. To the left of Loampit Hill is Sir Joseph Banks's Spring Grove House, off the map. Detail from a map by Roy, appended to "An Account of the Trigonometrical Operation."*

45. TO CHARLES BLAGDEN
[AFTER 16 SEPTEMBER 1787]

From the original draft letter in the Devonshire Collections, Chatsworth[1]

As the weather seems likely to be wet I have given up all thoughts of coming to you at present but be so good as to tell Gen[eral] Roy that if the weather grows fair I shall very likely accept his offer & pay him a visit while he is about his operations especially if the base is going on at the same time.

I was mistaken in supposing the angles could be reduced in Dr Maskelynes manner without taking into consideration the elevation or depression of the objects above the horizon. My mistake arose from supposing that if the objects were reduced to the level of the sea by lines drawn parellel to the direction of gravity at those places the reduced objects would subtend the same horizontal angle at the place of observation as the objects themselves which is true in the sphere but not in the spheroid.

M^r^ La Voisier has sent me the Nomenclature.

I do not know whether you have seen the sequel of Saussures journey.[2] The most remarkable circumstance is the effect of the rarity of the air on them which was such even after the fatigue of climbing was over that I wonder the French astronomers at Peru[3] did not observe it unless you suppose that this effect was made remarkably more sensible by their preceding fatigue.

He computed the height from his observations of the barom[eter] both according to De Lucs & Trembleys rule.[4] According to one it came out a little greater & by the other a little less than according to Sr G. Shuckburghs[5] measurement.[6]

I have been reading La V. preface.[7] It has only served the more to convince me of the impropriety of systematic names in Chemistry & the great mischief which will follow from his scheme if it should come into use. He says very justly that the only way to avoid false opinions is to suppress as much reasoning as much as possible unless of the most simple kind & reduce it perpetually to the test of experiment & can any thing tend more to rivet a theory in the minds of learners than to form all the names which they are to use upon that theory.

But the great inconvenience is the confusion which will arise from the different hypotheses entertaind by different people & the different notions which must be expected [to] arise from the improvements continually making. If the giving systematic names becomes the fashion it must be expected that other Chemists who differ from these in theory will give other names agreeing with their particular theories so that we shall have as many different sets of names <for the same substance> as there are theories. In order to understand the meaning of the names a person employs it will be necessary first to inform yourself what theories he adopts. An equal inconvenience too will arise from the necessity of altering the terms as often as new experiments point out inaccuracies in our notions or give us further knowledge of the composition of bodies. But to shew the ill consequence of what they are about, let them only consider what would be the present confusion if it had formerly been the fashion to give systematic names & that those names had been continually alterd as peoples opinions alterd. The great inconvenience is the fashion which so much prevails among philosophers of giving new names whenever they think the old ones improper as they call it. If a name is in use & its meaning well ascertained no inconvenience arises from its conveying an improper idea of its nature & the attempting to alter it serves only to make it more difficult to understand peoples meaning.

With regard to distinguishing the neutral salts of less common use by names expressive of the substances they are composed of the case is different for their number is so great that it would be endless to attempt to distinguish them otherwise. But as to those in common use or which are found naturally existing I think it would be better retaining the old names. And with regard to salts whose properties alter according to the manner of preparing them such as Corrosive sublimate Calomel &c I should in particular think it very wrong to attempt to give them names expressive of their compositon.

As I think this attempt a very mischievous one it has provoked me to go out of my usual way & give you a long sermon. I do not imagine indeed that their nomenclature will ever come into use but I am much afraid it will do mischief by setting peoples minds afloat & increasing the present rage of name making.[8]

Letter to Dr Mask[elyne]
Hatter Thursd at 3½[9]

---

1 Cavendish Mss Misc. This draft letter, which is in reply to one by Blagden on 16 Sep. 1787, letter 44, is published in *Sci. Pap.* 2:324–26.

2 Horace Bénédict de Saussure (1740–99), a Swiss scientific traveler, who observed geological formations, weather, and plant life, is best known for his *Voyages dans les Alpes, précédés d'un essai sur l'histoire naturelle des environs de Genève*, 4 vols. (Neuchâtel-Genève, 1779–96). Cavendish took considerable interest in volume 2, which appeared in 1786, and in its author. In June 1787 Saussure was proposed for foreign membership in the Royal Society; Cavendish and Blagden signed his certificate, which singled out his "treatise on hygrometry and travels into the Alps." In August 1787 Saussure climbed Mont Blanc, and within a month after returning to Geneva he published an account of the feat, remarking on the effect of the rarity of the air on the mountain: *Relation abrégée d'un voyage à la cime du Mont-Blanc* (Genève, 1787), 11. Other accounts appeared elsewhere, one of which Blagden saw. Writing to Sir Joseph Banks the day after writing to Cavendish, Blagden said that a sketch of Saussure's journey up and down Mont Blanc had appeared in the *Paris Journal* and that he was anxious to see Saussure's account of his experiments on top of the mountain. Carozzi, "Saussure," *DSB* 12:119–23. De Beer, "H.-B. de Saussure's Election into the Royal Society." 3 Apr. 1788, Royal Society Certificates, 5. Brown and De Beer, *First Ascent of Mont Blanc*, 8–9. Blagden to Banks, 17 Sep. 1787, draft, Blagden Letters, Royal Society, 7:73.

3 In 1735 the Paris Academy of Sciences sent an expedition to Peru to measure an arc of the meridian in the vicinity of the equator, while another expedition was sent to the arctic circle to make a similar measurement, the goal being to decide if the earth really is, as Newton said, flattened at the poles. The "Académiciens du Pérou" consisted of Pierre Bouguer, Charles Marie de La Con-

damine, and Louis Godin, who were accompanied by the natural historian Joseph de Jussieu. Middleton, "Bouguer," *DSB* 2:343–44. Laissus, "La Condamine," ibid., 15:269–73.

[4] Jean Trembley, "Analyse de quelques expériences faites pour la détermination des hauteurs par le moyen du baromètre," appendix to Saussure, *Voyages dans les Alpes*, vol. 2, beginning on p. 616. Jean Trembley (1749–1811), Swiss mathematician. "Trembley," Poggendorff 2: cols. 1130–31.

[5] Sir George Shuckburgh (1751–1804), mathematician and specialist in scientific instruments, F.R.S. 1774. Taylor, *Mathematical Practitioners*, 296.

[6] Sir George Shuckburgh, *Observations Made in Savoy, in Order to Ascertain the Height of Mountains by Means of the Barometer; Being an Examination of Mr. De Luc's Rules, Delivered in His Recherches sur les Modifications de l'Atmosphere. Read at the Royal Society, May 8 and 15, 1777* (London, 1777). In 1786 Cavendish calculated the height of Mont Blanc by Shuckburgh's rule: "Observations of Thermom. on Mont Blank," Cavendish Mss Misc. Charles Blagden to Sir Joseph Banks, 5 and 12 Oct. 1786, BL Add Mss 33272, pp. 17–20.

[7] Preface to the *Nomenclature.*

[8] At the conclusion of the letter, there are several incomplete sentences, crossed out: "Though you have seen this performance I have sent you the copy presented you by You will find in this packet a copy sent you by the authors."

[9] Cavendish jotted what appears to be a reminder list at the bottom of the second page turned upside down.

46. FROM CHARLES BLAGDEN

23 SEPTEMBER 1787

From the original letter in the Devonshire Collections, Chatsworth[1]

Dover (City of London)
Sep. 23, 1787

Dear Sir,

Having now finished the perusal of the Nomenclature chimique, of which I had only part before, I can make no other conclusion than that the authors have been seduced by the success of Linnaeus[2] in natural history, to apply the same kind of reformation in a case that is not analogous; as the objects of nature remain, at least during our time, always the same, whereas those of chemistry must be perpetually changing as new discoveries are made. There seems to me little danger that the systematic names will be adopted, and chiefly because so many of them have been brought forward at once; which will not only discourage people by presenting at the first appearance so great a load for the memory, but likewise, from the time it must necessarily take to become familiar with them, will probably afford an opportunity for further discoveries to render some of them improper, & to shew that a new change of nomenclature would be equally necessary. In page 204 of the book I see that they expect to prove that the different qualities of many vegetable acids, depend on the different quantities of d^{d} [dephlogisticated] air joined to the same basis; which would be a real improvement in chemistry. In the report upon the new characters, Lavoisier has ably combated the arguments of the phlogistic chemists who reported upon the nomenclature;[3] but I perceive that he has adopted (page 302) M. de Saussure's opinion of the quantity of water held in the air, & that all the rain is furnished by it, without taking any notice of De Luc's arguments to the contrary, though they were then well known in France.–I have had an opportunity of seeing here the sequel of M. de Saussure's journey up the Alps; & the only reason that occurs to me why this party were so much more affected in their breathing than the Gentlemen of Peru is, that being near ice, & in an air generally colder, their lungs were kept in the habit of consuming more d^{d} air, especially as they had ascended to the top so suddenly from the plain; whereas probably the Academicians had, from more favourable circumstances, better accommodated themselves to their new situation. And the symptoms Saussure describes are remarkably like what are felt in the *souterains* of fortifications & other places of the same nature, where the air is bad only from not being often renewed. By a note to Saussure's account it appears that he has declared open war against De Luc on the subject of hygrometry in general, & particularly of his whalebone hygrometer.[4]

It is fortunate for your own convenience that you did not come here on our speculation of the French Commissioners'[5] motions; for they are not yet arrived. Yesterday, however, Gen. Roy received a letter from Cassini, to announce that they were at Calais, & would come over as soon as they should know he was here: the answer to that letter they probably rec'd last night, & therefore we expect them in the course of this day. The weather has been blowing, & I suspect this foolish letter was in part meant to gain time till the sea should look pleasanter.

Some extraordinary facts have occurred relative to the refraction over the sea. Gravelines[6] by curvature with the ordinary allowance for refraction, should be near 100 feet under the surface, reckoning the steeple 150 feet; but we see it from the Castle not only very plain, but down far below the spire, & we see the houses of the town. They also assert at the Castle that Dunkirk is sometimes visible to them, tho' between 4 & 500 feet below the sea. Likewise we are informed that at the Pierhead in particular weather they distinguish all the steeples of Calais as it were lifted up into the air; though usually nothing of the kind can be seen; and indeed hitherto Calais has always been invisible to us from that spot, tho' plainly to be perceived at a little elevation. They say the weather in which this extraordinary refraction takes place most, is that of an easterly wind, or even the wind far to the southward, with a cloudy sky.[7]– Great inconvenience has been found in joining Dover to the other triangles, on account of its lying so behind the chalk hills that few distant objects can be perceived except to the northward. It will be necessary to have recourse to triangles of no more than 3 miles one side, & even then I fear one acute intersection cannot be avoided. This might have been prevented by carrying the series of triangles on the other side of the chalk Hills toward the Thames, but perhaps there inconveniences of another kind might have occurred. The first triangle from Dover westward seems already fixed at 5 miles on the road to Folkstone, & the village of Padlesworth (see your Survey of Kent) but what the next will be remains doubtful.–At Wrotham[8] I tried the Well, about 32 fathoms deep, & found the temperature of a bucket of water that had been raised about 5 minutes, 49⅓, the air being then 54°.[9]–I hope you got Mr Heydinger to read Crell's letter;[10] there was something about your subscription for his journal which he allows to have been all [duly] paid,[11] & an account of the freezing of ☿ by natural cold in Russia, perfectly conformable to Mr. Hutchins's experiments.[12] Be so good as to open & read or get read any letters [th]at you think may contain news.

The French [---] are arrived, & a la mode de France, have brought with t[hem] a 3^d person n[eve]r mentioned before, & much abler as a mathematician t[han] [ei]ther of the others; namely, M. le Gendre.[13] They pretend to have an instrument with which they can determine angles to 1/10″![14] I shall probably go over tuesday, but will write an exact account of the state of our business before I set out.– War seems inevitable: the French have been smuggling troops into Holland from Dunkirk in small parties; & it is said have now a force upon the sea, under M. de Bouillié,[15] to attack Jamaica.

Your faithful friend and Servant CBlagden

[address]:
The Honble
Henry Cavendish
Bedford Square[16]
London.

---

1 Cavendish Mss X(b), 14. This letter is in response to letter 45.

2 Linnaeus, or Carl von Linné, (1707–78), Swedish natural historian, who laid down a nomenclature for plants according to which each plant has two names, one for the genus and one for the species. Lindroth, "Linnaeus," *DSB* 8:374–81. The chemical nomenclature of Guyton de Morveau, Lavoiser, and their collaborators followed a similar logic: compound substances such as acids, bases, salts, and oxides were denoted by two names, one denoting their general nature, the other what is peculiar to each.

3 Blagden's wording suggests that he did not include Cavendish among the "phlogistic chemists." Cavendish's chemical researches had been guided by the phlogiston theory, but earlier that year he was reported as having renounced phlogiston. Richard Kirwan to Louis Bernard Guyton de Morveau, 2 Apr. 1787, in *A Scientific Correspondence During the Chemical Revolution: Louis-Bernard Guyton de Morveau and Richard Kirwan, 1782–1802*, 165–67.

4 The hygrometer is an instrument for measuring the humidity of the atmosphere, and although in Cavendish's time there were many attempts to make a better hygrometer, it was not as accurate as the barometer and the thermometer. Saussure invented a hygrometer based on the lengthening of a hair upon absorption of water from the air. Deluc preferred hygrometers based upon the expansion of a body not in the direction of the fibre, as with a hair, but across the fibre. His whalebone hygrometer was a slip of whalebone cut across the fibre. The two Genevans had a protracted disagreement over hygrometers and related questions, such as the quantity of water held in the air and its effect on the pressure of the air. For the Royal Society and for his own researches, Cavendish took considerable interest in hygrometers; starting in 1771, for ten years he experimented with hygrometers made of strings, ivory slips, and absorbing salts. Cavendish Mss IV, 5–9. Wolf, *History of Science* 1:325–41.

5 The three French commissioners, Jean-Dominique Cassini, Pierre-François-André Méchain, and Andrien-Marie Legendre, arrived on 23 September and stayed two days.

6 Town on the French coast near Calais.

7 In connection with observations of extraordinary refractions in Hudson Bay at the time of the transit of Venus in 1769, Cavendish had given an explanation of the phenomenon described by Blagden. "Some time ago," Cavendish wrote to an unspecified person, "in discoursing with you about the extraordinary refractions which Wales observed in Hudsons bay, I said that if the radius of curvature of a ray by refraction, was less than that of the earth, I did not see how it was possible for there to be any visible horizon: but on considering the matter further I find that it is possible." Cavendish Mss Misc.; *Sci. Pap.* 2:391–92. William Wales was at Hudson Bay to observe the transit of Venus of 1769; see letter 1. In the account of his journey to and from the observing site, he described "remarkable" refractions: "Journal of a Voyage," 115, 131.

8 The first ten stations of the series of triangles were completed from Hampton Poor-House to Wrotham Hill. The theodolite was then moved to Dover. Roy, "An Account of the Trigonometrical Operation," 113.

9 The measurements of well water belonged to Cavendish's project of determining average climates.

10 Lorenz Crell (1745–1816), German chemist, professor of medicine in Helmstedt. Hufbauer, "Crell," *DSB* 3:464–66. Crell wrote to Blagden in German about matters of concern to Cavendish. Cavendish had a German librarian who was probably "Mr. Heydinger."

[11] In 1784 Crell began the monthly journal *Chemische Annalen*, to which Cavendish subscribed but only after much delay received. Questions about the delivery and the method of payment dragged on for three years.

[12] See letters 15, note 3, 18, and 19.

[13] Adrien-Marie Legendre (1752–1833), French mathematician, member of the Paris Academy of Sciences, F.R.S. 1789. Itard, "Legendre," *DSB* 8:135–43.

[14] See next letter.

[15] François Claude Amour Bouillé (1739–1800), French general. *Encyclopaedia Britannica*, vol. 3 (Chicago: William Benton, 1962), 959.

[16] Before "Bedford Square," there is written in an unknown hand a large "4."

47. FROM CHARLES BLAGDEN

24 SEPTEMBER 1787

From the original letter in the Devonshire Collections, Chatsworth[1]

Dover Sep[r] 24, 1787.

Dear Sir,

One of the French Commissioners having brought me a parcel of Bertholletts Memoirs,[2] one copy for you, & others for some of our friends, I take the liberty of sending them to you, to be distributed, if you have an opportunity, among the Gentlemen to whom they are addressed.

I hop over to France with the Commissioners, (none of whom remain behind with General Roy) tomorrow, & expect to fire the first lights at Calais, Blancnez & Boulemberg, either the end of this week or the very beginning of next, which the General is to take from Dover. Dunkirk too will be attempted should the weather appear favorable.[3] Two days afterwards they will be fired at the same places for the General to take them from the Turnpike going down to Folkstone. After that he will be occupied at his stations of Livingfield & Padelsworth, (from neither of which lights are to be observed) and in removing the instrument to Ore, for about 10 days, when we are to shew the lights from Blancnez & Boulemberg, for him to observe at Ore; this will be perhaps the 15th of October. Thence he goes to Lydd, & there is to take the angles of lights on Blancnez & Boulemberg also, which will bring it to the 19 or 20th of October probably. He expects the measurement of the base to begin about the 10th but very probably it may be later. If you have any thoughts of joining him, you will I think be sure of finding him at or in the neighbourhood of Dover the 7th or 8th of October; & in the neighbourhood of Hastings on or soon after the 12th. He has promised me to let you know when the measurement of the base begins.

The French Gentlemen talk much of a great discovery they have made, of rendering the worst achromatic telescopes superior to the best now made of the same aperture, by insinuating a substance between the glasses of which the object-glass is composed. They say that white of egg will have the effect, & that it is wonderful; but that some less perishable substance is employed; I mentioned Blair's turpentine, & suspected from their manner it was either that, or some thing much like it. The thing may be worth attention, but Dolland[4] if I recollect right has been engaged upon it.–The fine instrument with which they take angles readily to a second & by long continuance to 1/10″, is a circle of one foot diameter, which they fix in the plane of the two objects whose angular distance is to be measured, & then take the angle a vast number of times on different parts of the circle, making the last point zero to the succeeding; they do not pretend that the circle is particularly well divided, but trust to the principle of subdividing the error till it be insensible.[5]

Probably nothing will occur on the other side of the Channel to make it worth while to trouble you with a letter. Should you have any commands for me, a[ddress] them to Calais à la poste restante. With great regard I remain

Dear Sir,

Your very faithful hble Serv.

CBlagden

[address]:

The Honble

Henry Cavendish

---

1 Cavendish Mss X(b), 12.

2 The commissioner was Legendre, who left several copies of Bertollet's memoirs for 1785 with Blagden at Dover. The *Nomenclature* was delivered by another member of the French party. Since Blagden was occupied with the triangulation project he could not deliver Berthollet's memoirs immediately to the persons for whom they were intended. Instead he sent them to Cavendish, who distributed them. Blagden to Berthollet, 17 Nov. 1787, draft, Blagden Letters, Royal Society, 7:85.

3 The lights were first fired on 29 September from all four places named by Blagden. If everything went according to plan, the last lights would have been fired on 17 October. Charles Blagden to Sir Joseph Banks, 30 Sep. 1787, BL Add Mss 33272, p. 47.

4 Peter Dolland (1730–1820), a well-known optical instrument-maker in London. Taylor, *Mathematical Practitioners*, 228–29.

5 The principle of the repeating transit was invented by Jean-Charles Borda. On his trip to France in connection with the Anglo-French triangulation, Blagden kept a journal in which he noted Borda's circle. On 29 September he described it carefully, two days later critically. He found "that the French circle was difficult to manage that the threads were not in the focus of the object glass that the stand was very unsteady & the whole instrument tottering." Cavendish copied out Blagden's journal. Cavendish Mss X(a), 1:2–3.

48. FROM JOHN HUNTER[1]

11 DECEMBER 1787

From the *Philosophical Transactions*[2]

Sir,

The following observations on the heat of springs and wells, and their application towards determining the mean temperature of the earth in different climates,[3] were suggested by you in some conversation on that subject, previous to my going to Jamaica[4] in 1780. If you think them deserving the attention of the Royal Society, I must beg the favour of you to lay them before that learned Body.

I have the honour to be, &c.

John Hunter

Charles-street
Dec. 11, 1787.

[1] John Hunter (1754–1809), physician, F.R.S. 1786. Wilkinson, "'The Other' John Hunter." At some point Hunter became Cavendish's physician.

[2] This letter prefaces Hunter, "Observations on the Heat of Wells and Springs in the Island of Jamaica, and on the Temperature of the Earth below the Surface in Different Climates," *PT* 78 (1788): 53–65.

[3] In the interest of his research on climates, Cavendish enlisted many observers in England and in other parts of the world.

[4] In 1781 Hunter was sent to Jamaica as superintendent of military hospitals, which post he held for two years. Wilkinson, "'The Other' John Hunter," 228.

49. FROM CHARLES BLAGDEN

2 FEBRUARY 1788

From the original draft letter in the Royal Society[1]

Mr Cavendish Feb 2, 1788

This day I *felt* myself under the necessity of sending [the] letter, of which the enclosed is a copy to Sir Jos. Banks. With^{t} such a detail of minute circumst^{ce} as it wo^{d} be almost impossible to give I can scarcely hope that you will approve my resolution;[2] but I perceived too plainly, either thro' my fault, or his, or both, unless some change was made we sho^{d} soon come to an open & perhaps a violent mixture; which by this step I hope to avoid.[3] At all events I have the satisfaction to think, that no one can be injurd by it but myself. I am, d^{r} Sir, y^{r} very faithful & affect. friend CB.

---

[1] Blagden Letters, B.39.

[2] On the same day he wrote to Cavendish, Blagden sent a letter to Sir Joseph Banks, from which we learn that his "resolution" was to resign as secretary of the Royal Society and to return all of the salary he had received. The letter to Banks is cool but guarded and not yet confrontational, as later letters to Banks would be, and as Blagden's letter to Cavendish portends. Blagden's letter to Banks begins:

> In conseq^{ce} of our conversation this morning, join^{d} [to] sev^{l} other circumst^{ces} that have occurred not conformable to the ideas which induced me to be a candidate for the office of Sec^{y} to the R.S. I am now come to the resolution of resigning that office, when it can be done with propriety. The time I leave entirely to you & the Council requesting that you would in that respect, consider nothing but the convenience of the Soc^{y}; and particularly, as the affair of Mr Planta is still in passage that you would not think it necessary to take any steps, till that gent^{n} shall either have [determ^{d}] to continue in his office, or another Sec^{y} shall have been chosen in his place. After my resignation, I shall be happy to assist & promote, as far as lies in my power, and as my situation will permit, the pursuits & interests of the Royal Society in the same manner as I used to do before I was Sec^{y}; but I perceive it must be a voluntary act, & not cons^{d} as a duty. I must now make you acquainted with an intention which I ment^{d} to my friend Mr Cavendish before my election to the office. It was & is my wish, that the Society would accept the different sums I have rec^{d} by way of salary, as the commencement of a fund for the purchase of books. You would oblige me very much by consulting with the Treasurer in what manner this money, amounting to about £250, can be so presented to the Society as to be appropriated to that use.

Charles Blagden to Sir Joseph Banks, 2 Feb. 1788, draft, Blagden Letters, Royal Society, B.38–39.

[3] See letters 60 and 61. Word of Blagden's disaffection spread. Three days after this first letter to Cavendish on the subject of Blagden's deteriorating relations with Banks, Blagden wrote to the physician William Watson, Jr., son of Cavendish's close friend William Watson. "Far from considering your interference on the present occasion as an intrusion I cannot but see it as a proof of the purest friendship. Be assured it will not be my fault if Sir Joseph Banks & myself do not meet upon the same terms as usual." Blagden said he did not bear Banks ill will and would continue to promote Banks's interests "short of an absolute sacrifice of myself." Charles Blagden to William Watson, Jr., 5 Feb. 1788, draft, Blagden Letters, Royal Society, 7:115.

50. FROM WILLIAM FARR[1]

2 MARCH [1788]

From the original letter in the Devonshire Collections, Chatsworth[2]

Dr Farr returns his respectful Comp^{ts} to Mr Cavendish, has rec^{d} his draught, & will take care to rectify any mistake in respect to the Registers, as he shall not leave town this week, hopes for the honor of meeting Mr Cavendish sometime in the course of it.[3]

N. 7 Steward street

[-----]

March 2^{d}

---

[1] William Farr, physician in the royal naval hospital at Plymouth, where he kept a meteorological journal, F.R.S. 1770. Munk, *Roll* 2:228.

[2] Cavendish Mss New Correspondence.

[3] We suppose that the "Registers" referred to in this letter were connected with a meteorological experiment on Dartmoor in 1787, which Cavendish directed with assistance from Blagden. Farr and two other men from the area participated. Charles Blagden to William Farr, 3 July 1787, draft, Blagden Letters, Royal Society, 7:335. See letter 55.

51. FROM RICHARD WALKER[1]

27 MARCH 1788

From the *Philosophical Transactions*[2]

The Royal Society having been pleased to insert, among their Transactions for last year, an account of some experiments of mine, relating to the production of artificial cold transmitted in a letter from Dr. Beddoes,[3] I am induced to mention a few I have made since.

Your zealous attention to this subject, under whose auspices this, as well as other branches of natural philosophy, hath received considerable improvement, will, I hope, apologize for the liberty I have taken in addressing myself to you,[4] especially since any new and useful facts I may have ascertained are principally owing to those endeavours your excellent Papers[5] have incited in me.

My most powerful frigorific mixture is the following:[6]

[...]

I have the honour to be, &c.
Rich. Walker.

Oxford, March 27, 1788.

---

[1] Richard Walker, apothecary to the Radcliffe Infirmary, Oxford.

[2] Walker's letter was published with his paper, "Experiments on the Production of Artificial Cold," *PT* 78 (1788): 395–402, on 402; read 5 June 1788.

[3] For upwards of three years, Walker had been performing experiments on artificial cold in the Radcliffe Infirmary in Oxford when they were made public by Thomas Beddoes, "An Account of Some Experiments on the Production of Artificial Cold," *PT* 77 (1787): 282–87. Beddoes (1760–1808), physician and chemist, that year, 1788, was appointed reader in chemistry at Oxford University. Knight, "Beddoes," *DSB* 1:563–64.

[4] See letter 56.

[5] Henry Cavendish, "An Account of Experiments Made by Mr. John McNab, at Henley House, Hudson's Bay, Relating to Freezing Mixtures," *PT* 76 (1786): 241–72; "An Account of Experiments Made by Mr. John McNab, at Albany Fort, Hudson's Bay, Relative to the Freezing of Nitrous and Vitriolic Acids," *PT* 78 (1788): 166–81. See letter 42.

[6] What follows, six pages of recipes for freezing mixtures and experiments made with them, reads not like a letter but like any other scientific commmunication in the journal.

52. FROM RICHARD WALKER

28 MAY 1788

From the *Philosophical Transactions*[1]

Extract from a Second Letter from Mr. Walker to Henry Cavendish, Esq. Dated Oxford, May 28, 1788.

A more intense cold may be produced by a solution of salts in water in summer, than can be produced by a mixture of snow and salt in winter.[2] [. . .]

I have since my last seen Fahrenheit's Experiments on the freezing of Water, related in Vol. XXXIII. of the Philosophical Transactions;[3] but as mine differ in degree I take no farther notice of them.

---

[1] This letter, written two months after the one above, was published as an afterword to Walker, "Experiments on the Production of Artificial Cold," 402.

[2] Walker would seem to have regarded his success in achieving low temperatures without adding snow to his mixtures as an important, or a principal, discovery of his. There follows a page containing a formula for mixing rain water, nitrated ammonia, and mineral alkali, resulting in a fall of the thermometer from +50° to –7° Fahrenheit.

[3] Evidently Daniel Gabriel Fahrenheit, "Experimenta & Observationes de Congelatione aquae in vacuo," *PT* 33 (1724): 78–84. Daniel Gabriel Fahrenheit (1686–1736), instrument-maker from Danzig. Gough, "Fahrenheit," *DSB* 4:516–18.

53. FROM JOHN MICHELL

14 AUGUST 1788

From the original letter in the Devonshire Collections, Chatsworth[1]

Dear Sir

Some observations, as I returned from London, having occur'd to me with regard to the Northamptonshire, Lincolnshire, &c. yellow limestone (viz Dr Blagden's, not my yellow limestone) I take the liberty of communicating them to you, though perhaps hardly worth your attention;[2] I could indeed have wished, I had been able to give them you with more precision. I lodged one night, in my road, at the Royal Oak, a new house built on Greetham Common about 7 or 8 years ago, 96 miles from London, which is in the midst of that set of strata, which constitute the yellow limestone; when, walking in the Garden there, I unexpectedly found it to be upon clay, & enquiring of the Master of the house about it, I found, that he had been obliged to sink a ditch between three & four feet deep at one side of his Garden, as well as to make two or three drains of about the same depth to carry the water into it, in order to prevent it from being so swampy, as to be unfit for that purpose, & the water at that time stood some inches deep in some parts of this ditch, though it was in the most droughty part of that time, when every thing about London was so much burnt up, which was also the case in a good measure, though not quite so much so, about Greetham. I the less expected to find things in this state, the land hereabout not being low & having a moderate declivity, sufficient, I should have thought, if it had not been retain'd by the clayeyness of the soil, to have carried of[f] the water, even of a wet season.

I also observed lying about two or three small heaps of pebbles, amongst which were some flints, & enquiring of the Master of the house, whence they came, he informed me, that they were pick'd up from the plough'd fields, which consisted of the same clay with the Garden: they were lodged, as I understood amongst the clay, being found here & there in digging into it. It was not till after you & Dr Blagden mention'd your having seen some specimens of chert, at some place on the coast, I think, amongst this set of strata,[3] that I was aware, that any flints were ever found belonging to them, & the flints, I met with at Greetham common, must I suppose be of the same kind with those, you consider'd as chert, though I should rather consider them as flints; for though they are opake, & had nothing of that horny look, when broken, that the flints from the chalky countries have, yet they have more of the glassy texture & want that appearance of toughness, which the cherts in general have, so that, I should not hesitate to call them flints rather than cherts. At the same time I can easily conceive, that our ideas of them may not so far coincide, but that you might well enough look on them as belonging to the cherts: I however met with, amongst the rest, two or three flints, that every body must look on as such, being, when broken, black & horny, & as perfect as the most perfect of the chalk country flints: they were also roundish like those & were cover'd with a dark brown coat, whereas the others had no coat, nor any appearance of ever having had one, that I could see, being rather angular, & somewhat irregularly shaped.

My Landlord also told me, he had been informed (for he had only kept the Inn a year or two himself) that, when the house was built, they had sunk a Well nine yards deep through this bed of clay, before they came to the stone; the clay may therefore, when compleat, very possibly have been of still greater thickness, but I had no opportunity of learning any farther particulars about it. My Landlord also informed me, that he had been told, that in sinking the above Well, they had met with in the clay a few small stragling bits of coal, but nothing, as far as he could make out, from the vague account, he had been able to procure, & which came through three or four hands, that seem'd to have any tendency towards a regular stratum; this story however seems to have induced the owner of the estate (Lord Winchelsea,[4] I think) to try for coal somewhere there abouts; for he had had people to bore in search of it, & they had gone to the depth of 130 yards without any success, as I could easily conceive.

This clay did not seem to compose a very uniform stratum, not only consisting of harder & softer parts, but having likewise these flints & pebbles scatter'd through it, in such manner, if I conceived rightly of the matter, as to shew, that though they might perhaps have been formed in it originally, yet supposing this to be the case they must however have been somewhat disturbed from their places after their formation, though I neither saw nor could learn circumstances sufficient to form any probable guess concerning the way, in which these flints, as well as the other pebbles, which seem'd to contain sand & some iron in their composition, were formed. May I not however consider the circumstances & company, in which they are found as rather tending to strengthen my conjecture concerning the origin of flints in general?

Besides this bed of clay of the existence of which I was not aware, before my last return from town, there is another pretty considerable bed of clay (for I think it is not the same, appearing again at another place) which I have often taken notice of, that shews itself in the side of the hill immediately descending towards Grantham, on the East side of it: What is the thickness of this bed, I dont know, but, from what I have been able to learn concerning it, I should suppose it is not less than the other: there are also found in it, in one part of the stratum some cornua ammonis, & in another part some selenities; but these last I pay no great regard to, as they are frequently of a very modern origin, being commonly formed in clay, where some little vitriolic water ouzes or trickles out, provided there is a little calcareous matter likewise for it to unite with. There are a great many Bricks & Tiles made out of this clay for the use of the town of Grantham, & I imagine, what might otherwise be very well, I think, supposed to be the case, that it is not an accidental mass of Clay in that place only, but part of a stratum of some extent for I observed some other Brick Kilns, at a mile or two distance, on the side of a hill, at about the same level. Whether there may not be still more beds of clay in some other parts of this set of strata, I dont know, though from these instances & general analogy, it is not very unlikely there should. Almost immediately to the Westward on this side Grantham, we again have clay, which is continued to the top of Gunnerby hill, but which however must no doubt consist in great part of some kind of stone; for it could not otherwise rise so much, as it does, in so short a space, viz. about 70 or 80 yards perpendicular, I apprehend, in the distance of a little more than a mile: there is likewise another set of strata, which form another ridge of lower hills, three or four miles still nearer this way, about Foston: all these probably contain several beds of clay, & under these are found the Lyas, which consists of a great many alternate beds of clay & blue limestone.

I believe, I have formerly mention'd it to yourself & Dr Blagden; but not recollecting whether I have before insisted so much upon it, as I might have done, I shall take this opportunity, which the country I have just been mentioning, suggests, of observing, that to the Westward of all that edge of Dr Blagden's yellow limestone, next our side of the sets of Strata, which run from North to South through the Island of Great Britain, as far as I am acquainted with them lies the Lyas at no very great distance, though indeed with two or three sets of strata, viz. those of Gunnerby & Foston, between them: these run into Leicestershire to the South, & to where the Trent falls into the Humber & the upper part of the Humber to the North, the Lyas being the lowest of all these sets of strata & all of them lying below the yellow limestone in order, but no where having any coal near them; whereas our yellow limestone has no Lyas any where under it or near it to the Westward of it, but, on the contrary, every where coal very near the Western edge of it all the way from Leicestershire by the edge of Nottinghamshire & Derbyshire, & a long way into Yorkshire, & how much farther I dont for certain know, & in many places, if not every where the coal is found under our yellow limestone, through which they sink in many places in order to come at it.

Since I began to write this letter I received from Mr Beatson of Rotheram a parcel of the substance, he was mentioning to you: he sent by the person, who brought it to me, an apology for not having sent it before, & saying at the same time that it was not yet so good a specimen, as he had wished to have sent. As it was directed to me, though it ought perhaps rather to be consider'd as your property, I have taken the liberty of reserving about half of it for my self, which however, if you want any more, than I have sent you, either to make experiments upon, or for any other purpose, I will send you, whenever you please. It seems to be in general a good deal harder than the black lead commonly used for pencils though some of the thin flakes seem to mark pretty well; probably the difference may be owing to too large a quantity of Iron contained in it; for it appears by it's applying so very strongly as it does to the Magnet to contain a great proportion of that metal. With best respects to yourself & due Comp^s^ to all friends, when you see them particularly those of the Crown & Anchor, & Cat & Bagpipes Clubs, I am, Dear Sir,

Your obed[t] humble Serv[t]

Thornhill J. Michell

14 Aug[st] 1788

---

1 Cavendish Mss X(b), 15. Published in Geikie, *Michell*, 47–58.

2 Beginning in 1785, Cavendish and Blagden made annual journeys to study the geology of Britain. Blagden wrote to Michell that on their way to Leicester, they saw nothing of "*your* yellow limestone." Blagden to Michell, 19 Sep. 1786, draft, Blagden Letters, 7:37.

3 In 1787 Cavendish and Blagden observed chert, a rock resembling flint, on the coast of Devonshire on their way to Cornwall. Cavendish Mss X(a), 7. See letter 54.

4 Probably George Finch, 9th earl of Winchilsea (1752–1826). *Burke's Peerage*, 2855.

54. TO JOHN MICHELL

[AFTER 14 AUGUST 1788]

From the original draft letter in the Devonshire Collections, Chatsworth[1]

I am much obliged to you & M^r B[eatson] for the plumbago & to you for your letter.

I have got some which I received from Wales part of which I think is purer than Mr Beatsons. But the rest consists of flakes of a more sparkling nature than Beatsons & less disposed to mark paper. I have also some which I received under the name of sulphur iron & which is much the same to appearance as the latter part of the Welch specimen. I analyzed this & found it to contain more silicious earth than plumbago besides a good deal of iron not so much in the state of plumbago but what it would dissolve in acids.

I suppose it must be the yellow limestone about Bridport in which D^r Bl[agden] told you we found Chert.[2] How far it deserves that name I can not say but to the best of my remembrance it was of a much coarser grain & had not at all the appearance of flint but my memory is too imperfect for me to attempt to describe it to you. As the circumstances relating to it are rather remarkable I will mention what we saw of it last year. On descending the chalk hills between Dorchester & Bridport by the time we got about ½ way to the bottom we came to the yellow limestone which seemed separated from the chalk only by a stratum of clay of no great thickness. A few miles further the stone though to appearance much the same was found to be of a silicious nature with very little calcarious matter in it. At Lyme the cliffs are blue clay & blue Lyas but the top of the hill which we pass over immediately before we come to Lyme consists of gravel composed of this Chert & about a mile to the west of Lyme was a hill with a steep bank towards the sea the foot of which was blue Lyas with yellow limestone over it mixed with veins of this Chert so much like the limestone that one could hardly distinguish them by the eye. But it must be observed that this as well as most [of] the limestone we saw is of a hard compact & rather brown kind.

From hence to Sidmouth the soil consisted chiefly of this Cherty gravel but the cliffs on each side of Sidmouth consisted of red rock (the sandy kind consisting of thick strata) only on the east side they were coverd by a great thickness of the same chert gravel as the hill by Lyme. From hence we had red rock & red soil with out any chert gravel to Hall down [Haldon][3] which is a hill extending from a little to the west of Exeter to near Teignmouth & the upper part of this hill consisted of the abovementiond chert gravel. So that it appears that the limestone of this country is very much mixed with Chert a great deal of which seems to have been reduced to gravel & deposited on strata of older formation & at a great distance from the limestone where it was formed.[4] Besides Hall down [Haldon] the top of which is coverd with this matter is I believe intirely separated from the rest of this country by a broad tract of the red rock country.

In the cliffs between Minehead & Watchett I saw the red rock lying immediately under the blue lyas.

In digging the tunnel for the canal in Gloucestershire they have found one or more beds of clay between the strata of yellow limestone & I believe the chalk is not free from them. A little to the west of Dunstable considerable springs of water break out on the N.W. side of the chalk hills about the level of Dunstable.

I believe you must be right in supposing your yellow limestone to be quite distinct from the other. From what I can learn I believe [the] N.W. edge of the other after running from Gunnerby hill on the E. side of the Trent crosses the Humber & runs under the Yorkshire chalk & appears again about Castle Howards, & so runs to Scarborough the chalk in that place lapping over or extending further west than the limestone.

D^{r} Bl. has sent me the miner[alogical] account of his journey as far as Paris. From Dieppe where he landed to some miles beyond Rouen it was intirely chalk except the valley of the Seine. He then came upon a pebbly gravelly soil which continued to a little beyond Lisieux where he met the yellow limestone so that he could not properly say where the chalk ended. From thence the yellow limestone continued to a little beyond Bayeux when on descending a hill he found the blue clay before he got to the bottom & met a lime kiln where they were burning lime with coal brought from about 2 leagues to west. From thence to S^{t} Lo the soil was at first clayey & afterwards in some places true slate. Between S^{t} Lo & Cherbourg he passed 2 or 3 ridges of hills which were composed of chiefly of what he calls silicious stone but in one place slate & Kellas. The plain country between these ridges was yellow limestone & blue lyas. The latter they burnt for lime & found it excellent for hardening under water. Some bits of the silicious stone had the appearance of grains of quartz or sand cemented together but not intirely filled up with quartzy matter. In other bits the grains were less distinguishable. They approached more to the Jasper appearance.

In his road from Cherbourg to Paris he went back the same way to between Lisieux & Rouen. At Evreux he again came upon the chalk which continued till he came into the valley of the Seine at Mante where he found freestone much like some of the Bath stone but he did not perceive any separation between this & the chalk. On going down into the valley of Passy (between Evreux & Mante) he also found this kind of freestone.

The information he received at Paris is remarkable. At Meudon the upper stratum consists of millstone like those of Picardy bedded in clay then some sand then the calcarious freestone of which Paris is built about 80 feet thick then a little sand & under that true chalk with flints in it. At Mont Martre they have millstone & sand at top & under that alternate layers of Marl & Gipsum. He was much out of order with a fever & Rheumatism at Paris but on the 20 of last month which is the date of my last letter was much better & was setting out for Geneva.

[1] Cavendish Mss X (b), 15. This letter, which is in response to letter 53, is published in part in Geikie, *Michell*, 59–63.

[2] This and the following two paragraphs contain geological observations from Cavendish and Blagden's journey in the southwest of England from mid-July to mid-August 1787. Cavendish Mss X(a), 6 and 7.

[3] Here we follow Geikie, *Michell*, who identifies Cavendish's "Hall down" with "Haldon."

[4] There is no punctuation here, and the next words are "& Besides Hall down the top of which . . . ," which is confusing; we have inserted a period and removed "&."

55. FROM THOMAS VIVIAN[1]

26 NOVEMBER 1788

From the original letter in the Devonshire Collections, Chatsworth[2]

Cornwood Novr 26. 1788.

Sir

Doctor Farr has Communicated to me Your intention to give me the Thermometer, Barometer, and Rain gage, which You sent to my house.[3] I return You many thanks for this present, & shall continue to keep a Register of the rain.

The Apparatus used by R. Wilson[4] is also here waiting your farther directions.

I desire my best respects to Doctor Blagden, and thank You both for the expence & pains in promoting Philosophick knowledge by experiments in this Neighborhood.

If either of You should come into this Country in future, I shall gladly embrace every opportunity of expressing my gratitude; being with the highest Esteem Your obedient & obliged Servant.

Thos Vivian.

---

1 Thomas Vivian, a clergyman, participated in Cavendish's meteorological experiment on Dartmoor. On a high elevation, Cavendish had a hut built for housing a rain-gage, barometer, and thermometer. Vivian's house, 950 feet lower in elevation, served as the other station of the experiment; there Vivian made observations with instruments of the same kind. William Watson, Jr., to William Herschel, 27 Aug. 1787, Royal Astronomical Society, Mss Herschel, W 1/13, W.49.

2 Cavendish Mss New Correspondence.

3 Blagden wrote to Farr that Cavendish wanted to discontinue the register. Farr no doubt informed Vivian. See letter 50.

4 R. Wilson, the other local man involved in the experiment, read the instruments in the hut.

56. FROM RICHARD WALKER

4 JANUARY 1789

From the original letter in the Devonshire Collections, Chatsworth[1]

Oxford Jan:ry 4th 1789

Sir

I have the satisfaction to inform You, that on Sunday last December the 28th I succeeded completely here, in an attempt to congeal Quicksilver; this being as I presume, the first instance upon record in Britain, of this metal being reduced by cold to a perfectly solid state;[2] it may perhaps be thought not unworthy to be communicated to the Royal Society: on the Tuesday following I froze some Quicksilver a second time, in the presence of Dr Thomson[3] Professor of Anatomy and Dr Sibthorp[4] Professor of Botany in this University,[5] and two more Gentlemen. In the latter experiment this effect was produced by the cold generated *immediately* from a frigorific mixture of my own without snows, the materials for this purpose being for economical reasons previously cooled by other means; [-----][6] for this purpose. By your permission Sir, I shall trouble You with the particulars of the above, and a few things I have to mention besides, the first opportunity.[7]

I have the honour to be Sir,
with the utmost respect, Your
most obedient, & very humble Servant
Richard Walker

[address]:
Henry Cavendish Esq:r
F:R:S: & A:S:
Royal Society House
London[8]

---

[1] Cavendish Mss New Correspondence.

[2] Cavendish himself froze mercury at his country house at Hampstead six years earlier. Charles Blagden, who assisted Cavendish in his thermometrical experiments, recorded that "Mr. Cavendish told me he had frozen ☿ the day before; sunk the thermr to −110." Entry for 27 Feb. 1783, Charles Blagden Diary, Royal Society, 1. In his history of the subject, Blagden noted the event: "Mr. Cavendish, by an ingenious artifice of diluting the nitrous acid to a proper degree, sunk the quicksilver in his thermometer to [minus] 110°, and consequently froze it in part. He then interrupted the experiment to try the cold of his frigorific mixture by a spirit thermometer, and found it nearly as great as Mr. Hutchins had ever produced at Hudson's Bay, that is, about equal to −45° of a standard mercurial thermometer." Blagden, "History of the Congelation of Quicksilver," 359–60. Beddoes, "Account of Some Experiments," 284, reported that Walker first froze mercury on 20 April 1787, using a freezing mixture without adding snow or ice; it contained diluted spirit of nitre, as described by Cavendish in 1786. Walker's claim of originality in this letter rested on the "completely solid" state of his frozen mercury, but by then this was not a particularly remarkable observation. In his publications on artificial cold, Walker did not repeat this claim of originality. See letters 51 and 52.

[3] William Thomson (1761–1803), Lee's reader and university reader in anatomy at Oxford University. Charles Webster, "The Medical Faculty and the Physic Garden," in *The History of the University of Oxford*, vol. 5: *The Eighteenth Century*, ed. L. S. Sutherland and L. G. Mitchell (Oxford: Clarendon Press, 1986), 683–724, on 707.

[4] John Sibthorp (1758–96), Sheridan professor of botany and keeper of the garden. Ibid., 708.

[5] The Radcliffe Infirmary, where Walker worked, was independent of Oxford University, but Sibthorpe and other members of the faculty served there as honorary physicians. Ibid., 708.

[6] Because of a tear in the letter, one and a half lines are missing.

[7] Walker published his third paper on the same subject several years later. This time he added snow to his freezing mixtures, noting that the "best and only way of trying or reducing any acid to its proper strength, is by adding snow, as Mr. Cavendish directs." Walker, "Observations on the Best Methods of Producing Artificial Cold," *PT* 85 (1795): 270–89, on 275. In 1801, by which time Walker had been experimenting on the means for producing cold for fifteen years, he published a fourth paper, which Cavendish again communicated to the Royal Society, "On the Production of Artificial Cold by Means of Muriate of Lime," *PT* 91 (1801): 120–38.

[8] This address is replaced in the handwriting of someone else by "Bedford Square."

57. FROM NEVIL MASKELYNE

16 APRIL 1789[1]

From the original letter in the Devonshire Collections, Chatsworth[2]

Remarks on Mr Cavendish Paper on Finding the Orbit of a Comet.

[. . .]

From this explanation of it, you will see what weight to give to this method. It goes on the supposition that the earth & Comet move uniformly in parallel lines during the interval of the 3 observations.

Instead of a globe covered with white paper, might not a planisphere be made use of, upon either the ort[h]ographic, or globular projection, in both [of] which great circles are represented by circles, an easy way of drawing which, be the radii ever so large, is done, as I am told, by an instrument made by Adams.[3]

As you said you would determine the orbit of the late Comet discovered by Miss Herschel,[4] by the help of a globe covered with white paper, if I would communicate some observations to you, I have set down the following.[5] [. . .] The first observation was Dr Herschel's. I have reduced it. The places of the Comet will be rendered more exact when I have settled the places of the stars with which the Comet was compared, but these are I suppose true to a minute. I had a few more observations, and there is another of D^r. Herschel's to be brought in viz. on Dec. 23^d as soon as I can settle the place of the star with which he compared the Comet. Greenwich April 16. 1788. N. M.–

---

[1] Maskelyne dated his letter 16 April 1788, but he gave observations of the comet discovered by Caroline Herschel on 21 December 1788. We assume that he meant to write 1789, the year we assign to this letter.

[2] Cavendish Mss VIII, 43. This letter is enclosed in a thirty-seven-page manuscript, "Method of Finding Comets Orbits Fair," which Cavendish gave to Maskelyne, who made corrections in it in pencil and then transferred them to a two-page letter of comments.

[3] George Adams, Jr. (1750–95), London instrument-maker. Taylor, *Mathematical Practitioners*, 277.

[4] Caroline Lucretia Herschel (1750–1848), astronomer renowned for her discoveries of comets, eight in all between 1786 and 1797. Hoskin, "Herschel," *DSB* 6:322–23.

[5] There follows a table of seven observations between 22 Dec. 1788 and 4 Feb. 1789.

112. *Nevil Maskelyne. Painting by John Downman. Courtesy of the National Maritime Museum.*

113. *Greenwich Royal Observatory. Lord Charles and Henry Cavendish made many inspections of this observatory as members of Royal Society visitation committees.*

58. TO NEVIL MASKELYNE

[AFTER 16 APRIL 1789]

From the original draft letter in the Devonshire Collections, Chatsworth[1]

D[ear] S[ir]

I have been trying the method I mention'd to you with the globe on the observations of the comet you was so good as to give me.[2] [. . .]

This method is rather more trouble than I imagined it would be before I tried it but on the whole seems as if it would prove an usefull method especially if proper tables were made which if I knew of any one that I could employ to compute them I would get done. I have been so much taken up about this & other matters that I have not been able to examine the remarks you made on my paper but hope to do it soon.

---

[1] Cavendish Mss VIII, 54. This letter is contained in a large bundle of papers, "Comets Orbits."

[2] Letter 57.

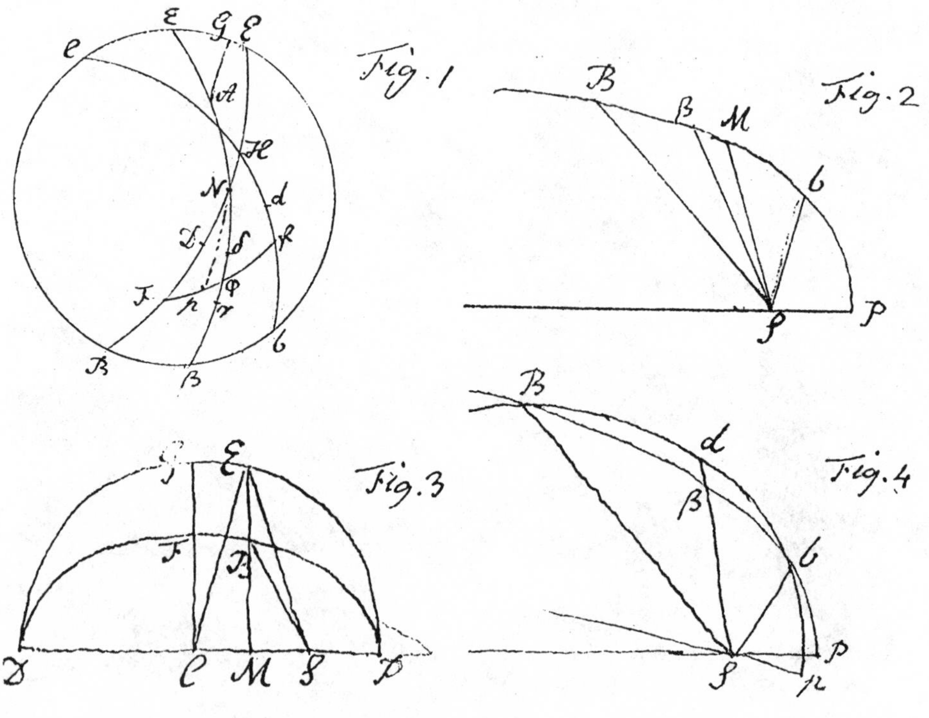

114. *Extract on Comet Orbits. These figures accompany a study of two methods of finding the orbit of a comet from three observations, the first method assuming a parabolic orbit, the second an elliptical. Fig. 1. Surface of a sphere centered on the sun with respect to which the earth and comet are described. Fig. 2. Parabolic path of the comet BbP. Figs. 3 and 4. Elliptical path. Cavendish Scientific Manuscripts VIII, 43. Reproduced by permission of the Chatsworth Settlement Trustees.*

59. FROM CHARLES BLAGDEN

9 JULY 1789

From the original draft letter in the Royal Society[1]

Mr Cavendish July 9, 1789.

Dr Sir,

Ld Palmerston[2] called upon me yesterday to make me a proposition of accompanying himself & L^{y} Palmerston[3] into Italy next winter.[4] They intend to set out the [2^{d}] week in Sept. & to return to England about midsummer next. I told his L^{d} <that> I was very much obliged to him for the offer, that the tour itself wo^{d} be highly agreeable to me, & that it would be a better opportunity than I was otherwise likely to find of seeing that country; but that as there were several reasons against my being absent a whole winter I wished to consider it for a day or two, & to ask your advice. The advantages & disadvantages seem to me, indeed, so nearly balanced, that I know not <what way to decide> how to form an opinion, & wish to refer the matter entirely to your decision: in which I beg that you will consider your own convenience as the first object.

---

[1] Blagden Letters, 7:271.

[2] Henry Temple, Viscount Palmerston (1739–1802), M.P., cabinet minister, F.R.S. 1776. G.E.C., *Complete Peerage* 4: cols. 294–95.

[3] Mary Mee, Lady Palmerston (d. 1805). Ibid.

[4] The Palmerstons made their house a center of social life in London. Fond of Europe, they were joined in their travels by Blagden. Blagden and the Palmerstons exchanged nearly a hundred letters between 1788 and 1804: Beinecke Rare Book and Manuscript Library, Yale. Geikie, *Annals of the Royal Society Club*, 148. Connell, *Portrait of a Whig Peer*, 18, 251–56, 260.

60. FROM CHARLES BLAGDEN

AUGUST 1789

From the original draft letter in the Royal Society[1]

Mr Cavendish Aug 1789.

Dear Sir

In the conversation I have had with you relative to the proposal of accompanying Ld Palmerston into Italy, the sole objection you have mentioned is that it will interfere with a pursuit which I have much more at heart than any object in life.[2] So indeed it appeared to me; but on farther reflexion, considering how much my former habits have thrown me out of the way of that pursuit in London, & the great number of English who resort every winter to Italy, I am doubtful whether the chances wo^{d} not be as at least as much in my favor with Ld Palmerston, as in my usual manner of life in town. Whatever good or agreeable company sho^{d} be in the diff^{t} places where we made any stay, the connexion with his Lordship would naturally lead me to know. As far therefore as personally regards myself, the more I think of his L$^{d's}$ offer the more I am inclined to accept it. Now I trust to the strict principles of <opennes> sincerity by which I know you are always guided <that you will fairly tell me> for an open & explicit answer to the question whether you have on your own part any objection to my going. If you have I entreat you by the confidence w^{h} ought guide [-----],[3] let no idea of delicacy, no supposed necessity[4] of caution, prevent you from telling me so <candidly> fairly at once. It is enough if my absence will be inconvenient to you, or retard any of your pursuits.[5] Moreover, I sho^{d} be much obliged to you as a friend that you w^{d} let me know if you think it w^{d} be attended with any inconvenience to yourself of which I am not at present aware. In case I go with Ld Palmerston it will be advisable that I should return speedily to London. You will receive this letter Thursday, and <I should beg an answer if you can find it convenient> if you co^{d} conveniently answer it the next day <which I sho^{d} receive Saturday. If it> [-----] be such as determines me to go, <I shall> return to town the beginning of next week, without going into Wales. I remain, d^{r} Sir, your very faithful friend & servant CB.

Perhaps too my absence for a winter may prevent an open rupture with Sir Jos. Banks, who [-----][6] & those corresponding [-----][7] not at all leading to reconciliation.[8]

---

[1] Blagden Letters, 7:694.

[2] Presumably to resume his practice as a physician.

[3] Illegible interlined five-word phrase.

[4] Blagden came to the end of the page here, beginning the next page with "of necessity," which we omit.

[5] For several years, Blagden had been assisting Cavendish in his scientific work.

[6] Four-word illegible interlined passage.

[7] Three words illegible.

[8] Beginning in February 1788, Blagden's relationship with Banks was strained; see letter 49. Accusations were made and rejected in their letters. Blagden gave his letters to Cavendish; see next letter.

61. FROM CHARLES BLAGDEN
16 AND 17 SEPTEMBER 1789

From the original draft letter in the Royal Society[1]

Sepr 16, 1789.

Dear Sir,

The inclosed key opens the drawers of my bureau, placed now in your bedroom Bedford Square, which contains several papers & letters. In case of my death be so good as to burn the latter, except there should be any among them which you would wish to keep.

I beg your acceptance of a couple of Gloucestershire cheeses sent me by my Brother:[2] & am, with the greatest esteem & regard,

Your very faithful friend & servant
CBlagden.

Sepr 17.

I have just received a letter from the Chevalier Landriani,[3] in which are the following items of news.

"Dans le courant de l'[-----] dernier j'ai fait la nouvelle poudre à tirer (I suppose with the muriate oxygené) pour Sa Majesté Imperiale. Elle a parfaitement bien réussi . . .

"Mr Klaproth[4] vient de decouvrir que les alkalis ne sont que de l'acide phosphorique saturé par l'acide carbonique . . . je doute encore."

"Mon ouvrage sur le feu et sur la chaleur (in which he was to give a very [result] of experiments from Dr Crawford's)[5] est dans un profond sommeil.[6]

———————

I inclose the late correspondence between Sir Joseph Banks & myself. Though it might be more prudent to keep one's secret, I did not find myself easy till I had let him know what I thought: and I have felt much pleasanter since. Be so good as to keep the letters.

[address]:

The Hon.
Henry Cavendish
Bedford Square.

---

[1] Blagden Letters, B.166b.

[2] John Blagden Hale. To qualify for the conditions of an inheritance, Charles Blagden's brother adopted the name Hale.

[3] Marsilio Landriani (1751–1816), Italian physical scientist best known for his work with the eudiometer, traveled widely in Europe. Belloni, "Landriani," *DSB* 7:620–21.

[4] Martin Heinrich Klaproth (1743–1817), German chemist. Hufbauer, "Klaproth," *DSB* 7:394–95.

[5] Adair Crawford (1748–95), London physician, acclaimed for his physical and physiological studies of heat, F.R.S. 1786. Donovan, "Crawford," *DSB* 15:94–96.

[6] In translation: In the course of last [-----] I made to extract the new powder for Her Imperial Majesty. It succeeded perfectly . . . Mr. Klaproth finds that alkalies are only phosphoric acid saturated by carbonic acid . . . I am still in doubt. My work on fire and heat . . . is in a deep sleep.

62. FROM WILLIAM HERSCHEL

1 FEBRUARY 1790

From the original letter in the Devonshire Collections, Chatsworth[1]

Dear Sir,

From my journal it appears that, on the 23^{d} of Feb. 1784, it was very clear in the night.[2] I had about 8 hours of observations, and find that from 7^{h} 26 to 9^{h} 59′ mean time my eyes were attentively fixed to the 20 feet telescope, which was directed to the south, and that of course I could not easily take notice of what might appear in other parts of the heavens.

Among other things I find a memorandum that (at 7^{h} 37′ sid, about 9^{h} 24′ mean time) a meteor passed thro' the field of view of my telescope which appeared like a star of the 10th magnitude and seemed to move not much faster than very small meteors appear to move to the naked eye. From the situation of the Sweep I infer the altitude of the meteor to have been between 45 and 47 degrees; and from the power, 157, of the telescope and the apparent size & velocity we may suppose its real distance & light to have been very considerable.

At 11^{h} 59′ sidereal time, about $1\frac{3}{4}^{h}$ after midnight the same evening, there passed a meteor thro' the field of view which had a visible diameter of 15 or 16″. Its motion was far from being quick when the power 157 is considered, so that I had even time enough to perceive that it contained a bright Lunula on the following side. A representation of it in my journal is as follows.[3]

Its altitude between 43° and 45°; in the meridian.

I have the honour to remain

Dear Sir

Slough near Windsor
Feb 1. 1790

Your faithful
humble $Serv^{t}$
Wm Herschel

---

[1] Cavendish Mss New Correspondence. There is a copy of the draft letter in the Royal Astronomical Society, Mss Herschel, W 1/1, p. 181.

[2] The night of 23 February 1784 was of particular interest to Cavendish, for then an uncommon aurora borealis had been observed in England, the subject of three reports read to the Royal Society in December 1786. Cavendish analyzed these reports in a paper read to the Royal Society on 25 February 1790. He urged others to observe auroras in order to test his hypothesis that they were streams of light shooting upwards. "On the Height of the Luminous Arch Which Was Seen on Feb. 23, 1784," *PT* 80 (1790): 101–5.

[3] There is a small drawing here.

115. *Sir William Herschel. Crayon portrait by John Russell, engraving by E. Scriven. Courtesy of Smith Image Collection, Van Pelt-Dietrich Library, University of Pennsylvania.*

116. *Herschel's Twenty-Foot Telescope. From a water color sketch probably made at Datchet.* The Scientific Papers of Sir William Herschel, *2 vols., ed. J. L. E. Dreyer (London: Royal Society and Royal Astronomical Society, 1912), facing p. xxxvii.*

63. FROM ROBERT HARRINGTON[1]

16 FEBRUARY 1790

From the original letter in the Devonshire Collections, Chatsworth[2]

Sir/

Sometime ago I wrote a Letter addressed to you and some other eminent men, adopting some different principles from what you have generally received. I am anxious to know in what light you look upon my labours; which will much oblige one, whose industry hitherto, has been very hardly treated by the world. From your high character both as a Philosopher and a Gentleman I make bold to write to you. An answer as soon as convenient would be gratefully received

by Your most humble &

Carlisle Febry 16th 1790 — Obedt Servt Robt Harrington

---

[1] Beginning in 1781 Robert Harrington, a surgeon practicing in Carlisle, published tracts on natural philosophy (one under the pseudonym Richard Bewley), culminating in *An Elucidation and Extension of the Harringtonian System of Chemistry, Explaining All the Phenomena Without One Single Anomaly* (London, 1819). He published two "letters" to Cavendish (which we have not included in this edition): *Letter Addressed to Dr. Priestley, Messers Cavendish, Lavoisier, and Kirwan; Endeavouring to Prove That Their Newly Adopted Opinions of Inflammable and Dephlogisticated Airs, Forming Water and the Acids Being Compounded of Different Airs, Are Fallacious* (London, 1788); *Some New Experiments, With Observations upon Heat . . . Also Letter to Henry Cavendish, Esq.* (London, 1798). "Harrington, Robert," *DNB* 8:1320–21. Harrington saw Cavendish and Banks as the main obstacle in his path. To Banks he wrote, "I received your Letter, & am not in the least disappointed; for I have seen all along a determined resolution, not to pay the least attention to my Labours. And I think I have likewise seen the motive, & who are the authors of it. . . . As to your repeated Observations, that any member has a right to present a paper; I must again repeat my answer that as you & Mr Cavendish are of the Council, no paper which contains my Philosophy, will be published as I know from experience, without your approbation." Harrington to Banks, 16 Nov. 1794, BL Add Mss 33979.

[2] Cavendish Mss New Correspondence.

64. TO CHARLES BLAGDEN

[BEFORE 12 MARCH 1790]

From the original letter in the Royal Society[1]

Dear Sir

Your computation[2] I think is not accurate on account of your having neglected the concentration. Let the concentration on mixing 100 gallons of Gilpins[3] spirit with 86,625 of water be β gallons. Then 100 of this spirit with 86,625 of water make 186,625–β of sp. 1/7 under proof. Let also the concentration on mixing 6 of proof with 1 of water be P; then

$$6 \text{ x } \frac{186{,}625-\beta}{7-P} \text{ of proof with } 6 \text{ x } \frac{186{,}625-\beta}{7-P} \text{ of water make}$$

186,625–β of spirit 1/7 under proof; & therefore

$$100 \text{ of Gilpins with } 86{,}625 \; \frac{-186{,}625+\beta}{7-P} \text{ of water makes proof.}$$

Another way of seeing whether Dicass specific gravity of proof is right is this. Let the specific gravity which he assigns to proof be β. [,972.][4] Then if this is right, 6β pound of proof will make 6β+1 pound of sp. 1/7 under proof; & therefore as

$$100 \text{ of Gilpins makes } 205 \text{ of sp. } 1/7 \text{ under proof, it will make } \frac{205 \text{ x } 6\beta}{6\beta+1} \text{ of}$$

proof.

Find therefore the specific gravity which Gilpins spt has when diluted in this proportion & see whether it agrees with that given by Dicas.[5]

The result of my fathers experiment was that a cubic foot of water weighs

$$76 \text{ Troy pound or } \frac{76 \text{ x } 12 \text{ x } 480}{7000} \text{ Avoirdupois pounds.}$$

Yours sincerely
H. Cavendish[6]

[address]:
Dr Blagden
No 45 Rathbone place
Oxford street

---

[1] Blagden Letters, C.23.

[2] The government asked the president of the Royal Society, Sir Joseph Banks, to determine the "best means of ascertaining the just proportion of duty to be paid by any kind of spiritous liquor that should come before the Officers of Excise." Banks turned to Blagden, one of the secretaries of the Society, to "assist in planning the proper experiments" and to "draw up the Report." Blagden, "Report on the Best Method of Proportioning the Excise upon Spiritous Liquors," *PT* 80 (1790): 321–45, on 321. Owing to a public criticism of the report by the instrument-maker Jesse Ramsden, and to an experimental error arising from the greater evaporation of spirits than of water, Blagden published a sequel two years later, "Supplementary Report on the Best Method of Proportioning the Excise upon Spiritous Liquors," *PT* 82 (1792): 425–38. Cavendish gave Blagden much assistance on this assignment from Banks.

[3] George Gilpin (1755–1810), clerk of the Royal Society, earlier assistant to Maskelyne at the Royal Observatory, a capable experimentalist. 17 Feb. 1785, Minutes of Council, Royal Society, 7:203–4. Poggendorff 1: col. 899. The Swiss chemist Johann Casper Dollfuss began the experiments to determine the method of deciding duty, and when he left the country, Gilpin, who had assisted Dollfuss, repeated them.

[4] This number, which is interlined, may be in Blagden's hand.

[5] The object of the investigation was to determine the quantity of alcohol in any given mixture at a given temperature. It was decided that the only accurate method was by measuring specific gravity, which required weighing. Equal volumes of pure water and pure spirits, or "alcohol," differ in weight by about one sixth of the weight of the water, and their mixture has a specific gravity somewhere in between. The problem would have had a straightforward solution if it were not for two effects, both requiring experimental investigation. One was the mutual penetration of spirits and water, their total bulk being less than the sum of the two bulks, increasing the specific gravity of a mixture. The other was the differential expansion of water and spirits by heat.

[6] Following the letter are some calculations by Blagden.

65. FROM CHARLES BLAGDEN

12 MARCH 1790[1]

From the original draft letter in the Royal Society[2]

Mr Cavendish Mar 12, 1790. Very much altered in transcribing.[3]

Dr Sir,

The result of my computation from the rule that

100 of Gilpins spirit (sp. gr. ,825 at 60) with $\frac{88{,}25-188{,}25-\beta}{7-P}$ of water make proof, was

100 grains with 74,36 grains (88,25 is the proportion in bulk of water to spirit 1/7 under proof, all reckoned at 60 degrees of heat.)

By your 2^d^ rule I find that if 922, the number given by Dicas is assumed, the weight of the proof spirit comes out 175,3: if I assume ,916, it comes out 175,1. The sp. gr [assuming] to which proportion namely 100 grains to 75 is ,91656 at 60.

Therefore ,916 must be very[4] nearly right. But then $\frac{75 \times 825}{1000} = 61{,}875$, the volume of the water.

Whence the computed sp. gr. of this mixture is ,892 but its real sp. gr. being ,916: the bulk of a mixture of 100 parts by measure of sp. with 61,875 of water is $\frac{61{,}875 \times 892}{916} = 157{,}634$. Dilute this with 1/6 of water, & the whole bulk of water is

$\frac{157{,}634}{6} + 61{,}875 = 88{,}147$. And $\frac{88{,}147 \times 1000}{825} = 107$ [----].

Therefore the true sp. gr. of proof spirit is 916 very nearly, rather above than under: the proportions of spirit in water in round numbers are 100 to 75 by weight or 100 to 62 parts by bulk.[5]

---

[1] This letter appears to be a reply to the preceding letter.

[2] Blagden Letters, 7:317.

[3] The difficulties Blagden experienced with the problem of excise duty on spirits would seem to be evident in this draft letter, which has many changes, and which Blagden changed further in the letter that was sent. To judge from letters that Blagden wrote to Banks at this time, this problem precipitated their open quarrel.

[4] Between "be" and "very" is "the," which Blagden neglected to strike out.

[5] The contents of this letter appear, slightly reworded, in Blagden's publication. Having found Dicas's value for the specific gravity of proof spirits inexact, 0.920 at 60°, he recommended his own, 0.916. "If, therefore, it be thought right to preserve the term proof-spirit in our Excise Laws, it may be understood to mean spirit, whose specific gravity is ,916, and which is composed of 100 parts of rectified spirit at ,825, and 62 parts of water by measure, or 75 by weight; the whole at 60 degrees of heat." Blagden recommended that the government levy duty strictly according to the quantity of rectified spirit. Upon being presented with a cask, a revenue officer would determine the quantity of its contents and their specific gravity and temperature, and then by reference to the new tables, he would deduce the quantity of rectified spirits, either in pounds or in gallons. "Report on the Best Method of Proportioning the Excise upon Spiritous Liquors," 339, 344.

66. TO CHARLES BLAGDEN

[BEFORE 26 MARCH 1790][1]

From the original letter in the Royal Society[2]

Dear Sir

As I think you had best reconsider what you say about the manner of proportioning the duty I send back the report[3] as soon as I can. I really cannot understand what you say in the latter part of P. 23 of the loss by concentration falling upon the distiller or importer nor do I see how any loss from thence falls upon anyone. On the other hand if the duty is not laid in proportion to the pure spirit artful persons will frequently have an advantage in importing or making the spirit on which the duty is to be laid of a different strength from that at which it is to be consumed & afterwards altering that strength to fit it for consumption.

H. Cavendish

---

[1] This letter is answered by letter 67, dated 26 Mar. 1790.

[2] Blagden Letters, C.21.

[3] Cavendish was referring to the manuscript of Blagden's report on the excise duty of spirits, which would be read before the Royal Society in four weeks, on 22 April.

67. FROM CHARLES BLAGDEN

26 MARCH 1790[1]

From the original draft letter in the Royal Society[2]

Mr Cavendish Mar 26, 1790.

Dr Sir,

What I mean by the loss from concentration falling upon the distiller is this. Suppose he had 100 gallons of rectified sp^{t} at ,825, upon which he paid 1 shilling only per gallon, amounting to £5. Let him dilute this with an equal volume of water, & he will obtain suppose 190 gallons. This spirit he would say is only half as strong as the former, being half water, & therefore should pay only 6^{d} duty per gallon; which wo^{d} be £4.15^{s}:0 upon the whole; whereas if the duty were based according to the gr of alcohol it contains, the amount wo^{d} be still £5. Allowing this to be in some measure sophistical <reasoning> (because the gallon of such dilute spirit should not be sold at half the price of rectified spirit, but at $^{1}/_{19}{}^{th}$ more) yet I doubt whether the distiller would easily be convinced that there is a fallacy, or persuaded that it is not his interest to pay the duty upon strong spirits rather than upon weak. However, since the other method strikes you as preferable, & upon the whole I think is so for the reason you assign of preventing frauds, I will adopt it in the report; it was the idea I originally entertained, & I abandoned it partly on the abovementioned account, & partly bec. in conversation with M^{r} [Shoss] he seemed to think it too abstract.

---

1 Reply to the preceding letter.

2 Blagden Letters, 7:695.

68. TO CHARLES BLAGDEN

[BEFORE 22 APRIL 1790][1]

From the original letter in the Royal Society[2]

Dear Sir

Great part of the diff[erence] between the 2 thermom[eters] proceeds from the vessel we tried them in being too short so that too much of the tube was out of water.[3]

In trying the upper degrees I believe that in $\begin{matrix}\text{long}\\ \text{short}\end{matrix}$ there were about $\begin{matrix}107^\circ\\ 51\end{matrix}$ out of water & therefore as the heat [of the] air was between 60 & 65 & these spirits expand about $\frac{1}{1700}$ for a degree the error in $\begin{matrix}\text{long}\\ \text{short}\end{matrix}$ was about $\left\{\begin{matrix}\frac{107 \times 55}{1700} = 3{,}5\\ \frac{51 \times 55}{1700} = 1{,}7\end{matrix}\right.$

In trying the degree of 90 the water reachd to the same height on [the] tube. Therefore the excess of degree shewn by $\begin{matrix}\text{long}\\ \text{short}\end{matrix}$ above that shewn by ☿ is $\begin{matrix}+2\\ +1{,}6\end{matrix}$ in heat of 120 & $\begin{matrix}-{,}8\\ -1{,}6\end{matrix}$ in heat 90.

Yours H. Cavendish

---

[1] Blagden discussed the material in this letter in his paper on the excise duty on spirits, on pp. 334–35, read on 22 April 1790.

[2] Blagden Letters, C.22.

[3] Carrying out experiments with Blagden on the problem of the excise duty, Cavendish put into practice the precautions in the use of thermometers he had recommended fifteen years before. Then he had written: "It has been too common a custom, both in making experiments with thermometers and in adjusting their fixed points, to pay no regard to the heat of that part of the quicksilver which is contained in the tube, though this is a circumstance which ought by no means to be disregarded." Because it was not always convenient to immerse the tube as well as the ball of a thermometer, Cavendish provided a table of corrections to compensate for the resulting error. "An Account of the Meteorological Instruments Used at the Royal Society's House," *PT* 66 (1776): 375–401; *Sci. Pap.* 2:112–26, on 112–13.

69. FROM CHARLES BLAGDEN

5 OCTOBER 1790

From the original draft letter in the Royal Society[1]

Mr Cavendish Oct 5, 1790.

Not having heard from Dr Crauford[2] at 10 last night, I sent a message to his house, & rec^{d} for answer that he co^{d} wait upon you either ♃ or ♄ next. In consequence I sent a note early this morning to Mr [Macie],[3] mentioning the business & telling him that Dr Crauford had appoint^{d} either ♃ or ♄ but that I knew the latter day wo^{d} be more agreeable to you; & that you wo^{d} be happy in his company to breakfast, if he could be at Clapham by 9 <o'clock> in the morning. His answer is inclosed; y^{r} name he has omitted, undoubtedly by mistake. Before receiving it I went to Dr Crauford's, & finding him at home, settled with him that he would attend you Saturday not later than 10 o'clock, & if possible at nine. I know not whether you intend to give them a dinner after the exp[erimen]t but if you do, it will be right to apprise them of the time. Most faithfully yours CBlagden.

---

[1] Blagden Letters, 7:702.

[2] At his house at Clapham Common, Cavendish was planning to perform experiments with, or in the presence of, Adair Crawford. There are two reasons why Cavendish might have wished to come together with Crawford in 1790. One is the recent publication, in 1788, of the second edition of Crawford's *Experiments and Observations on Animal Heat* . . . , which contained experiments on the specific heats of gases, a new field in which Cavendish was interested. The other reason is Crawford's publication earlier that year on gases extracted from distilled and putrefying animal matter, a subject which Cavendish had addressed incompletely in his first publication on gases. Crawford, "Experiments and Observations on the Matter of Cancer, and on Aëiral Fluids Extricated from Animal Substances by Distillation and Putrefaction; together with Some Remarks on Sulphureous Hepatic Air," *PT* 80 (1790): 391–426; read 17 June 1790.

[3] The name is partly effaced. A likely reading is James Louis Macie who later changed his name to Smithson (1765–1829), chemist and mineralogist, F.R.S. 1787. Macie's first scientific publication, which appeared the year after this letter, included experiments carried out by Cavendish at Macie's request. "An Account of Some Chemical Experiments on Tabasheer," *PT* 81 (1791): 368–88, on 370, 380. "Smithson," *DNB* 18:579–81.

70. FROM ISAAC DALBY[1]

13 NOVEMBER [1790]

From the original letter in the Devonshire Collections, Chatsworth[2]

Sir,

I take the liberty of informing you of a small Error in the bearing of Clapham Common from the meridian of St. Paul's, in Gen. Roy's Paper in the last Vol. of the Transactions.[3] And also of subjoining our manner of computing its Latitude and Longitude; as it is probable you may not think it of consequence enough to search for the data.

I am Sir

with great Respect

Your most obedient Servt

I. Dalby.

No. 28 Park Street.

Novr 13th [4]

---

[1] Isaac Dalby (1744–1821), mathematical teacher and surveyor, assistant to General Roy in the Anglo-French triangulation project of 1787–90. Taylor, *Mathematical Practitioners*, 258. When Roy died suddenly in 1790, Dalby was appointed by the Royal Society to correct the errors in Roy's final report. This letter to Cavendish came out of that work.

[2] Cavendish Mss Misc.

[3] In the conclusion of his account of the English half of the Anglo-French trigonometrical operation, Roy said that owing to superior instruments and to a "more accurate" method of measuring, the relative positions of the stations "may be said to be free from sensible error." The observations were, indeed, excellent. There were, however, many errors of another kind, those of calculation, Roy's own. They were discovered in time to spare the Royal Society the embarrassment of their being pointed out by foreigners. Roy began to correct his work but died suddenly in the middle of it. His capable assistant Dalby was appointed to complete the corrections. The error in the calculation of Cavendish's location at Clapham Common appeared in Roy, "An Account of the Trigonometrical Operation, Whereby the Distance between the Meridians of the Royal Observatories of Greenwich and Paris Has Been Determined," *PT* 80 (1790): 111–270, on 260–61.

[4] Below the close of this letter and continuing on a separate sheet are calculations and drawings of triangles, beginning with this correction: "Pag. 260 against Clapham Common 26° 29′ 56.1″ read 26° 29′ 52″." This correction appears in Dalby, "Remarks on Major-General Roy's Account of the Trigonometrical Operation, from Page 111. to Page 270. of This Volume," *PT* 80 (1790): 593–614, on 614.

71. FROM CHARLES BLAGDEN

27 NOVEMBER 1790

From the original draft letter in the Royal Society[1]

Mr Cavendish Nov 27, 1790.

Dr Sir,

As it is doubtful whether I shall be at Sir Joseph's this evening, I send you a small specimen of the sand from which Mr Gregor[2] obtains his supposed new mineral subs^{ce}, together with a copy of his letter to Mr Turner on that subject. The specimen may be shewn to any one, provided none of it be lost; but the letter must be read only by yourself, as I am told that Mr Turner is not to hear that it has been comm^{d} to you. Yours faithfully CB.

---

[1] Blagden Letters, 7:481.

[2] Almost certainly William Gregor (1762–1817), clergyman, who found a magnetic sand in Cornwall and who communicated mineralogical observations to the Royal Society. "Gregor," Poggendorff 1: col. 947.

72. FROM CHARLES BLAGDEN

8 JUNE 1791

From the original draft letter in the Royal Society[1]

Mr Cavendish June 8 1791.

Dear Sir,

I am sorry I was not in the way, when your servant called twice. The Committee,[2] I believe cannot avoid printing the paper, but Sir Joseph Banks has suggested the addition of grains *of quicksilver* in the one place, & omission of the paragraph about discovery in the other: if you think this would not be right, be so good as to send me word [----] *at the Council.* Sir Joseph I fear will not be there, being summoned to attend the [-----] of Trustees to the Museum. Dr Pearson[3] has sent his analysis of James's powder[4] part of wch will fill up the meeting tomorrow; but I have not opened any thing [misc] of Mr Macie's paper.[5] M. Hassenfratz[6] is just arrivd from France.

---

1 Blagden Letters, 7:523.

2 Committee of papers of the Royal Society.

3 George Pearson (1751–1828), chemist, London physician, F.R.S. 1791. Scott, "Pearson," *DSB* 10:445–47.

4 Pearson carried out a chemical analysis and synthesis of a popular medicine used to treat fever, "James's powder." He determined that the powder that made Robert James rich was composed of bone ash and antimony oxide. Ibid. "Experiments and Observations to Investigate the Composition of James's Powder," *PT* 81 (1791): 317–67; read 23 June 1791.

5 Macie's paper on tabasheer, cited in letter 69, note 3.

6 Jean-Henri Hassenfratz (1755–1827), French chemist. Birembaut, "Hassenfratz," *DSB* 6:164–65.

73. FROM CHARLES BLAGDEN

27 JULY 1791

From the original draft letter in the Royal Society[1]

July 27, 1791.

D^r^ B presents his compts to Mr Cavendish, and returns the Bergbaukunde,[2] for the use of which, as well as of several other books, he begs Mr Cavendish to accept his thanks. In the two volumes of the Bergbaukunde are letters from New Spain, giving a pretty good account of the mines & manner of treating the ore in that country.–Dr Blagden wishes Mr Cavendish his health, and a pleasant summer.

---

[1] Blagden Letters, 7:548.

[2] Societat der Bergbaukunde, *Bergbaukunde*, 2 vols. (Leipzig, 1789–90).

74. FROM BENJAMIN VAUGHAN[1]

25 OCTOBER 1791

From the original letter in the Devonshire Collections, Chatsworth.[2]

Mr B. Vaughan presents his respectful compliments to Mr Cavendish, & has the honor to send him the inclosed data & queries, upon which, as concerning so considerable an object, he hopes Mr Cavendish will have the goodness to favor the Bristol gentlemen with his opinion.–As it is also expressly wished that Dr Blagden should be consulted, Mr Cavendish is requested to oblige M^{r} V: by communicating the inclosed to him at his leisure for that purpose.–The earliest decision suiting Mr Cavendish's convenience will be esteemed a particular indulgence.[3]

Octr 25, 91,
Billiter Square.

---

[1] Benjamin Vaughan (1751–1835), politician. "Vaughan, Benjamin," *DNB* 20:158–59.

[2] Cavendish Mss New Correspondence.

[3] To make the port of Bristol competitive with other ports, the Society of Merchant Adventurers resolved to build a dam across the Frome River, and a number of well-known men of science served as consultants. Blagden, who had local connections and knowledge, was one of them. The port where ships loaded and unloaded was formed by the rivers Frome and Avon, both of which flowed through the city, and into which all the sewers ran. From the Severn River, daily a salt-water tide swept up the Avon and into the Frome, and on its retreat fresh water flowed down the rivers, cleansing them. The proposed dam would create a deeper harbor–ships in Bristol Harbor then cradled into deep mud–but it would also, its opponents argued, interfere with the outflow of filth and with the accompanying fresh wind, leaving the city at the mercy of the stench from both sewage and the fumes from lead smelting works and other industries skirting the city. The town fathers of Bristol were confronted with an environmental problem of a familiar kind, pitting economic progress against health. Sam Worrall to Charles Blagden, 8 Dec. 1791, Blagden Letters, Royal Society, W.24.

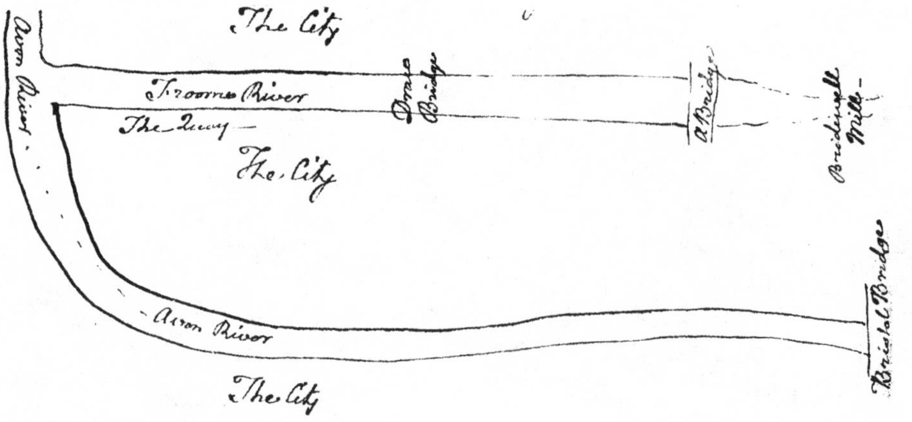

117. *Bristol Harbor. Drawing included in a letter from Sam Worrall to Charles Blagden, 8 December 1791, Blagden Letters, Royal Society, W.24. If the map of the Avon River were continued, the site of the dam would be about two thirds of the way to the top of the page. Reproduced by permission of the President and Council of the Royal Society.*

75. FROM BENJAMIN VAUGHAN

29 OCTOBER 1791

From the original letter in the Devonshire Collections, Chatsworth[1]

Mr B. Vaughan presents his respectful com^ts^ to Mr Cavendish, & has the pleasure to inform him, that Dr Higgins[2] has given his answers to the queries from Bristol, a copy of which Mr V. has desired may be sent to Mr Cavendish under a blank cover.

Dr H. recommends a main sewer, distinct from the Dock; but his answers are favorable in other respects, from the rapid view M^r^. V. took of them in Dr. Higgins's presence.

Qu^y^ What should prevent one or more principal sewers being made, running *within* or *without* the docks, as convenience shall direct?

Octr 29, 91.

[1] Cavendish Mss New Correspondence.

[2] Bryan or Bryant Higgins (b. 1737 or 1741, d. 1818), an Irish chemist who lived in London. Thackray, "Higgins," *DSB* 6:382–84.

76. TO BENJAMIN VAUGHAN

1 NOVEMBER [1791]

From the original letter in the Bristol Record Office.[1]

Clapham Nov. 1

Dear Sir

I must decline giving any answer to the queries you sent relating to the proposed undertaking at Bristol as none but Physicians are proper judges of many of them & the Engineers they have consulted are much better judges of the remainder than I can be.[2]

As the data which accompany the queries seem very imperfect I think it better to return them to you rather than send them to Dr Blagden that you may have an opportunity of looking at them again before they are sent to him.

The point in which they are most defective is that they do not mention what quantity of water passes down the Froom[3] nor what proportion of the sewers are discharged into the harbour so that there are no data for determining how the water in the harbour will be affected nor are there any data for determining the quantity of foul water discharged by the sewers.

I should have sent you my determination sooner had it not been that owing to the neglect of my servant in town I did not receive your letter of Oct. 25 so soon as I ought to have done & that I was in hopes of meeting you yesterday in the city.[4]

Yours sincerely
H. Cavendish

---

1 Reference 11168(3)t. A draft of this letter, which is in response to letters 74 and 75, is in Cavendish Mss New Correspondence.

2 Cavendish did not decline before he had made calculations of the flows with what data he had. "Data Extracted from Queries about Bristol Intended Harbour," Cavendish Mss Misc.

3 Spelled "Frome" today.

4 Yesterday being a Monday, Cavendish had expected to see Vaughan at the Monday Club, which met at the George and Vulture. At the next meeting of the club, Cavendish told Blagden that Vaughan had a communication from Bristol for him. Draft letter of 7 Nov. 1791, Blagden Letters, Royal Society, 7:581.

77. FROM CHARLES BLAGDEN

7 NOVEMBER 1791

From the original draft letter in the Royal Society[1]

Mr Cavendish Nov 7, 1791.

Dear Sir,

The inclosed papers, (being Mr Davis's's[2] answer to your question about the Hindoo astronomy) came to me from Sir Joseph Banks, with a letter[3] desiring, that when I had read them I had put them into y^{r} hands. They were sent down to me at Broadlands, whence I did not return till Sndy evening, which is the reason they have not been delivrd to you sooner. Y^{rs} very f^{ly} CB.

---

1 Blagden Letters, 7:579.

2 Samuel Davis (d. 1819), civil servant in Benares, F.R.S. 1792.

3 Probably Samuel Davis to Sir Joseph Banks, 10 Mar. 1791, Banks Correspondence, Kew, l.38. Davis apologized for the delay in answering a letter from Banks the previous August. He had been away, making it impossible to "attend sooner to the queries from Mr. Cavendish" about the astronomical knowledge of the Brahmins. At Davis's request Banks had shown Cavendish a paper by Davis on Hindu astronomy. Cavendish soon published a paper of his own on the subject, "On the Civil Year of the Hindoos, and Its Divisions; with an Account of Three Hindoo Almanacs Belonging to Charles Wilkins, Esq.," *PT* 82 (1792): 383–99; read 21 June 1792.

78. FROM CHARLES BLAGDEN

27 FEBRUARY 1792

From the original draft letter in the Royal Society[1]

Mr Cavendish Feb. 27, 1792

Dr Sir,

The smallest of the two parcels sent with this note is the book on the Cufic[2] Globe, in which the passage about the Sind Kend[3] occupies from p. xx to xxiii. Mr Aubert has not returned any answer to my inquiry about the disposal of this book; therefore, should you see him at the Club today,[4] be so good as let him know that I have sent it to you. The other parcel is Schröter's work on the moon[5] unbound as I rec^d^ it. If upon looking over the papers, there appears any thing about which you wish me to gave[6] you information, I shall [be] happy to do it, as far as my memory serves. This is to be returned to the R.S. Yours very f^ly^. CB.

---

[1] Blagden Letters, 7:621.

[2] From Cufa or Kufa, an ancient city near Babylon, a great seat of Muslim learning; the word also applies to a certain kind of Arabic writing. *Oxford English Dictionary.*

[3] Probably the *Sind Hind,* tables belonging to a Sanskrit Greco-Indian tradition in astronomy and astrology. Cavendish's paper on Sanskrit almanacs was read to the Royal Society four months after this letter.

[4] February 27 being a Monday, the "Club" referred to was the Monday Club.

[5] Johann Hieronymus Schröter (1745–1816), German astronomer, the first to study the surface of the moon systematically over a long period, making many drawings of its features. "Observations on the Atmospheres of Venus and the Moon, Their Respective Densities, Perpendicular Heights, and Twilight Occasioned by Them," *PT* 82 (1792): 309–61. Multhauf, "Schröter," *DSB* 12:226.

[6] Blagden obviously meant to write "give."

79. FROM CHARLES BLAGDEN

12 MARCH 1792

From the original draft letter in the Royal Society[1]

The H[ble] Henry Cavendish Mar 12, 1792.

D[r] Sir,

I am extremely sorry to hear of your illness, of which I rec[d] no intimation till I enquired at your house yesterday.[2] If you had chosen that I should wait upon you, I cannot doubt but you would have sent to me. Accept my best wishes for your speedy recovery; and believe me to remain always, y[r] f[l] friend CB.

The powder in the inclosed paper was given to me saturday by D[r] Pearson, as the purest kind of charcoal from the decomposition of fixed air.[3]

---

[1] Blagden Letters, 7:624.

[2] See letter 81. According to his friend Dalrymple, Cavendish was suffering from an attack of the "gravel," or difficult or painful urination with or without a deposit of urinary crystals.

[3] Pearson performed chemical experiments to prove that fixed air (carbon dioxide) decompounds into respirable air (oxygen) and carbon, the inverse of Lavoisier's synthesis of fixed air, or "carbonic acid." From fixed air, Pearson obtained a porous, fine, black powder, which he determined was carbon, a sample of which, we assume, Blagden delivered to Cavendish. "Experiments Made with the View of Decompounding Fixed Air, or Carbonic Acid," *PT* 82 (1792): 289–308, on 295; read 24 May 1792.

80. FROM CHARLES BLAGDEN

12 MARCH 1792

From the original draft letter in the Royal Society[1]

The Hon. Henry Cavendish Monday Mar 12, 4 o'clock, 1792.

Dr Sir,

It gives me great concern to hear that you are worse today. As a physician I know you have Dr Hunter,[2] & you could not do better: but is it agreeable to you that I sho^{d} visit you at Clapham as a friend?[3]

Faithfully y^{rs} CB.

---

[1] Blagden Letters, 7:625.

[2] The physician John Hunter; see letter 48.

[3] Blagden wrote to Sir Joseph Banks the next day that he was "engaged to be with Mr Cavendish (who is much disposed) at Clapham." Draft letter of 13 Mar. 1792, Blagden Letters, Royal Society, 7:626.

81. FROM ALEXANDER DALRYMPLE

16 MARCH 1792

From the original letter in the Devonshire Collections, Chatsworth[1]

Dr Sir

I was very sorry yesterday to hear that You were prevented from coming amongst us[2] by an attack of the Gravel: It brought to my recollection that Old Belchier[3] mentioned at the Club[4] one day, that nothing was more efficacious in that Complaint than *Lintseed Tea.* I hope however the Complaint is going off as it was said You were better. That You may soon come amongst us is the sincere wish of all Your Friends and of none more truely than of Dr Sir Your most affectionate

A. Dalrymple

16th March 1792
Hon. H. Cavendish

Rain from Bombay News Paper

Bombay average of 8 years observed by Mr Iveson 63,3/4 inches

Do to 31 July 1791 48,3 inches

Calcutta average of 11 years . . . Col Pearse 56

Maké on Malabar Coast average of 4 years . . . 127,1/4

[address]:
Hon. Henry Cavendish

---

1 Cavendish Mss X(b), 16. This letter is published in Wilson, *Cavendish*, 176.

2 As this letter was written on a Friday, Dalrymple would have been referring to the meeting of the Royal Society or to the dinner of the Royal Society Club or to both, as both met on Thursday.

3 John Belchier, F.R.S. 1732.

4 The Royal Society Club.

82. TO SIR JOSEPH BANKS

3 DECEMBER 1792

From a copy of the letter in the Natural History Museum, Botany Library[1]

Dec. 3^{d} 1792.

Dear Sir

I return the paper on Kempelin's machine[2] with many thanks, & enclose S^{r} C[harles] B[agden]s[3] letter[4] to me. I think it much most likely that your paper is right as to the principle on which it supposes Kempelin's machine was made, namely that magnets were enclosed in the Chess-men, & that moveable magnetical wires were placed under each square of the board, which were attracted by the chess men when set down, & thereby discovered to a concealed person his adversary's moves: but as to the rest of the explanation, I think it very doubtful; as it would be difficult to manage, & would hardly answer well, & besides I think one might easily contrive a better construction.

The explanation given in Sr C. B^{s} letter of the balls falling from the Tower, is by no means so bad as it at first appeared to me. If the Tower was 400 feet high, the balls would be 5″ in falling, & in that time the excess of the diurnal motion at the top of the Tower above that at the bottom is $^{1}/_{7}$ of a foot, so that the balls ought to fall $^{1}/_{7}$ of a foot to the East of the plumb line, & if the Tower is 200 feet high, should fall $^{1}/_{21}$ of a foot. Most likely, however, the irregularities arising from the resistance of the air & manner of letting fall the balls would be much greater than this, & would therefore make it difficult to distinguish the effect of the dirurnal motion.–

Yours sincerely
H. Cavendish

---

[1] DTC, 8:125–26.

[2] Wolfgang von Kempelen (1734–1804), privy councillor at the Hungarian chancery court in Vienna, published a book on the mechanism of human speech along with a description of his speaking machine. He exhibited a mechanical chess player that astonished and puzzled European audiences. The player was not a genuine automaton, for as Cavendish recognized, Kempelen had a concealed confederate. "Automaton," *Encyclopaedia Britannica* (Chicago: William Benton, 1961), 2:788B. Poggendorff 1: col. 1242.

[3] Blagden had just been knighted by George III for his services to science. Getman, "Blagden," 72.

[4] We do not have this letter, which would have been sent to Cavendish from abroad. Blagden left London in July 1792, spending the winter in Rome and Naples. De Beer, "Diary of Sir Charles Blagden," 89.

83. FROM J[OHN] CHURCHMAN[1]

12 JULY 1793

From the original letter in the Devonshire Collections, Chatsworth[2]

J. Churchman sends his best respects to Henry Cavendish Esquire, together with the printed proposals of a work which he is pursueing with Industry,[3] & altho he is about taking the variation himself at this place, as in his calculations that of Greenwich is considered the first Meridian, any observations near that observatory are highly interesting, & tend to prove the truth of each other. J. C. will be particularly thankful if he can be favoured by a note with the mean Variation at his own observatory at Clapham, for the present time, & for each year for a few years back if convenient. Dr Bradleys[4] observations he is already furnished with. He is very sorry to be the occasion of this trouble, & nothing but his desire of arriving as near to perfection as possible in his publication would urge him to take this Liberty. But having often understood that no one was more able & willing to furnish useful hints & assistance to the Enquirer, than the Gentleman to whom he now addresses himself, he was encouraged by these favourable reports to write the present Note.–

No 8 Providence Row, Finsbury Square.

July 12th 1793.

[address]:

Henry Cavendish Esquire

Clapham

---

[1] John Churchman (1753–1805), American author of books on terrestrial magnetism. "Churchman, John," *National Cyclopaedia of American Biography*, vol. 9 (New York, 1899), 287.

[2] Cavendish Mss New Correspondence.

[3] Churchman sent a memorandum to the Board of Longitude claiming the "true system of the magnetic variation of the needle" together with a method of determining longitude. Sir Joseph Banks, president of the Royal Society and member of the Board of Longitude, was told that Churchman was afraid that his idea might be stolen and therefore would appreciate prompt attention by the Board. William [Dillough] to Sir Joseph Banks, 25 May 1787, Banks Correspondence, Kew, 1.272. In 1792, upon an invitation by Banks, Churchman sailed to England to advance his work and to test his method of finding longitude at sea. "Churchman," *National Cyclopaedia*. Two years earlier he had published a book on magnetic variation, *An Explanation of the Magnetic Atlas, or Variation Chart, Hereunto Annexed: Projected on a Plan Entirely New, by Which the Magnetic Variation on Any Part of the Globe May Be Precisely Determined for Any Time Past, Present, or Future: and the Variation and Latitude Being Accurately Known, the Longitude Is of Consequence Truly Determined* (Philadelphia, 1790).

[4] James Bradley (1693–1762), F.R.S. 1718, from 1742 astronomer royal. Alexander, "Bradley," *DSB* 2:387–89.

84. TO JOHN CHURCHMAN

[AFTER 12 JULY 1793]

From the draft letter in the Devonshire Collections, Chatsworth[1]

S^r^

Last summer I found the variation 23°.50′. As there are many others who have observed the variation longer at the same place than I have I do not imagine the former observations can be of any use to you.[2]

---

[1] Cavendish Mss New Correspondence. This letter is in response to the preceding.

[2] Cavendish was more interested in the subject than his reply to Churchman would suggest. He may well have formed a negative opinion of Churchman's scheme, as did many men of science, and he may also have been wary of writing a fuller letter to Churchman, who had published letters from Banks and Thomas Jefferson in his book. Soon after moving to his new house on Clapham Common, Cavendish began to take readings there with his variation compass, which he continued to August 1809. For around three months in the summer and early fall, he took readings, at least one in the morning and one in the afternoon, and occasionally he took many readings on a single day. He calculated mean values of his readings for each year, which he then summarized. Cavendish Mss IX, 1 and 2. Churchman's inquiry came at a time of unusual interest, since from the mid 1770s, the variation increased every year with the exception of 1790 to 1791, when it decreased. Cavendish gave George Gilpin his observations for 1790 and 1791, which Gilpin discussed, "Observations on the Variation, and on the Dip of the Magnetic Needle, Made at the Apartments of the Royal Society, between the Years 1786 and 1805 Inclusive," *PT* 96 (1806): 385–419, on 391.

85. TO JOHN BROOKE AND JEREMIAH DIXON[1]

[1793]

From the original draft letter in the Devonshire Collections, Chatsworth[2]

Mr Cavendish presents his compliments to Mr Brooke & Dixon & sends back the account of the equatorial micrometer as Mr Lloyd[3] wanted to compare it with that in Mr Auberts possession[4] & said [he] would desire you to let him see it.

Mr C. cannot understand the account of the experiments made on the fire engine[5] for want of a description of the apparatus. If they have any account or drawing of it he would be glad to see it.

There is nothing among the papers at all in a state fit for publication.[6]

Perhaps it might be worth while giving some account of the experiments on the fire engine by way of appendix to his other things, but unless those should prove to be so he thinks he shall find very little if any thing else that would be so.

---

[1] This letter evidently concerns the papers of the civil engineer John Smeaton, who died in 1793. Mary, one of his daughters, married Jeremiah Dixon, a county magistrate and sometime mayor of Leeds and of Fell Foot, Windermere. Smiles, *Lives of the Engineers* 2:176. John Brooke was married to Smeaton's other daughter, Ann. As Smeaton's heirs, his two daughters and their husbands owned his papers. A.P. Woolrich, "John Farey and the Smeaton Manuscripts," *History of Technology* 10 (1985): 181–216. on 182–83.

[2] Cavendish Mss New Correspondence.

[3] John Lloyd, M.B., of Wygfair or Wickwer near St. Asaph, F.R.S. 1759, a friend of Alexander Aubert. "Aubert," *DNB* 1:715. Lloyd, "Account of an Earthquake," *PT* 73 (1783): 104–5.

[4] Alexander Aubert, whom Smeaton "greatly loved and respected," owned an equatorial micrometer constructed at his request by Smeaton. This micrometer was judged by his fellow astronomer Francis Wollaston as the "best instrument" for taking observations out of the meridian, "far superior" to any system of fixed wires or any equatorial sector. *Reports of the Late John Smeaton, F.R.S. Made on Various Occasions, in the Course of His Employment as a Civil Engineer*, 3 vols. (London, 1812), 1:xx. Wollaston, "A Description of a New System of Wires in the Focus of a Telescope, for Observing the Comparative Right Ascensions and Declinations of Coelestial Objects . . . ," *PT* 75 (1785): 346–52, on 348. Smeaton, "Account of an Observation of the Right Ascension and Declination of Mercury out of the Meridian, Near His Greatest Elongation, Sept. 1786, Made by Mr. John Smeaton, F.R.S. with an Equatorial Micrometer of His Own Invention and Workmanship . . . ," *PT* 77 (1787): 318–43, on 319.

[5] In addition to his work in civil engineering, Smeaton improved steam engines: a steam engine burning coal used for lifting water and rated at six horsepower, "Description of a Portable Fire-Engine, Invented by John Smeaton, F.R.S. at the Instance of the Right Honourable the Earl of Egmont, 1765," in *Reports of the Late John Smeaton* 1:223–29. Also "An Engine for Raising Water by Fire; Being an Improvement of Savery's Construction, to Render It Capable of Working Itself; Invented by M. De Moura, of Portugal, F.R.S., Described by Mr. Smeaton," *PT* 47 (1752): 436–38.

[6] It would seem that Cavendish was asked to advise on the publication of these papers by the estate. He was authorized to deliver the papers to Sir Joseph Banks, president of the Royal Society; see next letter. Banks for a large sum bought "all the manuscripts, designs, drawings of every sort, and all the papers of Mr Smeaton, from his executors and representatives." In the end the Society of Civil Engineers decided to publish only Smeaton's "reports," a judgment which agreed with Cavendish's. The project was overseen by a committee consisting of Banks and four engineers. *Reports of the Late John Smeaton* 1: ix–x. At the time of Cavendish's letter to Brooke and Dixon, Brooke was in correspondence with Banks and their go-between, Aubert, about the transfer of the papers. The business dragged on into the next year. In the end, Banks did not acquire "all" of Smeaton's papers. Woolrich, "John Farey," 182–83.

86. TO SIR JOSEPH BANKS

23 SEPTEMBER [1793]

From a copy of the letter in the Natural History Museum, Botany Library[1]

Clapham Septr 23rd

Dear Sir

I am sorry to inform you that Sir Charles Blagden is ill at Frankfort: Last saturday I received a letter from Dr de Neuf-ville, who it should seem attends him as physician, dated Septr 11th, saying that for near 13 days he had been ill of a continued remitting fever, which had attacked him with considerable violence, but that it appeared to diminish, & that there was the utmost reason to think that he would do well, that his strength kept up à merveille, & that his head was perfectly clear. He adds that the utmost care is taken of him.–

I received a letter about a week ago saying that he was ill, but I delayed informing you of it till I could mention something more precise.–

I have received authority from Mr Brooks to deliver Mr Smeaton's papers[2] to you, which I shall do when you come to town, unless you chuse to have them sent to you.

I called on Mr Lumsby[3] at Lincoln,[4] who shewed me every thing with great obligingness, but the weather was so bad the next day that I went straight to town without passing through Boston.

The white substance collected from your mine[5] is earth of Alum, not combined with silicious earth but mixed with a little calcarious earth, so that, from what Mr Kirwan says of lac luna, it should seem to be much the same as that substance only not yet hardened.

Yours sincerely
H. Cavendish

---

[1] DTC, 8:257.

[2] Discussed in last letter.

[3] Probably Banks's acquaintance William Lumby (d. 1804), master of Lincoln Gaol. *Banks Letters*, 558.

[4] Cavendish had just returned from a journey in August and September, his last (this time without Blagden), which took him through Lincolnshire on the return. Cavendish Mss X(a), 2. Lincolnshire is also the location of Banks's family estate, Revesby Abbey. Foote, "Banks," 433.

[5] The Gregory lead mine at Overton in Derbyshire was worked by Banks and several partners, who paid compensation to the duke of Devonshire among others. BL Add Mss 6679, ff. 5–10. On his recent journey, at Banks's request Cavendish had gone to the Gregory mine to inspect a new steam engine. "One of the hollows in this mine was found coverd with a soft substance in some places of an ochry colour & in others white," Cavendish noted. He collected a sample, dried it, powdered it, dissolved it in weak spirit of nitre, and found that "the solution had an aluminous taste." He concluded that the white part of the matter consisted of earth of alum mixed with a little calcarious earth, as he reported to Banks. "White Book," Cavendish Mss, p. 98.

87. FROM PAHIN DE LA BLANCHERIE[1]

23 SEPTEMBER 1794

From the original letter in the Devonshire Collections, Chatsworth[2]

Monsieur,

Je me suis fait addresser à votre Bibliothécaire pour jouir de la libéralité avec la quelle vous communiquez vos livres aux gens de Lettres.[3] La premiere fois que je l'ai vu, il ne m'a pas seulement aidé à faire les recherches qui m'etoient nécessaires, il m'a encore prèté chez moi un volume, en me disant, à ma grande admiration, que c'étoit selon le plan de votre munificence! J'ai eu depuis, besoin de parcourir l'Histoire de l'Astronomie par Bailly,[4] j'avois vu cet ouvrage au nombre de vos livres–Je me suis prèsenté avec confiance à votre Bibliothécaire[5]; il étoit alors dans la piece même du rét de chaussée où cet ouvrage a sa place attenant la porte, à gauche en entrant et en même temps que je la lui demandois, je la voyois, mais il s'est excusé de me le prêter, sur le pretexte que vous l'aviez pris à Clapham, depuis quelques jours........Je lui ai demandé à consulter le Dictionnaire historique des Grands hommes[6] qu'il m'avois dit être dans votre bibliothèque; mais il s'est trouvé que vous en aviez eu besoin en même temps que de l'histoire de l'Astronomie–Cependant il m'avoit prévenu qu'il auroit peut être ces livres à disposition, quelques jours aprės–Mais c'est en vain, que je n'ai pas manqué de revenir; les livres, quoique sans doute en place, n'étoient pas revenus et *vous en aviez le plus grand besoin à Clapham.*

J'ai été à portée, monsieur, depuis long temps, de savoir que l'on vous a beaucoup d'obligations pour le progrès des connoissances humaines tant par vos travaux particuliers que par l'encouragement que vous donnez à [ceux] des autres–J'ai donc lieu d'etre scandalisé ou du moins étonné qu'on se permette de m'exclure de cet encouragement et comme il n'est pas possible que vous autorisiez cette conduite, je crois entrer dans vos vues en vous la dénonçant pour en connoitre la cause.[7]

Ayant eprouvé toutes sortes de dégoûts au British Museum, il me sembloit que j'allois en être dédomagé, comme par la nation Angloise, dans votre Bibliotheque. Je me sens du moins le coeur anglois pour ne pas souffrir d'avantage, qu'on vexe de la maniere la plus scandaleuse en Angleterre, un étranger qui travaille à lui faire honneur. Au moment où je suis de demander justice au public à cet égard, j'ai cru, monsieur, ne devoir pas moins compter sur la votre.

Je suis avec bien du respect,
Monsieur

Votre trés humble
et trés obéissant serviteur
La Blancherie

Newton House, Londres ce 23. S[bre]
1794

[address]:
The Honble Henri Cavendish,
Clapham

[1] Mammès-Claude-Catherine Pahin Champlain de La Blancherie (1752–1811), journalist and author. Fearing harm or persecution in France, he took refuge in London, where he happened to lodge in a building having belonged to Newton, a situation he turned to his advantage, obtaining a pension from the English government. Léon, "La Blancherie," *Dictionnaire de biographie française* 18: col. 1344. Note the return address on this letter, "Newton House."

[2] Cavendish Mss New Correspondence.

[3] Cavendish made his large library available year round to persons who had need of it. To one who requested a book, Charles Blagden replied that his request had been conveyed to Cavendish, "who wishing to promote science by every measure in his power, will be very happy if his library can afford you assistance." Draft letter to Thomas Beddoes, 12 Mar. 1788, Blagden Letters, Royal Society, 7:129.

[4] Jean-Sylvain Bailly, *Histoire de l'astronomie ancienne, depuis son origine jusqu'à l'éstablissement de l'école d'Alexander* (Paris, 1775).

[5] Cavendish had a librarian. For a long while he was a German, probably named Heydinger.

[6] François-Xavier de Feller, *Dictionnaire historique des grands hommes* (Augsbourg, 1781).

[7] We are not so certain that Cavendish would have disapproved of his librarian's behavior, and indeed we suspect that he was behind it. Cavendish undoubtedly had an opinion about La Blancherie's use of his connection with Newton. He definitely would have had one about his character. In 1785, when he was a young journalist still living in France, La Blancherie wrote to Blagden, secretary of the Royal Society, making a gift to him and to the president, Banks, of issues of his journal, *Les Nouvelles de la république des lettres et des arts.* Blagden thanked him and offered his services should Blancherie want anything from England. Two months later Blagden received a letter from La Blancherie attacking a geologist, B. Faujas de Saint-Fond, on the basis of secondhand opinions originating with Blagden. Blagden was mortified. He wrote to La Blancherie that the latter had misunderstood his sources, left Blagden "completely exposed," and committed the "worst kind of indiscretion." La Blancherie had, in short, acted in an ungentlemanly fashion. In no uncertain terms, Blagden told him he wanted nothing to do with him or with his journal. "With regard to your proposal to make known your business in some public paper, I ask you to excuse me, for that accords neither with my ideas nor with my station." Blagden to La Blancherie, 21 May and 23 Aug. 1785, drafts, Blagden Letterbook, Yale.

87T. TRANSLATION OF THE LETTER FROM PAHIN DE LA BLANCHERIE

23 September 1794

From the original letter in the Devonshire Collections, Chatsworth

Sir,

I was presented to your librarian so that I might benefit from the freedom with which you lend your books to men of letters. The first time I saw him, he not only helped me to conduct research that was necessary to me, but he loaned me a volume telling me, to my great admiration, that this was in keeping with your munificence! I since had need to peruse l'Histoire de l'Astronomie by Bailly. I had seen this work among your many books–I presented myself with confidence to your librarian; he was then in the very room of the ground floor where this work is located–just by the door, to the left upon entering, and I saw the book at the moment I asked for it, but he excused himself from loaning it to me on the pretext that you had taken it to Clapham a few days before........ I asked to consult the Dictionnaire historique des Grands hommes which he told me was in your library; but it was the case that you had need of both it and l'Histoire de l'Astronomie. Nevertheless, he informed me that he might have these books at hand several days later. Of course I made certain to return, but in vain; the books, although without a doubt in place, "were not returned," and "*you had the greatest need of them at Clapham.*"

I have known for a long time, Sir, that we are greatly indebted to you for progress in human knowledge equally for your own work as for the encouragement that you give to that of others. I have the right therefore to be scandalized or at least astonished that [some]one takes the liberty of excluding me from this encouragement, and as it is not possible that you would allow this conduct, I believe I reflect your views by denouncing such behavior to you in order to know its cause.

Having felt all sorts of disgust at the British Museum, it seemed to me that I was going to be compensated for it in your library as I was by the English nation. I have, nonetheless, enough of an English disposition to suffer no further those who in the most scandalous manner in England vex a foreigner who works to honor England. At the moment when I must publicly demand justice in this matter, I thought, Sir, that I could count no less upon yours.

I am with the greatest respect,

Sir

Newton House, London 23 Sept.
1794

Your very humble
and very obedient servant
La Blancherie

[address]:
The Honble Henry Cavendish
Clapham

88. TO JOSEF DE MENDOZA Y RIOS[1]

JANUUARY 1795

From the *Philosophical Transactions*[2]

Extract of a Letter from Henry Cavendish, Esq. to Mr. Mendoza y Rios, January, 1795.

The methods in which the whole distance of the moon and star is computed, particularly yours, require fewer operations than those in which the difference of the true and apparent places is found; but yet, as in the former methods, it is necessary either to take proportional parts, or to use very voluminous tables; I am much inclined to prefer the latter. This induced me to try whether a convenient method of the latter kind might not be deduced from the fundamental proposition used in your paper, and I have obtained the following, which has the advantage of requiring only short tables, and wanting only one proportional part to be taken, and I think seems shorter than any of the kind I have met with.

[. . .]

Addition to the Foregoing Letter.

I have procured tables of the above-mentioned kind to be computed, which are intended to be inserted in a work now printing by Mr. Mendoza y Rios. [. . .]

---

[1] Josef de Mendoza y Rios (1762–1816), astronomer, Spanish naval officer who took up residence in England, F.R.S. 1793. Taylor, *Mathematical Practitioners*, 319.

[2] Cavendish's letter was published at the end of Mendoza y Rios, "Recherches sur les principaux problèmes de l'astronomie nautique," *PT* 87 (1797): 43–122. The author's object was to present general formulas from which the various methods of nautical astronomy could be deduced and compared. Cavendish, "Addition. Contenant une méthode pour réduire les distances lunaires," ibid., 119–22; *Sci. Pap.* 2:246–48.

89. TO SIR CHARLES BLAGDEN

22 JUNE [1796]

From the original letter in the Royal Society[1]

Clapham June 22

Dear Sir

On consideration I think the recommendation *that these & any other detached pieces of metal there may be in the building*[2] *be taken away or be made to communicate with the conductors & the earth* too indeterminate & such as might induce them to make communications which would be improper. For example let EBACD be the end of the building, & AF the conductor;[3] if there should be any piece of metal at G, the making a communication between that & the conductor might induce the lightning to strike the building at M & injure the wall in passing from thence to G. The making a communication from the hinges of the door N to the conductor may perhaps be in some measure liable to this objection, but not so much, but that if you think it of service I am ready to recommend it.

The most defective part of the defence is those side doors which have no conductors & no strap from the ridge of the roof. If you think it advisable to take notice of this I am ready to join in it. I will be at the R.S. tomorrow at ½ past 2, which I suppose will be time enough to settle any thing which can be wanted.

Yours sincerely

H. Cavendish

---

[1] Blagden Letters, C.25.

[2] In 1772–73 Cavendish was on a committee that recommended installing lightning rods made of iron on the then unprotected Purfleet powder magazines; see letter 4. The subject came up again in 1796, when the Board of Ordnance requested that the Royal Society appoint a committee to "examine into the state of the conductors" at Purfleet. Cavendish and Blagden were appointed to that committee on 17 Mar. 1796, and they delivered their report on 23 June 1796. Minutes of Council, Royal Society, 8:82.

[3] See sketch in extract, illustration 118, next page.

Clapham June 22

Dear Sir

On consideration I think the recommendation that these & any other detatched pieces of metal there may be in the building be taken away or be made to communicate with the conductor & the earth too indeterminate & such as might induce them to make communications which would be improper. For example let EBACD be the end of the building, & AF the conductor; if there should be any piece of metal at G, the making a communication between that & the conductor might induce the lightning to strike the building at M & injure the wall in passing from thence to G. The making a communication ~~between~~ from the hinges of the door N to the conductor may perhaps be in some measure liable to this objection, but not so much, but that if you think it of service I am ready to recommend it

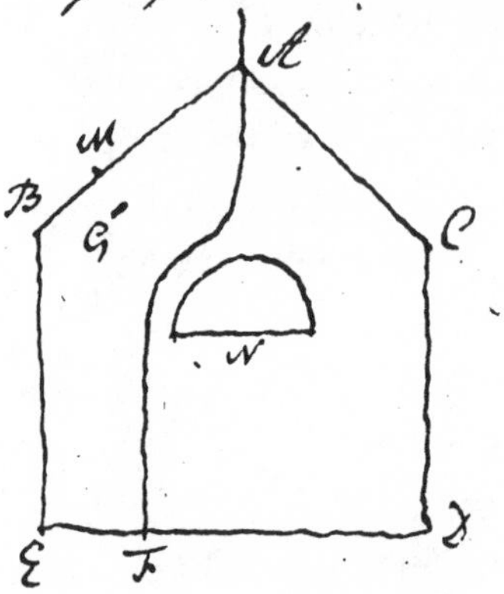

The most defective part of the defence is those side doors which have no conductors & no strap from the ridge of the roof. If you think it advisable to take notice of this I am ready to join in it. I will be at the R.S tomorrow at ½ past 2, which I suppose will be time enough to settle any thing which can be wanted

Your servant

H. Cavendish

118. *Extract on Lightning Conductors. Cavendish's sketch shows the Purfleet powder magazine, to be made safe from lightning. Henry Cavendish's letter to Charles Blagden, 22 June 1796, Blagden Letters, Royal Society, C.25. Reproduced by permission of the President and Council of the Royal Society.*

90. TO CHARLES JENKINSON, LORD LIVERPOOL[1]

6 APRIL [1798]

From the original letter in the British Library, Manuscript Department[2]

Clapham Apr. 6

Mr Cavendish presents his compliments to Lord Liverpool and will wait on his Lordship next Friday as appointed.[3]

---

[1] Charles Jenkinson, first earl of Liverpool (1727–1808), having held a variety of government positions including the relevant ones of lord of the treasury and master of the mint, was now in semi-retirement, serving as president of the privy council committee for coins. "Jenkinson," *DNB* 10:746–47.

[2] BL Add Mss 38232, f. 15.

[3] On 10 February 1798, a reconstituted committee of the privy council, headed by Liverpool and consisting of the officers of state, the chiefs of a number of courts, and Sir Joseph Banks, president of the Royal Society, was appointed to consider the "state of the coins of this kingdom" and the "establishment and constitution" of the Mint. Cavendish and Charles Hatchett were requested to perform experiments to decide if the considerable loss of gold in coins owing to wear was caused by any defect in the quality of the gold or in the figure or impression of the coins. The question demanded two investigations: 1) Whether soft or hard gold suffers the most by the friction that coins encounter in circulation; 2) Whether or not a smooth, flat, and broad coin wears less than one with protruberant parts. The experiments, which were carried out from late 1798 to April 1801, led to the conclusion, contrary to expectation, that the loss of gold to wear is trifling. Craig, *Mint*, 257. Chaston, "Wear Resistance of Gold Alloys for Coinage," 108. Charles Hatchett, "Experiments and Observations on the Various Alloys, on the Specific Gravity, and on the Comparative Wear of Gold. Being the Substance of a Report Made to the Right Honourable the Lords of the Committee of Privy Council, Apppointed to Take into Consideration the State of the Coins of This Kingdom, and the Present Establishment of His Majesty's Mint," *PT* 93 (1803): 43–194, on 44–45.

91. TO CHARLES JENKINSON, LORD LIVERPOOL

13 JULY [1798]

From the original letter in the British Library, Manuscript Department[1]

Clapham July 13

My Lord

I thank your Lordship for the sight of your draught of the report; & have the pleasure to agree in opinion with it very much; but there are 2 passages relating to the alloy (the first at the beginning of the 2nd sheet, in which it is said that the present alloy is supposed to render the gold hard & brittle, & the other at the end of the last sheet, in which it is recommended that the alloy which shall be put into gold hereafter coind shall be of silver) of the propriety of which I am in doubt, & which I am the more inclined to take notice of; as it would seem from the report that I had a share in recommending it

When the gold sent to the mint is of more than the proper fineness, so much Swedish copper is added as is sufficient to reduce it to standard; but as in all probability, the gold sent there is seldom much above standard, it will seldom happen that much copper will be added; & as copper does not much injure the ductility of gold, I do not think the coin can be made sensibly brittle by this addition, or that it would be sensibly less brittle, if silver were added instead of copper; & when the coin is brittle, I apprehend it to be owing to the substances which the gold is already mixed with when sent to the mint. If indeed the whole alloy was made to consist of silver, it is likely that the coin might be considerably improved; but as this could not be done without it being at the trouble of freeing the gold from the base metal in it, the expence of coinage would be much increased, & most likely in a much greater proportion than the durability of the coin

Though it seems likely that brittle gold wears faster than ductile, I do not know that it has ever been proved by experiment; & till more is known of the comparative wear of gold mixed with different kinds of alloy, it seems to me to be hardly advisable to make any alteration in this respect. But if your Lordship should think fit to order experiments to be made on the subject, it would enable us to form a better judgement, & perhaps might lead to some usefull improvement in the coin

I am
Your Lordships most
obedient servant
H. Cavendish

[1] BL Add Mss 38423, ff. 164–65.

92. FROM CHARLES JENKINSON, LORD LIVERPOOL

14 JULY 1798

From a copy of the letter in the British Library, Manuscript Department[1]

Addiscombe Place
14th July 1798

Sir

I have this Instant received the Favour of your Letter of the 13th.[2]–It affords me great Satisfaction to find, that you agree in Opinion with the Draft of the Report which I had prepared;–It is merely a Draft, and subject to any Alterations that may be suggested by You and my Brethern of the Committee;–I wrote it with a View of explaining to the Committee my general Ideas, and the Principles on which I proceeded, and particularly of learning thereby, from the Chancellor of the Exchequer, (who must ultimately execute this Business, and explain it to Parliament) whether He concurred in Opinion with me upon it; for it appeared to me to be useless to proceed in the Detail of the Business, till I was sure of his Concurrence:–He has since told me that He has considered the Subject; and begged that the Committee would proceed, from a Conviction that We were generally in the right.–I am far however from presuming to think that many Alterations must not still be made in this Draft of the Report.–With respect to the particular Passage at the End of the Draft, to which you appear to have some Objections, I only inserted it to shew the manner in which it would be proper to state the scientific Parts of the Report; for it occurred to me, that in this Part, the Opinion of the Committee, merely as Privy Councillors, could carry no Authority; and that the Judgment of the Publick would, in these Respects be directed by the Judgment of the scientific Persons who had favoured the Committee with their Assistance; and Sir Joseph Banks agreed with me in this Opinion.–I never entertained the smallest Idea of availing myself of your Name without having first obtained your Permission, and inserted it only in the Draft I gave you to exemplify the manner in which I meant to proceed.–It is right however that I should observe that when Mr Alchorne[3] was before the Committee, he gave it as his Opinion, that the Gold in the British Coin was made hard and brittle by being allayed solely with Copper, and recommended that half the Alloy should in future be Silver; but I never intended to rest solely on this Opinion, and I perfectly agree with you that some Experiments should be made; and as I am not a good Judge of this Part of the Subject, I shall trouble yourself and Sir Joseph Banks to suggest to me what those Experiments should be.–I shall be at the Committee on Thursday next at half past Eleven, when the Officers of the Mint and some of the Royal Academy are to attend, to consider on the future Fashion of the Coin, as far as related to Beauty and to the prevention of its Wearing to the Degree it has hitherto done, by which the Publick has been put to an enormous Expence;–and I will then consult Sir Joseph Banks on the Subject:–If it should be convenient and agreeable to you to call at the Office at that Time, We might discourse on this Subject together.–I shall in the mean time order Copies of three curious Reports, principally on the mechanical parts of Coining, made by Mr Rennie,[4] Mr Boulton,[5] and Mr Hatchett,[6] to be sent to you for your Consideration.

I am &c.
Liverpool

[address]:
Henry Cavendish Esqre

---

[1] BL Add Mss 38310, ff. 227b–228.

[2] Letter 91.

[3] Stanesby Alchorne, king's assay master, had a house at the Mint in the Tower of London, where he carried out experiments on the ductility of gold alloyed with tin, "Experiments on Mixing Gold With Tin," *PT* 74 (1784): 463–68. William Roy, "An Account of the Mode Proposed to Be Followed in Determining the Relative Situation of the Royal Observatories of Greenwich and Paris," *PT* 77 (1787): 188–228, on 204. Craig, *Mint*, 231.

[4] John Rennie (1761–1821), engineer and surveyor, known for his work on docks and canals, F.R.S. 1798. The Privy Council Committee on Coins inspected the Mint in April and May 1798, and it engaged Rennie to report on its machinery. Rennie's report was trenchant, advocating that the mint convert to steam. Taylor, *Mathematical Practitioners*, 322. Craig, *The Mint*, 268.

[5] Matthew Boulton (1728–1809), manufacturer and engineer, partner with James Watt in the manufacture of steam engines, F.R.S. 1785. In 1797 he established new copper coinage for Britain, setting up a rival mint in Soho, Birmingham. Lord Liverpool solicited reports from Boulton and Charles Hatchett. On Boulton's, Liverpool had this to say: "Mr Boulton's report contains no information whatever. His Sentiments of delicacy with respect to the officers of the mint are ridiculous: if he is to give us no better information than he has done, why was he sent for to Town?" Liverpool to Sir Joseph Banks, 10 May 1798, copy, BM (NH), DTC 10:279–80. *Webster's Biographical Dictionary* (Springfield, Mass.: G. & C. Merriam, 1970), 178.

[6] Charles Hatchett (1765–1847), chemist, F.R.S. 1797. Unlike Boulton's report, Hatchett's was well received by Liverpool, who called it "very able." Liverpool intended to give both reports, suitably corrected, to Rennie. Then all three reports would be considered by Banks and Cavendish, whose observations would be directed to the officers of the Mint. After this elaborate review, the Committee on Coins "assisted by Mr Cavendish" would then determine what parts should be adopted. Liverpool to Banks, 10 May 1798. Scott, "Hatchett," *DSB* 6:166–67.

93. TO CHARLES JENKINSON, LORD LIVERPOOL

[15 JULY 1798]

From the original letter in the British Library, Manuscript Department[1]

My Lord

I thank your Lordship for the favour of your letter;[2] & if I had known that Mr Alchorne who is so much better a judge than I am had recommended that in future the alloy should be silver, I believe I should hardly have troubled you with my letter. If he gave his opinion in writing & explaind his reasons for it I shall be obliged to your Lordship if you would let me have a copy of them. I will be sure to wait on your Lordship & the committee on Thursday

I am with much respect

Your Lordships most obedient Servant

H. Cavendish

[1] BL Add Mss 38423, f. 168.

[2] Letter 92.

94. TO SIR JOSEPH BANKS

23 JULY 1798

From a copy of the letter in the Natural History Museum, Botany Library[1]

Mr Cavendish to Sir Joseph Banks.

July 23. 1798

Dear Sir

I inclose a sketch of what seems to me the best manner of trying the experiments on the wear of coin. If Mr Hatchett would undertake the business, I shall be glad to give him any assistance I can; but I think the direction of it had best be left to his discretion. If he should not, I shall have no objection to the other way you mentioned of their being made by Cuthbertson[2] under my direction; but, if Mr H. would undertake it, it would be much more agreable to me.

It will be necessary for Lord Liverpool & you to consider about providing the pieces of gold.

I also inclose some queries, which, if Ld L. & you approve of, I could wish might be put to Mr Alchorne when he attends the committee. The 3 first you will perceive relate to 2 passages in L^d. L's report. The latter part relates to what I mentioned to him last Thursday.

Yours sincerely

H. Cavendish.

I have received an invitation to dine with him next Tuesday, but am prevented by engagement. I had already written this with intention to send it you when I received your letter.[3] I still think that it would not be doing justice to Mr Hatchett to put it on the footing mentioned in your letter, & think it would be better that the direction should be left to him. But, if he should wish to talk with me about the manner of trying them, I shall be ready to attend him any day he pleases after next Wednesday.

---

[1] DTC 11:19–20.

[2] John Cuthbertson, London instrument-maker, made the apparatus for testing the wear of coins, and the experiments were made at his house. Taylor, *Mathematical Practitioners*, 203. Chaston, "Wear Resistance of Gold Alloys for Coinage," 111.

[3] This letter we do not have.

95. TO SIR JOSEPH BANKS

6 AUGUST 1798

From a copy of the letter in the Natural History Museum, Botany Library[1]

Mr Cavendish to Sir Joseph Banks.

Clapham Aug 6, 1798.

Dear Sir

As you propose writing to Lord Liverpool,[2] I suppose you have deferred the visit to the Mint on Thursday, & our meeting at your house at one. If you have not, I shall be ready to attend you if you can give me notice by that morning's post or sooner.

I am very glad you intend to try to prevail on Lord L. to alter his arrangement; for, even though there should be a proper person at the mint, it is much better that the experiments should be made by one whose accuracy we can rely on than by one whom we know nothing of. As to the instrument, I see no reason why it may not be made as well by the workman for the mint as by any one else; so that, if L^d^ L likes better that it should be made by the Mint, it seems not worth objecting to.

Yours sincerely
H. Cavendish

---

[1] DTC 11:28.

[2] On this same day, Banks and Liverpool exchanged letters. In reply to Banks's letter, Liverpool wrote that he "agrees with Sir J. Banks, that the Experiments should be made in the way most approved by Mr Cavendish, and most agreeable to him." Charles Jenkinson, Lord Liverpool, to Sir Joseph Banks, 6 Aug. 1798, BM(NH), DTC 11:29.

96. FROM CHARLES HUTTON[1]

17 NOVEMBER 1798

From the original letter in the Devonshire Collections, Chatsworth[2]

Woolwich, Nov. 17, 1798.

Sir,

I have to return you thanks for a copy of your ingenious paper, on the Density of the Earth,[3] this day received from the Royal Society, which I suppose was ordered by yourself to be sent me.–Dr Maskelyne had before favoured me with a sight of the paper; in which I perceive you bring out the density in question to be 5.48 times that of water. And, in the paragraph at the bottom of pa. 54, you remark on the difference between this conclusion, and that of the Society's Experiment at Mount Schehallien,[4] in the calculation of which I bore so great a share.[5] I wish that paragraph had been a little differently worded; because, as it stands, some persons may think you meant those words as some disparagement of that experiment, or a hint concerning some inaccuracy in the calculations or observations. If there be any such inaccuracies, it will be easy to detect them, as the particulars are detailed in so particular a manner, in the printed papers giving a[n] Acco^{t} of the observations & calculations, that any person may go over the whole numbers again.

But it will be proper to remark, that the Schehallien experiment, as calculated in my paper, has not determined what is to be considered as the density of the earth, but only what is the ratio of that density to the density of the hill Schehallien, which it stated to be the ratio of 9 to 5. For the paper expressly states that we are ignorant as to the density of the hill, & consequently the real density of the earth also. All that was professed to be known, concerning the hill, was, that it is a mass of stone; but nothing as to the nature or density of that stone. I wish the Society had completed their experiment, by procuring a determination of the real density of the stone. And I wish they would now do it, that an accurate conclusion, as to the density of the earth, may be thence obtained. For want of the real density of the hill, we barely made a *supposition*, that it is of the density of common stone, or 2½, and on that supposition it followed, that the density of the earth would be 4½. But there is great reason to expect that the density of the stone of the hill Schehallien, is much more than 2½, probably more than 3, since the heavier stones, as granite, run as high as 3½; and I expect that the density of the earth, when it comes to be determined from the real density of the hill, will turn out to be between 5 and 6, but probably nearer the latter number.

I am, Sir,

Your most obed^{t} hble Servant

Cha. Hutton.

[address]:
Henry Cavendish Esq
at the Royal Society
Somerset Place[6]

---

[1] Charles Hutton (1737–1823), professor of mathematics at the Royal Academy, Woolwich, F.R.S. 1774. Baron, "Hutton," *DSB* 6:576–77.

[2] Cavendish Mss New Correspondence.

[3] Henry Cavendish, "Experiments to Determine the Density of the Earth," *PT* 88 (1798): 469–526.

[4] The preferred spelling of the mountain today is Schiehallion. Howse, *Maskelyne*, 37. In the eighteenth century, Cavendish, Hutton, and others spelled it variously.

[5] Hutton was referring to the experiment of the Royal Society on the gravitational attraction of a mountain, the object of which was to deduce the mean density of the earth; see letters 3 and 5. Cavendish, who was appointed to a committee of the Royal Society to measure this attraction, did much of the planning of the experiment. At its conclusion, Hutton was requested by Nevil Maskelyne to do the calculations leading to the density of the earth. Maskelyne, "An Account of Observations Made on the Mountain Schehallien for Finding Its Attraction," *PT* 65 (1775): 500–42. Hutton, "An Account of the Calculations Made from the Survey and Measures Taken at Schehallien, in Order to Ascertain the Mean Density of the Earth," *PT* 68 (1778): 689–788.

[6] Beneath the address, in another hand, it is written, "Through the hands of Dr Maskelyne."

97. TO CHARLES HUTTON

[AFTER 17 NOVEMBER 1798]

From the original draft memorandum in the Devonshire Collections, Chatsworth[1]

According to the experiments made by Dr Maskelyne on the attraction of the hill Shehallien the density of the earth is 4½ times that of water which differs rather more from the preceding determination than I should have expected but I forbear entering into any consideration of which determination is most to be depended on till I have examined more carefully how much the preceding determination is affected by irregularities whose quantity I cannot measure.

[1] Cavendish Mss New Correspondence. This draft response to Hutton's letter, letter 96, is identical to the last paragraph of Cavendish's paper on the density of the earth.

98. TO SIR CHARLES BLAGDEN

18 DECEMBER [1798]

From the original letter in the Royal Society[1]

Clapham Dec. 18

Dear Sir

I thank you for your letter on Humboldts paper,[2] though I am sorry you should have taken so much trouble about it. As his reasoning was not much detaild in your extract, I misunderstood it, but what you said on Sunday night was sufficient to point out to me my error.

I think however that the experiment is far from shewing that nitrous air destroys more pure air by being mixed with azote; & think, that if in his 2nd experiment, he had added 48 of pure nitrous air only, instead of a mixture of that with 52 of azote, the result might very likely have been nearly the same; for it appears from the experiments related in my paper on Eudiometers,[3] that when nitrous & common air are mixed, the acid produced contains much nitrous air, & contains much more in some methods of mixing than others, & that in consequence of it the same quantity of nitrous air goes much further in some methods than others; & in particular it seems likely that when a small quantity of nitrous air is added to much common air, the pure air destroyd bears a greater proportion to the nitrous air destroyd, than when the proportion of nitrous air is greater.

The trying the quantity of nitrous air remaining after the experiment, has the appearance of being a great improvement. The objection to it is that we are liable to the error of 2 operations instead of one, & perhaps the absorption of nitrous air by green vitriol may be liable to irregularities which we are not acquainted with. But however that may be, the great difference which he finds in the purity of common air convinces me that there must be some fault in his method; for though I tried the air of 60 different days, I could not find any difference; & though a faulty method of trying will make the purity of the air appear different at different times when in reality it is not, I do not see how it can make it appear always the same when in reality it is different.

Yours sincerely
H. Cavendish

[address]:
8/
Sir Charles Blagden
Upper Berkeley street

---

[1] Blagden Letters, C.24.

[2] Probably Alexander von Humboldt, "Abhandlung über die dreyfache Verbindung aus Phosphor, Stickstoff und Sauerstoff," *Allgemeines Journal der Chemie* 1 (1798): 573–89.

[3] Henry Cavendish, "An Account of a New Eudiometer," *PT* 73 (1783): 106–35.

99. FROM CHARLES JENKINSON, LORD LIVERPOOL

12 APRIL 1799

From a copy of the letter in the British Library, Manuscript Department[1]

Hertford Street 12th April 1799.

Dear Sir

I am much obliged to You for your Letter,[2] which I received last Night at my Return from the House of Lords.–I perfectly agree with You, that Mr Robertson's[3] Manner of taking the Deficiency of the Silver Coin is conformable to what was intended by me, and by the Committee; And I also agree with You, that it may also be proper to add some Words to the Report, which may make Our Intention clearer.–I am obliged to You for the Trouble You have been so good as to take on this Occasion.

I am with sincere, Regard &c.

Liverpool.

[address]:
H. Cavendish Esqre

---

[1] BL Add Mss 38311, f. 8.

[2] We do not have this letter.

[3] Abraham Robertson (1751–1826), astronomer and mathematician, Savilian professor of geometry (later of astronomy) at Oxford University, F.R.S. 1795. He did research, in part historical, on coinage for Liverpool. There are many letters from Robertson to Liverpool in vol. 235 of Liverpool Papers, BL Add Mss 38424. "Robertson," *DNB* 16:1284–85.

100. TO CHARLES HATCHETT

[AFTER 4 JULY 1799]

From the original draft letter in the Devonshire Collections, Chatsworth[1]

D. S.

I return you many thanks for you[r] exper[iments] on the substance I gave you. The paper which I gave you along with it containd only a general account of the manner in which that substance was procured but I here send a fuller account of it & of some other exper. I have made. They do not indeed shew any thing as to the nature of the substances which the platina is mixed with.

N1

Platina dissolved in aq[ua] reg[ia] & most of the superfluous acid driven off from the solution by distillation. Sal ammoniac was then added till ceased to make any precipitation. As the solution after separating this precipitate was still very red I supposed that it containd much platina & therefore tried whether I could separate it by ☿.

N.1 & 2

The ☿ quickly put on the appearance of an amalgam & by degrees was divided into a black powder. This was then separated & more ☿ added at different times till the whole quantity was many times greater than the metallic substance in the solution but yet the ☿ last added was as soon affected by the solution as the first & the colour of the solution was very little diminished.

N. 6

On letting this amalgam remain a few days in an open glass a great deal of running ☿ was found which to all appearance was perfectly pure. This was pourd off & the rest which I believe was 2 or 3000 was heated red hot in crucible. It left only 19 of reddish matter whose nature was not well examined.

During the heating some matter sublimed & stuck to the cover of the crucible but from a following experiment there is reason to suppose that was only ☿ united to the marine acid.

N 3

As the colouring matter of the solution was not separated by ☿ I tried what effect copper would have. It acquired a black coat on the surface but too thin to examine & as it seemed not disposed to separate the colouring matter it was taken out before much of it was dissolved.

Fixed alcali was then added by little at a time in hopes of separating the different component parts but without success as the colour of the part first precipitated was not different from the rest. It was dark colourd & acquired no ochry appearance.

The solution after the precipitate was made was blue & contain'd copper which perhaps might proceed only from the plate of copper put into the solution.

N 8

I then tried whether I could separate the different substances by a gradual addition of acid to this precipitate but without success. On adding a little spirit of salt [it][2] immediatly lost its acidity & produced heat but without any appearance of solution. On the addition of water a muddy fluid was produced which would not subside on standing but on the addition of more acid it grew clear & took a dark brown colour with a tinge of greenish yellow & by that means the rest of the precipitate was dissolved & made a solution of the same kind.

After some trials with some of this solution not worth mentioning fixed alcali was added to it & the precipitate heated in an earthen retort as mentiond in the paper I gave you.

In that paper I said that over the melted & vitrified part there lay a black powder which I shall call (A) & that this powder was not much affected by spirit of salt but dissolved with much effervescence in aqua regia & formed a brown solution. I did not examine whether the melted & vitrified parts were of the same nature as the powder A but from some circumstances not worth mentioning it seemed as if the solution of crude platina after the pure part is precipitated by sal ammon consists of a mixture of the substance A with another substance which I shall call B & which dissolves difficultly in acids but which when dissolved gives a deep red colour to a vast quantity of liquor & that on carefully evaporating the solution this matter was disposed to separate & fall to the bottom.

The better to examine how far this method of separation might be practicable I evaporated the solution of A at different times till it became thick & yielded strong acid fumes but yet on adding water to it in this state it intirely dissolved without forming any deposit so that unless the evaporation is carried to a great excess there seems little danger of much of this matter separating from the solution.

---

[1] This draft letter was inserted loosely in a bound volume of chemical experiments. Also inserted loosely was "Platina *1799*," minutes of experiments on platina, which contain the experiments reported in the letter. From a remark in Cavendish's account of the experiments, "black matter was given to Mr Hatchett his exper. with it are mentioned in his letter of July 4," we think this letter was probably a reply to Hatchett's letter, which we do not have. "White Book," Cavendish Mss.

[2] Cavendish wrote "to" instead of "it."

101. FROM NEVIL MASKELYNE

4 OCTOBER 1799

From the original letter in the Devonshire Collections, Chatsworth[1]

Dr Maskelyne's compliments to Mr Cavendish, in hopes he may be disposed to investigate the orbit of the Comet, which is still visible thro' the telescope & likely to continue so for some time, has sent him the following observations of it. Shall be obliged to him for the elements he may deduce. Saw it on 28th last month with short sighted spectacles on.–

Greenwich

Oct. 4. 1799

[. . .][2]

[1] Cavendish Mss VIII, 46. This letter and the next two letters by Maskelyne are enclosed in the manuscript, "Comet of 1799."

[2] There follow observations of the comet between 8 September and 4 October.

102. FROM NEVIL MASKELYNE

8 OCTOBER 1799

From the original letter in the Devonshire Collections, Chatsworth[1]

Dr Maskelyne's compliments to Mr Cavendish; has added the sun's longitudes to the paper which he has returned. The Long. & Lat. set down for the 28th Sept. are wrong, as he observes from the irregularity of the differences. Therefore the star was different from 49 Serpentis, & must be another star very near its parallel, & having its AR about a minute of time more, as he infers from the divisions of the instrument, which he shall examine into [at] first opportunity. Has since observed the Comet on the 4th not yet reduced. Observed it also on the 9th 15th 23^{d} Sept. & Oct.1. There are many stars omitted in the British Catalogue of equal brightness of those inserted viz 6 or 7th Magnitude. Thinks he remembers another star about that time.

Greenwich

Oct. 8. 1799–

[address]:

Henry Cavendish Esq.

Clapham

---

[1] Cavendish Mss VIII, 46.

103. FROM NEVIL MASKELYNE

9 OCTOBER 1799

From the original letter in the Devonshire Collections, Chatsworth[1]

Greenwich Oct. 9. 1799

Dear Sir,

Sir Henry Englefield[2], to whom I made the same communication of my observations as to yourself on the 4th instant, has in a letter of yesterday's date sent me the result of his work upon them, by his first trial. He says, as it was evident the comet was near its periheliem at first, he used the observations of Sept. 8, 14 & 19 near one another. From the elements partly by construction & partly by calculation he finds the error of the deduction from the elements on Sept. 29 to be −36′ in long. & +16′ in lat. & on Oct. 2 to be −22′¼ in long, and +32′ in latitude. He has sent its places deduced by construction to the 28th of this month, when its distance from us will be not much less than double the sun's, as we recede from each other nearly in a right line. Im astonished that nobody saw it sooner, as on the 22d August, it was in Long. 3s.24°.10′ & North Lat. 32°.25′ so that it might have been seen a fourtnight sooner with ease, & probably a month. Here follow the elements of its orbit.–[. . .]

They[3] have a distant resemblance to those of the Comet of 1299 except that the inclination & perihel. distance seem too remote–Also to that of 1784–that of 1787–Great perturbations, like that to which the Comet of 1779 was exposed from Jupiter might produce the variations. But these are vague remarks. I send these to save you unnecessary trouble; & that you may direct it with more advantage by commencing from the rough elements here given. Yesterday I sent you the sun's Longitudes you desired. The star observed on the 28th. had certainly a different place from 49th Serpentis in the Catalogue. I remain

Dear Sir,

Your obedient Servant
N. Maskelyne–

---

[1] Cavendish Mss VIII, 46.

[2] Sir Henry Englefield (1752–1822), F.R.S. 1778, antiquarian and writer on scientific subjects, especially astronomical. He was the author of *On the Determination of the Orbits of Comets* (London, 1793). "Englefield," *DNB* 6:792–93. From Englefield and two other astronomers, Maskelyne initially learned of the discovery of the comet of 1799. Maskelyne to William Herschel, 9 Sep. 1799, Royal Astronomical Society, Mss Herschel, W 1/13, M.62.

[3] The elements.

104. TO NEVIL MASKELYNE

[OCTOBER 1799]

From the original draft letter in the Devonshire Collections, Chatsworth[1]

[. . .][2]

Since my letter of last Thursday I have made a comput. to determine how nearly the geocentric distances I sent you would agree with the 3 observations used in finding them. [. . .] By comparing the 2 suppositions I used in the graphical method it appears that a small error in the log. of the distances makes 1,76 that error in the time & therefore the logs of the distances should each be dimin. by ,00188 or should be reduced to 9,68884 & 9,72054. If that was done I believe the orbit would be found to agree very nearly with observation but I have tired myself too much with the former comp. to do any more.

[. . .]

1 Cavendish Mss VIII, 46. This letter, like the three letters from Maskelyne in Oct. 1799, is enclosed in the manuscript, "Comet of 1799."

2 At the head of the letter is an arithmetic calculation giving ,00188, the number in the extract of the letter reproduced here.

105. FROM BENJAMIN VAUGHAN

21 DECEMBER 1799

From a copy of the letter in the Devonshire Collections, Chatsworth[1]

Honble Henry Cavendish

Hallowell, Decr 21, 1799.

Dear Sir/

(Copy.)

If the subject of the present letter should surprize you, it ought to be because I am the writer[2] & not because your pursuits, character, & station in life, do not indicate you as the person to whom it should be addressed.

[. . .][3]

It is in the neighborhood of this village,[4] that an observatory, a professorship of natural history, & perhaps an university may be established; & I am bold enough to say (this being the object of my letter) principally by your judgment & examples, and partly by your funds. Of the faculty of the operation, you may decide from what follows.

[. . .][5]

Observatories and cabinets of natural history not being common here, we[6] cannot look for many astronomers or naturalists, till the opportunities for forming a number have been first created; when emulation in the respective states will provide for every thing else. Talents here are as good as any where; but instructors, books, variety of company, literary rivalship, instruments, & collections of natural specimens, are less frequent than in Europe. Hence most Americans who have figured in natural knowledge, (as Dr Franklin & Count Rumford,[7] Mr Jefferson[8] & Dr Rush,[9]) have visited Europe. The present is proposed to be a mission from Europe to America; by which a nation may be taught, instead of individuals. But in any event, European advantages must be transformed here either by Americans passing to Europe, or by Europeans passing to America; & none would have been more anxious for the combination of human talents from every quarter, than Dr Rittenhouse;[10] who will be cited in vain as the produce of an American education solely; since he profited by company, books, & instruments from Europe.

[. . .][11]

One advantage may arise to you from a measure in this country in favor of science. You may be allowed to invest a sum in real property here equal to your benefactions; & congress may readily superadd the title of citizen to one, who shall have proved himself so deserving a member of the universal community of men. The convenience of this incidental consequence in favor of your person & a part of your property, in case of need; cannot be undesirable to one whose motto is *Cavendo tutus.*[12] In Europe, no umbrage can be conceived on the subject; because it will not have been the first object of your measures. Princes have directed expeditions of science to Lapland, the Andes, the South Seas, the North Pole, the Levant, & other places; without meaning unfavorably to the kingdoms they governed at home; & Mr Cavendish will not be thought the less of an Englishman for having philosophic views. The efforts of Mr Boyle,[13] Sir Isaac Newton,[14] B^{p} Berkeley,[15] Mr Peter Collinson,[16] Mr Thomas Hollis,[17] & others, in favor of learning on this continent separately considered, are on record here; & where known, have added to their estimation at home & in Europe.

[. . .][18]

I am with high respect,
Dear Sir, your sincere humble servant.
Benjn Vaughan

[address]:
To
The Honble Henry Cavendish, F.R.S.,
Bedford Square,
London.

---

1 Cavendish Mss New Correspondence. This long and detailed letter was not received by Cavendish until four years after it was written, forwarded to him by Benjamin Vaughan's brother William. See letters 110 and 111. Because of its length, we give only an extract of the letter. A draft of this letter, dated one day earlier, 20 December 1799, is in the Benjamin Vaughan Papers, American Philosophical Society.

2 Benjamin Vaughan, who in England had sought Cavendish's advice on Bristol Harbor, was now in America writing to Cavendish to help realize his "most extraordinary dream," which was to establish a university together with an astronomical observatory at Hallowell, Maine. Massachusetts had put up five townships in Maine to endow Bowdoin College, and Brunswick had been chosen as the site, but Vaughan was assured by James Bowdoin, Jr., and other promoters of the college that if Cavendish contributed, it could be located at Hallowell. Hallowell, however, was not essential, Vaughan said, for "a Cavendish observatory and Cavendish professors" could be established at another site. Murray, *Benjamin Vaughan*, 514–15.

3 There is a description of the setting of Hallowell.

4 Hallowell.

5 The foundation of Bowdoin College is described.

6 Americans.

7 Benjamin Thompson, Count Rumford (1753–1814), experimenter and inventor, F.R.S. 1779. Brown, "Thompson," *DSB* 13:350–52.

8 Thomas Jefferson (1743–1826).

9 Benjamin Rush (1746–1813), Philadelphia physician and chemist. Carlson, "Rush," *DSB* 11:616–18.

10 David Rittenhouse (1732–96), Philadelphia astronomer and instrument-maker, F.R.S. 1795. Hindle, "Rittenhouse," *DSB* 11:471–73.

11 Arguments are given for the superiority of Hallowell over Brunswick as the site of "Boudoin" College. Today Brunswick, Maine, is of course the location of Bowdoin College, founded in 1794.

12 *Cavendo tutus* is the motto on the coat of arms of the Devonshire Cavendish family, a play on words, meaning "Safe by being cautious." Pearson, *The Serpent and the Stag*, 54.

13 Robert Boyle (1627–91), founding member of the Royal Society, 1663.

[14] Sir Isaac Newton (1642–1727), F.R.S. 1671.

[15] George Berkeley (1685–1753), philosopher, bishop of Cloyne.

[16] Peter Collinson (1693–1768), natural historian, businessman, F.R.S. 1728. Frick, "Collinson," *DSB* 3:349–51.

[17] Thomas Hollis (1720–74), political author, F.R.S. 1757. "Hollis," *DNB* 9:1070–71.

[18] Financial matters are brought up, and confidentiality is requested.

106. TO THE PRIVY COUNCIL COMMITTEE FOR COINS

[1801]

From the original letter in the British Library, Manuscript Department[1]

My Lords

According to your Lordships intentions Mr Hatchett undertook the execution of the experiments,[2] which you directed to be made concerning the comparative wear of differently alloyed gold coins, & has performed them with great judgement & accuracy, & in the manner which to both of us seemed best adapted to the object proposed: He has also added many valuable experiments, concerning the effects of different alloys in diminishing the ductility of gold, & concerning the mixing them & casting the mixtures. As from his having undertaken the conduct of the experiments, he was best enabled to give an account of them; & as from the nature of the subject, the relation became in some measure mixed with the account of experiments peculiarly his own, I thought I could not do better than to request him to draw up the account & present it to your Lordships, which he has obligingly consented to. I have only to add that I have carefully read the account, & that I intirely agree with him in the conclusions which he draws from the experiments.

I am with the greatest respect
your Lordships most
obedient servant
H. Cavendish

---

[1] BL Add Mss 38426, f. 1.

[2] See letter 90, note 3.

107. FROM THOMAS YOUNG[1]

3 SEPTEMBER 1801

From the original letter in the Devonshire Collections, Chatsworth[2]

Dr. Young takes the liberty of sending for Mr. Cavendish's inspection a copy of what he means, with Mr. Cavendish's permission, to insert in his syllabus[3] respecting the teeth of wheels. He believes that the point of contact G will seldom, if ever, fall between E and F.

Wilbeck Street Thursday 3 Sept. 1801.

[address]:

Henry Cavendish Esq.

---

[1] Thomas Young (1773–1829), physician and author of scientific works, F.R.S. 1794. Morse, "Young," *DSB* 14:562–72, on 562.

[2] Cavendish Mss VI(b), 31. The letter, which is enclosed in a paper by Cavendish, labeled by him, "On the Shape of the Teeth in Rack Work," is accompanied by a discussion of the problem by Young and the acknowledgment: "For the substance of this demonstration I am indebted to Mr. Cavendish."

[3] Thomas Young, *A Syllabus of a Course of Lectures on Natural and Experimental Philosophy* (London, 1802). Young was professor of natural philosophy at the Royal Institution, London. Cavendish was a member of the standing committee that oversaw the syllabus of the Institution. Entry for 31 Mar. 1800, Minutes of the Meetings of Managers, Royal Institution Archive, pp. 39–41.

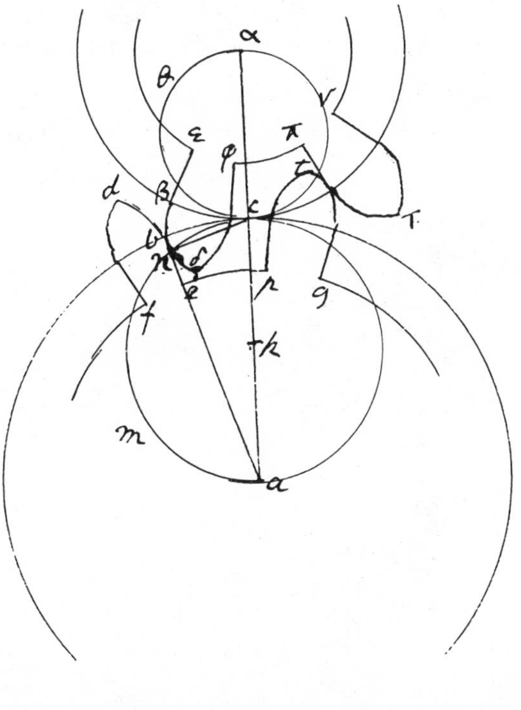

119. *Extract on Rackwork. This drawing is part of Cavendish's response to a question about rackwork from Thomas Young. Cavendish Scientific Manuscripts VI(b), 31. Reproduced by permission of the Chatsworth Settlement Trustees.*

108. TO CHARLES HATCHETT

15 OCTOBER 1802

From a copy of the letter in the Natural History Museum, Botany Library[1]

Copy of Mr Cavendish's Letter to C.H.–

Clapham October 15th 1802.

Dear Sir,

As you inform me that Lord Liverpool wishes to know whether I think any bad effect can result from the publication of your experiments relating to Coin,[2] you may assure his Lordship that I think there are many curious circumstances in them and such as well deserve publication, but that there is nothing in them which I think requires to be kept secret or which can cause any inconvenience to the publick if published.[3]

Yours sincerely
H. Cavendish

---

[1] DTC 13:283.

[2] Hatchett's report, "To the Right Honorable the Earl of Liverpool and the Right Honorable the Lords of the Select Committee for Coins," was signed by him on 28 April 1801. BL Add Mss 38426, ff. 2–276. Beginning on f. 25: "Experiments and Observations on the Various Alloys, on the Specific Gravity, and on the Comparative Wear of Gold."

[3] Hatchett wrote to Sir Joseph Banks, "Lord Liverpool is quite satisfied with Mr Cavendish's opinion (as enclosed) concerning the propriety of the communication; and, as the Members of the Coin Committee are at present so much dispersed that a Sufficient number cannot be collected, his Lordship has acquainted me that the permission shall be immediately granted, provided your opinion should accord with that of Mr Cavendish. I have therefore taken the liberty to trouble you with this, to beg the favor of a few lines to the above effect, which may be communicated to his Lordship; and, in that Case, it is my intention to have the papers ready for the Royal Society as soon as possible." Hatchett to Banks, 24 Oct. 1802, copy, BM(NH), DTC 13:281–82. With Banks's approval, Hatchett's paper was read to the Royal Society on 13 Jan. 1803.

109. TO CHARLES HATCHETT
7 MARCH 1803[1]

From the original letter in the Library of the University of Wales, Swansea[2]

Clapham Mar 7

Dear Sir

When I saw your paper this morning, I supposed that the 7th column had been the proportion which the expansion bore to the whole bulk, & therefore took it with me as I could not say without a little computation what number of cyphers there ought to be; but on examination I find that it is simply the difference of the bulk before & after combination. Consequently there is no absolute impropriety in the table as it now stands, though the method proposed in the morning is certainly a clearer & more natural way of expressing it.

For fear of mistake I have wrote down under the table the numbers of the first experiment in the manner I meant. To me the table seems clear enough without further explanation; but if you had a mind you might say that the 4th column was formed by dividing the weight of the metals employed by their specific gravity that the 6th was formed by dividing the sum of those weights by the specific gravity of the mixture & that that 7th column is the excess of the bulk after combination above that before.

Yours sincerely
H. Cavendish

[address]:
Charles Hatchett Esq
Lower Mall
Hammersmith

---

[1] The year 1803 is given by a stamp above the address and also by a label, in someone else's hand, which reads "H. Cavendish 1803 Mar 7." On the outside of the letter in yet another hand is another label, "Mr Cavendish."

[2] Library Archives, Hatchett A6.

110. FROM WILLIAM VAUGHAN[1]

27 OCTOBER 1803

From the original letter in the Devonshire Collections, Chatsworth[2]

Sir

In forwarding the inclosed letter from my Brother Benjamin I have to make many apologies for its not being delivered at the Time it was received. The Circumstances which occasioned that Delay I have not to trouble you having explained the same to my Brother. Late letters from him express a wish that I would present it and endeavour to see you and wait on you for an answer.[3] I have in my possession a new and an accurate Map of the Country if you should wish to see it. Since Dec 1799 there has been a great alteration and improvement of the Country and one of the most respectable characters in New England is presiding over the Institution. I have the honor to be

Sir

Your mo. ob. Ser^{t}

W. Vaughan

[Mineing] Lane

Oct 27 1803

---

1 William Vaughan (1752–1850), merchant and author, F.R.S. 1813. "Vaughan, William," *DNB* 20:187–88.

2 Cavendish Mss New Correspondence. This letter enclosed the letter by Benjamin Vaughan, William's brother, letter 105.

3 William Vaughan, who approached other friends of science to support his brother's plan, refused to deliver the letter to Cavendish until his (older) brother insisted. William forwarded Cavendish's refusal to Benjamin with the comment, "I never thought he would fall into the plan of improvement." Murray, *Benjamin Vaughan*, 515.

111. TO WILLIAM VAUGHAN

[AFTER 27 OCTOBER 1803]

From the original draft letter in the Devonshire Collections, Chatsworth[1]

S^r^

I have received your letter of Oct 27[2] with your brothers letter inclosed but there are many reasons to prevent my acceding to his proposal. As my mind is made up on the subject it is unnecessary to give yourself any further trouble on the subject.[3]

---

1 Cavendish Mss New Correspondence.

2 Letter 110.

3 Cavendish had a label for letters of which Benjamin Vaughan's may have been an instance, "begging letters." "Papers in Walnut Cabinet," Cavendish Mss Misc.

112. FROM JAMES HORSBURGH[1]

20 APRIL 1804

From the *Philosophical Transactions*[3]

Bombay, April 20, 1804.

Sir,

When I was in London at the conclusion of the year 1801, I had the pleasure of being introduced to you by my friend Mr. Dalrymple, at which time he presented you with some sheets of meteorological observations, with barometer and thermometer, made by me in India, and during a passage from India to England.

Being of opinion that few registers of the barometer are kept at sea, especially in low latitudes, I have been induced to continue my observations since I left England, judging that, even if they were found to be of no utility, they might at least be entertaining to you or other gentlemen, who have been making observations of a similar nature.[3]

[. . .]

P.S. Since I wrote the foregoing abstract, I have received a letter from my friend Mr. Dalrymple, intimating that a copy of the meteorological journal itself would be acceptable, which has induced me to transmit to him the original sheets, with a request to deliver them to you. I regret that I could not find leisure time to make out a fair copy, to have sent to you, in place of the original sheets in their rough state.

Bombay,
June 1st, 1804.

---

[1] James Horsburgh (1762–1836) was a hydrographer, ship commander, and F.R.S. 1806. "Horsburgh," *DNB* 9:1270.

[2] This letter to Cavendish was prefaced to James Horsburgh, "Abstract of Observations on a Diurnal Variation of the Barometer between the Tropics," *PT* 95 (1805): 177–85.

[3] There follow eight pages abstracted from his meteorological journal, covering twenty-two months, ending on 14 Feb. 1802.

113. FROM CHARLES JENKINSON, LORD LIVERPOOL

1805

From the original draft letter in the British Library, Manuscript Department[1]

1805

Sir

I recollect with great pleasure the short intercourse I had with you on the subject of the Coins of the Realm. I then shewed you some ideas which I had put upon paper, & of which you seemed to approve. In the course of the last winter I have finished what I intended to write on this subject, & have ordered it to be published.[2] I take the liberty of presenting you with a copy of it, & shall be happy if it affords any information & proves in the least satisfactory to a person of your knowledge & experience, particularly in subjects of an abstruse nature.

I am, with very high esteem & respect, Sir, your faithful humble Servant

Liverpool

[address]:
Draft of a letter
to Mr Cavendish–

---

1 BL Add Mss 38424, f. 278.

2 *A Treatise on the Coins of the Realm; in a Letter to the King* (Oxford, 1805). Liverpool acknowledged Hatchett and that "very eminent philosopher" Cavendish, p. 184.

PERMISSIONS

WE ACKNOWLEDGE permissions to reproduce images in the captions of the illustrations. Permissions to quote from published sources we acknowledge in footnotes.

For permission to publish Henry Cavendish's letters, we acknowledge the following owners: Trustees of the Chatsworth Settlement; Royal Society of London; British Library, Manuscript Department; Trustees of the Natural History Museum, London; Royal Astronomical Society; Society of Antiquaries of London; Bristol Record Office; Historical Society of Pennsylvania; Swansea Museum Collection.

For permission to quote from unpublished sources, we further acknowledge: Bedfordshire Record Office; Syndics of the Fitzwilliam Museum; Trustees of the Royal Botanic Gardens, Kew; Beinecke Rare Book and Manuscript Library (the James Marshall and Marie-Louise Osborn Collection), Yale University.

APPENDIX 1
FAMILY TREES

CAVENDISH

- William Cavendish, 2nd Duke of Devonshire (1672–1729) m. 1688 Rachel Russell 1674–1725)
  - Mary Cavendish (d. 1719)
  - William Cavendish, 3d Duke of Devonshire (1698–1755) m. 1718 Catherine Hoskins (d. 1777)
    - Carolina Cavendish (1719–60) m. 1739 William Ponsonby, 2nd Earl of Bessborough (1704–93)
      - Frederick Ponsonby, 3rd Earl of Bessborough (1758–1844) (His four brothers and four sisters all died young.) m. 1780 Henrietta-Frances Spencer (da. of John, 1st Earl Spencer) (1780–1821)
    - William Cavendish, 4th Duke of Devonshire (1720–64) m. 1748 Charlotte Elizabeth Boyle (1731–54)
      - William Cavendish, 5th Duke of Devonshire (1748–1811) m. 1774 Georgiana Spencer (da. of John, 1st Earl Spencer (1757–1806) m.2d 1809 Lady Elizabeth Foster (1759–1824)
      - Dorothy Cavendish (1750–94) m. 1766 William Henry Cavendish Bentinck, 3d Duke of Portland (1738–1809)
      - Richard Cavendish (1752–81)
      - George Augustus Henry Cavendish (1754–1834) m. 1782 Elizabeth Compton (da. of 7th Earl of Northampton) (1760–1835)
    - Elizabeth Cavendish (d. 1796) m. 1743 John Ponsonby (1713–87)
      - William Brabazon, 1st Baron Ponsonby (b. 1744) m. 1769 Louisa Molesworth (1749–1824)
    - Rachel Cavendish (1727–1805) m. 1748 Horatio Walpole Earl of Oxford (1723–1809)
      - Horatio Walpole Earl of Oxford (1752–1822) m. 1781 Sophia Churchill (d. 1797)
      - Mary Walpole (1754–1840) m. 1777 Thomas Hussey of Galtrim
      - George Walpole (1758–1835)
    - George Augustus Cavendish (1728–94)
    - Frederick Cavendish (1729–1803)
    - Daughter (d. 1731)
    - John Cavendish (1732–96)
  - Rachel Cavendish (1699 or 1700–1780) m. 1723 Sir William Morgan of Tredgar (1700-31)
    - William Morgan of Tredegar (1725–63)
    - Rachel Morgan (1726–39)
    - Edward Morgan (1727–43)
    - Elizabeth Morgan (1729–87) m. 1767 William Jones of Llanarthy (d. 1779)
  - Son, probably also William (d. 1697)
  - Elizabeth Cavendish (d. 1747) m. 1723 Sir Thomas Lowther of Marske (d. 1745)
    - Sir William Lowther (1727–56)
    - Elizabeth Lowther (b. 1728)
  - James Cavendish (1702 or 1703–1741) m.
    - Son (b. 1733)
  - Charles Cavendish (1704?–1783) m. 1729 Anne de Grey (1706–33)
    - Henry Cavendish (1731–1810)
    - Frederick Cavendish (1733–1812)
  - Catherine Cavendish (d. 1729)
  - Anne Cavendish (d. 1780)
  - Diana Cavendish (d. 1722)
  - John Cavendish (d. 1720)
- Henry Cavendish (1673–1700) m. Rhoda Cartwright (d. 1730)
  - Mary Cavendish (1699-1778) m. 1716 John Fane, 7th Earl of Westmorland (1686–1762)
- James Cavendish (d. 1751) m. 1708 Anne Yale (d. 1734)
  - Elizabeth Cavendish (1701–79) m. 1732 Richard Chandler-Cavendish (1703?–1769)
  - William Cavendish (1709?–1751) m. 1731 Barbara Chandler (d. 1786)
- Elizabeth Cavendish (d. 1741) m. Sir John Wentworth of Broadsworth
  - Sir Butler Cavendish Wentworth of Crambe (d. 1741)
  - Two more sons

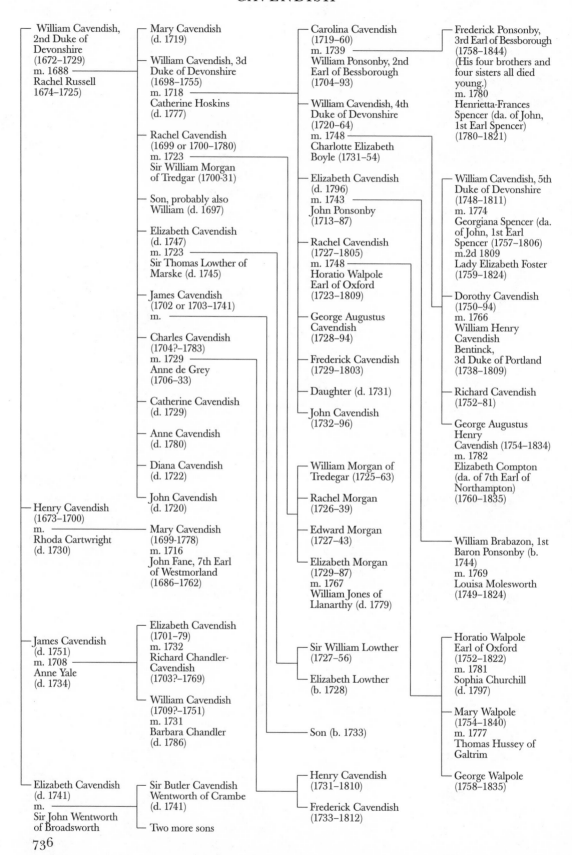

GREY

Henry de Grey,
Duke of Kent
(1671–1740)
m. 1695
Jemima Crewe
(1675–1728)
m.2d 1729
Sophia Bentinck
(d. 1748)

Amabell Grey

Anthony de Grey,
Earl of Harold
(1696–1723)
m. 1718
Mary Tufton
(1701–85)

Henry de Grey
(1697–1717)

Amabell de Grey
(1698–1727)
m. 1718
John Campbell, 3d
Earl of Breadalbane,
Lord Glenorchy
(d. 1782)

Jemima de Grey
(1700–31)
m. 1724
John, 1st Earl
of Ashburnham
(1688–1737)

Lucas de Grey
(1701–1704)

Henrietta de Grey
(1703–17)

Anne de Grey
(1706–33)
m. 1729
Charles Cavendish
(1704?–1783)

Jane de Grey
(1708–after 1723)

Stillborn boy

George de Grey
(1714–17)

Carolina de Grey
(b. and d. 1716)

Mary de Grey
(1719–62)
m.
David Gregory
(1696–1767)

Anne Sophia de Grey
(1730–80)
m. 1748
John Egerton,
Bishop of Durham
(1721–87)

George de Grey,
Earl of Harold
(1732–33)

Henry Campbell
(b. 1721)

Jemina Campbell
Marchioness of Kent,
Baroness Lucas of
Crudwell (1722–97)
m. 1740
Philip Yorke,
Viscount Royston,
later 2nd Earl
of Hardwicke
(1720–90)

John, 2d Earl of
Ashburnham
(1724–1812)
m. 1756
Elizabeth Crawley
of London (d. 1781)

Henry Cavendish
(1731–1810)

Frederick Cavendish
(1733–1812)

Amelia Egerton

John William Egerton,
7th Earl of Bridgewater
(1753–1823)
m. 1783
Charlotte Catherine
Anne Haynes

Francis Henry Egerton,
8th Earl of Bridgewater
(1756–1829)

Amabel,
Baroness Lucas
of Crudwell,
later Countess de Grey
of Wrest (1751–1833)
m. 1772
Alexander Hume-
Campbell
Lord Polwarth
(1751–81)

Mary Jemina Yorke
m.
Thomas Robinson, 2d
Baron Grantham
(d. 1786)

George Ashburnham,
Viscount St. Asaph
(b. and d. 1758)

Henrietta Theodosia
Ashburnham (b. 1759)

George, 3d Earl of
Ashburnham
(1760–1830)
m. 1784
Sophia (da. of 1st
Marquess of Bath)
(1763–91)
m.2d
Charlotte (da. of Earl
of Beverley)

Jemima Elizabeth
Ashburnham (1762–86)
m. 1785
James, 3d Duke of
Montrose
(1755)

Elizabeth Francis
Ashburnham (b. 1763)

Theodosia Maria
Ashburnham (b. 1765)
m. 1788
Robert Vyner, Esq.
of Gautby

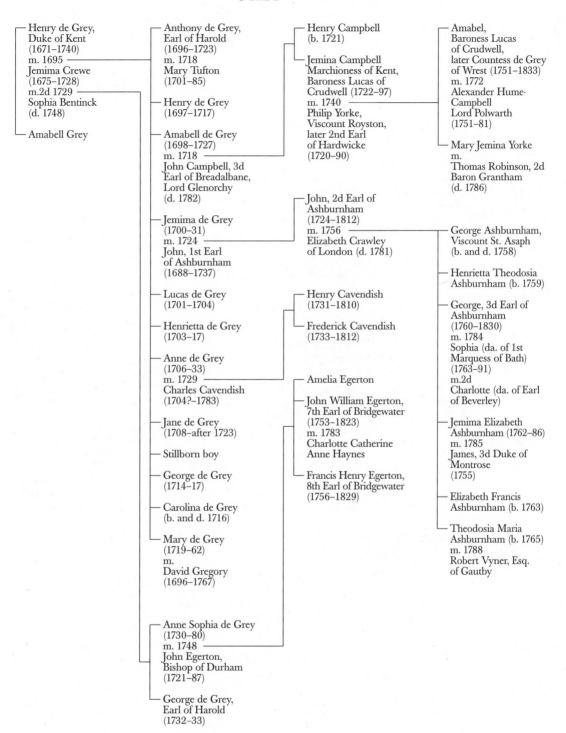

APPENDIX 2

HENRY CAVENDISH'S CHRONOLOGY AND PUBLICATIONS

Born Sunday 31 October 1731, in Nice, first child of Lord Charles Cavendish and Lady Anne (de Grey) Cavendish.

Death of his mother, Lady Anne, on 20 September 1733, at Putteridge.

Move of his father, Lord Charles, from Putteridge to Great Marlborough Street, Westminster, in 1738.

Entered Hackney Academy in 1742.

Entered St. Peter's College, or Peterhouse, Cambridge University, as a fellow-commoner, on 24 November 1749.

First publication, in Latin, "Luctus," in Cambridge University, *Academiae Cantabrigiensis Luctus in Obitum Frederici celsissimi Walliae Principis* (Cambridge, 1751). "Lament on the Death of Most Eminent Frederick, Prince of Wales."

Left Cambridge without taking a degree, having been in residence until 23 February 1753, nearly the full time required for a degree.

Subscribed to Felice Giardini's musical academy in London in 1758 or 1759.

Proposed 10 November 1757, and elected 31 July 1760, member of the Society of Royal Philosophers (Royal Society Dining Club).

Proposed 9 January 1760, and elected 16 January 1760, member of the Royal Society of Arts.

Proposed 31 January 1760, and elected 1 May 1760, Fellow of the Royal Society of London.

First published research, appearing in a paper by William Heberden, "Some Account of a Salt Found on the Pic of Teneriffe," *PT* 55 (1765): 57–60; read 7 February 1764.

Elected 30 November 1765 member of the council of the Royal Society, the first of many times.

First published research under his own name, "Three Papers, Containing Experiments on Factitious Air," *PT* 56 (1766): 141–84; read 29 May, 6 and 13 November 1766. For this work, he was awarded the Copley Medal of the Royal Society.

"Experiments on Rathbone-Place Water," *PT* 57 (1767): 92–108; read 19 February 1767.

"An Attempt to Explain Some of the Principal Phaenomena of Electricity, by Means of an Elastic Fluid," *PT* 61 (1771): 584–677; read 19 December 1771 and 9 January 1772.

Cavendish, listed first, together with the other members of the committee with the exception of Benjamin Wilson, "A Report of the Committee Appointed by the Royal Society, to Consider of a Method for Securing the Powder Magazines at Purfleet," *PT* 63 (1773): 42–47; dated 21 August 1772. The other members were William Watson, Benjamin Franklin, and John Robertson. Wilson published a dissenting opinion, which was answered by Cavendish and the other three members, "A Letter to Sir John Pringle, Bart. Pr. F.S. on Pointed Conductors," *PT* 63 (1773): 66; dated and read 17 December 1772.

Proposed 21 January 1773, and elected 25 February 1773, Fellow of the Society of Antiquaries.

Elected 8 December 1773 trustee of the British Museum.

"An Account of Some Attempts to Imitate the Effects of the Torpedo by Electricity," *PT* 66 (1776): 196–225; read 18 January 1775.

"An Account of the Meteorological Instruments Used at the Royal Society's House," *PT* 66 (1776): 375–401; read 14 March 1776.

Cavendish, listed first, together with the other members of the committee, "The Report of the Committee Appointed by the Royal Society to Consider the Best Method of Adjusting the Fixed Points of Thermometers; and of the Precautions Necessary to Be Used in Making Experiments with Those Instruments," *PT* 67 (1777): 816–57; read 19 June and 28 Dec. 1777. The other members were Heberden, Alexander Aubert, Jean-André Deluc, Nevil Maskelyne, Samuel Horsley, and Joseph Planta.

Acquired a country house, 34 Church Row, Hampstead, appearing on the Hampstead rate books beginning 3 January 1782.

"An Account of a New Eudiometer," *PT* 73 (1783): 106–35; read 16 January 1783.

Death of his father, Lord Charles, on or about 28 April 1783.

"Observations on Mr. Hutchins's Experiments for Determining the Degree of Cold at Which Quicksilver Freezes," *PT* 73 (1783): 303–28; read 1 May 1783.

"Experiments on Air," *PT* 74 (1784): 119–69; read 15 January 1784.

"Answer to Mr. Kirwan's Remarks upon the Experiments on Air," *PT* 74 (1784): 170–77; read 4 March 1784.

"Experiments on Air," *PT* 75 (1785): 372–84; read 2 June 1785.

Acquired a new country house on Clapham Common, leased 18 June 1785.

Acquired a new townhouse, 11 Bedford Square, on rate books from 1786.

"An Account of Experiments Made by Mr. John McNab, at Henley House, Hudson's Bay, Relating to Freezing Mixtures," *PT* 76 (1786): 241–72; read 23 February 1786.

"An Account of Experiments Made by Mr. John McNab, at Albany Fort, Hudson's Bay, Relative to the Freezing of Nitrous and Vitriolic Acids," *PT* 78 (1788): 166–81; read 28 February 1788.

"On the Conversion of a Mixture of Dephlogisticated and Phlogisticated Air into Nitrous Acid, by the Electric Spark," *PT* 78 (1788): 261–76; read 17 April 1788.

"On the Height of the Luminous Arch Which Was Seen on Feb. 23, 1784," *PT* 80 (1790): 101–5; read 25 February 1790.

"On the Civil Year of the Hindoos, and Its Divisions; with an Account of Three Hindoo Almanacs Belonging to Charles Wilkins," *PT* 82 (1792): 383–99; read 21 June 1792.

"Extract of a Letter from Henry Cavendish, Esq. to Mr. Mendoza y Rios, January, 1795," *PT* 87 (1797): 119–22; read 22 December 1796.

"Experiments to Determine the Density of the Earth," *PT* 88 (1798): 469–526; read 21 June 1798.

Became proprietor of the Royal Institution on 10 February 1800, elected manager on 1 May 1800.

Elected foreign associate of the Institute of France in 1803.

"On an Improvement in the Manner of Dividing Astronomical Instruments," *PT* 99 (1809): 221–45; read 18 May 1809.

Died 24 February 1810, at Clapham Common.

APPENDIX 3

OFFICERS OF THE ROYAL SOCIETY

Presidents:

1703. Sir Isaac Newton
1727. Sir Hans Sloane
1741. Martin Folkes
1752. George, Earl of Macclesfield
1764. James, Earl of Morton
1768. James West
1772. Sir John Pringle
1778. Sir Joseph Banks

Treasurers:

1700. Alexander Pitfield
1728. Roger Gale
1736. James West
1768. Samuel Wegg
1802. William Marsden

Secretaries (two):

1718–47. John Machin
1721–27. James Jurin
1727–30. William Rutty
1730–52. Cromwell Mortimer
1747–59. Peter Davall
1752–65. Thomas Birch
1759–73. Charles Morton
1765–76. Matthew Maty
1773–78. Samuel Horsley
1776–1804. Joseph Planta
1778–84. Paul Henry Maty
1784–97. Charles Blagden

1797–1807. Edward Whitaker Gray
1804–16. William Hyde Wollaston
1807–12. Sir Humphry Davy

Foreign Secretaries:

1723. Philip Henry Zollman
1728. Dr. Dillenius and Dr. Schuchzer
1748. Thomas Stack
1751. James Parson
1762. Matthew Maty
1766. John Bevis
1772. Paul Henry Maty
1774. Joseph Planta
1779. Charles Hutton
1784. Charles Peter Layard
1804. Thomas Young

Clerks and Assistant Secretaries:

1723. Francis Hawksbee
1763. Emanuel Mendez da Costa
1768. John Robertson
1777. John Robertson (son of above)
1785. George Gilpin

Source: Charles Richard Weld, *A History of the Royal Society*.

LIST OF ABBREVIATIONS

BL	British Library, Manuscript Department
Cavendish Mss	Cavendish Scientific Manuscripts, Devonshire Collections
Devon. Coll.	Devonshire Collections
DNB	*Dictionary of National Biography*
DSB	*Dictionary of Scientific Biography*
DTC	Dawson Turner Collection
HCJ	*House of Commons Journal*
JB	Journal Book of the Royal Society
Kew	Royal Botanic Gardens, Kew
BM(NH)	Natural History Museum, Botany Library
PT	*Philosophical Transactions of the Royal Society of London*
Sci. Pap.	*The Scientific Papers of the Honourable Henry Cavendish, F.R.S.*, 2 vols., ed. J. C. Maxwell, J. Larmor, E. Thorpe (Cambridge: Cambridge University Press, 1921).
Yale	Beinecke Rare Book and Manuscript Library, Yale University

BIBLIOGRAPHY

ARCHIVES

American Philosophical Society

Bank of England

Bedfordshire Record Office

Birmingham Assay Office

Birmingham University Library

Bristol Record Office

British Library, Department of Manuscripts

Cambridge University Library

Camden Archives

Cumbria County Record Office

Devonshire Collections, Chatsworth

Fitzwilliam Museum, Cambridge

Gloucester Record Office

Greater London Record Office

Historical Society of Pennsylvania

Holborn Public Library

Lambeth Archives

Lancashire Record Office

National Archives of Canada

Natural History Museum, Department of Botany

Public Record Office, Chancery Lane

Royal Astronomical Society

Royal Botanic Gardens, Kew

Royal Greenwich Observatory

Royal Institution of Great Britain

Royal Society of Arts

Royal Society of London

Scheffield Central Library

Society of Antiquaries

University of Wales, Swansea Library

Wellcome Historical Medical Library

Westminster Archives

Whitby Literary and Philosophical Society

Yale University Library

PRINTED SOURCES

Note: Because of their large number, scientific articles are not listed in this bibliography but are given in the notes.

Aarsleff, Hans. *The Study of Language in England, 1780–1860.* Minneapolis: University of Minnesota Press, 1983.

Adams, George. *A Catalogue of Mathematical, Philosophical, and Optical Instruments. . . .* London, 1746.

Adams, George, Jr. *An Essay on Electricity. . . .* 2d ed. London, 1785.

Aepinus, Franz Ulrich Theodorius. *Aepinus's Essay on the Theory of Electricity and Magnetism.* Notes and Introduction by R. W. Home. Translated by P. J. Connor. Princeton: Princeton University Press, 1979.

Albert, William. *The Turnpike Road System in England, 1663–1840.* Cambridge: Cambridge University Press, 1972.

Alexander, A. F. O'D. "Bradley, James." *DSB* 2:387–89.

Allan, D. G. C., and Robert E. Schofield. *Stephen Hales: Scientist and Philanthropist.* London: Scolar Press, 1980.

Allen, David Elliston. *The Naturalist in Britain: A Social History.* London: Allen Lane, 1976.

Allibone, T. E. *The Royal Society and Its Dining Clubs.* Oxford: Pergamon Press, 1976.

——. "The Thursday's Club Called the Club of the Royal Philosophers, and Its Relation to the Royal Society Club." *Notes and Records of the Royal Society London* 26 (1971): 73–80.

Antoine, Michel. "La cour de Lorraine dans l'Europe des lumières." In *La Lorraine dans l'Europe des lumières. Actes du colloque organisé par la Faculté des lettres et des sciences humaines de l'Université de Nancy, Nancy, 24–27 octobre 1966*, 69–76. Series *Annales de l'Est.* Mémoire 34. Nancy: Faculté des lettres et sciences humaines de l'Université, 1968.

Arnold, Matthew. *The Portable Matthew Arnold.* Edited by Lionel

Trilling. New York: Viking, 1949.

Ashton, T. S. *The Industrial Revolution, 1760–1830.* London: Oxford University Press, 1977.

"Aubert, Alexander." *DNB* 1:715.

Austen Leigh, R. A. *Eton College Lists 1678–1790.* Eton: Spottiswoode, 1907.

Austin, Jilian F., and Anita McConnell. "James Six, F.R.S.: Two Hundred Years of the Six's Self-Registering Thermometer." *Notes and Records of the Royal Society London* 35 (1980): 49–65.

Averley, Gwendoline. "English Scientific Societies of the Eighteenth and Early Nineteenth Centuries." Ph.D. diss., Teeside Polytechnic in collaboration with the University of Durham, 1989.

——. "The 'Social Chemists': English Chemical Societies in the Eighteenth and Early Nineteenth Century." *Ambix* 33 (1986): 99–128.

Badcock, A. W. "Physical Optics at the Royal Society, 1600–1800." *British Journal for the History of Science* 1 (1962): 99–116.

——. "Physics at the Royal Society, 1660–1800. 1. Change of State." *Annals of Science* 16 (1960): 95–115.

Baeyer, Hans Christian von. "Big G." *Discover*, March 1996, 96–101.

Baker, C. H. Collins, and Muriel I. Baker. *The Life and Circumstances of James Brydges, First Duke of Chandos, Patron of the Liberal Arts.* Oxford: Clarendon Press, 1949.

"Baker, Sir George." *DNB* 1:927–29.

Baker, Henry. *Employment for the Microscope. . . .* London, 1764.

Baker, John R. *Abraham Trembley of Geneva: Scientist and Philosopher, 1710–1784.* London: Edward Arnold, 1952.

Baker, Thomas. *History of the College of St. John the Evangelist, Cambridge.* Cambridge, 1869.

Baldwin, Thomas. *Aeropaidia: Containing the Narrative of a Balloon Excursion from Chester, the Eighth of September, 1785.* London, 1785.

Ball, W. W. Rouse. *History of the Study of Mathematics at Cambridge.* Cambridge, 1889.

Banks, Sir Joseph. *The Banks Letters. A Calendar of the Manuscript Correspondence of Sir Joseph Banks Preserved in the British Museum, the British Museum (Natural History) and Other Collections in Great Britain.* Edited by W. R. Dawson. London: British Museum (Natural History), 1958.

Barker, T. C., and M. Robbins. *A History of London Transport, Passenger Travel and the Development of the Metropolis.* Vol. 1. London: Allen & Unwin, 1963.

Baron, Margaret E. "Hutton, Charles." *DSB* 6:576–77.

Barrett, Thomas J. *The Annals of Hampstead.* 3 vols. London: Adam & Charles Black, 1912.

Barrow, John. *Sketches of the Royal Society and Royal Society Club.* London, 1849.

Baumé, Antoine. *Manuel de chymie, ou, exposé des opérations et des produits d'un cours de chymie. Ouvrage utile aux personnes qui veulent suivre un cours de cette science, ou qui ont dessein de se former un cabinet de chymie.* Paris, 1763.

Baxandall, David. "The Circular Dividing Engine of Edward Troughton, 1793." *Transactions of the Optical Society* 25 (1923–24): 135–40.

Baxter, Stephen B. *William III and the Defense of European Liberty 1650–1702.* New York: Harcourt, Brace & World, 1966.

Beaglehole, J. C. "Cook, James." *DSB* 3:396–97.

Beale, Catherine Hutton, ed. *Reminiscences of a Gentlewoman of the Last Century: Letters of Catherine Hutton.* Birmingham, 1891.

Beattie, John M. *The English Court in the Reign of George I.* Cambridge: Cambridge University Press, 1967.

Beatty, F. M. "The Scientific Work of the Third Earl Stanhope," *Notes and Records of the Royal Society of London* 11 (1955): 202–21.

Beckett, J. V. *The Aristocracy in England, 1660–1914.* Oxford: Basil Blackwell, 1986.

——. "Dr William Brownrigg, F.R.S.: Physician, Chemist and Country Gentleman." *Notes and Records of the Royal Society of London* 31 (1977): 255–71. .

——. "The Lowthers at Holker: Marriage, Inheritance and Debt in the Fortunes of an Eighteenth-Century Landowning Family." *Transactions of the Historic Society of Lancashire and Cheshire* 127 (1977): 47–64.

Beckinsale, Robert P. "Deluc, Jean André." *DSB* 4:27–29.

Beddoes, Thomas, ed. *Contributions to Physical and Medical Knowledge, Principally from the West of England.* Bristol, 1799.

Beddoes, Thomas, and James Watt. *Considerations on the Medicinal Use of Factitious Airs, and on the Manner of Obtaining Them in Large Quantities.* Bristol, 1794.

Bektas, Yakup, and Maurice Crosland. "The Copley Medal: The Establishment of a Reward System in the Royal Society, 1731–1839." *Notes and Records of the Royal Society of London* 46 (1992): 43–76.

Bell, Jr., Whitfield J. "Dixon, Jeremiah." *DSB* 4:131–32.

Belloni, Luigi. "Fontana, Felice." *DSB* 5:54–55.

——. "Landriani, Marsilio." *DSB* 7:620–21.

"Bentley, Richard." *DNB* 2:306–14.

Bergman, Torbern Olof. *Outlines of Mineralogy.* Translated by W. Withering. Birmingham, 1783.

——. *Physical and Chemical Essays . . . To Which Are Added Notes and Illustrations, by the Translator.* Translated by E. Cullen. 3 vols. London, 1784–91.

Berman, Morris. "The Early Years of the Royal Institution, 1799–1810: A Re-Evaluation." *Science Studies* 2 (1972): 205–40.

Berry, A. J. *Henry Cavendish: His Life and Scientific Work.* London: Hutchinson, 1960.

Berry, Mary. *Some Account of the Life of Rachael Wriothesley Lady Russell, . . . Followed by a Series of Letters. . . .* London, 1819.

Besant, Walter. *London in the Eighteenth Century.* London: Adean & Charles Black, 1902.

Bickley Francis. *The Cavendish Family.* London: Constable, 1911.

Biddle, Sheila. *Bolingbroke and Harley.* New York: Knopf, 1974.

A Bill Intitled an Act for the Encouragement of the British White Herring Industry. London, 1750.

Bingham, Hiram. *Elihu Yale: The American Nabob of Queen Square.* New York: Dodd, Mead, 1939.

Biot, J. B. "Cavendish (Henri)." *Biographie Universelle.* Vol. 7, pp. 272–73. Paris, 1813.

Birch, Thomas. *The History of the Royal Society of London for Improving of Natural Knowledge, from Its First Rise. . . .* Vol. 1. London, 1756.

——. *The Life of the Honourable Robert Boyle.* London, 1744.

Bird, John. *A Method of Constructing Mural Quadrants.* London, 1768.

——. *The Method of Dividing Astronomical Instruments.* London, 1767.

Birembaut, Arthur. "Hassenfratz, Jean-Henri." *DSB* 6:164–65.

Bishop, John. *Considerations on the Expediency of Making, and the Manner of Conducting the Late Regulations at Cambridge.* London, 1751.

Black, Joseph. *Experiments on Magnesia Alba, Quicklime, and Some Other Alcaline Substances.* No. 1. Edinburgh: Alembic Club Reprints, 1898.

——. *Lectures on the Elements of Chemistry.* 2 vols. Edited by J. Robison. Edinburgh, 1803.

——. *Notes from Doctor Black's Lectures on Chemistry 1767/8.* Edited by D. McKie. Wilmslow: Imperial Chemical Industries, Ltd. 1966.

Black, Joseph. See Thomas Cochrane.

Blagden, Charles. "The Diary of Sir Charles Blagden." Edited by Gavin De Beer. *Notes and Records of the Royal Society of London* 8 (1950): 6–89.

——. "Some Letters of Sir Charles Blagden." Edited by Gavin De Beer. *Notes and Records of the Royal Society of London* 8 (1951): 253–60.

Blanchard, Jean Pierre. *Journal of My Forty-Fifth Ascension. . . .* Philadelphia, 1793.

Bloomfield, Paul. *Uncommon People: A Study of England's Elite.* London: Hamish Hamilton, 1955.

Boerhaave, Hermann. *Elements of Chemistry: Being the Annual Lectures of Herman Boerhaave. . . .* 2 vols. in 1. Translated by T. Dallow. London, 1735.

——. *A New Method of Chemistry; Including the Theory and Practice of That Art; Laid Down on Mechanical Principles, and Accommodated to the Uses of Life. The Whole Making a Clear and Rational System of Chemistry. . . .* 2 vols. Translated by P. Shaw and E. Chambers. London, 1727.

Boklund, Uno. "Scheele, Carl Wilhelm." *DSB* 12:143–50.

Borgeaud, Charles. *Histoire de l'Université de Genève. L'Académie de Calvin 1559–1796.* Genève: Georg, 1900.

Bos, H. J. M. "Huygens, Christiaan." *DSB* 6:597–613.

Boscovich, Roger Joseph. *A Theory of Natural Philosophy.* Translated by J. M. Child from the 2d edition of 1763. Cambridge, Mass.: M.I.T. Press, 1966.

Boswell, James. *The Life of Samuel Johnson LL.D.* 3 vols. New York: Heritage, 1963.

Bouguer, Pierre. *La figure de la terre, déterminée par les observations de Messieurs de la Condamine et Bouguer, de l'Académie royale des sciences, envoyés par ordre du roy au Pérou pour observer aux environs de l'équateur. . . .* Paris, 1749.

——. *Pierre Bouguer's Optical Treatise on the Gradation of Light.* Translated with notes by W. E. Knowles Middleton. Toronto: University of Toronto Press, 1961.

"Boulton, Matthew." *DNB* 2: 916–17.

Boyé, Pierre. *Les Chateaux du Roi Stanislas en Lorraine.* Marseille: Laffitte Reprints, 1980.

Boyer, Carl B. *A History of Mathematics.* New York: Wiley, 1968.

Bradley, James. *Miscellaneous Works and Correspondence of the Rev. James Bradley, D.D., F.R.S.* Edited by S. P. Rigaud. Oxford, 1832.

Brazerman, Charles. *Shaping Written Knowledge: The Genre and Activity of the Experimental Article in Science.* Madison: University of Wisconsin Press, 1988.

Brewster, David. *Memoirs of the Life, Writings, and Discoveries of Isaac Newton.* 2 vols. Edinburgh, 1855.

Briggs, Jr., J. Morton. "Robins, Benjamin." *DSB* 11:493–94.

Briggs, Stephen R. See Jonathan M. Cheek.

Brimblecombe, Peter. "Earliest Atmospheric Profile." *New Scientist* 76 (1977): 364–65.

Brock, William H. *The Fontana History of Chemistry.* London: Fontana, 1992.

——. "The Society for the Perpetuation of Gmelin: The Cavendish Society, 1846–1872." *Annals of Science* 35 (1978): 599–617.

"Brocklesby, Richard." *DNB* 2:1282–83.

Brodie, Sir Benjamin Collins. *Autobiography of the Late Sir Benjamin Brodie, Bart.* 2d ed. London, 1865.

Brooke, John. See L. B. Namier.

Brooks, William Eric St. John. *Sir Hans Sloane, the Great Collector and His Circle.* London: Batchworth Press, 1954.

Brougham, Henry, Lord. *Lives of Men of Letters and Science Who Flourished in the Time of George III.* 2 vols. London, 1845–46. Vol. 1. Philadelphia, 1845.

Brown, Jennifer S. H. *Strangers in Blood: Fur Trade Company Families in Indian Country.* Vancouver: University of British Columbia Press, 1980.

Brown, Joyce. See A. W. Skempton.

Brown, Sanborn C. *Benjamin Thompson, Count Rumford.* Cambridge, Mass.: M.I.T. Press, 1979.

——. "Thompson, Benjamin (Count Rumford)." *DSB* 13: 350–52.

Brown, T. Graham, and Gavin de Beer. *The First Ascent of Mont Blanc.* London: Oxford University Press, 1957.

Bullen, Keith Edward. *The Earth's Density.* New York: Wiley, 1974.

Buller, Audley Cecil. *The Life and Works of Heberden.* London, 1879.

Burgess, J. H. Michael. *The Chronicles of Clapham [Clapham Common]. Being a Selection from the Reminiscences of Thomas Parsons, Sometime Member of the Clapham Antiquarian Society.* London: Ramsden, 1929.

Burke's Genealogical and Heraldic History of the Landed Gentry. London: Burke's Peerage Ltd, 1939.

Burke's Peerage and Baronetage. 150th ed. London: Burke's Peerage (Genealogical Books) Ltd., 1980.

Burney, Charles. *A General History of Music. From the Earliest Ages to the Present Period (1789).* Vol. 2. Edited by Frank Mercer. New York: Harcourt, Brace, 1935.

Bush, M. L. *The English Aristocracy: A Comparative Synthesis.* Manchester: Manchester University Press, 1984.

Buss, Arnold H. "A Conception of Shyness." In *Avoiding Communication: Shyness, Reticence and Communication Apprehension*, edited by J. A. Daley and J. C. McCroskey, 39–49. Beverley Hills: Sage, 1984.

——. "A Theory of Shyness." In *Shyness: Perspectives on Research and Treatment*, edited by Warren H. Jones et al., 39–46. New York: Plenum Press, 1986.

Bynum, W. F. "Health, Disease and Medical Care." In *Ferment of Knowledge: Studies in the Historiography of Eighteenth-Century Science*, edited by G. S. Rousseau and R. Porter, 221–53. Cambridge: Cambridge University Press, 1980.

Byrom, John. *The Private Journal and Literary Remains of John Byrom.* 2 vols. in 4 parts. Edited by R. Parkinson. Manchester, 1854–57.

"Call, Sir John." *DNB* 3:705–6.

Cambridge University. *Academiae Cantabrigiensis Luctus in Obitum Frederici celsissimi Walliae Principis.* Cambridge, 1751.

Cameron, Hector Charles. *Sir Joseph Banks, K.B., P.R.S. The Autocrat of the Philosophers.* London: Batchworth, 1952.

Canini, Gérard. See Michel Parisse.

Cannon, John Ashton. *Aristocratic Century. The Peerage of Eighteenth-Century England.* Cambridge: Cambridge University Press, 1984.

——. *The Fox-North Coalition: Crisis of the Constitution, 1782–4.* Cambridge: Cambridge University Press, 1969.

"Canton, John." *DNB* 3:908–9.

Cantor, G. N. *Optics After Newton: Theories of Light in Britain and Ireland, 1704–1840.* Manchester: Manchester University Press, 1983.

——. "Thomas Young's Lectures at the Royal Institution." *Notes and Records of the Royal Society of London* 25 (1970): 87–112.

Cantor, G. N., and M. J. S. Hodges, eds. *Conceptions of Ether: Studies in the History of the Ether Theories, 1740–1900.* Cambridge: Cambridge University Press, 1981.

Carlson, Eric T. "Rush, Benjamin." *DSB* 11:616–18.

Carmichael, Leonard, and J. C. Long. *James Smithson and the Smithsonian Story.* New York: G. P. Putnam's Sons, 1965.

Caroe, Gwendy. *The Royal Institution: An Informal History.* London: John Murray, 1985.

Carozzi, Albert V. "Saussure, Horace Bénédict de." *DSB* 12:119–23.

Carswell, John. *The South Sea Bubble.* Rev. ed. London: Alan Sutton, 1993.

Carter, Alice Clare. *The English Public Debt in the Eighteenth Century.* London: The Historical Association, 1968.

Carter, Edmund. *The History of the University of Cambridge, from Its Original, to the Year 1753. . . .* London, 1753.

Carter, Elizabeth, and Catherine Talbot. *A Series of Letters between Mrs. Elizabeth Carter and Miss Catherine Talbot from the Year 1741 to 1770. . . .* Vol. 1. London, 1809.

Cavallo, Tiberius. *A Complete Treatise of Electricity in Theory and Practice. . . .* London, 1777.

——. *A Treatise on the Nature and Properties of Air, and Other Permanently Elastic Fluids. To Which Is Prefixed, an Introduction to Chemistry*. London, 1781.

——. *A Treatise on Magnetism in Theory and Practice*. . . . London, 1787.

Cavendish, Elizabeth, Duchess of Devonshire, and Georgiana Cavendish, Duchess of Devonshire. *The Two Duchesses. Georgiana, Duchess of Devonshire. Elizabeth, Duchess of Devonshire. Family Correspondence*. Edited by V. Foster. London, 1898.

Cavendish, Georgiana, Duchess of Devonshire. *Georgiana: Extracts from the Correspondence of Georgiana, Duchess of Devonshire*. Edited by the Earl of Bessborough. London: John Murray, 1955.

Cavendish, Henry. *The Electrical Researches of the Honourable Henry Cavendish, F.R.S*. . . . Edited by J. C. Maxwell. 1879. Reprint, London: Frank Cass, 1967.

Cavendish, Henry. *The Scientific Papers of the Honourable Henry Cavendish, F.R.S.* Vol. I: *The Electrical Researches*. Edited with notes by James Clerk Maxwell. Revised with notes by Joseph Larmor. Cambridge: Cambridge University Press, 1921. Vol. II: *Chemical and Dynamical.* Edited with notes by Edward Thorpe. Contributions by Charles Chree, Frank Watson Dyson, Archibald Geikie, and Joseph Larmor. Cambridge: Cambridge University Press, 1921.

Cavendish, William, Fourth Duke of Devonshire. *The Devonshire Diary: William Cavendish, Fourth Duke of Devonshire, Memoranda on State of Affairs, 1759–1762*. Camden Fourth Series, Vol. 27. Edited by Peter D. Brown and Karl W. Schweizer. London: Royal Historical Society, 1982.

Chaldecott, J. A. *Handbook of the King George III Collection of Scientific Instruments*. London: His Majesty's Stationery Office, 1951.

Challinor, John. "Whitehurst, John," *DSB* 14:311–12.

Chambers, J. D. *Nottinghamshire in the Eighteenth Century: A Study of Life and Labour Under the Squirearchy*. 2d ed. London: Frank Cass, 1966.

Chancellor, E. Beresford. *The Romance of Soho; Being an Account of the District, Its Past Distinguished Inhabitants, Its Historic Houses, and Its Place in the Social Annals of London.* London: Country Life, 1931.

Chapin, Seymour L. "Bailly, Jean-Sylvain." *DSB* 1:400–2.

Chapman, Allan. "Pure Research and Practical Teaching: The Astronomical Career of James Bradley, 1693–1762." *Notes and Records of the Royal Society of London* 47 (1993): 205–12.

Chaston, J. C. "Wear Resistance of Gold Alloys for Coinage: An Early Example of Contract Research." *Gold Bulletin* 7 (1974): 108–12.

Cheek, Jonathan M., and Stephen R. Briggs, "Shyness as a Personality Trait." In *Shyness and Embarrassment: Perspectives from Social Psychology*, edited by W. Ray Crozier, 315–37. Cambridge: Cambridge University Press, 1990.

"Churchman, John." *National Cyclopaedia of American Biography* 9:287.

Clapham, John. *The Bank of England. A History*. 2 vols. Cambridge: Cambridge University Press, 1945.

Clare, Martin. *The Motion of Fluids, Natural and Artificial*. . . . 3d ed. London, 1747.

Clark, George N. *A History of the Royal College of Physicians of London.* 3 vols. Oxford: Clarendon Press, 1964–72.

Clark, John Willis. See Robert Willis.

Cleghorn, William. "William Cleghorn's *De igne* (1779)." Edited, annotated, and translated by Douglas McKie and Niels H. de V. Heathcote. *Annals of Science* 14 (1958): 1–82.

Clotfelter, B. E. "The Cavendish Experiment as Cavendish Knew It." *American Journal of Physics* 55 (1987): 210–13.

Clow, Archibald. "Some Notes on William Walker's 'Distinguished Men of Science.'" *Proceedings of the Royal Institution* 35 (1954): 890–94.

Clow, Archibald, and Nan L. Clow. *The Chemical Revolution: A Contribution to Social Technology.* London: Batchworth Press, 1952.

Cobbett's Parliamentary History of England. From the Norman Conquest, in 1066, to the Year 1803. Vol. 6: *Comprising the Period from the Accession of Queen Anne in 1702, to the Accession of King George the First in 1714.* London, 1810.

I. B. Cohen. "The Eighteenth-Century Origins of the Concept of Scientific Revolution." *Journal of the History of Ideas* 37 (1976): 257–88.

——. *Franklin and Newton: An Inquiry into Speculative Newtonian Experimental Science and Franklin's Work in Electricity as an Example Thereof.* Philadelphia: American Philosophical Society, 1956.

——. "Franklin, Benjamin." *DSB* 5:129–39.

——. *Introduction to Newton's Principia.* Cambridge: Cambridge University Press, 1971.

——. "Newton, Isaac." *DSB* 10: 42–101.

——. *The Newtonian Revolution.* Cambridge: Cambridge University Press, 1987.

Cohen, Murray. *Sensible Words: Linguistic Practice in England 1640–1785.* Baltimore: The Johns Hopkins University Press, 1977.

Cokayne, George Edward. *The Complete Peerage of England, Scotland, Ireland, Great Britain and the United Kingdom: Extant, Extinct, or Dormant.* Vols. 1–3. Gloucester: A. Sutton, 1982.

Coleby, L. J. M. "Isaac Milner and the Jacksonian Chair of Natural Philosophy." *Annals of Science* 10 (1954): 234–57.

——. "John Francis Vigani." *Annals of Science* 8 (1952): 46–60.

——. "John Hadley, Fourth Professor of Chemistry in the University of Cambridge." *Annals of Science* 8 (1952): 293–301.

——. "John Mickleburgh, Professor of Chemistry in the University of Cambridge, 1718–56." *Annals of Science* 8 (1952): 165–74.

——. "Richard Watson, Professor of Chemistry in the University of Cambridge, 1764–71." *Annals of Science* 9 (1953): 101–23.

Collins, A. S. *Authorship in the Days of Johnson, Being a Study of the Relation Between Author, Patron, Publisher and Public, 1726–1780.* New York: E. P. Dutton, 1929.

Collins's Peerage of England; Geneological, Biographical, and Historical. 9 vols. Edited by E. Brydges. London, 1812.

Collot, Claude. "La faculté de droit de l'Université de Pont-à-Mousson et de Nancy au XVIIIe siècle." *La Lorraine dans l'Europe des lumières. Actes du colloque organisé par la Faculté des lettres et des sciences humaines de l'Université de Nancy, Nancy, 24–27 octobre 1966*, 215–26. Séries *Annales de l'Est.* Mémoire 34. Nancy: Faculté des lettres et sciences humaines de l'Université, 1968.

"Colson, John." *DNB* 4:801–2.

Colvin, Howard Montagu. *A Biographical Dictionary of British Architects, 1600–1840.* Rev. ed. London: J. Murray, 197.

A Concise and Accurate Description of the University, Town, and County of Cambridge. . . . New ed. Cambridge, n.d. [1784].

Connell, Brian. *Portrait of a Whig Peer. Compiled from the Papers of the Second Viscount Palmerston, 1739–1802.* London: Andre Deutsch, 1957.

Conrady, A. E. See R. A. Sampson.

Cook, A. H. "Experiments on Gravitation." In *Three Hundred Years of Gravitation*, edited by S. W. Hawking and W. Israel, 51–79. Cambridge: Cambridge University Press, 1987.

Cooper, W. Durrant, ed. *Lists of Foreign Protestants, and Aliens, Resident in England 1618–1688.* London, 1862.

Copenhaver, Brian P. "Natural Magic, Hermeticism, and Occultism in Early Modern Science." In *Reappraisals of the Scientific Revolution*, edited by D. C. Lindberg and R. S. Westman, 261–301. Cambridge: Cambridge University Press, 1990.

Cornell, E. S. "Early Studies in Radiant Heat." *Annals of Science* 1 (1936): 217–25.

Costa, Jr., Paul T., and Robert R. McCrea. "Set Like Plaster? Evidence for the Stability of Adult Personality." In *Can Personality Change?* edited by T. F. Heatherton and J. L. Weinberger, 21–40. Washington, D.C.: American Psychological Association, 1994.

Costamagna, Henri. "Nice au XVIIIe siècle: présentation historique et géographique." *Annales de la Faculté des Lettres et Sciences Humaines de Nice*, no. 19, 1973, pp. 7–28.

Cotes, Roger. *Harmonia Mensurarum, sive Analysis & Synthesis per Rationum & Angulorum Mensuras Promotae: Accedunt alia Opuscula Mathematica.* Edited by Robert Smith. London, 1722.

——. *Hydrostatical and Pneumatical Lectures.* Edited by Robert Smith. 2d ed. Cambridge, 1747.

Cowper, Mary Clavering Cowper, Countess. *Diary of Mary Countess Cowper, Lady of the Bedchamber to the Princess of Wales 1714–1720.* Edited by C. S. Spencer Cowper. 2d ed. London, 1865.

Cowper, Spencer. *Letters of Spencer Cowper, Dean of Durham, 1746–74.* Edited by E. Hughes. Durham: Surtees Society, 1956.

Cox, R. T. "Electric Fish." *American Journal of Physics* 11 (1943): 13–22.

Coxe, William. *Memoirs of the Life and Administration of Sir Robert Walpole, Earl of Orford*. . . . 3 vols. London, 1798.

Craig, John. *The Mint: A History of the London Mint from A.D. 287 to 1948.* Cambridge: Cambridge University Press, 1953.

——. "The Royal Society and the Royal Mint." *Notes and Records of the Royal Society of London* 19 (1964): 156–67.

Crane, Verner W. "The Club of Honest Whigs: Friends of Science and Liberty." *William and Mary Quarterly* 23 (1966): 210–33.

Crawford, Adair. *Experiments and Observations on Animal Heat, and the Inflammation of Combustible Bodies; Being an Attempt to Resolve These Phaenomena into a General Law of Nature.* London, 1779.

Creighton, Charles. *A History of Epidemics in Britain.* Vol. 2: *From the Extinction of the Plague to the Present Time.* 2d ed. London: Frank Cass, 1965.

Crombie, A. C., ed. *Scientific Change; Historical Studies in the Intellectual, Social, and Technical Conditions for Scientific Discovery and Technical Invention, from Antiquity to the Present.* New York: Basic Books, 1963.

Cronstedt, Axel Fredric. *An Essay Towards a System of Mineralogy.* Translated by G. von Engestrom. Revised by E. M. Da Costa. London, 1770.

Crosland, Maurice. "The Development of Chemistry in the Eighteenth Century." *Studies on Voltaire* 24 (1963): 369–441.

——. "Explicit Qualifications as a Criterion for Membership of the Royal Society: A Historical Review." *Notes and Records of the Royal Society of London* 37 (1983): 167–87.

——. *Historical Studies in the Language of Chemistry.* London: Heinemann, 1962.

Crosland, Maurice. See Yakup Bektas.

Crowther, James Gerald. *Scientists of the Industrial Revolution: Joseph Black, James Watt, Joseph Priestley, Henry Cavendish.* London: Crescent Press, 1962.

Crozier, W. Ray. "Social Psychological Perspectives on Shyness, Embarrassment and Shame." In *Shyness and Embarrassment: Perspectives from Social Psychology*, edited by W. Ray Crozier, 19–50. Cambridge: Cambridge University Press, 1990.

Cuthbertson, John. *Description of an Improved Air-Pump, and an Account of Some Experiments Made with It. . . .* London, 1787.

Cuvier, Georges. "Henry Cavendish," 1812. Translated by D. S. Faber. In *Great Chemists*, edited by E. Faber, 227–38. New York: Interscience Publishers, 1961.

Dale, T. C. "History of Clapham." In *Clapham and the Clapham Sect*, edited by E. Baldwin, 1–28. Clapham: Clapham Antiquarian Sociey, 1927.

Dalrymple, Alexander. *General Introduction to the Charts and Memoirs.* London, 1772.

"Dalrymple, Alexander." *DNB* 5:402–3.

Darby, H. C. "The Draining of the Fens, A.D. 1600–1800." In *An Historical Geography of England Before A.D. 1800*, edited by H. C. Darby, 444–64. Cambridge: Cambridge University Press, 1936.

Daston, Lorraine. *Classical Probability in the Enlightenment.* Princeton: Princeton University Press, 1988.

Daumas, Maurice. "Precision of Measurement and Physical and Chemical Research in the Eighteenth Century." In *Scientific Change; Historical Studies in the Intellectual, Social, and Technical Conditions for Scientific Discovery and Technical Invention, from Antiquity to the Present*, edited by A. C. Crombie, 418–30. New York: Basic Books, 1963.

——. *Scientific Instruments of the Seventeenth and Eighteenth Centuries and Their Makers.* Translated by M. Holbrook. New York: Praeger, 1972.

Davies, J. D. Griffith. "The Banks Family." *Notes and Records of the Royal Society of London* 1 (1938): 85–87.

Davy, Humphry. *The Collected Works of Sir Humphry Davy, Bart.* Edited by J. Davy. Vol. 2. London, 1839.

——. *A Discourse, Introductory to a Course of Lectures on Chemistry.* . . . London, 1802.

——. *Elements of Chemical Philosophy.* Vol. 1. London, 1812.

——. *A Syllabus of a Course of Lectures on Chemistry Delivered at the Royal Institution of Great Britain.* London, 1802.

Davy, John. *Memoirs of the Life of Sir Humphry Davy, Bart.* 2 vols. London, 1836.

Day, Archibald. *The Admiralty Hydrographic Service 1795–1919.* London: Her Majesty's Stationery Office, 1967.

De Beer, Gavin. "H.-B. de Saussure's Election into the Royal Society." *Notes and Records of the Royal Society of London* 7 (1950): 264–67.

——. "The History of the Altimetry of Mont Blanc." *Annals of Science* 12 (1956): 3–29.

——. *Sir Hans Sloane and the British Museum.* London: Oxford University Press, 1953.

De Beer, Gavin. See Charles Blagden.

De Beer, Gavin. See T. Graham Brown.

De Beer, Gavin, and Max. H. Hey. "The First Ascent of Mont Blanc." *Notes and Records of the Royal Society of London* 11 (1955): 236–55.

De-la-Noy, Michael. *The King Who Never Was: The Story of Frederick, Prince of Wales.* London: Peter Owen, 1996.

Delaval, Edward Hussey." *DNB* 15:767.

Delorme, Edmond. *Lunéville et son arrondissement.* Marseille: Lafitte Reprints, 1977.

Deluc, Jean André. *An Elementary Treatise on Geology: Determining Fundamental Points in That Science, and Containing an Examination of Some Modern Geological Systems, and Particularly of the Huttonian Theory of the Earth.* Translated by H. de la Fite. London, 1809.

——. *Idées sur la météorologie*, 2 vols. Paris, 1786–87.

——. *Geological Travels in the North of Europe and in England.* 3 vols. Translated by H. de la Fite. London, 1810–11.

——. *Recherches sur les modifications de l'atmosphère.* . . . 2 vols. Genève, 1772.

Desaguliers, J. T. *A Course of Experimental Philosophy.* 2 vols. London, 1734–44.

——. *Physico-Mechanical Lectures.* . . . London, 1717.

——. *A System of Experimental Philosophy, Prov'd by Mechanicks.* . . . London, 1719.

Deutsch, Otto Erich. *Handel: A Documentary Biography.* New York: DaCapo Press, 1974.

Dickinson, H. T. *Bolingbroke.* London: Constable, 1970.

Dickson, P. G. M. *The Financial Revolution in England: A Study in the Development of Public Credit 1688–1756.* London: Macmillan, 1967.

Dictionary of National Biography. 22 vols. Edited by L. Stephen and S. Lee. New York: Macmillan, 1908–9.

Dictionary of Scientific Biography. 16 vols. Edited by C. C. Gillispie. New York: Charles Scribner's Sons, 1970–80.

Dobbs, Betty Jo. See Robert Siegfried.

Dodson, James. *The Anti-Logarithmic Canon. Being a Table of Numbers Consisting of Eleven Places of Figures, Corresponding to All Logarithms under 100000*. London, 1742.

——. *The Mathematical Repository. Containing Analytical Solutions of Five Hundred Questions, Mostly Selected from Scarce and Valuable Authors. Designed to Conduct Beginners to the More Difficult Properties of Numbers*. 3 vols. London, 1748–55.

Dolland, John. See Peter Dolland.

Dollond, Peter. *On Hadley's Quadrant & Sextant*. London, 1766.

——. *Some Account of the Discovery Made by the Late Mr. John Dollond, F.F.S. Which Led to the Grand Improvement of Refracting Telescopes*. . . . London, 1789.

Dolland, Peter, and John Dolland. *Description and Uses of the New Invented Universal Equatorial Instrument, or, Portable Observatory. With the Divided Object-Glass Micrometer*. London, [1772?].

Donovan, Arthur L. *Antoine Lavoisier: Science, Administration, and Revolution*. Oxford: Blackwell, 1993.

——. "Crawford, Adair." *DSB* 15:94–96.

——. *Philosophical Chemistry in the Scottish Enlightenment: The Doctrines and Discoveries of William Cullen and Joseph Black*. Edinburgh: Edinburgh University Press, 1975.

Dorling, Jon. "Henry Cavendish's Deduction of the Electrostatic Inverse Square Law from the Result of a Single Experiment." *Studies in the History and Philosophy of Science* 4 (1974): 327–48.

Dorn, Harold. "Smeaton, John." *DSB* 12:461–63.

"Douglas, James, Fourteenth Earl of Morton." *DNB* 5:1236–37.

Drew, Bernard. *The London Assurance, a Second Chronicle*. London: Printed for The London Assurance at the Curwen Press, Plaistow, 1949.

Dubbey, J. M. "Cotes, Roger." *DSB* 3:430–33.

Duncan, A. M. "The Functions of Affinity Tables and Lavoisier's List of Elements." *Ambix* 17 (1970): 26–42.

——. "Some Theoretical Aspects of Eighteenth-Century Tables of Affinity." Parts I and II. *Annals of Science* 18 (1962): 177–94, 217–32.

Dupree, A. Hunter. *Sir Joseph Banks and the Origins of Science Policy*. Minneapolis: The Associates of the James Ford Bell Library, University of Minnesota, 1984.

Dyment, S. A. "Some Eighteenth Century Ideas Concerning Aqueous Vapour and Evaporation." *Annals of Science* 2 (1937): 465–73.

Edelstein, Sidney M. "Priestley Settles the Water Controverswy." *Chymia* 1 (1948): 123–37.

Edwards, Edward. *Lives of the Founders of the British Museum; with Notices of Its Chief Augmentors and Other Benefactors, 1570–1870.* London, 1870.

Edwards, James. *A Companion from Lincoln to Brighthelmston, in Sussex; Consisting of a Set of Topographical Maps . . . .* London, 1789, 1801.

Ehrlich, Cyril. *The Music Profession in Britain since the Eighteenth Century: A Social History.* Oxford: Clarendon Press, 1985.

Eisenstaedt, J. "De l'influence de la gravitation sur la propagation de la lumière en théorie newtonienne. L'archéologie des trous noirs." *Archive for History of Exact Sciences* 42 (1991): 315–86.

Eklund, Jon. *The Incompleat Chymist. Being an Essay on the Eighteenth-Century Chemist in His Laboratory, with a Dictionary of Obsolete Chemical Terms of the Period.* Washington, DC: Smithsonian Institution, 1975.

Elkin, Robert. *The Old Concert Rooms of London.* London: Edward Arnold, 1955.

Ellis, Aytoun. *The Penny Universities: A History of Coffee-Houses.* London: Secker & Warburg, 1956.

Ellis, George E. *Memoir of Sir Benjamin Thompson, Count Rumford. With Notices of His Daughter.* Boston, 1871.

Ellis, Henry, ed. *Original Letters of Eminent Literary Men of the Sixteenth, Seventeenth, and Eighteenth Centuries.* London, 1843.

Emerson, William. *The Doctrine of Fluxions: Not Only Explaining the Elements Thereof, But Also Its Application and Use in the Several Parts of Mathematics and Natural Philosophy.* London, 1768.

Enfield, William. *Institutes of Natural Philosophy, Theoretical and Experimental . . . .* London, 1785.

"Englefield, Sir Henry Charles." *DNB* 6:792–93.

Esdaile, Arundell. *The British Museum Library: A Short History and a Survey.* London: George Allen & Unwin, 1946.

Evans, Joan. *A History of the Society of Antiquaries.* Oxford: Oxford University Press, 1956.

Everitt, C. W. F. "Gravitation, Relativity and Precise Experimentation." In *Proceedings of the First Marcel Grossmann Meeting on General Relativity*, edited by R. Ruffini, 545–615. Amsterdam: North-Holland, 1977.

Eyles, V. A. "The Extent of Geological Knowledge in the Eighteenth Century, and the Methods by Which It Was Diffused." In *Toward a History of Geology*, edited by Cecil J. Schneer, 159–83. Cambridge, Mass.: M.I.T. Press, 1969.

Fara, Patricia. *Sympathetic Attractions: Magnetic Practices, Beliefs, and Symbolism in Eighteenth-Century England.* Princeton: Princeton University Press, 1996.

Farrar, Kathleen R. "A Note on a Eudiometer Supposed to Have Belonged to Henry Cavendish." *British Journal for the History of Science* 1 (1963): 375–80.

Farrell, Maureen. *William Whiston.* New York: Arno, 1981.

Feigenbaum, L. "Brook Taylor and the Method of Increments." *Archive for History of Exact Sciences* 34 (1985): 1–140.

Feingold, Mordechai. See Dale Hoak.

Feldman, Theodore S. "Applied Mathematics and the Quantification of Experimental Physics: The Example of Barometric Hypsometry." *Historical Studies in the Physical Sciences* 15, no. 2 (1988): 127–97.

——. "Late Enlightenment Meteorology." In *The Quantifying Spirit in the Eighteenth Century*, edited by T. Frangsmyr, J. L. Heilbron, and R. E. Rider, 143–77. Berkeley: University of California Press, 1990.

Feliciangeli, Daniel. "Le développement de Nice au cours de la seconde moitié de XVIIIe siècle. Les Anglais à Nice." *Annales de la Faculté des Lettres et Sciences Humaines de Nice*, no. 19, 1973, pp. 45–67.

Ferguson, Donald N. *A History of Musical Thought*. 2d ed. New York and London: Appleton, Century, Crofts, 1935.

Ferguson, James. *An Introduction to Electricity*. . . . London, 1778.

Fiske, Roger. *English Theatre Music in the Eighteenth Century*. London: Oxford University Press, 1973.

Fiske, Roger. See H. Diack Johnstone.

Folkes, Martin. *A Table of English Silver Coins from the Norman Conquest to the Present Time. With Their Weights, Intrinsic Values, and Some Remarks upon the Several Pieces*. London, 1745.

Foote, George A. "Banks, Joseph." *DSB* 1:433–37.

Forbes, Eric G. "Mayer, Johann Tobias." *DSB* 9:232–35.

——. "The Origin and Development of the Marine Chronometer." *Annals of Science* 22 (1966): 1–25.

Force, James E. *William Whiston: Honest Newtonian*. Cambridge: Cambridge University Press, 1985.

Forster, E. M. *Marianne Thornton: A Domestic Biography, 1797–1887*. New York: Harcourt, Brace, 1956.

Foster, Joseph. *Alumni Oxoniensis: The Members of the University of Oxford, 1715–1886*. . . . 4 vols. London, 1891.

Fothergill, Brian. *Sir William Hamilton, Envoy Extraordinary*. New York: Harcourt, Brace & World, 1969.

Fox, Robert. *The Caloric Theory of Gases: From Lavoisier to Regnault*. Oxford: Clarendon Press, 1971.

Franklin, Benjamin. *Benjamin Franklin's Experiments. A New Edition of Franklin's Experiments and Observations on Electricity*. Edited with an historical introduction by I. B. Cohen. Cambridge, Mass.: Harvard University Press, 1941.

——. *Philosophical and Miscellaneous Papers*. London, 1787.

——. *The Papers of Benjamin Franklin*. Edited by L. W. Larabee (through vol. 14), W. R. Wilcox (through vol. 26), C. A. Lopez (vol. 27), and B. B. Oberg (from vol. 28). New Haven: Yale University Press, 1959-.

Fraser, Kevin J. "John Hill and the Royal Society in the Eighteenth Century." *Notes and Records of the Royal Society of London* 48 (1994): 43–67.

Freke, John. *An Essay to Shew the Cause of Electricity; and Why Some Things Are Non-Electricable*. London, 1746.

Freshfield, Douglas W., and H. F. Montagnier. *The Life of Horace Benedict de Saussure.* London: Edward Arnold, 1920.

Frick, George F. "Collinson, Peter." *DSB* 3:349–51.

Fry, Howard T. *Alexander Dalrymple (1737–1808) and the Expansion of British Trade.* London: Frank Cass, 1970.

Fullmer, J. Z. "Davy's Sketches of His Contemporaries." *Chymia* 12 (1966): 122–50.

Gaber, Stéphane. See Michel Parisse.

Garnett, Thomas. *Outlines of a Course of Lectures on Chemistry: Delivered at the Royal Institution of Great Britain, 1801.* London, 1801.

——. *Outlines of a Course of Lectures on Natural and Experimental Philosophy, Delivered at the Royal Institution of Great Britain, 1801.* London, 1801.

——. *Popular Lectures on Zoonomia, or the Laws of Animal Life, in Health and Disease.* London, 1804.

Garraty, John A. *The Nature of Biography.* New York: Knopf, 1957.

Gascoigne, John. *Cambridge in the Age of the Enlightenment: Science, Religion and Politics from the Restoration to the French Revolution.* Cambridge: Cambridge University Press, 1989.

——. *Joseph Banks and the English Enlightenment: Useful Knowledge and Polite Culture.* Cambridge: Cambridge University Press, 1994.

——. "Mathematics and Meritocracy: The Emergence of the Cambridge Mathematical Tripos." *Social Studies of Science* 14 (1984): 547–84.

Geikie, Archibald. *Annals of the Royal Society Club: The Record of a London Dining-Club in the Eighteenth and Nineteenth Centuries.* London: Macmillan, 1917.

——. *Founders of Geology.* 2d ed. London: Macmillan, 1905.

——. *Memoir of John Michell. . . .* Cambridge: Cambridge University Press, 1918.

George, M. Dorothy *London Life in the Eighteenth Century.* Harmondsworth: Penguin Books, 1966.

George III, King of Great Britain. *The Later Correspondence of George III.* Vol. 1: *December 1783 to January 1793,* edited by A. Aspinall. Cambridge: Cambridge University Press, 1962.

Getman, Frederick H. "Sir Charles Blagden, F.R.S." *Osiris* 3 (1937): 69–87.

Gibbs, F. W. *Joseph Priestley: Adventurer in Science and Champion of Truth.* London: T. Nelson, 1965.

——. "A Notebook of William Lewis and Alexander Chisholm." *Annals of Science* 8 (1952): 202–20.

Gilbert, L. F. "W. H. Wollaston Mss. at Cambridge." *Notes and Records of the Royal Society of London* 9 (1952): 311–32.

Gillespie, Richard. "Ballooning in France and Britain, 1783–1786: Aerostation and Adventurism." *Isis* 75 (1984): 249–68.

Gillispie, Charles Coulston. *Genesis and Geology: A Study in the Relations of Scientific Thought, Natural Theology, and Social Opinion in Great Britain, 1790–1850.* New York: Harper & Row, 1959.

——. "Laplace, Pierre-Simon, Marquis de." *DSB* 15: 273–403.

——. *The Montgolfier Brothers and the Invention of Aviation, 1783–1784.* Princeton: Princeton University Press, 1983.

——. *Science and Polity in France at the End of the Old Regime.* Princeton: Princeton University Press, 1980.

Gillmor, C. Stewart. *Coulomb and the Evolution of Physics and Engineering in Eighteenth-Century France.* Princeton: Princeton University Press, 1971.

"Gilpin, George." Poggendorff 1: col. 899.

Glass Works. Rotherham, 1751–1951. Rotherham: Beatson, Clark, 1952.

Godber, Joyce. *The Marchioness Grey of Wrest Park.* Vol. 47. Bedford: Bedfordshire Historical Record Society, 1968.

——. *Wrest Park and the Duke of Kent. Henry Grey (1671–1740).* 4th ed. Elstow Moot Hall: Bedfordshire County Council Arts and Recreation Department, 1982.

Golinski, Jan. "The Chemical Revolution and the Politics of Language." *The Eighteenth Century* 33 (1992): 238–51.

——. *Science as Public Culture: Chemistry and Enlightenment in Britain, 1760–1820.* Cambridge: Cambridge University Press, 1992.

Gooch, G. P. *Life of Charles, 3rd Earl Stanhope.* London: Longmans, 1914.

Goodfield, June. See Stephen Toulmin.

Gosse, Edmund William. *Gray.* New ed. London: Macmillan, 1906.

Gough, J. B. "Fahrenheit, Daniel Gabriel." *DSB* 4:516–17.

——. "Réaumur, René-Antione Ferchault de." *DSB* 11:327–35.

Gower, Leveson, Lord Granville. *Lord Granville Leveson Gower (First Earl Granville) Private Correspondence 1781 to 1821.* 2 vols. Edited by Castalia Countess Granville. London: John Murray, 1916.

Gowing, Ronald. *Roger Cotes, Natural Philosopher.* Cambridge: Cambridge University Press, 1983.

Grant, Francis. *A Letter to a Member of Parliament, Concerning the Free British Fisheries.* London, 1750.

'sGravesande, Willem Jacob van. *An Explanation of the Newtonian Philosophy, in Lectures Read to the Youth of the University of Leyden.* Translated by E. Stone. 2d edition. London, 1741.

——. *Mathematical Elements of Natural Philosophy, Confirmed by Experiments; or, an Introduction to Sir Isaac Newton's Philosophy,* Translated by J. T. Desagulier. 6th edition. London, 1747.

Great Britain. Historical Manuscripts Commission. *Calendar of the Stuart Papers Belonging to His Majesty the King Preserved at Windsor Castle.* Vol. 6. London: His Majesty's Stationery Office, 1916.

——. *The Manuscripts of the House of Lords.* Vol. 4: *1699–1702.* Vol. 7: *1706–1708.* London: His Majesty's Stationery Office, 1908, 1921.

——. *Report on Manuscripts in Various Collections.* Vol. 8: *The Manuscripts of the Hon. Frederick Lindley Wood; M. L. S. Clements, Esq.; Philip Unwin, Esq.* London: His Majesty's Stationery Office, 1913.

——. *Report on the Laing Manuscripts Preserved in the University of Edinborough* Vol. 2. London: His Majesty's Stationery Office, 1925.

——. *Report on the Manuscripts of J. B. Fortescue, Esq., Preserved at Dropmore.* Vol. 8. London: His Majesty's Stationery Office, 1912.

——. *Report on the Manuscripts of Lord Polwarth, Preserved at Mertoun House, Berwickshire.* Vols. 2 and 3. London: His Majesty's Stationery Office, 1916, 1931.

——. *Report on the Manuscripts of Sir William FitzHerbert, Bart., and Others.* London, 1893.

——. *Report on the Manuscripts of the Earl of Egmont. Diary of Viscount Percival Afterwards First Earl of Egmont.* Vols. 1–3. London: His Majesty's Stationery Office, 1920–23.

——. *Report on the Manuscripts of the Late Reginald Rawdon Hastings, Esq., of the Manor House, Ashby de la Zouche.* 4 vols. London: His Majesty's Stationery Office, 1928–47.

——. *Report on the Manuscripts of the Marquess of Downshire, Preserved at Easthampstead Park, Berks.* Vol. 1: *Papers of Sir William Trumbull.* Parts 1 and 2. London: His Majesty's Stationery Office, 1924.

Great Britain, Parliament. *House of Commons. Journals, 1547–1900.* New York: Readex Microprint, 1966.

Green, Frederick Charles. *Eighteenth-Century France: Six Essays.* New York: D. Appleton, 1931.

Green, George. *An Essay on the Application of Mathematical Analysis to the Theories of Electricity and Magnetism.* Nottingham, 1828.

Greene, John C. *American Science in the Age of Jefferson.* Ames: Iowa State University Press, 1984.

Greene, Mott T. *Geology in the Nineteenth Century: Changing Views of a Changing World.* Ithaca and London: Cornell University Press, 1982.

Gregory, David. *The Elements of Astronomy, Physical and Geometrical.* 2 vols. London, 1715.

Guerlac, Henry. "Black, Joseph." *DSB* 2:173–83.

——. "Chemistry as a Branch of Physics: Laplace's Collaboration with Lavoisier." *Historical Studies in the Physical Sciences* 7 (1976): 193–276.

——. "Joseph Black and Fixed Air: A Bicentenary Retrospective, with Some New or Little Known Material." *Isis* 48 (1957): 124–51.

——. "Lavoisier, Antoine-Laurent." *DSB* 8:66–91.

——. "Newton's Changing Reputation in the Eighteenth Century." In *Carl Becker's "Heavenly City" Revisited,* edited by Raymond O. Rockwood, 3–26. Ithaca: Cornell University Press, 1958.

——. "Quantification in Chemistry." *Isis* 52 (1961): 194–214.

——. "Where the Statue Stood: Divergent Loyalties to Newton in the Eighteenth Century." In *Aspects of the Eighteenth Century,* edited by Earl R. Wasserman, 317–34. Baltimore: The Johns Hopkins University Press, 1965.

Gunther, Albert E. *The Founders of Science at the British Museum, 1753–1900.* Halesworth: Halesworth Press, 1980.

——. *An Introduction to the Life of the Rev. Thomas Birch D.D., F.R.S., 1705–1766.* Halesworth: Halesworth Press, 1984.

——. "The Royal Society and the Foundation of the British Museum, 1753–1781." *Notes and Records of the Royal Society of London* 33 (1979): 207–16.

Gunther, Robert T. *Early Science in Cambridge.* Oxford: Clarendon Press, 1937.

Guyton de Morveau, Louis-Bernard, et al. *Method of Chymical Nomenclature.* Translated from the French edition of 1787 by James St. John. London, 1788.

Guyton de Morveau, Louis-Bernard, and Richard Kirwan. *A Scientific Correspondence During the Chemical Revolution: Louis-Bernard Guyton de Morveau and Richard Kirwan, 1782–1802.* Edited by E. Grison, M. Sadoun-Goupil, and P. Bret. Berkeley: Office for the History of Science and Technology, University of California at Berkeley, 1994.

Habakkuk, H. J. "England." In *The European Nobility in the Eighteenth Century*, edited by A. Goodwin, 1–21. London: Adam & Charles Black, 1953.

——. "Marriage Settlements in the Eighteenth Century." *Transactions of the Royal Historical Society* 32 (1950): 15–30.

Hacking, Ian. "Moivre, Abraham de." *DSB* 9:452–55.

Hackmann, Willem D. *Electricity from Glass: The History of the Frictional Electricity Machine 1600–1850.* Alphen aan den Rijn: Sijthoff & Noordhoff, 1978.

——. "The Relationship between Concept and Instrument Design in Eighteenth-Century Experimental Science." *Annals of Science* 36 (1979): 2–5=24.

——. "Swinden, Jan Hendrik van." *DSB* 13:183–84.

Hadcock, A. W. "Physical Optics at the Royal Society, 1660–1800." *British Journal for the History of Science* 1 (1962): 99–116.

Hadley, John. *A Plan of a Course of Chemical Lectures.* Cambridge, 1758.

"Hadley, John." *DNB* 8:879–80.

Hales, Stephen. *Vegetable Staticks: Or, an Account of Some Statical Experiments on the Sap in Vegetables . . . Also, a Specimen of an Attempt to Analyse the Air. . . .* 1727. Reprint, London: Macdonald, 1969.

Hall, A. Rupert. " 'sGravesande, Willem Jacob." *DSB* 5:509–11.

——. "Vigani, John Francis." *DSB* 14:26–27.

Hall, H., and F. T. J. Nicholas, eds. *Select Tracts and Table Books Relating to English Weights and Measures (1100–1742).* Camden Miscellany, vol. 15. London: Office of the Society, 1929.

Hall, Marie Boas. "Homberg, Wilhelm or Guillaume." *DSB* 6:477–78.

Hamilton, Hugh. *Four Introductory Lectures in Natural Philosophy.* London, 1774.

——. *A Geometrical Treatise of the Conic Sections. . . .* London, 1773.

——. *Philosophical Essays on the Following Subjects: I. On the Principles of Mechanics. II. On the Ascent of Vapours . . . III. Observations and Conjectures on the Nature of the Aurora Borealis, and the Tails of Comets.* London, 1766.

Hamilton, Max. "Symptoms and Assessment of Depression." In *Handbook of Affective Disorders*, edited by E. S. Paykel, 3–11. New York: Guilford, 1982.

Hankins, Thomas L. "Eighteenth-Century Attempts to Resolve the *Vis Viva* Controversy." *Isis* 56 (1965): 281–97.

——. *Science and the Enlightenment.* Cambridge: Cambridge University Press, 1985.

Hans, Nicholas A. *New Trends in Education in the Eighteenth Century.* London: Routledge & Kegan Paul, 1951.

Harcourt, W. Vernon. "Address," 3–45, with "Appendix," 45–68, followed by sixty pages of lithographed fascimiles of Cavendish's papers. *British Association Report,* 1839.

Hardin, Clyde L. "The Scientific Work of the Reverend John Michell." *Annals of Science* 22 (1966): 27–47.

Hardinge, George. *Biographical Anecdotes of Daniel Wray.* London, 1815.

Harrington, Robert. *A New System on Fire and Planetary Life . . . Also, an Elucidation of the Phaenomena of Electricity and Magnetism.* London, 1796.

"Harrington, Robert." *DNB* 8:1320–21.

Harris, John. *Lexicon Technicum; or, An Universal English Dictionary of Arts and Sciences* . . . Re-edited with a Supplement by a society of gentlemen. London, 1744.

Harris, Peter R. "Shyness and Embarrassment in Psychological Theory and Ordinary Language." In *Shyness and Embarrassment: Perspectives from Social Psychology,* edited by W. Ray Crozier, 59–86. Cambridge: Cambridge University Press, 1990.

Harris, William Snow. *Rudimentary Electricity.* . . . 4th ed. London, 1854.

Harrison, John. *An Account of the Proceedings, in Order to the Discovery of the Longitude.* London, 1763.

——. *The Principles of Mr. Harrison's Time-Keeper.* London, 1767.

Harvey, R. A. "The Private Library of Henry Cavendish (1731–1810)." *The Library* 2 (1980): 281–92.

Hatchett, Charles. *The Hatchett Diary: A Tour Through the Counties of England and Scotland in 1796 Visiting Their Mines and Manufactures.* Edited by Arthur Raistrick. Truro: D. Bradford Barton, 1967.

Hatton, Ragnhild Marie. *George I, Elector and King.* Cambridge, Mass.: Harvard University Press, 1978.

Hauksbee, Francis. *Physico-Mechanical Experiments on Various Subjects.* . . . 2d ed. London, 1719.

Haydn, Joseph Timothy. *The Book of Dignities: Continued to the Present Time (1894).* . . . Edited by N. and R. McWhirter. 3d ed. Baltimore: Genealogical Publishing Co., 1970.

Heathcote, Niels H. de V. See Douglas McKie.

Heathcote, Niels H. de V. See William Cleghorn.

Heberden, Ernest. "Correspondence of William Heberden, F.R.S. with the Reverend Stephen Hales and Sir Charles Blagden." *Notes and Records of the Royal Society of London* 39 (1985): 179–89.

Heberden, William. *Commentaries on the History and Cure of Diseases.* London, 1802.

"Heberden, William." *DNB* 7:359–60.

Heilbron, John L. "Aepinus, Franz Ulrich Theodosius." *DSB* 1:66–68.

———. *Electricity in the 17th and 18th Centuries: A Study of Early Modern Physics*. Berkeley: University of California Press, 1979.

———. *Physics at the Royal Society During Newton's Presidency*. Los Angeles: William Andrews Clark Memorial Library, 1983.

———. *Weighing Imponderables and Other Quantitative Science Around 1800*. Supplement to vol. 24, part 1 of *Historical Studies in the Physical and Biological Sciences*. Berkeley: University of California Press, 1993.

Heimann, P. M. "Ether and Imponderables." In *Conceptions of Ether: Studies in the History of Ether Theories, 1740–1900*, edited by G. N. Cantor and M. J. S. Hodge, 61–83. Cambridge: Cambridge University Press, 1981.

———. "'Geometry and Nature': Leibniz and Johann Bernoulli's Theory of Motion." *Centaurus* 21 (1977): 1–26.

———. "'Nature Is a Perpetual Worker': Newton's Aether and Eighteenth-Century Natural Philosophy." *Ambix* 20 (1973): 1–26.

———. "Newtonian Natural Philosophy and the Scientific Revolution." *History of Science* 11 (1973): 1–7.

Heimann, P. M., and J. E. McGuire. "Cavendish and the *Vis Viva* Controversy: A Leibnizian Postscript." *Isis* 62 (1970): 225–27.

Heimann, P. M., and J. E. McGuire. "Newtonian Forces and Lockean Powers: Concepts of Matter in 18th-Century Thought." *Historical Studies in the Physical Sciences* 3 (1971): 233–306.

Helsham, Richard. *A Course of Lectures in Natural Philosophy*. Edited by Bryan Robinson. 7th ed. Philadelphia, 1802.

Henderson, Alfred James. *London and the National Government, 1721–1742. A Study of City Politics and the Walpole Administration*. Durham: Duke University Press, 1945.

Hennell, Michael. *John Venn and the Clapham Sect*. London: Lutterworth, 1958.

Herschel, William. *The Scientific Papers of Sir William Herschel. . . .* 2 vols. Edited by J. L. E. Dreyer. London: Royal Society and Royal Astronomical Society, 1912.

"Herschel, Sir William." *DNB* 9:719–25.

Hervey, Lord John. *Memoirs of the Reign of George the Second from His Accession to the Death of Queen Caroline*. Edited by J. W. Croker. Vol. 1. London, 1848.

Hey, Max H. See Gavin De Beer.

Heyd, Michael. *Between Orthodoxy and the Enlightenment. Jean-Robert Chouet and the Introduction of Cartesian Science in the Academy of Geneva*. Boston: Martinus Nijhoff, 1982.

Hiebert, Erwin N. *Historical Roots of the Principle of Conservation of Energy*. Madison: State Historical Society of Wisconsin, 1962.

Higgins, Bryan. *Experiments and Observations Relating to Acetous Acid, Fixable Air, Dense Inflammable Air, Oils and Fuels; the Matter of Fire and Light. . . .* London, 1786.

Higgins, Bryan. *A Philosophical Essay Concerning Light*. London, 1776.

Hill, J. W. F. *The Letters and Papers of the Banks Family of Revesby Abbey, 1704–1760*. Hereford, England: Lincoln Record Society, 1952.

Hill, John. *Review of the Works of the Royal Society of London. . . .* London, 1751.

Hilts, Philip J. *Scientific Temperaments: Three Lives in Contemporary Science.* New York: Simon and Schuster, 1982.

Hindle, Brooke. *David Rittenhouse.* Princeton: Princeton University Press, 1964.

——. "Rittenhouse, David." *DSB* 11:471–73.

Hoak, Dale, and Mordechai Feingold, eds. *The World of William and Mary: Anglo-Dutch Perspectives on the Revolution of 1688–89.* Stanford: Stanford University Press, 1996.

Hobhouse, Hermione. *Lost London.* New York: Weathervane Books, 1971.

Hodges, M. J. S. See G. N. Cantor.

Holbrook, Mary. *Science Preserved: A Directory of Scientific Instruments in Collections in the United Kingdom and Eire.* London: Her Majesty's Stationery Office, 1992.

"Hollis, Thomas." *DNB* 9:1070–71.

Holmes, Geoffrey S. *Augustan England: Professions, State and Society, 1680–1730.* London: George Allen & Unwin, 1982.

——. *Britain After the Glorious Revolution 1689–1714.* New York: Macmillan, 1982.

——. *British Politics in the Age of Anne.* London: Macmillan, 1967.

——. *The Trial of Doctor Sacheverell.* London: Eyre Methuen, 1973.

Holmes, Geoffrey, and W. A. Speck, eds. *The Divided Society. Parties and Politics in England 1694–1716.* Documents of Modern History. New York: St. Martin's Press, 1968.

Holmes, Timothy. *Sir Benjamin Collins Brodie.* London, 1898.

Home, Roderick W. "Aepinus and the British Electricians: The Dissemination of a Scientific Theory." *Isis* 63 (1972): 190–204.

——. *Aepinus's Essay on the Theory of Electricity and Magnetism.* Translated by P. J. Connor. Princeton: Princeton University Press, 1979.

——. "Out of a Newtonian Straitjacket: Alternative Approaches to Eighteenth-Century Physical Science." In *Studies in the Eighteenth Century. IV. Papers Presented at the Fourth David Nichol Smith Memorial Seminar, Canberra 1976.* Edited by R. F. Brissenden and J. C. Eade, 235–49. Canberra: Australian National University Press, 1979.

——. "The Third Law in Newton's Mechanics." *British Journal for the History of Science* 4 (1968): 39–51.

"Horsburgh, James." *DNB* 9:1270.

Horwitz, Henry. *Parliament, Policy and Politics in the Reign of William III.* Newark: University of Delaware Press, 1977.

——. *Revolution Politicks. The Career of Daniel Finch, Second Earl of Nottingham, 1647–1730.* Cambridge: Cambridge University Press, 1968.

Hoskin, Michael A. "Herschel, Caroline Lucretia." *DSB* 6:322–23.

——. "Herschel, William," *DSB* 6:328–36.

——. *William Herschel and the Construction of the Heavens.* New York: American Elsevier, 1963.

——. *William Herschel. Pioneer of Sidereal Astronomy.* New York: Sheed & Hand, 1959.

Howse, Derek. "The Greenwich List of Observatories: A World List of Astronomical Observatories, Instruments and Clocks, 1670–1850." *Journal for the History of Astronomy* 17, pt. 4 (1986): 1–100.

——. *Greenwich Observatory*. Vol. 3: *The Buildings and Instruments*. London: Taylor & Francis, 1975.

——. *Nevil Maskelyne: The Seaman's Astronomer*. Cambridge: Cambridge University Press, 1989.

Hudson, Derek, and Kenneth W. Luckhurst. *The Royal Society of Arts, 1754–1954*. London: John Murray, 1954.

Hufbauer, Karl. "Crell, Lorenz Florenz Friedrich von." *DSB* 3:464–66.

——. "Klaproth, Martin Heinrich." *DSB* 7:394–95.

Hughes, Edward. "The Early Journal of Thomas Wright of Durham," *Annals of Science* 7 (1951): 1–24.

Hunter, John. *The Anthropological Treatises of Johann Friedrich Blumenbach . . . and the Inaugural Dissertation of John Hunter, MD. On the Varieties of Man*. Translated by T. Bendysche. London, 1865.

——. *Observations on the Diseases of the Army in Jamaica*. . . . 2d ed. London, 1796.

Hutton, Charles. *A Mathematical and Philosophical Dictionary* . . . . 2 vols. London, 1795–96.

——. *Tracts on Mathematical and Philosophical Subjects*. . . . 3 vols. London, 1812.

Hutton, James. *A Dissertation upon the Philosophy of Light, Heat, and Fire*. Edinburgh, 1794.

Irvine, William. *Essays, Chiefly on Chemical Subjects*. Edited by W. Irvine, Jr. London, 1805.

Irwin, Raymond. *The Origins of the English Library*. London: George Allen & Unwin, 1958.

Itard, Jean. "Legendre, Adrien-Marie." *DSB* 8:135–43.

Izard, Carroll E., and Marion C. Hyson. "Shyness as a Discrete Emotion." In *Shyness: Perspectives on Research and Treatment*, edited by W. H. Jones, T. M. Cheek, and S. R. Briggs, 147–60. New York: Plenum Press, 1986.

Jackman, W. T. *The Development of Transportation in Modern England*. 2 vols. Cambridge: Cambridge University Press, 1916.

Jacob, Margaret C. *The Cultural Meaning of the Scientific Revolution*. Philadelphia: Temple University Press, 1988.

——. *The Newtonians and the English Revolution 1689–1720*. Ithaca: Cornell University Press, 1976.

Jacquot, Jean. "Sir Charles Cavendish and His Learned Friends. A Contribution to the History of Scientific Relations between England and the Continent in the Earlier Part of the 17th Century. I. Before the Civil War. II. The Years of Exile." *Annals of Science* 8 (1952): 13–27, 175–91.

Janssens, Uta. *Matthieu Maty and the Journal Britannique, 1750–1755*. . . . Amsterdam: Holland University Press, 1975.

Jefferson, Thomas. *The Papers of Thomas Jefferson*. Vols. 11, 13, edited by Julian P. Boyd. Princeton: Princeton University Press, 1955, 1956.

Jenkinson, Charles, Lord Liverpool. *A Treatise on the Coins of the Realm; in a Letter to the King.* Oxford, 1805.

"Jenkinson, Charles, First Earl of Liverpool and First Baron Hawkesbury." *DNB* 10:746–47.

Johnstone, H. Diack, and Roger Fiske. *The Blackwell History of Music in Britain.* Vol. 4. *The Eighteenth Century.* Oxford: Basil Blackwell, 1988.

Jones, Henry Bence. *The Royal Institution: Its Founder and Its First Professors.* London, 1871.

Jones, Phillip S. "Cramer, Gabriel." *DSB* 3:459–62.

——. "Taylor, Brook." *DSB* 13:265–68.

Jones, William. *An Essay on the First Principles of Natural Philosophy. . . .* Oxford, 1762.

"Jones, William." *DNB* 10:1061–62.

Jorgensen, Bent Søren. "On a Text-Book Error: The Accuracy of Cavendish's Determination of the Oxygen Content of the Atmosphere." *Centarus* 12 (1968): 132–34.

Jungnickel, Christa, and Russell McCormmach. *Intellectual Mastery of Nature.* 2 vols. Chicago: University of Chicago Press, 1986.

Jurin, James. "An Essay upon Distinct and Indistinct Vision." In Robert Smith, *Opticks.* Vol. 2, appendix, pp. 115–170.

"Jurin, James." *DNB* 10:117–18.

Kagan, Jerome, J. Steven Reznick, and Nancy Snidman. "Biological Bases of Childhood Shyness." *Science* 240 (1988): 167–71.

Kaye, I. "Captain James Cook and the Royal Society." *Notes and Records of the Royal Society of London* 24 (1969): 7–18.

"Keene, Edmund." *DNB* 10:1191–92.

Keill, John. *An Introduction to the True Astronomy; or, Astronomical Lectures, Read in the Astronomical School of the University of Oxford.* London, 1721.

Kendrick, T. D. *The Lisbon Earthquake.* London: Methuen, 1956.

Kenyon, J. P. *Robert Spencer, Earl of Sunderland, 1641–1702.* London: Longmans, Green, 1958.

Kerridge, Eric. *The Agricultural Revolution.* London: Allen & Unwin, 1967.

Ketton-Cremer, Robert Wyndham. *Thomas Gray: A Biography.* Cambridge: Cambridge University Press, 1955.

King, Henry C. "Hadley, John." *DSB* 6:5–6.

——. *The History of the Telescope.* Cambridge, Mass.: Sky Publisher, 1955.

King, Lester S. "Stahl, Georg Ernst." *DSB* 12:599–606.

King-Hele, Desmond. *Doctor of Revolution: The Life and Genius of Erasmus Darwin.* London: Faber and Faber, 1977.

Kippis, Andrew. See John Pringle.

Kirwan, Richard. *An Essay on Phlogiston, and the Constitution of Acids.* New edition. London, 1789.

——. *An Estimate of the Temperature of Different Latitudes.* London, 1787.

——. *Geological Essays.* London, 1799.

Kirwan, Richard. See Louis-Bernard Guyton de Morveau.

Kisch, Bruno. *Scales and Weights: A Historical Outline.* New Haven: Yale University Press, 1965.

Kitchiner, William. *The Economy of the Eyes.* Pt. 2: *Of Telescopes; Being the Result of Thirty Years' Experiments with Fifty-One Telescopes, of from One to Nine Inches in Diameter.* London, 1825.

Kline, Morris. *Mathematical Thought from Ancient to Modern Times.* New York: Oxford University Press, 1972.

Knight, David M. "Beddoes, Thomas." *DSB* 1:563–64.

——. "Davy, Humphry," *DSB* 3:598–604.

Knight, Gowin. *An Attempt to Demonstrate, That All the Phaenomena in Nature May Be Explained by Two Simple Active Principles, Attraction and Repulsion: Wherein the Attractions of Cohesion, Gravity and Magnetism, Are Shewn to Be One and the Same; and the Phaenomena of the Latter Are More Particularly Explained.* London, 1748.

Koyré, Alexander. *Newtonian Studies.* London: Chapman & Hall, 1965.

Kryzhanovsky, Leonid N. "Why Cavendish Kept 'Coulomb's' Law a Secret." *Electronics World and Wireless World* 98 (1992): 847–48.

——. "The Fishy Tale of Early Electricity." *Electronics World and Wireless World* 99 (1993): 119–21.

Kuhn, Thomas S. "Mathematical Versus Experimental Traditions in the Development of Physical Science." In Kuhn, *The Essential Tension: Selected Studies in Scientific Tradition and Change,* 31–65. Chicago: Chicago University Press, 1977.

Kula, Witold. *Measures and Men.* Translated by R. Szreter. Princeton: Princeton University Press, 1986.

Labelye, Charles. *A Description of Westminster Bridge. . . .* London, 1751.

——. *The Present State of Westminster Bridge. . . .* London, 1743.

"La Blancherie (Mammès-Claude-Catherine Pahin Champlain de)." *Dictionnaire de biographie française.* Vol. 18, col. 1344. Paris: Librairie Letouzey et Ané, 1989.

Laissus, Yves. "La Condamine, Charles-Marie de." *DSB* 15:269–73.

Laplace, S. P. *Mécanique céleste.* Translated by N. Bowditch. Vol. 4. Boston, 1839.

Larmor, Joseph. *Mathematical and Physical Papers.* 2 vols. Cambridge: Cambridge University Press, 1929.

Laudan, Rachel. *From Mineralogy to Geology: The Foundations of a Science, 1630–1830.* Chicago: University of Chicago Press, 1987.

Lavoisier, Antoine Laurent. *Elements of Chemistry, in a New Systematic Order, Containing All the Modern Discoveries.* Translated from the French by R. Kerr. Edinburgh, 1790.

——. *Essays on the Effects Produced by Various Processes on Atmospheric Air; with a Particular View to an Investigation of the Constitution of the Acids.* Translated by T. Henry. Warrington, 1783.

Laymon, Ronald. "Demonstrative Induction, Old and New Evidence and the Accuracy of the Electrostatic Inverse Square Law." *Synthese* 99 (1994): 23–58.

LeFanu, William. "Home, Everard." *DSB* 6:478–79.

Leslie, John. *An Experimental Inquiry into the Nature and Propagation of Heat.* London, 1804.

Leslie, Peter Dugud. *A Philosophical Inquiry into the Cause of Animal Heat. . . .* London, 1778.

Lewis, William. *Commercium Philosophico-Technicum; or, The Philosophical Commerce of Arts: Designed as an Attempt to Improve Arts, Trades, and Manufactures.* London, 1763.

Lillywhite, Bryant. *London Coffee Houses. A Reference Book of Coffee Houses of the Seventeenth, Eighteenth, and Nineteenth Centuries.* London: George Allen & Unwin, 1963.

Lindeboom, G. A. *Boerhaave and Great Britain.* Leyden: Brill, 1974.

Lindroth, Sten. "Linnaeus (or von Linné), Carl." *DSB* 8:374–81.

London and the Advancement of Science. London: British Association for the Advancement of Science, 1931.

London County Council. *Survey of London.* Edited by F. H. W. Sheppard. Vol. 31: *The Parish of St. James Westminster.* Part 1: *South of Piccadilly.* Part 2: *North of Picadilly.* London: Athlone, 1960 and 1963.

——. *Survey of London.* Edited by Sir L. Gomme and P. Norman. Vol.5: *The Parish of St. Giles-in-the-Fields.* Part 2. London, 1914.

Long, J. C. See Leonard Carmichael.

Long, Roger. *Astronomy, In Five Books.* 2 vols. Cambridge, 1742, 1764, 1784.

"Long, Roger, D.D." *DNB* 12:109.

Lovett, Richard. *The Electrical Philosopher. Containing a New System of Physics Founded upon the Principle of an Universal Plenum of Elementary Fire. . . .* Worcester, 1774.

——. *Philosophical Essay, in Three Parts. . . .* Worcester, 1766.

"Lowther, James, Earl of Lonsdale." *DNB* 12: 217–20.

Lubbock, Constance A. *The Herschel Chronicle. The Life-Story of William Herschel and His Sister, Caroline Herschel.* Cambridge: Cambridge University Press, 1933.

Luckhurst, Kenneth W. See Derek Hudson.

Ludlam, William. *Astronomical Observations Made in St. John's College, Cambridge in the Years 1767 and 1768: With an Account of Several Astronomical Instruments.* London, 1769.

——. *Directions for the Use of Hadley's Quadrant, with Remarks on the Construction of That Instrument.* London, 1771.

——. *The Rudiments of Mathematics; Designed for the Use of Students at the Universities. . . .* Cambridge, 1785.

"Ludlam, William." *DNB* 12:254–55.

Lundgren, Anders. "The Changing Role of Numbers in 18th-Century Chemistry." In *The Quantifying Spirit in the 18th Century*, edited by T. Frangsmyr, J. L. Heilbron, and R. E. Rider, 245–66. Berkeley: University of California Press, 1990.

Luttrell, Narcissus. *A Brief Historical Relation of State Affairs from September 1678 to April 1714.* 6 vols. Oxford, 1857.

Lyon, John. *Experiments and Observations Made with a View to Point Out the Errors of the Present Received Theory of Electricity. . . .* London, 1780.

Lyons, Henry. "The Officers of the Society (1662–1860)." *Notes and Records of the Royal Society of London* 3 (1941): 116–40.

——. *The Royal Society, 1660–1940: A History of Its Administration under Its Charters.* Cambridge: Cambridge University Press, 1944.

Lysons, Daniel. *Environs of London; Being an Historical Account of the Towns, Villages, and Hamlets, within Twelve Miles of That Capital.* Vol. 1: *County of Surrey*. London, 1792. Vol. 2: *County of Middlesex*. London, 1795.

Lyte, H. C. Maxwell. *A History of Eton College 1440–1884.* Revised edition. London, 1889. Fourth edition, London: Macmillan, 1911.

McCann, H. Gilman. *Chemistry Transformed: The Paradigmatic Shift from Phlogiston to Oxygen.* Norwood: Ablex, 1978.

McClellan, James E., III. *Science Reorganized: Scientific Societies in the Eighteenth Century*. New York: Columbia University Press, 1985.

McClure, Ruth K. *Coram's Children: The London Foundling Hospital in the Eighteenth Century.* New Haven: Yale University Press, 1981.

McCormmach, Russell. "Cavendish, Henry." *DSB* 3 (1971): 155–59.

——"The Electrical Researches of Henry Cavendish." Ph.D. diss., Case Institute of Technology, 1967.

——. "Henry Cavendish: A Study of Rational Empiricism in Eighteenth-Century Natural Philosophy." *Isis* 60 (1969): 293–306.

——. "Henry Cavendish on the Proper Method of Rectifying Abuses." In *Beyond History of Science: Essays in Honor of Robert E. Schofield*, edited by E. Garber, 35–51. Bethlehem, PA: Lehigh University Press, 1990.

——. "Henry Cavendish on the Theory of Heat." *Isis* 79 (1988): 37–67.

——. "John Michell and Henry Cavendish: Weighing the Stars." *British Journal for the History of Science* 4 (1968): 126–55.

——. "The Last Experiment of Henry Cavendish." In *'No Truth Except in Details': Essays in Honor of Martin J. Klein.* Edited by A. J. Kox and Daniel M. Siegel, 1–30. Dordrecht: Kluwer Academic Publishers, 1995.

McCormmach, Russell. See Christa Jungnickel.

McCrae, Robert R., and Paul T. Costa, Jr. *Personality in Adulthood.* New York and London: The Guilford Press, 1990.

McCrea, Robert R. See Paul T. Costa, Jr.

McDonald, E. "Baumé, Antoine." *DSB* 1:527.

McEvoy, John G. "Continuity and Discontinuity in the Chemical Revolution." In *The Chemical Revolution: Essays in Reinterpretation.* Vol. 4, new series of *Osiris.* Edited by A. L. Donovan, 195–213. History of Science Society, 1988.

McEvoy, John G., and J. E. McGuire. "God and Nature: Priestley's Way of Rational Dissent." *Historical Studies in the Physical Sciences* 6 (1975): 325–404.

McGrath, Patrick. *The Merchant Adventurers of Bristol.* Bristol: The Society of Merchant Adventurers, 1975.

McGuire, J. E. See P. M. Heimann.

McKie, Douglas. "Priestley's Laboratory and Library and Other of His Effects." *Notes and Records of the Royal Society of London* 12 (1956): 114–36.

McKie, Douglas, and Niels H. de V. Heathcote. *The Discovery of Specific and Latent Heats.* London: Edward Arnold, 1935.

McKie, Douglas. See William Cleghorn.

McKie, Douglas. See J. R. Partington.

Maclaurin, Colin. *An Account of Sir Isaac Newton's Philosophical Discoveries.* . . . London, 1748.

——. *The Collected Letters of Colin Maclaurin.* Edited by S. Mills. Nanturch, Cheshire: Shiva, 1982.

Macquer, Pierre Joseph. *A Dictionary of Chemistry. Containing the Theory and Practice of That Science; Its Applications to Natural Philosophy, Natural History, Medicine, and Animal Economy.* . . . Translated by J. Keir. 2 vols. London, 1771. 2d ed. 3 vols. London, 1777.

——. *Elements of the Theory and Practice of Chemistry.* 2 vols. Translated from the French edition of 1756 by A. Reid. London, 1758.

Magellan, J.-H. de. *Essai sur la nouvelle théorie du feu élementaire, et de la chaleur des corps.* . . . London, 1780.

Marlborough, John Churchill, Duke of. *The Marlborough-Godolphin Correspondence.* 2 vols. Edited by H. L. Snyder. Oxford: Clarendon Press, 1975.

Marshall, Dorothy. *Dr. Johnson's London.* New York: John Wiley & Sons, 1968.

Marshall, John R. *Social Phobia: From Shyness to Stage Fright.* New York: Basic Books, 1995.

Martin, Benjamin. *A Catalogue of Philosophical, Optical, and Mathematical Instruments.* . . . London, n.d.

——. *A Course of Lectures in Natural and Experimental Philosophy, Geography and Astronomy . . . Exhibited and Explain'd on the Principles of the Newtonian Philosophy.* Reading, 1743.

——. *Description and Use of a Case of Mathematical Instruments.* . . . London, 1771.

——. *Description of a New, Portable Air-Pump and Condensing Engine.* London, 1766.

——. *A Description of the Nature, Construction, and Use of the Torricellian, or Simple Barometer. With a Scale of Rectification.* London, 1778.

——. *An Essay on Electricity: Being an Enquiry into the Nature, Cause and Properties Thereof on the Principles of Sir Isaac Newton's Theory of Vibrating Motion, Light and Fire.* Bath, 1746.

——. *A New and Comprehensive System of Mathematical Institutions, Agreeable to the Present State of the Newtonian Mathesis.* 2 vols. London, 1759–64.

——. *The New Art of Surveying by the Goniometer.* London, 1766.

——. *Philosophia Britannica: or a New and Comprehensive System of the Newtonian Philosophy, Astronomy, and Geography, in a Course of Twelve Lectures.* . . . 2 vols. Reading, 1747.

——. *A Plain and Familiar Introduction to the Newtonian Philosophy.* . . . London, 1751.

Martin, D. C. "Former Homes of the Royal Society." *Notes and Records of the Royal Society of London* 22 (1967): 12–19.

Martin, Thomas. "Origins of the Royal Institution." *British Journal for the History of Science* 1 (1962): 49–63.

Martine, George. *Essays on the Construction and Graduation of Thermometers, and on the Heating and Cooling of Bodies.* new ed. Edinburgh, 1792.

——. *Essays Medical and Philosophical.* London, 1740.

"Maskelyne, Nevil." *DNB* 12:1299–1301.

Matsuo, Yukitoshi. "Henry Cavendish: A Scientist in the Age of the *Révolution chimique.*" *Japanese Studies in the History of Science* 14 (1975): 83–94.

Maty, Matthew. *Memoire sur la vie et sur les ecrits de Mr. Abraham de Moivre.* The Hague, 1760.

"Maty, Matthew." *DNB* 13:76–79.

[Maty, Paul]. *An Authentic Narrative of the Dissentions and Debates in the Royal Society. Containing the Speeches at Large of Dr. Horsley, Dr. Maskelyne, Mr. Maseres, Mr. Poore, Mr. Glenie, Mr. Watson, and Mr. Maty.* London, 1784.

Maxwell, James Clerk. "On the Unpublished Electrical Papers of the Hon. Henry Cavendish." *Proc. Camb. Phil. Soc.* 3 (1877): 86–89.

——. *The Scientific Letters and Papers of James Clerk Maxwell.* Vol. 2: *1862–1873,* edited by P. M. Harman. Cambridge: Cambridge University Press, 1995.

Meacham, Standish. *Henry Thornton of Clapham, 1760–1815.* Cambridge, Mass.: Harvard University Press, 1964.

"Memoirs of the Late Frederick Cavendish, Esq." *Gentleman's Magazine* 82 (1812): 289–91.

Metzger, Hélène. *Newton, Stahl, Boerhaave et la doctrine chimique.* Paris: Librairie Felix Alcan, 1930.

Meyer, Gerald Dennis. *The Scientific Lady in England, 1650–1760.* . . . Berkeley: University of California Press, 1955.

Michell, John. *A Treatise of Artificial Magnets; in Which Is Shewn an Easy and Expeditious Method of Making Them, Superior to the Best Natural Ones.* . . . Cambridge, 1750.

"Michell, John." *DNB* 13:333–34.

Middleton, William E. Knowles. "Bouguer, Pierre." *DSB* 2:343–44.

——. *The History of the Barometer.* Baltimore: The Johns Hopkins University Press, 1964.

——. *A History of the Thermometer and Its Use in Meteorology.* Baltimore: The Johns Hopkins University Press, 1966.

——. *Invention of the Meteorological Instruments.* Baltimore: The Johns Hopkins University Press, 1969.

Millburn, John R. "Benjamin Martin and the Royal Society." *Notes and Records of the Royal Society of London* 28 (1973): 15–23.

——. *Benjamin Martin: Author, Instrument-Maker, and "Country Showman."* Leyden: Noordhoff, 1976.

Miller, David Philip. "The 'Hardwicke Circle': The Whig Supremacy and Its Demise in the Eighteenth-Century Royal Society." Forthcoming in *Notes and Records of the Royal Society of London.*

——. "'Into the Valley of Darkness': Reflections on the Royal Society in the Eighteenth Century." *History of Science* 27 (1989): 155–66.

——. "Sir Joseph Banks: An Historiographical Perspective." *History of Science* 19 (1981): 284–92.

Miller, Edward. *That Noble Cabinet: A History of the British Museum*. London: Deutsch, 1973. Athens, Ohio: Ohio University Press, 1974.

Miller, Jean A. "Enlightenment: Error and Experiment. *Henry Cavendish's Electrical Researches*." M.A. diss., Virginia Polytechnic and State University, 1997.

Mintz, Samuel I. "Hobbes, Thomas." *DSB* 6:444–51.

Mitchell, L. G., and L. S. Sutherland, ed. *The History of the University of Oxford*, vol. 5: *The Eighteenth Century*. Oxford: Clarendon Press, 1986.

Moivre, Abraham de. *The Doctrine of Chances: or, A Method of Calculating the Probability of Events in Play*. London, 1718.

——. *Miscellanea analytica de seriebus et quadraturis*. . . . London, 1730.

——. *A Treatise of Annuities on Lives*. London, 1725.

"Mongez (Jean-André)." *Biographie universelle*. New ed. Vol. 28, p. 622. Paris, 1813.

Monk, James Henry. *The Life of Richard Bentley*. . . . 2d ed. 2 vols. London, 1833.

Montagnier, H. F. See Douglas W. Freshfield.

Montagu of Beaulier, Edward John B. D. S., Lord. *More Equal Than Others: The Changing Fortunes of the British and European Aristocracies*. London: Michael Joseph, 1970.

Morse, E. W. "Smith, Robert." *DSB* 12:477–78.

——. "Young, Thomas." *DSB* 14:562–72.

"Morton, Charles." *DNB* 13:1047–48.

Multhauf, Lettie S. "Schröter, Johann Hieronymus." *DSB* 12:226.

Munk, W. *The Roll of the Royal College of Physicians of London. Comprising Biographical Sketches of All the Eminent Physicians Whose Names Are Recorded in the Annals*. 4 vols. London, 1878.

Muntendam, Alida M. "Marum, Martin (Martinus) van." *DSB* 9:151–53.

Murray, Craig C. *Benjamin Vaughan (1751–1835). The Life of an Anglo-American Intellectual*. New York: Arno, 1982.

Musschenbroek, Petrus van. *The Elements of Natural Philosophy. Chiefly Intended for the Use of Students in Universities*. 2 vols. Translated by J. Colson. London, 1744.

Musson, A. E., and E. Robinson. *Science and Technology in the Industrial Revolution*. Toronto: University of Toronto Press, 1969.

Nairne, Edward. *Directions for Using the Electrical Machine, As Made and Sold by Edward Nairne, Optical, Philosophical, and Mathematical Instrument-Maker*. London, 1764.

Namier, L. B. *Crossroads of Power: Essays on Eighteenth-Century England*. London: H. Hamilton, 1962.

——. *The Structure of Politics at the Accession of George III*. London: Macmillan, 1929. 2d ed. London: Macmillan, 1957.

Namier, L. B. and John Brooke. *The History of Parliament: The House of Commons 1754–1790*. 3 vols. London: Her Majesty's Stationery Office, 1964.

Neumann, Caspar. *The Chemical Works . . . Abridged and Methodized. With Large Additions, Containing the Later Discoveries and Improvements Made in Chemistry and the Arts Depending Thereon.* Translated by W. Lewis. London, 1759.

Newton, Isaac. *Mathematical Papers of Isaac Newton.* 8 vols. Edited by D. T. Whiteside. Cambridge: Cambridge University Press, 1967–81.

——. *Opticks; or A Treatise of the Reflections, Refractions, Inflections and Colours of Light.* Based on the 4th ed. 1730. Reprint, New York: Dover Publications, 1952.

——. *Sir Isaac Newton's Mathematical Principles of Natural Philosophy and His System of the World.* Translated by Andrew Motte in 1729 from the 3d ed. 1726. 2 vols. Revised translation and notes by Florian Cajori. Berkeley and Los Angeles: University of California Press, 1962.

——. *Universal Arithmetick; or, A Treatise of Arithmetical Composition and Resolution. . . .* Translated by J. Raphson. London, 1720.

Nichols, John. *Illustrations of the Literary History of the Eighteenth Century. . . .* 8 vols. London, 1817–58.

——. *Literary Anecdotes of the Eighteenth Century. . . .* 9 vols. London, 1812–16.

Nichols, R. H., and F. A. Wray. *The History of the Foundling Hospital.* London: Oxford University Press, 1935.

Nicholson, William. *A Dictionary of Chemistry, Exhibiting the Present State of the Theory and Practice of That Science. . . .* 2 vols. in 1. London, 1795.

——. *The First Principles of Chemistry.* London, 1790.

——. *An Introduction to Natural Philosophy.* 2 vols. London, 1781.

Nicolson, William. *The London Diaries of William Nicolson, Bishop of Carlisle 1702–1718.* Edited by C. Jones and G. Holmes. Oxford: Clarendon Press, 1985.

Nishikawa, Sugiko. "The Vaudois Baptism of Henry Cavendish." *Proceedings of the Huguenot Society* 26 (1997): 660–63.

"Norris, William." *DNB* 14:591.

North, J. D. "Hornsby, Thomas." *DSB* 6:511–12.

——. *The Norton History of Astronomy and Cosmology.* New York: W. W. Norton, 1995.

O'Donoghue, Yolande. *William Roy 1726–1790. Pioneer of the Ordnance Survey.* London: British Museum, 1977.

Oliver, J. "William Borlase's Contributions to Eighteenth-Century Meteorology and Climatology." *Annals of Science* 25 (1969): 275–317.

Palter, Robert. "Early Measurements of Magnetic Force." *Isis* 63 (1972): 544–58.

Pannekoek, A. *A History of Astronomy.* New York: Interscience, 1961.

Pares, Richard. *King George III and the Politicians.* Oxford: Clarendon Press, 1953.

Paris, John Ayrton. *The Life of Sir Humphry Davy.* London, 1831.

Parisse, Michel, Stéphane Gaber, and Gérard Canini. *Grandes dates de l'histoire lorraine.* Nancy, France: Service des Publications de l'Université de Nancy II, 1982.

"Parker, George, Second Earl of Macclesfield." *DNB* 15:234–35.

"Parker, Thomas, First Earl of Macclesfield." *DNB* 15:278–82.

Partington, J. R. *A History of Chemistry*. Vols. 2 and 3. London: Macmillan; New York: St. Martin's Press, 1961–62.

——. *A Short History of Chemistry*. 3d edition. New York: Harper & Brothers, 1960.

Partington, J. R., and Douglas McKie. "Historical Studies on the Phlogiston Theory. 1. The Levity of Phlogiston; 2. The Negative Weight of Phlogiston; 3. Light and Heat in Combustion; 4. Last Phases of the Theory." *Annals of Science* 2 (1937): 361–404; 3 (1938): 1–58, 337–71; 4 (1939): 113–49.

Partington, J. R. See T. S. Wheeler.

Pas, P. W. van der. "Ingen-Housz, Jan." *DSB* 7:11–16.

Peacock, George. *Life of Thomas Young, M.D., F.R.S.* . . . London, 1855.

"Pearson, George." See J. C. Poggendorff. Vol. 2, cols. 383–84.

Pearson, John. *The Serpent and the Stag: The Saga of England's Powerful and Glamourous Cavendish Family from the Age of Henry the Eighth to the Present.* New York: Holt, Rinehart & Winston, 1983.

Pemberton, Henry. *A Course of Chemistry, Divided into Twenty-Four Lectures*. . . . London, 1771.

——. *A View of Sir Isaac Newton's Philosophy*. Dublin, 1728.

Perkins, James Breck. *France under the Regency with a Review of the Administration of Louis XIV*. Boston and New York, 1892.

Perrin, Carleton E. "Joseph Black and the Absolute Levity of Phlogiston." *Annals of Science* 40 (1983): 109–37.

Pfister, Christian. *Histoire de Nancy*. Tome III. Paris and Nancy: Berger-Levrault, 1908.

Philip, Alex J. *Hampstead, Then and Now. An Historical Topography*. London: George Routledge, 1912.

Philippovich, Eugen von. *History of the Bank of England, and Its Financial Services to the State*. 2d ed. Translated by C. Meredith. Washington, DC: Government Printing Office, 1911.

Philosophical Magazine. *Natural Philosophy Through the Eighteenth Century and Allied Topics*. Commemoration number to mark the 150th anniversary of the foundation of the magazine. Edited by Allen Ferguson. London: Taylor & Francis, 1948.

Phipps, Constantine John. *A Voyage Towards the North Pole, Undertaken by His Majesty's Command, 1773*. London, 1774.

Pilet, P. E. "Senebier, Jean." *DSB* 12:308–9.

Playfair, John. *Outlines of Natural Philosophy, Being Heads of Lectures Delivered in the University of Edinburgh*. 2 vols. Edinburgh, 1812, 1814.

——. *The Works of John Playfair*. 4 vols. Edited by J. G. Playfair. Edinburgh, 1822.

Plumb, J. H. *Men and Centuries*. Boston: Houghton Mifflin, 1963.

——. *Sir Robert Walpole*. Vol. 1: *The Making of a Statesman*. London: Cresset, 1956. Vol. 2: *The King's Minister*. London: Cresset, 1960.

Poggendorff, J. C. *Biographisch-Literarisches Handwörterbuch zur Geschichte der exacten Wissenschaften*. 2 vols. Leipzig, 1863.

Pollock, John. *Wilberforce*. London: Constable, 1977.

Porter, Roy. *English Society in the Eighteenth Century*. Harmondsworth: Penguin, 1982.

——. "The Enlightenment in England." In *The Enlightenment in National Context*. Edited by Roy Porter and Mikulás Teich, 1–18. Cambridge: Cambridge University Press, 1981.

——. *The Making of Geology: Earth Science in Britain, 1660–1815*. Cambridge: Cambridge University Press, 1977.

——. "Science, Provincial Culture, and Public Opinion in Enlightenment England." *British Journal of 18th-Century Studies* 3 (1980): 20–46.

Poynting, J. H. *The Mean Density of the Earth*. London, 1894.

Priestley, Joseph. *Experiments and Observations Relating to Various Branches of Natural Philosophy*. . . . London, 1781.

——. *The History and Present State of Discoveries Relating to Vision, Light, and Colours*. 2 vols. London, 1772.

——. *The History and Present State of Electricity, with Original Experiments*. London, 1767.

——. *A Scientific Autobiography of Joseph Priestley (1733–1804)*. Edited by Robert E. Schofield. Cambridge, Mass.: M.I.T. Press, 1966.

Pringle, John. *A Discourse on the Attraction of Mountains, Delivered at the Anniversary Meeting of the Royal Society, November 30, 1775*. London, 1775.

——. *A Discourse on the Torpedo Delivered at the Anniversary Meeting of the Royal Society, November 30, 1774*. London, 1775.

——. *Six Discourses, Delivered by Sir John Pringle, Bart. When President of the Royal Society; on Occasion of Six Annual Assignments of Sir Godfrey Copley's Medal. To Which Is Prefixed the Life of the Author. By Andrew Kippis, D.D. F.R.S. and S.A.* London, 1783.

"Pringle, Sir John." *DNB* 16:386–88.

Quill, Humphrey. *John Harrison: The Man Who Found Longitude*. London: Baker, 1966.

Ramsay, William. *The Gases of the Atmosphere: The History of Their Discovery*. London, 1896.

——. *The Life and Letters of Joseph Black, M.D.* London: Constable, 1918.

Ramsden, Jesse. *An Account of Experiments to Determine the Specific Gravity of Fluids*. London, 1792.

——. *Description of an Engine for Dividing Mathematical Instruments*. London, 1771.

Rappaport, Rhoda. "Rouelle, Hilaire-Marin." *DSB* 11:564.

Ravetz, J. "The Representation of Physical Quantities in Eighteenth-Century Mathematical Physics." *Isis* 52 (1961): 7–20.

Read, John. *A Summary View of the Spontaneous Electricity of the Earth and Atmosphere*. . . . London, 1793.

Roberts, Lissa. "The Death of the Sensuous Chemist: The 'New' Chemistry and the Transformation of Sensuous Technology." *Studies in History and Philosophy of Science* 26 (1995): 503–29.

"Robertson, Abraham." *DNB* 16:1284–85.

Robins, Benjamin. *Mathematical Tracts of the Late Benjamin Robins*. . . . 2 vols. Edited by James Wilson. London, 1761.

Robinson, Bryan. *A Dissertation on the Aether of Sir Isaac Newton.* Dublin, 1743.

Robinson, Eric. "James Watt, Engineer and Man of Science." *Notes and Records of the Royal Society of London* 24 (1969): 221–32.

Robinson, Eric. See Musson, A. E.

Robinson, Mary. *Beaux and Belles of England.* London: Grolier Society, n.d.

Robison, John. *A System of Mechanical Philosophy.* . . . 4 vols. Edited with notes by David Brewster. Edinburgh, 1822.

Roger, Jacques. "Whiston, William." *DSB* 14:295–96.

Rolleston, Humphry. "The Two Heberdens." *Annals of Medical History* 5 (1933): 409–24, 566–83.

Ronan, Colin A. "Halley, Edmond." *DSB* 6:67–72.

——. *Edmund Halley.* New York: Doubleday, 1969.

Rowley, William. *A Treatise on Madness and Suicide, with the Modes of Determining With Precision Mental Affections, in a Legal Point of View, and Containing Objections to Vomiting, Opium, and Other Mal-Practices, &c. &c.* London, 1804.

Rowning, John. *A Compendious System of Natural Philosophy. With Notes Containing Mathematical Demonstrations, and Some Occasional Remarks.* 4th ed. London, 1745.

"Roy, William." *DNB* 17:371–73.

Royal Institution of Great Britain. *The Archives of the Royal Institution of Great Britain in Facsimile. Minutes of Managers' Meetings 1799–1900.* Vols. 1 and 2 (in one volume), edited by F. Greenaway. Ilkley, Yorkshire: Published in association with the Royal Institution of Great Britain by the Scolar Press Limited, 1971.

Royal Society of London. *The Record of the Royal Society at London for the Promotion of Natural Knowledge.* 4th ed. London: Royal Society of London, 1940.

Rubini, Dennis. *Court and Country 1688–1702.* London: Rupert Hart-Davis, 1967.

Rudé, George. *Hanoverian London 1714–1808.* Berkeley: University of California Press, 1971.

Rudolf, R. de M. "The Clapham Sect." In *Clapham and the Clapham Sect,* edited by E. Baldwin, 89–142. Clapham: Clapham Antiquarian Society, 1927.

Ruestow, Edward G. *Physics at Seventeenth and Eighteenth-Century Leiden: Philosophy and the New Science in the University.* The Hague: Martinus Nijhoff, 1973.

Ruffini, R., ed. *Proceedings of the First Marcel Grossmann Meeting on General Relativity.* Amsterdam: North-Holland, 1977.

Russell, Lord John, Fourth Duke of Bedford. *Correspondence of John, Fourth Duke of Bedford.* 3 vols. Edited by Lord John Russell. London, 1842–46.

Russell, Lady Rachel. *Letters of Lady Russell; from the Manuscript in the Library at Woburn Abbey.* 5th ed. London 1793.

Russell-Wood, J. "The Scientific Work of William Brownrigg, M.D., F.R.S. (1711–1800)–I." *Annals of Science* 6 (1950): 436–47.

Rutherforth, Thomas. *A System of Natural Philosophy, Being a Course of Lectures in Mechanics, Optics, Hydrostatics, and Astronomy; Which Are Read in St Johns College Cambridge. . . .* 2 vols. Cambridge, 1748.

"Rutherforth, Thomas." *DNB* 17:499–500.

Sachse, William L. *Lord Somers: A Political Portrait.* Manchester: Manchester University Press, 1975.

Salmon. *A Short View of the Families of the Present Nobility.* 3d ed. London, 1761.

Sampson, R. A., and A. E. Conrady. "On Three Huygens Lenses in the Possession of the Royal Society of London." *Proceedings of the Royal Society of Edinburgh* 49 (1928–29): 289–99.

Saunderson, Nicholas. *Elements of Algebra. . . .* 2 vols. Cambridge, 1740.

——. *The Method of Fluxions Applied to a Select Number of Useful Problems; . . . and an Explanation of the Principal Propositions of Sir Isaac Newton's Philosophy.* London, 1756.

"Saunderson or Sanderson, Nicholas." *DNB* 17:820–22.

Saussure, Horace Bénédict de. *Relation abrégée d'un voyage à la cime du Mont-Blanc.* Genève, 1787.

——. *Voyages dans les Alpes, précédés d'un essai sur l'histoire naturelle des environs de Genève.* 4 vols. Neuchâtel, 1779–96.

Schaffer, Simon. "Natural Philosophy and Public Spectacle in the 18th Century." *History of Science* 21 (1983): 1–43.

Scheele, Karl Wilhelm. *The Chemical Essays of Charles-William Scheele.* Translated with additions by T. Beddoes. London, 1786.

——. *Chemical Observations and Experiments on Air and Fire.* Translated by J. R. Forster, with notes by Richard Kirwan. London, 1780.

Schneider, Ivo. "Der Mathematiker Abraham de Moivre (1667–1754)." *Archive for History of Exact Sciences* 5 (1968): 177–317.

Schofield, Robert E. "The Counter-Reformation in Eighteenth-Century Science, Last Phase." *Perspectives in the History of Science and Technology*, edited by Duane H. D. Roller, 39–54. Norman: University of Oklahoma Press, 1971.

——. "Electrical Researches of Joseph Priestley." *Archives Internationales d'Histoire des Sciences*, No. 64 (1963): 277–86.

——. "Joseph Priestley, Natural Philosopher." *Ambix* 14 (1967): 1–15.

——. "Joseph Priestley, the Nature of Oxidation and the Nature of Matter." *Journal of the History of Ideas* 25 (1964): 285–94.

——. *The Lunar Society of Birmingham. A Social History of Provincial Science and Industry in Eighteenth-Century England.* Oxford: Oxford University Press, 1963.

——. *Mechanism and Materialism: British Natural Philosophy in an Age of Reason.* Princeton: Princeton University Press, 1970.

——. "Priestley, Joseph." *DSB* 11:139–47.

——. "Priestley Settles the Water Controversy." *Chymia* 9 (1964): 71–76.

Schofield, Robert E. See D. G. C. Allan.

Schofield, Robert E. See Joseph Priestley.

Schwoerer, Lois G. *Lady Rachel Russell. "One of the Best of Women"*. Baltimore: The Johns Hopkins University Press, 1988.

Scott, E. L. "Blagden, Charles." *DSB* 2:186.

——. "Hatchett, Charles." *DSB* 6:166–67.

——. "Kirwan, Richard." *DSB* 7:387–90.

——. "The 'Macbridean Doctrine' of Air; an Eighteenth-Century Explanation of Some Biochemical Processes Including Photosynthesis." *Ambix* 17 (1970): 43–57.

——. "Pearson, George." *DSB* 10L 445–47.

——. "Richard Kirwan, J. H. de Magellan, and the Early History of Specific Heat." *Annals of Science* 38 (1981): 141–53.

——. "Rutherford, Daniel." *DSB* 12:24–25.

"Scott, George Lewis." *DNB* 17:961–62.

Scott, Wilson L. *The Conflict Between Atomism and Conservation Theory, 1644–1860.* New York: Elsevier, 1970.

Sedgwick, Romney. *The History of Parliament: The House of Commons 1715–1754.* 2 vols. New York: Oxford University Press, 1970.

Shapin, Steven. "The House of Experiment in Seventeenth-Century England." *Isis* 79 (1988): 373–404.

——. "'A Scholar and a Gentleman': The Problematic Identity of the Scientific Practitioner in Early Modern England." *History of Science* 29 (1991): 279–327.

——. *A Social History of Truth: Civility and Science in Seventeenth-Century England.* Chicago: Chicago University Press, 1994.

Sheets-Pyenson, Susan. "New Directions for Scientific Biography: The Case of Sir William Dawson." *History of Science* 28 (1990): 399–410.

Shepherd, Anthony. *The Heads of a Course of Lectures in Experimental Philosophy Read at Christ College.* Cambridge, n.d.

Shuckburgh, George. *Observations Made in Savoy, in Order to Ascertain the Height of Mountains by Means of the Barometer; Being an Examination of Mr. De Luc's Rules, Delivered in His Récherches sur les Modifications de l'Atmosphere. Read at the Royal Society, May 18 and 15, 1777.* London, 1777.

"Shuckburgh-Evelyn, Sir George Augustus William." *DNB* 18:167–68.

Sichel, Walter. *Bolingbroke and His Times. The Sequel.* New York: Greenwood, 1968.

Sidgwick, J. B. *William Herschel: Explorer of the Heavens.* London: Faber and Faber, 1953.

Siegfried, Robert. "The Chemical Revolution in the History of Science." In *The Chemical Revolution: Essays in Reinterpretation.* Vol. 4, new series of *Osiris*, edited by A. L. Donovan, 34–50. History of Science Society, 1988.

Siegfried, Robert, and Betty Jo Dobbs. "Composition, a Neglected Aspect of the Chemical Revolution." *Annals of Science* 24 (1968): 275–93.

Sime, James. *William Herschel and His Work.* New York: Charles Scribner's Sons, 1900.

Simpson, Thomas. *The Doctrine and Application of Fluxions.* 2 vols. London, 1750.

——. *Miscellaneous Tracts on Some Curious and Very Interesting Subjects in Mechanics, Physical-Astronomy, and Speculative Mathematics, Wherein the Precession of the Equinox, the Nutation of the Earth's Axis, and the Motion of the Moon in Her Orbit Are Determined.* London, 1757.

——. *The Nature and Doctrine of Chance.* London, 1740.

Singer, Dorothea Waley. "Sir John Pringle and His Circle–Part I. Life." ". . .–Part III. Copley Discourses." *Annals of Science* 6 (1949): 127–80 and 6 (1950): 248–61.

Sivin, Nathan. "William Lewis (1708–1781) as a Chemist." *Chymia* 8 (1962): 63–88.

Six, James. *Construction and Use of a Thermometer for Shewing the Extremes of Temperature in the Atmosphere, During the Observer's Absence. . . .* London, 1794.

Skempton, A. W., and Joyce Brown. "John and Edward Troughton, Mathematical Instrument Makers." *Notes and Records of the Royal Society of London* 27 (1973): 233–49.

Skempton, A. W., ed. *John Smeaton, FRS.* London: Telford, 1981.

Sloan, W. R. "Sir Hans Sloan, F.R.S.: Legend and Lineage." *Notes and Records of the Royal Society of London* 35 (1980): 125–33.

Smeaton, John. *Experimental Enquiry Concerning the Natural Powers of Wind and Water.* London, 1794.

——. *Reports of the Late John Smeaton, F.R.S. Made on Various Occasions, in the Course of His Employment as a Civil Engineer.* 4 vols. Edited by the Society of Civil Engineers. London, 1812–14.

Smeaton, W. A. "Bergman, Torbern Olof." *DSB* 2:4–8.

——. "Guyton de Morveau, Louis Bernard." *DSB* 5:600–4.

——. "Macquer, Pierre Joseph." *DSB* 8:618–24.

——. "Montgolfier, Étienne Jacques de; Montgolfier, Michel Joseph de," *DSB* 9:492–94.

Smiles, Samuel. *The Huguenots: Their Settlements, Churches, and Industries in England and Ireland.* New York, 1868.

——. *Lives of the Engineers. Harbors–Lighthouses–Bridges. Smeaton and Rennie.* Rev. ed. London, 1874.

Smith, Edward. *The Life of Sir Joseph Banks.* London: John Lane, 1911.

Smith, Eric E. F. *Clapham.* London: London Borough of Lambeth, 1976.

Smith, James Edward. *Memoir and Correspondence of the Late Sir James Edward Smith, M.D.* 2 vols. Edited by Lady Smith. London, 1832.

Smith, James Edward, ed. *A Selection of the Correspondence of Linnaeus, and Other Naturalists.* 2 vols. London, 1821.

Smith, Robert. *A Compleat System of Opticks in Four Books, viz. A Popular, a Mathematical, a Mechanical, and a Philosophical Treatise. To Which Are Added Remarks upon the Whole.* 2 vols. Cambridge, 1738.

——. *Harmonics, or The Philosophy of Musical Sounds.* 2d ed. Cambridge, 1759.

"Smith, Robert." *DNB* 18:517–19.

Smithson, James. *The Scientific Writings of James Smithson.* Washington, 1879.

"Smithson, James." *DNB* 18:579–81.

Snelders, H. A. M. "Troostwijk, Adriaan Paets van." *DSB* 133:468–69.

Sorrenson, Richard John. "Scientific Instrument Makers at the Royal Society of London, 1720–1780." Ph.D. diss., Princeton University, 1993.

——. "Towards a History of the Royal Society in the Eighteenth Century." *Notes and Records of the Royal Society of London* 50 (1996): 29–46.

Sparrow, W. J. *Knight of the White Eagle*. London: Hutchinson, 1964.

Speck, W. A. *Tory & Whig. The Struggle in the Constituencies 1701–1715*. New York: St. Martin's Press, 1970.

Spencer, Ross L. "If Coulomb's Law Were Not Inverse Square: The Charge Distribution Inside a Solid Conducting Sphere." *American Journal of Physics* 58 (1990): 385–90.

Spray, W. A. "Alexander Dalrymple, Hydrographer." *American Neptune* 30 (1970): 200–16.

Stanhope, Charles, Lord Mahon. *Principles of Electricity, Containing Divers New Theorems and Experiments. . . .* London, 1779.

Stanhope, Philip Dormer, Earl of Chesterfield. *Letters Written by the Late Right Honourable Philip Dormer Stanhope, Earl of Chesterfield, to His Son, Philip Stanhope, Esq; Late Envoy Extraordinary at the Court of Dresden: Together with Several Other Pieces on Various Subjects.* Edited by E. Stanhope. Vol. 2. Dublin, 1774.

Stearns, Raymond Phineas. *Science in the British Colonies of America.* Urbana: University of Illinois Press, 1970.

Steffens, Henry John. *The Development of Newtonian Optics in England.* New York: Science History Publications, 1977.

Steiner, George. "The Retreat from the Word." In *George Steiner: A Reader*, 283–304. New York: Oxford University Press, 1984.

Steiner, Lewis H. *Henry Cavendish and the Discovery of the Chemical Composition of Water*. New York, 1855.

Stelling-Michaud, Sven, and Suzanne Stelling-Michaud, eds. *Le livre du recteur de l'Académie de Genève*. Vols. 1–3. Geneva: Droz, 1959–72.

Stephenson, R. J. "The Electrical Researches of the Hon. Henry Cavendish, F.R.S." *The American Physics Teacher* 6 (1938): 55–58.

Sterne, Laurence. *A Sentimental Journey Through France and Italy*. Originally published in 1768. Introduction by V. Woolf. London: Milford, 1951.

Stewart, John. *Sir Isaac Newton's Two Treatises of the Quadrature of Curves, and Analysis by Equations of an Infinite Number of Terms, Explained. . . .* London, 1745.

Stewart, Larry. "Public Lectures and Private Patronage in Newtonian England." *Isis* 77 (1986): 47–58.

——. *The Rise of Public Science: Rhetoric, Technology, and Natural Philosophy in Newtonian Britain, 1660–1750.* Cambridge: Cambridge University Press, 1992.

Stimson, Dorothy. *Scientists and Amateurs. A History of the Royal Society*. New York: Schuman, 1948.

Stirling, James. *The Differential Method: or, a Treatise Concerning Summation and Interpolation of Infinite Series*. London, 1749.

Stokes, Hugh. *The Devonshire House Circle*. London: Herbert Jenkins, 1917.

Stone, Edmund. *The Construction and Principal Uses of Mathematical Instruments. Translated from the French of M. Bion, Chief Instrument-Maker to the French King. . . .* London, 1723.

Stone, Lawrence. *The Family, Sex and Marriage in England 1500–1800.* Abr. ed. Harmondsworth: Penguin, 1982.

Struik, D. J. "Musschenbroek, Petrus van." *DSB* 9:594–97.

Summerson, John. *Georgian London.* Rev. ed. Harmondsworth: Penguin, 1978.

Supplement to Friend to Dr. Hutton. *An Appeal to the Fellows of the Royal Society, Concerning the Measures Taken by Sir Joseph Banks, Their President, to Compel Dr. Hutton to Resign the Office of Secretary to the Society for Their Correspondence.* London, 1784.

Supplement to the Appeal to the Fellows of the Royal Society: Being Letters Taken from the Public Advertiser and Morning Post. London, 1784.

Susskind, Charles. "Henry Cavendish, Electrician." *Journal of the Franklin Institute* 249 (1950): 181–87.

Sutherland, L. S. See L. G.. Mitchell.

Sykes, Norman. *Church and State in England in the XVIIIth Century.* Cambridge: Cambridge University Press, 1934.

Taton, René. "Cassini, Jean-Dominique (Cassini IV)." *DSB* 3:106–7.

——. "Cassini de Thury, César-François (Cassini III)." *DSB* 3:107–9.

——. "Monge, Gaspard." *DSB* 9:469–78.

Taylor, Brook. *Contemplatio Philosophica: A Posthumous Work of the Late Brook Taylor, L.L.D. F.R.S. Some Time Secretary of the Royal Society to Which Is Prefixed a Life of the Author by His Grandson, Sir William Young, Bart., F.R.S. A.S.S. . . .* London, 1793.

Taylor, E. G. R. *The Mathematical Practitioners of Hanoverian England, 1714–1840.* Cambridge: Cambridge University Press, 1966.

——. *The Mathematical Practitioners of Tudor and Stuart England.* Cambridge: Cambridge University Press, 1954.

Thackray, Arnold W. *Atoms and Powers: An Essay on Newtonian Matter-Theory and the Development of Chemistry.* Cambridge, Mass.: Harvard University Press, 1970.

——. "Dalton, John." *DSB* 3:537–47.

——. "Higgins, Bryan." *DSB* 6:382–84.

——. "Natural Knowledge in Cultural Context: The Manchester Model." *American Historical Review* 79 (1974): 672–709.

Thomas, Keith. *Man and the Natural World: A History of the Modern Sensibility.* New York: Pantheon, 1983.

Thomas, Lewis. *The Medusa and the Snail: More Notes of a Biology Watcher.* New York: Bantam, 1980.

——. *The Youngest Science: Notes of a Medicine-Watcher.* New York: Viking, 1983.

Thomas, P. D. G. *The House of Commons in the Eighteenth Century.* Oxford: Clarendon Press, 1971.

Thompson, Benjamin, Count Rumford. *The Complete Works of Count Rumford.* 4 vols. Boston, 1870–75.

Thompson, Francis. *A History of Chatsworth: Being a Supplement to the Sixth Duke of Devonshire's Handbook.* London: Country Life Limited, 1949.

Thompson, F. M. L. *Hampstead: Building a Borough, 1650–1964.* London: Routledge & Kegan Paul, 1974.

Thomson, Gladys Scott. *Life in a Noble Household, 1641–1700.* London: Jonathan Cape, 1937.

Thomson, John. *An Account of the Life, Lectures, and Writings of William Cullen, M.D., Professor of the Practice of Physic in the University of Edinburgh.* 2 vols. Edinburgh, 1832–59.

Thomson, S. P. *The Life of William Thomson, Baron Kelvin of Largs.* 2 vols. London, 1901.

Thomson, Thomas. *The History of Chemistry.* 2 vols. London, 1830–31.

——. *History of the Royal Society from Its Institution to the End of the Eighteenth Century.* London, 1812.

Thornton, William. *The New, Complete, and Universal History, Description, and Survey of the Cities of London and Westminster . . . Likewise the Towns, Villages, Palaces, Seats, and Country, to the Extent of Above Twenty Miles Round.* Rev. ed. London, 1784.

Titchmarsh, P. F. "The Michell-Cavendish Experiment." *The School Science Review*, no. 162 (Mar. 1966): 320–30.

——. "Temperature Effects in the Michell-Cavendish Experiment." *The School Science Review*, no. 163 (June 1966): 678–93.

Todhunter, Isaac. *A History of the Mathematical Theories of Attraction and the Figure of the Earth, from the Time of Newton to That of Laplace.* London, 1873.

——. *A History of the Mathematical Theory of Probability from the Time of Pascal to That of Laplace.* Cambridge, 1865.

Tompkins, Herbert W. *Highways and Byways in Hertfordshire.* London: Macmillan, 1902.

Toulmin, Stephen, and June Goodfield. *The Discovery of Time.* New York: Harper & Row, 1965.

Travers, Morris W. *A Life of Sir William Ramsay, K.C.B., F.R.S.* London: Edward Arnold, 1956.

Treasures from Chatsworth. The Devonshire Inheritance. A Loan Exhibition from the Devonshire Collection, by Permission of the Duke of Devonshire and the Trustees of the Chatsworth Settlement. Organized and Circulated by the International Exhibitions Foundation, 1979–1980.

"Trembley, Jean." Poggendorff 2: cols. 1130–31.

Trengove, Leonard. "Chemistry at the Royal Society of London in the Eighteenth Century." *Annals of Science* 19 (1963): 183–237; 20 (1964): 1–57; 21 (1965): 81–130, 75–201; 26 (1970): 331–53.

Troughton, John. *A Catalogue of Mathematical, Philosophical, and Optical Instruments. . . .* London, 1782–84.

Truesdell, Clifford. "A Program Toward Rediscovering the Rational Mechanics of the Age of Reason." *Archive for History of Exact Sciences* 1 (1960): 1–36.

Trumbach, Randolph. *The Rise of the Egalitarian Family: Aristocratic Kinship and Domestic Relations in Eighteenth-Century England.* New York: Academic Press, 1978.

Tunbridge, Paul A. "Jean André De Luc, F.R.S. (1727–1817)." *Notes and Records of the Royal Society of London* 26 (1971): 15–33.

Turberville, A. S., ed. *Johnson's England: An Account of the Life & Manners of His Age*. Vol. 2. Oxford: Clarendon Press, 1933.

Turner, A. J. "Mathematical Instruments and the Education of Gentlemen." *Annals of Science* 30 (1973): 51–88.

Turner, G. l'E. "The Auction Sale of the Earl of Bute's Instruments, 1793." *Annals of Science* 23 (1967): 213–42.

Tweedie, Charles. *James Stirling. A Sketch of His Life and Works Along with His Scientific Correspondence*. Oxford: Clarendon Press, 1922.

Twigg, John. *A History of Queens' College, Cambridge, 1448–1986*. Woodbridge, Suffolk: Boydell Press, 1987.

"Vaughan, Benjamin." *DNB* 20:158–59.

"Vaughan, William." *DNB* 20:187–88.

Venn, John, and J. A. Venn. *Alumni Cantabrigiensis* . . . Part 1. *From the Earliest Times to 1751*. 4 vols. Cambridge: Cambridge University Press, 1922, 1954.

Vernon, Kenneth D. C. *The Foundation and Early Years of the Royal Institution*. London: Royal Institution, 1963. Reprinted from *Proceedings of the Royal Institution* 39 (1963): 364–402.

The Victoria History of the Counties of England. Cambridge and the Isle of Ely. London: Published for the University of London, Institute of Historical Research by Dawsons of Pall Mall, 1967. Reprinted from the original edition of 1948.

———. *Derbyshire*. London: Published for the University of London, Institute of Historical Research by Dawsons of Pall Mall, 1970. Reprinted from the original edition of 1907.

The Victoria History of the County of Hertford. Vol. 2. Folkestone and London: Published for the University of London, Institute of Historical Research by Dawsons of Pall Mall, 1971. Reprinted from the original edition of 1902.

The Victoria History of the County of Lancaster. Edited by W. Farrer and J. Brownbill. Vol. 8. London: Constable, 1914.

Vince, Samuel. *The Heads of a Course of Lectures on Experimental Philosophy*. . . . Cambridge, 1795.

———. *A Plan of a Course of Lectures on the Principles of Natural Philosophy*. Cambridge, 1793.

"Vince, Samuel." *DNB* 20:355–56.

Walker, R. J. B. *Old Westminster Bridge: The Bridge of Fools*. Newton Abbot: David and Charles, 1979.

Walker, Thomas Alfred. *Admissions to Peterhouse or S. Peter's College in the University of Cambridge. A Biographical Register*. Cambridge: Cambridge University Press, 1912.

———. *Peterhouse*. Cambridge: W. Heffer, 1935.

Walker, W. Cameron. "Animal Electricity Before Galvani." *Annals of Science* 2 (1937): 84–113.

Wallis, P. J. "The MacLaurin 'Circle': The Evidence of Subscription Lists." *Bibliotheck* 11 (1982): 38–54.

——. "Stirling, James." *DSB* 13:67–70.

Wallis, R. V., and P. J. Wallis. *Biobibliography of British Mathematics and Its Applications.* Part 2: *1701–1760.* Newcastle upon Tyne: Epsilon Press, 1986.

Walpole, Horace. *Horace Walpole's Correspondence.* 48 vols. Edited by W. S. Lewis. New Haven: Yale University Press, 1937–83.

"Walsh, John." *DNB* 20:671–72.

Walters, Alice Nell. "Tools of Enlightenment: The Material Culture of Science in Eighteenth-Century England." Ph.D. diss., University of California at Berkeley, 1992.

Watermann, Rembert. "Eudiometrie (1772–1805)." *Technik-Geschichte* 35 (1968): 293–319.

Watson, John Steven. *Reign of George III, 1760–1815.* Oxford: Clarendon Press, 1960.

Watson, Richard. *Anecdotes of the Life of Richard Watson, Bishop of Landaff; Written by Himself at Different Intervals, and Revised in 1814.* 2d ed. Vol. 1. London, 1818.

"Watson, Sir William." *DNB* 20:956–58.

Watson, William. *An Account of a Series of Experiments Instituted with a View of Ascertaining the Most Successful Method of Inoculating the Smallpox.* London, 1768.

Watt, James. *Correspondence of the Late James Watt on His Discovery of the Theory of the Composition of Water.* Edited by James Patrick Muirhead. London, 1846.

——. *Partners of Science: Letters of James Watt and Joseph Black.* Edited by Eric Robinson and Douglas McKie. Cambridge, Mass.: Harvard University Press, 1970.

Watt, James. See Thomas Beddoes.

Webb, Sidney, and Beatrice Webb. *English Local Government: The Story of the King's Highway.* London: Longmans, Green, 1920.

Webster, Roderick S. "Nairne, Edward." *DSB* 9:607–8.

——. "Troughton, Edward." *DSB* 13:470–71.

Weiss, Leonard. *Watch-Making in England, 1760–1820.* London: Robert Hale, 1982.

Weld, Charles Richard. *A History of the Royal Society. . . .* 2 vols. 1848. Reprint, New York: Arno Press, 1975.

Wells, Ellen B. "Scientists' Libraries: A Handlist of Printed Sources," *Annals of Science* 40 (1983): 317–89.

Wells, Samuel. *The History of the Drainage of the Great Level of the Fens, Called Bedford Level; with the Constitution and Laws of the Bedford Level Corporation.* 2 vols. London, 1830.

Wentworth, Thomas. *The Wentworth Papers 1705–1739. Selected from the Private and Family Correspondence of Thomas Wentworth, Lord Raby, Created in 1711 Earl of Strafford, of Stainborough, Co. York.* Edited by James J. Cartwright. London, 1883.

Westfall, Richard. *Never at Rest. A Biography of Isaac Newton.* Cambridge: Cambridge University Press, 1980.

Wheatley, Henry B. *London, Past and Present. A Dictionary of Its History, Associations, and Traditions.* 3 vols. London, 1891.

Wheeler T. S., and J. R. Partington. *The Life and Work of William Higgins, Chemist (1763–1825).* New York: Pergamon, 1960.

Whiston, William. *Astronomical Lectures, Read in the Publick Schools of Cambridge*. . . . London, 1715.

——. *Memoirs of the Life and Writings of Mr. William Whiston*. London, 1749.

——. *A New Theory of the Earth*. . . . 5th ed. Cambridge, 1737.

——. *Sir Isaac Newton's Mathematic Philosophy More Easily Demonstrated*. Translated from the Latin edition of 1710. London, 1716.

Whitehurst, John. *An Inquiry into the Original State and Formation of the Earth; Deduced from Facts and the Laws of Nature. To Which Is Added an Appendix, Containing Some General Observations on the Strata in Derbyshire*. . . . London, 1778.

Whittaker, Sir Edmund. *A History of the Theories of Aether and Electricity*. Vol. I: *The Classical Theories*. New York: Harper & Bros., 1960.

Widmalm, Sven. "Accuracy, Rhetoric, and Technology: The Paris-Greenwich Triangulation, 1784–88." In *The Quantifying Spirit in the Eighteenth Century*, edited by T. Frangsmyr, J. L. Heilbron, and R. E. Rider, 179–206. Berkeley: University of California Press, 1990.

Wightman, William P. D. "The Copley Medal and the Work of Some of the Early Recipients." *Physis* 3 (1961): 344–55.

Wilkinson, Lise. "'The Other' John Hunter, M.D., F.R.S. (1754–1809): His Contributions to the Medical Literature, and to the Introduction of Animal Experiments into Infectious Disease Research." *Notes and Records of the Royal Society of London* 36 (1982): 227–41.

Will, Clifford M. "Henry Cavendish, Johann von Soldner, and the Deflection of Light." *American Journal of Physics* 56 (1988): 413–15.

Willey, Basil. *The Eighteenth Century Background: Studies on the Idea of Nature in the Thought of the Period*. Boston: Beacon, 1940.

Williams, Basil. *The Whig Supremacy, 1714–1760*. 2d rev. ed. Edited by C. H. Stuart. Oxford: Clarendon Press, 1962.

Willson, Beckles. *The Great Company (1667–1871); Being a History of the Honourable Company of Merchants-Adventurers Trading into Hudson's Bay*. Vol. 2. London: Smith, Elder, 1900.

Wilson, Alexander. *Thoughts on General Gravitation, and Views Thence Arising as to the State of the Universe*. London, 1777.

Wilson, Benjamin. *An Essay Towards an Explication of the Phaenomena of Electricity, Deduced from the Aether of Sir Isaac Newton*. . . . London, 1746.

Wilson, George. *The Life of the Honourable Henry Cavendish*. . . . London, 1851.

——. *Religio chemici. Essays*. Edited by J. A. Wilson. London, 1862.

Wilson, Jessie Aitken. *Memoir of George Wilson*. London and Cambridge, 1862.

Winstanley, Denys Arthur. *Unreformed Cambridge*. Cambridge: Cambridge University Press, 1935.

Wolf, A. *A History of Science, Technology, and Philosophy in the 16th and 17th Centuries*. 2 vols. 2d ed. Edited by D. McKie. New York: Harper & Bros., 1961.

——. *A History of Science, Technology, and Philosophy in the 18th Century*. 2 vols. 2d ed. Edited by D. McKie. New York: Harper & Bros., 1961.

"Wollaston, Francis." *DNB* 21:778–79.

Woolf, Harry. "Chappe d'Auteroche, Jean-Baptiste." *DSB* 3:197–98.

——. "Theories of the Universe in the Late Eighteenth Century." In *Biology, History, and Natural Philosophy*, edited by Allen D. Breck and Wolfgang Youngrau, 263–89. New York: Plenum, 1972.

——. *The Transits of Venus: A Study of Eighteenth-Century Science*. London: Oxford University Press, 1959.

Woolley, Richard. "Captain Cook and the Transit of Venus of 1769." *Notes and Records of the Royal Society of London* 24 (1969): 19–32.

Wordsworth, Christopher. *Scholae Academicae: Some Account of the Studies at the English Universities in the Eighteenth Century*. 1877. Reprint, London: Frank Cass, 1968.

Worster, Benjamin. *A Compendious and Methodical Account of the Principles of Natural Philosophy*. 2d ed. London, 1730.

Wray, R. A. See R. H. Nichols.

Wright, Thomas. *An Original Theory or New Hypothesis of the Universe, Founded upon the Laws of Nature. . . .* London, 1750.

Yorke, Philip Chasney. *The Life and Correspondence of Philip Yorke, Earl of Hardwicke, Lord High Chancellor of Great Britain*. 3 vols. Cambridge: Cambridge University Press, 1913.

Young, Robert. *An Essay on the Powers and Mechanism of Nature. . . .* London, 1788.

Young, Thomas. *A Course of Lectures on Natural Philosophy and the Mechanical Arts*. 2 vols. London, 1807.

——. "Life of Cavendish." *Encyclopaedia Britannica*, Supplement (1816–24). Reprinted in Henry Cavendish, *The Scientific Papers of the Honourable Henry Cavendish* 1:435–47.

——. *A Syllabus of a Course of Lectures on Natural and Experimental Philosophy*. London, 1802.

Zimbardo, Philip G. *Shyness: What It Is, What to Do About It*. Reading: Addison-Wesley, 1977.

INDEX